The Novel

For Jeffrey and Madeline

Edited By

DOROTHY J. HALE

An Anthology of Criticism and Theory
1900–2000

Blackwell
Publishing

The Novel

Editorial material and organization © 2006 by Blackwell Publishing Ltd

BLACKWELL PUBLISHING
350 Main Street, Malden, MA 02148-5020, USA
9600 Garsington Road, Oxford OX4 2DQ, UK
550 Swanston Street, Carlton, Victoria 3053, Australia

First published 2006 by Blackwell Publishing Ltd

1 2006

Library of Congress Cataloging-in-Publication Data

The novel : an anthology of criticism and theory, 1900–2000 / edited by Dorothy J. Hale.
    p. cm.
  Includes bibliographical references and index.
  ISBN-13: 978-1-4051-0773-0 (hardcover : alk. paper)
  ISBN-10: 1-4051-0773-1 (hardcover : alk. paper)
  ISBN-13: 978-1-4051-0774-7 (pbk. : alk. paper)
  ISBN-10: 1-4051-0774-X (pbk. : alk. paper)
1. Fiction—History and criticism—Theory, etc. I. Hale, Dorothy J.

PN3331.N66 2006
809.3—dc22
                             2005011205

A catalogue record for this title is available from the British Library.

Set in 10/12.5 pt Janson
by SPI Publisher Services, Pondicherry, India

For further information on
Blackwell Publishing, visit our website:
www.blackwellpublishing.com

CONTENTS

Acknowledgments   ix

General Introduction   1

Part I: Form and Function   17

1   *Viktor Shklovsky,* "Sterne's *Tristram Shandy*"   31

2   *Vladimir Propp,* from *Morphology of the Folktale*   54

3   *Henry James,* Prefaces to the New York Edition   65
    Preface to *The Portrait of a Lady*
    Preface to *The Ambassadors*

4   *Percy Lubbock,* from *The Craft of Fiction*   86

5   *Northrop Frye,* from *Anatomy of Criticism*   97
    "Rhetorical Criticism: Theory of Genres"

Part II: The Chicago School   **107**

6   *R. S. Crane*, from "The Concept of Plot and the Plot of *Tom Jones*"   119

7   *Ralph W. Rader*, "Richardson to Austen"   140

8   *Wayne C. Booth*, from *The Rhetoric of Fiction*   154

Part III: Structuralism, Narratology, Deconstruction   **185**

9   *Tzvetan Todorov*, from *The Poetics of Prose*
"Language and Literature"
"The Grammar of Narrative"   205

10   *Seymour Chatman*, from *Story and Discourse*
"Discourse: Covert versus Overt Narrators"   219

11   *Roland Barthes*, "The Reality Effect"   229

12   *Roland Barthes*, "From Work to Text"   235

13   *J. Hillis Miller*, from *Reading Narrative*
"Indirect Discourses and Irony"   242

14   *Barbara Johnson*, from *A World of Difference*
"Metaphor, Metonymy, and Voice in *Their Eyes Were Watching God*"   257

Part IV: Psychoanalytic Approaches   **271**

15   *René Girard*, from *Deceit, Desire, and the Novel*
" 'Triangular' Desire"   294

16   *Shoshana Felman*, from "Turning the Screw of Interpretation"
"The Turns of the Story's Frame: A Theory of Narrative"   315

17   *Peter Brooks*, "Freud's Masterplot"   329

Part V: Marxist Approaches   **343**

18   *Walter Benjamin*, "The Storyteller"   361

19   *György Lukács*, from *Studies in European Realism*   379

20   *György Lukács*, "The Ideology of Modernism"   394

21 *Fredric Jameson,* from *The Political Unconscious*   413

Part VI: The Novel as Social Discourse   435

22 *Ian Watt,* from *The Rise of the Novel*   462
    "Realism and the Novel Form"

23 *M. M. Bakhtin,* from "Discourse in the Novel"   481

24 *Henry Louis Gates, Jr.,* from *The Signifying Monkey*   511
    "Zora Neale Hurston and the Speakerly Text"

25 *Jane Tompkins,* from *Sensational Designs*   535
    "Introduction: The Cultural Work of American Fiction"

26 *D. A. Miller,* from *The Novel and the Police*   541

Part VII: Gender, Sexuality, and the Novel   559

27 *Virginia Woolf,* "Women and Fiction"   579

28 *Eve Kosofsky Sedgwick,* from *Between Men*   586

29 *Eve Kosofsky Sedgwick,* "Queer Performativity:
    Henry James's *The Art of the Novel*"   605

30 *Nancy Armstrong,* from *Desire and Domestic Fiction*   621
    "Introduction: The Politics of Domesticating Culture,
    Then and Now"

31 *Catherine Gallagher,* from *Nobody's Story*   644

Part VIII: Post-Colonialism and the Novel   653

32 *Gayatri Chakravorty Spivak,* "Three Women's Texts and
    a Critique of Imperialism"   674

33 *Edward W. Said,* from *Culture and Imperialism*   691
    "Consolidated Vision"

34   *Homi K. Bhabha*, from *The Location of Culture*   716
       "DissemiNation: Time, Narrative, and the Margins
       of the Modern Nation"

35   *Franco Moretti*, from *Atlas of the European Novel, 1800–1900*   734
       "The Novel, the Nation-State"

Part IX: Novel Readers   747

36   *Wolfgang Iser*, from *The Implied Reader*   763
       "The Reader as a Component Part of the Realistic Novel"

37   *Nina Baym*, from *Novels, Readers, and Reviewers*   779
       "The Triumph of the Novel"

38   *Garrett Stewart*, from *Dear Reader*   792
       "In the Absence of Audience: Of Reading and Dread
       in Mary Shelley"

Index   803

Acknowledgments

The biographical headnotes included in this anthology are written by Avilah Getzler. Avilah has for many years and for many projects been a research assistant extraordinaire. Her enthusiasm for this particular book sustained me over the long haul, while her efficiency kept my efforts on track. From the first version of the table of contents to the final copy-editing and proofreading, Avilah has participated in all phases of the anthology's design and execution. An insightful first reader of my own writing for the volume, she has clarified my ideas as well as their presentation. I can't imagine having undertaken this project without her assistance – and I know the research, writing, and revising would not have been nearly so enjoyable without our shared interest in novels and narrative.

I count myself lucky to have friends who made time to read and comment upon one or more of the essays I wrote for the volume. Victoria Kahn, Jeffrey Knapp, Sharon Marcus, Samuel Otter, Nancy Ruttenburg, and Cindy Weinstein showed exceptional generosity in their willingness to respond to my work in detail and on short notice. Their own intellectual vitality and capacity for alterity make them the best of interlocutors, even when my obsessions left me with little to talk about other than this book. Deirdre D'Albertis, Julia Bader, Dorri Beam, Margit Stange, and Lynn Wardley all helped launch the volume. Their response to the book's prospectus and my first introductions led me to imagine the anthology as more than the sum of its parts.

Many students and colleagues joined me in the happy conundrum of settling on the readings for the volume. I was first and foremost guided by my sense of which texts held the most interest for my students in the novel theory courses that I have taught at

Berkeley. Those class discussions provided the framework for the volume design and for the analytic work I do in the introductions. The Society for the Study of Narrative Literature has been both an invaluable scholarly resource and an enabling intellectual community. My warm thanks to Narrative Society colleagues for their lively interest in this anthology. I am particularly grateful for the opportunity to have presented my work at the 2003 Narrative Conference. On that occasion, I received suggestions about how to modify my table of contents to suit the interests and needs of colleagues who might find the volume useful for their teaching. Franco Moretti generously sponsored the 2003 panel through the Stanford Center for the Study of the Novel. Here at Berkeley, I profited from the expertise and intellectual generosity of Ian Duncan, who looked over a first draft of the table of contents. John McGowan and Martin Klepper, during visiting stints at Berkeley, also commented upon early versions of the table of contents. I have tried in my choice of readings to distill the expert advice I received from all quarters. If my final table of contents doesn't perfectly reflect all that others would like to have seen in the volume, no one, it's safe to say, would want the book any bigger.

From start to finish, Blackwell has wonderfully supported my large-scale vision for the anthology. I am grateful to Richard Hutson for putting Andrew McNeillie in touch with me. Andrew's wit and wisdom inspired me to take up the project. Unfailingly kind, patient, and efficient, Emma Bennett, Karen Wilson, and Sandra Raphael all saw me through the writing and production of the volume. My thanks also go to the anonymous readers who vetted the book's prospectus as well as to those who reviewed the completed manuscript.

The University of California, Berkeley, has nurtured this project both intellectually and materially. Ralph Hexter and Janet Adelman, as dean and department chair respectively, supported my pursuit of research funding. The Townsend Center's Associate Professor Initiative Grant provided teaching release that enabled me to bring the project to completion. I am indebted to David Hollinger for his willingness to participate in the Townsend colloquium and, more generally, for his generous mentoring of younger colleagues. Catherine Gallagher has fostered my work both in her capacity as department chair and through the example of her own scholarship. Ian Duncan, Susan Maslan, Alex Zwerdling, Florence Elon, and George Starr talked with me about the volume over dinner, in coffee shops, at cocktail parties, and in the halls of Wheeler. Eric Naiman advised me on editions and translations of the Russian formalists. The teaching and scholarship of Ralph Rader and Seymour Chatman provided my own introduction to the theory of the novel. In the deepest sense, their work has made mine possible. I am grateful for their friendship, encouragement, and inspiration over the years – not to mention the conversations that keep me learning from them.

Special thanks go to friends and family who had little or no professional interest in novel theory but who were always willing to discuss this book – or, the height of friendship, to give me the solitude I needed to write it. These include James Astorga, Suzy Bodor, Paul Billings, Caverlee Cary, Christopher Cavanagh, Milena Edwards, Elisabeth Garst, Walter Greenblatt, Donna Marie Grethen, John Hale, Raluca Iuster, Doreen Klein, Maria Mavroudi, Panos Papadopoulos, Susan Reider, Helene Silverberg, Paul Tong, Susan Vernon, and Henry Wigglesworth.

Jeffrey Knapp and Madeline Hale cheered me on, cheered me up, and gave me time. They never asked me to leave my work at the office, although they often helped me get

ACKNOWLEDGMENTS

there to write. Jeff willingly lent a hand to untangle any theoretical concept that I might have wound myself up in. His enthusiasm for this project increased my own pleasure in it. Jeff remains, always, my own best reader. I am grateful for his ability to see my point, often before I do, and to find its interest. Madeline, who, in an everyday miracle, learned to read while I was writing this book, is now my own favorite out-loud reader. She is promised the "first" copy of this book.

The editor and publisher wish to thank the following for permission to use copyright material.

Nancy Armstrong for "Introduction: Politics of Domesticating Culture. Then and Now," from *Desire and Domestic Fiction: A Political History of the Novel* by Nancy Armstrong. New York: Oxford University Press, 1987, pp. 3–27. Copyright © 1987 by Oxford University Press, Inc. Used by permission of Oxford University Press, Inc.

M. M. Bakhtin for *The Dialogic Imagination: Four Essays* by M. M. Bakhtin, edited by Michael Holquist, translated by Caryl Emerson and Michael Holquist. Austin: University of Texas Press, 1981, pp. 259–300. Copyright © 1981 by the University of Texas Press Reprinted by permission of the University of Texas Press.

Roland Barthes for "The Reality Effect" and "From Work to Text" from *The Rustle of Language* by Roland Barthes, translated by Richard Howard. New York: Hill and Wang, 1986, pp. 141–8, 56–64. Translation copyright © 1986 by Farrar, Straus and Giroux, Inc. Reprinted by permission of Hill and Wang, a division of Farrar, Straus and Giroux, LLC.

Nina Baym for *Novels, Readers and Reviewers: Responses to Fiction in Antebellum America* by Nina Baym. Ithaca, NY, and London: Cornell University Press, 1984, pp. 26–43. Copyright © 1984 by Cornell University. Used by permission of the publisher, Cornell University Press.

Walter Benjamin for "The Storyteller: Reflections on the Works of Nikolai Leskov" from *Illuminations*, translated by Harry Zohn, edited by Hannah Arendt. New York: Schocken Books, 1969, pp. 83–109. Copyright © 1955 by Suhrkamp Verlag, Frankfurt am Main, on behalf of Walter Benjamin. Translation copyright © 1968, renewed 1996, by Harcourt, Inc. Reprinted by permission of Harcourt, Inc.

Homi K. Bhabha for *The Location of Culture*. London and New York: Routledge, 1994, pp. 139–57. © 1994 Homi K. Bhabha. Reprinted by permission of Homi K. Bhabha.

Wayne C. Booth for *The Rhetoric of Fiction*, second edition. Chicago and London: University of Chicago Press, 1983 (first edition 1961), pp. 16–20, 67–77, 121–44, 391–8. © University of Chicago Press. Reprinted by permission of Princeton University Press and by permission of the author, Wayne Booth.

Peter Brooks for "Freud's Masterplot," from *Literature and Psychoanalysis* edited by Shoshana Felman (*Yale French Studies* 55/56, 1977). Baltimore and London: Johns Hopkins University Press, 1980, pp. 280–300. Reprinted by permission of *Yale French Studies*.

Seymour Chatman for *Story and Discourse: Narrative Structure in Fiction and Film*. Ithaca, NY, and London: Cornell University Press, 1978, pp. 196–209.

R. S. Crane for "The Concept of Plot and the Plot of Tom Jones" from *Critics and Criticism: Ancient and Modern*, edited by R. S. Crane. Chicago and London: University of Chicago Press, 1952, pp. 616–24, 631–47. © University of Chicago Press. Reprinted by permission of the University of Chicago Press.

Shoshana Felman for "Turning the Screw of Interpretation," from *Literature and Psychoanalysis*, ed. Felman (Yale French Studies 55/56, 1977). Baltimore and London: Johns Hopkins University Press, 1980, pp. 94–207. Reprinted by permission of *Yale French Studies*.

Northrop Frye for *Anatomy of Criticism: Four Essays*. Princeton, NJ: Princeton University Press, 1957, pp. 303–14. Copyright © 1957, renewed 1985, by Princeton University Press. Reprinted by permission of Princeton University Press.

Catherine Gallagher for *Nobody's Story: The Vanishing Acts of Women Writers in the Marketplace 1670–1820*. Oxford: Clarendon Press, 1994, pp. 162–75. Copyright © 1994 Catherine Gallagher. Reprinted by permission of Catherine Gallagher.

Henry Louis Gates Jr., for *The Signifying Monkey: A Theory of African-American Literary Criticism* by Henry Louis Gates, Jr. New York: Cambridge University Press, 1988, pp. 193–216. Copyright © 1988 by Henry Louis Gates, Jr. Used by permission of Oxford University Press, Inc.

René Girard for *Deceit, Desire, and the Novel: Self and Other in Literary Structure* by René Girard, translated by Yvonne Frecco. Baltimore and London: Johns Hopkins University Press, 1966, pp. 1–26, 41–52. © 1966 by the Johns Hopkins University Press. Reprinted with permission of the Johns Hopkins University Press.

Wolfgang Iser for *The Implied Reader: Patterns of Communication in Prose Fiction from Bunyan to Beckett*. Baltimore and London: Johns Hopkins University Press, 1974, pp. 101–20. Copyright © 1974 by the Johns Hopkins University Press. Reprinted with permission of the Johns Hopkins University Press.

Fredric Jameson for *The Political Unconscious: Narrative as a Socially Symbolic Act*. Ithaca, NY: Cornell University Press, 1987, pp. 17–23, 151–69, 296–9. Copyright © 1981 by Cornell University. Used by permission of the publisher, Cornell University Press.

Barbara Johnson for *A World of Difference* by Barbara Johnson. Baltimore and London: Johns Hopkins University Press, 1987, pp. 155–71. © 1987 by the Johns Hopkins University Press. Reprinted with permission of the Johns Hopkins University Press.

Percy Lubbock for *The Craft of Fiction*. London: Jonathan Cape, 1921, pp. 14-25, 251–64. Copyright © Percy Lubbock (1957), reprinted by the kind permission of the Estate of Percy Lubbock and the Sayle Literary Agency.

George Lukács for *The Meaning of Contemporary Realism*, translated by John and Necke Mander. London: Merlin Press, 1962, pp. 17–46. Reprinted by permission of Merlin Press Ltd.

George Lukács for *Studies in European Realism: A Sociological Survey of the Writings of Balzac, Stendhal, Zola, Tolstoy, Gorki and Others*, translated by Edith Bone. London: Hillway, 1950, pp. 1–19.

D. A. Miller for *The Novel and the Police*. Berkeley: University of California Press, 1988, foreword pp. vii–xiii, pp. 1–21. Copyright © 1988 by the University of California Press. Reprinted by permission of the Regents of the University of California and by the University of California Press.

J. Hillis Miller for *Reading Narrative* by J. Hillis Miller. Norman: University of Oklahoma Press, 1988, pp. 158–77, 247–9 Copyright © 1998 by the University of Oklahoma Press, Norman. Reprinted by permission. All rights reserved.

Franco Moretti for *Atlas of the European Novel, 1800–1900.* London and New York: Verso, 1998, pp. 12–29. Copyright © 1998 by Franco Moretti. Reprinted by permission of Verso.

Vladímir Propp, for *Morphology of the Folktale,* second edition, by Vladímir Propp, translated by Laurence Scott, revised and edited with a Preface by Louis A. Wagner. Austin: University of Texas Press, 1968, pp. 19–29, 66–70. Copyright © 1968 by the University of Texas Press. Reprinted by permission of the University of Texas Press.

Ralph W. Rader for "From Richardson to Austen" from *Johnson and His Age,* edited by James Engell. Cambridge, Mass., and London: Harvard University Press, 1984, pp. 461–83. Reprinted by permission of Harvard University, Department of English and American Literature and Language.

Edward Said for *Culture and Imperialism* by Edward W. Said. New York: Vintage, 1993, pp. 70–97. Copyright © 1993 by Edward W. Said. Used by permission of Alfred A. Knopf, a division of Random House, Inc.

Eve Kosofsky Sedgwick for *Between Men: English Literature and Male Homosocial Desire.* New York: Columbia University Press, 1985, pp. 1–15, 21–7. Reprinted by permission of Columbia University Press.

Eve Kosofsky Sedgwick for "Queer Performativity: Henry James's *The Art of the Novel*" from *GLQ: Journal of Lesbian and Gay Studies,* vol. 1, no. 1, 1993, pp. 1–16. Copyright © 1993 by Gordon and Breach Science Publishers SA. All rights reserved. Used with permission.

Víktor Shklovsky, for "Sterne's *Tristram Shandy:* Stylistic Commentary" from *Russian Formalist Criticism: Four Essays,* translated by Lee T. Lemon and Marion J. Reis. Lincoln: University of Nebraska Press, 1965, pp. 27–57. © University of Nebraska Press. Reprinted by permission of University of Nebraska Press.

Gayatri Chakravorty Spivak for "Three Women's Texts and a Critique of Imperialism" from *Critical Inquiry, 12* (Autumn 1985) pp. 243–61. © 1985 Gayatri Chakrovorty Spivak. Reprinted by permission of Gayatri Chakravorty Spivak.

Garrett Stewart for *Dear Reader: The Conscripted Audience in Nineteenth-Century British Fiction.* Baltimore and London: Johns Hopkins University Press, 1946, pp. 113–26 and 417–18. © 1996 Johns Hopkins University Press. Reprinted with permission of the Johns Hopkins University Press.

Tzvetan Todorov for *The Poetics of Prose* by Tzvetan Todorov, transalated by Richard Howard. Ithaca, NY: Cornell University Press, 1997, pp. 20–8, 108–19. © 1977 by Cornell University. Originally published in French as *La Poétique de la Prose.* Copyright © 1971 by Editions du Seuil. Reprinted by permission of Georges Borchardt, Inc. for Editions du Seuil and Blackwell Publishers.

Jane Tompkins for *Sensational Designs: The Cultural Work of American Fiction, 1790–1860* by Jane Tompkins. New York: Oxford University Press, 1985, pp. xi–xix. Copyright © 1985 by Oxford University Press, Inc. Used by permission of Oxford University Press, Inc.

Ian Watt for *The Rise of the Novel: Studies in Defoe, Richardson and Fielding.* Berkeley: University of California Press, 1957, pp. 9–34. Copyright © 1957, renewed 1985, by the University of California Press. Reprinted by permission of the Regents of the University of California and by the University of California Press.

General Introduction

This volume has emerged from a course called "The Novel in Theory" that I have taught at Berkeley over the past ten years. I have devised this seminar to be a genuine introduction, a starting point for undergraduates and graduates who have had no prior instruction in literary theory. My classroom experience has taught me that many students are intimidated by literary theory. They regard it almost as a foreign language, riddled with ugly jargon and originating from esoteric philosophical homelands to which they feel they have been given no intellectual passport. Students sign up for the course almost as an inoculation: I'll get my theory here, and build up resistance to future infections. But my seminar has also proven to me that students are disarmed when they learn that the study of literary theory need not be a move away from the kind of close reading that inspired them to become literature majors in the first place. Students are excited to learn that they can work through theoretical texts as they would any difficult piece of literature, relying on their training as readers to determine what is significant, what is confusing, what makes sense and what doesn't. Students will be intimidated and alienated by theory as long as they view it as a meta-discourse, mastered by the high priests of the discipline and disseminated from on high to the uninitiated. But if students can instead be taught to read theoretical texts as they would literary texts – as both paradigmatic and problematic, limpidly clear in some paragraphs and excruciatingly opaque in other passages, redundant about some issues and silent about others – then students are truly beginning to "do" theory: they are becoming imaginative and creative readers of imaginative and creative texts that also happen to be analytic and argumentative texts.

My own immersion in the field of novel theory has also taught me to do theory this way – precisely because the field itself has been made and remade over the course of the twentieth century, emerging as a rich problematic rather than a monolithic idea. Positioning novel theory in relation to larger theoretical movements, studying the novel "in" theory, allows us to understand how the study of the novel develops in answer to philosophical problems at the heart of twentieth-century literary theory more generally. Formalism, structuralism, narratology, deconstruction, psychoanalysis, Marxism, social discourse, gender and sexuality, post-colonialism, reader response – the section headings of this volume might be found in any introduction to literary theory. But when we pose the novel as a question, when we ask why the novel has been so important to the theoretical work of each school, we discover not only a new basis of connection among these schools but also something about the novel's importance to literary theory that is itself theorizable only through a examination of the field as a whole.

One of the first things a reader of this volume might notice is how few of the anthologized essays in fact use the term "novel theory." The Hungarian György Lukács, who published *The Theory of the Novel* (*Die Theorie des Romans*) in 1920, might be credited for putting the term into general circulation. But in a powerful example of how the field gets made and remade, Lukács repudiates in his famous 1962 preface the argument advanced by that early work. In particular, he critiques the Hegelian philosophical premises that led him to undertake a theory of the novel. Throwing off the "abstract synthesis" that for him defines theory as theory, Lukács champions instead the "concrete" historical analysis he has subsequently come to value.[1]

What the example of Lukács suggests, and what this volume more generally seeks to show, is that the theory of the novel can be practiced under other names. The theory of the novel develops as a problematic precisely through its vexed relation to theory narrowly understood – whether that understanding comes from Hegel or from other intellectual antecedents. Lukács' preface to *The Theory of the Novel* makes it seem as if the new work he does, the work of concrete historical analysis, is the opposite of theory, theory free, as it were. But in fact his historiography is underwritten by a different kind of theory: Marxist social theory. And although his later titles subtly mark this shift (*The Historical Novel* [first published in 1937]; *Studies in European Realism* [first published in 1948]; *The Meaning of Contemporary Realism* [first published in 1958]), they notably name an object of literary study rather than a theoretical approach. It is by following out the actual arguments that Lukács puts forward in these books that we can discover what counts as Marxist inquiry for him. And as we work to identify the ideas he directly imports from Marxist social theory, we also will appreciate the ways that Lukács advances the field of Marxist literary study through his own conceptual innovations, particularly through his new account of the novel. Such analysis will no doubt return us to the 1962 preface with at least one new insight: the account Lukács gives there of his career, the narrative of personal development achieved through self-critique, and more particularly the narrative of Marxist revelation arrived at through Hegelianism, is itself scripted by Marxist theory. We find that Lukács' account of his development through and beyond novel theory is as theoretical as it is personal. We could even go so far as to say that what counts as personal experience – just as what counts as the novel – is a product of the interpretative paradigm brought to bear on it.

To understand that the theory of the novel can be conducted under other names, in the service of different types of theories, leads to another, equally important, insight into the field: that even when the term theory is used by different thinkers to mean the same thing, even when it connotes a shared understanding of how theoretical inquiry is distinguished from other types of analytic practices, such shared understanding can nonetheless generate profoundly different types of novel study. For example, due to the climate of scientism that pervades the first half of the twentieth century, we find Percy Lubbock in 1921 using the term "theory" in ways that anticipate Roland Barthes' usage of the term in 1966.[2] Although Barthes explicitly imports the idea of theory from the American linguists who have inspired him to undertake the structural analysis of narrative,[3] Lubbock and Barthes are both more generally responding to the methodologies popularized by the new human sciences that rose to prominence in the first half of the twentieth century, to the point where we can find Lubbock using a phrase in 1921 that might describe the project that Barthes undertakes at mid-century: the attempt to give a "scientific account of the structure of the simplest book."[4] Lubbock himself doubts that the novel can in fact be studied scientifically, can in fact be theorized in this sense. But he is compelled by the attempt, enough to embark upon a project that, although not scientific in its methods, shares an endpoint of science: to name the objective properties of a work of fiction. By entitling his study *The Craft of Fiction*, Lubbock emphasizes, on the one hand, the limits of scientific methods and, on the other hand, the power of art: on his view, any objective account of the nature of fiction, of the "arts and devices" a novelist uses to bring his scenes and characters to life, derives from a reader response that is itself creative and imaginative, even artistic (*Craft*, 89). Barthes, on the other hand, turns to scientific methods precisely to challenge this sort of privileging of literary effects. Literature, as a linguistic activity, should not be regarded as qualitatively different from any other language use. Producing a scientific account of the structure of the simplest book is not only a worthy endeavor for Barthes, but also one that begins by simplifying literature itself, identifying its most basic linguistic components.

This brief comparison of Lubbock and Barthes suggests the productive sorts of comparisons that can be made when theory is understood as something to be discovered through the readings in this volume, rather than something we bring to the volume, thinking that we already know all about it. In tracing out the full problematic of Lubbock and Barthes, we would also want to note that Barthes finally ends up, if not (like Lukács) repudiating his early position, then working through and beyond the influence of sociological science to help found a radically new type of theory, deconstruction. Studying the theory of the novel as a problematic puts in significant relation thinkers who might otherwise seem to occupy different critical universes. Any reader will, of course, bring to this anthology a working sense of what theory is and, for that matter, what the novel is. But a full understanding of both the novel and novel theory requires us to pluralize and historicize these notions.

This volume charts the uneven development of the field across the twentieth century by putting into relation the different philosophical projects conducted through the study of the novel – whether these bear the name of novel theory or not. I have attempted to work out some of these larger connections in *Social Formalism: The Novel in Theory from Henry James to the Present* (Stanford University Press, 1998). There I argue that the fate of novel theory is tied to the rise and fall of literary theory as an academic discipline. Before the twentieth century, the novel was considered a popular entertainment, unworthy of a poetics of its own. But while novelists sought to develop the novel into a high art form (especially through the influential work of Gustave Flaubert, Leo Tolstoy, Henry James, Marcel Proust, Virginia Woolf, Edith Wharton, and James Joyce), academic scholarship was moving away from poetics to something that was increasingly called theory. On the one hand, the challenge to poetics came from formalists, structuralists, and narratologists who all sought (in their different ways) to separate questions of literary value from the scientific examination of the literary object, to analyze how a novel works, rather than arguing for its merit as a work of art. On the other hand, the challenge to poetics came from critical theory. From Lukács and M. M. Bakhtin to Fredric Jameson and Nancy Armstrong, the category of aesthetics has, along with the category of the literary, undergone political critique, been exposed as a covert ideological category. But if it can thus be said that novel theory lost its aesthetic grounding – its grounding as an aesthetic theory – almost before that foundation was fully laid, this is also to begin to explain why current academic interest in the novel has never been stronger. Studies of the novel have never been so prolific or so influential. The last thirty years have shown us that even cultural critics who think they have nothing to do with literary theory (and less to do with novel theory) have more than ever to do with novel studies. Especially in the sections on "Marxist Approaches," "The Novel as Social Discourse," "Gender, Sexuality, and the Novel," and "Post-Colonialism and the Novel," we can see that the very qualities that had previously disqualified the novel for serious scholarship – its popularity, discursive heterogeneity, commercialism, mimeticism, lack of stylistic density – now make it the genre of choice for cultural critics, within English departments and across disciplines. Especially for scholars who believe that the understanding of a culture lies in an understanding of its choice of popular entertainment, the novel's "rise" (to use Ian Watt's famous term) provides a rationale for privileging it as an object of cultural study. For post-Marxist ideological critics in particular, the novel's status as an early form of mass entertainment makes it a preeminent instrument for the operation of social power. Thus, by the end of the twentieth century the novel has derived its exceptionalism not through arguments defending its aesthetic accomplishments, but from those championing its social power. Political theory has, by understanding the novel as the most social of literary forms, done for the genre what poetic theory never quite succeeded in accomplishing – made it the preeminent literary genre of academic study, within the humanities and beyond.

My sense of the large-scale development of novel studies across the century has directed the sequence of this anthology. The first three sections of the volume – "Form and Function," "The Chicago School," and "Structuralism, Narratology, Deconstruction" – show how the progress from formalism to deconstruction is imagined primarily as an act of supersession: there is a shared sense among thinkers writing before 1980 that the project of advancing knowledge about the novel requires the invention of a whole new theoretical approach. Wayne Booth, for example, works out his theory of "the rhetoric of fiction" by tinkering with the premises of the Chicago School (of which he counts himself a member) – but more radically, he rounds up the contemporary truisms about fiction (including those derived from the work of James and Lubbock) in order to question their authority. He seeks more particularly to replace

DOROTHY HALE

dicta about good and bad novel writing with reasoned argument – what counts for him as theory. Whereas dicta lend themselves to epigraphic quotation, theory, it turns out, is a lengthy pursuit. Booth's new way of thinking about the novel runs to more than 400 pages (with the second edition adding another 100 pages). A less grand but no less dramatic example of theoretical innovation can be found in the work of Tzvetan Todorov, a Bulgarian living in France at mid-century. Todorov cites the Russian formalist Víktor Shklovsky and the Anglo-American formalist, Henry James, as twin inspirations for a new theoretical approach that he will name "narratology." And in Barthes' work we can see the move from structuralism to deconstruction enacted over the course of a single career.

The supersessivist logic of Parts I through III moves novel theory into the social approaches to the novel that are collected in Parts IV through VIII. Part IV presents the turn to psychoanalysis as an early and influential attempt to apply the methods of deconstruction to social disciplines outside of literature and linguistics. Part V establishes the long-standing Marxist counter-tradition to formalism, structuralism, and deconstruction. Parts VI, VII, and VIII highlight the major post-Marxist approaches to the novel that arose in the 1980s as an answer to deconstruction. I devote more than half the volume to such relatively recent theories because these schools have not just dominated the last two decades of the twentieth century, but have carried over into the next. They provide the contemporary critic with the immediate context for novel studies today. The relationship of Parts VI through VIII is more synchronic than diachronic: one school of social theory did not oust the other, nor, for the most part, did they/do they spend much time engaging in acts of repudiation or critique. In my introductions to these three sections I suggest why these social theories are more interested in finding grounds of compatibility than defining themselves through contestation. In part the answer lies in the overwhelming unanimity of their shared political commitments. But the intellectual tradition that they have inherited has made argumentation itself, as an appeal to reason, something difficult to defend. These thinkers turn to social theory as a way beyond deconstruction, in other words, but at the heart of their enterprise is an engagement with the epistemological problems with which deconstruction has left them.

The large-scale developmental logic of the anthology's design will, I hope, allow readers who have time to spend with the volume as a whole to notice on a smaller scale how the field advances through its return to foundational texts, texts whose influence is felt across the century and within different schools. For example, we might fully expect that Jameson would locate his own Marxist theory of the novel in relation to founding fathers of Marxist literary studies such as Lukács and Walter Benjamin; but we might not have anticipated that he would credit two different kinds of formalists, Vladímir Propp and Northrop Frye, as enabling him to develop a better theory of how "ideological consciousness" gets represented in novels.[5] In the unit "Gender, Sexuality, and the Novel," Eve Sedgwick in one essay develops her theory of queer identity by returning us to James, and, in a different essay, works out her own theoretical position as a post-Marxist feminist through the insights of a novel theorist who is neither: René Girard.

Following out these inter-references, the expected and the unexpected, helps us constellate novel theory as a braid of traditions. But even as we strive to comprehend novel theory through narratives of development (explicit or implicit), even as we chart the progress of the field across the century, we also want to keep in play other types of connections – the diachronic development within each Part, for example. The century seems astonishingly short when we consider that some of the scholars included in this volume have been contributing to the field of novel theory for three or four decades. Booth's *The Rhetoric of Fiction* was first published in 1961. The second edition appeared in 1983. In between, his theory is refined in works such as *A Rhetoric of Irony* (1974) and *Critical Understanding: The Powers and Limits of Pluralism* (1979). His thinking continues to develop in *The Company We Keep: An Ethics of Fiction* (1988) – and, in one of those exciting and unexpected moments of inter-reference, Booth writes an important introduction to a new English translation of M. M. Bakhtin's *Problems of Dostoevsky's Poetics* (1984). Bakhtin himself ends up having what we might call the career of the century. A vital figure in Russian culture in the 1920s, Bakhtin faced political opposition that delayed the publication of his major work. Studies that he authored in the twenties and thirties were reissued (sometimes in revised editions) in Russia in the 1960s. Bakhtin's work enjoyed yet another afterlife when it was translated into English in the 1980s, exploding onto the Anglo-American scene and taking novel studies in what was regarded as a significantly new direction. In his introduction to *Problems of Dostoevsky's Poetics*, Booth credits Bakhtin for providing a "clear and deep" challenge to his own views about the novel, a challenge that prompts him to engage in a wholesale reconsideration of the philosophical premises that inform the work of the Chicago School.[6] Henry Louis Gates, embarking in 1988 on a project related to the new theoretical field of identity politics that could not be more different from Booth's in method and spirit, likewise finds Bakhtin's work to be formative to his thinking, so much so that he cites a passage from Bakhtin's "Discourse in the Novel" as an epigraph to the first chapter of *The Signifying Monkey* (1988). Although Bakhtin is a rough chronological contemporary of his fellow countryman Shklovsky, the complexity of Bakhtin's publication and reception history situate him within the development of novel theory as *both* an early- and a late-century novel theorist.

A survey works by being representative, which means that the dynamism and complexity of these careers can be suggested only through the supplementary biographical notes included in each section. For readers of this volume, the anthologized essays will come to stand for a certain "ism": formalism, Marxism, post-colonialism, etc. While the making of intellectual historical categories should never be too tidy, my selection of essays has been guided by the influence each has had in helping to bring these rubrics into being. Because it is one of the explicit goals of this anthology to clarify the tenets of these major schools of literary theory, I have deliberately selected essays that fulfill that representative function. I have gathered together what is generally regarded to be the most famous or influential work produced by a particular thinker, whatever direction his or her own career may have taken before or after writing that work. And in order to try to detail the complexity of a particular approach, I try in my introductions to each Part to stay as focused as possible on the works included in the volume – to refer to D.A. Miller, for example, only as the Foucauldian author of *The Novel and the Police* (1988) and not mention his earlier contribution to narrative studies (*Narrative and Its Discontents: Problems of Closure in the Traditional Novel*, 1981); his later book on Roland Barthes, the novel, and gay sexuality (*Bringing Out Roland Barthes*, 1992); or his recently published

DOROTHY HALE

study of Jane Austen's style (*Jane Austen: or The Secret of Style,* [2003]). Catherine Gallagher is presented as a feminist cultural historian, but in essays such as "Formalism and Time" (2000) she makes an important contribution to literary history. Peter Brooks, represented in this volume as a deconstructive psychoanalytic theorist, has, in works such as *Troubling Confessions: Speaking Guilt in Law and Literature* (2000), moved into the field of legal studies. Franco Moretti's presence is regrettably limited to a small selection from his recent *Atlas of the European Novel, 1800–1900* (1998); but one wants also to recognize not just early, groundbreaking studies such as *The Way of the World: The Bildungsroman in European Culture* (1987) and *Modern Epic* (1994), but, more recently, his role as general editor of the five-volume *Il romanzo* (2001), whose encyclopedic reach remaps the novel as a world phenomenon.

If an anthology that surveys a field must accept the selectivity that enables representativeness, it can more actively work against a different type of partiality. The interest in organizing a field through narratives of development – across the century, within a school, over a career – can blind us to an important fact of intellectual history: it is one thing for a theorist to be the object of critique and another for him or her to accept that critique. Each school of theory represented in this volume has its twenty-first-century practitioners. How does one persist as a narratologist in the face of deconstructive critique? In the same way, presumably, that one persists as a deconstructionist in the face of social and political critique. Or that one persists as a Marxist in the face of the infinitely postponed day of revolution. The interest of Parts V through IX of this volume thus lies in seeing the way founding approaches to literary theory are refurbished to preserve a school *as* a school, as well as in appreciating how foundational ideas are picked up and put to work on the behalf of emergent social theories. An especially powerful example of the latter case is Homi Bhabha's trumpeted recovery of deconstruction for the sake of post-colonial studies (*The Location of Culture,* 1993). Bhabha's important concept of hybridity arguably develops from a theoretical approach that is itself self-consciously hybrid, grafting an older definition of literature onto new thinking about the nation-state. But one wants to contrast this sort of staged return to and incorporation of past theoretical work to more immanent defenses of a theoretical school, defenses that are offered as a working through rather than a working beyond. Bhabha's embrace of deconstruction might be, for example, fruitfully compared to what we might call the renewal of vows undertaken by Barbara Johnson in *A World of Difference* (1987). Her aim is to show that deconstruction has always at its heart been a political theory, and that it can give us the best account of the politics of social identity, even if its political potential has been missed by interpreters who mistake deconstructive play for aestheticism.

One wants to appreciate, in other words, the persistence of certain schools across the century: the way, for example, Nancy Armstrong's "materialist" feminism sees itself carrying forward the work of Virginia Woolf (*Desire and Domestic Fiction* [1987], 622); or the way Garrett Stewart's theory of the conscripted reader moves reader response theory into the twenty-first century by addressing the major critiques that have been leveled at this school over the past three decades. I regret that limitations of space have prevented me from doing justice to recent developments in narratology, especially narratological projects that reach out in interesting ways to the topics of ideology and history in works such as *Gendered Interventions: Narrative Discourse in the Victorian Novel* (1989) by Robyn

Warhol; *Fictions of Authority: Women Writers and Narrative Voice* (1992) by Susan Sniader Lanser; *Narrative as Rhetoric: Technique, Audiences, Ethics, Ideology* (1996) by James Phelan; and *The Distinction of Fiction* (1999) by Dorrit Cohn.

I have concluded the volume with a unit on "Novel Readers" to highlight how novel theory moves forward through acts of return. In making this the volume's concluding section, I do not mean to imply that the novel reader is the culminating chapter in the narrative of how novel theory develops over the twentieth century. I do not mean to suggest, in other words, that novel theory has ended – or should end – here. On the contrary, the book chapters collected in this Part (none published earlier than 1974) are meant to remind us that the reader has never not been a category of investigation for novel theory. The end of the volume is thus an invitation to rethink the volume across schools, to connect this latest wave of work to the theories of the reader (both explicit and implicit) that have gone before.

I hope that the reader of this anthology will more generally come to understand the progress of novel theory by identifying its constants, to develop a sense of what changes in novel theory by appreciating what recurs. In addition to pointing out the acts of tradition-making engaged in by the theorists themselves, my introductions call attention to the persistence of key concepts that have not as yet been generally acknowledged as abiding preoccupations in the twentieth-century study of the novel. Perhaps the most dominant of these is what I call the novel's referential lure. Throughout the century, theorists who disagree with one another on just about everything else all agree that the novel's extraordinary mimeticism is at once seductive and unsettling – and that no understanding of the novel can be complete without taking this generic doubleness into account. The referential lure is, I show, at stake in Shklovsky's theory of defamiliariza-tion; Lubbock's valorization of "showing"; Todorov's notion of the grammatical subject; Barthes' analysis of the sign (and his application of that understanding to realist fiction); Barbara Johnson's account of narrative as an endless "fishing expedition"; J. Hillis Miller's understanding of the relation between story and discourse; Shoshana Felman's description of narrative as grounded in the psychology of "disavowal"; and D. A. Miller's conceptualization of the liberal subject as politically and psychically constituted by the false belief in self-presence.

Almost as pervasive as the referential lure is the more recognized problem of point of view. For James, the novel's capacity to present rich characterological consciousnesses is one of its most distinctive generic resources. Later theorists make it their project to work out the ethical consequences of this generic capacity. If one is allowed into the mind of a character, does one have a responsibility to understand that mind in a certain way? Should one sympathize, identify – or do such acts compromise the alterity of the other, overwriting all the qualities that make that consciousness different from one's self? Bakhtin believes that the novel can promote social understanding precisely by allowing its reader to inhabit points of view different from her own. But for someone like Stewart, the reader's felt experience of characterological identification produces not an expanded social perspective but self-division and alienation: the fact that points of view can only be inhabited through the act of novel reading means that such understanding is only fictional, produced by the particular practices of novel reading, which are marked by their difference from the social practices that guide our knowledge about people who exist outside of novels. For Marxists, the social effects of characterological point of view

DOROTHY HALE

are understood to be of major political importance. Jameson, for example, believes that James's valorization of novelistic point of view is itself a symptom of late capitalist ideology. On Jameson's view, James's infatuation with private consciousness actively fosters a repressive political ideology. Under capitalism, people are encouraged to imagine themselves not as the social and communal beings that they are, but as unique and isolated individuals. Jameson argues that this false ideology effectively masks the social, historical, and material realities that are the true source of social identity and political power, and thus serves as an effective tool for class domination.

In Jameson's case, the theoretical account of novelistic point of view dovetails with his understanding of the novel as a referential lure: the novel gives its reader a picture of the world, organized through individualized points of view that she mistakes for social reality. Shklovsky similarly sees the referential lure and point of view as mutually entailed, but, given the apoliticism of his own theoretical stance, he believes that the professional reader can escape the seduction of both: point of view is correctable and the referential lure is avoidable simply by right reading. Shklovsky advises the reader not to adopt the point of view of one character or another nor the point of view of one narratorial agent or another – but to resist the lure of fictional subjectivity altogether, taking on instead the impersonal point of view of the work itself.

Another issue that is never laid to rest, that intrigues thinkers at the end of the century as much as at the beginning, is the problem of the novel's unity. This problem is posed in different registers, in keeping with the different philosophical concerns of each theoretical school. For some, the novel's unity is a matter of achieved aesthetic power: can the novel be theorized as its own literary genre or is it instead distinguished by a discursive heterogeneity that is antithetical to high art forms? For the theorists who decide in favor of latter, the problem of unity reemerges as another sort of question: if the novel is indeed a discursive heterogeneity, can it perform cultural work that is itself unified in its social effects? The problem of whether unity can and should be imputed to the novel is a question that we find taken up in every unit, and by almost every theorist. Henry James famously tries to tame the Victorian baggy monster through the unifying effects of composition and style. If we fast-forward to the other end of the century, we find post-colonial critics arguing that the novel is distinguished as a literary form – in fact projects itself as form – due to its unique capacity for spatial effects. The novel reader's experience of text as space can unify, so these theorists argue, even the most multi-plotted or digressive of narratives. For members of the Chicago School, a particular novel finds its unity as form through its successful control over readerly emotion and ethical judgment. And we will be interested to note more generally how often in this volume the novel's unity is defined in terms of the philosophical truth it offers its reader, a truth that is defined differently by each school. For Bakhtin, the novel's unity lies in the ethical condition of achieved alterity. Lukács, Jameson, Armstrong, D. A. Miller, and Edward Said all stress the unity of the ideological mystification performed by the novel. Jane Tompkins believes that the novel can provide a unified "blueprint" for social reform. Girard finds in the novel a unified path out of self-blindness and into authentic self-awareness. Johnson, Felman, and J. Hillis Miller imagine this same dynamic as a unified process of oscillation: the novel moves its reader into insight only to return her to blindness – and then back again.

The referential lure, point of view, novelistic unity – when taken together, do these persistent topics of inquiry add up to a meta-issue that might lie at the heart of the theory of the novel? Perhaps so. One of the primary concerns of the theorists in this volume is how the seeming social heterogeneity achieved in the pages of high realist novels (most often cited are works by Jane Austen, Charles Dickens, Honoré de Balzac, George Eliot, and Leo Tolstoy) is covertly mediated by unifying value. Value is, of course, defined variously – semantically, ideologically, ethically, politically, rhetorically, formally, or psychoanalytically. Wolfgang Iser, for example, formulates the split between the novel's visible story world and the invisible operation of value as the tension between the ostensible empirical world represented by the novel and the hidden principles of selectivity that underlie this seemingly mimetic presentation. Iser rightly sees his theory as compatible with James's view of the novel as an indirect expression of authorial identity. For James, novel reading refers us back to the author, whose vision of life is sincerely represented through its successful manifestation as an independent social world. Felman's deconstructive reading of James leads her to argue that the seemingly independent life of fictional characters is an emblem of the blindness upon which any act of knowledge is built. The value that mediates the novelistic world is, for Felman, a philosophical truth about the epistemological inadequacy of reference – and yet also a confession of our psychological dependence upon reference, our inability to pursue truth claims without it.

I have already indicated how this meta-issue plays out in the Marxist tradition. The understanding of the novel world as a referential lure, covertly mediated by point of view, working in the service of a unified political effect, is characterized by Jameson as one of capitalism's most effective tools of ideological indoctrination. But as we bring this problematic forward for closer study, we will need to shade our sense of how it functions within Marxism more generally. By Lukács' lights, the mimetic world of the novel can be imagined as working on behalf of social reform. Lukács argues that a gifted realist like Balzac can expose the hegemonic operation of social power, its mediation of a life that is experienced as free or empirical, without being guilty of carrying forward this cultural indoctrination through the novelistic act of mediation. Balzac's depiction of a heterogeneous social world lends itself to a Marxist counter-vision of human identity; and his portrayal of characters as social types manifests this alternative scale of values within the world of the novel.

Other social approaches in this volume follow the Marxist tradition in theorizing the split between the story world the novel makes visible and the mediating value that it hides as a representational disjunction that has powerful political effects. Post-colonialists, for example, come down hard on a writer like Jane Austen. Her critique of pride and prejudice on the home front distracts attention from other social sins practiced abroad. The somewhere brought into being by her novel worlds, in other words, authorizes the English imperialism conducted elsewhere. But from the feminist perspective of Virginia Woolf, the story worlds of Jane Austen's novels are triumphs of female self-empowerment. Rather than succumbing to the ideology of her age, Austen, according to Woolf, possessed a mind that "consumed all impediments."[7] Austen's ability to create a story world that seems wholly autonomous, that provides no trace of the biographical author who conceived that world, is for Woolf a political act of revolution. Austen's mimetic achievement represents for Woolf nothing less than the liberation of the female author from patriarchal mediation. While the political stakes of these Marxist and post-Marxist social theories (hegemonic or subversive, repressive or liberating) may be all too familiar to anyone practicing literary criticism today, I show in my introductions how the particular – and unexpected – arguments made about the way value is manifested in and through novelistic form open a fresh area of inquiry for the theory of the novel.

Of course, in working out the larger significance of this or another potential meta-issue within the field, we need to keep in mind that, while all the essays in this anthology take novels as their primary literary examples, not all have equal stakes in theorizing the novel *as* a genre. We especially want to notice the different types of conceptual work performed by the terms novel, fiction, story, literature, narrative, story/discourse, text, writing, and social discourse. I hope my introductions make clear the different provenances of these terms – the deconstructive and then Foucauldian context for writing, for example, or the structural linguistic and then deconstructive context for narrative. Of course many of these terms have more than one provenance. Storytelling, for example, is the term used by the Marxist Walter Benjamin to denote a supremely human act of communication. But for the narratologist, story is wholly nonevaluative: it is simply the word used to designate a basic component of narrative structure. The term fiction similarly has a descriptive and prescriptive role to play in novel theory. On the one hand, it is the term of choice for formalist studies that present themselves as classificatory, as devoted to labeling the elements or techniques basic to any prose fiction, from a Hemingway vignette to *War and Peace*. On the other hand, fiction is the preferred term for political thinkers such as Armstrong, who believe that novels perform the cultural work of creating false ideology, specifically the grand illusion that human desire is "independent of political history" (*Desire*, 626). Peter Brooks uses fiction to express a more universal distrust of any knowledge claim: in his post-structuralist version of psychoanalysis, he finds any assertion of interpretative authority to be an act of fiction – the fiction that meaning is knowable.

Brooks's theory of knowledge leads him to rely on another key term, one that is of overwhelming importance not just to his project but the field as a whole: narrative. Narrative is the name he gives (along with Felman, Johnson, and Hillis Miller) to knowledge reconceived experientially, as a dynamic and temporal process. Structured by the desire to obtain meaning, what Brooks calls the desire for the end, narrative provides only temporary satisfactions. Meaning culminates – but never holds. With each collapse, the search for meaning is renewed. Brooks's psychoanalytic account of narrative derives as much from formalist and narratological studies of narrative as from Freudian and deconstructive accounts of desire. But in appropriating the term narrative from these formalist and narratological studies, Brooks takes a concept that had been derived as a neutral category of semiotic classification (to enable the cross-disciplinary study of narrative in fiction, poetry, nonfictional narrative, film, dance, comic strips, or any other media) and finds it to hold nothing less than the foundational structure of the human mind. We can see this logic replayed in Jameson's ambitious attempt to refurbish psychoanalytic concepts (such as the unconscious) for Marxist theory. He believes that narrative is not just one semiotic mode but the "the central function or *instance* of the human mind."[8] On his view, form equates with content: structural centrality is understood as human essence. In a move that brings us back to Benjamin, Jameson declares that "storytelling is the supreme function of the human mind." For Jameson, the human essence that is storytelling provides a justification for studying the novel as a socio-political form. In modernity, the central instance of the human mind manifests itself through the culturally significant invention and development of the novel as a genre.

The theorists in this volume who have the most to say about the novel as a genre are those who, like Jameson, define genre as essentially a sociohistorical phenomenon. Some of the formalists (such as Frye and some members of the Chicago School) are arguably exceptions to this trend, since their explicit inquiries into genre are conducted with minimal historicization. Yet we want to note that even their analytic approach to genre is less prescriptive (what a good novel should be) and more descriptive (how the novel as a genre has evolved as a form or evolved in relation to other literary forms), which is why some of these formalist theories of genre have been successfully incorporated into historical approaches (such as Jameson's). Especially from Part VI on, however, theorists tend to follow the Marxist example explicitly: to avoid theories of genre that smack of abstract synthesis and instead to pursue concrete historicization. The historical studies in Parts VI through VIII thus tend to focus on a particular cultural moment of novelistic production: the eighteenth-century English novel; the antebellum American novel; the twentieth-century African American novel; the advent of the female novelist in England.

With this move to historical specificity, there is in Parts VI through VIII a move away from the comparative study of national literatures. In the first half of the century, theorists routinely draw from the canon of European and Russian novels. Shklovsky and Bakhtin conduct readings of Lawrence Sterne and Charles Dickens (respectively) as well as Tolstoy and Dostoevsky. The English Lubbock is as interested in Tolstoy, Flaubert, and Balzac as he is in Samuel Richardson, William Thackeray, and Henry James. But although later sociohistorical approaches to the novel generally refrain from crossing national and period boundaries, there is one important exception to this trend. Interestingly, Lukács and Jameson, the Marxists who played such an influential role in encouraging literary studies to, in Jameson's words, "Always historicize," are themselves able to meet this goal while maintaining a comparativist perspective.[9] The practice of concrete historicization is not, for these thinkers, at all compromised by the opening of the historical field through national border-crossing. For both of these Marxists, the ideological homogenization that takes place under late capitalism unifies modernity and allows modernism to be studied as a unified field. The specific national responses to global change thus become the focus for comparative analysis: Lukács undertakes a study of European realism that includes novels from France and Russia; and Jameson's work brings together Emily Brontë, Balzac, Joseph Conrad, as well as writers in between.

Other non-Marxist thinkers in the volume share the view that modernity is defined by an epistemic shift. The difference between the modern and the nonmodern is thus unbreachable in a way that the differences among modern cultural productions are not. Girard notably holds this view of modernity; but he attributes the cause of this historical shift not to the rise of a particular mode of production, but, more generally, to the decline of monarchy and the advent of individualism. He thus treats as a unified field the novels of Miguel de Cervantes, Stendhal, Flaubert, Proust, and Dostoevsky in his study of the modern condition of triangular desire. For a thinker such as Bhabha, however, the same historical shift (the decline of monarchy and the rise of nationalism) produces a universal modern condition that, on his view, only has meaning through its specific historical manifestations, what he calls the locality of culture. The kind of reading that

Girard undertakes, one that treats novels as autonomous works of art, is thus an impossibility for Bhabha.

Bhabha's belief in the value of thick descriptions of cultural practices is shared by other thinkers in this volume, leading some to pursue what might be called the comparative study of social discourses. Tompkins, studying antebellum American fiction, and Armstrong, studying eighteenth-century British fiction, both believe that the cultural work performed by the novel is best understood when compared to that performed by conduct books and homemaker manuals. Gates conducts his study of the twentieth-century African American novel by turning, on the one hand, to African mythology and, on the other, to African American folklore. Gayatri Spivak exhorts us to investigate government files in order to understand the novel's relation to English imperialism. Gallagher believes that the emergence and development of the English novel can best be understood in relation to legal and economic changes that created new discourses about fiction, female identity, and the market.

It would have been possible to represent the shift to cultural history that begins in the 1980s by organizing the second half of this volume under the rubrics of different national traditions: Chinese, British, Russian, European, American, Anglophone, etc. While such a study of the novel would be interesting in its own way, I have instead chosen rubrics that allow for the investigation of important philosophical differences among sociohistorical approaches that in spirit seem so compatible, especially in their political views. The essays gathered together in "Post-Colonialism and the Novel," for example, deal exclusively with English cultural production – and it is precisely this common focus that enables subtle theoretical differences to come into focus. Spivak, Said, and Moretti all understand themselves as refining one another's insights; but when we examine closely, for example, Said's analysis of Austen and Spivak's reading of Charlotte Brontë, we find that there are huge differences in the conceptualization of ideology. These conceptual differences have significant ramifications for understanding the novel as an ideological agent not just within these three essays, and not just for our understanding of English imperialism, but for the field of post-colonial theory more generally.

In the anthology as a whole, the discussion of British fiction far outweighs that of any other national tradition. This directly reflects the profound engagement that theorists of all schools have had with the British novel. Said offers an historical explanation for the dominance of British fiction. He argues that the "steady rise and gradually undisputed dominance of the British novel" gave it global hegemony. As other nations developed their own novel tradition, they looked to the English novel as a model. On Said's view, the "eminence" of the British novel cannot be understood apart from English world power: the rise and fall of the hegemony of the English novel is directly related, he argues, to the rise and fall of English imperialism (*Culture*, 693). While other theorists may not agree with Said's political argument, an extraordinary number agree that the novel did in fact rise first in England – and that this historical fact in and of itself makes the British novel of central concern to novel studies more generally. Ian Watt's *The Rise of the Novel* (1957) helped popularize this view of the English novel. His title has been the basis of citation and/or revision ever since. Nina Baym echoes it in her chapter title "The Triumph of the Novel." Armstrong explicitly takes Watt to task in her *Desire and Domestic Fiction*. And Gallagher encourages us to better understand the rise of the novel by asking a related question: when did fiction arise as a popular cultural form?

The enduring theoretical interest in the rise of the British novel will, I hope, work heuristically for the reader of this anthology. The repeated citation of particular novels across the volume will allow those works to serve as tutor texts for many of the theories in this book. When we are looking to make comparisons across theoretical schools, it is useful to be able to put into relation, say, Spivak's post-colonial interpretation of *Frankenstein* and Stewart's reader-response analysis of the same novel. If one has read *Frankenstein* for oneself, these literary repetitions might carry additional power: one knows intimately which features of the novel are emphasized or omitted – and further knows how one's preestablished interpretation of the novel is overthrown or confirmed by these different approaches to the same novel. But at the risk of sounding perverse, I would also make a case for the heuristic value of reading theoretical accounts that focus on novels that one has never read for oneself. Theoretical claims can sometimes come more clearly into view when one has no particular stake in the novels under discussion. This is not, of course, to say that one should read theory instead of novels or to say that knowing the novels spoils theory. It is only to point out that both types of relation (knowing and not knowing a particular novel under discussion) have their value. It is also to encourage readers of the volume to accept the fact that doing theory is always a process of finding one's moorings: there will be ideas in each essay that inevitably elude one's understanding, especially on a first reading, and the reader of literary theory needs to find a way of charting these waters. This applies equally to readers who are new to the field and readers who make the field their research specialty. For those who become interested in novel theory, this volume is an invitation to read more. Some readers may, for example, want to investigate the philosophical texts that provide the background for much literary theory: Aristotle, Marx, Freud, Saussure, Lacan, Derrida, and Foucault – to mention the names cited most frequently in this volume. Other readers may want to deepen their knowledge of a particular school by reading more deeply within that school. And all of us, one hopes, will be left wanting to read more novels, perhaps in new ways.

I have been talking thus far as if the novel and theory inhabit separate realms, the literary and the logical, perhaps, or the artistic and the argumentative. But I want to make a case for the literary pleasure that many of the essays in this volume provide through their own acts of style. Such literary pleasure does not have one critical modality. It may be found, for example, in the dazzling originality of the close readings performed by Eve Sedgwick. Or it can lie in the high lucidity that Barbara Johnson and D. A. Miller bring to the most abstruse concepts. Roland Barthes might be counted a theorist of the literary pleasures of criticism – and his own narrative and stylistic experiments with the genre culminate in *S/Z* (1970), his masterwork of narrative theory which, precisely because of its literariness is, alas, unexcerptable. If Barthes gives literary criticism a new literary form, Franco Moretti, by contrast, cultivates a conversational style, the projection of an individualized voice whose charm lies in its wit and seeming informality. Or some readers may be moved by the highly wrought sentences of Felman, whose key terms accrue meaning through repetition, making theory inseparable from narrative. Felman's technique actually performs the conceptual relation between her two masters, wedding the theory of Lacan to the style of James. James, himself, of course, culminated his own novel career with the turn to theory. Although after writing the Prefaces for the New York edition of his work (the body of work that is credited with

DOROTHY HALE

inaugurating Anglo-American novel theory), he did return to fiction-writing, the Prefaces stand as the epitome of his late style (to some a crowning sublimity, to others, the apex of over-refinement and super-subtlety).

In my introductions I suggest that such acts of literary critical style have their own theoretical importance: they are conducted, in many cases, in accordance with a particular thinker's sense of the function of literary criticism – as description, persuasion, or signification; philosophy, history, aesthetics, or politics. But there is also a more immediate and direct point to be made about the power of literary critical style. The writers in this volume have earned their status as foundational figures in the field of novel theory not just because of their innovative and influential arguments but also because of their own abilities as writers. The rereading that is required to understand the full complexity of any of these thinkers is made attractive in part by the pleasure of reengaging with the style. This literariness allows me to press a point I have already made: that such theory is most fully understood through close reading.

To display theoretical argument in all of its complexity, I have made every attempt to include in this volume book chapters or free-standing essays that are either unedited or very lightly edited. In this regard, the selections in this volume contrast with the sound-bite approach to literary theory, the belief that schools of thought can be understood through a brief excerpt, chosen to highlight a major concept. In my own experience with theory, I could no more understand, say, James's notion of the house of fiction by reading only the passage from the Prefaces in which he defines that idea than I could understand *The Portrait of a Lady* by reading only chapter 42. A theory comes philosophically alive when we see a thinker working it out, when we can see an argument develop narratively, across a chapter and through a book as a whole. Is a key idea formulated and then dropped? Does it accrue new meaning as it is applied? Do other ideas seem to mitigate its truth value or even to contradict its claims?

I have attempted to pose such questions consistently and fairly across the volume. In my discussion of each essay, I try to draw out the major thesis claims and to identify what is particularly innovative, controversial, and influential about the argument as a whole. By working out the developmental logic of each argument, I show how these essays actively *generate* the rubrics by which they came to be known. For the thinkers gathered here, the affiliation with a certain approach to the novel is a starting point rather than an end point for theoretical inquiry. Belonging to a theoretical school doesn't provide them with prefabricated answers, with a conceptual grid through which any particular novel can be processed. On the contrary, affiliation with a certain theoretical tradition is a means of generating important new questions about the novel, as well as a way of looking for new answers.

Part of what it means to keep open the dynamism of novel theory is to appreciate the ideas that have been taken from the field. Terms such as defamiliarization, triangular desire, and double voice have become clichés of academic parlance. Indeed, they have appealed to the popular imagination to the point where they enjoy an intellectual life outside the academy. We can find them routinely deployed in journalism and other popular discourses. I call these ideas the portable concepts of novel theory. They may have begun as applied concepts within literary study, but now, even in academic settings, the use of portable concepts may or may not be guided by the original meaning given to the term (in these examples the meaning given by, respectively, Shklovsky, Girard, and

Bakhtin). To study the origin of these concepts, to recapture them as conceptual problematics, does not mean that all later usages should be dismissed as misappropriations. On the contrary, knowing what, say, Shklovsky did and did not mean by defamiliarization puts us in a better position to understand how the act of application can result in theoretical permutation.

I am acutely aware that the kind of analysis that I offer in this volume is not itself a neutral endeavor – nor would I want it to be. My introductions are themselves arguments, attempts at persuasion. The stakes are higher at some moments than others. There are some thinkers that I especially admire and therefore want you to admire, too, preferably in the same way. There are others whose lapses in logic frustrate me – and others whose lapses in logic strike me as a theoretical tour de force. These investments will no doubt be clearer to my reader than to myself – and I hope they will be a spur to dialogue, a way of encouraging debate that will further enrich our understanding of the double problematic: novel theory. This anthology is not, despite its headstone dates (1900–2000), a memorial to twentieth-century novel theory. If I have done my job, this anthology will be one of the ways that novel theory gets carried forward into the twenty-first century, introducing readers of a new generation to these foundational texts.

NOTES

1 György Lukács, *The Theory of the Novel*, trans. Anna Bostock (1920; Cambridge, MA: MIT Press, 1971) 14, 17.
2 Percy Lubbock, *The Craft of Fiction* (London: Jonathan Cape, 1921) 9.
3 Roland Barthes, "Introduction to the Structural Analysis of Narratives" (1966), *Image-Music-Text*, ed. and trans. Stephen Heath (New York: Hill and Wang, 1977) 81.
4 Lubbock, *The Craft of Fiction* 11.
5 Fredric Jameson, *The Political Unconscious: Narrative as a Socially Symbolic Act* (Ithaca, NY: Cornell University Press, 1981) 47.
6 Wayne C. Booth, introduction, *Problems of Dostoevsky's Poetics*, by Mikhail Bakhtin, ed. and trans. Caryl Emerson, Theory and History of Literature, vol. 8 (Minneapolis: Minnesota University Press 1984) xxiv.
7 Virginia Woolf, *A Room of One's Own* (1929; New York: Harcourt Brace Jovanovich, 1957) 73.
8 Jameson, *The Political Unconscious* 13, 123.
9 Ibid. 9.

Form and Functio

Introduction

What distinguishes the novel as a literary form? It is not just the asking of this question that makes thinkers like Víktor Shklovsky and Percy Lubbock "formalists"; it is their shared belief that literary form should be studied as an autonomous entity, able to be isolated from social, political, and historical contexts. For Russian and Anglo-American formalists, form is an aesthetic property intrinsic to, and therefore varying among, literary genres. To ask what distinguishes the novel as a literary form thus already implies what was, at the beginning of the twentieth century, a controversial claim about the novel: that the novel should be considered neither a "baggy monster" (to use Henry James's phrase) nor disposable entertainment for the masses, but an art form with compositional strategies all its own. Accompanying this new confidence in the novel as a serious aesthetic accomplishment are new serious methods of studying the novel. By devoting unprecedented close attention to the narrative technique of individual novels, formalists seek to unearth what had so far been hidden from view: that novels are (or should be) more than exciting stories or even accurate pictures of life; novels are strategically composed works of art whose formal complexity and importance rival the aesthetic achievement of epic, drama, and the lyric as well as that of fine arts such as painting, sculpture, and music.

The belief that the art of the novel can be discussed and evaluated only after its narrative techniques or "devices" have been identified and enumerated launches novel theory into an Adamic ecstasy of naming. The first thing to notice about the essays in

DOROTHY HALE

this section is how many terms they coin, how the novel's particular literary form seems to require a new literary-critical vocabulary. The aesthetics of the novel have been missed, it seems, not because the novel isn't an aesthetic form, but because critical language derived from other literary genres can't register the novel's distinguishing formal features. James's Prefaces to the New York edition of his work (1907–9) offer plain-speech terms like "picture," "scene," and "center of consciousness" to describe the compositional effects he most valued. This rough vocabulary only whets the appetite of Percy Lubbock, James's most influential follower, who almost twenty years later is driven to write *The Craft of Fiction* (1921) because of his felt "want of a received nomenclature" (90) in the Anglo-American study of fiction. The Russian tradition derives its classificatory practice from a scientific paradigm that would have been anathema to James and Lubbock; but the catalogues generated by Vladímir Propp and Shklovsky are, like the work of the Anglo-Americans, derived from the text-based, empirical examination of specific novels and actual narrative practices.

The terms and grounds of this compatibility, however, should in no way be taken for granted: one of the interests in studying the formalist roots of novel theory is to gauge the conceptual cross-hatching of aesthetic positions that derives from such different intellectual and historical traditions. Although the cross-fertilization of the Russian and Anglo-American traditions is apparent in the theorists' overlapping sense of a novel canon (James quotes Turgenev, Tolstoy is a major figure for Lubbock, and Shklovsky has chapters on Dickens as well as Sterne), there is no evidence that Shklovsky read James's Prefaces (even though he does refer to William James's theory of the emotions) – and even if Shklovsky had read Henry James, he no doubt would have considered their projects far removed from one another. Shklovsky initiates his work on prose fiction in reaction to the poetic experiments being undertaken in Russia at the time, particularly those conducted by the symbolist and futurist poets. His preface to the *Theory of Prose* (1925) makes a bold and controversial statement, one that he will feel obliged to retract in 1930 under Stalinism: "As a literary critic, I've been engaged in the study of the internal laws that govern literature. If I may bring up the analogy of a factory, then I would say that neither the current state of the world cotton market nor the politics of cotton trusts interests me. One thing alone concerns me: the number of strands that make up the cotton plant and the different ways of weaving them."[1]

Whatever the long-term political ramifications of such inflammatory functionalism, Shklovsky's desire to isolate literature from the social world is in fact problematized more immediately by the internal logic of his own argument. In "Art as Technique," an essay that would become the first chapter of *Theory of Prose*, he implicitly establishes the difference between cotton and poetry by asserting the vital human value of literature. According to Shklovsky, literature restores the primacy and vivacity of human perception – and thus makes life worth living. Arguing against influential Russian scholars of the time who, in their own attempt to define the essence of literary language, declare poetry to be "a special way of thinking…precisely, a way of thinking in images," Shklovsky believes that to think in images is in fact not to think at all: poetic images function as symbols; symbols, he believes, express perception that has been robbed of its primacy by becoming habitual, and thus abstract.[2] Whereas his contemporaries praise poetic expression for its "economy," Shklovsky believes that such condensations of thought and expression in fact attenuate life itself. The "algebraic" substitution of symbols for things ultimately fosters a pernicious false knowledge: the partial representation of objects by their salient characteristics (rather than in their full complexity). As he dramatically puts it,

> Habitualization devours works, clothes, furniture, one's wife, and the fear of war... [A]rt exists that one may recover the sensation of life; it exists to make one feel things, to make the stone *stony.* The purpose of art is to impart the sensation of things as they are perceived and not as they are known. The technique of art is to make objects "unfamiliar," to make forms difficult, to increase the difficulty and length of perception because the process of perception is an aesthetic end in itself and must be prolonged. *Art is a way of experiencing the artfulness of an object; the object is not important.*[3]

This crux passage introduces the theoretical concept that has perhaps been Shklovsky's most portable and enduring legacy: the idea of defamiliarization. But although defamiliarization (meaning simply that the familiar has suddenly been made strange) is now a standard vocabulary word in literary study, scholars have never ceased to be perplexed by the logical tensions expressed in this passage. If art exists to restore perception, to make us perceive the stone's essential "stoniness," then what relation does the object's intrinsic identity have to the "artfulness" bestowed upon it through representation? Is the object unimportant, in other words, because no object is too trivial not to be worth restoring? (On this view, stones, clothes, one's wife, and the fear of war are all equatable because all are elemental to human life.) Or is the object unimportant because artistic representation supersedes the real-world importance (or triviality) of the thing it depicts? (On this view, the practice of art bestows significance, even on so lowly an object as a stone.) One may further feel that Shklovsky is trying to have it both ways when he describes perception as "an aesthetic end in itself" without taking into full account the profound real-life consequences he has in fact attributed to defamiliarized perception.

We can see in Shklovsky's reading of *Tristram Shandy* how literary defamiliarization has certain consequences for our understanding of wives, wars, and the perception of life more generally – and why for Shklovsky the novel is the literary genre best suited to the sustained practice of defamiliarization. Shklovsky argues that, on the one hand, Sterne employs defamiliarization to teach the reader something about the normative social values that produce her vision of the "natural" world: according to Shklovsky, Sterne's verbal practices of euphemism and erotic double entendre, for example, draw attention to the "normal" names for body parts (and the conventional social values those names imply) by denaturalizing these names. On the other hand, Sterne defamiliarizes the novel itself by exposing the "artificiality" and literary conventionality of the plot devices that structure the story world. He thus forces the reader to see how she has naturalized the novel as a genre by attending to its realist content and ignoring its antirealist formal practices. Sterne makes it impossible to read through literary form; and he does this by juxtaposing the "realist" logic that governs the story world with the "literary" logic that governs all novelistic representation. If characters in a novel live in a world where causes precede effects, where space is mapable and time chronological, where people come to know one another through shared social decorum, readers of *Tristram Shandy* find that novelistic plot structures operate by different laws. Sterne's narration puts effect before cause, willfully expands and contracts time, plays with Euclidian space, and overthrows the social conventions that regulate interpersonal intimacy in "real life." For Shklovsky, Sterne's flamboyant disruption of the story world is not a novelistic anomaly; on the contrary, it is a vivid display of the normative operation of all prose fiction: "*Tristram Shandy*," Shklovsky (with deliberate perversity) declares, "is the most typical novel in world literature" (52).

But if the highlighted difference in Sterne's novel between story world and plot structure exposes the "device," makes palpable to the reader the alternative logic governing literary form, for Shklovsky it also throws into question the normative categories that govern life in the story world. Sterne's outlandish narrative practices, his refusal to let his story world be taken as an unmediated referent, defamiliarize the conventional assumption that narrative can be neatly divided into content and form: *Tristram Shandy* allows the reader to reconceptualize the relation between story and narrative technique, representational content and representational form, as a dynamic, complex, and, above all, performative relationship. The reader cannot read the novel without normative expectations about the life it seems to depict – and the function of plot is to disrupt those conventions even as its story world invokes them. The story world is thus not what the novel is "about"; it is one element in a process, the referential lure, the "familiar," whose defamiliarization through the novel's literary techniques leads the reader to see how thoroughly his habits of perception have constructed his world – which he then mistakes for natural.

The logical tension that attends Shklovsky's theorization of the "stoniness of the stone" thus carries over to his conceptualization of the "literariness" of the literary work. On the one hand, defamiliarization is a readerly effect, an overturning of readerly habits of interpretation that yields a new perception of reality. But on the other hand, defamiliarization teaches the reader something new about the novel itself: that as an art form it is governed by laws different from those of the social world. Although a theory that emphasizes the reader's restored perception of "life" might ultimately have more to say about the political and ethical dimensions of "habituation," Shklovsky instead emphasizes perception's function within the art work as "an aesthetic end in itself." In keeping with his interest in "the number of strands that make up the cotton plant and the different ways of weaving them," he studies an art work only to see how it works: to understand the interrelation of the literary properties internal to it. To his mind, the analysis of the art work's internal functioning has nothing to do with "interpretation"; he is not concerned with what the novel might mean or how it might communicate. He does not, in other words, analyze individual novels for either thematic or symbolic meaning. Instead he strives to give a purely descriptive account of the "strands of the plant," the parts of the literary whole.

Shklovsky thus attenuates his account of readerly perception by focusing on its functional position as a part of the literary whole. And we can see in his opinions about other types of reader response how strictly Shklvosky construes "restored perception" as a response that leads the reader back to the literary text and not off into the social world. Restored perception is qualitatively different, on this view, from any emotional response a reader might have to the events in the story world. Shklovsky notes approvingly, for example, that "For Sterne, the death of Bobby Shandy is chiefly motivation for expansion of the material [i.e. the technique]" (45). If art restores perception to the reader, then this does not mean for Shklovsky that art produces emotion: in one of his most extreme formulations he declares that "Art…is unsympathetic – or beyond sympathy…In discussing such emotion we have to examine it from the point of view of the composition itself, in exactly the same way that a mechanic must examine a driving belt to understand the details of a machine; he certainly would not study the driving belt as if he were a vegetarian" (43). In this rejection of readerly affective response, we see Shklovsky's abiding valorization of the intrinsic identity of the object of perception. On this view the readerly emotion inspired by the story world is itself part of the novel's literary function, a drive belt that helps the novel as an art work to work. To understand this emotion in any other way is, for Shklovsky, to misunderstand it. The right perception of the art work thus is always only immanent and impersonal, "from the point of view of the composition itself." To see it from a different point view is to not see it at all – as is implied by the mechanic who adopts the perspective of the machine itself rather than that of a "vegetarian." This notion of a closed and integrated functionality allows Shklovsky to claim that the artfulness of the art object lies wholly in its composition or form: "awareness of form constitutes the subject matter of the novel" (34), he declares, as well as that "The story is, in fact, only material for plot formation" (52). To be moved by the art object would mean that the reader had mistaken its functional purpose, was in fact distorting this purpose by attending too naively to the action of the story world: an emotional response to the story world would mean that the reader had failed to respond to defamiliarization and therefore wrongly imagined that the literary work required a human response to a story about other human beings.

As the example of the driving belt emphasizes, Shklovsky's definition of the literariness of prose fiction is one based upon the elemental or basic operations of storytelling. For Shklovsky, Sterne is not revolutionary because he has invented something new; rather he is revolutionary in making visible the literariness of the novel's covert literariness, a complexity which for Shklovsky works more quietly in the ordinary narrative practices of any novel. Although Shklovsky implies that Sterne's self-consciousness adds to the power of his achievement, Shklovsky's notion of the literary is based upon a functionality in which neither artistic genius nor authorial intention plays any part. For these reasons, Shklovsky's theory of literature inspired other formalists to study narrative texts that traditionally have been considered beneath scholarly notice. Shklovsky's theory of prose fiction thus helped to elevate the novel to a high art form by enabling readers to see the novel's literariness, to see that it had a form; but it simultaneously weakened the concept of high art by finding formal complexity in just about any narrative performance. Since the greatness of *Tristram Shandy* lies not in its exceptionalism but in its typicality, then why shouldn't typicality itself become a positive literary value? Scholars who believed that it should and could turned their attention not only to works of art that had been dismissed precisely on the grounds of their unoriginality but also to extraliterary narrative modes such as journalism, history, and autobiography.

The belief that subliterary genres could have complex narrative forms is one inspiration folklorist Vladímir Propp took from Shklovsky's work. If Shklovsky could uncover the underlying literary laws that gave order to the surface chaos of Sterne's novel, and if he could further speculate about the common plot elements that unite all novels, then

Propp believed a similar method could work for the study of folk tales, whose multi-formity seemed overwhelming to the empirical researcher. Propp breaks down the chaotic archive of the Russian fairy tale into a typology that includes seven large spheres of action (performed by the dramatis personae) and thirty-one subcategories. He is able to achieve such a streamlined system of classification because, he believes, the wide differences in the story's "content" are simply differences in detail, epiphenomena that prevent the common generic identity of these tales from being readily grasped. Past researchers have been led astray, he maintains, in part because they have paid too much attention to the proliferation and variability of dramatis personae; his method looks past this superficial difference (the difference, say, between an old man and a princess as protagonists) to examine the actions these characters perform – and he finds astonishing uniformity in tales that otherwise might seem uncomparable.

Like Shklovsky's theory of plot, Propp's *Morphology* of the fairy-tale form begins with the conviction that form is essentially active. In answer to the question "how many functions are known to the tale?"(55), Propp interestingly defines a specific tale's function as a subset of a larger functional unit. Reading each individual tale in relation to the larger body of folk tales, Propp expresses this dynamic concept of form through the analogy of an extended sentence: the "functions" of any particular tale operate as parts of speech by virtue of the larger grammar of fairy tales that Propp's synthetic study has decoded. Propp's belief that this grammar is "dictated by the tale itself" (58) – that the grammar of the fairy tale is a closed set, isolated from social context and legible through a representational logic intrinsic to this set – thus resonates with Shklovsky's desire to understand art intrinsically, from "the point of view of the composition itself." But for Propp this intrinsic functionality is illegible if one were to try to derive it from a single text. The functions of any particular folk tale are noticeable only when detected as repetitions within an intertextual pattern. The formal similarities among individual folk tales thus reveal to the analyst the grammar of the folk tale, a structure that in turn makes legible the salient formal elements of each tale. But we can quickly see in Propp's need to consider the "double morphological meaning of a single function" (60) how the tale's intrinsic "dictation" of function might contain a certain latitude for interpretation: if the model can be complicated so a single function can serve two morphological meanings, why not three or four or more? The introduction of such complexity also suggests that two different decoders might disagree not only about how many functions are being performed but what exactly these functions might be. And yet such potential for interpretive disagreement does not enter Propp's theory – and so we cannot look to him to find a way of resolving potential debates about morphological meaning.

Whereas for Shklovsky the readerly experience of defamiliarization leads to the study of literature in its own terms, from the point of view of the composition itself, for Propp readerly subjectivity simply plays no part. Functions are unambiguous, interpretation is not required, and readers/anthropologists come to the literary text with a seemingly natural capacity for impersonality. And for Shklovsky as for Propp, within the story world "character" is not a privileged locus of human experience; it is a literary (Shklovsky) or grammatical (Propp) property, the function of which distinguishes one kind of textual practice from another and thus becomes the basis of generic (rather than human) identity. If anything, the apparent individuality of characters is a snare of the story world that each theorist learns to read through. For Shklovsky characters function as referential lures, familiarisms whose mimeticism is integral to the ultimate disruption of social habit performed by narrative structure. For Propp, the apparent heterogeneity and diversity of folkloric characters is accidental or superficial, but in either case insignificant to the common sets of *actions* they perform, actions that for Propp define their identity as functional elements in the larger grammar of the folk tale. As we will see more fully in Part III of this anthology, the Russian formalists' defamiliarization of character will later in the century be picked up by structuralists and contribute to a sweeping, post-humanist reconceptualization of personhood itself. What are the habits of thought about persons that are broken by the disruption of characterological mimeticism by narrative laws? If literary characters are defined by their position within a linguistic structure, and if that position is more important to identity than a name, gender, or occupation, then might the same be true for real persons?

Perhaps the most profound distinction between early Russian and early Anglo-American formalism lies in the treatment of subjective agents. The Jamesian formalist tradition places the representation of consciousness – and ultimately the problem of point of view – at the heart of novel studies. For James the novel is first and foremost a representation of the author's sensibility, his "vision of life." And at times it seems that this is the only quality James requires the novel to possess. In an early essay called "The Art of Fiction" (1888), James argues against an English contemporary, Walter Besant, who believes the "laws of fiction may be laid down and taught with as much precision and exactness as the laws of harmony, perspective, and proportion."[4] James insists instead that there are no laws of fiction, other than the grounding imperative that the novel be true to "life": "the only reason for the existence of a novel is that it does attempt to represent life."[5] This represented life is necessarily mediated for James by authorial consciousness: "A novel is in its broadest definition a personal, a direct impression of life."[6]

In an odd way, James and Shklovsky thus both imagine the same origin for prose fiction: human perception. But whereas Shklovsky's notion of human perception is essentially social, grounded in norms established through the shared experience of habituation, James thinks of perception as radically individualistic, based in his belief that each person's "impression of life" is unique. To invoke one of James's most famous figures from the Prefaces, each viewer in the house of fiction looks out onto the same scene, but they enjoy entirely different prospects: "one seeing more where the other sees less, one seeing black where the other sees white" (*Portrait* Preface, 69). For Shklovsky, habituated perception is a universal social condition, one that is worked through and ultimately resisted through the help of literature and its practice of defamiliarization; for James, the individual can resist conformity independently through the practice of authentic self-reference, the attempt to be true to one's own private sensibility, whether one writes a novel or not. And because the novel's only purpose is to express this unique sensibility, then, as James declares in his letter to the students at Deerfield Academy, "Any point of view is interesting that is a direct impression of life."[7] For James it is thus the authentic expression of unique individual experience that becomes not only the defining indication of the author's character – the amount of "felt life" of which he is capable – but also the sole imperative for the writing of fiction. In "The Art of Fiction" James declares, "But the only condition that I can think of attaching to the composition of the novel is…that it be sincere."[8]

"Sincere" perception resembles defamiliarized perception in that both are opposed to a conventionalized way of regarding "life." But if conventionalized thinking and feeling are anathema to James, the achievement of sincere experience is also a source of artistic difficulty – a happy problem about life that the novel's form can happily appear to solve. For James, sincere experience entails perceptual abundance: individual "experience is never limited, and it is never complete; it is an immense sensibility, a kind of huge spider-web of the finest silken threads suspended in the chamber of consciousness, and catching every air-borne particle in its tissue."[9] For James, literary form is the answer to this perceptual plentitude; the artist can compose his sensibility through the practice of art – and one of his most artful practices is to impose a limit upon experience without seeming to do so. As he puts it in his first Preface, the Preface to *Roderick Hudson*, "Really, universally, relations stop nowhere, and the exquisite problem of the artist is eternally but to draw, by a geometry of his own, the circle within which they shall happily *appear* to do so."[10] Thus, although James posits a model of the relation between story and structure that is more cooperative than Shklovsky's ("the story and the novel, the idea and the form, are the needle and the thread"[11]), the novel is in its very essence distinguished from life by having a compositional form – and for James the degree to which a novelist can successfully delimit the life he depicts is the degree to which he turns his vision of life into a work of art: "the painter of life...wishes both to treat his chosen subject and to confine his necessary picture. It is only by doing such things that art becomes exquisite, and it is only by positively becoming exquisite that it keeps clear of becoming vulgar."[12] James repeats this point in his Preface to *The Ambassadors*: "One's work should have composition, because composition alone is positive beauty" (*Ambassadors* Preface, 82). James's radical mimeticism, his belief that fiction's only charge is to represent an individual's sincere impression of life, is thus tempered by the practical necessity and aesthetic value of achieved literary composition.

When James discusses composition, then, a set of rules for fiction writers is the last thing on his mind. Composition is most frequently described in the Prefaces as the disciplined confinement of unfurling authorial sensibility to the productively "tight place" of fictional form. Fittingly, James's primary metaphor for the novelist is one that denotes spatial restriction: the portrait- or picture-painter. As a novelist, James thus strives to invent narrative techniques that will seem to spatialize writing, that will promote the illusion of the novel's plastic or organic integrity. By successfully creating the illusion that individual experience is encompassable, novels can also promote the illusion of their own representational economy, a symbiosis of internal elements in which all parts contribute to the whole. For example, James writes in the Preface to *The Ambassadors* that he is disinclined to use first-person narration purely for reasons of representational economy: it foredooms the novel to a "looseness" of self-revelation and thus "wastes" point of view as a potential element of literary form. James vastly prefers third-person narration because it promotes the illusion of formal integrity and representational economy. Third-person narration avoids the first-person narrator's unanchored commentary upon the story world by making such descriptions functions of the story world itself: background description or exposition thus unites form and content by carrying the added value of character revelation. The novel thereby accomplishes a representational efficiency that will enable it to seem fully composed, the needle and the thread working as one. James thus approvingly describes Lambert

Strether as "encaged and provided for" by third-person narration (*Ambassadors* Preface, 83). If James can create the illusion that Strether's consciousness is in fact a point of view, a sensibility delimited by its own immanent identity (the view), then this compositional technique can help the novelist succeed first of all in seeming "to draw the circle" around the "spider-web" of sensibility; and second of all in making consciousness seem solid enough (a point) to enhance the novel's goal of illusionary spatialization.

As we can see in this example, James's passion for economy can make him sound if not exactly exploitative then at least utilitarian in regard to the characters that he creates – and this kind of functionalism can seem at odds with the subjective primacy he bestows upon these beings in his actual novels. To the degree that James wants us to be moved by Lambert Strether's moral choices and complex consciousness, in other words, we may object to James's dehumanized description of him in the Preface as "encaged and provided for." Similarly, we might balk at the description of Isabel Archer as a "precious object…all curiously at [her author's] disposal" (*Portrait* Preface, 70) – however breath-taking it might be also to consider her the "corner-stone" of a novel whose structure is so vast and palpable that it compels James to think of it not just as portraiture but as inhabitable architecture. While James thus diminishes the subjectivity of his characters by theorizing them as compositional elements (and the concept of the *ficelle*[13] is precisely invented to describe certain characters as pure formal necessities), this theor-etical position is complicated by the real alterity – the subjective autonomy and otherness – he also feels his characters possess. As he says of Christopher Newman, "the interest of everything is all that it is *his* vision, *his* conception, *his* interpretation: at the window of his wide, quite sufficiently wide, consciousness we are seated, from that admirable position we 'assist.' He therefore supremely matters; all the rest matters only as he feels it, treats it, meets it."[14] James's sense of his characters' alterity is so strong that he more often than not describes the creative process as hinging on the imaginative appearance of a character whose complexities of sensibility and character "impose" upon the author the rest of the story. The person who can so magnanimously express his own vision of life through the realization of another's point of view seems at odds with the artist who finds point of view a convenient way of establishing a compositional "center" to unify his work of art.

In writing the Prefaces to the New York edition of his work, James did not sit down with the intention to invent a theory of fiction – and one of the interests of reading a Preface is to understand it as a narrative performance, to see how meditations upon the problems of technique emerge through the genre of authorial autobiography. James's disciple, Percy Lubbock, is more eager to systematize James's insights, and he begins by trying to put the problem of literary form on a philosophical footing, a philosophy that is grounded in his own empirical experience as a novel reader. This experience is, according to Lubbock, fundamentally double: novels are "objects, yes, completed and detached, but I recall them also as tracts of time during which Clarissa and Anna moved and lived and endured in my view… [A] critic seems to shift from this one to that, from the thing carved in the stuff of thought to the passing movement of life" (*Craft*, 87). The work of *The Craft of Fiction* is to make visible the novel as object, the solid form underlying the genre's evanescent representation of "life." And although Lubbock's notion of novelistic structure is fundamentally different from Shklovsky's, Lubbock is closer to Shklovsky than to James in positing an adversarial relation between "story" and

DOROTHY HALE

"form." For Lubbock, lifelike characters are not ruses or snares; they are integral to the novel's aim to represent life. But for all of its human value, the mimetic power of fiction does distract us, according to Lubbock, from the authentic grounds of its artistry. The novel is, he contends, not just a "piece of life"; it is a work of art – and it is the goal of *The Craft of Fiction* to theorize the particular kind of materiality that distinguishes the art as work. For Lubbock, the "devices" (89) of novelistic composition are what bestow "shape" upon the life that the novel represents (87); "many different substances, as distinct to the practised eye as stone and wood, go to the making of a novel" (89). Once the reader is properly trained to recognize the compositional techniques that give form to the novel, he becomes the co-constructor of the novel: "He must know how to handle the stuff which is continually forming in his mind while he reads; he must be able to recognize its fine variations and take them into account" (89). While Shklovsky's paradigmatic novel reader is a receiver of literary effects, is continually upset or thrown off balance by defamiliarization, Lubbock's paradigmatic reader is a producer of literary form: "the man of letters is a craftsman and the critic cannot be less" (89).

Lubbock's conception of the reader thus grants her more constructive power than Shklovsky's; but in other ways the Lubbockian reader seems strangely hollow. Lacking the socialization (through habitualization) of Shklovsky's reader, the Lubbockian reader possesses no identity other than that conferred upon him as a novel reader. In assuming the role of novelistic craftsman, the Lubbockian reader divests himself of all other subjective or social identities. Lubbock's initial theorization of the reader as the author's equal and partner turns into an altogether stranger notion: the reader's empty and receptive consciousness becomes for Lubbock the productive medium for the instanti-ation of literary form. The abstract activity of linguistic representation is, as Lubbock describes it, made material through the reader's imagination. And once granted this substantiality, fiction can prove itself equal to the formal accomplishments of any of the other plastic arts.

Throughout *The Craft of Fiction* we see Lubbock struggling with the problem of how to make the subjective objective, how to imagine not just an "author's vision" as material-ized through an art object but more particularly how to restrict the content of subjective identity, be it authorial, readerly, or characterological. Lubbock's belief that "The whole intricate question of method, in the craft of fiction [is] governed by the question of the point of view" (*Craft*, 91) shows how vital the problem of subjectivity is to his theoriza-tion of the novel as an art object. Unlike James, who could object to first-person narration on practical and aesthetic grounds of formal economy, Lubbock finds himself philosophically opposed to any "visible" subjective mediation of the novelistic world, arguing that it prevents the novel from cohering as an *objective* form. For Lubbock, the novel does not create the "appearance" of objectifiable sensibility, but actually creates characters whose autonomous consciousnesses possess the formal integrity of objects. Although he pays lip-service to James in saying that there are many "proper" methods for writing fiction and the choice depends upon the author's goals, his own analysis of point of view betrays his belief that one method is clearly superior: the technique of "oblique," third-person point of view perfected by James and other modernists. Lubbock prefers this technique because it diminishes the felt presence of an authorial "voice" (94). Used properly, oblique point of view diminishes the subjectivity of the narrating agent to the point where it can seem to represent the novelistic world wholly impersonally – and thus (on Lubbock's view) truly materially. We thus have formulated by Lubbock – not by James – the invidious distinction between showing and telling. James's aesthetic suggestion that the novelist "dramatize, dramatize" becomes Lubbock's ontological insistence that narrators always show and never "report" (95), that narration mask its subjective origins, transforming the individuality implied by narrative voice into the objectively visible world of the novel.

Lubbock's attempt to place James's study of form on a more rigorous philosophical and technical footing thus ultimately turns James's ideas about the novel upside down. Lubbock's objectivism effectively eliminates what for James was the novel's only generic imperative – that it represent the author's unique sensibility, his subjective vision of life. It is thus perhaps not surprising that *The Craft of Fiction* also opens the way for the rule-bound approach to fiction that James himself rejected. And if Lubbock uses the metaphor of "craft" as a halfway house between individualized artistic performance and universalizable standards of technical accomplishment, we can also see in Lubbock's objectivism an inclination that is not wholly incompatible with the Russian formalists. This movement towards scientific classification and systematization develops within the Anglo-American tradition to find explicit expression later in the century in the work of Northrop Frye. In his "Polemical Introduction" to the *Anatomy of Criticism* (1957), Frye declares, "[I]t is time for criticism to leap to a new ground from which it can discover what the organizing or containing forms of its conceptual framework are. Criticism seems to be badly in need of a coordinating principle, a central hypothesis which, like the theory of evolution in biology, will see the phenomena it deals with as parts of a whole."[15]

The *Anatomy of Criticism* offers a "system" for studying literature that is composed of four categories: modes, symbols, myths, and genres. These categories, Frye believes, are not imposed on literature from without but generated immanently by literature itself, their dominance ebbing and flowing in the development of literary history. In contrast to Propp, who believes the narrative elements of fairy tales could best be distinguished by their function within the larger narrative syntax of the fable as a whole, Frye's model is relatively static: it divides fiction into four basic building blocks (novel, confession, anatomy, and romance) and then identifies the degree to which any particular work of fiction apportions these elements. It might thus be said that Frye's own scientific system of classification possesses the functionalism that Propp ascribes to tales themselves: Frye's categories have so tight a logical relation to one another that the terms of his typology themselves function as a dynamic and yet closed literary grammar. Compare, for example, James's informal discussion of the difference between romance and realism with Frye's. For James the use of one mode over another is purely a matter of authorial temperament;[16] but for Frye the two modes are symmetrical corners in the perfect square of fictional possibilities: romance and the novel are carefully defined as systematic inversions of one another, with confession and anatomy closing the square. All four categories are in turn defined as degrees of one another, nodal points in a closed system: the novel is extroverted and personal; romance introverted and personal; confession introverted and intellectualized; and the anatomy extroverted and intellectual. And we may feel that Frye's "inductive" method is compromised by the neat closure this system demands – however brilliant his discussion of each genre may itself be.

In a formalist pattern of logic that is by now familiar to us, Frye's belief that literature should be studied immanently, in its own terms, requires a concomitant conceptualization of the critic as an agent whose capacity for impersonality qualifies him to realize, to bring into view, the literary identity of the art work. For the critic to become a scientist he must first, in a version of the subjectively empty Lubbockian reader, learn to separate his perception of "life" from his perception of literary works like the novel. In the same way that Lubbock exhorts the reader to become an equal in the craft of fiction, an expert in the "substances" of literature, Frye maintains,

> [T]he skill developed from constant practice in the direct experience of literature is a special skill, like playing the piano, not the expression of a general attitude to life, like singing in the shower. The critic has a subjective background of experience formed by his temperament and by every contact with words he has made, including newspapers, advertisements, conversations, movies, and whatever he read at the age of nine. He has a specific skill in responding to literature which is no more like this subjective background, with all its private memories, associations, and arbitrary prejudices, than reading a thermometer is like shivering.[17]

This position of course also resonates with Shklovsky's admonition that the work of art should be looked at intrinsically, from the perspective of its "literariness," that the critic should be a mechanic, taking the point of view of the machine rather than that of a vegetarian. But Lubbock and Frye put greater emphasis on the creative power of skilled reading. The craftsman and piano player do more than the mechanic: they do more than recognize the driving belt as a driving belt – to extend the analogy, they drive the car. For the art work to function fully, the "perceiver" must make it go. For Lubbock and Frye, only the skilled reader of literature has the training to perceive the authentic terms of the literary work's literariness – and the self-discipline not to project upon the literary work what Lubbock calls voice and what Frye calls the reader's "general attitude to life." Thus Frye's professional critic can never fall prey to the readerly effect of defamiliarization: to have the mimetic world defamiliarized by literature would mean that one first made the mistake of confusing novelistic mimeticism with the real world. Frye's professional reads from a position of bracketed or transcended subjectivity: he understands from the outset that literature is not life. But Frye's professional analyst is no passive consumer: he is a skilled performer who keeps the art work safely removed from subjective and social life by bringing it to life as a literary form.

NOTES

1 Víktor Shklovsky, *Theory of Prose*, trans. Benjamin Sher (1925; Elmwood Park: Dalkey Archive Press, 1990) vii.
2 Shklovsky, "Art as Technique," *Russian Formalist Criticism: Four Essays*, ed. and trans. Lee T. Lemon and Marion J. Reis (1917; Lincoln: University of Nebraska Press, 1965) 5.
3 Ibid. 12.
4 Quoted in Henry James, "The Art of Fiction" (1888), in *The Future of the Novel: Essays on the Art of Fiction*, ed. Leon Edel (New York: Vintage, 1956) 11.
5 Ibid. 5.

6 Ibid. 9.
7 James, Henry James to the Deerfield Summer School (1889), *The Future of the Novel: Essays on the Art of Fiction* 29.
8 James, "The Art of Fiction" 26.
9 Ibid. 12.
10 James, *Roderick Hudson* Preface, in *The Art of the Novel: Critical Prefaces*, ed. R. P. Blackmur (New York: Scribner, 1962) 5.
11 James, "The Art of Fiction" 21.
12 James, *Roderick Hudson* Preface 14.
13 James uses *ficelle* to describe the way novelistic characters can function as elements of form, (depersonalized) threads for artful composition. But significantly, the phrase also carries the colloquial sense of indirect control – as in "pulling strings." Once a character is imagined as a *ficelle*, a component of form, it becomes hard not to think of him or her as a marionette, as puppets the author pulls for his own self-expression.
14 James, *The American* Preface, *The Art of the Novel: Critical Prefaces* 37.
15 Northrop Frye, *Anatomy of Criticism: Four Essays* (Princeton: Princeton University Press, 1957) 16.
16 James, *The American* Preface 30–1.
17 Frye, *Anatomy of Criticism* 28.

FURTHER READING

Carroll, David. *The Subject in Question: The Languages of Theory and the Strategies of Fiction.* Chicago: University of Chicago Press, 1982.

Erlich, Victor. *Russian Formalism: History–Doctrine.* 3rd edn. New Haven: Yale University Press, 1981. [First published in 1965.]

Hart, Jonathan Lock. *Northrop Frye: The Theoretical Imagination.* London: Routledge, 1994.

Jameson, Fredric. *The Prison-House of Language: a Critical Account of Structuralism and Russian Formalism.* Princeton, NJ: Princeton University Press, 1972.

Naiman, Eric. "Shklovsky's Dog and Mulvey's Pleasure: The Secret Life of Defamiliarization." *Comparative Literature* 50:4 (1998): 333–352.

Rowe, John Carlos. *The Theoretical Dimensions of Henry James,* Madison: University of Wisconsin Press, 1984.

1

Sterne's *Tristram Shandy*: Stylistic Commentary

Víktor Shklovsky

Víktor Borísovich Shklovsky (1893–1984)

Víktor Shklovsky was born in St. Petersburg, Russia, and studied philology at the University of St. Petersburg (renamed, along with the city, Petrograd [1914] and then Leningrad [1924]). In 1916, a year before the Russian Revolution, Shklovsky co-founded OPOYAZ (the Society for the Study of Poetic Language), which gave rise to the formalist movement. Like many of his peers, Shklovsky's career was closely tied to Joseph Stalin's rise and fall: he responded to early Marxist attacks by integrating sociological analysis into articles such as "*Voyna I mir* Lva Tolstovo: Formalno-sotsiologicheskoye issledovaniye" (1928; "*War and Peace* of Leo Tolstoy: A Formal-istic-Sociological Study"); officially recanted formalism in a January 1930 *Litera-turnaya Gazeta* article; and, after Stalin's death in 1953, returned to his roots with books such as *Tetiva: o neskhodstve skhodnogo* (1970; *The Bow-String: On Incompatibility of the Compatible*). A prolific and versatile writer, Shklovsky published 46 books: in addition to literary and film criticism, he also penned biographies, autobiographies, novels, plays, and children's books. Shklovsky tried to put his formalist

From *Russian Formalist Criticism: Four Essays*, translated by Lee T. Lemon and Marion J. Reis. Lincoln: University of Nebraska Press, 1965 (1921), pp. 27–57. Copyright © 1965 by the University of Nebraska Press. Reprinted by permission of the University of Nebraska Press.

principles into practice in his creative writing, including his novel *Zoo: Pis'-mane o lyubvi, ili Tret'ya Eloiza* (1923; translated as *Zoo: or, Letters not about Love*, 1971), and his autobiography *Tret'ya fabrika* (1926; translated as *Third Factory*, 1977). "Stern's *Tristram Shandy*: Stylistic Commentary" was originally published in 1921 as "*Tristram Shandy* Sterna i teoriya romana" (translated 1965); Shklovsky reprinted the essay in his 1925 study *O teorii prozy*, which itself was revised and reprinted in 1929 (translated as *Theory of Prose*, 1990).

In this essay I do not propose to analyze Laurence Sterne's novel, but rather to illustrate general laws of plot. Formalistically, Sterne was an extreme revolutionary; it was characteristic of him to "lay bare" his technique. The artistic form is presented simply as such, without any kind of motivation. The difference between a novel by Sterne and the ordinary kind of novel is exactly that between ordinary poetry with its phonetic instrumentation and the poetry of the Futurists, written in obscure language.[1] Yet nothing much is written about Sterne any more; or, if it is, it consists only of a few banalities.

The first impression upon taking up Sterne's *Tristram Shandy* and beginning to read it is one of chaos. The action is continually interrupted; the author repeatedly goes backward or leaps forward; whole ten-page passages are filled with whimsical discussions about fortifications or about the influence of a person's nose or name on his character. Such digressions are unrelated to the basic narrative.

Although the beginning of the book has the tone of an autobiography, it drifts into a description of the hero's ancestors. In fact, the hero's birth is long delayed by the irrelevant material squeezed into the novel. The description of a single day takes up much of the book; I quote Sterne himself:

> I will not finish that sentence till I have made an observation upon the strange state of affairs between the reader and myself, just as things stand at present – an observation never applicable before to any one biographical writer since the creation of the world, but to myself – and I believe will never hold good to any other, until its final destruction – and therefore, for the very novelty of it alone, it must be worth your worships attending to.
>
> I am this month one whole year older than I was this time twelve-month; and having got, as you perceive, almost into the middle of my fourth volume – and no farther than to my first day's life – 'tis demonstrative that I have three hundred and sixty-four days more life to write just now, than when I first set out; so that instead of advancing, as a common writer, in my work with what I have been doing at it – on the contrary, I am just thrown so many volumes back – [pp. 285–286].[2]

But when you begin to examine the structure of the book, you see first of all that the disorder is intentional and, in this case, poetic. It is strictly regulated, like a picture by Picasso. Everything in the book is displaced; everything is transposed. The dedication occurs on page 15, contrary to the three basic requirements of content, form, and place. Nor is the Preface in its usual position. It takes up approximately a quire, not at the beginning of the book but rather in Volume III, Chapter 20, pages 192 through 203. Sterne justifies the Preface in this way: "All my heroes are off my hands; – 'tis the first time I have had a moment to spare, – and I'll make use of it, and write my preface" (p. 192). The Preface contains, of course, as many entanglements as ingenuity permits. But the most radical of the displacements is the transposition of entire chapters (Chapters 18 and 19 of Volume IX are placed after Chapter 25). Sterne justifies the transposition so: "All I wish is, that it may be a lesson to the world, 'to let people tell their stories their own way'" (p. 633).

But this transposition of chapters reveals another of Sterne's basic techniques – that of impeding the flow of the action. In the beginning, Sterne introduces an anecdote about an act of sexual intercourse interrupted by a woman's question (p. 5). Here is how the anecdote is brought in. Tristram Shandy's mother sleeps with his father only on the first Sunday of each month and on precisely that evening Mr. Shandy winds the clock in order to get both of these domestic duties "out of the way at one time, and be no more plagued and pester'd with them the rest of the month" (p. 8). As a result, an unavoidable association has formed in his wife's mind, so that she "could never hear the said clock wound up, – but the thoughts of some other things unavoidably popp'd into her head, – & vice versa" (p. 9). Here is the exact question with which Tristram's mother interrupted the activity of his father: "Pray, my dear, ... have you not forgot to wind up the clock?" (p. 5).

This anecdote is introduced into the work first by a general comment upon the inattentiveness of the parents (pp. 4–5), then by the mother's question, the context of which we do not yet know. At first we think she had merely interrupted the father's conversation. Sterne plays with our error:

> Good G—! cried my father, making an exclamation, but taking care to moderate his voice at the same time, – Did ever woman, since the creation of the world, interrupt a man with such a silly question? Pray, what was your father saying? – Nothing [p. 5].

Then his remarks about the homunculus (fetus) are spiced with anecdotal references to its right to legal defense (pp. 5–6). Only on pages 8 through 9 do we get an explanation of this whole passage and a description of the odd punctiliousness of the father in his family affairs.

Thus, from the very beginning, we find displacement of time in Tristram Shandy. The causes follow the consequences, and the author himself prepares the groundwork for erroneous assumptions. This is one of Sterne's characteristic techniques. The quibbling about the coitus motif itself, related to a definite day and referring back to what has already happened in the novel, reappears from time to time and ties together the various sections of this masterfully constructed and unusually complicated work.

If we visualize the digressions schematically, they will appear as cones representing an event, with the apex representing the causes. In an ordinary novel such a cone is joined to the main story line at its apex; in Tristram Shandy the base of the cone is joined to the main story line, so that all at once we fall into a swarm of allusions.

As we know, this same technique occurs in one of Andrey Bely's last novels, Kotik Latayev; it is motivated by the fact that the novel shows the formation of a world from chaos. Out of the swarming mass appears an established order, with layers of puns on the names of the substances in the order stratifying and giving form to the mass.

Such time shifts occur often enough in the poetics of the novel. Consider, for example, the time shift in [Turgenev's] *A Nest of Gentlefolk* (the shift is motivated by Lavertsky's reminiscence) or in [Goncharov's] "The Dream of Oblomov."[3] In Gogol's *Dead Souls* no reasons are given for the time shifts (back to Chichikov's childhood and Tentetnikov's upbringing). Sterne, however, spread the technique throughout the entire work.

Exposition, preparation for a new character, always occurs after we have paused in perplexity over a strange word or an exclamation from that character. Here we have the exposure of the technique. In *Tales of Belkin* – in "The Shot," for example – Pushkin made extensive use of time shifts. In "The Shot" we first see Silvio practicing his marksmanship; next we hear Silvio's story about the unfinished duel; then we meet the Count, Silvio's enemy, and learn the outcome of the story. The parts are in a II–I–III order, and we see a reason for the shift; Sterne, however, simply lays bare the technique.

As I have said already, Sterne thought such [aesthetic] motivation an end in itself.[4] He wrote:

> What I have to inform you, comes, I own, a little out of its due course; – for it should have been told a hundred and fifty pages ago, but that I foresaw then 'twould come in pat hereafter, and be of more advantage here than elsewhere [p. 144].

Sterne even lays bare the technique of combining separate story lines to make up the novel. In general, he accentuates the very structure of the novel. By violating the form, he forces us to attend to it; and, for him, this awareness of the form through its violation constitutes the content of the novel.

In my little book on *Don Quixote*,[5] I have already noted several conventional methods of splicing story lines to form a novel. Sterne used still other methods or, using an old one, did not hide its conventionality but rather thrust it out protrudingly and toyed with it. In an ordinary novel digressions are cut off by a return to the main story. If there are two, or only a few story lines in the novel, their fragments alternate with one another – as in *Don Quixote*, where the scenes showing the adventures of the knight in the court of the Duke alternate with scenes depicting the governorship of Sancho Panza. Zielinski notes something entirely different in Homer. Homer never shows two simultaneous actions. If by force of circumstances they ever had to be simultaneous, they were reported as happening in sequence. Only the activity of one character and the "standing pat" (that is, the inactivity) of another can occur simultaneously. Sterne allowed actions to occur simultaneously, and he even parodied the development of the story line and the instrusions of the new material into it.

The description of Tristram Shandy's birth is the subject of the story line developed in the first part. The topic covers 203 pages, which nevertheless contain almost nothing about the actual birth of Tristram Shandy. For the most part, they deal with the conversation between the hero's father and his uncle Toby. Here is how the development takes place:

> – I wonder what's all that noise, and running backwards and forwards for, above stairs, quoth my father, addressing himself, after an hour and a half's silence, to my uncle *Toby*, –

VÍKTOR SHKLOVSKY

who you must know, was sitting on the opposite side of the fire, smoking his social pipe all the time, in mute contemplation of a new pair of black-plush-breeches which he had got on; – What can they be doing brother? quoth my father, – we can scarce hear ourselves talk.

I think, replied my uncle *Toby*, taking his pipe from his mouth, and striking the head of it two or three times upon the nail of his left thumb, as he began his sentence, – I think, says he: – But to enter rightly into my uncle *Toby's* sentiments upon this matter, you must be made to enter first a little into his character, the out-lines of which I shall just give you, and then the dialogue between him and my father will go on as well again [p. 63].

Then begins a discussion of inconstancy so whimsical that it would have to be quoted to be communicated properly. On page 65 Sterne remembers, "But I forget my uncle *Toby*, whom all this while we have left knocking the ashes out of his tobacco pipe." Then begins a sketch of Uncle Toby into which the story of Aunt Dinah is inserted. On page 72, Sterne remembers: "I was just going, for example, to have given you the great out-lines of my uncle *Toby's* most whimsical character; – when my aunt *Dinah* and the coachman came a-cross us, and led us a vagary...." Unfortunately, I cannot include everything Sterne has written, so I shall continue with a large omission:

from the beginning of this, you see, I have constructed the main work and the adventitious parts of it with such intersections, and have so complicated and involved the digressive and progressive movements, one wheel within another, that the whole machine, in general, has been kept a-going; – and, what's more, it shall be kept a-going these forty years, if it pleases the fountain of health to bless me so long with life and good spirits [pp. 73–74].

So ends Chapter 22; Chapter 23 continues: "I have a strong propensity in me to begin this chapter very nonsensically, and I will not balk my fancy. – Accordingly I set off thus." And new digressions are in store for us. On page 77 there is a further reminder: "If I was not morally sure that the reader must be out of all patience for my uncle *Toby's* character,..." and further down the page we find a description of Uncle Toby's "Hobby-Horse," his mania. It seems that Uncle Toby, wounded in the groin at the siege of Namur, was drawn into the erection of toy fortifications. Finally, on page 99, Uncle Toby can finish the activity he began on page 63:

I think, replied my uncle *Toby*, – taking, as I told you, his pipe from his mouth, and striking the ashes out of it as he began his sentence; – I think, replied he, – it would not be amiss, brother, if we rung the bell.

Sterne repeatedly resorts to this technique; and, as we see from his facetious reminders about Uncle Toby, not only is he fully aware of the exaggerations in his use of it, but he even enjoys playing around with it.

This manner of development, as I have already noted, is the characteristic pattern of Sterne's work. For example, on page 144, uncle Toby says, "I wish,... you had seen what prodigious armies we had in *Flanders*." Further on, the material about the mania of Tristram's father begins to develop. In fact, Tristram's father has attached to himself the following manias: on the harmful influence of the pressure brought to bear on the head of an infant when a woman experiences labor pains (pp. 149–154), on the influence of a man's name upon his character (a motif developed in great detail), and on the influence of the size of a man's nose on his potential greatness (this motif is developed in an unusually ostentatious way, approximately from page 217, when, after a short break, curious stories about noseology begin to develop). The Tale of Slawkenbergius is especially remarkable; Tristram's father knows ten decades of ten tales each, all with stories about Slawkenbergius. The development of the noseology ends on page 272.

Mr. Shandy's other manias also play a part in this particular development – that is, Sterne sidetracks our attention to talk about them.

The main story resumes on page 157:

> – "*I wish*, Dr. *Slop*," quoth my uncle *Toby* (repeating his wish for Dr. *Slop* a second time, and with a degree of more zeal and earnestness in his manner of wishing, than he had wished it at first) – "*I wish*, Dr. *Slop*," quoth my uncle *Toby*, "*you had seen what prodigious armies we had in Flanders*."

Once again the expansion of the material interrupts. And on page 163: "What prodigious armies you had in *Flanders!*" In Sterne, conscious exaggeration of the expansion frequently occurs without the use of a transitional sentence.

> The moment my father got up into his chamber, he threw himself prostrate across his bed in the wildest disorder imaginable, but at the same time, in the most lamentable attitude of a man borne down with sorrows, that ever the eye of pity dropp'd a tear for [pp. 215–216].

An exact description of his posture follows; such descriptions are very characteristic of Sterne:

> The palm of his right hand, as he fell upon the bed, receiving his forehead, and covering the greatest part of both his eyes, gently sunk down with his head (his elbow giving way backwards) till his nose touch'd the quilt; – his left arm hung insensible over the side of the bed, his knuckles reclining upon the handle of the chamber pot, which peep'd out beyond the valance, – his right leg (his left being drawn up towards his body) hung half over the side of the bed, the edge of it pressing upon his shin-bone.

Mr. Shandy's despondency is brought on by the fact that the bridge of his son's nose had been crushed by the obstetrical tongs during delivery and, as I have already said, an entire literary cycle on noses follows. On page 273 we finally return to the man we left lying on the bed:

> My father lay stretched across the bed as still as if the hand of death had pushed him down, for a full hour and a half, before he began to play upon the floor with the toe of that foot which hung over the bed-side.

I cannot help saying a few words in general about the postures we find in Sterne. The first to introduce the description of postures into the novel, he always portrayed them strangely – or, more exactly, he defamiliarized them. I shall cite an example: "Brother *Toby*, replied my father, taking his wig from off his head with his right hand, and with his *left* pulling a striped *India* handkerchief from his right coat pocket,..." (p. 158). I go directly to page 159:

> It was not an easy matter in any king's reign, (unless you were as lean a subject as myself) to have forced your hand diagonally, quite across your whole body, so as to gain the bottom of your opposite coat-pocket.

The method of portraying postures passed from Sterne to Leo Tolstoy,[6] who used it more flexibly and with psychological motivation.

I now return to Sterne's technique of plot development with several examples which clearly establish the fact that awareness of form constitutes the subject matter of the novel.

> What a chapter of chances, said my father, turning himself about upon the first landing, as he and my uncle *Toby* were going down stairs – what a long chapter of chances do the events of this world lay open to us! [p. 279].

(Then follows a discussion containing an erotic element which I shall say more about later.)

> Is it not a shame to make two chapters of what passed in going down one pair of stairs? for we are got no farther yet than to the first landing, and there are fifteen more steps down to the bottom; and for aught I know, as my father and my uncle *Toby* are in a talking humour, there may be as many chapters as steps [p. 281].

Sterne devotes all of this chapter to a discussion of chapters.

The next chapter begins: "We shall bring all things to rights, said my father, setting his foot upon the first step from the landing –" (p. 283). And the next: "And how does your mistress? cried my father, taking the same step over again from the landing,..." (p. 284). And the next:

> Holla! – you chairman! – here's sixpence – do step into that book-seller's shop, and call me a *day-tall* critick. I am very willing to give any one of 'em a crown to help me with his tackling, to get my father and my uncle *Toby* off the stairs, and to put them to bed....
>
> I am this month one whole year older than I was this time twelvemonth; and having got, as you perceive, almost into the middle of my fourth volume – and no farther than to my first day's life – 'tis demonstrative that I have three hundred and sixty-four days more to write just now, than when I first set out; so that instead of advancing, as a common writer, in my work with what I have been doing at it – on the contrary, I am just thrown so many volumes back – [pp. 285–286].

The conventionality of this organization of the form is reminiscent of those octaves and sonnets filled with the description of how they were composed.

Here is one last example of such expansion in Sterne:

> My mother was going very gingerly in the dark along the passage which led to the parlour, as my uncle *Toby* pronounced the word *wife*. – 'Tis a shrill, penetrating sound of itself, and

---

Obadiah had helped it by leaving the door a little a-jar, so that my mother heard enough of it, to imagine herself the subject of the conversation: so laying the edge of her finger across her two lips – holding in her breath, and bending her head a little downwards, with a twist of her neck – (not towards the door, but from it, by which means her ear was brought to the chink) – she listened with all her powers: – the listening slave, with the Goddess of Silence at his back, could not have given a finer thought for an intaglio.

In this attitude I am determined to let her stand for five minutes: till I bring up the affairs of the kitchen (as *Rapin* does those of the church) to the same period [pp. 357–358].

And on page 367: "I am a *Turk* if I had not as much forgot my mother, as if Nature had plaistered me up, and set me down naked upon the banks of the river Nile,...." But there is another digression even after this reminder. The reminder is necessary merely to renew our awareness of the "forgotten mother" in order to prevent the impression of the expansion from fading.

At last, on page 370, the mother shifts her position: "Then, cried my mother, opening the door,...."

In this case Sterne expands the material by including a second parallel story; in such cases in novels, ordinary time is usually thought to be suspended, or at least not considered, as opposed to showing the passage of time by explicit appeals to our reason. Shakespeare used his interpolated scenes to suspend time – that is, to divert attention from the normal flow of time; and even if the entire inserted dialogue (invariably with new characters) continued only a few minutes, Shakespeare felt it permissible to carry on the action as if hours or even a whole night had gone by. (We assume that curtains were not lowered, for it is very likely that curtains were not used in the Shakespearean theater because of the projecting stage.) Sterne, by repeatedly mentioning and reminding us of the fact that the mother has been standing in a stooped position for the whole time, forces us to notice his handling of it.

It is interesting, in a general way, to study the role time plays in Sterne's works. "Literary time" is clearly arbitrary; its laws do not coincide with the laws of ordinary time. If one studies, for example, the numerous tales and events concentrated in *Don Quixote*, he will see that the beginning of day and the beginning of night play no compositional role in the sequence of events – that, in general, the slow, lingering passage of the day does not exist. L'Abbé Prévost narrates *Manon Lescaut* in precisely the same way. Chevalier des Grieux tells the whole first part (seven folios) without a break; then, after a slight respite, continues for another seven folios. Such a conversation would have lasted sixteen hours, even under conditions allowing for rapid speech.

I have already spoken of the arbitrariness of time on the stage. But Sterne conceived of and used the arbitrariness of "literary time" as material for a game, as in Volume II, Chapter 8:

It is about an hour and a half's tolerable good reading since my uncle *Toby* rung the bell, when *Obadiah* was order'd to saddle a horse, and go for Dr. *Slop* the man-midwife; – so that no one can say, with reason, that I have not allowed *Obadiah* time enough, poetically speaking, and considering the emergency too, both to go and come; – tho', morally and truly speaking, the man, perhaps, has scarce had time to get on his boots.

If the hypercritic will go upon this; and is resolved after all to take a pendulum, and measure the true distance betwixt the ringing of the bell, and the rap at the door; – and, after finding it to be no more than two minutes, thirteen seconds, and three fifths, – should take upon him to insult over me for such a breach in unity, or rather probability, of time; – I would remind him, that the idea of duration and of its simple modes, is got merely from the train and succession of our ideas, – and is the true scholastic pendulum, – and by which, as a scholar, I will be tried in this matter, – adjuring and detesting the jurisdiction of all other pendulums whatever.

I would, therefore, desire him to consider that it is but poor eight miles from *Shandy-Hall* to Dr. *Slop*, the man mid-wife's house; – and that whilst *Obadiah* has been going those said miles and back, I have brought my uncle *Toby* from *Namur*, quite across all *Flanders*, into *England*. – That I have had him ill upon my hands near four years; – and have since travelled him and Corporal *Trim*, in a chariot and four, a journey of near two hundred miles down into *Yorkshire*, – all which put together, must have prepared the reader's imagination for the entrance of Dr. *Slop* upon the stage, – as much, at least (I hope) as a dance, a song, or a concerto between the acts.

If my hypercritic is intractable, alledging, that two minutes and thirteen seconds are no more than two minutes and thirteen seconds, – when I have said all I can about them; – and that this plea, tho' it might save me dramatically, will damn me biographically, rendering my book, from this very moment, a profess'd Romance, which, before was a book aprocryphal: – If I am thus pressed – I then put an end to the whole objection and controversy about it all at once, – by acquainting him, that *Obadiah* had not got above three-score yards from the stable-yard before he met with Dr. *Slop*,... [pp. 103–104].

Sterne took the device of the "discovered manuscript" almost unchanged from among the old literary devices. Thus we find Yorick's sermon in the novel. But, of course, the reading of this discovered manuscript does not of itself represent a long digression from the novel, for the sermon is repeatedly interrupted, chiefly by emotional ejaculations. The course of the sermon occupies pages 125 through 140, but it is greatly expanded by insertions of the usual Sternean kind.

The reading of the sermon begins with a description of Corporal Trim's posture, depicted in Sterne's usual purposely awkward way:

He stood before them with his body swayed, and bent forward just so far, as to make an angle of 85 degrees and a half upon the plain of the horizon; – which sound orators, to whom I address this, know very well, to be the true persuasive angle of incidence [p. 122].

And so it continues to:

He stood, – for I repeat it, to take the picture of him in at one view, with his body sway'd, and somewhat bent forwards, – his right-leg firm under him, sustaining seven-eighths of his whole weight, – the foot of his left-leg, the defect of which was no disadvantage to his attitude, advanced a little, – not laterally, nor forwards, but in a line betwixt them;....

And so on. The entire description continues for more than a page. The sermon itself is interrupted by a story about Corporal Trim's brother. Then come the theological protests of a Roman Catholic (pp. 125, 126, 128, 129, etc.) and Uncle Toby's remarks on fortifications (pp. 133, 134, etc.). Thus while following the course of the manuscript, Sterne also integrates it into the novel to a far greater degree than does Cervantes.

Sterne made the "discovered manuscript" a favorite technique in his *Sentimental Journey*. He finds, as he sets out to do, a manuscript by Rabelais; but, as is quite typical of Sterne, he interrupts the manuscript with a discussion about wrapping merchandise. (Sterne has made the unfinished tale acceptable in both its motivated and unmotivated forms.) The interruption of the introduced manuscript is motivated by the fact that its conclusion has been lost. On the other hand, nothing motivates the conclusion of *Tristram Shandy*, which ends with a simple cutting off of the narrative:

> L—d! said my mother, what is all this story about? –
> A COCK and a BULL, said *Yorick* – and one of the best of its kind, I ever heard.
> The END of the NINTH VOLUME.

So also ends *Sentimental Journey.* "So that when I stretch'd out my hand, I caught hold of the Fille de Chambre's –" and it ends there.

This, of course, is a specific stylistic device based upon a variety of things. Sterne worked against a background of the adventure novel with its extraordinarily strict forms and with its formal rule to end with a wedding in the offing. In Sterne's novels the usual forms are changed and violated; it is not surprising that he handled the conclusions of his novels in the same way. We seem to stumble upon them, as if we found a trap door on a staircase where we had expected a landing. Gogol's "Ivan Fyodorovich Shponka and His Aunt"[7] is a short story concluded in the same way; but the conclusion is motivated, for the end of the manuscript was "lost" while baking pies (Sterne wraps currant jam in his). The notes comprising E. T. A. Hoffmann's *Kater Murr* depend upon the same technique, with the nonexistent conclusion motivated by complicated time shifts and parallelism (justified by the fact that the pages are not in order).

Sterne introduces the story of Le Fever in his usual way: During a conversation about the choice of a tutor for Tristram, at the time of Tristram's birth, Uncle Toby suggests the son of poor Le Fever, and the story immediately begins, narrated not by Toby but by Tristram Shandy himself:

> Then, brother *Shandy*, answered my uncle *Toby*, raising himself off the chair, and laying down his pipe to take hold of my father's other hand, – I humbly beg I may recommend poor *Le Fever's* son to you; – a tear of joy of the first water sparkled in my uncle *Toby's* eye, – and another, the fellow to it, in the corporal's, as the proposition was made; – you will see why when you read *Le Fever's* story: – fool that I was! nor can I recollect, (nor perhaps you) without turning back to the place, what it was that hindered me from letting the corporal tell it in his own words; – but the occasion is lost, – I must tell it now in my own [pp. 415–416].

The story about Le Fever, which runs from page 416 to page 432, then begins.

A separate cycle of stories (pp. 479–538) describes Tristram's travels. Sterne later developed this episode, step by step and motif by motif, into his *Sentimental Journey.*

Sterne also inserts a story about the Abbess of Andoüillets into the account of Tristram's journey (pp. 504–510).

All of this diverse material, which is augmented by extensive excerpts from the works of various pedants, would undoubtedly tear the novel to bits were it not drawn together by crisscrossing motifs.[8] A stated motif is never fully developed, never actually realized, but is only recalled from time to time; its fulfillment is continually put off to a more and more remote time. Yet its very presence in all the dimensions of the novel ties the episodes together.

There are several such motifs, one of them concerning knots. Here is how it appears – Dr. Slop's bag of obstetrical instruments is tied up in several knots:

'Tis God's mercy, quoth he [Dr. Slop], (to himself) that Mrs. *Shandy* has had so bad a time of it, – else she might have been brought to bed seven times told, before one half of these knots could have got untied [p. 167].

In the next chapter, same page:

In the case of *knots*, – by which, in the first place, I would not be understood to mean slip-knots, – because in the course of my life and opinions, – my opinions concerning them will come in more properly when I mention....

And so on. Then begins a discussion about knots, hitches, fastenings, bows, and so on endlessly. Meanwhile, Dr. Slop gets a little knife and cuts the knots, but accidentally wounds his hand. Then he begins to swear, but the elder Shandy "with Cervantes-like seriousness" suggests he not swear in vain, but rather curse in accordance with the rules of art and, in lieu of a handbook, hands him the formula of excommunication from the Roman Catholic church. Slop takes it and reads; the formula occupies two pages. The curious thing here is the motivation Sterne uses to develop the material. Usually such material has to do with medieval scholarship, which by Sterne's time was already considered laughable (just as, in stories about foreigners, it is thought funny when they pronounce words according to their own dialectical peculiarities). These medieval materials are usually introduced into the story merely as manias of Tristram's father. In this case, however, the motivation is more complicated. The material about baptizing a child prior to its birth and the droll argument of the lawyers about whether a mother is her son's relative is quite removed from Sterne's usual characterization of father *Shandy*.

On page 363 the knots motif appears again,[9] with the chambermaid motif. Sterne suggests that instead of devoting a chapter to those subjects, he would rather substitute one on chambermaids, green gowns, and old hats. But the unsettled account of the knots and packages is not forgotten and comes up again near the very end of page 617 as a promise to write a special chapter about knots.

The references to Jenny are another motif which runs through the novel. Jenny first appears in this way:

it is no more than a week from this very day, in which I am now writing this book for the edification of the world, – which is *March 9, 1759*, – that my dear, dear *Jenny* observing

I look'd a little grave, as she stood cheapening a silk of five-and-twenty shillings a yard, – told the mercer, she was sorry she had given him so much trouble; – and immediately went and bought herself a yard-wide stuff of ten-pence a yard [p. 44].

On pages 48 and 49 Sterne plays with the reader's curiosity concerning the kind of relationship that exists between Jenny and the narrator.

I own the tender appellation of my dear, dear *Jenny*, – with some other strokes of conjugal knowledge, interspersed here and there, might, naturally enough, have misled the most candid judge in the world into such a determination against me. – All I plead for, in this case, Madam, is strict justice, and that you do so much of it, to me as well as to yourself, – as not to prejudge or receive such an impression of me, till you have better evidence, than I am positive, at present, can be produced against me: – Not that I can be so vain or unreasonable, Madam, as to desire you should therefore think, that my dear, dear *Jenny* is my kept mistress; – no, – that would be flattering my character in the other extream, and giving it an air of freedom, which, perhaps, it has no kind of right to. All I contend for, is the utter impossibility for some volumes, that you, or the most penetrating spirit upon earth, should know how this matter really stands. – It is not impossible, but that my dear, dear *Jenny*! tender as the appellation is, may be my child. – Consider, – I was born in the year eighteen. – Nor is there any thing unnatural or extravagant in the supposition, that my dear *Jenny* may be my friend. – Friend! – My friend. Surely, Madam, a friendship between the two sexes may subsist, and be supported without – Fy! Mr. *Shandy*. – Without anything, Madam, but that tender and delicious sentiment, which ever mixes in friendship, where there is a difference of sex.

The Jenny motif appears again on page 337:

I shall never get all through in five minutes, that I fear – and the thing I *hope* is, that your worships and reverences are not offended – if you are, depend upon't I'll give you something, my good gentry, next year, to be offended at – that's my dear *Jenny's* way – but who my *Jenny* is – and which is the right and which the wrong end of a woman, is the thing to be *concealed* – it will be told you the next chapter but one, to my chapter of button-holes, – and not one chapter before.

And on page 493: "I love the Pythagoreans (much more than ever I dare tell my dear *Jenny*)." There are other references to Jenny on pages 550 and 610 through 611. This last (I have let several pass) has a sentimentality seldom equalled in Sterne:

I will not argue the matter: Time wastes too fast: every letter I trace tells me with what rapidity Life follows my pen; the days and hours of it, more precious, my dear *Jenny*! than the rubies about thy neck, are flying over our heads like light clouds of a windy day, never to return more – every thing presses on – whilst thou art twisting that lock, – see! it grows grey; and every time I kiss thy hand to bid adieu, and every absence which follows it, are preludes to that eternal separation which we are shortly to make. –
– Heaven have mercy upon us both!

CHAP. IX.

Now, for what the world thinks of that ejaculation – I would not give a groat.

and so ends Chapter 9.[10]

A few words about sentimentality in general are appropriate here. Sentimentality cannot serve as the mainstay of art, since art has no mainstay. The presentation of things from "a sentimental point of view" is a special method of presentation, like the presentation of them from the point of view of a horse (as in Tolstoy's "Kholstomer") or of a giant (as in Swift's *Gulliver's Travels*).

Art is essentially trans-emotional, as in stories told of persons rolled into the sea in a barrel spiked inside like an iron maiden. In the Russian version of "Tom Thumb"[11] children will not permit the omission even of the detail of the cannibal cutting off the heads of his daughters, not because children are cruel, but because the detail is part of the legend. Professor Anichkov's *Ceremonial Songs of Spring* includes vernal dancing songs which deal with ugly, quarrelsome husbands; maggots; and death. Although these are unpleasant, they are part of the songs. Gore in art is not necessarily gory; it rhymes with *amor*—it is either the substance of the tonal structure or material for the construction of figures of speech.

Art, then, is unsympathetic – or beyond sympathy – except where the feeling of compassion is evoked as material for the artistic structure. In discussing such emotion we have to examine it from the point of view of the composition itself, in exactly the same way that a mechanic must examine a driving belt to understand the details of a machine; he certainly would not study the driving belt as if he were a vegetarian.

Of course, even Sterne is beyond sympathy, as I shall show. The elder Shandy's son Bobby died at his home the very moment the father was deciding whether to use money, which he had acquired accidentally, either for sending his son abroad or for improving his estate:

my uncle *Toby* hummed over the letter.

———————— ———————— ———————— ———————— ———————— ———————— ———————— ————
———————— ———————— ———————— ———————— ———————— ———————— ———————— ————
———————— ———————— ———————— ———————— ———————— ———————— —————— he's

gone! said my uncle *Toby* – Where – Who? cried my father. – My nephew, said my uncle *Toby* – What – without leave – without money – without governor? cried my father in amazement. No: – he is dead, my dear brother, quoth my uncle *Toby* [p. 350].

Sterne here has used death to put his characters at "cross-purposes," a common literary device using two persons talking about two different things and thinking they are talking about one and the same thing. Gogol uses the device in *The Inspector General*, in the first conversation between the Mayor and Khlestakov:

MAYOR: Pardon me –
KH.: Not at all.
MAYOR: As Chief Magistrate of this town, my duty is to see that neither transients nor people of standing are oppressed....
KH.: (first stammering a bit, then towards the end speaking quite loudly) What can be done?... It's not my fault.... Really, I shall pay.... They're sending me some money from home. (Bobchinsky stares in at the door.) He is far more to blame than I; the

beef he serves me is as tough as a board and the devil knows what he puts in his soups – I just had to throw some out the window. He starves me for days. And such odd tea! it smells like fish, not tea. Why should I? ... It's unheard of!

MAYOR: (taken aback) Forgive me, really, I'm not to blame. The beef I inspect at the markets is always good; it's brought in by reliable merchants, sober, well-behaved people. I wouldn't know where his comes from. But if things are not just as they should be, then ... let me suggest that you accompany me to other quarters.

KH.: No, I'd rather not. I know those "other quarters" – the jail. And just what kind of authority do you have? ... How dare you? I ... I work at Petersburg! (Acting boldly) I ... I ... I ...

MAYOR: (aside) Oh! Good Lord, how angry he is. He knows everything; those damned shopkeepers have told him everything.

KH.: (blustering) Even if you come here with all your men, I won't go. I'll go directly to the Prime Minister! (Pounding the table) Who do you think you are? Who?

MAYOR: (Standing at attention, his whole body trembling) Please, don't ruin me. My wife! My little children! Don't set misfortune on a man!

KH.: No, I don't want to. But still! What's that to me? I should go to prison just because you have a wife and children – that's lovely! (Bobchinsky, peeking through the door and thoroughly frightened, hides.) No. Thanks a lot, but I will not.

MAYOR: (trembling) It's my inexperience, honest to God, my inexperience. The shortage of funds ... judge for yourself – my official salary won't keep me in tea and sugar. And if I have taken anything, they were the smallest trifles. Something for the table, enough cloth for a suit. About that corporal's widow who runs a shop and whom I'm said to have flogged – that is slander, by God, slander. It's from people who think evil of me, people ready to take my life.

KH.: So what? They are nothing to me. (Thoughtfully.) Yet I don't know why you talk of those who wish you ill and of some corporal's widow or other. A corporal's wife is something quite different. But you dare not flog me. We're a long way from that. But still.... Look at what we have here! I'll pay the bill, but I don't have the cash yet. That's why I'm stuck here, because I don't have a kopeck.

The same talking at cross-purposes occurs in Griboyedov's *Wit Works Woe.*

ZAGORETSKY:	On Chatsky's score this outcry has arisen.
COUNTESS GRANDMOTHER:	Chatsky was escorted out to prison?
ZAGORETSKY:	Was clubbed in the Carpathians, went muzzy from the wound.
COUNTESS GRANDMOTHER:	Has clubbed with the Freemasons and Musselman Mahound?[12]

We find the same technique with the same motivation (deafness) in Russian folk drama, but it arises from a series of puns because of the folk drama's usually loose plot. [A long quotation from the most popular of Russian folk dramas, *Czar Maximilian*, has been omitted here; it consists of one long misunderstanding based upon a series of puns.] These punning misunderstandings are typical of folk drama. Sometimes the device supplants the plot structure itself and leaves the drama without a trace of plot. Roman

Jakobson and Peter Bogatyrev analyze the technique in their work on Russian folk themes.[13]

But Sterne's own puns on death do not astonish us as much as the puns made by the father. For Sterne, the death of Bobby Shandy is chiefly motivation for expansion of the material: "Will your worships give me leave to squeeze in a story between these two pages?" (p. 351). And he inserts a fragment from the letter of consolation from Servius Sulpicius Rufus to Cicero. The introduction of this fragment is motivated by what Father Shandy has himself uttered. Later a collection of classical anecdotes about the disdain of death begins. Curiously, Sterne himself tells of Father Shandy's eloquence:

> My father was as proud of his eloquence as Marcus Tullius Cicero could be for his life, and for aught I am convinced of to the contrary at present, with as much reason: it was indeed his strength – and his weakness too. – His strength – for he was by nature eloquent, – and his weakness – for he was hourly a dupe to it; and provided an occasion in life would but permit him to shew his talents, or say either a wise thing, a witty, or a shrewd one – (bating the case of a systematick misfortune) – he had all he wanted. – A blessing which tied up my father's tongue, and a misfortune which set it loose with good grace, were pretty equal: sometimes, indeed, the misfortune was the better of the two; for instance, where the pleasure of the harangue was as *ten*, and the pain of the misfortune but as *five* – my father gained half in half, and consequently was as well again off, as it never had befallen him [p. 352].

Here Sterne shows with unusual clarity the difference between the "happiness" and "unhappiness" of life taken as an everyday occurrence and as material for art.

Later the mother has to learn about the death of her son. Sterne handles it by having her overhear the news at the door; then he takes it into his head to build a simultaneous action in the kitchen. As I have already pointed out, he plays around with the action while the poor mother is left standing in an uncomfortable pose. At this time, a conversation about the son's death is going on in the study. The thread of conversation has already passed from a discussion of death in general, through a discussion about voyages and the general diffusion of ancient learning (p. 369), and moved on to Socrates' oration before his judges:

> though my mother was a woman of no deep reading, yet the abstract of *Socrates'* oration, which my father was giving my uncle *Toby*, was not altogether new to her. – She listened to it with composed intelligence, and would have done so to the end of the chapter, had not my father plunged (which he had no occasion to have done) into that part of the pleading where the great philosopher reckons up his connections, his alliances, and children; but renounces a security to be so won by working upon the passions of his judges. – "I have friends – I have relations, – I have three desolate children," – says *Socrates*. –
> – Then, cried my mother, opening the door, – you have one more, Mr. *Shandy*, than I know of.
> By heaven! I have one less, – said my father, getting up and walking out of the room [p. 370].

Erotic defamiliarization, which is generally presented euphemistically (with genteel wording), is a very important part of Sterne's expansion of the material. I have already treated the basis of this phenomenon in "Art as Technique." In Sterne we find a remarkable diversity of methods of erotic defamiliarization; they are quite numerous, and I shall cite several. I shall begin with one dealing with the recognition of characters:

> I am not ignorant that the *Italians* pretend to a mathematical exactness in their designations of one particular sort of character among them, from the *forte* or *piano* of a certain wind instrument they use, – which they say is infallible. – I dare not mention the name of the instrument in this place; – 'tis sufficient we have it amongst us, – but never think of making a drawing by it; – this is aenigmatical, and intended to be so, at least, *ad populum.* – And therefore I beg, Madam, when you come here, that you read on as fast as you can, and never stop to make any inquiry about it[14] [pp. 75–76].

Or here is another:

> Now whether it was physically impossible, with half a dozen hands all thrust into the napkin at a time – but that some one chestnut, of more life and rotundity than the rest, must be put in motion – it so fell out, however, that one was actually sent rolling off the table; and as *Phutatorius* sat straddling under – it fell perpendicularly into that particular aperture of *Phutatorius's* breeches, for which, to the shame and indelicacy of our language be it spoke, there is no chaste word throughout all *Johnson's* dictionary – let it suffice to say – it was that particular aperture, which in all good societies, the laws of decorum do strictly require, like the temple of *Janus* (in peace at least) to be universally shut up [p. 320].

Two further episodes in *Tristram Shandy* are especially typical of Sterne's game of erotic defamiliarization. The two are similar, although one is simply an episode, while the other expands into one of those plots that continually interrupts the others and even becomes one of the major plot strands in the novel. The more important of these is Uncle Toby's wound, a severe wound in the groin. A widow courting him and waiting to marry him does not know whether or not he is castrated and at the same time hesitates to ask. This situation greatly slows the progress of the novel. Sterne comments upon it:

> There is not a greater difference between a single-horse chair and madam *Pompadour's* vis-à-vis, than betwixt a single amour, and an amour thus nobly doubled, and going upon all fours, prancing throughout a grand drama [p. 209].

Hints and allusions repeatedly interrupt the novel. Approximately in Volume VI, Chapter 34, the hints begin to thicken, even though the introductory motif of the journey intrudes. In Volume VII, Chapter 43, Sterne refers to the newly introduced material as if this vein were exhausted:

> I danced it along through *Narbonne, Carcasson*, and *Castle Naudairy*, till at last I danced myself into *Perdrillo's* pavillion, where pulling a paper of black lines, that I might go on straight forwards, without digressions of parenthesis, in my uncle *Toby's* amours – [p. 538].

Thus the wound in the groin and the impossibility of the woman's asking about it in detail is introduced into the romance of Uncle Toby and the widow Wadman as a

VÍKTOR SHKLOVSKY

delaying action. I shall show in several supporting quotations how Sterne impedes the action.

After a solemn promise to continue the story of Toby's amorous adventures without digression, Sterne then delays the action with digressions on digressions tied together by the repetition of such phrases as, "It is with love as with Cuckoldom" (pp. 540, 542). Then come the love metaphors: love is an old hat; love is a pie. The story proceeds with the attacks of the widow Wadman on Uncle Toby, but their description is again interrupted by a long "importunate story," narrated by Trim – "The Story of the King of Bohemia and his seven castles" (pp. 560–569). This story is like the one Sancho Panza tells his master on the night of the adventure with the fulling mill, when he had tied Rosinante's legs. Uncle Toby repeatedly interrupts with remarks on the nature of military techniques and on the style; I have already analyzed the method in *Don Quixote*. Like any "importunate tale," it is based upon the recognition of the stalling tactics. It must be interrupted by a listener. In some cases its function is to hold the flow of the novel in check. Later, Trim abandons his telling of the story of the King of Bohemia and takes up the story of his own love (pp. 568–575); and at last the widow Wadman reappears on the scene. Here the motif of the wound also reappears:

> I am terribly afraid, said widow *Wadman*, in case I should marry him, *Bridget* – that the poor captain will not enjoy his health, with the monstrous wound upon his groin –
> It may not, Madam, be so very large, replied *Bridget*, as you think – and I believe besides, added she – that 'tis dried up –
> – I would like to know – merely for his sake said Mrs. *Wadman* –
> – We'll know the long and the broad of it, in ten days – answered Mrs. *Bridget*, for whilst the captain is paying his addresses to you – I'm confident Mr. Trim will be for making love to me – and I'll let him as much as he will – added *Bridget* – to get it all out of him – [pp. 581–582].

In Volume VIII, Chapter 31, the new material is introduced in the form of a metaphor of the kind frequently found in Sterne. He brings into play the lexically accepted metaphor "hobby-horse" in the sense of a whim and refers it to a real horse, then introduces the "ass" (part of the body) figure of speech. (Perhaps the origin of this metaphor is found in St. Francis of Assisi's phrase about his own body, "My brother ass.") This figure of speech is also developed, and a "situation based on a misconception" is built from it.

The father asks Uncle Toby about his "ass," and the latter thinks this is a euphemistic name for the back part of his anatomy (pp. 583–584). [Shklovsky, apparently misled by the Russian, misinterprets the wordplay here as euphemistic.] A detail of the further development is interesting – Father Shandy's speech to Uncle Toby is nothing other than a parody of the speech of Don Quixote to Sancho Panza about the governorship. I shall not show parallel extracts from both speeches here, especially since the widow Wadman awaits us. Uncle Toby and Trim are going to her, along with Mr. Shandy and his wife, who glance behind them and talk about the coming marriage.

The motif of the impotent husband who has his wife only on the first Sunday of each month crops up again here; the motif had been stated at the very beginning of the novel.

Unless she should happen to have a child – said my mother –
But she must persuade my brother *Toby* first to get her one –
– To be sure, Mr. *Shandy*, quoth my mother.
– Though if it comes to persuasion – said my father – Lord have mercy upon them.
Amen: said my mother, *piano*.
Amen: cried my father, *fortissimè*.

Amen: said my mother again – but with such a sighing cadence of personal pity at the end of it, as discomfited every fibre about my father – he instantly took out his almanack; but before he could untie it, *Yorick's* congregation coming out of church, became a full answer to one half of his business with it – and my mother telling him it was a sacrament day – left him as little in doubt, as to the other part – He put his almanack into his pocket.

The first Lord of the Treasury thinking of *ways and means*, could not have returned home, with a more embarrassed look [pp. 613–614].

I let myself quote this passage at length because I want to show how the material Sterne introduces comes not merely from the outside, but rather belongs to one of the threads which tie up all the compositional strands of the novel. Again, as the digressions along the other strands progress, the knot motif reappears (p. 617). At last the wound motif returns, presented, as is typical of Sterne, from the middle:

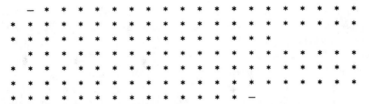

– You shall see the very place, Madam; said my uncle *Toby*.

Mrs. *Wadman* blush'd – look'd towards the door – turn'd pale – blush'd slightly again – recovered her natural colour – blush'd worse than ever; which for the sake of the unlearned reader, I translate thus –

> "*L – d! I cannot look at it –*
> *What would the world say if I look'd at it?*
> *I should drop down, if I look'd at it –*
> *I wish I could look at it –*
> *There can be no sin in looking at it.*
> *– I will look at it*" [p. 623].

But a new development occurs. Uncle Toby thinks the widow is interested in the geographical locality where he was wounded, not in the actual place of the wound on his body. As a result, not even the reader understands the dialogue. The whole movement of the plot is affected here; it is slowed down.

Trim brings a map of Namur (Uncle Toby was wounded at Namur) to the disappointed widow, and once more the play on Uncle Toby's wound is permitted to continue. Sterne repeatedly inserts it into the digressions (pages 625–629). And then comes the famous transposition of time; the previously bypassed Chapters 18 and 19 appear after Chapter 25. The scene resumes with Chapter 26:

It was just as natural for Mrs. *Wadman*, whose first husband was all his time afflicted with a Sciatica, to wish to know how far from the hip to the groin; and how far she was likely to suffer more or less in her feelings, in the one case than in the other.

She accordingly read *Drake's* anatomy from one end to the other. She had peeped into *Wharton* on the brain, and had borrowed[15] *Graaf* upon the bones and muscles; but could make nothing of it....

To clear up all, she had twice asked Doctor *Slop*, "if poor captain *Shandy* was ever likely to recover of his wound – ?"

– He is recovered, Doctor *Slop* would say –

What! quite?

– Quite: madam –

But what do you mean by a recovery? Mrs. *Wadman* would say.

Doctor *Slop* was the worst man alive at definitions [pp. 636–637].

Mrs. Wadman interrogates Captain Shandy himself about the wound:

" – Was it without remission? –

" – Was it more tolerable in bed?

" – Could he lie on both sides alike with it?

" – Was he able to mount a horse? [p. 637]

And so on. The business is finally settled when Trim speaks about Captain Shandy's wound with Bridget, the widow's maid:

and in this cursed trench, Mrs. *Bridget*, quoth the Corporal, taking her by the hand, did he receive the wound which crush'd him so miserable *here* – In pronouncing which he slightly press'd the back of her hand towards the part he felt for – and let it fall.

We thought, Mr. *Trim*, it had been more in the middle – said Mrs. *Bridget* –

That would have undone us for ever – said the Corporal.

– And left my poor mistress undone too – said *Bridget*....

Come – come – said Bridget – holding the palm of her left-hand parallel to the plane of the horizon, and sliding the fingers of the other over it, in a way which could not have been done, had there been the least wart or protuberance – 'Tis every syllable of it false, cried the Corporal, before she had half finished the sentence – [p. 639].

It is interesting to compare the symbolism of the hand motions with the erotic euphemism in the same novel.

A small preliminary observation. For the dramatis personae in the novel as well as for Sterne himself, the technique of decorous conversation becomes material for art in the sense that it is a method of defamiliarization. It is curious that this manual symbolism occurs in particularly masculine and "obscene" anecdotal folklore where we know the only rule of decency is the desire to speak as lewdly as possible. There too we find euphemistic material – in particular manual symbolism; once again, it is a technique of defamiliarization.

Let us turn to Sterne and a simple instance of erotic defamiliarization; again I have to quote almost an entire chapter, fortunately a short one:

> – 'Twas nothing, – I did not lose two drops of blood by it – 'twas not worth calling in a surgeon, had he lived next door to us.... The chamber-maid had left no ✱✱✱✱✱✱✱ ✱✱✱ under the bed: – Cannot you contrive, master, quoth *Susannah*, lifting up the sash with one hand, as she spoke, and helping me up into the window seat with the other, – cannot you manage, my dear, for a single time to ✱✱✱✱ ✱✱✱ ✱✱ ✱✱✱ ✱✱✱✱✱✱?
>
> I was five years old. – *Susannah* did not consider that nothing was well hung in our family, – so slap came the sash down like lightening upon us; – Nothing is left, – cried *Susannah*, – nothing is left – for me, but to run my country – [p. 376].

She flees to the home of Uncle Toby, who takes the blame in this case since his servant Trim had removed the hook-leads from the window sash for casting toy cannons.

Again, this is Sterne's usual technique: He gives the results before he gives the causes. In this case the cause is given on pages 377–378. Trim tells the story of the accident, with the aid of hand gestures:

> *Trim*, by the help of his forefinger, laid flat upon the table, and the edge of his hand striking a-cross it at right angles, made a shift to tell his story so, that priests and virgins might have listened to it; – and the story being told, – the dialogue went on as follows [p. 379].

Later, with digressions, discussions of digressions, etc., Sterne expands an episode about the rumors which spread among the people concerning what had happened.

It is interesting that Father Shandy, having learned what happened, runs to his son – with a book – and begins a talk about the general subject of circumcisions; it is also interesting that at this point Sterne parodies the motivation of interjected parts:

> – was *Obadiah* enabled to give him a particular account of it, just as it had happened. – I thought as much, said my father, tucking up his night-gown; – and so walked up stairs.
>
> One would imagine from this – (though for my own part I somewhat question it) – that my father before that time, had actually wrote that remarkable chapter in the *Tristrapædia*, which to me is the most original and entertaining one in the whole book; – and that is the *chapter upon sash-windows*, with a bitter *Philippick* at the end of it, upon the forgetfulness of chamber-maids. – I have but two reasons for thinking otherwise.
>
> First, had the matter been taken into consideration, before the event happened, my father certainly would have nailed up the sash-window for good an' all; – which, considering with what difficulty he composed books, – he might have done with ten times less trouble, than he could have wrote the chapter: this argument I foresee holds good against his writing the chapter, even after the event; but 'tis obviated under the second reason, which I have the honour to offer to the world in support of my opinion, that my father did not write the chapter upon sash-windows and chamber-pots, at the time supposed, – and it is this.
>
> – That, in order to render the *Tristrapædia* complete, – I wrote the chapter myself [pp. 383–384].

I have not even the slightest wish to follow Sterne's novel to the end because that is not what interests me; I am interested, rather, in the theory of the plot. I shall now remark on the abundance of quotations. It certainly would have been possible to have made fuller use of the material introduced in each quotation because almost no technique is represented anywhere in its pure form; but such an approach would have transformed my work into something like an interlinear translation with grammatical remarks. I would have forgotten the material and so exhausted it that I would have deprived the reader of the possibility of understanding it.

In order to follow the course of the novel in my analysis, I have had to show the whole of its "inconsistency." The unusualness of the general plan and the order of the novel, even of the frequently extraordinary handling of the most ordinary elements, is what is characteristic here.

By way of a conclusion and as a demonstration of Sterne's awareness of his work and his exaggerated violations of the usual plot structure, I introduce his very own graphs of the flow of the story of *Tristram Shandy*.

> I am now beginning to get fairly into my work; and by the help of a vegitable diet, with a few of the cold seeds, I make no doubt but I shall be able to go on with my uncle *Toby's* story, and my own, in a tolerable straight line. Now,

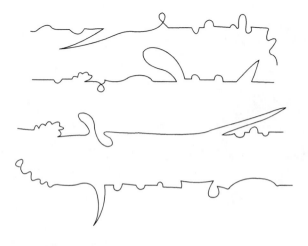

[p. 473][16]

These were the four lines I moved in through my first, second, third, and fourth volumes. – In the fifth volume I have been very good, – the precise line I have described in it being this:

[p. 474]

By which it appears, that except at the curve, marked A. where I took a trip to *Navarre*, – and the indented curve B. which is the short airing when I was there with the Lady *Baussiere* and her page, – I have not taken the least frisk of a digression, till *John de la Casse's* devils led me the round you see marked D. – for as for *c c c c c* they are nothing but parentheses, and the common *ins* and *outs* incident to the lives of the greatest ministers of state; and when compared with what men have done, – or with my own transgressions at the letters A B D – they vanish into nothing [pp. 473–474].

Sterne's diagrams are approximately accurate, but they do not call attention to the crosscurrent of motifs.

The idea of *plot* is too often confused with the description of events – with what I propose provisionally to call the *story*. The story is, in fact, only material for plot formulation. The plot of *Evgeny Onegin* is, therefore, not the romance of the hero with Tatyana, but the fashioning of the subject of this story as produced by the introduction of interrupting digressions. One sharp-witted artist (Vladimir Miklashevsky) proposed to illustrate *Evgeny Onegin* mainly through the digressions (the "small feet," for example); considering it as a composition of motifs, such a treatment would be proper.

The forms of art are explainable by the laws of art; they are not justified by their realism. Slowing the action of a novel is not accomplished by introducing rivals, for example, but by simply *transposing* parts. In so doing the artist makes us aware of the aesthetic laws which underlie both the transposition and the slowing down of the action.

The assertion that *Tristram Shandy* is not a novel is common; for persons who make that statement, opera alone is music – a symphony is chaos.

Tristram Shandy is the most typical novel in world literature.

NOTES

1   That is, in ordinary poetry the "phonetic instrumentation" – rhyme, meter, alliteration, etc. – is often said to accompany a "meaning," to which it is subordinate; Futurist poetry called attention to, or "laid bare," the devices of instrumentation. *Tristram Shandy* is like Futurist poetry in that it also calls attention to technical devices that are usually subordinated. *L&R note.*

2   Shklovsky read the Russian version of *Tristram Shandy* published in the journal *Panteon Literatury* [*Pantheon of Literature*] in 1982. Our quotations are taken from *The Life and Opinions of Tristram Shandy, Gentleman*, ed. James Aiken Work (New York: Odyssey Press, 1940); all page and chapter references are to this edition. *L&R note.*

3   A section of Goncharov's novel *Oblomov* (Part I, Chap. 9), originally published separately. *L&R note.*

4   "Motivation" as used by the Formalists is a complex concept. Generally, motivation is the reason governing the use of a particular device and may include everything from the author's desire to shock his readers, to the necessity of including specific props required by the action. *L&R note.*

5   Victor Shklovsky, *Kak sledan* Don Quixote [*How Don Quixote Was Made*], reprinted in *O teorii prozy*. *L&R note.*

6   Shklovsky here has a one-word parenthetical insertion "Eichenbaum," perhaps indicating that he saw Eichenbaum's *Molodoy Tolstoy* [*Young Tolstoy*] (Petrograd and Berlin, 1922), before its publication. *L&R note.*

7   From Nicholas Gogol's *Evenings on a Farm Near Dikanka*. *L&R note.*

8   This passage is interesting because it is one of the few in which Shklovsky shows his sense of the importance of unity in fiction. It can be said in Shklovsky's defense that he felt he had to take the novel apart before he could know how it worked. Moreover, he was usually interested

either in a particular technique in itself or in showing departures from such norms as unity. *L&R note.*

9   Actually, there is no reference to knots on p. 363, but there is a reference to buttonholes; in Russian both are *petlya.* Shklovsky may have been misled by the Russian, or he may have had in mind a more general "fastening" motif. The point makes little difference, however, since Sterne joins both the knot and the buttonhole motifs on p. 617. *L&R note.*

10 Shklovsky mistakenly has, "And so ends Chapter 8." *L&R note.*

11 "Malchik s palchik," a Russian variant of the Tom Thumb story. *L&R note.*

12 Trans. by Sir Bernard Pares in *Masterpieces of the Russian Drama*, ed. George Rapall Noyes (New York: Dover Publications, Inc., 1960), I, 133–134. Reprinted through permission of the publisher. *L&R note.*

13 Roman Jakobson and Peter Bogatyrev, "K probleme razmezhevaniya folkloristiki i literatur-ovedeniya," ["On the Problem of the Demarcation Between Folklore and Literary Studies"], *Lud Slowianski*, II, No. 2 (1931). *L&R note.*

14 "This passage probably alludes, with purposed equivocation, to the Italian *castrati*, some of whom had been imported into England, in the face of considerable popular opposition, to aid in the presentation of operas" (note by James Aiken Work, p. 76). *L&R note.*

15 This must be a mistake in Mr. *Shandy;* for *Graaf* wrote upon the pancreatick juice, and the parts of generation. *Sterne's note.*

16 These four diagrams are inverted in the Russian text. We have set them aright. *L&R note.*

Morphology of the Folktale

Vladímir Propp

From *Morphology of the Folktale*, second edition, translated by Laurence Scott, revised and edited with a preface by Louis A. Wagner. Austin: University of Texas Press, 1968 (1928), from ch. 2, pp. 19–24, ch. 3, pp. 25–9, ch. 4, 66–70. Copyright © 1968 by the University of Texas Press. Reprinted by permission of the University of Texas Press.

The Method and Material

Let us first of all attempt to formulate our task. As already stated in the foreword, this work is dedicated to the study of *fairy* tales. The existence of fairy tales as a special class is assumed as an essential working hypothesis. By "fairy tales" are meant at present those tales classified by Aarne under numbers 300 to 749. This definition is artificial, but the occasion will subsequently arise to give a more precise determination on the basis of resultant conclusions. We are undertaking a comparison of the themes of these tales. For the sake of comparison we shall separate the component parts of fairy tales by special methods; and then, we shall make a comparison of tales according to their components. The result will be a morphology (i.e., a description of the tale according to its component parts and the relationship of these components to each other and to the whole).

What methods can achieve an accurate description of the tale? Let us compare the following events:

1. A tsar gives an eagle to a hero. The eagle carries the hero away to another kingdom.[1]
2. An old man gives Súčenko a horse. The horse carries Súčenko away to another kingdom.
3. A sorcerer gives Iván a little boat. The boat takes Iván to another kingdom.
4. A princess gives Iván a ring. Young men appearing from out of the ring carry Iván away into another kingdom, and so forth.[2]

Both constants and variables are present in the preceding instances. The names of the dramatis personae change (as well as the attributes of each), but neither their actions nor functions change. From this we can draw the inference that a tale often attributes identical actions to various personages. This makes possible the study of the tale *according to the functions of its dramatis personae.*

We shall have to determine to what extent these functions actually represent recurrent constants of the tale. The formulation of all other questions will depend upon the solution of this primary question: how many functions are known to the tale?

Investigation will reveal that the recurrence of functions is astounding. Thus Bába Jagá, Morózko, the bear, the forest spirit, and the mare's head test and reward the stepdaughter. Going further, it is possible to establish that characters of a tale, however varied they may be, often perform the same actions. The actual means of the realization of functions can vary, and as such, it is variable. Morózko behaves differently than Bába Jagá. But the function, as such, is a constant. The question of *what* a tale's dramatis personae do is an important one for the study of the tale, but the questions of *who* does it and *how* it is done already fall within the province of accessory study. The functions of characters are those components which could replace Veselóvskij's "motifs," or Bédier's "elements." We are aware of the fact that the repetition of functions by various characters was long ago observed in myths and beliefs by historians of religion, but it was not observed by historians of the tale (cf. Wundt and Negelein[3]). Just as the characteristics and functions of deities are transferred from one to another, and, finally, are even carried over to Christian saints, the functions of certain tale personages are likewise transferred to other personages. Running ahead, one may say that the number of functions is extremely small, whereas the number of personages is extremely large. This explains the two-fold quality of a tale: its amazing multiformity, picturesqueness, and color, and on the other hand, its no less striking uniformity, its repetition.

Thus the functions of the dramatis personae are basic components of the tale, and we must first of all extract them. In order to extract the functions we must define them. Definition must proceed from two points of view. First of all, definition should in no case depend on the personage who carries out the function. Definition of a function will most often be given in the form of a noun expressing an action (interdiction, interrogation, flight, etc.). Secondly, an action cannot be defined apart from its place in the course of narration. The meaning which a given function has in the course of action must be considered. For example, if Iván marries a tsar's daughter, this is something entirely different than the marriage of a father to a widow with two daughters. A second example: if, in one instance, a hero receives money from his father in the form of 100 rubles and subsequently buys a wise cat with this money, whereas in a second case, the hero is rewarded with a sum of money for an accomplished act of bravery (at which point the tale ends), we have before us two morphologically different elements – in spite of the identical action (the transference of money) in both cases. Thus, identical acts can have different meanings, and vice versa. *Function is understood as an act of a character, defined from the point of view of its significance for the course of the action.*

The observations cited may be briefly formulated in the following manner:

1. *Functions of characters serve as stable, constant elements in a tale, independent of how and by whom they are fulfilled. They constitute the fundamental components of a tale.*
2. *The number of functions known to the fairy tale is limited.*

If functions are delineated, a second question arises: in what classification and in what sequence are these functions encountered?

A word, first, about sequence. The opinion exists that this sequence is accidental. Veselóvskij writes, "The selection and *order* of tasks and encounters (examples of motifs) already presupposes a certain *freedom.*" Šklóvskij [Shklovsky] stated this idea in even sharper terms: "It is quite impossible to understand why, in the act of adoption, the *accidental* sequence [Šklóvskij's italics] of motifs must be retained. In the testimony of witnesses, it is precisely the sequence of events which is distorted most of all." This reference to the evidence of witnesses is unconvincing. If witnesses distort the sequence of events, their narration is meaningless. The sequence of events has its own laws. The short story too has similar laws, as do organic formations. Theft cannot take place before the door is forced. Insofar as the tale is concerned, it has its own entirely particular and specific laws. The sequence of elements, as we shall see later on, is strictly *uniform.* Freedom within this sequence is restricted by very narrow limits which can be exactly formulated. We thus obtain the third basic thesis of this work, subject to further development and verification:

3. *The sequence of functions is always identical.*

As for groupings, it is necessary to say first of all that by no means do all tales give evidence of all functions. But this in no way changes the law of sequence. The absence of certain functions does not change the order of the rest. We shall dwell on this phenomenon later. For the present we shall deal with groupings in the proper sense of the word. The presentation of the question itself evokes the following assumption: if functions are singled out, then it will be possible to trace those tales which present identical functions. Tales with identical functions can be considered as belonging to one type. On this foundation, an index of types can then be created, based not upon theme features, which are somewhat vague and diffuse, but upon exact structural features. Indeed, this will be possible. If we further compare structural types among themselves, we are led to the following completely unexpected phenomenon: functions cannot be distributed around mutually exclusive axes. This phenomenon, in all its concreteness, will become apparent to us in the succeeding and final chapters of this book. For the time being, it can be interpreted in the following manner: if we designate with the letter A a function encountered everywhere in first position, and similarly designate with the letter B the function which (if it is at all present) *always follows A*, then all functions known to the tale will arrange themselves within a *single* tale, and none will fall out of order, nor will any one exclude or contradict any other. This is, of course, a completely unexpected result. Naturally, we would have expected that where there is a function A, there cannot be certain functions belonging to other tales. Supposedly we would obtain several axes, but only a single axis is obtained for all fairy tales. They are of the same type, while the combinations spoken of previously are subtypes. At first glance, this conclusion may appear absurd or perhaps even wild, yet it can be verified in a most exact manner. Such a typological unity represents a very complex problem on which it will be necessary to dwell further. This phenomenon will raise a whole series of questions.

In this manner, we arrive at the fourth basic thesis of our work:

4. *All fairy tales are of one type in regard to their structure.*

We shall now set about the task of proving, developing, and elaborating these theses in detail. Here it should be recalled that the study of the tale must be carried on strictly deductively, i.e., proceeding from the material at hand to the consequences (and in effect it is so carried on in this work). But the *presentation* may have a reversed order, since it is easier to follow the development if the general bases are known to the reader beforehand.

Before starting the elaboration, however, it is necessary to decide what material can serve as the subject of this study. First glance would seem to indicate that it is necessary to cover all extant material. In fact, this is not so. Since we are studying tales according to the functions of their dramatis personae, the accumulation of material can be suspended as soon as it becomes apparent that the new tales considered present no new functions. Of course, the investigator must look through an enormous amount of reference material. But there is no need to inject the entire body of this material into the study. We have found that 100 tales constitute more than enough material. Having discovered that no new functions can be found, the morphologist can put a stop to his work, and further study will follow different directions (the formation of indices, the complete systemization, historical study). But just because material can be limited in quantity, that does not mean that it can be selected at one's own discretion. It should be dictated from without. We shall use the collection by Afanás'ev, starting the study of tales with No. 50 (according to his plan, this is the first fairy tale of the collection), and finishing it with No. 151.[4] Such a limitation of material will undoubtedly call forth many objections, but it is theoretically justified. To justify it further, it would be necessary to take into account the degree of repetition of tale phenomena. If repetition is great, then one may take a limited amount of material. If repetition is small, this is impossible. The repetition of fundamental components, as we shall see later, exceeds all expectations. Consequently, it is theoretically possible to limit oneself to a small body of material. Practically, this limitation justifies itself by the fact that the inclusion of a great quantity of material would have excessively increased the size of this work. We are not interested in the quantity of material, but in the quality of its analysis. Our working material consists of 100 tales. The rest is reference material, of great interest to the investigator, but lacking a broader interest.

The Functions of Dramatis Personae

In this chapter we shall enumerate the functions of the dramatis personae in the order dictated by the tale itself.

For each function there is given: (1) a brief summary of its essence, (2) an abbreviated definition in one word, and (3) its conventional sign. (The introduction of signs will later permit a schematic comparison of the structure of various tales.) Then follow examples. For the most part, the examples far from exhaust our material. They are given only as samples. They are distributed into certain groups. These groups are in relation to the definition as *species* to *genus*. The basic task is the extraction of *genera*. An examination of *species* cannot be included in the problems of general morphology. Species can be further subdivided into *varieties*, and here we have the beginning of systemization. The arrangement given below does not pursue such goals. The citation of examples should only illustrate and show the presence of the function as a certain *generic* unit. As was already mentioned, all functions fit into one consecutive story. The series of functions given below represents the morphological foundation of fairy tales in general.[5]

A tale usually begins with some sort of initial situation. The members of a family are enumerated, or the future hero (e.g., a soldier) is simply introduced by mention of his name or indication of his status. Although this situation is not a function, it nevertheless is an important morphological element. The species of tale beginnings can be examined only at the end of the present work. We shall designate this element as the *initial situation*, giving it the sign α.

After the initial situation there follow functions:

I. ONE OF THE MEMBERS OF A FAMILY ABSENTS HIMSELF FROM HOME. (Definition: *absentation*. Designation: β.)

1. *The person absenting himself can be a member of the older generation* (β^1). Parents leave for work (113). "The prince had to go on a distant journey, leaving his wife to the care of strangers" (265). "Once, he (a merchant) went away to foreign lands" (197). Usual forms of absentation: going to work, to the forest, to trade, to war, "on business."
2. *An intensified form of absentation is represented by the death of parents* (β^2).

3. *Sometimes members of the younger generation absent themselves* (β^3). They go visiting (101), fishing (108), for a walk (137), out to gather berries (244).

II. AN INTERDICTION IS ADDRESSED TO THE HERO. (Definition: *interdiction.* Designation: γ.)

1. (γ^1). "You dare not look into this closet" (159). "Take care of your little brother, do not venture forth from the courtyard" (113). "If Bába Jagá comes, don't you say anything, be silent" (106). "Often did the prince try to persuade her and command her not to leave the lofty tower," etc. (265). Interdiction not to go out is sometimes strengthened or replaced by putting children in a stronghold (201). Sometimes, on the contrary, an interdiction is evidenced in a weakened form, as a request or bit of advice: a mother tries to persuade her son not to go out fishing: "you're still little," etc. (108). The tale generally mentions an absentation at first, and then an interdiction. The sequence of events, of course, actually runs in the reverse. Interdictions can also be made without being connected with an absentation: "don't pick the apples" (230); "don't pick up the golden feather" (169); "don't open the chest" (219); "don't kiss your sister" (219).
2. *An inverted form of interdiction is represented by an order or a suggestion.* (γ^2) "Bring breakfast out into the field" (133). "Take your brother with you to the woods" (244).

Here for the sake of better understanding, a digression may be made. Further on the tale presents the sudden arrival of calamity (but not without a certain type of preparation). In connection with this, the initial situation gives a description of particular, sometimes emphasized, prosperity. A tsar has a wonderful garden with golden apples; the old folk fondly love their Ivášečka, and so on. A particular form is agrarian prosperity: a peasant and his sons have a wonderful hay-making. One often encounters the description of sowing with excellent germination. This prosperity naturally serves as a contrasting background for the misfortune to follow. The spectre of this misfortune already hovers invisibly above the happy family. From this situation stem the interdictions not to go out into the street, and others. The very absentation of elders prepares for the misfortune, creating an opportune moment for it. Children, after the departure or death of their parents, are left on their own. A command often plays the role of an interdiction. If children are urged to go out into the field or into the forest, the fulfillment of this command has the same consequences as does violation of an interdiction not to go into the forest or out into the field.

III. THE INTERDICTION IS VIOLATED (Definition: *violation.* Designation: δ.)

The forms of violation correspond to the forms of interdiction. Functions II and III form a *paired* element. The second half can sometimes exist without the first (the tsar's daughters go into the garden [β^3]; they are *late* in returning home). Here the interdiction of tardiness is omitted. A fulfilled order corresponds, as demonstrated, to a violated interdiction.

At this point a new personage, who can be termed the *villain*, enters the tale. His role is to disturb the peace of a happy family, to cause some form of misfortune, damage, or harm. The villain(s) may be a dragon, a devil, bandits, a witch, or a stepmother, etc. (The question of how new personages, in general, appear in the course of action has been relegated to a special chapter.) Thus, a villain has entered the scene. He has come on foot, sneaked up, or flown down, etc., and begins to act.

IV. THE VILLAIN MAKES AN ATTEMPT AT RECONNAISSANCE. (Definition: *reconnaissance.* Designation: ε.)

1. *The reconnaissance has the aim of finding out the location of children, or sometimes of precious objects, etc.* (ε^1). A bear says: "Who will tell me what has become of the tsar's children? Where did they disappear to?" (201); a clerk: "Where do you get these precious stones?" (197);[6] a priest at confession: "How were you able to get well so quickly?" (258);[7] a princess: "Tell me, Iván the merchant's son, where is your wisdom?" (209);[8] "What does the bitch live on?" Jágišna thinks. She sends One-Eye, Two-Eye and Three-Eye on reconnaissance (101).[9]
2. *An inverted form of reconnaissance is evidenced when the intended victim questions the villain* (ε^2). "Where is your death, Koščéj?" (156). "What a swift steed you have! Could one get another one somewhere that could outrun yours?" (160).
3. *In separate instances one encounters forms of reconnaissance by means of other personages* (ε^3).

V. THE VILLAIN RECEIVES INFORMATION ABOUT HIS VICTIM. (Definition: *delivery.* Designation: ζ.)

1. *The villain directly receives an answer to his question.* (ζ^1) The chisel answers the bear: "Take me out into the courtyard and throw me to the ground; where I stick, there's the hive." To the clerk's question about the precious stones, the merchant's wife replies: "Oh, the hen lays them for us," etc. Once again we are confronted with paired functions. They often occur in the form of a dialogue. Here, incidentally, also belongs the dialogue between the stepmother and the mirror. Although the stepmother does not directly ask about her step-daughter, the mirror answers her: "There is no doubt of your beauty; but you have a stepdaughter, living with knights in the deep forest, and she is even more beautiful." As in other similar instances, the second half of the paired function can exist without the first. In these cases the delivery takes the form of a careless act: A mother calls her son home in a loud voice and thereby betrays his presence to a witch (108). An old man has received a marvelous bag; he gives the godmother a treat from the bag and thereby gives away the secret of his talisman to her (187).
2-3. *An inverted or other form of information-gathering evokes a corresponding answer.* (ζ^2-ζ^3) Koščéj reveals the secret of his death (156), the secret of the swift steed (159), and so forth.

* * *

Assimilations: Cases of the Double Morphological Meaning of a Single Function

It has already been shown that functions must be defined independently of the characters who are supposed to fulfill them. In following the enumeration of the functions, one becomes convinced that they must also be defined independently of how and in what manner they are fulfilled. This sometimes complicates the definition of individual cases, since different functions may be fulfilled in exactly the same way. Apparently we are confronted here with the influence of certain forms upon others. This phenomenon may be termed the assimilation of the means of fulfillment of functions.

This complicated phenomenon cannot be fully illuminated here. It can be examined only to the extent that this is necessary for subsequent analyses.

Let us examine a case in point (160): Iván asks a witch for a horse. She proposes that he select the best from a herd of identical colts. He chooses accurately and takes the horse. The action at the witch's house is a test of the hero by the donor, followed by the receipt of a magical agent. But in another tale (219), we see that the hero desires to wed the daughter of the water spirit who requires the hero to choose his bride from among twelve identical maidens. Can this case, as well, be defined as a *donor's* test? It is clear that in spite of the identical quality of the actions, we are confronted with a completely different element, namely, a difficult task connected with matchmaking. Assimilation of one form with another has taken place. Without concerning ourselves with the question of the priority of this or that particular meaning, we must nevertheless find the criterion which in all such cases would permit us to differentiate among elements without respect to similarity of actions. In these instances it is always possible to be governed by the principle of defining a function *according to its consequences*. If the receiving of a magical agent follows the solution of a task, then it is a case of the donor testing the hero (D^1). If the receipt of a bride and a marriage follow, then we have an example of the difficult task (M).

A difficult task can be distinguished from a dispatch of a complicational nature by the same method. The dispatch of someone in search of a deer with golden antlers, etc., also might be termed a "difficult task," but morphologically such a dispatch is a different element from a task set by a princess or a witch. If a dispatch gives rise to a departure, prolonged search ($C\uparrow$), the meeting with a donor, etc., we have a complicational element (a, B, lack and dispatch). If a task is immediately solved and leads directly to marriage, we have M-N (a difficult task and its solution).

If marriage follows the fulfillment of a task, this means that the bride is earned or obtained through fulfillment of the task. In this manner the consequence of the task (and an element is defined according to its consequences) is the *acquisition of a sought-for person* or object (but not of a magical agent). Difficult tasks may be attested with matchmaking and apart from it. The latter case occurs very rarely (only twice in our material, tales 249, 239[10]). The obtaining of a person sought follows the solution of a task. Thus we come to the following summation: all tasks giving rise to a search must be considered in terms of B; all tasks giving rise to the receipt of a magical agent are considered as D. *All other tasks* are considered as M, with two varieties: tasks connected with match-making and marriage, and tasks not linked with matchmaking.

Let us look at a few more cases of simpler assimilations. Difficult tasks are the richest source for the most varied assimilations. A princess sometimes requires the building of a magical palace which the hero usually constructs immediately, with the help of a magical agent. Yet the building of a magical palace may also figure within the context of an entirely different meaning. After all his feats the hero builds a palace in the twinkling of an eye, and is revealed as a prince. This is a special type of transformation, apotheosis, and not the solution of a difficult task. One form has become assimilated with another, while the question of the primacy of the form, in either meaning, here again must remain open.

Finally, tasks may also be assimilated with dragon fighting. The fight with a dragon which has either kidnapped a girl or is ravaging a kingdom and the tasks given by a princess are completely different elements. But in a certain tale the princess demands that the hero conquer the dragon if he wants to obtain her hand in marriage. Should this case be considered as M (difficult task), or as H (struggle, fight)? This case amounts to a task since, first of all, a marriage follows, and secondly, struggle has been defined above as struggle *with a villain*, and the dragon in this instance is not the villain, but is introduced *ad hoc* and, without the slightest detriment to the course of the action, may be replaced by another kind of creature which must be either slain or tamed (compare the tasks of taming a horse, defeating a rival).

Other elements which also frequently assimilate are initial villainy and pursuit of the villain. Tale No. 93 begins with Iván's sister (a witch, also called a she-dragon) striving to devour her brother.[11] He flees from the house, and from this point the action develops. The sister of a dragon (a common pursuing character) is here transformed into the sister of the hero, and pursuit is transferred to the beginning of the tale and is used as A (villainy) – in particular, as A^{xvii}. If one compares in general how she-dragons act while giving chase with how a stepmother acts at the beginning of a tale, one will obtain parallels which shed a certain amount of light upon tale beginnings in which a stepmother torments her stepdaughter. Such a comparison becomes particularly sharp if one adds to it a study of the attributes of these characters. By introducing more material it can be shown that the stepmother is a she-dragon transferred to the beginning of the tale, who has taken on some traits of a witch and some ordinary characteristics. Persecution is sometimes directly comparable to pursuit. We will point out that the case of a she-dragon who transforms herself into an apple tree standing along the route travelled by the hero, attracting him with her exquisite but deadly fruit, may be readily compared with the stepmother's offer of poisoned apples which are sent to her stepdaughter. One can compare the transformation of a she-dragon into a beggar, and the transformation of a sorceress (sent by the stepmother) into a market woman, etc.

Another phenomenon resembling assimilation is the double morphological meaning of a single function. The simplest example of this is found in case No. 265. A prince sets off on a journey and forbids his wife to leave the house. There comes "a little old lady who seemed so sweet and simple. 'Why' says she, 'are you bored? If you would just have a look at God's world! If only you would walk through the garden!'" etc. (the persuasions of the villain, η^1). The princess goes out into the garden, thereby heeding the persuasions of the villain (θ^1), and simultaneously breaking an interdiction (δ^1). Thus the princess' exit from the house has a double morphological meaning. A second, more complicated example is found in tale No. 180,[12] and in others: Here, a difficult task (to kiss the princess while riding at full gallop) is transferred to the beginning of the tale. It gives rise to the hero's departure (i.e., falls into the class of the connective moment, B). It is characteristic that this task, given in the form of a call, is similar to the one uttered by the father of kidnapped princesses (cf.: "Who will kiss my daughter, Princess Milolíka, at full gallop…" etc.; "Who will seek out my daughters…" etc.). The call in both cases represents the same element (B^1); but in addition to this, the call in tale No. 180[13] is simultaneously a difficult task. Here, as in several similar cases, a difficult task is transferred to the complication and is used as element B, while at the same time still remaining M.

We consequently see that the means by which functions are fulfilled influence one another, and that identical forms adapt themselves to different functions. A certain form is transferred to a different position, acquiring a new meaning, or simultaneously retaining an old one. All of these phenomena complicate the analysis and require special attention when being compared to one another.

NOTES

1 *"Car' daet udal'cu orla. Orel unosit udal'ca v inoe carstvo"* (p. 28). Actually, in the tale referred to (old number 104a = new number 171), the hero's future bride, Poljuša, tells her father the tsar that they have a *ptica-kolpalica* (technically a spoonbill, although here it may have meant a white stork), which can carry them to the bright world. For a tale in which the hero flies away on an eagle, see 71a (= new number 128). *L.A.W. note.*

2 See Afanás'ev, Nos. 171, 139, 138, 156.

3 W. Wundt, "Mythus und Religion," *Völkerpsychologie*, II, Section I; Negelein, *Germanische Mythologie*. Negelein creates an exceptionally apt term, *Depossedierte Gottheiten.*

4 Tales numbered 50 to 151 refer to enumeration according to the older editions of Afanás'ev. In the new system of enumeration, adopted for the fifth and sixth editions and utilized in this translation (cf. the Preface to the Second Edition, and Appendix V), the corresponding numbers are 93 to 270. *L.A.W. note.*

5 It is recommended that, prior to reading this chapter, one read through all the enumerated functions in succession without going into detail, taking note only of what is printed in capital letters. Such a cursory reading will make it easier to understand the thread of the account.

6 " 'Gde vy èti samocvetnye kamni berete?' (114)" (p. 38). The textual reference should be 115 (= new no. 197). *L.A.W. note.*

7 " 'Otčego tak skoro sumel ty popravit'sja?' (114)" (p. 38). The textual reference should be 144 (= new no. 258). *L.A.W. note.*

8 " 'Skaži, Ivan—kupečeskij syn, gde tvoja mudrost'?' (120)" (p. 38). The textual reference should be 120b (= new no. 209). *L.A.W. note.*

9 " 'Čem suka živet? dumaet Jagišna.' Ona posylaet na razvedku Odnoglazku, Dvuglazku, Treglazku (56)." Texts 56 and 57 (= new nos. 100 and 101) have been somewhat confused. The three daughters named are present in tale 56, but their mother is not called Jagišna, and the indicated question does not appear. On the other hand, in tale 57 Jagišna asks, "Čem suka živa živet?" but here she has only two daughters to send out, a two-eyed one and a three-eyed one. *L.A.W. note.*

10 "(v našem materiale liš' dva raza, No. 140, 132)" (p. 75). Although it is true that tale 140 (= new no. 249) contains difficult tasks not connected with matchmaking, tale 132 (= new no. 239) is not a clear illustration of the same thing. The latter contains at least a tacit assumption of matchmaking, since Iván marries the princess at the end of the tale, after she has failed to guess a third riddle posed by him. Also, a footnote at the beginning of the tale suggests that the princess will marry the man whose riddles she cannot guess. (There is the possibility here, of course, that the numerical reference is incorrect.) *L.A.W. note.*

11 "Skazka No. 50 načinaetsja s togo, čto sestra Ivana (ved'ma, nazvana takže zmeixoj) stremitsja s"est' brata" (p. 76). This statement provokes two comments: first, in the tale itself (= new no. 93), the villain is everywhere referred to as the sister (*sestra*) or the witch (*ved'ma*) except in the last line, where she is called a *ved'ma-zmeja* (literally, "witch-serpent"). Apparently the author's contention that Iván's sister is really the sister of a dragon, transferred to the

beginning of the tale, explains his referring to her in various places as a she-dragon (*zmeixa*): cf. pp. 52, 57, 86 in this translation.

Secondly, it should be noted that the tale does not begin with pursuit as such, but rather with a warning to Iván that his mother will soon give birth to a daughter who will be a terrible witch, etc. and that he had better flee. He does, and some time later (two-thirds of the way through the tale) he returns home and confronts his sister. It is from this point that the actual pursuit begins, as Iván flees again and his sister gives chase. *L.A.W. note.*

12 The tale cited here (p. 77) is 105. More correctly, it should be 105b (= new no. 180). *L.A.W. note.*

13 The tale cited here (p. 77) is 105. More correctly, it should be 105b (= new no. 180). *L.A.W. note.*

Prefaces to the New York Edition

Henry James

From *The Art of the Novel: Critical Prefaces*, edited by Richard P. Blackmur. New York and London: Charles Scribner's Sons, 1962 (1907–9), pp. 40–58, 307–26.

Preface to *The Portrait of a Lady*

(VOLUME III IN THE NEW YORK EDITION)

"The Portrait of a Lady" was, like "Roderick Hudson," begun in Florence, during three months spent there in the spring of 1879. Like "Roderick" and like "The American," it had been designed for publication in "The Atlantic Monthly," where it began to appear in 1880. It differed from its two predecessors, however, in finding a course also open to it, from month to month, in "Macmillan's Magazine"; which was to be for me one of the last occasions of simultaneous "serialisation" in the two countries that the changing conditions of literary intercourse between England and the United States had up to then left unaltered. It is a long novel, and I was long in writing it; I remember being again much occupied with it, the following year, during a stay of several weeks made in Venice. I had rooms on Riva Schiavoni, at the top of a house near the passage leading off to San Zaccaria; the waterside life, the wondrous lagoon spread before me, and the ceaseless human chatter of Venice came in at my windows, to which I seem to myself to have been constantly driven, in the fruitless fidget of composition, as if to see whether, out in the blue channel, the ship of some right suggestion, of some better phrase, of the next happy twist of my subject, the next true touch for my canvas, mightn't come into sight. But I recall vividly enough that the response most elicited, in general, to these restless appeals was the rather grim admonition that romantic and historic sites, such as the land of Italy abounds in, offer the artist a questionable aid to concentration when they themselves are not to be the subject of it. They are too rich in their own life and too charged with their own meanings merely to help him out with a lame phrase; they draw him away from his small question to their own greater ones; so that, after a little, he feels, while thus yearning toward them in his difficulty, as if he were asking an army of glorious veterans to help him to arrest a peddler who has given him the wrong change.

There are pages of the book which, in the reading over, have seemed to make me see again the bristling curve of the wide Riva, the large colour-spots of the balconied houses and the repeated undulation of the little hunchbacked bridges, marked by the rise and drop again, with the wave, of foreshortened clicking pedestrians. The Venetian footfall and the Venetian cry – all talk there, wherever uttered, having the pitch of a call across the water – come in once more at the window, renewing one's old impression of the delighted senses and the divided, frustrated mind. How can places that speak *in general* so to the imagination not give it, at the moment, the particular thing it wants? I recollect again and again, in beautiful places, dropping into that wonderment. The real truth is, I think, that they express, under this appeal, only too much – more than, in the given case, one has use for; so that one finds one's self working less congruously, after all, so far as the surrounding picture is concerned, than in presence of the moderate and the neutral, to which we may lend something of the light of our vision. Such a place as Venice is too proud for such charities; Venice doesn't borrow, she but all magnificently gives. We profit by that enormously, but to do so we must either be quite off duty or be on it in her service alone. Such, and so rueful, are these reminiscences; though on the whole, no doubt, one's book, and one's "literary effort" at large, were to be the better for them. Strangely fertilising, in the long run, does a wasted effort of attention often prove. It all depends on *how* the attention has been cheated, has been squandered. There are high-handed insolent frauds, and there are insidious sneaking ones. And there is, I fear, even on the most designing artist's part, always witless enough good faith, always anxious enough desire, to fail to guard him against their deceits.

Trying to recover here, for recognition, the germ of my idea, I see that it must have consisted not at all in any conceit of a "plot," nefarious name, in any flash, upon the fancy, of a set of relations, or in any one of those situations that, by a logic of their own, immediately fall, for the fabulist, into movement, into a march or a rush, a patter of quick steps; but altogether in the sense of a single character, the character and aspect of a particular engaging young woman, to which all the usual elements of a "subject," certainly of a setting, were to need to be super-added. Quite as interesting as the young woman herself, at her best, do I find, I must again repeat, this projection of memory upon the whole matter of the growth, in one's imagination, of some such apology for a motive. These are the fascinations of the fabulist's art, these lurking forces of expansion, these necessities of upspringing in the seed, these beautiful determin-ations, on the part of the idea entertained, to grow as tall as possible, to push into the light and the air and thickly flower there; and, quite as much, these fine possibilities of recovering, from some good standpoint on the ground gained, the intimate history of the business – of retracing and reconstructing its steps and stages. I have always fondly remembered a remark that I heard fall years ago from the lips of Ivan Turgenieff in regard to his own experience of the usual origin of the fictive picture. It began for him almost always with the vision of some person or persons, who hovered before him, soliciting him, as the active or passive figure, interesting him and appealing to him just as they were and by what they were. He saw them, in that fashion, as *disponibles*, saw them subject to the chances, the complications of existence, and saw them vividly, but then had to find for them the right relations, those that would most bring them out; to imagine, to invent and select and piece together the situations most useful and favour-able to the sense of the creatures themselves, the complications they would be most likely to produce and to feel.

"To arrive at these things is to arrive at my 'story,'" he said, "and that's the way I look for it. The result is that I'm often accused of not having 'story' enough. I seem to myself to have as much as I need – to show my people, to exhibit their relations with each other; for that is all my measure. If I watch them long enough I see them come together, I see them *placed*, I see them engaged in this or that act and in this or that difficulty. How they look and move and speak and behave, always in the setting I have found for them, is my account of them – of which I dare say, alas, *que cela manque souvent d'architecture*. But I would rather, I think, have too little architecture than too much – when there's danger of its interfering with my measure of the truth. The French of course like more of it than I give – having by their own genius such a hand for it; and indeed one must give all one can. As for the origin of one's wind-blown germs themselves, who shall say, as you ask, where *they* come from? We have to go too far back, too far behind, to say. Isn't it all we can say that they come from every quarter of heaven, that they are *there* at almost any turn of the road? They accumulate, and we are always picking them over, selecting among them. They are the breath of life – by which I mean that life, in its own way, breathes them upon us. They are so, in a manner prescribed and imposed – floated into our minds by the current of life. That reduces to imbecility the vain critic's quarrel, so often, with one's subject, when he hasn't the wit to accept it. Will he point out then which other it should properly have been? – his office being, essentially *to* point out. *Il en serait bien embarrassé.* Ah, when he points out what I've done or failed to do with it, that's another matter: there he's on his ground. I give him up my 'architecture,'" my distinguished friend concluded, "as much as he will."

So this beautiful genius, and I recall with comfort the gratitude I drew from his reference to the intensity of suggestion that may reside in the stray figure, the unattached character, the image *en disponibilité.* It gave me higher warrant than I seemed then to have met for just that blest habit of one's own imagination, the trick of investing some conceived or encountered individual, some brace or group of individuals, with the germinal property and authority. I was myself so much more antecedently conscious of my figures than of their setting – a too preliminary, a preferential interest in which struck me as in general such a putting of the cart before the horse. I might envy, though I couldn't emulate, the imaginative writer so constituted as to see his fable first and to make out its agents afterwards: I could think so little of any fable that it didn't need its agents positively to launch it; I could think so little of any situation that didn't depend for its interest on the nature of the persons situated, and thereby on their way of taking it. There are methods of so-called presentation, I believe – among novelists who have appeared to flourish – that offer the situation as indifferent to that support; but I have not lost the sense of the value for me, at the time, of the admirable Russian's testimony to my not needing, all superstitiously, to try and perform any such gymnastic. Other echoes from the same source linger with me, I confess, as unfadingly – if it be not all indeed one much-embracing echo. It was impossible after that not to read, for one's uses, high lucidity into the tormented and disfigured and bemuddled question of the objective value, and even quite into that of the critical appreciation, of "subject" in the novel.

One had had from an early time, for that matter, the instinct of the right estimate of such values and of its reducing to the inane the dull dispute over the "immoral" subject and the moral. Recognising so promptly the one measure of the worth of a given subject, the question about it that, rightly answered, disposes of all others – is it valid, in a word, is it genuine, is it sincere, the result of some direct impression or perception of life? – I had found small edification, mostly, in a critical pretension that had neglected from the first all delimitation of ground and all definition of terms. The air of my earlier time shows, to memory, as darkened, all round, with that vanity – unless the difference to-day be just in one's own final impatience, the lapse of one's attention. There is, I think, no more nutritive or suggestive truth in this connexion than that of the perfect dependence of the "moral" sense of a work of art on the amount of felt life concerned in producing it. The question comes back thus, obviously, to the kind and the degree of the artist's prime sensibility, which is the soil out of which his subject springs. The quality and capacity of that soil, its ability to "grow" with due freshness and straightness any vision of life, represents, strongly or weakly, the projected morality. That element is but another name for the more or less close connexion of the subject with some mark made on the intelligence, with some sincere experience. By which, at the same time, of course, one is far from contending that this enveloping air of the artist's humanity – which gives the last touch to the worth of the work – is not a widely and wondrously varying element; being on one occasion a rich and magnificent medium and on another a comparatively poor and ungenerous one. Here we get exactly the high price of the novel as a literary form – its power not only, while preserving that form with closeness, to range through all the differences of the individual relation to its general subject-matter, all the varieties of outlook on life, of disposition to reflect and project, created by conditions that are never the same from man to man (or, so far as that goes, from man to woman), but positively to appear more true to its character in proportion as it strains, or tends to burst, with a latent extravagance, its mould.

The house of fiction has in short not one window, but a million – a number of possible windows not to be reckoned, rather; every one of which has been pierced, or is still pierceable, in its vast front, by the need of the individual vision and by the pressure of the individual will. These apertures, of dissimilar shape and size, hang so, all together, over the human scene that we might have expected of them a greater sameness of report than we find. They are but windows at the best, mere holes in a dead wall, disconnected, perched aloft; they are not hinged doors opening straight upon life. But they have this mark of their own that at each of them stands a figure with a pair of eyes, or at least with a field-glass, which forms, again and again, for observation, a unique instrument, insuring to the person making use of it an impression distinct from every other. He and his neighbours are watching the same show, but one seeing more where the other sees less, one seeing black where the other sees white, one seeing big where the other sees small, one seeing coarse where the other sees fine. And so on, and so on; there is fortunately no saying on what, for the particular pair of eyes, the window may *not* open; "fortunately" by reason, precisely, of this incalculability of range. The spreading field, the human scene, is the "choice of subject"; the pierced aperture, either broad or balconied or slit-like and low-browed, is the "literary form"; but they are, singly or together, as nothing without the posted presence of the watcher – without, in other words, the consciousness of the artist. Tell me what the artist is, and I will tell you of what he has *been* conscious. Thereby I shall express to you at once his boundless freedom and his "moral" reference.

All this is a long way round, however, for my word about my dim first move toward "The Portrait," which was exactly my grasp of a single character – an acquisition I had made, moreover, after a fashion not here to be retraced. Enough that I was, as seemed to me, in complete possession of it, that I had been so for a long time, that this had made it familiar and yet had not blurred its charm, and that, all urgently, all tormentingly, I saw it in motion and, so to speak, in transit. This amounts to saying that I saw it as bent upon its fate – some fate or other; *which*, among the possibilities, being precisely the question. Thus I had my vivid individual – vivid, so strangely, in spite of being still at large, not confined by the conditions, not engaged in the tangle, to which we look for much of the impress that constitutes an identity. If the apparition was still all to be placed how came it to be vivid? – since we puzzle such quantities out, mostly, just by the business of placing them. One could answer such a question beautifully, doubtless, if one could do so subtle, if not so monstrous, a thing as to write the history of the growth of one's imagination. One would describe then what, at a given time, had extraordinarily happened to it, and one would so, for instance, be in a position to tell, with an approach to clearness, how, under favour of occasion, it had been able to take over (take over straight from life) such and such a constituted, animated figure or form. The figure has to that extent, as you see, *been* placed – placed in the imagination that detains it, preserves, protects, enjoys it, conscious of its presence in the dusky, crowded, heterogeneous back-shop of the mind very much as a wary dealer in precious odds and ends, competent to make an "advance" on rare objects confided to him, is conscious of the rare little "piece" left in deposit by the reduced, mysterious lady of title or the speculative amateur, and which is already there to disclose its merit afresh as soon as a key shall have clicked in a cupboard door.

That may be, I recognise, a somewhat superfine analogy for the particular "value" I here speak of, the image of the young feminine nature that I had had for so considerable a time all curiously at my disposal; but it appears to fond memory quite to fit the fact – with the recall, in addition, of my pious desire but to place my treasure right. I quite remind myself thus of the dealer resigned not to "realise," resigned to keeping the precious object locked up indefinitely rather than commit it, at no matter what price, to vulgar hands. For there *are* dealers in these forms and figures and treasures capable of that refinement. The point is, however, that this single small corner-stone, the conception of a certain young woman affronting her destiny, had begun with being all my outfit for the large building of "The Portrait of a Lady." It came to be a square and spacious house – or has at least seemed so to me in this going over it again; but, such as it is, it had to be put up round my young woman while she stood there in perfect isolation. That is to me, artistically speaking, the circumstance of interest; for I have lost myself once more, I confess, in the curiosity of analysing the structure. By what process of logical accretion was this slight "personality," the mere slim shade of an intelligent but presumptuous girl, to find itself endowed with the high attributes of a Subject? – and indeed by what thinness, at the best, would such a subject not be vitiated? Millions of presumptuous girls, intelligent or not intelligent, daily affront their destiny, and what is it open to their destiny to *be*, at the most, that we should make an ado about it? The novel is of its very nature an "ado," an ado about something, and the larger the form it takes the greater of course the ado. Therefore, consciously, that was what one was in for – for positively organising an ado about Isabel Archer.

One looked it well in the face, I seem to remember, this extravagance; and with the effect precisely of recognising the charm of the problem. Challenge any such problem with any intelligence, and you immediately see how full it is of substance; the wonder being, all the while, as we look at the world, how absolutely, how inordinately, the Isabel Archers, and even much smaller female fry, insist on mattering. George Eliot has admirably noted it – "In these frail vessels is borne onward through the ages the treasure of human affection." In "Romeo and Juliet" Juliet has to be important, just as, in "Adam Bede" and "The Mill on the Floss" and "Middlemarch" and "Daniel Deronda," Hetty Sorrel and Maggie Tulliver and Rosamond Vincy and Gwendolen Harleth have to be; with that much of firm ground, that much of bracing air, at the disposal all the while of their feet and their lungs. They are typical, none the less, of a class difficult, in the individual case, to make a centre of interest; so difficult in fact that many an expert painter, as for instance Dickens and Walter Scott, as for instance even, in the main, so subtle a hand as that of R. L. Stevenson, has preferred to leave the task unattempted. There are in fact writers as to whom we make out that their refuge from this is to assume it to be not worth their attempting; by which pusillanimity in truth their honour is scantly saved. It is never an attestation of a value, or even of our imperfect sense of one, it is never a tribute to any truth at all, that we shall represent that value badly. It never makes up, artistically, for an artist's dim feeling about a thing that he shall "do" the thing as ill as possible. There are better ways than that, the best of all of which is to begin with less stupidity.

It may be answered meanwhile, in regard to Shakespeare's and to George Eliot's testimony, that their concession to the "importance" of their Juliets and Cleopatras and Portias (even with Portia as the very type and model of the young person intelligent and presumptuous) and to that of their Hettys and Maggies and Rosamonds and Gwendolens, suffers the abatement that these slimnesses are, when figuring as the main props of the theme, never suffered to be sole ministers of its appeal, but have their inadequacy eked out with comic relief and underplots, as the playwrights say, when not with murders and battles and the great mutations of the world. If they are shown as "mattering" as much as they could possibly pretend to, the proof of it is in a hundred other persons, made of much stouter stuff, and each involved moreover in a hundred relations which matter to *them* concomitantly with that one. Cleopatra matters, beyond bounds, to Antony, but his colleagues, his antagonists, the state of Rome and the impending battle also prodigiously matter; Portia matters to Antonio, and to Shylock, and to the Prince of Morocco, to the fifty aspiring princes, but for these gentry there are other lively concerns; for Antonio, notably, there are Shylock and Bassanio and his lost ventures and the extremity of his predicament. This extremity indeed, by the same token, matters to Portia – though its doing so becomes of interest all by the fact that Portia matters to *us*. That she does so, at any rate, and that almost everything comes round to it again, supports my contention as to this fine example of the value recognised in the mere young thing. (I say "mere" young thing because I guess that even Shakespeare, preoccupied mainly though he may have been with the passions of princes, would scarce have pretended to found the best of his appeal for her on her high social position.) It is an example exactly of the deep difficulty braved – the difficulty of making George Eliot's "frail vessel," if not the all-in-all for our attention, at least the clearest of the call.

Now to see deep difficulty braved is at any time, for the really addicted artist, to feel almost even as a pang the beautiful incentive, and to feel it verily in such sort as to wish the danger intensified. The difficulty most worth tackling can only be for him, in these conditions, the greatest the case permits of. So I remember feeling here (in presence, always, that is, of the particular uncertainty of my ground), that there would be one way better than another – oh, ever so much better than any other! – of making it fight out its battle. The frail vessel, that charged with George Eliot's "treasure," and thereby of such importance to those who curiously approach it, has likewise possibilities of importance to itself, possibilities which permit of treatment and in fact peculiarly require it from the moment they are considered at all. There is always the escape from any close account of the weak agent of such spells by using as a bridge for evasion, for retreat and flight, the view of her relation to those surrounding her. Make it predominantly a view of *their* relation and the trick is played: you give the general sense of her effect, and you give it, so far as the raising on it of a superstructure goes, with the maximum of ease. Well, I recall perfectly how little, in my now quite established connexion, the maximum of ease appealed to me, and how I seemed to get rid of it by an honest transposition of the weights in the two scales. "Place the centre of the subject in the young woman's own consciousness," I said to myself, "and you get as interesting and as beautiful a difficulty as you could wish. Stick to *that* – for the centre; put the heaviest weight into *that* scale, which will be so largely the scale of her relation to herself. Make her only interested enough, at the same time, in the things that are not herself, and this relation needn't fear to be too limited. Place meanwhile in the other scale the lighter weight (which is usually the one that tips the balance of interest): press least hard, in short, on the consciousness of your heroine's satellites, especially the male; make it an interest contributive only to the greater one. See, at all events, what can be done in this way. What better field could there be for a due ingenuity? The girl hovers, inextinguishable, as a charming creature, and the job will be to translate her into the highest terms of that formula, and as nearly as possible moreover into *all* of them. To depend upon her and her little concerns wholly to see you through will necessitate, remember, your really 'doing' her."

So far I reasoned, and it took nothing less than that technical rigour, I now easily see, to inspire me with the right confidence for erecting on such a plot of ground the neat and careful and proportioned pile of bricks that arches over it and that was thus to form, constructionally speaking, a literary monument. Such is the aspect that to-day "The Portrait" wears for me: a structure reared with an "architectural" competence, as Turgenieff would have said, that makes it, to the author's own sense, the most proportioned of his productions after "The Ambassadors" – which was to follow it so many years later and which has, no doubt, a superior roundness. On one thing I was determined; that, though I should clearly have to pile brick upon brick for the creation of an interest, I would leave no pretext for saying that anything is out of line, scale or perspective. I would build large – in fine embossed vaults and painted arches, as who should say, and yet never let it appear that the chequered pavement, the ground under the reader's feet, fails to stretch at every point to the base of the walls. That precautionary spirit, on re-perusal of the book, is the old note that most touches me: it testifies so, for my own ear, to the anxiety of my provision for the reader's amusement. I felt, in view of the possible limitations of my subject, that no such provision could be excessive, and the development of the latter was simply the general form of that earnest quest. And I find indeed that this is the only account I can give myself of the evolution of the fable: it is all under the head thus named that I conceive the needful accretion as having taken place, the right complications as having started. It was naturally of the essence that the young woman should be herself complex; that was rudimentary – or was at any rate the light in which Isabel Archer had originally dawned. It went, however, but a certain way, and other lights, contending, conflicting lights, and of as many different colours, if possible, as the rockets, the Roman candles and Catherine-wheels of a "pyrotechnic display," would be employable to attest that she was. I had, no doubt, a groping instinct for the right complications, since I am quite unable to track the footsteps of those that constitute, as the case stands, the general situation exhibited. They are there, for what they are worth, and as numerous as might be; but my memory, I confess, is a blank as to how and whence they came.

I seem to myself to have waked up one morning in possession of them – of Ralph Touchett and his parents, of Madame Merle, of Gilbert Osmond and his daughter and his sister, of Lord Warburton, Caspar Goodwood and Miss Stackpole, the definite array of contributions to Isabel Archer's history. I recognised them, I knew them, they were the numbered pieces of my puzzle, the concrete terms of my "plot." It was as if they had simply, by an impulse of their own, floated into my ken, and all in response to my primary question: "Well, what will she *do?*" Their answer seemed to be that if I would trust them they would show me; on which, with an urgent appeal to them to make it at least as interesting as they could, I trusted them. They were like the group of attendants and entertainers who come down by train when people in the country give a party; they represented the contract for carrying the party on. That was an excellent relation with them – a possible one even with so broken a reed (from her slightness of cohesion) as Henrietta Stackpole. It is a familiar truth to the novelist, at the strenuous hour, that, as certain elements in any work are of the essence, so others are only of the form; that as this or that character, this or that disposition of the material, belongs to the subject directly, so to speak, so this or that other belongs to it but indirectly – belongs intimately to the treatment. This is a truth, however, of which he rarely gets the benefit – since it could be assured to him, really, but by criticism based upon perception, criticism which is too little of this world. He must not think of benefits, moreover, I freely recognise, for that way dishonour lies: he has, that is, but one to think of – the benefit, whatever it may be, involved in his having cast a spell upon the simpler, the very simplest, forms of attention. This is all he is entitled to; he is entitled to nothing, he is bound to admit, that can come to him, from the reader, as a result on the latter's part of any act of reflexion or discrimination. He may *enjoy* this finer tribute – that is another affair, but on condition only of taking it as a gratuity "thrown in," a mere miraculous windfall, the fruit of a tree he may not pretend to have shaken. Against reflexion, against discrimination, in his interest, all earth and air conspire; wherefore it is that, as I say, he must in many a case have schooled himself, from the first, to work but for a "living wage." The living wage is the reader's grant of the least possible quantity of attention required for consciousness of a "spell." The occasional charming "tip" is an act of his intelligence over and beyond this, a golden apple, for the writer's lap, straight from the wind-stirred tree. The artist may of course, in wanton moods, dream of some Paradise (for art) where the direct appeal to the intelligence might be legalised; for to such extravagances as these his yearning mind can scarce hope ever completely to close itself. The most he can do is to remember they *are* extravagances.

All of which is perhaps but a gracefully devious way of saying that Henrietta Stackpole was a good example, in "The Portrait," of the truth to which I just adverted – as good an example as I could name were it not that Maria Gostrey, in "The Ambassadors," then in the bosom of time, may be mentioned as a better. Each of these persons is but wheels to the coach; neither belongs to the body of that vehicle, or is for a moment accommodated with a seat inside. There the subject alone is ensconced, in the form of its "hero and heroine," and of the privileged high officials, say, who ride with the king and queen. There are reasons why one would have liked this to be felt, as in general one would like almost anything to be felt, in one's work, that one has one's self contributively felt. We have seen, however, how idle is that pretension, which I should be sorry to make too much of. Maria Gostrey and Miss Stackpole then are cases, each, of the light *ficelle*, not of the true agent; they may run beside the coach "for all they are worth," they may cling to it till they are out of breath (as poor Miss Stackpole all so vividly does), but neither, all the while, so much as gets her foot on the step, neither ceases for a moment to tread the dusty road. Put it even that they are like the fishwives who helped to bring back to Paris from Versailles, on that most ominous day of the first half of the French Revolution, the carriage of the royal family. The only thing is that I may well be asked, I acknowledge, why then, in the present fiction, I have suffered Henrietta (of whom we have indubitably too much) so officiously, so strangely, so almost inexplicably, to pervade. I will presently say what I can for that anomaly – and in the most conciliatory fashion.

A point I wish still more to make is that if my relation of confidence with the actors in my drama who *were*, unlike Miss Stackpole, true agents, was an excellent one to have arrived at, there still remained my relation with the reader, which was another affair altogether and as to which I felt no one to be trusted but myself. That solicitude was to be accordingly expressed in the artful patience with which, as I have said, I piled brick upon brick. The bricks, for the whole counting-over – putting for bricks little touches and inventions and enhancements by the way – affect me in truth as well-nigh innumerable and as ever so scrupulously fitted together and packed-in. It is an effect of detail, of the minutest; though, if one were in this connexion to say all, one would express the hope that the general, the ampler air of the modest monument still survives. I do at least seem to catch the key to a part of this abundance of small anxious, ingenious illustration as I recollect putting my finger, in my young woman's interest, on the most obvious of her predicates. "What will she 'do'? Why, the first thing she'll do will be to come to Europe; which in fact will form, and all inevitably, no small part of her principal adventure. Coming to Europe is even for the 'frail vessels,' in this wonderful age, a mild adventure; but what is truer than that on one side – the side of their independence of flood and field, of the moving accident, of battle and murder and sudden death – her adventures are to be mild? Without her sense of them, her sense *for* them, as one may say, they are next to nothing at all; but isn't the beauty and the difficulty just in showing their mystic conversion by that sense, conversion into the stuff of drama or, even more delightful word still, of 'story'?" It was all as clear, my contention, as a silver bell. Two very good instances, I think, of this effect of conversion, two cases of the rare chemistry, are the pages in which Isabel, coming into the drawing-room at Gardencourt, coming in from a wet walk or whatever, that rainy afternoon, finds Madame Merle in possession of the place, Madame Merle seated, all absorbed but all serene, at the piano, and deeply recognises, in the striking of such an hour, in the presence there, among the gathering shades, of this personage, of whom a moment before she had never so much as heard, a turning-point in her life. It is dreadful to have too much, for any artistic demonstration, to dot one's i's and insist on one's intentions, and I am not eager to do it now; but the question here was that of producing the maximum of intensity with the minimum of strain.

The interest was to be raised to its pitch and yet the elements to be kept in their key; so that, should the whole thing duly impress, I might show what an "exciting" inward life may do for the person leading it even while it remains perfectly normal. And I cannot think of a more consistent application of that ideal unless it be in the long statement, just beyond the middle of the book, of my young woman's extraordinary meditative vigil on the occasion that was to become for her such a landmark. Reduced to its essence, it is but the vigil of searching criticism; but it throws the action further forward than twenty "incidents" might have done. It was designed to have all the vivacity of incident and all the economy of picture. She sits up, by her dying fire, far into the night, under the spell of recognitions on which she finds the last sharpness suddenly wait. It is a representation simply of her motionlessly *seeing*, and an attempt withal to make the mere still lucidity of her act as "interesting" as the surprise of a caravan or the identification of a pirate.

It represents, for that matter, one of the identifications dear to the novelist, and even indispensable to him; but it all goes on without her being approached by another person and without her leaving her chair. It is obviously the best thing in the book, but it is only a supreme illustration of the general plan. As to Henrietta, my apology for whom I just left incomplete, she exemplifies, I fear, in her superabundance, not an element of my plan, but only an excess of my zeal. So early was to begin my tendency to *overtreat*, rather than undertreat (when there was choice or danger) my subject. (Many members of my craft, I gather, are far from agreeing with me, but I have always held overtreating the minor disservice.) "Treating" that of "The Portrait" amounted to never forgetting, by any lapse, that the thing was under a special obligation to be amusing. There was the danger of the noted "thinness" – which was to be averted, tooth and nail, by cultivation of the lively. That is at least how I see it to-day. Henrietta must have been at that time a part of my wonderful notion of the lively. And then there was another matter. I had, within the few preceding years, come to live in London, and the "international" light lay, in those days, to my sense, thick and rich upon the scene. It was the light in which so much of the picture hung. But that *is* another matter. There is really too much to say.

Preface to *The Ambassadors*

(VOLUME XXI IN THE NEW YORK EDITION)

Nothing is more easy than to state the subject of "The Ambassadors," which first appeared in twelve numbers of "The North American Review" (1903) and was published as a whole the same year. The situation involved is gathered up betimes, that is in the second chapter of Book Fifth, for the reader's benefit, into as few words as possible – planted or "sunk," stiffly and saliently, in the centre of the current, almost perhaps to the obstruction of traffic. Never can a composition of this sort have sprung straighter from a dropped grain of suggestion, and never can that grain, developed, overgrown and smothered, have yet lurked more in the mass as an independent particle. The whole case, in fine, is in Lambert Strether's irrepressible outbreak to little Bilham on the Sunday afternoon in Gloriani's garden, the candour with which he yields, for his young friend's enlightenment, to the charming admonition of that crisis. The idea of the tale resides indeed in the very fact that an hour of such unprecedented ease should have been felt by him *as* a crisis, and he is at pains to express it for us as neatly as we could desire. The remarks to which he thus gives utterance contain the essence of "The Ambassadors," his fingers close, before he has done, round the stem of the full-blown flower; which, after that fashion, he continues officiously to present to us. "Live all you can; it's a mistake not to. It doesn't so much matter what you do in particular so long as you have your life. If you haven't had that what *have* you had? I'm too old – too old at any rate for what I see. What one loses one loses; make no mistake about that. Still, we have the illusion of freedom; therefore don't, like me to-day, be without the memory of that illusion. I was either, at the right time, too stupid or too intelligent to have it, and now I'm a case of reaction against the mistake. Do what you like so long as you don't make it. For it *was* a mistake. Live, live!" Such is the gist of Strether's appeal to the impressed youth, whom he likes and whom he desires to befriend; the word "mistake" occurs several times, it will be seen, in the course of his remarks – which gives the measure of the signal warning he feels attached to his case. He has accordingly missed too much, though perhaps after all constitutionally qualified for a better part, and he wakes up to it in conditions that press the spring of a terrible question. *Would* there yet perhaps be time for reparation? – reparation, that is, for the injury done his character; for the affront, he is quite ready to say, so stupidly put upon it and in which he has even himself had so clumsy a hand? The answer to which is that he now at all events *sees*, so that the business of my tale and the march of my action, not to say the precious moral of everything, is just my demonstration of this process of vision.

Nothing can exceed the closeness with which the whole fits again into its germ. That had been given me bodily, as usual, by the spoken word, for I was to take the image over exactly as I happened to have met it. A friend had repeated to me, with great appreciation, a thing or two said to him by a man of distinction, much his senior, and to which a sense akin to that of Strether's melancholy eloquence might be imputed – said as chance would have, and so easily might, in Paris, and in a charming old garden attached to a house of art, and on a Sunday afternoon of summer, many persons of great interest being present. The observation there listened to and gathered up had contained part of the "note" that I was to recognise on the spot as to my purpose – had contained in fact the greater part; the rest was in the place and the time and the scene they sketched: these constituents clustered and combined to give me further support, to give me what I may call the note absolute. There it stands, accordingly, full in the tideway; driven in, with hard taps, like some strong stake for the noose of a cable, the swirl of the current roundabout it. What amplified the hint to more than the bulk of hints in general was the gift with it of the old Paris garden, for in that token were sealed up values infinitely precious. There was of course the seal to break and each item of the packet to count over and handle and estimate; but somehow, in the light of the hint, all the elements of a situation of the sort most to my taste were there. I could even remember no occasion on which, so confronted, I had found it of a livelier interest to take stock, in this fashion, of suggested wealth. For I think, verily, that there are degrees of merit in subjects – in spite of the fact that to treat even one of the most ambiguous with due decency we must for the time, for the feverish and prejudiced hour, at least figure its merit and its dignity as *possibly* absolute. What it comes to, doubtless, is that even among the supremely good – since with such alone is it one's theory of one's honour to be concerned – there is an ideal *beauty* of goodness the invoked action of which is to raise the artistic faith to its maximum. Then truly, I hold, one's theme may be said to shine, and that of "The Ambassadors," I confess, wore this glow for me from beginning to end. Fortunately thus I am able to estimate this as, frankly, quite the best, "all around," of my productions; any failure of that justification would have made such an extreme of complacency publicly fatuous.

I recall then in this connexion no moment of subjective intermittence, never one of those alarms as for a suspected hollow beneath one's feet, a felt ingratitude in the scheme adopted, under which confidence fails and opportunity seems but to mock. If the motive of "The Wings of the Dove," as I have noted, was to worry me at moments by a sealing-up of its face – though without prejudice to its again, of a sudden, fairly grimacing with expression – so in this other business I had absolute conviction and constant clearness to deal with; it had been a frank proposition, the whole bunch of data, installed on my premises like a monotony of fine weather. (The order of composition, in these things, I may mention, was reversed by the order of publication; the earlier written of the two books having appeared as the later.) Even under the weight of my hero's years I could feel my postulate firm; even under the strain of the difference between those of Madame de Vionnet and those of Chad Newsome, a difference liable to be denounced as shocking, I could still feel it serene. Nothing resisted, nothing betrayed, I seem to make out, in this full and sound sense of the matter; it shed from any side I could turn it to the same golden glow. I rejoiced in the promise of a hero so mature, who would give me thereby the more to bite into – since it's only into thickened motive and accumulated character, I think, that the painter of life bites more than a little. My poor friend should have accumulated character, certainly; or rather would be quite naturally and handsomely possessed of it, in the sense that he would have, and would always have felt he had, imagination galore, and that this yet wouldn't have wrecked him. It was immeasurable, the opportunity to "do" a man of imagination, for if *there* mightn't be a chance to "bite," where in the world might it be? This personage of course, so enriched, wouldn't give me, for his type, imagination in *predominance* or as his prime faculty, nor should I, in view of other matters, have found that convenient. So particular a luxury – some occasion, that is, for study of the high gift in *supreme* command of a case or of a career – would still doubtless come on the day I should be ready to pay for it; and till then might, as from far back, remain hung up well in view and just out of reach. The comparative case meanwhile would serve – it was only on the minor scale that I had treated myself even to comparative cases.

I was to hasten to add however that, happy stopgaps as the minor scale had thus yielded, the instance in hand should enjoy the advantage of the full range of the major; since most immediately to the point was the question of that *supplement* of situation logically involved in our gentleman's impulse to deliver himself in the Paris garden on the Sunday afternoon – or if not involved by strict logic then all ideally and enchantingly implied in it. (I say "ideally," because I need scarce mention that for development, for expression of its maximum, my glimmering story was, at the earliest stage, to have nipped the thread of connexion with the possibilities of the actual reported speaker. *He* remains but the happiest of accidents; his actualities, all too definite, precluded any range of possibilities; it had only been his charming office to project upon that wide field of the artist's vision – which hangs there ever in place like the white sheet suspended for the figures of a child's magiclantern – a more fantastic and more moveable shadow.) No privilege of the teller of tales and the handler of puppets is more delightful, or has more of the suspense and the thrill of a game of difficulty breathlessly played, than just this business of looking for the unseen and the occult, in a scheme half-grasped, by the light or, so to speak, by the clinging scent, of the gage already in hand. No dreadful old pursuit of the hidden slave with bloodhounds and the rag of association can ever, for "excitement," I judge, have bettered it at its best. For the dramatist always, by the very law of his genius, believes not only in a possible right issue from the rightly-conceived tight place; he does much more than this – he believes, irresistibly, in the necessary, the precious "tightness" of the place (whatever the issue) on the strength of any respectable hint. It being thus the respectable hint that I had with such avidity picked up, what would be the story to which it would most inevitably form the centre? It is part of the charm attendant on such questions that the "story," with the omens true, as I say, puts on from this stage the authenticity of concrete existence. It then *is*, essentially – it begins to be, though it may more or less obscurely lurk; so that the point is not in the least what to make of it, but only, very delightfully and very damnably, where to put one's hand on it.

In which truth resides surely much of the interest of that admirable mixture for salutary application which we know as art. Art deals with what we see, it must first contribute full-handed that ingredient; it plucks its material, otherwise expressed, in the garden of life – which material elsewhere grown is stale and uneatable. But it has no sooner done this than it has to take account of a *process* – from which only when it's the basest of the servants of man, incurring ignominious dismissal with no "character," does it, and whether under some muddled pretext of morality or on any other, pusillanimously edge away. The process, that of the expression, the literal squeezing-out, of value is another affair – with which the happy luck of mere finding has little to do. The joys of finding, at this stage, are pretty well over; that quest of the subject as a whole by "matching," as the ladies say at the shops, the big piece with the snippet, having ended, we assume, with a capture. The subject is found, and if the problem is then transferred to the ground of what to do with it the field opens out for any amount of doing. This is precisely the infusion that, as I submit, completes the strong mixture. It is on the other hand the part of the business that can least be likened to the chase with horn and hound. It's all a sedentary part – involves as much ciphering, of sorts, as would merit the highest salary paid to a chief accountant. Not, however, that the chief accountant hasn't *his* gleams of bliss; for the felicity, or at least the equilibrium, of the artist's state dwells less, surely, in the further delightful complications he can smuggle in than in those he succeeds in keeping out. He sows his seed at the risk of too thick a crop; wherefore yet again, like the gentlemen who audit ledgers, he must keep his head at any price. In consequence of all which, for the interest of the matter, I might seem here to have my choice of narrating my "hunt" for Lambert Strether, of describing the capture of the shadow projected by my friend's anecdote, or of reporting on the occurrences subsequent to that triumph. But I had probably best attempt a little to glance in each direction; since it comes to me again and again, over this licentious record, that one's bag of adventures, conceived or conceivable, has been only half-emptied by the mere telling of one's story. It depends so on what one means by that equivocal quantity. There is the story of one's hero, and then, thanks to the intimate connexion of things, the story of one's story itself. I blush to confess it, but if one's a dramatist one's a dramatist, and the latter imbroglio is liable on occasion to strike me as really the more objective of the two.

The philosophy imputed to him in that beautiful outbreak, the hour there, amid such happy provision, striking for him, would have been then, on behalf of my man of imagination, to be logically and, as the artless craft of comedy has it, "led up" to; the probable course to such a goal, the goal of so conscious a predicament, would have in short to be finely calculated. Where has he come from and why has he come, what is he doing (as we Anglo-Saxons, and we only, say, in our foredoomed clutch of exotic aids to expression) in that *galère?* To answer these questions plausibly, to answer them as under cross-examination in the witness-box by counsel for the prosecution, in other words satisfactorily to account for Strether and for his "peculiar tone," was to possess myself of the entire fabric. At the same time the clue to its whereabouts would lie in a certain *principle* of probability: he wouldn't have indulged in his peculiar tone without a reason;

it would take a felt predicament or a false position to give him so ironic an accent. One hadn't been noting "tones" all one's life without recognising when one heard it the voice of the false position. The dear man in the Paris garden was then admirably and unmistakeably *in* one – which was no small point gained; what next accordingly concerned us was the determination of *this* identity. One could only go by probabilities, but there was the advantage that the most general of the probabilities were virtual certainties. Possessed of our friend's nationality, to start with, there was a general probability in his narrower localism; which, for that matter, one had really but to keep under the lens for an hour to see it give up its secrets. He would have issued, our rueful worthy, from the very heart of New England – at the heels of which matter of course a perfect train of secrets tumbled for me into the light. They had to be sifted and sorted, and I shall not reproduce the detail of that process; but unmistakeably they were all there, and it was but a question, auspiciously, of picking among them. What the "position" would infallibly be, and why, on his hands, it had turned "false" – these inductive steps could only be as rapid as they were distinct. I accounted for everything – and "everything" had by this time become the most promising quantity – by the view that he had come to Paris in some state of mind which was literally undergoing, as a result of new and unexpected assaults and infusions, a change almost from hour to hour. He had come with a view that might have been figured by a clear green liquid, say, in a neat glass phial; and the liquid, once poured into the open cup of *application*, once exposed to the action of another air, had begun to turn from green to red, or whatever, and might, for all he knew, be on its way to purple, to black, to yellow. At the still wilder extremes represented perhaps, for all he could say to the contrary, by a variability so violent, he would at first, naturally, but have gazed in surprise and alarm; whereby the *situation* clearly would spring from the play of wildness and the development of extremes. I saw in a moment that, should this development proceed both with force and logic, my "story" would leave nothing to be desired. There is always, of course, for the story-teller, the irresistible determinant and the incalculable advantage of his interest in the story *as such*; it is ever, obviously, overwhelmingly, the prime and precious thing (as other than this I have never been able to see it); as to which what makes for it, with whatever headlong energy, may be said to pale before the energy with which it simply makes for itself. It rejoices, none the less, at its best, to seem to offer itself in a light, to seem to know, and with the very last knowledge, what it's about – liable as it yet is at moments to be caught by us with its tongue in its cheek and absolutely no warrant but its splendid impudence. Let us grant then that the impudence is always there – there, so to speak, for grace and effect and *allure*; there, above all, because the Story is just the spoiled child of art, and because, as we are always disappointed when the pampered don't "play up," we like it, to that extent, to look all its character. It probably does so, in truth, even when we most flatter ourselves that we negotiate with it by treaty.

All of which, again, is but to say that the *steps*, for my fable, placed themselves with a prompt and, as it were, functional assurance – an air quite as of readiness to have dispensed with logic had I been in fact too stupid for my clue. Never, positively, none the less, as the links multiplied, had I felt less stupid than for the determination of poor Strether's errand and for the apprehension of his issue. These things continued to fall together, as by the neat action of their own weight and form, even while their commentator scratched his head about them; he easily sees now that they were always well in advance of him. As the case completed itself he had in fact, from a good way behind, to catch up with them, breathless and a little flurried, as he best could. *The* false position, for our belated man of the world – belated because he had endeavoured so long to escape being one, and now at last had really to face his doom – the false position for him, I say, was obviously to have presented himself at the gate of that boundless menagerie primed with a moral scheme of the most approved pattern which was yet framed to break down on any approach to vivid facts; that is to any at all liberal appreciation of them. There would have been of course the case of the Strether prepared, wherever presenting himself, only to judge and to feel meanly: but *he* would have moved for me, I confess, enveloped in no legend whatever. The actual man's note, from the first of our seeing it struck, is the note of discrimination, just as his drama is to become, under stress, the drama of discrimination. It would have been his blest imagination, we have seen, that had already helped him to discriminate; the element that was for so much of the pleasure of my cutting thick, as I have intimated, into his intellectual, into his moral substance. Yet here it was, at the same time, just here, that a shade for a moment fell across the scene.

There was the dreadful little old tradition, one of the platitudes of the human comedy, that people's moral scheme *does* break down in Paris; that nothing is more frequently observed; that hundreds of thousands of more or less hypocritical or more or less cynical persons annually visit the place for the sake of the probable catastrophe, and that I came late in the day to work myself up about it. There was in fine the *trivial* association, one of the vulgarest in the world; but which gave me pause no longer, I think, simply because its vulgarity is so advertised. The revolution performed by Strether under the influence of the most interesting of great cities was to have nothing to do with any *bêtise* of the imputably "tempted" state; he was to be thrown forward, rather, thrown quite with violence, upon his lifelong trick of intense reflexion: which friendly test indeed was to bring him out, through winding passages, through alternations of darkness and light, very much *in* Paris, but with the surrounding scene itself a minor matter, a mere symbol for more things than had been dreamt of in the philosophy of Woollett. Another surrounding scene would have done as well for our show could it have represented a place in which Strether's errand was likely to lie and his crisis to await him. The *likely* place had the great merit of sparing me preparations; there would have been too many involved – not at all impossibilities, only rather worrying and delaying difficulties – in positing elsewhere Chad Newsome's interesting relation, his so interesting complexity of relations. Strether's appointed stage, in fine, could be but Chad's most luckily selected one. The young man had gone in, as they say, for circumjacent charm; and where he would have found it, by the turn of his mind, most "authentic," was where his earnest friend's analysis would most find *him*; as well as where, for that matter, the former's whole analytic faculty would be led such a wonderful dance.

"The Ambassadors" had been, all conveniently, "arranged for"; its first appearance was from month to month, in "The North American Review" during 1903, and I had been open from far back to any pleasant provocation for ingenuity that might reside in one's actively adopting – so as to make it, in its way, a small compositional law – recurrent breaks and resumptions. I had made up my mind here regularly to exploit and enjoy these often rather rude jolts – having found, as I believed, an admirable way to it; yet every question of form and pressure, I easily remember, paled in the light of the major propriety, recognised as soon as really weighed; that of employing but one centre and keeping it all within my hero's compass. The thing was to be so much this worthy's intimate adventure that even the projection of his consciousness upon it from beginning to end without intermission or deviation would probably still leave a part of its value for him, and *a fortiori* for ourselves, unexpressed. I might, however, express every grain of it that there would be room for – on condition of contriving a splendid particular economy. Other persons in no small number were to people the scene, and each with his or her axe to grind, his or her situation to treat, his or her coherency not to fail of, his or her relation to my leading motive, in a word, to establish and carry on. But Strether's sense of these things, and Strether's only, should avail me for showing them; I should know them but through his more or less groping knowledge of them, since his very gropings would figure among his most interesting motions, and a full observance of the rich rigour I speak of would give me more of the effect I should be most "after" than all other possible observances together. It would give me a large unity, and that in turn would crown me with the grace to which the enlightened story-teller will at any time, for his interest, sacrifice if need be all other graces whatever. I refer of course to the grace of intensity, which there are ways of signally achieving and ways of signally missing – as we see it, all round us, helplessly and woefully missed. Not that it isn't, on the other hand, a virtue eminently subject to appreciation – there being no strict, no absolute measure of it; so that one may hear it acclaimed where it has quite escaped one's perception, and see it unnoticed where one has gratefully hailed it. After all of which I am not sure, either, that the immense amusement of the whole cluster of difficulties so arrayed may not operate, for the fond fabulist, when judicious not less than fond, as his best of determinants. That charming principle is always there, at all events, to keep interest fresh: it is a principle, we remember, essentially ravenous, without scruple and without mercy, appeased with no cheap nor easy nourishment. It enjoys the costly sacrifice and rejoices thereby in the very odour of difficulty – even as ogres, with their "Fee-faw-fum!" rejoice in the smell of the blood of Englishmen.

Thus it was, at all events, that the ultimate, though after all so speedy, definition of my gentleman's job – his coming out, all solemnly appointed and deputed, to "save" Chad, and his then finding the young man so disobligingly and, at first, so bewilderingly not lost that a new issue altogether, in the connexion, prodigiously faces them, which has to be dealt with in a new light – promised as many calls on ingenuity and on the higher branches of the compositional art as one could possibly desire. Again and yet again, as, from book to book, I proceed with my survey, I find no source of interest equal to this verification after the fact, as I may call it, and the more in detail the better, of the scheme of consistency "gone in" for. As always – since the charm never fails – the retracing of the process from point to point brings back the old illusion. The old intentions bloom again and flower – in spite of all the blossoms they were to have dropped by the way. This is the charm, as I say, of adventure *transposed* – the thrilling ups and downs, the intricate ins and outs of the compositional problem, made after such a fashion admirably objective, becoming the question at issue and keeping the author's heart in his mouth. Such an element, for instance, as his intention that Mrs. Newsome, away off with her finger on the pulse of Massachusetts, should yet be no less intensely than circuitously present through the whole thing, should be no less felt as to be reckoned with than the most direct exhibition, the finest portrayal at first hand could make her, such a sign of artistic good faith, I say, once it's unmistakeably there, takes on again an actuality not too much impaired by the comparative dimness of the particular success. Cherished intention too inevitably acts and operates, in the book, about fifty times as little as I had fondly dreamt it might; but that scarce spoils for me the pleasure of recognising the fifty ways in which I had sought to provide for it. The mere charm of seeing such an idea constituent, in its degree; the fineness of the measures taken – a real extension, if successful, of the very terms and possibilities of representation and figuration – such things alone were, after this fashion, inspiring, such things alone were a gage of the probable success of that dissimulated calculation with which the whole effort was to square. But oh the cares begotten, none the less, of that same "judicious" sacrifice to a particular form of interest! One's work should have composition, because composition alone is positive beauty; but all the while – apart from one's inevitable consciousness too of the dire paucity of readers ever recognising or ever missing positive beauty – how, as to the cheap and easy, at every turn, how, as to immediacy and facility, and even as to the commoner vivacity, positive beauty might have to be sweated for and paid for! Once achieved and installed it may always be trusted to make the poor seeker feel he would have blushed to the roots of his hair for failing of it; yet, how, as its virtue can be essentially but the virtue of the whole, the wayside traps set in the interest of muddlement and pleading but the cause of the moment, of the particular bit in itself, have to be kicked out of the path! All the sophistications in life, for example, might have appeared to muster on behalf of the menace – the menace to a bright variety – involved in Strether's having all the subjective "say," as it were, to himself.

Had I meanwhile, made him at once hero and historian, endowed him with the romantic privilege of the "first person" – the darkest abyss of romance this, inveterately, when enjoyed on the grand scale – variety, and many other queer matters as well, might have been smuggled in by a back door. Suffice it, to be brief, that the first person, in the long piece, is a form foredoomed to looseness, and that looseness, never much my affair, had never been so little so as on this particular occasion. All of which reflexions flocked to the standard from the moment – a very early one – the question of how to keep my form amusing while sticking so close to my central figure and constantly taking its pattern from him had to be faced. He arrives (arrives at Chester) as for the dreadful purpose of giving his creator "no end" to tell about him – before which rigorous mission the serenest of creators might well have quailed. I was far from the serenest; I was more than agitated enough to reflect that, grimly deprived of one alternative or one substitute for "telling," I must address myself tooth and nail to another. I couldn't, save by implication, make other persons tell *each other* about him – blest resource, blest necessity, of the drama, which reaches its effects of unity, all remarkably, by paths absolutely opposite to the paths of the novel: with other persons, save as they were primarily *his* persons (not he primarily but one of theirs), I had simply nothing to do. I had relations for him none the less, by the mercy of Providence, quite as much as if my exhibition *was* to be a muddle; if I could only by implication and a show of consequence make other persons tell each other about him, I could at least make him tell *them* whatever in the world he must; and could so, by the same token – which was a further luxury thrown in – see straight into the deep differences between what that could do for me, or at all events for *him*, and the large ease of "autobiography." It may be asked why, if one so keeps to one's hero, one shouldn't make a single mouthful of "method," shouldn't throw the reins on his neck and, letting them flap there as free as in "Gil Blas" or in "David Copperfield," equip him with the double privilege of subject and object – a course that has at least the merit of brushing away questions at a sweep. The answer to which is, I think, that one makes that surrender only if one is prepared *not* to make certain precious discriminations.

The "first person" then, so employed, is addressed by the author directly to ourselves, his possible readers, whom he has to reckon with, at the best, by our English tradition, so loosely and vaguely after all, so little respectfully, on so scant a presumption of exposure to criticism. Strether, on the other hand, encaged and provided for as "The Ambassadors" encages and provides, has to keep in view proprieties much stiffer and more salutary than any our straight and credulous gape are likely to bring home to him, has exhibitional conditions to meet, in a word, that forbid the terrible *fluidity* of self-revelation. I may seem not to better the case for my discrimination if I say that, for my first care, I had thus inevitably to set him up a confidant or two, to wave away with energy the custom of the seated mass of explanation after the fact, the inserted block of merely referential narrative, which flourishes so, to the shame of the modern impatience, on the serried page of Balzac, but which seems simply to appal our actual, our general weaker, digestion. "Harking back to make up" took at any rate more doing, as the phrase is, not only than the reader of to-day demands, but than he will tolerate at any price any call upon him either to understand or remotely to measure; and for the beauty of the thing when done the current editorial mind in particular appears wholly without sense. It is not, however, primarily for either of these reasons, whatever their weight, that Strether's friend Waymarsh is so keenly clutched at, on the threshold of the book, or that no less a pounce is made on Maria Gostrey – without even the pretext, either, of *her* being, in essence, Strether's friend. She is the reader's friend much rather – in consequence of dispositions that make him so eminently require one; and she acts in that capacity, and *really* in that capacity alone, with exemplary devotion, from beginning to end of the book. She is an enrolled, a direct, aid to lucidity; she is in fine, to tear off her mask, the most unmitigated and abandoned of *ficelles*. Half the dramatist's art, as we well know – since if we don't it's not the fault of the proofs that lie scattered about us – is in the use of *ficelles*; by which I mean in a deep dissimulation of his dependence on them. Waymarsh only to a slighter degree belongs, in the whole business, less to my subject than to my treatment of it; the interesting proof, in these connexions, being that one has but to take one's subject for the stuff of drama to interweave with enthusiasm as many Gostreys as need be.

The material of "The Ambassadors," conforming in this respect exactly to that of "The Wings of the Dove," published just before it, is taken absolutely for the stuff of drama; so that, availing myself of the opportunity given me by this edition for some prefatory remarks on the latter work, I had mainly to make on its behalf the point of its scenic consistency. It disguises that virtue, in the oddest way in the world, by just *looking*, as we turn its pages, as little scenic as possible; but it sharply divides itself, just as the composition before us does, into the parts that prepare, that tend in fact to over-prepare, for scenes, and the parts, or otherwise into the scenes, that justify and crown the preparation. It may definitely be said, I think, that everything in it that is not scene (not, I of course mean, complete and functional scene, treating *all* the submitted matter, as by logical start, logical turn, and logical finish) is discriminated preparation, is the fusion and synthesis of picture. These alternations propose themselves all recogniseably, I think, from an early stage, as the very form and figure of "The Ambassadors"; so that, to repeat, such an agent as Miss Gostrey, pre-engaged at a high salary, but waits in the draughty wing with her shawl and her smelling-salts. Her function speaks at once for itself, and by the time she has dined with Strether in London and gone to a play with him her intervention as a *ficelle* is, I hold, expertly justified. Thanks to it we have treated scenically, and scenically alone, the whole lumpish question of Strether's "past," which has seen us more happily on the way than anything else could have done; we have strained to a high lucidity and vivacity (or at least we hope we have) certain indispensable facts; we have seen our two or three immediate friends all conveniently and profitably in "action"; to say nothing of our beginning to descry others, of a remoter intensity, getting into motion, even if a bit vaguely as yet, for our further enrichment. Let my first point be here that the scene in question, that in which the whole situation at Woollett and the complex forces that have propelled my hero to where this lively extractor of his value and distiller of his essence awaits him, is normal and entire, is really an excellent *standard* scene; copious, comprehensive, and accordingly never short, but with its office as definite as that of the hammer on the gong of the clock, the office of expressing *all that is in* the hour.

The "*ficelle*" character of the subordinate party is as artfully dissimulated, throughout, as may be, and to that extent that, with the seams or joints of Maria Gostrey's ostensible connectedness taken particular care of, duly smoothed over, that is, and anxiously kept from showing as "pieced on," this figure doubtless achieves, after a fashion, something of the dignity of a prime idea: which circumstance but shows us afresh how many quite incalculable but none the less clear sources of enjoyment for the infatuated artist, how many copious springs of our never-to-be-slighted "fun" for the reader and critic susceptible of contagion, may sound their incidental plash as soon as an artistic process begins to enjoy free development. Exquisite – in illustration of this – the mere interest and amusement of such at once "creative" and critical questions as how and where and why to make Miss Gostrey's false connexion carry itself, under a due high polish, as a real one. Nowhere is it more of an artful expedient for mere consistency of form, to mention a case, than in the last "scene" of the book, where its function is to give or to add nothing whatever, but only to express as vividly as possible certain things quite other than itself and that are of the already fixed and appointed measure. Since, however, all art is *expression*, and is thereby vividness, one was to find the door open here to any amount of delightful dissimulation. These verily are the refinements and ecstasies of method – amid which, or certainly under the influence of any exhilarated demonstration of which, one must keep one's head and not lose one's way. To cultivate an adequate intelligence for them and to make that sense operative is positively to find a charm in any produced ambiguity of appearance that is not by the same stroke, and all helplessly, an ambiguity of sense. To project imaginatively, for my hero, a relation that has nothing to do with the matter (the matter of my subject) but has everything to do with the manner (the manner of my presentation of the same) and yet to treat it, at close quarters and for fully economic expression's possible sake, as if it were important and essential – to do that sort of thing and yet muddle nothing may easily become, as one goes, a signally attaching proposition; even though it all remains but part and parcel,

HENRY JAMES

I hasten to recognise, of the merely general and related question of expressional curiosity and expressional decency.

I am moved to add after so much insistence on the scenic side of my labour that I have found the steps of re-perusal almost as much waylaid here by quite another style of effort in the same signal interest – or have in other words not failed to note how, even so associated and so discriminated, the finest proprieties and charms of the non-scenic may, under the right hand for them, still keep their intelligibility and assert their office. Infinitely suggestive such an observation as this last on the whole delightful head, where representation is concerned, of possible variety, of effective expressional change and contrast. One would like, at such an hour as this, for critical license, to go into the matter of the noted inevitable deviation (from too fond an original vision) that the exquisite treachery even of the straightest execution may ever be trusted to inflict even on the most mature plan – the case being that, though one's last reconsidered production always seems to bristle with that particular evidence, "The Ambassadors," would place a flood of such light at my service. I must attach to my final remark here a different import; noting in the other connexion I just glanced at that such passages as that of my hero's first encounter with Chad Newsome, absolute attestations of the non-scenic form though they be, yet lay the firmest hand too – so far at least as intention goes – on representational effect. To report at all closely and completely of what "passes" on a given occasion is inevitably to become more or less scenic; and yet in the instance I allude to, *with* the conveyance, expressional curiosity and expressional decency are sought and arrived at under quite another law. The true inwardness of this may be at bottom but that one of the suffered treacheries has consisted precisely, for Chad's whole figure and presence, of a direct presentability diminished and compromised – despoiled, that is, of its *proportional* advantage; so that, in a word, the whole economy of his author's relation to him has at important points to be redetermined. The book, however, critically viewed, is touchingly full of these disguised and repaired losses, these insidious recoveries, these intensely redemptive consistencies. The pages in which Mamie Pocock gives her appointed and, I can't but think, duly felt lift to the whole action by the so inscrutably-applied side-stroke or short-cut of our just watching, and as quite at an angle of vision as yet untried, her single hour of suspense in the hotel salon, in our partaking of her concentrated study of the sense of matters bearing on her own case, all the bright warm Paris afternoon, from the balcony that overlooks the Tuileries garden – these are as marked an example of the representational virtue that insists here and there on being, for the charm of opposition and renewal, other than the scenic. It wouldn't take much to make me further argue that from an equal play of such oppositions the book gathers an intensity that fairly adds to the dramatic – though the latter is supposed to be the sum of all intensities; or that has at any rate nothing to fear from juxtaposition with it. I consciously fail to shrink in fact from that extravagance – I risk it, rather, for the sake of the moral involved; which is not that the particular production before us exhausts the interesting questions it raises, but that the Novel remains still, under the right persuasion, the most independent, most elastic, most prodigious of literary forms.

The Craft of Fiction

Percy Lubbock

From *The Craft of Fiction*. London: Jonathan Cape, 1921, from ch. 2, pp. 14–25, ch. 17, pp. 251–64. Copyright © Percy Lubbock (1957). Reprinted by the kind permission of the Estate of Percy Lubbock and the Sayle Literary Agency.

II

A book has a certain form, we all agree; what the form of a particular book may be, whether good or bad, and whether it matters – these are points of debate; but that a book *has* a form, this is not disputed. We hear the phrase on all sides, an unending argument is waged over it. One critic condemns a novel as "shapeless," meaning that its shape is objectionable; another retorts that if the novel has other fine qualities, its shape is unimportant; and the two will continue their controversy till an onlooker, pardonably bewildered, may begin to suppose that "form" in fiction is something to be put in or left out of a novel according to the taste of the author. But though the discussion is indeed confusingly worded at times, it is clear that there is agreement on this article at least – that a book is a thing to which a shape is ascribable, good or bad. I have spoken of the difficulty that prevents us from ever seeing or describing the shape with perfect certainty; but evidently we are convinced that it is there, clothing the book.

Not as a single form, however, but as a moving stream of impressions, paid out of the volume in a slender thread as we turn the pages – that is how the book reaches us; or in another image it is a procession that passes before us as we sit to watch. It is hard to think of this lapse and flow, this sequence of figures and scenes, which must be taken in a settled order, one after another, as existing in the condition of an immobile form, like a pile of sculpture. Though we readily talk of the book as a material work of art, our words seem to be crossed by a sense that it is rather a process, a passage of experience, than a thing of size and shape. I find this contradiction dividing all my thought about books; they are objects, yes, completed and detached, but I recall them also as tracts of time, during which Clarissa and Anna moved and lived and endured in my view. Criticism is hampered by the ambiguity; the two books, the two aspects of the same book, blur each other; a critic seems to shift from this one to that, from the thing carved in the stuff of thought to the passing movement of life. And on the whole it is the latter aspect of the two which asserts itself; the first, the novel with its formal outline, appears for a moment, and then the life contained in it breaks out and obscures it.

But the procession which passes across our line of sight in the reading must be marshalled and concentrated somewhere; we receive the story of Anna bit by bit, all the numerous fragments that together make Tolstoy's book; and finally the tale is complete, and the book stands before us, or should stand, as a welded mass. We have been given the material, and the book should now be there. Our treacherous memory will have failed to preserve it all, but that disability we have admitted and discounted; at any rate an imposing object ought to remain, Tolstoy's great imaginative sculpture, sufficiently representing his intention. And again and again, at this point, I make the same discovery; I have been watching the story, that is to say, forgetful of the fact that there was more for me to do than to watch receptively and passively, forgetful of the novel that I should have been fashioning out of the march of experience as it passed. I have been treating it as life; and that is all very well, and is the right manner as far as it goes, but my treatment of life is capricious and eclectic, and this life, this story of Anna, has suffered accord-ingly. I have taken much out of it and carried away many recollections; I have omitted to think of it as matter to be wrought into a single form. What wonder if I search my mind in vain, a little later, for the book that Tolstoy wrote?

But how is one to construct a novel out of the impressions that Tolstoy pours forth from his prodigious hands? This is a kind of "creative reading" (the phrase is Emerson's) which comes instinctively to few of us. We know how to imagine a landscape or a conversation when he describes it, but to gather up all these sights and sounds into a compact fabric, round which the mind can wander freely, as freely as it strays and contemplates and loses its way, perhaps, in Tolstoy's wonderful world – this is a task which does not achieve itself without design and deliberation on the part of the reader. It is an effort, first of all, to keep the world of Anna (I cling to this illustration) at a distance; and yet it must be kept at a distance if it is to be impressed with the form of art; no artist (and the skilful reader is an artist) can afford to be swayed and beset by his material, he must stand above it. And then it is a further effort, prolonged, needing practice and knowledge, to recreate the novel in its right form, the best form that the material, selected and disposed by the author, is capable of accepting.

The reader of a novel – by which I mean the critical reader – is himself a novelist; he is the maker of a book which may or may not please his taste when it is finished, but of a book for which he must take his own share of the responsibility. The author does his part, but he cannot transfer his book like a bubble into the brain of the critic; he cannot make sure that the critic will possess his work. The reader must therefore become, for his part, a novelist, never permitting himself to suppose that the creation of the book is solely the affair of the author. The difference between them is immense, of course, and so much so that a critic is always inclined to extend and intensify it. The opposition that he conceives between the creative and the critical task is a very real one; but in modestly belittling his own side of the business he is apt to forget an essential portion of it. The writer of the novel works in a manner that would be utterly impossible to the critic, no doubt, and with a liberty and with a range that would disconcert him entirely. But in one quarter their work coincides; both of them make the novel.

Is it necessary to define the difference? That is soon done if we picture Tolstoy and his critic side by side, surveying the free and formless expanse of the world of life. The critic has nothing to say; he waits, looking to Tolstoy for guidance. And Tolstoy, with the help of some secret of his own, which is his genius, does not hesitate for an instant. His hand is plunged into the scene, he lifts out of it great fragments, right and left, ragged masses of life torn from their setting; he selects. And upon these trophies he sets to work with the full force of his imagination; he detects their significance, he disengages and throws aside whatever is accidental and meaningless; he re-makes them in conditions that are never known in life, conditions in which a thing is free to grow according to its own law, expressing itself unhindered; he liberates and completes. And then, upon all this new life – so like the old and yet so different, *more* like the old, as one may say, than the old ever had the chance of being – upon all this life that is now so much more intensely living than before, Tolstoy directs the skill of his art; he distributes it in a single, embracing design; he orders and disposes. And thus the critic receives his guidance, and *his* work begins.

No selection, no arrangement is required of him; the new world that is laid before him is the world of art, life liberated from the tangle of cross-purposes, saved from arbitrary distortion. Instead of a continuous, endless scene, in which the eye is caught in a thousand directions at once, with nothing to hold it to a fixed centre, the landscape that opens before the critic is whole and single; it has passed through an imagination, it has shed its irrelevancy and is compact with its own meaning. Such is the world in the book – in Tolstoy's book I do not say; but it is the world in the book as it may be, in the book where imagination and execution are perfectly harmonized. And in any case the critic accepts this ordered, enhanced display as it stands, better or worse, and uses it all for the creation of the book. There can be no picking and choosing now; that was the business of the novelist, and it has been accomplished according to his light; the critic creates out of life that is already subject to art.

But his work is not the less plastic for that. The impressions that succeed one another, as the pages of the book are turned, are to be built into a structure, and the critic is missing his opportunity unless he can proceed in a workmanlike manner. It is not to be supposed that an artist who carves or paints is so filled with emotion by the meaning of his work – the story in it – that he forgets the abstract beauty of form and colour; and though there is more room for such sensibility in an art which is the shaping of thought and feeling, in the art of literature, still the man of letters is a craftsman, and the critic cannot be less. He must know how to handle the stuff which is continually forming in his mind while he reads; he must be able to recognize its fine variations and to take them all into account. Nobody can work in material of which the properties are unfamiliar, and a reader who tries to get possession of a book with nothing but his appreciation of the life and the ideas and the story in it is like a man who builds a wall without knowing the capacities of wood and clay and stone. Many different substances, as distinct to the practised eye as stone and wood, go to the making of a novel, and it is necessary to see them for what they are. So only is it possible to use them aright, and to find, when the volume is closed, that a complete, coherent, appraisable book remains in the mind.

And what are these different substances, and how is a mere reader to learn their right use? They are the various forms of narrative, the forms in which a story may be told; and while they are many, they are not indeed so very many, though their modifications and their commixtures are infinite. They are not recondite; we know them well and use them freely, but to use them is easier than to perceive their demands and their qualities. These we gradually discern by using them consciously and questioningly – by reading, I mean, and reading critically, the books in which they appear. Let us very carefully follow the methods of the novelists whose effects are incontestable, noticing exactly the manner in which the scenes and figures in their books are presented. The scenes and figures, as I have said, we shape, we detach, without the smallest difficulty; and if we pause over them for long enough to see by what arts and devices, on the author's part, we have been enabled to shape them so strikingly – to see precisely how this episode has been given relief, that character made intelligible and vivid – we at once begin to stumble on many discoveries about the making of a novel.

Our criticism has been oddly incurious in the matter, considering what the dominion of the novel has been for a hundred and fifty years. The refinements of the art of fiction have been accepted without question, or at most have been classified roughly and summarily – as is proved by the singular poverty of our critical vocabulary, as soon as we pass beyond the simplest and plainest effects. The expressions and the phrases at our disposal bear no defined, delimited meanings; they have not been rounded and hardened by passing constantly from one critic's hand to another's. What is to be understood by a "dramatic" narrative, a "pictorial" narrative, a "scenic" or a "generalized" story? We must use such words, as soon as we begin to examine the structure of a novel; and yet they are words which have no technical acceptation in regard to a novel, and one cannot be sure how they will be taken. The want of a received nomenclature is a real hindrance, and I have often wished that the modern novel had been invented a hundred years sooner, so that it might have fallen into the hands of the critical schoolmen of the seventeenth century. As the production of an age of romance, or of the eve of such an age, it missed the advantage of the dry light of academic judgement, and I think it still has reason to regret the loss. The critic has, at any rate; his language, even now, is unsettled and unformed.

And we still suffer from a kind of shyness in the presence of a novel. From shyness of the author or of his sentiments or of his imagined world, no indeed; but we are haunted by a sense that a novel is a piece of life, and that to take it to pieces would be to destroy it. We begin to analyse it, and we seem to be like Beckmesser, writing down the mistakes of the spring-time upon his slate. It is an obscure delicacy, not clearly formulated, not admitted, perhaps, in so many words; but it has its share in restraining the hand of criticism. We scarcely need to be thus considerate; the immense and necessary difficulty of closing with a book at all, on any terms, might appear to be enough, without adding another; the book is safe from rude violation. And it is not a piece of life, it is a piece of art like another; and the fact that it is an ideal shape, with no existence in space, only to be spoken of in figures and metaphors, makes it all the more important that in our thought it should be protected by no romantic scruple. Or perhaps it is not really the book that we are shy of, but a still more fugitive phantom – our pleasure in it. It spoils the fun of a novel to know how it is made – is this a reflection that lurks at the back of our minds? Sometimes, I think.

But the pleasure of illusion is small beside the pleasure of creation, and the greater is open to every reader, volume in hand. How a novelist finds his subject, in a human being or in a situation or in a turn of thought, this indeed is beyond us; we might look long at the very world that Tolstoy saw, we should never detect the unwritten book he found there; and he can seldom (he and the rest of them) give any account of the process of discovery. The power that recognizes the fruitful idea and seizes it is a thing apart. For this reason we judge the novelist's eye for a subject to be his cardinal gift, and we have nothing to say, whether by way of exhortation or of warning, till his subject is announced. But from that moment he is accessible, his privilege is shared; and the delight of treating the subject is acute and perennial. From point to point we follow the writer, always looking back to the subject itself in order to understand the logic of the course he pursues. We find that we are creating a design, large or small, simple or intricate, as the chapter finished is fitted into its place; or again there is a flaw and a break in the development, the author takes a turn that appears to contradict or to disregard the subject, and the critical question, strictly so called, begins. Is this proceeding of the author the right one, the best for the subject? Is it possible to conceive and to name a better? The hours of the author's labour are lived again by the reader, the pleasure of creation is renewed.

So it goes, till the book is ended and we look back at the whole design. It may be absolutely satisfying to the eye, the expression of the subject, complete and compact. But with the book in this condition of a defined shape, firm of outline, its form shows for what it is indeed – not an attribute, one of many and possibly not the most important, but the book itself, as the form of a statue is the statue itself. If the form is to the eye imperfect, it means that the subject is somehow and somewhere imperfectly expressed, it means that the story has suffered. Where then, and how? Is it because the treatment has not started from the heart of the subject, or has diverged from the line of its true development – or is it that the subject itself was poor and unfruitful? The question ramifies quickly. But anyhow here is the book, or something that we need not hesitate to regard as the book, recreated according to the best of the reader's ability. Indeed he knows well that it will melt away in time; nothing can altogether save it; only it will last for longer than it would have lasted if it had been read uncritically, if it had not been deliberately recreated. In that case it would have fallen to pieces at once, Anna and Clarissa would have stepped out of the work of art in which their authors had so laboriously enshrined them, the book would have perished. It is now a single form, and let us judge the effect of it while we may. At best we shall have no more time than we certainly require.

* * *

XVII

The whole intricate question of method, in the craft of fiction, I take to be governed by the question of the point of view – the question of the relation in which the narrator stands to the story. He tells it as *he* sees it, in the first place; the reader faces the story-teller and listens, and the story may be told so vivaciously that the presence of the minstrel is forgotten, and the scene becomes visible, peopled with the characters of the tale. It may be so, it very often is so for a time. But it is not so always, and the story-teller himself grows conscious of a misgiving. If the spell is weakened at any moment, the listener is recalled from the scene to the mere author before him, and the story rests only upon the author's direct assertion. Is it not possible, then, to introduce another point of view, to set up a fresh narrator to bear the brunt of the reader's scrutiny? If the story-teller is *in* the story himself, the author is dramatized; his assertions gain in weight, for they are backed by the presence of the narrator in the pictured scene. It is advantage scored; the author has shifted his responsibility, and it now falls where the reader can see and measure it; the arbitrary quality which may at any time be detected in the author's voice is disguised in the voice of his spokesman. Nothing is now imported into the story from without; it is self-contained, it has no associations with anyone beyond its circle.

Such is the first step towards dramatization, and in very many a story it may be enough. The spokesman is there, in recognizable relation with his matter; no question of his authority can arise. But now a difficulty may be started by the nature of the tale that he tells. If he has nothing to do but to relate what he has seen, what anyone might have seen in his position, his account will serve very well; there is no need for more. Let him unfold his chronicle as it appears in his memory. But if he is himself the subject of his story, if the story involves a searching exploration of his own consciousness, an account in his own words, after the fact, is not by any means the best imaginable. Far better it would be to see him while his mind is actually at work in the agitation, whatever it may be, which is to make the book. The matter would then be objective and visible to the reader, instead of reaching him in the form of a report at second hand. But how to manage this without falling back upon the author and *his* report, which has already been tried and for good reasons, as it seemed, abandoned? It is managed by a kind of repetition of the same stroke, a further shift of the point of view. The spectator, the listener, the reader, is now himself to be placed at the angle of vision; not an account or a report, more or less convincing, is to be offered him, but a direct sight of the matter itself, while it is passing. Nobody expounds or explains; the story is enacted by its look and behaviour at particular moments. By the first stroke the narrator was brought into the book and set before the reader; but the action appeared only in his narrative. Now the action is there, proceeding while the pages are turned; the narrator is forestalled, he is watched while the story is in the making. Such is the progress of the writer of fiction towards drama; such is his method of evading the drawbacks of a mere reporter and assuming the advantages, as far as possible, of a dramatist. How far he may choose to push the process in his book – that is a matter to be decided by the subject; it entirely depends upon the kind of effect that the theme demands. It may respond to all the dramatization it can get, it may give all that it has to give for less. The subject dictates the method.

And now let the process be reversed, let us start with the purely dramatic subject, the story that will tell itself in perfect rightness, unaided, to the eye of the reader. This story never deviates from a strictly scenic form; one occasion or episode follows another, with no interruption for any reflective summary of events. Necessarily it must be so, for it is only while the episode is proceeding that no question of a narrator can arise; when the scene closes the play ceases till the opening of the next. To glance upon the story from a height and to give a general impression of its course – this is at once to remove the point of view from the reader and to set up a new one somewhere else; the method is no longer consistent, no longer purely dramatic. And the dramatic story is not only scenic, it is also limited to so much as the ear can hear and the eye see. In rigid drama of this kind there is naturally no admission of the reader into the private mind of any of the characters; their thoughts and motives are transmuted into action. A subject wrought to this pitch of objectivity is no doubt given weight and compactness and authority in the highest degree; it is like a piece of modelling, standing in clear space, casting its shadow. It is the most finished form that fiction can take.

But evidently it is not a form to which fiction can aspire in general. It implies many sacrifices, and these will easily seem to be more than the subject can usefully make. It is out of the question, of course, wherever the main burden of the story lies within some particular consciousness, in the study of a soul, the growth of a character, the changing history of a temperament; there the subject would be needlessly crossed and strangled by dramatization pushed to its limit. It is out of the question, again, wherever the story is too big, too comprehensive, too widely ranging, to be treated scenically, with no opportunity for general and panoramic survey; it has been discovered, indeed, that even a story of this kind *may* fall into a long succession of definite scenes, under some hands, but it has also appeared that in doing so it incurs unnecessary disabilities, and will likely suffer. These stories, therefore, which will not naturally accommodate themselves to the reader's point of view, and the reader's alone, we regard as rather pictorial than dramatic – meaning that they call for some narrator, somebody who *knows*, to contemplate the facts and create an impression of them. Whether it is the omniscient author or a man in the book, he must gather up his experience, compose a vision of it as it exists in his mind, and lay *that* before the reader. It is the reflection of an experience; and though there may be all imaginable diversity of treatment within the limits of the reflection, such is its essential character. In a pictorial book the principle of the structure involves a point of view which is not the reader's.

It is open to the pictorial book, however, to use a method in its picture-making that is really no other than the method of drama. It is somebody's experience, we say, that is to be reported, the general effect that many things have left upon a certain mind; it is a fusion of innumerable elements, the deposit of a lapse of time. The straightforward way to render it would be for the narrator – the author or his selected creature – to view the past retrospectively and discourse upon it, to recall and meditate and summarize. That is picture-making in its natural form, using its own method. But exactly as in drama the subject is distributed among the characters and enacted by them, so in picture the effect may be entrusted to the elements, the reactions of the moment, and *performed* by these. The mind of the narrator becomes the stage, his voice is no longer heard. His voice *is* heard so long as there is narrative of any sort, whether he is speaking in person or is reported obliquely; his voice is heard, because in either case the language and the intonation are his, the direct expression of his experience. In the drama of his mind there is no personal voice, for there is no narrator; the point of view becomes the reader's once more. The shapes of thought in the man's mind tell their own story. And that is the art of picture-making when it uses the dramatic method.

But it cannot always do so. Constantly it must be necessary to offer the reader a summary of facts, an impression of a train of events, that can only be given as somebody's narration. Suppose it were required to render the general effect of a certain year in a man's life, a year that has filled his mind with a swarm of many memories. Looking into his consciousness after the year has gone, we might find much there that would indicate the nature of the year's events without any word on his part; the flickers and flashes of thought from moment to moment might indeed tell us much. But we shall need an account from him too, no doubt; too much has happened in a year to be wholly acted, as I call it, in the movement of the man's thought. He must narrate – he must make, that is to say, a picture of the events as he sees them, glancing back. Now if he speaks in the first person there can, of course, be no uncertainty in the point of view; he has his fixed position, he cannot leave it. His description will represent the face that the facts in their sequence turned towards *him*; the field of vision is defined with perfect distinctness, and his story cannot stray outside it. The reader, then, may be said to watch a reflection of the facts in a mirror of which the edge is nowhere in doubt; it is rounded by the bounds of the narrator's own personal experience.

This limitation may have a convenience and a value in the story, it may contribute to the effect. But it need not be forfeited, it is clear, if the first person is changed to the third. The author may use the man's field of vision and keep as faithfully within it as though the man were speaking for himself. In that case he retains this advantage and adds to it another, one that is likely to be very much greater. For now, while the point of view is still fixed in space, still assigned to the man in the book, it is free in *time*; there no longer stretches, between the narrator and the events of which he speaks, a certain tract of time, across which the past must appear in a more or less distant perspective. All the variety obtainable by a shifting relation to the story in time is thus in the author's hand; the safe serenity of a far retrospect, the promising or threatening urgency of the present, every gradation between the two, can be drawn into the whole effect of the book, and all of it without any change of the seeing eye. It is a liberty that may help the story indefinitely, raising this matter into strong relief, throwing that other back into vaguer shade.

And next, still keeping mainly and ostensibly to the same point of view, the author has the chance of using a much greater latitude than he need appear to use. The seeing eye is with somebody in the book, but its vision is reinforced; the picture contains more, becomes richer and fuller, because it is the author's as well as his creature's, both at once. Nobody notices, but in fact there are now two brains behind that eye; and one of them is the author's, who adopts and shares the *position* of his creature, and at the same time supplements his wit. If you analyse the picture that is now presented, you find that it is not all the work of the personage whose vision the author has adopted. There are touches in it that go beyond any sensation of his, and indicate that some one else is looking over his shoulder – seeing things from the same angle, but seeing more, bringing another mind to bear upon the scene. It is an easy and natural extension of the personage's power of observation. The impression of the scene may be deepened as much as need be; it is not confined to the scope of one mind, and yet there is no blurring of the focus by a double point of view. And thus what I have called the sound of the narrator's voice (it is impossible to avoid this mixture of metaphors) is less insistent in oblique narration, even while it seems to be following the very same argument that it would in direct, because another voice is speedily mixed and blended with it.

So this is another resource upon which the author may draw according to his need; sometimes it will be indispensable, and generally, I suppose, it will be useful. It means that he keeps a certain hold upon the narrator *as an object*; the sentient character in the story, round whom it is grouped, is not utterly subjective, completely given over to the business of seeing and feeling on behalf of the reader. It is a considerable point; for it helps to meet one of the great difficulties in the story which is carefully aligned towards a single consciousness and consistently so viewed. In that story the man or woman who acts as the vessel of sensation is always in danger of seeming a light, uncertain weight compared with the other people in the book – simply because the other people are objective images, plainly outlined, while the seer in the midst is precluded from that advantage, and must see without being directly seen. He, who doubtless ought to bulk in the story more massively than any one, tends to remain the least recognizable of the company, and even to dissolve in a kind of impalpable blur. By his method (which I am supposing to have been adopted in full strictness) the author is of course forbidden to look this central figure in the face, to describe and discuss him; the light cannot be turned upon him immediately. And very often we see the method becoming an embarrassment to the author in consequence, and the devices by which he tries to mitigate it, and to secure some reflected sight of the seer, may even be tiresomely obvious. But the resource of which I speak is of a finer sort.

It gives to the author the power of imperceptibly edging away from the seer, leaving his consciousness, ceasing to use his eyes – though still without substituting the eyes of another. To revert for a moment to the story told in the first person, it is plain that in that case the narrator has no such liberty; his own consciousness must always lie open; the part that he plays in the story can never appear in the same terms, on the same plane, as that of the other people. Though he is not visible in the story to the reader, as the others are, he is at every moment *nearer* than they, in his capacity of the seeing eye, the channel of vision; nor can he put off his function, he must continue steadily to see and to report. But when the author is reporting *him* there is a margin of freedom. The author has not so completely identified himself, as narrator, with his hero that he can give him no objective weight whatever. If necessary he can allow him something of the value of a detached and phenomenal personage, like the rest of the company in the story, and that without violating the principle of his method. He cannot make his hero actually visible – there the method is uncompromising; he cannot step forward, leaving the man's point of view, and picture him from without. But he can place the man at the same distance from the reader as the other people, he can almost lend him the same effect, he can make of him a dramatic actor upon the scene.

And how? Merely by closing (when it suits him) the open consciousness of the seer – which he can do without any look of awkwardness or violence, since it conflicts in no way with the rule of the method. That rule only required that the author, having decided to share the point of view of his character, should not proceed to set up another of his own; it did not debar him from allowing his hero's act of vision to lapse, his function as the sentient creature in the story to be intermitted. The hero (I call him so for convenience – he may, of course, be quite a subordinate onlooker in the story) can at any moment become impenetrable, a human being whose thought is sealed from us; and it may seem a small matter, but in fact it has the result that he drops into the plane of the people whom he has hitherto been seeing and judging. Hitherto subjective, communicative in solitude, he has been in a category apart from them; but now he may mingle with the rest, engage in talk with them, and his presence and his talk are no more to the fore than theirs. As soon as some description or discussion of them is required, then, of course, the seer must resume his part and unseal his mind; but meanwhile, though the reader gets no direct view of him, still he is there in the dialogue with the rest, his speech (like theirs) issues from a hidden mind and has the same dramatic value. It is enough, very likely, to harden our image of him, to give precision to his form, to save him from dissipation into that luminous blur of which I spoke just now. For the author it is a resource to be welcomed on that account, and not on that account alone.

For besides the greater definition that the seer acquires, thus detached from us at times and relegated to the plane of his companions, there is much benefit for the subject of the story. In the tale that is quite openly and nakedly somebody's narrative there is this inherent weakness, that a scene of true drama is impossible. In true drama nobody *reports* the scene; it *appears*, it is constituted by the aspect of the occasion and the talk and the conduct of the people. When one of the people who took part in it sets out to report the scene, there is at once a mixture and a confusion of effects; for his own contribution to the scene has a different quality from the rest, cannot have the same crispness and freshness, cannot strike in with a new or unexpected note. This weakness may be well disguised, and like everything else in the whole craft it may become a positive and right effect in a particular story, for a particular purpose; it is always there, however, and it means that the full and unmixed effect of drama is denied to the story that is rigidly told from the point of view of one of the actors. But when that point of view is held in the manner I have described, when it is open to the author to withdraw from it silently and to leave the actor to play his part, true drama – or something so like it that it passes for true drama – is always possible; all the figures of the scene are together in it, one no nearer than another. Nothing is wanting save only that direct, unequivocal sight of the hero which the method does indeed absolutely forbid.

Finally there is the old, immemorial, unguarded, unsuspicious way of telling a story, where the author entertains the reader, the minstrel draws his audience round him, the listeners rely upon his word. The voice is then confessedly and alone the author's; he imposes no limitation upon his freedom to tell what he pleases and to regard his matter from a point of view that is solely his own. And if there is anyone who can proceed in this fashion without appearing to lose the least of the advantages of a more cautious style, for him the minstrel's licence is proper and appropriate; there is no more to be said. But we have yet to discover him; and it is not very presumptuous in a critic, as things are, to declare that a story will never yield its best to a writer who takes the easiest way with it. He curtails his privileges and chooses a narrower method, and immediately the story responds; its better condition is too notable to be forgotten, when once it has caught the attention of a reader. The advantages that it gains are not nameless, indefinable graces, pleasing to a critic but impossible to fix in words; they are solid, we can describe and recount them. And I can only conclude that if the novel is still as full of energy as it seems to be, and is not a form of imaginative art that, having seen the best of its day, is preparing to give place to some other, the novelist will not be willing to miss the inexhaustible opportunity that lies in its treatment. The easy way is no way at all; the only way is that by which the most is made of the story to be told, and the most was never made of any story except by a choice and disciplined method.

Anatomy of Criticism

Northrop Frye

Herman Northrop Frye (1912–1991)

Northrop Frye was born in the province of Quebec, Canada. He received his education at Victoria College of the University of Toronto, the theological college of the United Church of Canada (he was ordained in 1936, but never served as a minister), and Merton College, Oxford. In 1939 Frye returned to Victoria College to teach, and in 1978 he became Chancellor, a position he held until his death. He has been honored with the Royal Bank Award and as a Companion of the Order of Canada (two of the country's most prestigious cultural prizes), and, in 1988, the establishment of the Northrop Frye Centre at Victoria College. Frye's 30 books reflect the range of his interests: in addition to his literary criticism, he also wrote on public education and Canadian culture, and successfully worked to introduce literature and literary studies to a general audience. Published in 1957, *Anatomy of Criticism* developed out of a 1954 lecture series delivered at Princeton University.

From *Anatomy of Criticism: Four Essays*. Princeton: Princeton University Press, 1957, from Essay 4, pp. 303–14. Copyright © 1957, renewed 1985, by Princeton University Press. Reprinted by permission of Princeton University Press.

Rhetorical Criticism: Theory of Genres

Specific Continuous Forms (Prose Fiction)

In assigning the term fiction to the genre of the written word, in which prose tends to become the predominating rhythm, we collide with the view that the real meaning of fiction is falsehood or unreality. Thus an autobiography coming into a library would be classified as non-fiction if the librarian believed the author, and as fiction if she thought he was lying. It is difficult to see what use such a distinction can be to a literary critic. Surely the word fiction, which, like poetry, means etymologically something made for its own sake, could be applied in criticism to any work of literary art in a radically continuous form, which almost always means a work of art in prose. Or, if that is too much to ask, at least some protest can be entered against the sloppy habit of identifying fiction with the one genuine form of fiction which we know as the novel.

Let us look at a few of the unclassified books lying on the boundary of "non-fiction" and "literature." Is *Tristram Shandy* a novel? Nearly everyone would say yes, in spite of its easygoing disregard of "story values." Is *Gulliver's Travels* a novel? Here most would demur, including the Dewey decimal system, which puts it under "Satire and Humor." But surely everyone would call it fiction, and if it is fiction, a distinction appears between fiction as a genus and the novel as a species of that genus. Shifting the ground to fiction, then, is *Sartor Resartus* fiction? If not, why not? If it is, is *The Anatomy of Melancholy* fiction? Is it a literary form or only a work of "non-fiction" written with "style"? Is [George] Borrow's *Lavengro* fiction? Everyman's Library says yes; the World's Classics puts it under "Travel and Topography."

The literary historian who identifies fiction with the novel is greatly embarrassed by the length of time that the world managed to get along without the novel, and until he reaches his great deliverance in Defoe, his perspective is intolerably cramped. He is compelled to reduce Tudor fiction to a series of tentative essays in the novel form, which works well enough for [Thomas] Deloney but makes nonsense of Sidney. He postulates a great fictional gap in the seventeenth century which exactly covers the golden age of rhetorical prose. He finally discovers that the word novel, which up to about 1900 was still the name of a more or less recognizable form, has since expanded into a catchall term which can be applied to practically any prose book that is not "on" something. Clearly, this novel-centered view of prose fiction is a Ptolemaic perspective which is now too complicated to be any longer workable, and some more relative and Copernican view must take its place.

When we start to think seriously about the novel, not as fiction, but as a form of fiction, we feel that its characteristics, whatever they are, are such as make, say, Defoe, Fielding, Austen, and James central in its tradition, and Borrow, Peacock, Melville, and Emily Brontë somehow peripheral. This is not an estimate of merit: we may think *Moby Dick* "greater" than *The Egoist* and yet feel that Meredith's book is closer to being a typical novel. Fielding's conception of the novel as a comic epic in prose seems fundamental to the tradition he did so much to establish. In novels that we think of as typical, like those of Jane Austen, plot and dialogue are closely linked to the conventions of the comedy of manners. The conventions of *Wuthering Heights* are linked rather with

NORTHROP FRYE

the tale and the ballad. They seem to have more affinity with tragedy, and the tragic emotions of passion and fury, which would shatter the balance of tone in Jane Austen, can be safely accommodated here. So can the supernatural, or the suggestion of it, which is difficult to get into a novel. The shape of the plot is different: instead of manoeuvring around a central situation, as Jane Austen does, Emily Bronte tells her story with linear accents, and she seems to need the help of a narrator, who would be absurdly out of place in Jane Austen. Conventions so different justify us in regarding *Wuthering Heights* as a different form of prose fiction from the novel, a form which we shall here call the romance. Here again we have to use the same word in several different contexts, but romance seems on the whole better than tale, which appears to fit a somewhat shorter form.

The essential difference between novel and romance lies in the conception of characterization. The romancer does not attempt to create "real people" so much as stylized figures which expand into psychological archetypes. It is in the romance that we find Jung's libido, anima, and shadow reflected in the hero, heroine, and villain respectively. That is why the romance so often radiates a glow of subjective intensity that the novel lacks, and why a suggestion of allegory is constantly creeping in around its fringes. Certain elements of character are released in the romance which make it naturally a more revolutionary form than the novel. The novelist deals with personality, with characters wearing their *personae* or social masks. He needs the framework of a stable society, and many of our best novelists have been conventional to the verge of fussiness. The romancer deals with individuality, with characters *in vacuo* idealized by revery, and, however conservative he may be, something nihilistic and untamable is likely to keep breaking out of his pages.

The prose romance, then, is an independent form of fiction to be distinguished from the novel and extracted from the miscellaneous heap of prose works now covered by that term. Even in the other heap known as short stories one can isolate the tale form used by Poe, which bears the same relation to the full romance that the stories of Chekhov or Katherine Mansfield do to the novel. "Pure" examples of either form are never found; there is hardly any modern romance that could not be made out to be a novel, and vice versa. The forms of prose fiction are mixed, like racial strains in human beings, not separable like the sexes. In fact the popular demand in fiction is always for a mixed form, a romantic novel just romantic enough for the reader to project his libido on the hero and his anima on the heroine, and just novel enough to keep these projections in a familiar world. It may be asked, therefore, what is the use of making the above distinction, especially when, though undeveloped in criticism, it is by no means unrealized. It is no surprise to hear that Trollope wrote novels and William Morris romances.

The reason is that a great romancer should be examined in terms of the conventions he chose. William Morris should not be left on the side lines of prose fiction merely because the critic has not learned to take the romance form seriously. Nor, in view of what has been said about the revolutionary nature of the romance, should his choice of that form be regarded as an "escape" from his social attitude. If Scott has any claims to be a romancer, it is not good criticism to deal only with his defects as a novelist. The romantic qualities of *The Pilgrim's Progress*, too, its archetypal characterization and its revolutionary approach to religious experience, make it a well-rounded example of a literary form: it is not merely a book swallowed by English literature to get some religious bulk in its diet. Finally, when Hawthorne, in the preface to *The House of the Seven Gables*, insists that his story should be read as romance and not as novel, it is possible that he meant what he said, even though he indicates that the prestige of the rival form has induced the romancer to apologize for not using it.

Romance is older than the novel, a fact which has developed the historical illusion that it is something to be outgrown, a juvenile and undeveloped form. The social affinities of the romance, with its grave idealizing of heroism and purity, are with the aristocracy (for the apparent inconsistency of this with the revolutionary nature of the form just mentioned, see the introductory comment on the *mythos* of romance in the previous essay). It revived in the period we call Romantic as part of the Romantic tendency to archaic feudalism and a cult of the hero, or idealized libido. In England the romances of Scott and, in less degree, the Brontes, are part of a mysterious Northumbrian renaissance, a Romantic reaction against the new industrialism in the Midlands, which also produced the poetry of Wordsworth and Burns and the philosophy of Carlyle. It is not surprising, therefore, that an important theme in the more bourgeois novel should be the parody of the romance and its ideals. The tradition established by *Don Quixote* continues in a type of novel which looks at a romantic situation from its own point of view, so that the conventions of the two forms make up an ironic compound instead of a sentimental mixture. Examples range from *Northanger Abbey* to *Madame Bovary* and *Lord Jim*.

The tendency to allegory in the romance may be conscious, as in *The Pilgrim's Progress*, or unconscious, as in the very obvious sexual mythopoeia in William Morris. The romance, which deals with heroes, is intermediate between the novel, which deals with men, and the myth, which deals with gods. Prose romance first appears as a late development of Classical mythology, and the prose Sagas of Iceland follow close on the mythical Eddas. The novel tends rather to expand into a fictional approach to history. The soundness of Fielding's instinct in calling *Tom Jones* a history is confirmed by the general rule that the larger the scheme of a novel becomes, the more obviously its historical nature appears. As it is creative history, however, the novelist usually prefers his material in a plastic, or roughly contemporary state, and feels cramped by a fixed historical pattern. *Waverley* is dated about sixty years back from the time of writing and *Little Dorrit* about forty years, but the historical pattern is fixed in the romance and plastic in the novel, suggesting the general principle that most "historical novels" are romances. Similarly a novel becomes more romantic in its appeal when the life it reflects has passed away: thus the novels of Trollope were read primarily as romances during the Second World War. It is perhaps the link with history and a sense of temporal context that has confined the novel, in striking contrast to the worldwide romance, to the alliance of time and Western man.

Autobiography is another form which merges with the novel by a series of insensible gradations. Most autobiographies are inspired by a creative, and therefore fictional, impulse to select only those events and experiences in the writer's life that go to build up an integrated pattern. This pattern may be something larger than himself with which he has come to identify himself, or simply the coherence of his character and attitudes. We may call this very important form of prose fiction the confession form, following

St. Augustine, who appears to have invented it, and Rousseau, who established a modern type of it. The earlier tradition gave *Religio Medici*, *Grace Abounding*, and Newman's *Apologia* to English literature, besides the related but subtly different type of confession favored by the mystics.

Here again, as with the romance, there is some value in recognizing a distinct prose form in the confession. It gives several of our best prose works a definable place in fiction instead of keeping them in a vague limbo of books which are not quite literature because they are "thought," and not quite religion or philosophy because they are Examples of Prose Style. The confession, too, like the novel and the romance, has its own short form, the familiar essay, and Montaigne's *livre de bonne foy* is a confession made up of essays in which only the continuous narrative of the longer form is missing. Montaigne's scheme is to the confession what a work of fiction made up of short stories, such as Joyce's *Dubliners* or Boccaccio's *Decameron*, is to the novel or romance.

After Rousseau – in fact in Rousseau – the confession flows into the novel, and the mixture produces the fictional autobiography, the *Künstler-roman*, and kindred types. There is no literary reason why the subject of a confession should always be the author himself, and dramatic confessions have been used in the novel at least since *Moll Flanders*. The "stream of consciousness" technique permits of a much more concentrated fusion of the two forms, but even here the characteristics peculiar to the confession form show up clearly. Nearly always some theoretical and intellectual interest in religion, politics, or art plays a leading role in the confession. It is his success in integrating his mind on such subjects that makes the author of a confession feel that his life is worth writing about. But this interest in ideas and theoretical statements is alien to the genius of the novel proper, where the technical problem is to dissolve all theory into personal relationships. In Jane Austen, to take a familiar instance, church, state, and culture are never examined except as social data, and Henry James has been described as having a mind so fine that no idea could violate it. The novelist who cannot get along without ideas, or has not the patience to digest them in the way that James did, instinctively resorts to what Mill calls a "mental history" of a single character. And when we find that a technical discussion of a theory of aesthetics forms the climax of Joyce's *Portrait*, we realize that what makes this possible is the presence in that novel of another tradition of prose fiction.

The novel tends to be extroverted and personal; its chief interest is in human character as it manifests itself in society. The romance tends to be introverted and personal: it also deals with characters, but in a more subjective way. (Subjective here refers to treatment, not subject-matter. The characters of romance are heroic and therefore inscrutable; the novelist is freer to enter his characters' minds because he is more objective.) The confession is also introverted, but intellectualized in content. Our next step is evidently to discover a fourth form of fiction which is extroverted and intellectual.

We remarked earlier that most people would call *Gulliver's Travels* fiction but not a novel. It must then be another form of fiction, as it certainly has a form, and we feel that we are turning from the novel to this form, whatever it is, when we turn from Rousseau's *Emile* to Voltaire's *Candide*, or from Butler's *The Way of All Flesh* to the Erewhon books, or from Huxley's *Point Counterpoint* to *Brave New World*. The form thus has its own traditions, and, as the examples of Butler and Huxley show, has preserved some integrity even under the ascendancy of the novel. Its existence is easy enough to demonstrate, and no one will challenge the statement that the literary ancestry of *Gulliver's Travels* and *Candide* runs through Rabelais and Erasmus to Lucian. But while much has been said about the style and thought of Rabelais, Swift, and Voltaire, very little has been made of them as craftsmen working in a specific medium, a point no one dealing with a novelist would ignore. Another great writer in this tradition, Huxley's master Peacock, has fared even worse, for, his form not being understood, a general impression has grown up that his status in the development of prose fiction is that of a slapdash eccentric. Actually, he is as exquisite and precise an artist in his medium as Jane Austen is in hers.

The form used by these authors is the Menippean satire, also more rarely called the Varronian satire, allegedly invented by a Greek cynic named Menippus. His works are lost, but he had two great disciples, the Greek Lucian and the Roman Varro, and the tradition of Varro, who has not survived either except in fragments, was carried on by Petronius and Apuleius. The Menippean satire appears to have developed out of verse satire through the practice of adding prose interludes, but we know it only as a prose form, though one of its recurrent features (seen in Peacock) is the use of incidental verse.

The Menippean satire deals less with people as such than with mental attitudes. Pedants, bigots, cranks, parvenus, virtuosi, enthusiasts, rapacious and incompetent professional men of all kinds, are handled in terms of their occupational approach to life as distinct from their social behavior. The Menippean satire thus resembles the confession in its ability to handle abstract ideas and theories, and differs from the novel in its characterization, which is stylized rather than naturalistic, and presents people as mouthpieces of the ideas they represent. Here again no sharp boundary lines can or should be drawn, but if we compare a character in Jane Austen with a similar character in Peacock we can immediately feel the difference between the two forms. Squire Western belongs to the novel, but Thwackum and Square have Menippean blood in them. A constant theme in the tradition is the ridicule of the *philosophus gloriosus*, already discussed. The novelist sees evil and folly as social diseases, but the Menippean satirist sees them as diseases of the intellect, as a kind of maddened pedantry which the *philosophus gloriosus* at once symbolizes and defines.

Petronius, Apuleius, Rabelais, Swift, and Voltaire all use a loose-jointed narrative form often confused with the romance. It differs from the romance, however (though there is a strong admixture of romance in Rabelais), as it is not primarily concerned with the exploits of heroes, but relies on the free play of intellectual fancy and the kind of humorous observation that produces caricature. It differs also from the picaresque form, which has the novel's interest in the actual structure of society. At its most concentrated the Menippean satire presents us with a vision of the world in terms of a single intellectual pattern. The intellectual structure built up from the story makes for violent dislocations in the customary logic of narrative, though the appearance of carelessness that results reflects only the carelessness of the reader or his tendency to judge by a novel-centered conception of fiction.

The word "satire," in Roman and Renaissance times, meant either of two specific literary forms of that name, one (this one) prose and the other verse. Now it means a structural principle or attitude, what we have called a *mythos*. In the Menippean satires we have been discussing, the name of the form also applies to the attitude. As the name of an attitude, satire is, we have seen, a combination of fantasy and morality. But as the name of a form, the term satire, though confined to literature (for as a *mythos* it may appear in any art, a cartoon, for example), is more flexible, and can be either entirely fantastic or entirely moral. The Menippean adventure story may thus be pure fantasy, as it is in the literary fairy tale. The Alice books are perfect Menippean satires, and so is *The Water-Babies*, which has been influenced by Rabelais. The purely moral type is a serious vision of society as a single intellectual pattern, in other words a Utopia.

The short form of the Menippean satire is usually a dialogue or colloquy, in which the dramatic interest is in a conflict of ideas rather than of character. This is the favorite form of Erasmus, and is common in Voltaire. Here again the form is not invariably satiric in attitude, but shades off into more purely fanciful or moral discussions, like the *Imaginary Conversations* of Landor or the "dialogue of the dead." Sometimes this form expands to full length, and more than two speakers are used: the setting then is usually a *cena* or symposium, like the one that looms so large in Petronius. Plato, though much earlier in the field than Menippus, is a strong influence on this type, which stretches in an unbroken tradition down through those urbane and leisurely conversations which define the ideal courtier in Castiglione or the doctrine and discipline of angling in Walton. A modern development produces the country-house weekends in Peacock, Huxley, and their imitators in which the opinions and ideas and cultural interests expressed are as important as the love-making.

The novelist shows his exuberance either by an exhaustive analysis of human rela-tionships, as in Henry James, or of social phenomena, as in Tolstoy. The Menippean satirist, dealing with intellectual themes and attitudes, shows his exuberance in intellec-tual ways, by piling up an enormous mass of erudition about his theme or in over-whelming his pedantic targets with an avalanche of their own jargon. A species, or rather sub-species, of the form is the kind of encyclopaedic farrago represented by Athenaeus' *Deipnosophists* and Macrobius' *Saturnalia*, where people sit at a banquet and pour out a vast mass of erudition on every subject that might conceivably come up in a conversa-tion. The display of erudition had probably been associated with the Menippean tradition by Varro, who was enough of a polymath to make Quintilian, if not stare and gasp, at any rate call him *vir Romanorum eruditissimus*. The tendency to expand into an encyclopaedic farrago is clearly marked in Rabelais, notably in the great catalogues of torcheculs and epithets of codpieces and methods of divination. The encyclopaedic compilations produced in the line of duty by Erasmus and Voltaire suggest that a magpie instinct to collect facts is not unrelated to the type of ability that has made them famous as artists. Flaubert's encyclopaedic approach to the construction of *Bouvard et Pecuchet* is quite comprehensible if we explain it as marking an affinity with the Menippean tradition.

This creative treatment of exhaustive erudition is the organizing principle of the greatest Menippean satire in English before Swift, Burton's *Anatomy of Melancholy*. Here human society is studied in terms of the intellectual pattern provided by the conception of melancholy, a symposium of books replaces dialogue, and the result is the most comprehensive survey of human life in one book that English literature had seen since Chaucer, one of Burton's favorite authors. We may note in passing the Utopia in his introduction and his "digressions," which when examined turn out to be scholarly distillations of Menippean forms: the digression of air, of the marvellous journey; the digression of spirits, of the ironic use of erudition; the digression of the miseries of scholars, of the satire on the *philosophus gloriosus*. The word "anatomy" in Burton's title means a dissection or analysis, and expresses very accurately the intellectualized approach of his form. We may as well adopt it as a convenient name to replace the cumbersome and in modern times rather misleading "Menippean satire."

The anatomy, of course, eventually begins to merge with the novel, producing various hybrids including the *roman à thèse* and novels in which the characters are symbols of social or other ideas, like the proletarian novels of the thirties in this century. It was Sterne, however, the disciple of Burton and Rabelais, who combined them with greatest success. *Tristram Shandy* may be, as was said at the beginning, a novel, but the digressing narrative, the catalogues, the stylizing of character along "humor" lines, the marvellous journey of the great nose, the symposium discussions, and the constant ridicule of philosophers and pedantic critics are all features that belong to the anatomy.

A clearer understanding of the form and traditions of the anatomy would make a good many elements in the history of literature come into focus. Boethius' *Consolation of Philosophy*, with its dialogue form, its verse interludes and its pervading tone of contemplative irony, is a pure anatomy, a fact of considerable importance for the understanding of its vast influence. *The Compleat Angler* is an anatomy because of its mixture of prose and verse, its rural *cena* setting, its dialogue form, its deipnosophistical interest in food, and its gentle Menippean raillery of a society which considers everything more important than fishing and yet has discovered very few better things to do. In nearly every period of literature there are many romances, confessions, and anatomies that are neglected only because the categories to which they belong are unrecognized. In the period between Sterne and Peacock, for example, we have, among romances, *Melmoth the Wanderer*; among confessions, Hogg's *Confessions of a Justified Sinner*; among anatomies, Southey's *Doctor*, Amory's *John Buncle*, and the *Noctes Ambrosianae*.

To sum up then: when we examine fiction from the point of view of form, we can see four chief strands binding it together, novel, confession, anatomy, and romance. The six possible combinations of these forms all exist, and we have shown how the novel has combined with each of the other three. Exclusive concentration on one form is rare: the early novels of George Eliot, for instance, are influenced by the romance, and the later ones by the anatomy. The romance-confession hybrid is found, naturally, in the autobiography of a romantic temperament, and is represented in English by the extroverted George Borrow and the introverted De Quincey. The romance-anatomy one we have noticed in Rabelais; a later example is *Moby Dick*, where the romantic theme of the wild hunt expands into an encyclopaedic anatomy of the whale. Confession and anatomy are united in *Sartor Resartus* and in some of Kierkegaard's strikingly original experiments in prose fiction form, including *Either/Or*. More comprehensive fictional schemes usually employ at least three forms: we can see strains of novel, romance, and confession in *Pamela*, of novel, romance, and anatomy in *Don Quixote*, of novel, confession, and anatomy in Proust, and of romance, confession, and anatomy in Apuleius.

I deliberately make this sound schematic in order to suggest the advantage of having a simple and logical explanation for the form of, say, *Moby Dick* or *Tristram Shandy*. The usual critical approach to the form of such works resembles that of the doctors in Brobdingnag, who after great wrangling finally pronounced Gulliver a *lusus naturae*. It is the anatomy in particular that has baffled critics, and there is hardly any fiction writer deeply influenced by it who has not been accused of disorderly conduct. The reader may be reminded here of Joyce, for describing Joyce's books as monstrous has become a nervous tic. I find "demogorgon," "behemoth," and "white elephant" in good critics; the bad ones could probably do much better. The care that Joyce took to organize *Ulysses* and *Finnegans Wake* amounted nearly to obsession, but as they are not organized on familiar principles of prose fiction, the impression of shapelessness remains. Let us try our formulas on him.

If a reader were asked to set down a list of the things that had most impressed him about *Ulysses*, it might reasonably be somewhat as follows. First, the clarity with which the sights and sounds and smells of Dublin come to life, the rotundity of the character-drawing, and the naturalness of the dialogue. Second, the elaborate way that the story and characters are parodied by being set against archetypal heroic patterns, notably the one provided by the *Odyssey*. Third, the revelation of character and incident through the searching use of the stream-of-consciousness technique. Fourth, the constant tendency to be encyclopaedic and exhaustive both in technique and in subject matter, and to see both in highly intellectualized terms. It should not be too hard for us by now to see that these four points describe elements in the book which relate to the novel, romance, confession, and anatomy respectively. *Ulysses*, then, is a complete prose epic with all four forms employed in it, all of practically equal importance, and all essential to one another, so that the book is a unity and not an aggregate.

This unity is built up from an intricate scheme of parallel contrasts. The romantic archetypes of Hamlet and Ulysses are like remote stars in a literary heaven looking down quizzically on the shabby creatures of Dublin obediently intertwining themselves in the patterns set by their influences. In the "Cyclops" and "Circe" episodes particularly there is a continuous parody of realistic patterns by romantic ones which reminds us, though the irony leans in the opposite direction, of *Madame Bovary*. The relation of novel and confession techniques is similar; the author jumps into his characters' minds to follow their stream of consciousness, and out again to describe them externally. In the novel-anatomy combination, too, found in the "Ithaca" chapter, the sense of lurking antagonism between the personal and intellectual aspects of the scene accounts for much of its pathos. The same principle of parallel contrast holds good for the other three combinations: of romance and confession in "Nausicaa" and "Penelope," of confession and anatomy in "Proteus" and "The Lotos-Eaters," of romance and anatomy (a rare and fitful combination) in "Sirens" and parts of "Circe."

In *Finnegans Wake* the unity of design goes far beyond this. The dingy story of the sodden HCE and his pinched wife is not contrasted with the archetypes of Tristram and the divine king: HCE is himself Tristram and the divine king. As the setting is a dream, no contrast is possible between confession and novel, between a stream of consciousness inside the mind and the appearances of other people outside it. Nor is the experiential world of the novel to be separated from the intelligible world of the anatomy. The forms we have been isolating in fiction, and which depend for their existence on the commonsense dichotomies of the daylight consciousness, vanish in *Finnegans Wake* into a fifth and quintessential form. This form is the one traditionally associated with scriptures and sacred books, and treats life in terms of the fall and awakening of the human soul and the creation and apocalypse of nature. The Bible is the definitive example of it; the Egyptian Book of the Dead and the Icelandic Prose Edda, both of which have left deep imprints on *Finnegans Wake*, also belong to it.

PART II

The Chicago Sch

Introduction

The Chicago School might have been included in Part I, but the type of American formalism that this tradition represents has been so influential for the study of fiction that it merits expanded attention. R. S. Crane, chair of the English department at the University of Chicago from 1930 to 1942, helped to found a theoretical approach to novels that has attracted at least three generations of followers. Some of these students, such as Ralph Rader, did not actually study at Chicago but became elective members of the school as they sought to absorb and extend the teachings of Crane, especially in dialogue with Chicago Ph.D.s who, as they assumed their own faculty posts, exported Crane's influence to English departments across the US. The institutional identity and academic lineage of the Chicago School thus distinguish it from the Anglo-American approaches discussed in Part I. And this institutional affiliation carries with it a shared intellectual foundation: the Chicago School follows Crane in its admiration of Aristotle as a theorist of literature. Members of the Chicago School who are interested in the novel thus look for a way of theorizing this modern literary genre by extrapolating from the insights of classical poetics. The longevity and vitality of the Chicago School stem as much from its ability to accommodate – even to provoke – ways of adapting Aristotle to modern literary forms as from its self-conscious status as a distinct, literary-critical movement. As we can see in the selections that follow, Crane inspired his students to extend and complicate his work: Rader and Wayne Booth, for example, share an intellectual family resemblance, but their powerful critical imaginations lead them to

DOROTHY HALE

invent theories that are distinctively their own, the former emphasizing the novel's evolution as a genre and the latter investigating its rhetorical power.

In his preface to the second edition of *Critics and Criticism: Ancient and Modern* (1952), Crane credits his friend Kenneth Burke with coining the appellation "neo-Aristotelian" to describe the intellectual project of the Chicago School. According to Crane, Burke was a friendly observer of the group's determination "to begin where Aristotle left off and to pursue similar lines of study in the poetics of modern literature, using the distinctions he had suggested where these were relevant but attempting to enlarge his analysis in various ways in the light of the new things modern writers have achieved."[1] The return to Aristotle is motivated by the group's dissatisfaction with the current state of Anglo-American literary criticism. Crane first of all objects to the interdisciplinary procedures of the dominant critics of the period. On Crane's view, interdisciplinary work had not expanded the range and potential of literary criticism but contracted it; literary criticism had ossified into a "narrow set of ideas and interests which the critics of the thirties had derived from Eliot, Hulme, and Richards or had taken over from the psychoanalysis, analytical psychology, and cultural anthropology of the first years of the century."[2] Crane bemoans not just the predictability and conventionality of the concepts used by these critics, but also the lack of professionalism that characterizes literary criticism as a field. Crane accuses critics of practicing "unscholarly improvisation"; and he believes that this lack of theoretical self-consciousness results in the deployment of the same few analytic tools, the "fashionable" but "unexamined" categories of symbolism, irony, complexity, and archetype that, according to Crane, dominated literary analysis at the time.[3]

The return to Aristotle is, by this logic, a way to establish American literary criticism as a discipline. Literary criticism can be made coherent by regrouping; instead of modeling literary study on the rapidly proliferating new fields of social science (such as psychology, anthropology, and, one could add, linguistics), and instead of deriving its key analytic concepts casually from these far-flung disciplines, literary criticism should consolidate itself in relation to the ideas of a proven authority, an originator of literary criticism, extending the insights of this master thinker in a systematic way. The return to Aristotle thus helps constitute literary studies as a discipline by making the modern critic a more disciplined professional. The modern critic should be a scholar of literary criticism as well as a reader of literature; in fact he should be a scholar in order to be a competent reader. As a scholar, he will learn about the "essential problems of literature" not by plundering new fields of knowledge and not by the appeal to good taste (which Crane considered elitist), but by learning from thinkers who had for centuries made literature their explicit "object of critical attention."[4]

With the benefit of this training from past masters, the modern critic is qualified to bestow upon a particular literary object his own expert attention and thereby see for himself what makes the object literary. In keeping with the views we have encountered in Part I, Crane believes that the study of the literary is first and foremost a study of form, which is defined as an intrinsic property of the art work. In a statement that resonates with Víktor Shklovsky's recommendation that the art work be studied "from the point of view of the composition itself" ("*Tristram Shandy*," 43), Crane asserts that the trained literary critic is qualified to adopt "the point of view of their peculiar principles of construction and the special artistic problems which these presented to their writers" ("Plot," 647). For Crane the immanent point of view, the point of view of the form itself, rescues the literary work from either "dogmatic" evaluation or the superficial account of form provided by literary histories. But perhaps what brings Crane closest to Shklovsky is the difficulty each has in theorizing reader response as an intrinsic component of literary form. We can work up to an understanding of why this is the case for Crane by first noting the different ways Crane and Shklovsky theorize reader response as a formal element of fiction. As we saw through our analysis of Shklovsky's concept of defamiliarization, the "restored perception" offered to the reader through her experience of literature is ambiguously formulated as both a social and an aesthetic condition. Although Shklovsky's theory might inspire a political or ethical critique of the social conditions that produce habituation, Shklovsky himself emphasizes the insights gained into literary form itself. For Shklovsky, the reader's response to the novel's content, its mimeticism, is corrected by the operation of literary form. The reader thus comes to expect that any emotional response to the story world is a means to an end, the same end: the perception about literary form offered by literary form. For Crane, reader response is similarly vital to the successful operation of literary form. But on Crane's view, readerly emotion inspired by events in the story world is not undercut by literary form: on the contrary, this emotional response is itself the definition of literary form.

We should note here that Crane is not wholly clear about the relationship between the professionalized literary critic and the ordinary reader. For the most part, Crane seems to imply that the professional critic simply is more self-conscious and better able to articulate the formal dimension of a reading experience that in other ways is identical to that of the ordinary reader. For Crane, reader response is the objective basis of literary form: the more successful the work of art, the more uniform the emotional response of its readers. In this regard it is interesting to contrast Crane with Percy Lubbock, who sought to establish the novel as an objective form by *eliminating* what he felt was the reader's distracting emotional response to the story world and imagining the reader as purely a formal craftsman. Neo-Aristotelians believe instead that literary forms objectively solicit and control certain types of reader response, specifically the interplay of readerly knowledge and desire, a complex readerly response dictated by the representational logic of the work itself. For Crane, following Aristotle, different literary genres and modes within genres condition reader response by establishing different evaluative norms. In his essay on *Tom Jones*, Crane wants to know what kind of literary form this work is – which for him means, what kind of judgments about the story world does Henry Fielding's literary form elicit from its reader? He chooses *Tom Jones* as a test case not only because it is a novel written at the dawn of the English tradition, before novelistic modes could be routinely classified, but also to show that the famously complicated plot of this novel, burgeoning with event and incident, is unified by an overarching, meticulously formulated representational logic. What Crane calls the "form of the plot" ("Plot," 124) is the carefully calibrated positioning of reader response that is shaped by Fielding's meaningful and strategic representation of each story-world incident. The form of the plot is the author's controlled positioning of the reader in a progressive process of interpretation that leads the reader finally to a single, unified perception of the work's particular scale of value. This coherent scale of value that controls the reader's emotional response to the story world also serves as a stable criterion for the reader's apprehension of the generic character of the literary work itself. Crane's study of *Tom Jones* thus seeks to update Aristotle's catalogue of forms so it can accommodate the plots of modern genres like novels. If the aim of classical tragedy, for example, is to produce a catharsis in the reader, then what emotion, Crane asks, does the plot of *Tom Jones* aim to elicit?

The answer to this question is inseparable, according to Crane, from the reader's evaluation of Tom – and Crane's explicit critical task is to analyze the way Fielding directs the reader's "judgments" through the solicitation of emotion. For Crane, plot is the key formal element in the synthesis of readerly judgment with readerly feeling since it has the power to link knowledge with desire: the unfolding of the novel's plot incrementally increases the reader's knowledge (at the plot's end the reader knows all); but this knowledge is never abstract or academic, linked as it is with our "desires" for the characters' success or failure, reward or punishment. The achieved artistic unity that for Crane is a requirement of the successful literary work is thus, interestingly, the culmination of a reading process that itself is temporal and sequential. The best plot forms, the ones that most powerfully move us, are those that involve the reader at every moment in a coherent process of emotionalized interpretation; that elicit the right degree and kind of desire from the reader through the strategic manipulation of his interests and expectations; and that develop such emotions "consistently and progressively," establishing in the reader a confidence that her expectations for the characters will be rewarded, moment to moment, by the plot's coherent and satisfying representational logic. Read rightly, with the proper "attenuation" of "fear, pity, and indignation," *Tom Jones* yields "a peculiar comic pleasure" which Crane identifies as Fielding's primary artistic intention and thus the key to classifying it as a literary form (127). *Tom Jones* succeeds in achieving this unified affective response not only from Fielding's expert control of comic distance (which, Crane argues, effectively attenuates the reader's fear, pity, and indignation on Tom's behalf), but also from the astonishing homogeneity of his constructive intention: with only a few notable exceptions, every incident in the story world, no matter how seemingly detached or trivial, contributes to the reader's experience of the "peculiar comic pleasure" that Fielding's artistry creates – and it is Crane's task as a literary critic to describe how each representational choice contributes to the effect of the whole.

Although Crane would thus agree with Shklovsky that the form of the novel is what distinguishes it from the life it depicts, Crane's theory of the "form of the plot" is grounded in assumptions about the value of human experience that forge a continuum rather than a rupture between art and life. Crane follows Aristotle in believing that the "imitation" of life is the essential activity of literature. Since for Aristotle "life" consists of human beings engaged in meaningful action, then literary works accordingly make meaningful human action the subject of representation. In Aristotle's system, genres are classified according to the type and degree of meaningful human action they depict, and this scale is based on an absolute judgment of human achievement: by the nobility or baseness of the social types represented as well as by the achievement or failure of their actions. In the following passage from Aristotle, we may be reminded of Vladímir Propp's theory of "character" as a function of action – but for Aristotle this is a truth of life as well as art:

Both happiness and misery consist in a kind of action; and the end of life is some action, not some quality. Now, according to their characters men have certain qualities; but according to their actions they are happy or the opposite. Poets do not, therefore, create action in order to imitate character; but character is included on account of the action. Thus the end of tragedy is the presentation of the individual incidents and of the plot; and the end is, of course, the most significant thing of all. Furthermore, without action tragedy would be impossible, but without character it would still be possible.[5]

Achieved action is plot, whether it is accomplished by real men or fictional characters. In either case an individual life is given meaning by the teleology of his or her moral and ethical choices, without which subjective experiences would be discrete or incoherent. In Aristotle's theory, the artist's achievement of plot, the teleology he creates for his protagonist, entails a concomitant artistic goal: the elicitation of a coherent, unified emotional response from the reader. For the reader, as for the character, the "end" culminates in her emotionalized judgment of the character's success or failure, and thus is the "most significant thing of all." The scale of value that allows this final judgment also comes into view as a completed whole, thereby enabling the perspective of the generic character the work of art, the reader's crystallizing recognition of its distinct literary form.

Thus for the neo-Aristotelians the literary work is structured by four different types of unity. The first unity is derived from a philosophical belief in the achieved unity of subjective experience through accomplished action. This same philosophical belief allows Crane to posit a second unity, the plot of the novel. Focused around the fate of its protagonist, the plot of the novel is unified by the human action that it imitates. Following Aristotle, Crane calls this overarching unity the novel's "action" structure, by which he also means the unified creative intention that dictates the artist's depiction of his story world – and thereby introduces a third type of unity, that of authorial intention. It may be confusing to think of a creative intention as an "action," but the term is compatible with Crane's sense, derived from Aristotle, that authorial consciousness is important only as it is manifested through his action as an author. In the case of the novel, the author's intention is meaningful to the degree that he successfully expresses it through the representational choices he makes, which is to say by the shaping of the reader's response to the story world's mimetic content through the objectifying power of literary form. And the belief that reader response is thus contained and shaped by the teleology of her experience of the literary form makes reader response the fourth type of compositional unity.

Crane's theory of reader response raises a host of questions, some of which are taken up by other members of the Chicago School. Most pressingly, we might wonder what relation readerly emotion has to other types of human emotion: is catharsis or comic pleasure distinguishable from the emotions inspired in us by "real" life? Does the aestheticism of the reading experience, particularly our sense of the author's controlling hand, yield a kind of fear, pity, admiration, or satisfaction that is qualitatively different from our feelings and judgments about our family or our neighbors? As Ralph Rader points out, Crane believes that Aristotle decisively answers this question by putting didactic works in a different category from dramatic works. This means that, on Crane's view, despite their moral content, we can infer nothing about an author's personal beliefs

DOROTHY HALE

from reading works of fiction. The reward and punishment administered by the author through his fictional plots have no bearing on the values by which he directs his own life; it only expresses the formal economy necessary to produce a successful action plot. In Crane's model, the emotional effects entailed by these forms are ahistorical, noncontingent, and infinitely repeatable: every competent reader, regardless of her social identity, will respond to the work in the same way – and it is the aesthetic nature of this choice, its limitation by and reference to the work's strategic synthesis of plot elements, which, on his reading of *Tom Jones*, produces the "peculiar comic pleasure," the readerly emotion, that defines this literary genre.

Other members of the Chicago School were not so sure, however, that Aristotle meant to imply that the moral judgments elicited by dramatic forms were in fact separable from the everyday beliefs held by readers and authors when they were not engaged in reading or writing. Rader, for example, accepts the objectivism of Crane's model, but challenges its strict intrinsicality. Rader opens up neo-Aristotelianism to historical and biographical contexts, albeit ones that are themselves carefully restricted and defined. For Rader, when the English eighteenth-century novelist sits down to write, her representational choices are driven by three constructive imperatives. First of all, she strives to make a unified work of art by creating a coherent action structure (in the service of a particular emotional effect). This imperative derives from Crane, but the next is Rader's own addition to Crane's model: the nondidactic artist (i.e. the dramatic artist) strives not just to conceive an action plot, but also to follow the representational conventions particular to her chosen genre. To write a novel is not to write a play, even though they both are dramatic forms built through action structures. On Rader's view, the novel comes to be distinguished by generic features (such as characterological autonomy) that supplement and combine with the formal requirements of the action plot. Since genres are modified through time, Rader also adds a literary-historical dimension to neo-Aristotelianism, arguing that to write a novel in the eighteenth century is substantially different from writing a novel in the next. Rader's third imperative reaches even further beyond the work itself to take into account the dominant cultural values that, in any given period, help to define literature as an activity worth pursuing. In the eighteenth century, according to Rader, this value is epitomized by what he calls "Johnson's Rule": namely, Samuel Johnson's belief that the new form of imitation inaugurated by Samuel Richardson and Fielding should be used to model "the highest and purest" behavior that "humanity can reach" (Rader, quoting Johnson, 143). In other words, according to Rader the English novel is born in the belief that it should strive to represent morally superior actions that are themselves imitable, accomplished as they are by model, but not ideal, protagonists. Thus Rader, *contra* Crane, would argue for the eighteenth-century novel's necessary engagement with moral judgments that have personal and social consequences, consequences outside the aesthetic realm. But because Rader accepts in theory the distinction between imitative and didactic genres, he understands this duality – the self-contained aesthetic emotions and the real world consequences of aesthetic effects – as a source of productive creative tension for eighteenth-century novelists.

Rader examines the representational choices made by authors as much for the conflicts they reveal as for the formal unity they accomplish. In Rader's theory, the novelist's attempt to reconcile the conflicting demands of the three constructive imperatives leads to stronger or weaker artistic achievements, whose relative success is determinable not by the critic's taste but by the objective analysis of the author's formal choices in a given novel. Masterpieces, like *Clarissa* and *Pride and Prejudice*, find innovative resolutions to the three constructive imperatives; these novels succeed in creating moral paragons who nonetheless fill the novel's generic requirement of characterological autonomy by making the protagonists maximally responsible for their actions. And in keeping with the neo-Aristotelian requirements of the action structure, Richardson and Jane Austen both make representational choices that effectively involve the reader of each work in the incremental process of emotionalized judgment, leaving her satisfied at the end that the protaganist's fate and dessert are appropriately aligned.

Rader's approach can yield fascinating insights into the evolution of literary forms. For example, his understanding of the literary challenge undertaken by Austen seeks to explain both her formal contribution (her technical innovations) to the development of the novel as a genre as well as the division among literary scholars about the value of her artistic achievement. According to Rader, Austen succeeds in advancing the genre by her competitive desire to improve on *Tom Jones*. She thus succeeds in representing morally superior actions by giving her protagonists "imperfections" but not "moral faults" (which Tom Jones has been accused of having). Her solution to Johnson's Rule is simultaneously advanced by outdoing Fielding's narrative strategies for the representation of characterological autonomy: Austen's innovations in the representation of characterological point of view yield "a relative closeness of psychological transcription" that could "maintain moral interest and significance without imperiling the sacrosanct status of the paragons." Austen's particular synthetic solution to the three constructive imperatives thus for Rader explains why Austen's critical reception through the ages has been mixed. From her first publication some critics have found Austen's work to be nothing more than "a tempest in a teapot," while for others it is "a wonder of fine psychological and moral analysis" (148). This mixed critical judgment does not express ambiguity about her objective artistic achievement; according to Rader, it simply shows the different aesthetic criteria by which that objective achievement can be measured.

Rader's map of the evolution of the English novel does not stop with the eighteenth century; in other essays he carries the analysis from Brontë, Dickens, and Hardy through to Joyce and Woolf. In his later work, Rader becomes increasingly interested in consulting authorial lives for what he calls the "unique biographical situation,"[6] what he elsewhere terms the "uncreated core," an overriding personal attachment or belief that "would generate and give significance" to the novel's fictional world. He likewise turns away from the literary work to find empirical support for the objectivity both he and Crane attribute to the reading experience. Rader believes that the historical record of reader response reveals unified patterns of novel reception that confirm a particular novel's formal effects. In other words, he is interested not only in the professional critic's estimation in and over time of Austen as an artist, but also the popular reader response to her works through the ages. In an interesting reversal of the impulse that inaugurates Crane's initial turn to Aristotle – the desire to make the field of literary criticism more disciplined by creating trained readers – Rader suggests that academics do not always give the best accounts of their own reading experiences. Between 1952 (when Crane publishes his preface to *Critics and Criticism*) and 1993 (when Rader publishes "The

Emergence of the Novel in England: Genre in History vs. History of Genre"), Anglo-American literary criticism had become deeply professionalized, in large part due to the kind of theoretical self-consciousness engaged in and promoted by the thinkers in this volume. In ways that Crane could not expect, the successful professionalism of literary criticism thus poses a problem for the neo-Aristotelian: it creates a community of super-subtle interpreters who risk losing touch with what Rader calls the "intuitive impressions," the "pre-analytic registration" of formal effects, that are common to "every reader's imaginative experience" of literary form. Rader thus carries on Crane's project of returning to the "essential problems of literature," but with the understanding that what is most essential to the novel is that which is most often missed by professional critics, whose "variation in theoretical assumptions" causes them to overlook the stability of the reader's "underlying experience" of a literary work.[7] For Rader, the neo-Aristotelian thus makes his case for the novel's objectivity as a literary form by invoking the objective record of reader reception, which is handed down through the shared cultural knowledge that all readers have about novels, enduring commonplaces about specific masterpieces as well as the novel's overall generic character.

Wayne Booth, by contrast, is wholly determined to maintain the line between life and art, "real" people and literary agents. He insists that the literary work itself is the one and only objective source for its meaning and value. To use Booth's own vivid example, the confidence in humankind expressed by Faulkner in his Nobel Prize speech has no relevance to the tragic vision of southern society that we experience in reading a novel like *Absalom, Absalom!* Even when Faulkner speaks *as* an author, he is not *being* an author. Booth extends this logic to claim that the reader becomes a different kind of self when he sits down to read, in this case, shedding the ordinary self – the "self who goes about paying bills, repairing leaky faucets, and failing in generosity and wisdom" (172). As did Lubbock and Northrop Frye, Booth imagines the activity of reading to require and enable an identity wholly different from our everyday personhood. On Booth's account, the experience of literary form focuses and streamlines the reader's interests into three types of concerns (the intellectual, qualitative, and practical), categories that Booth derives directly from Aristotle.

Although Booth is committed to the intrinsicality of literary works as well as to the autonomy of the aesthetic experience, he ultimately deviates from Crane in a funda-mental way: he emphasizes exactly what Crane – following Aristotle – sought to diminish: individual character as a source of personal identity. Although Booth would agree that character cannot be understood apart from action, that character is in fact best understood as the sum of an agent's chosen actions, he has more trouble than either Crane or Aristotle in relying upon an ethical scale that would make possible the absolute judgment of human action, the objective classification of the nobility or baseness of either a protagonist's or an author's accomplishment. Booth thus attempts to locate absolute moral standards within specific generic forms and modes. The novel, on his account, promotes the values of democracy and humanism because it enables characters of any sort, from any walk of life, to speak in their own voices.[8] But some modalities of the novel can realize these values better than others: omniscient narrators, for example, may choose to recreate the world they represent in the image of their own point of view, and thus dominate the characters they depict rather than liberate them. The moral character of each genre and modality thus for Booth is a kind of formal potentiality whose ultimate value is decided by the author who takes up this form as his own means of self-expression. Booth's title, *The Rhetoric of Fiction*, emphasizes his engagement with Aristotle as a rhetorician as well as an aesthetician: Booth believes that novels should be studied not through a science of "forms," and not even through an evolutionary model of generic development (as is Rader's goal), but as acts of communication, specifically as strategies of persuasion.

But how can Booth reconcile his view of literature as communication with a formalism that insists that the beliefs of "ordinary" people are irrelevant to the activity of reading literature? His solution to this problem produces what is arguably his most influential contribution to literary studies: the concept of "implied" reader and author. In a move that reveals the ambiguity of the Craneian position (the tension in his theory between readerly judgments and emotions objectified by the literary work and subjective judgments and emotions held by authors and readers as persons), Booth interprets the achieved unity of art works as the expression of a morally unified *self*: the reader's progressive response to the implied author's technical choices result in her culminating "apprehension of a completed artistic whole; the chief value to which *this* implied author is committed, regardless of what party his creator belongs to in real life, is that which is expressed by the total form" (161). Jamesian sincerity, the notion that a successful art work expresses the unique sensibility of its author, may seem to be dismissed by Booth because he believes, in a Craneian way, that "Just as one's personal letters imply different versions of oneself, depending on the differing relationships with each correspondent and the purpose of each letter, so the writer sets himself out with a different air depending on the needs of particular works" (159). But Booth's desire to make the people who write literature the ultimate source of value, intention, and communication shows that he is not wholly willing to relinquish the Jamesian notion that a work of art expresses the author's sincere values, even if this author is in Booth's theory a shadow figure, an "implied" person, knowable only through the works he has written. Ultimately, the shaping power of genre in Booth's model does not so much do away with authorial sincerity as reformulate it into an objective quality intrinsic to literary works: "we have only the work as evidence for the only kind of sincerity that concerns us: Is the implied author in harmony with himself – that is, are his other choices in harmony with his explicit narrative character?" (161).

Because Booth understands the representational choices made by authors as reflections of their beliefs, he has an easier time maintaining the intrinsicality of the implied author than that of the reader. In "Emotions, Beliefs, and the Reader's Objectivity" (chapter 5 of *The Rhetoric of Fiction*), he qualifies the separation between ordinary man and reader by saying, "the divorce between my ordinary self and the selves I am willing to become as I read is not complete" (172). He goes on to detail the kinds of ruptures a reader might feel between the moral position the implied author asks him to occupy, the kinds of emotionalized judgments he establishes as normative, and the actual felt emotions and evaluative judgments that the reader feels and makes as she reads. In Booth's model, then, the reader falls short of taking the work's point of view – and this is because once form is reattached to subjective agents, points of view cannot be neutral "formal" positions; aesthetic effects "required" by the work of art cannot be so easily isolated from the "real" emotions that might disrupt even the most disciplined reading of literary texts. Thus to read the work objectively, "on its own terms," becomes for

Booth a negotiation between value systems (the implied author's and the real reader's) that are always potentially in conflict. Crane's aesthetic view, that the best plots are those that are most unified, is transmogrified in Booth to a moral directive: that the values of an implied author be clear and unambiguous so they may best be made "accessible to a public" (178), who can then, presumably, through normative evaluation, most clearly judge them. And because Booth thinks that the aesthetic power of the literary work depends upon the harmony between implied author and real reader, he believes that the success or failure of a literary work depends upon the convergence of belief, the real reader's sincere assent to the (sincere) values of the implied reader.

Thus Crane's attempt to found a school of literary criticism that would first and foremost be focused upon literary form ends up as an ethical criticism grounded in the standard of public judgment. The "unities" of authorial intention, reader response, and literary form can be sustained as intrinsic properties of the art work only in a social world whose shared values are so strong, so uniform, as to make the values expressed through the dramatic action of the story world seem wholly unified – and, by extension, able to be universalized to any reader at any time and in any place. But without the undergirding belief in such unifying cultural values, the categories of unity themselves lose stability: rather than seeming the objective product of successful literary form, a reader's response to an authorial intention may in fact simply be the reader's own projection – with no guarantee that another reader, with a different set of values, won't also call the mirror image of her response "author" as well. Despite criticism along these lines, the attempt to theorize an objective basis for the study of literary forms remains the enduring project of the Chicago School. And Chicago School critics are not the only ones who carry forward this dimension of the formalist endeavor. Structuralists likewise participate in the search for the objective basis of literary form, and they, too, believe that the first step toward this end is to distinguish the (neutral) study of literary form from, in Crane's neo-Aristotelian phrase, "the criticism of qualities." The structuralists will pursue this goal, however, by rejecting the notion that literary criticism must have its own intrinsic disciplinary practices. They will instead draw upon insights and methods from the new social sciences that Crane deplores – but doing in so in a professionalized way that he might have admired.

NOTES

1 R. S. Crane, preface, *Critics and Criticism: Essays in Method*, ed. Crane (1952; Chicago: University of Chicago Press, abridged 1957) iii.
2 Ibid. v.
3 Ibid.
4 Ibid.
5 Aristotle, *Poetics*, trans. Leon Golden (Englewood Cliffs, NJ: Prentice Hall, 1968) 12.
6 Ralph W. Rader, "The Emergence of the Novel in England: Genre in History vs. History of Genre," *Narrative* I (1993): 78.
7 Ibid. 72.
8 Wayne Booth, introduction, *Problems of Dostoevsky's Poetics*, by Mikhail Bakhtin, ed. and trans. Caryl Emerson, Theory and History of Literature Series vol. 8 (Minneapolis: University of Minnesota Press, 1984) xxii.

Rader, Ralph W. "Defoe, Richardson, Joyce and the Concept of Form in the Novel." In *Autobiography, Biography, and the Novel*, ed. William Matthews and Rader. Los Angeles: University of California Press, 1973, 31–72.

Richter, David. "The Second Flight of the Phoenix: Neo-Aristotelianism Since Crane." *The Eighteenth Century* 23.1 (1982): 27–48.

Sprinker, Michael. "What is Living and What is Dead in Chicago Criticism." *Boundary 2: A Journal of Postmodern Literature and Culture* 13.2–3 (1985): 189–212.

Wimsatt, W. K. "The Chicago Critics: The Fallacy of the Neoclassical Species." In *The Verbal Icon: Studies in the Meaning of Poetry*, ed. Wimsatt and Monroe Beardsley. Lexington: University of Kentucky Press, 1954, 41–65.

The Concept of Plot and the Plot of *Tom Jones*[1]

R. S. Crane

Ronald Salmon Crane (1886–1967)

Born in Tecumseh, Michigan, R. S. Crane attended the University of Michigan at Ann Arbor and the University of Pennsylvania, where he received his doctorate in 1911. After 14 years teaching at Northwestern University, and working as a biographer and philologist, Crane moved to the University of Chicago. By 1935 he had rejected the historical scholarship he had previously practiced and embraced a new aesthetic approach to literature. As chair of the English Department, and an influential and exacting teacher, Crane effectively shaped what was to be known as the Chicago School of literary studies; *The Languages of Criticism and the Structure of Poetry* (1953) and *Critical and Historical Principles of Literary History* (1967) formed the foundation for this movement. A selection of his essays was also published in the two-volume set *The Idea of the Humanities and Other Essays Critical and Historical* (1967). "The Concept of Plot and the Plot of *Tom Jones*" is an expanded version of an article originally published in 1950, entitled "The Plot of *Tom Jones*."

From *Critics and Criticism: Ancient and Modern*, edited by R. S. Crane. Chicago and London: University of Chicago Press, 1952, pp. 616–24, 631–47. Copyright © 1952 by the University of Chicago Press. Reprinted by permission of the University of Chicago Press.

Of all the plots constructed by English novelists that of *Tom Jones* has probably elicited the most unqualified praise. There is "no fable whatever," wrote Fielding's first biographer, that "affords, in its solution, such artful states of suspence, such beautiful turns of surprise, such unexpected incidents, and such sudden discoveries, sometimes apparently embarrassing, but always promising the catastrophe, and eventually promoting the completion of the whole."[2] Not since the days of Homer, it seemed to James Beattie, had the world seen "a more artful epick fable." "The characters and adventures are wonderfully diversified: yet the circumstances are all so natural, and rise so easily from one another, and co-operate with so much regularity in bringing on, even while they seem to retard, the catastrophe, that the curiosity of the reader...grows more and more impatient as the story advances, till at last it becomes downright anxiety. And when we get to the end...we are amazed to find, that of so many incidents there should be so few superfluous; that in such variety of fiction there should be so great probability; and that so complex a tale should be perspicuously conducted, and with perfect unity of design."[3] These are typical of the eulogies that preceded and were summed up in Coleridge's famous verdict in 1834: "What a master of composition Fielding was! Upon my word, I think the Oedipus Tyrannus, The Alchemist, and Tom Jones, the three most perfect plots ever planned."[4] More recent writers have tended to speak less hyperbolically and, like Scott, to insist that "even the high praise due to the construction and arrangement of the story is inferior to that claimed by the truth, force, and spirit of the characters,"[5] but it is hard to think of any important modern discussion of the novel that does not contain at least a few sentences on Fielding's "ever-to-be-praised skill as an architect of plot."[6]

I

The question I wish to raise concerns not the justice of any of these estimates but rather the nature and critical adequacy of the conception of plot in general and of the plot of *Tom Jones* in particular that underlies most if not all of them. Now it is a striking fact that in all the more extended discussions of Fielding's masterpiece since 1749 the consideration of the plot has constituted merely one topic among several others, and a topic, moreover, so detached from the rest that once it is disposed of the consideration of the remaining elements of character, thought, diction, and narrative technique invariably proceeds without further reference to it. The characters are indeed agents of the story, but their values are assessed apart from this, in terms sometimes of their degrees of conformity to standards of characterization in literature generally, sometimes of the conceptions of morality they embody, sometimes of their relation to Fielding's experiences or prejudices, sometimes of their reflection, taken collectively, of the England of their time. The other elements are isolated similarly, both from the plot and from one another: what is found important in the thought, whether of the characters or of the narrator, is normally not its function as an artistic device but its doctrinal content as a sign of the "philosophy" of Fielding; the style and the ironical tone of the narrative are frequently praised, but solely as means to the general literary satisfaction of the reader; and, what is perhaps more significant, the wonderful comic force of the novel, which all have delighted to commend, is assumed to be independent of the plot and a matter

R. S. CRANE

exclusively of particular incidents, of the characters of some, but not all, of the persons, and of occasional passages of burlesque or witty writing.[7]

All this points to a strictly limited definition of plot as something that can be abstracted, for critical purposes, from the moral qualities of the characters and the operations of their thought. This something is merely the material continuity of the story considered in relation to the general pleasure we take in any fiction when our curiosity about the impending events is aroused, sustained, and then satisfied to a degree or in a manner we could not anticipate. A plot in this sense – the sense in which modern novelists pride themselves on having got rid of plot – can be pronounced good in terms simply of the variety of incidents it contains, the amount of suspense and surprise it evokes, and the ingenuity with which all the happenings in the beginning and middle are made to contribute to the resolution at the end. Given the definition, indeed, no other criteria are possible, and no others have been used by any of the critics of *Tom Jones* since the eighteenth century who have declared its plot to be one of the most perfect ever planned. They have uniformly judged it as interesting story merely – and this whether, as by most of the earlier writers, "the felicitous contrivance and happy extrication of the story" is taken to be the chief "beauty" of the novel or whether, as generally nowadays, preference is given to its qualities of character and thought. It is clearly of plot in no completer sense than this that Oliver Elton is thinking when he remarks that, although some "have cared little for this particular excellence, and think only of Partridge, timorous, credulous, garrulous, faithful, and an injured man; of Squire Western, and of the night at Upton, and of wit and humour everywhere," still "the common reader, for whom Fielding wrote, cares a great deal, and cares rightly, for plot; and so did Sophocles."[8]

When plot is conceived thus narrowly, in abstraction from the peculiar characters and mental processes of the agents, it must necessarily have, for the critic, only a relatively external relation to the other aspects of the work. That is why, in most discussions of *Tom Jones*, the critical treatment of the plot (as distinguished from mere summary of the happenings) is restricted to the kind of enthusiastic general appreciation of which I have given some examples, supplemented by more particular remarks on various episodes, notably those of the Man of the Hill and of Mrs. Fitzpatrick, which appear to do little to advance the action. The plot, in these discussions, is simply one of several sources of interest and pleasure afforded by a novel peculiarly rich in pleasurable and interesting things, and the problem of its relation to the other ingredients is evaded altogether. Occasionally, it is true, the question has been faced; but even in those critics, like W. L. Cross and Oliver Elton, who have made it most explicit, the formulas suggested never give to the plot of *Tom Jones* the status of more than an external and enveloping form in relation to which the rest of the novel is content. It is not, as they see it, an end but a means, and they describe it variously, having no language but metaphor for the purpose, as a "framework" in which character (which is Fielding's "real 'bill of fare'") is "set"; as a device, essentially "artificial," for bringing on the stage "real men and women"; as a "mere mechanism," which, except now and then in the last two books, "does not obtrude," for keeping readers alert through six volumes.[9]

I do not believe, however, that it is necessary to remain content with this very limited and abstract definition of plot or with the miscellaneous and fragmentized criticism of works like *Tom Jones* that has always followed from it. I shall assume that any novel or drama not constructed on didactic principles is a composite of three elements, which unite to determine its quality and effect – the things that are imitated (or "rendered") in it, the linguistic medium in which they are imitated, and the manner or technique of imitation; and I shall assume further that the things imitated necessarily involve human beings interacting with one another in ways determined by, and in turn affecting, their moral characters and their states of mind (i.e., their reasonings, emotions, and attitudes). If this is granted, we may say that the plot of any novel or drama is the particular temporal synthesis effected by the writer of the elements of action, character, and thought that constitute the matter of his invention. It is impossible, therefore, to state adequately what any plot is unless we include in our formula all three of the elements or causes of which the plot is the synthesis; and it follows also that plots will differ in structure according as one or another of the three causal ingredients is employed as the synthesizing principle. There are, thus, plots of action, plots of character, and plots of thought. In the first, the synthesizing principle is a completed change, gradual or sudden, in the situation of the protagonist, determined and effected by character and thought (as in *Oedipus* and *The Brothers Karamazov*); in the second, the principle is a completed process of change in the moral character of the protagonist, precipitated or molded by action, and made manifest both in it and in thought and feeling (as in James's *The Portrait of a Lady*); in the third, the principle is a completed process of change in the thought of the protagonist and consequently in his feelings, conditioned and directed by character and action (as in Pater's *Marius the Epicurean*). All these types of construction, and not merely the first, are plots in the meaning of our definition; and it is mainly, perhaps, because most of the familiar classic plots, including that of *Tom Jones*, have been of the first kind that so many critics have tended to reduce plot to action alone.[10]

If this is granted, we may go farther. For a plot, in the enlarged sense here given to the term, is not merely a particular synthesis of particular materials of character, thought, and action, but such a synthesis endowed necessarily, because it imitates in words a sequence of human activities, with a power to affect our opinions and emotions in a certain way. We are bound, as we read or listen, to form expectations about what is coming and to feel more or less determinate desires relatively to our expectations. At the very least, if we are interested at all, we desire to know what is going to happen or how the problems faced by the characters are going to be solved. This is a necessary condition of our pleasure in all plots, and there are many good ones – in the classics of pure detective fiction, for example, or in some modern psychiatric novels – the power of which depends almost exclusively on the pleasure we take in inferring progressively, from complex or ambiguous signs, the true state of affairs. For some readers and even some critics this would seem to be the chief source of delight in many plots that have obviously been constructed on more specific principles: not only *Tom Jones*, as we have seen, but *Oedipus* has been praised as a mystery story, and it is likely that much of Henry James's popularity is due to his remarkable capacity for provoking a superior kind of inferential activity. What distinguishes all the more developed forms of imitative literature, however, is that, though they presuppose this instinctive pleasure in learning, they go beyond it and give us plots of which the effects derive in a much more immediate way from the particular ethical qualities manifested in their agents' actions and thoughts vis-à-vis the human situations in which they are engaged. When this is the case, we cannot help becoming, in a greater or less degree, emotionally involved; for some of the characters we wish good, for others ill, and, depending on our inferences as to the events, we feel hope or fear, pity or satisfaction, or some modification of these or similar emotions. The peculiar power of any plot of this kind, as it unfolds, is a result of our state of knowledge at any point in complex interaction with our desires for the characters as morally differentiated beings; and we may be said to have grasped the plot in the full artistic sense only when we have analyzed this interplay of desires and expectations sequentially in relation to the incidents by which it is produced.

It is, of course, an essential condition of such an effect that the writer should so have combined his elements of action, character, and thought as to have achieved a complete and ordered whole, with all the parts needed to carry the protagonist, by probable or necessary stages, from the beginning to the end of his change: we should not have, otherwise, any connected series of expectations wherewith to guide our desires. In itself, however, this structure is only the matter or content of the plot and not its form; the form of the plot – in the sense of that which makes its matter into a definite artistic thing – is rather its distinctive "working or power," as the form of the plot in tragedy, for example, is the capacity of its unified sequence of actions to effect through pity and fear a cartharsis of such emotions.

But if this is granted, then certain consequences follow for the criticism of dramas and novels. It is evident, in the first place, that no plot of this order can be judged excellent *merely* in terms of the unity of its action, the number and variety of its incidents, or the extent to which it produces suspense and surprise. These are but properties of its matter, and their achievement, even to a high degree, in any particular plot does not inevitably mean that the emotional effect of the whole will not still be diffused or weak. They are, therefore, necessary, but not sufficient, conditions of a good plot, the positive excellence of which depends upon the power of its peculiar synthesis of character, action, and thought, as inferable from the sequence of words, to move our feelings powerfully and pleasurably in a certain definite way.

But this power, which constitutes the form of the plot, is obviously, from an artistic point of view, the most important virtue any drama or novel can have; it is that, indeed, which most sharply distinguishes works of imitation from all other kinds of literary productions. It follows, consequently, that the plot, considered formally, of any imitative work is, in relation to the work as a whole, not simply a means – a "framework" or "mere mechanism" – but rather the final end which everything in the work, if that is to be felt as a whole, must be made, directly or indirectly, to serve. For the critic, therefore, the form of the plot is a first principle, which he must grasp as clearly as possible for any work he proposes to examine before he can deal adequately with the questions raised by its parts. This does not mean that we cannot derive other relevant principles of judgment from the general causes of pleasure operative in all artistic imitations, irrespective of the particular effect, serious or comic, that is aimed at in a given work. One of these is the imitative principle itself, the principle that we are in general more convinced and moved when things are "rendered" for us through probable signs than when they are given merely in "statement," without illusion, after the fashion of a scenario.[11] Critical judgments, valid enough if they are not taken absolutely, may also be drawn from considerations of the general powers of language as a literary medium, of the known potentialities or requirements of a given manner of representation (e.g., dramatic or narrative), and of the various conditions of suspense and surprise. We are not likely to feel strongly the emotional effect of a work in which the worse rather than the better alternatives among these different expedients are consistently chosen or chosen in crucial scenes. The same thing, too, can be said of works in which the thought, however clearly serving an artistic use, is generally uninteresting or stale, or in which the characters of the agents, though right enough in conception for the intended effect, are less than adequately "done" or fail to impress themselves upon our memory and imagination, or in which we perceive that the most has not been made of the possibilities implicit in the incidents. And there is also a kind of judgment, distinct from any of these, the object of which is not so much the traits of a work that follow from its general character as an imitative drama or novel as the qualities of intelligence and moral sensibility in its author which are reflected in his conception and handling of its subject and which warrant us in ascribing "greatness," "seriousness," or "maturity" to some products of art and in denying these values to others no matter how excellent, in a formal sense, the latter may be.

Such criticism of parts in the light of general principles is indispensable, but it is no substitute for – and its conclusions, affirmative as well as negative, have constantly to be checked by – the more specific kind of criticism of a work that takes the form of the plot as its starting point and then inquires how far and in what way its peculiar power is maximized by the writer's invention and development of episodes, his step-by-step rendering of the characters of his people, his use and elaboration of thought, his handling of diction and imagery, and his decisions as to the order, method, scale, and point of view of his representation.

All this is implied, I think, in the general hypothesis about plot which I have been outlining here and which I now propose to illustrate further in a re-examination of the "ever-to-be-praised" plot of *Tom Jones*.

* * *

III

In stating this principle for any plot, we must consider three things: (1) the general estimate we are induced to form, by signs in the work, of the moral character and deserts of the hero, as a result of which we tend, more or less ardently, to wish for him either good or bad fortune in the end; (2) the judgments we are led similarly to make about the nature of the events that actually befall the hero or seem likely to befall him, as having either painful or pleasurable consequences for him, and this in greater or less degree and permanently or temporarily; and (3) the opinions we are made to entertain concerning the degree and kind of his reponsibility for what happens to him, as being either little or great and, if the latter, the result either of his acting in full knowledge of what he is doing or of some sort of mistake. The form of a given plot is a function of the particular correlation among these three variables which the completed work is calculated to establish, consistently and progressively, in our minds; and in these terms we may say that the plot of *Tom Jones* has a pervasively comic form. The precise sense, however, in which the form is comic is a rather special one, which needs to be carefully defined.

R. S. CRANE

To begin with, it is obviously a plot in which the complication generates much pain and inner suffering for the hero, as a result of misfortunes which would seem genuinely serious to any good person. He is schemed against by a villain who will not stop even at judicial murder to secure his ends, and, what is worse in his eyes, he loses the good will of the two people whom he most loves, and loses it as a consequence not simply of the machinations of his enemies but of his own mistaken acts. From near the beginning until close to the end, moreover, he is made to undergo an almost continuous series of distressing indignities: to be insulted on the score of his birth, to be forbidden the sight of Sophia, to see her being pushed into a hated marriage with Blifil and persecuted when she refuses, to be banished abruptly from home, to be reduced to poverty and forced to take money from Lady Bellaston, to be laid in wait for by a press gang, to be compelled to run a man through in self-defense, and finally, in prison, to be faced with the prospect of a disgraceful death.

The hero, furthermore, to whom all this happens is a naturally good man – not notably virtuous, but, for all his faults, at least the equal of ourselves and of any other character in the novel in disinterestedness, generosity, and tender benevolent feeling. These traits are impressed upon us in the third book and are never obscured even in the worst of Tom's troubles in London; they are, in fact, revivified for us, just at the point when we might be most tempted to forget them, by the episodes of Anderson and of Mrs. Miller's daughter. We favor Tom, therefore, even if we do not admire him, and we wish for him the good fortune with Allworthy and Sophia which he properly wishes for himself and which, in terms of his basic moral character, he deserves to get. We follow him through his troubles and distresses, consequently, with a desire that he will eventually be delivered from them and reunited to his friend and mistress, and this all the more when, at the climax of his difficulties, we see him acting, for the first time, in a way we can entirely approve; in the end, when our wishes for him are unexpectedly realized, and to a fuller degree than we had anticipated, we feel some of the satisfaction which Fielding says (XVIII, xiii) was then felt by the principal characters themselves. "All were happy, but those the most who had been most unhappy before. Their former sufferings and fears gave such a relish to their felicity as even love and fortune, in their fullest flow, could not have given without the advantage of such a comparison."

Having conceived a plot in which so sympathetic a character is subjected in the complication to experiences so painful, it would have been relatively easy for Fielding to write a novel similar in form to his *Amelia*, that is to say, a tragicomedy of common life designed to arouse and then to dissipate, by a sudden happy resolution, emotions of fear and pity for his hero and of indignation toward his enemies. There is, indeed, an even greater material basis for such an effect in *Tom Jones* than in the later novel: the evils that threaten Tom and the indignities he undergoes are, in the abstract, more serious than anything Booth has to fear, and the same thing is true of the persecutions endured by Sophia as compared with those which Amelia is made to suffer. And yet nothing is more evident than that, whereas the emotions awakened in us by the distresses of Booth and Amelia are the graver emotions of anxiety and compassion that yield what Fielding calls "the pleasure of tenderness,"[12] our feelings for Tom and Sophia, as we anticipate or view in actuality the greater evils that befall them prior to the final discovery, partake only in the mildest degree of this painful quality. We do not actively fear for or pity

---

either of them, and our indignation at the actions of their enemies – even the actions of Blifil – never develops into a sustained punitive response.

Nor is the reason for this hard to find. It is generally the case that whatever tends to minimize our fear in a plot that involves threats of undeserved misfortune for the sympathetic characters tends also to minimize our pity when the misfortune occurs and likewise our indignation against the doers of the evil; and fear for Tom and Sophia as they move toward the successive climaxes of their troubles is prevented from becoming a predominant emotion in the complication of *Tom Jones* chiefly by two things.[13]

The first is our perception, which in each case grows stronger as the novel proceeds, that the persons whose actions threaten serious consequences for the hero and heroine are all persons for whom, though in varying degrees, we are bound to feel a certain contempt. The most formidable of them all is of course Blifil. As a villain, however, he is no Iago but merely a clever opportunist who is likely to overreach himself (as the failure of his first schemes shows) and whose power of harm depends entirely on the blindness of Allworthy; he deceives Tom only temporarily and Sophia and Mrs. Miller not at all; and after we have seen the display of his personal ineptitude in the proposal scene with Sophia, we are prepared to wait, without too much active suspense, for his final showing-up. Blifil is too coldly selfish, perhaps, to strike us as positively ridiculous, but in the characters of the other agents of misfortune the comic strain is clear. It is most obvious, needless to say, in Squire Western and his sister: who can really fear that the persecutions directed against the determined and resourceful Sophia by such a blundering pair of tyrants can ever issue in serious harm? For Allworthy, too, in spite of his excellent principles, it is hard for us to maintain entire respect; we should certainly take more seriously his condemnation of Tom in Book VI had we not become accustomed, as a result of earlier incidents in the novel, to smile at a man who could believe in the goodness of the two Blifils and whose pride in his own judgment could make him dispose so precipitously of Jenny and Partridge. There are evident comic traits also in all the persons who cause trouble for Tom and Sophia in the later part of the action: in Dowling, the man always in a hurry; in Lady Bellaston, the great dame who pursues a plebeian with frenzied letters and nocturnal visits to his lodgings; in Lord Fellamar, the half-hearted rake; in Fitzpatrick, the unfaithful but jealous husband who will not believe the evidence of his own eyes. In respect of her relations with Tom, though not otherwise, Sophia, too, must be added to the list, as a virtuous girl with a proper amount of spirit (not to say vanity) whose good resolutions against Tom never survive for long in the presence of her lover. These are all manifestations of the ineffectual or ridiculous in a plot in which the impending events are materially painful, and they contribute, on the principle that we fear less or not at all when the agents of harm to a hero are more or less laughable persons, to induce in us a general feeling of confidence that matters are not really as serious as they appear.

A second ground of security lies in the nature of the probabilities for future action that are made evident progressively as the novel unfolds. From the beginning until the final capitulation of Sophia, the successive incidents constantly bring forth new and unexpected complications, each seemingly fraught with more suffering for Tom than the last; but as we read we instinctively infer from past occurrences to what will probably happen next or in the end, and what steadily cumulates in this way, in spite

R. S. CRANE

of the gradual worsening of Tom's situation, is an opinion that, since nothing irreparable has so far happened to him, nothing ever will. In one sense – that which relates to its material events – the action becomes more and more serious as it moves to its climax, in another sense – that which relates to our expectations – less and less serious; and I think that any close reader who keeps in mind the earlier parts of the novel as he attends to the later is inevitably made aware of this, with the result that, though his interest mounts, his fear increasingly declines. We come thus to the first climax in Book VI recalling such things as Jenny's assurance to Allworthy that she will someday make known the whole truth, the sudden reversal of the elder Blifil's sinister plans, the collapse, after initial success, of young Blifil's first scheme against Tom, and Tom's return to favor with Allworthy after the incident of Molly's arrest; and all these memories inevitably operate to check the rise of any long-range apprehensions. And it is the same, too, with the second and apparently much more serious climax at the end of Book XVI, when Tom, dismissed by Sophia, lies in prison awaiting the death of Fitzpatrick, who has been given up by his surgeon: we cannot but remember how, in the affairs of Molly and then of Mrs. Waters, Sophia has more than once demonstrated her inability to inflict any great or prolonged punishment on Tom for his sins with other women and how, on the occasion of Allworthy's illness in Book V, the outcome had completely disappointed the gloomy predictions of the doctor.

The attenuation, in these ways, of fear, pity, and indignation is a necessary condition of the peculiar comic pleasure which is the form of the plot in *Tom Jones*, but it is only a negative and hence not a sufficient condition. A comic effect of any kind would be impossible if we took Tom's increasingly bad prospects with the same seriousness as he himself takes them, but what in a positive sense makes Fielding's plot comic is the combination of this feeling of security with our perception of the decisive role which Tom's own blunders are made to play, consistently, in the genesis of all the major difficulties into which he is successively brought – always, of course, with the eager assistance of Fortune and of the malice or misunderstanding of others. The importance of this becomes clear when we consider how much trouble he would have spared himself had he not mistaken his seduction by Molly for a seduction of her by him; had he not got drunk when he learned of Allworthy's recovery or fought with Blifil and Thwackum; had he not suggested to Western that he be allowed to plead Blifil's case with Sophia; had he not allowed himself to be seduced by Jenny at Upton; had he not thought that his very love for Sophia, to say nothing of his gallantry, required him "to keep well" with the lady at the masquerade; and, lastly, had he not accepted so uncritically Nightingale's scheme for compelling her to break off the affair.

The truth is that each successive stage of the plot up to the beginning of the denouement in Book XVII is precipitated by a fresh act of imprudence or indiscretion on the part of Tom, for which he is sooner or later made to suffer not only in his fortune but his feelings, until in the resolution of each sequence, he discovers that the consequences of his folly are after all not so serious as he has feared. This characteristic pattern emerges, even before the start of the complication proper, in the episode of Tom's relations with Molly and Sophia in Book IV and the first part of Book V; it dominates the prolonged suspense of his relations with Allworthy from the time of the latter's illness to the final discovery; and it determines the course of his troubles with

Sophia from Upton to the meeting in London and from the ill-conceived proposal scheme to her sudden surrender at the end.

The comic pleasure all this gives us is certainly not of the same kind as that produced by such classic comic plots as (say) Ben Jonson's *The Silent Woman* or, to take a more extreme instance of the type, his *Volpone*, in which a morally despicable person is made, by reason of his own folly or lapse from cleverness, to suffer a humiliating and, to him, though not to others, painful reversal of fortune. The comedy of Blifil is indeed of this simple punitive kind,[14] but our suspense concerning Blifil is only in a secondary way determinative of the effect of Fielding's novel, and the comedy of Tom and hence of the plot as a whole is of a different sort. It is not simple comedy but mixed, the peculiar power of which depends upon the fact that the mistaken acts of the hero which principally excite our amusement are the acts of a man for whom throughout the plot we entertain sympathetic feelings because of the general goodness of his character: we do not want, therefore, to see him suffer any permanent indignity or humiliation, and we never cease to wish good fortune for him. This favorable attitude, moreover, is not contradicted by anything in the acts themselves from which his trouble springs. We perceive that in successive situations, involving threats to his fortune or peace of mind, he invariably does some imprudent or foolish thing, which cannot fail, the circumstances being what, in our superior knowledge, we see them to be, to result for him in painful embarrassment and regret; but we realize that his blunders arise from no permanent weakness of character but are merely the natural errors of judgment, easily corrigible in the future, of an inexperienced and too impulsively generous and gallant young man. We look forward to the probable consequences of his indiscretions, therefore, with a certain anticipatory reluctance and apprehension – a kind of faint alarm which is the comic analogue of fear; it is some such feeling, I think, that we experience, if only momentarily, when Tom gets drunk and goes into the wood with Molly and when, much later, he sends his proposal letter to Lady Bellaston. We know that trouble, more trouble than the young man either foresees or deserves, is in store for him as a result of what he has done, and since, foolish as he is, we favor him against his enemies, the expectation of his inevitable suffering cannot be purely and simply pleasant.

And yet the expectation is never really painful in any positive degree, and it is kept from becoming so by our counter-expectation, established by the devices I have mentioned, that, however acute may be Tom's consequent sufferings, his mistakes will not issue in any permanent frustration of our wishes for his good. In this security that no genuine harm has been done, we can view his present distresses – as when he anguishes over the wrong he thinks he has done to Molly, or finds Sophia's muff in his bed at Upton, or receives her letter – as the deserved consequences of erroneous actions for which any good man would naturally feel embarrassment or shame. We do not therefore pity him in these moments, for all his self-accusations and cries of despair, but rather laugh at him as a man who has behaved ridiculously or beneath himself and is now being properly punished. And our comic pleasure continues into the subsequent resolving scenes – the discovery of Molly in bed with Square, the meeting with Sophia in London, and the final anticlimax of her agreement to marry him the next morning – when it appears that Tom has after all worried himself overmuch; for we now see that he has been doubly ridiculous, at first in not taking his situation seriously enough and then in

R. S. CRANE

taking it more seriously than he should. But Tom is a good man, and we expect him to get better, and so our amused reaction to his sufferings lacks entirely the punitive quality that characterizes comedy of the Jonsonian type. If the anticipatory emotion is a mild shudder of apprehension, the climactic emotion – the comic analogue of pity – is a kind of friendly mirth at his expense ("poor Tom," we say to ourselves), which easily modulates, in the happy denouement, into unsentimental rejoicing at his not entirely deserved good fortune.

This, however, is not quite all; for not only does Tom's final good fortune seem to us at least partly undeserved in terms of his own behavior, but we realize, when we look back from the end upon the long course of the action, that he has, in truth, needed all the luck that has been his. Again and again he has been on the verge of genuinely serious disaster; and, though we expect him to survive and hence do not fear for him in prospect, we perceive, at the resolution of each of his major predicaments, that there has been something of a hair's breadth quality in his escape. The cards have indeed been stacked against him; from the beginning to the ultimate discovery, he has been a young man whose lack of security and imprudence more than offset his natural goodness, living in a world in which the majority of people are ill-natured and selfish, and some of them actively malicious, and in which the few good persons are easily imposed upon by appearances. It is against this background of the potentially serious – more than ever prominent in the London scenes – that the story of Tom's repeated indiscretions is made to unfold, with the result that, though the pleasure remains consistently comic, its quality is never quite that of the merely amiable comedy, based likewise upon the blunders of sympathetic protagonists, of such works as *She Stoops To Conquer* or *The Rivals*. We are not disposed to feel, when we are done laughing at Tom, that all is right with the world or that we can count on Fortune always intervening, in the same gratifying way, on behalf of the good.

IV

This or something very close to this, I think, is the intended "working or power" of *Tom Jones*, and the primary question for the critic concerns the extent to which Fielding's handling of the constituent parts of the novel is calculated to sustain and maximize this special pleasure which is its form.

It must be said that he sometimes fails. There are no perfect works of art, and, though many of the faults that have been found in *Tom Jones* are faults only on the supposition that it should have been another kind of novel, still enough real shortcomings remain to keep one's enthusiasm for Fielding's achievement within reasonable bounds. There are not infrequent *longueurs*, notably in the Man of the Hill's story (whatever positive values this may have), in Mrs. Fitzpatrick's narrative to Sophia (useful as this is in itself), in the episode of Tom's encounter with the gypsies, and in the final complications of the Nightingale affair. With the best will in the world, too, it is impossible not to be shocked by Tom's acceptance of fifty pounds from Lady Bellaston on the night of his first meeting with her at the masquerade and his subsequent emergence as "one of the best-dressed men about town"; it is necessary, no doubt, that he should now fall lower than ever before, but surely not so low as to make it hard for us to infer his act from our previous knowledge of his character and of the rather modest limits hitherto of his financial need; for the moment at least, a different Tom is before our eyes. And there are also more general faults. The narrator, for one thing, though it is well that he should intrude, perhaps intrudes too much in a purely ornamental way; the introductory essays, thus, while we should not like to lose them from the canon of Fielding's writings, serve only occasionally the function of chorus, and the returns from them, even as embellishment, begin to diminish before the end. What chiefly strikes the modern reader, however, is the extent of Fielding's reliance, in the novel as a whole, on techniques of narrative now largely abandoned by novelists who have learned their art since the middle of the nineteenth century. It could be shown, I think, that as compared with most of his predecessors, the author of *Tom Jones* had moved a long way in the direction of the imitative and dramatic. Yet it cannot be denied that in many chapters where he might better have "rendered" he merely "states" and that even in the most successful of the scenes in which action and dialogue predominate he leaves far less to inference than we are disposed to like.[15]

Despite all this, however, there are not many novels of comparable length in which the various parts are conceived and developed with a shrewder eye to what is required for a maximum realization of the form.[16] A few examples of this will have to serve, and it is natural to start with the manner in which Fielding handles the incidents that follow directly from Tom's mistakes. The pattern of all of these is much the same. Tom first commits an indiscretion, which is then discovered, and the discovery results in his immediate or eventual embarrassment. Now it is clear that the comic pleasure will be enhanced in proportion as, in each incident, the discovery is made unexpectedly and by precisely those persons whose knowledge of what Tom has done will be most damaging to him, and by as many of these as possible so that the consequences for him are not simple but compounded. Fielding understood this well, and the effects of his understanding are repeatedly evident in *Tom Jones*, from Book IV to the end of the complication. Consider, for example, how he manages the discovery of Tom's original entanglement with Molly. It is necessary, of course, when Molly is arrested after the fight in the churchyard, that Tom should at once rush to Allworthy with his mistaken confession; but it is not necessary – only highly desirable – that he should intervene in the fight himself as Molly's champion, that Blifil and Square should be with him at the time, that the news of the arrest should reach him while he is dining with Western and Sophia, whose charm he is just beginning to perceive, and that, when he leaves in a hurry, the Squire should joke with his daughter about what he suspects. Or, again, there is the even more complicated and comically disastrous sequence that begins with Tom's drunkenness after Allworthy's recovery. This in itself is ridiculous, since we know the illness has never been serious; but observe how the succeeding embarrassments are made to pile up: Tom's hilarious joy leading to his fight with Blifil; this to his retirement to the grove, his romantic meditation on Sophia, and his surrender to Molly; this to the discovery of his new folly by Blifil and Thwackum; this to the second fight, much bloodier than the first; and this in turn, when the Westerns unexpectedly appear on the scene, to Sophia's fresh discovery of Tom's wildness and, what is much more serious, to the misconstruction of her fainting fit by her aunt, with results that lead presently to the proposal of a match with Blifil, the foolish intervention of Tom, the discovery by Western of the true state of affairs, his angry appeal to Allworthy, Blifil's distorted version of what has happened, Tom's expulsion from home, and Sophia's imprisonment. All this is probable enough, but there is something of the comically wonderful in the educing of so many appropriately extreme consequences from a cause in itself so apparently innocent and trivial. And the same art of making the most out of incidents for the sake of the comic suspense of the plot can be seen at work through the rest of the novel: in the great episode at Upton, for example, where all the happenings are contrived to produce, immediately or remotely, a maximum of pseudo-serious suffering for Tom, and also in the various later scenes in which the discovery to Sophia of Tom's intrigue with her cousin is first narrowly averted, with much embarrassment to him, and then finally made under circumstances that could hardly be worse for the young man. A less accomplished artist seeking to achieve the same general effect through his plot would certainly have missed many of these opportunities.

A less accomplished artist, again, would never have been able to invent or sustain characters so good for the form, as well as so interesting in themselves, as the two Westerns and Partridge. We need not dwell on the multiple uses to which these great humorists are put; it is more important, since the point has been less often discussed, or discussed in part to Fielding's disadvantage, to consider what merits can be found in his handling of the other characters, such as Tom himself, Allworthy, Sophia, and Blifil, who are intended to seem morally sympathetic or antipathetic to us and comically inferior only by virtue of their erroneous acts. With the exception of Sophia, who is made charming and lively enough to constitute in herself good fortune for Tom, they are not endowed with any notably particularized traits, and the question for criticism is whether, given the comic form of the novel as a whole, any more lifelike "doing" would not have entailed a departure from the mean which this imposed. I think the answer is clear for Blifil: he must be made to seem sufficiently formidable in the short run to arouse comic apprehension for Tom but not so formidable as to excite in us active or prolonged feelings of indignation; and any further individualizing of him than we get would almost certainly have upset this balance to the detriment of the whole. The answer is clear also, I think, for Tom. We must consistently favor him against his enemies and think it probable that he should suffer acute embarrassment and remorse when he discovers the consequences of his mistakes; but, on the other hand, any appreciably greater particularizing of his sympathetic traits than is attempted would inevitably have made it difficult for us not to feel his predicaments as seriously as he does himself, and that would have been an error; it is not the least happy of Fielding's inventions, for example, that he repeatedly depicts Tom, especially when he is talking to Sophia or thinking about her, in terms of the clichés of heroic romance. There remains Allworthy, and concerning him the chief doubt arises from a consideration of the important part he is given, along with Sophia, in the definition of Tom's final good fortune. For the purposes of the comic complication it is sufficient that we should see him acting in the character of a severely just magistrate who constantly administers injustice through too great trust in his knowledge of men; it is not for this, however, but for his "amiability" that Tom loves him and cherishes his company in the end; yet of Allworthy's actual possession of that quality we are given few clear signs.

A whole essay, finally, could be written on the masterly way in which Fielding exploited the various devices implicit in his third-person "historical" mode of narration in the service of his comic form. Broadly speaking, his problem was twofold: first, to establish and maintain in the reader a general frame of mind appropriate to the emotional quality of the story as a whole and, second, to make sure that the feelings aroused by his characters at particular moments or stages of the action were kept in proper alignment with the intended over-all effect.

That the first problem is adequately solved there can be little doubt; long before we come to the incidents in which Tom's happiness is put in jeopardy by his own blunders and the malice of Blifil, we have been prepared to expect much unmerited calamity and distress for him, and at the same time to view the prospect without alarm. Our security would doubtless have been less had not Fielding chosen to represent at length the events contained in Books I and II, with the vivid impressions they give of the fallibility of Allworthy on the one hand and of the impotence for permanent harm of the elder Blifil on the other: we cannot but look forward to a repetition of this pattern in the later parts of the novel. This is less important, however, as a determinant of our frame of mind than the guidance given us by the clearly evident attitude of Fielding's narrator. He is, we perceive, a man we can trust, who knows the whole story and still is not deeply concerned; one who understands the difference between good men and bad and who can yet speak with amused indulgence of the first, knowing how prone they are to weakness of intellect, and with urbane scorn, rather than indignation, of the second, knowing that most of them, too, are fools. This combination of sympathetic moral feeling with ironical detachment is bound to influence our expectations from the first, and to the extent that it does so, we tend to anticipate the coming troubles with no more than comic fear.

It is when the troubles come, in Book V and later, that Fielding's second problem emerges; for, given the kinds of things that then happen to Tom and especially the seriousness with which, as a good man, he necessarily takes them, there is always a danger that our original comic detachment may give way, temporarily, to tragicomic feelings of fear, pity, and indignation. That this seldom happens is another sign of how successfully, in *Tom Jones*, the handling of the parts is kept consonant with the formal demands of the whole. It is a question primarily of maximizing the general comic expectations of the reader by minimizing the possible noncomic elements in his inferences about particular situations; and the devices which Fielding uses for the purpose are of several kinds. Sometimes the result is achieved by preventing our attention from concentrating long or closely on potential causes of distress for Tom; it is notable, for example, that we are given no representation of Blifil scheming Tom's ruin before his speech to Allworthy in Book VI, chapter xi, and that from this point until Book XVI Blifil and his intentions are not again brought to the fore. Sometimes the device consists in slurring over a painful scene by generalized narration and then quickly diverting us to an obviously comic sequence in another line of action: this is what Fielding does, to excellent effect, with the incident of Tom's condemnation and banishment; we should feel much more keenly for him if, in the first place, we were allowed to hear more of his talk with Allworthy and, in the second place, were not plunged so soon after into the ridiculous quarrels of the Westerns. Or, again, the expedient may take the simple form of a refusal by the narrator to describe feelings of Tom which, if they were represented directly and at length, might easily excite a non-comic response; as in the accounts of his "madness" at Upton after he finds Sophia's muff and of the torments he endures ("such that even Thwackum would almost have

R. S. CRANE

pitied him") when her message of dismissal comes to him in prison. And the same general minimizing function is also served by the two episodes in the middle part of the novel which have occasioned so much discussion among critics. Both the story told to Tom by the Man of the Hill and that recounted to Sophia by Mrs. Fitzpatrick, however much they owe to the convention of interpolated narratives which Fielding had inherited, along with other devices, from the earlier writers of "comic romance," are clearly designed as negative analogies to the moral state of the listeners, from which the reader is led to infer, on the eve of the most distressing part of the complication for the hero and heroine, that nothing that may happen to them will be, in comparison, very bad.

The controlling influence of the form can be seen in all these expedients, and it is no less apparent in Fielding's handling of the intrigue upon which the action of the novel ultimately depends – Bridget's affair with Summer, her scheme of temporary conceal-ment and eventual disclosure of Tom's parentage, and the frustration of the second of these intentions, until the denouement, by Blifil. Without this series of events and the consequences they entail in the opinions and acts of the characters, the plot as we have it could not have existed; but there was nothing in the nature of the events themselves to prescribe the particular manner in which they must be brought before the reader. At least two alternative modes of procedure were open to Fielding besides the one he actually chose. He could, on the one hand, have let the reader into the secret, either from the beginning or at the point in Book V where Bridget's dying message is brought by Dowling: in the former case a brief statement by the narrator would have been sufficient (since he plainly knows the facts); in the latter case, a brief report, for which there are precedents elsewhere in the novel, of Blifil's thoughts. Or, on the other hand, he could have contrived to keep our curiosity regarding the mystery more continuously and actively awake, especially in the long stretches of the story between Book III and the final scenes in London: this need not again have required any invention of new incidents, but only manipulations of the narrative discourse, such as an explicit direction of the reader's mind to the circumstance that Dowling brought a letter from Bridget as well as the news of her death, a hint that Blifil now had some new and surprising information about Tom, and an occasional reminder thereafter that the full truth concerning Tom's birth was still to be learned and that it might, when known, have important bearings, for good or possibly for ill, upon his fortunes.

Given, however, the form which Fielding, according to our hypothesis, was at-tempting to impose on the materials of his plot, with its distinctive line of seriocomic expectations and desires, either of these two courses would clearly have been incorrect. The second would have injected into the middle sections of the narrative a competing principle of suspense, diverting our attention unduly from the question of what is likely to befall Tom as a result of his mistakes to the question of who he is; the novel would then have become in fact the mystery story which, on a partial and erroneous view, it has sometimes been taken to be. And the consequences of the other course would have been equally, perhaps more, disruptive. For the complication in that case would have become, in large part, the story of a completely foreseen and wished-for discovery repeatedly deferred, with the result, on the one hand, that our complacency about the eventual outcome would have been increased to such a degree as sensibly to lessen our comic fear and hence our comic mirth in the successive anticlimactic reversals and, on the other hand, that our preoccupation with the comic aspects of Tom's well-intentioned blunderings would have tended to give way excessively to a concern with the original injustice done him by Bridget and with the villainy of Blifil. A mean between emphasis on the existence of a mystery and full revelation of the secret to the reader was therefore indicated as the right technique, and it was his perception of this that guided Fielding's procedure both in Books I and II, where the question of Tom's parentage is formally inquired into by Allworthy and settled to his own satisfaction, and in Books V–XVII, where the question is reopened, in intent but not in result, first by the confession of Bridget and then by the advances of Dowling to Tom. Something close to the proper mean is achieved by concentrating the narrative in the opening books on the objective acts and declarations of Bridget, Jenny, and Partridge subsequent to the finding of Tom in Allworthy's bed and representing these by signs sufficiently ambiguous so that, although we discount the inferences drawn by Allworthy from the behavior of the two supposed parents, we are yet given no adequate premises from which to reason to any particular alternative explanation. We surmise that one will ultimately be forthcoming, but in the meantime we are easily persuaded by the narrator to suspend our curiosity, especially since we perceive that neither of Allworthy's discoveries will make any difference in his treatment of Tom. We are predisposed therefore to yield our attention to the events recounted in the middle books of the novel without active speculation concerning their remoter causes or growing impatience for further disclosures. Ambiguous disclosures do indeed continue to be made. There is the pervasive irony (in the world of this novel) of a young man assumed by nearly everyone in his circle, including himself, to be base-born who yet manifests all the signs, in appearance and sensibility, of being a gentleman and is regularly taken as one by strangers until they learn his story; and there are also the more specific clues to the real state of affairs afforded by Bridget's increasing preference for Tom as he grows up, the suddenly intensified animosity of Blifil toward the foundling after he learns the content of Bridget's message, Partridge's disavowal of the role in which he has been cast as Tom's father, and, most pointed of all, Dowling's sly reference to "your uncle" in the interview which he forces on Tom in Book XII. But though hints of the truth are thus given in the events themselves, it is only in retrospect, at the moment of the discovery scene in Book XVIII, that we grasp their cumulative import; so effectively, in the narrator's discourse up to the very eve of this scene, has the question of who Tom is been kept subordinate to the question, upon which the main comic effect depends, of what will immediately follow from his imprudent acts.

V

These are only a few of the things that can be said, in the light of our general hypothesis about plot, concerning the plot of *Tom Jones* and the relation to it of the other parts of the novel. I have given no consideration, thus, either to the functions served by the minor characters and by the many passages of extradramatic thought in defining the moral quality of the "world" in which the action takes place, or to the formal purposes governing Fielding's highly selective use of dialogue, or to the manner in which the diction and imagery of the narrative parts help to hold our responses to the right comic line even when the incidents themselves seem most serious.

R. S. CRANE

An adequate study of the plot of *Tom Jones* considered as a first principle of artistic construction would require answers to these and possibly still other questions, all of them of a kind which the traditional ways of discussing works with "plots" have tended to leave out of account. My intention, however, has been not so much to attempt a revaluation of *Tom Jones* as to make clear the assumptions and illustrate some of the possibilities for practical criticism of a kind of whole-part analysis of narrative compositions such as has not too often, I think, been undertaken. Like all critical methods it has its limitations, and it must be judged, accordingly, in terms not only of the problems it is peculiarly fitted to deal with but of those which lie beyond its scope. Its distinctive character derives, in the first place, from the fact that it views a work of art as a dynamic whole which affects our emotions in a certain way through the functioning together of its elements in subordination to a determinate poetic form. It is better suited, therefore, to exhibit the degree of efficiency with which the parts of a work or section thereof contribute to the maximum achievement of its effect than to do full justice to the qualities over and above this which characterize, in all fine works, the development of the parts themselves: there are many strokes in the representation of Partridge, for instance, which no one would wish away, yet which are bound to seem gratuitous when considered merely in the light of his somewhat minor role in the evolution of the comic action.[17] The method, again, is specific, in the sense that it seeks to appraise a writer's performance in a given work in relation to the nature and requirements of the particular task he has set himself, the assumed end being the perfection of the work as an artistic whole of the special kind he decided it should be. It is a method better adapted, consequently, to the appreciation of success or failure in individual works than it is to the making of comparative judgments based on criteria of literary "greatness" or "seriousness" that transcend differences of kind: we clearly need other terms and distinctions than those provided by a poetics of forms if we are to talk discriminatingly about the general qualities of intelligence and feeling reflected in *Tom Jones* or even be able to defend Fielding against the recent, and surely somewhat insensitive, judgment that his "attitudes and his concern with human nature, are simple, and not such as to produce an effect of anything but monotony (on a mind, that is, demanding more than external action) when exhibited at the length of an 'epic in prose.'"[18] Finally, the method is one which depends on the analytical isolation of works of art, as finished products, from the circumstances and processes of their origin. It is therefore better fitted to explain those effects in a work which would be specifically the same in any other work, of whatever date, that was constructed in accordance with the same combination of artistic principles, than those effects which must be attributed to the fact that the work was produced by a given artist, in a given period, at a given stage in the evolution of the species or tradition to which it belongs: we have obviously to go beyond formal criticism if we would assess Fielding's originality as a writer of "comic romance" or account for that peculiarly eighteenth-century flavor in *Tom Jones* which causes us to reflect that, unique and unrepresentative as Fielding's novel is when considered as a whole, it could yet have been written at no other time.

The criticism of forms needs thus to be supplemented by the criticism of qualities, in both of the senses just indicated, and also by historical inquiries of various sorts. This granted, however, two things can be said, the first of which is that, although the criticism of forms is only one among a number of valid and useful critical methods, it is still the sole method capable of dealing adequately – i.e., with a minimum of unanalyzed terms – and at the same time literally – i.e., in terms of causes and effects rather than analogies – with those characteristics and values in any literary work which derive from its construction as a self-contained whole endowed with a power of affecting us in a particular way by virtue of the manner in which its internal parts are conceived and fitted together. It is a method, therefore, which ought to have a strong appeal to the many students of literature in our time who wish to consider their subject, in a now famous phrase, "as literature and not another thing," but who are temperamentally averse to analogical procedures and intellectually dissatisfied with those modern critical systems which, however literal, provide no analysis of any except one or two of the internal causes of literary effects. And the second point is perhaps equally clear: namely, that although the criticism of qualities and the investigation of historical origins and significances may achieve important results independently of the criticism of forms, as the past history of practical criticism and literary scholarship shows, both of these modes of judging literary productions would gain considerably in rigor and scope if they were founded on, and hence controlled by, a prior analysis of works from the point of view of their peculiar principles of construction and the special artistic problems which these presented to their writers. We should then, perhaps, have less qualitative criticism of the dogmatic sort which reproaches writers of poems, dramas, and novels perfect enough in their respective kinds for not exhibiting virtues of language or thought incompatible with the specific tasks these writers chose to undertake, and likewise fewer literary histories in which the achievements of authors are discussed exclusively in terms of materials and techniques without reference to the formal ends that helped to determine how these were used.

NOTES

1 Reprinted, with alterations and additions, from the *Journal of General Education*, January, 1950.
2 Arthur Murphy (1762), quoted in Frederic T. Blanchard, *Fielding the Novelist: A Study in Historical Criticism* (New Haven, 1927), p. 161.
3 *Dissertations Moral and Critical* (1783), quoted in Blanchard, pp. 222–23.
4 Ibid., pp. 320–21.
5 Ibid., p. 327.
6 The phrase is Oliver Elton's in *A Survey of English Literature, 1730–1780* (New York, 1928), I, 195. See also Wilbur L. Cross, *The History of Henry Fielding* (New Haven, 1918), II, 160–61; Aurélien Digeon, *Les Romans de Fielding* (Paris, 1923), pp. 210–16; Elizabeth Jenkins, *Henry Fielding* (London, 1947), pp. 57–58; and George Sherburn, in *A Literary History of England*, ed. Albert C. Baugh (New York and London, 1948), pp. 957–58; cf. his interesting Introduction to the "Modern Library College Editions" reprint of *Tom Jones* (New York, 1950), pp. ix–x.
7 The explanation of this procedure lies, partly at least, in a still unwritten chapter in the history of criticism. When works of prose fiction became objects of increasingly frequent critical attention in the eighteenth century, it was natural that the new form should be discussed in terms of its obvious analogies, both positive and negative, to drama and epic and that critics of novels should avail themselves, consequently, of the familiar categories of "fable," "characters," "sentiments," and "language" which had been long established, in the neoclassical tradition, as standard devices for the analysis of tragedies, comedies, and heroic poems. In remote origin

these distinctions derived from the four qualitative "parts" which Aristotle had shown to be common to tragedy and epic (cf. *Poetics* 5. 1449^{b}15 ff.; 24. 1459^{b}8–11). In the course of their transmission to the eighteenth century, however – as a result partly of the influence of Horace and partly of a complex of more general causes operative from the beginnings of Aristotelian commentary in the Renaissance – the analytical significance of the scheme had undergone a radical change. For Aristotle, concerned with the construction of poetic wholes that afford "peculiar pleasures" through their imitations of different species of human actions, the four terms had designated the essential elements upon the proper handling and combination of which, relatively to the intended over-all effect, the quality of a tragedy or epic necessarily depends. They are distinct parts in the sense of being variable factors in the complex problem of composing works which, when completed, will produce their effects, synthetically, as organic wholes. Hence it is that in the *Poetics* they are treated, not discretely as co-ordinate topics, but hierarchically in a causal sequence of form-matter or end-means relationships in which plot is the most inclusive or architectonic of the four, subsuming all the others as its poetic matter; in which character, while subordinated materially to plot and effect, is similarly a formal or organizing principle with respect to thought and diction; in which thought, while functioning as matter relatively to character, incident, and effect, is the form which immediately controls the choice and arrangement of language in so far as this is employed as a means to imitative rather than ornamental ends; and in which diction, though necessarily having a form of its own by virtue of its rhythmical, syntactical, and "stylistic" figuration, is the underlying matter which, as significant speech, at once makes possible all the other "parts" and is in turn, mediately or immediately, controlled by them. The nature of the four elements is such, in short, that, although a critic in his analysis of a given tragedy or epic may take any one of them as his primary object of attention, he can make no adequate judgment of the poet's success or failure with respect to it without bringing into his discussion all the others to which it is related, directly or indirectly, either as matter or as form.

Of this causal scheme only the general outlines survived in the doctrines of subsequent critics in the "Aristotelian" line. The distinction of the four parts was retained and, along with it, the substance of the rules which Aristotle had formulated for their handling; what disappeared was precisely the rationale which in the *Poetics* had justified not only the rules but the discrimination, definition, and ordering of the parts themselves. In its place various new principles and schemes of analysis were substituted by different theorists and critics, the general tendency of which was to make of poetics a practical rather than a productive art and hence to reduce tragedy and epic to modes of ethical or rhetorical discourse designed to serve, each in its specialized way, the common purposes of all such discourse, namely, the delight and instruction of mankind. The consequence was that, although critics continued to distinguish aspects of tragedies and epics that corresponded roughly with the Aristotelian "parts" and although these served to determine the framework of the discussion at least in the most systematic treatises and essays, the discussion itself no longer turned on the nature and functional interrelations of the four parts as elements in an artistic synthesis of a particular kind but on the general qualities which the poet ought to aim at in each, in order to enhance its independent power of pleasing, moving, and edifying spectators or readers. And when this apparatus was carried over from the statement of tragic or epic theory to the practical criticism of tragedies or epics (as in Addison's papers on *Paradise Lost* or Pope's Preface to the *Iliad*), the disjunction of the four elements tended to become still more marked. They were no longer functional parts in an organic whole but so many relatively discrete *loci* of critical praise and blame; and critics could write *seriatim* of the beauties or defects in the fable, characters, sentiments, and language of a given tragedy or heroic poem without assuming any synthesizing principles more specific than the decorum of the genre or the necessity (e.g.) that the sentiments expressed should be consonant with the characters of the persons who uttered them (many illustrations of the procedure may be found in H. T. Swedenberg, Jr., *The Theory of the Epic in England, 1650–1800* [Berkeley and Los Angeles, 1944]; cf. The Index under "Fable or action," "Characters," "Sentiments in the epic," and "Language of the epic").

It was at this stage in the history of the Aristotelian "parts" that they entered into the criticism, both general and applied, of modern prose fiction. See, for example, besides many notices of novels in the *Monthly Review* and the *Critical Review*, the anonymous *Critical Remarks on Sir Charles Grandison, Clarissa, and Pamela* (1754); Arthur Murphy's "Essay on the Life and Genius of Henry Fielding," in *The Works of Henry Fielding* (1762); James Beattie's "On Fable and Romance," in his *Dissertations* (1783); and John More's "View of the Commencement and Progress of Romance," in *The Works of Tobias Smollett* (1797). In spite of the general indifference of criticism since about 1750 to questions specific to the various poetic kinds (see above, pp. 14, 459), the tradition of method thus established has persisted, especially in academic circles, to the present day; its influence still lingers in the topical divisions of treatises or textbooks dealing with the technique of fiction; and it still provides the commonplaces of a good many "studies" of novelists and novels (e.g., the pages on *Tom Jones*, already referred to, in Elton's *Survey*). The undoubted deficiencies of the scheme (in its neoclassical degradation) as an instrument of critical analysis and judgement have not passed unnoticed in recent years, particularly among critics of the *Scrutiny* group, who point out, justly enough, that "plot" and "character" are treated in a fashion that abstracts them unduly from the continuum of the novelist's language through which alone they affect us. These critics, however, are usually content to offer, as a positive substitute for the traditional scheme, only a still more extreme reduction of Aristotle's principles, in which everything in the discussion of a novel is made to turn on the relations between diction, in the sense of the author's "verbal arrangements," and thought, in the sense of the "experience" which he communicates by imposing "the pattern of his own sensibility" on the reader through the medium of language. See, for example, Martin Turnell, "The Language of Fiction," *Times Literary Supplement*, August 19, 1949, pp. 529–31; reprinted in his *Novel in France* (New York, 1951).

8   Elton, *Survey*, I, 195.

9   Cross, *The History of Henry Fielding*, II, 159–61; Elton, *Survey* I, 195–96.

10 This accounts in large part, I think, for the depreciation of "plot" in E. M. Forster's *Aspects of the Novel*, and for his notion of a rivalry between "plot" and "character," in which one or the other may "triumph." For a view much closer to that argued in this essay see Elizabeth Bowen, "Notes on Writing a Novel," *Orion*, II (1945), 18 ff.

11 The meaning and force of this will be clear to anyone who has compared in detail the text of *The Ambassadors* with James's preliminary synopsis of the novel (*The Notebooks of Henry James* [New York, 1947], pp. 372–415). See also the excellent remarks of Allen Tate, apropos of *Madame Bovary*, in his "Techniques of Fiction" (*Forms of Modern Fiction*, ed. William Van O'Connor [Minneapolis, 1948], esp. pp. 37–45).

12 *Amelia*, Book III, chap. i.

13 I confine myself here to devices in some sense implicit in the plot itself as distinguished from devices, serving the same purpose, which involve Fielding's manner of representation; on the latter, see Section IV, below. A full solution of the problem would also have to take into account, as one of my friends reminds me, such things as the choice of names for the characters and the general nonserious expectations suggested by the title of the work.

14 I borrow this term from Elder Olson's "An Outline of Poetic Theory," from 'Critics and Criticism" pp. 3–23.

15 Perhaps the chief exception to this, in its relatively large use of "intimation," is the scene of Tom's conversation with Dowling in Book XII, chap. x.

16 I am indebted for several points in what follows to an unpublished essay by one of my students, Mr. Melvin Seiden.

17 The kind of thing I have in mind is well illustrated by the late George Orwell's remarks on the "unnecessary detail" in Dickens (see his *Dickens, Dali & Others* [New York, 1946], pp. 59–65). Of the same order is the following sentence from the account of the fight with the captain in *Joseph Andrews*, Book III, chap. xi (italics mine): "The uplifted hanger dropped from his hand, and he fell prostrated on the floor with a lumpish noise, *and his halfpence rattled in his pocket...*" It is difficult to conceive of any functional analysis, however refined its principles, that would afford premises for the discussion of such traits; and yet their presence or absence is obviously an important factor in our discrimination between distinguished and undistinguished writing.

18 F. R. Leavis, *The Great Tradition* (New York, [1949]), p. 4.

From Richardson to Austen: "Johnson's Rule" and the Development of the Eighteenth-Century Novel of Moral Action

Ralph W. Rader

Ralph Wilson Rader (b. 1930)

Ralph Rader was born in 1930 in Muskegon, Michigan; he received his bachelor's degree from Purdue University in 1952, and his doctorate from Indiana University in 1958. Rader, now professor emeritus, began teaching at the University of California, Berkeley, in 1956, and twice served as chair of the English department. He has been an American Council of Learned Societies grantee and a Guggenheim fellow. Rader's most significant contributions to novel theory are found in a series of separately published essays, covering the evolution of the English novel from the eighteenth to the twentieth century. He has also published *Tennyson's Maud: The Biographical Genesis* (1963), and co-authored *Autobiography, Biography, and the Novel* (1972).

From *Johnson and His Age*, edited by James Engell (Harvard English Studies 12). Cambridge, Mass., and London: Harvard University Press, 1984, pp. 461–83. Reprinted by permission of Harvard University, Department of English and American Literature and Language.

The neo-Aristotelian approach to the novel from which my own approach in part derives – I refer specifically to the work of R. S. Crane and Sheldon Sacks[1] – has tended to identify the novel with the action structure first described by Aristotle and long employed in the drama before its appearance in *Pamela* and, subsequently, in Richardson's later novels and those of Fielding, Burney, and Austen. Since I shall be referring to the action structure throughout, let me define it here by saying, more simply than would my predecessors, that it is an affective structure designed to induce, develop, and finally cathartically resolve in the reader an active concern for a protagonist which results from the tension between what the reader is led to think will happen to the protagonist (his fate) and what he is led to think ought to happen to him (his desert). Thus stated, the concept corresponds pretty much to what we might call the novel of plotted suspense, and, intelligently applied to such novels, it can yield consistent insight. But it does not provide any really satisfactory basis for analyzing a number of works unequivocally registered as novels – for instance, in the eighteenth century, *Tristram Shandy* and *Humphry Clinker* – and this points to the more general fact that our possession of the intuitive concept "novel" is stronger than our intuitive notion of the action structure. We are more aware of *Tom Jones*, *Tristram Shandy*, and *Ulysses* as novels than we are of the fact that the first is a novel of plotted suspense while the other two are not.

The plain implication of such reflections is that the action structure is not the definitive characteristic of the novel. The most fundamental thing that Richardson in *Pamela* borrowed from the drama was, I think, not the action structure but, as Mark Kinkead-Weekes has suggested, the dramatic mode itself.[2] In watching a play we seem to see the actors as characters acting out of their own purposes, while more fundamentally our imaginations register and respond to the fact that their actions are fictive, designed to realize the playwright's artistic purpose in the play. Now it is this same kind of illusion that the novel, using mere words and not actors, contrives with largely covert art to present. We may say for the sake of precision and clarity, using Michael Polanyi's helpful terms, that the novel presents to our imagination a focal illusion of characters acting autonomously as if in the real world, within our subsidiary awareness of an underlying authorial purpose which gives their story, virtually real, implicit significance and affective force.[3] This formulation is meant to locate the basis of the universal impression that the novel is "realistic," that it is "dramatic," that it shows rather than tells, or rather tells by showing, in contrast with earlier narratives which may be said to tell in order to show.

Crane's and Sacks's formulations do not directly express the realistic mode of the novel as independent of the action structure, in large part I think because of their tendency to think of that structure as an integral and unmalleable formal principle and of the transition from the drama to the novel as a mere change in the manner of representation – in drama, in prose – conceived as a repertory of logical possibilities in principle available to artists at any time. This almost structuralist tendency to think in terms of fixed and timeless forms deflected their attention from the evidence which suggests that the novel needs to be conceived as a unique, historically emergent construction, something entirely new under the literary sun. Nevertheless, I believe that the concept of the action structure is accurately applicable to the novel as historically the most important of the subsidiary organizations used to give the realistic surface of novels their significance and force, and I have already implied my agreement with Crane and Sacks that it characterizes the main line of development in the eighteenth-century novel from Richardson to Austen. But the attempt to explain the structural peculiarities of these novels individually and as a developmental sequence immediately again raises the problem whether the action novel, any more than the novel form as a whole, can be thought of as fixed and timeless rather than as mixed and historically adapted to the purposes and preconceptions of its users, specifically in the present instance to the didactic purposes of the eighteenth-century novelists who employed it. Crane was quite sure that didactic aims had no part in actions, the essence of which for him was just that they *were* mimetic and not didactic, and in his famous essay on *Tom Jones* he made no mention of Fielding's explicitly announced didactic intention, just as in his account of neoclassical criticism he tended to think of critics who spoke of incorporating morals into actions as misunderstanding Aristotle rather than as formulating viable conceptions of mixed forms which fell well within the possibilities of free human creation.

Following Crane and clearly recognizing that Fielding's and other eighteenth-century action novels do in fact incorporate didactic material, Sacks redefined the action so as to make the expression of an author's belief not only permissible but necessary. In doing this I think he blurred the distinction between two different claims: (1) that the aesthetic requirements of the action structure put no pressure on an author to falsify his beliefs in building into his work the moral judgments of characters necessary to develop and resolve the tension of suspense; and (2) that the expression of doctrinal or other didactic material was inherently compatible with the action conceived as a strictly integral form. The first claim I take to be indubitable, but the second dubious. Sacks's own demonstration of the brilliantly inventive ways in which didactic material is built into *Tom Jones* and *Amelia* is more easily interpreted to the opposite conclusion, that such material is *not* inherently compatible with the action structure but requires special accommodation. Sacks did not draw this conclusion because he was committed, as I say, to an almost structuralist view that principles of literary form must be conceived as fixed, unitary, and finite if they are to be capable of explaining the facts of our literary experience, but it seems to me just the facts of our literary experience – that *Amelia*, for instance, seems manifestly weakened by formal contradictions – that suggest the usefulness of thinking of literary works not as embodiments of *a priori* principles of literary form but as constructions in which the author's attempt to realize his aesthetic and allied aims may produce conflicts which leave on the works the marks of their solutions.

My specific thesis in this paper is that we can get maximum insight into what I will call the eighteenth-century novel of moral action if we think of its employment of the action structure, with its inherent need to develop and cathartically resolve concern for a protagonist, as under the constraint of a commitment to moral instruction imposed by the most fundamental critical assumptions of the time, assumptions which the novelists shared and positively accepted as the basis of their work. My aim may be considered an intention to explore, in relation to the novel, the concrete critical implications of Ralph Cohen's much larger argument that "neo-classical forms were mixed and interrelated, dominated by didactic models."[4]

Fielding's example shows that ideas and messages as such can be built into action structures, sometimes, as with *Amelia*, at a heavy formal price. But the didactic pressures of the time exerted an even more fundamental influence on the substance of the action structure itself by restricting the novelist's freedom to develop the character of his protagonist solely on the basis of aesthetic considerations, for cathartic effect alone.

In implicit reproof of current novelistic practice, Dr. Johnson asserted in his famous *Rambler* 4, that "In narratives, where historical veracity has no place, I cannot discover why there should not be exhibited the most perfect idea of virtue; of virtue not angelical, nor above probability, for what we cannot credit we shall never imitate, but the highest and purest that humanity can reach, which, exercised in such trials as the various revolutions of things shall bring upon it, may, by conquering some calamities, and enduring others, teach us what we may hope, and what we can perform."[5] Now we may take this prescription not as laying down a principle (let us call it "Johnson's Rule") which the novelists ignored but one which they consciously accepted and attempted to embody in their works, with results, as I shall attempt to show, that have much to do with the problematic qualities of their individual novels and with the progressively different forms which emerged in this series.

I have elsewhere described the specific action structure of *Pamela* by saying that the concern we are made to feel for her is a serious fear which results from the fact that her desert and fate develop along a line of branching alternatives where one branch always leads to an ethically unacceptable or materially undesirable safety (respectively either refused by Pamela or closed by circumstance), while the other, ethically impeccable and always chosen by Pamela, leads overtly and immediately to greater danger but covertly and ultimately to the most desirable resolution of her difficulties.[6]

It can be predicted from this model that the impeccable moral choices which lead Pamela immediately to her greatest danger but ultimately to her greatest reward will constitute her a moral paragon but will also involve the danger that she will be viewed as a hypocrite, since the dramatic presentation through her consciousness makes the reader's awareness of the potential positive outcome of her morally defensive action seem, contrary to Richardson's intention, part of her implicit calculation; and, indeed, whatever her motivation, the dynamic equation of virtue and reward which the novel offers the reader is inherently ambiguous and vulgar.

I will not detail here the full structural account of *Pamela* which this model can generate, since I have already done so in another essay (see footnote 6) but will turn at once to *Clarissa*, a novel which has as its structural core the same contest between the sexually libertine male and the female paragon, or perfect "exemplar," as Richardson himself calls Clarissa.[7] We may assume that Richardson, sensitive to criticism of the have-your-cake-and-eat-it-too morality of *Pamela*, decided to alter its desert-fate structure so as to create a novel of contrasting moral stringency and grandeur. We may precisely locate the great moral difference within close structural similarity of *Pamela* and *Clarissa* by saying that Clarissa's fate and merit develop along a line of alternatives where one branch, always refused by Clarissa or closed by circumstance, is defined as ethically acceptable but not as impeccable, and apparently promises earthly felicity, while the other, always chosen by Clarissa, is defined as ethically impeccable and increasingly excludes the possibility of her earthly felicity.

The model appears cold and taciturn, but if we question it in the right spirit it will grow articulate and tell us that *Clarissa* is the story of a woman who is constrained, or constrains herself, to give up all objects of earthly desire in order to remain virtuous, since the only outcome of the sequence envisaged in the model is the heroine's death. Such a story is inherently painful and is made more so by the basic principle of its structure, which forces us to be aware, as Clarissa makes her impeccably virtuous choices, that to make a self-regarding choice would be very easy, since an alternative temptation is always present and defined as ethically acceptable. Our participation in the book may be described by saying that we fully empathize with Clarissa's plight and in a way (a crucial way) feel its pain more sharply than she does, since we are more attracted than she is to the earthly goods she gives up with such relatively clear-sighted ease; she suffers, but she does not suffer agonies of indecision. On the other hand, we are reassured about her sacrificial choices and do not judge them as capricious or overly nice, since we are made more aware than she can be that if she did make the self-regarding acceptable choices, she would not by such means actually achieve earthly happiness. She is restrained by principle alone from choices that full knowledge would define as imprudent. The emotion that develops and is discharged as we witness this struggle is an admiring and indignant pity quite in contrast with the hopeful fear gradually turning to fearful hope with which we follow the career of Pamela.

The inherent moral grandeur of *Clarissa*, however, is not quite the tragic grandeur envisaged by Aristotle and achieved by the Greek tragedians and, in a somewhat altered form, by Shakespeare. Superficially considered, *Clarissa* is that kind of tragedy proscribed by Aristotle when he asserted that in effective tragedy "a good man must not be seen passing from happiness to misery" because such a spectacle "is not fear-inspiring or piteous but simply odious to us."[8] Aristotle has in mind a situation where a good man is externally deprived of the happiness he desires and deserves and that we desire for him, a situation merely frustrating or shocking. But *Clarissa* is not shocking in an aesthetically unpleasant way, because it does not fulfill Aristotle's implicit conditions. Clarissa is not deprived of but, at the behest of an ethical imperative which forbids self-gratification, voluntarily gives up all objects of earthly desire. But more than that, she gives up desire itself; she wills finally, as her commitment to principle demands, not to will, not to desire anything earthly, even life itself. Rather, she actively desires death as a positive, pleasurable good, and we are made to believe in and at an admiring distance to sympathize with that desire. She is not a good person, then, whose desires are frustrated, but a good person whose desires, in a strange way, are fully realized. Unlike the usual tragic situation, Clarissa's involves her conscious, willed choice, at every step along the way, of her own personal moral good, clearly perceived as it is present in the situation in which she finds herself. She *chooses* her fate as the true tragic protagonist does not, without moral mistake (except in a token sense), and she remains ethically impeccable to the end, blaming herself but free of blame.

Despite Clarissa's positive choice of her fate and lack of blame in it, her story would still be unsatisfactory if the reader did not also take satisfaction in the outcome, and to secure that satisfaction was Richardson's primary problem in constructing the ending. His solution was simple: to make it appear that Clarissa would find her full and proper reward in heaven. But this appearance was difficult to achieve within the limits of a form which could display only the phenomena of this world. One dimension of Richardson's solution was his successful representation of Clarissa's own serene conviction, expatiated upon and dramatized in her long renunciation of life, that her destiny was indeed her Father's house in heaven. But the most brilliant part of the solution was the development of a possibility latent in Richardson's use of the letter form as a story-telling vehicle. By presenting posthumously Clarissa's long will and a number of her letters to various persons, Richardson achieved the wonderful effect of giving Clarissa's afterlife a seemingly concrete manifestation, whereas if her voice had ceased at her death, the effect would have been far different. In her letters she seems to speak fully, easily, and serenely after her death from the achieved perspective of immortality. At the same time that Richardson gives this affective proof of her afterlife, he concurrently represents other characters in a way that will enhance that sense. Even the best of those who remain after her death have no positive happiness, while those responsible for her death are punished with condign severity; everyone seems to have no thought but of Clarissa and her merits and her life beyond, so that the whole world of the novel seems to give a kind of negative testimony to her transcendent significance and existence.

The climax of this aspect of the book is Lovelace's death scene, which is narrated as follows by the valet De La Tour:

> *Blessed* – said he [Lovelace], addressing himself no doubt to Heaven; for his dying eyes were lifted up. A strong convulsion prevented him for a few moments saying more, but recovering, he again, with great fervour (lifting up his eyes and his spread hands), pronounced the word *blessed*. Then, in a seeming ejaculation, he spoke inwardly, so as not to be understood: at last, he distinctly pronounced these three words, LET THIS EXPIATE! And then, his head sinking on his pillow, he expired, at about half an hour after ten.[9]

The scene is constructed so as to give the most persuasive testimony possible to Clarissa's presence in heaven. Here the great prevaricator – speaking in pain, at the point of death, and only for himself, since he is indifferent to De La Tour's presence – is seen for once to be absolutely sincere. Through Lovelace's words, much more through his gesture and attitude, which imply his thorough and undoubted conviction of Clarissa's presence in beatitude above, the imagination of the reader is led to experience the fact of Clarissa's immortality, all the more since De La Tour does not understand the implications of the scene, which is left to the reader's own active inference and hence to his implicit belief.

Richardson's maintenance of that impeccability in Clarissa's choices which ultimately justifies her apotheosis presented him with some special problems of which I may briefly notice those surrounding first her elopement and then the rape. In order to free Clarissa of fault in the elopement, Richardson first develops a situation where it appears that Clarissa may not be able to resist the nefarious pressures or even forged processes that may be brought upon her to marry Solmes, and thus he makes acceptable but not impeccable the choice Lovelace offers of rescuing her and depositing her in some safe place. But Clarissa decides to withdraw from this choice (more dangerous than she knows, as *we* know) only to be obliged by Lovelace's contrivance to meet him in the garden to revoke her tentative consent in person. Once there, Lovelace tricks her into his carriage by making it appear that her brother and father are about to burst out upon them, to their great danger at the hands of Lovelace. Thus, at last, Clarissa chooses to run away not for her own salvation but for the sake of the others she is bound to hold dear. But now Richardson has contrived to maintain her impeccability while bringing her by choice into the moral bind he needs to generate her fate. From this point on, her freedom, though actual, is almost an illusion; she cannot thereafter really choose to profit by her choice, marry Lovelace, and live, without appearing retrospectively to have made in leaving a self-interested choice and thus being less than impeccable. When she steps into the carriage her doom is, as the melodramatic phrase goes, sealed.

But even as that doom develops against the apparent but always receding possibility that she and Lovelace can accept each other, we become more and more aware of the absolute opposition between their characters that prevents any actual rapprochement. Their characters are designed so as to be mutually exclusive in their potential choices. She will do nothing which, not dictated by principle, has the least hint of self-gratification about it, while he seeks from her, in gratification of his pride, a fearful, self-regarding acknowledgment of his power. (It is important to note that his desire is not basically sensual, as is consistently suggested by the fact that he remains indifferent to the other women available in Mrs. Sinclair's house.) His primary wish is that she show herself less than an angel, acknowledging her fleshliness toward him. He wants to validate in respect of himself the proposition of Satan in Job 2:4, "Skin for skin, yea all that a man hath will he give for his life." But she will give nothing, will not violate principle even for her life, and he will not spare her unless she does. For that matter, we understand clearly that he would not spare her even if she did, because she would then be less than perfect, and he would not want her. He can neither accept her perfection without the ultimate test which makes his possession of it impossible, nor would he have been able to accept her had she proved imperfect in the test.

Admiration and pity for Clarissa thus grow as the action leads inevitably toward the rape. But a difficulty for Richardson emerges with and in the rape. It is necessary that the violation which makes it impossible for Clarissa to live be a rape and that she be unconscious while it is perpetrated, or else she might seem in some sense to have assented, which would mar her perfection, as of course would marriage after the fact, an ethically acceptable temptation which all England seems to urge upon her. But in being raped, she emphatically does not choose and maintain her moral responsibility for her fate, and hence the principle of form of the book seems to fail: internal moral development is replaced by melodrama, with Clarissa a passive victim of external force. Richardson's solution is the famous pen-knife scene, in which, after the pathos of Clarissa's postrape situation has been fully developed, Clarissa splendidly faces Lovelace down, persuading both him and the reader that she will take her life rather than suffer further indignity. With this scene she has taken her fate once more into her own hands and afterwards is spiritually free of Lovelace, so that when she escapes the house a few hours later she is henceforward free of his physical presence and control.

This following out of the constructive logic implicit in the formal principle I have hypothesized locates something of *Clarissa*'s moral magnitude and cathartic power. It can also suggest the limits of its effectiveness as they derive from the same source, the need to sustain unto death Clarissa's program of impeccable obedience to principle by means of which she seeks to contravene her natural desires, selfishness, and pride. Her implicit motto is "I will not do what I will; I will not gratify my selfish pride." But that she will not gratify her pride is, of course, just her pride; in its own self-immolation her ego (or rather the reader's) finds the gratification she has pervasively denied herself; her self-denial is the ground of the reader's moral self-indulgence. Clarissa is cut off from responsibility and causally separated from the devastation wreaked by the rocket blast of her ascent to heaven. She forgives Lovelace and does not desire his punishment; she forgives all her enemies. Yet Lovelace dies miserably and they die, satisfying in the reader the vengeance which he has admired Clarissa for giving up. In this sense, *Clarissa* is affectively similar to *Pamela* in that it requires the reader to tolerate in himself a moral ambiguity from which the heroine is represented as being free. But *Clarissa*, though it falls short of the agapemenous sublimity displayed in a Cordelia, achieves grandeur just because, unlike *Pamela*, it does dramatize the full price for moral pride, renouncing the earthly vanities which in *Pamela* are cherished. In essence it is an enactment of the you'll-be-sorry-when-I'm-dead fantasy, but it is the grandest and most scarifying version of it imaginable in the stringency and relentlessness with which it carries the moral will to the extremity of death. It is an epic of righteousness, or rather self-righteousness, with the virtues and defects proper to such a work; but with its defects it is still a novelistic action of nearly incomparable massiveness and power.

Richardson's last novel, *Sir Charles Grandison*, presents for explanation, within the terms I have used to consider its predecessors, the fact of its great critical popularity in its own and immediately succeeding times as compared with its marked neglect in our own era and in contrast with *Clarissa*. Why the great loss in power from the earlier to the later work? Space permits only a brief and schematic answer. Envious as always of Fielding, Richardson had been particularly scornful of *Tom Jones* and of the low and immoral adventures in which Fielding was willing to display his hero. Yet his own Lovelace, though antagonist and not protagonist, fell as much as Tom Jones under Johnson's condemnation of mixed characters whose sympathetic attractions masked vice and made it seem attractive. Looking back on Lovelace and Mr. B., Richardson felt the point of his friends who urged him to paint a truly good man to put Fielding's flawed hero in his proper light. And so, as is well-known, it became Richardson's specific intention in *Grandison* to present "the Example of a Man acting uniformly well thro' a Variety of trying Scenes."[10]

There was only one difficulty with Richardson's plan. His decision to make a perfect hero meant that he could not develop an effective action. In his previous novels he could generate powerfully dynamic action structures through his impeccable heroines' acts of moral resistance to the threatening advances of the male antagonists, thus creating a mounting sense of moral danger registered against a mounting sympathy. But a hero cannot be put in such a posture of passive resistance leading increasingly to danger without making him seem unheroically weak or ludicrous. And to make a successful action out of his positive choices would require either that he make mistakes inconsistent with his moral perfection or that the grounds of his acts be merely external and the action therefore melodramatic and independent of his internal moral state. An action based on a courtship, as Richardson's was, was even more limited: a morally perfect hero can only be attracted by and rewarded with a morally perfect heroine, but between two such paragons there cannot be any morally significant differences that can serve as the dynamic basis of a truly fateful separation between them. Richardson's solution, such as it was, was to separate his hero Grandison from his heroine Harriet Byron by means of a prior semi-commitment Grandison has unblameably made to a third paragon, Lady Clementina della Poretta. The situation is artificial and not productive of morally dynamic action, but it does permit a semblance of action, while the real emotional effect lies in the episodes, Richardson's "Variety of trying Scenes," as occasions for displaying at large Grandison's moral perfection. Richardson does all that he can to offset the inherent and essential dullness of a story in which the principals can make no real mistake and be in no real distress, by using novelistic means to lend interest to his characters and by using the resources of his genius to reconcile, as Jocelyn Harris says, "an inert mass of instruction with the demands of entertainment."[11]

But no degree of genius could truly vitalize an action stultified by its initial commitment to display its leading characters as moral paragons. And saying no more than this, we can find the solution to the first half of the problem noted above: the eighteenth century loved *Sir Charles Grandison* because, triply observing Johnson's Rule, it was so full of beautiful conduct, an orgy of impeccabilities and delicacies, whereas later audiences are wearied by its lack of organic movement. The choices of the characters create and resolve no tension, and there is no catharsis. In short, we may say that its structure is such that eighteenth-century audiences were edified but that we are not delighted.

Richardson's tripartite engagement with Johnson's Rule left a distinct problem for his successors: how to construct an effective action in which both male and female protagonists were moral paragons. The solution was begun by Fanny Burney and completed by Jane Austen, with some help from Fielding. Fielding's own struggle with the demands of moral action and related problems requires the attention of another essay, but for my purposes here I may say briefly that in his most relevant work, *Tom Jones*, he did present a hero who, despite the long history of moral complaints about him, was intended as a moral paragon – a man incapable of acts inconsistent with his perfect natural benevolence. The defects of Tom Jones's virtues are flaws sufficient to generate an exemplary moral action of the comic kind, in which those defects are displayed as the partial cause of an apparently adverse fate before the actually happy fate generated by his virtues themselves finally appears. The hero's internal activity is thus made causally integral with his external career, but Jones's defects were too gross to pass muster by most eighteenth-century and even later standards (as already noticed), and the comic attenuation Fielding employs to reduce our sense of the seriousness both of Jones's lapses and his potential fate prevents us from having anything like the close view of his internal moral life that Richardson offers in his novels. But with the resource of the comic action provided by Fielding, new solutions were possible to the dilemma which had stultified *Grandison*. If in a comic novel the fateful issues were made less materially serious than in *Tom Jones*, and the hero and heroine given correlated imperfections not amounting to moral faults, a relative closeness of psychological transcription would be possible which could maintain moral interest and significance without imperiling the sacrosanct status of the paragons. The closer and more sensitive the transcription, the less materially momentous the separating moral issue would have to be to achieve affective balance, and here we see the basis of two apparently contradictory views of the Jane Austen novel as on the one hand a tempest in a teapot and on the other a wonder of fine psychological and moral analysis.

The halfway house to Austen was, of course, Fanny Burney. We need be concerned here only with her first novel, *Evelina*, for only in that novel, written in obscure anonymity, was she able to be free from the burdens of propriety which increasingly crushed the life out of her late novels. Borrowing from *Grandison* her paragon hero and heroine, Lord Orville and Evelina, Burney reduced their dignity and the high seriousness of their moral concerns in a way appropriate to the reduced scope of the comic action in which she placed them. In the early stages of the story she allows Evelina's choices to create her own fate in somewhat the same manner as Tom Jones's do. We are in general assured that Evelina, beautiful and impeccable but provincial and naive, will eventually, though we know not how, be rewarded by marriage to Orville, but in the meantime we are treated to the spectacle of Evelina in her naivete committing faux pas which would seem to doom her romantic hopes but which are nevertheless overcome with perfect aplomb by the endlessly considerate Orville. By reducing the heroine's defect to a merely social ineptitude, Burney is able to present her as a moral paragon while still organically creating a suspense in which we closely participate. But this solution was imperfect. The defect attributed to Evelina was lacking in moral significance and, accidental and circumstantial as it was, could not be used to generate the whole action. If Evelina had continued the line of inept social choices with which the action so effectively begins, she would increasingly have seemed a fool, unworthy of Orville's love and the reader's sympathy. The result was that Burney was forced to relocate the sources of the separating embarrassments outside the heroine in the Branghtons, a band of low bourgeois relatives to whom Evelina is not affectionally committed but whose association she cannot for various reasons, including those of propriety, escape. The result is a wonderfully excruciating series of embarrassments, but the point of her predicament is that she is *not* responsible for her relatives' vulgarity and other shortcomings, though she seems doomed to suffer from them.

The climax of this development comes when the Branghtons, in Evelina's name, crudely demand the use of Lord Orville's carriage from his servants and, after setting her down, become involved in an accident that damages the carriage. The sequel is narrated to Evelina next morning by an egregiously conceited vulgarian cousin, who tells her of his visit to ask Lord Orville's pardon, gaining entree again by use of Evelina's name. Lord Orville receives the visit with characteristic politeness, whereupon the cousin offers a further encroachment as follows:

> "…so it come into my head, as he was so affable, that I'd ask him for his custom. So I says, says I, my Lord, says I, if your Lordship i'n't engaged particularly, my father is a silversmith, and he'll be very proud to serve you, says I; and Miss Anville, as danced with you, is his cousin, and she's my cousin too, and she'd be very much obliged to you, I'm sure."
>
> "You'll drive me wild," cried I, starting from my seat, "you have done me an irreparable injury; – but I will hear no more!" – and then I ran into my own room.
>
> I was half frantic, I really raved; the good opinion of Lord Orville seemed now irretrievably lost;…for the rest of my life, he would regard me as an object of utter contempt.[12]

This is as far as the secondary line of development can be taken, and Burney immediately after develops out of this the first of a number of largely external melodramatic devices to maintain and increase suspense until such time as she can dramatize the closing fullness of mutual understanding which Orville and Evelina achieve as a prelude to their union. Thus Burney was able neither to generate her action from within her characters nor to make morally significant the internal dimension of the action which she did manage to realize. Her location of her heroine's embarrassments outside of her control but impinging on her sense of responsibility – she suffers from them because she *appears* responsible for them – is the characteristic feature of her work. Considering the matter a little more closely, we can see that the external embarrassments through which Evelina suffers constitute an appeal to that side of our self which locates the source of our social insecurities in persons or situations other than ourself. It is not I but the others, my relatives, who are so vulgar (our weaker self says), and I am not responsible for them. The nightmare of social embarrassment is exquisitely realized in the book, but it *is* nightmare and, despite the degree to which it is brought to objective dramatization, requires a kind of indulgence of the insecure, snobbish part of our nature against the other side of mature responsibility. The psyche is flattered but not forced to self-knowledge and confrontation of the submerged moral issues involved, which is why we find *Evelina* today still amusing where it does not seem stilted, but not deeply moving.

We can begin to understand Jane Austen's contribution to the development I have been tracing by setting against the episode of Evelina's outrageous cousin an episode from *Northanger Abbey* remarkably similar in structure but significantly different in quality. The Thorpes in concert with Catherine's brother have renewed plans to visit Blaize Castle but discover that Catherine has engaged herself (for a second time) to walk with Miss Tilney. Her friends urge her to cancel the engagement for the sake of their collective pleasure: "she *must* and *should* retract, was instantly the eager cry of both the Thorpes; they must go to Clifton tomorrow, they would not go without her, it would be nothing to put off a mere walk for one day longer, and they would not hear of a refusal."[13] But Catherine will not be moved: "do not urge me, Isabella. I am engaged to Miss Tilney. I cannot go." Still her friends press her, making every unfair and selfish appeal, and her brother joins his voice strongly to theirs. "I did not think you had been so obstinate, Catherine;…you once were the kindest, best-tempered of my sisters" (pp. 99–100). "I hope I am not less so now," she replied, very feelingly; "but indeed I cannot go. If I am wrong, I am doing what I believe is right." But external circumstance in the person of John Thorpe intervenes to shape her fate (as he had on the previous day deflected her from her first date to walk with Miss Tilney). He has left the discussion for a few minutes and rejoins them with a gay look, saying:

"Well, I have settled the matter, and now we may all go tomorrow with a safe conscience. I have been to Miss Tilney and made your excuses."

"You have not!" cried Catherine.

"I have, upon my soul. Left her this moment. Told her you had sent me to say, that having recollected a prior engagement of going to Clifton with us to-morrow, you could not have the pleasure of walking with her till Tuesday. She said very well, Tuesday was just as convenient to her; so there is an end of all our difficulties. – A pretty good thought of mine – hey?" (p. 100)

Isabella and James are pleased but Catherine is not. "This will not do," she says, and sets off, despite efforts to restrain her, to find Miss Tilney. "I will go after them," said Catherine; "wherever they are I will go after them. It does not signify talking. If I could not be persuaded into doing what I thought wrong, I never will be tricked into it" (p. 101). The analogy of the scene with that where young Branghton speaks to Lord Orville about the carriage is close, but how different the effect. Austen has built into her scene of social embarrassment a dimension of moral agency and responsibility that serves to integrate a serious moral intention with her need to develop an organic and affectively potent action, and this serves to raise the pleasure of the scene into a range of moral value that Burney never touches but that is Austen's characteristic register.

Further consideration of the principle of structural difference in similarity of the scenes from *Evelina* and *Northanger Abbey* allows us to describe a striking relation between *Evelina* and the first drafted of Austen's novels, *Pride and Prejudice*. The title of Austen's novel is, of course, taken from Burney's second novel, *Cecilia*, a fact that helps us to direct our attention to the initial change which Austen made in the paired paragons she drew from *Evelina* as Burney had taken them from *Grandison*. Darcy and Elizabeth are given imperfections not amounting to moral faults – pride and prejudice, in short but adequate description – which serve as the beginning but not the full substance of their separation, a substance which can be seen to derive so remarkably, not from *Cecilia* but from *Pride and Prejudice*, that one might almost say that *Pride and Prejudice* is *Evelina* transformed according to the principle already specified for the scene in *Northanger Abbey*, namely, that those characters represented as responsible for the paragon's adverse fate but as having no claim upon her affections and thus her sense of moral responsibility, be represented as having such a claim and requiring such responsibility.

Evelina is committed early to the unwanted chaperonage of Mme. Duval, her grandmother, a volubly vulgar, aggressive, and déclassé woman, through circumstances scarcely known to Evelina and, except for the fact of kinship, alien to her in every respect. Thus developed, Mme. Duval is calculated to be a powerful source of social embarrassment and distress to Evelina without posing any real threat to her intrinsic status or any real problem in moral accommodation to either Evelina or Orville. Austen modulates the almost surrealistic stridencies of this figure into Mrs. Bennet, a normally vulgar mother whose propinquity Elizabeth must from the first acknowledge and respect, while within that respect ultimately conceding that her mother's deficiencies offer Darcy reasonable grounds for his misjudged advice to Bingley. In parallel fashion, the tradesmen cousins of *Evelina*, the Branghtons, become Elizabeth's city cousins, the Gardiners, but whereas the Branghtons are occasions of embarrassment whom Evelina can snobbishly scorn and reject, the Gardiners exemplify fully the cultivated values on which the evaluations of the book are based, so that the values are thus emphatically defined as more than class values, as Darcy's easy acceptance of the Gardiners under-lines. Austen makes the same point from another direction with Lady Catherine de Bourgh, a second upper-class relative of Mme. Duval, whose boorishness also bears witness against the identification made in *Evelina* (though to some extent dramatically qualified) of manners with class, and so provides a full expression of the barriers of class pride which Darcy in moral autonomy must cross to claim Elizabeth. The result of this system of transpositions is, like that in *Northanger Abbey*, to bring within the range of consciousness and dramatized moral responsibility elements of feeling which are re-pressed in *Evelina* and thus to strengthen probability and morally enrich the suspense structure of the book.

A further borrowing involves the conversion of Sir Clement Willoughby into Wick-ham. In *Evelina*, Willoughby is used as a melodramatic threat to the heroine, a covert external expression of internal sexual feeling. Wickham's sexual attractiveness to

Elizabeth is directly represented in an early episode where her muted physical infatuation is expressed in an implicit but distinct fashion that permits psychological honesty but preserves her status as a paragon. The full reality of Wickham's sexual threat is deflected to expression in his off-stage elopement with Lydia; thus the sexual dimension of courtship is acknowledged without compromising either the moral purity or realistic integrity of the story. And these characters are then nicely reintegrated into the main action as a final barrier to the marriage of Elizabeth and Darcy. By this means Darcy can be presented with an opportunity to display with gratifying probability and surprise the full resources of his moral character and intelligence, as Elizabeth had earlier done in revising, against the grain and in response to good evidence, her mistaken estimate of *him*.

In short, Austen in *Pride and Prejudice* achieves a solution to the problems presented to the action novelist by the didactic demands reflected in what I have called Johnson's Rule. She does this by creating a morally impeccable, yet entirely natural, hero and heroine who are first separated from each other, not by circumstance but by significant misjudgments not amounting to moral error, defects deriving from appropriate strengths of their splendid characters – Darcy's pride in his inherited station, and Elizabeth's prejudice against Darcy which arises from a proper pride in herself. Austen then amplifies and supports this original rift by means of the protagonists' relationships to characters whose qualities and actions are themselves morally problematical, without damaging the essential impeccability of the protagonists. She thus achieves a novelistic action which is fully and honestly edifying and completely delightful.[14]

Austen's other two early novels, *Sense and Sensibility* and *Northanger Abbey*, also repay analysis as structures resulting from conflicts between the action structure and didactic intentions less specific than those expressed in the requirements of Johnson's Rule. Austen's creative intention in *Northanger Abbey* was not to parody the gothic novel but rather to incorporate in a comic action a reference to it that would define a corrigible defect in the heroine's understanding of the world so as to measure the realistic or confrontational fantasy of the Austenian novel against the deceptive and indulgent fantasy of the gothic mode. Though the incorporation of the alien matter is as complete as the nature of the constructional situation allows, the final effect is to render the action a bit top-heavy and lacking in the full substance of the other books.[15] *Sense and Sensibility* is a work with which few of Austen's readers are fully satisfied, yet whose precise formal deficiencies are hard to define. Some see the formal rationale of the work in an intention to contrast the systems of thought and value of the two sisters, as indicated in the title. But this merely didactic or thematic conception does not do justice to the actual dramatic power of the work, which can be analyzed quite effectively as developed in action terms. The precise formal situation can be expressed if we say that, though the work is entirely developed as an action, the first choice of a structural core for the book, the choice of the contrasting sisters, cannot be explained as being inherently appropriate to an action as are the choices of Pamela and Mr. B., for instance, or Elizabeth and Darcy, but only as appropriate to a didactic intention. We have in *Sense and Sensibility*, then, a different kind of example of the impingement upon the action form of the requirement that novels be morally instructive. The idea that Austen in this instance built an action novel on a didactic base I believe can be used to develop an analysis which will explain quite well its feel to us and its puzzlements.

Austen's later novels – except perhaps *Persuasion*, where, eyes to the sea, her art looks toward fresher formal possibilities – are touched in fairly obvious ways by the pressures of eighteenth-century didacticism. After her the action novel was to undergo new lines of development, but the novel of moral action and its concomitant formal problems came to an end with her, partly because the line had reached its perfection, but more largely because later novelists threw Johnson's Rule and related didactic baggage out the window, as Becky Sharp did his *Dictionary*, en route from the restraints of the academy to new and less trammeled pleasures.

NOTES

1   See Crane's "The Concept of Plot and the Plot of *Tom Jones*," in *Critics and Criticism: Ancient and Modern*, ed. R. S. Crane (Chicago: University of Chicago Press, 1952), pp. 616–647; [see also pp. 119–39 in this book]; and Sacks's *Fiction and the Shape of Belief* (Berkeley: University of California Press, 1964), esp. pp. 26–27 and 268–269.

2   Mark Kinkead-Weekes, *Samuel Richardson: Dramatic Novelist* (Ithaca, New York: Cornell University Press, 1973), p. 395.

3   See Michael Polanyi, *Personal Knowledge: Towards a Post-Critical Philosophy* (Chicago: University of Chicago Press, 1974), pp. 55–56.

4   See Ralph Cohen, "On the Interrelations of Eighteenth-Century Literary Forms," in *New Approaches to Eighteenth-Century Literature* (New York: Columbia University Press, 1974), p. 75.

5   Samuel Johnson, *The Rambler*, ed. W. J. Bate and Albrecht B. Strauss, Vol. 3 of *The Yale Edition of the Works of Samuel Johnson* (New Haven: Yale University Press, 1969), p. 24.

6   See the author's "Defoe, Richardson, Joyce and the Concept of Form in the Novel," in *Autobiography, Biography, and the Novel* by Will Matthews and Ralph W. Rader (Los Angeles: William Andrews Clark Memorial Library, 1973), pp. 34–35.

7   Preface to *Clarissa; or, The History of a Young Lady*, Everyman Edition, 1902 (reprint, London: J. M. Dent and Sons, 1967), I, xiv. Subsequent references by page number in text.

8   Aristotle, *Poetics*, trans. Ingham Bywater, in *The Basic Works of Aristotle*, ed. Richard McKeon (New York: Random House, 1941), p. 1466.

9   Samuel Richardson, *Clarissa*, IV, 530.

10   Preface to *The History of Sir Charles Grandison*, ed. Jocelyn Harris, 3 vols. (London: Oxford University Press, 1972), I, 4.

11   Jocelyn Harris, Introduction to *Sir Charles Grandison*, p. xxiii.

12   *Evelina; or, The History of a Young Lady's Entrance into the World* (New York: Norton, 1965), p. 234.

13   *Northanger Abbey and Persuasion*, Vol. 3 of The Novels of Jane Austen, ed. R. W. Chapman (London: Oxford University Press, 1933), p. 97. Subsequent references by page number in text.

14   My view of the structure of *Pride and Prejudice* has been significantly influenced by that of Sheldon Sacks as briefly sketched in his "Golden Birds and Dying Generations," *Comparative Literature Studies*, 6 (September 1969), 285–287. See also Walter Anderson's cognate but more extended analysis in "Plot, Character, Speech, and Place in *Pride and Prejudice*," *Nineteenth-Century Fiction*, 30 (December 1975), 367–382.

15   For a cogent and much fuller account of the interrelation of the action structure and gothic material in *Northanger Abbey*, see Walter Anderson, "From Northanger Abbey to Woodston: Catherine's Education in Common Life," *Philological Quarterly*, 63 (Fall 1984), 493–509.

The Rhetoric of Fiction

Wayne C. Booth

Wayne Clayson Booth (b. 1921)

Born in American Fork, Utah, Wayne Booth attended Brigham Young University, and, after three years of military service, the University of Chicago. After receiving his Ph.D. in 1950, Booth taught at Haverford and Earlham Colleges, returning to teach at Chicago in 1962. As George M. Pullman Distinguished Service Professor, Booth has served as Dean of Chicago's Undergraduate College, and as President of the Modern Language Association. Booth's honors include election to the American Academy of Arts and Sciences and the American Philosophical Society, as well as fellowships from the Guggenheim Foundation and the National Endowment for the Humanities. *The Rhetoric of Fiction*, originally published in 1961, was reissued in 1983 with a new afterword and an expanded bibliography. It received the Phi Beta Kappa Christian Gauss Award and the National Council of Teachers of English David H. Russell Award for Distinguished Research. Additional books include *A Rhetoric of Irony* (1974); *Critical Understanding: The Powers and Limits of Pluralism* (1979); *The Craft of Research* (1995); *The Company We Keep: An Ethics of Fiction* (1988); and *Rhetoric of Rhetoric: The Quest for Effective Communication* (2004).

From *The Rhetoric of Fiction*, second edition. Chicago and London: University of Chicago Press, 1983, from ch. 1, pp. 16–20, ch. 3, pp. 67–77, ch. 5, pp. 121–44, ch. 13, pp. 391–8. Copyright © 1961, 1983 by the University of Chicago Press. Reprinted by permission of the author and the University of Chicago Press.

Telling and Showing

The Author's Many Voices

In the next… chapters I shall look in detail at some of the more important arguments for authorial objectivity or impersonality. Most of these call for eliminating certain overt signs of the author's presence. As we might expect, however, one man's objectivity is another man's bête noire. If we are to have any degree of clarity as we make our way through attacks on the author's voice, we must have some preliminary notion of the variety of forms that voice can take, both in fiction and in attacks on fiction. What is it, in fact, that we might expunge if we attempted to drive the author from the house of fiction?

First, we must erase all direct addresses to the reader, all commentary in the author's own name. When the author of the *Decameron* speaks to us directly, in both the introduction and conclusion, whatever illusion we may have had that we are dealing immediately with Fiammetta and her friends is shattered. An astonishing number of authors and critics since Flaubert have agreed that such direct, unmediated commentary will not do. And even those authors who would allow it have often, like E. M. Forster, forbidden it except on certain limited subjects.[1]

But what, really, is "commentary"? If we agree to eliminate all personal intrusions of the kind used by Fielding, do we then agree to expunge less obtrusive comment? Is Flaubert violating his own principles of impersonality when he allows himself to tell us that in such and such a place one finds the worst Neufchatel cheeses of the entire district, or that Emma was "incapable of understanding what she didn't experience, or of recognizing anything that wasn't expressed in conventional terms"?[2]

Even if we eliminate all such explicit judgments, the author's presence will be obvious on every occasion when he moves into or out of a character's mind – when he "shifts his point of view," as we have come to put it. Flaubert tells us that Emma's little attentions to Charles were "never, as he believed, for his sake… but for her own, out of exasperated vanity" (p. 69). It is clearly Flaubert who constructs this juxtaposition of Emma's motive with Charles' belief about the motive, and the same obtrusive "voice" is evident whenever a new mind is introduced. When Emma's father bids farewell to Emma and Charles, he remembers "his own wedding, his own earlier days.… He, too, had been very happy.… He felt dismal, like a stripped and empty house" (pp. 34–35). This momentary shift to Rouault is Flaubert's way of providing us with an evaluation of the marriage and a sense of what is to come. If we are troubled by all reminders of the author's presence, we shall be troubled here.

But if we are to object to this, why not go the next step and object to all inside views, not simply those that require a shift in point of view. In life such views are not to be had. The act of providing them in fiction is itself an obtrusion by the author.[3]

For that matter, we must object to the reliable statements of any dramatized character, not just the author in his own voice, because the act of narration as performed by even the most highly dramatized narrator is itself the author's presentation of a prolonged "inside view" of a character. When Fiammetta says "the love she bore the boy carried the day," she is giving us a reliable inside view of Monna, and she is also giving a view of her own evaluation of events. Both are reminders of the author's controlling hand.

But why stop here? The author is present in every speech given by any character who has had conferred upon him, in whatever manner, the badge of reliability. Once we know that God is God in Job, once we know that Monna speaks truth in "The Falcon," the authors speak whenever God and Monna speak. Introducing the great Doctor Larivière, Flaubert says:

> He belonged to that great surgical school created by Bichat – that generation, now vanished, of philosopher-practitioners, who cherished their art with fanatical love and applied it with enthusiasm and sagacity. Everyone in his hospital trembled when he was angry; and his students so revered him that the moment they set up for themselves they imitated him as much as they could.... Disdainful of decorations... hospitable, generous, a father to the poor, practicing Christian virtues although an unbeliever, he might have been thought of as a saint if he hadn't been feared as a devil because of the keenness of his mind [pp. 363–64].

This unambiguous bestowal of authority contributes greatly to the power of the next few pages, in which Larivière judges for us everything that we see. But helpful as he is, he must go – if the author's voice is a fault.

Even here we cannot stop, though many of the critics of the author's voice have stopped here. We can go on and on, purging the work of every recognizably personal touch, every distinctive literary allusion or colorful metaphor, every pattern of myth or symbol; they all implicitly evaluate. Any discerning reader can recognize that they are imposed by the author.[4]

Finally, we might even follow Jean-Paul Sartre and object, in the name of "durational realism," to all evidences of the author's meddling with the natural sequence, proportion, or duration of events. Earlier authors, Sartre says, tried to justify "the foolish business of storytelling by ceaselessly bringing to the reader's attention, explicitly or by allusion, the existence of an author." The existentialist novels, in contrast, will be "toboggans, forgotten, unnoticed," hurling the reader "into the midst of a universe where there are no witnesses." Novels should "exist in the manner of things, of plants, of events, and not at first like products of man."[5] If this is so, the author must never summarize, never curtail a conversation, never telescope the events of three days into a paragraph. "If I pack six months into a single page, the reader jumps out of the book" (p. 229).

Sartre is certainly right in claiming that all these things are signs of the author's manipulating presence. In *The Brothers Karamazov*, for example, the story of Father Zossima's conversion could logically be placed anywhere. The events of Zossima's story took place long before the novel begins; unless they are to be placed at the beginning, which is out of the question, there is no natural reason for giving them in one place rather than another. Wherever they are placed, they will call attention to the author's selecting presence, just as Homer is glaringly present to us whenever the *Odyssey* takes one of its many leaps back and forth over a nineteen-year period. It is not accident but Dostoevski's careful choice that gives us Zossima's story as the sequel to Ivan's dream of the Grand Inquisitor. It is intended as a judgment on the values implied by that dream, just as everything that happens to Ivan afterward is an explicit criticism of his own ideas. Since the sequence is obviously not dictated by anything other than the author's purposes, it betrays the author's voice, and according to Sartre, it presumably will not do.

But, as Sartre woefully admits (see "All Authors should be Objective," below), even with all these forms of the author's voice expunged, what we have left will reveal to us a shameful artificiality. Unless the author contents himself with simply retelling The Three Bears or the story of Oedipus in the precise form in which they exist in popular accounts – and even so there must be some choice of *which* popular form to tell – his very choice of what he tells will betray him to the reader. He chooses to tell the tale of Odysseus rather than that of Circe or Polyphemus. He chooses to tell the cheerful tale of Monna and Federigo rather than a pathetic account of Monna's husband and son. He chooses to tell the story of Emma Bovary rather than the potentially heroic tale of Dr. Larivière. The author's voice is as passionately revealed in the decision to write the *Odyssey*, "The Falcon," or *Madame Bovary* as it is in the most obtrusive direct comment of the kind employed by Fielding, Dickens, or George Eliot. Everything he *shows* will serve to *tell*; the line between showing and telling is always to some degree an arbitrary one.

In short, the author's judgment is always present, always evident to anyone who knows how to look for it. Whether its particular forms are harmful or serviceable is always a complex question, a question that cannot be settled by any easy reference to abstract rules. As we begin now to deal with this question, we must never forget that though the author can to some extent choose his disguises, he can never choose to disappear.

* * *

"All Authors Should Be Objective"

A second type of general criterion common to many of the founders of modern fiction deals with the author's state of mind or soul. A surprising number of writers, even those who have thought of their writing as "self-expression," have sought a freedom from the tyranny of subjectivity, echoing Goethe's claim that "Every healthy effort...is directed from the inward to the outward world."[6] From time to time others have risen to defend commitment, engagement, involvement. But, at least until recently, the predominant demand in this century has been for some sort of objectivity.

Like all such terms, however, *objectivity* is many things. Underlying it and its many synonyms – impersonality, detachment, disinterestedness, neutrality, etc. – we can distinguish at least three separate qualities: neutrality, impartiality, and *impassibilité*.

Neutrality and the Author's "Second Self"

Objectivity in the author can mean, first, an attitude of neutrality toward all values, an attempt at disinterested reporting of all things good and evil. Like many literary enthusiasms, the passion for neutrality was imported into fiction from the other arts relatively late. Keats was saying in 1818 the kind of thing that novelists began to say only with Flaubert. "The poetical character...has no character....It lives in gusto, be it foul or fair, high or low, rich or poor, mean or elevated. It has as much delight in conceiving an Iago as an Imogen. What shocks the virtuous philosopher, delights the camelion Poet.

It does not harm from its relish of the dark side of things any more than from its taste for the bright one; because they both end in speculation."[7] Three decades later Flaubert recommended a similar neutrality to the novelist who would be a poet. For him the model is the attitude of the scientist. Once we have spent enough time, he says, in "treating the human soul with the impartiality which physical scientists show in studying matter, we will have taken an immense step forward."[8] Art must achieve "by a pitiless method, the precision of the physical sciences."[9]

It should be unnecessary here to show that no author can ever attain to this kind of objectivity. Most of us today would, like Sartre, renounce the analogy with science even if we could admit that science is objective in this sense. What is more, we all know by now that a careful reading of any statement in defense of the artist's neutrality will reveal commitment; there is always some deeper value in relation to which neutrality is taken to be good. Chekhov, for example, begins bravely enough in defense of neutrality, but he cannot write three sentences without committing himself. "I am afraid of those who look for a tendency between the lines, and who are determined to regard me either as a liberal or as a conservative. I am not a liberal, not a conservative, not a believer in gradual progress, not a monk, not an indifferentist. I should like to be a free artist and nothing more.... I have no preference either for gendarmes, or for butchers, or for scientists, or for writers, or for the younger generation. I regard trade-marks and labels as a superstition."[10] Freedom and art are good, then, and superstition bad? Soon he is carried away to a direct repudiation of the plea for "indifference" with which he began. "My holy of holies is the human body, health, intelligence, talent, inspiration, love, and the most absolute freedom – freedom from violence and lying, whatever forms they may take" (p. 63). Again and again he betrays in this way the most passionate kind of commitment to what he often calls objectivity.

> The artist should be, not the judge of his characters and their conversations, but only an unbiassed witness. I once overheard a desultory conversation about pessimism between two Russians; nothing was solved, – and my business is to report the conversation exactly as I heard it, and let the jury, – that is, the readers, estimate its value. My business is merely to be talented, i.e., to be able ... to illuminate the characters and speak their language [pp. 58–59].

But "illuminate" according to what lights? "A writer must be as objective as a chemist; he must abandon the subjective line; he must know that dung-heaps play a very respectable part in a landscape, and that evil passions are as inherent in life as good ones" (pp. 275–76). We have learned by now to ask of such statements: Is it *good* to be faithful to what is "inherent"? Is it good to include every part of the "landscape"? If so, why? According to what scale of values? To repudiate one scale is necessarily to imply another.

It would be a serious mistake, however, to dismiss talk about the author's neutrality simply because of this elementary and understandable confusion between neutrality toward *some* values and neutrality toward *all*. Cleansed of the polemical excesses, the attack on subjectivity can be seen to rest on several important insights.

To succeed in writing some kinds of works, some novelists find it necessary to repudiate all intellectual or political causes. Chekhov does not want himself, *as artist*, to be either liberal or conservative. Flaubert, writing in 1853, claims that even the artist who recognizes the demand to be a "triple-thinker," even the artist who recognizes the

WAYNE C. BOOTH

need for ideas in abundance, "must have neither religion, nor country, nor social conviction."[11]

Unlike the claim to complete neutrality, this claim will never be refuted, and it will not suffer from shifts in literary theory or philosophical fashion. Like its opposite, the existentialist claim of Sartre and others that the artist should be totally *engagé*, its validity depends on the kind of novel the author is writing. Some great artists have been committed to the causes of their times, and some have not. Some works seem to be harmed by their burden of commitment (many of Sartre's own works, for example, in spite of their freedom from authorial comment) and some seem to be able to absorb a great deal of commitment (*The Divine Comedy, Four Quartets, Gulliver's Travels, Darkness at Noon, Bread and Wine*). One can always find examples to prove either side of the case; the test is whether the particular ends of the artist enable him to do something with his commitment, not whether he has it or not.

Everyone is against everyone else's prejudices and in favor of his own commitment to the truth. All of us would like the novelist somehow to operate on the level of our own passion for truth and right, a passion which by definition is not in the least prejudiced. The argument in favor of neutrality is thus useful in so far as it warns the novelist that he can seldom afford to pour his untransformed biases into his work. The deeper he sees into permanency, the more likely he is to earn the discerning reader's concurrence. The author as he writes should be like the ideal reader described by Hume in "The Standard of Taste," who, in order to reduce the distortions produced by prejudice, considers himself as "man in general" and forgets, if possible, his "individual being" and his "peculiar circumstances."

To put it in this way, however, is to understate the importance of the author's individuality. As he writes, he creates not simply an ideal, impersonal "man in general" but an implied version of "himself" that is different from the implied authors we meet in other men's works. To some novelists it has seemed, indeed, that they were discovering or creating themselves as they wrote. As Jessamyn West says, it is sometimes "only by writing the story that the novelist can discover − not his story − but its writer, the official scribe, so to speak, for that narrative."[12] Whether we call this implied author an "official scribe," or adopt the term recently revived by Kathleen Tillotson − the author's "second self"[13] − it is clear that the picture the reader gets of this presence is one of the author's most important effects. However impersonal he may try to be, his reader will inevitably construct a picture of the official scribe who writes in this manner − and of course that official scribe will never be neutral toward all values. Our reactions to his various commitments, secret or overt, will help to determine our response to the work.... Our present problem is the intricate relationship of the so-called real author with his various official versions of himself.

We must say various versions, for regardless of how sincere an author may try to be, his different works will imply different versions, different ideal combinations of norms. Just as one's personal letters imply different versions of oneself, depending on the differing relationships with each correspondent and the purpose of each letter, so the writer sets himself out with a different air depending on the needs of particular works.

These differences are most evident when the second self is given an overt, speaking role in the story. When Fielding comments, he gives us explicit evidence of a modifying process from work to work; no single version of Fielding emerges from reading the satirical *Jonathan Wild*, the two great "comic epics in prose," *Joseph Andrews* and *Tom Jones*, and that troublesome hybrid, *Amelia*. There are many similarities among them, of course; all of the implied authors value benevolence and generosity; all of them deplore self-seeking brutality. In these and many other respects they are indistinguishable from most implied authors of most significant works until our own century. But when we descend from this level of generality to look at the particular ordering of values in each novel, we find great variety. The author of *Jonathan Wild* is by implication very much concerned with public affairs and with the effects of unchecked ambition on the "great men" who attain to power in the world. If we had only this novel by Fielding, we would infer from it that in his real life he was much more single-mindedly engrossed in his role as magistrate and reformer of public manners than is suggested by the implied author of *Joseph Andrews* and *Tom Jones* – to say nothing of *Shamela* (what would we infer about Fielding if he had never written anything but *Shamela*!). On the other hand, the author who greets us on page one of *Amelia* has none of that air of facetiousness combined with grand insouciance that we meet from the beginning in *Joseph Andrews* and *Tom Jones*. Suppose that Fielding had never written anything but *Amelia*, filled as it is with the kind of commentary we find at the beginning:

> The various accidents which befel a very worthy couple after their uniting in the state of matrimony will be the subject of the following history. The distresses which they waded through were some of them so exquisite, and the incidents which produced these so extraordinary, that they seemed to require not only the utmost malice, but the utmost invention, which superstition hath ever attributed to Fortune: though whether any such being interfered in the case, or, indeed, whether there be any such being in the universe, is a matter which I by no means presume to determine in the affirmative.

Could we ever infer from this the Fielding of the earlier works? Though the author of *Amelia* can still indulge in occasional jests and ironies, his general air of sententious solemnity is strictly in keeping with the very special effects proper to the work as a whole. Our picture of him is built, of course, only partly by the narrator's explicit commentary; it is even more derived from the kind of tale he chooses to tell. But the commentary makes explicit for us a relationship which is present in all fiction, but which, in fiction without commentary, may be overlooked.

It is a curious fact that we have no terms either for this created "second self" or for our relationship with him. None of our terms for various aspects of the narrator is quite accurate. "Persona," "mask," and "narrator" are sometimes used, but they more commonly refer to the speaker in the work who is after all only one of the elements created by the implied author and who may be separated from him by large ironies. "Narrator" is usually taken to mean the "I" of a work, but the "I" is seldom if ever identical with the implied image of the artist.

"Theme," "meaning," "symbolic significance," "theology," or even "ontology" – all these have been used to describe the norms which the reader must apprehend in each work if he is to grasp it adequately. Such terms are useful for some purposes, but they can be misleading because they almost inevitably come to seem like purposes for which the works exist. Though the old-style effort to find the theme or moral has been generally repudiated, the new-style search for the "meaning" which the work "commu-nicates" or "symbolizes" can yield the same kinds of misreading. It is true that both types of search, however clumsily pursued, express a basic need: the reader's need to know where, in the world of values, he stands – that is, to know where the author *wants* him to stand. But most works worth reading have so many possible "themes," so many possible mythological or metaphorical or symbolic analogues, that to find any one of them, and to announce it as what the work is *for*, is to do at best a very small part of the critical task. Our sense of the implied author includes not only the extractable meanings but also the moral and emotional content of each bit of action and suffering of all of the characters. It includes, in short, the intuitive apprehension of a completed artistic whole; the chief value to which *this* implied author is committed, regardless of what party his creator belongs to in real life, is that which is expressed by the total form.

Three other terms are sometimes used to name the core of norms and choices which I am calling the implied author. "Style" is sometimes broadly used to cover whatever it is that gives us a sense, from word to word and line to line, that the author sees more deeply and judges more profoundly than his presented characters. But, though style is one of our main sources of insight into the author's norms, in carrying such strong overtones of the merely verbal the word *style* excludes our sense of the author's skill in his choice of character and episode and scene and idea. "Tone" is similarly used to refer to the implicit evaluation which the author manages to convey behind his explicit presentation,[14] but it almost inevitably suggests again something limited to the merely verbal; some aspects of the implied author may be inferred through tonal variations, but his major qualities will depend also on the hard facts of action and character in the tale that is told.

Similarly, "technique" has at times been expanded to cover all discernible signs of the author's artistry. If everyone used "technique" as Mark Schorer does,[15] covering with it almost the entire range of choices made by the author, then it might very well serve our purposes. But it is usually taken for a much narrower matter, and consequently it will not do. We can be satisfied only with a term that is as broad as the work itself but still capable of calling attention to that work as the product of a choosing, evaluating person rather than as a self-existing thing. The "implied author" chooses, consciously or unconsciously, what we read; we infer him as an ideal, literary, created version of the real man; he is the sum of his own choices.

It is only by distinguishing between the author and his implied image that we can avoid pointless and unverifiable talk about such qualities as "sincerity" or "seriousness" in the author. Because Ford Madox Ford thinks of Fielding and Defoe and Thackeray as the unmediated authors of their novels, he must end by condemning them as insincere, since there is every reason to believe that they write "passages of virtuous aspirations that were in no way any aspirations of theirs."[16] Presumably he is relying on external evidences of Fielding's lack of virtuous aspirations. But we have only the work as evidence for the only kind of sincerity that concerns us: Is the implied author in harmony with himself – that is, are his other choices in harmony with his explicit narrative character? If a narrator who by every trustworthy sign is presented to us as a reliable spokesman for the author professes to believe in values which are never realized in the structure as a whole, we can then talk of an insincere work. A great work establishes the "sincerity" of its implied author, regardless of how grossly the man who created that author may belie in his *other* forms of conduct the values embodied in his work. For all we know, the only sincere moments of his life may have been lived as he wrote his novel.

What is more, in this distinction between author and implied author we find a middle position between the technical irrelevance of talk about the artist's objectivity and the harmful error of pretending that an author can allow direct intrusions of his own immediate problems and desires. The great defenders of objectivity were working on an important matter and they knew it. Flaubert is right in saying that Shakespeare does not barge clumsily into his works. We are never plagued with his undigested personal problems. Flaubert is also right in rebuking Louise Colet for writing "La Servante" as a personal attack on Musset, with the personal passion destroying the aesthetic value of the poem (January 9–10, 1854). And he is surely right when he forces the hero of the youthful version of *The Sentimental Education* (1845) to choose between the merely confessional statement and the truly rendered work of art.

But is he right when he claims that we do not know what Shakespeare loved or hated?[17] Perhaps – if he means only that we cannot easily tell from the plays whether the man Shakespeare preferred blondes to brunettes or whether he disliked bastards, Jews, or Moors. But the statement is most definitely mistaken if it means that the implied author of Shakespeare's plays is neutral toward all values. We do know what *this* Shakespeare loved and hated; it is hard to see how he could have written his plays at all if he had refused to take a strong line on at least one or two of the seven deadly sins. I return in chapter V to the question of beliefs in literature, and I try there to list a few of the values to which Shakespeare is definitely and obviously committed. They are for the most part not personal, idiosyncratic; Shakespeare is thus not recognizably subjective. But they are unmistakable violations of true neutrality; the implied Shakespeare is thoroughly engaged with life, and he does not conceal his judgment on the selfish, the foolish, and the cruel.

Even if all this were denied, it is difficult to see why there should be any necessary connection between neutrality and an absence of commentary. An author might very well use comments to warn the reader against judging. But if I am right in claiming that neutrality is impossible, even the most nearly neutral comment will reveal some sort of commitment.

> Once upon a time there lived in Berlin, Germany, a man called Albinus. He was rich, respectable, happy; one day he abandoned his wife for the sake of a youthful mistress; he loved; was not loved; and his life ended in disaster.
>
> This is the whole of the story and we might have left it at that had there not been profit and pleasure in the telling; and although there is plenty of space on a gravestone to contain, bound in moss, the abridged version of a man's life, detail is always welcome.[18]

Nabokov may here have purged his narrator's voice of all commitments save one, but that one is all-powerful: he believes in the ironic interest – and as it later turns out, the poignancy – of a man's fated self-destruction. Maintaining the same detached tone, this author can intrude whenever he pleases without violating our conviction that he is as objective as it is humanly possible to be. Describing the villain, he can call him both a "dangerous man" and "a very fine artist indeed" without reducing our confidence in

WAYNE C. BOOTH

his open-mindedness. But he is not neutral toward all values, and he does not pretend to be.

* * *

Emotions, Beliefs, and the Reader's Objectivity

Many of the attacks on allegedly non-aesthetic matters like plot and emotional involvement have been based on the modern rediscovery of "aesthetic distance." After an unrestrained binge of romantic emotionalism and literal naturalism, authors began to discover, as the nineteenth century moved to an end, that in removing the various artificialities of earlier literature they had raised more problems than they had solved; it became more and more clear that if the gap between art and reality were ever fully closed, art would be destroyed. But it was not until this century that men began to take seriously the possibility that the power of artifice to keep us at a certain distance from reality could be a virtue rather than simply an inevitable obstacle to full realism. In 1912 Edward Bullough formulated the problem of what he called "psychic distance" as that of making sure that a work is neither "over-distanced" nor "under-distanced." If it is over-distanced, it will seem, he said, improbable, artificial, empty, or absurd, and we will not respond to it. Yet if it is "under-distanced," the work becomes too personal and cannot be enjoyed as art. For example, if a man who believes that he has reason to be jealous of his wife attends *Othello*, he will be moved too deeply and in a manner not properly aesthetic.[19] It is this second danger that was really an expression of something new in the air; when Bullough suggested that the artist should take steps to prevent under-distancing, he was in the vanguard of a great parade of authors and critics who have become enthusiastic for this or that "alienation effect," or who have deplored the common reader's demand that he should be deeply and emotionally involved in what he reads. Bertolt Brecht's effort to produce plays "of a non-Aristotelian kind," "plays which are not based on empathy," is only an extreme form of what many artists have sought, in their effort to break the bond with tyrannical reality.[20]

The emphasis on the need for control of distance is obviously sound. But the novelist will find himself in difficulties if he tries to discover some ideal distance that all works ought to seek. "Aesthetic distance" is in fact many different effects, some of them quite inappropriate to some kinds of works. More important, distance is never an end in itself; distance along one axis is sought for the sake of increasing the reader's involvement on some other axis. When Chikamatsu, for example, urges that poets avoid all emotional epithets, he does so in order to increase the emotional effect in the reader. "I take pathos to be entirely a matter of restraint. . . . It is essential that one not say of a thing that 'it is sad,' but that it be sad of itself."[21] When Brecht, on the other hand, asks for a "pervading coolness" (p. 71), he may seem at first to desire an increase in distance of all kinds. But what he really wants is to increase the emotional distance in order to involve the reader's social judgment more deeply.

The closer we look at the concept of distance the more complicated it appears. Of course, if we were content to see all literature as aspiring to one kind of involvement and one kind only – a sense of realism, an ecstatic contemplation of pure form, or whatever – we could feel comfortable about seeking one kind of distance as well. Each critic could then offer his formula and try to convert readers to it: As much realism as possible, but enough distance from reality to preserve a sense of form; As close to pure form as possible, with only so much of impurities like plot as cannot be done without; and so on. But is our experience with actual works ever as simple as this approach suggests? Every literary work of any power – whether or not its author composed it with his audience in mind – is in fact an elaborate system of controls over the reader's involvement and detachment along *various* lines of interest. The author is limited only by the range of human interests.

Resisting, then, the natural temptation to substitute my own universal rules about which interests should be heightened and which suppressed to make the greatest literature, I must develop here an elementary – and perhaps to some readers rather obvious – catalogue of the interests that novelists have, in fact rather than in theory, played upon in constructing their works. Once the catalogue is completed, we may still be convinced that one type of interest is far superior to all others, but even so our legislations in its favor should be based on a fairly comprehensive look at the range of interests or appetites[22] which our rules would forbid. The various kinds of purge – whether of unrealistic author's voice, of impure human emotions, or of the moral judgments which help to produce them – can be understood only in the context of what cannot be purged: some kind of interest that will grasp and sustain the reader throughout the work.

In setting up interest as a general criterion, I am aware of indulging in what may look like the apriorism that I have criticized. Why must all works be interesting? And interesting to whom? Cannot a work be simply "true" or "expressive" or "finely composed" – with the reader left to make of it what he can? To answer these questions properly would lead me far afield. Perhaps it will be sufficient to say here that *interest* is dictated to me by the nature of my topic: if I am to deal with literature as it affects readers, some kind of interest will always be central. Different general values would be dictated if I were trying to deal with works as reflections of reality, in which case truth would probably be my over-all term; or as expressions of the author's mind or soul, in which case some general term like sincerity or expressiveness might be central; or, finally, as realizations of formal excellence, in which case general terms like coherence, complexity, unity, or harmony would prove central. Literary works are, in fact, all of these things; one's choice of which aspect to emphasize is largely determined by the kind of question one wants to answer. What is more, there are unavoidable limitations in any one choice, as Abrams has shown so persuasively in *The Mirror and the Lamp.* There are also dangers and temptations that are avoidable – but only by the critic who can resist imposing his general commitment arbitrarily upon the rich variety of actual authors, works, and audiences. Whether I have done so in what follows is not, unfortunately, a question I can settle simply by laying my hand on my heart and swearing that I have tried.

Types of Literary Interest (and Distance)

The values which interest us, and which are thus available for technical manipulation in fiction, may be roughly divided into three kinds. (1) Intellectual or cognitive: We have, or can be made to have, strong intellectual curiosity about "the facts," the true interpretation, the true reasons, the true origins, the true motives, or the truth about life itself. (2) Qualitative: We have, or can be made to have, a strong desire to see any pattern or form completed, or to experience a further development of qualities of any kind. We might call this kind "aesthetic," if to do so did not suggest that a literary form using this interest was necessarily of more artistic value than one based on other interests. (3) Practical: We have, or can be made to have, a strong desire for the success or failure of those we love or hate, admire or detest; or we can be made to hope for or fear a change in the quality of a character. We might call this kind "human," if to do so did not imply that 1 and 2 were somehow less than human. This hope or fear may be for an intellectual change in a character or for a change in his fortune; one finds this practical aspect even in the most uncompromising novel of ideas that might seem to fall entirely under 1. Our desire may, second, be for a change of quality in a character; one finds this practical aspect even in the purely "aesthetic" novel of sensibility that might seem to fall entirely under 2. Finally, our desire may be for a moral change in a character, or for a change in his fortune – that is, we can be made to hope for or to fear particular moral choices and their results.

Intellectual interests. – We always want to find out the facts of the case, whether the simple material circumstances, as in most mystery stories, or psychological or philosophical truths which explain the external circumstances. Even in so-called plotless works we are pulled forward by the desire to discover the truth about the world of the book. In works relying heavily on this interest, we know that the book is completed when we once see the complete picture. In Hermann Hesse's *Siddhartha*, for example, our major interest is in Siddhartha's quest for the truth about how a man should live. If we do not think that the question of how a man should live is important, or that this author's insights on the question are likely to prove valuable, we can never care very much for this novel, even though we may enjoy some of the lesser pleasures offered by it. In many serious modern novels we look for an answer to the question, "What do these lives *mean*?" In others we look for completed patterns of theme, image, or symbol.

Very few imaginative works, however, rely entirely on a desire for intellectual completion. The pure literary forms that belong properly to this kind of suspense are the philosophical treatise which arouses our curiosity about an important question and the purely ratiocinative detective novel.

Completion of qualities. – Most imaginative works, even those of a kind that might seem to be cognitive or didactic in the sense of being built only on speculative or intellectual interests, rely in part on interests very different from intellectual curiosity; they make us desire a quality. Though some of the qualities which some works provide are often discussed under cognitive terms like "truth" and "knowledge," clearly the satisfaction we receive from the following qualities is to some degree distinct from the pleasure of learning.

(a) *Cause-effect*. – When we see a causal chain started, we demand – and demand in a way that is only indirectly related to mere curiosity – to see the result. Emma meddles, Tess is seduced, Huck runs away – and we demand certain consequences. This kind of sequence, so strongly stressed by Aristotle in his discussion of plot, is, as we have seen, often underplayed or even deplored by modern critics and novelists. Yet our desire for causal completion is one of the strongest of interests available to the author. Not only do we believe that certain causes do in life produce certain effects; in literature we believe that they should. Consequently, we ordinary readers will go to great lengths, once we have been caught up by an author who knows how to make use of this interest, to find out whether our demands will be met.

The suspension from cause to effect is of course closely related, on the one hand, to curiosity – that is, to a cognitive interest; we know that whatever fulfilment of our expectations we are given will be given with a difference, and we are inevitably curious about what the difference will be. All good works surprise us, and they surprise us largely by bringing to our attention convincing cause-and-effect patterns which were earlier played down. We can predict that disaster will result from Achilles' anger; we could never predict the generosity to Priam as a crucial part of the "disaster," even though when it comes it can be seen to follow properly as a result from other causes in Achilles' nature and situation.

On the other hand, this interest is easily confused with practical interests, which are described below. It is qualitative, nonetheless, because it operates quite independently of our interests in the welfare of human beings. In fact it can conflict with those interests. The hero commits a crime – and we are torn between our appetite for the proper effect, discovery and punishment, and our practical desire for his happiness.

(b) *Conventional expectations.* – For experienced readers a sonnet begun calls for a sonnet concluded; an elegy begun in blank verse calls for an elegy completed in blank verse. Even so amorphous a genre as the novel, with hardly any established conventions, makes use of this kind of interest: when I begin what I think is a novel, I expect to read a novel throughout, unless the author can, like Sterne, transform my idea of what a novel can be.

We seem to be able to accept almost anything as a literary convention, no matter how inherently improbable. Even the most outlandish of mannerisms, like Euphuism or Finneganswakism, can perform the essential task of maintaining our sense of the artistic integrity of *this work* as distinct from all others and as distinct from life. Again, authors may surprise us by violating conventions, but only so long as conventional expectations are available in a given public to be played upon. When everyone prides himself on violating conventions, there is nothing left to violate; the fewer the conventions the fewer the surprises.

(c) *Abstract forms.* – There seems to lie behind each convention some more general pattern of desires and gratifications that it serves. Balance, symmetry, climax, repetition, contrast, comparison – some pattern derived from our experience is probably imitated by every successful convention. The conventions which continue to give pleasure when they are no longer fashionable are based on patterns of reaction that lie very deep. Fashions in verse form come and go, for example, but meter and rhyme and the other musical devices of poetry do not lose their importance.

With the surrender of verse, and with no conventional agreement whatever about what is good narrative prose style, writers of longer narratives have been forced to engage in a constant search for new ways of giving body to abstract forms.

(d) *"Promised" qualities.* – In addition to these qualities, common to many works, each work promises in its early pages a further provision of distinctive qualities exhibited in those pages. Whether the quality is a peculiar stylistic or symbolic brilliance, an original kind of wit, a unique sublimity, irony, ambiguity, illusion of reality, profundity, or convincing character portrayal, there is an implied promise of more to come.

Our interest in these qualities may be static; we do not hope for or find a change in the quality but simply move forward looking for more of the same. Some good works rely heavily on this kind of interest (Montaigne's *Essays*, Burton's *Anatomy of Melancholy*, collections of table talk and facetiae, modern novels of stylistic experimentation like Gertrude Stein's *Melanctha*). Many of the realistic and naturalistic novels which were once popular and which now seem tedious relied somewhat too heavily on the sustained appeal of what was often called truth. Reading for the first time a novel dealing in the new vivid way with any new subject matter – whether the social reality about prostitution, slums, or the wheat market or the psychological reality about Irish Jews or American psychopaths – many readers were so fascinated by the new sense of reality, quite aside from the appeal of the facts as information, that little else was needed to carry them through to the end. But once this quality had become common, its appeal faded. Now that most commercial writers know how to portray violent physical reality, for example, with a vividness that would at one time have established an international reputation, only those novels which provide something more than physical reality survive.

The same danger threatens interest in any technique, even when the inherently more interesting procedure is adopted of providing some progressive change in the quality. Following James's masterful explorations of what "composition" could do for the novel, it was easy to believe that the reader's interest in technique was an adequate substitute for other interests, rather than at best a useful adjunct and at worst a harmful distraction. And some novels were written which encouraged this interest. When James and his eleven colleagues wrote *The Whole Family: A Novel by Twelve Authors* (1908), each author writing one chapter, each chapter using a different central intelligence to throw a different light on the events, no reader could help being mainly interested in the point of view rather than in what the point of view revealed: "I wonder what James will make of *his* chapter?"[23] But even with this much "suspense" introduced, interest in technique alone is likely to prove trivial.

Practical interests. – If we look closely at our reactions to most great novels, we discover that we feel a strong concern for the characters as people; we care about their good and bad fortune. In most works of any significance, we are made to admire or detest, to love or hate, or simply to approve or disapprove of at least one central character, and our interest in reading from page to page, like our judgment upon the book after reconsideration, is inseparable from this emotional involvement. We care, and care deeply, about Raskolnikov and Emma, about Father Goriot and Dorothea Brooke. Whatever happens to them, we wish them well. It is of course true that our desires concerning the fate of such imagined people differ markedly from our desires in real life. We will accept destruction of the man we love, in a literary work, if destruction is required to satisfy our other interests; we will take pleasure in combinations of hope and fear which in real life would be intolerable. But hope and fear are there, and the destruction or salvation is felt in a manner closely analogous to the feelings produced by such events in real life.

Any characteristic, mental, physical, or moral, which in real life will make me love or hate other men will work the same effect in fiction. But there is a large difference. Since we are not in a position to profit from or be harmed by a fictional character, our judgment is disinterested, even in a sense irresponsible. We can easily find our interests magnetized by characters who would be intolerable in real life. But the fact remains that what I am calling practical interests, and particularly moral qualities as inferred from characteristic choices or as stated directly by the author, have always been an important basis for literary form. Our interest in the fate of Oedipus and Lear, of David Copperfield and Richard Feverel, of Stephen Dedalus and Quentin Compson, springs in part from our conviction that they are people who matter, people whose fate concerns us not simply because of its meaning or quality, but because we care about them as human beings.

Such concerns are not simply a necessary but impure base, as Ortega would have it, to "make contemplation possible" but "with no aesthetic value or only a reflected or secondary one" (pp. 80, 76). In many first-rate works they are the very core of our experience. We may refuse assent when an author tries to manipulate us too obviously or cheaply with a casual bestowal of goodness or intellectual brilliance or beauty or charm. We all have use for epithets like "melodramatic" to apply against abuses of this kind. But this does not mean that human interest in itself is cheap. It is true that our involvement in the fate of Raskolnikov is not different in kind from the involvement sought by the most sentimental of novels. But in the great work we surrender our emotions for reasons that leave us with no regrets, no inclination to retract, after the immediate spell is past. They are, in fact, reasons which we should be ashamed *not* to respond to.

The best of these has always been the spectacle of a good man facing moral choices that are important. Our current neglect of moral terms like "good man" and "bad man" is really unfortunate if it leads us to overlook the role that moral judgment plays in most of our worthwhile reading. There is a story of the psychoanalyst who listened patiently and without judgment to the criminal self-revelations of his patient – until suddenly, as the patient was leaving, the analyst was filled with surprised revulsion. Try as we will to avoid terms like "moral" and "good" – and despite the mounting chorus against relativism, many still do try – we cannot avoid judging the characters we know as morally admirable or contemptible, any more than we can avoid judgments on their intellectual ability. We may tell ourselves that we do not condemn stupidity and viciousness, but we believe that men ought not to be stupid and vicious nonetheless. We may explain the villain's behavior by relating him to his environment, but even to explain away is to admit that something requires excuse.

Actually, there has been less of a retreat from moral judgment than appears on the surface, because of the shift, in modern fiction, to new terms for goodness and wickedness. Modern literature is in fact full of conventionally "virtuous" villains, fatally flawed by their blind adherence to outmoded norms, or by their intolerance of true but unconventional goodness (the missionaries in Maugham's "Rain," the "quiet American" in Greene's novel). Perhaps the prototype is Huck Finn's Miss Watson, who is determined to "live so as to go to the good place." It is easy for the author to make us agree with Huck, who "couldn't see no advantage in going where she was going, so I made up my mind I wouldn't try for it." But few have ever made the mistake of thinking that Huck has repudiated virtue in repudiating Miss Watson's idea of virtue.

Much of what looks like purely aesthetic or intellectual quality in a character may in fact have a moral dimension that is highly effective, though never openly acknowledged between author and reader. When compared with Dickens, for example, James Joyce may seem explicitly amoral. Joyce's overt interests are entirely in matters of truth and beauty. Conventional moral judgments never occur in his books except in mockery. And yet the full force of *A Portrait of the Artist* depends on the essentially moral quality of Stephen's discovery of his artistic vocation and of his integrity in following where it leads. His repudiations of conventional morality – his refusal to enter the priesthood, his rejection of communion, his decision to become an exile – are in fact read as signs of aesthetic integrity – that is, of superior morality. Joyce would probably never call him a "good" boy, though later an older and mellower Joyce was willing to describe Bloom as "a good man," a "complete man."[24] For us Stephen is, in part, a good boy. His pursuit of his own vision is uncompromising; he is headed for Joyce's heaven.[25] We may pretend that we read Joyce objectively and disinterestedly, without the sentimental involvements required of us in Victorian fiction. But most of us would never get beyond page one if the novel were only a portrait of an aesthetic sensibility receiving its Joycean epiphanies.[26]

Whatever Joyce's intentions, for example, with such episodes as the cruel pandybatting of the innocent Stephen, Joyce clearly profits from our irresistible sympathy for the innocent victim. Once such sympathy is established, each succeeding episode is felt deeply, not simply contemplated. The Victorian hero often enough won our sympathies because his heart was in the right place. Many modern heroes win our allegiance because their aesthetic sensibilities will not be denied, or because they live life to the hilt, or simply because they are victims of their surroundings. This is indeed a shift of emphasis, but we should not let popular talk about the "affective fallacy" deceive us: the very structure of fiction and, hence, of our aesthetic apprehension of it is often built of such practical, and in themselves seemingly "non-aesthetic," materials.

Combinations and Conflicts of Interests

Since men do have strong intellectual, qualitative, and practical interests, there is no reason why great novels cannot be written relying primarily on any one kind. But it is clear that no great work is based on only one interest. Whenever a work tends toward an exclusive reliance on intellectual interests, on the contemplation of qualities, or on practical desires we all look for adjectives to whip the offender with; a mere "novel of ideas," a mere "desiccated form," a mere "tear-jerker" will offend all but the small handful of critics and authors who are momentarily absorbed in pushing one interest to the limit.[27] But it is a rare critic who can distinguish the novels that are really marred by narrowness from those "narrow" novels which, like Jane Austen's, develop a wide range of interests within a narrow social setting.

In any case, for good or ill, we all seem convinced that a novel or play which does justice to our interest in truth, in beauty, and in goodness is superior to even the most successful "novel of ideas," "well-made play," or "sentimental novel" – to name only a selection from the partialities that conventional labels describe. Our emotional concern in Shakespeare is firmly based on intellectual, qualitative, and moral interests. It is a serious mistake to talk as if this richness were simply a matter of stuffing in something for the pit and something else for the gallery. To separate the plot, the manifold qualitative pleasures (including the patterns of imagery and the rich bawdry), or the profound intellectual import and to erect one of the fragments as superior to the others is precisely what a direct experience of the plays teaches us not to do. We experience a miraculous unity of what might have remained dissociated but for Shakespeare's ability to involve our minds, hearts, and sensibilities simultaneously.

Another master of the same kind of richness is Dostoevski. In *Crime and Punishment* we experience a wide variety of intellectual appeals. We are curious about the philosophical and religious and political battle between nihilism and relativism on the one hand and salvation on the other. We are also simply curious about whether Porphyry will catch his mouse. We are curious about a thousand and one details that are resolved in the course of the work. Second, we are constantly titillated with qualitative hungers: we have seen the crime and we demand the punishment; we would like more of this remarkably profound use of dreams, and we are given more; we would like more of this skill in transforming disagreeable characters into sympathetic portraits, and Dostoevski does not disappoint us. Finally, our *practical* judgments and the resulting emotions are powerfully involved. We sympathize with Raskolnikov in a peculiarly intense fashion from beginning to end; we wish passionately, though without much hope, for his happiness, and we fear the very punishment which our interest in cause-and-effect patterns demands. We sympathize also with many others, particularly with Sonia. Those aesthetic frauds, tears and laughter, are prominent throughout, but we do not experience them as isolated, sentimental moments, divorced from our intellectual and aesthetic hungers and rewards.

So far, so good. It would be a mistake, however, to make a simple plea for authors to enrich their palettes, as if all appeals had to be in all works, the more the better. The danger is not so much that enough interests won't be packed in, but that pursuit of secondary interests may diminish interests that the author most desires. Even though most great works embody to some degree all three types of interest, some of the particular interests under each type are incompatible with each other and with some types of rhetoric. It was, in fact, a recognition of this incompatibility of interests that led to the notion that overt rhetoric, useful as it was in heightening some practical interests, hampered some qualitative interests, particularly the qualities of realism or purity. But there are other incompatibilities that have not been so fully described.

An author may want, for instance, to cultivate the reader's interest in the quality of ambiguity. He cannot do so, however, and at the same time convey the full intellectual pleasure of gratified curiosity or use fully the reader's moral and emotional interests. There is a pleasure in seeing someone whom we like triumph over difficulties and there is a pleasure in recognizing that life is so complex that no one ever triumphs unambiguously. Both pleasures cannot be realized to the full in the same work. If I am to rejoice, for example, in Stephen's flight into exile as the final sign of his growth into the true artist, I cannot at the same time delight fully in his creator's cleverness in leaving the meaning of that flight ambiguous; the more ambiguity the less triumph.

If he is clear about where his focus lies, a great artist can of course do some justice to the complexities of the world and still achieve a high degree of emotional involvement. Dostoevski, like Shakespeare, derives some of his pre-eminence from his ability to show what a murky business the moral world really is while still keeping the lines of our moral sympathies clear. His criminals remain deeply sympathetic because he knows, and makes us know, why they are criminals and why they are still sympathetic. Not genuine ambiguity, but rather complexity with clarity, seems to be his secret. If he were to leave the basic worth of Raskolnikov or Dmitri ambiguous, or if he were to leave us in doubt concerning Ivan's sincerity in his dialectic with Alyosha, we could never be moved as deeply as we are by their fate.

The real world is of course ambiguous. When my king goes to his doom, I am never sure whether to weep or cheer; or if I am sure, I find out soon that I may very well have been wrong. My true love turns out to have, not a heart of stone – as might very well have happened in the older fiction and drama – but a heart that leaves me baffled. Like myself, she is neither good nor bad, but a puzzling mixture. If literature is to deal realistically with life, then, must it not dwell on the neutral tones rather than the scarlets and deep sky blues? Yes – if verisimilitude and naturalness are more important than anything else. But high dramatic effects depend on heightening. Demigods, heroes, villains, poetic Othellos and Iagos – these are not realistic in the sense of being like our everyday reality. And, on the other hand, Maggie, the girl of the streets, will not appear as a queen, even potentially, if she is treated with strict realism; only if the narrator feels free to manipulate his materials in order to show what she might have been or how her fate is representative of a society – in short, why it is more significant than the disasters one reads about in today's paper – will we care about her with anything like the concern we grant willingly to the unrealistic Desdemona. A Joyce may provide enough other interests to be able to risk our question, "Who cares about the fate of Molly Bloom?" but what is Farrell to reply when I ask, "Who cares about the unheroic hero of *Gas-House McGinty*?"[28]

Similarly, if an author wishes to take me on a long quest for the truth and finally present it to me, I will feel the quest as a boring triviality unless he gives me unambiguous signs of what quest I am on and of the fact that I have found my goal when I get there; his private conviction that the question, the goal, and their importance are clear, or that clarity is unimportant, will not be sufficient. For his purposes a direct authorial comment, destroying the illusion that the story is telling itself, may be what will serve his desired effect rather than kill it.

There is a pleasure from learning the simple truth, and there is a pleasure from learning that the truth is not simple. Both are legitimate sources of literary effect, but they cannot both be realized to the full simultaneously. In this respect, as in all others, the artist must choose, consciously or unconsciously. To write one kind of book is always to some extent a repudiation of other kinds. And regardless of an author's professed indifference to the reader, every book carves out from mankind those readers for which its peculiar effects were designed.

The Role of Belief

With this broadened spectrum of interests in mind, we should now be in a somewhat more favorable position to consider the question of the author's and reader's beliefs. "Most contemporary students of literature would agree that a writer's ideas have as little to do with his artistic talent as his personal morals.... Not many people would agree with the views of man held by Homer, Dante, Baron Corvo, or Ezra Pound; but whether or not we agree with them should have little to do with whether or not we accept or reject their art." So writes Maurice Beebe, editor of *Modern Fiction Studies*,[29] expressing once more a position that has been repeated again and again since the famous claim by I. A. Richards that "we need no beliefs, and indeed we must have none, if we are to read *King Lear*."[30] On the other hand, the editor of a recent symposium on belief in literature finds common ground among all the participants in the conviction that literature "involves assumptions and beliefs and sympathies with which a large measure of concurrence is indispensable for the reading of literature as literature and not another thing."[31]

The seeming disagreement here is striking. But it is partly dissolved when we remember the distinction we have made between the real author and the implied author, the second self created in the work. The "views of man" of Faulkner and E. M. Forster, as they go about making their Stockholm addresses or writing their essays, are indeed of only peripheral value to me as I read their novels. But the implied author of each novel is someone with whose beliefs on all subjects I must largely agree if I am to enjoy his work. Of course, the same distinction must be made between myself as reader and the often very different self who goes about paying bills, repairing leaky faucets, and failing in generosity and wisdom. It is only as I read that I become the self whose beliefs must coincide with the author's. Regardless of my real beliefs and practices, I must subordinate my mind and heart to the book if I am to enjoy it to the full. The author creates, in short, an image of himself and another image of his reader; he makes his reader, as he makes his second self, and the most successful reading is one in which the created selves, author and reader, can find complete agreement.

This distinction, however, only partly dissolves the contradiction about the role of beliefs, because the divorce between my ordinary self and the selves I am willing to become as I read is not complete. Walker Gibson, in an excellent essay on "Authors, Speakers, Readers, and Mock Readers,"[32] says that the book we reject as bad is often simply a book in whose "mock reader we discover a person we refuse to become, a mask we refuse to put on, a role we will not play." We may exhort ourselves to read tolerantly, we may quote Coleridge on the willing suspension of disbelief until we think ourselves totally suspended in a relativistic universe, and still we will find many books which postulate readers we refuse to become, books that depend on "beliefs" or "attitudes" – the term we choose is unimportant here[33] – which we cannot adopt even hypothetically as our own.

We can see that from this standpoint the trouble I had with Lawrence's implied second self can equally well be described as my inability or refusal to take on the characteristics he requires of his "mock reader." Whatever may be said by Laurentians of the weaknesses in my own real character that might account for my refusal, I simply cannot read his polemic without smiling when I should be panting, scoffing when I should be feeling awe. Whether I should blame myself or Lawrence for this, I can never be quite sure. Perhaps we are both partly at fault. Even if I cannot resist blaming him, at least a little, it is difficult to know whether his failure to carry me along is a failure of craftsmanship or a fundamental incompatibility that no amount of craftsmanship could overcome. But it is impossible for me to conclude that incompatibility of beliefs is irrelevant to my judgment of Lawrence.

We cannot fully enjoy James's *Ambassadors*, for another example, if we insist as we read that spontaneity of consciousness must always be subordinated to the puritan conscience – if we refuse, that is, to entertain the implied author's values at something like his own estimate. Strether's discovery in Paris of what it means to *live* will be for us a fall rather than a triumph, and the book will be for us less effective. His discovery must seem a good thing, not just in his or James's views, in which we can take an interest, but in our own. And afterwards, if the book is to maintain our respect, if it is to be remembered as something more than a pleasant experience based on ephemeral trickery, we must be able to entertain the beliefs on which Strether's discovery is based as among the intellectually and morally defensible views of life. One of our most common reading experiences is, in fact, the discovery on reflection that we have allowed ourselves to become a "mock reader" whom we *cannot* respect, that the beliefs which we were temporarily manipulated into accepting cannot be defended in the light of day.

It is true, as Beebe reminds us, that we can read with pleasure the works of a great many authors, some of whose beliefs we reject: Dante, Milton, Hopkins, Yeats, Eliot, Pound – the list varies, of course, with the position of the critic. But is it really true that the serious Catholic or atheist, however sensitive, tolerant, diligent, and well-informed about Milton's beliefs he may be, enjoys *Paradise Lost* to the degree possible to one of Milton's contemporaries and co-believers, of equal intelligence and sensitivity? Can a devout Protestant or Jew who abhors clerical celibacy enjoy Hopkins' "The Habit of Perfection" as a devout Catholic of equal literary sensibility and experience enjoys it? We must be very clear that we are talking now about literary experience, not about the pleasures of finding one's prejudices echoed. The question is whether the enjoyment of literature as literature, and not as propaganda, inevitably involves our beliefs, and I think that the answer is inescapable. Anyone who has ever read the same novel "before and after," noticing that strange loss of power a novel betrays when one has repudiated its norms, whether of Church or Party, of faith in progress, nihilism, existentialism, or whatever, knows that our convictions even about the most purely intellectual matters cannot help fundamentally affecting our literary responses.

Purists may reply that, even though all readers do in fact allow their beliefs to get in the way of an objective view of the work, they should not do so. Which puts us right back where we started: if we want to deal with an ideal literature that has never existed on land or sea, and postulate an ideal reader who could never possibly exist, and then judge all books and all readers as they more or less approximate to this pure state, that is our privilege. But as the facts are, even the greatest of literature is radically dependent on the concurrence of beliefs of authors and readers. In an excellent discussion of this problem, M. H. Abrams says what would not need to be said at all if a generation of exhortation to "objectivity" had not led us astray:

> Is an appreciation of the Ode [on a Grecian Urn], then, entirely independent of the reader's beliefs? Surely not. As it evolves, the poem makes constant call on a complex of beliefs which are the product of ordinary human experiences with life, people, love, mutability, age, and art. These subsist less in propositional form than in the form of unverbalized attitudes...; but they stand ready to precipitate into assertions the moment they are radically challenged....If the poem works, our appreciation of the matters it

presents is not aloofly contemplative, but actively engaged.... We are interested in a fashion that brings into play our entire moral economy and expresses itself continuously in attitudes of approval or disapproval, sympathy or antipathy.[34]

This does not mean, of course, that Catholics cannot enjoy *Paradise Lost* more than they might a second-rate Catholic epic, or that Protestants cannot enjoy "The Habit of Perfection" more than they might a second-rate Protestant hymn. It means simply that differences of belief, even in the sense of abstract, speculative systems, are always to some extent relevant, often seriously hampering, and sometimes fatal. Imagine a beautifully written tragedy with a convinced Nazi SS man as hero, his tragic error consisting of a temporary, and fatal, toying with bourgeois democratic ideals. Is there any one of us, regardless of our commitment to objectivity, who could seriously claim that agreement or disagreement with the author's ideas in such a work would have nothing to do with our accepting or rejecting his art?

It is true that some great works seem to rise above differences of speculative system and to win readers of all camps. Shakespeare is the pre-eminent example. The norms in his plays are indeed compatible with more philosophies than are comprehended in most of our dogmas; it is precisely this centrality, this lack of bias, this capacity to cut to the heart of problems which all philosophies attempt to deal with in conceptual terms, that makes his plays what we call universal. Great art can bring men of different convictions together by translating, as it were, their different vocabularies into a tangible experience that incorporates what they mean. It thus mediates among philosophies: Platonist and Aristotelian, Catholic and Protestant, liberal and conservative, can agree that these lives are comic and those tragic, that this behavior is vicious and that admirable, that somehow, in fact, these plays express existentially, as the current fashion puts it, what life means.

But this is far from saying that great literature is compatible with *all* beliefs. Though Shakespeare seems, when looked at superficially, to "have no beliefs," though it is indeed impossible to extract from the plays any one coherent philosophical or religious or political formulation that will satisfy all readers, it is not difficult to list innumerable norms which we must accept if we are to comprehend particular plays, and some of these do run throughout his works. It is true that these beliefs are for the most part self-evident, even commonplace – but that is precisely because they are acceptable to most of us. Shakespeare requires us to believe that it is right to honor our fathers, and that it is wrong to kill off old men like Lear or grind out the eyes of old men like Gloucester. He insists that it is always wrong to use other people as instruments to one's own ends, whether by murder or slander, that it is good to love, but wrong to love selfishly, that helpless old age is pitiable, and that blind egotism deserves punishment. He never lets us forget that the world is made up of good and evil in very strange and frightening mixtures or that suffering is an essential part of the world's constitution, but he also remembers that it can produce a ripeness which in a sense justifies all: in his plays, suffering, like everything else, makes a kind of sense in an ordered universe. Such a list of persistent norms is surprisingly similar to the norms derived from other really great authors, as well as those found in many very mediocre ones. Certainly, to work in accordance with such universals is not enough to make an author great. But to accept them in the works where they are pertinent is a fundamental step before greatness can be experienced.

We seldom talk in these terms about great literature only because we take them for granted or because they seem old-fashioned.[35] Only a maniac, presumably, would side with Goneril and Regan against Lear. It is only when a work seems explicitly doctrinaire, or when reasonable men can be in serious disagreement about its values, that the question of belief arises for discussion. Even when it does arise, it is often misleading if we think of beliefs in terms of speculative theories. The great "Catholic" or "Protestant" works are not, in their essentials, Catholic or Protestant at all. Even though a Catholic may be presumed to derive additional pleasures and insights not available to the non-Catholic in reading Mauriac's *Knot of Vipers*, the picture it gives of a man made miserable through his own spiritual confusion depends for its effect on values common to most views of man's fate. Any reader who believes that human misery is pitiable and that to feel constant envy and fear and mistrust is to be miserable must pity this man. Anyone who believes that it is good, or important, for a miserable, loveless man to find some repentance and love, however slight, before he dies, cannot help responding to this conclusion. The non-Catholic reader's lack of concern over whether the protagonist will receive extreme unction – a problem that plays a minor role in the book – will no doubt reduce his response to some degree. But the knot of vipers gnaws as excruciatingly for an unbeliever as for the most orthodox reader.

Although such universals inevitably operate to some extent in all successful literature, it is true that most works whose authors have asked the reader to be "objective" have in fact depended strongly on the substitution of unconventional or private values – often in modern criticism called "myths" – for more conventional or public standards. Far from asking for objectivity, their authors have really asked for commitment on an unusual axis. The strangeness of much modern literature when it is first encountered comes in large part from this substitution – often unacknowledged and unsupported by any clarification or intensification – of a new and peculiar scale of norms for the old.

Thus the "novel of sensibility," as written by Virginia Woolf and others, deliberately rejected most of the values on which the effects of older fiction were based. In *To the Lighthouse* there is little effort to engage our feelings strongly for or against one or more characters on the basis of their moral or intellectual traits. Instead, the value of "sensibility" has been placed at the core of things; those characters who, like Mrs. Ramsey, have a highly developed sensibility are sympathetic; the "villains" are those who, like Mr. Ramsey, are insensitive. We read forward almost as much to discover further instances of sensibility as to discover what happens to the characters. The revelation of the whole, such as it is, is of the overall *feeling* rather than the meaning of events.[36] But this, of course, does not mean that belief is irrelevant. The reader who does not value sensibility as highly as Virginia Woolf will fail to enjoy much of her work unless he is persuaded by it, as he reads, to shift his judgment.

Similarly, if I say to myself, as I read *Ulysses*, "Bloom is a bad man because he masturbates in public," or "Camus' Stranger is wicked because he commits murder," I am obviously barred from any complete experience of *Ulysses* or *The Stranger*. It is true, I think, that moral values of another kind are in operation in both works.[37] But it is also true that neither Joyce nor Camus cares very much whether his characters are good in any sense of the word except the author's own. On the other hand, in the later works of Tolstoy, the chief value is a narrowly moral one; a host of beliefs that one must accept to read Joyce or Camus, Faulkner or Hemingway properly are not only ignored but actively combated by the rhetoric of a story like "Where Love Is, God Is Also."

The problem for the reader is thus really that of discovering which values are in abeyance and which are genuinely, though in modern works often surreptitiously, at work. To pass judgment where the author intends neutrality is to misread. But to be neutral or objective where the author requires commitment is equally to misread, though the effect is likely to be less obvious and may even be overlooked except as a feeling of boredom. At the beginning of the modern period, no doubt the danger of dogmatic overjudgment was the greater one. But for at least two decades now, I am convinced, far more misreading has resulted from what I can only call dogmatic neutrality.

* * *

The Morality of Impersonal Narration

The Morality of Elitism

We have noted that many of the works in the unreliable mode depend for their effects on ironic collusion between the author and his readers. The line between such effects legitimately pursued and the pleasures of snobbery is difficult to draw, but impersonal, ironic narration lends itself neatly, far too neatly, to disguised expressions of snobbery which would never be tolerated if expressed openly in commentary. Chesterton once attributed part of the decline of Dickens' popularity to "that basest of all artistic indulgences (certainly far baser than the pleasure of absinthe or the pleasure of opium), the pleasure of appreciating works of art which ordinary men cannot appreciate."[38] Even baser would be the pleasure of writing works *so that* only the select few can understand. The author who sets out to appeal by his impersonality to "the most alert young people of two successive generations – in Berlin, Paris, London, New York, Rome, Madrid," regardless of the needs of the work in hand, is as inartistic as the author who plants irrelevant appeals to the prejudices of the buying public.

We do not judge the finished work, of course, according to the motives of the author. But the prohibition works both ways: If I cannot condemn a work simply because I know that its author was a snob, neither can I praise it simply because its author refused to be commercial, or condemn another because its author set out to write a best seller. The work itself must be our standard, and if the reader can see no reason for its difficulties except that critical fashion dictates an anti-commercial pose, he is bound to condemn it fully as much as he would if he discovered cheap appeals to temporary prejudices in a popular audience. In both cases the test is whether everything has been done that ought to be done – nothing more, nothing less – to make the work fundamentally accessible, realized in the basic etymological sense of being made into a thing that has its own existence, no longer tied to the author's ego. And if it was the peculiar temptation of Victorian novelists to give a false air of sentimental comradeship through their commentary, impersonal novelists are strongly tempted to give the reader less help than they know they should, in order to make sure that they are seen to be "serious."

A frequent explanation of the snobbish air that sometimes results is that there is no serious audience left for art except the precious, saving remnant. Virginia Woolf, for example, was haunted by the sense that older writers could depend upon an audience with public norms, while she must construct her private values as she went, and then impose them, without seeming to do so, on the reader. Neither Austen nor Scott, she says, has much to say about the matter of judgment of conduct outright, "but everything depends on it.... To believe that your impressions hold good for others is to be released from the cramp and confinement of personality."[39] We are told again and again that the novelist could not help turning inward to his own private world of values because there was no outer world left to which he could appeal.[40] But even if consensus has declined – something in itself hard to prove, in spite of our ready clichés about it – surely artists must accept some of the responsibility for the decline themselves. If the loss of consensus forced them into private value systems, private myths, it hardly could be said to have forced them into the kind of private techniques I have discussed in the latter part of this book. One possible reaction to a fragmented society may be to retreat to a private world of values, but another might well be to build works of art that themselves help to mold a new consensus.[41]

There have been philosophical and psychological obstacles to facing the presumed decline of consensus in this positive way. The philosophical obstacle at its most destructive is nihilism, with the temptations to subjectivism or even solipsism that it always brings in its train. If the novelist really believes that there is no objective meaning to existence, then his only motive for writing is that he wants to write – a motive that is no better and no worse in the ultimate scheme than would be the motive of a Hitler, or, let us say, of a scrawler of graffiti. To worry about the reader would be absurd in a genuinely absurd universe.

Most so-called nihilisms stop far short, however, of this complete negation; almost all writers think there is some meaning, at least in the act of artistic creation. The more common philosophical assumption of unphilosophical writers since Kant has been a kind of subjective art-ism: there is value, but it is only what the artist creates out of the chaos.

Now it is possible, I think, to derive even from such a position inescapable arguments in favor of the artist's making an effort to communicate his vision. But often enough it has been used in defense of an aesthetic solipsism almost as radical as would be dictated by nihilism. Dujardin, whom Joyce claimed as the father of stream-of-consciousness technique, said that "the whole of reality consists in the clear or confused consciousness one has of it." And he quotes Joyce with approval as saying that "the soul, in one sense, is all there is."[42]

Even this position might be extended to require of the author that he do everything possible to make his consciousness of reality clear, not simply to "himself" but to that part of himself which lives in relation to a public; if a work is really clear to the author-as-reader, we might argue, it will be accessible to his proper public. But in practice it has tended to produce a pose of indifference to all readers. We need not be philistines to believe that even the purest of artists can be victimized by human pride, and we must be blind devotees of modern literature indeed to ignore the destructive, though often amusing, cultism that has marked discussions of certain novelists since Joyce.

It is hard to see how anything can be done about such a situation short of rejecting the subjectivism on which it is based. Though I cannot argue the case philosophically here, it seems clear that this one aspect of our rhetorical difficulties cannot be corrected simply by working for more intelligent discrimination in readers. The author himself must achieve a kind of objectivity far more difficult and far more profound than the "objectivity" of surface hailed in many discussions of technique. He must first plumb to universal values about which his readers can really care. But it is not enough, I suspect, that he operate on some kind of eternal ground, as recommended by our religious critics.[43] He must be sufficiently humble to seek for ways to help the reader to accept his view of that ground. The artist must in this sense be willing to be both a seer and a revelator; though he need not attempt to discover new truths in the manner of the prophet-novelists like Mann and Kafka, and though he certainly need not include explicit statement of the norms on which his work is based, he must know how to transform his private vision, made up as it often is of ego-ridden private symbols, into something that is essentially public.

It is at this point that the philosophical problem becomes a psychological problem. The artist must, like all men, wrestle constantly with the temptation of false pride. Hard as it may be for him to accept the fact, his private vision of things is not great art simply through being his. It is made into great art, if at all, only by being given an objective existence of its own — that is, by being made accessible to a public.

But of course as soon as the vision is made accessible, it subjects itself to being judged; one of the nicest of ironies is that of the writer who loses more and more stature the better we understand him, because the better we understand him the more of his egotistical weakness we see untransformed in the work.

In short, the writer should worry less about whether his *narrators* are realistic than about whether the *image he creates of himself*, his implied author, is one that his most intelligent and perceptive readers can admire. Nothing will so certainly consign a work to ultimate oblivion as an implied author who detests his readers[44] or who thinks that his work is better than it is. And nothing is so certain to lead an author into creating such a picture of himself as the effort to appear brighter, more esoteric, less commercial than he really is. The convenient but ultimately ridiculous notions that all concessions to the public are equally base, that the public itself is base, and that the author himself is not a member of "the public," can be as harmful as the desire to become a best seller at all costs.

The ultimate problem in the rhetoric of fiction is, then, that of deciding for whom the author should write. We saw earlier that to answer, "He writes for himself," makes sense only if we assume that the self he writes for is a kind of public self, subject to the limitations that other men are subject to when they come to his books. Another answer often given is that he writes for his peers. True enough. The hack is, by definition, the man who asks for responses he cannot himself respect. But no one is ever the peer of any author in the sense of needing no help in viewing the author's world. If the novelist waits passively on his pedestal for the occasional peer whose perceptions are already in

WAYNE C. BOOTH

harmony with his own, then it is hard to see why he should not leave everything to such readers. Why bother to write at all? If the reader were really the artist's peer in this sense, he would not need the book. In a world made up of such readers, we could stop worrying about the problem of communication entirely and simply write each his own books. But if such a world is recognized as ridiculous, however close it may seem to some of the facts of our present one, then the novelist cannot be excused from providing the judgment upon his own materials which alone can lift them from being what Faulkner has called the mere "record of man" and turn them into the "pillars" that can help him be fully man. We may scoff at the southern gentleman's rhetoric in the Stockholm address, but the greatest living novelist means – for once – what he says.

Since the war we have seen many pleas for a return to the older, pre-Flaubertian models, not only in the matter of point of view but in the general structure and interests built into the novel.[45] The false restrictions imposed by various forms of objectivity have been attacked frequently, sometimes with great acumen based on personal experience in writing novels. But it would be a serious mistake to think that what we need is a return to Balzac, or to the English nineteenth century, or to Fielding and Jane Austen. We can be sure that traditional techniques will find new uses, just as the epistolary technique, declared dead many times over, has been revived to excellent effect again and again.[46] But what is needed is not any simple restoration of previous models, but a repudiation of all arbitrary distinctions among "pure form," "moral content," and the rhetorical means of realizing for the reader the union of form and matter. When human actions are formed to make an art work, the form that is made can never be divorced from the human meanings, including the moral judgments, that are implicit whenever human beings act. And nothing the writer does can be finally understood in isolation from his effort to make it all accessible to someone else – his peers, himself as imagined reader, his audience. The novel comes into existence as something communicable, and the means of communication are not shameful intrusions unless they are made with shameful ineptitude.

The author makes his readers. If he makes them badly – that is, if he simply waits, in all purity, for the occasional reader whose perceptions and norms happen to match his own, then his conception must be lofty indeed if we are to forgive him for his bad craftsmanship. But if he makes them well – that is, makes them see what they have never seen before, moves them into a new order of perception and experience altogether – he finds his reward in the peers he has created.

NOTES

1   Forster would not allow the author to take "the reader into his confidence about his charac-
    ters," since "intimacy is gained but at the expense of illusion and nobility." But he allows the
    author to take the reader into his confidence "about the universe" (*Aspects of the Novel* [London,
    1927], pp. 111–12).

2   *Madame Bovary*, trans. Francis Steegmuller (New York, 1957), p. 80.

3   Such obtrusions are especially obvious in narration that purports to be historical. And yet
    intelligent men were until quite recently able to read ostensibly historical accounts, like the
    Bible, packed with such illicit entries into private minds, with no distress whatever. For us it

may seem strange that the writers of the Gospels should claim so much knowledge of what Christ is feeling and thinking. "Moved with pity, he stretched out his hand and touched him" (Mark 1:41). "And Jesus, perceiving in himself that power had gone forth from him..." (5:30). Who reported to the authors these internal events? Who told them what occurs in the Garden, when everyone but Jesus is asleep? Who reported to them that Christ prays to God to "let this cup pass"? Such questions, like the question of how Moses could have written an account of his own death and burial, may be indispensable in historical criticism, but they can easily be overdone in literary criticism.

4   Speaking of Joyce's *Ulysses*, Edmund Wilson once complained that as soon as "we are aware of Joyce himself systematically embroidering on his text," packing in puzzles, symbols, and puns, "the illusion of the dream is lost" ("James Joyce," *Axel's Castle* [New York, 1931], p. 235).

5   "Situation of the Writer in 1947," *What Is Literature?* trans. Bernard Frechtman (London, 1950), p. 169.

6   "Conversations with Eckerman," January 29, 1826, trans. John Oxenford, as reprinted in *Criticism: The Major Texts*, ed. Walter Jackson Bate (New York, 1952), p. 403.

7   Letter to Richard Woodhouse, October 27, 1818, *The Poetical Works and Other Writings of John Keats*, ed. H. Buxton Forman (New York, 1939), VII, 129.

8   *Correspondence* (October 12, 1853) (Paris, 1926–33), III, 367–68. For some of the citations from Flaubert in what follows I am indebted to the excellent monograph by Marianne Bonwit, *Gustave Flaubert et le principe d'impassibilité* (Berkeley, Calif., 1950). My distinction among the three forms of objectivity in the author is derived in part from her discussion.

9   Ibid. (December 12, 1857), IV, 243.

10   *Letters on the Short Story, the Drama and other Literary Topics*, selected and edited by Louis S. Friedland (New York, 1924), p. 63.

11   *Corr.* (April 26–27, 1853), III, 183: "...ne doit avoir ni religion, ni patrie, ni même aucune conviction sociale...."

12   "The Slave Cast Out," in *The Living Novel*, ed. Granville Hicks (New York, 1957), p. 202. Miss West continues: "Writing is a way of playing parts, of trying on masks, of assuming roles, not for fun but out of desperate need, not for the self's sake but for the writing's sake. 'To make any work of art,' says Elizabeth Sewell, 'is to make, or rather to unmake and remake one's self.'"

13   In her inaugural lecture at the University of London, published as *The Tale and the Teller* (London, 1959). "Writing on George Eliot in 1877, Dowden said that the form that most persists in the mind after reading her novels is not any of the characters, but 'one who, if not the real George Eliot, is that second self who writes her books, and lives and speaks through them.' The 'second self,' he goes on, is 'more substantial than any mere human personality' and has 'fewer reserves'; while 'behind it, lurks well pleased the veritable historical self secure from impertinent observation and criticism'" (p. 22).

14   E.g., Fred B. Millett, *Reading Fiction* (New York, 1950): "This tone, the general feeling which suffuses and surrounds the work, arises ultimately out of the writer's attitude toward his subject.... *The subject derives its meaning from the view of life which the author has taken*" (p. 11).

15   "When we speak of technique, then, we speak of nearly everything. For technique is the means by which the writer's experience, which is his subject matter, compels him to attend to it; technique is the only means he has of discovering, exploring, developing his subject, of conveying its meaning, and finally of evaluating it.... Technique in fiction is, of course, all those obvious forms of it which are usually taken to be the whole of it, and many others" ("Technique as Discovery," *Hudson Review*, I [Spring, 1948], 67–87, as reprinted in *Forms of Modern Fiction*, ed. Wm. Van O'Connor [Minneapolis, Minn., 1948], pp. 9–29; see esp. pp. 9–11).

16 *The English Novel* (London, 1930), p. 58. See Geoffrey Tillotson, *Thackeray the Novelist* (Cambridge, 1954), esp. chap. iv, "The Content of the Authorial 'I'" (pp. 55–70), for a convincing argument that the "I" of Thackeray's works should be carefully distinguished from Thackeray himself.

17 "Qu'est qui me dira, en effet ce que Shakespeare a aimé, ce qu'il a haï, ce qu'il a senti?" (Corr., I, 386).

18 Vladimir Nabokov, *Laughter in the Dark* (New York, 1938), p. 1.

19 "'Psychical Distance' as a Factor in Art and an Aesthetic Principle," *British Journal of Psychology*, V (1912), 87–98, as reprinted in *The Problems of Aesthetics*, ed. Eliseo Vivas and Murray Krieger (New York, 1953), pp. 396–405.

20 See, for example, Brecht's "Chinese Acting," trans. Eric Bentley, in *Furioso* (Fall, 1949). A history should be written of the concept of aesthetic distance. One element in such a history would be the growing knowledge, early in the century, of oriental literature, with its extremely unrealistic setting, costumes, and acting manners. Donald Keene shows some similarities between anti-realist theories of the eighteenth-century puppet dramatist, Chika-matsu, and certain western theories, beginning with the Imagists (*Japanese Literature* [London, 1953], esp. chap. iii). Brecht's so-called epic theatre, with its emphasis on unrealistic "alienation effects," is explicitly patterned upon certain effects in the Chinese theatre. "In the Chinese theatre," Brecht says, "the alienation effect is achieved in the following way. The Chinese performer does not act as if, in addition to the three walls around him, there were also a fourth wall. *He makes it clear that he knows he is being looked at.... The actor looks at himself*" (p. 69). But such external influences by no means account for the readiness with which serious artists pursued the very sense of distance which the preceding generations had struggled to overcome.

21 Keene, *Japanese Literature*, p. 8.

22 See Kenneth Burke, "Psychology and Form," *Counter-Statement* (Los Altos, Calif., 1953), p. 31. Readers who know Burke's *Lexicon Rhetoricae* will notice in my threefold classification as I develop it below some similarities to his "five aspects of form": syllogistic progression, qualitative progression, repetitive form, conventional form, and minor or incidental forms. But I am classifying interests, not forms; forms are almost always built upon several interests.

23 See also *The Affair at the Inn* (London, 1904) by Kate Douglas Wiggin, Mary Findlater, Jane Findlater, Allan McAuley. Each author "did" one character. Protests against this tendency to let interest in the quality of the telling replace interest in what is told can be found throughout modern criticism. Beach claimed that the net effect of *The Awkward Age* depended too much on "the recognition of the author's cleverness" (*The Method of Henry James* [New Haven, Conn., 1918; Philadelphia, 1954], p. 249). David Daiches finds that the pleasure in Virginia Woolf's *The Years* "derives more from a recognition of virtuosity, let us say, than from our complete domination by the novel as an integrated work of art"; though he tries to allow for the former recognition as a legitimate literary pleasure, it is clear that for him it is inferior to what is really "an integrated work of art" (*Virginia Woolf* [Norfolk, Conn., 1942], p. 120).

Compare Faulkner's complaint about Sherwood Anderson: "His was that fumbling for exactitude, the exact word and phrase within the limited scope of a vocabulary controlled and even repressed by what was in him almost a fetish of simplicity, to milk them both dry, to seek always to penetrate to thought's uttermost end. He worked so hard at this that it finally became just style: an end instead of a means: so that he presently came to believe that, provided he kept the style pure and intact and unchanged and inviolate, what the style contained would have to be first rate: it couldn't help but be first rate, and therefore himself too" (*Atlantic Monthly* [June, 1953], p. 28).

24 Quoted from Frank Budgen in R. Ellmann, *James Joyce* (New York, 1959), p. 449.

25 For a contrary view, see Caroline Gordon, *How To Read a Novel* (New York, 1957), p. 213. For a convincing argument that Joyce is interested in moral satire, not simply in aesthetic values,

see Lawrance Thompson, *A Comic Principle in Sterne – Meredith – Joyce* (Oslo, 1954). "There's moral indignation, even though both Stuart Gilbert and David Daiches insist that Joyce's concern is not moral, only aesthetic" (p. 26). See also Joyce's letter to Grant Richards about *Dubliners*, "My intent was to write a chapter of the moral history of my country, and I chose Dublin for the scene, because that city seemed to be the center of paralysis…" (quoted in Thompson, p. 25).

26 To see how essential judgment was to Joyce's conception of his work, see Ellmann, *James Joyce*, pp. 380 ff.

27 Cf. David Daiches' distinction between the "intellectual fallacy, where the most 'real' facts about men and women are considered to be their states of mind rather than of heart," and the "sentimental fallacy" of constructing novels or plays "out of purely emotional patterns" (*Virginia Woolf*, pp. 27–28). Though Daiches explicitly denies that works committing either "fallacy" are necessarily inferior, it seems clear that he would rate a work which somehow avoided both of these "exaggerations" above even the best work committing one or the other fallacy.

28 What I am saying here is related to the case made by E. E. Stoll about the artificial, and hence unrealistic, heightening of sympathy in Shakespeare's characters. "To sympathize you must know the facts; when you don't know them, your interest is of another sort; and while the incentive of suspense in Shakespeare and the ancients is an anxious sympathy, in Ibsen and the moderns it is an excited curiosity" (*Shakespeare and Other Masters* [Cambridge, Mass., 1940], p. 14; see also pp. 27, 28, 240).

29 Summer, 1958, p. 182.

30 "Poetry and Beliefs," *Science and Poetry* (1926), as reprinted in R. W. Stallman (ed.), *Critiques and Essays* (New York, 1949), pp. 329–33. A short bibliography of criticism of Richards' position is given in Stallman, p. 333. It should be noted that in the context of his distinction between "statement" and "pseudo-statement" the word *belief* does not mean what Richards' critics have generally taken it to mean; rather it means something like "convictions about ultimate reality based on solid evidence."

31 *Literature and Belief: English Institute Essays*, 1957, ed. M. H. Abrams (New York, 1958), p. x.

32 *College English*, XI (February, 1950), 265–69.

33 Many writers have rejected "beliefs" only to bring them back under another term like "attitudes." See "Poetry and Belief," *T.L.S.* (August 17, 1956), pp. xvi–xvii.

34 *Literature and Belief*, pp. 16–17.

35 After a similar, though more comprehensive, listing of Shakespeare's values, Alfred Harbage seems to hear in the background, as I do, a chorus of very modern voices protesting that he has got it all wrong. He turns, as it were, and faces them, and to me he has it all right: "If anyone can ask how an artist of the intelligence postulated above could have accepted the values described in this book – so cribbed and 'Victorian,' so bourgeois and grubby – …. [I answer that] A great poet could accept the values because they were great values. They represented a synthesis of such products of Judaic and Hellenistic philosophy as had shown the highest power of survival – literally, the best that had been known and thought in the world. Nothing since Shakespeare's time has impeached the evidence of an ordered universe, however more diffidently it must now be defined, or of the superiority of an ethic of love…" (*Shakespeare and the Rival Traditions* [New York, 1952], p. 296).

36 "The new philosophy opened up sources of interest for the novel which allowed it to dispense with whatever values such writers as George Eliot and Henry James had depended on in a still remoter period. Like naturalism, it brought with it its own version of an esthetic; it supplied a medium which involved no values other than the primary one of self-expression" (William Troy, "Virginia Woolf: The Novel of Sensibility," *The Symposium*, III [January–March, 1932], 53–63; and [April–June, 1932], 153–66, as reprinted in Zabel, *Literary Opinion in America* [rev. ed.; New York, 1951], p. 324).

37 For a convincing argument that morality is important in *Ulysses*, see Lawrance Thompson, *A Comic Principle in Sterne – Meredith – Joyce.* See also p. 183, above.

38 Introduction to Everyman edition of *Bleak House* (n.d.), p. ix.

39 Virginia Woolf, *The Common Reader* (London, 1925), pp. 301–2.

40 Robert Liddell talks of the same contrast between the chaotic present and the ordered past. "People are not [at the present time] necessarily less moral but there is no universal standard of Moral Taste – even among Principled persons – to which a writer can appeal" (*Some Principles of Fiction* [London, 1953], p. 110). Alex Comfort, contrasting the traditional drama and the nineteenth-century novel, on the one hand, with the modern novel on the other, says that the latter "can make no assumptions about [the reader's] beliefs or activities comparable with those which the early nineteenth-century novel, addressed to a section of society, could make....An entire world has to be created and peopled separately in each book which is written." "For the first time in recent history we have a totally fragmented society" (*The Novel and Our Time* [London, 1948], pp. 13, 11).

41 For a persuasive statement of a less hopeful view of the possibilities open to the novelist, see Earl H. Rovit, "The Ambiguous Modern Novel," *The Yale Review* (Spring, 1960), pp. 413–24: "The modern novelist...seems to have no choice between simplicity and directness on the one hand or complexity and ambiguity on the other. If he tries to deal honestly with the fearful intangibilities of his own experience and the chaos of the twentieth-century human condition, he must, in some sense, invent his own peculiar form. If he attempts to employ the traditional story-telling forms...he will run an overwhelming danger of accepting some of the sureties of the past inherent in the form, and, consequently, of dissipating into the mood of sentimentality and the mode of melodrama. The serious modern novelist is thus obliged to plunge into the abyss of value-creation, and his resultant novel, if successful, will necessarily communicate reflexively and symbolically [that is, without direct authorial statement of the values on which the work depends]. And if he is successful in crystallizing his alienation in an aesthetically satisfying metaphor, the chances are excellent that his work will be politely ignored by the mass audience" (p. 424).

42 Edouard Dujardin, *Le Monologue intérieur: Son apparition, ses origines, sa place dans l'œuvre de James Joyce* (Paris, 1931), p. 99.

43 See Edwin Muir, "The Decline of the Novel," *Essays on Literature and Society* (London, 1949), pp. 144–50.

44 The case of Henry de Montherlant is one of the most interesting in this regard. The aristocratic "ethic of quality," the "virtue of contempt," that his novels seem to advocate has led to widespread protest. Whether Montherlant himself really stands for what his characters advocate is hard to determine, but it is clear that to the extent he does so, our admiration for his work suffers. As a recent reviewer said, we cannot believe that a character like Pierre Costals in *Les jeunes filles* is intended to be sympathetic and at the same time fully respect the author. "Might it not be better," he suggests, "for M. de Montherlant's reputation as an intelligent writer if Pierre Costals were looked upon as a character who has as little of his author's complete approval as Georges Carrion, Alissa, or Jean-Baptiste Clamence?" (*T.L.S.*, January 6, 1961, p. 8). Surely it would be better. But must we not ask *of the novels themselves* whether they will justify the exoneration? In any case, his stature will rise and fall depending on what they tell us.

45 See, for example, Angus Wilson, *The Observer*, April 7, 1957, p. 16: "Balzac...is once again one of the great masters of the traditional form to which novelists are returning...."

46 The most recent is Mark Harris' delightful comic novel, *Wake Up, Stupid* (New York, 1959).

Structuralism, Narratology, Deconstruction

Introduction

Theorists in this chapter explicitly build upon the ground-breaking work of the Russian and Anglo-American formalists, even as they themselves seek to redefine the very idea of literary form. Thus the initial formalist forays into questions of the novel's identity as a literary form, the disparate and localized beginnings of novel theory, converge into an international literary-critical tradition, one that self-consciously imagines its own progress as an engagement with and refinement of scholarly work that has preceded it. We can see this second wave of novel studies gaining force and direction at mid-century in the work of Tzvetan Todorov. Todorov, a Bulgarian who settled in Paris, recovered and translated into French the work of Víktor Shklovsky, Vladímir Propp, and other Russian Formalists; in the essays he wrote between 1964 and 1969, which became chapters in *The Poetics of Prose* (first published in 1971, translated 1977), he frequently cites these Russian formalists alongside Henry James. James is both a fiction writer whose literary productions inspire Todorov to undertake the most subtle theoretical analysis, and a founding theorist of fictional form whose conceptualization of point of view (*Poetics*, 210–11) influences Todorov's own attempt to articulate a comprehensive narrative theory. Even though, as we have seen, formalists such as Shklvosky and James are motivated by profoundly different philosophical views of human subjectivity and language, the generation who saw themselves as their inheritors believed that insights into the complexities of fictional form might be detached from these differing philosophical bases and grafted into a new and more inclusive theory of literature. Seymour Chatman,

DOROTHY HALE

for example, in his *Story and Discourse: Narrative Structure in Fiction and Film* (1978), explicitly describes his project as a synthesis of international sources: he cites Wayne Booth, Todorov, and Roland Barthes among his chief influences and refers within his study not only to Shklovsky, Propp, James, Percy Lubbock, and Northrop Frye, but to Aristotle and R. S. Crane as well. When we consider that Barthes served as Todorov's dissertation director, we can appreciate how the field of novel theory is becoming consolidated through this scholarly dialogue, even as the centers of its production multiply, extending from Moscow, to Paris, Prague, London, Chicago, and Berkeley.

It is crucial to note, however, that the project of genre theory per se was not the explicit aim of this movement. These second-wave scholars of the novel fervently believed that they were answering the call for a truly scientific study of literature, a call that, as we have seen, had been issued in different quarters and contexts since the beginning of the twentieth century. The call could finally be met, these critics thought, by applying the discoveries made by the new field of linguistic science to literature – to understand literature more precisely and more thoroughly as itself a particular type of linguistic activity. The linguistic study of literature was not by any means limited to the novel; in the true spirit of scientific inquiry, it strove to comprehend all varieties of literary performance. But in point of fact theorists found the novel to be so fruitful for linguistic study that it became their privileged example. As we work through the essays included in this unit, we will come to understand more specifically which aspects of novelistic representation attracted structuralists. But we can mention right away the most fundamental one: the belief that the linguistic features of narrative fiction resonate, in obvious and illuminating ways, with the analytic categories used by linguists to describe the operation of ordinary language. The apparent discursive compatibility between fictional narratives and real-life narratives becomes a theoretical basis for extrapolating the normative categories of ordinary language to these literary perform-ances. Thus the minimalist or covert nature of the novel's literary identity – precisely the quality that caused it to be discounted or ignored by poetic theories based upon traditional aesthetic values – is considered a signal virtue for linguistic literary theory. By the 1970s, the novel not only enjoys the validation of widespread scholarly regard but can, for the first time, stand as the norm for all other literary performances.

To understand fully the novel's ascendance in literary study, we need to appreciate the sweeping influence of structuralist theory at mid-century. In its range and scope, structuralism stands as nothing less than an epistemic shift in western culture. Pursued interdisciplinarily as well as internationally, just about every branch of learning contrib-uted to its development, including social anthropology, mathematics, physics, psych-ology, philosophy, and linguistics. Structuralists interested in literature drew from all of this work, but especially from the seminal teachings of Swiss linguist, Ferdinand de Saussure (1857–1913), and the American and European linguists he inspired. Roland Barthes credits structuralist linguistics with providing the term "theory" to describe the synchronic analysis that they have undertaken, a term that Barthes himself then applies to his own methodology in "Introduction to the Structural Analysis of Narratives"[1] (81, first published in 1966). The hallmark of Saussure's structuralist method is its determin-ation to look at language as a self-enclosed and self-generating system. Saussure turns attention away from the empirical study of individual speakers communicating in specific social contexts (away from what he calls *parole*) and instead inductively "theorizes" the laws that govern the construction of language itself, that enable words (which he calls signs) to mean. Saussure's first radical contribution, then, was to conceptualize language as an autonomous totality: by bracketing the specificity of individual utterances and the historical (or diachronic) development of language, Saussure could imagine a linguistic system whose elements were all equally present and dynamically interrelated (what he calls *langue*). On this model, the rules of language work like the rules of a game: it might be interesting to compare different soccer matches or to contemplate why the same game is called soccer in the US and football in Europe; but this knowledge is not strictly necessary to play a game of soccer. The rules of soccer – not the history of soccer or the abilities of a particular player of soccer or any other "external" contingencies – determine both the possibilities of behavior and the meaning of that behavior in any actual game being scored.

Saussure's structuralist theory of language thus contrasts profoundly with an empirical model that imagines language to be a second-order cultural activity, an abstract way of referring to a material and concrete "real world" that seems prior to and thus generative of language. Although common sense may tell us that language is primarily referential – that, for example, babies learn language by pointing at things (referents) and then memorizing the word that their particular society gives to that thing – in fact Saussure's work asks us to consider the possibility that such a commonsensical view is no more reliable than the "self-evident" belief that the world is flat or that the sun moves around the earth. If reference seems to drive language, and if, as a consequence, the connection between word and referent is so intimate as to appear natural, then commonsensical intuition needs to be corrected by scientific theory. Saussure thus posits a comprehensive system of meaning that is wholly linguistic, and he seeks to discover the logical laws that govern this system, that give it a self-defining autonomy of its own. He thus provocatively upends the empiricists' model of cause and effect: it is not the "real" world referent that gives rise to language; but rather the human cognitive ability to produce language (language as a signifying system) that dictates the very conditions for knowing the "real world."

What are these internal laws? Saussure argues first of all that the differences within the system create the possibility for meaning. In his famous phrase, "in language there are only differences."[2] One way to understand this is to think about words as sounds or, if written down, "sound images." Sounds become recognizable as words only when they can be perceived as differing from other sounds. The word tree has meaning not because it has a necessary relation to the thing that in English is called a tree, but because it is distinguishable within a linguistic system from other sounds that are similar to or different from "tree." The word tree is not flea, knee, tea, or tee: the fact that these sounds can be compared with one another and distinguished by a salient aural or graphic difference (the signifying difference) makes form an active element in the signifying process. The sound or graphic mark is thus arbitrary but not passive or static. It has the power to mean, to signify, because it can only mean within a system where meaning is dynamic and relational. In structuralist linguistics, form is not a vehicle that carries content, an empty shell filled up with referential substance. On the contrary, form carries a meaning of its own, one derived by its active and dynamic relation to other forms in the system. The signifying difference between tree and tee is different from the signifying difference between tree and three. Because the relationality among forms is in no way predetermined, even if it is systematic, each contrast (tree/tee, tree/three) establishes a new signifying relation. If I compare tree to tee I might then be led by the logic of similar but different to compare tee to tea. But if I compare tree to tray, I might then compare tray to hay and then hay to hey and then hey to grey. This is what Saussure means when he says that form itself produces significance. Saussure calls the generative logic of dyadic association a "chain of signification." What is important is not the endpoint of the chain, but the logical linkage from one word in the chain to the next. In fact there can be no endpoint because the couplings are infinite.

The associational logic of this model, its "horizontal" functioning, is complemented in Saussure's theory by the "vertical" production of meaning. Every sign is composed of two elements: the signifier (or sound image) and the signified (the concept associated with the signifier by social convention). The sound image thus derives its signifying power not only from its relation to other sound images, but also from its link to a signified. The signified is not the referent, not the actual tree that you might touch as you stand under it, talking; rather the signified is the idea of a tree, understood abstractly in relation to other concepts, allowing the notion of "tree" to come into focus within and against a field of semantic possibilities. The idea of a tree is created by its difference from the idea of a shrub, plant, vine, or flower. And thus the meaning of a signified is produced through its own signifying chain. The meaning of a sign, then, comes from two kinds of linguistic activity: meaning is produced horizontally through the respective chain of associations established by the signifier and signified; and it is produced vertically through the coupling of a particular signifier to a particular chain of signifieds. The logical division between signifier and signified becomes, on this view, the dynamic structural condition through which the unification between signifier and signified is achieved: "an idea is fixed in a sound and a sound becomes the sign of an idea."[3] The signifier, Saussure emphasizes, is not the passive, "material phonic means for expressing ideas,"[4] but a contributing force in the active unification of thought and sound achieved through the combinative power of the linguistic sign. Yet this achieved combination does not, in Saussure's theory, mitigate the arbitrariness of the relation between any particular signifier and its signified. There is no necessary reason why in English the concept of a tree is linked to the particular sound image "tree" (in French it would be tied to *arbre*, another sound image, equally as arbitrary), except that society has established such conventions.

Narratology was born – and christened by Todorov in 1971 – in the belief that the scientific study of narrative was the logical next step in the Saussurian project. Since structuralist linguistics had identified the sentence as the largest unit of its own grammatical investigation, literary study could expand the field by moving to the next larger unit: the unit of narrative.[5] Since there is no way to prove this claim empirically – how can we prove that narrative is the next larger unit after the sentence? – the move to narrative must be understood as theoretically driven, a starting hypothesis whose efficacy would be judged by the insights about language it enabled. While narratologists scrupulously acknowledge the speculative nature of their work, they also attempt to characterize the assumptions that link their theory of narrative to structuralist linguistics. Roland Barthes argues, for example, that narratives are similar to sentences in their infinite variety. Taken empirically, they are seemingly inexhaustible as a linguistic class. If this very pervasiveness has hitherto made narrative seem so ordinary as to be an unworthy object of literary critical attention, narratologists would, following the methods of Saussure, reverse this judgment: Barthes argues that the very ubiquity of narrative distinguishes it as a basic operation of the human mind, an essential structure of human understanding.[6] The understanding of narrative, like the understanding of language, thus helps to illuminate the semiotic systems that produce human knowledge. The structuralist's task is to theorize the underlying rules that govern the production of narrative and to identify its basic components. And any study of literature modeled on structuralist linguistics necessarily postulates a multilevel signifying system, whose components are not discrete and static entities but dynamic parts of a unified whole.

Thus for many theorists, the validation for narratology as a scientific field came from the seeming ease with which the grammatical terms used by linguists to describe sentences could be transferred to narrative. In Barthes' words,

> Structurally, narrative shares the characteristics of the sentence without ever being redu-cible to the simple sum of its sentences: a narrative is a long sentence, just as every constative sentence is in a way the rough outline of a short narrative. Although there provided with different signifiers (often extremely complex), one does find in narrative, expanded and transformed proportionately, the principal verbal categories: tenses, aspects, moods, persons.[7]

This theory of narrative is built upon, as structuralists themselves are quick to admit, an analogical or, even more precisely, a homological identity between sentence structure and narrative structure. Narrative can be studied as a sentence because its component parts match the categories of sentence syntax. Narrative can be studied as a sentence because on this view it *is* a sentence, differing from other types of sentences only in length. We can at this point appreciate why structuralists such as Todorov felt such a strong affinity with the Russian formalists. What had Propp done but unified the seemingly endless variety of folk tales by identifying the large-scale signifiers, the syntactical categories of narrative that functioned as analogic equivalents to sentence elements? And hadn't Shklovsky insisted upon the normative representational logic of seemingly unique literary works? His analysis of *Tristram Shandy* takes a novel that seems wholly unclassifiable, sui generis, and discovers it to be instead completely typical of the internal laws that govern all literary production.

In *The Poetics of Prose* (1977), Todorov explicitly locates his structuralist project as an extension of Shklvosky's and Propp's ideas about prose fiction. In the same way that these Russian formalists tested their theories through the study of texts whose story worlds teem with what seemed to be a limitless variety of unclassifiable detail, Todorov takes Boccaccio's *Decameron* as his theoretical challenge. Is there an underlying structure, a syntactic "sequence," that organizes this multifarious collection of stories into logically related components? Todorov, like Propp before him, abstracts the story details until they achieve a level of conceptual generality that enables him to compare them as repeating and repeatable grammatical "forms." The achievement of this coherent narrative syntax depends heavily on the regulation of characterological motivation by the possibilities for characterological action that Todorov, following Propp, believes is dictated by the grammar of narrative itself. Thus, in Todorov's reading of Boccaccio, crucial developments in the story content, such as Peronella's response to her husband's discovery, must, according to Todorov's homological model, be decoded as grammatical functions, formal units that have determined possibilities within the development of the overarching narrative sentence. Although as readers we may imagine many different choices that might lie before the adulterer, Peronella, the only possibilities allowable within the logic of Todorov's narrative grammar are "punishment" and "disguise" (214). These two choices are, Todorov believes, extrapolations from the nature of narrative itself: since he defines narrative as a logical category by the quality of duration or temporality, any particular narrative must either move forward or remain static. In the example of Peronella, punishment would "re-establish the initial equilibrium" of the narrative by reinstating the authority of family law (214). "Disguise," on the other hand, is Peronella's means of making disequilibrium appear to be equilibrium – while covertly establishing a "new law," "according to which the wife can follow her own inclinations" (214). Todorov believes that all the stories in the *Decameron* can be schematized by their relation to one of the two essential qualities of narrative: its tendency toward either equilibrium or disequilibrium. He concludes his analysis of Boccaccio's stories by identifying two master plots, both of which result in the final achievement of narrative equilibrium: plots of "conversion" (disequilibrium – equilibrium) or plots of "punishment evaded" (equilibrium – disequilibrium – equilibrium) (218).

In "Language and Literature" (chapter 1 of *The Poetics of Prose*), Todorov ventures beyond the strict homology between sentence structure and narrative structure –which was, of course, a speculative assumption to begin with. He posits here a looser linguistic unit, one derived from the field of rhetoric: the "narrative figure." The narrative figure, Todorov tells us, does not differ from the rhetorical figures from which it is derived, except for its extent: in the same way that narrative could be theorized as a long "sentence," narrative figure is defined as the underlying structure of the text as a whole. Discovering the rhetorical figure that organizes a given literary work – or by extension, a given literary genre – allows the analyst to name the most comprehensive formal identity of that class of linguistic performance. Todorov credits Shklovsky with first recognizing the value of the narrative figure and first cataloguing its varieties. Todorov adds to Shklovsky's typology through figures such as "sustenation," which he sees as the formal key for the detective novel. But it is not just works with relatively thin content – what we call genre fiction – that can profit, according to Todorov, from such analysis: he argues that there is a figural structure for even highly realistic or idiosyncratic literary masterworks. As in Shklovsky's analysis of Sterne, Todorov thus points out the unified figural structure that underpins even Dostoyevsky's most complex characterological effects ("occupation").

Todorov explicitly considers the identification of narrative figures – and the work of narratology generally – to be a classificatory activity that is distinct and different from what he calls "interpretation" (*Poetics*, 209). Like the scientist who identifies the basic building block of water through the formula H_2O, the goal of the narratologist is purely descriptive. He or she thus offers neither a close reading of a particular narrative, in the sense of attending to representational details and idiosyncrasies of style, nor what Todorov calls a "translation" of narrative form into a particular value system – humanism, for example, or psychoanalysis, or historicism. The belief that a scientific (i.e. noninterpretative) description of literature is possible becomes the hallmark of narratology as a field and is carried forward into the twenty-first century, despite, as we shall see, strong criticism from the rival line of structuralist inheritors: the deconstructionists. In his own major contribution to the field, *Story and Discourse* (1978), Seymour Chatman succinctly articulates his confidence in the distinction between narratology and literary criticism: "Narrative theory has no critical axe to grind. Its objective is a grid of possibilities, through the establishment of the minimal narrative constitutive features."[8] And almost a decade later we hear the same belief echoed by the Dutch narratologist Mieke Bal. In *Narratology: Introduction to the Theory of Narrative* (1985), Bal describes narratology as providing "a set of tools" for literary interpretation. Literary interpretation can best take place if we first have, writes Bal, an accurate and fundamental apprehension of the object of study, in this case narrative. For Bal the "tools" are the basic components of narrative that have been identified and described by narratologists; these tools may then be, she believes, put to "varied uses"; possessing no interpretative value of their own, they provide the critic – a feminist or a Marxist or a psychoanalyst – with a formal vocabulary that helps him or her better "specify" his or her "interpretative reactions" to the text.[9]

As we will see in other parts of this anthology, it is certainly debatable whether interpretative criticism in practice needs or cares about any sort of literary basis – formal or otherwise. But it is nonetheless true that the narratologist's scientific rage for order generated a technical vocabulary for the study of narrative that built upon but ultimately superseded the terms invented by the Russian and American formalists. Gérard Genette fashions a new vocabulary for narrative out of old Greek words (anachrony, analepses, prolepsis, etc). Dorrit Cohn attempts to add to and refine literary-critical vocabularies that already are in play. For example, stream of consciousness and interior monologue, terms that had been used roughly and sometimes interchangeably, are systematized by Cohn into subcategories like quoted monologue and narrated monologue.[10] But if the terminology of narratology proliferates, this abundance of nomenclature remains grounded in the linguistic theory carried forward from Saussure, specifically the notion that linguistic narratives operate by linguistic laws.

Whether conceptualized as a long sentence or an extended rhetorical figure, narrative functions for narratologists as a sign. As we have seen in our analysis of Todorov, narratologists follow Saussure in their belief that the formal units of narrative do not just have a horizontal relation (in the sense of being related to other formal units through syntax); each of these signifiers also functions vertically in relation to a signified, the representational content of the story world. The dual nature of narrative is so fundamental to narratology that most major languages have attempted to coin appropriate terminological equivalents: in English story and discourse; in Russian *fabula* and *sjuzhet*; and in French *histoire* and *récit*.

The story is, in the words of Chatman, the "what" or "content" of the narrative; and the discourse is, again in Chatman's words, the "how" of narrative. The "how" of narrative is, as in structuralist linguistic theory, the "expression, the means by which the content is communicated."[11] The "what" is the mimetic story world whose events, characters, and settings operate by the logic of natural laws. The laws of narrative discourse dictate how this mimetic content can be represented as and through narrative. The meaning produced by the relation between story and discourse is, in keeping with the Saussurian linguistic paradigm, *narrative* meaning – not "interpretation." It is the meaning made possible by the particular relation between the two components (story and discourse) of the closed system, meaning that is produced both on parallel levels (as story and as discourse) and between levels (story and discourse in relation to each other). As in Saussurian theory, discourse is not the passive vehicle for the expression of rich content: rather the dynamic relation between story and discourse is itself the form of narrative, while the laws that determine this interaction are the laws of narrative.

Thus at the heart of "the grid of possibilities" that narratologists seek to chart is what we might call the ratio of representation between story elements and discourse elements. For example, in the story world, ten years may pass between two different actions performed by the protagonist. The discourse may represent that passing of time in a variety of ways: it may contextualize and seem to fill in the time period by giving a long summary of other happenings during this period; it may denote the passage of time in a single phrase ("Ten years later George went home"); or it may refrain from noting the passage of time altogether by a formal device such as a chapter break. In the same way that the word tree has no necessary or natural relation to the signified "tree," the representation of story time in narrative discourse can never be "natural" in the sense of reproducing story time; even if some techniques seem more mimetic, more designed to make the reader experience what it is like for ten years to go by, these effects are themselves dictated by the laws governing narrative language. They can never be unmediated citations of story-world time. The relation between discourse time and story time is thus structured by the necessary difference between the natural laws that underlie the story world and the laws of representation that guide discursive representation. Narratology thereby reconceptualizes an old Lubbockian tenet of novelistic realism. Lubbock had insisted in 1921 that good fiction shows rather than tells. But, as Genette points out, in fiction, language can never "show; as language it can only ever tell – and if it seems to show, then that effect is produced in and through the operation of language."[12]

In theory, then, narratology builds itself around Saussure's linguistic law: in the relation between story and discourse "there are only differences." But if we step outside the account that narratology gives of itself, we can see that there are some obvious ways that the narratological distinction between story and discourse deviates from Saussure's theory of the linguistic sign. In Saussure's system, the signifier as a sound image clearly has no necessary relation to its signified; as we have seen, tree or *arbre*, the sound image is wholly arbitrary, established by social convention and differing among national languages. But in narratology, the relation between story and discourse is structured by a system of differences that is not arbitrary because there are elements that occur in both domains and thus forge a logical connection between "signified" and "signifier." The overlapping elements that bring story and discourse in relation thus relocate the productive unification between the "what" and the "how" that Saussure attributes wholly to the operation of the sign. For example, the story world takes place in time; discourse unfolds in time, the amount of time it takes to read a sentence, a chapter, a book. Thus the unity forged by the narrative as "sign" is one that itself brings into being a significant basis of comparison and contrast. We would not ask how the concept of a tree, produced as it is through the field of signifieds, logically relates to the arbitrary sound "tree" – it is in fact the lack of logical connection between these two elements that defines it as arbitrary. But in narratology, the laws of narrative become legible through such comparison: the difference between overlapping attributes (in this example, time) is what allows narratologists to chart their "grid of possibilities." The comparability of story and discourse as structural elements is at the heart of their narrative functionality.

Chatman's chapter on "Covert versus Overt Narrators" stands as a powerful example of how much narratology can teach us about narrative technique, how subtle and precise the description of the form of fiction has become since James and Shklovsky opened up the field. But the particular topic Chatman takes on in this chapter also provides an important example of the difficulty narratology sometimes encounters in distinguishing between the "what" and the "how" of narrative. Chatman's project is to catalogue the ways narrative discourse represents characterological language. Language that appears in quotation marks and is assigned ("tagged") to a character belongs, by literary convention, to the story world: readers understand such quotations as direct transcriptions of the characters' words (whether spoken or thought). The narrator, even a first-person narrator, belongs logically to the level of discourse (although he or she might also represent herself as a character in the story she tells and thus provide another interesting category of overlap between story and discourse worlds). It is the narrator's report of the character's quotation that represents it within the story that he or she relates. Chatman thus extrapolates from these examples the laws of narrative that put characterological and narratorial language into functional relation. While the logic of narrative demands that some sort of narrator be posited, there are narratives that seem so little informed by a narrator's subjective presence that we may mistake them as pure story, as "nonnarrated." The degree and kind of subjective presence thus becomes for Chatman the category by which to chart the functional relation between character and narrator. To accomplish this task, he creates categories based upon the amount and kind of language attributable to each agent, language that is present – on both levels – to direct readerly inspection.

We can thus trace a line of development from Percy Lubbock's early interest in the novel's capacity for what he called "double point of view" and narratology's linguistic analysis of the narrative laws governing quotation. Lubbock sought to explain moments in third-person narrative when the points of view of the author and, to use Lubbock's term, "his creature," are simultaneously distinguishable and yet unified. These moments, according to Lubbock, give the reader the impression that the author is "looking over the shoulder" of his character, "bringing another mind to bear upon the scene," a mind able to see "more" on behalf of the character, without distracting the reader with his own mediating presence (*Craft*, 94). Narratology refines and complicates the narrative technique that interests Lubbock by investigating the grammatical basis of such doubling, focusing in particular on the differences between quoted characterological language and summarized characterological language. If a narrator reports that George says, "I want to go home," the reader understands the quotation as a direct reproduction of language uttered in the story world. If the narrator says instead, "George said that he wanted to go home," the language that George actually used is obscured to us: he may have said "I want to go home" or he may have said something like it, perhaps "Let us go home then, you and I." Narratology reveals that indirect report – especially when it is not "tagged" to a character but is combined more loosely with statements that clearly belong to the narrator alone – is the grammatical basis for the doubling effect prized by Lubbock.

Chatman's investigation of an element of narrative discourse, the "how" that represents the "what" of characterological language, is structured by the comparability of characterological and narratorial language: the calibration of narratorial audibility is determined by the ratio of narratorial language to characterological language. In the case of indirect report, the reader decides whether or not the words might plausibly be attributed to the character in "real life," or whether they sound more in keeping with the normative language practices attributable to the narrator as they have been deduced from the language of the narrative discourse. The same criteria govern the reader's detection of free indirect discourse (FID), words that plausibly belong to a character but which are neither tagged nor within quotation marks. The putative equality between story and discourse as neutral and equal components of narrative structure is thereby mitigated by the convention of quotation, which positions the story world as both prior to and the basis of narrative discourse.

Reference, bracketed in Saussurian linguistics, thus reemerges as an element in the narratologist's structuralist equation. In narratological theory, the seeming priority of story language is encouraged by the convention of quotation. Direct quotation establishes the possibility of an unmediated representation of characterological language, a mimetic baseline by which to gauge narrative discourse as a mediating and distorting presence – not simply a neutral (and arbitrary) signifier. Thus an evaluative vocabulary enters even a theory that has no axe to grind: even though narratorial mediation is a necessary function of narrative, it is hard for Chatman not to describe covert narrators in invidious terms. They hide themselves in "discursive shadows" [sic]; they are "shadowy" presences "lurking in the wings" (220–1). In many applications of narratological theory, the "autonomy" of characterological quotation comes not simply to describe a formal feature of narrative (quoted language stands out from the text as an autonomous entity), but is caught up in an ideology of liberal selfhood. It is not just the "autonomy" of the character's language that is compromised by narratorial mediation. Since quoted language is understood as the character's "own" language, as his or her authentic utterance, quotation thus becomes valued as free speech. The formal autonomy of quotation – its being set off by quotation marks – becomes equated with the autonomy of individual identity. The neutral relation between story and discourse, one of the "tools" offered to us by the narratologist, is thus metaphorized into a value-laden interpretative category. The relation between character and narrator is understood by narratologists as a rivalry for self-representation. Will the free speech of the character be compromised by a self-displaying narrator? Or will the narrator enact his role as representative, subordinating his own subjective interests to enable the voice of the other to be heard? For the narratologist, narrative structure thus pits discourse world against story world, narrators against characters, in an economy of presence whereby one subject can be represented only at the expense of another. Especially in narratological analyses of free indirect discourse, the battle for subjective presence, for ownership of the word, plays out sentence by sentence, word by word. Todorov's notion of narrative equilibrium is reconceptualized as an economy of power relations.

For the narratologist, such problems do not invalidate the spirit of narratological inquiry: they are an inducement to go back to the drawing board and rectify the error – in this case to search for terms that might more neutrally describe the narrative laws that govern quoted language. And narratology has developed into the twenty-first century through this belief in its progressive refinement. But to a different kind of critical mind the slide from scientific objectivism into the realm of interpretation shows instead that the narratological project itself is doomed from within: its very premises, logically pursued, necessarily result not in a grid of possibilities but in the collapse of its defining categories. Story and discourse, character and narrator, story time and discourse time can no more be distinguished as "autonomous" entities than tools can be separated from their interpretative uses. In this critique of the stability of binary relations, the post-structuralist theory of deconstruction is born.

J. Hillis Miller's essay "Indirect Discourses and Irony" (chapter 13 of *Reading Narrative*, 1998) provides a vivid demonstration of deconstruction's spirit of critique, its desire to turn narratological categories inside out, keeping them in play even as their collapsibility is constantly held before our eyes. The first pages of Miller's essay might in fact be mistaken for a narratological project: the long quotations from three Victorian novelists remind us of Shklovsky's engagement with Sterne; and the kinds of questions that Miller asks about narrative technique, particularly the functional relation established between the narrator's discourse and characterological discourse, are certainly at the heart of Chatman's *Story and Discourse*. But in Miller's hands the complexities of narrative form are not mappable units on the structural grid of story and discourse; in the deconstructive enterprise, the very attempt to chart the relation between the "what" and the "how" of narrative results in the collapse of this fundamental distinction. On Miller's view, the distinction between narrator and character establishes the expectation of two distinct logical levels (what Miller calls "lines"); but the violations of this distinction – the tendency of narrative discourse to shift pronouns, the blurring of characterological and narratorial language in free indirect discourse, the partial disappearance of an omniscient narrator into texts he claims to have recovered and to quote verbatim – are not for Miller variations of narrative discourse to be calibrated and catalogued. They instead drive him to a more global, theoretical conclusion: that the referential power of the story world is not a mistake about the (arbitrary) relation of signifier and signified within the otherwise sound project of narratology, but rather a necessary illusion promoted by narrative itself, an illusion that narratologists can't see because it would fundamentally change their understanding of the closed system, the grid of possibilities, that enables their descriptive project.

Narrative structure does indeed have its own story to tell; but this story is, for deconstructionists, nothing less than the truth of the human experience. It is not the covert structuralist story of the subjective rivalry between narrators and characters, but a philosophical account of the universal human struggle for truth against desire and illusion. As Miller's essay argues, to read a narrative is to engage in a universal psychological condition: to follow the sequence of hope and loss, to discover at the end "of the line" a lesson that can never be finally learned but must be always repeated. The persistence of the desire for reference is in no sense a "tool" for studying narrative; it becomes a topic of philosophical inquiry as unabashedly speculative as any other in the deconstructive project.

In Miller's analysis, narrative's seeming ability to distinguish the "what" from the "how" initiates the reader into the search for reference. She accepts the referential bait because the literary work encourages her to believe that the story world is primary, a coherent and autonomous presence to be represented by narrative discourse. Like the

DOROTHY HALE

narratologist, she engages in the project of categorization, she attempts to distinguish signified from signifier, story from discourse. But she discovers instead, unlike the narratologist, all that is missing from these categories. Discourse and story seem to be autonomous worlds, but in fact their respective "substance" is an illusion created through their interreference and mutual mediation. The reader comes to realize this larger truth especially as she chases the illusion of subjective autonomy produced through the narrative convention of quotation. As she attempts to distinguish narratorial language from characterological language (by tracking the ownership of language through quotation, direct discourse, and free indirect discourse), the reader becomes aware that neither narrator nor character can be fully represented by the language ascribed to each. The logic of presence will always disappoint: language will always be missing, there is always more language that belongs to the character and the narrator, language that is not recorded by the narrative text. The standard for authentic identity, the quotations and direct discourse that seem to represent character and narrator without mediation and in their own words, are revealed as fundamentally insufficient, always only a partial reference of identity. The standard of linguistic self-presence, in other words, is always potentially invalidated by the language that has been left out of the narrative record.

Thus all narrative representation of subjectivity will always reveal itself to be partial and incomplete, even as narrative creates the illusion that it is full and complete. According to Miller, this contradictory quality of narrative objectively structures the reading experience as a psychological journey through philosophical terrain. Following the referential cues of narrative, the reader searches to define narrators and characters as autonomous agents and complete wholes. Yet she discovers instead that narrators and characters collapse into one another, that they won't cohere as distinct and stable presences. She likewise discovers that the story world cannot be securely distinguished from the narrative discourse that represents it, that the signified and signifier collapse in upon each other as well. The failure of categorization thus leads to her philosophical revelation: the discovery that reference and presence, along with subjective autonomy and wholeness, are themselves illusions. But this new knowledge can be gained, on this model, only through the experience of the failure and collapse of the old ways of knowing: reference can be rejected, autonomous subjects can be abandoned, thanks to the debunking power of narrative.

Miller's theory of narrative performance begs for comparison to Shklovsky's notion of defamiliarization. For Shklovsky, we remember, the difference between content and form, the story world and its literary representation, similarly upset the reader's conventional expectations about reality, paving the way for a truer perception of life and literature. But whereas for Shklovsky defamiliarization restores reference, allowing the reader to know the world through her experience of its phenomenological essences (the stoniness of the stone and the literariness of the literary work), for Miller the reader's failure ever to access such essence problematizes the notion of reference itself, even as reference is kept in play as a psychic need. What is more, on Miller's view it is not just the objects of the reader's perception that fail her, but her own subjectivity as well. As Miller describes it, as the reader attempts to sort out character and narrator, imagining that each will cohere as an autonomous presence, she learns that her own subjectivity is itself unstable, that it, too, lacks presence. Character refers her to narrator;

narrator refers her to character in a never-ending, because never resolvable, attempt to establish each as a discrete entity. The reader's own subjectivity is thus constituted in and through the characters' and narrators' capacity never to be formed, never to be complete; and the unfinalizability of their subjectivity induces the unfinalizability of the reader's subjectivity, as she engages in the endless attempt to stabilize, to pin down, the subjectivity of the other (see p. 360, note 4). This vital circuit of relation becomes for Miller the essence of a self-definition that works ironically, because paradoxically, through interpersonal projection: "Each language source is the mirror image of the other, but which is the shadow, which the substance, which the real thing, which the simulacrum or mimesis, is impossible to tell" (248). Miller coins the term "dialogology" to describe both this self-doubling and its ironic subversion: "It is a specular or speculative relationship in which, as one might say, the mirror is empty when I seek my face in the glass, or in which, perhaps, the face I see is more original than my own and so depersonalizes me when I copy it in order to achieve or affirm my own substance" (249). When the reader becomes aware of all that is not there, i.e. the autonomous self-presence that she has mistakenly assumed to be the basis of comparison between herself and another person, the door is open for Miller's deconstructed understanding of subjectivity as a process rather than a thing, an energy of circulating relationality rather than a personal essence.

We can understand, then, why for Miller narrative meaning *is* human experience. The search for knowledge, the understanding of how narrative works, cannot be separated from the reading experience, an experience that puts the reader inside the very equation she seeks to articulate, the "objective" laws she seeks to define. To read narrative is thus to know narrative because there is no knowledge beyond or outside of subjective experience. But for Miller the subjectivity of knowledge does not lead to the kind of radical individualism that we saw in Henry James's model of identity. On the contrary, because subjective experience is itself objectively structured through narrative, it is both universalizable and knowable as narrative experience. On Miller's view, philosophical knowledge thus stands in dynamic relation to psychological experience. The philosophical knowledge obtained by the reader at the end of the line, as the culmination of narrative, does not fundamentally alter her experience of narrative – or of the world. Narrative is the journey to self-knowledge, but it is also a journey that starts each time in the same place. The reader opens each narrative in the pursuit of stable reference and autonomous selves, no matter how many other narrative experiences may have taught her that originary and coherent selves are projections of desire. According to Miller, narrative fiction dramatizes for the reader the fiction created by her desires: each novel, any narrative that pits narrator against character, teaches us that "however hard one tries, one cannot speak in one's own voice" (251). But for Miller it is equally our inability to act upon this knowledge, to relinquish those illusions once and for all, that makes philosophical truth dependent upon the never-ending story of narrative's mystification, demystification, and remystification.

If Miller's account of narrative upset resonates with Shklovsky's notion of defamiliarization, his description of subjectivity as an activity rather than an entity may also remind us of Propp and Todorov. Their narrative analyses led, we remember, to the devaluation of the subject, first by considering subjectivity itself only as a grammatical category (an element of a sentence rather than the speaker or originator of the sentence);

DOROTHY HALE

and secondly, within this grammatical model, by theorizing the grammatical subject as an empty category. In Todorov's words, the grammatical subject is always empty, "always devoid of internal properties, for these derive only from a temporary junction with a predicate" (*Poetics*, 213). Although we might think that nouns, especially proper names, refer to entities defined by a distinct set of attributes, for Todorov nomination is distinguished by an absence within the signifying system: "The agent cannot be endowed with any property, but is rather a blank form which is complete by different predicates" (213). It is, in other words, the narrative sentence as a whole, particularly the action performed by the agent, that defines the narrative subject as an agent. As we saw in relation to Propp, this definition of the agent as a product of his action begs comparison with Aristotle's poetics; but the grammatical definition of subjectivity – especially the dramatic way in which the grammatical subject is first posited as a grammatical unit equal to other grammatical units, only to be revealed to be a "blank form" – ultimately suggests values that could not be farther away from ancient Greece. Aristotle's definition of subjects in terms of the actions they performed is part of his larger humanist vision of social identity. But for Todorov, the grammatical description of the subject works to diminish human agency altogether, first exposing the false plenitude of human subjects, the fallacy of imagining that subjects are the source of their attributes; and then, on a larger analogic level, suggesting that human subjects do not speak a language but that language speaks through human subjects.

Roland Barthes' work shows how much power could be attributed to language through post-structuralist analysis – and how the concepts that govern the linguistic study of narrative move far beyond the homology with sentence structure. As we have seen, with essays such as "Introduction to the Structural Analysis of Narratives," Barthes helped to invent the field of narratology. And yet what makes Barthes' later work so interesting is its suspension between structuralism and deconstruction. By examining the relation between "The Reality Effect" and "From Work to Text," we can see how Barthes arrives in this quintessential post-structuralist position. "The Reality Effect" begins with the seeming intention simply to add to the structuralist project, to continue the kind of work that Barthes himself has already pursued in earlier essays. He points out that structuralist analysis concerns itself with identifying large-scale narratological functions, the most basic building blocks of narrative structure. But over the course of the essay, Barthes throws into question our ability to distinguish, by any appeal to common sense or even by way of the hierarchies of sentence syntax, the "basic" from the nonbasic. By the end of "The Reality Effect" what is basic has been turned upon its head: we learn that it is the "details" hitherto overlooked by narratology which are most crucial to the signifying practices of modern literature. If even self-evident opposites like "structure" and "detail" prove to be reversible, then how can we trust any of our analytic tools?

Barthes argues that the seemingly gratuitous detail in Flaubert's fiction partakes of an age-old tradition of verisimilitude, even as it attempts to distinguish itself from that tradition through its attempt at purification, its desire for the real to be uncorrupted by representation, to be represented by nothing other than itself. Barthes shows that this desire for the thing itself (similar to the desire for an original voice that drives Miller's analysis of subjectivity) is logically impossible to achieve through representation – and the necessary failure of this desire to be satisfied leads to the exposure and deployment of the "absence" that is for Barthes at the heart of language itself, part of its signifying structure. According to Barthes, the gratuitous realistic detail, in its attempt to be a nonsignifying object within a field of signs, presents itself as a signifier without a signified. Seemingly united to no concept, no idea, the signifier thus appears to lose any referentiality: it refers to nothing other than itself. But in striving to present itself as form qua form, materiality qua materiality, the signifier ultimately fails to free itself from representational meaning. According to Barthes, the signifier's success in detaching itself from the signified leads to the creation of a new signifier, one that is produced through this sequential process of revision and redefinition. Barthes goes on to argue that the *absence* of the signified becomes the new signifier. The signifier, which had in structuralism been distinguished from the signified as form, is now conceptualized as anti-form, as an "absence." Barthes achieves this inversion by emphasizing the functional meaning Saussure ascribes to form. If absence is the opposite of materiality, if it seems common-sensically disqualified from the position of signifier because it is not in any way a "form," it is nonetheless, according to Barthes, capable of fulfilling the function of a signifier, capable, that is, of expressing a signified. Barthes argues that the signified expressed by the "absent signified" is the "category of the real." Details like Flaubert's barometer may seem endlessly various and endlessly specific if we think of their meaning as tied to their thingness. But once established in their proper place within the signifying system, their meaning is shown to be wholly detached from their individuality. In fact, all these details mean only one thing, the same thing: they signify "the real" as a category of signification. Thus their final meaning is to deconstruct the authority of reference, of identity, by revealing reference itself to be not outside of language but an effect of language – even as the narrative of signification that these details themselves perform also display a desire for extra-linguistic reference that cannot be fully banished.

In Barthes' work it can be difficult to tell if the need to overthrow reference, to do away with the notion of meaning as presence, the self as a coherent substance, is something that will wither away (thanks in part to the light shed upon such fallacies by deconstruction) or if such a dynamic is an essential part of language's signifying structure, one of the ways language speaks humans. Concluding "The Reality Effect," he implies that the understanding of language has been diachronic and progressive, that modernists are more willing to confront the absence at the heart of realist signification: "the goal today is to empty the sign and infinitely to postpone its object so as to challenge, in a radical fashion, the age-old aesthetic of 'representation'" (239). But in "From Work to Text" he emphasizes instead that the desire for closure and the desire for openness are equal elements of a synchronic system. On one end of this ahistorical spectrum is the "work," the attempt to limit signification to a finite number of meanings or to interpret its one meaning. On the other end of the spectrum is the "text" – which seems a more extended conceptualization of the signifier as "absent signified." But whereas in "The Reality Effect," the absent signified ultimately served as the signifier for a new signified, in "From Work to Text," the text resists even this connection with reference. However, in throwing out the signified, the text then does not seek to accomplish the goal of nonmeaningfulness, of pure materiality. The text is produced, in Barthes' words, first by the signifier's work of semantic subversion, its rejection of the conventions of meaning established through society's conjunction of signifiers and signifieds; and secondly by its active generation of other signifiers.

We can better understand what Barthes has in mind by this notion if we think of the plurality he ascribes to the text. The Chicago School formalists, we remember, believed that the object of literary analysis was singular and objective while its interpretations were plural and evaluative. Barthes reverses this distinction, arguing instead that all attempts at interpretation are equally constricting and delimiting; they reduce the multiplicity of the text to a consumable object. Narratologists understand the dynamic nature of language, its status as an activity, not a thing; but they, too, ultimately have an impoverished conception of linguistic activity. The text's plurality, Barthes claims, is both endless and essentially active. The text is thus not an object for investigation and not even a grammatical unit: it is a "network" of endless semantic possibility. The signifiers lead not just horizontally but in multiple vectors, any of which might be pursued by the reader. Socially established codes of meaning will suggest a chain of association to the reader; but the reader does not appeal to these codes for "interpretation," a move that would reintroduce the signified as a "referent," whose discovery would necessarily put an end to the activity of meaning-making. Instead, Barthes argues, cultural codes refer the reader in turn to other codes, each as authoritative or non-authoritative as the next. A Marxist understanding of economy might, for example, refer us to a Lacanian understanding of psychic exchange, which might in turn contrast with a Freudian understanding of Oedipal desire, which might lead us to consider the emergence of childhood development as a clinical field – and so on, in an endless chain of signification, no different from that which linked tree to tee to tea. Importantly, Barthes believes his understanding of "the text" is compatible with, is in fact a better fulfillment of, structuralist linguistics: the logical conclusion of Saussure's "system without end or center" (238) is deconstruction.

If the reader does not read to get to the end, to arrive at interpretation, then what does she do? According to Barthes, she reads for an emotional gratification, for her own pleasure. The reader's job is to "play" the text, to follow out the associative logic set in motion by the signifiers. The reader thus "produces" the text; it is her interest that leads her to pursue some signifiers and not others. There can be no loss to meaning in this practice because there is no end to be accomplished other than the reader's engagement with the text. This, according to Barthes, is secured by the pleasure of reading, which she feels only as long as she enjoys an active participation in the chain of signification. The "theory" that was to be a hallmark of new science now becomes a term for deliberately "irresponsible" speculation. At the beginning of "From Work to Text," Barthes insists that his purpose is to formulate "propositions" and "hints" (236–7), an interpretative approach that could not be more removed from the methodical and objective nature of scientific inquiry. Barthes' refusal to put himself forward as master of the text is the logical conclusion of his understanding of how language works. Texts cannot be comprehended, but only approached. There is no "meta-language" (241) for textual mastery; every description of a text is more textual "activity," another signifier. Thus the homology of the sentence that served as a tool for the science of narratology is ultimately superseded, for the deconstructionists, by "writing" (241): the active condition of semantic play.

It is not surprising that deconstruction has been accused of promoting a new type of aestheticism: the play of language and the pleasure of the reader reveling in their uselessness, locked in a self-perpetuating and never-ending embrace. But to a critic like Barbara Johnson, the political and social implications of deconstruction have been underestimated. Barthesian play may seem to take place in a world of its own, far away from the social referents it has deconstructed; but in fact, Johnson argues, the deconstructive understanding of language illuminates the signifying strategies through which social power itself operates. Barthes' philosophical insights enable Johnson to speculate about *why* knowledge has been conceptualized as a universal tool for human understanding – and she concludes that such a conceptualization serves the political interest of those who themselves wield knowledge as an instrument of power. Johnson's project in *A World of Difference* (1987) is to explore the political ramifications of such knowledge about knowledge. The paradoxicality of the project does not prevent her from lucidly framing the questions that guide her study: "How can the study of suppressed, disseminated, or marginalized messages within texts equip us to intervene against oppression and injustice in the world? Is a willingness to carry an inquiry to the point of undecidability necessarily at odds with political engagement?"[13]

Through her reading of Zora Neale Hurston's *Their Eyes Were Watching God*, Johnson gives us an idea of what deconstructionist politics look like. She begins with a brief discussion of Roman Jakobson's classic distinction between metaphor and metonymy, which leads her to the conclusion that rhetorical figures, while seeming to be neutral classifications of linguistic practices, turn out to be instruments of power. As Jakobson argues, metaphor and metonymy allow language users to conduct comparison in two different ways, either by establishing identification between two different things or by representing a thing by the attributes it shares with another thing (contiguity). But, according to Johnson, through their history of usage, the neutrality of this relation has been compromised: metaphor has come to seem a superior form of expression, one that captures the hidden essence that joins two seemingly dissimilar things, that sees through meaningless detail to discover the significant basis of identity. Thus we can understand what Johnson means when she says that metaphor has been a privileged trope – but what does she mean when she also says that it is the trope of privilege?

It is important for Johnson's political analysis that the truth uncovered by metaphor is one of identity. Metaphor is the trope of privilege because it promotes essence as the best way of understanding identity; it thus suppresses the logic of predication, the truth of the empty subject. Metaphor thus implements the will to "unification and simplification" ("Metaphor," 266) practiced by groups of people who hold power. These groups will try to repress or deny social difference, as well as the social privilege unfairly bestowed upon them by their race and gender, by a belief in and appeal to universality. In other words, differences in race and gender will be falsely dismissed as "details" even as they provide the deep structure of a racist and sexist social system. On Johnson's view, the social disempowerment of women and racial minorities, their structural inability to occupy the hegemonic point of view, brings with it a kind of compensation: their alienation allows first of all insight into the operation of hegemony and secondly the deployment of language (freed from the false referent of rationalist knowledge) in the service of subversion, manipulating it as the instrument of power that, according to Johnson, it in fact is.

DOROTHY HALE

If the will to metaphor expresses the identity of the white male, then the capacity to balance metaphor and metonymy expresses the identity of the subaltern as inherently self-divided, as constituted through the vacillation between the poles of metaphor and metonymy. For Johnson the political and social division thrust upon the minority subject by virtue of hegemonic alienation allows him or her a purer relation to what is in fact the true universal human condition, the condition described by deconstruction as the endless play of meaning. The minority subject knows the fallacy of the liberal subject, the snare of presence, and the delusion of originary voice. The voice of the minority writer (such as Hurston) thus can "articulate its own, ever-differing self-difference" (269) by expressing its own fundamental "self-difference," its structure as a "figure," not a presence or a substance (264). Through such self-expression, minority voice resists the false identifications (and covert subordinations) of hegemony. In the overthrow of metaphor, narrative comes into being: narrative is, for Johnson, exactly the vacillation between metaphor and metonymy, the "ever-differing self-difference" between competing human desires: presence and absence, universality and fragmentation, totalization and particularity, public and private, similarity and difference.

A movement that begins in the scientific study of narrative thus ends in the conceptualization of knowledge itself as always only narrative. For Barthes, Miller, and Johnson, knowledge is an experience rather than a possession, the repetitive enactment of an objective psychological dynamic, rather than the obtainment of an atemporal and objective truth. But if deconstruction relies on assertions about the subjective experience of the pursuit of knowledge, it notably sketches its psychological claims in the most generalized terms, relying on hugely underdeveloped accounts of affect. Barthesian "play" describes a process of belief and disappointment that is similar to Johnson's understanding of narrative as an endless "fishing expedition" (290). But readers may wonder how Johnson manages to transmogrify DuBoisian psychic pain into something at all resembling Barthesian pleasure. It is precisely this difference, the difference affect makes to narrative theory, that is left out of Johnson's account of deconstruction's political value. Her description of Janie's (and Hurston's) liberating vacillation between metaphor and metonymy provides a feel-good, happy-ever-after ending to the novel – but we may be troubled by the homological happy ending this reading of Hurston's final paragraph supplies for the final paragraph of Johnson's own essay. Johnson's conclusion implies that the social plight of minority social discrimination contains the objective conditions of its own amelioration. Without the need to alter social conditions, the liberation of the minority subject can take place simply by going fishing, in and through narrative. The DuBoisian subject, agonized by his psychic split, is transformed by Johnson into the triumphant deconstructionist. Hurston, empowered by her discovery of "ever-differing self-difference," seeks not to repair rent subjectivity (as DuBois desired) but to revel in it. The happy-ever-after ending to Johnson's analysis of minority experience is thus derived from the Barthesian belief that the never-ending subjective condition of ever-differing self-difference is itself a happy condition, the condition for pleasure. On Johnson's view, the serious business of expressing the "appeal and injustice of universalization" (269) amounts to an endless fishing expedition because, in this deconstructionist theory, politics are play.

NOTES

1   Roland Barthes "Introduction to the Structural Analysis of Narratives" (1966), *Image-Music-Text* , ed. and trans. Stephen Heath (New York: Hill and Wang, 1977) 81.
2   Ferdinand de Saussure, *Course in General Linguistics*, trans. Wade Baskin (1916; New York: McGraw-Hill, 1959) 120.
3   Ibid. 113.
4   Ibid. 112.
5   Roland Barthes, "Introduction to the Structural Analysis of Narratives" 82.
6   Ibid. 84.
7   Ibid.
8   Seymour Chatman, *Story and Discourse: Narrative Structure in Fiction and Film* (Ithaca, NY: Cornell University Press) 18–19.
9   Mieke Bal, *Narratology: Introduction to the Theory of Narrative*, trans. Christine van Boheemen (Toronto: University of Toronto Press, 1985) x.
10   Dorrit Cohn, *Transparent Minds: Narrative Modes for Presenting Consciousness in Fiction* (Princeton, NJ: Princeton University Press, 1978). See Cohn Part I for her full categorization of "consciousness in a third-person context."
11   Chatman, *Story and Discourse* 19.
12   Gérard Genette, *Narrative Discourse: An Essay in Method*, trans. Jane E. Lewin (1977; Ithaca, NY: Cornell University Press, 1980) 164.
13   Barbara Johnson, introduction, *A World of Difference* (Baltimore: Johns Hopkins University Press 1987) 7.

FURTHER READING

Barthes, Roland. *S/Z*. Trans. Richard Miller. 1970. New York: Hill and Wang, 1974.
Chatman, Seymour. *Coming to Terms: The Rhetoric of Narrative in Fiction and Film*. Ithaca, NY: Cornell University Press, 1990.
Culler, Jonathan. *Structuralist Poetics: Structuralism, Linguistics, and the Study of Literature*. Ithaca, NY: Cornell University Press, 1975.
—— *On Deconstruction: Theory and Criticism after Structuralism*. Ithaca, NY: Cornell University Press, 1982.
Eco, Umberto. *A Theory of Semiotics*. Bloomington: Indiana University Press, 1976.
Hawkes, Terence. *Structuralism and Semiotics*. Berkeley: University of California Press, 1977.
Jameson, Fredric. *The Prison-House of Language: A Critical Account of Structuralism and Russian Formalism*. Princeton, NJ: Princeton University Press, 1972.
Johnson, Barbara. *The Critical Difference: Essays in the Contemporary Rhetoric of Reading*. Baltimore, MD: Johns Hopkins University Press, 1980.
Miller, J. Hillis. *Fiction and Repetition: Seven English Novels*. Cambridge, MA: Harvard University Press, 1982.
Norris, Christopher. *Deconstruction: Theory and Practice*. 3rd edn. New York: Routledge, 2002.
Prince, Gerald. *Narratology: The Form and Functioning of Narrative*. Berlin: Mouton, 1982.
Scholes, Robert, and Robert Kellogg. *The Nature of Narrative*. New York: Oxford University Press, 1966.

The Poetics of Prose

Tzvetan Todorov

Tzvetan Todorov (b. 1939)

Born in Sofia, Bulgaria, Tzvetan Todorov attended the University of Sofia and the University of Paris, where he completed his doctoral degree in 1966, under Roland Barthes' direction. Todorov has been at the Centre National de la Recherche Scientifique (CNRS) since 1963, and served as the editor of *Poétique* from 1970 to 1979. His awards include the first Maugean Prize of the Académie Française and appointment as an officer of the Ordre des Arts et des Lettres; in 2004, the First International Tzvetan Todorov Conference was held to honor his sixty-first birthday. His structuralist works include: *Introduction à la littérature fantastique* (1970; translated as *The Fantastic: A Structural Approach to a Literary Genre*, 1973); and *Poétique de la prose* (1971; translated as *The Poetics of Prose*, 1977). Since the 1980s Todorov has primarily written on issues of ethics and history, including in *La Conquête de l'Amérique: La question de l'autre* (1982; translated as *The Conquest of America: The Question of the Other*, 1984); *Face à l'extrême* (1991; translated as

From *The Poetics of Prose*, translated by Richard Howard. Ithaca, NY: Cornell University Press, 1977 (1966, 1968), pp. 20–8, 108–19. First published in French as *La Poétique de la prose*, 1971. Copyright © 1971 by Editions du Seuil. Reprinted by permission of Georges Borchardt Inc. for Editions du Seuil and Blackwell Publishers.

Facing the Extreme: Moral Life in the Concentration Camps, 1996); and *Mémoire du mal, tentation du bien* (2000, translated as *Hope and Memory: Lessons from the Twentieth Century*, 2003). He has also written a study of M. M. Bakhtin, entitled *Mikhail Bakhtine: Le principe dialogique* (1981; translated as *Mikhail Bakhtin: The Dialogical Principle*, 1984).

Language and Literature

My undertaking is epitomized by Valéry's remark which I shall try to make both exemplary and explicit: "Literature is, and cannot be anything but, a kind of extension and application of certain properties of language."

What allows us to assert such a relationship? The very fact that the literary work is a "verbal work of art" has long provoked investigators to speak of language's "leading role" in literature; an entire discipline – stylistics – has been created on the borderline between literary studies and linguistics; many theses have been written on the "language" of this or that writer. Language is defined here as the material substance of the poet or of the work.

This too-obvious relationship is far from exhausting the many connections between language and literature. Perhaps Valéry was not concerned with language as material, but rather with language as model. Language performs this function in many cases outside literature. Man has constituted himself out of language, as the philosophers of our century have so often observed, and we are likely to discover its schema in all social activity. Or, in Emile Benveniste's phrase, "the configuration of language determines all semiotic systems." Since art is one of these systems, we can be sure of finding it marked by the abstract forms of language.

Literature enjoys, therefore, a particularly privileged status among semiotic activities. It has language as both its point of departure and its destination; language furnishes literature its abstract configuration as well as its perceptible material – it is both mediator and mediatized. Hence literature turns out to be not only the first field whose study takes language as its point of departure, but also the first field of which a knowledge can shed new light on the properties of language itself.

This special position of literature determines our relation to linguistics. It is obvious that in dealing with language we are not entitled to ignore the knowledge accumulated by that science, or by any other investigations of language. Yet, like every science, linguistics often proceeds by reduction and simplification of its object in order to manipulate it more readily; it sets aside or provisionally ignores certain features of language so that it can establish the homogeneity of others and permit their logic to show through. A procedure doubtless justified in the internal development of this science, but one which those who extrapolate its results must thereby regard with a certain suspicion: the features left out of consideration may be precisely those which have the greatest importance in another "semiotic system." The unity of the human sciences abides less in the methods elaborated by linguistics that are beginning to be employed in other fields than in the very object common to them all – language itself.

Our image of language today, an image derived from certain studies of linguists must be enriched by what we have learned from these other sciences.

From this point of view, it becomes obvious that all knowledge of literature will follow a path parallel to that of the knowledge of language – more than that, these two paths will tend to coincide. An enormous field lies open to such investigation; only a relatively limited part of it has been explored hitherto in the brilliant pioneer studies of Roman Jakobson and his followers. Such studies have dealt with poetry, and they try to demonstrate the existence of a structure formed by the distribution of certain linguistic elements within a poem. I propose to indicate here, apropos of literary prose, several points where the relationship between language and literature seems particularly noticeable. Of course, because of the present state of our knowledge in this field, I shall limit myself to remarks of a general nature, without the slightest claim to "exhausting the subject."

Indeed, such a relationship has already been explored, with similar hopes. The Russian Formalists, pioneers in more than one field, had already sought to exploit this analogy. They located it, more specifically, between the devices of style and the procedures of narrative organization; one of Victor Shklovsky's first articles was in fact called "The Link between the Devices of Composition and General Stylistic Devices." This author noted that "staircase construction occurred in the same series as repetitions of sounds, tautology, tautological parallelism, repetitions." The three blows Roland strikes upon the rock were for Shklovsky of the same nature as the lexical ternary repetitions in folk poetry.

I do not wish to undertake a historical study here, and I shall confine myself to reviewing briefly several other results of the Formalist investigations, giving them the form which will be useful here. In his studies of narrative typology, Shklovsky had come to distinguish two major types of combination among stories: on the one hand, an open form in which new peripeties can always be added to the end, for instance the adventures of some such hero as Rocambole; and on the other, a closed form which begins and ends with the same motif, while inside it we are told other stories, for instance the story of Oedipus: at the beginning a prediction, at the end its fulfillment, between the two the attempts to evade it. Shklovsky did not realize, however, that these two forms represent the rigorous projection of two fundamental syntactic figures, used in the combination of two propositions between them, coordination and subordination. We may note that contemporary linguistics gives this second operation a name borrowed from the old poetics: embedding (*enchâssement*).

In the passage quoted above, it was *parallelism* that was investigated; this procedure is only one of those observed by Shklovsky. In his analysis of *War and Peace*, he points out, for instance, the *antithesis* formed by pairs of characters: "1. Napoleon – Kutuzov; 2. Pierre Bezukov – André Bolkonsky and at the same time Nicholas Rostov who serves as an axis of reference to one and the other." Shklovsky also notes *gradation:* several members of a family share the same character traits, but to varying degrees. Thus in *Anna Karenina*, "Stiva is located on a lower step in relation to his sister."

But parallelism, antithesis, gradation and repetition are just so many rhetorical figures. We may then formulate as follows the underlying thesis of Shklovsky's remarks: there exist certain narrative figures which are projections of rhetorical figures. Starting from this supposition, we might verify what forms are taken by other, less familiar figures of rhetoric on the level of narrative.

Consider, for example *association*, a figure relating to the use of an inadequate person of the verb. Here is a linguistic example – this sentence which a teacher might say to his pupils: "What do we have for today?" Michel Butor has given an interesting demonstration of the uses of this figure in literature apropos of Descartes; he has also employed it himself in his novel *A Change of Heart* (*La Modification*).

Here is another figure which might be taken for a definition of the detective novel, if we had not borrowed it from Fontanier's study of rhetoric, written early in the nineteenth century. The figure is *sustentation*, and "consists in keeping the reader or listener in suspense for a long time, and then surprising him by something he was far from expecting." The figure can thus be transformed into a literary genre.

Mikhail Bakhtin, the great Soviet literary critic, has studied Dostoyevsky's particular use of another figure, *occupation*, which Fontanier defines as follows: "It consists in forestalling or rejecting in advance an objection which might be raised." Any utterance of Dostoyevsky's characters implicitly encompasses that of their interlocutor, whether imaginary or real. Monologue is always a dissimulated dialogue, which determines the profound ambiguity of Dostoyevsky's characters.

Finally, I shall review several figures based on one of language's essential properties: the absence of a one-to-one relation between the sounds and the meaning. This absence gives rise to two well-known linguistic phenomena, synonymy and polysemy. Synonymy, the basis of some kinds of wordplay, takes the form of a literary device we call "recognition." The fact that the same character can have two appearances – or, one might say, the existence of two forms for the same content – recalls the phenomenon which results from the comparison of two synonyms.

Polysemy gives rise to several rhetorical figures of which I shall discuss only one: *syllepsis*. A notorious example occurs in this line by Racine:

> Brûlé de plus de feux que je n'en allumai.

> Burnt by more fires than any I lighted.

Where does the figure come from? From the fact that the word *feux* (fires), which occurs in each proposition, is taken, in each, in a different sense. The *feux* of the first proposition are imaginary, they burn the character's soul, whereas those of the second correspond to very real flames.

This figure has had a great extension in narrative; we may observe it in the example of one of Boccaccio's novellas. Here we are told that a monk had paid a visit to his mistress, wife of a prosperous townsman. Suddenly the husband returns: what is to be done? The monk and the wife, who had shut themselves up in the baby's room, pretend to be taking care of the child who they say is sick. The reassured husband thanks them warmly. Here the movement of the narrative follows a form similar to syllepsis. The same fact, the monk and the wife in the bedroom, receives one interpretation in the part of the narrative which precedes it and another in the part which follows. According to the first part, the event is a lovers' meeting; according to the second, the care of a sick child. This figure occurs quite frequently in Boccaccio – in such stories as those of the nightingale, the cask, and so forth.

Till now our comparison – following the practice of the Formalists – has juxtaposed certain manifestations of language with certain literary ones. In other words, we have observed only forms. I should now like to sketch another possible approach which would explore the categories underlying these two universes, that of language and that of literature. For this we must depart from the level of forms and turn to that of structures. Thereby, we shall leave literature in order to treat that discourse on literature which is criticism.

The problems of signification could be treated if not successfully, at least promisingly once we come closer to defining the notion of meaning. Linguistics has long neglected this phenomenon, hence it is not in linguistics that we shall find our categories, but among the logicians. We can take as our point of departure Frege's tripartite division: a sign has a reference, a meaning, and an associated image (*Bedeutung, Sinn, Vorstellung*). Only the meaning can be apprehended with the help of rigorous linguistic methods, for only the meaning depends on language alone and is controlled by the power of usage, of linguistic habits. What is the meaning? According to Benveniste, it is the capacity of a linguistic unit to integrate a higher-level unit. A word's meaning is delimited by the combinations in which it can fulfill its linguistic function. A word's meaning is the sum of its possible relations with other words.

To isolate meaning in the sum of significations is a procedure which might greatly aid the work of description, in literary studies. In literary discourse, as in everyday speech, meaning can be isolated from a set of other significations which we might call *interpretations*. In literature the problem of meaning is more complex: whereas in speech, the integration of units does not exceed the level of the sentence, in literature the sentences are once again integrated into utterances and the utterances, in their turn, are integrated into units of larger dimensions, until we reach the work as a whole. The meaning of a monologue or of a description can be grasped and verified by its relations with the other elements of the work: the characterization of a hero, the preparation of a reversal or suspension in the plot. Conversely the *interpretations* of each unit are countless, for they depend on the system in which that unit will be included in order to be understood. According to the type of discourse into which we project the element of the work, we will be dealing with a sociological, psychoanalytical, or philosophical criticism. But this will always be an interpretation of literature in another type of discourse, whereas the investigation of meaning does not lead us outside literary discourse itself. It is here perhaps that we may trace the borderline between those two related and nonetheless distinct activities, poetics and criticism.

Now let us turn to another pair of basic categories. They have been formulated by Benveniste in his studies of verb tenses. He has shown the existence, within language, of two distinct levels of the speech-act: that of discourse and that of the story. These levels refer to the integration of the subject of the speech-act within what is spoken. In the case of the story, Benveniste tells us, "we are dealing with the presentation of phenomena which occurred at a certain moment of time without any intervention on the part of the speaker in the story." Discourse, on the other hand, is defined as "any speech-act supposing a speaker and a listener, and in the speaker an intention to influence the listener in some way." Each language possesses a certain number of elements which serve to inform us exclusively about the subject and the other elements of the speech-act and which effect the conversion of language into discourse; the others serve exclusively to "present the phenomena which have occurred."

We must, then, make an initial distribution within the literary texture according to the level of speech-act manifest there. Let us take these sentences by Proust: "He lavished upon me a kindness as superior to Saint-Loup's as the latter's to the affability of a tradesman. Compared to that of a great artist, the friendliness of *grand seigneur*, however charming, seems like play-acting, a pretense." In this text, only the first proposition (up to "kindness") concerns the level of narrative. The comparison which follows as well as the general reflection contained in the second sentence belong to the level of discourse, which is marked by specific linguistic indices (for instance, the change in tense). But the first proposition, too, is linked to discourse, for the subject of the speech-act is indicated in it by the personal pronoun. Hence there is an intersection of means in order to indicate the relation to discourse: they may be either external (direct or indirect style) or internal (when speech does not refer to an exterior reality). The proportion of the two speech-act levels determines the degree of opacity of the literary language: a discourse has a superior autonomy for it assumes its entire signification starting from itself, without the intermediary of an imaginary reference. The fact that Elstir has lavished his kindness refers to an external representation, that of the two characters and of an action. But the comparison and the reflection which follows are representations in themselves, they refer only to the subject of the speech-act, and they thereby assert the presence of language itself.

The interpenetration of these two categories is, we realize, considerable, and in itself raises many problems which have not yet been touched. The situation is further complicated if we realize that this is not the sole form such categories assume in literature. The possibility of considering any speech as, above all, a communication concerning reality or as a subjective speech-act leads us to another important observation. We can see in it not only the characteristics of two types of speech, but also two complementary aspects of all speech, literary or not. In any utterance, we can temporarily separate these two aspects – which are on the one hand an action on the part of a speaker, a linguistic manipulation; and on the other, the evocation of a certain reality – and this reality has in the case of literature no other existence than that conferred by the utterance itself.

Here again, the Russian Formalists had noted the opposition, though without being able to show its linguistic bases. In any narrative, they distinguished the *fable* (the story), that is, the series of events represented as they would have occurred in life, from the *subject* (the plot), the special arrangement given to these events by the author. Temporal inversions were the example they preferred: it is obvious that the posterior communication of an event which had actually occurred before another event betrays the author's intervention, in other words the intervention of the subject of the speech-act. We now realize that this opposition does not correspond to a dichotomy between the book and represented life, but to two ever-present aspects of an utterance, to its double nature as utterance and speech-act. These two aspects give life to two realities, each as linguistic as the other: the world of the characters and the world of the narrator-reader couple.

The distinction between discourse and narrative affords us a better understanding of another problem of literary theory, that of "point of view." Here we are concerned with the transformations which the notion of "person" undergoes in literary narrative. This problem raised by Henry James has been treated a number of times subsequently – in France, notably by Jean Pouillon, Claude-Edmonde Magny, and Georges Blin. Those studies which failed to take into account the linguistic nature of the phenomenon have not managed to make its nature entirely explicit, though they have described its most important aspects.

Literary narrative, which is a mediatized, not an immediate language and which moreover is subject to the constraints of fiction, knows only one "personal" category, the third person: that is, impersonality. The one who says *I* in the novel is not the *I* of discourse, that is, the subject of the speech-act. He is only a character, and the status of his words (direct style) gives them a maximum objectivity, instead of bringing them closer to the subject of the actual speech-act. But there exists another *I*, an *I* generally invisible, which refers to the narrator, that "poetic personality" we apprehend through the discourse. Hence there is a dialectic of personality and impersonality, between the *I* of the narrator (implicit) and the *he* of the character (which can be an explicit *I*), between discourse and story. Here is the whole problem of "point of view": in the degree of transparency of the impersonal *he* of the story in relation to the *I* of discourse.

It is easy to see, from this perspective, what classification of "point of view" we can adopt; it corresponds closely to the one Jean Pouillon proposes in his book *Temps et Roman:*

—either the *I* of the narrator appears constantly through the *he* of the hero, as in the case of classical narrative, with an omniscient narrator; here discourse supplants story;

—or the *I* of the narrator is entirely effaced by the *he* of the hero; this is the famous "objective narration," a type used chiefly by American authors between the two world wars, in which the narrator knows nothing about his character, but merely sees his movements and gestures, hears his words; here story supplants discourse;

—or else the *I* of the narrator is on a basis of equality with the *he* of the hero, both are informed in the same way as to the development of the action; this type of narrative, which first appeared in the eighteenth century, dominates contemporary literary production; the narrator attaches himself to one of the characters and observes everything through his eyes; in this type, the fusion of *I* and *he* into a narrating *I* makes the presence of the real *I*, that of the narrator, still more difficult to grasp.

This is only a first rough outline; every narrative combines several "points of view"; moreover, there exist many intermediary forms. The character may deceive himself in telling the story, just as he may confess all he knows about it; he may analyze it down to the last detail or be content with the appearance of things; we may be given a dissection of his consciousness ("stream of consciousness") or an articulated speech; all these varieties belong to the point of view which puts the narrator and the character on a basis of equality. Analyses based on linguistic categories will be able to grasp these nuances more surely.

I have tried to sketch the most obvious manifestations of a linguistic category in literary narrative. Other categories await their turn: we must some day discover what time, person, aspect, and voice have become in literature, for they will certainly be present in it if literature is, as Valéry believed, only an "extension and application of certain properties of language."

* * *

The Grammar of Narrative

The metaphorical usage enjoyed by certain terms – "language," "grammar," "syntax," and so forth – makes us habitually forget that these words might have a precise meaning, even when they do not refer to a natural language. In proposing a discussion of "the grammar of narrative," we must first specify what meaning the word "grammar" will assume.

In the very earliest reflections on language, a hypothesis appears according to which there may be discovered a common structure that transcends the obvious differences among languages. Investigations of this common structure, a kind of universal grammar, have been pursued, with varying degrees of success, for more than twenty centuries. Before our own period, their apogee was doubtless reached by the "modists" of the thirteenth and fourteenth centuries. Here is how one of them, Robert Kilwardby, formulated their credo: "Grammar can constitute a science only if it is one and the same for all men. It is by accident that grammar lays down rules proper to a particular language, such as Latin or Greek; for just as geometry is not concerned with concrete lines or surfaces, so grammar established the correctness of discourse insofar as the latter ignores actual language [current usage would here invert the terms *discourse* and *language*]. The object of grammar is the same for all men."

But if we admit the existence of a universal grammar, we must no longer limit it to languages alone. It will have, evidently, a psychological reality; here we might quote George Boas, whose testimony is all the more valuable in that its author has inspired an antiuniversalist linguistics: "The appearance of the most fundamental grammatical concepts in every language must be regarded as the proof of the unity of certain fundamental psychological processes." This psychological reality makes plausible the existence of the same structure elsewhere than in speech.

Such are the premises which permit us to search for this same universal grammar by studying other symbolic activities besides natural language. Since this grammar still remains a hypothesis, it is obvious that the results of a study of such an activity will be at least as pertinent to its knowledge as the results of a study of, say, French. Unfortunately there exist very few extended explorations of the grammar of symbolic activities; one of the rare examples we might cite is Freud's study of oneiric language. Yet linguists have failed to consider it when they inquire into the nature of a universal grammar.

A theory of narrative will also contribute, then, to the knowledge of this grammar, insofar as narrative is such a symbolic activity. Here a two-way relation is set up: we can borrow categories from the rich conceptual apparatus of linguistic studies, but at the same time we must avoid following the prevailing theories of language too docilely. Perhaps the study of narration will permit us to correct the image of discourse as we find it in the grammars.

I should like to illustrate here, by several examples from the *Decameron* (roman numerals indicate the day, arabic numbers the tale), the problems which arise in the attempt to describe narrative, when this attempt is placed in a similar perspective.

1. Let us consider first the problem of the parts of speech. Any semantic theory of the parts of speech must be based on the distinction between description and denomination.

Language performs these two functions equally well, and their interpenetration in the lexicon often makes us forget this distinction. If I say "the child," this word serves to describe an object, to enumerate its characteristics (age, size, and so forth); but at the same time it permits me to identify a spatio-temporal unit, to give it a name (particularly, here, by means of the article). These two functions are irregularly distributed within language: proper nouns, pronouns (personal, demonstrative, and so forth), and articles are chiefly denominative, whereas common nouns, verbs, adjectives, and adverbs are chiefly descriptive. Yet this is only a matter of predominance, which is why it is useful to conceive of description and denomination as detached, so to speak, from proper nouns and common nouns; these parts of speech are a quasi-accidental form of description and denomination. This explains why common nouns can easily become proper nouns (Hotel "Universe") and conversely ("a Svengali"): each of the two forms serves the two processes, but to different degrees.

To study the structure of a narrative's plot, we must first present this plot in the form of a summary, in which each distinct action of the story has a corresponding proposition. The opposition between denomination and description will appear much more clearly here than in language. The agents (subjects and objects) of the propositions will always be ideal proper nouns (we may usefully recall that the first meaning of "*proper* noun" is not "a name which is someone's property" but "a name in the proper sense," "a name par excellence"). If the agent of a proposition is a common noun (a substantive), we must subject it to an analysis which will distinguish, within the word itself, its denominative and descriptive aspects. To say, as Boccaccio often does, "the king of France" or "the widow" or "the servant" is both to identify a unique person and to describe certain of his properties. Such an expression is equivalent to an entire proposition: its descriptive aspects form the predicate of the proposition, whereas its denominative aspects constitute the subject. "The king of France sets out on a journey" actually contains two propositions – "X is king of France" and "X sets out on a journey" – in which X plays the part of the proper noun, even if this noun is absent from the tale. The agent cannot be endowed with any property, but is rather a blank form which is complete by different predicates. The agent has no more meaning than a pronoun such as "he" in "he who runs" or "he who is brave." The grammatical subject is always devoid of internal properties, for these derive only from a temporary junction with a predicate.

We shall therefore keep description solely within the predicate. In order now to distinguish several classes of predicates, we must consider the construction of narratives more closely. The minimal complete plot consists in the passage from one equilibrium to another. An "ideal" narrative begins with a stable situation which is disturbed by some power or force. There results a state of disequilibrium; by the action of a force directed in the opposite direction, the equilibrium is re-established; the second equilibrium is similar to the first, but the two are never identical.

Consequently there are two types of episodes in a narrative: those which describe a state (of equilibrium or of disequilibrium) and those which describe the passage from one state to the other. The first type will be relatively static and, one might say, iterative; the same kind of actions can be repeated indefinitely. The second, on the other hand, will be dynamic and in principle occurs only once.

This definition of the two types of episodes (and hence of propositions designating them) permits us to relate them to two parts of speech, the adjective and the verb. As has often been remarked, the opposition between verb and adjective is not that of an action having no common denominator with a quality, but that of two aspects, probably iterative and noniterative. Narrative "adjectives" will therefore be those predicates which describe states of equilibrium or disequilibrium, narrative "verbs" those which describe the passage from one to the other.

It may seem surprising that our list of parts of speech does not include substantives. But the substantive can always be reduced to one or more adjectives, as some linguists have already pointed out. For example, H. Paul writes: "The adjective designates a simple property, or one which is represented as simple; the substantive contains a complex of properties." In the *Decameron*, substantives are almost always reduced to an adjective; thus "gentleman" (II,6; II,8; III,9), "king" (X,6; X,7), and "angel" (IV,2) all reflect a single property, which is "to be well born." It should be noted here that the words – in French, or in English – by which we designate some property or action are not pertinent to determining the part of (narrative) speech. A property can just as well be designated by an adjective as by a substantive or even by a whole locution. We are here concerned with adjectives or verbs of the grammar of narrative, and not with those of the grammar of French or English.

Let us take an example which will let us illustrate these parts of (narrative) speech. Peronella receives her lover when her husband, a poor mason, is away from home. But one day the husband returns early. Peronella hides her lover in a cask and tells her husband that someone wants to buy it – that this someone is in fact examining the cask right now. The husband believes her and is delighted by the prospect of the sale. He climbs inside the cask in order to scrape it out, and while he does so the lover makes love to Peronella, who has thrust her head and arms into the opening of the cask to keep her husband from seeing what is going on (VII,2).

Peronella, the lover, and the husband are the agents of this story. All three are narrative proper nouns, though the last two are not named; we can designate them by X, Y, and Z. The words lover and husband further indicate a certain state (it is the legality of the relation with Peronella which is here in question); they therefore function as adjectives. These adjectives describe the initial equilibrium: Peronella is the mason's wife, hence she is not entitled to make love with other men.

Then comes the transgression of this law: Peronella receives her lover. Here we are obviously dealing with a "verb" which we might designate as to violate, to transgress (a law). It produces a state of disequilibrium, for the family law is no longer respected.

From this moment on, two possibilities exist by which equilibrium can be re-established. The first would be to punish the unfaithful wife, but this action would serve to re-establish the initial equilibrium. Now, the novella (or at least Boccaccio's novellas) never describes such a repetition of the initial order. The verb "to punish" is therefore present within the tale (it is the danger which hangs over Peronella) but it is not realized – it remains in a virtual state. The second possibility consists in finding a means of avoiding punishment; this is what Peronella will do. She succeeds by disguising the situation of disequilibrium (the transgression of the law) into a situation of equilibrium (the purchase of a cask does not violate the family law). Hence there is a third verb here: "to disguise." The final result is again a state, hence an adjective; a new law is established, though it is not an explicit one, according to which the wife can follow her natural inclinations.

Thus analysis of narrative permits us to isolate formal units which present striking analogies with the parts of speech: proper noun, verb, adjective. Since no account is taken here of the verbal substance which supports these units, it becomes possible to give descriptions of them which may be clearer than those we could produce in the study of a language.

2. We habitually distinguish in a grammar the *primary* categories, which permit us to define the parts of speech, from the *secondary* categories, which are the properties of these parts: for instance, voice, aspects, mood, tense, and so forth. Here let us take the example of one of these secondary categories, mood, in order to observe its transformations within the grammar of narrative.

The mood of a narrative proposition makes explicit the relation which the character concerned sustains with it; hence this character takes the role of the subject of the utterance. First we shall distinguish two classes: the indicative on the one hand, and all the other moods on the other. These two groups stand in opposition, as real to unreal. Propositions uttered in the indicative are perceived as designating actions which have really taken place; if the mood is different, it is because the action has not been performed but exists in potentiality, virtually (Peronella's virtual punishment has provided us an example of this).

The former grammars accounted for the existence of modal propositions by the fact that language serves not only to describe and therefore to refer to reality, but also to express our will. Whence too the close relation, in some languages, between the moods and the future tense, which habitually signifies only an intention. We shall not follow these grammars all the way: we may establish a first dichotomy between the moods proper to the *Decameron*, of which there are four, by discovering whether or not they are linked to a human will. This dichotomy gives us two groups: moods of *will* and moods of *hypothesis*.

There are two moods of will: the obligative and the optative. The *obligative* is the mood of a proposition which must occur; it is a coded, nonindividual will which constitutes the law of a society. For this reason, the obligative has a special status; the laws are always implied, never named (it is unnecessary), and risk passing unnoticed by the reader. In the *Decameron*, punishment must be written in the obligative mood – it is a direct consequence of the laws of the society, and it is present even if it does not take place.

The *optative* corresponds to the actions desired by the character. In a certain sense, any proposition can be preceded by the same proposition in the operative mood, insofar as each action in the *Decameron* – though to different degrees – results from someone's desire to see this action realized. *Renunciation* is a special case of the optative: it is an optative initially affirmed, subsequently denied. Thus Gianni renounces his initial desire to transform his wife into a mare when he learns the details of the transformation (IX, 10). Similarly, Ansaldo renounces his desire to possess Dianora when he learns of her husband's generosity (X,5). One novella also demonstrates a second-degree optative: in III,9, Giletta not only wants to sleep with her husband, but even wants her husband to love her, to become the subject of an optative proposition: she desires another's desire.

The other two moods, conditional and predictive, not only offer a common semantic characteristic (hypothesis) but are distinguished by a special syntactic structure: they refer to a succession of two propositions and not to an isolated proposition. More precisely, they concern the relation between these two propositions, which is always implied but with which the subject of the utterance may sustain varying relations.

The *conditional* is defined as the mood which puts two attributive propositions into an implied relation, so that the subject of the second proposition and whoever makes the condition are one and the same character (the conditional has sometimes been designated as a *test*). Hence in IX,1, Francesca makes it a condition of granting her love that Rinuccio and Alessandro must each perform a heroic deed; if the proof of their courage is forthcoming, she will yield to their claims. Similarly in X,5, Dianora demands of Ansaldo "a garden which will bloom in January even as in the month of May"; if he succeeds, he can possess her. One novella takes the test itself as a central theme. Pyrrhus demands that Lidia, as a proof of her love, perform three actions: kill her husband's favorite falcon before his eyes, tear out a tuft of her husband's beard, and finally, extract one of his best teeth. Once Lidia has passed the test, he will agree to sleep with her (VII, 9).

Last, the *predictive* has the same structure as the conditional, but the subject who predicts need not be the subject of the second proposition (the consequence); whereby the predictive approaches what Benjamin Whorf has identified as the *transrelative mood*. No restriction burdens the subject of the first proposition. Hence that subject can be the same as the subject of the prediction (in I, 3: if I cause Melchisedech discomfort, Saladin decides, he will give me money; in X,10: if I am cruel to Griselda, Gautier muses, she will try to do me harm). The two propositions can have the same subject (IV,8: if Girolamo leaves the city, his mother speculates, he will no longer love Salvestra; VII,7: if my husband is jealous, Beatrice supposes, he will get up and leave). These predictions are sometimes highly elaborated. Thus in this last novella, in order to sleep with Ludovico, Beatrice tells her husband that Ludovico has been flirting with her; similarly, in III,3, in order to provoke a knight's love, a lady complains to the knight's friend that he does nothing but flirt with her. The predictions in these two novellas (which both turn out to be accurate) are not a matter of course: here words create things instead of reflecting them.

This phenomenon allows us to see that the predictive is a special manifestation of the logic of verisimilitude. We suppose that one action will lead to another, because such causality corresponds to a common probability. Yet we must take care not to confuse this verisimilitude of the *characters* with the verisimilitude of the *reader*. Such a confusion would lead us to seek the probability of each individual action; whereas the verisimilitude of the characters has a precise formal reality, the predictive.

If we try to articulate more clearly the relations presented by the four moods, we will have, as well as the opposition, presence-of-will/absence-of-will, another dichotomy which will oppose the optative and the conditional to the obligative and the predictive. The first pair is characterized by an identity of the author of the verbal act with the subject of the utterance: here one puts oneself in question. The second pair, on the other hand, reflects actions external to the speaking subject: they are social and not individual laws.

3. If we seek to go beyond the level of propositions, more complex problems appear. For hitherto we could compare the results of our analysis with those of linguistic studies. But

there is hardly any linguistic theory of discourse; hence we shall not make the attempt to refer to it. Here are some general conclusions which can be drawn from the analysis of the *Decameron* about the structure of narrative discourse.

The relations established between propositions can be of three kinds. The simplest is the *temporal* relation in which events follow one another in the text because they follow one another in the imaginary world of the book. The *logical* relation is another type of relation; narratives are habitually based on implications and presuppositions, whereas texts more remote from fiction are characterized by the presence of a movement from the general to the particular, and vice versa. Finally, a third relation is of a *spatial* type, insofar as the two propositions are juxtaposed because of a certain resemblance between them, thereby indicating a space proper to the text. Here we are dealing, evidently, with parallelism and its many subdivisions; this relation seems dominant in poetry. Narrative possesses all three types of relations, but in a constantly varying proportion and according to a hierarchy proper to each individual text.

We may establish a syntactic unit superior to the proposition; let us call it the *sequence.* The sequence will have different characteristics, according to the type of relation between propositions. But in each case, an incomplete repetition of the initial proposition will mark its end. Moreover, the sequence provokes an intuitive reaction on the reader's part, that is, that he is faced with a complete story, an integral anecdote. A novella coincides frequently, though not always, with a sequence; the novella may contain several sequences or only a part of one.

From the perspective of the sequence, we may distinguish several types of propositions. These types correspond to the logical relations of exclusion (either-or), of disjunction (and-or), and of conjunction (and-and). We shall call the first type of propositions *alternative*, for only one among them can appear at one point of the sequence; this appearance, moreover, is obligatory. The second type will be that of *optional* propositions whose place is not specified and whose appearance is not obligatory. Last, a third type will be formed by the *obligatory* propositions; these must always appear at a specific place.

Let us take a novella which will permit us to illustrate these various relations. A Gascony lady is "abused by several lewd fellows" during her sojourn in Cyprus. She wishes to lodge a complaint with the king of the island, but is told that her efforts would be futile, for the king remains indifferent to the insults he himself receives. Nonetheless, she meets the king and makes several bitter remarks to him. The king is touched and abandons his indifferent attitude (I,9).

A comparison between this novella and the other texts which form the *Decameron* will permit us to identify the status of each proposition. There is first of all the obligatory proposition: this is the lady's desire to modify the preceding situation. We encounter this desire in all the novellas of the collection. Further, two propositions contain the causes of this desire (the abuse by the boys and the unhappiness of the lady), and we may label them as optional. Here we are dealing with a psychological motivation for our heroine's modifying action, a motivation which is frequently absent from the *Decameron* (contrary to what occurs in the nineteenth-century tale). In the story of Peronella (VII,2), there is no psychological motivation, but here we also find an optional proposition: this is the fact that the lovers once again make love behind the husband's back. Let there be no mistake: by labeling this proposition optional, we mean that it is not necessary to our perception of the novella's plot as a completed whole. The novella itself certainly needs it, it is in fact the "salt of the story," but we must be able to separate the concept of plot from the concept of tale.

Finally there exist alternative propositions. Let us take for instance the lady's action which modifies the king's character. From the syntactic point of view, it has the same function as Peronella's in concealing her lover in the cask; both aim at establishing a new equilibrium. Yet here this action is a direct verbal attack, whereas Peronella made use of disguise. "To attack" and "to disguise" are therefore two verbs which appear in alternative propositions; in other words, they form a paradigm.

If we try to establish a typology of narratives, we can do so only by relying on the alternative elements: neither the obligatory propositions which must always appear, nor the optional ones which can always appear, will help us here. Further, the typology might be based on purely syntactic criteria. We said earlier that the narrative consisted in a passage from one equilibrium to another. But a narrative can also present only a portion of this trajectory. Hence it can describe only the passage from an equilibrium to a disequilibrium, or conversely.

The study of the novellas of the *Decameron* has led us, for example, to discern in this collection only two types of story. The first, of which the tale about Peronella was an example, could be called "punishment evaded." Here the complete trajectory is followed (equilibrium – disequilibrium – equilibrium); moreover, the disequilibrium is provoked by the transgression of a law, an act which deserves punishment. The second type of story, illustrated by the novella about the Gascony lady and the king of Cyprus, can be designated as a "conversion." Here, only the second part of the narrative is present; we start from a state of disequilibrium (a weak king) to arrive at the final equilibrium. Further, this disequilibrium is caused not by a particular action (a verb) but by the very qualities of the character (an adjective).

These few examples may suffice to give some notion of the grammar of narrative. One could object that, in doing so, we have not managed to "explicate" narrative, to draw general conclusions from it. But the state of studies of narrative implies that our first task is the elaboration of a descriptive apparatus; before being able to explain the facts, we must learn to identify them.

Imperfections may (and should) also be found in the concrete categories proposed here; my purpose was to raise questions rather than to provide answers. It seems to me, nonetheless, that the notion itself of a grammar of narrative cannot be contested. This notion rests on the profound unity of language and narrative, a unity which obliges us to revise our ideas about both. We shall understand narrative better if we know that the character is a noun, the action a verb. But we shall understand noun and verb better by thinking of the role they assume in the narrative. Ultimately, language can be understood only if we learn to think of its essential manifestation – literature. The converse is also true: to combine a noun and a verb is to take the first step toward narrative. In a sense, what the writer does is to read language.

Story and Discourse: Narrative Structure in Fiction and Film

Seymour Chatman

Seymour Chatman (b. 1928)

Seymour Chatman was born in Detroit, Michigan, and attended Wayne State University and the University of Michigan. Chatman has taught at the University of Pennsylvania, the University of Melbourne, Zurich University, and the University of Venice; he joined the Rhetoric department at the University of California, Berkeley, in 1960, where he is now professor emeritus of Rhetoric and Film. Chatman has been honored with a National Endowment for the Humanities Senior Fellowship, a Fulbright Fellowship, and a Guggenheim Fellowship. He has co-edited numerous books of narrative theory, including *Essays on the Language of Literature* (1967); *Approaches to Poetics: Selected English Institute Essays* (1973); *Reading Narrative Fiction* (1993); and *New Perspectives on Narrative Perspective* (2001). Chatman's books include *Story and Discourse: Narrative Structure in Fiction and Film* (1978); *Antonioni, or, The Surface of the World* (1985); *Coming to Terms: The Rhetoric of Narrative in Fiction and Film* (1990); and *Michelangelo Antonioni: The Investigation* (2004).

From *Story and Discourse: Narrative Structure in Fiction and Film*. Ithaca, NY, and London: Cornell University Press, 1978, from ch. 5, pp. 196–209.

Discourse: Covert versus Overt Narrators

A clear sonorous voice, inaudible
To the vast multitude.
William Wordsworth,
The Excursion

I was in the Spirit on the Lord's day,
and heard behind me a great voice,
as of a trumpet.
The Revelation

It is less important to categorize types of narrators than to identify the features that mark their degrees of audibility. A quantitative effect applies: the more identifying features, the stronger our sense of a narrator's presence.[1] The "non" or minimally narrated story is simply one in which no or very few such features occur.

Still, a fundamental distinction can be made between covert and overt narrators, and that is the task of this chapter. Not every feature can be discussed in detail, so the focus is on the salient and particularly the problematic features.

Three matters are of preliminary concern: the nature of indirect discourse, the manipulation of the surface of the text for covert narrative purposes, and the limitation of point of view to a particular character or characters. The first two are very much open topics, as recent research has shown. The complexities of indirect discourse have spawned a large literature that is not yet conclusive. Contemporary linguistics has challenged the traditional formulations and raised some fascinating questions about indirect style. It has also begun to analyze the mechanisms for placing special emphasis on certain elements in sentences – by which the covert narrator may "surreptitiously" manipulate his sentence structures, thus backgrounding or foregrounding narrative elements of varying degrees of importance. The mechanism of "presupposition" is discussed here by way of example. Closely related to covertness, indeed often confused with it, is the limitation placed by the implied author on the narrator's knowledge.

Shifting to the overt narrator, we consider a spectrum of features, ranging from least to most obtrusive markers: from set descriptions and reports of what characters did *not* say or think, to the various kinds of commentary – interpretation, judgment, generalization. This chapter (and the book) concludes with some observations about the narrator's interlocutor, the narratee.

Covert Narrators

Covert or effaced narration occupies the middle ground between "nonnarration" and conspicuously audible narration. In covert narration we hear a voice speaking of events, characters, and setting, but its owner remains hidden in the discursive shadows. Unlike the "nonnarrated" story, the covertly narrated one can express a character's speech or thoughts in indirect form. Such expression implies an interpretive device or mediator qualitatively different from the simple mindreading stenographer of nonnarrated narra-

SEYMOUR CHATMAN

tives. Some interpreting person must be converting the characters' thoughts into indirect expression, and we cannot tell whether his own slant does not lurk behind the words: "John said that he would come" may transmit more than "John said 'I will come,'" since there can be no guarantee that John used those exact words. Hence our intuition of a shadowy narrator lurking in the wings.

The terrain of covert narration is bewildering, and it is easy to lose one's bearings. I was disconcerted to hear in a lecture recently that Joyce's "narrators" included most of his major characters – Eveline, Lenehan, Gabriel, Stephen Dedalus, Leopold and Molly Bloom. The impropriety of assigning the term "narrator" to the character's own mental voice in interior monologue was demonstrated in Chapter 4.[2] The point is even clearer where characters' thoughts are expressed by covert narrators. It is simply a mistake to argue that Lenehan is in any sense the "narrator" of "Two Gallants." When he speculates, reminisces, or whatever, he is not telling a story to anybody, not even himself. It is an outside speaker who is reporting ("internally analyzing") his thoughts:

> In his imagination he beheld the pair of lovers walking along some dark road; he heard Corley's voice in deep energetic gallantries and saw again the leer of the young woman's mouth. This vision made him feel keenly his own poverty of purse and spirit. He was tired of knocking about, of pulling the devil by the tail, of shifts and intrigues.

Clearly Lenehan's vocabulary does not include "deep energetic gallantries," "his own poverty of purse and spirit," "shifts and intrigues." And since these are not his words, he cannot be the narrator of the story which they recount. The narrator is *imputing* the feeling of "poverty of purse and spirit" to Lenehan, but it is only an imputation, an internal analysis or report by a covert narrator. When words and phrases that could be part of Lenehan's vocabulary appear – "tired of knocking about," "pulling the devil by the tail" – we are conscious of quotation in indirect free form.

Indirect Tagged and Free Style

Any analysis of the complex relations between the speech acts of characters and narrators requires an understanding of the ways of communicating speech (external voice) or thought (internal voice). A basic distinction is that between quotation and report, or in more traditional terms, "direct" and "indirect" forms, a distinction that has been commonplace for centuries. Usually formulated in terms of speech – the difference between "'I have to go,' she said" and "She said that she had to go" – it obviously applies to thinking as well: "'I have to go,' she thought" and "She thought that she had to go."

The surface differences between the two forms are quite clear-cut. In both cases there are two clauses, one optional and the other obligatory. For clarity's sake I shall call the introductory or optional clause the "tag" ("she said") and the second the "reference." The tag clause signals that it is the reference clause which contains what is reported or quoted ("I have to go" or "She had to go"). In English, the differences between direct and indirect style involve (1) the tense of the predicate of the reference clause, (2) the person of the subject of the clause, and (3) the (optional) presence of "that." In indirect style the tense of the reference clause is generally one tense *earlier* than that of its direct counterpart. And the pronoun is changed from first to third person.

The deeper semantic relations of the two forms, however, are more obscure. Until recently, it was thought that they were straightforward variants of each other, that "She said she had to go" meant the same as "She said 'I have to go'". But linguists have shown that important differences discredit that easy assumption.[3] For example, some sentences can only appear in direct form. "Egbert blurted out, 'How I have loved it!'" cannot be transformed to "Egbert blurted out how he had loved it" and still preserve its original meaning. In the first sentence "how" means "how much," while in the second it means "in what manner." Similarly, "Clarissa whispered, 'There!'" cannot occur in indirect form – *"Clarissa whispered that there." Perhaps the most interesting restriction, from the narrative point of view, is that only direct forms can cite the speaker's exact words; indirect forms give no such guarantee. Thus it is possible to question only the language of indirect report clauses; we can say "Oedipus cried out that he had done something horrible with his mother, but I won't repeat what he actually said," but not *"Oedipus cried out, 'I have done something horrible with my mother,' but I won't repeat what he actually said."

The indirect form in narratives implies a shade more intervention by a narrator, since we cannot be sure that the words in the report clause are precisely those spoken by the quoted speaker. Of course, they may be, as when they differ radically in diction and/or syntax from the established "well-spoken" style of the narrator: for example in "Eveline" the sentence "...latterly he [Eveline's father] had begun to threaten her and say what he would do *only* for her dead mother's sake." The context clearly indicates that the italicized portion is the lower-class Irish dialect counterpart of "*if it were not* for her dead mother's sake." But the well-spoken narrator is not speaking in lower-class dialect. There are several other kinds of expressive effects which suggest that the character's speech or thoughts are being directly quoted. For instance, parts of the sentence can be shifted around and elements deleted to give them more prominence, as someone might do in the heat of actual expression: "John shouted out that how Mary could behave so badly was beyond his comprehension." Interjections can be introduced: "Richard protested that Lord! he didn't like it." Or hesitations: "He protested that he, God help him, he could not be held responsible." Or special emphasis: "He protested that *he* could not be held responsible."[4]

On the other hand there may be good evidence that the words are not exactly quoted, as in the Oedipus example cited above. We sense that the "I" has paraphrased Oedipus' original words. The "I" may equally summarize, epitomize, interpret, or otherwise alter the exact words of the quoted speaker. And, of course, the "I," the reporter, who must be the narrating subject of such sentences, may not refer to himself, so that the *pronoun* "I" need not actually appear.

In the nineteenth century there arose in most European languages another distinction which crosscuts that between direct and indirect speech and thought, namely that between "tagged" and "free" style (*style indirect libre, erlebte Rede*).[5] Free style deletes the tag. Thus:

	Tagged	Free
Direct:		
Speech	"I have to go," she said	I have to go
Thought	"I have to go," she thought	I have to go

SEYMOUR CHATMAN

Indirect:

Speech	She said that she had to go	She had to go
Thought	She thought that she had to go	She had to go

Free speech and thought are expressed identically, and thus ambiguously, unless the context clarifies.

Direct free forms, I have argued, characterize interior monologue. Indirect free forms do not, precisely because a narrator is presupposed by the third person pronouns and the anterior tense. They may, of course, co-occur with direct free forms: examples abound in *Ulysses*. But often, as in Virginia Woolf's major novels, they co-occur only with indirect-tagged forms.

Still, the meaning of the indirect free form is not the simple remainder of indirect tagged form minus the tag. It has a greater degree of autonomy, and though ambiguity may persist, the absence of the tag makes it sound more like the character speaking or thinking than a narrator's report. A sentence like "She felt that John, bless his soul! would provide for the family" could mean that either the character or the narrator, or both, were blessing John's soul. Whereas in context the indirect free counterpart "John, bless his soul, would provide for the family" seems more exclusively the blessing of the character. This is true of a whole host of expressive features: exclamations, questions, expletives, imperatives, repetitions and similar emphases, interruptions, the words "yes" and "no," colloquialisms, and other forms of "unnarrative" diction (for example, pet names, technical jargon, foreign language elements, etc.). A narrator could hardly remain covert if he himself were to use such forms.

Take exclamations, for example. A covert narrator is hard put to use them because they express strong feelings – deprecation, enthusiasm, or whatever. Such expression would call undue attention to those feelings: we would begin to wonder about them and particularly whether "thereby hangs a tale" about *him*. Exclamations do not suit the role of effaced or transparent mediator. The logic of covert narration permits only the character to exclaim. In Joyce's "The Dead":

> Gabriel's warm trembling fingers tapped the cold pane of the window. How cool it must be outside! How pleasant it would be to walk out alone, first along by the river and then through the park! The snow would be lying on the branches of the trees and forming a bright cap on the top of the Wellington Monument. How much more pleasant it would be there than at the supper-table!

We assume that the exclamations are exclusively Gabriel's, a direct quotation of his mind's speech. We have no reason to believe that the narrator is exclaiming.[6]

Stylistically, the reference clause can be either identical with or clearly distanced from the surmisable words of the character, indeed, so distanced as to seem only the narrator's paraphrase. I can present indirectly the statement of a fired streetcleaner in language which is or is not evidently his: "He said he was canned and it was the goddamned foreman's fault." Or "He said that his resignation was enforced, implying that questions of a distinctly jurisdictional nature had been raised." And either of these can occur in free indirect style. Thus free indirect style divides into subclasses, attributable to character or to narrator. In between, there are statements of varying degrees of ambiguity. For language that is clearly the character's, a suitable label, recently proposed, is *narrated monologue*.[7] "Narrated" accounts for the indirect features – third person and prior tense – while "monologue" conveys the sense of hearing the very words of the character. Narrated monologue is clearly distinguished from narrative report (internal analysis), where the character's thinking or speech is communicated in words that are recognizably the narrator's. Finally, there is the relatively common ambiguous situation, discussed below, where it is difficult to know whose voice speaks.

The kind of indirect mode considered so far is purely verbal, that is, an account of *words* spoken or thought by the character. But there is clearly another kind of report, whose basis is, rather, perceptions. From the end of Chapter IV and the beginning of Chapter V of *Madame Bovary*:

> The old servant appeared, presented her respects, apologized for not having dinner ready and suggested that Madame look over her new house in the meantime.

V

> The brick front of the house was flush with the street, or rather the road. Behind the door hung a coat with a short cape, a bridle and a black leather cap....

And so on through a description of the parlor, the hall, Charles's office, a large room used as a woodshed and storeroom, and the garden. Then

> Emma went up to the bedrooms. The first one was not furnished, but the second one, the conjugal chamber, had a mahogany bed standing in an alcove hung with red draperies....

This is not a mere description of the house at Tostes by an outside narrator, but a sense of how the place struck Emma on her first view of it. Though no verb refers to Emma's perceptions, they are clearly implied – that is, we infer that the second sentence is really a shortened form of "She saw that the brick front of the house was flush with the street," and so on. This cannot be called "indirect free thought": the full form is not "Emma thought that the brick front of the house was flush with the street'." It is rather a "free indirect perception."[8]

Let me illustrate the distinctions between narrated monologue and internal analysis with two quotations. Here is something of the logic by which I think we decide whose voice it is that we hear in indirect discourse. The opening sentences of "Eveline" again:

(1) "She sat at the window watching the evening invade the avenue." At first we are uncertain that there is a narrator. The discourse may be only an enactment, the narrative equivalent of an actress sitting on-stage by a window painted on the backdrop. "Sitting at the window" could clearly pass as "nonnarrated," but "watching" is ambiguous. A character may be described as watching something from an external vantage, hence no narrator. Or the verb may verbalize her perception, hence a covert narrator.

Then we encounter the phrase "evening invade the avenue." The metaphor clearly presupposes a mind capable of its invention; if it is not Eveline who does so, the speaker can only be the narrator. Later evidence validates this hypothesis (number five below).

(2) "Her head was leaned against the window curtains and in her nostrils was the odor of dusty cretonne." The first part of this sentence again might seem to present a simple enactment. But in the jelling context it seems more like a covert narrator's pronouncement, a free indirect perception.

(3) "She was tired." This is ambiguous: either "She felt [that she was] tired," or "My [the narrator's] report is that she was tired," whatever she thought. (Or *both*: the ambiguity of free indirect forms.)

(4) "Few people passed." Ditto: "She saw few people pass" or "On my [the narrator's] authority few people passed." Or both.

(5) "The man out of the last house passed on his way home." Here clearly we distinguish two vocalic styles. "Out of" is a class dialect form of "from." The voice that speaks of the evening "invading" the avenue is clearly not the one that speaks of a man "out of" the last house; clearly the former belongs to an "author"-narrator and the latter to the character. The basic form of the sentence is indirect free perception but the phrase "out of the last house" is a direct quotation, hence narrated monologue.[9] (Corroboration occurs later in the text in usages like "used to" as iterative instead of the more literary "would," "she always had an edge on her," "hunt them in," "not so bad," including forms that indicate that Eveline is still very young: "grownup," "keep nix," and so on.)

Several changes that Joyce made when "Eveline" was republished in *The Dubliners* (it had originally appeared in the *Irish Homestead*, September 10, 1904) are obvious attempts to make her mental voice more prominent. In the revision, she wonders where "all the dust came from"; in the original, her room is said to "secrete" dust. A subjunctive is replaced by a dialectal form: her father's "saying what he would do if it were not for her dead mother's sake," becomes "what he would do to her only for her dead mother's sake." Perhaps the most interesting change is the dropping of the quotation marks that originally embraced the word "edge" in the sentence about Miss Gavan: "Miss Gavan had an 'edge' on her...." Deleting the quotation marks turns the sentence into narrated monologue. (The quotation marks would mean not direct free thought but a narrator's "Jamesian" self-consciousness about slang.)

So we distinguish the simple colloquial voice of the character Eveline from the voice of a covert narrator of literary ability. The distinction, of course, is supported by the story's content. We have now read enough to sense that her environment is poor (the curtains are dusty because they hang in a decrepit building in a neighborhood where the atmosphere is smoky), that she has lived in that neighborhood since she was a child, playing in empty lots with the other children of the neighborhood (not in the green fields of an exclusive boarding school), and so on. Even without the evidence from diction, these recognitions would make it unlikely that she is "literary," say a would-be author struggling in a loft. Later sentences confirm our judgments about the first two sentences: they are clearly a narrator's report.[10]

This laborious and unnatural way of reading is not, of course, what the reader actually does, but only a suggestion of what his logic of decision must be like. As narratee he *hears* the narrator's report; the snatches of the character's actual verbiage he *overhears*.

Sometimes it is not possible to decide whether the words in indirect free form are the character's or the narrator's, for example, if both speak in a highly literate manner. This is not a negative characterization, since the merging of the two voices may well be an intended aesthetic effect. The implication is "It doesn't matter who says or thinks this; it is appropriate to both character and narrator." The ambiguity may strengthen the bond between the two, make us trust still more the narrator's authority. Perhaps we should speak of "neutralization" or "unification," rather than ambiguity.

Thus, the covert narrator can describe from a clear external vantage point, dip down to quote from the character's thoughts in his own or the character's very words, or plant an ambiguity about a locution, indistinguishably telling and showing, narrating and enacting the character's inner life.

Brilliant examples of the "neutralized" indirect free style occur in Virginia Woolf's *Mrs. Dalloway.* The first sentences:

> Mrs. Dalloway said she would buy the flowers herself. For Lucy had her work cut out for her. The doors would be taken off their hinges; Rumplemayer's men were coming.

A "sympathetic" effect arises because there is no reason to assume that Clarissa's idiolect differs significantly from the narrator's. Such statements imply that character and narrator are so close, in such sympathy, that it does not matter to whom we assign the statement. Indifferently "For you see, dear reader, Lucy had her work cut out for her" (that is, "I, the narrator observe that"), or "[Mrs. Dalloway remembered that] Lucy had her work cut out for her." Indeed the ambiguity goes further, since a *speech* could as easily be implied: "[Mrs. Dalloway *said* that] Lucy had her work cut out for her." All three possibilities hover above the sentence. A feeling is established that the narrator possesses not only access to but an unusual affinity or "vibration" with the character's mind. There is the suggestion of a kind of "in"-group psychology: "It was understood by all parties, including 'myself' (the narrator), that Lucy had her work cut out for her." The content of the first sentence prepares us for this consensus: Mrs. Dalloway is reported simply as saying that she would buy the flowers, not saying that to any particular person. It seems more pronouncement than dialogue. There arises a sense of the broader social context: Mrs. Dalloway is accustomed to having a cooperative audience, maids, cooks, and butlers. The same kind of consensus operates at the beginning of Katherine Mansfield's "The Garden Party." "And after all the weather was ideal. They could not have had a more perfect day for a garden-party if they had ordered it": indistinguishably the thought of one or all of the family, or what one of them said to the others, or the narrator's judgment of the situation.

But the indirect free style is by no means committed to sympathy. It may work ironically.[11] In a beautifully conceived passage Flaubert plays the dreams of Charles and Emma Bovary against each other:

> When he came home in the middle of the night he did not dare to wake her. . . . Charles looked at his wife and daughter. . . . How pretty she would be later, at fifteen! She would look just like her mother, and they would both wear wide straw hats in summer; from a distance they would look like two sisters . . . they would think about her marriage: they would find her some fine young man with a good position; he would make her happy, and it would last forever.
>
> Emma was not asleep, but only pretending to be; and while he sank into sleep beside her she lay awake, dreaming different dreams.

SEYMOUR CHATMAN

She and Rodolphe had been traveling for a week, drawn by four galloping horses toward a new country from which they would never return. They went on and on, their arms intertwined, without speaking. Often from the top of a mountain they would suddenly catch sight of some magnificent city, with domes, bridges, ships, forests of lemon trees and white marble cathedrals with storks' nests on their pointed steeples.

The irony lies in the juxtaposition of the indirect free plunges into the two disparate fantasy worlds. The minds are a million miles apart, though the bodies are separated only by inches.

As I have argued, indirect tagged forms go further toward illuminating a narrator's presence. Indeed, the tag may directly interpret the character's thought, feeling or speech: "John concluded that he was right" implies a greater degree of narrator-mediation than "John thought that he was right" precisely because the mental process through which John has achieved his certainty is characterized by the narrator.

Also interpretive are sentences in which the thought or sensation is not couched in a *that*-clause, but in a nominal phrase. This further syntactic move underlines a kind of epitomization, hence greater narrator audibility. "John concluded the correctness of his position" is more evidently the internal analysis of the situation by a narrator, since it is even less certain that John had in fact uttered to himself the precise words "the correctness of my position."

"Internal analysis" or "narrator's report" is what critics doubtless mean by "limited third person narration," though, as I argue above, "third person" is improperly used. In pure covert narration, the narrator does not refer to himself at all, so there is no real parallelism with "first person narration." In the latter the narrator indeed refers to *himself* through the first person pronoun. But in the former it is the *character* who is referred to by the third person pronoun: the narrator simply does not refer to himself at all. It is no more meaningful to call him "he" than "I" or "you."

NOTES

1   There is a hierarchy of "degrees of narratorhood" implicit in Wayne Booth's *reductio ad absurdum* of the dogma of "objective" argument in narratives (*Rhetoric of Fiction*, 1961, pp. 16–19). But I take the notion of degree of narratorhood seriously.

2   Dorrit Cohn, "Narrated Monologue: Definition of a Fictional Style," *Comparative Literature*, 18 (1966), 102, ventures an explanation of the reason for this kind of mistake: "The arguments in favor of an internal angle of vision, so forcefully stated by Henry James, Percy Lubbock, and Joseph Warren Beach, have led to the belief that the separate narrator is absent from the dramatized novel, and that therefore the 'central intelligence' is himself the narrator, in the same sense as the 'I' is the narrator of a story told in the first person. Lubbock may have started this misapprehension when he referred to the character in whom the vision rests by such names as 'dramatized author,' 'spokesman for the author,' or 'fresh narrator.' But despite these misleading metaphors, Lubbock himself was fully aware that in all third-person novels the figural psyche is supplemented by 'someone else...looking over his shoulder....' "

3   See Ann Banfield, "Narrative Style and the Grammar of Direct and Indirect Speech," *Foundations of Language*, 10 (1973), 1–39 (and the literature quoted therein); see also the important study by Roy Pascal, *The Dual Voice* (Totowa, N.J., 1977). The examples are taken

from Banfield's article, which I find challenging even as I disagree with it. Asterisks mark un-English forms.

4   Despite Banfield, who asterisks them, these are eminently possible in fiction. But not all expressive elements can occur. Banfield is right in arguing that the indirect counterpart of sentences like "Clarissa exclaimed, 'What a lark!'" is not possible (p. 7).

5   See the bibliography in footnotes to Dorrit Cohn's article and that in Stephen Ullmann's "Reported Speech and Internal Monologue in Flaubert," *Style in the French Novel* (Cambridge, 1957). The first reference to "*style direct libre*" that I know, cited by Derek Bickerton, "Modes of Interior Monologue: A Formal Definition," *Modern Language Notes*, 28 (1976), 233, occurred in L. C. Harmer, *The French Language Today* (Melbourne, 1954), p. 301.

6   Why exclamations must mark the indirect free discourse of a character is argued in a subtle article by Pierre Guiraud, "Modern Linguistics Looks at Rhetoric: Free Indirect Style," in Joseph Strelka, ed., *Patterns of Literary Style*, Yearbook of Comparative Criticism, Vol. III (University Park, Penn., 1971), p. 83.

7   Cohn, "Narrated Monologue," p. 98. Among the many other terms that have been suggested are "substitutionary speech," *verschleierte Rede, erlebte Rede*, "independent form of indirect discourse," *uneigentlich direkte Rede*, "represented speech," "narrative mimicry," *Rede als Tatsache, monologue intérieur indirect*. See Paul Hernadi, *Beyond Genre* (Ithaca, N.Y., 1972), pp. 187–205, and Edward Versluis, "Narrative Mimicry and the Representation of the Mental Processes" (Ph.D. dissertation, University of Chicago, 1972).

8   Or "substitutionary perception," in the phrase of Bernard Fehr, "Substitutionary Narration and Description: A Chapter in Stylistics," *Von Englands geistigen Bestanden* (Frauenfeld, 1944), pp. 264–279. Fehr notes some interesting features of substitutionary perception, for instance that it is regularly followed by progressive rather than simple verb forms: "He saw one of the men who had returned with Silva. *He was standing* in his boat...."

9   Graham Hough has identified the convention of the "well-spoken" narrator and its importance as a norm against which the voices of the characters are placed. He points out that the contrast is characteristic of the novel but not the epic ("Narrative and Dialogue in Jane Austen," *Critical Quarterly*, 12 [1970], 201).

10 Thus the incorrectness of Clive Hart's assumption (in "Eveline," *James Joyce's Dubliners: Critical Essays*, London, 1969, p. 51) that the "invasion" figure of the first sentence is "just the sort of hyperbole that a girl like Eveline might be expected to use."

11 Dorrit Cohn too has noted that the free indirect style "implies two basic possibilities: fusion with the subject, in which the actor identifies with, 'becomes' the person he imitates; or distance from the subject, a mock-identification that leads to caricature. Accordingly there are two divergent directions open to the narrated monologue, depending on which imitative tendency prevails: the lyric and the ironic" (110–111). "Lyric" strikes me as less descriptive of the effect than "sympathetic," in its root sense of the word – "in agreement with another's taste, mood, feeling, disposition, etc."

SEYMOUR CHATMAN

The Reality Effect

Roland Barthes

Roland Barthes (1915–1980)

Born in Cherbourg, France, Roland Barthes died at the age of 64 after being hit by a laundry truck. He earned degrees in classical literature (1939) and grammar and philosophy (1943) from the University of Paris, all the while battling tuberculosis (a disease which also exempted him from military service). After he was cured in 1950, Barthes' academic career took off: two years later he became a researcher at the Centre National de la Recherche Scientifique (CNRS), in 1960 he moved to the École des Hautes Études (School for Advanced Studies), and in 1976 became chair of Literary Semiology at the Collège de France. The breadth of Barthes' interests can be seen in his first three books: *Le Degré zéro de l'écriture* (1953; translated as *Writing Degree Zero*, 1967) covers the history of French literary styles; *Michelet par lui-même* (1954; translated as *Michelet*, 1987) considers the imagery in the work of nineteenth-century historian Jules Michelet; and *Mythologies* (1957; translated 1972) explores mass culture. With his 1963 study *Sur Racine* (translated as *On Racine*, 1964), Barthes entered into a spirited conflict with a more traditional scholar, Raymond Picard, and became aligned with structuralism; however, Barthes turned towards deconstruction with his publication of *S/Z* (1970; translated 1974) and *Le Plaisir de texte* (1973; translated as *The Pleasure of the Text*, 1975). Barthes' final shift was towards increasingly imaginative autobiographical pieces, including *Roland Barthes par Roland Barthes* (1975; translated as *Roland Barthes by Roland Barthes*, 1977), *Fragments d'un discours amoureux* (1977, translated as *A Lover's Discourse: Fragments*, 1979), and *La Chambre claire* (1980; translated as *Camera Lucida: Reflections on Photography*, 1981). The essays reprinted here are taken from *Le Bruissement de la langue* (1984; translated as *The Rustle of Language*, 1986): "The Reality Effect" was originally published in *Communications* (1968), and "From Work to Text" in *Revue d'esthétique* (1971).

W hen Flaubert, describing the room occupied by Mme Aubain, Félicité's employer, tells us that "an old piano supported, under a barometer, a pyramidal heap of boxes and cartons" ("A Simple Heart," from *Three Tales*); when Michelet, recounting the death of Charlotte Corday and reporting that, before the executioner's arrival, she was visited in prison by an artist who painted her portrait, includes the detail that "after an hour and a half, there was a gentle knock at a little door behind her" (*Histoire de France: La Révolution*) – these authors (among many others) are producing notations which structural analysis, concerned with identifying and systematizing the major articulations of narrative, usually and heretofore has left out, either because its inventory omits all details that are "superfluous" (in relation to structure) or because these same details are treated as "filling" (catalyses), assigned an indirect functional value insofar as, cumulatively, they constitute some index of character or atmosphere and so can ultimately be recuperated by structure.

It would seem, however, that if analysis seeks to be exhaustive (and what would any method be worth which did not account for the totality of its object, i.e., in this case, of the entire surface of the narrative fabric?), if it seeks to encompass the absolute detail, the indivisible unit, the fugitive transition, in order to assign them a place in the structure, it inevitably encounters notations which no function (not even the most indirect) can justify: such notations are scandalous (from the point of view of structure), or, what is even more disturbing, they seem to correspond to a kind of narrative *luxury*, lavish to the point of offering many "futile" details and thereby increasing the cost of narrative information. For if, in Flaubert's description, it is just possible to see in the notation of the piano an indication of its owner's bourgeois standing and in that of the cartons a sign of disorder and a kind of lapse in status likely to connote the atmosphere of the Aubain household, no purpose seems to justify reference to the barometer, an object neither incongruous nor significant, and therefore not participating, at first glance, in the order of the *notable*; and in Michelet's sentence, we have the same difficulty in accounting structurally for all the details: that the executioner came after the painter is all that is necessary to the account; how long the sitting lasted, the dimension and location of the door are useless (but the theme of the door, the softness of death's knock have an indisputable symbolic value). Even if they are not numerous, the "useless details" therefore seem inevitable: every narrative, at least every Western narrative of the ordinary sort nowadays, possesses a certain number.

Insignificant notation[1] (taking this word in its strong sense: apparently detached from the narrative's semiotic structure) is related to description, even if the object seems to be denoted only by a single word (in reality, the "pure" word does not exist: Flaubert's barometer is not cited in isolation; it is located, placed in a syntagm at once referential and syntactic); thus is underlined the enigmatic character of all description, about which a word is necessary: the general structure of narrative, at least as it has been occasionally analyzed till now, appears as essentially *predictive*; schematizing to the extreme, and without taking into account numerous detours, delays, reversals, and disappointments which narrative institutionally imposes upon this schema, we can say that, at each articulation of the narrative syntagm, someone says to the hero (or to the reader, it does not matter which): if you act in this way, if you choose this alternative, this is what will happen (the *reported* character of these predictions does not call into question their practical nature). Description is entirely different: it has no predictive mark; "analogical," its structure is purely summary and does not contain that trajectory of choices and alternatives which gives narration the appearance of a huge traffic-control center, furnished with a referential (and not merely discursive) temporality. This is an opposition which, anthropologically, has its importance: when, under the influence of von Frisch's experiments, it was assumed that bees had a language, it had to be realized that, while these insects possessed a predictive system of dances (in order to collect their food), nothing in it approached a *description*. Thus, description appears as a kind of characteristic of the so-called higher languages, to the apparently paradoxical degree that it is justified by no finality of action or of communication. The singularity of description (or of the "useless detail") in narrative fabric, its isolated situation, designates a question which has the greatest importance for the structural analysis of narrative. This question is the following: Is everything in narrative significant, and if not, if insignificant stretches subsist in the narrative syntagm, what is ultimately, so to speak, the significance of this insignificance?

First of all, we must recall that Western culture, in one of its major currents, has certainly not left description outside meaning, and has furnished it with a finality quite "recognized" by the literary institution. This current is Rhetoric, and this finality is that of the "beautiful": description has long had an aesthetic function. Very early in antiquity, to the two expressly functional genres of discourse, legal and political, was added a third, the epideictic, a ceremonial discourse intended to excite the admiration of the audience (and no longer to persuade it); this discourse contained in germ – whatever the ritual rules of its use: eulogy or obituary – the very idea of an aesthetic finality of language; in the Alexandrian neo-rhetoric of the second century A.D., there was a craze for ecphrasis, the detachable set piece (thus having its end in itself, independent of any general function), whose object was to describe places, times, people, or works of art, a tradition which was maintained throughout the Middle Ages. As Curtius has emphasized, description in this period is constrained by no realism; its truth is unimportant (or even its verisimilitude); there is no hesitation to put lions or olive trees in a northern country; only the constraint of the descriptive genre counts; plausibility is not referential here but openly discursive: it is the generic rules of discourse which lay down the law.

Moving ahead to Flaubert, we see that the aesthetic purpose of description is still very strong. In *Madame Bovary*, the description of Rouen (a real referent if ever there was one) is subject to the tyrannical constraints of what we must call aesthetic verisimilitude, as is attested by the corrections made in this passage in the course of six successive rewritings. Here we see, first of all, that the corrections do not in any way issue from a closer consideration of the model: Rouen, perceived by Flaubert, remains just the same, or more precisely, if it changes somewhat from one version to the next, it is solely because he finds it necessary to focus an image or avoid a phonic redundancy condemned by the rules of *le beau style*, or again to "arrange" a quite contingent felicity of expression;[2] next we see that the descriptive fabric, which at first glance seems to grant a major importance (by its dimension, by the concern for its detail) to the object *Rouen*, is in fact only a sort of setting meant to receive the jewels of a number of rare metaphors, the neutral, prosaic excipient which swathes the precious symbolic substance, as if, in Rouen, all that mattered were the figures of rhetoric to which the sight of the city lends itself – as if Rouen were notable only by its substitutions (*the masts like a forest of needles, the islands like huge motionless black fish, the clouds like aerial waves silently breaking against a cliff*); last, we see that the whole description is *constructed* so as to connect Rouen to a painting: it is a painted scene which the language takes up ("Thus, seen from above, the whole landscape had the motionless look of a painting"); the writer here fulfills Plato's definition of the artist as a maker in the third degree, since he imitates what is already the simulation of an essence. Thus, although the description of Rouen is quite irrelevant to the narrative structure of *Madame Bovary* (we can attach it to no functional sequence nor to any characterial, atmospheric, or sapiential signified), it is not in the least scandalous, it is justified, if not by the work's logic, at least by the laws of literature: its "meaning" exists, it depends on conformity not to the model but to the cultural rules of representation.

All the same, the aesthetic goal of Flaubertian description is thoroughly mixed with "realistic" imperatives, as if the referent's exactitude, superior or indifferent to any other function, governed and alone justified its description, or – in the case of descriptions reduced to a single word – its denotation: here aesthetic constraints are steeped – at least as an alibi – in referential constraints: it is likely that, if one came to Rouen in a diligence, the view one would have coming down the slope leading to the town would not be "objectively" different from the panorama Flaubert describes. This mixture – this interweaving – of constraints has a double advantage: on the one hand, aesthetic function, giving a meaning to "the fragment," halts what we might call the vertigo of notation; for once, discourse is no longer guided and limited by structural imperatives of the anecdote (functions and indices), nothing could indicate why we should halt the details of the description here and not there; if it were not subject to an aesthetic or rhetorical choice, any "view" would be inexhaustible by discourse: there would always be a corner, a detail, an inflection of space or color to report; on the other hand, by positing the referential as real, by pretending to follow it in a submissive fashion, realistic description avoids being reduced to fantasmatic activity (a precaution which was supposed necessary to the "objectivity" of the account); classical rhetoric had in a sense institutionalized the fantasmatic as a specific figure, *hypotyposis*, whose function was to "put things before the hearer's eyes," not in a neutral, constative manner, but by imparting to representation all the luster of desire (this was the vividly illuminated

ROLAND BARTHES

sector of discourse, with prismatic outlines: *illustris oratio*); declaratively renouncing the constraints of the rhetorical code, realism must seek a new reason to describe.

The irreducible residues of functional analysis have this in common: they denote what is ordinarily called "concrete reality" (insignificant gestures, transitory attitudes, insignificant objects, redundant words). The pure and simple "representation" of the "real," the naked relation of "what is" (or has been) thus appears as a resistance to meaning; this resistance confirms the great mythic opposition of the *true-to-life* (the lifelike) and the *intelligible*; it suffices to recall that, in the ideology of our time, obsessive reference to the "concrete" (in what is rhetorically demanded of the human sciences, of literature, of behavior) is always brandished like a weapon against meaning, as if, by some statutory exclusion, what is alive cannot not signify – and vice versa. Resistance of the "real" (in its written form, of course) to structure is very limited in the fictive account, constructed by definition on a model which, for its main outlines, has no other constraints than those of intelligibility; but this same "reality" becomes the essential reference in historical narrative, which is supposed to report "what really happened": what does the non-functionality of a detail matter then, once it denotes "what took place"; "concrete reality" becomes the sufficient justification for speaking. History (historical discourse: *historia rerum gestarum*) is in fact the model of those narratives which consent to fill in the interstices of their functions by structurally superfluous notations, and it is logical that literary realism should have been – give or take a few decades – contemporary with the regnum of "objective" history, to which must be added the contemporary development of techniques, of works, and institutions based on the incessant need to authenticate the "real": the photograph (immediate witness of "what was here"), reportage, exhibitions of ancient objects (the success of the Tutankhamen show makes this quite clear), the tourism of monuments and historical sites. All this shows that the "real" is supposed to be self-sufficient, that it is strong enough to belie any notion of "function," that its "speech-act" has no need to be integrated into a structure and that the *having-been-there* of things is a sufficient principle of speech.

Since antiquity, the "real" has been on History's side; but this was to help it oppose the "lifelike," the "plausible," to oppose the very order of narrative (of imitation or "poetry"). All classical culture lived for centuries on the notion that reality could in no way contaminate verisimilitude; first of all, because verisimilitude is never anything but *opinable*: it is entirely subject to (public) opinion; as Nicole said: "One must not consider things as they are in themselves, nor as they are known to be by one who speaks or writes, but only in relation to what is known of them by those who read or hear"; then, because History was thought to be general, not particular (whence the propensity, in classical texts, to functionalize all details, to produce strong structures and to justify no notation by the mere guarantee of "reality"); finally, because, in verisimilitude, the contrary is never impossible, since notation rests on a majority, but not an absolute, opinion. The motto implicit on the threshold of all classical discourse (subject to the ancient idea of verisimilitude) is: *Esto* (*Let there be, suppose…*). "Real," fragmented, interstitial notation, the kind we are dealing with here, renounces this implicit intro-duction, and it is free of any such postulation that occurs in the structural fabric. Hence, there is a break between the ancient mode of versimilitude and modern realism; but hence, too, a new verisimilitude is born, which is precisely *realism* (by which we mean any discourse which accepts "speech-acts" justified by their referent alone).

Semiotically, the "concrete detail" is constituted by the *direct* collusion of a referent and a signifier; the signified is expelled from the sign, and with it, of course, the possibility of developing a *form of the signified*, i.e., narrative structure itself. (Realistic literature is narrative, of course, but that is because its realism is only fragmentary, erratic, confined to "details," and because the most realistic narrative imaginable develops along unrealistic lines.) This is what we might call the *referential illusion*.[3] The truth of this illusion is this: eliminated from the realist speech-act as a signified of denotation, the "real" returns to it as a signified of connotation; for just when these details are reputed to *denote* the real directly, all that they do – without saying so – is *signify* it; Flaubert's barometer, Michelet's little door finally say nothing but this: *we are the real*; it is the category of "the real" (and not its contingent contents) which is then signified; in other words, the very absence of the signified, to the advantage of the referent alone, becomes the very signifier of realism: the *reality effect* is produced, the basis of that unavowed verisimilitude which forms the aesthetic of all the standard works of modernity.

This new verisimilitude is very different from the old one, for it is neither a respect for the "laws of the genre" nor even their mask, but proceeds from the intention to degrade the sign's tripartite nature in order to make notation the pure encounter of an object and its expression. The disintegration of the sign – which seems indeed to be modernity's grand affair – is of course present in the realistic enterprise, but in a somewhat regressive manner, since it occurs in the name of a referential plenitude, whereas the goal today is to empty the sign and infinitely to postpone its object so as to challenge, in a radical fashion, the age-old aesthetic of "representation."

NOTES

1   In this brief account, we shall not give examples of "insignificant" notations, for the insignificant can be revealed only on the level of an immense structure: once cited, a notion is neither significant nor insignificant; it requires an already analyzed context.
2   A mechanism distinguished by Valéry, in *Littérature*, commenting on Baudelaire's line "*La servante au grand coeur...*": "This line *came* to Baudelaire...And Baudelaire continued. He buried the cook out on the lawn, which goes against the custom, but goes with the rhyme," etc.
3   An illusion clearly illustrated by the program Thiers assigned to the historian: "To be simply true, to be what things are and nothing more than that, and nothing except that."

From Work to Text

Roland Barthes

From *The Rustle of Language*, translated by Richard Howard. New York: Hill and Wang, 1986 (1971), pp. 56–64. Translation copyright © 1986 by Farrar, Straus and Giroux, Inc. Reprinted by permission of Hill and Wang, a division of Farrar, Straus and Giroux, LLC.

scholar, Raymond Picard, and became aligned with structuralism; however, Barthes turned towards deconstruction with his publication of *S/Z* (1970; translated 1974) and *Le Plaisir de texte* (1973; translated as *The Pleasure of the Text*, 1975). Barthes' final shift was towards increasingly imaginative autobiographical pieces, including *Roland Barthes par Roland Barthes* (1975; translated as *Roland Barthes by Roland Barthes*, 1977), *Fragments d'un discours amoureux* (1977, translated as *A Lover's Discourse: Fragments*, 1979), and *La Chambre claire* (1980; translated as *Camera Lucida: Reflections on Photography*, 1981). The essays reprinted here are taken from *Le Bruissement de la langue* (1984; translated as *The Rustle of Language*, 1986): "The Reality Effect" was originally published in *Communications* (1968), and "From Work to Text" in *Revue d'esthétique* (1971).

A change has lately occurred, or is occurring, in our idea of language and consequently of the (literary) work which owes to that language at least its phenomenal existence. This change is obviously linked to the present development of (among other disciplines) linguistics, anthropology, Marxism, psychoanalysis (the word *link* is used here in a deliberately neutral manner: no determination is being invoked, however multiple and dialectical). The transformation of the notion of the work does not necessarily derive from the internal renewal of each of these disciplines, but rather from their intersection at the level of an object which traditionally proceeds from none of them. We might say, as a matter of fact, that *interdisciplinary* activity, today so highly valued in research, cannot be achieved by the simple confrontation of specialized branches of knowledge; the interdisciplinary is not a comfortable affair: it begins *effectively* (and not by the simple utterance of a pious hope) when the solidarity of the old disciplines breaks down – perhaps even violently, through the shocks of fashion – to the advantage of a new object, a new language, neither of which is precisely this discomfort of classification which permits diagnosing a certain mutation. The mutation which seems to be affecting the notion of the work must not, however, be overestimated; it is part of an epistemological shift, more than of a real break of the kind which in fact occurred in the last century upon the appearance of Marxism and Freudianism; no new break has occurred since, and we might say that for the last hundred years we have been involved in a repetition. What History, our History, allows us today is merely to displace, to vary, to transcend, to repudiate. Just as Einsteinian science compels us to include within the object studied the *relativity of reference points*, so the combined action of Marxism, Freudianism, and structuralism compels us, in literature, to relativize the relations of *scriptor*, reader, and observer (critic). Confronting the *work* – a traditional notion, long since, and still today, conceived in what we might call a Newtonian fashion – there now occurs the demand for a new object, obtained by a shift or a reversal of previous categories. This object is the *Text*. I know that this word is fashionable (I myself am compelled to use it frequently), hence suspect in some quarters; but this is precisely why I should like to review the main propositions at whose intersection the Text is located, as I see it; the word *proposition* must here be understood more grammatically

ROLAND BARTHES

than logically: these are speech-acts, not arguments, "hints," approaches which agree to remain metaphorical. Here are these propositions: they concern method, genres, the sign, the plural, filiation, reading, pleasure.

1. The text must not be understood as a computable object. It would be futile to attempt a material separation of works from texts. In particular, we must not permit ourselves to say: the work is classical, the text is avant-garde; there is no question of establishing a trophy in modernity's name and declaring certain literary productions *in* and *out* by reason of their chronological situation: there can be "Text" in a very old work, and many products of contemporary literature are not texts at all. The difference is as follows: the work is a fragment of substance, it occupies a portion of the spaces of books (for example, in a library). The Text is a methodological field. The opposition may recall (though not reproduce term for term) a distinction proposed by Lacan: "reality" is shown [*se montre*], the "real" is proved [*se démontre*]; in the same way, the work is seen (in bookstores, in card catalogues, on examination syllabuses), the text is demonstrated, is spoken according to certain rules (or against certain rules); the work is held in the hand, the text is held in language: it exists only when caught up in a discourse (or rather it is Text for the very reason that it knows itself to be so); the Text is not the decomposition of the work, it is the work which is the Text's imaginary tail. Or again: *the Text is experienced only in an activity, in a production.* It follows that the Text cannot stop (for example, at a library shelf); its constitutive moment is *traversal* (notably, it can traverse the work, several works).

2. Similarly, the Text does not stop at (good) literature; it cannot be caught up in a hierarchy, or even in a simple distribution of genres. What constitutes it is on the contrary (or precisely) its force of subversion with regard to the old classifications. How to classify Georges Bataille? Is this writer a novelist, a poet, an essayist, an economist, a philosopher, a mystic? The answer is so uncertain that handbooks of literature generally prefer to leave Bataille out; as a matter of fact, Bataille has written texts, or even, perhaps, always one and the same text. If the Text raises problems of classification (moreover, this is one of its "social" functions), it is because it always implies a certain experience of limits. Thibaudet used to speak (but in a very restricted sense) of limit-works (such as Chateaubriand's *Life of Rancé*, a work which indeed seems to us to be a "text"): the Text is what is situated at the limit of the rules of the speech-act (rationality, readability, etc.). This notion is not rhetorical, we do not resort to it for "heroic" postures: the Text attempts to locate itself very specifically *behind* the limit of the *doxa* (is not public opinion, constitutive of our democratic societies, powerfully aided by mass communications – is not public opinion defined by its limits, its energy of exclusion, its *censorship?*); taking the word literally, we might say that the Text is always *paradoxical*.

3. The text is approached and experienced in relation to the sign. The work closes upon a signified. We can attribute two modes of signification to this signified: either it is claimed to be apparent, and the work is then the object of a science of the letter, which is philology; or else this signified is said to be secret and final, and must be sought for, and then the work depends upon a hermeneutics, an interpretation (Marxist,

psychoanalytic, thematic, etc.); in short, the work itself functions as a general sign, and it is natural that it should represent an institutional category of the civilization of the Sign. The Text, on the contrary, practices the infinite postponement of the signified, the Text is dilatory; its field is that of the signifier; the signifier must not be imagined as "the first part of the meaning," its material vestibule, but rather, on the contrary, as its *aftermath*; similarly, the signifier's *infinitude* does not refer to some notion of the ineffable (of an unnamable signified) but to a notion of *play*; the engendering of the perpetual signifier (in the fashion of a perpetual calendar) in the field of the Text is not achieved by some organic process of maturation, or a hermeneutic process of "delving deeper," but rather by a serial movement of dislocations, overlappings, variations; the logic governing the Text is not comprehensive (trying to define what the work "means") but metonymic; the activity of associations, contiguities, cross-references coincides with a liberation of symbolic energy (if it failed him, man would die). The work (in the best of cases) is *moderately* symbolic (its symbolics runs short, i.e., stops); the Text is *radically* symbolic: *a work whose integrally symbolic nature one conceives, perceives, and receives is a text.* The Text is thus restored to language; like language, it is structured but decentered, without closure (let us note, to answer the scornful suspicion of "fashion" sometimes lodged against structuralism, that the epistemological privilege nowadays granted to language derives precisely from the fact that in it [language] we have discovered a paradoxical idea of structure: a system without end or center).

4. The Text is plural. This does not mean only that it has several meanings but that it fulfills the very plurality of meaning: an *irreducible* (and not just acceptable) plurality. The Text is not coexistence of meaning, but passage, traversal; hence, it depends not on an interpretation, however liberal, but on an explosion, on dissemination. The plurality of the Text depends, as a matter of fact, not on the ambiguity of its contents, but on what we might call the stereographic plurality of the signifiers which weave it (etymologic-ally, the text is a fabric): the reader of the Text might be compared to an idle subject (who has relaxed his image-repertoire): this fairly empty subject strolls (this has happened to the author of these lines, and it is for this reason that he has come to an intense awareness of the Text) along a hillside at the bottom of which flows a wadi (I use the word to attest to a certain alienation); what he perceives is multiple, irreducible, issuing from heterogeneous, detached substances and levels: lights, colors, vegetation, heat, air, tenuous explosions of sound, tiny cries of birds, children's voices from the other side of the valley, paths, gestures, garments of inhabitants close by or very far away; all these incidents are half identifiable: they issue from known codes, but their combinative operation is unique, it grounds the stroll in a difference which cannot be repeated except *as difference*. This is what happens in the Text: it can be Text only in its difference (which does not mean its individuality); its reading is semelfactive (which renders any induct-ive-deductive science of texts illusory: no "grammar" of the text) and yet entirely woven of quotations, references, echoes: cultural languages (what language is not cultural?), antecedent or contemporary, which traverse it through and through, in a vast stereoph-ony. The intertextuality in which any text is apprehended, since it is itself the intertext of another text, cannot be identified with some *origin* of the text: to seek out the "sources," the "influences" of a work is to satisfy the myth of filiation; the quotations a text is made of are anonymous, irrecoverable, and yet *already read*: they are quotations

without quotation marks. The work disturbs no monistic philosophy (there are antagonistic ones, as we know); for such a philosophy, plurality is Evil. Hence, confronting the work, the Text might indeed take for its motto the words of the man possessed by devils: "My name is legion, for we are many" (Mark 5:9). The plural or demonic texture which sets the Text in opposition to the work may involve profound modifications of reading, precisely where monologism seems to be the law: certain "texts" of Scripture, traditionally adopted by theological (historical or anagogical) monism, may lend themselves to a diffraction of meanings (i.e., finally, to a materialist reading), while the Marxist interpretation of the work, hitherto resolutely monistic, may become more materialist by pluralizing itself (if, of course, Marxist "institutions" permit this).

5. The work is caught up in a process of filiation. What is postulated are a *determination* of the world (of the race, then of History) over the work, a *consecution* of works among themselves, and an *appropriation* of the work to its author. The author is reputed to be the father and the owner of his work; literary science thus teaches us to *respect* the manuscript and the author's declared intentions, and society postulates a legality of the author's relation to his work (this is the "author's rights," actually a recent affair, not legalized in France until the time of the Revolution). The Text, on the other hand, is read without the Father's inscription. The metaphor of the Text is here again detached from the metaphor of the work; the latter refers to the image of an *organism* which grows by vital expansion, by "development" (a significantly ambiguous word: biological and rhetorical); the metaphor of the Text is that of the *network*; if the Text expands, it is by the effect of a combinative operation, of a systematics (an image, moreover, close to the views of contemporary biology concerning the living being); no vital "respect" is therefore due to the Text: it can be *broken* (moreover, this is what the Middle Ages did with two nonetheless authoritarian texts: Scripture and Aristotle); the Text can be read without its father's guarantee; the restoration of the intertext paradoxically abolishes inheritance. It is not that the Author cannot "return" in the Text, in his text, but he does so, one might say, as a guest; if he is a novelist, he inscribes himself there as one of his characters, drawn as a figure in the carpet; his inscription is no longer privileged, paternal, alethic, but ludic: he becomes, one can say, a paper author; his life is no longer the origin of his fables, but a fable concurrent with his life; there is a reversion of the work upon life (and no longer the contrary); the work of Proust and Genet permits us to read their lives as a text: the word *bio-graphy* regains a strong, etymological meaning; and thereby the sincerity of the speech-act, a veritable "cross" of literary ethics, becomes a false problem: the *I* that writes the text is never anything but a paper *I.*

6. The work is ordinarily the object of consumption; I intend no demagoguery by referring to what is called a consumer culture, but we must recognize that today it is the work's "quality" (which ultimately implies an appreciation of "taste") and not the actual operation of reading which can make differences between books: "cultivated" reading is not structurally different from reading on trains. The Text (if only by its frequent "unreadability") decants the work (if it permits it at all) from its consumption and recuperates it as play, task, production, practice. This means that the Text requires an attempt to abolish (or at least to diminish) the distance between writing and reading, not by intensifying the reader's projection into the work, but by linking the two together

into one and the same signifying practice. The distance that separates reading from writing is historical. In the period of strongest social division (before the instauration of democratic cultures), reading and writing were *equally* class privileges: Rhetoric, the great literary code of that time, taught *writing* (even if what was ordinarily produced were discourses, not texts); it is significant that the advent of democracy reversed the watchword: the (secondary) school prides itself on teaching *reading* and no longer writing. In fact, *reading*, in the sense of *consuming*, is not *playing* with the text. "Playing" must be taken here in all the polysemy of the term: the text itself "plays" (like a door that "plays" back and forth on its hinges; like a fishing rod in which there is some "play"); and the reader plays twice over: he *plays at* the Text (ludic meaning), he seeks a practice which reproduces it; but, so that this practice is not reduced to a passive, interior *mimesis* (the Text being precisely what resists this reduction), he *plays* the Text; we must not forget that *play* is also a musical term; the history of music (as practice, not as "art") is, moreover, quite parallel to that of the Text; there was a time when, active amateurs being numerous (at least within a certain class), "to play" and "to listen" constituted a virtually undifferentiated activity; then two roles successively appeared: first of all, that of the *interpreter*, to which the bourgeois public (though it could still play a little itself: this is the entire history of the piano) delegated its playing; then that of the (passive) amateur who listens to music without being able to play it (the piano has effectively been replaced by the record); we know that today post-serial music has disrupted the role of the "interpreter," who is asked to be in a sense the co-author of the score which he completes rather than "expresses." The Text is a little like a score of this new kind: it solicits from the reader a practical collaboration. A great novation this, for who *executes* the work? (Mallarmé raised this question: he wanted the audience to *produce* the book.) Today only the critic executes the work (pun intended). The reduction of reading to consumption is obviously responsible for the "boredom" many feel in the presence of the modern ("unreadable") text, the avant-garde film or painting: to be bored means one cannot produce the text, play it, release it, *make it go*.

7. This suggests one final approach to the Text: that of pleasure. I do not know if a hedonist aesthetic ever existed (eudaemonist philosophies are certainly rare). Of course, a pleasure of the work (of certain works) exists; I can enjoy reading and rereading Proust, Flaubert, Balzac, and even — why not? — Alexandre Dumas; but this pleasure, however intense, and even when it is released from any prejudice, remains partly (unless there has been an exceptional critical effort) a pleasure of consumption: for, if I can read these authors, I also know that I cannot *rewrite* them (that one cannot, today, write "like that"); and this rather depressing knowledge suffices to separate me from the production of these works, at the very moment when their distancing founds my modernity (to be modern — is this not really to know that one cannot begin again?). The Text is linked to delectation, i.e., to pleasure without separation. Order of the signifier, the Text participates in its way in a social utopia; before History (supposing that History does not choose barbarism), the Text fulfills if not the transparency of social relations, at least the transparency of language relations: it is the space in which no language prevails over any other, where the languages circulate (retaining the *circular* meaning of the word).

ROLAND BARTHES

These few propositions do not necessarily constitute the articulation of a Theory of the Text. This is not merely the consequence of the presenter's inadequacies (moreover, in many points he has merely recapitulated what is being investigated and developed around him). This is a consequence of the fact that a Theory of the Text cannot be satisfied with a meta-linguistic exposition: the destruction of meta-language, or at least (for it may be necessary to resort to it provisionally) calling it into question, is part of the theory itself: discourse on the Text should itself be only text, research, textual activity, since the Text is that *social* space which leaves no language safe, outside, and no subject of the speech-act in a situation of judge, master, analyst, confessor, decoder: the theory of the Text can coincide only with a practice of writing.

13

Reading Narrative

J. Hillis Miller

Joseph Hillis Miller (b. 1928)

Born in Newport News, Virginia, J. Hillis Miller attended Oberlin College and Harvard University, where he received his doctoral degree at the age of 24. After 19 years teaching at Johns Hopkins University, Miller went to Yale University in 1972. There he joined Paul de Man, Geoffrey Hartman, Harold Bloom, and Jacques Derrida to form what became known as the Yale School of deconstruction. Miller moved to the University of California at Irvine in 1986, where he is now professor emeritus. Miller is a member of the American Academy of Arts and Sciences and the American Philosophical Society, and has been honored as a Guggenheim Fellow and a National Endowment for the Humanities Senior Fellow. He has also served as editor of *Modern Language Notes* and *ELH,* and president of the Modern Language Association. Miller's books include: *The Form of Victorian Fiction* (1968); *Fiction and Repetition: Seven English Novels* (1982); *The Ethics of Reading* (1987); *Ariadne's Thread: Story Lines* (1992); *Reading Narrative* (1998); *Speech Acts in Literature* (2001); and *On Literature* (2002).

From *Reading Narrative.* Norman: University of Oklahoma Press, 1998, from ch. 13, pp. 158–77, notes, 247–9. Copyright © 1998 by the University of Oklahoma Press. Reprinted by permission. All rights reserved.

Indirect Discourses and Irony

I turn now to indirect discourse, one of the major resources of story-telling in novels and one of the most important sources of disquieting perturbations in narrative middles. This chapter, which also will focus more closely on irony in narrative, is the penultimate essay before the extended discussion of works by [Walter] Pater and Gaskell that makes up the final chapter in *Reading Narrative*. I take as examples three innocent-looking passages of indirect discourse, one from Anthony Trollope's *The Warden*, one from Elizabeth Gaskell's *Cranford*, one from the opening of Dickens's *Pickwick Papers*. It is necessary to cite each at some length in order to give the full flavor of the vibrating meaning generated by the play between different superimposed languages. I ask the reader to read each with patient attention to the different quality of irony in each:

> In the meantime the warden sat alone, leaning on the arm of his chair; he had poured out a glass of wine, but had done so merely from habit, for he left it untouched; there he sat gazing at the open window, and thinking, if he can be said to have thought, of the happiness of his past life. All manner of past delights came before his mind, which at the time he had enjoyed without considering them; his easy days, his absence of all kind of hard work, his pleasant shady home, those twelve old neighbours whose welfare till now had been the source of so much pleasant care, the excellence of his children, the friendship of the dear old bishop, the solemn grandeur of those vaulted aisles, through which he loved to hear his own voice pealing; and then that friend of friends, that choice ally that had never deserted him, that eloquent companion that would always, when asked, discourse such pleasant music, that violoncello of his – ah, how happy he had been! but it was over now; his easy days and absence of work had been the crime which brought on him his tribulation; his shady home was pleasant no longer; maybe it was no longer his; the old neighbours, whose welfare had been so desired by him, were his enemies; his daughter was as wretched as himself; and even the bishop was made miserable by his position. He could never again lift up his voice boldly as he had hitherto done among his brethren, for he felt that he was disgraced; and he feared even to touch his bow, for he knew how grievous a sound of wailing, how piteous a lamentation, it would produce.[1]

> Cranford had so long piqued itself on being an honest and moral town, that it had grown to fancy itself too genteel and well-bred to be otherwise, and felt the stain upon its character at this time doubly. But we comforted ourselves with the assurance which we gave to each other, that the robberies could never have been committed by any Cranford person; it must have been a stranger or strangers who brought this disgrace upon the town, and occasioned as many precautions as if we were living among the Red Indians or the French.

> This last comparison of our nightly state of defence and fortification was made by Mrs. Forrester, whose father had served under General Burgoyne in the American war, and whose husband had fought the French in Spain. She indeed inclined to the idea that, in some way, the French were connected with the small thefts, which were ascertained facts, and the burglaries and highway robberies, which were rumours. She had been deeply impressed with the idea of French spies, at some time in her life; and the notion could never be fairly eradicated, but sprung up again from time to time. And now her theory was this: the Cranford people respected themselves too much, and were too grateful to the aristocracy who were so kind as to live near the town, ever to disgrace their bringing up by being dishonest or immoral; therefore, we must believe that the robbers were strangers – if

strangers, why not foreigners? – if foreigners, who so likely as the French? Signor Brunoni spoke broken English like a Frenchman, and, though he wore a turban like a Turk, Mrs. Forrester had seen a print of Madame de Staël with a turban on, and another of Mr. Denon in just such a dress as that in which the conjuror had made his appearance; showing clearly that the French, as well as the Turks, wore turbans: there could be no doubt Signor Brunoni was a Frenchman – a French spy, come to discover the weak and undefended places of England; and, doubtless, he had his accomplices; for her part, she, Mrs. Forrester, had always had her own opinion of Miss Pole's adventure at the George Inn – seeing two men where only one was believed to be: French people had ways and means, which she was thankful to say, the English knew nothing about; and she had never felt quite easy in her mind about going to see that conjuror; it was rather too much like a forbidden thing, though the Rector was there. In short, Mrs. Forrester grew more excited than we had ever known her before; and, being an officer's daughter and widow, we looked up to her opinion, of course.

Really, I do not know how much was true or false in the reports which flew about like wildfire just at this time; but it seemed to me then that there was every reason to believe that at Mardon (a small town about eight miles from Cranford) houses and shops were entered by holes made in the walls, the bricks being silently carried away in the dead of night, and all done so quietly that no sound was heard either in or out of the house. Miss Matty gave it up in despair when she heard of this. "What was the use," said she, "of locks and bolts, and bells to the windows, and going round the house every night? That last trick was fit for a conjuror. Now she did believe that Signor Brunoni was at the bottom of it."[2]

The first ray of light which illumines the gloom, and converts into a dazzling brilliancy that obscurity in which the earlier history of the public career of the immortal Pickwick would appear to be involved, is derived from the perusal of the following entry in the Transactions of the Pickwick Club, which the editor of these papers feels the highest pleasure in laying before his readers, as a proof of the careful attention, indefatigable assiduity, and nice discrimination, with which his search among the multifarious documents confided to him has been conducted.

"May 12, 1827. Joseph Smiggers, Esq., P.V.P.M.P.C.,* presiding. The following resolutions unanimously agreed to: –

"That this Association has heard read, with feelings of unmingled satisfaction, and unqualified approval, the paper communicated by Samuel Pickwick, Esq., G.C.M.P.C.,† entitled "Speculations on the Source of the Hampstead Ponds, with some Observations on the Theory of Tittlebats"; and that this Association does hereby return its warmest thanks to the said Samuel Pickwick, Esq., G.C.M.P.C., for the same...."

A casual observer, adds the secretary, to whose notes we are indebted for the following account – a casual observer might possibly have remarked nothing extraordinary in the bald head, and circular spectacles, which were intently turned towards his (the secretary's) face, during the reading of the above resolutions: to those who knew that the gigantic brain of Pickwick was working beneath that forehead, and that the beaming eyes of Pickwick were twinkling behind those glasses, the sight was indeed an interesting one. There sat the man who had traced to their source the mighty ponds of Hampstead, and agitated the scientific world with his Theory of Tittlebats, as calm and unmoved as the deep waters of the one on a frosty day, or as a solitary specimen of the other in the inmost recesses of an

---

* Perpetual Vice-President – Member Pickwick Club.
† General Chairman – Member Pickwick Club.

J. HILLIS MILLER

earthen jar. And how much more interesting did the spectacle become, when starting into full life and animation, as a simultaneous call for "Pickwick" burst from his followers, that illustrious man slowly mounted into the Windsor chair, on which he had been previously seated, and addressed the club he himself had founded. What a study for an artist did that exciting scene present! The eloquent Pickwick, with one hand gracefully concealed behind his coat tails, and the other waving in air, to assist his glowing declamation; his elevated position revealing those tights and gaiters, which, had they clothed an ordinary man, might have passed without observation, but which, when Pickwick clothed them – if we may use the expression – inspired involuntary awe and respect; surrounded by the men who had volunteered to share the perils of his travels, and who were destined to participate in the glories of his discoveries.[3]

Passages, *topoi*, places, *lieux de passage*, crossings, examples, samples, each cut from its context and cited here, sewn into a new context, like a prosthetic limb or organ to repair, replace, or stand in for something that might otherwise be missing in my own argument. At this point that argument cannot pass from here to there without the help of these quotations. This happens according to the law of each text's dependence on other texts that Jacques Derrida formulates: "Every thesis is (bands erect) a prosthesis; what affords reading affords reading by citations (necessarily truncated, clippings, repetitions, suctions, sections, suspensions, selections, stitchings, scarrings, grafts, postiches, organs without their own proper body, proper body covered with cuts...."[4]

Would not the passage I have cited cease to be problematic if they were reinserted in their originating contexts and related back to the authorizing sources that first wrote them, the minds that generated them and were their places of emission? Would not each context determine a stable, monological program according to which the passage in question should be read? Does not citation perhaps always do violence to what it cites, always quote too little or too much, or too little and too much at once, so that the passage is neither completely free of its paternal or maternal source nor sufficiently provided with it? These are just the questions here, questions that lead to other questions. Do the passages cohere with their contexts, the whole narrative lines of which they are segments? What happens in repetition or citation? When I cite these passages here I do something oddly violent to them, or allow them to do something odd and violent to me by citing them. The act of citation changes them radically, if only by putting implicit "scare quotes" around them. They are themselves, however, already, in part at least, citations, already therefore themselves acts of violence, like the ironic undermining that is performed by repeating exactly, with the same intonation, what someone has just said to you. My citations repeat in indirect discourse, with a change of person and tense, previous states of mind or acts of language that are imagined as having already occurred for the characters. These are at a later time iterated by the narrator. This form makes possible my reiteration of them later still, here in my own text, where the passages are grafted or tipped in to help me out as examples.

The critic of a given work must begin somewhere. He or she must establish some passage or other, not necessarily the first in the text in question, as a firm foundation, open to being solidly and unequivocally interpreted. On the basis of that the movement forward on the spirals of the hermeneutical corkscrew may proceed. This positing of a beginning can, however, never securely happen, neither in a reading that keeps the founding passage fully attached to its surrounding context, if that could ever happen, nor in a reading, like mine here, that detaches citations from their original places and sews them together in juxtaposed incongruity within a critical or theoretical text, making something like Robinson Crusoe's patched garment of many skins.

The name for the oscillation of meaning in the passages quoted above is irony. All the passages vibrate with one form or another of radical irony. Since irony is a form of endless looping or feedback, this instability suggests that the interpreter can never go beyond any passage she or he takes as a starting place, if the problem of interpreting it is taken as a serious task. The interpreter remains, rather, suspended interminably in an impossible attempt to still the passage's internal movement so that it can be used as a firm stepping-off place for a more complete journey of interpretation.

There is no apparent difficulty in understanding any of these passages. Each is pellucidly clear. Each of the first two conveys the strong illusion of two personalities in particular "life situations," that of the character, that of the narrator recreating at a later time the character's words or inner state. Word and inner state seem each the perfect match, mirror, or vehicle of the other. In the passage from *Cranford* Mary Smith reports, for the understanding of her urban readers, who do not know provincial village life, Mrs. Forrester's words and the way her mind works. In the passage from Trollope the anonymous narrator of *The Warden* records not so much Mr. Harding's words as his state of mind at a certain moment of his ordeal. The opening of *Pickwick Papers* establishes the narrator as only an editor, a transparent medium through which is transmitted the words (whether formal minutes or informal notes) of the secretary of the Pickwick Club. The narrator's opening words, however, are his own, and, within a few paragraphs, the "editor" is not quoting but reporting what the characters said in the same odd form of language, indirect discourse, that is used in the other two passages.

In spite of these complications, the reader has no difficulty following in all three citations the shifts from person to person. The reading is aided by changes in person, number, and tense, and by quotation marks. It is only when the reader begins to ask questions of the passages' language, rather than taking for granted the phantasmal illusions of the personalities created by language, that the words start to become problematic. This happens according to that law Paul Valéry formulates by the example of an innocent little word like "time." The word "time" functions splendidly as a plank-walk over an abyss so long as you do not begin to jump up and down on the plank, interrogating it, testing it, in this case by asking, as Saint Augustine did long ago, "What is time?" Then the plank breaks, and you fall.[5]

Such risky questions might include the following: In the passages I have quoted, who is speaking, from what place, and to whom? Whose language or idiom is the reader given, that of the character, that of the narrator, or a mixture of the two? How can one tell, in a given sentence, where the language of the character stops and that of the narrator begins? The two languages must be constantly superimposed, the reader supposes, not so much in an anacoluthon, or switching in the middle, as in a constant doubling or displacement in which the language of the character is said over again in a shift from "I" or "we" to "he," "she," or "they" and in a shift from present tense to past tense: "He could never again lift up his voice boldly as he had hitherto done among his brethren." "[F]or her part, she, Mrs. Forrester, had always had her own opinion of Miss Pole's adventures at the George Inn...: French people had ways and means, which she

J. HILLIS MILLER

was thankful to say, the English knew nothing about." "The bald head, and circular spectacles, which were intently turned towards his (the secretary's) face...." Such language would be spoken by no one in any conceivable "real life" situation, unless in the situation of oral storytelling that is, it may be, the origin of all narrative. Indirect discourse is primarily a convention of printed narrative, though it may be borrowed from the habits of oral narrative. In either oral or written forms indirect discourse is an artifice of language. It is always at a remove from speech used in its own immediate context.

What exactly, however, is the significance of the shift from "we" to "she" to "I" in the passage from *Cranford*? Why is the indirect discourse reporting Miss Matty's speech put in quotation marks ("Now she did believe that Signor Brunoni was at the bottom of it"), whereas the same kind of indirect discourse used for Mrs. Forrester is not put inside quotation marks? What is the significance of the phrase "thinking, if he can be said to have thought," in the passage in *The Warden?* In the opening of *Pickwick Papers*, what is the basic idiom from which the others are comic deviations? Let me try to answer these questions or at least show why they cannot be answered.

In the passage from *Cranford*, the speaker, Mary Smith, the narrator of the whole novel, unmarried, a little over thirty years old by the end of the novel, occasional visitor to Cranford from the large neighboring city of Drumble, speaks at first as a collective "we" for all the Cranford ladies. She then uses, apparently almost by accident, a comparison that has been made by one of those ladies, Mrs. Forrester: "as if we were living among the Red Indians or the French." The narrator's memory of this ("This last comparison...was made by Mrs. Forrester") leads to a sequence in which the "we" of the narrator allows a single voice, a single idiom, a single way of speaking to emerge from the group of Cranford ladies. This is mimed in the third person past tense by that narrative we (or is it a narrative I?): "French people had ways and means, which she was thankful to say, the English knew nothing about." At the end of this sequence there is a shift back to the first person plural, that is, a plunge back into the surrounding collective consciousness of the Cranford ladies as a group: "[she] being an officer's daughter and widow, we looked up to her opinion, of course." Then the present "I" of the narrator, drily skeptical now, though caught up then in the collective "panic,"[6] separates itself out: "Really I do not know how much was true or false in the reports...; but it seemed to me then...." Finally this "I" reports, oddly within quotation marks, Miss Matty's words, but transposes them again to the third person past tense. "Now I do believe" (which is what Miss Matty presumably said) is changed to "Now she did believe." Do these quotation marks function to grant Miss Matty's mind and her idiom greater respect than Mrs. Forrester's "thoughts"? The latter are Mrs. Forrester's own or at any rate they are the unique form a powerful ideology takes within her mind. These thoughts are then swallowed up in the collective mind of the panicked "all." They are, moreover, not supposed to be cited from a single continuous speech but to be a summary of the sort of thing Mrs. Forrester said over and over at that time. The passage moves from "we" to "she" to "we" to "I" to another "she," widening and narrowing its focus constantly. The narrative line bends, stretches, vibrates to an invisible blur, divides itself into two, into three, into a multitude that is yet one, comes together again into an unequivocal or univocal one, breaks, begins again, after a brief, almost imperceptible hiatus between paragraphs, and so on throughout the novel.

What is the original line of continuous consciousness (in the sense of the constant presence to itself of a self expressed in a single idiom, an idiolect, a proper language) that is the "source" of all these doublings and redoublings, and to which the line would safely return if its oscillations were allowed to die down or could be damped? The author? The narrator? The author's memory of her younger self and its language? The characters, one by one? The "consciousness of the community," the collective "we"? What attitude does Elizabeth Gaskell have, or does the text have, or are we as readers supposed to have, of judgment, sympathy, understanding, or condescending laughter toward these various imaginary persons? No verifiable answer can be given to these questions. The irony intrinsic to indirect discourse suspends or fragments the narrative line, making it irreducible to any unitary trajectory.

The passage from *The Warden* does not quite work in the same way. In *Cranford* a multiplicity of minds are matched to a multiplicity of different idiolects. In the passage from *The Warden*, there are only two lines, that of the narrator and that of Mr. Harding. Or perhaps there is only one language, the narrator's, since the warden, we are told, may not even be thinking. The narrator may be giving language to Harding's wordless revery. Trollope apparently means, by questioning whether or not the warden was thinking, that he may not have been articulating his wordless global state of mind in distinct language. The warden, says the narrator, sat "thinking, if he can be said to have thought, of the happiness of his past life." Nevertheless, the language that ensues, as it follows the various images that are said to pass through Mr. Harding's mind, appears to be much more the warden's language, ironized by being mimed with slight hyperbole in the third person past tense by the narrator, than it is the narrator's or Trollope's. At any rate, the passage, as it progresses, rapidly comes to seem Harding's language or its corresponding consciousness transposed into the sort of language we know from elsewhere in the novel he habitually uses: "– ah, how happy he had been! but it was over now...." This is a translation of: "– ah, how happy I have been! but it is over now."

The difficulty comes when the reader tries to separate out the two sources of the language line, the language-producing foyer that is the narrator, the language-producing foyer that is the character. The relation between the two is elided, elliptical, specular, but in an equivocal way. Something is always missing that would make it possible to make a firm distinction and say, "This is the narrator's language; that is the warden's." The line of language is produced in the manner of a strange ellipse, a closed circuit with two foci or centers of gravity, like a planet that moves both around the sun as focus and around another focus in empty space. In the case of the passage from *The Warden*, however, each focus, when you go to seek it out, is absent, virtual, empty, an imaginary locus that seems to be generated by the substantiality of the other one. The other one, however, is missing too when you seek it out. Harding has at this point no language but that ascribed to him by the narrator, but the narrator can speak or write only language that ironically mimes language Harding would have used. Each language source is the mirror image of the other, but which is the shadow, which the substance, which the real thing, which the simulacrum or mimesis, is impossible to tell. The language of the narrator is no stable base. It is an anonymous, neutral, collective power of representing the language of the characters by miming them ironically in indirect discourse. The character, however, has, in this case at least, no language of his own, only a wordless state of mind to which language is ascribed by the narrator. This speech act conjures that

J. HILLIS MILLER

state of mind into existence for the reader by waving the magic wand of a performative language that says in effect, "Let there be the Reverend Septimus Harding, and let his wordless mind be granted speech." The narrator depends on the character for his existence, the character depends on the narrator, in a constant oscillation that is characteristic both of what I am calling – in a deliberately self-doubling word – dialogology and also of the subversion of dialogue's apparent stability by irony. This doubling is an odd mirroring. It is a specular or speculative relationship in which, as one might say, the mirror is empty when I seek my face in the glass, or in which, perhaps, the face I see is more original than my own and so depersonalizes me when I copy it in order to achieve or affirm my own substance. That is what happens in Thomas Hardy's poem "The Pedigree."[7] To cite another parallel, an insight similar to Hardy's is expressed in Shakespeare's brilliant play on the double sense of "speculation" – as mirroring and as self-affirming doubling dialectical thought, thought that must go out from itself in order to become itself. The wordplay occurs in the speech of Ulysses to Achilles in *Troilus and Cressida*:

> For speculation turns not to itself
> Till it hath traveled and is married[8] there
> Where it may see itself. (3.3.109–11)

Speculum, speculation, narcissism, dialogue, ellipsis – each of these models involves a doubling that can become ultimately an annihilation. The search for a substance of the self outside the self leads to the absurdity of a bifold authority, as in the two Cressidas, each the source of the other and yet each nothing without the other. The passage I have cited from *The Warden* contains a parable for this annihilating bifurcation in the relation between Septimus Harding and his cello. This relation functions throughout the novel as an emblem for the doubling within the warden between his "consciousness" and his "conscience": "and then that friend of friends, that choice ally that had never deserted him, that eloquent companion that would always, when asked, discourse such pleasant music, that violoncello of his...." The violoncello is a faithful friend, ally, and eloquent speaker, but not one that exists independent, as a power of speaking, of *its* friend, ally, and player, Harding himself. The cello "discourses" only "when asked." Mr. Harding calls its language into being by a performative request or demand. The cello's language, in return, answers and reaffirms the asking language of Mr. Harding, in a reciprocal, specular, or narcissistic relation. It is narcissistic because the cello is of course no more alive than Narcissus's reflection in the pool. Harding gives the cello life by personifying it. The echoing of Harding by his cello is not a true "marriage" or "mirroring" of two separate beings. It is an attempt at self-generation by auto-affection. In this act twoness, oneness, and nothingness are mixed. Each language has its origin in the other language source. Mr. Harding can only speak from his conscience by way of his cello, but the cello can only speak when asked by Mr. Harding. The intimate relation between Mr. Harding and his cello matches parabolically the relation of the narrator's language to that of the character in all three of the passages quoted here. It matches also the relation between the language of the author and that of the narrator. It matches, finally, the relation of the language of criticism to that of the text criticized. In each case a supplementary ironizing displacement redoubles an already acentered and duplicitous language.

The latter two relations, that between author and narrator, that between text and critic, are articulated with special clarity in the passage from *Pickwick Papers*. In *Pickwick*, moreover, the way all three examples exploit properties more salient in written, not spoken, language is made explicit. The narrator of *Pickwick Papers* is not a speaker but an editor of written documents. This follows a convention that has a long history in seventeenth- and eighteenth-century novels. Dickens's use of this convention is one of the "archaic" aspects of *Pickwick Papers*, as opposed to the use of an omniscient narrator in, say, *Middlemarch* or *Our Mutual Friend*. Nevertheless, the device of having a novel described as a manuscript found in a bottle or in an old trunk has of course continued to our own day. Dickens, however, employs this already old convention by ironically parodying it. The "editor" of *The Posthumous Papers of the Pickwick Club* at first asserts that he is entirely dependent on the manuscripts in his possession for his reconstruction of Pickwick's adventures. This pretense is then rapidly forgotten. The novel becomes straightforward narrative with a narrator not unlike the storyteller in Dickens's later novels. What matters for my purposes here is the process whereby that narrative voice gets started and established. It begins as the fiction of a citation from the minutes of a meeting of the Pickwick Club. The editor, speaking of himself in the third person, claims to be quoting these verbatim, "as a proof of the careful attention, indefatigable assiduity, and nice discrimination, with which his search among the multifarious documents confided to him has been conducted." The next section, after the extended formal citation, is in a curious kind of indirect discourse. One written document, that of the editor, paraphrases another written document, the notes of the recording secretary at the meeting: "A casual observer, adds the secretary, to whose notes we are indebted for the following account – a casual observer might possibly have remarked nothing extraordinary in the bald head, and circular spectacles...." The editor's language is dependent on the language of his documents, in the same way as the language of the narrator in *Cranford* or of *The Warden* is dependent on the language or on the "thoughts" of Mrs. Forrester or of Septimus Harding. Who is the "we," however, who speaks toward the end of my citation: "which, when Pickwick clothed them – if we may use the expression..." Is this the "we" of the secretary who is mimed by the editor, or is it the "we" of the editor already interpolating his language into the language of the secretary's notes, or is it the language of the irrepressible Boz, that is, of Dickens himself, bursting through the parody of a pompous editor like a sun penetrating the clouds? Boz's own heteroglossic, hyperbolic, linguistic high jinks, in *Pickwick Papers*, come rapidly to efface the simple one-dimensional parody of editorial language, for example, in Jingle's elliptical wildly exuberant lying stories or in Sam Weller's fecundity in inventing "Wellerisms," to which I shall return. There is no ascertainable answer to the question whose language this is. The "we" is all these voices at once and so no one particular identifiable voice. It is several superimposed idioms at once, in ironic proliferating multiplicity.

What, then, about the first language the reader encounters in *Pickwick Papers*? Whose language is it that opens the novel, at the very beginning, before the first citation? "The first ray of light which illumines the gloom, and converts into a dazzling brilliancy that obscurity in which the earlier history of the public career of the immortal Pickwick would appear to be involved, is derived from the perusal of the following entry in the Transactions of the Pickwick Club...." Is this Dickens's own idiom, or that of Boz, his invented persona, or that of the "editor," or what? Since, as Steven Marcus has recognized,[9] this sentence is virtually the moment of Boz's birth, the answer is of some importance. I say "virtually," since *Pickwick Papers* was preceded by the *Sketches by Boz*. The *Sketches*, however, for all their interest, hardly belong to world literature in the way *Pickwick Papers* does. The moment of Dickens's appearance as a great creative writer happens in a pseudoperformative fiat or "let there be light." The opening sentence, with its pompous hyperbole and awkward syntax, is not Dickens himself speaking or writing. It parodies the style of adulatory biography. Dickens adopts this style in order to ridicule it: "The first ray of light which illumines the gloom"!

Dickens begins his career as a writer by pretending to be a pedantic editor who is in turn dependent on the language of the documents "confided to him" in order to be able to tell his story. Those documents themselves parody the language of parliamentary reporting. Dickens got his start as an extraordinarily facile parliamentary reporter. He was a genius at shorthand. *Pickwick Papers* is another example of a dialogical doubling. The reader can nowhere identify language that has straightforwardly emerged, without irony, from an emitting source in a "real" consciousness. Each distinguishable voice is ironically undermined. Nowhere in *Pickwick Papers* is an unironic language to be found against which other language may be measured. Even when Dickens seems most to be speaking in "his own voice," as in the political or moralizing asides by the narrator later on in *Pickwick*, or even in the direct interventions by Dickens himself, speaking in the first person, as in the farewell to his readers at the end of the novel, the wary reader suspects that this may be just another assumed voice. There is no way to be sure that this is not the case. This uncertainty happens according to a law that says any piece of language may be taken as literature, that is, as fictional, as "nonserious." This makes Wellerisms possible. I shall return to this point about literature later.

The reader is presented throughout *Pickwick Papers* with parodies of alternative ways to write, to speak, or to tell a story: picaresque language, journalistic, scientific, political, sentimental, sensational, Carlylean language, the language of travel literature, and so on. There is no personal idiom of Dickens as such, any more than there is a personal idiom in the fictional writings by Thackeray or Trollope or George Eliot. Becoming a novelist means inventing a narrative voice. Far from being a secure performative affirmation of one's hitherto precarious selfhood, this speech act is depersonalizing, in that, however hard one tries, one cannot speak in one's own voice. To put this another way, remembering the root metaphor in the word "person" (it comes from the Latin "persona," mask[10]), to become a storyteller is personalizing as if one were covering whatever personality was already there with a mask. Innumerable other masks may be superimposed over that first mask, according to a propensity for duplicitous multiplying intrinsic to signs. This is like Miss Matty's two hats simultaneously worn, one on top of another, in *Cranford*, to which I shall return in the last chapter.

The linguistic structure of all three of the cited passages is similar. In each case, though in a different way each time, the author goes outside himself or herself, doubles himself or herself, in order to affirm the self through a language that will be mirrored in the eyes of others, recognized by them, mirrored or married there where it may see itself. Elizabeth Gaskell, née Stevenson, became "Mrs. Gaskell," the well-known author of *Mary Barton, North and South, Cranford*, et cetera, by the act of inventing the language of narration in these works. The mute youth Anthony Trollope ("with all a stupid boy's slowness, I said nothing"[11]), guilty of the secret vice of daydreaming ("There can,

I imagine," he said in his autobiography, "hardly be a more dangerous mental practice" [*Autobiography*, 33]), became himself through the invention of the narrative voice that speaks in those forty-seven novels and through their recognition by the reading public. Charles Dickens transcended the depersonalizing experience of the blacking-factory episode of his life[12] and had his selfhood spectacularly affirmed by hundreds of thousands of readers through the detour of his externalization of himself. He traveled out of himself into the language of Boz. In each case, however, this doubling, by an unavoidable law, became a redoubling to infinity, a multiplication of images of the self. Such a multiplication ultimately undermines the notion of fixed selfhood, even of double or triple selfhood. The self becomes vibrating, ambiguous, unstable, ironic. Such a self is not a single language-emitting consciousness or ego. The detour outside the self becomes an endless wandering, the permanent suspension of any single narratable life line.

One name we give to this wandering or suspension is "literature." Literature depends on the possibility of detaching language from its firm embeddedness in a social or biographical context and allowing it to play freely as fiction. A Wellerism is a joke that depends on the way a given utterance can have radically different meanings in different contexts. Wellerisms brilliantly identify the propensity of any utterance to become literature or to become ironic by a simple displacement into a fictional context. Wellerisms are thus related to the ironic suspension that is performed by indirect discourse. A example is what Sam Weller's father says when he hears that Sam is to be married: " 'Nev'r mind, Sammy,' replied Mr Weller, 'it'll be a wery agonizin' trial to me at my time of life, but I'm pretty tough, that's vun consolation, as the wery old turkey remarked wen the farmer said he wos afeerd he should be obliged to kill him for the London market.' "[13]

I say literature is "the possibility of detaching language" from its pragmatic context in order to stress that no piece of language in itself is either literature or not literature. It depends on how you take it. That we take the three novels from which I have quoted as literary works is the result of a complex historical happening that began at a certain time in Europe. On the one hand, any piece of language can be "taken as literature." On the other hand, the so-called novels I have cited could be taken as nonliterature. No distinctive marks identify a given piece of language as literature, nor do different features allow us to say of another piece of language that it is not literature, that it is a serious use of language to refer to things as they are or to make something happen through a felicitous speech act surrounded by an enabling context in "the real world." One could imagine an imaginary telephone book, complete with Yellow Pages. It would look just like a real one, that is, like an effectively referential telephone book. We might be beguiled into taking it as such. Defoe has the preliminary "editor" of *Moll Flanders* use the same sort of language attesting to the authenticity of Moll's autobiographical account (altered, says the editor, only to make it "modester") as the editor of a genuine autobiography would use. Even if I say, "The following is fictional," I may be lying to hide the reality of the account.

Much work in literary study as a university-based institutionalized endeavor, including so-called cultural studies, has been an attempt to treat what could be taken as literary works as though they were historical, social, or autobiographical documents, that is, as though they were not literature. The institution of literary study, including of course most journalistic reviewing, is, paradoxically, a vigorous and multifaceted attempt to suppress, efface, cover over, ignore, and forget the properly literary in literature, that is, what is

J. HILLIS MILLER

improper about literary language or about any language when it is taken as literature. By "improper" I mean detached from its proper referential or performative use.

Dialogue, in Bakhtin's sense, is a powerful tool for putting in question the deeply rooted ideological assumption that a literary text should be thought of as emerging monologically from a single consciousness. If the work were monological then it could be returned to its author and to the subject position of the author as a person of a certain gender, race, and class in a certain country at a certain moment in history. Dialogue has been my instrument of analysis in this section on indirect discourse, as well as in what I said earlier about citations, letters, epigraphs, interpolations – all those doublings of the narrative line. "Dialogue," however, when applied to a text, is a metaphor. It still presupposes the guiding principle of monologism: selfhood, consciousness, logos in the sense of mind. Dialogue substitutes two voices or consciousnesses for one, the ellipse for the circle. When the meaning of "dialogue" shifts from mind to word, however, as it does for Bakhtin, it deconstructs dialogism as double consciousness in the same act in which it deconstructs monologue. The assumption that "dialogue" means two minds interacting, exchanging words, nevertheless constantly reasserts itself, since that is the primary sense of the word. When dialogue comes to mean two forms of language, however, and one of those becomes a neutral, anonymous power of narration, speaking as who knows who from who knows where, then one focus of the ellipse of dialogue vanishes. The ellipse becomes hyperbolic, "thrown beyond" itself, or, in the geometric meaning of "hyperbole," an ellipse turned inside out. Hyperbole names in this case the ironic excess with which one voice mimes the other. The specular look of one consciousness at another in dialogue in its usual sense becomes a look not at the other, but at an absence.

Hyperbole in turn then becomes parable or parabola ("thrown beside," as, in a geometric parabola, the curve is "thrown beside" the line that controls it). In parable the figure of dialogue, even with one of its foci hyperbolically at infinity, is replaced by the figure of one voice or language that is controlled by an absent or allegorical meaning, at an unapproachable distance from the narrative line of language whose literal meaning functions as a visible center. This may be figured in the way a comet of parabolic orbit swings around the sun and sweeps out again to disappear forever, whereas a comet of elliptical orbit returns periodically, for example, Halley's comet.

Parable, finally, gives way in its turn to irony. Irony is the suspension of both line and any center or centers of meaning, even at infinity. Irony cannot be expressed by any geometric figure. Both subjectivity and intersubjectivity are abolished by irony. Irony belongs to no voice or voices, neither to two nor to one. Ironic language functions mechanically in detachment from any controlling center or centers, just as indirect discourse, which is irony as an operative principle of narration, can no longer be certainly identified as spoken or written by anyone in particular. Irony suspends any possible ordering according to some sequence controlled by a governing principle of meaning. Even the neat narrative sequence I have established here, from circle to ellipse to hyperbole to parable to irony as permanent parabasis is undermined from beginning to end by the possibility of being taken ironically. Rather than being a culmination or guiding telos, irony is present at the beginning, middle, and end of any narrative line. Irony can only be stabilized by an arbitrary act of the interpreter stilling the unstillable and ignoring other possibilities of meaning. No passage in a narrative, short or long, partial or complete, will stay motionless long enough, unless killed by the critic, in her or his rage for certainty, to form the stable base for a further journey or line of interpretation.

My investigation of the narrative line has constantly approached and receded from the recognition of irony as a pervasive element of undecidability making both narrative and the analysis of narrative in principle impossible, if verifiable certainty of meaning is demanded. This does not keep both narrative and the interpretation of narrative from continuing imperturbably, in defiance of this impossibility. I, Anthony Trollope, or Elizabeth Gaskell, or Charles Dickens, driven by some sense of lack or deprivation, double myself. I invent another voice, a narrator, and then other voices, "characters," beyond that, for the first speaker to repeat in indirect discourse or in citation of spoken words. I double or split my tongue to give myself, in my muteness, a tongue, but in this act I deprive myself of any tongue, idiom, voice, logos proper to me. I depersonalize myself. As Rousseau says in the second preface to *La Nouvelle Héloïse*, "Wishing to be what one is not, one comes to believe oneself to be other than one is, and that is how one goes mad."[14] The doubling of storytelling becomes madness, as Friedrich Schlegel said irony is.[15]

If one associates univocal sense-making with some masculine principle of authority, which Derrida has dubbed "phallogocentrism," then irony can be defined as a species of castration. This happens according to the Freudian law that says the doubling of the phallus signifies its absence, the vanishing of phallocentrism along with logocentrism. Phallus goes when logos goes. If it seems absurd to ascribe phallogocentrism to Elizabeth Gaskell, Jacques Lacan, in "Le Séminaire sur 'la Lettre volée,'" and Jacques Derrida, on Lacan on Poe, in "Le Facteur de la vérité," in their quite different outlinings of the rules for the game of "phallus, phallus, who's got the phallus," have identified the mother in one way or another as the phallus's keeper or, what comes to the same thing, as keeping the secret of its eternal absence. The card game of "Old Maid" is a version of that interplay.[16]

The metaphor of dialogue destroys that of monologue, and destroys the unity of the narrative line by doubling it, but it destroys itself at the same time. It destroys the phenomenological implications, the references to consciousness, of its own model. This leaves only the invisible blur of the vibrations of irony, language as a machine working without the control of any logos, the mirror empty of any face. Plato (that is, Socrates) was right. Mimesis, in the sense of double diegesis, is an extreme danger to single diegesis and to the phallogocentric idea behind diegesis. "Or can you think of anything more frightful," asks the "Or" of Kierkegaard's *Either/Or*, "than that it might end with your nature being resolved into a multiplicity, that you really might become many, become, like those unhappy demoniacs, a legion, and you thus would have lost the inmost and holiest thing of all in man, the unifying power of personality?"[17] Unity becomes duplicity becomes a multiplicity that is legion, demoniac, alogical. That dissolves ultimately not only any concept of a stable authoring mind but also dissolves the mind, the self-possession, of any reader who yields himself or herself fully to the corrosive irony implicit in any storytelling or narrative line, however strait or straight it tries to be. It is the fascination of this danger that makes even the simplest story or narrative fragment seem inexhaustible, fathomless in its power and perfection, as Franz Kafka discovered in 1911:

J. HILLIS MILLER

The special nature of my inspiration in which I, the most fortunate and unfortunate of men, now go to sleep at 2 A.M. (perhaps, if I can only bear the thought of it, it will remain, for it is loftier than all before [denn sie ist höher als alle früheren]), is such that I can do everything, and not only what is directed to a definite piece of work [ist die, daß ich alles kann, nicht nur auf eine bestimmte Arbeit hin]. When I arbitrarily write a single sentence, for instance, "He looked out of the window," it already has perfection. [Wenn ich wahllos einen Satz hinschreibe, zum Beispiel "Er schaute aus dem Fenster," so ist er schon vollkommen.]"[18]

This exploration by way of selected "segments," beginnings, middles, and ends in the narrative line has constantly encountered impasses, interruptions, doublings, suspensions. Starting, continuing, and concluding all occur, but they are constantly, from beginning to end, suspended over the abyss of their own impossibility. The most inclusive name for this impossibility is "irony." Irony is in one way or another the pervasive trope of narrative. Irony is another name for literature as a constant possibility of the fictional within language. The difficulty in analyzing the narrative line is the difficulty, or rather the impossibility, of mastering the unmasterable, the trope that is no trope, the figure not figurable as a turning, crossing, displacement, detour, or as any other line, the trope-no-trope of irony. I shall, in the concluding chapter, exemplify this impossibility and the way it is does not prevent interpretation from occurring by a more complete reading of two narratives.

NOTES

1   Anthony Trollope, *The Warden* (World's Classics edn. London: Oxford University Press, 1963), 123.
2   Elizabeth Gaskell, *Cranford; The Cage at Cranford; The Moorland Cottage* (World's Classics edn. London: Oxford University Press, 1965), 135–37.
3   Charles Dickens, *The Posthumous Papers of the Pickwick Club* (Harmondsworth, England: Penguin, 1972), 67, 68–69.
4   Jacques Derrida, *Glas*, trans. cit., 168; "toute thèse est (bande) une prothèse; ce qui se donne à lire se donne à lire par citations (nécessairement tronquées, coupures, répétitions, succions, sections, suspensions, sélections, coutures, greffes, postiches, organes sans corps propre, corps propre couvert de coups …)" (Jacques Derrida, *Glas*, trans. John P. Leavey, Jr. and Richard Rand [Lincoln: University of Nebraska Press, 1986], 189).
5   If I just use the word "time" in a sentence, says Valéry, I have no problem with it, but as soon as I detach the word from its familiar linguistic surroundings and ask what it means, then "il se change en énigme, en abîme, en tourment de la pensée [it changes into an enigma, an abyss, a torment of thought]" (Paul Valéry, "Poésie et pensée abstraite," *Oeuvres*, ed. Jean Hytier, Pléiade ed. [Paris: Gallimard, 1957], 1:1314–37, my trans.). In a celebrated passage in book 11 of *The Confessions*, Saint Augustine asks, "What then is time? [quid est enim tempus?]" (*The Confessions*, trans. Edward B. Pusey [New York: Pocket Books, 1952], 224). The whole of Augustine's chapter 11 is one of the great meditations on time in the Western tradition. For a full discussion of it in the context of narrative theory, see Paul Ricoeur, *Temps et récit* (Paris: Seuil, 1983), 1:19–53; Ricoeur, *Time and Narrative*, trans. Kathleen McLaughlin and David Pellauer (Chicago: University of Chicago Press, 1984), 5–30.
6   The chapter is entitled "The Panic."

7   Thomas Hardy, *Complete Poems*, ed. James Gibson (London: Macmillan, 1976), 460–61. See my discussion of this poem in "Prosopopoeia in Hardy and Stevens," *Tropes, Parables, Performatives* (New York: Harvester Wheatsheaf, 1990), 248–54.

8   Other texts have "mirror'd" in place of "married," which seems more plausible, though both words work to generate meaning. "Mirror'd" and "married" are like the two words in "Ariachnes," divided in this case into two versions of the text. I have cited the version of *Troilus and Cressida*, ed. Daniel Seltzer, in *The Complete Signet Classic Shakespeare* (New York: Harcourt Brace Jovanovich, 1972). For the most part this version follows the quarto.

9   Steven Marcus, *Dickens: From Pickwick to Dombey* (New York: Basic Books, 1965).

10 "Persona" meant, more specifically, the mask worn by the actors in Greek and Latin drama, or the part, character, or person represented by the actor, or the character that someone sustains before the world.

11 Anthony Trollope, *An Autobiography*, ed. David Skilton (London: Penguin, 1996) 10.

12 "No words can express the secret agony of my soul as I sunk into this companionship; compared these every day associates with those of my happier childhood; and felt my early hopes of growing up to be a learned and distinguished man, crushed in my breast. The deep remembrance of the sense I had of being utterly neglected and hopeless; of the shame I felt in my position; of the misery it was to my young heart to believe that, day by day, what I had learned, and thought, and delighted in, and raised my fancy and my emulation up by, was passing away from me, never to be brought back any more; cannot be written." Quoted in John Forster, *The Life of Charles Dickens*, 3 vols. (London: Chapman and Hall, 1872), 1:33.

13 *Pickwick Papers*, 539.

14 My trans.: "Voulant être ce qu'on n'est pas, on parvient à se croire autre chose que ce qu'on est, et voilà comment on devient fou" (Rousseau, *Oeuvres complètes*, ed. Bernard Gagnebin and Marcel Raymond. Pléiade ed. [Paris: Gallimard, 1964], 2:21).

15 Discussing irony in Cervantes and Shakespeare, Schlegel speaks of the "Schein des Verkehrten und Verrückten order des Einfältigen und Dummen [the semblance of the absurd and of madness, of simplicity and foolishness]" in irony (Friedrich Schlegel, "Rede über die Mythologie," *Gespräch über die Poesie, Kritische Schriften*, 501–502; "Talk on Mythology," *Dialogue on Poetry and Literary Aphorisms*, 86).

16 Jacques Lacan, *Ecrits* (Paris: Seuil, 1966), 11–61; Jacques Derrida, *La Carte postale* (Paris: Aubier-Flammarion, 1980), 439–524. Translations of both essays are conveniently collected in *The Purloined Poe: Lacan, Derrida, and Psychoanalytic Reading*, ed. John P. Muller and William J. Richardson (Baltimore: Johns Hopkins University Press, 1988), 28–54, 173–212.

17 Sören Kierkegaard, *Either/Or*, trans. David F. Swenson and Lillian Marvin Swenson. (Princeton: Princeton University Press, 1971), 2:164.

18 Franz Kafka, *Tagebücher 1910–23*, ed. Max Brod (Frankfurt am Main: S. Fischer, 1986), 29; *The Diaries ... 1910–1913*, ed. Max Brod, trans. Joseph Kresh (London: Secker and Warburg, 1948), 45. "Vollkommen" means complete, entire, finished, full, as well as perfect. Kafka's first great story, "The Judgment," which he finished in a single burst of inspiration during one long night in 1912, opens showing the protagonist "with his elbows propped on the writing table ... gazing out of the window at the river, the bridge and the hills on the farther bank with their tender green" (Franz Kafka, "The Judgment," *Selected Short Stories*, trans. Willa and Edwin Muir [New York: Modern Library, 1952], 3). Kafka's "arbitrarily" chosen examplary sentence is by no means fortuitous, nor is the fact that the protagonist of "The Judgment" sits with his elbows propped on the writing table. Writing opens a window to a magical land on the other shore, a land that can be reached only through just those words, each sentence of which contains the whole, in perfection and completeness: "Er schaute aus dem Fenster."

A World of Difference

Barbara Johnson

Barbara E. Johnson (b. 1947)

Barbara Johnson was born near Boston, Massachusetts, and received her education at Oberlin College and Yale University, where she worked under Paul de Man. After receiving her doctoral degree in 1977, Johnson remained at Yale to teach; in 1983 she moved to Harvard University, where she is the Frederic Wertham Professor of Law and Psychiatry in Society. Her honors include a Guggenheim Fellowship. The range of Johnson's theoretical interests is reflected in the titles of her published works: she translated, and wrote a much lauded introduction to, Jacques Derrida's *Dissemination* (1981); co-edited *The Consequences of Theory* (1991); and authored *The Critical Difference: Essays in the Contemporary Rhetoric of Reading* (1981); *A World of Difference* (1987); *The Wake of Deconstruction* (1994); *The Feminist Difference* (1998); and *Mother Tongues: Sexuality, Trials, Motherhood, Translation* (2003).

Metaphor, Metonymy, and Voice in *Their Eyes Were Watching God*

Not so very long ago, metaphor and metonymy burst into prominence as the salt and pepper, the Laurel and Hardy, the Yin and Yang, and often the Scylla and Charybdis of literary theory. Then, just as quickly, this cosmic couple passed out of fashion again. How did it happen that such an arcane rhetorical opposition was able to acquire the brief but powerful privilege of dividing and naming the whole of human reality, from Mommy and Daddy or Symptom and Desire all the way to God and Country or Beautiful Lie and Sober Lucidity?[1]

The contemporary sense of the opposition between metaphor and metonymy was first formulated by Roman Jakobson in an article entitled "Two Aspects of Language and Two Types of Aphasic Disturbances."[2] That article, first published in English in 1956, derives much of its celebrity from the central place accorded by the French structuralists to the 1963 translation of a selection of Jakobson's work entitled *Essais de linguistique générale*, which included the aphasia study. The words *metaphor* and *metonymy* are not, of course, twentieth-century coinages: they are classical tropes traditionally defined as the substitution of a figurative expression for a literal or proper one. In metaphor, the substitution is based on resemblance or analogy; in metonymy, it is based on a relation or association other than that of similarity (cause and effect, container and contained, proper name and qualities or works associated with it, place and event or institution, instrument and user, etc.). The use of the name "Camelot" to refer to King Arthur's world is a metonymy (of place), while the same word applied to John Kennedy's Washington is a metaphor, since it implies an analogy between Kennedy's world and King Arthur's.

Jakobson's use of the two terms is an extension and polarization of their classical definitions. Jakobson found that patterns of aphasia (speech dysfunction) fell into two main categories: similarity disorders and contiguity disorders. In the former, grammatical contexture and lateral associations remain while synonymity drops out; in the latter, heaps of word substitutes are kept while grammar and connectedness vanish. Jakobson concludes:

> The development of a discourse may take place along two different semantic lines: one topic may lead to another either through their similarity or through their contiguity. The metaphoric way would be the most appropriate term for the first case and the metonymic way for the second, since they find their most condensed expression in metaphor and metonymy respectively. In aphasia one or the other of these two processes is restricted or totally blocked – an effect which makes the study of aphasia particularly illuminating for the linguist. In normal verbal behavior both processes are continually operative, but careful observation will reveal that under the influence of a cultural pattern, personality, and verbal style, preference is given to one of the two processes over the other.
>
> In a well-known psychological test, children are confronted with some noun and told to utter the first verbal response that comes into their heads. In this experiment two opposite linguistic predilections are invariably exhibited: the response is intended either as a substitute for, or as a complement to the stimulus. In the latter case the stimulus and the response together form a proper syntactic construction, most usually a sentence. These two types of reaction have been labeled substitutive and predicative.

To the stimulus *hut* one response was *burnt out*; another, *is a poor little house*. Both reactions are predicative; but the first creates a purely narrative context, while in the second there is a double connection with the subject *hut*: on the one hand, a positional (namely, syntactic) contiguity, and on the other a semantic similarity.

The same stimulus produced the following substitutive reactions: the tautology *hut*; the synonyms *cabin* and *hovel*; the autonym *palace*; and the metaphors *den* and *burrow*. The capacity of two words to replace one another is an instance of positional similarity, and, in addition, all these responses are linked to the stimulus by semantic similarity (or contrast). Metonymical responses to the same stimulus, such as *thatch*, *litter*, or *poverty*, combine and contrast the positional similarity with semantic contiguity.

In manipulating these two kinds of connection (similarity and contiguity) in both their aspects (positional and semantic) – selecting, combining, and ranking them – an individual exhibits his personal style, his verbal predilections and preferences. (pp. 76–77)

Two problems immediately arise that render the opposition between metaphor and metonymy at once more interesting and more problematic than at first appears. The first is that there are not two poles here, but four: similarity, contiguity, semantic connection, and syntactic connection. A more adequate representation of these oppositions can be schematized (see figure 14.1). Jakobson's contention that poetry is a syntactic extension of metaphor ("The poetic function projects the principle of equivalence from the axis of selection into the axis of combination"),[3] while realist narrative is an extension of metonymy, can be added to the graph (see figure 14.2).

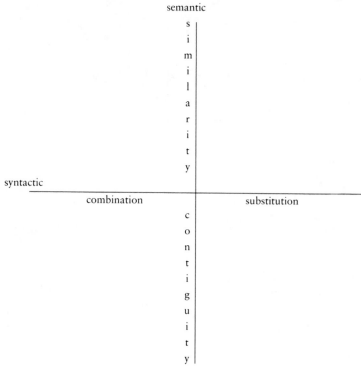

Figure 14.1

The second problem that arises in any attempt to apply the metaphor/metonymy distinction is that it is often very hard to tell the two apart. In Ronsard's poem "Mignonne, allons voir si la rose," the speaker invites the lady to go for a walk with him (the walk being an example of contiguity) to see a rose which, once beautiful (like the lady), is now withered (as the lady will eventually be): the day must therefore be seized. The metonymic proximity to the flower is designed solely to reveal the metaphoric point of the poem: enjoy life while you still bloom. The tendency of contiguity to become overlaid by similarity, and vice versa, may be summed up in the proverb "Birds of a feather flock together" – "qui se ressemble s'assemble." One has only to think of the applicability of this proverb to the composition of neighborhoods in America to realize that the question of the separability of similarity from contiguity may have considerable political implications. The controversy surrounding the expression "Legionnaires' disease" provides a more comical example: while the name of the disease derives solely from the contingent fact that its first victims were at an American Legion Convention, and is thus a metonymy, the fear that it will take on a metaphoric color – that a belief in some natural connection or similarity may thereby be propagated between Legionnaires and the disease – has led spokesmen for the Legionnaires to attempt to have the malady renamed. And finally, in the sentence "the White House denied the charges," one might ask whether the place name is a purely contiguous metonymy for the presidency, or whether the whiteness of the house isn't somehow metaphorically connected to the whiteness of its inhabitant.

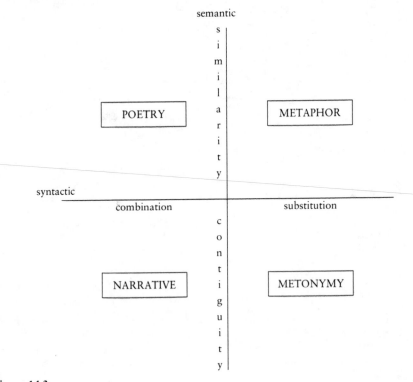

Figure 14.2

BARBARA JOHNSON

One final prefatory remark about the metaphor/metonymy distinction: far from being a neutral opposition between equals, these two tropes have always stood in hierarchical relation to each other. From Artistotle to George Lakoff, metaphor has always, in the Western tradition, had the privilege of revealing unexpected truth.[4] As Aristotle puts it, "Midway between the unintelligible and the commonplace, it is a metaphor which most produces knowledge" (*Rhetoric* 3.1410). Paul de Man summarizes the preference for metaphor over metonymy by aligning analogy with necessity and contiguity with chance: "The inference of identity and totality that is constitutive of metaphor is lacking in the purely relational metonymic contact: an element of truth is involved in taking Achilles for a lion but none in taking Mr. Ford for a motor car."[5] De Man then goes on to reveal this "element of truth" as the product of a purely rhetorical – and ultimately metonymical – sleight of hand, thus overturning the traditional hierarchy and deconstructing the very basis for the seductiveness and privilege of metaphor.

I would like now to turn to the work of an author acutely conscious of, and superbly skilled in, the seductiveness and complexity of metaphor as privileged trope and trope of privilege. Zora Neale Hurston – novelist, folklorist, essayist, anthropologist, and Harlem Renaissance personality – cut her teeth on figurative language during the tale-telling, or "lying," sessions that took place on a store porch in the all-black town of Eatonville, Florida, where she was born around 1901.[6] She devoted her life to the task of recording, preserving, novelizing, and analyzing the patterns of speech and thought of the rural black South and related cultures. At the same time, she deplored the appropriation, dilution, and commodification of black culture (through spirituals, jazz, etc.) by the pre-Depression white world, and she constantly tried to explain the difference between a reified "art" and a living culture in which the distinctions between spectator and spectacle, rehearsal and performance, experience and representation, are not fixed. "Folklore," she wrote, "is the arts of the people before they find out that there is such a thing as art."

> Folklore does not belong to any special area, time, nor people. It is a world and an ageless thing, so let us look at it from that viewpoint. It is the boiled down juice of human living and when one phase of it passes another begins which shall in turn give way before a successor.
> Culture is a forced march on the near and the obvious.... The intelligent mind uses up a great part of its lifespan trying to awaken its consciousness sufficiently to comprehend that which is plainly there before it. Every generation or so some individual with extra keen perception grasps something of the obvious about us and hitches the human race forward slightly by a new "law." Millions of things had been falling on men for thousands of years before the falling apple hit Newton on the head and he saw the law of gravity.[7]

Through this strategic description of the folkloric heart of scientific law, Hurston dramatizes the predicament not only of the anthropologist but also of the novelist: both are caught between the (metaphorical) urge to universalize or totalize and the knowledge that it is precisely "the near and the obvious" that will never be grasped once and for all, but only (metonymically) named and renamed as different things successively strike different heads. I will return to this problem of universality at the end of this essay, but first I would like to take a close look at some of the figurative operations at work in Hurston's best-known novel, *Their Eyes Were Watching God*.[8]

The novel presents, in a combination of first- and third-person narration, the story of Janie Crawford and her three successive husbands. The first, Logan Killicks, is chosen by Janie's grandmother for his sixty acres and as a socially secure harbor for Janie's awakening sexuality. When Janie realizes that love does not automatically follow upon marriage and that Killicks completely lacks imagination, she decides to run off with ambitious, smart-talking, stylishly dressed Joe Starks, who is headed for a new all-black town, where he hopes to become what he calls a "big voice." Later, as store owner and mayor of the town, he proudly raises Janie to a pedestal of property and propriety. Because this involves her submission to his idea of what a mayor's wife should be, Janie soon finds her pedestal to be a straitjacket, particularly when it involves her exclusion – both as speaker and as listener – from the tale-telling sessions on the store porch and at the mock funeral of a mule. Little by little, Janie begins to talk back to Joe, finally insulting him so profoundly that, in a sense, he dies of it. Some time later, into Janie's life walks Tea Cake Woods, whose first act is to teach Janie how to play checkers. "Somebody wanted her to play," says the text in free indirect discourse; "Somebody thought it natural for her to play" (p. 146). Thus begins a joyous liberation from the rigidities of status, image, and property – one of the most beautiful and convincing love stories in any literature. In a series of courtship dances, appearances, and disappearances, Tea Cake succeeds in fulfilling Janie's dream of "a bee for her blossom" (p. 161). Tea Cake, unlike Joe and Logan, regards money and work as worth only the amount of play and enjoyment they make possible. He gains and loses money unpredictably until he and Janie begin working side by side picking beans on "the muck" in the Florida everglades. This idyll of pleasure, work, and equality ends dramatically with a hurricane, during which Tea Cake, while saving Janie's life, is bitten by a rabid dog. When Tea Cake's subsequent hydrophobia transforms him into a wild and violent animal, Janie is forced to shoot him in self-defense. Acquitted of murder by an all-white jury, Janie returns to Eatonville, where she tells her story to her friend Phoeby Watson.

The passage on which I would like to concentrate both describes and dramatizes, in its figurative structure, a crucial turning point in Janie's relation to Joe and to herself. The passage follows an argument over what Janie has done with a bill of lading, during which Janie shouts, "You sho loves to tell me whut to do, but Ah can't tell you nothin' Ah see!"

"Dat's 'cause you need tellin'," he rejoined hotly. "It would be pitiful if Ah didn't. Somebody got to think for women and chillun and chickens and cows. I god, they sho don't think none theirselves."

"Ah knows uh few things, and womenfolks thinks sometimes too!"

"Aw naw they don't. They just think they's thinkin'. When Ah see one thing Ah understands ten. You see ten things and don't understand one."

Times and scenes like that put Janie to thinking about the inside state of her marriage. Time came when she fought back with her tongue as best she could, but it didn't do her any good. It just made Joe do more. He wanted her submission and he'd keep on fighting until he felt he had it.

So gradually, she pressed her teeth together and learned how to hush. The spirit of the marriage left the bedroom and took to living in the parlor. It was there to shake hands whenever company came to visit, but it never went back inside the bedroom again. So she put something in there to represent the spirit like a Virgin Mary image in a church. The bed was no longer a daisy-field for her and Joe to play in. It was a place where she went and laid down when she was sleepy and tired.

She wasn't petal-open anymore with him. She was twenty-four and seven years married when she knew. She found that out one day when he slapped her face in the kitchen. It happened over one of those dinners that chasten all women sometimes. They plan and they fix and they do, and then some kitchen-dwelling fiend slips a scrochy, soggy, tasteless mess into their pots and pans. Janie was a good cook, and Joe had looked forward to his dinner as a refuge from other things. So when the bread didn't rise and the fish wasn't quite done at the bone, and the rice was scorched, he slapped Janie until she had a ringing sound in her ears and told her about her brains before he stalked on back to the store.

Janie stood where he left her for unmeasured time and thought. She stood there until something fell off the shelf inside her. Then she went inside there to see what it was. It was her image of Jody tumbled down and shattered. But looking at it she saw that it never was the flesh and blood figure of her dreams. Just something she had grabbed up to drape her dreams over. In a way she turned her back upon the image where it lay and looked further. She had no more blossomy openings dusting pollen over her man, neither any glistening young fruit where the petals used to be. She found that she had a host of thoughts she had never expressed to him, and numerous emotions she had never let Jody know about. Things packed up and put away in parts of her heart where he could never find them. She was saving up feelings for some man she had never seen. She had an inside and an outside now and suddenly she knew how not to mix them. (pp. 110–13)

This opposition between an inside and an outside is a standard way of describing the nature of a rhetorical figure. The vehicle, or surface meaning, is seen as enclosing an inner tenor, or figurative meaning. This relation can be pictured somewhat facetiously as a gilded carriage – the vehicle – containing Luciano Pavarotti, the tenor. Within the passage cited from *Their Eyes Were Watching God*, I would like to concentrate on the two paragraphs that begin respectively "So gradually…" and "Janie stood where he left her…." In these two paragraphs Hurston plays a number of interesting variations on the inside/outside opposition.

In both paragraphs, a relation is set up between an inner "image" and outward, domestic space. The parlor, bedroom, and store full of shelves already exist in the narrative space of the novel: they are figures drawn metonymically from the familiar contiguous surroundings. Each of these paragraphs recounts a little narrative of, and within, its own figurative terms. In the first, the inner spirit of the marriage moves outward from the bedroom to the parlor, cutting itself off from its proper place, and replacing itself with an image of virginity, the antithesis of marriage. Although Joe is constantly exclaiming, "I god, Janie," he will not be as successful as his namesake in uniting with the Virgin Mary. Indeed, it is his godlike self-image that forces Janie to retreat to virginity. The entire paragraph is an externalization of Janie's feelings onto the outer surroundings in the form of a narrative of movement from private to public space. While the whole of the figure relates metaphorically, analogically, to the marital situation it is designed to express, it reveals the marriage space to be metonymical, a movement through a series of contiguous rooms. It is a narrative not of union but of separation, centered on an image not of conjugality but of virginity.

In the second passage, just after the slap, Janie is standing, thinking, until something "fell off the shelf inside her." Janie's "inside" is here represented as a store that she then goes in to inspect. While the former paragraph was an externalization of the inner, here we find an internalization of the outer: Janie's inner self resembles a store. The material for this metaphor is drawn from the narrative world of contiguity: the store is the place where Joe has set himself up as lord, master, and proprietor. But here, Jody's image is broken and reveals itself never to have been a metaphor, but only a metonymy, of Janie's dream: "Looking at it she saw that it never was the flesh and blood figure of her dreams. Just something she had grabbed up to drape her dreams over."

What we find in juxtaposing these two figural mininarratives is a kind of chiasmus, or crossover, in which the first paragraph presents an externalization of the inner, a metaphorically grounded metonymy, while the second paragraph presents an internalization of the outer, or a metonymically grounded metaphor. In both cases, the quotient of the operation is the revelation of a false or discordant "image." Janie's image, as Virgin Mary, acquires a new intactness, while Joe's lies shattered on the floor. The reversals operated by the chiasmus map out a reversal of the power relations between Janie and Joe. Henceforth, Janie will grow in power and resistance, while Joe deteriorates both in his body and in his public image.

The moral of these two figural tales is rich with implications: "She had an inside and an outside now and suddenly she knew how not to mix them." On the one hand, this means that she knew how to keep the inside and the outside separate without trying to blend or merge them into one unified identity. On the other hand it means that she has stepped irrevocably into the necessity of figurative language, where inside and outside are never the same. It is from this point on in the novel that Janie, paradoxically, begins to speak. And it is by means of a devastating figure – "You look like the change of life" – that she wounds Jody to the quick. Janie's acquisition of the power of voice thus grows not out of her identity but out of her division into inside and outside. Knowing how not to mix them is knowing that articulate language requires the co-presence of two distinct poles, not their collapse into oneness.

This, of course, is what Jakobson concludes in his discussion of metaphor and metonymy. For it must be remembered that what is at stake in the maintenance of both sides – metaphor and metonymy, inside and outside – is the very possibility of speaking at all. The reduction of a discourse to oneness, identity – in Janie's case, the reduction of woman to mayor's wife – has as its necessary consequence aphasia, silence, the loss of the ability to speak: "She pressed her teeth together and learned to hush."

What has gone unnoticed in theoretical discussions of Jakobson's article is that behind the metaphor/metonymy distinction lies the much more serious distinction between speech and aphasia, between silence and the capacity to articulate one's own voice. To privilege either metaphor or metonymy is thus to run the risk of producing an increasingly aphasic *critical* discourse. If both, or all four, poles must be operative in order for speech to function fully, then the very notion of an "authentic voice" must be redefined. Far from being an expression of Janie's new wholeness or identity as a character, Janie's increasing ability to speak grows out of her ability not to mix inside with outside, not to pretend that there is no difference, but to assume and articulate the incompatible forces involved in her own division. The sign of an authentic voice is thus not self-identity but self-difference.

The search for wholeness, oneness, universality, and totalization can nevertheless never be put to rest. However rich, healthy, or lucid fragmentation and division may be, narrative seems to have trouble resting content with it, as though a story could not recognize its own end as anything other than a moment of totalization – even when what is totalized is loss. The ending of *Their Eyes Were Watching God* is no exception:

> Of course [Tea Cake] wasn't dead. He could never be dead until she herself had finished feeling and thinking. The kiss of his memory made pictures of love and light against the wall. Here was peace. She pulled in her horizon like a great fish-net. Pulled it from around the waist of the world and draped it over her shoulder. So much of life in its meshes! She called in her soul to come and see.

The horizon, with all of life caught in its meshes, is here pulled into the self as a gesture of total recuperation and peace. It is as though self-division could be healed over at last, but only at the cost of a radical loss of the other.

This hope for some ultimate unity and peace seems to structure the very sense of an ending as such, whether that of a novel or that of a work of literary criticism. At the opposite end of the "canonical" scale, one finds it, for example, in the last chapter of Erich Auerbach's *Mimesis*, perhaps the greatest of modern monuments to the European literary canon. That final chapter, entitled "The Brown Stocking" after the stocking that Virginia Woolf's Mrs. Ramsay is knitting in *To the Lighthouse*, is a description of certain narrative tendencies in the modern novel: "multipersonal representation of consciousness, time strata, disintegration of the continuity of exterior events, shifting of narrative viewpoint," and so on.[9] "Let us begin with a tendency which is particularly striking in our text from Virginia Woolf. She holds to minor, unimpressive, random events: measuring the stocking, a fragment of a conversation with the maid, a telephone call. Great changes, exterior turning points, let alone catastrophes, do not occur" (p. 483). Auerbach concludes his discussion of the modernists' preoccupation with the minor, the trivial, and the marginal by saying:

> It is precisely the random moment which is comparatively independent of the controversial and unstable orders over which men fight and despair.... The more numerous, varied, and simple the people are who appear as subjects of such random moments, the more effectively must what they have in common shine forth.... So the complicated process of dissolution which led to fragmentation of the exterior action, to reflection of consciousness, and to stratification of time seems to be tending toward a very simple solution. Perhaps it will be too simple to please those who, despite all its dangers and catastrophes, admire and love our epoch for the sake of its abundance of life and the incomparable historical vantage point which it affords. But they are few in number, and probably they will not live to see much more than the first forewarnings of the approaching unification and simplification. (p. 488)

Never has the desire to transform fragmentation into unity been expressed so succinctly and authoritatively – indeed, almost prophetically. One cannot help but wonder, though, whether the force of this desire has not been provoked by the fact that the primary text it wishes to unify and simplify was written by a woman. What Auerbach calls "minor, unimpressive, random events" – measuring a stocking, conversing with the maid, answering the phone – can all be identified as conventional *women's* activities. "Great changes, exterior turning points," and "catastrophes" have been the stuff of heroic *male* literature. Even plot itself – up until *Madame Bovary*, at least – has been conceived as the doings of those who do *not* stay at home, in other words, men. Auerbach's urge to unify and simplify is an urge to resubsume female difference under the category of the universal, which has always been unavowedly male. The random, the trivial, and the marginal will simply be added to the list of things all *men* have in common.

If "unification and simplification" is the privilege and province of the male, it is also, in America, the privilege and province of the white. If the woman's voice, to be authentic, must incorporate and articulate division and self-difference, so, too, has Afro-American literature always had to assume its double-voicedness. As Henry Louis Gates, Jr., puts it in "Criticism in the Jungle":

> In the instance of the writer of African descent, her or his texts occupy spaces in at least two traditions – the individual's European or American literary tradition, and one of the three related but distinct black traditions. The "heritage" of each black text written in a Western language, then, is a double heritage, two-toned, as it were.... Each utterance, then, is double-voiced.[10]

This is a reformulation of W. E. B. Dubois's famous image of the "veil" that divides the black American in two:

> The Negro is a sort of seventh son, born with a veil, and gifted with second sight in this American world, – a world which yields him no true self-consciousness, but only lets him see himself through the revelation of the other world. It is a peculiar sensation, this double-consciousness, this sense of always looking at one's self through the eyes of others, of measuring one's soul by the tape of a world that looks on in amused contempt and pity. One ever feels his twoness – an American, a Negro; two souls, two thoughts, two unreconciled strivings; two warring ideals in one dark body, whose dogged strength alone keeps it from being torn asunder.
>
> The history of the American Negro is the history of this strife, – this longing to attain self-conscious manhood, to merge his double self into a better and truer self.[11]

James Weldon Johnson, in his *Autobiography of an Ex-Colored Man*, puts it this way:

> This is the dwarfing, warping, distorting influence which operates upon each and every colored man in the United States. He is forced to take his outlook on all things, not from the view-point of a citizen, or a man, or even a human being, but from the view-point of a *colored* man.... This gives to every colored man, in proportion to his intelectuality, a sort of dual personality.[12]

What is striking about the above two quotations is that they both assume without question that the black subject is male. The black woman is totally invisible in these descriptions of the black dilemma. Richard Wright, in his review of *Their Eyes Were Watching God*, makes it plain that for him, too, the black female experience is nonexistent. The novel, says Wright, lacks "a basic idea or theme that lends itself to significant interpretation.... [Hurston's] dialogue manages to catch the psychological movements of the Negro folk-mind in their pure simplicity, but that's as far as it goes.... The sensory sweep of her novel carries no theme, no message, no thought."[13]

No message, no theme, no thought: the full range of questions and experiences of Janie's life are as invisible to a mind steeped in maleness as Ellison's Invisible Man is to minds steeped in whiteness. If the black *man*'s soul is divided in two, what can be said of the black woman's? Here again, what is constantly seen exclusively in terms of a binary opposition – black versus white, man versus woman – must be redrawn at least as a tetrapolar structure (see figure 14.3). What happens in the case of a black woman is that the four quadrants are constantly being collapsed into two. Hurston's work is often called nonpolitical simply because readers of Afro-American literature tend to look for confrontational *racial* politics, not sexual politics. If the black woman voices opposition to male domination, she is often seen as a traitor to the cause of racial justice. But if she sides with black men against white oppression, she often winds up having to accept her position within the Black Power movement as, in Stokely Carmichael's words, "prone." This impossible position between two oppositions is what I think Hurston intends when, at the end of the novel, she represents Janie as acquitted of the murder of Tea Cake by an all-white jury but condemned by her fellow blacks. This is not out of a "lack of bitterness toward whites," as one reader would have it,[14] but rather out of a knowledge of the standards of male dominance that pervade both the black and the white worlds. The black crowd at the trial murmurs: "Tea Cake was a good boy. He had been good to that woman. No nigger woman ain't never been treated no better" (p. 276). As Janie's grandmother puts it early in the novel:

> "Honey, de white man is de ruler of everything as fur as Ah been able tuh find out. Maybe it's some place way off in de ocean where de black man is in power, but we don't know nothin' but what we see. So de white man throw down de load and tell de nigger man tuh pick it up. He pick it up because he have to, but he don't tote it. He hand it to his womenfolks. De nigger woman is de mule uh de world so fur as Ah can see." (p. 29)

In a very persuasive book on black women and feminism entitled *Ain't I a Woman*, Bell Hooks (Gloria Watkins) discusses the ways in which black women suffer from both sexism and racism within the very movements whose ostensible purpose is to set them free. Watkins argues that "black woman" has never been considered a separate, distinct category with a history and complexity of its own. When a president appoints a black woman to a cabinet post, for example, he does not feel he is appointing a person

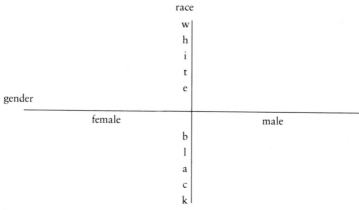

Figure 14.3

belonging to the category "black woman"; he is appointing a person who belongs *both* to the category "black" *and* to the category "woman," and is thus killing two birds with one stone. Watkins says of the analogy often drawn – particularly by white feminists – between blacks and women:

> Since analogies derive their power, their appeal, and their very reason for being from the sense of two disparate phenomena having been brought closer together, for white women to acknowledge the overlap between the terms "blacks" and "women" (that is, the existence of black women) would render this analogy unnecessary. By continuously making this analogy, they unwittingly suggest that to them the term "women" is synonymous with "white women" and the term "blacks" synonymous with "black men."[15]

The very existence of black women thus disappears from an analogical discourse designed to express the types of oppression from which black women have the most to suffer.

In the current hierarchical view of things, this tetrapolar graph can be filled in as in figure 14.4. The black woman is both invisible and ubiquitous: never seen in her own right but forever appropriated by the others for their own ends.

Ultimately, though, this mapping of tetrapolar differences is itself a fantasy of universality. Are all the members of each quadrant the same? Where are the nations, the regions, the religions, the classes, the professions? Where are the other races, the interracial subdivisions? How can the human world be totalized, even as a field of divisions? In the following quotation from Zora Neale Hurston's autobiography, we see that even the same black woman can express self-division in two completely different ways:

> Work was to be all of me, so I said.... I had finished that phase of research and was considering writing my first book, when I met the man who was really to lay me by the heels....
>
> He was tall, dark brown, magnificently built, with a beautifully modeled back head. His profile was strong and good. The nose and lips were especially good front and side. But his looks only drew my eyes in the beginning. I did not fall in love with him just for that. He had a fine mind and that intrigued me. When a man keeps beating me to the draw mentally, he

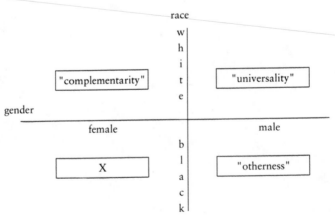

Figure 14.4

BARBARA JOHNSON

begins to get glamorous.... His intellect got me first for I am the kind of woman that likes to move on mentally from point to point, and I like for my man to be there way ahead of me....

His great desire was to do for me. *Please* let him be a *man!*....

That very manliness, sweet as it was, made us both suffer. My career balked the completeness of his ideal. I really wanted to conform, but it was impossible. To me there was no conflict. My work was one thing, and he was all the rest. But I could not make him see that. Nothing must be in my life but himself.... We could not leave each other alone, and we could not shield each other from hurt.... In the midst of this, I received my Guggenheim Fellowship. This was my chance to release him, and fight myself free from my obsession. He would get over me in a few months and go on to be a very big man. So I sailed off to Jamaica [and] pitched in to work hard on my research to smother my feelings. But the thing would not down. The plot was far from the circumstances, but I tried to embalm all the tenderness of my passion for him in *Their Eyes Were Watching God.*[16]

The plot is indeed far from the circumstances, and, what is even more striking, it is lived by what seems to be a completely different woman. While Janie struggles to attain equal respect *within* a relation to a man, Zora readily submits to the pleasures of submission yet struggles to establish the legitimacy of a professional life *outside* the love relation. The female voice may be universally described as divided, but it must be recognized as divided in a multitude of ways.

There is no point of view from which the universal characteristics of the human, or of the woman, or of the black woman, or even of Zora Neale Hurston, can be selected and totalized. Unification and simplification are fantasies of domination, not understanding.

The task of the writer, then, would seem to be to narrate both the appeal and the injustice of universalization, in a voice that assumes and articulates its own, ever-differing self-difference. In the opening pages of *Their Eyes Were Watching God* we find, indeed, a brilliant and subtle transition from the seduction of a universal language through a progressive de-universalization that ends in the exclusion of the very protagonist herself. The book begins:

Ships at a distance have every man's wish on board. For some they come in with the tide. For others they sail forever on the horizon, never out of sight, never landing until the Watcher turns his eyes away in resignation, his dreams mocked to death by Time. That is the life of men.

Now, women forget all those things they don't want to remember, and remember everything they don't want to forget. The dream is the truth. Then they act and do things accordingly.

So the beginning of this was a woman, and she had come back from burying the dead. Not the dead of sick and ailing with friends at the pillow and the feet. She had come back from the sodden and the bloated; the sudden dead, their eyes flung wide open in judgment. The people all saw her come because it was sundown. (p. 9)

At this point Janie crosses center stage and goes out, while the people, the "bander log," pass judgment on her. The viewpoint has moved from "every man" to "men" to "women" to "a woman" to an absence commented on by "words without masters," the gossip of the front porch. When Janie begins to speak, even the universalizing category of standard English gives way to the careful representation of dialect. The narrative voice in this novel expresses its own self-division by shifts between first and third person, standard English and dialect. This self-division culminates in the frequent use of free indirect discourse, in which, as Henry Louis Gates, Jr., points out, the inside/outside boundaries between narrator and character, between standard and individual, are both transgressed and preserved, making it impossible to identify and totalize either the subject or the nature of discourse.[17]

Narrative, it seems, is an endless fishing expedition with the horizon as both the net and the fish, the big one that always gets away. The meshes continually enclose and let escape, tear open and mend up again. Mrs. Ramsay never finishes the brown stocking.[18] A woman's work is never done. Penelope's weaving is nightly re-unraveled. The porch never stops passing the world through its mouth. The process of de-universalization can never, universally, be completed.

NOTES

1 For an excellent discussion of the importance of the metaphor/metonymy distinction, see Maria Ruegg, "Metaphor and Metonymy: The Logic of Structuralist Rhetoric," in *Glyph 6: Johns Hopkins Textual Studies* (Baltimore: Johns Hopkins University Press, 1979).

2 Roman Jakobson, "Two Aspects of Language and Two Types of Aphasic Disturbances," in Roman Jakobson and Morris Halle, *Fundamentals of Language* (The Hague: Mouton, 1956).

3 Roman Jakobson, "Linguistics and Poetics," in *The Structuralists from Marx to Lévi-Strauss* (Garden City, N. Y.: Doubleday Anchor, 1972), p. 95.

4 See George Lakoff and Mark Johnson, *Metaphors We Live By* (Chicago: University of Chicago Press, 1980).

5 Paul de Man, *Allegories of Reading* (New Haven: Yale University Press, 1979), p. 14.

6 It now appears, according to new evidence uncovered by Professor Cheryl Wall of Rutgers University, that Hurston was born as much as ten years earlier than she claimed. See Robert Hemenway's Introduction to the re-edition of *Dust Tracks on a Road* (Urbana: University of Illinois Press, 1984), pp. x–xi.

7 "Folklore Field Notes from Nora Neale Hurston," introduced by Robert Hemenway, *The Black Scholar* 7, no. 7 (1976): 41–42.

8 Zora Neale Hurston, *Their Eyes Were Watching God* (1937), Illini Book Edition (Urbana: University of Illinois Press, 1978).

9 Erich Auerbach, *Mimesis* (New York: Doubleday Anchor, 1957), pp. 482–83.

10 Henry Louis Gates, Jr., "Criticism in the Jungle," introduction to *Black Literature and Literary Theory* (New York: Methuen, 1984), pp. 4, 8.

11 W. E. B. DuBois, *The Souls of Black Folk*, in *Three Negro Classics* (New York: Avon, 1965), pp. 214–15.

12 James Weldon Johnson, *The Autobiography of an Ex-Colored Man*, in *Three Negro Classics*, p. 403.

13 Richard Wright, "Between Laughter and Tears," *New Masses*, October 5, 1937, pp. 25–26.

14 Arthur P. Davis, *From the Dark Tower* (Washington, D. C.: Howard University Press, 1974), p. 116.

15 Bell Hooks, *Ain't I a Woman* (Boston: South End Press, 1981), p. 8.

16 Zora Neale Hurston, *Dust Tracks on a Road*, pp. 252–60.

17 See Gates' discussion of *Their Eyes Were Watching God* as what he calls (à la Barthes) a "speakerly text," in *The Signifying Monkey* (New York: Oxford University Press, 1988), pp. 193–216. [See also pp. 511–34 in this book.]

18 I wish to thank Patti Joplin of Stanford University for calling this fact to my attention.

Psychoanalytic Approache

Introduction

Some readers might turn to a unit on psychoanalysis with the reasonable expectation of finding an alternative to structuralist and post-structuralist critiques of humanism, a way of reclaiming the individual personality as a category worthy of investigation in life as well as art. In the previous sections of this volume, we have seen that, as novel theory consolidates itself as a field around the study of narrative, it provocatively calls into question the very thing many readers turn to novels for: the enjoyment of highly individual characters. We may feel that it is one thing for Vladímir Propp to reduce the multiformity of fairy-tale characters (princesses, ogres, etc.) to their positionality within a constitutive folk-tale grammar and another for Tzvetan Todorov to find the interest of Dostoyevsky's extended and detailed representation of highly individualized psyches to lie only in the large-scale rhetorical structures to which they can be analogized. Is there a way of conceptualizing the human subject as something other than a depersonalized sentence function? And if there is an alternative model, does it also allow the human subject to be something other than, in Todorov's words, a "blank form which is complete by different predicates" (*Poetics*, 213)?

Asking such questions might also be a way of turning from theories about narrative (with the novel serving as prime example) to a theory more particularly about the novel as a genre. After all, for many literary critics as well as general readers, the novel's capacity for sustained psychological realism is arguably its most distinctive generic feature. *Clarissa, Evelina, Emma, Oliver Twist, Jane Eyre, Madame Bovary, Anna Karenina,*

DOROTHY HALE

Daniel Deronda, Lord Jim, Lucky Jim – for these major novels the project of representing an individualized identity is so dominant that the book title itself is a proper name. From Pamela's epistolary representation of her emotional perturbations to Quentin Compson's flashbacks and free-thought association, the novel has been interested in presenting a microscopic look at the dynamic working of an individual's consciousness in and through time. The narratologist Dorrit Cohn, who seeks in *Transparent Minds* (1978) to catalogue the different novelistic techniques for representing consciousness, declares that "fictional consciousness is the special preserve of narrative fiction."[1] And Cohn further argues that the paradoxical status of psychological realism is the source of the novel's artistry, its distinctive accomplishment as a literary form: "the most real, the 'roundest' characters of fiction are those we know most intimately, precisely in ways we could never know people in real life." The novel uses its particular artistic resources either to tell us, by way of an authoritative narrator, or to show us, by creating the illusion of quoted mind content, "how another mind thinks, another body feels."[2]

The humanistic terms of Cohn's formulation echo Percy Lubbock's vivid description of novelistic intimacy put forward fifty years earlier. Using *Clarissa* as an example, Lubbock declares that "on the first page of Richardson's book ... it is so easy to construct the idea of the exquisite creature, that she seems to step from the pages of her own accord; I, as I read, am aware of nothing but that a new acquaintance is gradually becoming better and better known to me."[3] For Lubbock the fictiveness of a novelistic character is hardly an impediment to personal engagement. The literary conditions under which this stranger comes to be known to the reader establish an affective relation that rivals our real-life social relations. In support of Lubbock, we might note the way novels inspire detailed analysis about individual motive and choice. It is indeed a striking tribute to the novel's powers of realism that when readers of, for example, *The Portrait of a Lady* pause to consider, "Should Isabel Archer marry Lord Warburton?" they frequently formulate their answer in terms that have little or no reference to Isabel as a fictional character in a work of art: instead they talk about her choice as they would that of a sister or roommate. If the artistry of James's portrayal is considered in such discussions, it may be to determine why fictional characters can sometimes seem even more "real" to us than, say, our actual next-door neighbor. In addition to Cohn's emphasis on our exceptional access to a fictional character's deepest thoughts and feelings, we might also want to consider in this regard the coherence of their lives (plot); the one-sidedness of our affective relation to them (we know them, but they do not know us); and the extraordinariness or "exquisite" qualities of character that make their lives or minds worth narrating.

For readers with such investments in the affective power of novelistic character, the surprise of this unit will lie in the determination of psychoanalytic theorists *not* to imagine psychoanalytic theory as an alternative to post-structuralist conceptions of the subject – but, if anything, to regard psychoanalysis as the logical next step in the refinement of post-structuralist theory. Although there is indeed throughout the century a body of critical work that concerns itself with the surface psychologies of novelistic characters and speculates on the ethical effect these characters have on novel readers (see for example, Martha C. Nussbaum's *Love's Knowledge*, 1990), the psychoanalytic approaches to the novel that have had the most influence on the development of novel theory as a field treat these topics as inseparable from the larger philosophical truths taught by post-structuralism. The theorists included in this section – René Girard, Peter Brooks, and Shoshana Felman – follow Víktor Shklovsky, Todorov, Roland Barthes, J. Hillis Miller, and Barbara Johnson in regarding the full and self-present subjectivities associated with realist novels as referential lures, as one component in a dynamic and temporal signifying relation. For Girard, Brooks, and Felman, post-structuralist psychology is a means of explaining the persistence of the referential lure: why humans can't help but feel themselves as self-present and autonomous – and the complex psychic apparatus that is generated in the maintenance of this primary human need.

For Felman in particular, psychoanalysis carries forward the post-structuralist project by imagining language as not just a component of the mind, one among many functions, but the structure of the mind itself. This important idea will become clearer as we examine in more detail Felman's work, but in a general way it will already be familiar to us from a popular understanding of the Freudian unconscious. For Freud the split between the conscious and the unconscious means that the self can never be wholly present to itself. The unconscious is, by Freud's definition, that which can never be known by consciousnesses but which expresses itself indirectly through its effects on consciousness. Put in linguistic terms, the unconscious functions as a transcendental signified, the basis of meaningful human experience that is not itself directly apprehensible but whose effects are legible in the performance of consciousness (the signifier). Freud's theory of split subjectivity means that identity is thus produced as narrative: through the noncoincidence of signifier and signified, identity is always enacted rather than known, displayed rather than self-described. No amount of introspection, not even the *experience* of self-reflection, will yield definitive self-knowledge. But the conscious quest for self-knowledge is not a logic error, something to be corrected by reason. It is in fact essential to the operation of the unconscious: the belief in reason and self-will produces the unconscious.

For Felman, the work of Jaques Lacan crucially connects Freud's account of the unconscious with Saussurian linguistic theory. In his famous seminar, "The Instance of the Letter in the Unconscious" (first published in 1966), Lacan argues that Saussure's chain of signification should be rightly understood as the psychic vacillation between self-presence and self-noncoincidence; between knowing oneself to be oneself and knowing that this knowledge is nonetheless partial, contingent, itself in process. The lure of self-presence is embodied for Lacan in the Cartesian *cogito*: I think therefore I am. But for Lacan it is precisely the ambiguity of "I think" in this phrase that expresses the full complexity of human experience. On the one hand, "I think therefore I am" can mean "I think, I know my thoughts and am therefore present to myself" (what Lacan calls "metaphoric" totality or "tautology"). On the other hand, "I think therefore I am" can mean "My thoughts think me, I am produced by my thoughts," or in Lacan's words, "I am thinking where I am not, therefore I am where I am not thinking" (what he calls the metonymic denial of tautology and the pursuit of "coming into being").[4]

For Felman and Girard, novels are especially important cultural products precisely because they so vividly display the belief in self-presence as a necessary self-delusion. Novelistic characters (especially, one might argue, those represented as thinking for themselves, as present to themselves through their thinking) dramatically expose the appeal of conscious thought as the basis of self-knowledge – and also expose the inadequacy of this basis. Thus it can be said that Girard and Felman do turn to the novel for the psychological realism it offers. But their notion of how the psyche functions leads them not to relish but to read through the particularities of individual personality; they see the novel's contribution as lying in its revelation of the psychic structures that produce the illusion of individuality. The critic's job is to identify these structures and to classify the various types of self-deceptions that unify human experience, specifically the kinds of projections, distortions, or transformations that enable a subject to sustain the illusion of self-presence and autonomy. If questions about the appropriateness of Isabel's marriage choices can serve to represent the interest of a school of psychology that takes seriously the power of characterological presence, then the following quotation from *The Turn of the Screw*, James's most gothic work, the work that Felman takes as the departure point for her theory of narrative, might serve to capture the interest in the dynamics of noncoincidence characteristic of the psychoanalytic approaches to the novel in this unit: "Nothing was more natural than that these things should be the other things they absolutely were not."[5]

Peter Brooks's essay, "Freud's Masterplot" (1977), is a useful place to chart the interpenetration of post-structuralism and psychoanalysis since it explicitly begins by emphasizing the psychological claims at work in the narrative theories put forward by Todorov and especially Barthes. If Barthes is right, if "the passion that animates us as readers of narrative is the passion for (of) meaning," what, Brooks asks, should we make of Barthes' related assertion: that "this passion appears to be finally a desire for the end" (Barthes quoted by Brooks, "Masterplot," 331)? Within structuralist linguistics, a speaker's attempt to reach "the end" of signification is simply a fact of language use, a nonaffective component of the signifying chain. But by introducing the emotions of passion and desire, Barthes suggests that the quest for the transcendental signifier, for knowledge as a stable referent, is not a neutral fact of language but a psychological compulsion.

Brooks's project is not to question Barthes' psychologized account of signification but to find in Freud's work a way of elucidating its claims. The interest and sometimes the difficulty of Brooks's essay is that it walks a double line in its engagement with Freud. "Freud's Masterplot" aims to accomplish a discursive reversal: to show not that Freud explains or authorizes Barthes' account of the desiring post-structuralist subject, but that Barthes' theory of signification underlies Freud's theory of life, that Freud's "masterplot" is a narrative theory. But although this is the explicit thesis of Brooks' essay, and an interesting one in its own right, we see at key moments the appeal to psychoanalysis as not just an alternative discourse for explaining human motivation and identity but a theory with a fuller account of human motivation and identity, one that would allow us to understand human subjectivity as more than the radically reduced emotional states of "passion" and "desire" invoked by Barthes.

Brooks's attempt to align Barthes and Freud begins with his gloss of Barthes' phrase "the desire for the end" by way of Freud's "the aim of all life is death" (Freud quoted by Brooks, 335). According to Freud, all organisms are animated by two rival energies: the pleasure principle moves the organism "forward," as it seeks external gratification or "discharge," while the death instinct strives to move the organism "backward," to eliminate desire altogether, to end the "tension" and "irritation" of its demand, to reachieve lost stasis (336). For Brooks, Freud's masterplot of organic life is structured by a binary opposition that is comparable to that which underlies Barthes' description of the psychology of human signification. The questing subject moves energetically "forward" from one signifier to the next as he or she seeks to "discharge" meaning; but this search is itself produced by the equally powerful desire for, in Barthes' phrase, "the end": to be at rest, to be outside of the chain, to have achieved meaning. The struggle in the Freudian model between the pleasure and death instincts, and in the Barthesian model between the pleasure of semantic play and the desire for semantic satiation, generates "life," a repetition through time that Brooks also calls the "narrative middle." In the Freudian model, the narrative middle is the life span of the organism. In the Barthesian model, the narrative middle is the chain of signification, the subject's move through infinitely substitutable, because equally interchangeable, signifiers.

How does Brooks apply the concept of the masterplot to the novel and why is he interested in thinking about literature in these terms? It is significant that Brooks himself does not explicitly theorize the concept of the masterplot as a specifically literary or novelistic phenomenon. In fact, he seems careful *not* to offer a theory of the novel or a theory of narrative literature. Instead he portrays as deliberately ungrounded the comparison he is making between Freud's theory of the organism and literary texts. He insists that he is "superimposing" the "model of the functioning of the mental apparatus on the functioning of the text" (341). Brooks thus implies that there is nothing necessary about the relation between mental apparatus and text, that their connection is created through his own playful gesture. Presumably this decision is dictated by the truths about meaning that he has learned from deconstruction: that there is no master key to knowledge, only the unquenchable desire for master texts and the inevitable failure of authority. Brooks's gesture of superimposition is meant to distinguish the concept of the masterplot from the authority of the psychoanalytic master. It also preserves the intrinsicality of literature and psychoanalysis as separate discourses, their equality as arbitrary signifiers in the chain of signification.

And he seems happy to carry out the project of superimposition with a handful of metaphoric terms that stress the arbitrary relation between Freudian theory and literary texts through the purely figurative connections they establish between the two dis-courses. But the sheer intellectual surprise and excitement of Brooks's execution of this superimposition, the imaginative way he negotiates similarity and difference, and the range of literary texts he calls upon may convince the reader that Brooks has in fact mounted a powerful theory of narrative, despite his philosophical opposition to such authoritative discourse. If this theory is born through the play of Brooks's intelligence and imagination, if it comes into being through figurative connections that we might typically associate more with literary texts than literary-critical texts, then it is in keeping with Brooks's deconstructive position that theory itself may need to be more self-consciously redefined as an activity that is as speculative as it is argumentative, whose "science" is a hypothetical knowledge.

But if Brooks thus believes he has suggestively established a playful relation between Barthes' phrase, "the desire for the end," and Freud's phrase, "the aim of all life is death," and if he further believes that his own theoretical stance is in keeping with this relativized view of knowledge as narrative performance, it is crucial to note that Brooks can hold this position only because he leaves untheorized the ways his use of Freud's biology in fact restricts Barthes' notion of free play. For Barthes the interplay between signifier and signified, metonymy and metaphor, endlessly generates signification; for

DOROTHY HALE

Brooks (via Freud) this vacillation is itself structured by the way pleasure functions as a psychological condition. As Freud explains it, if the pleasure principle were to satisfy itself too early and too completely it would be indistinguishable from the death drive. It is only the inadequacy of its external gratifications and the temporariness of its discharges that enable the organism to move itself forward in the quest for more satisfactory gratification. Freud theorizes that this delay becomes crucial to obtaining satisfactory pleasure. As Brooks puts it, the pleasure principle seeks not just any discharge, but "significant discharge" (335). The organism's mastery of time is thus crucial to Freud's masterplot: through strategic self-impediment, the organism achieves not just any end but the satisfying end, the "right death, the correct end" (336) to "follow its own path to death" (335). The endless chain of signification thus reemerges in Brooks's theory via Freud as "a perfect and self-regulatory economy which makes both end and *detour* perfectly necessary and interdependent," structuring life with a beginning, middle, and end that stand not just in temporal but in meaningful relation, symbiotic parts of an organic whole (338). Barthes' view of knowledge as an endless performance of meaning becomes for Brooks a theory of the "right ending." For Barthes, metonymic association is infinite; for Brooks metonymy is a means to an end: "We must have metonymy in order to reach metaphor" (338). Barthes' description of the endless vacillation between the desire for achieved meaning (metaphor) and the perceived inadequacy of all referents (metonymy) thus is reordered by the evaluative nature of Freudian pleasure as a teleological development. Freud's phrase, "the aim of all life is death," glosses Barthes's phrase "the desire for the end" by turning free play into plot.

Brooks's skepticism about authoritative discourse thus does not prevent him from having a theory about literature, but it does prevent him from being able to make explicit the contradictory nature of his philosophical beliefs. In his essay, knowledge claims stand in tension with his explicit commitment to interpretative relativism. When we look closely at the way Brooks extends the concept of the masterplot to literary texts, we can see how the gesture of superimposition quickly yields to the assertion of meaningful relation. For example, on the one hand we can vividly see Brooks forging the figurative relation between the mental apparatus and the literary text through his flexible use of the word "meaning": texts function like minds in that they develop their "meanings" in time (331). But, on the other hand, we can also see that for Brooks the play of the word "meaning" is not endless; on the contrary, the ending provided by Freud is ultimately what Brooks imports so that the text, like the organism, can have an ending. Freud's theory of intrinsic organic identity is recuperated specifically as semantic meaning: as in the operation of the pleasure principle, so for narrative texts "the very possibility of meaning plotted through time depends on the anticipated structuring force of the ending" (332), the satisfying discharge that allows mere incidents to become "promises and annunciations" of satisfied, semantic desire. Although for Brooks it is sometimes the reader who derives his satisfaction from the text's self-delay, it is more often the text itself that pursues its own meaningful satisfaction. But in either case, the "meanings" developed in time and achieved through the right end are always valuable only in terms of their meaningfulness for the text's identity as an intrinsic organism. On Brooks's account, the semantic meaning of texts is no more or less than their functioning as organisms. Thus Brooks's act of playful superimposition yields a knowledge claim about literary texts, one that could not be made without the act of superimposition.

In Brooks's theory of plot, "the very possibility of meaning plotted through time" is always only the quality of "necessity" (333) that the right ending gives to the text, allowing it to be analogized to the life span of a living organism.

When Brooks refers to literary texts, we find that he uses the terms "narrative" plot, "fictional" plot, "novelistic" plot, and "literary" text in a free-floating way. But he most often has in mind the novel, since novels can be easily analogized to organisms in the terms that Brooks has derived from Freud. The teleology of the novel's plot structure, the seemingly necessary entailment of end from beginning and beginning from end, creates the impression of a textual life span, of the novel's culmination in and through its ending. Brooks is thus most concerned with what we might call the life of the novel itself – which is to say, the temporal life of the novel as a narrative. In fact, his theory focuses on the life of the novel to the exclusion of more obvious novelistic human agents: he gives no theoretical attention to the living characters associated with the genre; and he mentions only by the way the passionate "reader of narrative" invoked by Barthes.

In the few places where Brooks does meditate upon the literariness of literary texts, he significantly defines that quality as simply and only a high degree of strategic temporal mastery. Within the explicit terms afforded him by the concept of the masterplot, literature is worth studying only because it excels at meaningful repetition. Poetry, he says, is based upon the masterful repetitions of "rhyme, alliteration, assonance, meter, refrain"; while "all the mnemonic elements" of fiction, "and indeed most of its tropes are in some manner repetitions which take us back in the text, which allow the ear, the eye, the mind to make connections between different textual moments, to see past and present as related and as establishing a future which will be noticeable as some variation in the pattern" (334). The literary text establishes through masterful repetition the meaningful play of similarity and difference, the expectation that narrative meaning will ultimately cohere in a satisfying whole at the end of the text; and the irritation (both the reader's and the text's) produced by the delay will be orgasmically rewarded through significant discharge.

Yet although Brooks's explicit theoretical terms allow him to emphasize the purely formal intensity of literature – its ability to create a "necessary middle" through thick repetition – at key moments he implies that the content of these literary texts also matters. It is not simply that their textual strategies of repetition make them seem organic; and it is not that their repetitions make them seem semantically significant, offering "the possibility (or the illusion) of 'meaning' wrested from 'life'" (338); but that these formal devices can be interpreted figuratively or metaphorically as versions of the human conflicts and social struggles depicted as the content of literature. For example, Brooks sees the inauguration of expectation in text and reader as shared by the novelistic character whose career is frequently launched as "an awakening, an arousal, the birth of an appetency, ambition, desire, or intention" (336). Brooks thus implies that the novel's characters serve as formal expressions of the text's organic life: he explicitly understands Pip's life as a mirror for the life of the text. At the end of *Great Expectations* Pip is "the image of a 'life' cured of 'plot'" (340). But in other descriptions Brooks gives us of Charles Dickens's protagonist, he mobilizes untheorized Freudian concepts ("the return of the repressed," "the spell of childhood," the "primal scene") that provide psychic content to Pip's motives and choices, making him seem far less an allegory of the life of the text and more like a living psychological subject. Brooks's theory of narrative meaning as meta-meaning, his belief that the temporal structure of life constitutes the meaning of life, is haunted by its own return of the repressed: whenever Brooks moves from theorizing narrative generally to discussing particular novels, his post-structuralist commitment to moral and epistemological relativism is compromised by his untheorized invocation of social and psychological truths about the human condition.

Brooks may feel that he has in "Freud's Masterplot" put Barthes and Freud together to suggest why the impulse to death is no more than the condition for meaning. Yet his superimposition leaves unstated the psychic difference between the desire for meaning and the fact of death. Brooks may be attracted to the Freud of "Beyond the Pleasure Principle" because the essay seems to normalize by making structural what otherwise seems aberrant, perverse, irrational, or inexplicable (the desire for death). But if this neutralized view of death enables him to put psychology and signification in relation, it also is what causes Brooks to neglect the signal difference between linguistic and Freudian models: organisms, unlike the play of meaning, do die. To imagine psychic repetition as so many versions of the "doomed" attempt to master originary loss leaves Brooks with no way to acknowledge the different psychic registers this anxiety takes. As in Freud's essay, for Brooks the trauma that inaugurates the study of the death drive (the soldiers who gain no peace from their recurring nightmares) simply drops out. But in the same way that Brooks covertly invokes Freudian concepts that describe psychological functions in more human ways, he also reaches out to nonpsychoanalytic thinkers to supply the social content forbidden by his theoretical position. Brooks opens and closes his essay with two Marxist thinkers, Walter Benjamin and György Lukács (both included in Part V of this anthology). Through Benjamin, Brooks introduces "fiction" (332) as the cultural practice used by humans to grapple with the fact of death; and through Lukács he derives the notion of the modern condition as one of "transcendental homelessness" (340). Such allusions seem to allow Brooks to have his deconstructed signification and his social meaning, too. But although Brooks implies through these references that his argument is compatible with the Marxist social project, although he seems to think that transcendental homelessness is equitable to the collective yearning for the transcendental signifier, it is doubtful that Benjamin and Lukács would agree. For these Marxist thinkers, the psychological question necessarily entails a moral and ethical dimension: why humans are "shivering" or why, in Lukács's case, the "work of memory" (340) cannot be understood outside the work of social history. In the strict logic of Brooks's deconstructive position, the Marxist belief in society and history would be just another example of the dream of semantic fulfillment, the desire to worship false referents – part of the dream of achieved human meaning that makes any assertion of interpretative authority (even his own) the ultimate "fiction" for Brooks. And only as "fiction" can Brooks incorporate into this deconstructive position the beliefs that challenge this definition of knowledge as fiction.

Shoshana Felman, in her "Turning the Screw of Interpretation" (first published in 1977) takes on many of the same topics as Brooks; but rather than playfully superimposing a psychoanalytic masterplot onto novelistic narratives, Felman seeks to explain logically why a psychoanalytic theory of narrative is also a narrative theory of psychoanalysis. Elements of Brooks's theory that seem in logical tension (for example, the openness of signification and the closure of plot) are thus worked out more explicitly by Felman as contradictions inherent to the operation of narrative/the mind. Her theory, like Brooks's, takes as a foundational principle that an original loss – the loss of origin itself – initiates psychic repetition. In Felman's theory, however, psychic repetition in human beings is not an abstracted analogue to an organism's life span, not "masterful" delay in service of a satisfying "discharge." The signal difference between Felman and Brooks lies in the sociality that is fundamental to her theory of narrative: for Felman the distinguishing quality of narrative is not time but interpersonal relation: every story is told to someone and for someone. Every teller/author posits an addressee whom she hopes will understand her; every listener/reader projects an author whose meaning she seeks to know.

Felman's complete essay is really a short book, 113 pages long. But "The Turns of the Story's Frame: A Theory of Narrative" presents many of her most important ideas. We can, for example, immediately see Felman's social revision of the Barthesian notion of signification when she writes, "The narrators, in fact, constitute not only a self-relaying *chain* of narrative transmissions, but also a series of pairs or *couples*" (322). For Felman, human beings narrate not to "tell" or to "show," but to perform: they tell their stories in the hopes of eliciting an emotionally gratifying reaction from their listener/reader, of creating positive terms of relationship between self and other. In her words, "couples... become couples by virtue of a constitutive situation of dialogue and of *interlocution*, whose discursiveness subtly develops into a discreet game of *seduction*" (323). For Felman the referent, "the story" (324) is, as it was for Shklovsky, Propp, and the structuralists influenced by these Russian formalists, a ruse, a "mask" (323), a "disguise" (324). It is the ostensible object of and motive for communication, the "what" that is passed from teller/author to listener/reader. The term "seduction," of course, further implies that the fascinating referent is also a distraction, a way of doing one thing while pretending to do another – in Felman's theory, of deploying reference itself as a cover for emotional performance.

Yet in the psychoanalytic model Felman develops, tellers/authors are unaware that they are initiating a game of seduction. On a conscious level, they themselves believe that the referent *is* the object of narration, that their purpose in telling is to serve as a link in the chain of transmission: to pass on a story from themselves to someone else. The transferential structure thus is something that can never itself be the subject of narration; it is expressed through and can be known only by its effects on the story: "The transferential structure will, however, not only motivate, but also modify the narrative, becoming at once its *motive* and its *mask*: putting the narrative in motion as its dynamic, moving force, it will also hide, distort it through the specular mirages of its numerous mirrors of seduction" (323). The desire to believe that the referent is the reason and purpose of narration is thus the way consciousness sustains an idealized view of self-identity: to communicate or transfer a story is also to pass on its meaning, and the belief that meaning is conscious meaning – the narrator's proffered interpretation of the meaning and value of the story she passes on, the lesson to be learned, the moral that is drawn – actively works to mask the power of unconscious forces. What one *can* say about one's meaning, in other words, is necessarily (in this psychoanalytic model) only always what is morally acceptable to consciousness. For Felman, the narrative investment in the referent is thus also the psychic investment in literal meaning, in knowledge as consciousness and in the experience of self-consciousness (self-presence) as the touchstone of self-knowledge.

For Felman, then, transference structures self-presence along two lines of dynamic relation. The relation between consciousness and unconsciousness is, in a primary

DOROTHY HALE

way, itself both a transferal relation and an interpersonal relation. Since the unconscious is, as we have discussed above, always that which cannot be known by consciousness and yet can be known by its effects on consciousness, the split subject is itself constituted by the mediation of self by a force that is always "other" to it. Freud himself declares that the unconscious and conscious are like two people in conversation: "one person who was dependent upon a second person had to make a remark which was bound to be disagreeable in the ears of this second one." For the unconscious to express itself it must thus find mediated forms of expression that represent a "compromise between the intentions of one agency and the demands of the other."[6] For Freud, this compromise results most spectacularly in the symbolic language of dream work: through rhetorical techniques such as displacement, condensation, and visual punning, the unconscious covertly sneaks by the censoring conscious the expression of taboo desires.

But putting it this way might make it sound as if the analyst has a privileged access to the latent content of the unconscious, that, by the power of his wisdom and authority, he and he alone can decode the unmediated content of the unconscious. In Freud's early work, especially in his opus *The Interpretation of Dreams* (first published in 1899), he certainly displays such interpretative self-confidence. But in later essays such as "The Unconscious" (1915), he formulates the problem as a phenomenological one: "Just as Kant warned us not to overlook the fact that our perceptions are subjectively conditioned and must not be regarded as identical with what is perceived though unknowable, so psycho-analysis warns us not to equate perceptions by means of consciousness with the unconscious mental processes which are their object. Like the physical, the psychical is not necessarily in reality what it appears to us to be." Freud goes on in this passage to reassert optimism about the knowledge base of psychoanalysis (declaring that "internal objects are less unknowable than the external world").[7] Felman would agree with this assertion, but would find the objective grounding for the analyst's knowledge of the unconscious to lie in the analyst's own social relationship with his patient. In the same way that consciousness is mediated by the unconscious, so too is the patient's conversation with her analyst mediated by her attempts to "seduce" him, to win his interest and his approval by mediating her "story" in ways that will please him. Yet this remains an unconscious motive; the patient believes that she offers her narrative to the analyst as an object for authoritative analysis. The only hidden meaning that she considers is the one that the analyst will find through his expertise, authority, and objectivity as a professional psychoanalyst. The patient remains unaware that the doctor's role as a professional masks the social and emotional relationship between them. Nor does the patient consider that her belief in the analyst's authority is itself simply another version of the belief in reference, in literal meaning. The full story, Felman insists, is always unknown – and the difference between the psychoanalyst and the patient is simply that the psychoanalyst knows that it is unknowable (325).

What does the psychoanalyst do, then? While the patient's fantasy imagines that the analyst will find her real story beneath the masks and disguises her unconscious deploys, the Felmanian post-structuralist psychoanalyst (via Lacan and deconstruction) knows that there is in fact no end to interpretation. The relation between the unconscious and consciousness instead produces an endlessly signifying text, one that the analyst is "always reading, deciding, *interpreting*" (327). In one of Felman's most provocative assertions, she likens the analyst's interpretative position to the unconscious itself. The analyst is like the unconscious because of his belief in the unconscious. The belief in the unconscious authorizes the analyst to "interfere" with the manifest content of the patient's narrative. The analyst's understanding (I see) is thus always itself an act of mediation (I transfer). The analyst reads, like the unconscious itself, "not literally but rhetorically" (327). The analyst, according to Felman, becomes the author of the patient's text through "*an effect of reading*" (320). Because the analyst reads not just dreams but any patient narrative as mediated by the unconscious, he invests all "conscious, daylight signifiers with an unconscious energy" (327). Felman thus transmogrifies Barthesian play (the endlessness of signification) into a psychoanalytic basis for human potentiality. The theory of the unconscious assures that human thought and action do mean, that there is a coherent motive for human behavior, a transcendental signified, that produces both the patient's narrative and the analyst's authoring. But the theory also requires that unconscious meaning will always be ungraspable, will elude conscious understanding. The patient thus transfers her story to the analyst who dignifies it not by finding its meaning but by finding it to be endlessly significant. Psychoanalysis can never be completed because the patient's text is endlessly expressive of the unconscious. The analyst authors the patient's text, and thereby authorizes the patient's subjectivity, by attributing to it more meaning than he can possibly say.

One might expect Felman to discuss the analyst's emotional relation to the patient, especially since she has detailed the patient's emotional expectations of the analyst. But if she refrains from the explicit treatment of this topic, we can fill in her position by extrapolating from the discussion that leads up to her description of the patient's transferential fantasy. And we can also see how her understanding of the patient and analyst as an interlocutionary relation clarifies the emotional dynamics that are at work between any teller/author and listener/reader. Narration may begin in the narrator's "very act" of "*referring to the Other*" (322), but this reach outward is also an act of self-authorization. The narrator hopes that if she successfully charms her listener, he will in turn refer to her, and thus authorize her ability to refer, to mean. Felman uses the term seduction to connote the eroticism of this activity, but for Felman eroticism is interpretation; there is no sexuality apart from the meaning of sexuality. For Felman this is one of the most crucial teachings of psychoanalysis. Sexuality is not the referent of identity, not the drive that gives meaning to life, not the "literal," the key to the human psyche. But the fact that sex seems to drive us, seems all these things, stages the "*problematization of literality as such.*"[8] In the case of the interpersonal structure of transference, the erotics are "primarily discursive and linguistic" (322). And, according to Felman, the "play of seduction" through narration is itself the "play of *belief*": a belief in the other as other, a play that is mutually self-defining, and mutually reinforcing. As Felman describes it, the "charmed" listener "*adds faith* to the literality of her narrative and to the authority of [the speaker's] own idealized mirror-image of herself" (323). It is thus the listener/reader who imputes credibility to the speaker/author rather than the mastery or wisdom of the author herself. The listener/reader's imputation of authority is thus itself a symptom of his "love." The belief that there is a literal meaning, self-presence, authorial mastery, is itself a signifier of what remains unspeakable between the couple. Felman thus declares that "'seeing' is *interpreting*; it is *interpreting love*; and it is also interpreting *by means of love*" (324).

DOROTHY HALE

In such formulations Felman seems to be providing us with the complex affective content of psychological experience ignored by Brooks and Barthes. But the specific valence of terms such as "love" and "charm" are not sustained in her argument and quickly become indistinguishable from seduction, erotics, and sexuality as versions of the abstracted nature of reference itself. If the psychoanalyst is himself engaged in the reciprocal exchange of "passionate glances" (324), if he is seduced and also seduces, this "emotive look" is ultimately the source of the patient's fantasy of his aloofness and impersonality. Without the emotive look, the analyst would not "see" the patient, would not take on her story as his object of interpretation. According to Felman, the analyst's relation to the patient is thus not unique but paradigmatic: the special circumstances of the psychoanalytic relation simply make vivid what is true of any and all narrative performance. For Felman all interpersonal relations are driven by the subject's un-quenchable desire for mastery, for master interpreters of the subject's own personhood. The love relation is, on Felman's view, a process of self-authorization through the narrator's depersonalization of the addressee. The relation between self and other thus is structured, on her view, by the subject's need to be interpreted by an authoritative other, even though, according to Felman, this authoritative other is a social impossibility.

Felman's social and interpersonal theory of narrative thus is grounded in a hypothesis about the mutually depersonalizing and self-projecting social activity of narrators and readers. The sociality that distinguishes her psychoanalytic theory turns out to be itself an agent of depersonalization and objectification. The other that the narrator begins by speaking to is "by virtue of the storyteller's transference on the reader," the addressee of the narrator's unconscious (325). The other ultimately possesses no constitutive charac-teristics except "otherness"; in Felman's provocative formulation, the other thus ultim-ately functions more as a place than a person. Even the analyst's belief in the endless significance of the patient's subjectivity is due to his conceptualization of that subjectiv-ity as a signifier, a vehicle for the expression of unconscious energy, rather than a source of intrinsic value.

Felman's explanation of why narration takes place within an affective, interpersonal relation thus ultimately theorizes not just sexuality but sociality itself as a "rhetorical" activity. The other is an instrument of psychical performance, a means for the "acting-out of the unconscious" (324). If the theory of the unconscious provides grounds for belief in the meaning of human activity, the operation of the unconscious effectively eliminates the social content of alterity, and thus sociality itself becomes a merely formal relation. Each agent in the transferal chain eventually "becomes a ghost" (325). The self–other relation that structures psychical activity turns out to be itself a "reading effect." The social life of narrative for Felman ultimately has always only one activity to perform: the telling "of transference…through transference" (325). Because this story is performed through the "active operation of *substitution*" (324), it is ultimately indistin-guishable for Felman from the Barthesian play of the signifier – except that the dramatic interplay of "love, death, and substitution" changes in Felman's theory the affect of play, which may be why she prefers the term rhetoric. Because the emotional components in this cluster are experienced sequentially or unconsciously by the humans engaged in transference, we might go so far as to say that Felman theorizes an affect of rhetoric, which she calls the "uncanny" (325).

The universalism underlying Felman's theory of narrative means in one regard that the type and varieties of narrative performance are wholly negligible: fiction or nonfiction, tragedy or comedy, newspaper report or lyric poem – all require that the teller/author position herself in relation to a listener/reader. Felman is drawn to Henry James's gothic tale, "The Turn of the Screw," she writes elsewhere in her essay, because it is a paradigmatic expression of the psychoanalytic theory she is advancing. On her view, the critical reception of "The Turn of the Screw" illuminates the role of sexuality in psychoanalytic theory, distinguishing her Lacanian model from the old-fashioned Freudians. Felman argues that these old-fashioned Freudians are themselves literalists: they believe they have discovered the real meaning of James's story, the forbidden sexual desires that remain unspoken and even unthought by the characters. But Felman contends that this appearance of a "solution" to the mystery only contributes to James's cultivation of a more profound interpretative ambiguity. James sets a trap for the reader: he invites critics like Edmund Wilson to feel that they can "master" his story by uncovering its interpretative key. Wilson thus believes that one "is on the *outside*, that one *can* be on the outside."[9] According to Felman, Wilson thus puts himself in the position of a pseudo-professional, an interpretative authority who knows nothing because he does not know that he cannot know:

> And what James in effect *does* in *The Turn of the Screw*, what he undertakes through the performative action of his text, is precisely to mislead us…In attempting to escape the reading-error constitutive of rhetoric, in attempting to escape the rhetorical error constitutive of literature, in attempting to master literature in order *not to be its dupe*, psychoanalysis, in reality, is *doubly duped*: unaware of its own inescapable participation *in* literature and *in* the errors and the traps of rhetoric, it is blind to the fact that it itself exemplifies no less than the *blind spot* of rhetoricity, the spot where any affirmation of mastery in effect amounts to a self-subversion and to a self-castration.[10]

Does James himself escape such self-mutilation? Henry James enacts his mastery by, in Felman's words, his "*disappearance* from the scene." "James's mastery consists in knowing that mastery as such is but a *fiction*"; by "dispossessing himself of his own story," James hands over interpretative authority to the reader.[11] But the very condition of the master's death is what reveals to the reader that graspable meaning is a projection; that the meaning of literature per se is that which, like the unconscious, exceeds interpretation. The terms of Jamesian mastery may on this account be paradoxical – he is a master because he voluntarily relinquishes mastery – but nonetheless he, like the post-structuralist psychoanalyst, seems to know more than others and behave differently because of this knowledge.

We might feel that Felman's punning deployment of "mastery" in this context allows her to preserve the notion of Jamesian genius, even if genius itself is defined as the barely registerable difference between voluntary, self-conscious self-dispossession and unwitting self-castration. Felman's theory gives no direct account of why James in particular achieves the insight of a post-structuralist psychoanalyst. She does, however, imply that literary authors generally are specially positioned for such insight since they work in a discourse defined by its semantic ungraspability, its ability to exceed interpretation. Felman does not explain why she believes literature has this power, but we might conjecture that she is thinking of literature as a dramatic form of expression, one that tells through its showing – and therefore whose telling can never be directly accessed. But in granting literature a privileged position, in holding it up as the master discourse of relinquished semantic mastery, Felman does not then imagine the literary to be an autonomous and isolated realm. On the contrary, Felman's essay culminates in the search for literary values that might be said to belong, in lesser or greater degrees, to all narrative performances. For Felman, literary value is found not in the "what" but in the "how" of the story. She asks, "How does the meaning of the story, whatever it may be, rhetorically take place through permanent displacement, textually take shape and take effect: *take flight?*"[12] These are of course the same questions asked by the psychoanalyst of the narrative that is presented to him by his patient – and in this sense for Felman psychoanalytic and literary interpretation are one and the same, made so by their shared insight into the functioning of the human mind.

In a turn of the screw of her own theoretical project, Felman goes even further to conclude that the knowledge claims put forward by her theory, the psychoanalytic assumptions about subjective motive and the operation of the unconscious through transference, may themselves belong to a tale told to someone and for a purpose. If the tale of transference told by psychoanalysis establishes interpretation as objective through its interpersonal structures, there is always on the meta-level the concern that these objective structures may themselves be disguises for false mastery. Felman authoritatively declares that "the tale of transference thus turns out to be the tale of the transference of a tale," but she also by the end of her essay encourages us to ask if "the tale of the tale of transference" may itself be a fiction. If so, then psychoanalysis is in another way no different than literature: its participation in the fiction of mastery makes it an art rather than a science. In Felman's vivid formulation, the structural "exteriority" psychoanalysis imagines for itself may be a necessary cover for the "very madness of our own art staring back at us."[13]

"Freud's Masterplot" and "Turning the Screw of Interpretation" are enormously useful in helping us understand why post-structuralist psychoanalytic theory cannot finally mount a theory of literature but instead proposes that theory is literature. Brooks and Felman are driven to conclude that all knowledge, even the postulates of psychoanalysis, is "fiction," may be a "tale." When we turn to the last selection in this unit, an excerpt from René Girard's *Deceit, Desire, and the Novel* (first published in 1961), and discover a psychological theory that is not only entirely confident about its truth claims but also willing to make truth claims about the novel as a particular literary mode, we may be tempted to explain this difference as one of chronology. Girard's book appears almost two decades before Felman and Brooks publish their work. Whereas the later theorists self-consciously fashion their psychoanalytic theories within post-structuralist thought, Girard is interested in disassociating himself from many of the theoretical models for understanding life and literature that were popular at his moment of writing. For example, whereas Brooks and Felman draw in a sustained way from Freud and Lacan, Girard refers only to Freud – and then to dismiss him in a footnote.[14] But although Girard enjoys presenting himself as an innovator and an iconoclast, his psychological account of what he calls the modern self has strong resonances with the deconstructed subject put forward by Brooks and Felman. This conceptual overlap is perhaps even more interesting since Girard offers them in service of a theory whose ultimate vision of life and literature is grounded explicitly in religious values (and implicitly in a conservative politics) that would be anathema to Brooks and Felman.

Girard's theory starts where Felman's starts: in the belief that the complex interpersonal dynamic between self and other is the constitutive structure of the human psyche. Girard also resembles Felman in his belief that the socially mediated psyche is only one component in a two-part psychological dynamic: the self is unwilling to accept the fact of its social mediation, dedicated as it is to imagining itself as autonomous and self-defined. This sentence from Girard might almost have been found in Felman: "Let us note that contradictions which in reality are the very basis of our psychic life always appear as 'differences' between Others and ourselves."[15] But rather than explaining this divided self in terms of the psychoanalytic concepts of transference and the unconscious, Girard instead believes the split self to be a specifically modern phenomenon, not (as in Brooks's view) "transhistorical" but historically contingent – and thus, perhaps, repairable.

Girard's historical claims are easy to sum up because they do not pretend to be exhaustive. Instead he intentionally appeals to truisms about modernity, believing that the more uncontested such generalities can be, then the more they will provide the evidentiary basis for his psychological theory. How did the "illusion of autonomy to which modern man is passionately devoted" (302) become the dominant belief? Girard considers this belief the product of social equalization, conducted simultaneously by different kinds of historical changes. The social revolutions that abolished the divine right of monarchs; the technological revolution that leveled the physical distinctions between men; and the death of God – all are factors that produced modern man as a "free agent," an individual equal to any other individual and wholly responsible (physically, emotionally, and socially) for and to himself.[16]

But if historical forces have constructed individuality and social equality as positive values, for Girard this is a "truth" that creates an intolerable burden for the modern psyche. According to Girard, the modern split subject is born in his inability to live up to his introjected self-expectations: he feels he should be wholly "original," be wholly himself – and because he believes that everyone else is precisely this, he finds himself turning to others for models of self-direction and autonomy. The anxiety produced by this feeling of exceptionalism further isolates the modern subject and further self-divides him. He must imitate the putative "originality" of the other in order to mask his own lack of originality. But because he also cannot admit to himself this dependence upon others, he becomes caught in psychic strategies of self-delusion, of masking and distortion, that attempt to "camouflage the essential role which the Other plays in his desires" (302). As we saw in Part III, J. Hillis Miller uses a more explicit Lacanian vocabulary to describe a similar phenomenon: "It is a specular or speculative relationship in which, as one might say, the mirror is empty when I seek my face in the glass, or in which, perhaps, the face I see is more original than my own and so depersonalizes me when I copy it in order to achieve or affirm my own substance" ("Indirect Discourses," 249). But whereas for Miller the psychological dimension of this social projection was attenuated by the linguistic notion of "dialogy," Girard elaborates this psychological structure by way of the historical phenomenon of secularized religious experience:

Each individual discovers in the solitude of his consciousness that the promise is false but no one is able to universalize his experience. The promise remains true for Others. Each one believes that he alone is excluded from the divine inheritance and takes pains to hide this misfortune. Original sin is no longer the truth about all men as in a religious universe but rather each individual's secret, the unique possession of that subjectivity which broadcasts its omnipotence and its dazzling supremacy.[17]

Deceit, Desire and the Novel seeks to contribute to psychological theory by identifying this psychic condition – which Girard christens triangular desire – and then proving its scope and reach. Most of his 300-page book is devoted to laying out a typology of triangular desire, to displaying its operation within and between people who on the surface seem radically different from one another. In an interpretative move that is by now familiar to us, Girard reads through the surface differences of character to uncover the underlying structure of identity. And as with so many of the theories in this anthology, this structure itself is essentially dynamic, constituted in its relation to the surface that seems to disguise it. Despite the metaphor of the triangle, Girard's model of identity is grounded in the reversible binary opposition between self and other that creates the psychic disguises that establish the illusion of surface differences.

What exactly is triangular desire? Girard opposes the concept of triangular desire to spontaneous desire. In spontaneous desire, a subject imagines that he will achieve psychic satisfaction if he can obtain a specific object that lies outside of the self. Triangular desire is mediated desire: the subject learns what to desire by imitating the desire of another person. Within the typology of triangular desire, Girard establishes two large categories: external mediation and internal mediation. The difference between these categories is a difference in self-honesty. In external desire the mediator is an ideal who can be freely imitated because he is perceived as essentially superior to the subject. In self-consciously striving to imitate his idol, the subject knows that he can never possibly become the idol; rather his explicit position of subordination is what enables him to admit his dependency upon the other and regard the idol as an inspiration and spur to achievement. The subject knows what to do, how to act, what to desire, because he can copy his idol. In this way, external mediation is a vestige of the old order of social hierarchy – and in the overall typology Girard charts, external mediation occupies one end of the spectrum. More prolific because more authentically modern are the various types of internal mediation Girard identifies. If we start with Girard's description of the *vaniteux*, we can get a good idea of how triangular desire operates through internal mediation. According to the ethos of individuality, the individual knows who he is, knows that he is an individual, by knowing what he wants. He believes in Girard's words that he "chooses the objects of his own desire" (295). This already is a mildly deconstructed definition of autonomy: the individual could not desire an object if he or she were indeed wholly complete. But what motivates action is the need for something that is not already one's self (the metonymic chain). The autonomous self is thus the lacking self who seems "spontaneously" to know how to know what will make the self whole, what will satisfy.

Girard derives his term *vaniteux*, which he defines as "vain person," from Stendhal's description of the person who cannot "draw his desires from his own resources" (*Deceit*, 297). In the operation of triangular desire, the subject first of all projects spontaneity onto the others around him. He thus cannot see that the autonomy of the other is his own subjective projection, a mirror of his own psychic anxiety. What he takes as an essential quality of the other is that bestowed upon the other by the self. But the effect of this projection is to intensify his feelings of failure. He needs to convince himself that he is wholly original, just like the others he has projected. He thus covertly attempts to imitate the spontaneous individuals, and pretends to himself that he, too, "chooses the objects of his own desire" (295). The triangle is thus born: the individual deceives himself that he desires an object that will satisfy him and that he can possess – when in truth he desires something that he can never be: the autonomous subject the mediator seems to be. The "object" is thus itself a disguise, a mask to hide the subject's dependence upon another person. But we should also remember that the mediator himself is in some ways simply an "object" to begin with, the screen upon which the subject projects the initial fantasy of achieved individuality. He is projected first as the autonomous individual and then as the "rival" who possesses or seeks to possess the object that the subject believes himself to desire.

The reversals at work in the model of the *vaniteux* are only the base for Girard's description of other kinds of mediated desire, types such as the snob, the coquette, and the sadomasochist. As in Felman's work, part of the thrill of reading Girard is to feel one is walking through a hall of mirrors where anything that might appear to be genuinely different is actually a version of the same thing, and any illusion of difference is in fact produced by that originary thing. For example, in what Girard calls double mediation the "person who is a mediator…may…be tempted to copy the copy of his own desire."[18] And the coquette in imitating her lover's desire for her will come to desire herself: precisely because the desire she arouses makes her feel precious, she must work to arouse that desire yet never surrender to it.[19] Girard's spectrum of types of internally mediated desire also charts the kinds and intensities of emotion produced by each triangulated relationship. The snob is one for whom all love is jealousy (305) and whose slavish thrall to those he admires is more explicit than in the case of the *vaniteux*. The height of internal mediation is the subject whose emotions are so ambivalent as to be wholly contradictory, leading to an emotional intensity and a seesaw of activity that verge on the explosive. For this apocalyptic subject, "there is no longer any love without jealousy, any friendship without envy, any attraction without repulsion" (307) – and this conflict is not hidden but completely transparent. He will, to use Girard's example, insult the other and then instantly beg for mercy.

Girard's psychological theory is thus structuralist in the sense that he posits, as did Felman, an intersubjective psychic structure that underlies – that in fact produces – the illusion of self-presence and autonomy. But unlike Felman – and unlike Brooks as well – Girard does not invoke this structuralist paradigm to show the ways that it itself operates *as* narrative: that it preserves its status as a structure through a process of destabilization and restabilization. Girard explicitly positions himself against this particular post-structuralist conception of knowledge by defending what he calls the "intelligibility" of "human reality" (295). But this does not mean that Girard returns to the confidence in science that buoyed the projects of the structuralists we studied in Part III. On the contrary, in a startling departure from all the theories we have thus far examined in this volume, Girard turns to sources for epistemological stability that could be considered the opposite of the formal and scientific approaches we have been studying: artistic genius and Christian humanism.

How is it that some can come to know the hidden structure of psychology, even while those people are themselves subjected to the illusions of modernity? For Girard the

DOROTHY HALE

answer is as clear as it is elitist: those who come to know triangular desire are privileged and special beings. They have themselves experienced triangular desire – and they have come out the other side. They have lived through it, in both senses of the term: by having had the full experience of internal mediation they can then live beyond it. The man of insight is the one who "More or less surreptitiously, more or less openly... crosses the barrier between Self and Other"; "he discovers a *man like himself* in the mediator who fascinates him."[20] The spiritual difference between Girard and the other psychoanalytic theorists we have been discussing is made clear by Girard when, in an important footnote, he discusses the Oedipal Triangle. For Girard the story of Oedipus is not the Freudian story of sexual repression, nor is it the Lacanian story of necessary interpretative blindness. For Girard the Oedipus story is, on the contrary, a story of achieved alterity, the revelation of an authentic human equality through the universal condition of shared psychological self-deceit. In Girard's words, Oedipus discovers that "the Other, who has become the hated Double, is really identical to himself in those very features which make him appear most hateful." The self, says Girard in a later formulation, learns about the self by recognizing "the sin of which he is accusing his mediator. The curse which Oedipus hurls at Others falls on his own head." "This profound Self is also a universal Self."[21]

Girard's invocation of Oedipus not only marks his differences from Freud but also supports another aspect of his theory – that which makes it a literary theory as well as a psychological theory. In another radical assertion, Girard proposes that the man of insight is first and foremost an author of imaginative writing. Girard does not say that other people are incapable of discovering and representing the truth of triangular desire; but he does make a distinct case for why imaginative writers are particularly qualified to achieve this insight – and which modes of imaginative writing enable this insight: "A basic contention of this essay is that the great writers apprehend intuitively and concretely, through the medium of their art, if not formally, the system in which they were first imprisoned together with their contemporaries" (296). For Girard, the process of artistic expression itself contributes to the author's self-revelation. And the works that most allow for this psychic development are, according to Girard, novels.

Girard's articulation of his psychological theory is conducted by way of fictional characters – and he does not feel that the ontological differences between characters and real people disable his analysis in any way. On the contrary, he understands these fictional characters as authorial self-portraits, vivid representations of the experience of triangular desire that the author has not made up but undergone. In Girard's theory, novel writing itself is the final and last stage of triangular desire. The great novelists are those who begin their novels in the belief that they are representing characters who are inferior to themselves, perhaps who are even "enemies" in the sense that their values seem wholly other.[22] But in part through what Girard calls the "detached" vision afforded him through the form of the novel itself, the novelist comes to see his hero as a projection of himself, and the failings he had attributed to his character as his own. The novel enables the novelist "to *view his characters from different perspectives* and, with the third dimension, give them true freedom and motion."[23] The characterological autonomy allowed by the novel thus effects a change in the relationship between the novelist and his protagonist: "the hero of the novel gradually merges with the novelist in the course of creation." Great characters are thus for Girard the "result of a synthesis of the two halves of existence which pride usually succeeds in keeping separate." The epitome of this relation is expressed for Girard by Flaubert's famous phrase: "Mme Bovary, c'est moi."[24]

Girard's psychological theory thus is also an aesthetic theory, with the value of aesthetics being defined by the privileged insight into the human condition achieved by an author through the imaginative practice of novel writing. For Girard, the novel is not just a significant literary form but the most profound and systematic representation of the absolute truth of the modern condition. When Girard states that he is not offering a traditional genre theory, he simply means that he is offering one based on the standard of content as well as form. In his terms, the "novelistic" (or the French "romanesque") is in a dialectical relationship with the romantic (302–3). The difference between the romantic and the novelistic is a difference of self-consciousness. Both represent the workings of triangular desire, but only the novelistic makes explicit the presence and importance of the mediator. Girard's own analysis of the relation between characters serves as a model for the application of his theory to novels he does not discuss. What does one do if one wants to perform a Girardian reading of Henry James? Girard encourages literary critics to fill out the spectrum of possibility that he roughly charts from Cervantes, Stendhal, Flaubert, Proust, and Dostoevsky. A Girardian analysis of *The Portrait of a Lady* would analyze the relationship between characters, applying or extending Girard's typology of triangular forms (the relation between Lord Warburton, Isabel, and Pansy immediately suggests itself as an example of triangular desire). The literary critic would then try to ascertain the degree of "romantic" and "novelistic" revelation within *Portrait* as well as the comparative degree of self-consciousness about triangular desire possessed by James himself.

In the last chapter of *Deceit, Desire and the Novel*, Girard reveals that the attainment of self-consciousness is not simply the random play of genius, but a result of a very specific crisis that the author has personally experienced – one that is replayed in the novel itself. On Girard's view, the career of the protagonist culminates in the meeting of character and author, which is to say at the moment when the character is shown to become capable of being an author, when he transcends mimetic desire and knows that authentic "passion is inseparable from aesthetic happiness" (305). Aesthetic happiness first and foremost lies in the satisfaction that comes from obtaining true knowledge: the revelation of triangular desire (305). It is also the "delight of creation which wins out over desire and anguish" (305). The delight of creation is what enables the author to write a novel, for the character to become the author. The happiness felt by the novelist "frees" him from the social world, the world of triangular desire. He ceases to be a participant in this world and becomes instead the creator of the novelistic world. His entry into the aesthetic realm enables him to transcend self-satisfaction; he devotes himself to the representation of a hero, an other whose connection to himself is not a mendacious subjective projection but is based upon the novelist's self-conscious understanding of the shared plight of the human condition.

The novelist thus according to Girard earns a freedom that is genuine – but importantly this freed self is itself never directly represented. It is in fact what removes the author from the social world, allowing him to act only in his writing. His revelation, in other words, cannot serve as an instrument of social reform, nor can it even be the source of more satisfying social relations. Instead it displaces the author from the social world of "vanity and desire" (305), reconstituting his identity in the no-place of the novel. This displacement is the source of the creator's "more detached vision" which "enables the novelist *to view his characters from different perspectives.*"[25] Although Girard himself refers only in a general way to the formal properties of the novel as a genre, his notion of "different perspectives" implies that the novel offers the novelist a more inclusive vision of life because it allows him to occupy more points of view than he could occupy in real life. Girard's allusion to the objectivity allowed by the novel's form might also encourage us to extend his claim about novelistic point of view to another common aspect of novelistic narration: the quasi-human presences that are produced through omniscient and retrospective narration. As with the omniscient narrator in *The Portrait of a Lady*, these narratorial presences seem suggestive of a specific individual identity but lack the full attributes of personhood. They thus might be understood as representing the author's double nature as social and aesthetic being, as a social being who has been transmogrified into an aesthetic being.

But Girard leaves it to his reader to develop his stray insights into narrative technique. His theory remains focused on the philosophical and religious dimensions of aesthetic achievement. The novelist's discovery of "aesthetic happiness," Girard believes, is akin to worldly renunciation. The Christian overtones of this idea become clear as Girard insists upon a common feature of the authentic novelistic masterplot: "The title of hero of a novel must be reserved for the character who triumphs over [triangular] desire in a tragic conclusion and thus becomes *capable of writing the novel*."[26] The hero is he who "looks despair and nothingness in the face," who verges on psychic death – and who often is portrayed as confronting or enduring physical death as well. Girard insists that "a reconciliation between hero and the world" occurs only "at the moment of death. It is at the conclusion, and only then, that the hero speaks in the name of the author." The protagonist is thus both continuous with the author and yet qualitatively different: he must die as a person in order to become a novelist. He "triumphs in defeat" through "conversion."[27]

Thus we are oddly back to the claim that "the aim of all life is death." And we may further be struck by the similarities between Girard's "disappeared" novelist and Felman's ghostly one – both types of dissolution praised as triumphs brought on by insight into the true nature of human desire. But on Felman's view, all narrative is "literature," including the narrative of literary criticism; while in Girard's paradigm there is no such deconstructive collapse. For Girard the literary critic completes the work of the novelist; what is expressed through narrative in the novel is fully realizable by the critic through the language of philosophical argument. Girard believes that the critic enjoys the light of novelistic understanding to the degree that he is able to "formalize implicit or already half-explicit systems" in the novels themselves (296). He prides himself in thus being able to show that texts that seem to have nothing to do with each other in terms of their content in fact are versions of one another. Don Quixote is a version of Marcel who is a version of Ivan Karamazov. Girard's literary structuralism thus opposes itself to a literary-historical tradition of authorial influence (313) and instead credits the critic with the power to establish, through systematic analysis, "an unbroken chain" (313) of novels that are united by the shared belief that is their "essence" (313): that "one can rediscover everything" in triangular desire (313). If Girard's study of the novel is devoted to showing that surface differences mask a shared essence, then one would want to say that, in the case of the psychoanalytic theories we have studied in this section, surface similarities should not mask differences of essence. Girard in fact would not agree that "the aim of all life is death" but instead explicitly counters such thinking with a reversal made possible by the aesthetic privilege he accords to the novel: "The ultimate meaning of desire is death but death is not the novel's ultimate meaning."[28] The difference for Girard is not a signifying one but a spiritual one: in his version of the novel's masterplot, the "sense of beginning... is determined by the sense of an ending" ("Masterplot," 332) because this meaning is "an almost miraculous descent of novelistic grace."[29]

NOTES

1 Dorrit Cohn, *Transparent Minds: Narrative Modes for Presenting Consciousness in Fiction* (Princeton, NJ: Princeton University Press, 1978) vi.
2 Ibid. 5–6.
3 Percy Lubbock, *The Craft of Fiction* (London: Jonathan Cape, 1921) 7–8.
4 Jacques Lacan, "The Instance of the Letter in the Unconscious, or Reason Since Freud" (1966). In *Écrits: A Selection*, trans. Bruce Fink, with Héloise Fink and Russell Grigg (New York: Norton, 2002) 157.
5 Henry James, *The Turn of the Screw* (1898; New York: Norton Critical, 1966) 30.
6 Sigmund Freud, "On Dreams" (1911), in *The Freud Reader*, ed. Peter Gay (New York: Norton, 1989) 166.
7 Freud, "The Unconscious" (1915), in *The Freud Reader* 577.
8 Shoshana Felman, "Turning the Screw of Interpretation." In *Literature and Psychoanalysis: The Question of Reading – Otherwise*, ed. Felman (1977; Baltimore, MD: Johns Hopkins University Press, 1982) 110.
9 Ibid. 199.
10 Ibid. 199–200.
11 Ibid. 206.
12 Ibid. 119.
13 Ibid. 207.
14 René Girard, *Deceit, Desire, and the Novel: Self and Other in Literary Structure*, trans. Yvonne Freccero (1961; Baltimore, MD: Johns Hopkins University Press, 1965) 186.
15 Ibid. 183.
16 Ibid. 119, 138, 56.
17 Ibid. 57.
18 Ibid. 99.
19 Ibid. 105.
20 Ibid. 146.
21 Ibid. 187, 299, 298.
22 Ibid. 300.
23 Ibid. 146.
24 Ibid. 300.
25 Ibid. 297, 146.
26 Ibid. 296.
27 Ibid. 146, 294, 292.
28 Ibid. 290.
29 Ibid. 310.

Brooks, Peter. *Reading for the Plot: Design and Intention in Narrative.* 1984. Cambridge, MA: Harvard University Press, 1992.

Clayton, Jay. "Narrative and Theories of Desire." *Critical Inquiry* 16.1 (1989): 33–53.

Davis, Robert Con, ed. *Lacan and Narration: The Psychoanalytic Difference in Narrative Theory.* Baltimore, MD: Johns Hopkins University Press, 1983.

Dumouchel, Paul, ed. *Violence and Truth: On the Work of René Girard.* 1985. London: Athlone Press, 1987.

Felman, Shoshana. *Jacques Lacan and the Adventure of Insight: Psychoanalysis in Contemporary Culture.* Cambridge, MA: Harvard University Press, 1987.

Gallop, Jane. *Reading Lacan.* Ithaca, NY: Cornell University Press, 1985.

Moi, Toril. "The Missing Mother: The Oedipal Rivalries of René Girard." *Diacritics* 12.2 (1982): 21–31.

White, Hayden. "Ethnological 'Lie' and Mythical 'Truth.'" *Diacritics* 8.1 (1978): 2–9.

15

Deceit, Desire, and the Novel

René Girard

René Noël Girard (b. 1923)

René Girard was born in Avignon, France, and studied at the *lycée* of Avignon, the École des Chartes in Paris, and Indiana University, where he received his doctorate in history in 1950. Girard taught at Johns Hopkins University (1957–70) and the State University of New York at Buffalo (1971–5), before returning to teach at Indiana; in 1981 he went to Stanford University, where he was Andrew B. Hammond Professor of French Language, Literature, and Civilization until his retirement in 1995. Girard formed the Colloquium on Violence and Religion in 1990, which began publishing the annual *Contagion: Journal of Violence, Mimesis, and Culture* in 1994. He has won election to the American Academy of Arts and Sciences and a Guggenheim Fellowship. Girard's books include: *Mensonge romantique et vérité romanesque* (1961, translated as *Deceit, Desire, and the Novel*, 1965); *La Violence et le sacre* (1972; translated as *Violence and the Sacred*, 1977); *Des choses cachées depuis la fondation du monde* (1978; translated as *Things Hidden Since the Foundation of the World*, 1987); and books on Proust, Dostoevsky, Shakespeare, and the story of Job. Selected essays are available in *The Girard Reader* (1996).

From *Deceit, Desire, and the Novel: Self and Other in Literary Structure*, translated by Yvonne Freccero. Baltimore and London: Johns Hopkins University Press, 1966 (1961), from ch. 1, pp. 1–26, 41–52. Translation copyright © 1965 by the Johns Hopkins University Press.

"Triangular" Desire

"I want you to know, Sancho, that the famous Amadis of Gaul was one of the most perfect knight errants. But what am I saying, one of the most perfect? I should say the only, the first, the unique, the master and lord of all those who existed in the world.... I think... that, when a painter wants to become famous for his art he tries to imitate the originals of the best masters he knows; the same rule applies to most important jobs or exercises which contribute to the embellishment of republics; thus the man who wishes to be known as careful and patient should and does imitate Ulysses, in whose person and works Homer paints for us a vivid portrait of carefulness and patience, just as Virgil shows us in the person of Aeneas the valor of a pious son and the wisdom of a valiant captain; and it is understood that they depict them not as they are but as they should be, to provide an example of virtue for centuries to come. In the same way Amadis was the pole, the star, the sun for brave and amorous knights, and we others who fight under the banner of love and chivalry should imitate him. Thus, my friend Sancho, I reckon that whoever imitates him best will come closest to perfect chivalry."

Don Quixote has surrendered to Amadis the individual's fundamental prerogative: he no longer chooses the objects of his own desire – Amadis must choose for him. The disciple pursues objects which are determined for him, or at least seem to be determined for him, by the model of all chivalry. We shall call this model the *mediator* of desire. Chivalric existence is the *imitation* of Amadis in the same sense that the Christian's existence is the imitation of Christ.

In most works of fiction, the characters have desires which are simpler than Don Quixote's. There is no mediator, there is only the subject and the object. When the "nature" of the object inspiring the passion is not sufficient to account for the desire, one must turn to the impassioned subject. Either his "psychology" is examined or his "liberty" invoked. But desire is always spontaneous. It can always be portrayed by a simple straight line which joins subject and object.

The straight line is present in the desire of Don Quixote, but it is not essential. The mediator is there, above that line, radiating toward both the subject and the object. The spatial metaphor which expresses this triple relationship is obviously the triangle. The object changes with each adventure but the triangle remains. The barber's basin or Master Peter's puppets replace the windmills; but Amadis is always present.

The triangle is no *Gestalt*. The real structures are intersubjective. They cannot be localized anywhere; the triangle has no reality whatever; it is a systematic metaphor, systematically pursued. Because changes in size and shape do not destroy the identity of this figure, as we will see later, the diversity as well as the unity of the works can be simultaneously illustrated. The purpose and limitations of this structural geometry may become clearer through a reference to "structural models." The triangle is a model of a sort, or rather a whole family of models. But these models are not "mechanical" like those of Claude Lévi-Strauss. They always allude to the mystery, transparent yet opaque, of human relations. All types of structural thinking assume that human reality is intelligible; it is a *logos* and, as such, it is an incipient *logic*, or it degrades itself into a logic. It can thus be systematized, at least up to a point, however unsystematic, irrational, and chaotic it may appear even to those, or rather especially to those who operate the system. A basic contention of this essay is that the great writers apprehend intuitively and concretely, through the medium of their art, if not formally, the system in which they were first imprisoned together with their contemporaries. Literary interpretation must be systematic because it is the continuation of literature. It should formalize implicit or already half-explicit systems. To maintain that criticism will never be systematic is to maintain that it will never be real knowledge. The value of a critical thought depends not on how cleverly it manages to disguise its own systematic nature or on how many fundamental issues it manages to shirk or to dissolve but on how much literary substance it really embraces, comprehends, and makes articulate. The goal may be too ambitious but it is not outside the scope of literary criticism. It is the very essence of literary criticism. Failure to reach it should be condemned but not the attempt. Everything else has already been done.

Don Quixote, in Cervantes' novel, is a typical example of the victim of triangular desire, but he is far from being the only one. Next to him the most affected is his squire, Sancho Panza. Some of Sancho's desires are not imitated, for example, those aroused by the sight of a piece of cheese or a goatskin of wine. But Sancho has other ambitions besides filling his stomach. Ever since he has been with Don Quixote he has been dreaming of an "island" of which he would be governor, and he wants the title of duchess for his daughter. These desires do not come spontaneously to a simple man like Sancho. It is Don Quixote who has put them into his head.

This time the suggestion is not literary, but oral. But the difference has little importance. These new desires form a new triangle of which the imaginary island, Don Quixote, and Sancho occupy the angles. Don Quixote is Sancho's mediator. The effects of triangular desire are the same in the two characters. From the moment the mediator's influence is felt, the sense of reality is lost and judgment paralyzed.

Since the mediator's influence is more profound and constant in the case of Don Quixote than in that of Sancho, romantic readers have seen in the novel little more than the contrast between Don Quixote the *idealist* and the *realist* Sancho. This contrast is real but secondary; it should not make us overlook the analogies between the two characters. Chivalric passion defines a desire *according to Another*, opposed to this desire *according to Oneself* that most of us pride ourselves on enjoying. Don Quixote and Sancho borrow their desires from the Other in a movement which is so fundamental and primitive that they completely confuse it with the will to be Oneself.

One might object that Amadis is a fictitious person – and this we must admit, but Don Quixote is not the author of this fiction. The mediator is imaginary but not the mediation. Behind the hero's desires there is indeed the suggestion of a third person, the inventor of Amadis, the author of the chivalric romances. Cervantes' work is a long meditation on the baleful influence that the most lucid minds can exercise upon one another. Except in the realm of chivalry, Don Quixote reasons with a great deal of common sense. Nor are his favorite writers mad: perhaps they do not even take their fiction seriously. The illusion is the fruit of a bizarre marriage of two lucid consciousnesses. Chivalric literature, ever more widespread since the invention of the printing press, multiplies stupendously the chances of similar unions.

Desire according to the Other and the "seminal" function of literature are also found in the novels of Flaubert. Emma Bovary desires through the romantic heroines who fill her imagination. The second-rate books which she devoured in her youth have destroyed all her spontaneity. We must turn to Jules de Gaultier for the definition of this "bovarysm" which he reveals in almost every one of Flaubert's characters: "The same ignorance, the same inconsistency, the same absence of individual reaction seem to make them fated to obey the suggestion of an external milieu, for lack of an auto-suggestion from within." In his famous essay, entitled *Bovarysm*, Gaultier goes on to observe that in order to reach their goal, which is to "see themselves as they are not," Flaubert's heroes find a "model" for themselves and "imitate from the person they have decided to be, all that can be imitated, everything exterior, appearance, gesture, intonation, and dress."

The external aspects of imitation are the most striking; but we must above all remember that the characters of Cervantes and Flaubert are imitating, or believe they are imitating, the *desires* of models they have freely chosen. A third novelist, Stendhal, also underscores the role of suggestion and imitation in the personality of his heroes. Mathilde de la Mole finds her models in the history of her family; Julien Sorel imitates Napoleon. *The Memoirs of Saint-Helena* and the *Bulletins* of the Grand Army replace the tales of chivalry and the romantic extravagances. The Prince of Parma imitates Louis XIV. The young Bishop of Agde practices the benediction in front of a mirror; he mimics the old and venerable prelates whom he fears he does not sufficiently resemble.

Here history is nothing but a kind of literature; it suggests to all Stendhal's characters feelings and, especially, desires that they do not experience spontaneously. When he enters the service of the Rênal family, Julien borrows from Rousseau's *Confessions* the desire to eat at his master's table rather than at that of the servants. Stendhal uses the word "vanity" (*vanité*) to indicate all these forms of "copying" and "imitating." The *vaniteux* – vain person – cannot draw his desires from his own resources; he must borrow them from others. Thus the *vaniteux* is brother to Don Quixote and Emma Bovary. And so in Stendhal we again find triangular desire.

In the first pages of *The Red and the Black* we take a walk through Verrières with the mayor of the village and his wife. Majestic but tormented, M. de Rênal strolls along his retaining walls. He wants to make Julien Sorel the tutor of his two sons, but not for their sake nor from love of knowledge. His desire is not spontaneous. The conversation between husband and wife soon reveals the mechanism: "Valenod has no tutor for his children – he might very well steal this one from us."

Valenod is the richest and most influential man in Verrières, next to M. de Rênal himself. The mayor of Verrières always has the image of his rival before his eyes during his negotiations with old M. Sorel. He makes the latter some very favorable propositions but the sly peasant invents a brilliant reply: "We have a better offer." This time M. de Rênal is completely convinced that Valenod wishes to engage Julien and his own desire is redoubled. The ever-increasing price that the buyer is willing to pay is determined by the imaginary desire which he attributes to his rival. So there is indeed an imitation of this imaginary desire, and even a very scrupulous imitation, since everything about the desire which is copied, including its intensity, depends upon the desire which serves as model.

At the end of the novel, Julien tries to win back Mathilde de la Mole and, on the advice of the dandy Korasof, resorts to the same sort of trick as his father. He pays court to the Maréchale de Fervacques; he wishes to arouse this woman's desire and display it before Mathilde so that the idea of imitating it might suggest itself to her. A little water is enough to prime a pump; a little desire is enough to arouse desire in the creature of vanity.

Julien carries out his plan and everything turns out as expected. The interest which the Maréchale takes in him reawakens Mathilde's desire. And the triangle reappears – Mathilde, Mme de Fervacques, Julien – M. de Rênal, Valenod, Julien. The triangle is present each time that Stendhal speaks of vanity, whether it is a question of ambition, business, or love. It is surprising that the Marxist critics, for whom economic structures provide the archetype of all human relations, have not as yet pointed out the analogy between the crafty bargaining of old man Sorel and the amorous maneuvers of his son.

A *vaniteux* will desire any object so long as he is convinced that it is already desired by another person whom he admires. The mediator here is a *rival*, brought into existence as a rival by vanity, and that same vanity demands his defeat. The rivalry between mediator and the person who desires constitutes an essential difference between this desire and that of Don Quixote, or of Emma Bovary. Amadis cannot vie with Don Quixote in the protection of orphans in distress, he cannot slaughter giants in his place. Valenod, on the other hand, can steal the tutor from M. de Rênal; the Maréchale de Fervacques can take Julien from Mathilde de la Mole. In most of Stendhal's desires, the mediator himself desires the object, or could desire it: it is even this very desire, real or presumed, which makes this object infinitely desirable in the eyes of the subject. The mediation begets a second desire exactly the same as the mediator's. This means that one is always confronted with two *competing* desires. The mediator can no longer act his role of model without also acting or appearing to act the role of obstacle. Like the relentless sentry of the Kafka fable, the model shows his disciple the gate of paradise and forbids him to enter with one and the same gesture. We should not be surprised if the look cast by M. de Rênal on Valenod is vastly different from that raised by Don Quixote toward Amadis.

In Cervantes the mediator is enthroned in an inaccessible heaven and transmits to his faithful follower a little of his serenity. In Stendhal, this same mediator has come down to earth. The clear distinction between these two types of relationship between mediator and subject indicates the enormous spiritual gap which separates Don Quixote from the most despicably vain of Stendhal's characters. The image of the triangle cannot remain valid for us unless it at once allows this distinction and measures this gap for us. To achieve this double objective, we have only to vary the *distance*, in the triangle, separating the mediator from the desiring subject.

Obviously this distance is greatest in Cervantes. There can be no contact whatsoever between Don Quixote and his legendary Amadis. Emma Bovary is already closer to her Parisian mediator. Travelers' tales, books, and the press bring the latest fashions of the capital even to Yonville. Emma comes still closer to her mediator when she goes to the ball at the Vaubyessards'; she penetrates the holy of holies and gazes at the idol face to face. But this proximity is fleeting. Emma will never be able to desire that which the incarnations of her "ideal" desire; she will never be able to be their rival; she will never leave for Paris.

Julien Sorel does all that Emma cannot do. At the beginning of *The Red and the Black* the distance between the hero and his mediator is as great as in *Madame Bovary*. But Julien spans this distance; he leaves his province and becomes the lover of the proud Mathilde; he rises rapidly to a brilliant position. Stendhal's other heroes are also close to their mediators. It is this which distinguishes Stendhal's universe from those we have already considered. Between Julien and Mathilde, between Rênal and Valenod, between Lucien Leuwen and the nobles of Nancy, between Sansfin and the petty squires of Normandy, the distance is always small enough to permit the rivalry of desires. In the novels of Cervantes and Flaubert, the mediator remained beyond the universe of the hero; he is now within the same universe.

Romantic works are, therefore, grouped into two fundamental categories – but within these categories there can be an infinite number of secondary distinctions. We shall speak of *external mediation* when the distance is sufficient to eliminate any contact between the two spheres of *possibilities* of which the mediator and the subject occupy the respective centers. We shall speak of *internal mediation* when this same distance is sufficiently reduced to allow these two spheres to penetrate each other more or less profoundly.

Obviously it is not physical space that measures the gap between mediator and the desiring subject. Although geographical separation might be one factor, the *distance* between mediator and subject is primarily spiritual. Don Quixote and Sancho are always close to each other physically but the social and intellectual distance which separates them remains insuperable. The valet never desires what his master desires. Sancho covets the food left by the monks, the purse of gold found on the road, and other objects which Don Quixote willingly lets him have. As for the imaginary island, it is from Don Quixote himself that Sancho is counting on receiving it, as the faithful vassal holds everything in the name of his lord. The mediation of Sancho is therefore an external mediation. No rivalry with the mediator is possible. The harmony between the two companions is never seriously troubled.

The hero of external mediation proclaims aloud the true nature of his desire. He worships his model openly and declares himself his disciple. We have seen Don Quixote himself explain to Sancho the privileged part Amadis plays in his life. Mme Bovary and Léon also admit the truth about their desires in their lyric confessions. The parallel between *Don Quixote* and *Madame Bovary* has become classic. It is always easy to recognize analogies between two novels of external mediation.

Imitation in Stendhal's work at first seems less absurd since there is less of that divergence between the worlds of disciple and model which makes a Don Quixote or an Emma Bovary so grotesque. And yet the imitation is no less strict and literal in internal mediation than in external mediation. If this seems surprising it is not only because the imitation refers to a model who is "close," but also because the hero of internal mediation, far from boasting of his efforts to imitate, carefully hides them.

The impulse toward the object is ultimately an impulse toward the mediator; in internal mediation this impulse is checked by the mediator himself since he desires, or perhaps possesses, the object. Fascinated by his model, the disciple inevitably sees, in the mechanical obstacle which he puts in his way, proof of the ill will borne him. Far from declaring himself a faithful vassal, he thinks only of repudiating the bonds of mediation. But these bonds are stronger than ever, for the mediator's apparent hostility does not diminish his prestige but instead augments it. The subject is convinced that the model considers himself too superior to accept him as a disciple. The subject is torn between two opposite feelings toward his model – the most submissive reverence and the most intense malice. This is the passion we call *hatred*.

Only someone who prevents us from satisfying a desire which he himself has inspired in us is truly an object of hatred. The person who hates first hates himself for the secret admiration concealed by his hatred. In an effort to hide this desperate admiration from others, and from himself, he no longer wants to see in his mediator anything but an obstacle. The secondary role of the mediator thus becomes primary, concealing his original function of a model scrupulously imitated.

In the quarrel which puts him in opposition to his rival, the subject reverses the logical and chronological order of desires in order to hide his imitation. He asserts that his own desire is prior to that of his rival; according to him, it is the mediator who is responsible for the rivalry. Everything that originates with this mediator is systematically belittled although still secretly desired. Now the mediator is a shrewd and diabolical enemy; he tries to rob the subject of his most prized possessions; he obstinately thwarts his most legitimate ambitions.

All the phenomena explored by Max Scheler in *Ressentiment*[1] are, in our opinion, the result of internal mediation. Furthermore, the word *ressentiment* itself underscores the quality of reaction, of repercussion which characterizes the experience of the subject in this type of mediation. The impassioned admiration and desire to emulate stumble over the unfair obstacle with which the model seems to block the way of his disciple, and then these passions recoil on the disciple in the form of impotent hatred, thus causing the sort of psychological self-poisoning so well described by Scheler.

As he indicates, *ressentiment* can impose its point of view even on those whom it does not dominate. It is *ressentiment* which prevents us, and sometimes prevents Scheler himself, from recognizing the part played by imitation in the birth of desire. For example, we do not see that jealousy and envy, like hatred, are scarcely more than traditional names given to internal mediation, names which almost always conceal their true nature from us.

Jealousy and envy imply a third presence: object, subject, and a third person toward whom the jealousy or envy is directed. These two "vices" are therefore triangular; however we never recognize a model in the person who arouses jealousy because we always take a jealous person's attitude toward the problem of jealousy. Like all victims of internal mediation, the jealous person easily convinces himself that his desire is spontaneous, in other words, that it is deeply rooted in the object and in this object alone. As a result he always maintains that his desire preceded the intervention of the mediator. He would have us see him as an intruder, a bore, a *terzo incomodo* who interrupts a delightful tête-à-tête. Jealousy is thus reduced to the irritation we all experience when one of our desires is accidentally thwarted. But true jealousy is infinitely more profound and complex; it always contains an element of fascination with the insolent rival. Furthermore, it is always the same people who suffer from jealousy. Is it possible that they are all the victims of repeated accidents? Is it *fate* that creates for them so many rivals and throws so many obstacles in the way of their desires? We do not believe it ourselves, since we say that these chronic victims of jealousy or of envy have a "jealous temperament" or an "envious nature." What exactly then does such a "temperament" or "nature" imply if not an irresistible impulse to desire what Others desire, in other words to imitate the desires of others?

Max Scheler numbers "envy, jealousy, and rivalry" among the sources of *ressentiment*. He defines envy as "a feeling of impotence which vitiates our attempt to acquire

RENÉ GIRARD

something, because it belongs to another." He observes, on the other hand, that there would be no envy, in the strong sense of the word, if the envious person's imagination did not transform into concerted opposition the passive obstacle which the possessor puts in his way by the mere fact of possession. "Mere regret at not possessing something which belongs to another and which we covet is not enough in itself to give rise to envy, since it might also be an incentive for acquiring the desired object or something similar. . . . *Envy* occurs only when our efforts to acquire it fail and we are left with a feeling of impotence."

The analysis is accurate and complete; it omits neither the envious person's self-deception with regard to the cause of his failure, nor the paralysis that accompanies envy. But these elements remain isolated; Scheler has not really perceived their relationship. On the other hand everything becomes clear, everything fits into a coherent structure if, in order to explain envy, we abandon the object of rivalry as a starting point and choose instead the rival himself, i.e., the mediator, as both a point of departure for our analysis and its conclusion. Possession is a merely passive obstacle; it is frustrating and seems a deliberate expression of contempt only because the rival is secretly revered. The demigod seems to answer homage with a curse. He seems to render evil for good. The subject would like to think of himself as the victim of an atrocious injustice but in his anguish he wonders whether perhaps he does not deserve his apparent condemnation. Rivalry therefore only aggravates mediation; it increases the mediator's prestige and strengthens the bond which links the object to this mediator by forcing him to affirm openly his right or desire of possession. Thus the subject is less capable than ever of giving up the inaccessible object: it is on this object and it alone that the mediator confers his prestige, by possessing or wanting to possess it. Other objects have no worth at all in the eyes of the envious person, even though they may be similar to or indeed identical with the "mediated" object.

Everything becomes clear when one sees that the loathed rival is actually a mediator. Max Scheler himself is not far from the truth when he states in *Ressentiment* that "the fact of choosing a model for oneself" is the result of a certain tendency, common to all men, to compare oneself with others, and he goes on to say, "all jealousy, all ambition, and even an ideal like the 'imitation of Christ' is based on such comparisons." But this intuition remains isolated. Only the great artists attribute to the mediator the position usurped by the object; only they reverse the commonly accepted hierarchy of desire.

In *The Memoirs of a Tourist*, Stendhal warns his readers against what he calls the *modern* emotions, the fruits of universal vanity: "envy, jealousy, and impotent hatred." Stendhal's formula gathers together the three triangular emotions; it considers them apart from any particular object; it associates them with that imperative need to imitate by which, according to the novelist, the nineteenth century is completely possessed. For his part, Scheler asserts, following Nietzsche – who acknowledged a large debt to Stendhal – that the romantic state of mind is pervaded by "*ressentiment*." Stendhal says precisely this, but he looks for the source of this spiritual poison in the passionate imitation of individuals who are fundamentally our equals and whom we endow with an arbitrary prestige. If the *modern* emotions flourish, it is not because "envious natures" and "jealous temperaments" have unfortunately and mysteriously increased in number, but because *internal* mediation triumphs in a universe where the differences between men are gradually erased.

The great novelists reveal the imitative nature of desire. In our days its nature is hard to perceive because the most fervent imitation is the most vigorously denied. Don Quixote proclaimed himself the disciple of Amadis and the writers of his time proclaimed themselves the disciples of the Ancients. The romantic *vaniteux* does not want to be anyone's disciple. He convinces himself that he is thoroughly *original*. In the nineteenth century spontaneity becomes a universal dogma, succeeding imitation. Stendhal warns us at every step that we must not be fooled by these individualisms professed with fanfare, for they merely hide a new form of imitation. Romantic revulsion, hatred of society, nostalgia for the desert, just as gregariousness, usually conceal a morbid concern for the Other.

In order to camouflage the essential role which the Other plays in his desires, Stendhal's *vaniteux* frequently appeals to the clichés of the reigning ideology. Behind the devotion, the mawkish altruism, the hypocritical *engagement* of the *grandes dames* of 1830, Stendhal finds not the generous impulse of a being truly prepared to give itself but rather the tormented recourse of vanity at bay, the centrifugal movement of an ego powerless to desire by itself. The novelist lets his characters act and speak; then, in the twinkling of an eye, he reveals to us the mediator. He re-establishes covertly the true hierarchy of desire while pretending to believe in the weak reasoning advanced by his character in support of the contrary hierarchy. This is one of the perpetual methods of Stendhal's irony.

The romantic *vaniteux* always wants to convince himself that his desire is written into the nature of things, or, which amounts to the same thing, that it is the emanation of a serene subjectivity, the creation *ex nihilo* of a quasi-divine ego. Desire is no longer rooted in the object perhaps, but it is rooted in the subject; it is certainly not rooted in the Other. The objective and subjective fallacies are one and the same; both originate in the image which we all have of our own desires. Subjectivisms and objectivisms, romanticisms and realisms, individualisms and scientisms, idealisms and positivisms appear to be in opposition but are secretly in agreement to conceal the presence of the mediator. All these dogmas are the aesthetic or philosophic translation of world views peculiar to internal mediation. They all depend directly or indirectly on the lie of spontaneous desire. They all defend the same illusion of autonomy to which modern man is passionately devoted.

It is this same illusion which the great novel does not succeed in shattering although it never ceases to denounce it. Unlike the romantics and neoromantics, a Cervantes, a Flaubert, and a Stendhal reveal the truth of desire in their great novels. But this truth remains hidden even at the heart of its revelation. The reader, who is usually convinced of his own spontaneity, applies to the work the meanings he already applies to the world. The nineteenth century, which failed completely to understand Cervantes, continually praised the "originality" of his hero. The romantic reader, by a marvelous misinterpretation which fundamentally is only a superior truth, identifies himself with Don Quixote, the supreme imitator, and makes of him the *model individual*.

Thus it should not surprise us that the term *romanesque*[2] still reflects, in its ambiguity, our unawareness of all mediation. The term denotes the chivalric romances and it denotes *Don Quixote*; it can be synonymous with *romantic* and it can indicate the destruction of romantic pretentions. In the future we shall use the term *romantic* for

RENÉ GIRARD

the works which reflect the presence of a mediator without ever revealing it and the term *novelistic* for the works which reveal this presence. It is to the latter that this book is primarily devoted.

The mediator's prestige is imparted to the object of desire and confers upon it an illusory value. Triangular desire is the desire which transfigures its object. *Romantic* literature does not disregard this metamorphosis; on the contrary, it turns it to account and boasts of it, but never reveals its actual mechanism. The illusion is a living being whose conception demands a male and a female element. The poet's imagination is the female which remains sterile as long as it is not fertilized by the mediator. The novelist alone describes this actual genesis of the illusion for which romanticism always makes the poet alone responsible. The romantic insists on a "parthenogenesis" of the imagination. Forever in love with autonomy, he refuses to bow before his own gods. The series of solipsistic theories of poetry produced during the past century and a half are an expression of this refusal.

The romantics congratulate Don Quixote on mistaking an ordinary barber's basin for Mambrino's helmet, while they themselves secretly feel they refrain from such folly. They are mistaken. The Parisian world of "envy," "jealousy," and "impotent hatred" is no less illusory and no less desired than the helmet of Mambrino. All of its desires are based on abstractions; Stendhal tells us they are "cerebral desires." Joys and especially suffering are not rooted in things; they are "spiritual," but in an inferior sense which must be explained. From the mediator, a veritable artificial sun, descends a mysterious ray which makes the object shine with a false brilliance. There would be no illusion if Don Quixote were not imitating Amadis. Emma Bovary would not have taken Rudolph for a Prince Charming had she not been imitating romantic heroines. All of Stendhal's art is aimed at persuading us that the values of vanity, nobility, money, power, reputation only *seem* to be concrete...

It is this abstract character which allows the comparison of the desire stemming from vanity with Don Quixote's desire. The illusion is not the same but there is still an illusion. Desire projects a dream universe around the hero. In both cases the hero escapes from his fantasies only on his deathbed. If Julien seems more lucid than Don Quixote it is because the people who surround him, with the exception of Mme de Rênal, are even more bewitched than he.

The metamorphosis of the desired object occurred to Stendhal long before his novelistic period. In *De l'Amour* he gives a famous description of it based on the image of crystallization. The later novelistic developments appear faithful to the ideology of 1822. They diverge from it, however, on one essential point. According to the preceding analyses crystallization should be the result of vanity. But it is not under the heading of vanity that Stendhal presents this phenomenon to us in *De l'Amour* – it is under the heading of "passion."

Passion, in Stendhal, is the opposite of vanity. Fabrice del Dongo is the perfect example of the passionate person; he is distinguished by his emotional autonomy, by the spontaneity of his desires, by his absolute indifference to the opinion of Others. The passionate person draws the strength of his desire from within himself and not from others.

Can it be that we are mistaken? Could it be authentic passion, in the novels, which is accompanied by crystallization? All Stendhal's great pairs of lovers contradict this point of view. True love, such as that of Fabrice for Clélia and that which Julien finally knows with Mme de Rênal, does not transfigure. The qualities which this love discovers in its object, the happiness it expects from it, are not illusory. Love-passion is always accompanied by esteem, in Corneille's sense of the word. It is based on a perfect agreement among reason, will, and sensibility. The real Mme de Rênal is the one desired by Julien. The real Mathilde is the one he does not desire. In the first case it is a question of passion, in the second of vanity. It is indeed, therefore, vanity which transforms its object.

There is a radical difference between the essay of 1822 and the novelistic masterpieces which is not always easy to perceive because in both cases a distinction is made between passion and vanity. In *De l'Amour* Stendhal describes for us the subjective effects of triangular desire but he attributes them to spontaneous desire. The real criterion of spontaneous desire is the intensity of that desire. The strongest desires are the passionate desires. The desires of vanity are tarnished reflections of authentic desires. Thus it is always Others' desires which derive from vanity, for we are all under the impression that we desire more intensely than Others. The distinction between passion and vanity serves to vindicate Stendhal — and his reader — of the charge of vanity. The mediator remains hidden precisely where his revelation is of the utmost significance, in the existence of the author himself, and so the point of view of 1822 must be characterized as romantic. The passion-vanity dialectic remains "individualistic." It reminds one a little of Gide's dialectic of the natural Self and the social Self in *The Immoralist*.

The Stendhal of whom the critics speak, especially Paul Valéry in his preface to *Lucien Leuwen*, is almost always this "Gide-like" Stendhal of the youthful period. It is obvious that the youthful Stendhal would have been in vogue during the heyday of the ethics of desire of which he himself was the precursor. This first Stendhal, who triumphed at the end of the nineteenth century and the beginning of the twentieth century, offers us a contrast between the spontaneous being who desires intensely and the gregarious man who desires feebly by copying Others.

One might maintain, basing one's view on *The Italian Chronicles* and a few sentences taken from the *écrits intimes*, that the vanity-passion opposition has kept its original meaning in the mature Stendhal. But neither *The Italian Chronicles* nor the *écrits intimes* belong to the pattern of the great novelistic works. A close look at the structure of the latter will readily show that in them vanity becomes at once the transfiguring desire and the most intense desire.

Even in the texts of his youth the vanity-passion opposition never coincided with Gide's opposition of the social and the natural Self such as it is shown, for example, in the contrast between Fleurissoire and Lafcadio in *Lafcadio's Adventures*. Already in *De l'Amour* Stendhal asserts that "vanity gives birth to rapture." He does not therefore totally conceal from himself the prodigious strength of imitated desire. And he is only at the beginning of an evolution which will end in the pure and simple overturning of the initial hierarchy. The further one goes in his work, the more the strength of desire is associated with vanity. It is vanity which causes Julien's suffering when Mathilde turns away from him and this suffering is the most violent the hero has ever known. All the intense desires of Julien are imitated desires. His ambition is a triangular sentiment

RENÉ GIRARD

nourished by hatred for the members of the "establishment." As he places his feet on the ladder, the lover's ultimate thoughts go to the husbands, fathers, and fiancés, i.e., the rivals – never to the woman who is waiting for him on the balcony. The evolution which makes of vanity the stronger desire is completed in the prodigious Sansfin of *Lamiel*, in whom vanity is a veritable frenzy.

As for passion, in these great novels it begins only with that *silence* which Jean Prévost discusses so ably in his *La Création chez Stendhal*. This passion which keeps silent is hardly desire. As soon as there is really desire, even in the passionate characters, we find the mediator. And so we shall find the triangle of desire even in heroes less impure and less complex than Julien. In Lucien Leuwen the thought of the mythical Colonel Busant de Sicile stirs a vague desire for Mme de Chasteller, a vague desire of desiring which could just as well have settled on another young lady of the Nancy aristocracy. Mme de Rênal herself is jealous of Elisa, jealous too of the unknown person whose portrait she thinks Julien is hiding in his mattress. In the birth of desire, the third person is always present.

We must yield to the evidence. In the later Stendhal there is no longer spontaneous desire. Every "psychological" analysis is an analysis of vanity, in other words, a revelation of triangular desire. True passion eventually supplants this madness in the best of Stendhal's heroes. It comes to them with the calm of the summits which these heroes attain in their supreme moments. In *The Red and the Black* the peace before Julien's execution is in marked contrast with the morbid agitation of the preceding period. Fabrice and Clélia enjoy peace and tranquility in the Tour Farnèse, above desires and vanity which always threaten them but never harm them.

Why does Stendhal still speak of passion when desire has disappeared? Perhaps because these moments of ecstasy are always the result of a feminine mediation. For Stendhal woman can be the mediatrix of peace and serenity after mediating desire, anguish, and vanity. As in Nerval, it is not so much a question of opposition between two types of women as two antinomic functions exercised by the feminine element in the existence and the creation of the novelist.

In the great works, the transition from vanity to passion is inseparable from aesthetic happiness. It is the delight of creation which wins out over desire and anguish. The transition always takes place under the sign of the deceased Mathilde, the woman who had rejected him in Milan, and, as it were, as a result of her intercession. Stendhalian passion cannot be understood without taking into account the problems of aesthetic creation. It is to the full and complete revelation of triangular desire, in other words, to his own liberation, that the novelist owes these moments of happiness. Even though it is the novelist's supreme reward, passion is scarcely present in the novel itself. Freed, it rises out of a novelistic world totally given over to vanity and desire.

It is the transfiguration of the desired object which constitutes the unity of external and internal mediation. The hero's imagination is the mother of the illusion but the child must still have a father: the mediator. Proust's work also bears witness to this marriage and this birth. The concepts so far developed should enable us to perceive the unity of certain works of genius, which Proust himself did not fear to assert. The idea of mediation encourages literary comparisons at a level which is no longer that of *genre* criticism or thematic criticism. It may illuminate the works through each other; it may unite them without destroying their irreducible singularity.

The analogies between Stendhalian vanity and Proustian desire strike the least critical reader. But they strike only him, for it seems that critical reflection never begins from such elementary intuitions. The resemblance is taken for granted by those interpreters who are fond of "realism": the novel is a photograph of a reality external to the novelist; observation bears on a substratum of psychological truth which has neither time nor place. For existentialist or aesthetic criticism, however, the "autonomy" of the novelistic world is an untouchable dogma; it is dishonorable to suggest the slightest connection between one's own novelist and that of one's neighbor.

It is clear nevertheless that features of Stendhalian vanity reappear, emphasized and intensified, in Proustian desire. The metamorphosis of the desired object is more radical now than before, jealousy and envy are even more frequent and intense. It is not an exaggeration to say that, in all of the characters of *Remembrance of Things Past*, love is strictly subordinated to jealousy, to the presence of the rival. The privileged role of the mediator in the genesis of desire is therefore more obvious than ever. Again and again the Proustian narrator defines clearly a triangular structure which remains more or less implicit in *The Red and the Black*:

> In love, our successful rival, that is our enemy, is our benefactor. To a person who aroused in us only an insignificant physical desire, he adds an immense prestige and value, which we immediately recognize in him. If we had no rivals, if we were to believe there were none....
> For it is not necessary for them really to exist.

The triangular structure is no less obvious in social snobbism than it is in love-jealousy. The snob is also an imitator. He slavishly copies the person whose birth, fortune, or stylishness he envies. Proustian snobbism could be defined as a caricature of Stendhalian vanity; it could also be defined as an exaggeration of Flaubertian bovarysm. Jules de Gaultier terms this shortcoming "bovarysm triumphant" and quite rightly dedicates a passage in his book to it. The snob does not dare trust his own judgment, he desires only objects desired by others. That is why he is the slave of the fashionable.

For the first time, moreover, we come across a term in current usage, "snobbism," which does not conceal the truth of triangular desire. Just to call a desire snobbish is enough to underscore its imitative character. The mediator is no longer hidden; the object is relegated to the background for the very reason that snobbism, unlike jealousy for example, is not limited to a particular category of desires. One can be a snob in aesthetic pleasure, in intellectual life, in clothes, food, etc. To be a snob in love is to doom oneself to jealousy. Proustian love therefore is synonomous with snobbism and we have only to give a slightly broader meaning to the term than is normally done in order to discern in it the unity of Proustian desire. The mimetic nature of desire in *Remembrance of Things Past* is such that the characters can be called jealous or snobbish depending on whether their mediator is a lover or a member of high society. The triangular conception of desire gives us access to what is most central in Proust, to the conjunction of love-jealousy and snobbism. Proust continually asserts that these two "vices" are identical. "Society," he writes, "is only a reflection of what happens in love."

This is an example of those "psychological laws" to which the novelist refers constantly but which he did not always manage to formulate with sufficient clarity. Most critics do not bother with these laws. They attribute them to out-of-date psychological theories which are supposed to have influenced Proust. They think that the essence of novelistic genius is foreign to any *law* because inevitably it is on the side of *beauty*, or *liberty*. We believe that the critics are mistaken. Proust's laws are identical with the laws of triangular desire. They define a new type of internal mediation which occurs when the distance between mediator and desiring subject is even less than in Stendhal.

One might object that Stendhal celebrates passion while Proust denounces it. This is true, but the opposition is purely verbal. What Proust denounces under the name of passion, Stendhal denounces under the name of vanity. And what Proust praises under the name of *The Past Recaptured* is not always so far from what Stendhal's heroes celebrate in the solitude of their prisons.

Differences of novelistic tonality frequently hide from us the close relationship of structure between Stendhalian vanity and Proustian desire. Stendhal is almost always external to the desire which he describes; he throws an ironic light on phenomena which in Proust are bathed in a light of anguish. And even this difference of perspective is not constant. Proustian tragedy does not exclude humor, especially in the case of secondary characters. Stendhalian comedy, on the other hand, sometimes borders on tragedy. Julien suffered more, the author tells us, during his brief and vain passion for Mathilde than during the darkest hours of his childhood.

Nevertheless it must be recognized that psychological conflicts are more aggravated in Proust's work than in Stendhal's. The differences of perspective reflect essential oppositions. We do not wish to minimize these in order to guarantee a mechanical unity of the writers we consider. On the contrary, we want to emphasize contrasts which will bring out one of our fundamental data: the distance between mediator and subject, whose variations shed light on the most diverse aspects of novelistic works.

The closer the mediator gets to the desiring subject, the more the possibilities of the two rivals merge and the more insuperable becomes the obstacle they set in each other's way. Thus we should not be surprised that human experience in Proust is even more "negative" and painful than the experience of Stendhal's *vaniteux*.

* * *

In *De l'Amour* Stendhal had already noticed that there is a crystallization of hatred. One step further and the two crystallizations become one. Proust constantly reveals hatred in desire, desire in hatred. But he remains faithful to the traditional language; he never eliminates the "like"s and the "as much as"s which are strewn through the preceding quotation. He will never reach the highest level of internal mediation. This last stage was reserved for another novelist, the Russian, Dostoyevsky, who precedes Proust chronologically but succeeds him in the history of triangular desire.

Except for a few characters who entirely escape imitated desire, in Dostoyevsky there is no longer any love without jealousy, any friendship without envy, any attraction without repulsion. The characters insult each other, spit in each other's faces, and minutes later they fall at the enemy's feet, they abjectly beg mercy. This fascination coupled with hatred is no different in principle from Proustian snobbism and Stendhalian vanity. The inevitable consequences of desire copied from another desire are "envy, jealousy, and impotent hatred." As one moves from Stendhal to Proust and from Proust to Dostoyevsky, and the closer the mediator comes, the more bitter are the fruits of triangular desire.

In Dostoyevsky hatred is so intense it finally "explodes," revealing its double nature, or rather the double role of model and obstacle played by the mediator. This adoring hatred, this admiration that insults and even kills its object, are the paroxysms of the conflict caused by internal mediation. In his words and gestures, Dostoyevsky's hero constantly reveals a truth which remains a secret in the consciousness of previous heroes. The "contradictory" feelings are so violent that the hero can no longer control them.

Western readers sometimes feel a little lost in Dostoyevsky's universe. Internal mediation exerts its dissolving power at the very heart of the family itself. It affects a dimension of existence which remains more or less inviolable in the French novelists. The three great novelists of internal mediation each have their own privileged territory. In Stendhal public and political life are threatened by borrowed desire. In Proust the evil spreads to private life but usually excludes the family circle. In Dostoyevsky this intimate circle itself is contaminated. Thus we find within internal mediation one can distinguish *exogamic* mediation in Stendhal and Proust from *endogamic* mediation in Dostoyevsky.

This is not, however, a strict division. Stendhal encroaches on Proustian territory when he describes the extreme forms of cerebral love and even on Dostoyevskian territory when he shows us the hatred of son for father. Similarly Marcel's relations with his parents are sometimes "pre-Dostoyevskian." The novelists often venture out of their own domain, but the further they wander, the more hurried, schematic, and uncertain they are.

This rough division of the existential domain among our novelists represents an invasion of the vital centers of the individual by triangular desire, a desecration which gradually infects the most intimate parts of being. This desire is a corrosive disease which first attacks the periphery and then spreads toward the center; it is an *alienation* which grows more complete as the distance between model and disciple diminishes. This distance is smallest in familial mediation of father to son, brother to brother, husband to wife, or mother to son, as in Dostoyevsky and many contemporary novelists.

In terms of mediation, the Dostoyevskian universe is "this side of" – one might also say "beyond" – that of Proust, just as Proust is "this side of" or "beyond" Stendhal. The Dostoyevskian universe differs from those of his predecessors in the same way that they differ from each other. This difference does not imply an absence of relationships and points of contact. If Dostoyevsky were as "autonomous" as is sometimes claimed, we would never be able to understand his works. They would be as meaningless to us as the words of a foreign language: we could spell them out but we would be unable to grasp their significance.

Dostoyevsky's "admirable monsters" should not be considered as so many meteorites with unpredictable trajectories. In the time of the Marquis de Vogüé people often said that Dostoyevsky's characters were too "Russian" to be completely accessible to the French Cartesian mind. His mysterious work would by definition elude our rational, Western criteria. Today it is no longer Dostoyevsky the Russian who seems most important to us, but rather the apostle of "liberty," the brilliant innovator, the iconoclast who smashed the molds in which novels and previously been cast. The Dostoyevskian man and his free existence are constantly opposed to the simplistic analyses of our own novelists who are seen as old fashioned, bourgeois, and psychologizing. This fanatic cult, as much as the mistrust of times past, prevents us from seeing in Dostoyevsky the final and supreme stage of the development of the modern novel.

The relative esoterism of Dostoyevsky makes him neither superior nor inferior to our own novelists. It is not the writer but the reader who creates the obscurity here. Our hesitations would not surprise Dostoyevsky, convinced as he was that Russian forms of experience were in advance of those in the West. Russia has passed, without any transitional period, from traditional and feudal structures to the most *modern* society. She has not known any bourgeois interregnum. Stendhal and Proust are the novelists of this interregnum. They occupy the upper regions of internal mediation, while Dostoyevsky occupies its lowest.

A Raw Youth gives a very good illustration of the characteristics peculiar to Dostoyevskian desire. The relations between Dolgorouki and Versilov can be interpreted only in terms of mediation. Son and father love the same woman. Dolgorouki's passion for Akhmakova, the general's wife, is copied from that of his father. This mediation of father for son is not the *external* mediation of Proustian childhood, which we defined in talking of Combray, but an *internal* mediation, which turns the mediator into a loathed rival. The unfortunate bastard is both the equal of a father who does not fulfill his obligations and the fascinated victim of this being who has rejected him for some unknown reason. To understand Dolgorouki one should not therefore compare him with the children and parents of previous novels, but rather with the Proustian snob obsessed by the person who *refuses to accept him.* Nevertheless this comparison is not entirely exact, for the distance between father and son is less than the distance between the two snobs. Dolgorouki's ordeal therefore is even more painful than that of the Proustian snob or lover.

The closer the mediator comes, the greater his role becomes and the smaller that of the object. Dostoyevsky by a stroke of genius places the mediator in the foreground and relegates the object to the background. At last novelistic composition reflects the real hierarchy of desire. Had Stendhal or Proust written *A Raw Youth*, everything would be centered on the principal hero, or on Akhmakova, the general's wife. Dostoyevsky puts the mediator, Versilov, at the center of his novel. But, from our point of view, *A Raw Youth* is not the most daring of Dostoyevsky's works. It is a compromise between several solutions. The transfer of the novelistic center of gravity is best and most spectacularly illustrated by *The Eternal Husband.* Veltchaninov, a rich bachelor, is a middle-aged Don Juan who is beginning to give in to weariness and boredom. For several days he has been obsessed by the fleeting apparitions of a man, at once mysterious and familiar, disturbing and odd. The character's identity is soon revealed. It seems he is a certain Pavel Pavlovitch Troussotzki, whose wife, a former mistress of Veltchaninov's, has just died. Pavel Pavlovitch has left his province in order to find in St. Petersburg the lovers of his dead wife. One of the lovers also dies, and Pavel Pavlovitch, in deep mourning, follows the funeral procession. There remains Veltchaninov on whom he heaps the most grotesque attentions and whom he wears out by his constant presence. The deceived husband makes very strange statements concerning the past. He pays his rival a visit in the middle of the night, drinks to his health, kisses him on the lips, and very cleverly tortures him, using an unfortunate little girl whose father remains unknown.

The woman is dead and the lover remains. There is no longer an object but the mediator, Veltchaninov, still exerts an irresistible attraction. This mediator makes an ideal narrator since he is the center of the action and yet scarcely participates in it. He describes events all the more carefully since he does not always succeed in interpreting them and is afraid of neglecting some important detail.

Pavel Pavlovitch considers a second marriage. Fascinated, he goes again to his first wife's lover; he asks him to help him choose a present for his latest choice; he begs him to go with him to her house. Veltchaninov demurs but Pavel Pavlovitch insists, begs, and ends by getting his way.

The two "friends" are given a warm reception at the young lady's house. Veltchaninov's conversation is entertaining and he plays the piano. His social ability arouses admiration: the whole family crowds around him, including the young lady whom Pavel Pavlovitch already looks on as his fiancée. The scorned suitor tries to be seductive without success. No one takes him seriously. He reflects on this new disaster, trembling with anguish and desire. Some years later Veltchaninov meets Pavel Pavlovitch again in a railroad station. The eternal husband is not alone; a charming lady, his wife, accompanies him, along with a dashing young soldier...

The Eternal Husband reveals the essence of internal mediation in the simplest and purest form possible. No digression distracts or misleads the reader. The text seems enigmatic only because it is too clear. It throws on the novelistic triangle a light so brilliant it dazzles us.

Confronted with Pavel Pavlovitch we can have no more doubts about the priority of the Other in desire, a principle first laid down by Stendhal. The hero is always trying to convince us that his relationship to the object of desire is independent of the rival. Here we clearly see that the hero is deceiving us. The mediator is immobile and the hero turns around him like a planet around the sun. The behavior of Pavel Pavlovitch seems strange to us but it is completely consistent with the logic of triangular desire. Pavel Pavlovitch can desire only through the mediation of Veltchaninov, *in* Veltchaninov as the mystics would say. He drags Veltchaninov along to the house of the lady he has chosen, so that he might desire her and thus guarantee her erotic value.

Some critics would like to see in Pavel Pavlovitch a "latent homosexual." But the homosexuality, whether it is latent or not does not explain the structure of desire. It puts a distance between Pavel Pavlovitch and the so-called normal man. Nothing is gained by reducing triangular desire to a homosexuality which is necessarily opaque to the heterosexual. If one turned the explanation around, the results would be much more interesting. An attempt should be made to *understand* at least some forms of homosexuality from the standpoint of triangular desire. Proustian homosexuality, for example, can be defined as a gradual transferring to the mediator of an erotic value which in "normal" Don Juanism remains attached to the object itself. This gradual transfer is not, a priori, impossible; it is even likely, in the acute stages of internal mediation, characterized by a noticeably increased preponderance of the mediator and a gradual obliteration of the object. Certain passages in *The Eternal Husband* clearly show the beginning of an erotic deviation toward the fascinating rival.

The novels considered here illuminate each other and the critic should borrow from the novels themselves his methods, concepts, and even the direction of his efforts. We must turn to the Proust of *The Captive*, who is close enough to Dostoyevsky to let us understand what it is that Pavel Pavlovitch desires:

> It would fall to our lot, were we better able to analyse our loves, to see that often women rise in our estimation only because of the dead weight of men with whom we have to compete for them, although we can hardly bear the thought of that competition; the counterpoise removed, the charm of the woman declines. We have a painful and salutary example of this…in the man who, conscious of a decline in his affection for the woman whom he loves, spontaneously applies the rules that he has deduced, and, to make sure of his not ceasing to love the woman, places her in a dangerous environment from which he is obliged to protect her daily.

Beneath the casual tone is the fundamental Proustian anguish which is also the anguish of Pavel Pavlovitch. Dostoyevsky's hero, too, applies "spontaneously," if not serenely, rules which he has not really "analyzed" but which only control his miserable existence all the more.

Triangular desire is *one*. We can start with Don Quixote and end with Pavel Pavlovitch, or we can begin with *Tristan and Isolde* as Denis de Rougemont does in *Love in the Western World* and quickly reach that "psychology of jealousy" which pervades our analyses. When he defines this psychology as a "profanation of the myth" embodied in the poem of Tristan, De Rougemont explicitly acknowledges the bond uniting the most "noble" forms of passion with morbid jealousy, such as Proust or Dostoyevsky describe for us: "Jealousy, desired, provoked, and cunningly encouraged." De Rougemont correctly observes: "One reaches the point of wanting the beloved to be unfaithful so that one can court her again."

Such is – or very close to it – the desire of Pavel Pavlovitch. The eternal husband cannot do without jealousy. Trusting our analyses and the testimony of De Rougemont, we shall now see behind all forms of triangular desire the same diabolic trap into which the hero slowly sinks. Triangular desire is *one* and we think we are able to furnish a striking proof of its unity precisely where skepticism seems most justified. The two "extremes" of desire, one illustrated by Cervantes, the other by Dostoyevsky, seem the hardest to incorporate in the same structure. We can accept that Pavel Pavlovitch is a brother to Proust's snob and even to Stendhal's *vaniteux*, but who would recognize in him a distant cousin of the famous Don Quixote? The impassioned eulogists of that hero cannot help but consider our comparison sacrilegious. For them Don Quixote lives only on the summits. How could the creator of this sublime being have an inkling of the swamps in which the eternal husband wallows?

The answer is to be found in one of the short stories with which Cervantes padded *Don Quixote*. Although they were all cast in a pastoral or chivalric mold these texts do not all fall back into the "romantic," non-novelistic pattern. One of them, "The Curious Impertinent," portrays a triangular desire exactly like that of Pavel Pavlovitch.

Anselmo has just married the pretty young Camilla. The marriage was arranged with the help of Lothario, a very dear friend of the happy husband. Some time after the wedding Anselmo makes a curious request to Lothario. He begs him to pay court to Camilla, claiming that he wishes "to test" her faithfulness. Lothario refuses indignantly but Anselmo does not give up. He entreats his friend in a thousand different ways and in all his suggestions reveals the obsessive nature of his request. For a long time Lothario manages to put him off and finally pretends to accept in order to put him at ease. Anselmo arranges for the two young people to be alone together. He leaves on a journey, returns without warning, bitterly reproaches Lothario for not taking his role seriously. In short his behavior is so mad that he finally drives Lothario and Camilla into each other's arms. Learning that he has been betrayed, Anselmo kills himself in despair.

When one rereads the story in the light of *The Eternal Husband* and *The Captive* it is no longer possible to consider it artificial and lacking in interest. Dostoyevsky and Proust enable us to dig down to its true meaning. "The Curious Impertinent" is Cervantes' *Eternal Husband;* the only difference between the two stories is in technique and the details of the intrigue.

Pavel Pavlovitch entices Veltchaninov to his fiancée's house; Anselmo asks Lothario to pay court to his wife. In both cases only the prestige of the mediator can certify the excellence of a sexual choice. Cervantes, at the beginning of his story, describes at length the friendship between the two protagonists, Anselmo's high opinion of Lothario, and the role of go-between which Lothario played with the two families on the occasion of the marriage.

It is clear that their ardent friendship is accompanied by a sharp feeling of rivalry. But this rivalry remains in the shadows. In *The Eternal Husband* the other side of the "triangular" feeling remains hidden. The hatred of the betrayed husband is obvious; we gradually guess at the admiration which this hatred hides. Pavel Pavlovitch asks Veltchaninov to choose the jewel he will give to his fiancée because to him Veltchaninov enjoys immense sexual prestige.

In both stories the hero seems to offer the beloved wife freely to the mediator, as a believer would offer a sacrifice to his god. But the believer offers the object in order that the god might enjoy it, whereas the hero of internal mediation offers his sacrifice to the god in order that he might not enjoy it. He pushes the loved woman into the mediator's arms in order to arouse his desire and then triumph over the rival desire. He does not desire *in* his mediator but rather *against* him. The hero only desires the object which will frustrate his mediator. Ultimately all that interests him is a decisive victory over his insolent mediator. Anselmo and Pavel Pavlovitch are driven by sexual pride, and it is this pride which plunges them into the most humiliating defeats.

"The Curious Impertinent" and *The Eternal Husband* suggest a nonromantic interpretation of Don Juan. Anselmo and Pavel Pavlovitch are the very opposite of the prattling, conceited, "Promethean" fops with which our century abounds. Pride creates Don Juan and it is pride which sooner or later makes us a slave to someone else. The real Don Juan is not autonomous; on the contrary, he is incapable of doing without Others. This truth is not apparent today. But it can be seen in some of Shakespeare's seducers and in Molière's *Don Juan:*

By chance I saw this pair of lovers three or four days before their journey. I have never seen two people more happy with one another or who shone so with their love. The obvious tenderness of their passion for one another moved me; I was struck to the heart and my love began through jealousy. Yes, I could not bear to see them so happy together; resentment

RENÉ GIRARD

aroused my desires, and I foresaw great pleasure in being able to upset their understanding and break this engagement which offended my delicate feelings.

No literary influence can explain the points of contact between "The Curious Impertin- ent" and *The Eternal Husband*. The differences are all differences of form, while the resemblances are resemblances of essence. No doubt Dostoyevsky never realized these similarities. Like so many nineteenth-century readers he saw the Spanish masterpiece only through romantic exegeses and probably had a most inaccurate picture of Cer- vantes. All his remarks on *Don Quixote* betray a romantic influence.

The existence of "The Curious Impertinent" next to *Don Quixote* has always intrigued critics. The question arises of whether the short story is compatible with the novel; the unity of the masterpiece seems somewhat compromised. It is this unity which is revealed by our journey through novelistic literature. Having begun with Cervantes, we return to Cervantes and ascertain that this novelist's genius has grasped the extreme forms of imitated desire. No small distance separates the Cervantes of Don Quixote and the Cervantes of Anselmo since it encompasses all the novels we have considered in this chapter. Yet the distance is not insuperable since all the novelists are linked to each other; Flaubert, Stendhal, Proust, and Dostoyevsky form an unbroken chain from one Cervantes to the other.

The simultaneous presence of external and internal mediation in the same work seems to us to confirm the unity of novelistic literature. And in turn, the unity of this literature confirms that of *Don Quixote*. One is proved by the other, just as one proves that the earth is round by going around it. The creative force of Cervantes is so great that it is exerted effortlessly throughout the whole novelistic "space." All the ideas of the Western novel are present in germ in *Don Quixote*. And the idea of these ideas, the idea whose central role is constantly being confirmed, the basic idea from which one can rediscover everything is triangular desire. And triangular desire is the basis of the theory of the *novelistic* novel for which this first chapter serves as an introduction.

NOTES

1   The author quotes from the French translation, *L'Homme du Ressentiment*. There is an English translation by William H. Holdheim, *Ressentiment* (New York: Free Press, 1960). The word *ressentiment* is used by Scheler in the original German text as the most accurate term for the feeling described. (*Translator's note.*)

2   In the French original, constant association and opposition of "romantique" and "roman- esque", with their same radical and different endings, tried to convey something of an essential, yet elusive, difference between the works which passively reflect and those which actively reveal "mediated" desire. The two words are not interchangeable, to be sure, but their opposition alone is fully significant. The essay must not be read as the indictment of a narrowly, or even broadly defined literary *school*. Neither is it an effort to circumscribe the *genre* of the novel. The author is aware that *Jean Santeuil is* a novel and should be classified as such if classifications were the order of the day. *Jean Santeuil* can nevertheless be viewed as "romantic" within the context of the essay, in other words by contrast with the "romanesque" – novelistic – *Remembrance of Things Past*. Similarly, Chateaubriand's *Mémoires d'outre-tombe* are not a novel but they partake somewhat of the "romanesque" by contrast with the romantic *René*.

Unlike the categories of literary historians which are mechanistic and positivistic, the present categories, even though they are not Hegelian, are still dialectical. They are not independent labels stuck once and for all on a fixed amount of static and objective literary material. Neither are they literature-proof receptacles in which that same material would be contained. They have no value in themselves; no single category can be appraised separately. Oppositions are essential; their terms should not be dissociated. The whole *system* alone is truly significant and self-sufficient, in accordance with a *structural* hypothesis.

16

Turning the Screw of Interpretation

Shoshana Felman

Shoshana Felman (b. 1942)

Born in Tel Aviv, Israel, Shoshana Felman received her bachelor's and master's degrees at the Hebrew University of Jerusalem, and her doctorate from the University of Grenoble (France). After receiving her Ph.D. in 1970, she joined the faculty at Yale University; in 2004 she moved to Emory University, where she is Robert W. Woodruff Professor of Comparative Literature and French. Her honors include Guggenheim and Ford Foundation fellowships, American Council of Learned Societies grants, and, in 1982, decoration as an Officier des Palmes Académiques by the French government. Her books include *Folie et la chose littéraire* (1978; *Writing and Madness (Literature/Philosophy/Psychoanalysis)*, 1985); *Jacques Lacan and the Adventure of Insight: Psychoanalysis in Contemporary Culture* (1987); *What Does a Woman Want? Reading and Sexual Difference* (1993); *Testimony: Crises of Witnessing in Literature, Psychoanalysis, and History* (with Dori Laub, 1991); and *Juridical*

From *Literature and Psychoanalysis: The Question of Reading – Otherwise*, edited by Shoshana Felman (*Yale French Studies* 55/56, 1977). Baltimore and London: Johns Hopkins University Press, 1980, pp. 119–38. Reprinted by permission of *Yale French Studies*.

Unconscious: Trials and Traumas in the Twentieth Century (2002). ''Turning the Screw of Interpretation'' is taken from *Literature and Psychoanalysis: The Question of Reading – Otherwise*, edited by Felman; it appeared as a special issue of *Yale French Studies* (volume 55/56, 1977) before its 1982 publication in book form.

The Turns of the Story's Frame: a Theory of Narrative

It appeared that the narrative he had promised to read us really required for a proper intelligence a few words of prologue.

(The Turn of the Screw)

Literature is language (…); but it is language around which we have drawn a frame, a frame that indicates a decision to regard with a particular self-consciousness the resources language had always possessed.

(Stanley E. Fish)

The actual story of *The Turn of the Screw* (that of the governess and the ghosts) is preceded by a prologue which is both posterior and exterior to it, and which places it *as a story*, as a speech event, in the context of the "reality" in which the story comes to be told. With respect to the story's *content*, then, the prologue constitutes a sort of *frame*, whose function is to situate the *story's origin*.

The narrated story is thus presented as the *center* of the *frame* – the focal point of a narrative space which designates and circumscribes it from the outside as *its inside*. Placed *around* the story which becomes its center, the narrative frame, however, frames *another* center within its *literal* space:

> The story had held us, *round the fire*, sufficiently breathless (…) He began to read to our hushed *little circle*, (…) kept it, *round the hearth*, subject to a common thrill.[1]

Since the narrative space of the prologue organizes both a *frame around the story* and a *circle around the fire*, since the fire and the story are both placed at the very *center* of the *narration*, the question could arise as to whether they could be, in any way, considered *metaphors of each other* in the rhetorical constellation of the text. This hypothesis in turn opens up another question: if the content of the story and the fire in the hearth *are* metaphors of each other, how does this metaphorical relation affect the centrality of the two terms?

Before pursuing these questions further, let us take another look at the prologue's status as the story's "frame." The prologue, in fact, frames the story not only spatially but also temporally: while it takes place long *after* the governess's story, it also tells of events which had occurred *before* it: the meeting between the governess and the Master which sets up the determining conditions of the subsequent events. The frame picks up the story, then, both *after its end* and *before its opening*. If the function of the frame is to

SHOSHANA FELMAN

determine the story's *origin*, then that origin must somehow be both anterior and posterior to the story.

Anterior to the story but recounted and accounted for *a posteriori*, the story's origin seems to depend on the authority of the story teller, i.e., of the narrator, who is usually supposed to be both the story's literal source and the depositary of the knowledge out of which the story springs and which the telling must reveal. But while the prologue's function would thus seem to be to *relate* the story to its narrator, the prologue of *The Turn of the Screw* rather *disconnects* the story from the narrator since it introduces not *one* narrator, but *three*: 1) the person who says "I," the first person "general narrator" who transmits to *us* the story with which he himself had no direct connection, and which he heard from Douglas; 2) Douglas, who reads the story to the circle around the fire, but who did not participate in it himself. Douglas had known the governess, the story's heroine, as his sister's governess long after the story had taken place, and had been secretly in love with her although she was ten years his senior. It was, however, only later, on her deathbed, that the governess confided to him a written account of her story. 3) The third teller of the story is thus the governess herself, who is the first-person narrator of her own written narrative.

Having received and read the manuscript, Douglas has in turn kept the governess's story secret for forty years, until that night around the fire when at last, to his privileged circle of friends and most especially to the general narrator, he decided to reveal it. And finally, long after his own telling of the story around the fire, Douglas, on his own deathbed, confided the treasured manuscript to his friend the narrator, who tells us in the prologue that the story he is transmitting to us is his own transcription, made still later, of that manuscript, which he had heard Douglas read before the fire.

The existence of the story is thus assured only through the constitution of a *narrative chain*, in which the narrators relay the story from one to the other. The story's origin is therefore not assigned to any one voice which would assume responsibility for the tale, but to the deferred action of a sort of *echoing effect*, produced – "after the fact" – by voices which themselves re-produce previous voices. It is as though the frame itself could only multiply *itself*, repeat itself: as though, in its infinite reproduction of the very act of narration, the frame could only be its own self-repetition, its own self-framing. If the tale is thus introduced through its own reproduction, if the story is preceded and anticipated by a repetition of the story, then the frame, far from situating, as it first appeared, the story's *origin*, actually situates its *loss*, constitutes its infinite deferral. The story's origin is therefore situated, it would seem, in a *forgetting* of its origin: to tell the story's origin is to tell the story of that origin's obliteration. But isn't this forgetting of the story's origin and beginning, and the very story of this forgetting, constitutive, precisely, of the very story of psychoanalysis and of *analysis as a story*? *The Turn of the Screw* would seem to be very like a psychoanalytical tale. Through the spiral threads of its prologue, the story indeed originates in a frame through which it frames itself into losing its own origin: as is the case with the psychoanalytical story of the unconscious, it is here the very loss of the story's origin which *constitutes* the origin of the story. The New York Preface, in its turn, both underlines and illustrates this point: added *a posteriori* as a second preface to the beginning of the story, it is like a prologue to the prologue, an introduction to the introduction, as if to make up for the missing origin or beginning, but succeeding only in repeating, in beginning once again the tale of the constitutive loss of the tale's beginning.

The starting point itself – the sense (…) of the circle, one winter afternoon, round the hall-fire of a grave old country house where (…) the talk turned, *on I forget what homely pretext*, to apparitions and night-fears, to the marked and sad drop in the general supply (…). The good (…) ghost stories appeared all to have been told (…) Thus it was, I remember, that amid our lament for a beautiful *lost form*, our distinguished host expressed the wish *that he might but have recovered for us* one of the scantiest of *fragments* of this form at its best. He had never forgotten the impression made on him as a young man by the withheld glimpse, at it were, of a dreadful matter that had been reported years before, and with as few particulars, to a lady with whom he had youthfully talked. The story would have been thrilling *could she but find herself in better possession of it*, dealing as it did with a couple of small children in an out-of-the-way place, to whom the spirits of certain "bad" servants, dead in the employ of the house, were believed to have appeared with the design of "getting hold" of them. This was all, but *there had been more*, which my friend's old converser *had lost the thread of* (…). He himself could give us but *this shadow of a shadow* – my own appreciation of which, I need scarcely say, was exactly *wrapped up in that thinness* (*Norton*, pp. 117–118).

A narrative frame which thus incarnates the very principle of repetition of the story it contains, and, through that repetition, situates both the loss of the story's origin and the story's origin *as* its own loss, is clearly not a simple backdrop, staging, from the circumstancial *outside*, the *inside* of the story's content, but constitutes rather a complication, a problematization of the relationship itself between the inside and the outside of the textual space. On the one hand, as Alexander Jones points out, the "outside" frame expands the "inside" of the story, bringing into it both the storyteller and the reader:

> By placing himself within the confines of the story as "I," the narrator, James makes himself one of the characters rather than an omniscient author. *No one is left on the "outside" of the story*, and *the reader is made to feel that he and James are members of the circle around the fire.*[2]

In including not only the content of the story but also the figure of the reader within the fireside circle, the frame indeed leaves no one *out*: it pulls the outside of the story into its inside by enclosing in it what is usually outside it: its own readers. But the frame at the same time does the very opposite, pulling the inside outside: for in passing through the echoing chain of the multiple, repetitive narrative voices, it is the very *content*, the *interior* of the story which becomes somehow *exterior to itself*, reported as it is by a voice inherently alien to it and which can render of it but "the shadow of a shadow," a voice whose intrusion compromises the tale's secret intimacy and whose otherness violates the story's presence to itself. The frame is therefore not an outside contour whose role is to display an inside content: it is a kind of exteriority which permeates the very heart of the story's interiority, an internal cleft separating the story's content from itself, distancing it from its own referential certainty. With respect to the story's content, the frame thus acts both as an inclusion of the exterior and as an exclusion of the interior: it is a perturbation of the outside at the very core of the story's inside, and as such, it is a blurring of the very difference between inside and outside.

No one, then, is left on the "outside" of the story, except the story's inside. Like the circle round the fire, the story's frame thus encloses not only the story's content, but, equally, its readers and its reading. But what if the story's content *were* precisely *its own*

SHOSHANA FELMAN

reading? What if the *reading* (outside the text) were none other than the story's *content* (inside the text), being also, at the same time, that which compromises that content's inside, preventing it from coinciding with itself, making it ec-centric, exterior to itself? If we stop to consider that this non-presence of the story to itself, this self-exteriority, this ec-centricity and foreignness of the content to itself, can define, as such, precisely, the *unconscious*, we can see that reading, here, might be just the key to an understanding of the essential link between the story and the unconscious. "That is what analytical discourse is all about: reading," says Lacan.[3] For has it not become obvious that the chain of narrative voices which transmits *The Turn of the Screw* is also, at the same time, a chain of *readings?* Readings which re-read, and re-write, other readings? In the chain transmission of the story, each narrator, to relay the story, must first be a *receiver* of the story, a *reader* who at once records it and *interprets* it, simultaneously trying to make sense of it and *undergoing* it, as a lived experience, an "impression," a *reading-effect.*

> I asked him if the experience in question had been his own. To this his answer was prompt. "Oh, thank God, no!"
> "And is the record yours? You took the thing down?"
> "Nothing but the impression. I took it here —" he tapped his heart. "I've never lost it" (Prologue, p. 2).

"The safest arena," writes James elsewhere, "for the play of moving accidents and of mighty mutations and of strange encounters, or whatever odd matters, is the field, as I may call it, rather of their second than of their first exhibition":

> By which, to avoid obscurity. I mean nothing more cryptic than I feel myself show them best by showing almost exclusively the way they are felt, by recognising as their *main interest* some *impression strongly made by them* and intensely received. We but too probably break down (...) when we attempt the prodigy (...) in itself; with its "objective" side too emphasised the report (...) will practically run thin. We want it clear, goodness knows, but we also want it thick, and *we get the thickness in the human consciousness that entertains and records, that amplifies and interprets it.* That indeed, when the question is (...) of the "supernatural", constitutes the only thickness we do get; here *prodigies*, when they come straight, come with an effect imperilled; *they keep all their character*, on the other hand, *by looming through some other history* – the indispensable history of somebody's *normal* relation to something.[4]

The "main interest" of the story is thus the "thickness" it acquires through its own *reading* – through "the human consciousness that entertains and records, that amplifies and interprets it." The very subject-matter of the story of the "supernatural," its narrative condition, is, says James, its way of "*looming through some other history,*" its narration *in the other,* and *out of* the other. And that "other" here is the reader. The reader – i.e., also each one of the narrators: Douglas with respect to the governess's manuscript; "I" with respect to Douglas's account of it. The reader-narrator is here that "other," his personal story is the "other history," and his reading (i.e., his narrative, his telling) is significant to the extent that it *interferes* with the tale it tells. Each one of these superimposed stories, each act of narration and each narrative, is here a *reading of the other*; each reading is a *story in the other,* a story whose signification is interfered with but whose interference is significant, a story whose very meaning *interferes* but whose interference *means*. And this, of course, brings us back to the very question of the unconscious, for what, indeed, is the unconscious if not – in every sense of the word – a *reader?* "In analytical discourse," writes Lacan, "the unconscious subject is presumed to be able to read. And that's what the whole affair of the unconscious amounts to" (*Encore*, p. 38). The story of the unconscious thus resembles James's tale, insofar as they both come to us, constitutively, *through the reader.*

Thus it is that the narrator presents us with his own transcription of the manuscript which Douglas, "with *immense effect*, (...) began to *read* to our hushed little circle" (p. 4). Douglas's performance as storyteller, as author-narrator, consists, thereby, of a literal act of *reading.* And if the first-person narrator retransmits the story, communicates to us a reproduction and a reading of that reading, it is doubtless the result of the "immense effect" Douglas's reading produced on him, and which he hopes in turn to produce on us. The very act of telling, of narration, proceeds then from the potentially infinite repercussion of an *effect of reading*; an effect that, once produced, seeks to reproduce itself as an effect yet to be produced – an effect whose *effect* is an effect to produce. Narrative as such turns out to be the trace of the *action* of a reading; it is, in fact, *reading as action*. In Douglas's very first remarks, on the opening page of the prologue, the very *title* of the story is uttered as the mark, or the description, of its own *reading-effect:*

> "I quite agree – in regard to Griffin's ghost, or whatever it was – that its appearing first to the little boy, at so tender an age, adds a particular touch. (...) If the child gives the *effect* another *turn of the screw*, what do you say of two children?"
>
> "We say, of course," somebody exclaimed, "that they give two turns! Also that we want to hear about them." (Prologue, p. 1)

It is by virtue of the reading-effect it produces that the text receives its very name, its title. But that title, as a title, is not given to it by the original author of the manuscript: it is added to it "after the fact" – as the alien seal of the reader – by the third narrator, the last reader-receiver in the narrative chain of readings:

> The next night, by the corner of the hearth (...) [Douglas] opened the faded red cover of a thin old-fashioned gilt-edged album (...). On the first occasion the same lady put another question. "*What is your title?*"
>
> "*I haven't one.*"
>
> "Oh, *I** have"! *I said.* But Douglas, without heeding me, had begun to *read* with a fine clearness that was like a rendering to the ear of the beauty of his author's hand (Prologue, p. 14; *James's italics; remaining italics mine).

Not only does the title precisely name "the turn of the screw" of its own *effect:* the title is itself the *product* of such an effect, it is itself the *outcome* of a *reading* of the story (and is itself thereby a reading of the story), since the narrative is given its name and title by the reader and not by the author. In this manner the prologue, just as it displaced and dislocated the relationship between the inside and the outside, deconstructs as well the distinction and the opposition between reader and writer. The reader here becomes the author, and the author is in turn a reader. What the narrator perceives in Douglas's

SHOSHANA FELMAN

reading as "a rendering to the ear of the beauty of his author's hand" is nothing but Douglas's *performance* as a *reader*, which becomes a metaphor of the original author's writing *through* the very act of reading which that writing has inspired and produced as one of its effects. In essence, then, when Douglas answers the question "What is your title?" with "I haven't one," that answer can be understood in two different manners: he has no *name for* his own narrative; or else, he has no *title to* that narrative which is really not his own, he is not *entitled*, therefore, to give it a title, he has no right or authority over it, since he is not its author, since he can only "render the beauty of his author's hand," "represent" the story's author, to the extent that he is the story's reader.

The story, therefore, seems to frame itself into losing not only its origin but also its very title: having lost both its name and the authority of its author, the narrative emerges, out of the turns of its frame, not only authorless and nameless, but also unentitled to its own authority over itself, having no capacity to denominate, no right to *name itself.* Just as the frame's content, the governess's narrative, tells of the *loss of the proprietor* of the *house,* of the "Master" (by virtue of which loss the house becomes precisely *haunted,* haunted by the usurping ghosts of its *subordinates*), so does the framing prologue convey, through the reader's (vocal) rendering of an authorship to which he has no title, the *loss of the proprietor of the narrative.* And this strange condition of the narrative, this strange double insistence, in the frame as in the story, on the absence of the story's master, of the owner of the property, cannot but evoke, once more, the constitutive condition of the unconscious, itself a sort of obscure knowledge which is, precisely, authorless and ownerless, to the extent that it is a knowledge which no consciousness can *master* or *be in possession of,* a knowledge which no conscious subject can attribute to himself, assume as *his own* knowledge. "Any statement of authority," writes Lacan with respect to the discourse of the unconscious, but in terms which can equally describe the very narrative conditions of *The Turn of the Screw* – "Any statement of authority [in this discursive space] has no other guarantee than that of its own utterance."[5]

If the story has thus managed to lose at once its author, its authority, its title, and its origin, *without losing itself* – without being itself suppressed, obliterated or forgotten –, it is because its written record has been repeatedly and carefully *transferred* from hand to hand: bequeathed first by the dying governess to Douglas, and then by the dying Douglas to the narrator. It is thus *death* itself which moves the narrative chain forward, which *inaugurates* the manuscript's *displacements* and the process of the *substitution* of the narrators. By so doing, death paradoxically appears not as an end but rather as a starting point: the starting point of the *transferral* of the story, that is, of its *survival,* of its capacity to go on, to subsist, by means of the repeated *passages* which it effects *from death to life,* and which effect the narrative.

For each of the people who receive and keep the manuscript of the story, that manuscript constitutes, well beyond the death of the addresser – the person who bequeathed it to them –, the survival of the giver's language and the giver's own survival *in* his language: a *return* of the dead *within the text.* And we hardly need recall that it is precisely the return of the dead which provides the central moving force of the narrative being thus transferred: the story of the governess's struggles with the servants' ghosts. While the prologue contains nothing supernatural in itself, it curiously foreshadows the question of the return of the dead by making the manuscript itself into a ghost, speaking from beyond several graves.

What, however, is the motivation for the narrative's transmission? For what reason is the manuscript at all transferred? Douglas, quite discreetly, alludes to the reason.

> "Then your manuscript – ?"
>
> "(…) A woman's. She has been dead these twenty years. She sent me the pages in question before she died." They were all listening now, and of course there was somebody to be arch, or at any rate to draw the inference. But if he put the inference by without a smile it was also without irritation. "She was a most charming person, but she was ten years older than I. She was my sister's governess," he quietly said. "She was the most agreeable woman I've ever known in her position; she would have been worthy of any whatever. It was long ago, and this episode was long before. (…) We had, in her off-hours, some strolls and talks in the garden – talks in which she struck me as awfully clever and nice. Oh yes; don't grin: *I liked her extremely and am glad to this day to think she liked me too. If she hadn't she wouldn't have told me.* She had never told anyone (Prologue, p. 2).

In an understatement, Douglas lets it be understood that if the manuscript has survived "these twenty years" beyond the death of its author, it is because of the love which had once drawn him to her and which had prompted her in turn to confide to him her ultimate deathbed secret. The cause for the transferral of the manuscript is, therefore, not just death, but love. For Douglas, the manuscript commemorates his encounter with a woman, and with her writing: the story is as such the outcome, the result of love, of death, of writing, of transferring.

If the story's origin is lost, then it is not just because, by virtue of the author's death, it is buried in an unrecoverable, distant past: it is also because that origin cannot be situated as a *fixed point*, but only as a movement, a dynamics: the story's origin is *in transference.* The beginning of the tale, in other words, is not ascribable to any of the narrators, but to the relationship between the narrators. The story's origin is not a *referent*, but the very *act of reference*: the very act – through love and death – of *referring* to *the Other*, the gesture of the transference of a story.

The narrators, in fact, constitute not only a self-relaying *chain* of narrative transmissions, but also a series of pairs or *couples*: the governess and Douglas; Douglas and the first-person narrator. Before the triangular narrative chain comes into being – by means of the repeated and successive transfers of the manuscript due precisely to the disruption of the couples, to the death, each time, of one of the two partners, – the couples, during their lifetime, carry on a relationship which, in both cases, has a discreet erotic connotation but is primarily discursive and linguistic. Such is the relationship between the governess and Douglas:

> [and] we had, in her off-hours, some strolls and talks in the garden – talks in which she struck me as awfully clever and nice. Oh yes; don't grin: I liked her extremely and am glad to this day to think she liked me too (Prologue, p. 2).

Later on, it is the same sort of relationship which structures the rapport between Douglas narrating and the first-person narrator listening:

SHOSHANA FELMAN

It was *to me in particular* that he appeared to propound this – appeared almost to appeal for aid not to hesitate (…). The others resented postponement, but it was just his scruples that *charmed me* (Prologue, p. 2).

In both cases, the couples therefore become couples by virtue of a constitutive situation of dialogue and of *interlocution*, whose discursiveness subtly develops into a discreet game of *seduction*. Indeed, this structuring situation of the couples strikingly calls to mind the psychoanalytical situation *par excellence*, governed as it is by *transference*, in its most strictly analytical sense: it is quite clear that the narrator's fascination with Douglas, as well as Douglas's fascination with the governess, are both transferential fascinations – and so is the governess's fascination with the Master. The tale of transference thus turns out to be the tale of the transference of a tale. This transferential structure will, however, not only motivate, but also modify the narrative, becoming at once its *motive* and its *mask*: putting the narrative in motion as its dynamic, moving force, it will also hide, distort it through the specular mirages of its numerous mirrors of seduction.

The play of seduction is productive of mirages insofar as, inscribed within the very process of narration, it becomes a play of *belief* – belief in the narrator and therefore in the accuracy of his narrative. It is because Douglas is so charmed by the governess, on whom the discursive situation makes him transfer, with whom he becomes narcissistically infatuated, that he *adds faith* to the literality of her narrative and to the authority of her own idealized mirror-image of herself. Vouching for the governess, he grants her story the illusory authority of a delusive *credibility*. Douglas, in other words, endows the governess with a *narrative authority*. Authority as such, so crucial to *The Turn of the Screw*, nonetheless turns out to be itself a fiction, an error in perspective, created by and established through the illusions and delusions of the transferential structure.[6] In the same way, Douglas's account of the governess's story is in turn given authority and credibility by the play of mutual admiration and intuitive understanding between him and his charmed, privileged listener, who will himself become a narrator.

The transferential narrative chain thus consists not only of the echoing effect of voices reproducing other voices, but also of the specular effect of the seductive *play of glances*, of the visual exchange of specular reflections, of the mirror-repetition of a symmetrically – and therefore infinitely – self-reproducing, self-reflecting self-reflections. *The Turn of the Screw*, indeed, in every sense of the word, is a *reflection* of, and on, the act of *seeing*. The story's frame is nothing other than a *frame of mirrors*, in which the narrative is both reflected and deflected through a series of symmetrical, mutual glances of couples looking at themselves looking at themselves.

" … she liked me too. If she hadn't she wouldn't have told me. She had never told anyone. It wasn't simply that she said so, but that I knew she hadn't. I was sure; *I could see*. You'll easily judge why when you hear."

"Because the thing had been such a scare?"

He continued to fix me. "You'll easily judge," he repeated; "*you** will."

I fixed him too. "*I see.* She was in love."

He laughed for the first time. "You *are** acute. Yes, she was in love. That is she *had** been. That came out – she couldn't tell her story without its coming out. *I saw it*, and *she saw I saw it*; but neither of us spoke of it (…)" (Prologue, pp. 2–3; *James's italics; remaining italics mine)

What, however, is the nature of the act of "seeing"? This is the crucial question raised by the appearance of the ghosts, not simply because the ghosts only appear when the governess sees them, but also because each of their appearances enacts the same specular confrontation as that between the other couples: the same exchange of symmetrical, dual glances occurs between the governess and the supernatural intruder. In this play of "seeing oneself seen by the other" and of "seeing the other see," through which the prologue, once again, foreshadows the main story, what, then, does "seeing" mean? "I saw it, and she saw I saw it"; "I was sure; I could see"; "He continued to fix me (…) I fixed him too. 'I see. She was in love.'" Clearly, in the play of these Jamesian sentences, "seeing" is *interpreting*; it is *interpreting love*; and it is also interpreting *by means of love*. Thus, in several ways and on several levels, love has here become, in both senses of the word, the *subject* of interpretation. In this double transferential structure, in this double love-relation, between the narrator and Douglas, and between Douglas and the governess, love has become both what is *seen* and what "*can see*"; both what is *read* and what *is reading*; both what is *to be interpreted* in this intense exchange of glances, and what is actively, through that exchange, *doing the interpreting*. Love interprets. And inversely, the interpreter as such, whether or not he knows it, wants it, or intends it, is caught up in a love-relation, in a relationship constitutively transferential.

Transference, says Lacan, is "the acting-out of the reality of the unconscious."[7] On the basis of the literary evidence which we are analyzing, and within the framework of a theory of narrative, we are here prompted to raise the question whether the acting-out of the unconscious is always in effect the acting-out of a *story*, of a narrative; and whether, on the other hand, *all* stories and all narratives imply a transferential structure, that is, a love-relation which both organizes and disguises, deciphers and enciphers them, turning them into their own substitute and their own repetition. *The Turn of the Screw* at any rate would seem to confirm such a hypothesis.

It is therefore no coincidence that the *transferral* of the manuscript should be presided over by a pair of would-be *lovers*, nor that the story should be twice retold (and acted out) for love, precisely, of its previous narrator or teller. Nor is it a coincidence that the transferential couple is here identified with the couple *author-reader*. The love-relation, i.e., the acting out of the unconscious through a relation of performative interpretation, seems to inhere in, and to govern, the relationship between the addressor of the narrative ("author" or narrator) and its addressee (listener-receiver or reader-interpreter).

> I can see Douglas there before the fire (…) looking down at his converser with his hands in his pockets. "Nobody but me, till now, has ever heard. It's quite too horrible." (…) "It's beyond everything. Nothing at all that I know touches it."
> "For sheer terror?" I remember asking.
> He seemed to say that it wasn't so simple as that; to be really at a loss how to qualify it. *He passed his hand over his eyes*, made a little wincing grimace. "For dreadful – dreadfulness!"
> "Oh, how delicious!" cried one of the women.
> He took no notice of her; *he looked at me, but as if, instead of me, he saw what he spoke of.* "For general uncanny ugliness and horror and pain" (Prologue, pp. 1–2).

The play of passionate glances becomes even more complex when the act of looking is revealed to be not so much a passive observation but an active operation of *substitution*.

Paradoxically, the intensity of that emotive look directs both the seduction and the story, both the narrative and the emotion toward a rhetorical *place* rather than an individual object: "he looked at me, but *as if, instead of me,* he saw *what he spoke of.*" That sentence has two different implications: 1) "what the narrator *speaks of*" is equivalent to the *place* of the person he addresses, or *speaks to:* if the reader also finds himself in that place (spoken to), then the reader is indeed the *subject* of the story; 2) what Douglas actually "speaks of" is the "general uncanny ugliness and horror and pain" that has to do with *ghosts.* In becoming, by virtue of his *place* ("spoken *to*") the *subject* of the story ("spoken *of*"), the *reader* (as well as the first-person narrator) himself becomes a ghost, occupying the rhetorical *ghostly place,* bound up in the "uncanniness" of the odd relationship between love, death, and substitution.

If, by virtue of the storyteller's transference on the reader, the reader thus becomes the storyteller's *ghost* (the addressee of his unconscious), the reader, in his turn, transfers on the storyteller or the "author," to the extent that he invests the latter with the authority and prestige of the *"subject presumed to know."* "Transference," says Lacan, "is only understandable insofar as its starting point is seen in the subject presumed to know; he is presumed to know what no one can escape: meaning as such." It is, as we have seen, the first-person narrator who, in his role as fascinated reader and admiring interpreter, confers upon Douglas his prestige, upon the narrative its title, and upon the story the authority of the ultimate *knowledge* it is *presumed* to have of its own meaning: " 'The story will tell,' I took upon myself to reply" (p. 10). The "I" of the first-person narrator in his role of reader thus constitutes as the text's *knowledge* what his own reading does *not* know in precisely the same way as a psychoanalytical patient's transferential fantasy attributes to his analyst a knowledge which is really his own story as *unknown.*

In telling at once of transference and through transference, the story acts as a repetitive border-crossing, as a constant shuttle between opposed domains: speech and silence, life and death, inside and outside, consciousness and the unconscious, sleep and wakefulness:

> The case, I may mention, was that of an apparition in just such an old house as had gathered us for the occasion – an appearance, of a dreadful kind, to a little boy *sleeping* in the room with his mother and *waking her up* in the terror of it; *waking her not to dissipate his dread* and soothe him to sleep again, *but to encounter also, herself,* (...) *the same sight* that had shaken him. It was this observation that drew from Douglas – not immediately, but later in the evening – a reply that had the interesting consequence to which I call attention (Prologue, p. 1).

It is noteworthy that, in these opening lines of the prologue, it is a child who is at the origin both of the dream and of the dreamlike tale that follows. But if the child, indeed, *awakens* here his mother, it is only so as to *include her in his dream,* to wake her *into his own sleep.* In straddling, in this manner, the line between waking and sleeping, the child's story thus subverts or at least distorts the possibility of telling the two apart. Like the child, the narrator, too, through the dreamlike narrative which he puts in motion out of his own transferential illusions, can only *wake us* into *his own sleep:* into the transferential dream which becomes our own. What the tale awakens in us is finally nothing other than, precisely, *our own sleep.*

At this juncture, it could be illuminating to recall that the psychoanalytical notion of transference is for the first time brought up by Freud in *The Interpretation of Dreams*, precisely with respect to the question of the *relation between sleeping and waking*: in attempting to explain the interactions and exchanges which occur between sleep and wakefulness, Freud analyzes the role of the "day's residues" and their relation to the "dream wish":

> On this view dream might be described as *a substitute for an infantile scene modified by being TRANSFERRED on to a recent experience.* The infantile scene is unable to bring about its own revival and has to be content with returning as a dream.[8]

> *My supposition is that a conscious wish can only become a dream-instigator if it succeeds in AWAKENING an unconscious wish with the same tenor and in obtaining reinforcement from it* (Ibid., p. 591).

> It is only possible to do so [to explain the part played by the day's residues] if we bear firmly in mind the part played by the unconscious wish and then seek for information from the psychology of the neuroses. We learn from the latter that an unconscious idea is as such quite incapable of entering the preconscious and that it can only exercise any effect there by establishing a connection with an idea which already belongs to the preconscious, by TRANSFERRING ITS INTENSITY on to it and by getting itself "covered" by it. Here we have the fact of "TRANSFERENCE," which provides an explanation of so many striking phenomena in the mental life of neurotics (Ibid., p. 601).

> I will be seen, then, that the DAY'S RESIDUES (...) not only *borrow* something from the unconscious when they succeed in taking a share in the formation of a dream – namely the instinctual force which is at the disposal of the repressed wish – but that they also *OFFER THE UNCONSCIOUS* something indispensable – namely THE NECESSARY POINT OF ATTACHMENT FOR A TRANSFERENCE (Ibid., p. 603).

> Let us summarize what we have learnt so far. (...) The unconscious wish links itself up with the day's residues and effects a transference on to them; this may happen either in the course of the day or not until a state of sleep has been established. A wish now arises which has been transferred on to the recent material; or a recent wish, having been suppressed, gains fresh life by being reinforced from the unconscious. This wish seeks to force its way along the normal path taken by thought-processes, through the preconscious (...) to consciousness. But it comes up against the censorship. (...) At this point it takes on the distortion for which the way has already been paved by the transference of the wish on to the recent material. So far it is on the way to becoming an obsessive idea or a delusion or something of the kind – that is, *a thought* which has been intensified by transference and distorted in its expression by censorship. Its further advance is halted, however, by the sleeping state of the preconscious. (...) The dream-process consequently enters on a regressive path, which lies open to it precisely owing to the peculiar nature of the state of sleep, and it is led along that path by the attraction exercised on it by groups of memories; some of these memories themselves exist only in the form of visual cathexes and not as translations into the terminology of the later systems (....) In the course of its regressive path the dream-process acquires the attribute to representability. (...) It has now completed the second portion of its zigzag journey (Ibid., pp. 612–613).

SHOSHANA FELMAN

Freud's analysis of the movement of psychic energies back and forth between sleep and wakefulness *via* transference seems perfectly tailored to fit precisely the visual dream-like figures of the *ghosts*. *Seeing* is thus above all *transferring*. And if, as we have "seen" ourselves from the prologue, seeing is always reading, deciphering, *interpreting*, it is because reading is also transferring: just as a dream is a transference of energy between the "day's residue" and the unconscious wish, so does the act of reading invest the conscious, daylight signifiers with an unconscious energy, transfer on recent materials the intensity of an archaic sleep. Seeing, thus, is always in some manner sleeping, that is, looking with the very eyes of the unconscious – through the fabric of a dream, reading not literally but rhetorically.

Both senses of the term "transference" in Freud's text – transference as the main-spring of psychoanalysis, as the repetitive structural principle of the relation between patient and analyst, and transference as the rhetorical function of any signifying material in psychic life, as the movement and the energy of displacement through a chain of signifiers – thus come together in the prologue of *The Turn of the Screw*: it is their very interaction which gives rise to the story and carries out the narrative both as a *couple-relation* and as the displacement – the transferral – of a manuscript. The whole story is thus played out in the differential space between the transference of the narrators and the transference of the narrative, between an enterprise of seduction and of narcissistic capture and the displacement of a signifier, the transferral of a text, the work of an effect of writing:

> "Well then," I said, "just sit right down and begin."
>
> He turned round to the fire, gave a kick to a log, watched it an instant. Then as he faced us again: "I can't begin. I shall have to send to town. (...) *The story's written.* It's in a locked drawer – it has not been out for years" (Prologue, p. 2).

NOTES

1 *The Turn of the Screw*, ed. Robert Kimbrough, New York: Norton, 1966; pp. 1 and 4. Unless otherwise specified, all quotes from the New York Preface and *The Turn of the Screw* are taken from this edition, hereafter abbreviated *Norton*. As a rule, all italics within the quoted texts throughout this paper are mine; original italics alone will be indicated.

2 "Point of View in *Turn of the Screw*," in: *A Casebook on Henry James's "The Turn of the Screw*," ed. Gerald Willen, New York: Thomas Y. Crowell Company, 1969, 2nd edition; p. 299.

3 *Le Séminaire–Livre XX: Encore* (1972–73), Paris: Seuil, 1975, p. 29; translation mine. Unless otherwise indicated, all quotations from Lacan's works in this paper are in my translation. This work will henceforth be referred to as *Encore*.

4 Preface to "The Altar of the Dead," in Henry James, *The Art of the Novel, Critical Prefaces*, ed. R. P. Blackmur, New York: Charles Scribner's Sons, 1962, p. 256.

5 *Ecrits*, Paris: Seuil, 1966, p. 813.

6 Cf. James's own comments on the "authority" of the governess in the New York Preface: "I recall (...) a reproach made me by a reader capable evidently, for the time, of some attention, but not quite capable of enough, who complained that I hadn't sufficiently 'charac-terized' my young woman engaged in her labyrinth (...), hadn't in a word invited her to deal

with her own mystery as well as with that of Peter Quint (…) I remember well (…) my reply to that criticism. "(…) We have surely as much of her own nature as we can swallow in watching it reflect her anxieties and inductions. It constitutes no little of a character indeed, in such conditions, (…) that she is able to make her particular *credible* statement of such strange matters. She has "authority," which is a good deal to have given her, and I couldn't have arrived at so much had I clumsily tried for more" (*Norton*, pp. 120–121).

7   J. Lacan, *Le Séminaire – Livre XI: Les Quatre Concepts fondamentaux de la psychanalyse*, Paris: Seuil, 1973, p. 158.

8   S. Freud, *The Interpretation of Dreams* (trans. James Strachey), New York: Discus/Avon, 1967, p. 585. In this quotation and those that follow from *The Interpretation of Dreams*, the italics are Freud's; the capitalization is mine.

Freud's
Masterplot

Peter Brooks

Peter Brooks (b. 1938)

Peter Brooks was born in New York City and educated at Harvard University. After receiving his doctorate in 1965, Brooks joined the faculty at Yale University, where he remained until 2004. Brooks served as chair for the Department of Comparative Literature (1991–7) and the Department of French (1983–8), and was director of the Whitney Humanities Center at Yale (1980–91; 1996–2000). In 2005 he moved to the University of Virginia, where he is University Professor and the Director of the Program in Law and the Humanities. Brooks has been honored with election to the American Philosophical Society and the American Academy of Arts and Sciences; decorated as an Officier des Palmes Académiques; and received fellowships from the National Endowment for the Humanities, the American Council of Learned Societies, and the Guggenheim Foundation. Brooks's books include *The Melodramatic Imagination: Balzac, Henry James, Melodrama, and the Mode of Excess* (1976); *Reading for the Plot: Design and*

From *Literature and Psychoanalysis: The Question of Reading – Otherwise*, edited by Shoshana Felman (*Yale French Studies* 55/56, 1977). Baltimore and London: Johns Hopkins University Press, 1980, pp. 280–300. Reprinted by permission of *Yale French Studies*.

As if they would confine th' Interminable,
And tie him to his own prescript.

In one of his best essays in "narratology," where he is working toward a greater formalization of principles advanced by Vladimir Propp and Viktor Shklovsky, Tzvetan Todorov elaborates a model of narrative transformation whereby narrative plot *(le récit)* is constituted in the tension of two formal categories, difference and resemblance.[1] Transformation – a change in a predicate term common to beginning and end – represents a synthesis of difference and resemblance; it is, we might say, the same-but-different. Now "the same-but-different" is a common (and if inadequate, not altogether false) definition of metaphor. If Aristotle affirmed that the master of metaphor must have an eye for resemblances, modern treatments of the subject have affirmed equally the importance of difference included within the operation of resemblance, the chief value of the metaphor residing in its "tension." Narrative operates as metaphor in its affirmation of resemblance, in that it brings into relation different actions, combines them through perceived similarities (Todorov's common predicate term), appropriates them to a common plot, which implies the rejection of merely contingent (or unassimilable) incident or action. The plotting of meaning cannot do without metaphor, for meaning in plot is the structure of action in closed and legible wholes. Metaphor is in this sense totalizing. Yet it is equally apparent that the key figure of narrative must in some sense be not metaphor but metonymy: the figure of contiguity and combination, the figure of syntagmatic relations.[2] The description of narrative needs metonymy as the figure of movement, of linkage in the signifying chain, of the slippage of the signified under the signifier. That Jacques Lacan has equated metonomy and desire is of the utmost pertinence, since desire must be considered the very motor of narrative, its dynamic principle.

The problem with "the same-but-different" as a definition of narrative would be the implication of simultaneity and stasis in the formulation. The postulation of a static model indeed is the central deficiency of most formalist and structuralist work on narrative, which has sought to make manifest the structures of narrative in spatial and atemporal terms, as versions of Lévi-Strauss' "atemporal matrix structure."[3] Todorov is an exception in that, faithful to Propp, he recognizes the need to consider sequence and succession as well as the paradigmatic matrix. He supplements his definition with the remark: "Rather than a 'coin with two faces,' [transformation] is an operation in two directions: it affirms at once resemblance and difference; it puts time into motion and suspends it, in a single movement; it allows discourse to acquire a meaning without this meaning becoming pure information; in a word, it makes narrative possible and reveals its very definition."[4] The image of a double operation upon time has the value of returning us to the evident but frequently eluded fact that narrative meanings are developed in time, that any narrative partakes more or less of what Proust called "un jeu formidable ... avec le Temps," and that this game of time is not merely in the world of reference (or in the *fabula*) but as well in the narrative, in the *sjužet*, be it only that the meanings developed by narrative *take time*: the time of reading.[5] If at the end of a narrative we can suspend time in a moment where past and present hold together in a metaphor which may be the very recognition which, said Aristotle, every good plot should bring, that moment does not abolish the movement, the slidings, the errors and partial recognitions of the middle. As Roland Barthes points out, in what so far must be counted our most satisfactory dynamic analysis of plot, the proairetic and hermeneutic codes − code of actions, code of enigmas and answers − are irreversible: their interpretation is determined linearly, in sequence, in one direction.[6]

Ultimately − Barthes writes elsewhere − the passion that animates us as readers of narrative is the passion for (of) meaning.[7] Since for Barthes meaning (in the "classical" or "readable" text) resides in full predication, completion of the codes in a "plenitude" of signification, this passion appears to be finally a desire for the end. It is at the end − for Barthes as for Aristotle − that recognition brings its illumination, which then can shed retrospective light. The function of the end, whether considered syntactically (as in Todorov and Barthes) or ethically (as in Aristotle) or as formal or cosmological closure (as in Barbara H. Smith or Frank Kermode) continues to fascinate and to baffle. One of the strongest statements of its determinative position in narrative plots comes in a passage from Sartre's *La Nausée* which bears quotation once again. Roquentin is reflecting on the meaning of "adventure" and the difference between living and narrating. When you narrate, you appear to start with a beginning. You say, "It was a fine autumn evening in 1922. I was a notary's clerk in Marommes." But, says Roquentin:

In reality you have started at the end. It was there, invisible and present, it is what gives these few words the pomp and value of a beginning. "I was out walking, I had left the town without realizing it, I was thinking about my money troubles." This sentence, taken simply for what it is, means that the man was absorbed, morose, a hundred miles from an adventure, exactly in a mood to let things happen without noticing them. But the end is there, transforming everything. For us, the man is already the hero of the story. His moroseness, his money troubles are much more precious than ours, they are all gilded by the light of future passions. And the story goes on in the reverse: instants have stopped piling themselves up in a haphazard way one on another, they are caught up by the end of the story which draws them and each one in its turn draws the instant preceding it: "It was night, the street was deserted." The sentence is thrown out negligently, it seems superfluous; but we don't let ourselves be duped, we put it aside: this is a piece of information whose value we will understand later on. And we feel that the hero has lived all the details of this night as annunciations, as promises, or even that he has lived only those that were promises, blind and deaf to all that did not herald adventure. We forget that the future wasn't yet there; the man was walking in a night without premonitions, which offered him in disorderly fashion its monotonous riches, and he did not choose.[8]

The beginning in fact presupposes the end. The very possibility of meaning plotted through time depends on the anticipated structuring force of the ending: the interminable would be the meaningless. We read the incidents of narration as "promises and annunciations" of final coherence: the metaphor reached through the chain of metonymies. As Roquentin further suggests, we read only those incidents and signs which can be construed as promise and annunciation, enchained toward a construction of significance – those signs which, as in the detective story, appear to be *clues* to the underlying intentionality of event.

The sense of beginning, then, is determined by the sense of an ending. And if we inquire further into the nature of the ending, we no doubt find that it eventually has to do with the human end, with death. In *Les Mots*, Sartre pushes further his reflection on ends. He describes how in order to escape contingency and the sense of being unjustified he had to imagine himself as one of the children in *L'Enfance des hommes illustres*, determined, as promise and annunciation, by what he would become for posterity. He began to live his life retrospectively, in terms of the death that alone would confer meaning and necessity on existence. As he succinctly puts it, "I became my own obituary."[9] All narration is obituary in that life acquires definable meaning only at, and through, death. In an independent but convergent argument, Walter Benjamin has claimed that life assumes transmissible form only at the moment of death. For Benjamin, this death is the very "authority" of narrative: we seek in fictions the knowledge of death, which in our own lives is denied to us. Death – which may be figural but in the classic instances of the genre is so often literal – quickens meaning: it is the "flame," says Benjamin, at which we warm our "shivering" lives.[10]

We need to know more about this death-like ending which is nonetheless animating of meaning in relation to initiatory desire, and about how the interrelationship of the two determines, shapes, necessitates the middle – Barthes' "dilatory space" of retard, postponement – and the kinds of vacillation between illumination and blindness that we find there. If the end is recognition which retrospectively illuminates beginning and middle, it is not the exclusive truth of the text, which must include the processes along the way – the processes of "transformation" – in their metonymical complexity. If beginning is desire, and is ultimately desire for the end, between lies a process we feel to be necessary (plots, Aristotle tells us, must be of "a certain length") but whose relation to originating desire and to end remains problematic. It is here that Freud's most ambitious investigation of ends in relation to beginnings may be of help – and may suggest a contribution to a properly dynamic model of plot.

We undertake, then, to read *Beyond the Pleasure Principle* as an essay about the dynamic interrelationship of ends and beginnings, and the kind of processes that constitute the middle. The enterprise may find a general sort of legitimation in the fact that *Beyond the Pleasure Principle* is in some sense Freud's own masterplot, the text in which he most fully lays out a total scheme of how life proceeds from beginning to end, and how each individual life in its own way repeats the masterplot. Of Freud's various intentions in this text, the boldest – and most mysterious – may be to provide a theory of comprehension of the dynamic of the life-span, its necessary duration and its necessary end, hence, implicitly, a theory of the very narratability of life. In his pursuit of his "beyond," Freud is forced to follow the implications of argument – "to throw oneself into a line of thought and follow it wherever it leads," as he says late in the essay – to ends that he had

PETER BROOKS

not originally or consciously conceived.[11] *Beyond the Pleasure Principle* shows the very plotting of a masterplot made necessary by the structural demands of Freud's thought, and it is in this sense that we shall attempt to read it as a model for narrative plot.

Narrative always makes the implicit claim to be in a state of repetition, as a going over again of a ground already covered: a *sjužet* repeating the *fabula*, as the detective retraces the tracks of the criminal.[12] This claim to an act of repetition – "I sing," "I tell" – appears to be initiatory of narrative. It is equally initiatory of *Beyond the Pleasure Principle*; it is the first problem and clue that Freud confronts. Evidence of a "beyond" that does not fit neatly into the functioning of the pleasure principle comes first in the dreams of patients suffering from war neuroses, or from the traumatic neuroses of peace: dreams which return to the moment of trauma, to relive its pain in apparent contradiction of the wish-fulfillment theory of dreams. This "dark and dismal" example is superseded by an example from "normal" life, and we have the celebrated moment of child's play: the toy thrown away, the reel on the string thrown out of the crib and pulled back, to the alternate exclamation of *fort* and *da*. When he has established the equivalence between making the toy disappear and the child's mother's disappearance, Freud is faced with a set of possible interpretations. Why does the child repeat an unpleasurable experience? It may be answered that by staging his mother's disappearance and return, the child is compensating for his instinctual renunciation. Yet the child has also staged disappearance alone, without reappearance, as a game. This may make one want to argue that the essential experience involved is the movement from a passive to an active role in regard to his mother's disappearance, claiming mastery in a situation which he has been compelled to submit to.

Repetition as the movement from passivity to mastery reminds us of "The Theme of the Three Caskets," where Freud, considering Bassanio's choice of the lead casket in *The Merchant of Venice* – the correct choice in the suit of Portia – decides that the choice of the right maiden in man's literary play is also the choice of death; by this choice, he asserts an active mastery of what he must in fact endure. "Choice stands in the place of necessity, of destiny. In this way man overcomes death, which he has recognized intellectually."[13] If repetition is mastery, movement from the passive to the active; and if mastery is an assertion of control over what man must in fact submit to – choice, we might say, of an imposed end – we have already a suggestive comment on the grammar of plot, where repetition, taking us back again over the same ground, could have to do with the choice of ends.

But other possibilities suggest themselves to Freud at this point. The repetition of unpleasant experience – the mother's disappearance – might be explained by the motive of revenge, which would yield its own pleasure. The uncertainty which Freud faces here is whether repetition can be considered a primary event, independent of the pleasure principle, or whether there is always some direct yield of pleasure of another sort involved. The pursuit of this doubt takes Freud into the analytic experience, to his discovery of patients' need to repeat, rather than simply remember, repressed material: the need to reproduce and to "work through" painful material from the past as if it were present. The analyst can detect a "compulsion to repeat," ascribed to the unconscious repressed, particularly discernible in the transference, where it can take "ingenious" forms. The compulsion to repeat gives patients a sense of being fatefully subject to a "perpetual recurrence of the same thing"; it suggests to them pursuit by a daemonic power. We know also, from Freud's essay on "The Uncanny," that this feeling of the daemonic, arising from involuntary repetition, is a particular attribute of the literature of the uncanny.[14]

Thus in analytic work (as also in literary texts) there is slim but real evidence of a compulsion to repeat which can over-ride the pleasure principle, and which seems "more primitive, more elementary, more instinctual than the pleasure principle which it overrides" (23). We might note at this point that the transference itself is a metaphor, a substitutive relationship for the patient's infantile experiences, and thus approximates the status of a text. Now repetition is so basic to our experience of literary texts that one is simultaneously tempted to say all and to say nothing on the subject. To state the matter baldly: rhyme, alliteration, assonance, meter, refrain, all the mnemonic elements of fictions and indeed most of its tropes are in some manner repetitions which take us back in the text, which allow the ear, the eye, the mind to make connections between different textual moments, to see past and present as related and as establishing a future which will be noticeable as some variation in the pattern. Todorov's "same but different" depends on repetition. If we think of the trebling characteristic of the folk tale, and of all formulaic literature, we may consider that the repetition by three constitutes the minimal repetition to the perception of series, which would make it the minimal intentional structure of action, the minimum plot. Narrative must ever present itself as a repetition of events that have already happened, and within this postulate of a generalized repetition it must make use of specific, perceptible repetitions in order to create plot, that is, to show us a significant interconnection of events. Event gains meaning by repeating (with variation) other events. Repetition is a *return* in the text, a doubling back. We cannot say whether this return is a return *to* or a return *of*: for instance, a return to origins or a return of the repressed. Repetition through this ambiguity appears to suspend temporal process, or rather, to subject it to an indeterminate shuttling or oscillation which binds different moments together as a middle which might turn forward or back. This inescapable middle is suggestive of the daemonic. The relation of narrative plot to story may indeed appear to partake of the daemonic, as a kind of tantalizing play with the primitive and the instinctual, the magic and the curse of reproduction or "representation." But in order to know more precisely the operations of repetition, we need to read further in Freud's text.

"What follows is speculation" (24). With this gesture, Freud, in the manner of Rousseau's dismissal of the facts in the *Discourse on the Origins of Inequality*, begins the fourth chapter and his sketch of the economic and energetic model of the mental apparatus: the system Pcpt-Cs and Ucs, the role of the outer layer as shield against excitations, and the definition of trauma as the breaching of the shield, producing a flood of stimuli which knocks the pleasure principle out of operation. Given this situation, the repetition of traumatic experiences in the dreams of neurotics can be seen to have the function of seeking retrospectively to master the flood of stimuli, to perform a mastery or binding of mobile energy through developing the anxiety whose omission was the cause of the traumatic neurosis. Thus the repetition compulsion is carrying out a task that must be accomplished *before* the dominance of the pleasure principle can begin. Repetition is hence a primary event, independent of the pleasure principle and more primitive. Freud now moves into an exploration of the theory of the instincts.[15] The instinctual is the realm of freely mobile, "unbound" energy: the "primary process,"

PETER BROOKS

where energy seeks immediate discharge, where no postponement of gratification is tolerated. It appears that it must be "the task of the higher strata of the mental apparatus to bind the instinctual excitation reaching the primary process" before the pleasure principle can assert its dominance over the psychic economy (34–35). We may say that at this point in the essay we have moved from a postulate of repetition as the assertion of mastery (as in the passage from passivity to activity in the child's game) to a conception whereby repetition works as a process of *binding* toward the creation of an energetic constant-state situation which will permit the emergence of mastery, and the possibility of postponement.

That Freud at this point evokes once again the daemonic and the uncanny nature of repetition, and refers us not only to children's play but as well to their demand for exact repetition in storytelling, points our way back to literature. Repetition in all its literary manifestations may in fact work as a "binding," a binding of textual energies that allows them to be mastered by putting them into serviceable form within the energetic economy of the narrative. Serviceable form must in this case mean perceptible form: repetition, repeat, recall, symmetry, all these journeys back in the text, returns to and returns of, that allow us to bind one textual moment to another in terms of similarity or substitution rather than mere contiguity. Textual energy, all that is aroused into expectancy and possibility in a text – the term will need more definition, but corresponds well enough to our experience of reading – can become usable by plot only when it has been bound or formalized. It cannot otherwise be plotted in a course to significant discharge, which is what the pleasure principle is charged with doing. To speak of "binding" in a literary text is thus to speak of any of the formalizations (which, like binding, may be painful, retarding) that force us to recognize sameness within difference, or the very emergence of a *sjužet* from the material of *fabula*.

We need at present to follow Freud into his closer inquiry concerning the relation between the compulsion to repeat and the instinctual. The answer lies in "a universal attribute of instincts and perhaps of organic life in general," that "*an instinct is an urge inherent in organic life to restore an earlier state of things*" (36). Instincts, which we tend to think of as a drive toward change, may rather be an expression of "the conservative nature of living things." The organism has no wish to change; if its conditions remained the same, it would constantly repeat the very same course of life. Modifications are the effect of external stimuli, and these modifications are in turn stored up for further repetition, so that, while the instincts may give the appearance of tending toward change, they "are merely seeking to reach an ancient goal by paths alike old and new" (38). Hence Freud is able to proffer, with a certain bravado, the formulation: "*the aim of all life is death*." We are given an evolutionary image of the organism in which the tension created by external influences has forced living substance to "diverge ever more widely from its original course of life and to make ever more complicated *détours* before reaching its aim of death" (38–49). In this view, the self-preservative instincts function to assure that the organism shall follow its own path to death, to ward off any ways of returning to the inorganic which are not immanent to the organism itself. In other words, "the organism wishes to die only in its own fashion." It must struggle against events (dangers) which would help it to achieve its goal too rapidly – by a kind of short-circuit.

We are here somewhere near the heart of Freud's masterplot for organic life, and it generates a certain analytic force in its superimposition on fictional plots. What operates in the text through repetition is the death instinct, the drive toward the end. Beyond and under the domination of the pleasure principle is this baseline of plot, its basic "pulsation," sensible or audible through the repetitions which take us back in the text. Repetition can take us both backwards and forwards because these terms have become reversible: the end is a time before the beginning. Between these two moments of quiescence, plot itself stands as a kind of divergence or deviance, a postponement in the discharge which leads back to the inanimate. For plot starts (must give the illusion of starting) from that moment at which story, or "life," is stimulated from quiescence into a state of narratability, into a tension, a kind of irritation, which demands narration. Any reflection on novelistic beginnings shows the beginning as an awakening, an arousal, the birth of an appetency, ambition, desire or intention.[16] To say this is of course to say – perhaps more pertinently – that beginnings are the arousal of an intention in reading, stimulation into a tension. (The specifically erotic nature of the tension of writing and its rehearsal in reading could be demonstrated through a number of exemplary texts, notably Rousseau's account, in *The Confessions*, of how his novel *La Nouvelle Héloïse* was born of a masturbatory reverie and its necessary fictions, or the very similar opening of Jean Genet's *Notre-Dame des fleurs;* but of course the sublimated forms of the tension are just as pertinent.) The ensuing narrative – the Aristotelean "middle" – is maintained in a state of tension, as a prolonged deviance from the quiescence of the "normal" – which is to say, the unnarratable – until it reaches the terminal quiescence of the end. The development of a narrative shows that the tension is maintained as an ever more complicated postponement or *détour* leading back to the goal of quiescence. As Sartre and Benjamin compellingly argued, the narrative must tend toward its end, seek illumination in its own death. Yet this must be the right death, the correct end. The complication of the *détour* is related to the danger of short-circuit: the danger of reaching the end too quickly, of achieving the im-proper death. The improper end indeed lurks throughout narrative, frequently as the wrong choice: choice of the wrong casket, misapprehension of the magical agent, false erotic object-choice. The development of the subplot in the classical novel usually suggests (as William Empson has intimated) a different solution to the problems worked through by the main plot, and often illustrates the danger of short-circuit.[17] The subplot stands as one means of warding off the danger of short-circuit, assuring that the main plot will continue through to the right end. The desire of the text (the desire of reading) is hence desire for the end, but desire for the end reached only through the at least minimally complicated *détour*, the intentional deviance, in tension, which is the plot of narrative.

Deviance, *détour*, an intention which is irritation: these are characteristics of the narratable, of "life" as it is the material of narrative, of *fabula* become *sjužet*. Plot is a kind of arabesque or squiggle toward the end. It is like Corporal Trim's arabesque with his stick, in *Tristram Shandy*, retraced by Balzac at the start of *La Peau de chagrin* to indicate the arbitrary, transgressive, gratuitous line of narrative, its deviance from the straight line, the shortest distance between beginning and end – which would be the collapse of one into the other, of life into immediate death. Freud's text will in a moment take us closer to understanding of the formal organization of this deviance toward the end. But it also at this point offers further suggestions about the beginning. For when he has identified both the death instincts and the life (sexual) instincts as conservative, tending toward the restoration of an earlier state of things, Freud feels obliged to

PETER BROOKS

deconstruct the will to believe in a human drive toward perfection, an impulsion forward and upward: a force which – he here quotes *Faust* as the classic text of man's forward striving – "*ungebändigt immer vorwärts dringt.*" The illusion of the striving toward perfection is to be explained by instinctual repression and the persisting tension of the repressed instinct, and the resulting difference between the pleasure of satisfaction *demanded* and that which is *achieved*, a difference which "provides the driving factor which will permit of no halting at any position attained" (36). This process of subtraction reappears in modified form in the work of Lacan, where it is the difference between *need* (the infant's need for the breast) and *demand* (which is always demand for recognition) that gives as its result *desire*, which is precisely the driving power, of plot certainly, since desire for Lacan is a metonymy, the forward movement of the signifying chain. If Roman Jakobson is able, in his celebrated essay, to associate the metonymic pole with prose fiction (particularly the nineteenth-century novel) – as the metaphoric pole is associated with lyric poetry – it would seem to be because the meanings peculiar to narrative inhere (or, as Lacan would say, "insist") in the metonymic chain, in the drive of desire toward meaning in time.[18]

The next-to-last chapter of *Beyond the Pleasure Principle* cannot here be rehearsed in detail. In brief, it leads Freud twice into the findings of biology, first on the track of the origins of death, to find out whether it is a necessary or merely a contingent alternative to interminability, then in pursuit of the origins of sexuality, to see whether it satisfies the description of the instinctual as conservative. Biology can offer no sure answer to either investigation, but it offers at least metaphorical confirmation of the necessary dualism of Freud's thought, and encouragement to reformulate his earlier opposition of ego instincts to sexual instincts as one between life instincts and death instincts, a shift in the grouping of oppositional forces which then allows him to reformulate the libidinal instincts themselves as the Eros "of the poets and philosophers" which holds all living things together, and which seeks to combine things in ever greater living wholes. Desire would then seem to be totalizing in intent, a process tending toward combination in new unities: metonymy in the search to become metaphor. But for the symmetry of Freud's opposition to be complete, he needs to be able to ascribe to Eros, as to the death instinct, the characteristic of a need to restore an earlier state of things. Since biology will not answer, Freud, in a remarkable gesture, turns toward myth, to come up with Plato's Androgyne, which precisely ascribes Eros to a search to recover a lost primal unity which was split asunder. Freud's apologetic tone in this last twist to his argument is partly disingenuous, for we detect a contentment to have formulated the forces of the human masterplot as "philosopher and poet." The apology is coupled with a reflection that much of the obscurity of the processes Freud has been considering "is merely due to our being obliged to operate with the scientific terms, that is to say with the figurative language, peculiar to psychology" (60). *Beyond the Pleasure Principle*, we are to understand, is not merely metapsychology, it is also mythopoesis, necessarily resembling "an equation with two unknown quantities" (57), or, we might say, a formal dynamic the terms of which are not substantial but purely relational. We perceive that *Beyond the Pleasure Principle* is itself a plot which has formulated that dynamic necessary to its own *détour*.

The last chapter of Freud's text recapitulates, but not without difference. He returns to the problem of the relationship between the instinctual processes of repetition and the dominance of the pleasure principle. One of the earliest and most important functions of the mental apparatus is to bind the instinctual impulses which impinge upon it, to convert freely mobile energy into a quiescent cathexis. This is a preparatory act on behalf of the pleasure principle, which permits its dominance. Sharpening his distinction between a *function* and a *tendency*, Freud argues that the pleasure principle is a "tendency operating in the service of a function whose business it is to free the mental apparatus entirely from excitation or to keep the amount of excitation in it constant or to keep it as low as possible" (62). This function is concerned "with the most universal endeavour of all living substance – namely to return to the quiescence of the inorganic world." Hence one can consider "binding" to be a preliminary function which prepares the excitation for its final elimination in the pleasure of discharge. In this manner, we could say that the repetition compulsion and the death instinct serve the pleasure principle; in a larger sense, the pleasure principle, keeping watch on the invasion of stimuli from without and especially from within, seeking their discharge, serves the death instinct, making sure that the organism is permitted to return to quiescence. The whole evolution of the mental apparatus appears as a taming of the instincts so that the pleasure principle – itself tamed, displaced – can appear to dominate in the complicated *détour* called life which leads back to death. In fact, Freud seems here at the very end to imply that the two antagonistic instincts serve one another in a dynamic interaction which is a perfect and self-regulatory economy which makes both end and *détour* perfectly necessary and interdependent. The organism must live in order to die in the proper manner, to die the right death. We must have the arabesque of plot in order to reach the end. We must have metonymy in order to reach metaphor.

We emerge from reading *Beyond the Pleasure Principle* with a dynamic model which effectively structures ends (death, quiescence, non-narratability) against beginnings (Eros, stimulation into tension, the desire of narrative) in a manner that necessitates the middle as *détour*, as struggle toward the end under the compulsion of imposed delay, as arabesque in the dilatory space of the text. We detect some illumination of the necessary distance between beginning and end, the drives which connect them but which prevent the one collapsing back into the other: the way in which metonymy and metaphor serve one another, the necessary temporality of the same-but-different which to Todorov constitutes the narrative transformation. The model suggests further that along the way of the path from beginning to end – in the middle – we have repetitions serving to bind the energy of the text in order to make its final discharge more effective. In fictional plots, these bindings are a system of repetitions which are returns to and returns of, confounding the movement forward to the end with a movement back to origins, reversing meaning within forward-moving time, serving to formalize the system of textual energies, offering the possibility (or the illusion) of "meaning" wrested from "life."

As a dynamic-energetic model of narrative plot, then, *Beyond the Pleasure Principle* gives an image of how "life," or the *fabula*, is stimulated into the condition of narrative, becomes *sjužet*: enters into a state of deviance and *détour* (ambition, quest, the pose of a mask) in which it is maintained for a certain time, through an at least minimally complex extravagance, before returning to the quiescence of the non-narratable. The energy generated by deviance, extravagance, excess – an energy which belongs to the textual hero's career and to the readers' expectation, his desire of and for the text – maintains the plot in its movement through the vacillating play of the middle, where repetition as binding works toward the generation of significance, toward recognition and the retrospective illumination which will allow us to grasp the text as total metaphor, but not therefore to discount the metonymies that have led to it. The desire of the text is ultimately the desire for the end, for that recognition which is the moment of the death of the reader in the text. Yet recognition cannot abolish textuality, does not annul the middle which, in its oscillation between blindness and recognition, between origin and endings, is the truth of the narrative text.

It is characteristic of textual energy in narrative that it should always be on the verge of premature discharge, of short-circuit. The reader experiences the fear – and excitation – of the improper end, which is symmetrical to – but far more immediate and present than – the fear of endlessness. The possibility of short-circuit can of course be represented in all manner of threats to the protagonist or to any of the functional logics which demand completion; it most commonly takes the form of temptation to the mistaken erotic object choice, who may be of the "Belle Dame sans merci" variety, or may be the too-perfect and hence annihilatory bride. Throughout the Romantic tradition, it is perhaps most notably the image of incest (of the fraternal-sororal variety) which hovers as the sign of a passion interdicted because its fulfillment would be too perfect, a discharge indistinguishable from death, the very cessation of narrative movement. Narrative is in a state of temptation to over-sameness, and where we have no literal threat of incest (as in Chateaubriand, or Faulkner), lovers choose to turn the beloved into a soul-sister so that possession will be either impossible or mortal: Werther and Lotte, for instance, or, at the inception of the tradition, Rousseau's *La Nouvelle Héloïse*, where Saint-Preux's letter to Julie following their night of love begins: "Mourons, ô ma douce amie." Incest is only the exemplary version of a temptation of short-circuit from which the protagonist and the text must be led away, into *détour*, into the cure which prolongs narrative.

It may finally be in the logic of our argument that repetition speaks in the text of a return which ultimately subverts the very notion of beginning and end, suggesting that the idea of beginning presupposes the end, that the end is a time before the beginning, and hence that the interminable never can be finally bound in a plot. Analysis, Freud would eventually discover, is inherently interminable, since the dynamics of resistance and the transference can always generate new beginnings in relation to any possible end.[19] It is the role of fictional plots to impose an end which yet suggests a return, a new beginning: a rereading. A narrative, that is, wants at its end to refer us back to its middle, to the web of the text: to recapture us in its doomed energies.

One ought at this point to make a new beginning, and to sketch the possible operation of the model in the study of the plot of a fiction. One could, for instance, take Dickens' *Great Expectations*. One would have to show how the energy released in the text by its liminary "primal scene" – Pip's terrifying meeting with Magwitch in the graveyard – is subsequently bound in a number of desired but unsatisfactory ways (including Pip's "being bound" as apprentice, the "dream" plot of Satis House, the apparent intent of the "expectations"), and simultaneously in censored but ultimately more satisfying ways (through all the returns of the repressed identification of Pip and his convict). The most salient device of this novel's "middle" is literally the journey back – from London to

Pip's home town – a repeated return to apparent origins which is also a return of the repressed, of what Pip calls "that old spell of my childhood." It would be interesting to demonstrate that each of Pip's choices in the novel, while consciously life-furthering, forward oriented, in fact leads back, to the insoluble question of origins, to the palindrome of his name, so that the end of the narrative – its "discharge" – appears as the image of a "life" cured of "plot," as celibate clerk for Clarrikers.

Pip's story, while ostensibly the search for progress, ascension, and metamorphosis, may after all be the narrative of an attempted homecoming: of the effort to reach an assertion of origin through ending, to find the same in the different, the time before in the time after. Most of the great nineteenth-century novels tell this same tale. Georg Lukács has called the novel "the literary form of the transcendent homelessness of the idea," and argued that it is in the discrepancy between idea and the organic that time, the process of duration, becomes constitutive of the novel as of no other genre:

> Only in the novel, whose very matter is seeking and failing to find the essence, is time posited together with the form: time is the resistance of the organic – which possesses a mere semblance of life – to the present meaning, the will of life to remain within its own completely enclosed immanence.... In the novel, meaning is separated from life, and hence the essential from the temporal; we might almost say that the entire inner action of the novel is nothing but a struggle against the power of time.[20]

The understanding of time, says Lukács, the transformation of the struggle against time into a process full of interest, is the work of memory – or more precisely, we could say with Freud, of "remembering, repeating, working through." Repetition, remembering, reënactment are the ways in which we replay time, so that it may not be lost. We are thus always trying to work back through time to that transcendent home, knowing of course that we cannot. All we can do is subvert or, perhaps better, pervert time: which is what narrative does.[21]

To forgo any true demonstration on a novel, and to bring a semblance of conclusion, we may return to the assertion, by Barthes and Todorov, that narrative is essentially the articulation of a set of verbs. These verbs are no doubt ultimately all versions of desire. Desire is the wish for the end, for fulfillment, but fulfillment delayed so that we can understand it in relation to origin, and to desire itself. The story of Scheherezade is doubtless the story of stories. This suggests that the tale as read is inhabited by the reader's desire, and that further analysis should be directed to that desire, not (in the manner of Norman Holland) his individual desire and its origins in his own personality, but his transindividual and intertextually determined desire as a reader. Because it concerns ends in relation to beginnings and the forces that animate the middle in between, Freud's model is suggestive of what a reader engages when he responds to plot. It images that engagement as essentially dynamic, an interaction with a system of energy which the reader activates. This in turn suggests why we can read *Beyond the Pleasure Principle* as a text concerning textuality, and conceive that there can be a psychoanalytic criticism of the text itself that does not become – as has usually been the case – a study of the psychogenesis of the text (the author's unconscious), the dynamics of literary response (the reader's unconscious), or the occult motivations of the characters (postulating an "unconscious" for them). It is rather the superimposition of the model of the functioning of the mental apparatus on the functioning of the text that offers the possibility of a psychoanalytic criticism. And here the superimposition of Freud's psychic masterplot on the plots of fiction seems a valid and useful maneuver. Plot mediates meanings with the contradictory human world of the eternal and the mortal. Freud's masterplot speaks of the temporality of desire, and speaks to our very desire for fictional plots.

NOTES

1 Tzvetan Todorov, "Les Transformations narratives," in *Poétique de la prose* (Paris: Seuil, 1971), p. 240. Todorov's terms *récit* and *histoire* correspond to the Russian Formalist distinction between *sjužet* and *fabula*. In English, we might use with the same sense of distinctions: narrative *plot* and *story*.

I wish at the outset of this essay to express my debt to two colleagues whose thinking has helped to clarify my own: Andrea Bertolini and David A. Miller. It is to the latter that I owe the term "the narratable."

2 See Roman Jakobson, "Two Types of Language and Two Types of Aphasic Disturbances," in Jakobson and Halle, *Fundamentals of Language* (The Hague: Mouton, 1956). Todorov in a later article adds to "transformation" the term "succession," and sees the pair as definitional of narrative. He discusses the possible equation of these terms with Jakobson's "metaphor" and "metonymy," to conclude that "the connection is possible but does not seem necessary." (Todorov, "The Two Principles of Narrative," *Diacritics*, Fall, 1971, p. 42.) But there seem to be good reasons to maintain Jakobson's terms as "master tropes" referring to two aspects of virtually any text.

3 See Claude Lévi-Strauss, "La Structure et la forme," *Cahiers de l'Institut de science économique appliquée*, 99, série M, no. 7 (1960), p. 29. This term is cited with approval by A. J. Greimas in *Sémantique structurale* (Paris: Larousse, 1966) and Roland Barthes, in "Introduction à l'analyse structurale des récits," *Communications* 8 (1966).

4 Todorov, "Les Transformations narratives," *Poétique de la prose*, p. 240. Translations from the French, here and elsewhere, are my own.

5 Proust's phrase is cited by Gerard Genette in "Discours du récit," *Figures III* (Paris: Seuil, 1972), p. 182. Whereas Barthes maintains in "Introduction à l'analyse structurale des récits" that time belongs only to the referent of narrative, Genette gives attention to the time of reading and its necessary linearity. See pp. 77–78.

6 See Roland Barthes, *S/Z* (Paris: Seuil, 1970), p. 37.

7 "Introduction à l'analyse structurale des récits," p. 27.

8 Jean-Paul Sartre, *La Nausée* (Paris: Livre de Poche, 1957), pp. 62–63.

9 Sartre, *Les Mots* (Paris: Gallimard, 1968), p. 171.

10 Walter Benjamin, "The Storyteller," in *Illuminations*, translated by Harry Zohn (New York: Schocken Books, 1969), p. 101. [See also pp. 361–78 in this book.]

11 Sigmund Freud, "Beyond the Pleasure Principle" (1920), in *The Standard Edition of the Complete Psychological Works of Sigmund Freud*, ed. James Strachey (London: Hogarth Press, 1955), 18, 59. Subsequent page references will be given between parentheses in the text.

12 J. Hillis Miller, in "Ariadne's Web" (unpublished manuscript), notes that the term *diegesis* suggests that narrative is a retracing of a journey already made. On the detective story, see Tzvetan Todorov, "Typologie du roman policier," *Poétique de la prose*, pp. 58–59.

13 Freud, "The Theme of the Three Caskets" (1913), *Standard Edition*, 12, 299.

14 See Freud, "The Uncanny" *(Das Unheimliche)* (1919), in *Standard Edition*, 17, 219–52.

15 I shall use the term "instinct" since it is the translation of *Trieb* given throughout the Standard Edition. But we should realize that "instinct" is inadequate and somewhat misleading, since it loses the sense of "drive" associated with the word *Trieb*. The currently accepted French translation, *pulsion*, is more to our purposes: the model that interests me here might indeed be called "pulsional."

16 On the beginning as intention, see Edward Said, *Beginnings: Intention and Method* (New York: Basic Books, 1975). It occurs to me that the exemplary narrative beginning might be that of Kafka's *Metamorphosis:* waking up to find oneself transformed into a monstrous vermin.

17 See William Empson, "Double Plots," in *Some Versions of Pastoral* (New York: New Directions, 1960), pp. 25–84.

18 See Jakobson, "Two Types of Language...". See, in Lacan's work, especially "Le Stade du miroir" and "L'Instance de la lettre dans l'inconscient," in *Écrits* (Paris: Seuil, 1966).

19 See Freud, "Analysis Terminable and Interminable" (1937), in *Standard Edition*, 23, 216–53.

20 Georg Lukács, *The Theory of the Novel*, trans. Anna Bostock (Cambridge, Mass.: MIT Press, 1971), p. 122.

21 Genette discusses Proust's "perversion" of time in "Discours du récit," p. 182. "Remembering, Repeating, and Working Through" (*Erinnern, Wiederholen und Durcharbeiten*) (1914) is the subject of one of Freud's papers on technique. See *Standard Edition*, 12, 145–56.

PART V

Marxist Approach

Introduction

What perhaps most distinguishes Marxism as a theory of literature is the belief that it is the only true theory of literature. As Fredric Jameson boldly proclaims in the opening sentences of his first chapter of *The Political Unconscious* (1981), Marxist interpretation should be regarded not "as some supplementary method, not as an optional auxiliary to other interpretative methods current today – the psychoanalytic or the myth-critical, the stylistic, the ethical, the structural – but rather as the absolute horizon of all reading and all interpretation" (414). Jameson can insist upon the preeminence of Marxism because he believes that all other twentieth-century schools of literary theory are, to greater or lesser degrees, expressions of false ideology: their willingness to present themselves as one interpretation among many equally good possibilities is, on Jameson's view, an admission of partiality – and a symptom of the fragmentation of social value produced by capitalism. Jameson regards the endorsement of pluralism (expressed in the very notion of "schools of thought") as a reflection of the debilitating relativism of modern life. Marxists thus define their own belief in objective value as both a rejection of and a correction to the moral relativism of modern society. Even the self-styled scientific approaches to literature that we have studied in other parts of this volume would be viewed by Marxists as not truly objective. Most of those theories begin with the positivistic premise that interpretation is separable from the study of form: that the science of literature can be purely descriptive, prior to the evaluative activity of interpretation. For Marxists, there is no such thing as neutral description; every act of classification is rooted in social beliefs about value. Marxism prides itself in making this self-consciousness about social value the basis of its own theoretical position – and also in believing it has solved the problem of relativism since the values that inform Marxist theory have themselves an objective basis in material conditions that are, so Marxists argue, the source of true human value. Marxists thus devote themselves on the one hand to studying what Jameson (modifying Lacan) terms the "Real," the ultimate source of social value as revealed through sociohistorical development; and, on the other hand, to studying the material conditions of labor and economic production that are the localized determinants for human action and satisfaction within specific social formations at any particular historical moment. For the Marxist, then, the objective study of literature is fashioned from an objective knowledge of what it means to be authentically human along with an equally objective understanding of how ruling classes have generated false realities – ideologies – to pass for the Real.

All of the Marxists included in this section draw the connection between objective value and objective interpretation, but György Lukács in his preface to *Studies in European Realism* (written in 1948), perhaps puts the relation most succinctly. For Lukács, the whole point of literary criticism is to make judgments about worth, to be evaluative. He explicitly aims to distinguish true novelistic realism from "pseudo" objective naturalism and "mirage" subjectivism (383) – and, in so doing, to differentiate the great artist from the pretender. Lukács notes that, on strict aesthetic grounds, his critical judgments would seem completely indefensible: launching his analysis of what he calls Zola's biologism he freely admits, "there is no reason why, regarded merely from the point of view of good writing, erotic conflict with its attendant moral and social conflicts should be rated higher than the elemental spontaneity of pure sex" (384). But for Lukács, moral values are what make "good writing" a meaningful category for literary analysis. And these values are, according to Marxist doctrine, both unambiguous and specifiable:

> The central aesthetic problem of realism is the adequate presentation of the complete human personality...Only if we accept the concept of the complete human personality as the social and historical task humanity has to solve; only if we regard it as the vocation of art to depict the most important turning-points of this process with all the wealth of the factors affecting it; only if aesthetics assign to art the role of explorer and guide, can the content of life be systematically divided up into spheres of greater and lesser importance. (384)

The "complete human personality" is for Lukács a wholly knowable value. Its actualization is the goal of authentic social life and, therefore, the objective standard for judging artistic value. Great art depicts "the social and historical task humanity has to solve," revealing the sociohistorical possibilities for the realization of the complete human personality, as well as the conditions that have compromised or deterred its achievement. Lukács' belief that all art has the same ultimate goal gives the critic an objective basis for the judgment of the success or failure of what he calls the art work's social "content." To the degree that the artist has succeeded in portraying the "content of life" as "systematically divided up into spheres of greater and lesser importance," then he has successfully achieved what Lukács in "The Ideology of Modernism" will call "perspective" (405).

The concept of "perspective" seems a deliberate attempt on Lukács' part to correct the interpretative pluralism imported into literary studies through the valorization of "point of view," both as a narrative technique and as a symptom of modern society's increasing belief in the radical relativity of value. The Marxist concept of "perspective" stresses instead the achievement of uniform aesthetic judgments based upon shared, hierarchically ranked values. Perspective enables the critic and the artist "to choose between the important and the superficial, the crucial and the episodic" ("Ideology," 405). The novelist who possesses the Marxist social vision thus avoids the compositional dilemmas that Henry James confronted when he sat down to write a novel. As we saw in Part I, for James the problem of novelistic representation is the problem of limitation: the artist's experience of life is endlessly ramifying; yet the art work must create the illusion that subjective experience, the author's "vision of life," is unified and complete. As he says in "The Art of Fiction," "Experience is never limited, and it is never complete; it is an immense sensibility, a kind of huge spider-web of the finest silken threads suspended in the chamber of consciousness."[1] The successful novelist sets limits to experience through the sleight of hand he performs through composition. As James puts it in the Preface to *Roderick Hudson*, "Really, universally, relations stop nowhere, and the exquisite problem of the artist is eternally but to draw, by a geometry of his own, the circle within which they shall happily *appear* to do so."[2] And in the Preface to *What Maisie Knew*, James goes so far as to depict the form-giving artist as a happy capitalist: "life has no direct sense whatever for the subject and is capable, luckily for us, of nothing but splendid waste. Hence the opportunity for the sublime economy of art, which rescues, which saves, and hoards and 'banks,' investing and reinvesting these fruits of toil in wondrous useful 'works' and thus making up for us, desperate spendthrifts that we all naturally are, the most princely of incomes."[3] By contrast, life for Lukács is always already value-laden and socially formed. The job of the great novelist is to mirror this hierarchized social value, to represent faithfully these social formations, and the job of the critic is to judge the success of that attempt.

It is the opposite of surprising, then, that this clarity of "perspective" produces a Marxist understanding of the novel that is powerfully uniform. The influential Marxist tradition represented in this section – the line of inquiry systematically developed from the 1930s through the 1980s in the work of Walter Benjamin, Lukács, and Fredric Jameson – is in essential agreement about not only the social value of studying the novel's development as a genre but also what the salient features of that development might be. Each of these thinkers believes that the novel possesses overwhelming cultural importance as an instrument in the institution of capitalistic bourgeois values. For Benjamin, Lukács, and Jameson, the novel is at once a bad guy – the debased scion of more authentically human literary genres produced by better, less alienated societies in the past – and a golden key, a privileged site for the unveiling of ideological processes that work with insidious invisibility in other realms of modern culture.

Of the essays included in this section, Walter Benjamin's "The Storyteller" (1936) makes the most pessimistic case for the novel as a social form. Benjamin attributes to the invention of printing the rise of the novel and the fall of human community and communication. Although Benjamin believes that the social conditions that enabled the novel to become the most popular modern literary form developed gradually over the centuries, without a decisive change in the modes of production the novel could not finally have come into being as its own distinctive genre. Written in isolation, read in isolation, the novel as a cultural form helps to produce the lack of community that it also depicts within its pages. Benjamin feels that he himself writes from a historical moment where the value of storytelling is still able to be apprehended and where the practice of storytelling is still possible, but only as a rare achievement, a resistance to the hegemonic ideology of capitalism. Through his study of the Russian writer Nikolai Leskov, he details the attributes and value of storytelling as it has managed to survive within and despite print culture.

The ultimate value of storytelling for Benjamin lies in its ability to communicate what Benjamin calls human "experience," a notion that, with its grounding in the belief in the objectivity and knowability of what authentic human experience might be, has much in common with Lukács' "complete human personality." Benjamin's theory distinguishes itself from Lukács', though, in that it focuses on what Wayne Booth and Shoshana Felman call the rhetorical circumstances of the storyteller's act of communication. Benjamin is as concerned with the reception of the tale as with its telling: "The storyteller takes what he tells from experience – his own or that reported by others. And he in turn makes it the experience of those who are listening to his tale" (364). The forms of narration are, for Benjamin, generated in the service of this communicative function: how a story is told influences the listener's ability to receive the teller's experience as his own. On Benjamin's view, the authentic expression of the teller's subjectivity, expressed through effective narrative forms, becomes the objective condition of identification between self and other, the forging of the listener's subjectivity through the act of incorporating the teller's subjectivity as his or her own.

Benjamin's belief in the human value conveyed through and created by storytelling thus leads him to theorize a dialectical relation between the semantic "meaning" of a story and its meaning for and as an expression of subjectivity. We can see Benjamin making this interesting move when he praises Leskov for creating plots that are free "from explanation." Although this might at first sound as if Benjamin is endorsing the Anglo-American formalist preference for "showing" over "telling," in fact the narrative technique Benjamin most values is something more akin to inscrutability. To the degree that a story resists explanation, it engages the listener as an active agent of interpretation, a participant in the search for the story's meaning. But unlike Lubbockian "showing" which ideally results in the reader's confident reconstruction of authorial meaning, Benjamin sees the lack of explanation in Leskov as a permanent unfinalizability of meaning.[4] The activity of interpretation, unfinished (and unfinishable) for the listener, keeps the story alive long after the occasion of its reading has passed. As she herself attempts to explain what Leskov has not explained, different possibilities for meaning unfold for the reader at different times – within a particular day that the story comes back to mind and possibly even over a lifetime. According to Benjamin, the story's resistance to explanation thus defines the storyteller's craft in opposition to the information culture produced under capitalism. Whereas information is transparent in meaning and has value only in the present, the opaqueness of story-meaning insures that it cannot be used up or worn out. In fact, this opaqueness becomes the condition of the story's communal reproduction: taken in but not absorbed by the listener, it becomes part of the "life" of the listener, a life that is itself passed on when the story is retold by her to another listener. In Benjamin's figure, the story's connection to each teller's subjectivity is expressed as a material aspect of the story itself, becoming part of the story's form: the "traces of the storyteller cling to the story the way the handprints of the potter cling to the clay vessel" (367). Hermeneutic unfinalizability thus, on this view, does not spin off into the endlessness of deconstructive play, but instead becomes a condition for the communication of alterity, alterity conceived of as materialized subjectivity, made legible and transmissible as literary form.

Benjamin's desire to define the social value of storytelling in terms of the material qualities of handicraft production suggests how tempting it is for Marxists to establish a homological relationship between the conditions of production and the values of production – to the point where materiality itself may seem, in the Marxist hierarchy of value, the ultimate good. In Benjamin's case, the material conditions under which storytelling flourished (the guild system) bestow upon the story itself the material solidity and intricacy of a craft object. The ephemeral passing of a story from mouth to mouth makes it more rather than less tangible: according to Benjamin, it is the oral tradition which allows "that slow piling one on top of the other of thin, transparent layers which constitutes the most appropriate picture of the way in which the perfect narrative is revealed through the layers of a variety of retellings" (368). Paradoxically, then, the story's unfinalizability generates the story's materiality: the incompleteness of the story and the shortness of the storyteller's memory produce the story as a crafted object – an enduring and collective cultural production that contrasts with the consumability of the novel, despite (or rather because) of the novel's less metaphoric materiality. The novel is disposable first of all because it is literally hand-held (rather than figuratively bearing each teller's handprint). When one has finished reading a novel, one can simply leave it behind, knowing that its materiality, the fact that its pages are printed and bound, gives it an autonomous life of its own: since any interested reader can get a copy for herself, no particular reader need feel it necessary to preserve the existence of the tale by passing the story on.

According to Benjamin the conditions of novel production – both the materiality of the novel's form (which I have just discussed) and the solitary nature of novel-writing – contribute to the genre's disposability by creating a conceptual density and complexity that for Benjamin is the opposite of hermeneutic unfinalizability: less elliptical, more "done" than the story, novel-meaning is all too complete. Cut off from a live audience, printed works like the novel feel compelled to say everything, to leave nothing out – and the result is that no room is left for the reader's participation in the creation of meaning.

Benjamin believes that even the author is affected by the novel's capacity for finish. Rather than providing what Benjamin calls "counsel," the wisdom derived from a storyteller's lived experience, the novelist strives instead to impart generalized truth: the representation of character, so crucial to the novel, is undertaken in the effort to provide an absolute statement about the "meaning of life" (373). And the meaning of life, as presented by the novel, Benjamin goes on to argue, is itself reduced to a single category: the teleological coherence retrospectively achieved when a human life ends, the answer death allows us to give to the eternal human question, what did this person live for? The novel presents characterological experience as so unified, so comprehensible, as to seem fated; the reader reads with only one question in mind: "How do the characters make him understand that death is already waiting for them – a very definite death at a very definite place?" (373). Novelistic characters are thus in this sense supremely finalized, made whole by their end. In representing the meaning of life as fully culminated, novels present themselves to readers as consumable objects: once the fate of a character is revealed, there is nothing more to read for. Narratives that care only for the consummation of life function themselves as consumable commodities: in the same way that a character's life is used up by his death, so too does the reader's "consuming" interest end when the novel's suspense is over, when the character's fate is achieved. There is no reason to reread a particular novel; instead the reader picks up another, with the "hope of warming his shivering life with a death he reads about" (373). Novel reading thus fulfills a psychic compulsion: it confirms over and over again the reader's need to believe that his own death will bestow upon his life a similar coherence and meaning, presumably because capitalism offers no other way to make him feel that life as he lives it is valuable or useful.

As his citations indicate, Benjamin derives some of his most important ideas about the novel's form from a pre- (or, some critics would say, a proto-) Marxist work by Lukács, *The Theory of the Novel* (first published in 1920). In this influential study, Lukács evocatively describes the novel as "the epic of a world that has been abandoned by God," claiming that "the novel form is, like no other, an expression of... transcendental homelessness." [5] *The Theory of the Novel* shares with "The Storyteller" the view that the novel as a genre is distinguished by its excessive formal totality. Lukács is fully aware that the understanding of the novel as too finished, as being a closed form, runs against the common grain of opinion; but he believes critics who accuse the novel of being unruly, of needing the aesthetic discipline of formal composition, are simply missing the social meaning of generic forms. He protests that the novel "has been described as only half an art by many who equate *having a problematic* with *being problematic*." [6] Lukács' significant form is not a matter just of narrative technique or logical unity. The total aesthetic form of any genre represents the conception of social life made possible at a given moment in history. Aesthetic form is neither ornament, envelope, nor arbitrary signifier; generic forms are a social product, part of a particular society's attempt to negotiate the relation of individual experience to what Lukács in *The Theory of the Novel* calls "empirical life." [7]

We thus see Lukács conceptualizing the ideological value of cultural forms in a dynamic and complex way, even in this early work. A form such as the novel expresses social life as the individual understands it, through the objective possibilities for understanding allowed by his or her historical moment. Thanks to the security of his "perspective," Lukács believes that his own critical study of the novel can distinguish between these two ideological functions, the novel's objective representation of things as they are and its equally objective representation of things as the individual author understands them to be. On Lukács' view, the novel as a bourgeois genre reflects the capitalistic sources of modern alienation through its valorization of individual agency. The novel is defined as a genre by its attempt to make its meaning wholly at home, wholly immanent; and, according to Lukács, it accomplishes this goal most typically by deriving its own immanent meaning from the career of an individual life: "The inner form of the novel has been understood as the process of the problematic individual's journeying towards himself." [8] The achievement of the individual's self-recognition thus makes meaning seem wholly a product of individual insight, which in turn serves the novel's bourgeois attempt to compass the world through its formal totalization of it: "The novel comprises the essence of its totality between the beginning and the end, and thereby raises an individual to the infinite heights of one who must create an entire world through his experience and who must maintain that world in equilibrium – heights which no epic individual, not even Dante's, could reach, because the epic individual owed his significance to the grace accorded him, not to his pure individuality."[9]

Over the course of his career, as he fits his thinking about the novel into a more self-consciously Marxist framework, Lukács becomes increasingly interested in the complexies of ideological form, specifically in the possibilities for political resistance and reform that might be available through the novel "as a problematic." The novel's generic will to totality, its inadequate attempt to reenvision modern alienation as individual liberation, is modified in Lukács' later thinking by the deeper social vision of great realists. These gifted artists do not succumb to the novel's bourgeois penchant for valorizing the individual qua individual. They instead modify generic convention by portraying the individual as inherently a social being; and they do this through the representation of characters as "types" (*Studies*, 384). When truly conceived as a social type, novelistic characters are, according to Lukács, not only rebalanced through the "inner dialectic of their social and individual existence" (387), but are thereby understandable as truly independent and autonomous beings, freed through this objective social identity from even their creator's subjectivity. The force of Lukács' work on Balzac is to show how a gifted realist can represent things as they are in his society, the objective social conditions of his society, by adapting a literary genre like the novel so that it no longer functions as an instrument of bourgeois power – even if the full social reality depicted through his generic modifications exceeds his own self-conscious understanding of his authorial intention.

Lukács' important contribution to Marxist literary study is precisely the notion that to be effective literary realism need not, in fact should not, be propagandist. As he develops his ideas over the course of his career, his theory of the novel allows for a complex and even a contradictory relation between an author's consciously held political beliefs and the social vision expressed by his art work. For Lukács great art works are not politically didactic; on the contrary, they result from the failure of an author's conscious control, from the deep split within the author between his consciously held political beliefs and his unconscious awareness of the broader, politicized social context from which those beliefs have emerged. In Lukács' famous example, the radical Zola has better politics, but the royalist Balzac is the better literary realist. According to Lukács, Balzac's novels gain their breadth of vision first of all because he is conflicted: because his psyche is in contradiction it can structurally mirror the contradictions that for Marxists define social life. But the content of the psyche also matters for Lukács: Balzac is the better literary realist because the contradictions that structure his psyche match the defining social contradictions of the period. On the one hand, Balzac's royalist political views made him an opponent of capitalism, giving him the vision to see "the torments which the transition to the capitalist system of production inflicted on every section of the people" (*Studies*, 388). But "At the same time Balzac was also deeply aware of the fact that this transformation was not only socially inevitable, but at the same time progressive" (388). Thus the conflict between Balzac's consciously held political views and the "real depth" of his "*Weltanschauung*" (388) produces for Lukács a realistic vision of social life that ultimately speaks the Marxist truth about modern social reality: "Balzac's profound comprehension of the contradictorily progressive character of capitalist development" (388). According to Lukács, Balzac understands that "progress" as defined by capitalism is "contradictory" in the sense that it is a false value, that in fact human welfare has declined and not progressed; and Lukács also believes that Balzac further understands that despite the overwhelming negativity of life under capitalism, the class divisions it engenders establish the positive social conditions for a new world order.

Balzac's "profound comprehension" is thus made legible, in Lukács' theory, not through the political views he might express as a citizen, but through the art work he creates. It is the power of the novel as an ideological form that it can provide a deep and extensive vision of the dialectical totality of social life that is by definition unavailable to authorial self-consciousness. Lukács explicitly says that the author's "conscious opinions" (*Studies*, 390) – about art or politics – are never for the Marxist critic the authoritative source of evaluation but rather are only a component in the dialectical relation of literature and society. In his blueprint for Marxist literary criticism, Lukács lays out the steps of objective analysis: the critic must first establish the "real social foundations" that produced "the human and the literary personality of [the] author"; he will then be able to ascertain "the real spiritual and intellectual content" of the art work; and at that point will be able to analyze accurately how "the writer build[s] up his aesthetic forms in the struggle for the adequate expression of such contents" (*Studies*, 390).

The commitment to the study of social contexts is, of course, the pride of the Marxist literary method; but it is important to remember how much this social theory is also a theory of literary form – and how much Lukács' conceptualization of form as function resonates with other formalist theories included in this volume, even though the underlying philosophies of these theories would be unacceptable to Lukács. For example, Lukács' belief that the meaning of a novel lies in the form of the novel echoes Víktor Shklovsky's claim that "awareness of form constitutes the subject matter of the novel" ("*Tristram Shandy*," 37). But the explicit aim of Shklovsky's theory is to formulate the relation between story and plot as strictly aesthetic, established only by the laws of art, and having no reference beyond the work of art (see Part I). By contrast, for Lukács the study of novelistic story as ideological form redefines, and thereby revalidates, the "realism" that Shklovsky works so hard to dispel: as Lukács says in "The Ideology of Modernism" (1958), style "ceases to be a formalistic category. Rather it is rooted in content; it is the specific form of a specific content" (396). The variety and specificity of literary forms in a given period is, for the Marxist, an objective expression of the dynamic operation of ideology. And the way that ideology works in society (and therefore in literature) is to express interested views (for example, class values) as if they were facts of life. Thus form, in life and in art, is always for the Marxist critic, never neutral but part of the dynamic operation of ideology: to the degree that form seems neutral, that it seems a carrier of meaning rather than a creator of social meaning, it functions as a significant cultural form, successfully passing off its vested interests as universal truth.

Lukács' belief that works of art are the privileged expression of profound authorial "comprehension" might lead us in a very different way to compare the concept of ideological form to Wayne Booth's notion of the rhetoric of fiction, discussed in Part II of this volume. Wayne Booth's contention, for example, that the reader of a particular novel should be concerned with "the chief value to which *this* implied author is committed, regardless of what party his creator belongs to in real life, is that which is expressed by the total form" of his fiction (*Rhetoric*, 161) sounds similar to Lukács' belief that Balzac's explicit political views are secondary to the "picture conveyed by the work" (*Studies*, 387). But we can see the crucial difference between Lukács and Booth in Booth's insistence that we bracket the real-life author – and all social forces – and substitute "implied" subjectivities derived only from the ethical implications of the novelist's formal choices. For Booth, the art work is the only "evidence for the only kind of sincerity that concerns us" (*Rhetoric*, 162); but for Lukács, Balzac's political views remain a crucial component in the novel's dialectical representation of the contradictory forces that structure society. To attribute the complexity of this social vision to an "author," implied or real, would be for Lukács to reinstate the modernist mistake of privileging the individual subject, of confusing the objective totality of the Real with the formal unity of a particular art work; or, on the other hand, of mistaking the hierarchical and dialectical value produced by a social collectivity with the "mirage" unity of a single author's morality. For Lukács, Balzac's stated political views are not to be bracketed or in any other way discounted: they are a vital component in the dialectical social vision that makes great novels comprehensive ideological forms.

Lukács' belief in the capacity of ideological form to express objective social value through the dialectical interplay of conscious and unconscious beliefs is at the heart of Fredric Jameson's work. Jameson's engagement with Lukács is a career-long preoccupation, beginning with *Marxism and Form* (1971). *The Political Unconscious: Narrative as a Socially Symbolic Act* (1981) is arguably Jameson's attempt to sophisticate Lukács' notion of ideological form through a post-structuralist understanding of texuality. Jameson agrees with thinkers such as Roland Barthes, who believe that there are no objects of interpretation and no "works" of art, but only cultural "texts"; Jameson would further agree with Barbara Johnson's opinion, expressed in "Metaphor, Metonymy, and Voice in *Their Eyes Were Watching God*" (see pp. 257–70), that cultural texts are always already politically motivated, their reading and reception made possible by practices that may present themselves as hermeneutic but are in fact value-laden and socially strategic. Interpretation is, for Jameson as it is for Johnson, inseparable from the deployment of social power, the "rewriting [of] a given text in terms of a particular interpretative master code" to serve political interests.[10] For Jameson as for Johnson, "narrative" is the term that best describes the ideological production of meaning. The dynamism, multi-leveledness, self-division, and temporality of narrative are meant to contrast with the rationalist definition of knowledge as logical thought, the belief that truth is uncovered through philosophical contemplation or scientific experimentation. For Johnson and Jameson, the storytelling dimension to narrative, the story content, underscores the urgent political connection between representation and re-presentation; in fact for Jameson literary works qualify as socially symbolic acts of interpretation to the degree that they attempt to transform the world they ostensibly depict.

In the ambitious and densely argued first chapter of *The Political Unconscious*, Jameson marshals wide-ranging intellectual sources for his theory of the socially symbolic text, drawing especially upon the contribution of Louis Althusser, whom he credits generally for bringing deconstructive insights to bear on Marxist theory. Althusser's critique of the conventional Marxist distinction between base and superstructure, the modes of production (material causes) and the "ideal" effects they produce, rightly rids Marxism, so Jameson believes, of its tendency to naively equate objective value with physical objects.

Althusser infinitely complicates the conventional Marxist distinction between base and superstructure by theorizing how superstructural elements can themselves serve as objective determinants of social value. This is a controversial innovation in Marxist thought, since it threatens what had traditionally been the stable, material ground of Marxist objectivism: if the objective forces of production no longer enjoy the clear ontological distinction of their own materiality, if the forces of production are themselves texts indistinguishable from other texts, then how does the post-structuralist preserve his belief in the stability of Marxist perspective? Jameson's implicit goal in *The Political Unconscious* is to answer this question. He agrees with Johnson that all interpretation is textual, narrativized through the operation of social power, but he resists the deconstructive conclusion that the textualization of meaning leads to the endless play of signification. Narrative for Jameson is, to use Johnson's figure, "an endless fishing expedition"; but Jameson would disagree about what it means that "the big one...always gets away" ("Metaphor," 270). For Jameson, the "big one," the referent that grounds textualization, is History, what he unabashedly calls the Real. The Real is, Jameson asserts, not the reinstatement of a transcendental signified, but the reconceptualization of the transcendental signified as an "absent cause." As absent cause, History is the referent, the Real, that always gets away but nonetheless makes itself clearly felt, the "absolute horizon" that may be expressed, again to use Johnson's figure, as both "net and fish" but, which, for Jameson though not for Johnson, retains an objective integrity and a meaning independent and generative of any specific textual manifestation.

In Jameson's words, "history is *not* a text, not a narrative, master or otherwise, but that, as an absent cause, it is inaccessible to us except in textual form, and that our approach to it and to the Real itself necessarily passes through its prior textualization."[11] What is the nature of the Real that we might glimpse in our "approaches" to it? The "experience of Necessity," what "refuses desire and sets inexorable limits to individual as well as collective praxis." In one of Jameson's most famous formulations, "History is what hurts."[12] History is thus a ground for meaning that has experiential content (psychic pain) but makes no claim to transcendental signification – and thus cannot be easily deconstructed as a master code whose meaning is relativizable by an alternative master code with an alternative value system.

As the title of his book emphasizes, Jameson thus offers a Marxist theory of history that is indebted to the psychoanalytic understanding of the unconscious. As we saw in Part IV, in late essays such as "The Unconscious" (1915), Freud presents the unconscious as the source of meaning for human life, a source that is forever outside of conscious knowledge but whose presence is registerable through its effects upon consciousness. But although it might seem as if Jameson is proposing a theory of a cultural unconscious based on an analogy to Freud's model of the human psyche, Jameson has in fact significantly revised Freud, and psychoanalytic theory generally, by redefining the absent cause of human life as history rather than the unconscious. In Jameson's Marxist model, the political unconscious is a secondary function, an effect of history. The political unconscious is the textualization of history created through the collective social management of Necessity. It is the cultural "narrativization" of the Real which is the outcome of the social conflict between Necessity (things as they are) and desire (things as social beings wish they could be).[13] The psychic limits of Necessity are experienced in literary representation as narrative conventions: the signifiers that a culture does not choose, that are the necessary constraints upon ideological expression, their "*semantic* conditions of possibility."[14]

In revising Freud, Jameson makes the political unconscious a property of things rather than human minds: in his words, he modifies psychoanalysis "by relocating" the unconscious "within the [cultural] object." The political unconscious is produced in the attempt to "control or master"[15] the experience of social contradiction through narrative and thus is expressed most fully in narratives. Following both Benjamin and Lukács, Jameson views life under capitalism as a dark night for humanity, an era steeped in social contradiction: "Unfortunately, no society has ever been quite so mystified in quite so many ways as our own, saturated as it is with messages and information, the very vehicles of mystification...If everything were transparent, then no ideology would be possible, and no domination either: evidently that is not our case."[16] The job of the Marxist critic is to restore, to some degree, transparency (or perspective) by identifying "strong" ideological performances and articulating the dialectical complexity of their social vision.

But this job is arguably harder for Jameson than for Lukács because of the transformative power Jameson ascribes to the political unconscious: how can determinant social contradictions be represented in a text if the ideological work of these cultural texts is to overwrite the Real? How can the signifiers that a culture does not choose be distinguished from those that it deploys to achieve narrative mastery? The political unconscious, after all, performs, in Jameson's words, a "prestidigitation of narrative" that, unlike the compositional illusions accomplished by Henry James, does not attempt to impose false limits to experience but to overthrow the real limits that experience sets on desire.[17] In the attempt to overthrow the Real, the political unconscious produces socially symbolic texts that offer a compensatory "resolution" of deep social conflict through the creation of formally controlled narratives.

Significantly, Jameson solves this problem by reproducing the very move he criticizes naive Marxists for making: he gives objective value the quality of physicality. Jameson distinguishes himself from the naive Marxist in this regard only by the complexity he ascribes to materialized value. Whereas for Lukács the relation between literary form and content functioned as a dynamic expression of ideology, Jameson imagines gradations of materialized value *within* the cultural object. As Jameson conceives it, the political unconscious is an agent of hierarchical, semantic layering within the art work itself. The full meaning of narrative, its comprehensive social meaning, derives from the interplay of surface and depth within the cultural object – the attempt of a particular narrative to master its anxiety through the repression of the Real and the substitution of a compensatory "realism." But by the laws of the political unconscious, no prestidigitation, no matter how adept, can fully veil the Real; even the smoothest narrative surface will inevitably suffer lapses in coherence. Like Freudian slips, these lapses in logic are the analyst's key to what he cannot see, his proof that another layer of meaning lies below the one fully visible to him. Jameson finds in the "aporia" of surface narrative logic the "diagnostic revelation of terms or nodal points implicit in the ideological system which have, however, remained unrealized in the surface of the text, which have failed to become manifest in the logic of the narrative, and which we can therefore read as what the texts represses." The full socially symbolic meaning of a given narrative emerges through the "rifts and discontinuities within the work"; in Althusser's words, the cultural text is produced "as an *interference* between levels, as a subversion of one level by another." By enacting this clash of levels, the literary work "articulates its own situation and textualizes it, thereby encouraging and perpetuating the illusion that the situation itself did not exist before it, that there is nothing but a text, that there never was any extra- or con-textual reality before the text itself generated it in the form of a mirage."[18] Thus, like Benjamin's storyteller who passes on his own subjectivity in the handprints of crafted narrative, the Real is drawn by the socially symbolic narrative into its very "texture," and this attempt to "carry the Real within itself as its own intrinsic or immanent subtext" leads to the interiorization within the text of the objective basis for ideological hierarchy.

The political unconscious's creation of semantic stratification allows Jameson to read socially symbolic literary works as if they were geological formations: he finds he can distinguish conscious meaning from repressed meaning, surface logic from deep logic, compensatory ideological narratives from necessary expressions of the Real. He extends this logic to define generic identity itself, theorizing it as an internal property of the cultural object. Genre is legible as the "formal persistence of... archaic structures of alienation – and the sign systems specific to them – beneath the overlay of all the more recent and historically original types of alienation – such as political domination and commodity reification."[19]

Rather than recognizing how this theory of materialized meaning links him with the naive Marxists he criticizes, Jameson instead credits the field of narrative theory – especially the thinking of Vladímir Propp, Northrop Frye, and A. J. Greimas – for enabling him to conceptualize socially symbolic texts in terms of semantic "sedimenta-tion."[20] What especially interests Jameson about this body of work is its willingness to read narrative as a code: to establish a significant and uncollapsible relation between the ostensible content of a narrative and the hidden meaning embedded in its symbolic form or syntactical structures. As we can see in his interpretation of Balzac, he finds particularly useful Greimas's concept of narrative "antinomies," the notion that a text's underlying structure is identifiable through a set of logical contradictions that emerge as we attempt to read a narrative as a coherent hermeneutical statement. As Jameson puts this idea, the surface level of narrative significance is constructed as the "reading mind" (426) attempts to work out the authorial values expressed through the "antinomies," the irresolvable contradictions, in the text's representational logic. According to Jameson, that logical double bind "maps the limits of a specific ideological consciousness and marks the conceptual points beyond which that consciousness cannot go, and between which it is condemned to oscillate."[21] In the case of *La Vieille Fille*, Balzac attempts to "manage" the "irrevocable brute facts of empirical history" by re-presenting them in a way that will "empty" them of "their finality" (425). Drawing on Tzvetan Todorov's analogy of narrative structure to sentence structure (discussed in Part III), Jameson argues that Balzac's novel attempts to recast the operation of history into a conditional mode. Balzac thereby attempts to repress what he finds to be an unacceptable insight: the good reasons for the "palpable... failures" of the royalist regime (426). Motivated by wish-fulfillment, the desire for satisfaction that recoils from ideological necessity, the novel's political unconscious produces a "solution" to the logical double bind that plagues its surface narrative logic: Jameson reads the Count de Troisville as the text's representation of a Utopian ideal, the hope that it might still be possible for humanity to live "a history in which some genuine Restoration would still be possible, provided the aristocracy could learn this particular object-lesson, namely that it needs a strong man who combines aristocratic values with Napoleonic energy" (428).

Balzac's symbolic representation of individuals as complex social agents is what makes this author, for Jameson as well as Lukács, a great realist – however complicated Jameson has made Lukács' notion of the social type by expanding it to include the representation of unconscious processes like political wish-fulfillment (see 424). But for Jameson – as for Lukács – Balzac's accomplishment derives not from anything like authorial genius but from the good luck of historical positioning: Balzac's successful representation of novelistic characters as socially symbolic results from his significant experience of a cataclysmic social transition, his participation in the world-historical end of one social formation and the beginning of another. For Jameson – as for Lukács – the unique reification of society under capitalism makes novels like Balzac's virtually impossible to write: capitalism denies literary forms any authentic ideological dialectic. For all the Marxist theorists in this section, there is little to admire about late nineteenth- and twentieth-century literature. The Marxist tradition's shared sense of modern literature as a diminished thing has prompted some to declare that Marxist theory yearns to bring literature back to the future: to return the novel, if not to Benjamin's guilded age of storytelling, then at least to the early nineteenth-century's era of social transition.

In the "Ideology of Modernism" Lukács can find only one modern novelist, Thomas Mann, whose social vision resists the reification of everyday life produced by capitalism's debilitating fragmentation of the social totality and its concomitant over-valuation of individual, subjective experience. Faulkner, Joyce, Kafka, Musil – the ostentatious stylistic differences that seem to distinguish these novelists in fact bespeak what is for Lukács their overwhelming ideological unity: the loss of modern society's objective "perspective" (404) is registered in these writers' shared belief that "Man...is by nature solitary [and] asocial" (397). Whatever ideological complexity the modern novel might have lies in what Lukács calls a misguided "protest": the attempt to counter the alienation of modern social conditions through the romanticization of psychopathology. But since these novels present psychopathy and only psychopathy as the condition of modern life, to a Marxist way of thinking modern literature is thus complicit in the functioning of hegemonic ideology: it, too, renders "objective" social conditions "invisible." If these experimental novelists are not part of the solution they are part of the problem: "to present psychopathology as a way of escape from this distortion is itself a distortion" ("Ideology," 404).

Jameson's own account of late realists like Henry James and Theodore Dreiser interestingly adds to Lukács' critique of the twentieth-century novel by showing how an earlier and different kind of novelistic realism establishes the preconditions for high modernist psychopathy. According to Jameson, the novel is consolidated as a tool of capitalist hegemony precisely at the time novelists themselves begin to exercise more self-conscious aesthetic control over their fiction-writing. The production of the novel as a high art form, a form governed by principles of composition (like those articulated in Lubbock's *The Craft of Fiction*) is for Jameson the beginning of the novel's commodification, the death knell for its expressive possibilities as a socially symbolic form. A novel such as *Sister Carrie* (1900) does not mount a failed protest against capitalism but actively deploys formal devices like point of view to foster the goals of capitalism: on Jameson's view, "the newly centered subject of the age of reification" is expressed fully in this novel as a "point of view," a "closed monad, henceforth governed by the laws of 'psychology'" (*Unconscious*, 422). The understanding of psychology as a discrete mental universe is, of course, precisely what Jameson's theory of the political unconscious has been devised to critique. For Jameson, the novelistic construction of subjectivity as point of view is not just a reflection of the Freudian theory being worked out at the same historical moment; psychology as a discrete discipline and point of view as a novelistic technique are both powerful instruments of capitalist ideology. For Jameson, the modern psychological novel helps train the unruly power of wish-fulfillment into structured paths of desire, particularly through the reader's emotional "identification" with novelistic characters who think of themselves as wholly independent, free to choose their course of action and thus personally responsible for their life decisions. Whereas in Balzac the stratified layers of the political unconscious embody rich social contradictions, in Dreiser cultural wish-fulfillment becomes fully equal to, and no more complicated than, the reader's sympathetic investment in Carrie's desire for a nice, new jacket: "the Utopian impulse...now reified, is driven back inside the monad, where it assumes the status of some merely psychologized experience, private feeling, or relativized value" (*Unconscious*, 423).

The development of novelistic realism is, then, for all the Marxist theorists in this section, the fate of the Real under capitalism. Balzac's comprehensive social vision is simply unavailable to the modern novelist. From the *Communist Manifesto* forward, the Marxist story of the rise of capitalism retains an apocalyptic urgency. In Lukács' conclusion to the "Ideology of Modernism," he laments: "We see that modernism leads not only to the destruction of traditional literary forms; it leads to the destruction of literature as such" (412). This same regret over lost literary forms prompts Jameson to declare that the novel is the last genre, the genre that helps produce the "the end of genre." By this Jameson means that the novel is the last genre to offer a sedimentary expression of the deep contradictions that define society (417). As the novel develops, its formal refusal of history, its capacity for irony, quotation, and other destabilizing representational practices, becomes its dominant mode of expression – changing once and for all, according to Jameson, the relation of contemporary expression to inherited literary forms. Before the modern novel, genres came into being through a socially dialectical process: in response to social change, cultures would struggle to project new social meaning onto inherited forms, creating, according to Jameson, a "coexistence or tension" within genres "between several generic modes or strands."[22] These are distinguishable, as we have discussed, by the special legibility he grants to the semantic layering of narrative texts, in this case their ability to represent the present in active relation to the historical past, to bring the past forward as "objectified survivals," as "formal processes" which should be understood as "sedimented content in their own right, as carrying ideological messages of their own, distinct from the ostensible or manifest content of the works."[23] The modern novel's debased distinctiveness lies in its ability to eliminate or erase these historical legacies, converting social convention and cultural inheritance into "the raw material on which the novel works" (417) in its social production of a new world, defined as a wholly modern world. The realist novel thereby accomplishes for Jameson its "objective" function of

> producing as though for the first time that very life world, that very "referent" – the newly quantifiable space of extension and market equivalence, the new rhythms of measurable

time, the new secular and "disenchanted" object world of the commodity system, with its...bewilderingly empirical "meaninglessness," and contingent *Umwelt* – of which this new narrative discourse will then claim to be the "realistic" reflection. (152)

For Jameson the loss of genre thus means the loss of what we might call the good expressive materiality of socially symbolic formations (his equivalent to Benjamin's handcrafted object) and the inauguration of the bad materiality of modern cultural forms like the novel. Rather than serving as a vehicle of historical transmission, rather than conveying the full stratification of social meaning in relation to past social meaning, the form of the modern novel is, as Jameson theorizes it, one of the social structures that produces reification. We can see Jameson's abiding tendency to equate materiality with interpretative legibility when he argues that the narrative techniques of the modern novel (such as point of view) should themselves be regarded as a "textual determinant" of ideology. "Textual determinant" is a term Jameson invents to theorize a halfway house between material causes and their ideological effects. Certain techniques of the modern novel are such powerful instruments of ideology that they should be regarded, in Jameson's words, as a "quasi-material transmission point" in the production and institutionalization of modern psychologism (419). Good or bad, the capacity for interpretative legibility is what, in Jameson's theory, distinguishes literary texts as narrative performances. On his view, authentic literary genres memorialize ideological meaning as well as its objective social sources by locating these values all in one place, in one cultural object; the special materializing power of the cultural object then makes these layers of meaning distinct and visible (at least to the Marxist critic). Inauthentic cultural objects, such as the modern novel, do not display the complexity of social value but instead serve themselves as material causes of ideological effects. In either case, it is the ability of the narrative text to objectify value, to stabilize and make legible the social sources of ideology and their ideological effects, that privileges it as a cultural production.

Thus, although history may be the putative source of stable meaning in Jameson's theory, the unknowability of this ultimate referent for human experience is offset by all the Marxist critic can know about ideology, thanks to the interpretative legibility provided by textual materiality. Jameson is thereby able to prevent the deconstructive collapse into textual relativity not only because he believes in the grounding power of the Real, but because in his theory, even in the modern era, all texts are not the same: some are in fact more material than others – and so the objective ground for ideology remains legible, even when this ground is found within so mystified an ideological product as the modern novel itself.

To the degree that the modern novel can serve as a material basis for ideology, it can also, importantly, take on another function for Jameson, one that is central to his full political vision: it can be an agent of positive social change, aiding ultimately in the abolition of capitalism. Jameson believes that Lukács discounts "the Utopian vocation" of even debased cultural forms like the novel. If reification works by re-presenting the "isolated broken bits and pieces of older unities" as autonomous and independent wholes, it also preserves, Jameson believes, these lost communal values within those bits and pieces – and thus, one might be tempted to say, they function as fragments shored against humanity's ruin. On Jameson's view, these modern fragments, in their new form as reified wholes, can produce in their consumers a complex psychological effect that can have positive political consequences: they can "restore at least a symbolic experience of libidinal gratification to a world drained of it" and thus keep alive, even through the very vehicles of mystification, a trace of the complete human personality that will be restored with the demise of capitalism.[25]

In the conclusion to *The Political Unconscious*, Jameson worries that his own position might be too extreme, that he might rightly be accused of overestimating the utopian potential of novelistic reification. Yes, by writing *The Political Unconscious* he has furthered the Marxist project of exposing "the dark underside of even the most seemingly innocent and 'life-enhancing' masterpieces of the canon" (430); but as a result he may have attenuated the vital project of social critique by countering these dark realities with "a recovery of the Utopian impulses at work" even in instruments of capitalism like the novel. Benjamin and Lukács are, of course, writing in the wake of world conflicts, which for each made the notion of cultural survival, let alone progress, difficult to believe, even with the help of Marxist doctrine. Lukács declares in his introduction to *The Theory of the Novel* that the work was motivated by the outbreak of the First World War and "written in a mood of permanent despair over the state of the world."[26] Benjamin opens "The Storyteller" by voicing his sense of a world wholly and forever changed: "Every glance at a newspaper demonstrates that it has reached a new low, that our picture, not only of the external world but of the moral world as well, overnight has undergone changes which were never thought possible. With the [First] World War a process began to become apparent which has not halted since then" (362). For Jameson, writing in the US at the end of the twentieth century, those unthinkable changes can now be thought through as chapters in a unified narrative of historical progress. "Storytelling" is, for Jameson, not a lost rhetorical practice but an objective condition of human thought, "the supreme function of the human mind";[26] and, as we have seen, this objective condition of human thought holds for Jameson an objective meaning – one that is derived from the Marxist masterplot. In Jameson's words, the human condition is the "single great collective story…in however disguised and symbolic a form…sharing a single fundamental theme" (415). And so Jameson's conscious practice of his Marxist utopian vocation allows him to narrativize the absent cause that is History as the politically conscious narrative that Marxism tells about history. To see cultures past and present as "vital episodes in a single vast unfinished plot" (415) is also, for Jameson, to project a happy ending to this story. To the degree that his utopian belief can itself be viewed as a product of objective forces determining his own cultural moment, Jameson can feel that his literary theoretical work is itself effective political action, that it works toward the demise of capitalist ideology by exposing its covert operation in and through literary works – and thus hastens the day when collective human endeavor will successfully "wrest a realm of Freedom from a realm of Necessity" (415).

NOTES

1   Henry James, "The Art of Fiction" (1888), in *The Future of the Novel: Essays on the Art of Fiction*, ed. Leon Edel (New York: Vintage, 1956) 12.
2   James, *Roderick Hudson* Preface, in *The Art of the Novel: Critical Prefaces*, ed. R.P. Blackmur (New York: Scribners, 1934) 5.

3 James, *What Maisie Knew* Preface, *The Art of the Novel: Critical Prefaces*, 120.
4 See M. M. Bakhtin, "The Problem of Speech Genres," in *Speech Genres and Other Essays*, trans. Vern W. McGee, ed. Caryl Emerson and Michael Holquist (Austin: University of Texas Press, 1986) esp. 77–90 for an alternative social account of the unfinalizability of meaning. The term "unfinalizability" is Bakhtin's.
5 György Lukács, *The Theory of the Novel*, trans. Anna Bostock (1920; Cambridge, MA: MIT Press, 1971) 88, 41.
6 Ibid. 73.
7 Ibid. 71.
8 Ibid. 80.
9 Ibid. 83.
10 Fredric Jameson, *The Political Unconscious: Narrative as a Socially Symbolic Act* (Ithaca, NY: Cornell University Press, 1981) 10.
11 Ibid. 35.
12 Ibid. 102.
13 Ibid.
14 Ibid. 57.
15 Ibid. 34, 49.
16 Ibid. 60–1.
17 Ibid. 82.
18 Ibid. 48, 56, 82.
19 Ibid. 100.
20 Ibid. 99.
21 Ibid. 47.
22 Ibid. 141.
23 Ibid. 99.
24 Ibid. 63.
25 Ibid. 12.
26 Ibid. 123.

FURTHER READING

Bennett, Tony. *Formalism and Marxism.* 1979. London: Routledge, 2003.
Bernstein, J. M. *The Philosophy of the Novel: Lukács, Marxism, and the Dialectics of Form.* Minneapolis: University of Minnesota Press, 1984.
Dowling, William C. *Jameson, Althusser, Marx: An Introduction to* The Political Unconscious. Ithaca, NY: Cornell University Press, 1984.
Eagleton, Terry. *Marxism and Literary Criticism.* 1976. New York: Routledge, 2002.
Eagleton, Terry, and Drew Milne, eds. *Marxist Literary Theory: A Reader.* Oxford: Blackwell, 1996.
Green, Leonard, ed. *Fredric Jameson's* The Political Unconscious. Special issue of *Diacritics* 12 (1982).
Jacobs, Carol. *In the Language of Walter Benjamin.* Baltimore, MD: Johns Hopkins University Press, 1999.
Jameson, Fredric. *Marxism and Form: Twentieth-Century Dialectical Theories of Literature.* Princeton, NJ: Princeton University Press, 1971.
Jay, Martin. "Experience Without a Subject: Walter Benjamin and the Novel." In *The Actuality of Walter Benjamin*, ed. Laura Marcus and Lynda Nead. London: Lawrence and Wishart, 1998, 194–211.
Vološhinov, V.N. *Marxism and the Philosophy of Language*, trans. Ladislav Matejka and I. R. Titunik. 1929. Cambridge, MA: Harvard University Press, 1986.

DOROTHY HALE

The Storyteller: Reflections on the Works of Nikolai Leskov

Walter Benjamin

Walter Benedix Schönflies Benjamin (1892–1940)

Born in Berlin, Walter Benjamin studied philosophy, German literature, and psychology at universities in Freiburg, Berlin, Munich, and Bern; he received his doctorate in 1919. After Hitler came to power in 1933, Benjamin fled Germany for Paris, where he wrote for the Frankfurt School's journal while working on his magnum opus, *Das Passagen-Werk* (unfinished, published 1983; translated as *The Arcades Project*, 1999). Benjamin died trying to escape from Nazi-occupied France. He received a United States visa shortly after the 1940 invasion of Paris, but did not have the documents he needed to claim it; when he failed in his subsequent attempt to escape through Spain, Benjamin took a lethal dose of morphine. The Franco-Spanish border reopened shortly after his death. Largely unknown during his lifetime, Benjamin began to gain recognition in 1955, after his friend Theodor W. Adorno edited and published the first collected edition of his work. Among Benjamin's best-known books are *Der Begriff der Kunstkritik in der deutschen Romantik* (his doctoral dissertation, published 1920; translated as "The Concept of Criticism in German Romanticism" in *Selected Writings*, volume 1, 1996) and *Versuche über Brecht* (1971; translated as *Understanding Brecht*, 1973). The first selection of essays in English, *Illuminations: Essays and Reflections*, edited by Hannah Arendt (1968), includes the essay reprinted here: "The Story-Teller: Reflections on the Works of Nicolai Leskov" was first published in *Orient und Okzident*, October 1936.

I

Familiar though his name may be to us, the storyteller in his living immediacy is by no means a present force. He has already become something remote from us and something that is getting even more distant. To present someone like Leskov as a storyteller does not mean bringing him closer to us but, rather, increasing our distance from him. Viewed from a certain distance, the great, simple outlines which define the storyteller stand out in him, or rather, they become visible in him, just as in a rock a human head or an animal's body may appear to an observer at the proper distance and angle of vision. This distance and this angle of vision are prescribed for us by an experience which we may have almost every day. It teaches us that the art of storytelling is coming to an end. Less and less frequently do we encounter people with the ability to tell a tale properly. More and more often there is embarrassment all around when the wish to hear a story is expressed. It is as if something that seemed inalienable to us, the securest among our possessions, were taken from us: the ability to exchange experiences.

One reason for this phenomenon is obvious: experience has fallen in value. And it looks as if it is continuing to fall into bottomlessness. Every glance at a newspaper demonstrates that it has reached a new low, that our picture, not only of the external world but of the moral world as well, overnight has undergone changes which were never thought possible. With the [First] World War a process began to become apparent which has not halted since then. Was it not noticeable at the end of the war that men returned from the battlefield grown silent – not richer, but poorer in communicable experience? What ten years later was poured out in the flood of war books was anything but experience that goes from mouth to mouth. And there was nothing remarkable about that. For never has experience been contradicted more thoroughly than strategic experience by tactical warfare, economic experience by inflation, bodily experience by mechanical warfare, moral experience by those in power. A generation that had gone to school on a horse-drawn streetcar now stood under the open sky in a countryside in which nothing remained unchanged but the clouds, and beneath these clouds, in a field of force of destructive torrents and explosions, was the tiny, fragile human body.

II

Experience which is passed on from mouth to mouth is the source from which all storytellers have drawn. And among those who have written down the tales, it is

WALTER BENJAMIN

the great ones whose written version differs least from the speech of the many nameless storytellers. Incidentally, among the last named there are two groups which, to be sure, overlap in many ways. And the figure of the storyteller gets its full corporeality only for the one who can picture them both. "When someone goes on a trip, he has something to tell about," goes the German saying, and people imagine the storyteller as someone who has come from afar. But they enjoy no less listening to the man who has stayed at home, making an honest living, and who knows the local tales and traditions. If one wants to picture these two groups through their archaic representatives, one is embodied in the resident tiller of the soil, and the other in the trading seaman. Indeed, each sphere of life has, as it were, produced its own tribe of storytellers. Each of these tribes preserves some of its characteristics centuries later. Thus, among nineteenth-century German storytellers, writers like Hebel and Gotthelf stem from the first tribe, writers like Sealsfield and Gerstäcker from the second. With these tribes, however, as stated above, it is only a matter of basic types. The actual extension of the realm of storytelling in its full historical breadth is inconceivable without the most intimate interpenetration of these two archaic types. Such an interpenetration was achieved particularly by the Middle Ages in their trade structure. The resident master craftsman and the traveling journeymen worked together in the same rooms; and every master had been a traveling journeyman before he settled down in his home town or somewhere else. If peasants and seamen were past masters of storytelling, the artisan class was its university. In it was combined the lore of faraway places, such as a much-traveled man brings home, with the lore of the past, as it best reveals itself to natives of a place.

III

Leskov was at home in distant places as well as distant times. He was a member of the Greek Orthodox Church, a man with genuine religious interests. But he was a no less sincere opponent of ecclesiastic bureaucracy. Since he was not able to get along any better with secular officialdom, the official positions he held were not of long duration. Of all his posts, the one he held for a long time as Russian representative of a big English firm was presumably the most useful one for his writing. For this firm he traveled through Russia, and these trips advanced his worldly wisdom as much as they did his knowledge of conditions in Russia. In this way he had an opportunity of becoming acquainted with the organization of the sects in the country. This left its mark on his works of fiction. In the Russian legends Leskov saw allies in his fight against Orthodox bureaucracy. There are a number of his legendary tales whose focus is a righteous man, seldom an ascetic, usually a simple, active man who becomes a saint apparently in the most natural way in the world. Mystical exaltation is not Leskov's forte. Even though he occasionally liked to indulge in the miraculous, even in piousness he prefers to stick with a sturdy nature. He sees the prototype in the man who finds his way about the world without getting too deeply involved with it.

He displayed a corresponding attitude in worldly matters. It is in keeping with this that be began to write late, at the age of twenty-nine. That was after his commercial travels. His first printed work was entitled "Why Are Books Expensive in Kiev?"

A number of other writings about the working class, alcoholism, police doctors, and unemployed salesmen are precursors of his works of fiction.

IV

An orientation toward practical interests is characteristic of many born storytellers. More pronouncedly than in Leskov this trait can be recognized, for example, in Gotthelf, who gave his peasants agricultural advice; it is found in Nodier, who concerned himself with the perils of gas light; and Hebel, who slipped bits of scientific instruction for his readers into his *Schatzkästlein*, is in this line as well. All this points to the nature of every real story. It contains, openly or covertly, something useful. The usefulness may, in one case, consist in a moral; in another, in some practical advice; in a third, in a proverb or maxim. In every case the storyteller is a man who has counsel for his readers. But if today "having counsel" is beginning to have an old-fashioned ring, this is because the communicability of experience is decreasing. In consequence we have no counsel either for ourselves or for others. After all, counsel is less an answer to a question than a proposal concerning the continuation of a story which is just unfolding. To seek this counsel one would first have to be able to tell the story. (Quite apart from the fact that a man is receptive to counsel only to the extent that he allows his situation to speak.) Counsel woven into the fabric of real life is wisdom. The art of storytelling is reaching its end because the epic side of truth, wisdom, is dying out. This, however, is a process that has been going on for a long time. And nothing would be more fatuous than to want to see in it merely a "symptom of decay," let alone a "modern" symptom. It is, rather, only a concomitant symptom of the secular productive forces of history, a concomitant that has quite gradually removed narrative from the realm of living speech and at the same time is making it possible to see a new beauty in what is vanishing.

V

The earliest symptom of a process whose end is the decline of storytelling is the rise of the novel at the beginning of modern times. What distinguishes the novel from the story (and from the epic in the narrower sense) is its essential dependence on the book. The dissemination of the novel became possible only with the invention of printing. What can be handed on orally, the wealth of the epic, is of a different kind from what constitutes the stock in trade of the novel. What differentiates the novel from all other forms of prose literature – the fairy tale, the legend, even the novella – is that it neither comes from oral tradition nor goes into it. This distinguishes it from storytelling in particular. The storyteller takes what he tells from experience – his own or that reported by others. And he in turn makes it the experience of those who are listening to his tale. The novelist has isolated himself. The birthplace of the novel is the solitary individual, who is no longer able to express himself by giving examples of his most important concerns, is himself uncounseled, and cannot counsel others. To write a novel means to carry the incommensurable to extremes in the representation of human life. In the midst of life's fullness, and through the representation of this fullness, the novel gives evidence of the profound perplexity of the living. Even the first great book of the genre, *Don Quixote*, teaches how the spiritual greatness, the boldness, the helpfulness of one of the noblest of men, Don Quixote, are completely devoid of counsel and do not contain the slightest scintilla of wisdom. If now and then, in the course of the centuries, efforts have been made – most effectively, perhaps, in *Wilhelm Meisters Wanderjahre* – to implant instruction in the novel, these attempts have always amounted to a modification of the novel form. The *Bildungsroman*, on the other hand, does not deviate in any way from the basic structure of the novel. By integrating the social process with the development of a person, it bestows the most frangible justification on the order determining it. The legitimacy it provides stands in direct opposition to reality. Particularly in the *Bildungsroman*, it is this inadequacy that is actualized.

VI

One must imagine the transformation of epic forms occurring in rhythms comparable to those of the change that has come over the earth's surface in the course of thousands of centuries. Hardly any other forms of human communication have taken shape more slowly, been lost more slowly. It took the novel, whose beginnings go back to antiquity, hundreds of years before it encountered in the evolving middle class those elements which were favorable to its flowering. With the appearance of these elements, storytelling began quite slowly to recede into the archaic; in many ways, it is true, it took hold of the new material, but it was not really determined by it. On the other hand, we recognize that with the full control of the middle class, which has the press as one of its most important instruments in fully developed capitalism, there emerges a form of communication which, no matter how far back its origin may lie, never before influenced the epic form in a decisive way. But now it does exert such an influence. And it turns out that it confronts storytelling as no less of a stranger than did the novel, but in a more menacing way, and that it also brings about a crisis in the novel. This new form of communication is information.

Villemessant, the founder of *Le Figaro*, characterized the nature of information in a famous formulation. "To my readers," he used to say, "an attic fire in the Latin Quarter is more important than a revolution in Madrid." This makes strikingly clear that it is no longer intelligence coming from afar, but the information which supplies a handle for what is nearest that gets the readiest hearing. The intelligence that came from afar – whether the spatial kind from foreign countries or the temporal kind of tradition – possessed an authority which gave it validity, even when it was not subject to verification. Information, however, lays claim to prompt verifiability. The prime requirement is that it appear "understandable in itself." Often it is no more exact than the intelligence of earlier centuries was. But while the latter was inclined to borrow from the miraculous, it is indispensable for information to sound plausible. Because of this it proves incompatible with the spirit of storytelling. If the art of storytelling has become rare, the dissemination of information has had a decisive share in this state of affairs.

Every morning brings us the news of the globe, and yet we are poor in noteworthy stories. This is because no event any longer comes to us without already being shot through with explanation. In other words, by now almost nothing that happens benefits storytelling; almost everything benefits information. Actually, it is half the art of storytelling to keep a story free from explanation as one reproduces it. Leskov is a master at this (compare pieces like "The Deception" and "The White Eagle"). The most extraordinary things, marvelous things, are related with the greatest accuracy, but the psychological connection of the events is not forced on the reader. It is left up to him to interpret things the way he understands them, and thus the narrative achieves an amplitude that information lacks.

VII

Leskov was grounded in the classics. The first storyteller of the Greeks was Herodotus. In the fourteenth chapter of the third book of his *Histories* there is a story from which much can be learned. It deals with Psammenitus.

When the Egyptian king Psammenitus had been beaten and captured by the Persian king Cambyses, Cambyses was bent on humbling his prisoner. He gave orders to place Psammenitus on the road along which the Persian triumphal procession was to pass. And he further arranged that the prisoner should see his daughter pass by as a maid going to the well with her pitcher. While all the Egyptians were lamenting and bewailing this spectacle, Psammenitus stood alone, mute and motionless, his eyes fixed on the ground; and when presently he saw his son, who was being taken along in the procession to be executed, he likewise remained unmoved. But when afterwards he recognized one of his servants, an old, impoverished man, in the ranks of the prisoners, he beat his fists against his head and gave all the signs of deepest mourning.

From this story it may be seen what the nature of true storytelling is. The value of information does not survive the moment in which it was new. It lives only at that moment; it has to surrender to it completely and explain itself to it without losing any time. A story is different. It does not expend itself. It preserves and concentrates its strength and is capable of releasing it even after a long time. Thus Montaigne referred to this Egyptian king and asked himself why he mourned only when he caught sight of his servant. Montaigne answers: "Since he was already overfull of grief, it took only the smallest increase for it to burst through its dams." Thus Montaigne. But one could also say: The king is not moved by the fate of those of royal blood, for it is his own fate. Or: We are moved by much on the stage that does not move us in real life; to the king, this servant is only an actor. Or: Great grief is pent up and breaks forth only with relaxation. Seeing this servant was the relaxation. Herodotus offers no explanations. His report is the driest. That is why this story from ancient Egypt is still capable after thousands of years of arousing astonishment and thoughtfulness. It resembles the seeds of grain which have lain for centuries in the chambers of the pyramids shut up air-tight and have retained their germinative power to this day.

VIII

There is nothing that commends a story to memory more effectively than that chaste compactness which precludes psychological analysis. And the more natural the process by which the storyteller forgoes psychological shading, the greater becomes the story's claim to a place in the memory of the listener, the more completely is it integrated into his own experience, the greater will be his inclination to repeat it to someone else someday, sooner or later. This process of assimilation, which takes place in depth, requires a state of relaxation which is becoming rarer and rarer. If sleep is the apogee of physical relaxation, boredom is the apogee of mental relaxation. Boredom is the dream bird that hatches the egg of experience. A rustling in the leaves drives him away. His nesting places – the activities that are intimately associated with boredom – are already extinct in the cities and are declining in the country as well. With this the gift for listening is lost and the community of listeners disappears. For storytelling is always the art of repeating stories, and this art is lost when the stories are no longer retained. It is lost because there is no more weaving and spinning to go on while they are being listened to. The more self-forgetful the listener is, the more deeply is what he listens to impressed upon his memory. When the rhythm of work has seized him, he listens to the tales in such a way that the gift of retelling them comes to him all by itself. This, then, is the nature of the web in which the gift of storytelling is cradled. This is how today it is becoming unraveled at all its ends after being woven thousands of years ago in the ambience of the oldest forms of craftsmanship.

IX

The storytelling that thrives for a long time in the milieu of work – the rural, the maritime, and the urban – is itself an artisan form of communication, as it were. It does not aim to convey the pure essence of the thing, like information or a report. It sinks the thing into the life of the storyteller, in order to bring it out of him again. Thus traces of the storyteller cling to the story the way the handprints of the potter cling to the clay vessel. Storytellers tend to begin their story with a presentation of the circumstances in which they themselves have learned what is to follow, unless they simply pass it off as their own experience. Leskov begins his "Deception" with the description of a train trip on which he supposedly heard from a fellow passenger the events which he then goes on to relate; or he thinks of Dostoevsky's funeral, where he sets his acquaintance with the heroine of his story "À Propos of the Kreutzer Sonata"; or he evokes a gathering of a reading circle in which we are told the events that he reproduces for us in his "Interesting Men." Thus his tracks are frequently evident in his narratives, if not as those of the one who experienced it, then as those of the one who reports it.

This craftsmanship, storytelling, was actually regarded as a craft by Leskov himself. "Writing," he says in one of his letters, "is to me no liberal art, but a craft." It cannot come as a surprise that he felt bonds with craftsmanship, but faced industrial technology as a stranger. Tolstoy, who must have understood this, occasionally touches this nerve of Leskov's storytelling talent when he calls him the first man "who pointed out the inadequacy of economic progress.... It is strange that Dostoevsky is so widely read.... But I simply cannot comprehend why Leskov is not read. He is a truthful writer." In his artful and high-spirited story "The Steel Flea," which is midway between legend and farce, Leskov glorifies native craftsmanship through the silversmiths of Tula. Their masterpiece, the steel flea, is seen by Peter the Great and convinces him that the Russians need not be ashamed before the English.

The intellectual picture of the atmosphere of craftsmanship from which the story-teller comes has perhaps never been sketched in such a significant way as by Paul Valéry. "He speaks of the perfect things in nature, flawless pearls, full-bodied, matured wines, truly developed creatures, and calls them 'the precious product of a long chain of causes similar to one another.'" The accumulation of such causes has its temporal limit only at perfection. "This patient process of Nature," Valéry continues, "was once imitated by men. Miniatures, ivory carvings, elaborated to the point of greatest perfection, stones that are perfect in polish and engraving, lacquer work or paintings in which a series of thin, transparent layers are placed one on top of the other – all these products of sustained, sacrificing effort are vanishing, and the time is past in which time did not matter. Modern man no longer works at what cannot be abbreviated."

In point of fact, he has succeeded in abbreviating even storytelling. We have wit-nessed the evolution of the "short story," which has removed itself from oral tradition and no longer permits that slow piling one on top of the other of thin, transparent layers which constitutes the most appropriate picture of the way in which the perfect narrative is revealed through the layers of a variety of retellings.

X

Valéry concludes his observations with this sentence: "It is almost as if the decline of the idea of eternity coincided with the increasing aversion to sustained effort." The idea of eternity has ever had its strongest source in death. If this idea declines, so we reason, the face of death must have changed. It turns out that this change is identical with the one that has diminished the communicability of experience to the same extent as the art of storytelling has declined.

It has been observable for a number of centuries how in the general consciousness the thought of death has declined in omnipresence and vividness. In its last stages this process is accelerated. And in the course of the nineteenth century bourgeois society has, by means of hygienic and social, private and public institutions, realized a secondary effect which may have been its subconscious main purpose: to make it possible for people to avoid the sight of the dying. Dying was once a public process in the life of the individual and a most exemplary one; think of the medieval pictures in which the deathbed has turned into a throne toward which the people press through the wide-open doors of the death house. In the course of modern times dying has been pushed further and further out of the perceptual world of the living. There used to be no house, hardly a room, in which someone had not once died. (The Middle Ages also felt spatially what makes that inscription on a sun dial of Ibiza, *Ultima multis* [the last day for many], significant as the temper of the times.) Today people live in rooms that have never been touched by death, dry dwellers of eternity, and when their end approaches they are stowed away in sanatoria or hospitals by their heirs. It is, however, characteristic that not only a man's knowledge or wisdom, but above all his real life – and this is the stuff that stories are made of – first assumes transmissible form at the moment of his death. Just as a sequence of images is set in motion inside a man as his life comes to an end – unfolding the views of himself under which he has encountered himself without being aware of it – suddenly in his expressions and looks the unforgettable emerges and imparts to everything that concerned him that authority which even the poorest wretch in dying possesses for the living around him. This authority is at the very source of the story.

XI

Death is the sanction of everything that the storyteller can tell. He has borrowed his authority from death. In other words, it is natural history to which his stories refer back. This is expressed in exemplary form in one of the most beautiful stories we have by the incomparable Johann Peter Hebel. It is found in the *Schatzkästlein des rheinischen Hausfreundes*, is entitled "Unexpected Reunion," and begins with the betrothal of a young lad who works in the mines of Falun. On the eve of his wedding he dies a miner's death at the bottom of his tunnel. His bride keeps faith with him after his death, and she lives long enough to become a wizened old woman; one day a body is brought up from the abandoned tunnel which, saturated with iron vitriol, has escaped decay, and she recognizes her betrothed. After this reunion she too is called away by death. When Hebel, in the course of this story, was confronted with the necessity of making this long period of years graphic, he did so in the following sentences: "In the meantime the city of Lisbon was destroyed by an earthquake, and the Seven Years' War came and went, and Emperor Francis I died, and the Jesuit Order was abolished, and Poland was partitioned, and Empress Maria Theresa died, and Struensee was executed. America became independent, and the united French and Spanish forces were unable to capture Gibraltar. The Turks locked up General Stein in the Veteraner Cave in Hungary, and Emperor Joseph died also. King Gustavus of Sweden conquered Russian Finland, and the French Revolution and the long war began, and Emperor Leopold II went to his grave too. Napoleon captured Prussia, and the English bombarded Copenhagen, and the peasants sowed and harvested. The millers ground, the smiths hammered, and the miners dug for veins of ore in their underground workshops. But when in 1809 the miners at Falun..."

Never has a storyteller embedded his report deeper in natural history than Hebel manages to do in this chronology. Read it carefully. Death appears in it with the same regularity as the Reaper does in the processions that pass around the cathedral clock at noon.

XII

Any examination of a given epic form is concerned with the relationship of this form to historiography. In fact, one may go even further and raise the question whether historiography does not constitute the common ground of all forms of the epic. Then written history would be in the same relationship to the epic forms as white light is to the colors of the spectrum. However this may be, among all forms of the epic there is not one whose incidence in the pure, colorless light of written history is more certain than the chronicle. And in the broad spectrum of the chronicle the ways in which a story can be told are graduated like shadings of one and the same color. The chronicler is the history-teller. If we think back to the passage from Hebel, which has the tone of a chronicle throughout, it will take no effort to gauge the difference between the writer of history, the historian, and the teller of it, the chronicler. The historian is bound to explain in one way or another the happenings with which he deals; under no circumstances can he content himself with displaying them as models of the course of the world. But this is precisely what the chronicler does, especially in his classical representatives, the chroniclers of the Middle Ages, the precursors of the historians of today. By basing their historical tales on a divine plan of salvation – an inscrutable one – they have from the very start lifted the burden of demonstrable explanation from their own shoulders. Its place is taken by interpretation, which is not concerned with an accurate concatenation of definite events, but with the way these are embedded in the great inscrutable course of the world.

Whether this course is eschatologically determined or is a natural one makes no difference. In the storyteller the chronicler is preserved in changed form, secularized, as it were. Leskov is among those whose work displays this with particular clarity. Both the chronicler with his eschatological orientation and the storyteller with his profane outlook are so represented in his works that in a number of his stories it can hardly be decided whether the web in which they appear is the golden fabric of a religious view of the course of things, or the multicolored fabric of a worldly view.

Consider the story "The Alexandrite," which transports the reader into "that old time when the stones in the womb of the earth and the planets at celestial heights were still concerned with the fate of men, and not today when both in the heavens and beneath the earth everything has grown indifferent to the fates of the sons of men and no voice speaks to them from anywhere, let alone does their bidding. None of the undiscovered planets play any part in horoscopes any more, and there are a lot of new stones, all measured and weighed and examined for their specific weight and their density, but they no longer proclaim anything to us, nor do they bring us any benefit. Their time for speaking with men is past."

As is evident, it is hardly possible unambiguously to characterize the course of the world that is illustrated in this story of Leskov's. Is it determined eschatologically or naturalistically? The only certain thing is that in its very nature it is by definition outside all real historical categories. Leskov tells us that the epoch in which man could believe himself to be in harmony with nature has expired. Schiller called this epoch in the history of the world the period of naïve poetry. The storyteller keeps faith with it, and his eyes do not stray from that dial in front of which there moves the procession of creatures of which, depending on circumstances, Death is either the leader or the last wretched straggler.

XIII

It has seldom been realized that the listener's naïve relationship to the storyteller is controlled by his interest in retaining what he is told. The cardinal point for the unaffected listener is to assure himself of the possibility of reproducing the story. Memory is the epic faculty *par excellence*. Only by virtue of a comprehensive memory can epic writing absorb the course of events on the one hand and, with the passing of these, make its peace with the power of death on the other. It is not surprising that to a simple man of the people, such as Leskov once invented, the Czar, the head of the sphere in which his stories take place, has the most encyclopedic memory at his command. "Our Emperor," he says, "and his entire family have indeed a most astonishing memory."

Mnemosyne, the rememberer, was the Muse of the epic art among the Greeks. This name takes the observer back to a parting of the ways in world history. For if the record kept by memory – historiography – constitutes the creative matrix of the various epic forms (as great prose is the creative matrix of the various metrical forms), its oldest form, the epic, by virtue of being a kind of common denominator includes the story and the novel. When in the course of centuries the novel began to emerge from the womb of the epic, it turned out that in the novel the element of the epic mind that is derived from the Muse – that is, memory – manifests itself in a form quite different from the way it manifests itself in the story.

Memory creates the chain of tradition which passes a happening on from generation to generation. It is the Muse-derived element of the epic art in a broader sense and encompasses its varieties. In the first place among these is the one practiced by the storyteller. It starts the web which all stories together form in the end. One ties on to the next, as the great storytellers, particularly the Oriental ones, have always readily shown. In each of them there is a Scheherazade who thinks of a fresh story whenever her tale comes to a stop. This is epic remembrance and the Muse-inspired element of the narrative. But this should be set against another principle, also a Muse-derived element in a narrower sense, which as an element of the novel in its earliest form – that is, in the epic – lies concealed, still undifferentiated from the similarly derived element of the story. It can, at any rate, occasionally be divined in the epics, particularly at moments of solemnity in the Homeric epics, as in the invocations to the Muse at their beginning. What announces itself in these passages is the perpetuating remembrance of the novelist as contrasted with the short-lived reminiscences of the storyteller. The first is dedicated to *one* hero, *one* odyssey, *one* battle; the second, to *many* diffuse occurrences. It is, in other words, *remembrance* which, as the Muse-derived element of the novel, is added to reminiscence, the corresponding element of the story, the unity of their origin in memory having disappeared with the decline of the epic.

XIV

"No one," Pascal once said, "dies so poor that he does not leave something behind." Surely it is the same with memories too – although these do not always find an heir. The novelist takes charge of this bequest, and seldom without profound melancholy. For what Arnold Bennett says about a dead woman in one of his novels – that she had had almost nothing in the way of real life – is usually true of the sum total of the estate which the novelist administers. Regarding this aspect of the matter we owe the most important elucidation to Georg Lukács, who sees in the novel "the form of transcendental homelessness." According to Lukács, the novel is at the same time the only art form which includes time among its constitutive principles.

"Time," he says in his *Theory of the Novel*, "can become constitutive only when connection with the transcendental home has been lost. Only in the novel are meaning and life, and thus the essential and the temporal, separated; one can almost say that the whole inner action of a novel is nothing else but a struggle against the power of time.... And from this ... arise the genuinely epic experiences of time: hope and memory ....Only in the novel...does there occur a creative memory which transfixes the object and transforms it.... The duality of inwardness and outside world can here be overcome for the subject 'only' when he sees the...unity of his entire life...out of the past life-stream which is compressed in memory.... The insight which grasps this unity...becomes the divinatory-intuitive grasping of the unattained and therefore inexpressible meaning of life."

The "meaning of life" is really the center about which the novel moves. But the quest for it is no more than the initial expression of perplexity with which its reader sees himself living this written life. Here "meaning of life" – there "moral of the story": with these slogans novel and story confront each other, and from them the totally different historical co-ordinates of these art forms may be discerned. If *Don Quixote* is the earliest perfect specimen of the novel, its latest exemplar is perhaps the *Éducation sentimentale*.

In the final words of the last-named novel, the meaning which the bourgeois age found in its behavior at the beginning of its decline has settled like sediment in the cup of life. Frédéric and Deslauriers, the boyhood friends, think back to their youthful friendship. This little incident then occurred: one day they showed up in the bordello of their home town, stealthily and timidly, doing nothing but presenting the *patronne* with a bouquet of flowers which they had picked in their own gardens. "This story was still discussed three years later. And now they told it to each other in detail, each supplementing the recollection of the other. 'That may have been,' said Frédéric when they had finished, 'the finest thing in our lives.' 'Yes, you may be right,' said Deslauriers, 'that was perhaps the finest thing in our lives.'"

With such an insight the novel reaches an end which is more proper to it, in a stricter sense, than to any story. Actually there is no story for which the question as to how it continued would not be legitimate. The novelist, on the other hand, cannot hope to take the smallest step beyond that limit at which he invites the reader to a divinatory realization of the meaning of life by writing "Finis."

XV

A man listening to a story is in the company of the storyteller; even a man reading one shares this companionship. The reader of a novel, however, is isolated, more so than any other reader. (For even the reader of a poem is ready to utter the words, for the benefit of the listener.) In this solitude of his, the reader of a novel seizes upon his material more jealously than anyone else. He is ready to make it completely his own, to devour it, as it were. Indeed, he destroys, he swallows up the material as the fire devours logs in the fireplace. The suspense which permeates the novel is very much like the draft which stimulates the flame in the fireplace and enlivens its play.

It is a dry material on which the burning interest of the reader feeds. "A man who dies at the age of thirty-five," said Moritz Heimann once, "is at every point of his life a man who dies at the age of thirty-five." Nothing is more dubious than this sentence – but for the sole reason that the tense is wrong. A man – so says the truth that was meant here – who died at thirty-five will appear to *remembrance* at every point in his life as a man who dies at the age of thirty-five. In other words, the statement that makes no sense for real life becomes indisputable for remembered life. The nature of the character in a novel cannot be presented any better than is done in this statement, which says that the "meaning" of his life is revealed only in his death. But the reader of a novel actually does look for human beings from whom he derives the "meaning of life." Therefore he must, no matter what, know in advance that he will share their experience of death: if need be their figurative death – the end of the novel – but preferably their actual one. How do the characters make him understand that death is already waiting for them – a very definite death and at a very definite place? That is the question which feeds the reader's consuming interest in the events of the novel.

The novel is significant, therefore, not because it presents someone else's fate to us, perhaps didactically, but because this stranger's fate by virtue of the flame which consumes it yields us the warmth which we never draw from our own fate. What draws the reader to the novel is the hope of warming his shivering life with a death he reads about.

XVI

"Leskov," writes Gorky, "is the writer most deeply rooted in the people and is completely untouched by any foreign influences." A great storyteller will always be rooted in the people, primarily in a milieu of craftsmen. But just as this includes the rural, the maritime, and the urban elements in the many stages of their economic and technical development, there are many gradations in the concepts in which their store of experience comes down to us. (To say nothing of the by no means insignificant share which traders had in the art of storytelling; their task was less to increase its didactic content than to refine the tricks with which the attention of the listener was captured. They have left deep traces in the narrative cycle of *The Arabian Nights*.) In short, despite the primary role which storytelling plays in the household of humanity, the concepts through which the yield of the stories may be garnered are manifold. What may most readily be put in religious terms in Leskov seems almost automatically to fall into place in the pedagogical perspectives of the Enlightenment in Hebel, appears as hermetic tradition in Poe, finds a last refuge in Kipling in the life of British seamen and colonial soldiers. All great storytellers have in common the freedom with which they move up and down the rungs of their experience as on a ladder. A ladder extending downward to the interior of the earth and disappearing into the clouds is the image for a collective experience to which even the deepest shock of every individual experience, death, constitutes no impediment or barrier.

"And they lived happily ever after," says the fairy tale. The fairy tale, which to this day is the first tutor of children because it was once the first tutor of mankind, secretly lives on in the story. The first true storyteller is, and will continue to be, the teller of fairy tales. Whenever good counsel was at a premium, the fairy tale had it, and where the need was greatest, its aid was nearest. This need was the need created by the myth. The fairy tale tells us of the earliest arrangements that mankind made to shake off the nightmare which the myth had placed upon its chest. In the figure of the fool it shows us how mankind "acts dumb" toward the myth; in the figure of the youngest brother it shows us how one's chances increase as the mythical primitive times are left behind; in the figure of the man who sets out to learn what fear is it shows us that the things we are afraid of can be seen through; in the figure of the wiseacre it shows us that the questions posed by the myth are simple-minded, like the riddle of the Sphinx; in the shape of the animals which come to the aid of the child in the fairy tale it shows that nature not only is subservient to the myth, but much prefers to be aligned with man. The wisest thing – so the fairy tale taught mankind in olden times, and teaches children to this day – is to meet the forces of the mythical world with cunning and with high spirits. (This is how the fairy tale polarizes *Mut*, courage, dividing it dialectically into *Untermut*, that is, cunning, and *Übermut*, high spirits.) The liberating magic which the fairy tale has at its disposal does not bring nature into play in a mythical way, but points to its complicity with liberated man. A mature man feels this complicity only occasionally, that is, when he is happy; but the child first meets it in fairy tales, and it makes him happy.

XVII

Few storytellers have displayed so profound a kinship with the spirit of the fairy tale as did Leskov. This involves tendencies that were promoted by the dogmas of the Greek Orthodox Church. As is well known, Origen's speculation about *apokatastasis* – the entry of all souls into Paradise – which was rejected by the Roman Church plays a significant part in these dogmas. Leskov was very much influenced by Origen and planned to translate his work *On First Principles*. In keeping with Russian folk belief he interpreted the Resurrection less as a transfiguration than as a disenchantment, in a sense akin to the fairy tale. Such an interpretation of Origen is at the bottom of "The Enchanted Pilgrim." In this, as in many other tales by Leskov, a hybrid between fairy tale and legend is involved, not unlike that hybrid which Ernst Bloch mentions in a connection in which he utilizes our distinction between myth and fairy tale in his fashion.

"A hybrid between fairy tale and legend," he says, "contains figuratively mythical elements, mythical elements whose effect is certainly captivating and static, and yet not outside man. In the legend there are Taoist figures, especially very old ones, which are 'mythical' in this sense. For instance, the couple Philemon and Baucis: magically escaped though in natural repose. And surely there is a similar relationship between fairy tale and legend in the Taoist climate of Gotthelf, which, to be sure, is on a much lower level. At certain points it divorces the legend from the locality of the spell, rescues the flame of life, the specifically human flame of life, calmly burning, within as without."

"Magically escaped" are the beings that lead the procession of Leskov's creations: the righteous ones. Pavlin, Figura, the toupee artiste, the bear keeper, the helpful sentry – all of them embodiments of wisdom, kindness, comfort the world, crowd about the story-teller. They are unmistakably suffused with the *imago* of his mother.

This is how Leskov describes her: "She was so thoroughly good that she was not capable of harming any man, nor even an animal. She ate neither meat nor fish, because she had such pity for living creatures. Sometimes my father used to reproach her with this. But she answered: 'I have raised the little animals myself, they are like my children to me. I can't eat my own children, can I?' She would not eat meat at a neighbor's house either. 'I have seen them alive,' she would say; 'they are my acquaintances. I can't eat my acquaintances, can I?'"

The righteous man is the advocate for created things and at the same time he is their highest embodiment. In Leskov he has a maternal touch which is occasionally intensi-fied into the mythical (and thus, to be sure, endangers the purity of the fairy tale). Typical of this is the protagonist of his story "Kotin the Provider and Platonida." This figure, a peasant named Pisonski, is a hermaphrodite. For twelve years his mother raised him as a girl. His male and female organs mature simultaneously, and his bisexuality "becomes the symbol of God incarnate."

In Leskov's view, the pinnacle of creation has been attained with this, and at the same time he presumably sees it as a bridge established between this world and the other. For these earthily powerful, maternal male figures which again and again claim Leskov's skill as a storyteller have been removed from obedience to the sexual drive in the bloom of their strength. They do not, however, really embody an ascetic ideal; rather, the continence of these righteous men has so little privative character that it becomes the elemental counterpoise to uncontrolled lust which the storyteller has personified in *Lady Macbeth of Mzensk*. If the range between a Pavlin and this merchant's wife covers the breadth of the world of created beings, in the hierarchy of his characters Leskov has no less plumbed its depth.

XVIII

The hierarchy of the world of created things, which has its apex in the righteous man, reaches down into the abyss of the inanimate by many gradations. In this connection one particular has to be noted. This whole created world speaks not so much with the human voice as with what could be called "the voice of Nature" in the title of one of Leskov's most significant stories.

This story deals with the petty official Philip Philipovich who leaves no stone unturned to get the chance to have as his house guest a field marshal passing through his little town. He manages to do so. The guest, who is at first surprised at the clerk's urgent invitation, gradually comes to believe that he recognizes in him someone he must have met previously. But who is he? He cannot remember. The strange thing is that the host, for his part, is not willing to reveal his identity. Instead, he puts off the high personage from day to day, saying that the "voice of Nature" will not fail to speak distinctly to him one day. This goes on until finally the guest, shortly before continuing on his journey, must grant the host's public request to let the "voice of Nature" resound. Thereupon the host's wife withdraws. She "returned with a big, brightly polished, copper hunting horn which she gave to her husband. He took the horn, put it to his lips, and was at the same instant as though transformed. Hardly had he inflated his cheeks and produced a tone as powerful as the rolling of thunder when the field marshal cried: 'Stop, I've got it now, brother. This makes me recognize you at once! You are the bugler from the regiment of jaegers, and because you were so honest I sent you to keep an eye on a crooked supplies supervisor.' 'That's it, Your Excellency,' answered the host. 'I didn't want to remind you of this myself, but wanted to let the voice of Nature speak.'"

The way the profundity of this story is hidden beneath its silliness conveys an idea of Leskov's magnificent humor. This humor is confirmed in the same story in an even more cryptic way. We have heard that because of his honesty the official was assigned to watch a crooked supplies supervisor. This is what we are told at the end, in the recognition scene. At the very beginning of the story, however, we learn the following about the host: "All the inhabitants of the town were acquainted with the man, and they knew that he did not hold a high office, for he was neither a state official nor a military man, but a little supervisor at the tiny supply depot, where together with the rats he chewed on the state rusks and boot soles, and in the course of time had chewed himself together a nice little frame house." It is evident that this story reflects the traditional sympathy which storytellers have for rascals and crooks. All the literature of farce bears witness to it. Nor is it denied on the heights of art; of all Hebel's characters, the Brassenheim Miller, Tinder Frieder, and Red Dieter have been his most faithful companions. And yet for Hebel, too, the righteous man has the main role in the *theatrum mundi*. But because no one is actually up to this role, it keeps changing hands. Now it is the tramp, now the haggling Jewish peddler, now the man of limited intelligence who steps in to play this part. In every single case it is a guest performance, a moral improvisation. Hebel is a casuist. He will not for anything take a stand with any principle, but he does not reject it either, for any principle can at some time become the instrument of the righteous man. Compare this with Leskov's attitude. "I realize," he writes in his story "A Propos of the Kreutzer Sonata," "that my thinking is based much more on a practical view of life than on abstract philosophy or lofty morality; but I am nevertheless used to thinking the way I do." To be sure, the moral catastrophes that appear in Leskov's world are to the moral incidents in Hebel's world as the great, silent flowing of the Volga is to the babbling, rushing little millstream. Among Leskov's historical tales there are several in which passions are at work as destructively as the wrath of Achilles or the hatred of Hagen. It is astonishing how fearfully the world can darken for this author and with what majesty evil can raise its scepter. Leskov has evidently known moods – and this is probably one of the few characteristics he shares with Dostoevsky – in which he was close to antinomian ethics. The elemental natures in his *Tales from Olden Times* go to the limit in their ruthless passion. But it is precisely the mystics who have been inclined to see this limit as the point at which utter depravity turns into saintliness.

XIX

The lower Leskov descends on the scale of created things the more obviously does his way of viewing things approach the mystical. Actually, as will be shown, there is much evidence that in this, too, a characteristic is revealed which is inherent in the nature of the storyteller. To be sure, only a few have ventured into the depths of inanimate nature, and in modern narrative literature there is not much in which the voice of the anonymous storyteller, who was prior to all literature, resounds so clearly as it does in Leskov's story "The Alexandrite." It deals with a semi-precious stone, the chrysoberyl. The mineral is the lowest stratum of created things. For the storyteller, however, it is directly joined to the highest. To him it is granted to see in this chrysoberyl a natural prophecy of petrified, lifeless nature concerning the historical world in which he himself lives. This world is the world of Alexander II. The storyteller – or rather, the man to whom he attributes his own knowledge – is a gem engraver named Wenzel who has achieved the greatest conceivable skill in his art. One can juxtapose him with the silversmiths of Tula and say that – in the spirit of Leskov – the perfect artisan has access to the innermost chamber of the realm of created things. He is an incarnation of the devout. We are told of this gem cutter: "He suddenly squeezed my hand on which was the ring with the alexandrite, which is known to sparkle red in artificial light, and cried: 'Look, here it is, the prophetic Russian stone! O crafty Siberian. It was always green as hope and only toward evening was it suffused with blood. It was that way from the beginning of the world, but it concealed itself for a long time, lay hidden in the earth, and permitted itself to be found only on the day when Czar Alexander was declared of age, when a great sorcerer had come to Siberia to find the stone, a magician....' 'What nonsense are you talking,' I interrupted him; 'this stone wasn't found by a magician at all, it was a scholar named Nordenskjöld!' 'A magician! I tell you, a magician!' screamed Wenzel in a loud voice. 'Just look; what a stone! A green morning is in it and a bloody evening.... This is fate, the fate of noble Czar Alexander!' With these words old Wenzel turned to the wall, propped his head on his elbows, and...began to sob."

One can hardly come any closer to the meaning of this significant story than by some words which Paul Valéry wrote in a very remote context. "Artistic observation," he says in reflections on a woman artist whose work consisted in the silk embroidery of figures, "can attain an almost mystical depth. The objects on which it falls lose their names. Light and shade form very particular systems, present very individual questions which depend upon no knowledge and are derived from no practice, but get their existence and value exclusively from a certain accord of the soul, the eye, and the hand of someone who was born to perceive them and evoke them in his own inner self."

With these words, soul, eye, and hand are brought into connection. Interacting with one another, they determine a practice. We are no longer familiar with this practice. The role of the hand in production has become more modest, and the place it filled in storytelling lies waste. (After all, storytelling, in its sensory aspect, is by no means a job for the voice alone. Rather, in genuine storytelling the hand plays a part which supports what is expressed in a hundred ways with its gestures trained by work.) That old co-ordination of the soul, the eye, and the hand which emerges in Valéry's words is that of the artisan which we encounter wherever the art of storytelling is at home. In fact, one can go on and ask oneself whether the relationship of the storyteller to his material, human life, is not in itself a craftsman's relationship, whether it is not his very task to fashion the raw material of experience, his own and that of others, in a solid, useful, and unique way. It is a kind of procedure which may perhaps most adequately be exempli-fied by the proverb if one thinks of it as an ideogram of a story. A proverb, one might say, is a ruin which stands on the site of an old story and in which a moral twines about a happening like ivy around a wall.

Seen in this way, the storyteller joins the ranks of the teachers and sages. He has counsel – not for a few situations, as the proverb does, but for many, like the sage. For it is granted to him to reach back to a whole lifetime (a life, incidentally, that comprises not only his own experience but no little of the experience of others; what the storyteller knows from hearsay is added to his own). His gift is the ability to relate his life; his distinction, to be able to tell his entire life. The storyteller: he is the man who could let the wick of his life be consumed completely by the gentle flame of his story. This is the basis of the incomparable aura about the storyteller, in Leskov as in Hauff, in Poe as in Stevenson. The storyteller is the figure in which the righteous man encounters himself.

Studies in European Realism

György Lukács

From *Studies in European Realism: A Sociological Survey of the Writings of Balzac, Stendhal, Zola, Tolstoy, Gorki and Others*, translated by Edith Bone. London: Hillway, 1950 (1948), preface, pp. 1–19.

arrested one last time for his participation in the 1956 Hungarian revolution; released a year later but banned from official intellectual activities, Lukács continued to write until his death from cancer in 1971. Lukács' major contributions to novel theory are *Die Theorie des Romans* (1920; translated as *Theory of the Novel: A Historico-philosophical Essay on the Forms of Great Epic Literature*, 1971); *A történelmi regény* (1937; translated as *The Historical Novel*, 1962); and the two studies excerpted here: *Studies in European Realism: A Sociological Survey of the Writings of Balzac, Stendhal, Zola, Tolstoy, and Others* (introduction 1948, essays published in Hungarian and German 1935–9; translated 1950) and *Wider den missverstandenen Realismus* (1958, translated as *The Meaning of Contemporary Realism*, 1963).

Preface

The articles contained in this book were written some ten years ago. Author and reader may well ask why they should be republished just now. At first sight they might seem to lack all topicality. Subject and tone alike may appear remote to a considerable section of public opinion. I believe, however, that they have some topicality in that, without entering upon any detailed polemics, they represent a point of view in opposition to certain literary and philosophical trends still very much to the fore today.

Let us begin with the general atmosphere: the clouds of mysticism which once surrounded the phenomena of literature with a poetic colour and warmth and created an intimate and "interesting" atmosphere around them, have been dispersed. Things now face us in a clear, sharp light which to many may seem cold and hard; a light shed on them by the teachings of Marx. Marxism searches for the material roots of each phenomenon, regards them in their historical connections and movement, ascertains the laws of such movement and demonstrates their development from root to flower, and in so doing lifts every phenomenon out of a merely emotional, irrational, mystic fog and brings it to the bright light of understanding.

Such a transition is at first a disillusionment to many people and it is necessary that this should be so. For it is no easy matter to look stark reality in the face and no one succeeds in achieving this at the first attempt. What is required for this is not merely a great deal of hard work, but also a serious moral effort. In the first phase of such a change of heart most people will look back regretfully to the false but "poetic" dreams of reality which they are about to relinquish. Only later does it grow clear how much more genuine humanity – and hence genuine poetry – attaches to the acceptance of truth with all its inexorable reality and to acting in accordance with it.

But there is far more than this involved in such a change of heart. I am thinking here of that philosophical pessimism which was so deeply rooted in the social conditions of the period between the two world wars. It was not by accident that everywhere there arose thinkers who deepened this pessimism and who built up their *Weltanschauung* on some philosophical generalization of despair. The Germans, Spengler and Heidegger, and a considerable number of other influential thinkers of the last few decades embraced such views.

There is, of course, plenty of darkness around us now, just as there was between the two wars. Those who wish to despair can find cause enough and more in our everyday life. Marxism does not console anyone by playing down difficulties, or minimizing the material and moral darkness which surrounds us human beings today. The difference is only – but in this "only" lies a whole world – that Marxism has a grasp of the main lines of human development and recognizes it laws. Those who have arrived at such knowledge know, in spite of all temporary darkness, both whence we have come and where we are going. And those who know this find the world changed in their eyes: they see purposeful development where formerly only a blind, senseless confusion surrounded them. Where the philosophy of despair weeps for the collapse of a world and the destruction of culture, there Marxists watch the birth-pangs of a new world and assist in mitigating the pains of labour.

One might answer to all this – I have met with such objections myself often enough – that all this is only philosophy and sociology. What has all this to do with the theory and history of the novel? We believe that it has to do quite a lot. If we were to formulate the question in terms of literary history, it would read thus: which of the two, Balzac or Flaubert, was the greatest novelist, the typical classic of the 19th century? Such a judgment is not merely a matter of taste – it involves all the central problems of the æsthetics of the novel as an art form. The question arises whether it is the unity of the external and internal worlds or the separation between them which is the social basis of the greatness of a novel; whether the modern novel reached its culminating point in Gide, Proust and Joyce or had already reached its peak much earlier, in the works of Balzac and Tolstoy; so that today only individual great artists struggling against the current – as for instance Thomas Mann – can reach the heights already long attained.

These two æsthetic conceptions conceal the application of two opposite philosophies of history to the nature and historical development of the novel. And because the novel is the predominant art form of modern *bourgeois* culture, this contrast between the two æsthetic conceptions of the novel refers us back to the development of literature as a whole, or perhaps even culture as a whole. The question asked by the philosophy of history would be: does the road of our present-day culture lead upwards or downwards? There is no denying that our culture has passed and is passing through dark periods. It is for the philosophy of history to decide whether that darkening of the horizon which was adequately expressed for the first time in Flaubert's *Education Sentimentale* is a final, fatal eclipse or only a tunnel from which, however long it may be, there is a way out to the light once more.

Bourgeois æstheticists and critics, the author of the present book among them, saw no way out of this darkness. They regarded poetry merely as a revelation of the inner life, a clear-sighted recognition of social hopelessness or at best a consolation, an outward-reflected miracle. It followed with logical necessity from this historico-philosophical conception that Flaubert's *œuvre*, notably his *Education Sentimentale*, was regarded as the greatest achievement of the modern novel. This conception naturally extends to every sphere of literature. I quote only one instance: the real great philosophical and psychological content of the epilogue to *War and Peace* is the process which after the Napoleonic wars led the most advanced minority of the Russian aristocratic *intelligentsia* – a very small minority, of course – to the Decembrist rising, that tragically heroic prelude to the secular struggle of the Russian people for its liberation. Of all this my own old philosophy of history and æsthetics saw nothing. For me the epilogue held only the subdued colours of Flaubertian hopelessness, the frustration of the purposeless searchings and impulses of youth, their silting-up in the grey prose of *bourgeois* family life. The same applies to almost every detailed analysis of *bourgeois* æsthetics. The opposition of Marxism to the historical views of the last 50 years (the essence of which was the denial that history is a branch of learning that deals with the unbroken upward evolution of mankind) implied at the same time a sharp objective disagreement in all problems of *Weltanschauung* or æsthetics. No one can expect me to give even a skeleton outline of the Marxist philosophy of history within the limits of a preface. But we must nevertheless eliminate certain commonplace prejudices in order that author and reader may understand one another, that readers approach without bias this book with its application of Marxism to certain important problems of literary history and æsthetics and not pass judgment on it until they have compared this application with the facts. The Marxist philosophy of history is a comprehensive doctrine dealing with the necessary progress made by humanity from primitive communism to our own time and the perspectives of our further advance along the same road; as such it also gives us indications for the historical future. But such indications – born of the recognition of certain laws governing historical development – are not a cookery book providing recipes for each phenomenon or period; Marxism is not a Baedeker of history, but a signpost pointing the direction in which history moves forward. The final certainty it affords consists in the assurance that the developmnt of mankind does not and cannot finally lead to nothing and nowhere.

Of course, such generalizations do not do full justice to the guidance given by Marxism, a guidance extending to every topical problem of life. Marxism combines a consistent following of an unchanging direction with incessant theoretical and practical allowances for the deviousness of the path of evolution. Its well-defined philosophy of history is based on a flexible and adaptable acceptance and analysis of historical development. This apparent duality – which is in reality the dialectic unity of the materialist world-view – is also the guiding principle of Marxist æsthetics and literary theory.

Those who do not know Marxism at all or know it only superficially or at second-hand, may be surprised by the respect for the classical heritage of mankind which one finds in the really great representatives of this doctrine and by their incessant references to that classical heritage. Without wishing to enter into too much detail, we mention as an instance, in philosophy, the heritage of Hegelian dialectics, as opposed to the various trends in the latest philosophies. "But all this is long out of date," the modernists cry. "All this is the undesirable, outworn legacy of the nineteenth century," say those who – intentionally or unintentionally, consciously or unconsciously – support the Fascist ideology and its pseudo-revolutionary rejection of the past, which is in reality a rejection of culture and humanism. Let us look without prejudice at the bankruptcy of the very latest philosophies; let us consider how most philosophers of our day are compelled to pick up the broken and scattered fragments of dialectic (falsified and distorted in this decomposition) whenever they want to say something even remotely touching its essence about present-day life; let us look at the modern attempts at a philosophical synthesis and we shall find them miserable, pitiful caricatures of the old genuine dialectic, now consigned to oblivion.

GYÖRGY LUKÁCS

It is not by chance that the great Marxists were jealous guardians of our classical heritage in their æsthetics as well as in other spheres. But they do not regard this classical heritage as a reversion to the past; it is a necessary outcome of their philosophy of history that they should regard the past as irretrievably gone and not susceptible of renewal. Respect for the classical heritage of humanity in æsthetics means that the great Marxists look for the true highroad of history, the true direction of its development, the true course of the historical curve, the formula of which they know; and because they know the formula they do not fly off at a tangent at every hump in the graph, as modern thinkers often do because of their theoretical rejection of the idea that there is any such thing as an unchanged general line of development.

For the sphere of æsthetics this classical heritage consists in the great arts which depict man as a whole in the whole of society. Again it is the general philosophy, (here: proletarian humanism) which determines the central problems posed in æsthetics. The Marxist philosophy of history analyses man as a whole, and contemplates the history of human evolution as a whole, together with the partial achievement, or non-achievement of completeness in its various periods of development. It strives to unearth the hidden laws governing all human relationships. Thus the object of proletarian humanism is to reconstruct the complete human personality and free it from the distortion and dis-memberment to which it has been subjected in class society. These theoretical and practical perspectives determine the criteria by means of which Marxist æsthetics establish a bridge back to the classics and at the same time discover new classics in the thick of the literary struggles of our own time. The ancient Greeks, Dante, Shakespeare, Goethe, Balzac, Tolstoy all give adequate pictures of great periods of human development and at the same time serve as signposts in the ideological battle fought for the restoration of the unbroken human personality.

Such viewpoints enable us to see the cultural and literary evolution of the nineteenth century in its proper light. They show us that the true heirs of the French novel, so gloriously begun early in the last century, were not Flaubert and especially Zola, but the Russian and Scandinavian writers of the second half of the century. The present volume contains my studies of French and Russian realist writers seen in this perspective.

If we translate into the language of pure æsthetics the conflict (conceived in the sense of the philosophy of history) between Balzac and the later French novel, we arrive at the conflict between realism and naturalism. Talking of a conflict here may sound a paradox to the ears of most writers and readers of our day. For most present-day writers and readers are used to literary fashions swinging to and fro between the pseudo-objectivism of the naturalist school and the mirage-subjectivism of the psychologist or abstract-formalist school. And inasmuch as they see any worth in realism at all, they regard their own false extreme as a new kind of near-realism or realism. Realism, however, is not some sort of middle way between false objectivity and false subjectivity, but on the contrary the true, solution-bringing third way, opposed to all the pseudo-dilemmas engendered by the wrongly-posed questions of those who wander without a chart in the labyrinth of our time. Realism is the recognition of the fact that a work of literature can rest neither on a lifeless average, as the naturalists suppose, nor on an individual principle which dissolves its own self into nothingness. The central category and criterion of realist literature is the type, a peculiar synthesis which organically binds together the general and the particular both in characters and situations. What makes a type a type is not its average quality, not its mere individual being, however profoundly conceived; what makes it a type is that in it all the humanly and socially essential determinants are present on their highest level of development, in the ultimate unfolding of the possibilities latent in them, in extreme presentation of their extremes, rendering concrete the peaks and limits of men and epochs.

True great realism thus depicts man and society as complete entities, instead of showing merely one or the other of their aspects. Measured by this criterion, artistic trends determined by either exclusive introspection or exclusive extraversion equally impoverish and distort reality. Thus realism means a three-dimensionality, an all-roundness, that endows with independent life characters and human relationships. It by no means involves a rejection of the emotional and intellectual dynamism which necessarily develops together with the modern world. All it opposes is the destruction of the completeness of the human personality and of the objective typicality of men and situations through an excessive cult of the momentary mood. The struggle against such tendencies acquired a decisive importance in the realist literature of the nineteenth century. Long before such tendencies appeared in the practice of literature, Balzac had already prophetically foreseen and outlined the entire problem in his tragi-comic story *Le Chef d'œuvre inconnu*. Here experiment on the part of a painter to create a new classic three-dimensionality by means of an ecstasy of emotion and colour quite in the spirit of modern impressionism, leads to complete chaos. Fraunhofer, the tragic hero, paints a picture which is a tangled chaos of colours out of which a perfectly modelled female leg and foot protrude as an almost fortuitous fragment. Today a considerable section of modern artists has given up the Fraunhofer-like struggle and is content with finding, by means of new æsthetic theories, a justification for the emotional chaos of their works.

The central æsthetic problem of realism is the adequate presentation of the complete human personality. But as in every profound philosophy of art, here, too, the consistent following-up to the end of the æsthetic viewpoint leads us beyond pure aesthetics: for art, precisely if taken in its most perfect purity, is saturated with social and moral humanistic problems. The demand for a realistic creation of types is in opposition both to the trends in which the biological being of man, the physiological aspect of self-preservation and procreation are dominant (Zola and his disciples) and to the trends which sublimate man into purely mental psychological processes. But such an attitude, if it remained within the sphere of formal æsthetic judgments, would doubtless be quite arbitrary, for there is no reason why, regarded merely from the point of view of good writing, erotic conflict with its attendant moral and social conflicts should be rated higher than the elemental spontaneity of pure sex. Only if we accept the concept of the complete human personality as the social and historical task humanity has to solve; only if we regard it as the vocation of art to depict the most important turning-points of this process with all the wealth of the factors affecting it; only if æsthetics assign to art the role of explorer and guide, can the content of life be systematically divided up into spheres of greater and lesser importance; into spheres that throw light on types and paths and spheres that remain in darkness. Only then does it become evident that any description of mere biological processes – be these the sexual act or pain and sufferings, however detailed and from the literary point of view perfect it may be – results in a levelling-down of the social, historical and moral being of men and is not a means but an

GYÖRGY LUKÁCS

obstacle to such essential artistic expression as illuminating human conflicts in all their complexity and completeness. It is for this reason that the new contents and new media of expression contributed by naturalism have led not to an enrichment but to an impoverishment and narrowing-down of literature.

Apparently similar trains of thought were already put forward in early polemics directed against Zola and his school. But the psychologists, although they were more than once right in their concrete condemnation of Zola and the Zola school, opposed another no less false extreme to the false extreme of naturalism. For the inner life of man, its essential traits and essential conflicts can be truly portrayed only in organic connection with social and historical factors. Separated from the latter and developing merely its own immanent dialectic, the psychologist trend is no less abstract, and distorts and impoverishes the portrayal of the complete human personality no less than does the naturalist biologism which it opposes.

It is true that, especially regarded from the viewpoint of modern literary fashions, the position in respect of the psychologist school is at the first glance less obvious than in the case of naturalism. Everyone will immediately see that a description in the Zola manner of, say, an act of copulation between Dido and Aeneas or Romeo and Juliet would resemble each other very much more closely than the erotic conflicts depicted by Virgil and Shakespeare, which acquaint us with an inexhaustible wealth of cultural and human facts and types. Pure introspection is apparently the diametrical opposite of naturalist levelling-down, for what it describes are quite individual, non-recurring traits. But such extremely individual traits are also extremely abstract, for this very reason of non-recurrence. Here, too, Chesterton's witty paradox holds good, that the inner light is the worst kind of lighting. It is obvious to everyone that the coarse biologism of the naturalists and the rough outlines drawn by propagandist writers deform the true picture of the complete human personality. Much fewer are those who realize that the psychologists' punctilious probing into the human soul and their transformation of human beings into a chaotic flow of ideas destroy no less surely every possibility of a literary presentation of the complete human personality. A Joyce-like shoreless torrent of associations can create living human beings just as little as Upton Sinclair's coldly calculated all-good and all-bad stereotypes.

Owing to lack of space this problem cannot be developed here in all its breadth. Only one important and, at present, often neglected point is to be stressed here because it demonstrates that the live portrayal of the complete human personality is possible only if the writer attempts to create types. The point, in question is the organic, indissoluble connection between man as a private individual and man as a social being, as a member of a community. We know that this is the most difficult question of modern literature today and has been so ever since modern *bourgeois* society came into being. On the surface the two seem to be sharply divided and the appearance of the autonomous, independent existence of the individual is all the more pronounced, the more completely modern *bourgeois* society is developed. It seems as if the inner life, genuine "private" life, were proceeding according to its own autonomous laws and as if its fulfilments and tragedies were growing ever more independent of the surrounding social environment. And correspondingly, on the other side, it seems as if the connection with the community could manifest itself only in high-sounding abstractions, the adequate expression for which would be either rhetoric or satire.

An unbiased investigation of life and the setting aside of these false traditions of modern literature leads easily enough to the uncovering of the true circumstances to the discovery which had long been made by the great realists of the beginning and middle of the nineteenth century and which Gottfried Keller expressed thus: "Everything is politics." The great Swiss writer did not intend this to mean that everything was immediately tied up with politics; on the contrary, in his view – as in Balzac's and Tolstoy's – every action, thought and emotion of human beings is inseparably bound up with the life and struggles of the community, i.e., with politics; whether the humans themselves are conscious of this, unconscious of it or even trying to escape from it, objectively their actions, thoughts and emotions nevertheless spring from and run into politics.

The true great realists not only realized and depicted this situation – they did more than that, they set it up as a demand to be made on men. They knew that this distortion of objective reality (although, of course, due to social causes), this division of the complete human personality into a public and a private sector was a mutilation of the essence of man. Hence they protested not only as painters of reality, but also as humanists, against this fiction of capitalist society however unavoidable this spontan-eously formed superficial appearance. If as writers, they delved deeper in order to uncover the true types of man, they had inevitably to unearth and expose to the eyes of modern society the great tragedy of the complete human personality.

In the works of such great realists as Balzac we can again find a third solution opposed to both false extremes of modern literature, exposing as an abstraction, as a vitiation of the true poesy of life, both the feeble commonplaces of the well-intentioned and honest propagandist novels and the spurious richness of a preoccupation with the details of private life.

This brings us face to face with the question of the topicality today of the great realist writers. Every great historical period is a period of transition, a contradictory unity of crisis and renewal of destruction and rebirth; a new social order and a new type of man always come into being in the course of a unified though contradictory process. In such critical, transitional periods the tasks and responsibility of literature are exceptionally great. But only truly great realism can cope with such responsibilities; the accustomed, the fashionable media of expression, tend more and more to hamper literature in fulfilling the tasks imposed by history. It should surprise no one if from this point of view we turn against the individualistic, psychologist trends in literature. It might more legitimately surprise many that these studies express a sharp opposition to Zola and Zolaism.

Such surprise may be due in the main to the fact that Zola was a writer of the left and his literary methods were dominant chiefly, though by no means exclusively, in left-wing literature. It might appear, therefore, that we are involving ourselves in a serious contradiction, demanding on the one hand the politization of literature and on the other hand attacking insidiously the most vigorous and militant section of left-wing literature. But this contradiction is merely apparent. It is, however, well suited to throw light on the true connection between literature and *Weltanschauung*.

The problem was first raised (apart from the Russian democratic literary critics) by Engels, when he drew a comparison between Balzac and Zola. Engels showed that Balzac, although his political creed was legitimist royalism, nevertheless inexorably exposed the vices and weakness of royalist feudal France and described its death agony with magnificent poetic vigour. This phenomenon, references to which the reader will find more than once in these pages, may at first glance again – and mistakenly – appear contradictory. It might appear that the *Weltanschauung* and political attitude of serious great realists are a matter of no consequence. To a certain extent this is true. For from the point of view of the self-recognition of the present and from the point of view of history and posterity, what matters is the picture conveyed by the work; the question to what extent this picture conforms to the views of the authors is a secondary consideration.

This, of course, brings us to a serious question of æsthetics. Engels, in writing about Balzac, called it "the triumph of realism"; it is a problem that goes down to the very roots of realist artistic creation. It touches the essence of true realism: the great writer's thirst for truth, his fanatic striving for reality – or expressed in terms of ethics: the writer's sincerity and probity. A great realist such as Balzac, if the intrinsic artistic development of situations and characters he has created comes into conflict with his most cherished prejudices or even his most sacred convictions, will, without an instant's hesitation, set aside these his own prejudices and convictions and describe what he really sees, not what we would prefer to see. This ruthlessness towards their own subjective world-picture is the hall-mark of all great realists, in sharp contrast to the second-raters, who nearly always succeed in bringing their own *Weltanschauung* into "harmony" with reality, that is forcing a falsified or distorted picture of reality into the shape of their own world-view. This difference in the ethical attitude of the greater and lesser writers is closely linked with the difference between genuine and spurious creation. The characters created by the great realists, once conceived in the vision of their creator, live an independent life of their own; their comings and goings, their development, their destiny is dictated by the inner dialectic of their social and individual existence. No writer is a true realist – or even a truly good writer, if he can direct the evolution of his own characters at will.

All this is however merely a description of the phenomenon. It answers the question as to the ethics of the writer: what will he do if he sees reality in such and such a light? But this does not enlighten us at all regarding the other question: what does the writer see and how does he see it? And yet it is here that the most important problems of the social determinants of artistic creation arise. In the course of these studies we shall point out in detail the basic differences which arise in the creative methods of writers according to the degree to which they are bound up with the life of the community, take part in the struggles going on around them or are merely passive observers of events. Such differences determine creative processes which may be diametrical opposites; even the experience which gives rise to the work will be structurally different, and in accordance with this the process of shaping the work will be different. The question whether a writer lives within the community or is a mere observer of it, is determined not by psychological, not even by typological factors; it is the evolution of society that determines (not automatically, not fatalistically, of course), the line the evolution of an author will take. Many a writer of a basically contemplative type has been driven to an intense participation in the life of the community by the social conditions of his time; Zola, on the contrary, was by nature a man of action, but his epoch turned him into a mere observer and when at last he answered the call of life, it came too late to influence his development as a writer.

But even this is as yet only the formal aspect of this problem, although no longer the abstractly formal. The question grows essential and decisive only when we examine concretely the position taken up by a writer. What does he love and what does he hate? It is thus that we arrive at a deeper interpretation of the writer's true *Weltanschauung*, at the problem of the artistic value and fertility of the writer's world-view. The conflict which previously stood before us as the conflict between the writer's world-view and the faithful portrayal of the world he sees, is now clarified as a problem within the *Weltanschauung* itself, as a conflict between a deeper and a more superficial level of the writer's own *Weltanschauung*.

Realists such as Balzac or Tolstoy in their final posing of questions always take the most important, burning problems of the community for their starting point; their pathos as writers is always stimulated by those sufferings of the people which are the most acute at the time; it is these sufferings that determine the objects and direction of their love and hate and through these emotions determine also what they see in their poetic visions and how they see it. If, therefore, in the process of creation their conscious world-view comes into conflict with the world seen in their vision, what really emerges is that their true conception of the world is only superficially formulated in the consciously held world-view and the real depth of their *Weltanschauung*, their deep ties with the great issues of their time, their sympathy with the sufferings of the people can find adequate expression only in the being and fate of their characters.

No one experienced more deeply than Balzac the torments which the transition to the capitalist system of production inflicted on every section of the people, the profound moral and spiritual degradation which necessarily accompanied this transformation on every level of society. At the same time Balzac was also deeply aware of the fact that this transformation was not only socially inevitable, but at the same time progressive. This contradiction in his experience Balzac attempted to force into a system based on a Catholic legitimism and tricked out with Utopian conceptions of English Toryism. But this system was contradicted all the time by the social realities of his day and the Balzacian vision which mirrored them. This contradiction itself clearly expressed, however, the real truth: Balzac's profound comprehension of the contradictorily progressive character of capitalist development.

It is thus that great realism and popular humanism are merged into an organic unity. For if we regard the classics of the social development that determined the essence of our age, from Goethe and Walter Scott to Gorki and Thomas Mann, we find *mutatis mutandis* the same structure of the basic problem. Of course every great realist found a different solution for the basic problem in accordance with his time and his own artistic personality. But they all have in common that they penetrate deeply into the great universal problems of their time and inexorably depict the true essense of reality as they see it. From the French revolution onwards the development of society moved in a direction which rendered inevitable a conflict between such aspirations of men of letters and the literature and public of their time. In this whole age a writer could achieve greatness only in the struggle against the current of everyday life. And since Balzac the resistance of daily life to the deeper tendencies of literature, culture and art has grown ceaselessly stronger. Nevertheless there were always writers who in their life-work,

GYÖRGY LUKÁCS

despite all the resistance of the day, fulfilled the demand formulated by Hamlet: 'to hold the mirror up to nature,' and by means of such a reflected image aided the development of mankind and the triumph of humanist principles in a society so contradictory in its nature that it on the one hand gave birth to the ideal of the complete human personality and on the other hand destroyed it in practice.

The great realists of France found worthy heirs only in Russia. All the problems mentioned here in connection with Balzac apply in an even greater measure to Russian literary development and notably to its central figure Leo Tolstoy. It is not by chance that Lenin (without having read Engels' remarks about Balzac) formulated the Marxist view of the principles of true realism in connection with Tolstoy. Hence there is no need for us to refer to these problems again here. There is all the more need, however, to call attention to the erroneous conceptions current in respect of the historical and social foundations of Russian realism, errors which in many cases are due to deliberate distortion or concealment of facts. In Britain, as everywhere else in Europe, the newer Russian literature is well known and popular among the intelligent reading public. But as everywhere else, the reactionaries have done all they could to prevent this literature from becoming popular; they felt instinctively that Russian realism, even if each single work may not have a definite social tendency, is an antidote to all reactionary infection.

But however widespread familiarity with Russian literature may have been in the West, the picture formed in the minds of readers was nevertheless incomplete and largely false. It was incomplete because the great champions of Russian revolutionary democracy, Herzen and Bielinski, Chernyshevski and Dobrolyubov were not translated and even their names were known to very few outside the reach of the Russian language. And it is only now that the name of Saltykov-Shchedrin is getting to be known, although in him the newer Russian literature had produced a satirist unrivalled anywhere in the world since the days of Jonathan Swift.

What is more, the conception of Russian literature was not only incomplete, it was also distorted. The great Russian realist Tolstoy was claimed by reactionary ideologies for their own and the attempt was made to turn him into a mystic gazing into the past; into an "aristocrat of the spirit" far removed from the struggles of the present. This falsification of the image of Tolstoy served a second purpose as well; it helped to give a false impression of the tendencies predominant in the life of the Russian people. The result was the myth of a "holy Russia" and Russian mysticism. Later, when the Russian people in 1917 fought and won the battle for liberation, a considerable section of the *intelligentsia* saw a contradiction between the new, free Russia and the older Russian literature. One of the weapons of counter-revolutionary propaganda was the untrue allegation that the new Russian had effected a complete volte-face in every sphere of culture and had rejected, in fact was persecuting, older Russian literature.

These counter-revolutionary allegations have long been refuted by the facts. The literature of the White Russian émigrés, which claimed to be the continuation of the allegedly mystical Russian literature, quickly showed its own sterility and futility, once it was cut off from the Russian soil and the real Russian problems. On the other hand, it was impossible to conceal from the intelligent reading public that in the Soviet Union the vigorous treatment of the fresh issues thrown up by the rejuvenated life of the nation was developing a rich and interesting new literature and the discerning readers of this literature could see for themselves how deeply rooted were the connections between it and Russian classical realism. (It will suffice to refer here to Sholokhov, the heir to Tolstoy's realism.)

The reactionary campaign of misrepresentation directed against the Soviet Union reached its culminating point before and during the late war, and then collapsed in the course of the same war, when the liberated peoples of the Soviet Union in their struggle against German Nazi imperialism demonstrated to the world such strength and such achievements in the sphere of moral and material culture that the old-style slanders and misrepresentations ceased to be effective. On the contrary, a very large number of people began to ask: what was the source of the mighty popular forces, the manifest-ations of which were witnessed by the whole world during the war. Such dangerous thoughts required countermeasures and now we see a fresh wave of slander and misrepresentation breaking against the rock of Soviet civilization. Nevertheless the history of the internal and external evolution of the Russian people still remains an exciting and interesting problem for the reading public of every country.

In examining the history of the liberation of the Russian people and of the consoli-dation of its achievements, we must not overlook the important part played by literature in these historical events, – a part greater than the usual influence exercised by literature on the rising and falling fortunes of any civilized nation. On the one hand no other literature is as public-spirited as the Russian and on the other hand there has scarcely been any society in which literary works excited so much attention and provoked such crises as in Russian society in the classical realist period of Russian literature. Hence, although a very wide public is acquainted with Russian literature, it may not be superfluous to present this freshly arising problem in a new light. The new problems imperatively demand that our analysis penetrate, both from the social and the æsthetic viewpoint, to the true roots of Russian social development.

It is for this reason that our first study attempts to fill one of the greatest gaps in our knowledge of Russian literature by giving a characterization of the little-known great Russian revolutionary-democratic critics Bielinski, Chernyshevski and Dobrolyubov. Closely linked with this question is a revaluation of the well-known classical realists, or rather a characterization and appreciation which is somewhat more in accordance with historical truth. In the past, western critics and readers in their approach to Tolstoy and others took for their guide the views on society, philosophy, religion, art, and so on, which these great men had themselves expressed in articles, letters, diaries and the like. They thought to find a key to the understanding of the often unfamliar great works of literature in these conscious opinions. In other words reactionary criticism interpreted the works of Tolstoy and Dostoyevski by deriving the alleged spiritual and artistic content of these works from certain reactionary views of the authors.

The method employed in the present studies is the exact opposite of this. It is a very simple method: it consists in first of all examining carefully the real social foundations on which say Tolstoy's existence rested and the real social forces under the influence of which the human and the literary personality of this author developed. Secondly, in close connection with the first approach, the question is asked: what do Tolstoy's works represent, what is their real spiritual and intellectual content and how does the writer build up his æsthetic forms in the struggle for the adequate expression of such contents. Only if, after an unbiassed examination, we have uncovered and understood these objective relationships, are we in a position to provide a correct interpretation of the

GYÖRGY LUKÁCS

conscious views expressed by the author and correctly evaluate his influence on literature.

The reader will see later that in applying this method a quite new picture of Tolstoy will emerge. The revaluation will be new only to the non-Russian reading public. In Russian literature itself the method of appreciation outlined in the preceding has an old tradition behind it: Bielinski and Herzen were the precursors of the method, the culminating points of which are marked by the names of Lenin and Stalin. It is this method that the author of the present book is attempting to apply to an analysis of the works of Tolstoy. That Tolstoy is followed by Gorki in this book will surprise no one; the essay on Gorki is also a polemic against reactionary literary trends, is also to some extent a revaluation; and its main theme is the close link between Gorki the great innovator and his precursors in Russian literature and an examination of the question to what extent Gorki continued and developed classical Russian realism. The uncovering of these connections is at the same time the answer to the question: where is the bridge between old and new culture, between the old and the new Russian literature?

Finally the last paper gives a short outline of Tolstoy's influence on Western literature, discusses how Tolstoy came to be a figure of international stature and attempts to define the social and artistic significance of his influence on world literature. This paper, too, is an attack on the reactionary conception of Russian realism, but an attack which also marshals allies: it shows how the finest German, French, English and American writers opposed such reactionary distortions, and fought for a correct understanding of Tolstoy and of Russian literature. The reader will see from this that the opinions put forward in this book are not the idle speculations of a solitary and isolated writer but a world-wide trend of thought constantly gaining in strength.

In the remarks about method the social tendencies underlying the essays have been strongly stressed and their significance could scarcely be exaggerated. Nevertheless the main emphasis in these papers is on the æsthetic, not the social, analysis; investigation of the social foundations is only a means to the complete grasp of the æsthetic character of Russian classical realism. This point of view is not an invention of the author. Russian literature owed its influence not only to its new social and human content but chiefly to the fact of being a really great literature. For this reason it is not enough to eradicate the old firmly-rooted false notions regarding its historical and social foundations; it is also necessary to draw the literary and æsthetic conclusions from the correct evaluation of these social and historical foundations. Only then can it be understood why great Russian realism has played a leading part in world literature for three quarters of a century and has been a beacon of progress and an effective weapon in the struggle against open and covert literary reaction and against the decadence masquerading as innovation.

Only if we have a correct æsthetic conception of the essence of Russian classical realism can we see clearly the social and even political importance of its past and future fructifying influence on literature. With the collapse and eradication of Fascism a new life has begun for every liberated people. Literature has a great part to play in solving the new tasks imposed by the new life in every country. If literature is really to fulfil this role, a role dictated by history, there must be as a natural prerequisite, a philosophical and political rebirth of the writers who produce it. But although this is an indispensable prerequisite, it is not enough. It is not only the opinions that must change, but the whole emotional world of men; and the most effective propagandists of the new, liberating, democratic feeling are the men of letters. The great lesson to be learnt from the Russian development is precisely the extent to which a great realist literature can fructifyingly educate the people and transform public opinion. But such results can be achieved only by a truly great, profound and all-embracing realism. Hence, if literature is to be a potent factor of national rebirth, it must itself be reborn in its purely literary, formal, æsthetic aspects as well. It must break with reactionary, conservative traditions which hamper it and resist the seeping-in of decadent influences which lead into a blind alley.

In these respects the Russian writers' attitude to life and literature is exemplary, and for this, if for no other, reason it is most important to destroy the generally accepted reactionary evaluation of Tolstoy, and, together with the elimination of such false ideas, to understand the human roots of his literary greatness. And what is most important of all; to show how such greatness comes from the human and artistic identification of the writer with some broad popular movement. It matters little in this connection what popular movement it is in which the writer finds this link between himself and the masses; that Tolstoy sinks his roots into the mass of the Russian peasantry, and Gorki of the industrial workers and landless peasants. For both of them were to the bottom of their souls bound up with the movements seeking the liberation of the people and struggling for it. The result of such a close link in the cultural and literary sphere was then and is to-day that the writer can overcome his isolation, his relegation to the role of a mere observer, to which he would otherwise be driven by the present state of capitalist society. He thus becomes able to take up a free, unbiassed, critical attitude towards those tendencies of present-day culture which are unfavourable to art and literature. To fight against such tendencies by purely artistic methods, by the mere formal use of new forms, is a hopeless undertaking, as the tragic fate of the great writers of the West in the course of the last century clearly shows. A close link with a mass movement struggling for the emancipation of the common people does, on the other hand, provide the writer with the broader viewpoint, with the fructifying subject-matter from which a true artist can develop the effective artistic forms which are commensurate with the requirements of the age, even if they go against the superficial artistic fashions of the day.

These very sketchy remarks were required before we could express our final conclusion. Never in all its history did mankind so urgently require a realist literature as it does to-day. And perhaps never before have the traditions of great realism been so deeply buried under a rubble of social and artistic prejudice. It is for this reason that we consider a revaluation of Tolstoy and Balzac so important. Not as if we wished to set them up as models to be imitated by the writers of our day. To set an example means only: to help in correctly formulating the task and studying the conditions of a successful solution. It was thus that Goethe aided Walter Scott, and Walter Scott aided Balzac. But Walter Scott was no more an imitator of Goethe than Balzac was of Scott. The practical road to a solution for the writer lies in an ardent love of the people, a deep hatred of the people's enemies and the people's own errors, the inexorable uncovering of truth and reality, together with an unshakable faith in the march of mankind and their own people towards a better future.

There is to-day in the world a general desire for a literature which could penetrate with its beam deep into the tangled jungle of our time. A great realist literature could play the leading part, hitherto always denied to it, in the democratic rebirth of nations.

GYÖRGY LUKÁCS

If in this connection we evoke Balzac in opposition to Zola and his school, we believe that we are helping to combat the sociological and æsthetical prejudices which have prevented many gifted authors from giving their best to mankind. We know the potent social forces which have held back the development of both writers and literature: a quarter-century of reactionary obscurantism which finally twisted itself into the diabolical grimace of the Fascist abomination.

Political and social liberation from these forces is already an accomplished fact, but the thinking of the great masses is still bedevilled by the fog of reactionary ideas which prevents them from seeing clearly. This difficult and dangerous situation puts a heavy responsibility on the men of letters. But it is not enough for a writer to see clearly in matters political and social. To see clearly in matters of literature is no less indispensable and it is to the solution of these problems that this book hopes to bring its contribution.

The Ideology
of Modernism

György Lukács

György Lukács (1885–1971)

György Löwinger was born in Budapest in 1885 (his family changed their surname to the Hungarian Lukács in 1890, and György converted from Judaism to Christianity in 1907). Lukács studied at the Péter Pázmány University before getting his doctorate in aesthetics, English, and German philology at the University of Berlin in 1909. He joined the Hungarian Communist movement in 1918, and the rest of his life follows the party's tumultuous history. After the Hungarian commune was defeated in 1919, Lukács fled to Vienna, where, in 1928, he wrote the theses for the Second Congress of the Hungarian Communist Party (called the "Blum" theses after Lukács' Communist code name). When the theses were criticized by Lenin, the Communist party forced Lukács to make a public retraction and move to Moscow. In 1945 Lukács finally returned to Budapest, where he became a member of the Hungarian Provisional National Assembly, as well as a professor of aesthetics and philosophy at the University of Budapest. When a new Communist dictatorship came to power in 1948, Lukács was demoted, but he regained his position with the favorable reception of *Die Zerstörung der Vernunft* (1954; translated as *The Destruction of Reason*, 1980). Lukács was

From *The Meaning of Contemporary Realism*, translated by John and Necke Mander. London: Merlin Press, 1962 (1958), pp. 17–46. Reprinted by permission of Merlin Press Ltd.

arrested one last time for his participation in the 1956 Hungarian revolution; released a year later but banned from official intellectual activities, Lukács continued to write until his death from cancer in 1971. Lukács' major contributions to novel theory are *Die Theorie des Romans* (1920; translated as *Theory of the Novel: A Historico-philosophical Essay on the Forms of Great Epic Literature*, 1971); *A történelmi regény* (1937; translated as *The Historical Novel*, 1962); and the two studies excerpted here: *Studies in European Realism: A Sociological Survey of the Writings of Balzac, Stendhal, Zola, Tolstoy, and Others* (introduction 1948, essays published in Hungarian and German 1935–9; translated 1950) and *Wider den missverstandenen Realismus* (1958, translated as *The Meaning of Contemporary Realism*, 1963).

I t is in no way surprising that the most influential contemporary school of writing should still be committed to the dogmas of 'modernist' anti-realism. It is here that we must begin our investigation if we are to chart the possibilities of a bourgeois realism. We must compare the two main trends in contemporary bourgeois literature, and look at the answers they give to the major ideological and artistic questions of our time.

We shall concentrate on the underlying ideological basis of these trends (ideological in the above-defined, not in the strictly philosophical, sense). What must be avoided at all costs is the approach generally adopted by bourgeois-modernist critics themselves: that exaggerated concern with formal criteria, with questions of style and literary technique. This approach may appear to distinguish sharply between 'modern' and 'traditional' writing (i.e. contemporary writers who adhere to the styles of the last century). In fact it fails to locate the decisive formal problems and turns a blind eye to their inherent dialectic. We are presented with a false polarization which, by exaggerating the importance of stylistic differences, conceals the opposing principles actually underlying and determining contrasting styles.

To take an example: the *monologue intérieur*. Compare, for instance, Bloom's monologue in the lavatory or Molly's monologue in bed, at the beginning and at the end of *Ulysses*, with Goethe's early-morning monologue as conceived by Thomas Mann in his *Lotte in Weimar*. Plainly, the same stylistic technique is being employed. And certain of Thomas Mann's remarks about Joyce and his methods would appear to confirm this.

Yet it is not easy to think of any two novels more basically dissimilar than *Ulysses* and *Lotte in Weimar*. This is true even of the superficially rather similar scenes I have indicated. I am not referring to the – to my mind – striking difference in intellectual quality. I refer to the fact that with Joyce the stream-of-consciousness technique is no mere stylistic device; it is itself the formative principle governing the narrative pattern and the presentation of character. Technique here is something absolute; it is part and parcel of the aesthetic ambition informing *Ulysses*. With Thomas Mann, on the other hand, the *monologue intérieur* is simply a technical device, allowing the author to explore aspects of Goethe's world which would not have been otherwise available. Goethe's experience is not presented as confined to momentary sense-impressions.

The artist reaches down to the core of Goethe's personality, to the complexity of his relations with his own past, present, and even future experience. The stream of association is only apparently free. The monologue is composed with the utmost artistic rigour: it is a carefully plotted sequence gradually piercing to the core of Goethe's personality. Every person or event, emerging momentarily from the stream and vanishing again, is given a specific weight, a definite position, in the pattern of the whole. However unconventional the presentation, the compositional principle is that of the traditional epic; in the way the pace is controlled, and the transitions and climaxes are organized, the ancient rules of epic narration are faithfully observed.

It would be absurd, in view of Joyce's artistic ambitions and his manifest abilities, to qualify the exaggerated attention he gives to the detailed recording of sense-data, and his comparative neglect of ideas and emotions, as artistic failure. All this was in conformity with Joyce's artistic intentions; and, by use of such techniques, he may be said to have achieved them satisfactorily. But between Joyce's intentions and those of Thomas Mann there is a total opposition. The perpetually oscillating patterns of sense- and memory-data, their powerfully charged – but aimless and directionless – fields of force, give rise to an epic structure which is *static*, reflecting a belief in the basically static character of events.

These opposed views of the world – dynamic and developmental on the one hand, static and sensational on the other – are of crucial importance in examining the two schools of literature I have mentioned. I shall return to the opposition later. Here, I want only to point out that an exclusive emphasis on formal matters can lead to serious misunderstanding of the character of an artist's work.

What determines the style of a given work of art? How does the intention determine the form? (We are concerned here, of course, with the intention realized in the work; it need not coincide with the writer's conscious intention). The distinctions that concern us are not those between stylistic 'techniques' in the formalistic sense. It is the view of the world, the ideology or *Weltanschauung* underlying a writer's work, that counts. And it is the writer's attempt to reproduce this view of the world which constitutes his 'intention' and is the formative principle underlying the style of a given piece of writing. Looked at in this way, style ceases to be a formalistic category. Rather, it is rooted in content; it is the specific form of a specific content.

Content determines form. But there is no content of which Man himself is not the focal point. However various the *données* of literature (a particular experience, a didactic purpose), the basic question is, and will remain: what is Man?

Here is a point of division: if we put the question in abstract, philosophical terms, leaving aside all formal considerations, we arrive – for the realist school – at the traditional Aristotelian dictum (which was also reached by other than purely aesthetic considerations): Man is *zoon politikon*, a social animal. The Aristotelian dictum is applicable to all great realistic literature. Achilles and Werther, Oedipus and Tom Jones, Antigone and Anna Karenina: their individual existence – their *Sein an sich*, in the Hegelian terminology; their 'ontological being', as a more fashionable terminology has it – cannot be distinguished from their social and historical environment. Their human significance, their specific individuality cannot be separated from the context in which they were created.

The ontological view governing the image of man in the work of leading modernist writers is the exact opposite of this. Man, for these writers, is by nature solitary, asocial, unable to enter into relationships with other human beings. Thomas Wolfe once wrote: 'My view of the world is based on the firm conviction that solitariness is by no means a rare condition, something peculiar to myself or to a few specially solitary human beings, but the inescapable, central fact of human existence.' Man, thus imagined, may establish contact with other individuals, but only in a superficial, accidental manner; only, ontologically speaking, by retrospective reflection. For 'the others', too, are basically solitary, beyond significant human relationship.

This basic solitariness of man must not be confused with that individual solitariness to be found in the literature of traditional realism. In the latter case, we are dealing with a particular situation in which a human being may be placed, due either to his character or to the circumstances of his life. Solitariness may be objectively conditioned, as with Sophocles' Philoctetes, put ashore on the bleak island of Lemnos. Or it may be subjective, the product of inner necessity, as with Tolstoy's Ivan Ilyitsch or Flaubert's Frédéric Moreau in the *Education Sentimentale*. But it is always merely a fragment, a phase, a climax or anticlimax, in the life of the community as a whole. The fate of such individuals is characteristic of certain human types in specific social or historical circumstances. Beside and beyond their solitariness, the common life, the strife and togetherness of other human beings, goes on as before. In a word, their solitariness is a specific social fate, not a universal *condition humaine*.

The latter, of course, is characteristic of the theory and practice of modernism. I would like, in the present study, to spare the reader tedious excursions into philosophy. But I cannot refrain from drawing the reader's attention to Heidegger's description of human existence as a 'thrownness-into-being' (*Geworfenheit ins Dasein*). A more graphic evocation of the ontological solitariness of the individual would be hard to imagine. Man is 'thrown-into-being'. This implies, not merely that man is constitutionally unable to establish relationships with things or persons outside himself; but also that it is impossible to determine theoretically the origin and goal of human existence.

Man, thus conceived, is an ahistorical being. (The fact that Heidegger does admit a form of 'authentic' historicity in his system is not really relevant. I have shown elsewhere that Heidegger tends to belittle historicity as 'vulgar'; and his 'authentic' historicity is not distinguishable from ahistoricity). This negation of history takes two different forms in modernist literature. First, the hero is strictly confined within the limits of his own experience. There is not for him – and apparently not for his creator – any pre-existent reality beyond his own self, acting upon him or being acted upon by him. Secondly, the hero himself is without personal history. He is 'thrown-into-the-world': meaninglessly, unfathomably. He does not develop through contact with the world; he neither forms nor is formed by it. The only 'development' in this literature is the gradual revelation of the human condition. Man is now what he has always been and always will be. The narrator, the examining subject, is in motion; the examined reality is static.

Of course, dogmas of this kind are only really viable in philosophical abstraction, and then only with a measure of sophistry. A gifted writer, however extreme his theoretical modernism, will in practice have to compromise with the demands of historicity and of social environment. Joyce uses Dublin, Kafka and Musil the Hapsburg Monarchy, as the locus of their masterpieces. But the locus they lovingly depict is little more than a backcloth; it is not basic to their artistic intention.

This view of human existence has specific literary consequences. Particularly in one category, of primary theoretical and practical importance, to which we must now give our attention: that of *potentiality*. Philosophy distinguishes between *abstract* and *concrete* (in Hegel, 'real') *potentiality*. These two categories, their interrelation and opposition, are rooted in life itself. *Potentiality* – seen abstractly or subjectively – is richer than actual life. Innumerable possibilities for man's development are imaginable, only a small percentage of which will be realized. Modern subjectivism, taking these imagined possibilities for actual complexity of life, oscillates between melancholy and fascination. When the world declines to realize these possibilities, this melancholy becomes tinged with contempt. Hofmannsthal's Sobeide expressed the reaction of the generation first exposed to this experience:

The burden of those endlessly pored-over
And now forever perished possibilities...

How far were those possibilities even concrete or 'real'? Plainly, they existed only in the imagination of the subject, as dreams or day-dreams. Faulkner, in whose work this subjective potentiality plays an important part, was evidently aware that reality must thereby be subjectivized and made to appear arbitrary. Consider this comment of his: 'They were all talking simultaneously, getting flushed and excited, quarrelling, making the unreal into a possibility, then into a probability, then into an irrefutable fact, as human beings do when they put their wishes into words.' The possibilities in a man's mind, the particular pattern, intensity and suggestiveness they assume, will of course be characteristic of that individual. In practice, their number will border on the infinite, even with the most unimaginative individual. It is thus a hopeless undertaking to define the contours of individuality, let alone to come to grips with a man's actual fate, by means of potentiality. The *abstract* character of potentiality is clear from the fact that it cannot determine development – subjective mental states, however permanent or profound, cannot here be decisive. Rather, the development of personality is determined by inherited gifts and qualities; by the factors, external or internal, which further or inhibit their growth.

But in life potentiality can, of course, become reality. Situations arise in which a man is confronted with a choice; and in the act of choice a man's character may reveal itself in a light that surprises even himself. In literature – and particularly in dramatic literature – the denouement often consists in the realization of just such a potentiality, which circumstances have kept from coming to the fore. These potentialities are, then, 'real' or concrete potentialities. The fate of the character depends upon the potentiality in question, even if it should condemn him to a tragic end. In advance, while still a subjective potentiality in the character's mind, there is no way of distinguishing it from the innumerable abstract potentialities in his mind. It may even be buried away so completely that, before the moment of decision, it has never entered his mind even as an abstract potentiality. The subject, after taking his decision, may be unconscious of his own motives. Thus Richard Dudgeon, Shaw's Devil's Disciple, having sacrificed himself as Pastor Andersen, confesses: 'I have often asked myself for the motive, but I find no good reason to explain why I acted as I did.'

Yet it is a decision which has altered the direction of his life. Of course, this is an extreme case. But the qualitative leap of the denouement, cancelling and at the same time renewing the continuity of individual consciousness, can never be predicted. The concrete potentiality cannot be isolated from the myriad abstract potentialities. Only actual decision reveals the distinction.

The literature of realism, aiming at a truthful reflection of reality, must demonstrate both the concrete and abstract potentialities of human beings in extreme situations of this kind. A character's concrete potentiality once revealed, his abstract potentialities will appear essentially inauthentic. Moravia, for instance, in his novel *The Indifferent Ones*, describes the young son of a decadent bourgeois family, Michel, who makes up his mind to kill his sister's seducer. While Michel, having made his decision, is planning the murder, a large number of abstract – but highly suggestive – possibilities are laid before us. Unfortunately for Michel the murder is actually carried out; and, from the sordid details of the action, Michel's character emerges as what it is – representative of that background from which, in subjective fantasy, he had imagined he could escape.

Abstract potentiality belongs wholly to the realm of subjectivity; whereas concrete potentiality is concerned with the dialectic between the individual's subjectivity and objective reality. The literary presentation of the latter thus implies a description of actual persons inhabiting a palpable, identifiable world. Only in the interaction of character and environment can the concrete potentiality of a particular individual be singled out from the 'bad infinity' of purely abstract potentialities, and emerge as the determining potentiality of just this individual at just this phase of his development. This principle alone enables the artist to distinguish concrete potentiality from a myriad abstractions.

But the ontology on which the image of man in modernist literature is based invalidates this principle. If the 'human condition' – man as a solitary being, incapable of meaningful relationships – is identified with reality itself, the distinction between abstract and concrete potentiality becomes null and void. The categories tend to merge. Thus Cesare Pavese notes with John Dos Passos, and his German contemporary, Alfred Döblin, a sharp oscillation between 'superficial *verisme*' and 'abstract Expressionist schematism'. Criticizing Dos Passos, Pavese writes that fictional characters 'ought to be created by deliberate selection and description of individual features' – implying that Dos Passos' characterizations are transferable from one individual to another. He describes the artistic consequences: by exalting man's subjectivity, at the expense of the objective reality of his environment, man's subjectivity itself is impoverished.

The problem, once again, is ideological. This is not to say that the ideology underlying modernist writings is identical in all cases. On the contrary: the ideology exists in extremely various, even contradictory forms. The rejection of narrative objectivity, the surrender to subjectivity, may take the form of Joyce's stream of consciousness, or of Musil's 'active passivity', his 'existence without quality', or of Gide's *'action gratuite'*, where abstract potentiality achieves pseudo-realization. As individual character manifests itself in life's moments of decision, so too in literature. If the distinction between

---

abstract and concrete potentiality vanishes, if man's inwardness is identified with an abstract subjectivity, human personality must necessarily disintegrate.

T. S. Eliot described this phenomenon, this mode of portraying human personality, as

> Shape without form, shade without colour,
> Paralysed force, gesture without motion.

The disintegration of personality is matched by a disintegration of the outer world. In one sense, this is simply a further consequence of our argument. For the identification of abstract and concrete human potentiality rests on the assumption that the objective world is inherently inexplicable. Certain leading modernist writers, attempting a theoretical apology, have admitted this quite frankly. Often this theoretical impossibility of understanding reality is the point of departure, rather than the exaltation of subjectivity. But in any case the connection between the two is plain. The German poet Gottfried Benn, for instance, informs us that 'there is no outer reality, there is only human consciousness, constantly building, modifying, rebuilding new worlds out of its own creativity'. Musil, as always, gives a moral twist to this line of thought. Ulrich, the hero of his *The Man without Qualities*, when asked what he would do if he were in God's place, replies: 'I should be compelled to abolish reality.' Subjective existence 'without qualities' is the complement of the negation of outward reality.

The negation of outward reality is not always demanded with such theoretical rigour. But it is present in almost all modernist literature. In conversation, Musil once gave as the period of his great novel, 'between 1912 and 1914'. But he was quick to modify this statement by adding: 'I have not, I must insist, written a historical novel. I am not concerned with actual events.... Events, anyhow, are interchangeable. I am interested in what is typical, in what one might call the ghostly aspect of reality.' The word 'ghostly' is interesting. It points to a major tendency in modernist literature: the attenuation of actuality. In Kafka, the descriptive detail is of an extraordinary immediacy and authenticity. But Kafka's artistic ingenuity is really directed towards substituting his *angst*-ridden vision of the world for objective reality. The realistic detail is the expression of a ghostly un-reality, of a nightmare world, whose function is to evoke *angst*. The same phenomenon can be seen in writers who attempt to combine Kafka's techniques with a critique of society – like the German writer, Wolfgang Koeppen, in his satirical novel about Bonn, *Das Treibhaus*. A similar attenuation of reality underlies Joyce's stream of consciousness. It is, of course, intensified where the stream of consciousness is itself the medium through which reality is presented. And it is carried *ad absurdum* where the stream of consciousness is that of an abnormal subject or of an idiot – consider the first part of Faulkner's *Sound and Fury* or, a still more extreme case, Beckett's *Molloy*.

Attenuation of reality and dissolution of personality are thus interdependent: the stronger the one, the stronger the other. Underlying both is the lack of a consistent view of human nature. Man is reduced to a sequence of unrelated experiential fragments; he is as inexplicable to others as to himself. In Eliot's *Cocktail Party* the psychiatrist, who voices the opinions of the author, describes the phenomenon:

> Ah, but we die to each other daily.
> What we know of other people

Is only our memory of the moments
During which we knew them. And they have changed since then.
To pretend that they and we are the same
Is a useful and convenient social convention
Which must sometimes be broken. We must also remember
That at every meeting we are meeting a stranger.

The dissolution of personality, originally the unconscious product of the identification of concrete and abstract potentiality, is elevated to a deliberate principle in the light of consciousness. It is no accident that Gottfried Benn called one of his theoretical tracts 'Doppelleben'. For Benn, this dissolution of personality took the form of a schizophrenic dichotomy. According to him, there was in man's personality no coherent pattern of motivation or behaviour. Man's animal nature is opposed to his denaturized, sublimated thought-processes. The unity of thought and action is 'backwoods philosophy'; thought and being are 'quite separate entities'. Man must be either a moral or a thinking being – he cannot be both at once.

These are not, I think, purely private, eccentric speculations. Of course, they are derived from Benn's specific experience. But there is an inner connection between these ideas and a certain tradition of bourgeois thought. It is more than a hundred years since Kierkegaard first attacked the Hegelian view that the inner and outer world form an objective dialectical unity, that they are indissolubly married in spite of their apparent opposition. Kierkegaard denied any such unity. According to Kierkegaard, the individual exists within an opaque, impenetrable 'incognito'.

This philosophy attained remarkable popularity after the Second World War – proof that even the most abstruse theories may reflect social reality. Men like Martin Heidegger, Ernst Jünger, the lawyer Carl Schmitt, Gottfried Benn and others passionately embraced this doctrine of the eternal incognito which implies that a man's external deeds are no guide to his motives. In this case, the deeds obscured behind the mysterious incognito were, needless to say, these intellectuals' participation in Nazism: Heidegger, as Rector of Freiburg University, had glorified Hitler's seizure of power at his Inauguration; Carl Schmitt had put his great legal gifts at Hitler's disposal. The facts were too well-known to be simply denied. But, if this impenetrable incognito were the true 'condition humaine', might not – concealed within their incognito – Heidegger or Schmitt have been secret opponents of Hitler all the time, only supporting him in the world of appearances? Ernst von Salomon's cynical frankness about his opportunism in The Questionnaire (keeping his reservations to himself or declaring them only in the presence of intimate friends) may be read as an ironic commentary on this ideology of the incognito as we find it, say, in the writings of Ernst Jünger.

This digression may serve to show, taking an extreme example, what the social implications of such an ontology may be. In the literary field, this particular ideology was of cardinal importance; by destroying the complex tissue of man's relations with his environment, it furthered the dissolution of personality. For it is just the opposition between a man and his environment that determines the development of his personality. There is no great hero of fiction – from Homer's Achilles to Mann's Adrian Leverkühn or Sholochov's Grigory Melyekov – whose personality is not the product of such an opposition. I have shown how disastrous the denial of the distinction between abstract and concrete potentiality must be for the presentation of character. The destruction of the complex tissue of man's interaction with his environment likewise saps the vitality of this opposition. Certainly, some writers who adhere to this ideology have attempted, not unsuccessfully, to portray this opposition in concrete terms. But the underlying ideology deprives these contradictions of their dynamic, developmental significance. The contradictions co-exist, unresolved, contributing to the further dissolution of the personality in question.

It is to the credit of Robert Musil that he was quite conscious of the implications of his method. Of his hero Ulrich he remarked: 'One is faced with a simple choice: either one must run with the pack (when in Rome, do as the Romans do); or one becomes a neurotic.' Musil here introduces the problem, central to all modernist literature, of the significance of psychopathology.

This problem was first widely discussed in the Naturalist period. More than fifty years ago, that doyen of Berlin dramatic critics, Alfred Kerr, was writing: 'Morbidity is the legitimate poetry of Naturalism. For what is poetic in everyday life? Neurotic aberration, escape from life's dreary routine. Only in this way can a character be translated to a rarer clime and yet retain an air of reality.' Interesting, here, is the notion that the poetic necessity of the pathological derives from the prosaic quality of life under capitalism. I would maintain – we shall return to this point – that in modern writing there is a continuity from Naturalism to the Modernism of our day – a continuity restricted, admittedly, to underlying ideological principles. What at first was no more than dim anticipation of approaching catastrophe developed, after 1914, into an all-pervading obsession. And I would suggest that the ever-increasing part played by psychopathology was one of the main features of the continuity. At each period – depending on the prevailing social and historical conditions – psychopathology was given a new emphasis, a different significance and artistic function. Kerr's description suggests that in naturalism the interest in psychopathology sprang from an aesthetic need; it was an attempt to escape from the dreariness of life under capitalism. The quotation from Musil shows that some years later the opposition acquired a moral slant. The obsession with morbidity had ceased to have a merely decorative function, bringing colour into the greyness of reality, and become a moral protest against capitalism.

With Musil – and with many other modernist writers – psychopathology became the goal, the *terminus ad quem*, of their artistic intention. But there is a double difficulty inherent in their intention, which follows from its underlying ideology. There is, first, a lack of definition. The protest expressed by this flight into psychopathology is an abstract gesture; its rejection of reality is wholesale and summary, containing no concrete criticism. It is a gesture, moreover, that is destined to lead nowhere; it is an escape into nothingness. Thus the propagators of this ideology are mistaken in thinking that such a protest could ever be fruitful in literature. In any protest against particular social conditions, these conditions themselves must have the central place. The bourgeois protest against feudal society, the proletarian against bourgeois society, made their point of departure a criticism of the old order. In both cases the protest – reaching out beyond the point of departure – was based on a concrete *terminus ad quem*: the establishment of a new order. However indefinite the structure and content of this new order, the will towards its more exact definition was not lacking.

GYÖRGY LUKÁCS

How different the protest of writers like Musil! The *terminus a quo* (the corrupt society of our time) is inevitably the main source of energy, since the *terminus ad quem* (the escape into psychopathology) is a mere abstraction. The rejection of modern reality is purely subjective. Considered in terms of man's relation with his environment, it lacks both content and direction. And this lack is exaggerated still further by the character of the *terminus ad quem*. For the protest is an empty gesture, expressing nausea, or discomfort, or longing. Its content – or rather lack of content – derives from the fact that such a view of life cannot impart a sense of direction. These writers are not wholly wrong in believing that psychopathology is their surest refuge; it is the ideological complement of their historical position.

This obsession with the pathological is not only to be found in literature. Freudian psychoanalysis is its most obvious expression. The treatment of the subject is only superficially different from that in modern literature. As everybody knows, Freud's starting point was 'everyday life'. In order to explain 'slips' and day-dreams, however, he had to have recourse to psychopathology. In his lectures, speaking of resistance and repression, he says: 'Our interest in the general psychology of symptom-formation increases as we understand to what extent the study of pathological conditions can shed light on the workings of the normal mind.' Freud believed he had found the key to the understanding of the normal personality in the psychology of the abnormal. This belief is still more evident in the typology of Kretschmer, which also assumes that psychological abnormalities can explain normal psychology. It is only when we compare Freud's psychology with that of Pavlov, who takes the Hippocratic view that mental abnormality is a deviation from a norm, that we see it in its true light.

Clearly, this is not strictly a scientific or literary-critical problem. It is an ideological problem, deriving from the ontological dogma of the solitariness of man. The literature of realism, based on the Aristotelian concept of man as *zoon politikon*, is entitled to develop a new typology for each new phase in the evolution of a society. It displays the contradictions within society and within the individual in the context of a dialectical unity. Here, individuals embodying violent and extraordinary passions are still within the range of a socially normal typology (Shakespeare, Balzac, Stendhal). For, in this literature, the average man is simply a dimmer reflection of the contradictions always existing in man and society; eccentricity is a socially-conditioned distortion. Obviously, the passions of the great heroes must not be confused with 'eccentricity' in the colloquial sense: Christian Buddenbrook is an 'eccentric'; Adrian Leverkühn is not.

The ontology of *Geworfenheit* makes a true typology impossible; it is replaced by an abstract polarity of the eccentric and the socially-average. We have seen why this polarity – which in traditional realism serves to increase our understanding of social normality – leads in modernism to a fascination with morbid eccentricity. Eccentricity becomes the necessary complement of the average; and this polarity is held to exhaust human potentiality. The implications of this ideology are shown in another remark of Musil's: 'If humanity dreamt collectively, it would dream Moosbrugger.' Moosbrugger, you will remember, was a mentally-retarded sexual pervert with homicidal tendencies.

What served, with Musil, as the ideological basis of a new typology – escape into neurosis as a protest against the evils of society – becomes with other modernist writers an immutable *condition humaine*. Musil's statement loses its conditional 'if' and becomes a simple description of reality. Lack of objectivity in the description of the outer world finds its complement in the reduction of reality to a nightmare. Beckett's *Molloy* is perhaps the *ne plus ultra* of this development, although Joyce's vision of reality as an incoherent stream of consciousness had already assumed in Faulkner a nightmare quality. In Beckett's novel we have the same vision twice over. He presents us with an image of the utmost human degradation – an idiot's vegetative existence. Then, as help is imminent from a mysterious unspecified source, the rescuer himself sinks into idiocy. The story is told through the parallel streams of consciousness of the idiot and of his rescuer.

Along with the adoption of perversity and idiocy as types of the *condition humaine*, we find what amounts to frank glorification. Take Montherlant's *Pasiphae*, where sexual perversity – the heroine's infatuation with a bull – is presented as a triumphant return to nature, as the liberation of impulse from the slavery of convention. The chorus – i.e. the author – puts the following question (which, though rhetorical, clearly expects an affirmative reply): 'Si l'absence de pensée et l'absence de morale ne contribuent pas beaucoup à la dignité des bêtes, des plantes et des eaux…?' Montherlant expresses as plainly as Musil, though with different moral and emotional emphasis, the hidden – one might say repressed – social character of the protest underlying this obsession with psychopathology, its perverted Rousseauism, its anarchism. There are many illustrations of this in modernist writing. A poem of Benn's will serve to make the point:

> O that we were our primal ancestors,
> Small lumps of plasma in hot, sultry swamps;
> Life, death, conception, parturition
> Emerging from those juices soundlessly.
>
> A frond of seaweed or a dune of sand,
> Formed by the wind and heavy at the base;
> A dragonfly or gull's wing – already, these
> Would signify excessive suffering.

This is not overtly perverse in the manner of Beckett or Montherlant. Yet, in his primitivism, Benn is at one with them. The opposition of man as animal to man as social being (for instance, Heidegger's devaluation of the social as '*das Man*', Klages' assertion of the incompatibility of *Geist* and *Seele*, or Rosenberg's racial mythology) leads straight to a glorification of the abnormal and to an undisguised anti-humanism.

A typology limited in this way to the *homme moyen sensuel* and the idiot also opens the door to 'experimental' stylistic distortion. Distortion becomes as inseparable a part of the portrayal of reality as the recourse to the pathological. But literature must have a concept of the normal if it is to 'place' distortion correctly; that is to say, to see it as distortion. With such a typology this placing is impossible, since the normal is no longer a proper object of literary interest. Life under capitalism is, often rightly, presented as a distortion (a petrification or paralysis) of the human substance. But to present psychopathology as a way of escape from this distortion is itself a distortion. We are invited to measure one type of distortion against another and arrive, necessarily, at universal distortion. There is no principle to set against the general pattern, no standard by which the petty-bourgeois and the pathological can be seen in their social context. And these tendencies, far from being relativized with time, become ever more absolute.

Distortion becomes the normal condition of human existence; the proper study, the formative principle, of art and literature.

I have demonstrated some of the literary implications of this ideology. Let us now pursue the argument further. It is clear, I think, that modernism must deprive literature of a sense of *perspective*. This would not be surprising; rigorous modernists such as Kafka, Benn, and Musil have always indignantly refused to provide their readers with any such thing. I will return to the ideological implications of the idea of perspective later. Let me say here that, in any work of art, perspective is of overriding importance. It determines the course and content; it draws together the threads of the narration; it enables the artist to choose between the important and the superficial, the crucial and the episodic. The direction in which characters develop is determined by perspective, only those features being described which are material to their development. The more lucid the perspective – as in Molière or the Greeks – the more economical and striking the selection.

Modernism drops this selective principle. It asserts that it can dispense with it, or can replace it with its dogma of the *condition humaine*. A naturalistic style is bound to be the result. This state of affairs – which to my mind characterizes all modernist art of the past fifty years – is disguised by critics who systematically glorify the modernist movement. By concentrating on formal criteria, by isolating technique from content and exaggerating its importance, these critics refrain from judgment on the social or artistic significance of subject-matter. They are unable, in consequence, to make the aesthetic distinction between *realism* and *naturalism*. This distinction depends on the presence or absence in a work of art of a 'hierarchy of significance' in the situations and characters presented. Compared with this, formal categories are of secondary importance. That is why it is possible to speak of the basically *naturalistic* character of modernist literature – and to see here the literary expression of an ideological continuity. This is not to deny that variations in style reflect changes in society. But the particular form this principle of naturalistic arbitrariness, this lack of hierarchic structure, may take is not decisive. We encounter it in the all-determining 'social conditions' of Naturalism, in Symbolism's impressionist methods and its cultivation of the exotic, in the fragmentation of objective reality in Futurism and Constructivism and the German *Neue Sachlichkeit*, or, again, in Surrealism's stream of consciousness.

These schools have in common a basically static approach to reality. This is closely related to their lack of perspective. Characteristically, Gottfried Benn actually incorporated this in his artistic programme. One of his volumes bears the title, *Static Poems*. The denial of history, of development, and thus of perspective, becomes the mark of true insight into the nature of reality.

> The wise man is ignorant
> of change and development
> his children and children's children
> are no part of his world.

The rejection of any concept of the future is for Benn the criterion of wisdom. But even those modernist writers who are less extreme in their rejection of history tend to present social and historical phenomena as static. It is, then, of small importance whether this condition is 'eternal', or only a transitional stage punctuated by sudden catastrophes (even in early Naturalism the static presentation was often broken up by these catastrophes, without altering its basic character). Musil, for instance, writes in his essay, *The Writer in our Age*: 'One knows just as little about the present. Partly, this is because we are, as always, too close to the present. But it is also because the present into which we were plunged some two decades ago is of a particularly all-embracing and inescapable character.' Whether or not Musil knew of Heidegger's philosophy, the idea of *Geworfenheit* is clearly at work here. And the following reveals plainly how, for Musil, this static state was upset by the catastrophe of 1914: 'All of a sudden, the world was full of violence.... In European civilization, there was a sudden rift....' In short: thus static apprehension of reality in modernist literature is no passing fashion; it is rooted in the ideology of modernism.

To establish the basic distinction between modernism and that realism which, from Homer to Thomas Mann and Gorky, has assumed change and development to be the proper subject of literature, we must go deeper into the underlying ideological problem. In *The House of the Dead* Dostoevsky gave an interesting account of the convict's attitude to work. He described how the prisoners, in spite of brutal discipline, loafed about, working badly or merely going through the motions of work until a new overseer arrived and allotted them a new project, after which they were allowed to go home. 'The work was hard,' Dostoevsky continues, 'but, Christ, with what energy they threw themselves into it! Gone was all their former indolence and pretended incompetence.' Later in the book Dostoevsky sums up his experiences: 'If a man loses hope and has no aim in view, sheer boredom can turn him into a beast....' I have said that the problem of perspective in literature is directly related to the principle of selection. Let me go further: underlying the problem is a profound ethical complex, reflected in the composition of the work itself. Every human action is based on a presupposition of its inherent meaningfulness, at least to the subject. Absence of meaning makes a mockery of action and reduces art to naturalistic description.

Clearly, there can be no literature without at least the appearance of change or development. This conclusion should not be interpreted in a narrowly metaphysical sense. We have already diagnosed the obsession with psychopathology in modernist literature as a desire to escape from the reality of capitalism. But this implies the absolute primacy of the *terminus a quo*, the condition from which it is desired to escape. Any movement towards a *terminus ad quem* is condemned to impotence. As the ideology of most modernist writers asserts the unalterability of outward reality (even if this is reduced to a mere state of consciousness) human activity is, *a priori*, rendered impotent and robbed of meaning.

The apprehension of reality to which this leads is most consistently and convincingly realized in the work of Kafka. Kafka remarks of Josef K., as he is being led to execution: 'He thought of flies, their tiny limbs breaking as they struggle away from the fly-paper.' This mood of total impotence, of paralysis in the face of the unintelligible power of circumstances, informs all his work. Though the action of *The Castle* takes a different, even an opposite, direction to that of *The Trial*, this view of the world, from the perspective of a trapped and struggling fly, is all-pervasive. This experience, this vision of a world dominated by *angst* and of man at the mercy of incomprehensible terrors, makes Kafka's work the very type of modernist art. Techniques, elsewhere of merely formal significance, are used here to evoke a primitive awe in the presence of an utterly strange and hostile reality. Kafka's *angst* is the experience *par excellence* of modernism.

Two instances from musical criticism – which can afford to be both franker and more theoretical than literary criticism – show that it is indeed a universal experience with which we are dealing. The composer, Hanns Eisler, says of Schönberg: 'Long before the invention of the bomber, he expressed what people were to feel in the air raid shelters.' Even more characteristic – though seen from a modernist point of view – is Theodor W. Adorno's analysis (in *The Ageing of Modern Music*) of symptoms of decadence in modernist music: 'The sounds are still the same. But the experience of *angst*, which made their originals great, has vanished.' Modernist music, he continues, has lost touch with the truth that was its *raison d'être*. Composers are no longer equal to the emotional presuppositions of their modernism. And that is why modernist music has failed. The diminution of the original *angst*-obsessed vision of life (whether due, as Adorno thinks, to inability to respond to the magnitude of the horror or, as I believe, to the fact that this obsession with *angst* among bourgeois intellectuals has already begun to recede) has brought about a loss of substance in modern music, and destroyed its authenticity as a modernist art-form.

This is a shrewd analysis of the paradoxical situation of the modernist artist, particularly where he is trying to express deep and genuine experience. The deeper the experience, the greater the damage to the artistic whole. But this tendency towards disintegration, this loss of artistic unity, cannot be written off as a mere fashion, the product of experimental gimmicks. Modern philosophy, after all, encountered these problems long before modern literature, painting or music. A case in point is the problem of *time*. Subjective Idealism had already separated time, abstractly conceived, from historical change and particularity of place. As if this separation were insufficient for the new age of imperialism, Bergson widened it further. Experienced time, subjective time, now became identical with real time; the rift between this time and that of the objective world was complete. Bergson and other philosophers who took up and varied this theme claimed that their concept of time alone afforded insight into authentic, i.e. subjective, reality. The same tendency soon made its appearance in literature.

The German left-wing critic and essayist of the twenties, Walter Benjamin, has well described Proust's vision and the techniques he uses to present it in his great novel: 'We all know that Proust does not describe a man's life as it actually happens, but as it is remembered by a man who has lived through it. Yet this puts it far too crudely. For it is not actual experience that is important, but the texture of reminiscence, the Penelope's tapestry of a man's memory.' The connection with Bergson's theories of time is obvious. But whereas with Bergson, in the abstraction of philosophy, the unity of perception is preserved, Benjamin shows that with Proust, as a result of the radical disintegration of the time sequence, objectivity is eliminated: 'A lived event is finite, concluded at least on the level of experience. But a remembered event is infinite, a possible key to everything that preceded it and to everything that will follow it.'

It is the distinction between a philosophical and an artistic vision of the world. However hard philosophy, under the influence of Idealism, tries to liberate the concepts of space and time from temporal and spatial particularity, literature continues to assume their unity. The fact that, nevertheless, the concept of subjective time cropped up in literature only shows how deeply subjectivism is rooted in the experience of the modern bourgeois intellectual. The individual, retreating into himself in despair at the cruelty of the age, may experience an intoxicated fascination with his forlorn condition. But then a new horror breaks through. If reality cannot be understood (or no effort is made to understand it), then the individual's subjectivity – alone in the universe, reflecting only itself – takes on an equally incomprehensible and horrific character. Hugo von Hofmannsthal was to experience this condition very early in his poetic career:

> It is a thing that no man cares to think on,
> And far too terrible for mere complaint,
> That all things slip from us and pass away,
>
> And that my ego, bound by no outward force –
> Once a small child's before it became mine –
> Should now be strange to me, like a strange dog.

By separating time from the outer world of objective reality, the inner world of the subject is transformed into a sinister, inexplicable flux and acquires – paradoxically, as it may seem – a static character.

On literature this tendency towards disintegration, of course, will have an even greater impact than on philosophy. When time is isolated in this way, the artist's world disintegrates into a multiplicity of partial worlds. The static view of the world, now combined with diminished objectivity, here rules unchallenged. The world of man – the only subject-matter of literature – is shattered if a single component is removed. I have shown the consequences of isolating time and reducing it to a subjective category. But time is by no means the only component whose removal can lead to such disintegration. Here, again, Hofmannsthal anticipated later developments. His imaginary 'Lord Chandos' reflects: 'I have lost the ability to concentrate my thoughts or set them out coherently.' The result is a condition of apathy, punctuated by manic fits. The development towards a definitely pathological protest is here anticipated – admittedly in glamorous, romantic guise. But it is the same disintegration that is at work.

Previous realistic literature, however violent its criticism of reality, had always assumed the unity of the world it described and seen it as a living whole inseparable from man himself. But the major realists of our time deliberately introduce elements of disintegration into their work – for instance, the subjectivizing of time – and use them to portray the contemporary world more exactly. In this way, the once natural unity becomes a conscious, constructed unity (I have shown elsewhere that the device of the two temporal planes in Thomas Mann's *Doctor Faustus* serves to emphasize its historicity). But in modernist literature the disintegration of the world of man – and consequently the disintegration of personality – coincides with the ideological intention. Thus *angst*, this basic modern experience, this by-product of *Geworfenheit*, has its emotional origin in the experience of a disintegrating society. But it attains its effects by evoking the disintegration of the world of man.

To complete our examination of modernist literature, we must consider for a moment the question of allegory. Allegory is that aesthetic genre which lends itself par excellence to a description of man's alienation from objective reality. Allegory is a problematic genre because it rejects that assumption of an immanent meaning to human existence which – however unconscious, however combined with religious concepts of transcend-

GYÖRGY LUKÁCS

ence – is the basis of traditional art. Thus in medieval art we observe a new secularity (in spite of the continued use of religious subjects) triumphing more and more, from the time of Giotto, over the allegorizing of an earlier period.

Certain reservations should be made at this point. First, we must distinguish between literature and the visual arts. In the latter, the limitations of allegory can be the more easily overcome in that transcendental, allegorical subjects can be clothed in an aesthetic immanence (even if of a merely decorative kind) and the rift in reality in some sense be eliminated – we have only to think of Byzantine mosaic art. This decorative element has no real equivalent in literature; it exists only in a figurative sense, and then only as a secondary component. Allegorical art of the quality of Byzantine mosaic is only rarely possible in literature. Secondly, we must bear in mind in examining allegory – and this is of great importance for our argument – a historical distinction: does the concept of transcendence in question contain within itself tendencies towards immanence (as in Byzantine art or Giotto), or is it the product precisely of a rejection of these tendencies?

Allegory, in modernist literature, is clearly of the latter kind. Transcendence implies here, more or less consciously, the negation of any meaning immanent in the world or the life of man. We have already examined the underlying ideological basis of this view and its stylistic consequences. To conclude our analysis, and to establish the allegorical character of modernist literature, I must refer again to the work of one of the finest theoreticians of modernism – to Walter Benjamin. Benjamin's examination of allegory was a product of his researches into German Baroque drama. Benjamin made his analysis of these relatively minor plays the occasion for a general discussion of the aesthetics of allegory. He was asking, in effect, why it is that transcendence, which is the essence of allegory, cannot but destroy aesthetics itself.

Benjamin gives a very contemporary definition of allegory. He does not labour the analogies between modern art and the Baroque (such analogies are tenuous at best, and were much overdone by the fashionable criticism of the time). Rather, he uses the Baroque drama to criticize modernism, imputing the characteristics of the latter to the former. In so doing, Benjamin became the first critic to attempt a philosophical analysis of the aesthetic paradox underlying modernist art. He writes:

In Allegory, the *facies hippocratica* of history looks to the observer like a petrified primeval landscape. History, all the suffering and failure it contains, finds expression in the human face – or, rather, in the human skull. No sense of freedom, no classical proportion, no human emotion lives in its features – not only human existence in general, but the fate of every individual human being is symbolized in this most palpable token of mortality. This is the core of the allegorical vision, of the Baroque idea of history as the passion of the world; History is significant only in the stations of its corruption. Significance is a function of mortality – because it is death that marks the passage from corruptibility to meaningfulness.

Benjamin returns again and again to this link between allegory and the annihilation of history:

In the light of this vision history appears, not as the gradual realization of the eternal, but as a process of inevitable decay. Allegory thus goes beyond beauty. What ruins are in the physical world, allegories are in the world of the mind.

Benjamin points here to the aesthetic consequences of modernism – though projected into the Baroque drama – more shrewdly and consistently than any of his contemporaries. He sees that the notion of objective time is essential to any understanding of history, and that the notion of subjective time is a product of a period of decline. 'A thorough knowledge of the problematic nature of art' thus becomes for him – correctly, from his point of view – one of the hall-marks of allegory in Baroque drama. It is problematic, on the one hand, because it is an art intent on expressing absolute transcendence that fails to do so because of the means at its disposal. It is also problematic because it is an art reflecting the corruption of the world and bringing about its own dissolution in the process. Benjamin discovers 'an immense, anti-aesthetic subjectivity' in Baroque literature, associated with 'a theologically-determined subjectivity'. (We shall presently show – a point I have discussed elsewhere in relation to Heidegger's philosophy – how in literature a 'religious atheism' of this kind can acquire a theological character.) Romantic – and, on a higher plane, Baroque – writers were well aware of this problem, and gave their understanding, not only theoretical, but artistic – that is to say allegorical – expression. 'The image,' Benjamin remarks, 'becomes a rune in the sphere of allegorical intuition. When touched by the light of theology, its symbolic beauty is gone. The false appearance of totality vanishes. The image dies; the parable no longer holds true; the world it once contained disappears.'

The consequences for art are far-reaching, and Benjamin does not hesitate to point them out: 'Every person, every object, every relationship can stand for something else. This transferability constitutes a devastating, though just, judgment on the profane world – which is thereby branded as a world where such things are of small importance.' Benjamin knows, of course, that although details are 'transferable', and thus insignificant, they are not banished from art altogether. On the contrary. Precisely in modern art, with which he is ultimately concerned, descriptive detail is often of an extraordinary sensuous, suggestive power – we think again of Kafka. But this, as we showed in the case of Musil (a writer who does not consciously aim at allegory) does not prevent the materiality of the world from undergoing permanent alteration, from becoming transferable and arbitrary. Just this, modernist writers maintain, is typical of their own apprehension of reality. Yet presented in this way, the world becomes, as Benjamin puts it, 'exalted and depreciated at the same time'. For the conviction that phenomena are *not* ultimately transferable is rooted in a belief in the world's rationality and in man's ability to penetrate its secrets. In realistic literature each descriptive detail is both *individual* and *typical*. Modern allegory, and modernist ideology, however, deny the *typical*. By destroying the coherence of the world, they reduce detail to the level of mere particularity (once again, the connection between modernism and naturalism is plain). Detail, in its allegorical transferability, though brought into a direct, if paradoxical connection with transcendence, becomes an abstract function of the transcendence to which it points. Modernist literature thus replaces concrete typicality with abstract particularity.

We are here applying Benjamin's paradox directly to aesthetics and criticism, and particularly to the aesthetics of modernism. And, though we have reversed his scale of values, we have not deviated from the course of his argument. Elsewhere, he speaks out even more plainly – as though the Baroque mask had fallen, revealing the modernist skull underneath:

GYÖRGY LUKÁCS

Allegory is left empty-handed. The forces of evil, lurking in its depths, owe their very existence to allegory. Evil is, precisely, the non-existence of that which allegory purports to represent.

The paradox Benjamin arrives at – his investigation of the aesthetics of Baroque tragedy has culminated in a negation of aesthetics – sheds a good deal of light on modernist literature, and particularly on Kafka. In interpreting his writings allegorically I am not, of course, following Max Brod, who finds a specifically religious allegory in Kafka's works. Kafka refuted any such interpretation in a remark he is said to have made to Brod himself: 'We are nihilistic figments, all of us; suicidal notions forming in God's mind.' Kafka rejected, too, the gnostic concept of God as an evil demiurge: 'The world is a cruel whim of God, an evil day's work.' When Brod attempted to give this an optimistic slant, Kafka shrugged off the attempt ironically: 'Oh, hope enough, hope without end – but not, alas, for us.' These remarks, quoted by Benjamin in his brilliant essay on Kafka, point to the general spiritual climate of his work: 'His profoundest experience is of the hopelessness, the utter meaninglessness of man's world, and particularly that of present-day bourgeois man.' Kafka, whether he says so openly or not, is an atheist. An atheist, though, of that modern species who regard God's removal from the scene not as a liberation – as did Epicurus and the Encyclopedists – but as a token of the 'God-forsakenness' of the world, its utter desolation and futility. Jacobsen's *Niels Lyhne* was the first novel to describe this state of mind of the atheistic bourgeois intelligentsia. Modern religious atheism is characterized, on the one hand, by the fact that unbelief has lost its revolutionary *élan* – the empty heavens are the projection of a world beyond hope of redemption. On the other hand, religious atheism shows that the desire for salvation lives on with undiminished force in a world without God, worshipping the void created by God's absence.

The supreme judges in *The Trial*, the castle administration in *The Castle*, represent transcendence in Kafka's allegories: the transcendence of Nothingness. Everything points to them, and they could give meaning to everything. Everybody believes in their existence and omnipotence; but nobody knows them, nobody knows how they can be reached. If there is a God here, it can only be the God of religious atheism: *atheos absconditus*. We become acquainted with a repellent host of subordinate authorities; brutal, corrupt, pedantic – and, at the same time, unreliable and irresponsible. It is a portrait of the bourgeois society Kafka knew, with a dash of Prague local colouring. But it is also allegorical in that the doings of this bureaucracy and of those dependent on it, its impotent victims, are not concrete and realistic, but a reflection of that Nothingness which governs existence. The hidden, non-existence God of Kafka's world derives his spectral character from the fact that his own non-existence is the ground of all existence; and the portrayed reality, uncannily accurate as it is, is spectral in the shadow of that dependence. The only purpose of transcendence – the intangible *nichtendes Nichts* – is to reveal the *facies hippocratica* of the world.

That abstract particularity which we saw to be the aesthetic consequence of allegory reaches its high mark in Kafka. He is a marvellous observer; the spectral character of reality affects him so deeply that the simplest episodes have an oppressive, nightmarish immediacy. As an artist, he is not content to evoke the surface of life. He is aware that individual detail must point to general significance. But how does he go about the business of abstraction? He has emptied everyday life of meaning by using the allegorical method; he has allowed detail to be annihilated by his transcendental Nothingness. This allegorical transcendence bars Kafka's way to realism, prevents him from investing observed detail with typical significance. Kafka is not able, in spite of his extraordinary evocative power, in spite of his unique sensibility, to achieve that fusion of the particular and the general which is the essence of realistic art. His aim is to raise the individual detail in its immediate particularity (without generalizing its content) to the level of abstraction. Kafka's method is typical, here, of modernism's allegorical approach. Specific subject-matter and stylistic variation do not matter; what matters is the basic ideological determination of form and content. The particularity we find in Beckett and Joyce, in Musil and Benn, various as the treatment of it may be, is essentially of the same kind.

If we combine what we have up to now discussed separately we arrive at a consistent pattern. We see that modernism leads not only to the destruction of traditional literary forms; it leads to the destruction of literature as such. And this is true not only of Joyce, or of the literature of Expressionism and Surrealism. It was not André Gide's ambition, for instance, to bring about a revolution in literary style; it was his philosophy that compelled him to abandon conventional forms. He planned his *Faux-Monnayeurs* as a novel. But its structure suffered from a characteristically modernist schizophrenia: it was supposed to be written by the man who was also the hero of the novel. And, in practice, Gide was forced to admit that no novel, no work of literature could be constructed in that way. We have here a practical demonstration that – as Benjamin showed in another context – modernism means not the enrichment, but the negation of art.

The Political Unconscious

Fredric Jameson

Fredric Jameson (b. 1934)

Fredric Jameson was born in Cleveland, Ohio, and educated at Haverford College and Yale University, where he received his doctorate in French in 1960. Jameson taught at Harvard University (1959–67), the University of California, San Diego (1967–76), Yale University (1976–83), and the University of California, Santa Cruz (1983–5). In 1986 Jameson became the William A. Lane Professor of Comparative Literature and Romance Studies in the Department of Romance Studies at Duke University, where he has also served as the director for the Center for Critical Theory. Jameson's honors include membership of the American Academy of Arts and Sciences, and fellowships from the Woodrow Wilson Foundation, the Humanities Institute, and the Guggenheim Foundation. He is the chair of the editorial board of *South Atlantic Quarterly,* and past editor of *Social Text.* In addition to *The Political Unconscious: Narrative as a Socially Symbolic Act* (1981), Jameson also has published *Marxism and Form: Twentieth-Century Dialectical Theories of Literature* (1971);

From *The Political Unconscious: Narrative as a Socially Symbolic Act.* Ithaca, NY: Cornell University Press, 1981, from ch. 1, pp. 17–23, ch. 3, pp. 151–69, Conclusion, pp. 296–9.

The Prison-House of Language: A Critical Account of Structuralism and Russian Formalism (1972); *Postmodernism, or, The Cultural Logic of Late Capitalism* (1991); and *A Singular Modernity: Essay on the Ontology of the Present* (2002); selected essays are collected in *The Jameson Reader* (2000).

On Interpretation: Literature as a Socially Symbolic Act

This book will argue the priority of the political interpretation of literary texts. It conceives of the political perspective not as some supplementary method, not as an optional auxiliary to other interpretive methods current today – the psychoanalytic or the myth-critical, the stylistic, the ethical, the structural – but rather as the absolute horizon of all reading and all interpretation.

This is evidently a much more extreme position than the modest claim, surely acceptable to everyone, that certain texts have social and historical – sometimes even political – resonance. Traditional literary history has, of course, never prohibited the investigation of such topics as the Florentine political background in Dante, Milton's relationship to the schismatics, or Irish historical allusions in Joyce. I would argue, however, that such information – even where it is not recontained, as it is in most instances, by an idealistic conception of the history of ideas – does not yield interpretation as such, but rather at best its (indispensable) preconditions.

Today this properly antiquarian relationship to the cultural past has a dialectical counterpart which is ultimately no more satisfactory; I mean the tendency of much contemporary theory to rewrite selected texts from the past in terms of its own aesthetic and, in particular, in terms of a modernist (or more properly post-modernist) conception of language. I have shown elsewhere[1] the ways in which such "ideologies of the text" construct a straw man or inessential term – variously called the "readerly" or the "realistic" or the "referential" text – over against which the essential term – the "writerly" or modernist or "open" text, *écriture* or textual productivity – is defined and with which it is seen as a decisive break. But Croce's great dictum that "all history is contemporary history" does not mean that all history is *our* contemporary history; and the problems begin when your epistemological break begins to displace itself in time according to your own current interests, so that Balzac may stand for unenlightened representationality when you are concerned to bring out everything that is "textual" and modern in Flaubert, but turns into something else when, with Roland Barthes in *S/Z*, you have decided to rewrite Balzac as Philippe Sollers, as sheer text and *écriture*.

This unacceptable option, or ideological double bind, between antiquarianism and modernizing "relevance" or projection demonstrates that the old dilemmas of historicism – and in particular, the question of the claims of monuments from distant and even archaic moments of the cultural past on a culturally different present[2] – do not go away just because we choose to ignore them. Our presupposition, in the analyses that follow, will be that only a genuine philosophy of history is capable of respecting the specificity and radical difference of the social and cultural past while disclosing the solidarity of its

FREDRIC JAMESON

polemics and passions, its forms, structures, experiences, and struggles, with those of the present day.

But genuine philosophies of history have never been numerous, and few survive in workable, usable form in the contemporary world of consumer capitalism and the multinational system. We will have enough occasion, in the pages that follow, to emphasize the methodological interest of Christian historicism and the theological origins of the first great hermeneutic system in the Western tradition, to be permitted the additional observation that the Christian philosophy of history which emerges full blown in Augustine's *City of God* (A.D. 413–426) can no longer be particularly binding on us. As for the philosophy of history of a heroic bourgeoisie, its two principal variants – the vision of progress that emerges from the ideological struggles of the French Enlightenment, and that organic populism or nationalism which articulated the rather different historicity of the central and Eastern European peoples and which is generally associated with the name of Herder – are neither of them extinct, certainly, but are at the very least both discredited under their hegemonic embodiments in positivism and classical liberalism, and in nationalism respectively.

My position here is that only Marxism offers a philosophically coherent and ideo-logically compelling resolution to the dilemma of historicism evoked above. Only Marxism can give us an adequate account of the essential *mystery* of the cultural past, which, like Tiresias drinking the blood, is momentarily returned to life and warmth and allowed once more to speak, and to deliver its long-forgotten message in surroundings utterly alien to it. This mystery can be reenacted only if the human adventure is one; only thus – and not through the hobbies of antiquarianism or the projections of the modernists – can we glimpse the vital claims upon us of such long-dead issues as the seasonal alternation of the economy of a primitive tribe, the passionate disputes about the nature of the Trinity, the conflicting models of the *polis* or the universal Empire, or, apparently closer to us in time, the dusty parliamentary and journalistic polemics of the nineteenth-century nation states. These matters can recover their original urgency for us only if they are retold within the unity of a single great collective story; only if, in however disguised and symbolic a form, they are seen as sharing a single fundamental theme – for Marxism, the collective struggle to wrest a realm of Freedom from a realm of Necessity[3]; only if they are grasped as vital episodes in a single vast unfinished plot: "The history of all hitherto existing society is the history of class struggles: freeman and slave, patrician and plebeian, lord and serf, guild-master and journeyman – in a word, oppressor and oppressed – stood in constant opposition to one another, carried on an uninterrupted, now hidden, now open fight, a fight that each time ended, either in a revolutionary reconstitution of society at large or in the common ruin of the contending classes."[4] It is in detecting the traces of that uninter-rupted narrative, in restoring to the surface of the text the repressed and buried reality of this fundamental history, that the doctrine of a political unconscious finds its function and its necessity.

From this perspective the convenient working distinction between cultural texts that are social and political and those that are not becomes something worse than an error: namely, a symptom and a reinforcement of the reification and privatization of contemporary life. Such a distinction reconfirms that structural, experiential, and conceptual gap between the public and the private, between the social and the psychological, or the political and the poetic, between history or society and the "individual," which – the tendential law of social life under capitalism – maims our existence as individual subjects and paralyzes our thinking about time and change just as surely as it alienates us from our speech itself. To imagine that, sheltered from the omnipresence of history and the implacable influence of the social, there already exists a realm of freedom – whether it be that of the microscopic experience of words in a text or the ecstasies and intensities of the various private religions – is only to strengthen the grip of Necessity over all such blind zones in which the individual subject seeks refuge, in pursuit of a purely individual, a merely psychological, project of salvation. The only effective liberation from such constraint begins with the recognition that there is nothing that is not social and historical – indeed, that everything is "in the last analysis" political.

The assertion of a political unconscious proposes that we undertake just such a final analysis and explore the multiple paths that lead to the unmasking of cultural artifacts as socially symbolic acts. It projects a rival hermeneutic to those already enumerated; but it does so, as we shall see, not so much by repudiating their findings as by arguing its ultimate philosophical and methodological priority over more special-ized interpretive codes whose insights are strategically limited as much by their own situational origins as by the narrow or local ways in which they construe or construct their objects of study.

Still, to describe the readings and analyses contained in the present work as so many *interpretations*, to present them as so many exhibits in the construction of a new *hermeneutic*, is already to announce a whole polemic program, which must necessarily come to terms with a critical and theoretical climate variously hostile to these slogans.[5] It is, for instance, increasingly clear that hermeneutic or interpretive activity has become one of the basic polemic targets of contemporary post-structuralism in France, which – powerfully buttressed by the authority of Nietzsche – has tended to identify such operations with historicism, and in particular with the dialectic and its valorization of absence and the negative, its assertion of the necessity and priority of totalizing thought. I will agree with this identification, with this description of the ideological affinities and implications of the ideal of the interpretive or hermeneutic act; but I will argue that the critique is misplaced.

Indeed, one of the most dramatic of such recent attacks on interpretation – *The Anti-Oedipus*, by Gilles Deleuze and Félix Guattari – quite properly takes as its object not Marxian, but rather Freudian, interpretation, which is characterized as a reduction and a rewriting of the whole rich and random multiple realities of concrete everyday experi-ence into the contained, strategically pre-limited terms of the family narrative – whether this be seen as myth, Greek tragedy, "family romance," or even the Lacanian structural version of the Oedipus complex. What is denounced is therefore a system of allegorical interpretation in which the data of one narrative line are radically impover-ished by their rewriting according to the paradigm of another narrative, which is taken as the former's master code or Ur-narrative and proposed as the ultimate hidden or unconscious *meaning* of the first one. The thrust of the argument of the *Anti-Oedipus* is, to be sure, very much in the spirit of the present work, for the concern of its authors is to reassert the specificity of the political content of everyday life and of individual fantasy-experience and to reclaim it from that reduction to the merely subjective and to the status of psychological projection which is even more characteristic of American cultural and ideological life today than it is of a still politicized France. My point in mentioning this example is to observe that the repudiation of an older interpretive system – Freudian rewriting, overhastily assimilated to hermeneutics in general and as such – is in *The Anti-Oedipus* coupled with the projection of a whole new method for the reading of texts:

> The unconscious poses no problem of meaning, solely problems of use. The question posed by desire is not "What does it mean?" but rather *"How does it work?"*...[The unconscious] represents nothing, but it produces. It means nothing, but it works. Desire makes its entry with the general collapse of the question "What does it mean?" No one has been able to pose the problem of language except to the extent that linguists and logicians have first eliminated meaning; and the greatest force of language was only discovered once a *work* was viewed as a machine, producing certain effects, amenable to a certain use. Malcolm Lowry says of his work: it's anything you want it to be, so long as it works – "It works too, believe me, as I have found out" – a machinery. But on condition that meaning be nothing other than use, that it become a firm principle only if we have at our disposal *immanent criteria* capable of determining the legitimate uses, as opposed to the illegitimate ones that relate use instead to a hypothetical meaning and re-establish a kind of transcendence.[6]

From our present standpoint, however, the ideal of an immanent analysis of the text, of a dismantling or deconstruction of its parts and a description of its functioning and malfunctioning, amounts less to a wholesale nullification of all interpretive activity than to a demand for the construction of some new and more adequate, immanent or antitranscendent hermeneutic model, which it will be the task of the following pages to propose.[7]

* * *

Realism and Desire: Balzac and the Problem of the Subject

The novel is the end of genre in the sense in which it has been defined in the previous chapter: a narrative ideologeme whose outer form, secreted like a shell or exoskeleton, continues to emit its ideological message long after the extinction of its host. For the novel, as it explores its mature and original possibilities in the nineteenth century, is not an outer, conventional form of that kind. Rather, such forms, and their remains – inherited narrative paradigms, conventional actantial or proairetic schemata[8] – are the raw material on which the novel works, transforming their "telling" into its "showing," estranging commonplaces against the freshness of some unexpected "real," foregrounding convention itself as that through which readers have hitherto received their notions of events, psychology, experience, space, and time.

The "novel" as process rather than as form: such is the intuition to which apologists of this narrative structure have found themselves driven again and again, in an effort to characterize it as something that happens to its primary materials, as a specific but quite properly interminable set of operations and programming procedures, rather than a finished object whose "structure" one might model and contemplate. This process can be evaluated in a twofold way, as the transformation of the reader's subjective attitudes which is at one and the same time the production of a new kind of objectivity.

Indeed, as any number of "definitions" of realism assert, and as the totemic ancestor of the novel, *Don Quixote*, emblematically demonstrates, that processing operation variously called narrative mimesis or realistic representation has as its historic function the systematic undermining and demystification, the secular "decoding," of those pre-existing inherited traditional or sacred narrative paradigms which are its initial givens.[9] In this sense, the novel plays a significant role in what can be called a properly bourgeois cultural revolution – that immense process of transformation whereby populations whose life habits were formed by other, now archaic, modes of production are effectively reprogrammed for life and work in the new world of market capitalism. The "objective" function of the novel is thereby also implied: to its subjective and critical, analytic, corrosive mission must now be added the task of producing as though for the first time that very life world, that very "referent" – the newly quantifiable space of extension and market equivalence, the new rhythms of measurable time, the new secular and "disenchanted" object world of the commodity system, with its post-traditional daily life and its bewilderingly empirical, "meaningless," and contingent *Umwelt* – of which this new narrative discourse will then claim to be the "realistic" reflection.

The problem of the subject is clearly a strategic one for both dimensions of the novelistic process, particularly if one holds, as Marxists do, that the forms of human consciousness and the mechanisms of human psychology are not timeless and everywhere essentially the same, but rather situation-specific and historically produced. It follows, then, that neither the reader's reception of a particular narrative, nor the actantial representation of human figures or agents, can be taken to be constants of narrative analysis but must themselves ruthlessly be historicized. The Lacanian terminology and thematics in which much of the present chapter has been cast offer a tactical advantage here.[10] Lacan's work, with its emphasis on the "constitution of the subject," displaces the problematic of orthodox Freudianism from models of unconscious processes or blockages toward an account of the formation of the subject and its constitutive illusions which, though still genetic in Lacan himself and couched in terms of the individual biological subject, is not incompatible with a broader historical framework. Furthermore, the polemic thrust of Lacanian theory, with its decentering of the ego, the conscious subject of activity, the personality, or the "subject" of the Cartesian cogito – all now grasped as something like an "effect" of subjectivity – and its repudiation of the various ideals of the unification of the personality or the mythic conquest of personal identity, poses useful new problems for any narrative analysis which still works with naive, common-sense categories of "character," "protagonist," or "hero," and with psychological "concepts" like those of identification, sympathy, or empathy.

We have already touched…on the ways in which the Althusserian attack on "humanism" – on the categories of bourgeois individualism, and its anthropological myths of human nature – may be read as one powerful way of historicizing the Lacanian critique of the "centered subject." What becomes interesting in the present context is not the denunciation of the centered subject and its ideologies, but rather the study of its historical emergence, its constitution or virtual construction as a mirage which is also

FREDRIC JAMESON

evidently in some fashion an objective reality. For the lived experience of individual consciousness as a monadic and autonomous center of activity is not some mere conceptual error, which can be dispelled by the taking of thought and by scientific rectification: it has a quasi-institutional status, performs ideological functions, and is susceptible to historical causation and produced and reinforced by other objective instances, determinants, and mechanisms. The concept of reification which has been developed in these pages conveys the historical situation in which the emergence of the ego or centered subject can be understood: the dissolution of the older organic or hierarchical social groups, the universal commodification of the labor-power of individuals and their confrontation as equivalent units within the framework of the market, the *anomie* of these now "free" and isolated individual subjects to which the protective development of a monadic armature alone comes as something of a compensation.

Cultural study allows us to isolate a certain number of specific instances and mechanisms which provide concrete mediations between the "superstructures" of psychological or lived experience and the "infrastructures" of juridical relations and production process. These may be termed *textual determinants* and constitute quasi-material transmission points which produce and institutionalize the new subjectivity of the bourgeois individual at the same time that they themselves replicate and reproduce puely infrastructural requirements. Among such textual determinants in high realism are surely to be numbered narrative categories such as Jamesian point of view or Flaubertian *style indirect libre*, which are thus strategic loci for the fully constituted or centered bourgeois subject or monadic ego.

I

This is the context in which a crucial feature of an earlier "realism" – what is often designated as the "omniscient narrator" in Balzac – may usefully be reexamined. Omniscience is, however, the least significant thing about such authorial intervention, and may be said to be the aftereffect of the closure of classical *récit*, in which the events are over and done with before their narrative begins. This closure itself projects something like an ideological mirage in the form of notions of fortune, destiny, and providence or predestination which these *récits* seem to "illustrate," their reception amounting, in Walter Benjamin's words, to "warming our lives upon a death about which we read." Such *récits* – closed adventures, *unerhörte Begebenheiten*, the very idea of strokes of fortune and destinies touched off by chance – are among the raw materials upon which the Balzacian narrative process works, and with whose inherited forms it sometimes uneasily coexists. At the same time the gestures and signals of the storyteller (perpetuated in the English novel well beyond 1857, the year Flaubert abolishes them with a single stroke in France) symbolically attempt to restore the coordinates of a face-to-face storytelling institution which has been effectively disintegrated by the printed book and even more definitively by the commodification of literature and culture.

The constitutive feature of the Balzacian narrative apparatus, however, is something more fundamental than either authorial omniscience or authorial intervention, something that may be designated as libidinal investment or authorial wish-fulfillment, a form of symbolic satisfaction in which the working distinction between biographical subject, Implied Author, reader, and characters is virtually effaced. Description is one privileged moment in which such investments may be detected and studied, particularly when the object of the description, as in the following evocation of a provincial townhouse, is contested, and focuses antagonistic ambitions within the narrative itself:

> On the balustrade of the terrace, imagine great blue and white pots filled with wallflowers; envision right and left, along the neighboring walls, two rows of square-trimmed lime-trees; you will form an idea of this landscape filled with demure good humor, with tranquil chastity, and with modest homely [bourgeois] vistas offered by the other bank and its quaint houses, the trickling waters of the Brillante, the garden, two rows of trees lining its walls, and the venerable edifice of the Cormon family. What peace! what calm! nothing pretentious, but nothing transitory: here everything seems eternal. The ground-floor, then, was given over to reception rooms for visitors. Here everything breathed the Provincial, ancient but unalterable.[11]

The familiar mechanisms and characteristic rhetoric of Balzacian description are here reappropriated by a less characteristic function, or, to use a term which will be further developed in this chapter, are projected through a rather different *register* than the metonymic and connotative one of normal Balzacian exposition. The Cormon townhouse, along with its unwed heiress, is indeed the prize on which the narrative struggle or *agon* of *La Vieille Fille* turns. It is therefore quintessentially an object of desire; but we will not have begun to grasp its historical specificity until we sense the structural difference between this object and all those equally desirable goals, aims, or ends around which classical *récits* or quest narratives of the type studied by Propp are organized. The content, indifferently substitutable, of these last – gold, princess, crown or palace – suggests that the signifying value of such objects is determined by their narrative position: a narrative element becomes desirable whenever a character is observed to desire it.

In Balzac, as the heavily persuasive nature of the passage in question testifies, it has for whatever historical reason become necessary to secure the reader's consent, and to validate or accredit the object as desirable, before the narrative process can function properly. The priorities are therefore here reversed, and this narrative apparatus depends on the "desirability" of an object whose narrative function would have been a relatively automatic and unproblematical secondary effect of a more traditional narrative structure.

But the historical originality of the Balzacian object needs to be specified, not merely against the mechanisms of classical storytelling, but against the psychological and interpretive habits of our own period as well. For us, wishes and desires have become the traits or psychological properties of human monads; but more is at stake in this description than the simple "identification" with a plausible desire that we do not ourselves share, as when our films or bestsellers offer the proxy spectacles of a whole range of commodified passions. For one thing, we cannot attribute this particular desire (for the Cormon townhouse) to any individual subject. Biographical Balzac, Implied Author, this or that desiring protagonist: none of these unities are (yet) present, and desire here comes before us in a peculiarly anonymous state which makes a strangely absolute claim on us.

FREDRIC JAMESON

Such an evocation – in which the desire for a particular object is at one and the same time allegorical of all desire in general and of Desire as such, in which the pretext or theme of such desire has not yet been relativized and privatized by the ego-barriers that jealously confirm the personal and purely subjective experience of the monadized subjects they thus separate – may be said to reenact the Utopian impulse in the sense in which Ernst Bloch has redefined this term.[12] It solicits the reader not merely to reconstruct this building and grounds in some inner eye, but to reinvent it as Idea and as heart's desire. To juxtapose the depersonalized and retextualized provincial houses of Flaubert with this one is to become perhaps uncomfortably aware of the degree to which the Balzacian dwelling invites the awakening of a longing for possession, of the mild and warming fantasy of landed property as the tangible figure of a Utopian wish-fulfillment. A peace released from the competitive dynamism of Paris and of metropolitan business struggles, yet still imaginable in some existent backwater of concrete social history; a well-nigh Benjaminian preservation of the storehouse of the past, and of its quintessential experience, within the narrative present; a "chaste" diminution of the libidinal to its mildest and least afflictive murmur; a Utopia of the household, in whose courtyards, hallways, and garden paths the immemorial routines of daily life, of husbandry and domestic economy, are traced in advance, projecting the eternal cycle of meals and walks, marketing and high tea, the game of whist, the preparation of the daily menu and the commerce with faithful servants and with habitual visitors – this mesmerizing image is the "still point" around which the disorder and urgency of a properly novelistic time will turn. It is the modulation into Biedermeier of that more properly "sublime" wish-fulfillment of the magnificent opening description of the chateau of Les Aigues in *Les Paysans*, where this milder longing for landed property is magnified into the fantasy of feudal lordship and of the return of the great estate. Nor are the ideological conflicts of the later, more openly historical and political, master novel alien to this relatively minor comic *fabliau*: indeed, Mademoiselle Cormon's townhouse – an architectural monument to the splendor of an ancient patrician *Bürgertum* or merchant aristocracy – already "resolves" in advance, and in the recollected vividness of a tangible image, by its combination of the twin "semes" of bourgeois commercial activity and aristocratic tradition, the social and ideological contradiction around which the novel will turn.

The peculiarity of a Utopian libidinal investment of this kind can be underscored by shifting from the landed manifestation of this desire to its actantial personification in the figure of Mademoiselle Cormon herself, the old maid of the title. What is significant here is that, as with the house itself, no reconstruction of this character in a properly ironic perspective is possible. Mademoiselle Cormon is comic, grotesque, and desirable all at once (or in succession): her big feet, the "beauty" of her "force and abundance," her "embonpoint," her massive hips, "which made her seem cast in a single mould," her triple chin, with its "folds" rather than "wrinkles" – none of these features is inconsistent with the Utopian desire that takes her person as its focus. Nor is anything to be gained by referring the bewildered reader back to the documented peculiarities of Balzac's own sexual tastes, here reinscribed in the narrative in the passion of the unhappy young poet Athanase Granson for this corpulent older woman ("this ample person offered attributes capable of seducing a young man full of desires and longing, such as Athanase"). To be sure, *La Vieille Fille* is a comic novel, heavily and insistently punctuated by sexual innuendo and by undertones of the type of gross physical farce Balzac himself rehearsed in his *Contes drolatiques*; this essentially comic register of the narrative, is, then, presumably enough to account for a perspective in which the vicissitudes of carnal desire are observed with sympathetic detachment and malicious empathy.

Yet to insist on the Utopian dimension of this particular desire is evidently to imply that this particular comic narrative is also an *allegorical* structure, in which the sexual "letter" of the farce must itself be read as a figure for the longing for landed retreat and personal fulfillment as well as for the resolution of social and historical contradiction. The Silenus box – a grotesque and comical exterior which contains a wondrous balm – is, of course, the very emblem of the hermeneutic object;[13] but the relationship between farce and the Utopian impulse is not particularly clarified by this image.

Paradoxically, however, it is this very tension or inconsistency between levels which will vanish from expressions of the Utopian impulse in a later age of high reification. A passage from the American writer whose commodity lust and authorial investments and attitudinizing are most reminiscent of Balzac may give some sense of the transformation:

> At this time of the year the days are still comparatively short, and the shadows of the evening were beginning to settle down upon the great city. Lamps were beginning to burn with that mellow radiance which seems almost watery and translucent to the eye. There was a softness in the air which speaks with an infinite delicacy of feeling to the flesh as well as to the soul. Carrie felt that it was a lovely day. She was ripened by it in spirit for many suggestions. As they drove along the smooth pavement an occasional carriage passed. She saw one stop and the footman dismount, opening the door for a gentleman who seemed to be leisurely returning from some afternoon pleasure. Across the broad lawns, now first freshening into green, she saw lamps faintly glowing upon rich interiors. Now it was but a chair, now a table, now an ornate corner which met her eye, but it appealed to her as almost nothing else could. Such childish fancies as she had had of fairy palaces and kingly quarters now came back. She imagined that across these richly carved entrance-ways, where the globed and crystalled lamps shone upon panelled doors set with stained and designed panes of glass, was neither care nor unsatisfied desire. She was perfectly certain that here was happiness.[14]

Between the moment of Balzac and the moment of Dreiser, *bovarysme* has fallen, and the congealment of language, fantasy, and desire into Flaubertian *bêtise* and Flaubertian cliché transmutes Balzacian longing into the tawdriness of Carrie's hunger for trinkets, a tawdriness that Dreiser's language ambiguously represents and reflects all at once.[15]

Commodification is not the only "event" which separates Dreiser's text from Balzac's: the charges it has wrought in the object world of late capitalism have evidently been accompanied by a decisive development in the construction of the subject as well, by the constitution of the latter into a closed monad, henceforth governed by the laws of "psychology." Indeed, for all the caressing solicitations of this text, it clearly positions us outside Carrie's desire, which is represented as a private wish or longing to which we relate ourselves as readers by the mechanisms of identification and projection, and to which we may also adopt a moralizing stance, or what amounts to the same thing, an ironic one. What has happened is that "Carrie" has become a "point of view": this is in effect, as we have already suggested, the textual institution or determinant that expresses and reproduces the newly centered subject of the age of reification. Not coincidentally, the emergence of such narrative centers is then at once accompanied by the verbal or narrative equivalents of techniques characteristic of film (the tracking shot, the panning of the camera from Carrie's position as observer to that telescopic or keyhole glimpse of the ultimate interior, with its enclosed warmth and light) – that medium which will shortly become the hegemonic formal expression of late capitalist society. With this virtually fullblown appearance of filmic point of view, however, the Utopian overtones and intensities of desire are ever more faintly registered by the text; and the Utopian impulse itself, now reified, is driven back inside the monad, where it assumes the status of some merely psychological experience, private feeling, or relativized value.

It should not overhastily be concluded, however, that Dreiser's situation is only one of loss and constraint; as we will have occasion to observe in a later chapter, on Joseph Conrad, the effects of reification – the sealing off of the psyche, the division of labor of the mental faculties, the fragmentation of the bodily and perceptual sensorium – also determine the opening up of whole new zones of experience and the production of new types of linguistic content. In Dreiser, indeed, we witness the emergence of an incomparable sensory intensity, "that infinite delicacy of feeling to the flesh as well as to the soul," which marks the passage from Balzacian rhetoric to a more properly modern practice of *style* in Dreiser, a strange and alien bodily speech which, interwoven with the linguistic junk of commodified language, has perplexed readers of our greatest novelist down to the present day.[16]

Now it is time to examine the operation of a narrative apparatus about which we have implied that, antedating the emergence of the centered subject, it has not yet developed the latter's textual determinants, such as point of view or protagonists with whom the reader sympathizes in some more modern psychological sense. Yet it is evident that *La Vieille Fille* is by no stretch of the imagination a post-modern or "schizophrenic" text, in which traditional categories of character and narrative time are dissolved altogether. We will indeed want to suggest that the "decentering" of Balzacian narrative, if that is not an anachronistic term for it, is to be found in a rotation of character centers which deprives each of them in turn of any privileged status. This rotation is evidently a small-scale model of the decentered organization of the *Comédie humaine* itself. What interests us in the present context, however, is the glimpse this turning movement gives us into the semic production of characters, or in other words into what we will call a *character system*.

We have already mentioned the least important of the suitors for Mademoiselle Cormon's hand, the poet Athanase, who, unlike his more celebrated counterpart Lucien de Rubempré, finds no Vautrin to dissuade him from the suicide that removes him from this competition. Alongside this pitiable romantic, two more powerful but more grotesque figures emerge as the principal candidates for a prize that, as we have seen, is not merely matrimonial (or financial) but also Utopian: an elderly and penniless nobleman, who claims descent from the (extinct) House of Valois and worthily upholds the traditions of elegance of the *ancien régime*; and a bourgeois "Farnese Hercules," former profiteer of the Revolutionary armies and victim of Napoleon's animosity, who, as head of the liberal opposition to the Bourbon restoration, counts on the marriage with Mademoiselle Cormon not merely to reestablish his finances, but above all to carry him back to political power (he wants to be appointed Prefect of Alençon).

The reader does not need to wait for Lukács' theory of typification to grasp the social and historical figuration of these characters, since Balzac underscores it heavily and explicitly himself:

> The one [the Liberal Du Bousquier], abrupt, energetic, with loud and demonstrative manners, and brusque and rude of speech, dark in complexion, hair and look, terrible in appearance, in reality as impotent as an insurrection, might quite adequately be said to represent the Republic. The other [the Chevalier de Valois], mild and polished, elegant, carefully dressed, reaching his ends by the slow but infallible methods of diplomacy, and upholding good taste to the end, offered the very image of the old court aristocracy.[17]

Lukács' theory of typification, while confirmed by such a passage, can nonetheless be said to be incomplete on two counts; on the one hand, it fails to identify the typifying of characters as an essentially allegorical phenomenon, and thus does not furnish any adequate account of the process whereby a narrative becomes endowed with allegorical meanings or levels. On the other, it implies an essentially one-to-one relationship between individual characters and their social or historical reference, so that the possibility of something like a *system* of characters remains unexplored.

In fact, the reader's initial attentions are less absorbed by matters of social status here taken for granted, or by the struggle for Mademoiselle Cormon's hand, which will set in only later on, than directed to the solution of a group of puzzles and enigmas. Du Bousquier's secret is indeed no secret for the reader, since it is quickly made apparent to us that he is sexually impotent. What this revelation does to our reading, however, is to generate a systematic movement back and forth between what we know (and what poor Mademoiselle Cormon has to marry him to find out) and that external appearance by which the other characters are deceived: not merely his physical strength and his powerful deportment, but also his association with new industrial wealth and with the Jacobin traditions of the bourgeois political system. The "secret" no doubt underscores Balzac's own opinion of these ideals and traditions in a crude but effective manner; yet, unlike Poe's story, "The Man That Was Used Up," this "reality" never undermines the power and the objectivity of an "appearance" in which Du Bousquier has very real social and political importance, and which is indeed consecrated by his ultimate triumph over his rival.

As for the latter, the various enigmas that center on the Chevalier (those, in particular, of the legitimacy of his title and the true sources of his income) tend to be displaced in the direction of the sexual code. Thus, a series of gross allusions (the size of the Chevalier's nose, for instance) begin to make it clear that his "secret" is on the contrary one of unexpected potency and of a properly aristocratic capacity for gallant adventures.

The point to be made about this whole initial narrative movement – the operation of what Barthes somewhat improperly calls the "hermeneutic code" of a play of appearance and reality and a search for withheld secrets – is that, itself a preparation for the principal narrative, it is never fully resolved: the revelation of the sexual secret does not, in other words, spell a conclusion to the comedy, as it would in Boccaccio or in the *Contes drolatiques*, but is a means to a more unexpected end.[18] The function of the sexual comedy is essentially to direct our reading attention toward the relationship between sexual potency and class affiliation. Our assumption that it is the former which is the object of this particular game of narrative hide-and-seek is in fact the blind or subterfuge behind which the otherwise banal and empirical facts of social status and political prehistory are transformed into the fundamental categories in terms of which the narrative is interpreted. Our reading "set" toward the social and historical interpretations which can be allegorically derived from the narrative is thus something like a lateral by-product of our initial attention to the sexual comedy; but this allegorical by-product, once established, reorients the narrative around its new interpretive center, retroactively returning upon the sexual farce to assign it a henceforth marginalized place in the narrative structure, where it comes to seem a relatively inessential or arbitrary "bonus of pleasure."

Thus established, the allegorical reading becomes the dominant one, and the struggle for Mademoiselle Cormon's hand becomes the unavoidable figure not merely for the struggle for power over France, but also the conquest of legitimation and the appropriation of everything in the post-revolutionary state which remains the most authentically and quintessentially "French" by tradition and by inheritance: the old patrician values of a provincial merchant aristocracy with the slow eternity of its custom, as embodied in the houses and gardens of Alençon. But if this were all that was at stake, then the conclusion of the drama – Du Bousquier's triumph over his rival, precipitated by his Napoleonic decisiveness and by the Chevalier's complacent confidence in his own preponderancies – would amount to little more than a punctual allusion to an empirical event, namely, the failure of the restoration with the overthrow of the Bourbons, in 1830, by liberal middle-class forces. This would certainly be a reflection of historical reality in Lukács' sense, even though scarcely a prophetic one (the novel, whose action takes place in 1816, was written in 1836). Lukács' general point about Balzac is, of course, that this novelist's sense of historical realities inflects his own personal wishes (presumably they accompany the Chevalier) in the direction of social and historical verisimilitude (it is after all Du Bousquier who wins out).

The novel is, however, more complicated than this, and if it inscribes the irrevocable brute facts of empirical history – the July Revolution, for Balzac a fall into the secular corruption of a middle-class age – it does so in order the more surely to "manage" those facts and to open up a space in which they are no longer quite so irreparable, no longer quite so definitive. La Vieille Fille is indeed not merely a matrimonial farce, nor even only a social commentary on provincial life; it is above all a didactic work and a political object-lesson that seeks to transform the events of empirical history into an optional trial run against which the strategies of the various social classes can be tested. This peculiar shift in registers, in which the events of the narrative remain the same but yet somehow are emptied of their finality, is perhaps best conveyed by way of Todorov's conception of a "modal" poetics, and of a variety of modal realizations of narrative content in the surface of a narrative text.[19] If, as Greimas suggests, we suppose that a narrative can be modeled like an individual sentence, then it might well follow that, as with sentences themselves, each deep narrative structure could be actualized according to a number of different modes, of which the indicative, governing conventional narrative realism, is only the most familiar. Yet other possible narrative modalizations – the subjunctive, the optative, the imperative, and the like – suggest a heterogeneous play of narrative registers which will gradually, as we shall see in our next chapter, be recontained and reunified under the massive homogenization of a later high realism. On this view, the

---

didactic status of *La Vieille Fille* can be accounted for by a modalization in terms of the *conditional* (if this...then this), whose content must now be determined.

Now the entire sequence of our reading frameworks must be reversed. The earlier frameworks – the initial sexual "hermeneutic code" and the subsequent reading of the primary *agon* (who will finally win out?) – are now retroactively restructured in terms of a new kind of reading interest, namely the effort to assign responsibilities, and to determine what as yet undetermined advantage Du Bousquier (= impotent) can have had over his aristocratic rival (= potent). The establishment of these causes and responsibilities will ultimately make up the content of what has now become a history lesson.

This restructuration, however, confronts us not with answers or immediate ideological solutions, but rather with a set of determinate contradictions. What began by being a simple judgment – that the Revolution and its bourgeois values are essentially sterile, that is to say, *impotent*, but also, in Edmund Burke's sense artificial and non-organic – now turns into a problem or an antinomy. The *ancien régime*, coded as sexual gallantry through its stereotypical representations as Regency, Deer Park, Watteau, Fragonard, Louis XV, and the like, lends its positive sexual seme to the portrait of the Chevalier; yet even before the failure of his matrimonial attempt, the combination of semes which make up his portrait can be shown to be contradictory, and the reading mind must on some level worry the question: how is it possible for the graceful, effeminate, elderly Chevalier to be more "potent" than the rough-and-ready bourgeois speculator Du Bousquier? Meanwhile, the latter offers no less of a paradox, namely the relation to his sexual impotence of that principle of quasi-military initiative and decisiveness to which he owes his triumph and about whose historical reference the text leaves us in no doubt: it is the energy Balzac associates with Napoleon and with the whole history of the Revolutionary armies from Valmy to the anticlimax at Waterloo. Yet this seme is already historically ambiguous, for if such martial initiative is sharply dissociated from the culture, values, and practices of the *ancien régime*, neither can it be wholly identified with the business society that will come into its own after 1830.

Following the program we outlined in our initial chapter, we will wish to distinguish between the reconstruction of this particular inconsistency as a *contradiction* and its formulation in terms of an *antinomy* for the reading mind. We there suggested that whereas the former is governed by a properly dialectical thinking, the latter may be most appropriately mapped out by semiotic method, which is in this sense the privileged instrument of analysis of ideological closure. Greimas' semiotic rectangle[20] suggests an initial formulation of this antinomy or double bind as follows: sexual potency + languor versus energy + impotence. The underlying ideological contradiction here can evidently be expressed in the form of a meditation on history: Balzac as a royalist and an apologist for the essentially organic and decentered *ancien régime* must nonetheless confront the latter's palpable military failures and administrative inefficiencies, which are underscored by the inevitable juxtaposition with the power of the Napoleonic period, although that period itself, a kind of hybridization of Jacobin values and monarchic trappings, proved to be a dead end.

Faced with a contradiction of this kind – which it cannot think except in terms of a stark antinomy, an insoluble logical paradox – the historical *pensée sauvage*, or what we have called the political unconscious, nonetheless seeks by logical permutations and combinations to find a way out of its intolerable closure and to produce a "solution," something it can begin to do owing to the semic dissociations already implicit in the initial opposition formulated above. Thus, it would seem possible to disjoin the seme of "energy" from that of "impotence" or "sterility" (part of a larger ideologeme that denotes the world of bourgeois materialism and business generally); and, on the other side of this opposition, to disjoin the valorized seme of the "*ancien régime*" from its general debility which may perhaps be resumed under the theme of "culture" (manners, traditions, forms, aristocratic values, and the like). At this point, we can map these terms, and the possibilities of new combinations they suggest, as follows.

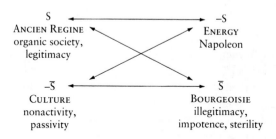

It now becomes clear that of the four chief logical combinations available here, we so far have only identified two. From this perspective, then, we can observe the way in which a semic system generates those anthropomorphic combinations that are narrative characters, and in particular, in the present instance, how the semes S and −S̄ produce the representation of the "Chevalier," while the combination −S and S̄ gives anthropomorphic content to that other proper name, "Du Bousquier." What is so far missing are the two combinations designated by Greimas as the complex and the neutral term respectively: the ideal synthesis which would "resolve" the initial binary opposition by subsuming it under a single unity, and that union of purely negative or privative terms which would subsume the simple contradictories of the two terms of the initial binary opposition. Our methodological hypothesis would be validated, and our demonstration of a character system fulfilled, if it could be shown that these two additional logical possibilities have their equivalent in the Balzacian text.

But we have already mentioned a likely candidate for the neutral or neuter term. Its apparently inconsistent synthesis of bourgeois origins and cultural values is indeed realized in the sorry young would-be poet Athanase, and beyond him by Romanticism itself: a movement of which Balzac's work, like that of Hegel, stands as a thoroughgoing critique.[21]

As for the complex term or ideal synthesis, we have omitted to mention until now the retarding episode that precipitates the crisis of the novel and impels Du Bousquier on to his climactic decision. This is the arrival, at Mademoiselle Cormon's house, of an exiled aristocratic officer, the Comte de Troisville, who, returning from Russia to reestablish himself in the region, is for a fond moment imagined by Mademoiselle Cormon to be the "solution" to her problems and a more appropriate match than either of the other contenders. Unfortunately, the Count is already married; this "solution," which would satisfactorily combine undoubted aristocratic "legitimacy" with documented military prowess of the Napoleonic type, is thus explicitly marked by the narrative as a merely "ideal" one, as a Utopian resolution in the narrower and empirically unrealizable sense.

The "Count de Troisville" thus figures as what we will call a horizon-figure in this narrative. He blocks out a place which is not that of empirical history but of a possible alternate one: a history in which some genuine Restoration would still be possible, provided the aristocracy could learn this particular object-lesson, namely that it needs a strong man who combines aristocratic values with Napoleonic energy (at some wish-fulfilling or fantasy level, Balzac obviously has himself in mind). This is then the ultimate sense in which the novel's comic yet rueful ending – the ultimate fate of Mademoiselle Cormon, married, *and* an old maid all at once! the very caricature of a dialectical resolution – is not truly a definitive one, but merely a horrible object-lesson.

In this light, *Les Paysans* – which is something like a transposition of these materials into a more somber and tragic register – can also be reread, and its well-known interpretation by Lukács shown to be a premature finalization.[22] For the doomed hero of *Les Paysans*, Count Montcornet, is, like Valois here, only ambiguously aristocratic; his title is in reality a Napoleonic one, and the doubtful legitimacy of his "feudal" authority over the chateau is underscored by the existence at the margins of the narrative of two other great estates, Ronquerolles and Soulanges, still in the possession of authentic noblemen. The implication is that where Montcornet failed, owing to the imperfection of his origins, these neighboring horizon-figures, the representatives of a more authentic nobility, have some chance of succeeding – provided they heed Balzac's narrative warning! The disaster of *Les Paysans* (like that of *La Vieille Fille*, a reflection of a certain empirical history) is thus emptied of its finality, its irreversibility, its historical inevitability, by a narrative register which offers it to us as merely conditional history, and transforms the indicative mode of historical "fact" into the less binding one of the cautionary tale and the didactic lesson.

* * *

Conclusion

One hesitates to defend the privileged position of cultural criticism in a self-serving way. Still, it is a historical fact that the "structuralist" or textual revolution – as, mainly through Althusserianism, it has transformed a whole range of other disciplines, from political science to anthropology, and from economics to legal and juridical studies – takes as its model a kind of decipherment of which literary and textual criticism is in many ways the strong form. This "revolution," essentially antiempiricist, drives the wedge of the concept of a "text" into the traditional disciplines by extrapolating the notion of "discourse" or "writing" onto objects previously thought to be "realities" or objects in the real world, such as the various levels or instances of a social formation: political power, social class, institutions, and events themselves. When properly used, the concept of the "text" does not, as in garden-variety semiotic practice today, "reduce" these realities to small and manageable written documents of one kind or another, but rather liberates us from the empirical object – whether institution, event, or individual work – by displacing our attention to its *constitution* as an object and its *relationship* to the other objects thus constituted.

The specific problems addressed by literary and cultural interpretation today may thus be expected to present suggestive analogies with the methodological problems of the other social sciences (it being understood that for Marxism, literary and cultural analysis *is* a social science). I would go even further and suggest that the solution outlined in this conclusion to those specifically cultural dilemmas has a good deal of relevance for other fields, where indeed analogous solutions are everywhere the order of the day. I will illustrate these analogies with brief reference to three such areas, namely the problem of the state, the constitution of radical legal studies, and the national question. We have already touched earlier on the first, in which a contemporary political science, particularly in the work of Nicos Poulantzas,[23] has sought to free the study of the state and of state power from the older Marxian view in which the state is little more than an instrument or vehicle of class domination. Such traditional reduction of the political corresponds clearly enough to what we have described above as the instrumental-functional view of ideology. As against this tradition, Poulantzas offers a view of the state as a semi-autonomous arena, which is not the vehicle of any one class but rather a space of class struggle generally. Such a view has evident political consequences, and reflects the immense expansion of the public sector in modern societies, as well as the dynamic of nonhegemonic forces such as pressure groups of unemployed or marginalized people and the more militant work of public-sector trade unions. This vision of the state or the public sector as a collectivity in its own right evidently corresponds to what we have called the Utopian reading or decipherment of the "text" of the state.

In radical legal studies, as well as in related areas of the study of public policy such as health care and housing, the problem of the "text" is even more vivid. There is, in the area of the juridical as the Left conceives it today, an open antithesis between a school based on ideological interpretation – which seeks to unmask existing law as the instrument of class domination – and one working in a Utopian perspective – which on the contrary sees its work as the conception and projection of a radically new form of some properly socialist legality that cannot be achieved within the existing institutions, or that is in them merely "emergent." Here too, then, the coordination of the ideological with the Utopian would seem to have a theoretical urgency which is accompanied by very real political and strategic consequences.

Finally, I will take Tom Nairn's pathbreaking book on the national questions, *The Break-up of Britain*, as an example of an analogous theoretical solution to that proposed here in an area which remains one of the fundamental ones of contemporary world politics but about which Nairn rightly observes that it stands as "Marxism's great historical failure," blocked precisely by a practice of the traditional Marxian negative hermeneutic for which the national question is a mere ideological epiphenomenon of the economic. "The task of a theory of nationalism ... must be to embrace both horns of the dilemma. It must be to see the phenomenon as a whole, in a way that rises above these 'positive' and 'negative' sides. ... [Such] distinctions do not imply the existence of two brands of nationalism, one healthy and one morbid. The point is that, as the most elementary comparative analysis will show, all nationalism is both healthy and morbid.

Both progress and regress are inscribed in its genetic code from the start."[24] Nor is this insistence on the simultaneously ideological and Utopian character of the national phenomenon a merely theoretical issue. On the contrary, it is increasingly clear in today's world (if it had ever been in doubt) that a Left which cannot grasp the immense Utopian appeal of nationalism (any more than it can grasp that of religion or of fascism) can scarcely hope to "reappropriate" such collective energies and must effectively doom itself to political impotence.

But at this point, we must restore Benjamin's identification of culture and barbarism to its proper sequence, as the affirmation not merely of the Utopian dimension of ideological texts, but also and above all of the ideological dimension of all high culture. So it is that a Marxist hermeneutic – the deciphering by historical materialism of the cultural monuments and traces of the past – must come to terms with the certainty that all the works of class history as they have survived and been transmitted to people the various museums, canons and "traditions" of our own time, are all in one way or another profoundly ideological, have all had a vested interest in and a functional relationship to social formations based on violence and exploitation; and that, finally, the restoration of the meaning of the greatest cultural monuments cannot be separated from a passionate and partisan assessment of everything that is oppressive in them and that knows complicity with privilege and class domination, stained with the guilt not merely of culture in particular but of History itself as one long nightmare.

Yet Benjamin's slogan is a hard saying, and not only for liberal and apoliticizing critics of art and literature, for whom it spells the return of class realities and the painful recollection of the dark underside of even the most seemingly innocent and "life-enhancing" masterpieces of the canon. For a certain radicalism also, Benjamin's formulation comes as a rebuke and a warning against the facile reappropriation of the classics as humanistic expressions of this or that historically "progressive" force. It comes, finally, as an appropriate corrective to the doctrine of the political unconscious which has been developed in these pages, reasserting the undiminished power of ideological distortion that persists even within the restored Utopian meaning of cultural artifacts, and reminding us that within the symbolic power of art and culture the will to domination perseveres intact. It is only at this price – that of the simultaneous recognition of the ideological and Utopian functions of the artistic text – that a Marxist cultural study can hope to play its part in political praxis, which remains, of course, what Marxism is all about.

NOTES

1 See "The Ideology of the Text," *Salmagundi*, No. 31–32 (Fall 1975/Winter 1976), pp. 204–246.
2 This is to my mind the relevance of a theory of "modes of production" for literary and cultural criticism; see, for further reflections on this issue and a more explicit statement on the "historicist" tendencies of Marxism, my "Marxism and Historicism," *New Literary History*, 11 (Autumn, 1979), 41–73.
3 "The realm of freedom actually begins only where labor which is in fact determined by necessity and mundane considerations ceases; thus in the very nature of things it lies beyond the sphere of actual material production. Just as the savage must wrestle with Nature to satisfy

his wants, to maintain and reproduce life, so must civilized man, and he must do so in all social formations and under all possible modes of production. With his development this realm of physical necessity expands as a result of his wants; but, at the same time, the forces of production which satisfy these wants also increase. Freedom in this field can only consist in socialized men, the associated producers, rationally regulating their interchange with Nature, bringing it under their common control, instead of being ruled by it as by the blind forces of Nature; and achieving this with the least expenditure of energy and under conditions most favorable to, and worthy of, their human nature. But it nonetheless still remains a realm of necessity. Beyond it begins that development of human energy which is an end in itself, the true realm of freedom, which, however, can blossom forth only with this realm of necessity as its basis." Karl Marx, *Capital* (New York: International Publishers, 1977), III, 820.

4   Karl Marx and Friedrich Engels, "The Communist Manifesto," in K. Marx, *On Revolution*, ed. and trans. S. K. Padover (New York: McGraw-Hill, 1971), p. 81.

5   See Michel Foucault, "The Retreat and Return of the Origin," chap. 9, part 6, of *The Order of Things* (New York: Vintage, 1973), pp. 328–335; as well as the same author's *Archeology of Knowledge*, trans. A. M. Sheridan Smith (New York: Pantheon, 1972), in particular, the introduction and the chapter on the "history of ideas"; Jacques Derrida, "The Exorbitant. Question of Method," in *Of Grammatology*, trans. Gayatri Spivak (Baltimore: Johns Hopkins University Press, 1976), pp. 157–164; as well as his "Hors livre," in *La Dissémination* (Paris: Seuil, 1972), pp. 9–67; Jean Baudrillard, "Vers une critique de l'économie politique du signe," in *Pour une critique de l'économie politique du signe* (Paris: Gallimard, 1972); along with his *Mirror of Production*, trans. Mark Poster (St. Louis: Telos, 1975); Gilles Deleuze and Félix Guattari, *The Anti-Oedipus*, trans. Robert Hurley, Mark Seem, and Helen R. Lane (New York: Viking, 1977), pp. 25–28, 109–113, 305–308; Jean-François Lyotard, *Economie libidinale* (Paris: Minuit, 1974), especially "Le Désir nommé Marx," pp. 117–188; and last but not least, Louis Althusser, et al., *Reading Capital*, trans. Ben Brewster (London: New Left Books, 1970), especially "Marx's Immense Theoretical Revolution," pp. 182–193.

6   Deleuze/Guattari, *Anti-Oedipus*, p. 109.

7   From the present perspective, in other words, Deleuze and Guattari's proposal for an *anti*interpretive method (which they call schizo-analysis) can equally well be grasped as a new hermeneutic in its own right. It is striking and noteworthy that most of the antiinter-pretive positions enumerated in note 5 above have felt the need to project new "methods" of this kind: thus, the archeology of knowledge, but also, more recently, the "political technol-ogy of the body" (Foucault), "grammatology" and deconstruction (Derrida), "symbolic exchange" (Baudrillard), libidinal economy (Lyotard), and "sémanalyse" (Julia Kristeva).

8   On the term *actant* see Greimas conception of the actant is based on a distinction between narrative syntax (or "deep structure") and that "surface" narrative discourse in which "actors" or recognizable "characters" are the visible unities: actants, which correspond to the necessarily far more limited functions of the narrative syntagm, are generally reduced by Greimas to three groups: Sender/Receiver, Subject-Hero/Object-Value, and Auxiliary/Vil-lain. See A. J. Greimas, *Sémantique structurale* (Paris: Larousse, 1966), pp. 172–191; or more recently, "Les Actants, les acteurs, et les figures," in C. Chabrol, ed., *Sémiotique narrative et textuelle* (Paris: Larousse, 1973), pp. 161–176. The "proairetic code" is Roland Barthes's designation for the terms or names of the conventional unities and actions of everyday life: "What is a series of actions? the unfolding of a name. To *enter?* I can unfold it into 'to appear' and 'to penetrate.' To *leave?* I can unfold it into 'to want to,' 'to stop,' 'to leave again.' To *give?*: 'to incite,' 'to return,' 'to accept.' Inversely, to establish the sequence is to find the name." *S/Z*, trans. R. Miller (New York: Hill and Wang, 1974), p. 82.

9 See in particular Roman Jakobson, "On Realism in Art," in K. Pomorska and L. Matejka, eds., *Readings in Russian Formalist Poetics* (Cambridge: MIT Press, 1971), pp. 38–46. "Decoding" is a term of Deleuze and Guattari: see the *Anti-Oedipus*, pp. 222–228.

10 For a fuller account of my own understanding and use, here and later on in this chapter, of Lacanian terminology, see my "Imaginary and Symbolic in Lacan," *Yale French Studies*, Nos. 55–56 (1977), pp. 338–395. The accredited exposition of the Lacanian "system" is Anika Rifflet-Lemaire, *Jacques Lacan* (Brussels: Dessart, 1970).

11 "Sur la balustrade de la terrasse imaginez de grands vases en faience bleue et blanche d'où s'élèvent des giroflées; à droite et à gauche, le long des murs voisins, voyez deux couverts de tilleuls carrément taillés; vous aurez une idée du paysage plein de bonhomie pudique, de chasteté tranquille, de vues modestes et bourgeoises qu'offraient la rive opposée et ses naïves maisons, les eaux rares de la Brillante, le jardin, ses deux couverts collés contre les murs voisins, et le vénérable édifice des Cormon. Quelle paix! quel calme! rien de pompeux, mais rien de transitoire: là, tout semble éternel. Le rez-de-chaussée appartenait donc à la réception. Là tout respirait la vieille, l'inaltérable province" (Honoré de Balzac, *La Comédie humaine* [Paris: La Pléiade, 1952], 11 vols., "La Vieille Fille," IV, 247).

12 In *Das Prinzip Hoffnung* (Frankfurt: Suhrkamp, 1959), 2 vols.; for a brief account, see my *Marxism and Form* (Princeton: Princeton University Press, 1971), pp. 116–158.

13 "Sileni of old were little boxes, like those we now may see in the shops of apothecaries, painted on the outside with wanton toyish figures, as harpies, satyrs, bridled geese, horned hares, saddled ducks, flying goats, thiller harts, and other such counterfeited pictures, at pleasure, to excite people unto laughter, as Silenus himself, who was the foster-father of good Bacchus, was wont to do; but within those capricious caskets called Sileni were carefully preserved and kept many rich and fine drugs, such as balm, ambergreese, amomon, musk, civet, with several kinds of precious stones, and other things of great price" (Author's Prologue, *Gargantua* [the Urquhart-Mortteux translation]).

14 Theodore Dreiser, *Sister Carrie* (New York: Norton, 1970), p. 86.

15 The axiological paradox about Dreiser – he is best at his worst – is peculiarly intensified by the problem of his style, which must be studied in terms of alienation and reification, rather than according to the usual positivist categories; see Sandy Petrey, "Language of Realism, Language of False Consciousness: A Reading of *Sister Carrie*," *Novel* 10 (1977), 101–113.

16 On the use of the distinction between rhetoric and style as a historical and periodizing concept, see Roland Barthes, *Writing Degree Zero*, trans. A. Lavers and C. Smith (London: Cape, 1967), pp. 10–13, 41–52. The distinction is that evoked by Genette, following Lubbock's differentiation of *picture* (or "report") from *scene*, as "the opposition between classical abstraction . . . and 'modern' *expressivity*" (Gérard Genette, *Figures III* [Paris: Seuil, 1972], p. 131); and see Percy Lubbock, *The Craft of Fiction* (New York: Viking, 1957), esp. pp. 251–254. [See also pp. 86–96 in this book.]

17 *La Vieille Fille*, p. 228.

18 See, for a more detailed reading of the opening section of the novel, the first version of the present chapter, "The Ideology of Form: Partial Systems in *La Vieille Fille*," *Sub-stance*, No. 15 (Winter, 1976), 29–49.

19 Tzvetan Todorov, "Poétique," in F. Wahl, ed., *Qu'est-ce que le structuralisme?* (Paris: Seuil, 1968), pp. 142–145. And see the special number of *Langages* devoted to "modalités" (No. 43, September 1976). The ultimate philosophical underpinnings are to be found in modal logic: see Georg Henrik von Wright, *An Essay in Modal Logic* (Amsterdam: North Holland Publishing Co., 1951), and *An Essay in Deontic Logic* (Amsterdam: North Holland Publishing Co., 1968). Properly formalized, the model of an ideological axiomatic proposed here may be described as a projection onto narrative and macrostructure of Oswald Ducros' account of presuppositions in individual propositions or sentences: Ducros expands the notion of the

performative or speech act into what he calls "the juridical act" in which, as in Mauss's conception of the gift, the act of reception structurally entails the receiver's consent to the ideological content presupposed by a given utterance (Oswald Ducros, *Dire et ne pas dire* [Paris: Hermann, 1972], pp. 69–80).

20 Briefly, the semiotic rectangle or "elementary structure of signification" is the representation of a binary opposition or of two contraries (S and −S), along with the simple negations or contradictories of both terms (the so-called subcontraries −$\bar{S}$ and $\bar{S}$): significant slots are constituted by the various possible combinations of these terms, most notably the "complex" term (or ideal synthesis of the two contraries) and the "neutral" term (or ideal synthesis of the two subcontraries). See A. J. Greimas and François Rastier, "The Interaction of Semiotic Constraints," *Yale French Studies*, No. 41 (1968), pp. 86–105; and F. Nef, ed., *Structures élémentaires de la signification* (Brussels: Complexe, 1976). See also my *Prison-House of Language* (Princeton: Princeton University Press, 1972), pp. 162–168.

21 On Balzac's antiromanticism, see Pierre Barbéris, *Balzac et le mal du siècle* (Paris: Gallimard, 1970), especially chap. 7.

22 In his essay on "Balzac: *The Peasants*," in *Studies in European Realism* (New York: Grosset and Dunlap, 1964), pp. 21–46.

23 E.g., *Political Power and Social Classes*, trans. Timothy O'Hagan (London: New Left Books, 1973), chap. 4, "The Relative Autonomy of the Capitalist State."

24 Tom Nairn, *The Break-up of Britain* (London: New Left Books, 1977), pp. 332, 347–348.

The Novel as Social Discourse

Introduction

Although Marxists were early and influential theorists of the novel, the interest in the social, historical, and political value of literary genre is by no means exclusive to Marxism. As Parts VI, VII, and VIII of this anthology demonstrate, other types of thinkers throughout the century are also deeply invested in the novel's cultural role – including scholars of national literatures, intellectual historians, sociologists, New Historicists, and cultural critics. "The Novel as Social Discourse" focuses on theorists who attempt to study the novel's social value without the anchor of Marxist objectivity, without, in Fredric Jameson's words, the belief that Marxism is "the absolute horizon of all reading and interpretation" (*Unconscious*, 414). With lesser or greater degrees of explicitness, the theorists in this unit and the two that follow either borrow or invent alternative conceptions of history and society to underwrite their study of the novel. Yet the profound influence of Marxist thought can be felt even in these alternative historical approaches. Although these theories resist Marxist orthodoxy, all are sympathetic to some aspect of the Marxist project – whether in the emphasis put on the material conditions of authorship, book production, and readership; the interest in the novel as a popular (rather than elite) literary form; the concern with the operation of social power; or the critic's own self-conscious awareness of literary scholarship itself as a politicized enterprise.

Ian Watt's *The Rise of the Novel* (1957), for example, makes the case for the novel as an essentially bourgeois genre – but without the political critique that György Lukács,

Walter Benjamin, and Fredric Jameson level at bourgeois ideology. As discussed in the introduction to Part V, in his *The Theory of the Novel* (first published in 1920) Lukács bemoans the cataclysmic shift in Western society which rendered the epic obsolete. Watt's overview of English history similarly posits the birth of modernism and the rise of the novel as an epistemic break with the past, but he casts his version in nonpolitical terms: the "vast transformation of Western Civilization since the Renaissance...has replaced the unified world picture of the Middle Ages with another very different one – one that presents us, essentially, with a developing but unplanned aggregate of particular individuals having particular experiences at particular times and at particular places" (*Rise*, 476–7). Lukács believes that the communal values and practices of ancient societies produced this "unified world picture"; and from his Marxist perspective the vast transformation of society is a tragic diminishment of human experience. By contrast, for Watt the social causes of the lost "unified world picture" are not a topic of investigation; the vast transformation of society provides a temporal starting point for his study of modernity. The values that Watt ascribes to the Middle Ages are formulated in highly general terms, functioning mainly as a point of contrast to the modern values that are detailed by his study. On Watt's view, the vast transformation has the status of a neutral historical fact: a momentous social change has occurred and there is no going back to the future. According to Watt, absolutes and universals have given way to a new philosophy of individualism that comes to dominate social attitudes in eighteenth-century England. This philosophy – epitomized for Watt by the writings of John Locke and René Descartes – is based upon the increasing cultural trust in what Watt calls the "truth of individual experience" (466). According to Watt, empiricism becomes in eighteenth-century England the new touchstone for ontology and epistemology – and thereby the impetus for a new kind of representation of real life accomplished through the invention of the novel. The philosophy of individualism is expressed by the novel in two fundamental ways: through the detailed depiction of the particular experience of fictional characters in their social worlds, and through the novel's positioning of its readers as witnesses to and interpreters of those fictional worlds.

As Watt elaborates the new philosophy of individualism, we might be reminded of Henry James's famous description of novelistic point of view, rendered through the extended metaphor of "the house of fiction" (see p. 69). According to Watt, the Lockean valorization of the senses leads to a belief in not just the primacy of individual experience but the uniqueness of individual perception. In James's figure, the viewers behind the windows of the house of fiction gaze at a common scene, but because of their differences in perspective (both material and subjective), what they see may be radically contradictory: "He and his neighbours are watching the same show, but one seeing more where the other sees less, one seeing black, where the other sees white, one seeing big where the other sees small" (Preface to *Portrait*, 69). Thus small locational differences can yield not just radically different value judgments (black and white, as polarized opinions), but disagreements about the phenomenal composition of the world itself (black and white, as differing perceptions of material reality). Watt's analysis of eighteenth-century philosophy encourages us to understand James's windows not just as a metaphor for the variety of authorial points of view accommodated by the novel as a literary form, but as a metonymy for the modern era's new conception of space and time as relativizing forces. Variations in order, duration, and environment (what one sees first, how long perception lasts, how the material shape and size of the "window" shape the view) not only make each viewer's perception unique but also make experience itself always "new," based as it is in sense experiences that are never exactly the same from moment to moment (*Rise*, 466, 470–3). In Watt's words, the valorization of perception results in a conception of personal identity as both essential and fluid, "subsisting through duration and yet being changed by the flow of experience" (472). The flow of experience, on this account, makes perception constitutive of individuality and also makes the individual ever-changing. These differences may be "only" those of detail; but the power of contingency in forming subjective perception means that individuality itself is in the details. Particular experience is the experience of the particular. The "show" is, in James's figure of the house of fiction, nothing more entertaining than the play of perception itself. And in Watt's theory of the rise of the novel, the new value accorded to the quotidian details of everyday life (the interest of big and small, black and white) is expressed by the invention of a new literary genre devoted to the mimetic representation of these ordinary details.

Although Watt does not comment explicitly upon the theoretical assumptions that guide his own scholarly method, his way of doing intellectual history is itself arguably an inheritance of the modern understanding of space and time that his book describes. Watt believes that the discipline of history is a modern invention, an outgrowth of the logic of individualism (465). This might at first seem a paradoxical claim: how can the valorization of unique personal identity be compatible with an understanding of societies defined by trans-individual forces? But for thinkers less radically subjectivist than James, the relativizing power of individual perception as expressed through the image of the house of fiction is tempered if one imagines the material and social commonalities that define the house itself as a location – on a particular street in a particular city in a particular country, with its watchers gathered at a particular time. The individual whose identity is defined through her particular experience of space and time lives in a society that itself is marked by its own particular spatial and temporal location. Eras or periods can by this logic be demarcated by an "individuality" that makes them clearly distinguishable from one another.

Thus Watt's conceptualization of the decisive break between the Middle Ages and modernity enables him to understand both as separate and distinct entities, defined by two radically different points of view. But there is another, more subtle aspect of Watt's own historical method that similarly seems underwritten by the philosophy of individualism that he describes as "rising" in the eighteenth century. In "Realism and the Novel Form," the first chapter of *The Rise of the Novel* and the excerpt included in this anthology, Watt seeks to analyze eighteenth-century England from its *own* point of view, as it were, to reconstruct the way that this particular culture at this particular time conceptualized the world and its place in that world. The desire to analyze a historical period in its own terms, to define its historical individuality as a culturally coherent point of view on life, leads Watt to focus upon what he takes to be the dominant beliefs held by eighteenth-century English society. But where are these defining statements to be found and upon what scale is their social typicality or influence to be evaluated? This is a key methodological problem that confronts all the historians in this section, and we will see how the different historical approaches here are distinguished by the different

DOROTHY HALE

answers provided to such methodological questions. Without the Marxist grounding in objective ethical and political values, the cultural theorists in this section all find themselves having to justify the criteria used to delimit what might otherwise be an endless sociohistorical field. They feel obliged to defend not only their focus upon a certain set of typifying social discourses or practices within a historical period, but also the act of historical periodization itself. What makes one century or decade distinguishable from another? What makes a particular historical era worthy of study at the present moment? And how do the values of that past age relate to our present-day values? Is the past past? Or is it the basis of the present?

For Watt, the difficulty of the theoretical problem results in a certain logical tension in his historical analysis. Early in his argument he confidently declares that the dominant values of the period are best articulated by the major philosophers of the time. The concept of individualism will, he claims, "be clarified by the help of those professionally concerned with the analysis of concepts, the philosophers" (*Rise*, 464). Watt implies that the philosophers of the era are the best spokespersons for the values of the period because, as professionally trained thinkers, they will provide the richest and fullest articulation of the era's intellectual and spiritual beliefs. But Watt is simultaneously aware that philosophy itself is a field of knowledge with its own conventions, regulations, and limitations. On this view, philosophy becomes apprehensible, to use M. M. Bakhtin's term, as a social "discourse": philosophy may present itself as a privileged mode of knowledge, knowledge about knowledge, but precisely to the degree that it belongs to "professionals," it also defines itself as a social practice, conducted in and through the shared values of a particular social group. As we will see more fully when we turn to Bakhtin, the goal of understanding a period intrinsically, from its own point of view, becomes considerably harder if that "point" is itself pluralized and relativized, redefined as dynamically interactive ideological positions, vying for political dominance, rather than as a culturally unifying philosophy about knowledge.

Watt himself does not address this theoretical problem; but we can see his uneasiness a few pages later when he abruptly dismisses the discursive hierarchy that he himself has just established. His transition from philosophy to the novel is in fact a logical break – if not a "vast transformation" then a mini leap – within his historical account of the period: "So much for the main analogies between realism in philosophy and literature. They are not proposed as exact; philosophy is one thing and literature is another" (476). Thus, although Watt begins by imagining the distinct, individual identity of his historical period to be decodable through the era's own discourse about knowledge, a discourse that presents itself as a master discourse about knowledge, he believes that individualism so permeates every aspect of English society during this period that ultimately philosophical discourse is simply one discursive site among many for its expression. According to Watt, we may want to look first at philosophy because it formulates the values of individualism in abstract ways that are useful for our general understanding; but to appreciate the historical specificity of individualism within English culture, we need to translate the terms and codes used by other social discourses to detect the ways that the philosophy of individualism is registered in ostensibly nonphilosophical social practices.

In *The Rise of the Novel* as a whole, Watt resists hierarchizing the many "new" social practices and instead tries to take them all together, seeing each as contributing

---

simultaneously to the cultural construction of individualism in the period. It is by studying the variety of new social discourses and practices, and finding their underlying commonality – in his words by analyzing them as "parallel manifestations of larger change" (476) – that the historian can apprehend the defining cultural belief of the age. For example, in later chapters of *The Rise of the Novel*, we find not only that the philosophy of the period resonates with the new realism invented by the novel, but also that both philosophy and literature are guided by the epistemological beliefs that underlie more far-flung social practices, such as the legal procedures governing jury trials and the rhetorical conventions of newspaper journalism. The power of Watt's analysis lies precisely in his ability to theorize a common cultural denominator – individualism – for these seemingly diverse and disjunctive social practices.

Watt's analogical historical method also extends to a consideration of material factors. Although his discussion of material conditions is in many ways compatible with the Marxist account of social change – especially in his analysis of the new technology that inaugurated modern modes of production – for Watt these material forces are no more or less primary, no more or less causal, than any of the other social practices and discourses he discusses. Thus, although sections of *The Rise of the Novel* focus on the modern metropolis, the technological changes in printing, the new importance of booksellers in the distribution of literature, the decline of court patronage of authors, and the economic forces that shaped the reading public (including the rise of manufacturing that relieved women of many household duties), these material factors are not invoked by Watt as either the root of social transformation or the ground of bourgeois ideology. On Watt's view, material forces and cultural attitudes reciprocally interact with one another, each possessing their own kind of social influence and each contributing to the same dominant cultural value. Puritanism is as important as capitalism, secularism and sexism are as important as copyright laws in registering the modern philosophy of individualism.[1] And if Watt's attempt to locate the defining social beliefs of the period leads him to look at a plurality of social discourses and practices, then his belief that these various social practices and discourses all amount to one thing (the expression of individualism) means that he also need not fear he has overlooked or left out of his study any particular discourse, since nothing has been missed that would substantially alter his account of the age.

Watt's description of the novel as one of the discourses of individualism is similarly characterized by its nonevaluative stance, its lack of interest in either making comparative judgments about the genre as an aesthetic accomplishment or attributing particular political power to its social effects. Instead, Watt sticks with the logic of his intellectual history, seeking to explain through close readings of particular novels the features of this new genre that made it the popular choice for the growing reading public in the age of individualism. He concludes that it is precisely the novel's lack of what is conventionally thought of as "literary" form that enables it to express the modern conception of reality. His study of the earliest English novels, works such as *Pamela* and *Moll Flanders*, shows how the novel's modernity lies in its achieved departure from recognizable literary conventions, indeed from the entire notion that the quality of literariness itself is recognizable and meaningful only in relation to traditional literary sources. In Watt's words, "What is often felt as the formlessness of the novel, as compared, say with the tragedy or the ode, probably follows from this: the poverty of the novel's formal conventions would seem to be the price it must pay for its realism" (466). According to Watt, the novel's disregard for formal convention serves the cultural project of individualism by making primary the representation of quotidian empirical experience, both the experience of the characters in the novel and that of the reader who feels that she has direct access to the characters' experiences as they unfold before her eyes. This new level of empirical mimeticism is what gives Charles Lamb the impression, according to Watt, that the novel reads more like "evidence in a court of Justice" than a poem or a play (478).

As Watt explains it, the novel's form was thus conceived as a representation of the structure of perception, registering the era's belief in the philosophical distinction between the means of perception and the values, beliefs, and opinions of the perceiver. The freedom from a strict poetics allows the genre, according to Watt, to be defined as a genre by its form rather than its content. If epic, tragedy, comedy, romance, georgic, and pastoral all are defined as much by their subject matter as their formal conventions, the novel's innovation, its newness, its novelty, its modernity as a literary genre lies in its purely formal generic identity. Watt coins the term "formal realism" to emphasize the distinction the novel as a genre establishes between form and content – and Watt further argues that formal realism is the defining feature of the novel as a literary genre, however minimalist and nontraditional the novel's formal conventions may seem (478). Watt thus explicitly opposes critics who argue that the novel's realism is connected to a grittier view of life, that as a genre it is devoted to exploding polite or mannered conventions of representation. Many novels do indeed fall into this category, but for Watt the genre as a whole cannot be equated with the project of social reform: "If the novel were realistic merely because it saw life from the seamy side, it would only be an inverted romance; but in fact it surely attempts to portray all the varieties of human experience, and not merely those suited to a particular literary perspective: the novel's realism does not reside in the kind of life it presents, but in the way it presents it" (464). "All the varieties of human experience" can be expressed only by a literary genre that is open to the point of view of any individual – and the minimal rules about form that the novel does have are, according to Watt, themselves in service of the relativity of point of view that defines the modern conception of life.

The Rise of the Novel has proven to be tremendously influential in novel studies, inspiring other critical investigations into all sorts of novelistic "rises," especially in other national traditions (the rise of the Indian novel, the rise of the American novel); by period (the modern novel); by social group (the Asian American novel); by gender (the rise of the woman novelist); and by mode (the historical novel, the self-conscious novel, the gothic novel). But an alternative register of Watt's influence lies in the number of critics who launch their study in either explicit or implicit disagreement with his work. D. A. Miller's *The Novel and the Police* (1988) is a powerful example of such critique: Miller's study of the Victorian novel builds on the historical account of individualism that Watt advances – but radically revises Watt's understanding of individualism's social function. For Miller, the social changes that produce the modern valorization of individualism lead in the nineteenth century to the political concept of the individual as a "liberal subject," defined by Miller as "the subject whose private life, mental or domestic, is felt to provide constant inarguable evidence of his constitutive 'freedom'" (*Police*, 573). We can find in Watt an explanation of why private life becomes the register of personal freedom:

By weakening communal and traditional relationships, [individualism] fostered not only the kind of private and egocentric mental life we find in Defoe's heroes, but also the later stress on the importance of personal relationships which is so characteristic both of modern society and of the novel – such relationships may be seen as offering the individual a more conscious and selective pattern of social life to replace the more diffuse, and as it were involuntary, social cohesions which individualism had undermined.[2]

But for Miller it is not that private life "*may be seen* as offering the individual a more conscious and selective pattern of social life"; this perception is itself a historical component of the liberal subject's belief about itself. And if it is necessary to the liberal subject to believe that she enjoys a conscious and selective pattern of social life, it is equally necessary to Miller's understanding of history to believe that the liberal subject does not in fact enjoy more personal and individual power than people in the past. For Miller the liberal subject is not an alternative to a model of identity determined by "diffuse" and "involuntary" "social cohesions" but is a symptom of the new way that social power operates in the modern era. The valorization of privacy and the belief in individual choice and efficacy is, on this view, produced by and in service of diffuse and decidedly involuntary social cohesions, which individualism seems to undermine as part of the larger project of maintaining them. Miller thus shares with the Marxists the belief that immanent history can take us only so far. The kind of intellectual history practiced by Watt, which attempts to understand a culture from its own point of view, its dominant social practices and beliefs, remains important for Miller as a kind of referent: the self-image projected by a culture that confirms its own sense of its self-presence. But for Miller that referent needs to be read against social forces that create the conditions for the belief in self-presence. His politicized understanding of social power makes him doubt the connection between self-description and true motive, between what a society says about itself through its discourses of knowledge and the cultural work which is in fact performed through such discourses of knowledge.

For Miller it is Michel Foucault rather than Karl Marx whose theory of social power best explains the operation of this necessary cultural self-deception. And Miller's concise summary of Foucault makes clear the elements of thought that are most important to him (*Police*, 553–4). While Marxism imagines social power as, throughout human history, always only hierarchical and repressive, a matter of antagonistic class interests, Foucault believes that the operation of social power fundamentally changes as part of the epistemic shift that historically differentiates modernity. By the end of the eighteenth century, with the decline of monarchies and the spread of democratic forms of government, social power ceases to work through corporal punishment and repression, ceases to be clearly located in the rule of privileged and visible agents, and is instead dispersed through every element of social life. Power, in other words, is no longer the possession of any particular social agent (either an individual, such as a king, or a collective social agent, such as the ruling class) and, according to Foucault, instead circulates through society impersonally, on behalf of social discipline itself. In Miller's words, "The aim of such regulation is to enforce not so much a norm as the normality of normativeness itself. Rather than in rendering all its subjects uniformly 'normal,' discipline is interested in putting in place a perceptual grid in which a division between the normal and the deviant inherently imposes itself. Concomitantly, discipline attenuates the role of actual supervisors by enlisting the consciousness of its subjects in the work of supervision" (554).

Miller's own cultural history focuses upon precisely this: the unwitting participation of liberal subjects in their own social discipline. And because Miller joins other post-Foucauldian (or New Historical) literary scholars in regarding the novel as the age's most effective "technology" of self-supervision, his examination of the ideological construction of liberal subjectivity in turn focuses on the tactics of social discipline practiced by the novel upon its readers (see Nancy Armstrong in this volume and, for an Americanist study, Richard Brodhead's "Sparing the Rod"). In many ways, the Foucauldian view of the novel is compatible with the ideological function ascribed to it by Marxists. As we saw in Part V, Walter Benjamin argues that novels cultivate private experience not just in the private lives that they take for their subject, but in the social practice of private reading, of imaginative absorption, that they make available to the reading public. But for Miller the privacy that the novel helps culturally to construct is only half of the historical story. This privacy (specifically the novel's construction of privacy as something opposed to and outside of public life) is what enables the novel to serve as an effective agent of social discipline. Thus, although Miller would agree with Watt that the novel moved us into "the private experience of characters," taking the reader "inside their minds as well as inside their houses,"[3] from Miller's Foucauldian position there is another party accompanying us inside: the police have moved "out of the streets [and] into the closet – I mean, into the private and domestic sphere on which the very identity of the liberal subject depends" (*Police"*, 542). Rejecting Watt's belief in the novel's formal minimalism and its openness to the varieties of human experience, Miller instead credits the genre with highly sophisticated and intricate narrative tactics of readerly seduction and indoctrination, pursued with the aim of creating a single type of social subject, a disciplined social subject.

Miller argues that in the Victorian period the novel consolidates its disciplinary tactics – and the most visible sign of this consolidation is the genre's explicit thematic dedication to social reform. In Miller's words, "perhaps no openly fictional form has ever sought to 'make a difference' in the world more than the Victorian novel, whose cultural hegemony and diffusion well qualified it to become the spiritual exercise of an entire age" (543). But, according to Miller, it is precisely through this explicit social criticism that the novel positions itself as standing outside of social power – and this "disavowal" (533) of its own participation in social power is, Miller maintains, its most effective (because most "discrete") tactic for enforcing social power. As Miller describes it, the novel deploys the strategy of disavowal by first, through its thematic content, depicting social power as the possession of professional social agents – the police, the court, etc. The reader thus is led to feel his own difference from the "lawless other" hunted by these holders of social power – and more generally the difference between a private life of middle-class integrity and personal freedom granted to the law-abiding citizen and the public world of crime and crime fighters. Thus for Miller the novel's thematic content functions as a version of the referential lure that has been so important to novel theorists from Víktor Shklovsky onward (see the General Introduction). But rather than "defamiliarizing" the representational function of literary language, on Miller's view the reader's belief in the image of power represented by the content of the novel is a necessary delusion fostered by the operation of real social power, which itself works in very different terms. In Miller's words, "Whenever the novel censures policing power, it has already reinvented it, in *the very practice of novelistic representation*" (555).

For Miller the work of "self-supervision" thus is grounded in the socially constructed belief in the projection of a public other (the criminal, the policeman) antithetical to oneself. This mediation of self-identity through what Miller calls the "fantasy of its otherness" (553) may remind us of René Girard's theory of the covert mediation of personal identity through its projection of the alien other (see pp. 299–301). But where as Girard emphasizes the emotional ambivalence that results from such self-deception and the attendant emotional *angst*, for Miller the "fantasy of otherness" cannot produce negative emotion in the individual because it cannot be brought to consciousness by the individual: the "liberal subject … recognize[s] himself most fully only when he forgets or disavows his functional implication in a system of carceral restraints or disciplinary injunctions" (543). The fantasy of otherness is thus not an ethical truth that, as for Girard, might become knowable and thus correctable; for Miller it is one tactic in the social construction of a self-disciplined modern subject, "a subject habituated to psychic displacements, evacuations, reinvestments," whose fluidity thus matches the "mobility" and "infinitely removed finality" of the social power that has produced it (544).

Foucault's social theory gives Miller a clear historical justification for studying the Victorian novel. On this view, the novel is not simply one important social discourse among many in the Victorian period, but a preeminent technology of power. Yet if Miller's theoretical approach seems more able than Watt's to hierarchize social practices and discourses within a given period – to identify those that are most "social" by their disciplinary effectiveness and reach – there are other moments in which Miller's interest in arguing for the specific characteristics that define a specific historical period and specific social discourse (the novel) within that period gives way to a more universalizing view of the political operation of social power in the modern world. In his introduction, Miller presents *The Novel and the Police*, his own scholarly work written at the end of the twentieth century, as itself potentially caught in the same epistemological ambiguity that defines the Victorian liberal subject.[4] He questions whether, by offering a series of essays rather than a more conventionally unified book, he has escaped the masking power of putative autonomous reference. But he also sees how the attempt to write in a way that would dislocate the illusion of autonomy might in fact reinscribe the illusion of autonomy in more subtle ways. He wonders if his own attempt to resist the unified narrative of a scholarly monograph might "play precisely into the ideology of the liberal subject who, never fixed in any of the determinations that he may provisionally entertain, is always free to remake himself; and whose now-fashionable lack of anguish or embarrassment before heterogeneity depends on an imperial state (of 'affairs') that has already unified the world in a total system."[5]

It may be that on Miller's view the historical differences between the present moment and Victorian England, between a Victorian novel and a contemporary work of American literary criticism, are ultimately negligible, given the overwhelming historical persistence of liberal subjectivity as a cultural construction into and throughout the twentieth century. And indeed Miller seems to suggest something like this when he explicitly declares that although in the twentieth century the novel is no longer the preeminent technology for the operation of social power (its popularity as a form of entertainment having been superseded by new media such as film, television, and, one might add, the internet), Miller nonetheless sees these later forms of mass entertainment as epiphenomena of the innovation in social control that begins with the novel: "The 'death of the novel' (of that novel, at any rate) has really meant the explosion everywhere of the novelistic, no longer bound in three-deckers, but freely scattered across a far greater range of cultural experience" (543).

But if on Miller's view neither liberal subjectivity nor the "novel" has substantively changed in over a century, we may begin to wonder if it is history or Foucauldian theory that is responsible for the homogeneity. As Miller himself is well aware, although Foucauldian theory is committed to the possibility and actuality of historical change, its theory of power is itself so all-encompassing that differences in material conditions, political formations, and social practices from era to era can themselves seem like mere epiphenomena of modern power, interchangeable from century to century, era to era. Although Foucault believes in the modification of social power through effective political reform, his theory makes it difficult to judge where and how social progress is to be found, especially since he deconstructs the conventional wisdom that civilization has been advanced in the move away from corporal punishment to criminal reform.

Jane Tompkins' desire to avoid such pessimism about social reform inspires her to offer a different account of the rise of the novel, one that aims to make Foucault's theory of power yield the political legibility that Marxism provides. *Sensational Designs* (1985) is explicitly Foucauldian in that it views literary works "not as works of art embodying enduring themes in complex forms" but as agents of "cultural work" (536). Novels should be regarded, she says, using a phrase from Foucault, as "'nodes within a network,' expressing what lay in the minds of many or most of their contemporaries" (539). For Tompkins this means that the cultural historian, in her case the historian of nineteenth-century US culture, should regard novels and the category of literature more generally as possessing the same amount and kind of social power as any other social discourse from the period. On her view, novels perform the same type of ideological work as nonfictional and nonliterary writing published during the period. When "set side by side with contemporary fiction," Tompkins argues, nonliterary social discourses such as "advice books, tract society reports, and hagiographic biographies…can be seen to construct the real world in the image of set of ideals and beliefs in *exactly the same way* that novels and stories do" (538, my emphasis). Foucault, she says, has taught her to interpret a social period by its "continuities" rather than its "ruptures," to look not for aberrations (be they of excellence or deficiency) but for "the strands that connected a novel to other similar texts" (538).

But Tompkins ultimately departs from her own account of Foucault by reprivileging the novel as an object of cultural study – and she is led to do so in order to accomplish her goal of political legibility. Tompkins credits the nineteenth-century American novel with an authentic capacity for social reform that she regards as an unambiguous political good, not a ruse or a self-deception, not a covert instrument of social discipline. On her view, although the novel is indistinguishable as an ideological form from other non-literary discourses, it is nonetheless a notable node in the web of cultural discourse because of the political value of the cultural work it performs. And, as she describes it, the novel accomplishes this political work through the narrative techniques that are particular to it, that in fact distinguish it from advice books, tract society reports, and hagiographic biographies. The novel's political power lies for Tompkins in its ability to imagine alternative social worlds and to bring them to life as possible realities. The novel can "construct the real world in the image of a set of ideals and beliefs" that may change the reigning social order, that may usher in a new and better common "mind" (539). Her claim to be interested in social discourse as normative rather than "aberrant" thus is compromised to the degree that she regards novelistic discourse as exceptionally able to envision, express, and enact social change. Tompkins' study may theoretically envision a social world in which all social discourses are equal, but her theory in fact assumes a new reason, a political reason, for the cultural historian to privilege the study of literature.

Tompkins's politics lead to an account of novelistic representation that could not be more different than Watt's theory of formal realism. She follows Fredric Jameson in arguing that the novel's political power lies in its anti-mimeticism, its power to explode the apparent autonomy and givenness of the quotidian world and so to expose the ideologies that promote the social belief in empiricism and individualism. For Tompkins it is the sentimental rather than the realist novel that most accurately depicts the everyday atrocities of social life. Susan Warner's *The Wide, Wide World* and Harriet Beecher Stowe's *Uncle Tom's Cabin* are, on her view, nothing less than potent "attempts to redefine the social order" (536). Tompkins thereby offers a new political explanation for a well-established literary-historical fact: she explains the paucity and belatedness of American realism not, as many literary critics have, by the relative lack of high culture in a young country, but by the authentic commitment of American novelists to social reform. According to Tompkins, the nineteenth-century US novel did not achieve formal realism only because it did not pursue it. Its formal anti-realism – improbable plots, stereotypical characters, excessive description, and sensationalism – are, according to Tompkins, integral to the project of reform. By deploying such anti-realist methods, these novels adopt the narrative strategies of radical political thinkers such as William Godwin, who in *Caleb Williams* (1794) attempts to change "things as they are" through a symbolic representation of the horror of social norms. Tompkins believes that if sentimental novels are read rightly, for their affective power as well as their political symbolism, they not only expose what is wrong with society but constructively remake "the social and political order in which events take place" (539). Tompkins goes so far to describe the decoded symbolic content of sentimental novels as a "blueprint for survival under a specific set of political, economic, social, or religious conditions" (540).

But if the novel on Tompkins' view is a "blueprint," it is one whose superior political effectiveness is due to its distinctively *novelistic* rhetorical power, the qualities that made it the reading matter of choice not just in England but the United States, too. Tompkins would agree with Miller that novels have what she calls "designs" upon their readers; but for Tompkins the novel's attempt to influence people to "think and act in a particular way" is an overt part of its reform project. Antebellum American novels, on her account, work not by seduction, disguise, or distraction but by the more positive solicitation of the reader's emotional engagement. The use of stereotypes, for example, allows sentimental novels to "convey enormous amounts of cultural information in an extremely condensed form," information that engages the reader because of its "strong emotional associations" (536). Tompkins would thus agree with Miller that people are shaped as social subjects by novel reading – but unlike Miller she believes that this change can be on behalf of authentic self-improvement and political betterment. On her view, social discourses are not "nodes in a network" because the totalizing operation of Foucauldian social power has equalized their function as disciplinary agents. For Tompkins this metaphor instead emphasizes the social and political power available to all discourses, even those, such as literature, that may seem unmotivated by political goals. We can say that Tompkins conceptualizes the novel not as a preeminent technology of power but as a preeminent tool of social reform, a social discourse whose narrative strategies are particularly effective for critiquing society and whose unprecedented popularity with the new reading public gives it the potential to effect mass political change.

In organizing her study of a particular historical period around "powerful examples of the way a culture thinks about itself" (536), Tompkins believes in the real opportunity for individual decision-making and political choice. Readers may come to a novel from a social position different from the author's only to find themselves emotionally acted upon by the novel and therefore made willing to change their political views. The historical account of "what lay in the minds of many or most of their contemporaries" (539) is for Tompkins not a single belief (like individualism or even the ideology of the liberal individual), but a plurality of contending political views, pitted in dynamic struggle for the hearts and minds of the reading public. The novelist enters this fray and sets about in good faith "to win the belief and influence the behavior of the widest possible audience" (536).

Tompkins thus solves the Millerian double bind by having it both ways – she imagines culturally constructed identity as a kind of soft determinism, essential in the construction of individual identity as social and ideological but open to alteration through individual control. It is this kind of faith in the distinguishability between cultural forces and individual decisions that allows her to imagine a methodology for her own historical project that is grounded in the limits she places on perspectival mediation. As a historian, Tompkins insists that the past is different from the present; she emphasizes that the common values of early nineteenth-century American culture are far removed from those that define postmodern American culture – a difference, she says, registered by the widely shared twentieth-century belief that the aesthetic pleasure and power of nineteenth-century sentimental novels are unavailable to today's readers. But Tompkins also believes that her historical research can bring forward the social context for these works and, instructed by this knowledge, the postmodern reader can directly experience the aesthetic pleasure of these novels: "The power of a sentimental novel to move its audience depends upon the audience's being in possession of the conceptual categories that constitute character and event."[6] Even more radically, Tompkins describes historical understanding per se as a function of readerly identification: to be "in possession of the conceptual categories" of the past is, for Tompkins, to be "sympathetic" to them. By reading nineteenth-century US culture not just immanently (Watt's goal), but sympathetically, the cultural critic can, according to Tompkins, actually "inhabit and make available to a modern audience the viewpoint from which their [own] politics made sense" (537). Tompkins imagines historical understanding as itself an act of identification, not just the identification of the dominant point(s) of view of the period, but the actual "inhabitation" of a past point of view by the modern literary critic. For Tompkins historical position is thus at once determining and also suspendable: the late twentieth-century reader lives in a world wholly different from the past but, informed by historical knowledge, is able, according to Tompkins, to bracket that postmodern self to become a sympathetic novel reader (the way that Wayne Booth's novel reader left behind the quotidian self who paid bills and fixed faucets), a recreated nineteenth-century reader.

But for Tompkins the temporal mobility enabled by historical understanding is not only a matter of present-day readers moving backward. She also believes that the history she writes has the power to reform the contemporary world. She wants postmodern readers not just to inhabit the past through sympathetic identification, but for that reconstructed past to itself come forward as a point of view, a point of view that can stand as a critique of and an alternative to the hegemonic social control operating in contemporary life:

> Because I am a woman in a field dominated by male scholars, I have been particularly sensitive to the absence of women's writing from the standard American literature curriculum. I chose to discuss two works of domestic, or "sentimental," fiction because I wanted to demonstrate the power and ambition of novels written by women, and specifically by women whose work twentieth-century criticism has repeatedly denigrated. (537)

A skeptic may wonder if this "power and ambition" is a projection of Tompkins' contemporary political agenda onto the past. But from Tompkins' perspective on her own work, it seems that the profound differences between nineteenth-century US culture and the present are bridgeable by at least one kind of continuity: the ideological continuity of class and gender. Tompkins is moved by the sentimental works she reads because she interprets their political commitments as continuous with hers. She explicitly states that the "sentimental novel represents the interests of middle-class women" – and she implies that these interests remain (like Miller's liberal subject or his concept of the "novelistic") substantially unchanged from one century to the next.[7] The instruction she finds in and through history thus confirms her own political beliefs, beliefs that place her in closer connection with women novelists of the past, she feels, than male literary critics in the present.

Although Tompkins does not list M. M. Bakhtin among the theorists who have influenced her work, Bakhtin's interest in defining social discourse as both ideologically determinant and individually chosen has strong resonances with Tompkins' project. "Discourse in the Novel" was written in Russia in the 1930s, but it was not until the 1970s that Bakhtin's work began to be translated into English, finding fans in Britain and the US. By the 1980s Bakhtin's ideas had become almost ubiquitous in the humanities; and this quick popularity suggests the compatibility of Bakhtin's theoretical investments with those of post-formalist, post-structuralist, post-Marxist academics looking for a fresh social theory. In part, Bakhtin met this contemporary need because his work also envisioned itself as moving beyond Formalism, structuralism, and Marxism – albeit at an earlier stage of the development of these schools of thought. Bakhtin's theory of literature and society is founded in a specific critique of a founding father of each school: the formalist Víktor Shklovsky; the structural linguist, Ferdinand de Saussure; and the Marxist, György Lukács. In *The Formal Method of Literary Scholarship* (1928), Bakhtin explicitly opposes Saussure's opposition between *langue* and *parole*, positing instead a social theory of language as it is lived and used by real people in specific communicative contexts (see the biographical note for the vexed publication history of works attributed to members of the Bakhtin Circle). The insistence on the social nature of language is also what distinguishes his theory from the poetics pursued by Shklovsky and the other Russian formalists, some of whom overlapped with Bakhtin at the University of St. Petersburg. When Lukács' *Theory of the Novel* was first published in 1920, Bakhtin was inspired to begin a Russian translation; although this project was never finished, his engagement with Lukács resulted in "Epic and Novel," Bakhtin's own conceptualization of the relation between the two genres, which comes to conclusions almost diametrically opposite to Lukács'.

Whereas Lukács bemoans the loss of social cohesion that made the epic meaningful in its time, Bakhtin makes a case for the ethical power of the "modern" values of process, inconclusiveness, relativity, diversity, subversion, and the quotidian. The novel is the modern genre par excellence for Bakhtin because it promotes these values. In an early work such as *Problems of Dostoevsky's Poetics* (1929), Bakhtin stresses the relativizing power of novelistic character, the force and persuasiveness given by the novel as a genre to individual points of view. But in contrast to Anglo-American thinkers such as Ian Watt and Henry James, who understand relativized point of view as a product of cultural individualism, Bakhtin defines point of view as essentially social and interactive: an individual knows that he has a particular point of view only when it is able to be contrasted with points of view different from his own. If points of view weren't comparable, then the individual would never know that his vision of the world was a point of view. In his figure of the house of fiction, James conceptualizes his watchers as engaged in parallel and yet wholly isolated acts of perception; by contrast, in *Dostoevsky's Poetics*, Bakhtin conceives of points of view as fundamentally interactive, what he in a mixed metaphor calls the "dialogic" (or conversational) relation of points of view. Characters are defined as points of view extopically and relationally, not hermetically and immanently.

In the later "Discourse in the Novel" (1934–5) Bakhtin expands his notion of intersubjective dialogism into a more general social theory of language. He invents the term "heteroglossia" to emphasize the larger ideological heterogeneity within which dialogic relations are established. On this view, the novel is conceptualized not just as individual, characterological points of view emerging in and through dialogic relation, but as the dialogic interactions between ideological points of view staged by language itself. According to Bakhtin, the novel distinguishes itself from other literary genres by its openness to the authentic ideological heterogeneity of social language. He thus finds positive value in a generic feature of the novel that other critics have attempted to downplay or dismiss, worried that it might compromise the novel's bid for high art status. For Bakhtin, the novel's generic distinctiveness lies exactly in its generic promiscuity, its ability to fashion itself out of and in relation to extra-literary discourses such as letters, newspaper articles, historical documents, autobiographies, religious confessions, as well as other artistic discourses – lyric poetry, the epic, even visual arts such as illustration, painting, and photography. In this discursive hybridity lies the novel's authentic social realism. According to Bakhtin, the novel does not artfully mimic or simulate reality through language. Like Watt, Bakhtin believes that the novel's generic form actually reproduces the structure of perception – but for Bakhtin the structure of perception is not based in empirical individualism but in linguistic sociality. The novel's heteroglossia is for Bakhtin no more and no less than a social act of language that communicates the linguistic sociality of human life itself.

For Bakhtin, all social discourses are distinguished by the point of view they express: each social language is, to use his term, "populated" with the communicative "intentions" and the ideological investments of the actual people who have used this language (504). Because we learn words within particular social situations, idiolects develop to the point where different social groups seem to speak completely different languages: they may use the same words, but the words have highly specific meanings, reflective of the shared attitudes uniting each social group. Bakhtin's concept of heteroglossia thus is predicated upon the cohesion of social values that give words different meanings in different social settings: the word "hot," for example, might be one thing to weather men, another to jazz musicians, and yet another to jewel thieves. As Bakhtin puts it, "We are taking language not as a system of abstract grammatical categories, but rather language conceived as ideologically saturated, language as a world view, even as a concrete opinion, insuring a *maximum* of mutual understanding in all spheres of ideological life" (489–90). An individual speaker does not possess one point of view, according to Bakhtin, but inhabits multiple "world views" through the various social discourses she speaks. A high-school senior, for example, might use one language when instant messaging her friends and another to address the admissions committee who will read her college application essay.

Bakhtin invents the term "internal dialogism" to denote the ability of different ideological discourses to distinguish themselves within a shared, overarching language – whether that overarching language is considered on the scale of a social group, a profession, a region, a nation, or an art work such as the novel. In a way, we can think of internal dialogism as an adaptation and extension of free indirect discourse (FID), the grammatical construction that is of such interest to narratologists such as Roy Pascal, Gerard Genette, and Seymour Chatman (see Part III). In his close reading of specific novels (his analysis of Charles Dickens's *Little Dorrit* being a prime example in a section of "Discourse in the Novel" not excerpted here), Bakhtin charts an intricate system of sociolinguistic norms, distinguishing, for example, the language of the law from the language of ceremonial speeches from the literary language of high epic style.[8] Bakhtin encourages the reader to notice not just the variety of social discourses activated in the novel but the novelist's own attitude to these discourses, the relative distance between the world view expressed through these languages and the novelist's estimation of that world view. Is the novelist attempting to make a word his own? Is the discourse of manners, for example, directly intentional? Or is he ironizing it, speaking though it, ventriloquizing it to display the lack of compatibility between the belief system that informs it and his own?

Bakhtin might be said to take the notion of ideological struggle from Marx and to reconceptualize it as part of the ordinary business of language. Ideology is a politically neutral term for Bakhtin, an inevitable aspect of life lived in any type of social community. The range and variety of social differences entertained by Bakhtin's theory mean that almost any speech act can become a site of social struggle. As Bakhtin puts it, the word is "private property," it "exists in other people's mouths, in other people's contexts, serving other people's intentions; it is from there that one must take the word,

DOROTHY HALE

and make it one's own" (505). Whereas for Marxists it takes social reform or revolution to redistribute private property, for Bakhtin such social struggle unfolds on the more ambiguously material ground of the individual utterance. Language is for Bakhtin not simply a container for social identity but is itself an ideological agent. He goes so far as to imagine that language itself can defy colonization: "many words stubbornly resist, others remain alien, sound foreign in the mouth of the one who appropriated them and who now speaks them; they cannot be assimilated into his context and fall out of it; it is as if they put themselves in quotation marks against the will of the speaker" (505).

But although Bakhtin entertains the possibility of discursive rebellion, more often in "Discourse in the Novel" speakers are able to overcome the ideological boundaries that define linguistic subgroups through an individual act of language. The determinism of ideology, in other words, is for Bakhtin (as it is for Tompkins as well) able to be modified through individual action. Bakhtin uses as his paradigmatic example two speakers who belong to radically different social groups and whose respective discourses thus are wholly incommensurate, entailing different "forms for conceptualizing the world in words...each characterized by its own objects, meanings and values" (503). As Bakhtin describes it, the gulf created by social position can be potentially transcended by the will of the speakers themselves. Through an ethical act of imagination, a speaker can adopt the point of view of the other, an act of alterity that for Bakhtin does not abolish the speaker's "own" discourse but relativizes his relationship to it:

> The speaker strives to get a reading on his own word, and on his own conceptual system that determines this word, within the alien conceptual system of the understanding receiver; he enters into dialogical relationships with certain aspects of this system. The speaker breaks through the alien conceptual horizon of the listener, constructs his own utterance on alien territory, against his, the listener's, apperceptive background. (497)

Although Bakhtin says that this kind of internal dialogism is fostered by certain historical eras more than others and thus is easier to pursue and achieve during particular historical moments, he also posits dialogic self-consciousness as an absolute human condition, a necessary feature of all social experience. Bakhtin's parable of the illiterate peasant sketches the cognitive evolution of the social everyman, who "sooner or later" (506) discovers that his various social practices require him to use heterogeneous social languages, each of which is constituted by "ideological systems and approaches to the world that...in no way could live in peace and quiet with one another" (506). In Bakhtin's theory, this discovery of self-consciousness brings with it the possibility of personal decision and control: the peasant can now begin the necessity "of actively choosing [his] orientation among [these discourses]" (506). The peasant does not make this choice by standing outside of language but by looking "at one of these languages through the eyes of another language" (506).

For Bakhtin, the novel distinguishes itself as a social discourse not just through the amount and variety of discourses it contains but through its capacity to place these discourses in dialogical relation. The novelist on Bakhtin's view is a genius of heteroglossia: his own superiority to the poet (his generic other) and the peasant (his illiterate other) is registered by the "welcome" he extends to "alien" social discourses (508). The novelist is, Bakhtin declares, "first and foremost" distinguished by his self-consciousness about the value of dialogized heteroglossia (503). The novelist is not simply open to heterogeneity; he is able to produce new heterogeneity by actively participating in the interanimation of social discourses, by performing through his representation of social discourse the act of looking "at one of these languages through the eyes of another language" (506). The novelist can, it seems, try out ideological points of view the way one would try out new pairs of glasses: seeing "through the eyes of another language" is a state of mediation that is not itself mediated by one's history or gender or class – or whatever social determinants constituted one's original point of view. In Bakhtin's theory, the "eyes" of another language are always legible and distinct; the perspective they give on other languages, including one's own language, is isolatable and unified. Heteroglossia does not blur discursive difference or make it ambiguous; it simply enables the complexity and intensity of dialogism. If anything, the novel seems to have for Bakhtin a heightened ability to clarify the author's investments and judgments by materializing them. Bakhtin describes the novelist's intentionality as a material aspect of novelistic language: "The intentions of the prose writer are refracted, and refracted *at different angles*, depending on the degree to which the refracted, heteroglot languages he deals with are socio-ideologically alien, already embodied and already objectivized" (508). The critic can confidently gauge the author's social attitudes by charting the type and degree of refraction made visible through the novel's objectified word. Authorial intentions may be fluctuating or ambivalent but can nonetheless be parsed out by the critic as distinct and separate angles of vision.

Given the superior capacity for dialogized heteroglossia that Bakhtin attributes both to the novel and to novelist, readers may understand Bakhtin as positing a qualitative distinction between the novel and other social or literary discourses. But the qualities that Bakhtin attributes to the novel ultimately function adjectivally. The issue for Bakhtin is always one of degree rather than kind. The "poetic" and the "novelistic" function for Bakhtin as two poles of a spectrum rather than absolute binary oppositions. The more self-conscious a speaker is about the social identities carried within the language he speaks, the more "dialogized" his own language use will become, the more he will express through his utterance his understanding of the ideological view-point that characterizes his language as a particular social discourse. Bakhtin does believe that the novel as a narrated form is especially suited to the representation of authentic dialogism, allowing as it does for the complexity of layered and embedded points of view; on Bakhtin's account it is precisely the novel's narration which makes it superior to more crudely dialogic literary genres, such as the drama. But Bakhtin is happy to call "novelistic" any sort of literary genre that reveals the operation of dialogized heteroglossia. Within a lyric poem one might find "novelistic" moments; and within a given novel one discovers lapses into "poetic" or monologic discourse. Bakhtin would even say that such dynamic fluctuation between degrees of dialogism characterizes most actual novels.

But in a different way "Discourse and the Novel" does harbor a utopian ideal of the novelist, one that grows out of Bakhtin's theory of social language even as it ultimately seems to call into question some of its premises about the foundational nature of positionality in forming social identity. As Bakhtin euphorically describes it, the novelist who takes full advantage of the ethical revelations made possible by the novel's relativization of social discourse is a person who "does not speak in a given language (from which he distances himself to a greater or lesser degrees), but he speaks, as it were, *through* language, a language that has somehow more or less materialized, become objectivized, that he merely ventriloquates" (508). The determining nature of social positionality, it seems, can be overcome by the self-consciousness and self-willed pursuit of social plurality. The novelist's self-consciousness about ideological pluralism, in other words, releases him from the social determinants of his own identity, allowing him to become first and foremost a "novelist" (rather than, say, a member of the middle class, or a resident of a certain town, or a speaker of a particular national language). His ability to look "at one…[language] through the eyes of another language" has so relativized the novelist's consciousness that all social points of view are objectifiable for him, no social language is his own even as all social languages are available to him. Infinitely mobile through the voluntary changeability of his social points of view, his identity is defined more by his capacity for heteroglossia per se than by his particular social investments or communicative intentions. Tied to no social discourse, he is thus able to ventriloquize all social discourse. If we invoke Miller's Foucauldian perspective, Bakhtin's novelist sounds eerily like that self-disciplined social subject, "a subject habituated to [the] psychic displacements, evacuations, reinvestments" required by modern power (*Police*, 544). But in Bakhtinian theory, the novelist's capacity for relativization is an absolute ethical good: his own transcendent position enables the novelist to display heteroglossia in action, allowing novel readers to share his insights into the sociality of the human condition: to understand the linguistic basis of ideological differences and the linguistic means by which these differences can be bridged.

Watt, Miller, Tompkins, and Bakhtin thus all, in their different ways, join the Marxists in arguing for the novel's historical importance in the inauguration of modernity. But unlike the Marxists, who generally blame the novel for its ethically and politically deficient representation of sociality, who chastise the genre for furthering the capitalist palliation of the historical and material sources of the modern social condition, the theorists in this chapter regard the novel as worthy of study precisely because of its preeminent sociality, its exceptional historical representativeness, in a phrase of Catherine Gallagher's, its "extreme typicality."[9] For Watt, this sociality lies in the novel's formal realism, which, as we have seen, on his view makes it the least literary genre, and thus the literary form most suited to represent the new empiricism of the modern age. For Miller, the novel's sociality lies in its status as the first mass cultural commodity, making it the first pop culture literary form and thus an important technology in the modern operation of social discipline. For Tompkins, the novel's superior sociality lies in its rhetorical power, the narrative techniques that she believes make it the literary form most suited to persuasion and therefore to social reform. And for Bakhtin, the novel is nothing other than a complex sociolinguistic performance that displays heteroglossia as the constitutive quality of human sociality, in the past as well as the present.

The combined influence of such arguments led in the 1980s to what we might call, modifying Miller's phrase, "the explosion everywhere of the novel" within humanist studies. If the novel had in the first half of the century been considered the illegitimate step-sister of high art forms worthy of serious academic study, now the very minimalism of the novel's aesthetic achievement became the key to its social function, its cultural representativeness, and thus made the novel a vital object of interest to scholars both within and outside of English departments. As we turn to post-colonialism and gender studies, we will find scholars who focus more particularly upon the opportunities for and barriers to social representation that the novel as a genre offers to the politically disempowered. But for the branch of subaltern studies known as identity politics, Bakhtin's work has been so crucial that it makes sense to turn to it now. By looking at a chapter from Henry Louis Gates's path-breaking study of African American identity, *The Signifying Monkey* (1988), we can see what happens when the privilege for ventriloquization that Bakhtin confers upon the novelist is appropriated on behalf of minority identity, when the exceptionalism Bakhtin attributes to a literary genre is claimed as the defining characteristic of a particular cultural group. Gates provocatively declares that it is not novelists but African Americans who are defined by their linguistic self-consciousness, their everyday cultural practice of ventriloquization and double voice.

Gates is highly self-conscious about his use of Bakhtin: the first chapter of *The Signifying Monkey* begins with an epigraph from "Discourse in the Novel," and Gates shows the seriousness and thoroughgoingness of his engagement with Bakhtin by quoting him at key moments throughout the book. Gates is careful to insist, however, that his theoretical account of African American identity is not "influenced" or "derived" from Bakhtin. Gates's primary commitment is to put forward a theory of African American identity that is, as he calls it, an "indigenous" theory, which means that it is wholly derived from African American cultural sources. In calling upon non-African thinkers such as Bakhtin, Gates seeks not to apply Bakhtin or to conduct a Bakhtinian reading of African American literature, but to demonstrate the cross-cultural resonance and translatability of certain theoretical concepts. On his view, European and African theories of language and identity exist in "parallel discursive universe[s]."[10] Bakhtin's terms thus, according to Gates, help to gloss for non-Africans the African American cultural, linguistic, and literary theories that have come into being through a black vernacular.

In Gates's work we can thus see how politicized the pursuit of intrinsicality has become for cultural historians. Watt's desire to represent modernism immanently, from the point of view of its own dominant cultural values, leads to a historicism that insists upon an identificatory relation with its subject. We have seen versions of this already in Tompkins and Bakhtin. Tompkins believes that past cultures must be understood "sympathetically" to be understood at all, and she encourages the reader to cultivate sympathy by, in her words, "inhabiting" that past point of view. For Bakhtin, the novelist can, to use Tompkins' word, "inhabit" points of view different from his own through an ethical act of imagination that has to do more with the extremity of his relativized consciousness than with sympathy per se; and for Bakhtin the novel can make these points of view available to its readers because the novel preserves through its stabilizing materiality the autonomy and intrinsicality of sociolinguistic point of view, even while displaying its mediated and dialogized condition. But whereas Watt, Bakhtin, and Tompkins are more or less content to leave untheorized the special dispensation that enables the interpreter (historian, novelist, or novel reader) to transcend her own historical and social position in order to accomplish an act of cultural identification, Gates questions the notion that identification stands outside or beyond historical and political determinates.

Integral to Gates's social theory is a thought expressed in passing by Tompkins: the notion that her own position as a middle-class woman links her ideologically to middle-class women of the past. Gates believes that he is qualified to write a cultural history of African American literature because, as an African American, he has direct knowledge about African American experience. Like the Bakhtinian novelist, Gates seeks to present African American social discourse in its own terms, "to allow the black tradition to speak for itself" rather than to "read it, or analyze it."[11] But unlike the Bakhtinian novelist whose relativized consciousness ultimately severs his ideological determinism, ultimately frees him from any group affiliation, Gates believes that his own practice of heteroglossia expresses an authentic African American voice that he himself possesses and that he strives to make more generally heard and understood. Bakhtin's investment in the value of heteroglossia thus is reformulated by Gates's identity politics as the value of the vernacular, the idiolect that is used for everyday communication among African Americans and which unites them as a cultural group. Spoken language, "voice," becomes in Gates's theory the authentic register of black indigenousness.[12] What most belongs to African Americans, and thus what most represents their identity, is the social discourse they share. Gates is qualified to study African American vernacular because he, too, talks the talk. And because Gates has, like the Bakhtinian novelist, also learned to speak other social discourses, he can, he believes, bring home to non-African American readers the meaning of African American identity by finding analogous expressions for this meaning in the languages of Western literary and social theory that, on his view, belong to a different cultural tradition, a "white" cultural tradition.

Yet even as Gates imagines himself as a cultural translator and a speaker of heteroglossia, he also insists on the limits of historical and cultural understanding, limits created by the specificity and autonomy of ethnic experience. Even if a reader can, with Gates's aid, find terms in his own language that will enable him to understand the defining myths, rituals, and values of African American culture, something will always be lost in translation. An indigenous tradition can, on this view, truly be understood only by those to whom the indigenous terms of its understanding belong. In contrast to Tompkins' account of sympathetic historical understanding, available to anyone in possession of accurate historical facts, Gates theorizes the African American cultural tradition as resistant to identificatory appropriation for anyone other than indigenous speakers. For non-African Americans the literary works of this tradition will, to use Bakhtin's phrase, "put themselves in quotation marks against the will of the speaker" ("Discourse," 505). The best a non-African American can do is to recognize her own outsiderness, to acknowledge the escaped meanings that the translator cannot bridge for those who merely study rather than live "black texts of being."[13] To the degree that Gates succeeds in his goal of presenting these texts in their own terms, from the African American point of view, he presents a model of knowledge that is delimited by a color line. If for Henry James "black and white" is a figure for the radically relativistic nature of all individual perception, for Gates the social difference between black and white experience is the source of relativized knowledge. Non-African American readers can know about African American texts, can find terms in their own language by which to relate to these texts, but they can never live these texts, never own them. In Gates's words, "These are *our* texts, to be delighted in, enjoyed, contemplated, explicated, and willed through repetition to our daughters and to our sons."[14]

But what makes the argument of *The Signifying Monkey* so complex is Gates's willingness to complicate identity politics through deconstructive theory. *The Signifying*

Monkey controversially argues that "black" experience is made legible by dominant values common to all African Americans – to go on to argue even more controversially that this essence is itself nothing other than the capacity for ambiguity, irony, plurality, and, in general, suspended linguistic referentiality. Gates thus defines African American identity as an essence, a trans-historical and fully legible constant, but aims to avoid the restrictiveness of such absolute definition by defining this essence as the capacity for relativization. In other words, Gates ascribes to African Americans as a social group all the qualities that Bakhtin attributes to the novelist. And although Gates uses Bakhtin's terms, especially ventriloquization, dialogization, and double voice, to characterize the performance of African American identity, in keeping with his larger commitment to indigenous theory, his primary term for African American linguistic relativization is derived from the black vernacular: "signifyin'."

Gates devotes a whole chapter (Chapter 2) to the complexity of signifyin' as a concept and a social practice, but we can see the most important elements of this definition at work in his close reading of Zora Neale Hurston's *Their Eyes Were Watching God*. Gates notes the unprecedented amount of space Hurston devotes to documenting signifyin' cultural practices among the townspeople of Eatonville: the Mule stories; the mock wooing; and the verbal sparring of Sam and Lige. Signifyin' is first and foremost a mock competition, a showing off of one's linguistic prowess in an act of play. The playfulness of these rituals intersects for Gates with the more specialized meaning of "play" within deconstructive theory. Gates emphasizes that these acts of signifyin' "produce nothing" (514), they defy the referential nature of ordinary communication by serving no purpose other than the intrinsic activity of signifyin'. Gates stresses that on the larger level of the novel's literary form, the characters' signifyin' practices are excessive – unnecessary to and therefore disruptive of – the cause and effect economy of traditional novelistic plotting. Since these scenes of signifyin' serve no literary purpose, their sociological value becomes all the more apparent, their value as free and autonomous vocal documents of African American identity. These extended dialogues conducted in dialect allow "a full range of characters' discourse to be heard" (519) without interruption or mediation. The literary inutility of this lengthy reported discourse, its nonintegration into the plot's economy of cause and effect, has ultimately a political value for Gates. On his view, to be free from the mastery of plot is to be free from social control per se. To be about nothing other than itself is for reported discourse to represent only itself, to serve as a social document of language performance. For Gates the documentary nature of reported discourse has in this context important political consequences. Gates understands the uselessness of signifyin' as an act of African American self-representation. The unmediated expression of African American voice, the articulation of black identity in its own terms, liberates African Americans from the oppressive emplotment of minority identity within the structures of hegemonic power.

This politicized understanding of reported discourse is, arguably, an extension of the narratological theory discussed in the introduction to Part III of this volume. There we noted the tendency of narratology to personify the relationship between character and narrator as a rivalrous struggle for self-representation. But it may be more difficult to grasp why Gates wants to make this particular argument in the context of what is, after all, a novel written by an African American woman, a novel distinguished, moreover, by its innovative choice not to represent black identity in relation to white identity, but to

DOROTHY HALE

depict instead the complexities of an all black social world. We may wonder about the type of social oppression from which reported discourse is escaping when it opposes itself to the plot of *Their Eyes Were Watching God*. The plot is, after all, Hurston's plot; and the other acts of language to which Gates contrasts reported discourse are arguably as African American (belonging as they do to Hurston) as the dialogue among characters. The answer to this problem seems to lie in Gates's methodology rather than in his theory per se. When he discusses the political value of narrative techniques he tends to stratify their effects, isolating, for example, in his analysis the formal relation of dialogue to plot from, say, his analysis of the social relation of characters in the story world, or the novelistic relation of author to narrator and character. Such analytic compartmentalization allows Gates to argue on the one hand that reported discourse liberates itself from a plot that would attempt to compromise the intrinsic expression of African American identity by putting it in the service of an extrinsic utility; and, on the other hand (as I will discuss in more detail) that Hurston's novel as a whole is itself an act of signification, deploying referential lures such as plot in order to accomplish its own political display of the intrinsic value and meaning of African American voice. Gates so thoroughly conceives novelistic representation as politically charged that almost all aspects of form are potentially acts of either oppression or liberation – and it can be difficult to sort out and keep straight the wars of power being waged at the different levels of the novel's discourse.

But at the heart of Gates's account of African American identity is a larger philosophical tension, an investment in two different models of subjectivity that ultimately obscures the exact politics of his theory, no matter how explicit he may seem to be about those politics. In his reading of Hurston's novel, Gates finds political efficacy in two completely different types of vocal performance: the definition of African American identity as the particular kind of playful self-display that is signifyin' seems at odds with the decisive social utility of voice conceived as self-conscious and self-willed self-expression. For example, Gates praises Hurston for her capacity for alterity and dialogism. Rather than dominating her novel with the monologic expression of her own voice, an act of self-expression that for Gates (and Bakhtin) would inhibit the novel's generic capacity for alterity, Hurston, Gates stresses, generously gives her novel over to her characters, even minor characters, enabling a "multiplicity of narrative voices to assume control of the text, if only for a few paragraphs on a few pages" (515). But if Gates lauds Hurston for her ability to "celebrate" the "play of black language" (513) and if it is this democratic characterological empowerment that for Gates makes *Eyes* a "paradigmatic Signifyin(g) text" (512), at other moments he stresses the personal and political need for individuals to speak in their own voice, in self-defense or for the achievement of individual agency. The key moment in Janie's journey toward self-empowerment is, in Gates's close reading of the scene, an act of signifyin' that has very specific social causes and effects, ones that prove not just useful but necessary to Janie's achievement of self-definition. Janie's public humiliation of Joe is not just a mock argument: it is deadly serious. In Gates's words, Janie's insult "has rewritten Joe's text of himself, and liberated herself in the process. Janie writes herself into being by naming, by speaking herself free" (524). This textual rewriting is, of course, nothing less than the literal death of Joe Starks. And Joe's death brings a decisive change in Janie's own material condition that makes it easier for her to continue to be self-defining, to continue to speak for herself. This conception of voice as the authentic expression of and means to independent and self-governing subjectivity seems the opposite of the playful gamesmanship of signifyin' – and the two paradigms of sociality seem difficult to reconcile in Gates's theory as a whole.

In his analysis of Janie's achievement of self-consciousness and autonomous individuality, Gates seems to advance the kind of humanist position that the rest of his theory has been designed to critique: that although social structures establish the positions of power, moral virtues such as personal courage can enable the victim to defeat her victimizer. This achievement of individual agency through individual action is actually enhanced, as Gates describes it, by the increased self-efficacy that attends the growth of self-consciousness through such acts of heroism. In the scene of epiphany that Gates focuses upon, Janie's act of rebellion is the outcome of independent and sudden self-consciousness: an epiphany, a flash of consciousness, shows her the truth of her relationship with Joe, providing simultaneously insight into the worth of her own self-identity. But rather than working out the implications of Janie's growth into self-understanding and self-autonomy, Gates instead cites Barbara Johnson's essay on Hurston (see Part III) as a way of making the case against such a reading of Janie. Through Johnson, Gates argues that Janie's newly achieved self-consciousness is nothing less than the deconstructive knowledge of self-division: "her newly found and apparently exhilarating double-consciousness, is that crucial event that enables her to speak and assert herself" (204). Yet Gates does not carry through Johnson's position, in part because he ultimately, like W. E. B. DuBois before him, understands double consciousness as a specifically African American condition, and thus one not wholly conflatable with the Barthesian notion of universal, psychic self-division. Double consciousness is not, as Gates works it out, a good in and of itself, a true insight about the inherent self-alienation of linguistic consciousness, registered by linguistic play. On the contrary, as Gates deploys the term in his reading of Janie, double consciousness is an individual attainment, an achieved self-consciousness about the victim's capacity for devictimization through the exercise of individual agency. In Gates's words, what Hurston demonstrates in Janie's act of signifyin' is the "killing timbre of Janie's *true inner voice*" (523, my emphasis). Double consciousness is for Gates an African American strategy for political efficacy, a means of gaining self-control over the potentially debilitating internal alienation produced by social discrimination, a way of gaining, in Gates's words, the "maximum of self-control over the [historically and politically produced] division between self and other" (531).

The theoretical difference between Gates and Johnson is vividly registered in the ways that each generalizes about the effects of narrative representation within Hurston's novel. Johnson's essay, we remember, ends with a claim about Hurston's discovery that knowledge itself is structured as *narrative*, an "endless fishing expedition." But for Gates, Hurston's accomplishment lies in a particular act of narrative performance, one that embodies her own insight into the specific politics that inform African American self-representation, an insight that could only be arrived at and expressed by an African American. On Gates's view, Hurston accomplishes real political reform through her novel by inventing a new type of narrative technique that has the potential of changing the criteria by which African American literature is evaluated. Through a new, hybrid mixture of black vernacular and lyrical language, Hurston, according to Gates, forges a "black" literary voice, one that upsets the white conventions of linguistic decorum and posits an alternative standard for judging aesthetic achievement. This black voice is, according to Gates, a double voice. Hurston's novel speaks from the perspective of black vernacular and from the perspective of the white audience that she imagines will be reading her, from the perspective of the black folklore tradition and from the perspective of the Anglo-American realist novel, from the perspective of her characters and from her own point of view.

Gates understands Hurston's double voice as a potent social intervention, one that attempts to dismantle the either/or economy of power that is registered by the narratological account of novelistic representation. He argues that Hurston's narration transcends the power play of either/or (the rivalry between black and white, author and character, one character's voice against another) by bringing into being an "anonymous, collective, free indirect discourse" (531) that is distinguished for Gates by its hybridity, its combination of literary diction and dialect, written and spoken discourses (208). It is a language that he says belongs as much to Janie as a character as to Hurston as an author (529) because, in the discursive world of the novel, double voice transcends and equalizes subjectivities that would otherwise be kept separated by the ontological distinction between, on the one hand, the novel's story and discourse worlds and, on the other, the novel as a literary artifact and the social world outside it. For Gates, Hurston reforms real world power relations by creating through her novel a new social language of political freedom and autonomy, a language owned by no one, whose "Words [walk] without masters" (526).

But in keeping with the tension in his theory between the determining power of social structures and the self-defining power of the individual, Gates's valorization of the enabling collectivity he finds in Hurston's narrative strategy, his admiration for the anonymous and (therefore shared) social voice articulated by her novel, is also on his view the creative achievement of a single individual: Zora Neale Hurston. This paradox, that a new model of collectivity can be brought into being by a single individual, is perhaps mitigated by the powers of signifyin' that he attributes to African Americans as a social group. Throughout *The Signifying Monkey*, the "extreme typicality," to use Gallagher's phrase again, of African American identity has been defined for Gates by linguistic exceptionalism. One way of making sense of Gates's view of Hurston's literary triumph is to understand the new collectivity that she brings into being as made possible by the attributes that already belong to African Americans: in other words, the African American practice of signifyin' is the precondition for the new, political application that Hurston makes of it. She is able to stage the unification of politically divided groups within the African American community and between individual African Americans because she imagines a new way to apply the double voice that is hers and therefore theirs, by right of cultural experience and inheritance, as African Americans. Out of the extreme typicality of her African American linguistic capabilities, she devises an innovative social remedy for the bad politics that have, on Gates's view, plagued the novel as a social discourse, a white social discourse.

1 Ian Watt, *The Rise of the Novel: Studies in Defoe, Richardson and Fielding* (Berkeley: University of California Press, 1957) 77.
2 Ibid. 177.
3 Ibid. 175.
4 D. A. Miller, *The Novel and the Police* (Berkeley: University of California Press, 1988) xiv.
5 Ibid.
6 Jane Tompkins, *Sensational Designs: The Cultural Work of American Fiction, 1760–1860* (New York: Oxford University Press, 1985) 126–7.
7 Ibid. 141.
8 M. M. Bakhtin, *The Dialogic Imagination: Four Essays*, "Discourse in the Novel," trans. Caryl Emerson and Michael Holquist, ed. Holquist (1975; Austin: University of Texas Press, 2000) 302–8.
9 Catherine Gallagher, *Nobody's Story: The Vanishing Acts of Women Writers in the Market Place, 1670-1820* (Berkeley: University of California Press,1994) xv.
10 Henry Louis Gates, Jr., *The Signifying Monkey: A Theory of African-American Literary Criticism* (New York: Oxford University Press, 1988) xxii.
11 Ibid. xix.
12 Ibid. xxii.
13 Ibid. xii.
14 Ibid.

FURTHER READING

Bakhtin, Mikhail. *Problems of Dostoevsky's Poetics*, ed. and trans. Caryl Emerson. Introduction by Wayne C. Booth. Theory and History of Literature, vol. 8. 1929. Minneapolis: Minnesota University Press, 1984.

Bakhtin, M.M./P.M. Medvedev. *The Formal Method in Literary Scholarship: A Critical Introduction to Sociological Poetics*, trans. Albert J. Wehrle. 1928. Cambridge, MA: Harvard University Press, 1985.

Brodhead, Richard H. *Cultures of Letters: Scenes of Reading and Writing in Nineteenth-Century America*. Chicago: Chicago University Press, 1993.

—— "Sparing the Rod: Discipline and Fiction in Antebellum America." *Representations* 21 (1988): 67–96.

Clark, Katerina, and Michael Holquist. *Mikhail Bakhtin*. Cambridge, MA: Harvard University Press, 1984.

Dreyfus, Hubert L., and Paul Rabinow. *Michel Foucault: Beyond Structuralism and Hermeneutics*. 2nd edn. Chicago: Chicago University Press, 1983.

Foucault, Michel. *Discipline and Punish: the Birth of the Prison*, trans. Alan Sheridan. 1975. New York: Vintage, 1995.

—— *The History of Sexuality*. Vol. 1: An Introduction, trans. Robert Hurley. 1976. New York: Vintage, 1978.

—— "What is an Author?" In *Language, Counter-Memory, Practice: Selected Essays and Interviews*, trans. Donald F. Bouchard and Sherry Simon, ed. Bouchard. Ithaca, NY: Cornell University Press, 1977.

Gates, Henry Louis, Jr. Afterword. In *Their Eyes Were Watching God*, by Zora Neale Hurston. New York: Perennial-Harper, 1998.

DOROTHY HALE

—— ed. *"Race," Writing, and Difference.* Chicago: Chicago University Press, 1986.

Hirschkop, Ken. *Mikhail Bakhtin: An Aesthetic for Democracy.* New York: Oxford University Press, 1999.

Hitchcock, Peter. *Dialogics of the Oppressed.* Minneapolis: University of Minnesota Press, 1993.

Johnson, Barbara. *A World of Difference.* Baltimore, MD: Johns Hopkins University Press, 1987.

—— "Bringing Out D.A. Miller." *Narrative* 10.1 (2002): 3–8.

Maslan, Mark. "Foucault and Pragmatisim." *Raritan* 7.3 (1988): 94–114.

McKeon, Michael. "Watt's *Rise of the Novel* within the Tradition of the Rise of the Novel." *Eighteenth-Century Fiction* 12.2–3 (2000): 253–76.

Morson, Gary Saul, ed. *Forum on Mikhail Bakhtin.* Special issue of *Critical Inquiry* 10.2 (1983): 225–319.

Todorov, Tzvetan. *Mikhail Bakhtin: The Dialogical Principle,* trans. Wlad Godzich. Theory and History of Literature, vol. 13. 1981. Minneapolis: University of Minnesota Press, 1984.

22

The Rise of the Novel

Ian Watt

Ian Watt (1917–1999)

Born in Windermere, in the Lake District of England, Ian Watt earned first-class honors in the English tripos from St. John's College, Cambridge, in 1948. His education was interrupted by his World War II military service (1939–46), which included three years as a prisoner of war in the labor camps on the River Kwai – during which time he read Shakespeare, Dante, and Swift. Watt taught at St. John's College (1948–52) and the University of California, Berkeley (1952–62), and served two years as Dean of the School of English at the newly founded University of East Anglia in Norwich; in 1964 he joined Stanford University, where he remained throughout the rest of his career. At Stanford, Watt was named Jackson Eli Reynolds Professor of English, served as department chair (1968–71), and was the founding director of the Stanford Humanities Center (1980–5). His honors include membership of the American Academy of Arts and Sciences, Commonwealth Fellowships, and a Guggenheim Fellowship. In addition to *The Rise of the Novel* (1957), Watt also wrote *Conrad in the Nineteenth Century* (1980) and *Myths of Modern Individualism* (1996).

Realism and the Novel Form

There are still no wholly satisfactory answers to many of the general questions which anyone interested in the early eighteenth-century novelists and their works is likely to ask: Is the novel a new literary form? And if we assume, as is commonly done, that it is, and that it was begun by Defoe, Richardson and Fielding, how does it differ from the prose fiction of the past, from that of Greece, for example, or that of the Middle Ages, or of seventeenth-century France? And is there any reason why these differences appeared when and where they did?

Such large questions are never easy to approach, much less to answer, and they are particularly difficult in this case because Defoe, Richardson and Fielding do not in the usual sense constitute a literary school. Indeed their works show so little sign of mutual influence and are so different in nature that at first sight it appears that our curiosity about the rise of the novel is unlikely to find any satisfaction other than the meagre one afforded by the terms 'genius' and 'accident', the twin faces on the Janus of the dead ends of literary history. We cannot, of course, do without them: on the other hand there is not much we can do with them. The present inquiry therefore takes another direction: assuming that the appearance of our first three novelists within a single generation was probably not sheer accident, and that their geniuses could not have created the new form unless the conditions of the time had also been favourable, it attempts to discover what these favourable conditions in the literary and social situation were, and in what ways Defoe, Richardson and Fielding were its beneficiaries.

For this investigation our first need is a working definition of the characteristics of the novel – a definition sufficiently narrow to exclude previous types of narrative and yet broad enough to apply to whatever is usually put in the novel category. The novelists themselves do not help us very much here. It is true that both Richardson and Fielding saw themselves as founders of a new kind of writing, and that both viewed their work as involving a break with the old-fashioned romances; but neither they nor their contemporaries provide us with the kind of characterisation of the new genre that we need; indeed they did not even canonise the changed nature of their fiction by a change in nomenclature – our usage of the term 'novel' was not fully established until the end of the eighteenth century.

With the help of their larger perspective the historians of the novel have been able to do much more to determine the idiosyncratic features of the new form. Briefly, they have seen 'realism' as the defining characteristic which differentiates the work of the early eighteenth-century novelists from previous fiction. With their picture – that of writers otherwise different but alike in this quality of 'realism' – one's initial reservation must surely be that the term itself needs further explanation, if only because to use it without qualification as a defining characteristic of the novel might otherwise carry the invidious suggestion that all previous writers and literary forms pursued the unreal.

The main critical associations of the term 'realism' are with the French school of Realists. 'Réalisme' was apparently first used as an aesthetic description in 1835 to denote the 'vérité humaine' of Rembrandt as opposed to the 'idéalité poétique' of neo-classical painting; it was later consecrated as a specifically literary term by the foundation in 1856 of *Réalisme*, a journal edited by Duranty.[1]

Unfortunately much of the usefulness of the word was soon lost in the bitter controversies over the 'low' subjects and allegedly immoral tendencies of Flaubert and his successors. As a result, 'realism' came to be used primarily as the antonym of 'idealism', and this sense, which is actually a reflection of the position taken by the enemies of the French Realists, has in fact coloured much critical and historical writing about the novel. The prehistory of the form has commonly been envisaged as a matter of tracing the continuity between all earlier fiction which portrayed low life: the story of the Ephesian matron is 'realistic' because it shows that sexual appetite is stronger than wifely sorrow; and the fabliau or the picaresque tale are 'realistic' because economic or carnal motives are given pride of place in their presentation of human behaviour. By the same implicit premise, the English eighteenth-century novelists, together with Furetière, Scarron and Lesage in France, are regarded as the eventual climax of this tradition: the 'realism' of the novels of Defoe, Richardson and Fielding is closely associated with the fact that Moll Flanders is a thief, Pamela a hypocrite, and Tom Jones a fornicator.

This use of 'realism', however, has the grave defect of obscuring what is probably the most original feature of the novel form. If the novel were realistic merely because it saw life from the seamy side, it would only be an inverted romance; but in fact it surely attempts to portray all the varieties of human experience, and not merely those suited to one particular literary perspective: the novel's realism does not reside in the kind of life it presents, but in the way it presents it.

This, of course, is very close to the position of the French Realists themselves, who asserted that if their novels tended to differ from the more flattering pictures of humanity presented by many established ethical, social, and literary codes, it was merely because they were the product of a more dispassionate and scientific scrutiny of life than had ever been attempted before. It is far from clear that this ideal of scientific objectivity is desirable, and it certainly cannot be realised in practice: nevertheless it is very significant that, in the first sustained effort of the new genre to become critically aware of its aims and methods, the French Realists should have drawn attention to an issue which the novel raises more sharply than any other literary form – the problem of the correspondence between the literary work and the reality which it imitates. This is essentially an epistemological problem, and it therefore seems likely that the nature of the novel's realism, whether in the early eighteenth century or later, can best be clarified by the help of those professionally concerned with the analysis of concepts, the philosophers.

I

By a paradox that will surprise only the neophyte, the term 'realism' in philosophy is most strictly applied to a view of reality diametrically opposed to that of common usage – to the view held by the scholastic Realists of the Middle Ages that it is universals, classes or abstractions, and not the particular, concrete objects of sense-perception, which are the true 'realities'. This, at first sight, appears unhelpful, since in the novel, more than in any other genre, general truths only exist *post res*; but the very unfamiliarity of the point of view of scholastic Realism at least serves to draw attention to a characteristic of the novel which is analogous to the changed philosophical meaning

IAN WATT

of 'realism' today: the novel arose in the modern period, a period whose general intellectual orientation was most decisively separated from its classical and mediaeval heritage by its rejection – or at least its attempted rejection – of universals.[2]

Modern realism, of course, begins from the position that truth can be discovered by the individual through his senses: it has its origins in Descartes and Locke, and received its first full formulation by Thomas Reid in the middle of the eighteenth century.[3] But the view that the external world is real, and that our senses give us a true report of it, obviously does not in itself throw much light on literary realism; since almost everyone, in all ages, has in one way or another been forced to some such conclusion about the external world by his own experience, literature has always been to some extent exposed to the same epistemological naïveté. Further, the distinctive tenets of realist epistemology, and the controversies associated with them, are for the most part much too specialised in nature to have much bearing on literature. What is important to the novel in philosophical realism is much less specific; it is rather the general temper of realist thought, the methods of investigation it has used, and the kinds of problems it has raised.

The general temper of philosophical realism has been critical, anti-traditional and innovating; its method has been the study of the particulars of experience by the individual investigator, who, ideally at least, is free from the body of past assumptions and traditional beliefs; and it has given a peculiar importance to semantics, to the problem of the nature of the correspondence between words and reality. All of these features of philosophical realism have analogies to distinctive features of the novel form, analogies which draw attention to the characteristic kind of correspondence between life and literature which has obtained in prose fiction since the novels of Defoe and Richardson.

(a)

The greatness of Descartes was primarily one of method, of the thoroughness of his determination to accept nothing on trust; and his *Discourse on Method* (1637) and his *Meditations* did much to bring about the modern assumption whereby the pursuit of truth is conceived of as a wholly individual matter, logically independent of the tradition of past thought, and indeed as more likely to be arrived at by a departure from it.

The novel is the form of literature which most fully reflects this individualist and innovating reorientation. Previous literary forms had reflected the general tendency of their cultures to make conformity to traditional practice the major test of truth: the plots of classical and renaissance epic, for example, were based on past history or fable, and the merits of the author's treatment were judged largely according to a view of literary decorum derived from the accepted models in the genre. This literary traditionalism was first and most fully challenged by the novel, whose primary criterion was truth to individual experience – individual experience which is always unique and therefore new. The novel is thus the logical literary vehicle of a culture which, in the last few centuries, has set an unprecedented value on originality, on the novel; and it is therefore well named.

This emphasis on the new accounts for some of the critical difficulties which the novel is widely agreed to present. When we judge a work in another genre, a recognition of its literary models is often important and sometimes essential; our evaluation depends to a large extent on our analysis of the author's skill in handling the appropriate formal conventions. On the other hand, it is surely very damaging for a novel to be in any sense an imitation of another literary work: and the reason for this seems to be that since the novelist's primary task is to convey the impression of fidelity to human experience, attention to any pre-established formal conventions can only endanger his success. What is often felt as the formlessness of the novel, as compared, say, with tragedy or the ode, probably follows from this: the poverty of the novel's formal conventions would seem to be the price it must pay for its realism.

But the absence of formal conventions in the novel is unimportant compared to its rejection of traditional plots. Plot, of course, is not a simple matter, and the degree of its originality or otherwise is never easy to determine; nevertheless a broad and necessarily summary comparison between the novel and previous literary forms reveals an important difference: Defoe and Richardson are the first great writers in our literature who did not take their plots from mythology, history, legend or previous literature. In this they differ from Chaucer, Spenser, Shakespeare and Milton, for instance, who, like the writers of Greece and Rome, habitually used traditional plots; and who did so, in the last analysis, because they accepted the general premise of their times that, since Nature is essentially complete and unchanging, its records, whether scriptural, legendary or historical, constitute a definitive repertoire of human experience.

This point of view continued to be expressed until the nineteenth century; the opponents of Balzac, for example, used it to deride his preoccupation with contemporary and, in their view, ephemeral reality. But at the same time, from the Renaissance onwards, there was a growing tendency for individual experience to replace collective tradition as the ultimate arbiter of reality; and this transition would seem to constitute an important part of the general cultural background of the rise of the novel.

It is significant that the trend in favour of originality found its first powerful expression in England, and in the eighteenth century; the very word 'original' took on its modern meaning at this time, by a semantic reversal which is a parallel to the change in the meaning of 'realism'. We have seen that, from the mediaeval belief in the reality of universals, 'realism' had come to denote a belief in the individual apprehension of reality through the senses: similarly the term 'original' which in the Middle Ages had meant 'having existed from the first' came to mean 'underived, independent, first-hand'; and by the time that Edward Young in his epoch-making *Conjectures on Original Composition* (1759) hailed Richardson as 'a genius as well moral as original',[4] the word could be used as a term of praise meaning 'novel or fresh in character or style'.

The novel's use of non-traditional plots is an early and probably independent manifestation of this emphasis. When Defoe, for example, began to write fiction he took little notice of the dominant critical theory of the day, which still inclined towards the use of traditional plots; instead, he merely allowed his narrative order to flow spontaneously from his own sense of what his protagonists might plausibly do next. In so doing Defoe initiated an important new tendency in fiction: his total subordination of the plot to the pattern of the autobiographical memoir is as defiant an assertion of the primacy of individual experience in the novel as Descartes's *cogito ergo sum* was in philosophy.

IAN WATT

After Defoe, Richardson and Fielding in their very different ways continued what was to become the novel's usual practice, the use of non-traditional plots, either wholly invented or based in part on a contemporary incident. It cannot be claimed that either of them completely achieved that interpenetration of plot, character and emergent moral theme which is found in the highest examples of the art of the novel. But it must be remembered that the task was not an easy one, particularly at a time when the established literary outlet for the creative imagination lay in eliciting an individual pattern and a contemporary significance from a plot that was not itself novel.

(b)

Much else besides the plot had to be changed in the tradition of fiction before the novel could embody the individual apprehension of reality as freely as the method of Descartes and Locke allowed their thought to spring from the immediate facts of consciousness. To begin with, the actors in the plot and the scene of their actions had to be placed in a new literary perspective: the plot had to be acted out by particular people in particular circumstances, rather than, as had been common in the past, by general human types against a background primarily determined by the appropriate literary convention.

This literary change was analogous to the rejection of universals and the emphasis on particulars which characterises philosophic realism. Aristotle might have agreed with Locke's primary assumption, that it was the senses which 'at first let in particular ideas, and furnish the empty cabinet' of the mind.[5] But he would have gone on to insist that the scrutiny of particular cases was of little value in itself; the proper intellectual task of man was to rally against the meaningless flux of sensation, and achieve a knowledge of the universals which alone constituted the ultimate and immutable reality.[6] It is this generalising emphasis which gives most Western thought until the seventeenth century a strong enough family resemblance to outweigh all its other multifarious differences; similarly when in 1713 Berkeley's Philonous affirmed that 'it is an universally received maxim, that *everything which exists is particular*',[7] he was stating the opposite modern tendency which in turn gives modern thought since Descartes a certain unity of outlook and method.

Here, again, both the new trends in philosophy and the related formal characteristics of the novel were contrary to the dominant literary outlook. For the critical tradition in the early eighteenth century was still governed by the strong classical preference for the general and universal: the proper object of literature remained *quod semper quod ubique ab omnibus creditum est*. This preference was particularly pronounced in the neo-Platonist tendency, which had always been strong in the romance, and which was becoming of increasing importance in literary criticism and aesthetics generally. Shaftesbury, for instance, in his *Essay on the Freedom of Wit and Humour* (1709), expressed the distaste of this school of thought for particularity in literature and art very emphatically: 'The variety of Nature is such, as to distinguish every thing she forms, by a *peculiar* original character; which, if strictly observed, will make the subject appear unlike to anything extant in the world besides. But this effect the good poet and painter seek industriously to prevent. They hate *minuteness*, and are afraid of *singularity*.'[8] He continued: 'The mere Face-Painter, indeed, has little in common with the Poet; but, like the mere Historian, copies what he sees, and minutely traces every feature, and odd mark'; and concluded confidently that "'Tis otherwise with men of invention and design'.

Despite Shaftesbury's engaging finality, however, a contrary aesthetic tendency in favour of particularity soon began to assert itself, largely as a result of the application to literary problems of the psychological approach of Hobbes and Locke. Lord Kames was perhaps the most forthright early spokesman of this tendency. In his *Elements of Criticism* (1762) he declared that 'abstract or general terms have no good effect in any composition for amusement; because it is only of particular objects that images can be formed';[9] and Kames went on to claim that, contrary to general opinion, Shakespeare's appeal lay in the fact that 'every article in his descriptions is particular, as in nature'.

In this matter, as in that of originality, Defoe and Richardson established the characteristic literary direction of the novel form long before it could count on any support from critical theory. Not all will agree with Kames that 'every article' in Shakespeare's descriptions is particular; but particularity of description has always been considered typical of the narrative manner of *Robinson Crusoe* and *Pamela*. Richardson's first biographer, indeed, Mrs. Barbauld, described his genius in terms of an analogy which has continually figured in the controversy between neo-classical generality and realistic particularity. Sir Joshua Reynolds, for example, expressed his neo-classical orthodoxy by preferring the 'great and general ideas' of Italian painting to the 'literal truth and...minute exactness in the detail of nature modified by accident' of the Dutch school;[10] whereas the French Realists, it will be remembered, had followed the 'vérité humaine' of Rembrandt, rather than the 'idéalité poétique' of the classical school. Mrs. Barbauld accurately indicated Richardson's position in this conflict when she wrote that he had 'the accuracy of finish of a Dutch painter...content to produce effects by the patient labour of minuteness'.[11] Both he and Defoe, in fact, were heedless of Shaftesbury's scorn, and like Rembrandt were content to be 'mere face-painters and historians'.

The concept of realistic particularity in literature is itself somewhat too general to be capable of concrete demonstration: for such demonstration to be possible the relationship of realistic particularity to some specific aspects of narrative technique must first be established. Two such aspects suggest themselves as of especial importance in the novel – characterisation, and presentation of background: the novel is surely distinguished from other genres and from previous forms of fiction by the amount of attention it habitually accords both to the individualisation of its characters and to the detailed presentation of their environment.

(c)

Philosophically the particularising approach to character resolves itself into the problem of defining the individual person. Once Descartes had given the thought processes within the individual's consciousness supreme importance, the philosophical problems connected with personal identity naturally attracted a great deal of attention. In England, for example, Locke, Bishop Butler, Berkeley, Hume and Reid all debated the issue, and the controversy even reached the pages of the *Spectator*.[12]

The parallel here between the tradition of realist thought and the formal innovations of the early novelists is obvious: both philosophers and novelists paid greater attention to the particular individual than had been common before. But the great attention paid in

IAN WATT

the novel to the particularisation of character is itself such a large question that we will consider only one of its more manageable aspects: the way that the novelist typically indicates his intention of presenting a character as a particular individual by naming him in exactly the same way as particular individuals are named in ordinary life.

Logically the problem of individual identity is closely related to the epistemological status of proper names; for, in the words of Hobbes, 'Proper names bring to mind one thing only; universals recall any one of many'.[13] Proper names have exactly the same function in social life: they are the verbal expression of the particular identity of each individual person. In literature, however, this function of proper names was first fully established in the novel.

Characters in previous forms of literature, of course, were usually given proper names; but the kind of names actually used showed that the author was not trying to establish his characters as completely individualised entities. The precepts of classical and renaissance criticism agreed with the practice of their literature in preferring either historical names or type names. In either case, the names set the characters in the context of a large body of expectations primarily formed from past literature, rather than from the context of contemporary life. Even in comedy, where characters were not usually historical but invented, the names were supposed to be 'characteristic', as Aristotle tells us,[14] and they tended to remain so until long after the rise of the novel.

Earlier types of prose fiction had also tended to use proper names that were characteristic, or non-particular and unrealistic in some other way; names that either, like those of Rabelais, Sidney or Bunyan, denoted particular qualities, or like those of Lyly, Aphra Behn or Mrs. Manley, carried foreign, archaic or literary connotations which excluded any suggestion of real and contemporary life. The primarily literary and conventional orientation of these proper names was further attested by the fact that there was usually only one of them – Mr. Badman or Euphues; unlike people in ordinary life, the characters of fiction did not have both given name and surname.

The early novelists, however, made an extremely significant break with tradition, and named their characters in such a way as to suggest that they were to be regarded as particular individuals in the contemporary social environment. Defoe's use of proper names is casual and sometimes contradictory; but he very rarely gives names that are conventional or fanciful – one possible exception, Roxana, is a pseudonym which is fully explained; and most of the main characters such as Robinson Crusoe or Moll Flanders have complete and realistic names or aliases. Richardson continued this practice, but was much more careful and gave all of his major characters, and even most of his minor ones, both a given name and a surname. He also faced a minor but not unimportant problem in novel writing, that of giving names that are subtly appropriate and suggestive, yet sound like ordinary realistic ones. Thus the romance-connotations of Pamela are controlled by the commonplace family name of Andrews; both Clarissa Harlowe and Robert Lovelace are in many ways appropriately named; and indeed nearly all Richardson's proper names, from Mrs. *Sin*clair to Sir Charles *Grand*ison, sound authentic and are yet suited to the personalities of the bearers.

Fielding, as an anonymous contemporary critic pointed out, christened his characters 'not with fantastic high-sounding Names, but such as, tho' they sometimes had some reference to the Character, had a more modern termination'.[15] Such names as Heartfree, Allworthy and Square are certainly modernised versions of the type name, although they are just credible; even Western or Tom Jones suggest very strongly that Fielding had his eye as much on the general type as on the particular individual. This, however, does not controvert the present argument, for it will surely be generally agreed that Fielding's practice in the naming, and indeed in the whole portrayal of his characters, is a departure from the usual treatment of these matters in the novel. Not, as we have seen in Richardson's case, that there is no place in the novel for proper names that are in some way appropriate to the character concerned: but that this appropriateness must not be such as to impair the primary function of the name, which is to symbolise the fact that the character is to be regarded as though he were a particular person and not a type.

Fielding, indeed, seems to have realised this by the time he came to write his last novel, *Amelia*: there his neo-classical preference for type-names finds expression only in such minor characters as Justice Thrasher and Bondum the bailiff; and all the main characters – the Booths, Miss Matthews, Dr. Harrison, Colonel James, Sergeant Atkinson, Captain Trent and Mrs. Bennet, for example – have ordinary and contemporary names. There is, indeed, some evidence that Fielding, like some modern novelists, took these names somewhat at random from a printed list of contemporary persons – all the surnames given above are in the list of subscribers to the 1724 folio edition of Gilbert Burnet's *History of His Own Time*, an edition which Fielding is known to have owned.[16]

Whether this is so or not, it is certain that Fielding made considerable and increasing concessions to the custom initiated by Defoe and Richardson of using ordinary contemporary proper names for their characters. Although this custom was not always followed by some of the later eighteenth-century novelists, such as Smollett and Sterne, it was later established as part of the tradition of the form; and, as Henry James pointed out with respect to Trollope's fecund cleric Mr. Quiverful,[17] the novelist can only break with the tradition at the cost of destroying the reader's belief in the literal reality of the character concerned.

(d)

Locke had defined personal identity as an identity of consciousness through duration in time; the individual was in touch with his own continuing identity through memory of his past thoughts and actions.[18] This location of the source of personal identity in the repertoire of its memories was continued by Hume: 'Had we no memory, we never should have any notion of causation, nor consequently of that chain of causes and effects, which constitute our self or person'.[19] Such a point of view is characteristic of the novel; many novelists, from Sterne to Proust, have made their subject the exploration of the personality as it is defined in the interpenetration of its past and present self-awareness.

Time is an essential category in another related but more external approach to the problem of defining the individuality of any object. The 'principle of individuation' accepted by Locke was that of existence at a particular locus in space and time: since, as he wrote, 'ideas become general by separating from them the circumstances of time and place',[20] so they become particular only when both these circumstances are specified. In the same way the characters of the novel can only be individualised if they are set in a background of particularised time and place.

IAN WATT

Both the philosophy and the literature of Greece and Rome were deeply influenced by Plato's view that the Forms or Ideas were the ultimate realities behind the concrete objects of the temporal world. These forms were conceived as timeless and unchanging,[21] and thus reflected the basic premise of their civilisation in general that nothing happened or could happen whose fundamental meaning was not independent of the flux of time. This premise is diametrically opposed to the outlook which has established itself since the Renaissance, and which views time, not only as a crucial dimension of the physical world, but as the shaping force of man's individual and collective history.

The novel is in nothing so characteristic of our culture as in the way that it reflects this characteristic orientation of modern thought. E. M. Forster sees the portrayal of 'life by time' as the distinctive role which the novel has added to literature's more ancient preoccupation with portraying 'life by values';[22] Spengler's perspective for the rise of the novel is the need of 'ultrahistorical' modern man for a literary form capable of dealing with 'the whole of life';[23] while more recently Northrop Frye has seen the 'alliance of time and Western man' as the defining characteristic of the novel compared with other genres.[24]

We have already considered one aspect of the importance which the novel allots the time dimension: its break with the earlier literary tradition of using timeless stories to mirror the unchanging moral verities. The novel's plot is also distinguished from most previous fiction by its use of past experience as the cause of present action: a causal connection operating through time replaces the reliance of earlier narratives on disguises and coincidences, and this tends to give the novel a much more cohesive structure. Even more important, perhaps, is the effect upon characterisation of the novel's insistence on the time process. The most obvious and extreme example of this is the stream of consciousness novel which purports to present a direct quotation of what occurs in the individual mind under the impact of the temporal flux; but the novel in general has interested itself much more than any other literary form in the development of its characters in the course of time. Finally, the novel's detailed depiction of the concerns of everyday life also depends upon its power over the time dimension: T. H. Green pointed out that much of man's life had tended to be almost unavailable to literary representation merely as a result of its slowness;[25] the novel's closeness to the texture of daily experience directly depends upon its employment of a much more minutely discriminated time-scale than had previously been employed in narrative.

The role of time in ancient, mediaeval and renaissance literature is certainly very different from that in the novel. The restriction of the action of tragedy to twenty-four hours, for example, the celebrated unity of time, is really a denial of the importance of the temporal dimension in human life; for, in accord with the classical world's view of reality as subsisting in timeless universals, it implies that the truth about existence can be as fully unfolded in the space of a day as in the space of a lifetime. The equally celebrated personifications of time as the winged chariot or the grim reaper reveal an essentially similar outlook. They focus attention, not on the temporal flux, but on the supremely timeless fact of death; their role is to overwhelm our awareness of daily life so that we shall be prepared to face eternity. Both these personifications, in fact, resemble the doctrine of the unity of time in that they are fundamentally ahistorical, and are therefore equally typical of the very minor importance accorded to the temporal dimension in most literature previous to the novel.

Shakespeare's sense of the historical past, for example, is very different from the modern one. Troy and Rome, the Plantagenets and the Tudors, none of them are far enough back to be very different from the present or from each other. In this Shakespeare reflects the view of his age: he had been dead for thirty years before the word 'anachronism' first appeared in English,[26] and he was still very close to the mediaeval conception of history by which, whatever the period, the wheel of time churns out the same eternally applicable *exempla*.

This a-historical outlook is associated with a striking lack of interest in the minute-by-minute and day-to-day temporal setting, a lack of interest which has caused the time scheme of so many plays both by Shakespeare and by most of his predecessors from Aeschylus onwards, to baffle later editors and critics. The attitude to time in early fiction is very similar; the sequence of events is set in a very abstract continuum of time and space, and allows very little importance to time as a factor in human relationships. Coleridge noted the 'marvellous independence and true imaginative absence of all particular space or time in the "Faerie Queene" ';[27] and the temporal dimension of Bunyan's allegories or the heroic romances is equally vague and unparticularised.

Soon, however, the modern sense of time began to permeate many areas of thought. The late seventeenth century witnessed the rise of a more objective study of history and therefore of a deeper sense of the difference between the past and the present.[28] At the same time Newton and Locke presented a new analysis of the temporal process;[29] it became a slower and more mechanical sense of duration which was minutely enough discriminated to measure the falling of objects or the succession of thoughts in the mind.

These new emphases are reflected in the novels of Defoe. His fiction is the first which presents us with a picture both of the individual life in its larger perspective as a historical process, and in its closer view which shows the process being acted out against the background of the most ephemeral thoughts and actions. It is true that the time scales of his novels are sometimes both contradictory in themselves, and inconsistent with their pretended historical setting, but the mere fact that such objections arise is surely a tribute to the way the characters are felt by the reader to be rooted in the temporal dimension. We obviously could not think of making such objections seriously to Sidney's *Arcadia* or *The Pilgrim's Progress*; there is not enough evidence of the reality of time for any sense of discrepancies to be possible. Defoe does give us such evidence. At his best, he convinces us completely that his narrative is occurring at a particular place and at a particular time, and our memory of his novels consists largely of these vividly realised moments in the lives of his characters, moments which are loosely strung together to form a convincing biographical perspective. We have a sense of personal identity subsisting through duration and yet being changed by the flow of experience.

This impression is much more strongly and completely realised in Richardson. He was very careful to locate all his events of his narrative in an unprecedentedly detailed time-scheme: the superscription of each letter gives us the day of the week, and often the time of the day; and this in turn acts as an objective framework for the even greater temporal detail of the letters themselves – we are told, for example, that Clarissa died at 6.40 P.M. on Thursday, 7th September. Richardson's use of the letter form also induced in the reader a continual sense of actual participation in the action which was until then unparalleled in its completeness and intensity. He knew, as he wrote in the 'Preface' to *Clarissa*, that it was 'Critical situations... with what may be called *instantan-*

IAN WATT

eous descriptions and reflections' that engaged the attention best; and in many scenes the pace of the narrative was slowed down by minute description to something very near that of actual experience. In these scenes Richardson achieved for the novel what D. W. Griffith's technique of the 'close-up' did for the film: added a new dimension to the representation of reality.

Fielding approached the problem of time in his novels from a more external and traditional point of view. In *Shamela* he poured scorn on Richardson's use of the present tense: 'Mrs. Jervis and I are just in bed, and the door unlocked; if my master should come – Ods-bobs! I hear him just coming in at the door. You see I write in the present tense, as Parson William says. Well, he is in bed between us...'[30] In *Tom Jones* he indicated his intention of being much more selective than Richardson in his handling of the time dimension: 'We intend...rather to pursue the method of those writers who profess to disclose the revolutions of countries, than to imitate the painful and voluminous historian, who, to preserve the regularity of his series, thinks himself obliged to fill up as much paper with the detail of months and years in which nothing remarkable happened, as he employs upon those notable eras when the greatest scenes have been transacted on the human stage'.[31] At the same time, however, *Tom Jones* introduced one interesting innovation in the fictional treatment of time. Fielding seems to have used an almanac, that symbol of the diffusion of an objective sense of time by the printing press: with slight exceptions, nearly all the events of his novel are chronologically consistent, not only in relation to each other, and to the time that each stage of the journey of the various characters from the West Country to London would actually have taken, but also in relation to such external considerations as the proper phases of the moon and the time-table of the Jacobite rebellion in 1745, the supposed year of the action.[32]

(e)

In the present context, as in many others, space is the necessary correlative of time. Logically the individual, particular case is defined by reference to two co-ordinates, space and time. Psychologically, as Coleridge pointed out, our idea of time is 'always blended with the idea of space'.[33] The two dimensions, indeed, are for many practical purposes inseparable, as is suggested by the fact that the words 'present' and 'minute' can refer to either dimension; while introspection shows that we cannot easily visualise any particular moment of existence without setting it in its spatial context also.

Place was traditionally almost as general and vague as time in tragedy, comedy and romance. Shakespeare, as Johnson tells us, 'had no regard to distinction of time or place';[34] and Sidney's *Arcadia* was as unlocalized as the Bohemian limbos of the Elizabethan stage. In the picaresque novel, it is true, and in Bunyan, there are many passages of vivid and particularised physical description; but they are incidental and fragmentary. Defoe would seem to be the first of our writers who visualised the whole of his narrative as though it occurred in an actual physical environment. His attention to the description of milieu is still intermittent; but occasional vivid details supplement the continual implication of his narrative and make us attach Robinson Crusoe and Moll Flanders much more completely to their environments than is the case with previous fictional characters. Characteristically, this solidity of setting is particularly noticeable in Defoe's treatment of movable objects in the physical world: in *Moll Flanders* there is much linen and gold to be counted, while Robinson Crusoe's island is full of memorable pieces of clothing and hardware.

Richardson, once again occupying the central place in the development of the technique of narrative realism, carried the process much further. There is little description of natural scenery, but considerable attention is paid to interiors throughout his novels. Pamela's residences in Lincolnshire and Bedfordshire are real enough prisons; we are given a highly detailed description of Grandison Hall; and some of the descriptions in *Clarissa* anticipate Balzac's skill in making the setting of the novel a pervasive operating force – the Harlowe mansion becomes a terrifyingly real physical and moral environment.

Here, too, Fielding is some way from Richardson's particularity. He gives us no full interiors, and his frequent landscape descriptions are very conventionalised. Nevertheless *Tom Jones* features the first Gothic mansion in the history of the novel:[35] and Fielding is as careful about the topography of his action as he is about its chronology; many of the places on Tom Jones's route to London are given by name, and the exact location of the others is implied by various other kinds of evidence.

In general, then, although there is nothing in the eighteenth-century novel which equals the opening chapters of *Le Rouge et le noir* or *Le Père Goriot*, chapters which at once indicate the importance which Stendhal and Balzac attach to the environment in their total picture of life, there is no doubt that the pursuit of verisimilitude led Defoe, Richardson and Fielding to initiate that power of 'putting man wholly into his physical setting' which constitutes for Allen Tate the distinctive capacity of the novel form;[36] and the considerable extent to which they succeeded is not the least of the factors which differentiate them from previous writers of fiction and which explain their importance in the tradition of the new form.

(f)

The various technical characteristics of the novel described above all seem to contribute to the furthering of an aim which the novelist shares with the philosopher – the production of what purports to be an authentic account of the actual experiences of individuals. This aim involved many other departures from the traditions of fiction besides those already mentioned. What is perhaps the most important of them, the adaptation of prose style to give an air of complete authenticity, is also closely related to one of the distinctive methodological emphases of philosophical realism.

Just as it was the Nominalist scepticism about language which began to undermine the attitude to universals held by the scholastic Realists, so modern realism soon found itself faced with the semantic problem. Words did not all stand for real objects, or did not stand for them in the same way, and philosophy was therefore faced with the problem of discovering their rationale. Locke's chapters at the end of the third Book of the *Essay Concerning Human Understanding* are probably the most important evidence of this trend in the seventeenth century. Much of what is said there about the proper use of words would exclude the great bulk of literature, since, as Locke sadly discovers, 'eloquence, like the fair sex', involves a pleasurable deceit.[37] On the other hand, it is interesting to note that although some of the 'abuses of language' which Locke specifies, such as figurative language, had been a regular feature of the romances, they are much rarer in the prose of Defoe and Richardson than in that of any previous writer of fiction.

The previous stylistic tradition for fiction was not primarily concerned with the correspondence of words to things, but rather with the extrinsic beauties which could be bestowed upon description and action by the use of rhetoric. Heliodorus's *Aethiopica* had established the tradition of linguistic ornateness in the Greek romances and the tradition had been continued in the Euphuism of John Lyly and Sidney, and in the elaborate conceits, or 'phébus', of La Calprenède and Madeleine de Scudéry. So even if the new writers of fiction had rejected the old tradition of mixing poetry with their prose, a tradition which had been followed even in narratives as completely devoted to the portrayal of low life as Petronius's *Satyricon*, there would still have remained a strong literary expectation that they would use language as a source of interest in its own right, rather than as a purely referential medium.

In any case, of course, the classical critical tradition in general had no use for the unadorned realistic description which such a use of language would imply. When the 9th *Tatler* (1709) introduced Swift's 'Description of the Morning' as a work where the author had 'run into a way perfectly new, and described things as they happen', it was being ironical. The implicit assumption of educated writers and critics was that an author's skill was shown, not in the closeness with which he made his words correspond to their objects, but in the literary sensitivity with which his style reflected the linguistic decorum appropriate to its subject. It is natural, therefore, that it is to writers outside the circle of wit that we should have to turn for our earliest examples of fictional narrative written in a prose which restricts itself almost entirely to a descriptive and denotative use of language. Natural, too, that both Defoe and Richardson should have been attacked by many of the better educated writers of the day for their clumsy and often inaccurate way of writing.

Their basically realistic intentions, of course, required something very different from the accepted modes of literary prose. It is true that the movement towards clear and easy prose in the late seventeenth century had done much to produce a mode of expression much better adapted to the realistic novel than had been available before; while the Lockean view of language was beginning to be reflected in literary theory – John Dennis, for example, proscribed imagery in certain circumstances on the ground that it was unrealistic: 'No sort of imagery can ever be the language of grief. If a man complains in simile, I either laugh or sleep.'[38] Nevertheless the prose norm of the Augustan period remained much too literary to be the natural voice of Moll Flanders or Pamela Andrews: and although the prose of Addison, for example, or Swift, is simple and direct enough, its ordered economy tends to suggest an acute summary rather than a full report of what it describes.

It is therefore likely that we must regard the break which Defoe and Richardson made with the accepted canons of prose style, not an incidental blemish, but rather as the price they had to pay for achieving the immediacy and closeness of the text to what is being described. With Defoe this closeness is mainly physical, with Richardson mainly emotional, but in both we feel that the writer's exclusive aim is to make the words bring his object home to us in all its concrete particularity, whatever the cost in repetition or parenthesis or verbosity. Fielding, of course, did not break with the traditions of Augustan prose style or outlook. But it can be argued that this detracts from the authenticity of his narratives. Reading *Tom Jones* we do not imagine that we are eavesdropping on a new exploration of reality; the prose immediately informs us that exploratory operations have long since been accomplished, that we are to be spared that labour, and presented instead with a sifted and clarified report of the findings.

There is a curious antinomy here. On the one hand, Defoe and Richardson make an uncompromising application of the realist point of view in language and prose structure, and thereby forfeit other literary values. On the other hand, Fielding's stylistic virtues tend to interfere with his technique as a novelist, because a patent selectiveness of vision destroys our belief in the reality of report, or at least diverts our attention from the content of the report to the skill of the reporter. There would seem to be some inherent contradiction between the ancient and abiding literary values and the distinctive narrative technique of the novel.

That this may be so is suggested by a parallel with French fiction. In France, the classical critical outlook, with its emphasis on elegance and concision, was not fully challenged until the coming of Romanticism. It is perhaps partly for this reason that French fiction from *La Princesse de Clèves* to *Les Liaisons dangereuses* stands outside the main tradition of the novel. For all its psychological penetration and literary skill, we feel it is too stylish to be authentic. In this Madame de La Fayette and Choderlos de Laclos are the polar opposites of Defoe and Richardson, whose very diffuseness tends to act as a guarantee of the authenticity of their report, whose prose aims exclusively at what Locke defined as the proper purpose of language, 'to convey the knowledge of things',[39] and whose novels as a whole pretend to be no more than a transcription of real life – in Flaubert's words, 'le réel écrit'.

It would appear, then, that the function of language is much more largely referential in the novel than in other literary forms; that the genre itself works by exhaustive presentation rather than by elegant concentration. This fact would no doubt explain both why the novel is the most translatable of the genres; why many undoubtedly great novelists, from Richardson and Balzac to Hardy and Dostoevsky, often write gracelessly, and sometimes with downright vulgarity; and why the novel has less need of historical and literary commentary than other genres – its formal convention forces it to supply its own footnotes.

II

So much for the main analogies between realism in philosophy and literature. They are not proposed as exact; philosophy is one thing and literature is another. Nor do the analogies depend in any way on the presumption that the realist tradition in philosophy was a cause of the realism of the novel. That there was some influence is very likely, especially through Locke, whose thought everywhere pervades the eighteenth-century climate of opinion. But if a causal relationship of any importance exists it is probably much less direct: both the philosophical and the literary innovations must be seen as parallel manifestations of larger change – that vast transformation of Western civilisation since the Renaissance which has replaced the unified world picture of the Middle Ages with another very different one – one which presents us, essentially, with a developing but unplanned aggregate of particular individuals having particular experiences at particular times and at particular places.

Here, however, we are concerned with a much more limited conception, with the extent to which the analogy with philosophical realism helps to isolate and define the distinctive narrative mode of the novel. This, it has been suggested, is the sum of literary techniques whereby the novel's imitation of human life follows the procedures adopted by philosophical realism in its attempt to ascertain and report the truth. These procedures are by no means confined to philosophy; they tend, in fact, to be followed whenever the relation to reality of any report of an event is being investigated. The novel's mode of imitating reality may therefore be equally well summarised in terms of the procedures of another group of specialists in epistemology, the jury in a court of law. Their expectations, and those of the novel reader coincide in many ways: both want to know 'all the particulars' of a given case – the time and place of the occurrence; both must be satisfied as to the identities of the parties concerned, and will refuse to accept evidence about anyone called Sir Toby Belch or Mr. Badman – still less about a Chloe who has no surname and is 'common as the air'; and they also expect the witnesses to tell the story 'in his own words'. The jury, in fact, takes the 'circumstantial view of life', which T. H. Green[40] found to be the characteristic outlook of the novel.

The narrative method whereby the novel embodies this circumstantial view of life may be called its formal realism; formal, because the term realism does not here refer to any special literary doctrine or purpose, but only to a set of narrative procedures which are so commonly found together in the novel, and so rarely in other literary genres, that they may be regarded as typical of the form itself. Formal realism, in fact, is the narrative embodiment of a premise that Defoe and Richardson accepted very literally, but which is implicit in the novel form in general: the premise, or primary convention, that the novel is a full and authentic report of human experience, and is therefore under an obligation to satisfy its reader with such details of the story as the individuality of the actors concerned, the particulars of the times and places of their actions, details which are presented through a more largely referential use of language than is common in other literary forms.

Formal realism is, of course, like the rules of evidence, only a convention; and there is no reason why the report on human life which is presented by it should be in fact any truer than those presented through the very different conventions of other literary genres. The novel's air of total authenticity, indeed, does tend to authorise confusion on this point: and the tendency of some Realists and Naturalists to forget that the accurate transcription of actuality does not necessarily produce a work of any real truth or enduring literary value is no doubt partly responsible for the rather widespread distaste for Realism and all its works which is current today. This distaste, however, may also promote critical confusion by leading us into the opposite error; we must not allow an awareness of certain shortcomings in the aims of the Realist school to obscure the very considerable extent to which the novel in general, as much in Joyce as in Zola, employs the literary means here called formal realism. Nor must we forget that, although formal realism is only a convention, it has, like all literary conventions, its own peculiar advantages. There are important differences in the degree to which different literary forms imitate reality; and the formal realism of the novel allows a more immediate imitation of individual experience set in its temporal and spatial environment than do other literary forms. Consequently the novel's conventions make much smaller demands on the audience than do most literary conventions; and this surely explains why the majority of readers in the last two hundred years have found in the novel the literary form which most closely satisfies their wishes for a close correspondence between life and art. Nor are the advantages of the close and detailed correspondence to real life offered by formal realism limited to assisting the novel's popularity; they are also related to its most distinctive literary qualities, as we shall see.

In the strictest sense, of course, formal realism was not discovered by Defoe and Richardson; they only applied it much more completely than had been done before. Homer, for example, as Carlyle pointed out,[41] shared with them that outstanding 'clearness of sight' which is manifested in the 'detailed, ample and lovingly exact' descriptions that abound in their works; and there are many passages in later fiction, from *The Golden Ass* to *Aucassin and Nicolette*, from Chaucer to Bunyan, where the characters, their actions and their environment are presented with a particularity as authentic as that in any eighteenth-century novel. But there is an important difference: in Homer and in earlier prose fiction these passages are relatively rare, and tend to stand out from the surrounding narrative; the total literary structure was not consistently oriented in the direction of formal realism, and the plot especially, which was usually traditional and often highly improbable, was in direct conflict with its premises. Even when previous writers had overtly professed a wholly realistic aim, as did many seventeenth-century writers, they did not pursue it wholeheartedly. La Calprenède, Richard Head, Grimmelshausen, Bunyan, Aphra Behn, Furetière,[42] to mention only a few, had all asserted that their fictions were literally true; but their prefatory asseverations are no more convincing than the very similar ones to be found in most works of mediaeval hagiography. The aim of verisimilitude had not been deeply enough assimilated in either case to bring about the full rejection of all the non-realistic conventions that governed the genre.

For reasons to be considered in the next chapter, Defoe and Richardson were unprecedentedly independent of the literary conventions which might have interfered with their primary intentions, and they accepted the requirements of literal truth much more comprehensively. Of no fiction before Defoe's could Lamb have written, in terms very similar to those which Hazlitt used of Richardson,[43] 'It is like reading evidence in a court of Justice'.[44] Whether that is in itself a good thing is open to question; Defoe and Richardson would hardly deserve their reputation unless they had other and better claims on our attention. Nevertheless there can be little doubt that the development of a narrative method capable of creating such an impression is the most conspicuous manifestation of that mutation of prose fiction which we call the novel; the historical importance of Defoe and Richardson therefore primarily depends on the suddenness and completeness with which they brought into being what may be regarded as the lowest common denominator of the novel genre as a whole, its formal realism.

NOTES

1   See Bernard Weinberg, *French Realism: the Critical Reaction 1830–1870* (London, 1937), p. 114.
2   See R. I. Aaron, *The Theory of Universals* (Oxford, 1952), pp. 18–41.

3   See S. Z. Hasan, *Realism* (Cambridge, 1928), chs. 1 and 2.

4   *Works* (1773), V, 125; see also Max Scheler, *Versuche zu einer Soziologie des Wissens* (München and Leipzig, 1924), pp. 104 ff.; Elizabeth L. Mann, 'The Problem of Originality in English Literary Criticism, 1750–1800', *PQ*, XVIII (1939), 97–118.

5   *Essay Concerning Human Understanding* (1690), Bk. I, ch. 2, sect. xv.

6   See *Posterior Analytics*, Bk. I, ch. 24; Bk. II, ch. 19.

7   First *Dialogue between Hylas and Philonous*, 1713 (Berkeley, *Works*, ed. Luce and Jessop (London, 1949), II, 192).

8   Pt. IV, sect. 3.

9   1763 ed., III, 198–199.

10 *Idler*, No. 79 (1759). See also Scott Elledge, 'The Background and Development in English Criticism of the Theories of Generality and Particularity', *PMLA*, LX (1945), 161–174.

11 *Correspondence of Samuel Richardson*, 1804, I, cxxxvii. For similar comments by contemporary French readers, see Joseph Texte, *Jean-Jacques Rousseau and the Cosmopolitan Spirit in Literature* (London, 1899), pp. 174–175.

12 No. 578 (1714).

13 *Leviathan* (1651), Pt. I, ch. 4.

14 *Poetics*, ch. 9.

15 *Essay on the New Species of Writing Founded by Mr. Fielding*, 1751, p. 18. This whole question is treated more fully in my 'The Naming of Characters in Defoe, Richardson and Fielding', *RES*, XXV (1949), 322–338.

16 See Wilbur L. Cross, *History of Henry Fielding* (New Haven, 1918), I, 342–343.

17 *Partial Portraits* (London, 1888), p. 118.

18 *Human Understanding*, Bk. II, ch. 27, sects. ix, x.

19 *Treatise of Human Nature*, Bk. I, pt. 4, sect. vi.

20 *Human Understanding*, Bk. III, ch. 3, sect. vi.

21 Plato does not specifically state that the Ideas are timeless, but the notion, which dates from Aristotle (*Metaphysics*, Bk. XII, ch. 6), underlies the whole system of thought with which they are associated.

22 *Aspects of the Novel* (London, 1949), pp. 29–31.

23 *Decline of the West*, trans. Atkinson (London, 1928), I, 130–131.

24 'The Four Forms of Fiction', *Hudson Review*, II (1950), 596.

25 'Estimate of the Value and Influence of Works of Fiction in Modern Times' (1862), *Works*, ed. Nettleship (London, 1888), III, 36.

26 See Herman J. Ebeling, 'The Word Anachronism', *MLN*, LII (1937), 120–121.

27 *Selected Works*, ed. Potter (London, 1933), p. 333.

28 See G. N. Clark, *The Later Stuarts, 1660–1714* (Oxford, 1934), pp. 362–366; René Wellek, *The Rise of English Literary History* (Chapel Hill, 1941), ch. 2.

29 See especially Ernst Cassirer, 'Raum und Zeit', *Das Erkenntnisproblem...* (Berlin, 1922–23), II, 339–374.

30 Letter 6.

31 Bk. II, ch. I.

32 As was shown by F. S. Dickson (Cross, *Henry Fielding*, II, 189–193).

33 *Biographia Literaria*, ed. Shawcross (London, 1907), I, 87.

34 'Preface' (1765), *Johnson on Shakespeare*, ed. Raleigh (London, 1908), pp. 21–22.

35 See Warren Hunting Smith, *Architecture in English Fiction* (New Haven, 1934), p. 65.

36 'Techniques of Fiction', in *Critiques and Essays on Modern Fiction, 1920–1951*, ed. Aldridge (New York, 1952), p. 41.

37 Bk. III, ch. 10, sects. xxxiii–xxxiv.

38 Preface, *The Passion of Byblis, Critical Works*, ed. Hooker (Baltimore, 1939–43), I, 2.

39 *Human Understanding*, Bk. III, ch. 10, sect. xxiii.

40 'Estimate', *Works*, III, 37.

41 'Burns', *Critical and Miscellaneous Essays* (New York, 1899), I, 276–277.

42 See A. J. Tieje, 'A Peculiar Phase of the Theory of Realism in Pre-Richardsonian Prose-Fiction', *PMLA*, XXVII (1913), 213–252.

43 'He sets about describing every object and transaction, as if the whole had been given in on evidence by an eye-witness' (*Lectures on the English Comic Writers* (New York, 1845), p. 138).

44 Letter to Walter Wilson, Dec. 16, 1822, printed in the latter's *Memoirs of the Life and Times of Daniel de Foe* (London, 1830, III, 428).

Discourse in the Novel

M. M. Bakhtin

Mikhail Mikhailovich Bakhtin (1895–1975)

Born in Orel, Russia, M. M. Bakhtin studied classics at Petrograd (St. Petersburg) University during the turbulent years of 1914 to 1918. Upon graduating he struggled to find gainful employment but thrived intellectually in the informal philosophical society which became known as the "Bakhtin Circle." The group's closeness is evinced by the difficulty of ascribing the authorship of several books published during this time. Major works emerging from the group include *Formal'nyi metod v literaturovedeni* (published under the name of P. N. Medvedev, 1928; translated as *The Formal Method in Literary Scholarship: A Critical Introduction to Sociological Poetics*, 1978), and *Marksizm i filosofiia iazyka* (published under the name of V. N. Vološinov, 1929; translated as *Marxism and the Philosophy of Language*, 1973). In 1929, Bakhtin, along with many other intellectuals, was arrested; spared a period in Siberia due to his ill-health (he suffered from typhoid and the bone disease, osteomyelitis), Bakhtin was exiled to what is now Kazakhstan. In 1936 he

From *The Dialogic Imagination: Four Essays*, translated by Caryl Emerson and Michael Holquist, edited by Michael Holquist. Austin: University of Texas Press, 1981 (1972), pp. 259–300. Copyright © 1981 by the University of Texas Press. Reprinted by permission of the University of Texas Press.

returned to teach at the Mordovia Pedagogical Institute in Saransk, but resigned a year later to avoid being purged, and spent the next eight years in Savelovo. During this period he wrote his doctoral dissertation (published 1965 as *Tvorchestvo Fransua Rable i narodnaia kul'tura srednevekov'ia i Renessansa*; translated as *Rabelais and His World*, 1968), but the controversial nature of his ideas kept him from receiving a degree until 1952. Bakhtin finally gained job stability in 1945, when he returned to the Mordovia Pedagogical Institute, where he remained until his 1961 retirement. Meanwhile, Bakhtin was beginning to gain a national following, especially among younger scholars, and particularly for his book on Dostoevsky (originally published as *Problemy tvorchestva Dostoevkogo*, 1929; revised and expanded as *Problemy poetiki Dostoevskogo*, 1963; translated as *Problems of Dostoevsky's Poetics*, 1973). In 1969 Bakhtin moved to Moscow; now suffering from severe emphysema as well as osteomyelitis, Bakhtin had only a few years to enjoy his long-awaited fame. The essay reprinted here comes from *Voprosy literatury i estetiki: Issledovaniia raznykh let* (1972; selected essays translated by Michael Holquist and Caryl Emerson as *The Dialogic Imagination: Four Essays*, 1981).

The principal idea of this essay is that the study of verbal art can and must overcome the divorce between an abstract "formal" approach and an equally abstract "ideological" approach. Form and content in discourse are one, once we understand that verbal discourse is a social phenomenon – social throughout its entire range and in each and every of its factors, from the sound image to the furthest reaches of abstract meaning.

It is this idea that has motivated our emphasis on "the stylistics of genre." The separation of style and language from the question of genre has been largely responsible for a situation in which only individual and period-bound overtones of a style are the privileged subjects of study, while its basic social tone is ignored. The great historical destinies of genres are overshadowed by the petty vicissitudes of stylistic modifications, which in their turn are linked with individual artists and artistic movements. For this reason, stylistics has been deprived of an authentic philosophical and sociological approach to its problems; it has become bogged down in stylistic trivia; it is not able to sense behind the individual and period-bound shifts the great and anonymous destinies of artistic discourse itself. More often than not, stylistics defines itself as a stylistics of "private craftsmanship" and ignores the social life of discourse outside the artist's study, discourse in the open spaces of public squares, streets, cities and villages, of social groups, generations and epochs. Stylistics is concerned not with living discourse but with a histological specimen made from it, with abstract linguistic discourse in the service of an artist's individual creative powers. But these individual and tendentious overtones of style, cut off from the fundamentally social modes in which discourse lives, inevitably come across as flat and abstract in such a formulation and cannot therefore be studied in organic unity with a work's semantic components.

M. M. BAKHTIN

Modern Stylistics and the Novel

Before the twentieth century, problems associated with a stylistics of the novel had not been precisely formulated — such a formulation could only have resulted from a recognition of the stylistic uniqueness of novelistic (artistic-prose) discourse.

For a long time treatment of the novel was limited to little more than abstract ideological examination and publicistic commentary. Concrete questions of stylistics were either not treated at all or treated in passing and in an arbitrary way: the discourse of artistic prose was either understood as being poetic in the narrow sense, and had the categories of traditional stylistics (based on the study of tropes) uncritically applied to it, or else such questions were limited to empty, evaluative terms for the characterization of language, such as "expressiveness," "imagery," "force," "clarity" and so on — without providing these concepts with any stylistic significance, however vague and tentative.

Toward the end of the last century, as a counterweight to this abstract ideological way of viewing things, interest began to grow in the concrete problems of artistic craftsmanship in prose, in the problems of novel and short-story technique. However, in questions of stylistics the situation did not change in the slightest; attention was concentrated almost exclusively on problems of composition (in the broad sense of the word). But, as before, the peculiarities of the stylistic life of discourse in the novel (and in the short story as well) lacked an approach that was both principled and at the same time concrete (one is impossible without the other); the same arbitrary judgmental observations about language — in the spirit of traditional stylistics — continued to reign supreme, and they totally overlooked the authentic nature of artistic prose.

There is a highly characteristic and widespread point of view that sees novelistic discourse as an extra-artistic medium, a discourse that is not worked into any special or unique style. After failure to find in novelistic discourse a purely poetic formulation ("poetic" in the narrow sense) as was expected, prose discourse is denied any artistic value at all; it is the same as practical speech for everyday life, or speech for scientific purposes, an artistically neutral means of communication.[1]

Such a point of view frees one from the necessity of undertaking stylistic analyses of the novel; it in fact gets rid of the very problem of a stylistics of the novel, permitting one to limit oneself to purely thematic analyses of it.

It was, however, precisely in the 1920s that this situation changed: the novelistic prose word began to win a place for itself in stylistics. On the one hand there appeared a series of concrete stylistic analyses of novelistic prose; on the other hand, systematic attempts were made to recognize and define the stylistic uniqueness of artistic prose as distinct from poetry.

But it was precisely these concrete analyses and these attempts at a principled approach that made patently obvious the fact that all the categories of traditional stylistics — in fact the very concept of a *poetic* artistic discourse, which lies at the heart of such categories — were not applicable to novelistic discourse. Novelistic discourse proved to be the acid test for this whole way of conceiving style, exposing the narrowness of this type of thinking and its inadequacy in all areas of discourse's artistic life.

All attempts at concrete stylistic analysis of novelistic prose either strayed into linguistic descriptions of the language of a given novelist or else limited themselves to those separate, isolated stylistic elements of the novel that were includable (or gave the appearance of being includable) in the traditional categories of stylistics. In both instances the stylistic whole of the novel and of novelistic discourse eluded the investigator.

The novel as a whole is a phenomenon multiform in style and variform in speech and voice. In it the investigator is confronted with several heterogeneous stylistic unities, often located on different linguistic levels and subject to different stylistic controls.

We list below the basic types of compositional-stylistic unities into which the novelistic whole usually breaks down:

(1) Direct authorial literary-artistic narration (in all its diverse variants);
(2) Stylization of the various forms of oral everyday narration (*skaz*);
(3) Stylization of the various forms of semiliterary (written) everyday narration (the letter, the diary, etc.);
(4) Various forms of literary but extra-artistic authorial speech (moral, philosophical or scientific statements, oratory, ethnographic descriptions, memoranda and so forth);
(5) The stylistically individualized speech of characters.

These heterogeneous stylistic unities, upon entering the novel, combine to form a structured artistic system, and are subordinated to the higher stylistic unity of the work as a whole, a unity that cannot be identified with any single one of the unities subordinated to it.

The stylistic uniqueness of the novel as a genre consists precisely in the combination of these subordinated, yet still relatively autonomous, unities (even at times comprised of different languages) into the higher unity of the work as a whole: the style of a novel is to be found in the combination of its styles; the language of a novel is the system of its "languages." Each separate element of a novel's language is determined first of all by one such subordinated stylistic unity into which it enters directly – be it the stylistically individualized speech of a character, the down-to-earth voice of a narrator in *skaz*, a letter or whatever. The linguistic and stylistic profile of a given element (lexical, semantic, syntactic) is shaped by that subordinated unity to which it is most immediately proximate. At the same time this element, together with its most immediate unity, figures into the style of the whole, itself supports the accent of the whole and participates in the process whereby the unified meaning of the whole is structured and revealed.

The novel can be defined as a diversity of social speech types (sometimes even diversity of languages) and a diversity of individual voices, artistically organized. The internal stratification of any single national language into social dialects, characteristic group behavior, professional jargons, generic languages, languages of generations and age groups, tendentious languages, languages of the authorities, of various circles and of passing fashions, languages that serve the specific sociopolitical purposes of the day, even of the hour (each day has its own slogan, its own vocabulary, its own emphases) – this internal stratification present in every language at any given moment of its historical existence is the indispensable prerequisite for the novel as a genre. The novel orchestrates all its themes, the totality of the world of objects and ideas depicted and expressed in it, by means of the social diversity of speech types [*raznorečie*] and by the differing individual voices that flourish under such conditions. Authorial speech, the speeches of narrators, inserted genres, the speech of characters are merely those fundamental compositional unities with whose help heteroglossia [*raznorečie*] can enter the novel; each of them permits a multiplicity of social voices and a wide variety of their links and interrelationships (always more or less dialogized). These distinctive links and interrelationships between utterances and languages, this movement of the theme through different languages and speech types, its dispersion into the rivulets and droplets of social heteroglossia, its dialogization – this is the basic distinguishing feature of the stylistics of the novel.

Such a combining of languages and styles into a higher unity is unknown to traditional stylistics; it has no method for approaching the distinctive social dialogue among languages that is present in the novel. Thus stylistic analysis is not oriented toward the novel as a whole, but only toward one or another of its subordinated stylistic unities. The traditional scholar bypasses the basic distinctive feature of the novel as a genre; he substitutes for it another object of study, and instead of novelistic style he actually analyzes something completely different. He transposes a symphonic (orchestrated) theme on to the piano keyboard.

We notice two such types of substitutions: in the first type, an analysis of novelistic style is replaced by a description of the language of a given novelist (or at best of the "languages" of a given novel); in the second type, one of the subordinated styles is isolated and analyzed as if it were the style of the whole.

In the first type, style is cut off from considerations of genre, and from the work as such, and regarded as a phenomenon of language itself: the unity of style in a given work is transformed either into the unity of an individual language ("individual dialect"), or into the unity of an individual speech (*parole*). It is precisely the individuality of the speaking subject that is recognized to be that style-generating factor transforming a phenomenon of language and linguistics into a stylistic unity.

We have no need to follow where such an analysis of novelistic style leads, whether to a disclosing of the novelist's individual dialect (that is, his vocabulary, his syntax) or to a disclosing of the distinctive features of the work taken as a "complete speech act," an "utterance." Equally in both cases, style is understood in the spirit of Saussure: as an individualization of the general language (in the sense of a system of general language norms). Stylistics is transformed either into a curious kind of linguistics treating individual languages, or into a linguistics of the utterance.

In accordance with the point of view selected, the unity of a style thus presupposes on the one hand a unity of language (in the sense of a system of general normative forms) and on the other hand the unity of an individual person realizing himself in this language.

Both these conditions are in fact obligatory in the majority of verse-based poetic genres, but even in these genres they far from exhaust or define the style of the work. The most precise and complete description of the individual language and speech of a poet – even if this description does choose to treat the expressiveness of language and speech elements – does not add up to a stylistic analysis of the work, inasmuch as these elements relate to a system of language or to a system of speech, that is, to various linguistic unities and not to the system of the artistic work, which is governed by a completely different system of rules than those that govern the linguistic systems of language and of speech.

But – we repeat – in the majority of poetic genres, the unity of the language system and the unity (and uniqueness) of the poet's individuality as reflected in his language and speech, which is directly realized in this unity, are indispensable prerequisites of poetic style. The novel, however, not only does not require these conditions but (as we have said) even makes of the internal stratification of language, of its social heteroglossia and the variety of individual voices in it, the prerequisite for authentic novelistic prose.

Thus the substitution of the individualized language of the novelist (to the extent that one can recover this language from the "speech" and "language" systems of the novel) for the style of the novel itself is doubly imprecise: it distorts the very essence of a stylistics of the novel. Such substitution inevitably leads to the selection from the novel of only those elements that can be fitted within the frame of a single language system and that express, directly and without mediation, an authorial individuality in language. The whole of the novel and the specific tasks involved in constructing this whole out of heteroglot, multi-voiced, multi-styled and often multi-languaged elements remain outside the boundaries of such a study.

Such is the first type of substitution for the proper object of study in the stylistic analysis of the novel. We will not delve further into the diverse variations of this type, which are determined by the different ways in which such concepts as "the speech whole," "the system of language," "the individuality of the author's language and speech" are understood, and by a difference in the very way in which the relationship between style and language is conceived (and also the relationship between stylistics and linguistics). In all possible variants on this type of analysis, which acknowledge only one single language and a single authorial individuality expressing itself directly in that language, the stylistic nature of the novel slips hopelessly away from the investigator.

The second type of substitution is characterized not by an orientation toward the language of the author, but rather toward the style of the novel itself – although style thus understood is narrowed down to mean the style of merely one out of the several subordinated unities (which are relatively autonomous) within the novel.

In the majority of cases the style of the novel is subsumed under the concept of "epic style," and the appropriate categories of traditional stylistics are applied to it. In such circumstances only those elements of epic representation (those occurring predominantly in direct authorial speech) are isolated from the novel for consideration. The profound difference between novelistic and purely epic modes of expression is ignored. Differences between the novel and the epic are usually perceived on the level of composition and thematics alone.

In other instances, different aspects of novelistic style are selected out as most characteristic of one or another concrete literary work. Thus the narrational aspect can be considered from the point of view not of its objective descriptive mode, but of its subjective expression mode (expressiveness). One might select elements of vernacular extraliterary narration (*skaz*) or those aspects that provide the information necessary to further the plot (as one might do, for example, in analyzing an adventure novel).[2] And it is possible, finally, to select those purely dramatic elements of the novel that lower the narrational aspect to the level of a commentary on the dialogues of the novel's characters. But the system of languages in drama is organized on completely different principles, and therefore its languages sound utterly different than do the languages of the novel. There is no all-encompassing language, dialogically oriented to separate languages, there is no second all-encompassing extra-plot (not dramatic) dialogue.

All these types of analysis are inadequate to the style not only of the novelistic whole but even of that element isolated as fundamental for a given novel – inasmuch as that element, removed from its interaction with others, changes its stylistic meaning and ceases to be that which it in fact had been in the novel.

The current state of questions posed by a stylistics of the novel reveals, fully and clearly, that all the categories and methods of traditional stylistics remain incapable of dealing effectively with the artistic uniqueness of discourse in the novel, or with the specific life that discourse leads in the novel. "Poetic language," "individuality of language," "image," "symbol," "epic style" and other general categories worked out and applied by stylistics, as well as the entire set of concrete stylistic devices subsumed by these categories (no matter how differently understood by individual critics), are all equally oriented toward the single-languaged and single-styled genres, toward the poetic genres in the narrow sense of the word. Their connection with this exclusive orientation explains a number of the particular features and limitations of traditional stylistic categories. All these categories, and the very philosophical conception of poetic discourse in which they are grounded, are too narrow and cramped, and cannot accommodate the artistic prose of novelistic discourse.

Thus stylistics and the philosophy of discourse indeed confront a dilemma: either to acknowledge the novel (and consequently all artistic prose tending in that direction) an unartistic or quasi-artistic genre, or to radically reconsider that conception of poetic discourse in which traditional stylistics is grounded and which determines all its categories.

This dilemma, however, is by no means universally recognized. Most scholars are not inclined to undertake a radical revision of the fundamental philosophical conception of poetic discourse. Many do not even see or recognize the philosophical roots of the stylistics (and linguistics) in which they work, and shy away from any fundamental philosophical issues. They utterly fail to see behind their isolated and fragmented stylistic observations and linguistic descriptions any theoretical problems posed by novelistic discourse. Others – more principled – make a case for consistent individualism in their understanding of language and style. First and foremost they seek in the stylistic phenomenon a direct and unmediated expression of authorial individuality, and such an understanding of the problem is least likely of all to encourage a reconsideration of basic stylistic categories in the proper direction.

However, there is another solution of our dilemma that does take basic concepts into account: one need only consider oft-neglected rhetoric, which for centuries has included artistic prose in its purview. Once we have restored rhetoric to all its ancient rights, we may adhere to the old concept of poetic discourse, relegating to "rhetorical forms" everything in novelistic prose that does not fit the Procrustean bed of traditional stylistic categories.[3]

Gustav Shpet,[4] in his time, proposed such a solution to the dilemma, with all due rigorousness and consistency. He utterly excluded artistic prose and its ultimate realization – the novel – from the realm of poetry, and assigned it to the category of purely rhetorical forms.[5]

Here is what Shpet says about the novel: "The recognition that contemporary forms of moral propaganda – i.e., the *novel* – do not spring from *poetic creativity* but are purely rhetorical compositions, is an admission, and a conception, that apparently cannot arise without immediately confronting a formidable obstacle in the form of the universal recognition, despite everything, that the novel *does* have a certain aesthetic value."[6]

Shpet utterly denies the novel any aesthetic significance. The novel is an extra-artistic rhetorical genre, "the contemporary form of moral propaganda"; artistic discourse is exclusively poetic discourse (in the sense we have indicated above).

Viktor Vinogradov[7] adopted an analogous point of view in his book *On Artistic Prose*, assigning the problem of artistic prose to rhetoric. While agreeing with Shpet's basic philosophical definitions of the "poetic" and the "rhetorical," Vinogradov was, however, not so paradoxically consistent: he considered the novel a syncretic, mixed form ("a hybrid formation") and admitted that it contained, along with rhetorical elements, some purely poetic ones.[8]

The point of view that completely excludes novelistic prose, as a rhetorical formation, from the realm of poetry – a point of view that is basically false – does nevertheless have a certain indisputable merit. There resides in it an acknowledgment in principle and in substance of the inadequacy of all contemporary stylistics, along with its philosophical and linguistic base, when it comes to defining the specific distinctive features of novelistic prose. And what is more, the very reliance on rhetorical forms has a great heuristic significance. Once rhetorical discourse is brought into the study with all its living diversity, it cannot fail to have a deeply revolutionizing influence on linguistics and on the philosophy of language. It is precisely those aspects of any discourse (the internally dialogic quality of discourse, and the phenomena related to it), not yet sufficiently taken into account and fathomed in all the enormous weight they carry in the life of language, that are revealed with great external precision in rhetorical forms, provided a correct and unprejudiced approach to those forms is used. Such is the general methodological and heuristic significance of rhetorical forms for linguistics and for the philosophy of language.

The special significance of rhetorical forms for understanding the novel is equally great. The novel, and artistic prose in general, has the closest genetic, family relationship to rhetorical forms. And throughout the entire development of the novel, its intimate interaction (both peaceful and hostile) with living rhetorical genres (journalistic, moral, philosophical and others) has never ceased; this interaction was perhaps no less intense than was the novel's interaction with the artistic genres (epic, dramatic, lyric). But in this uninterrupted interrelationship, novelistic discourse preserved its own qualitative uniqueness and was never reducible to rhetorical discourse.

The novel is an artistic genre. Novelistic discourse is poetic discourse, but one that does not fit within the frame provided by the concept of poetic discourse as it now exists. This concept has certain underlying presuppositions that limit it. The very concept – in the course of its historical formulation from Aristotle to the present day – has been oriented toward the specific "official" genres and connected with specific historical tendencies in verbal ideological life. Thus a whole series of phenomena remained beyond its conceptual horizon.

M. M. BAKHTIN

Philosophy of language, linguistics and stylistics [i.e., such as they have come down to us] have all postulated a simple and unmediated relation of speaker to his unitary and singular "own" language, and have postulated as well a simple realization of this language in the monologic utterance of the individual. Such disciplines actually know only two poles in the life of language, between which are located all the linguistic and stylistic phenomena they know: on the one hand, the system of a *unitary language*, and on the other the *individual* speaking in this language.

Various schools of thought in the philosophy of language, in linguistics and in stylistics have, in different periods (and always in close connection with the diverse concrete poetic and ideological styles of a given epoch), introduced into such concepts as "system of language," "monologic utterance," "the speaking *individuum*," various differing nuances of meaning, but their basic content remains unchanged. This basic content is conditioned by the specific sociohistorical destinies of European languages and by the destinies of ideological discourse, and by those particular historical tasks that ideological discourse has fulfilled in specific social spheres and at specific stages in its own historical development.

These tasks and destinies of discourse conditioned specific verbal-ideological move-ments, as well as various specific genres of ideological discourse, and ultimately the specific philosophical concept of discourse itself – in particular, the concept of poetic discourse, which had been at the heart of all concepts of style.

The strength and at the same time the limitations of such basic stylistic categories become apparent when such categories are seen as conditioned by specific historical destinies and by the task that an ideological discourse assumes. These categories arose from and were shaped by the historically *aktuell* forces at work in the verbal-ideological evolution of specific social groups; they comprised the theoretical expression of actualizing forces that were in the process of creating a life for language.

These forces are *the forces that serve to unify and centralize the verbal-ideological world.*

Unitary language constitutes the theoretical expression of the historical processes of linguistic unification and centralization, an expression of the centripetal forces of language. A unitary language is not something given [*dan*] but is always in essence posited [*zadan*] – and at every moment of its linguistic life it is opposed to the realities of heteroglossia. But at the same time it makes its real presence felt as a force for overcoming this heteroglossia, imposing specific limits to it, guaranteeing a certain maximum of mutual understanding and crystallizing into a real, although still relative, unity – the unity of the reigning conversational (everyday) and literary language, "correct language."

A common unitary language is a system of linguistic norms. But these norms do not constitute an abstract imperative; they are rather the generative forces of linguistic life, forces that struggle to overcome the heteroglossia of language, forces that unite and centralize verbal-ideological thought, creating within a heteroglot national language the firm, stable linguistic nucleus of an officially recognized literary language, or else defending an already formed language from the pressure of growing heteroglossia.

What we have in mind here is not an abstract linguistic minimum of a common language, in the sense of a system of elementary forms (linguistic symbols) guaranteeing a *minimum* level of comprehension in practical communication. We are taking language not as a system of abstract grammatical categories, but rather language conceived as ideologically saturated, language as a world view, even as a concrete opinion, insuring a *maximum* of mutual understanding in all spheres of ideological life. Thus a unitary language gives expression to forces working toward concrete verbal and ideological unification and centralization, which develop in vital connection with the processes of sociopolitical and cultural centralization.

Aristotelian poetics, the poetics of Augustine, the poetics of the medieval church, of "the one language of truth," the Cartesian poetics of neoclassicism, the abstract grammatical universalism of Leibniz (the idea of a "universal grammar"), Humboldt's insistence on the concrete – all these, whatever their differences in nuance, give expression to the same centripetal forces in sociolinguistic and ideological life; they serve one and the same project of centralizing and unifying the European languages. The victory of one reigning language (dialect) over the others, the supplanting of languages, their enslavement, the process of illuminating them with the True Word, the incorporation of barbarians and lower social strata into a unitary language of culture and truth, the canonization of ideological systems, philology with its methods of studying and teaching dead languages, languages that were by that very fact "unities," Indo-European linguistics with its focus of attention, directed away from language plurality to a single proto-language – all this determined the content and power of the category of "unitary language" in linguistic and stylistic thought, and determined its creative, style-shaping role in the majority of the poetic genres that coalesced in the channel formed by those same centripetal forces of verbal-ideological life.

But the centripetal forces of the life of language, embodied in a "unitary language," operate in the midst of heteroglossia. At any given moment of its evolution, language is stratified not only into linguistic dialects in the strict sense of the word (according to formal linguistic markers, especially phonetic), but also – and for us this is the essential point – into languages that are socio-ideological: languages of social groups, "professional" and "generic" languages, languages of generations and so forth. From this point of view, literary language itself is only one of these heteroglot languages – and in its turn is also stratified into languages (generic, period-bound and others). And this stratification and heteroglossia, once realized, is not only a static invariant of linguistic life, but also what insures its dynamics: stratification and heteroglossia widen and deepen as long as language is alive and developing. Alongside the centripetal forces, the centrifugal forces of language carry on their uninterrupted work; alongside verbal-ideological centralization and unification, the uninterrupted processes of decentralization and disunification go forward.

Every concrete utterance of a speaking subject serves as a point where centrifugal as well as centripetal forces are brought to bear. The processes of centralization and decentralization, of unification and disunification, intersect in the utterance; the utterance not only answers the requirements of its own language as an individualized embodiment of a speech act, but it answers the requirements of heteroglossia as well; it is in fact an active participant in such speech diversity. And this active participation of every utterance in living heteroglossia determines the linguistic profile and style of the utterance to no less a degree than its inclusion in any normative-centralizing system of a unitary language.

M. M. BAKHTIN

Every utterance participates in the "unitary language" (in its centripetal forces and tendencies) and at the same time partakes of social and historical heteroglossia (the centrifugal, stratifying forces).

Such is the fleeting language of a day, of an epoch, a social group, a genre, a school and so forth. It is possible to give a concrete and detailed analysis of any utterance, once having exposed it as a contradiction-ridden, tension-filled unity of two embattled tendencies in the life of language.

The authentic environment of an utterance, the environment in which it lives and takes shape, is dialogized heteroglossia, anonymous and social as language, but simultaneously concrete, filled with specific content and accented as an individual utterance.

At the time when major divisions of the poetic genres were developing under the influence of the unifying, centralizing, centripetal forces of verbal-ideological life, the novel – and those artistic-prose genres that gravitate toward it – was being historically shaped by the current of decentralizing, centrifugal forces. At the time when poetry was accomplishing the task of cultural, national and political centralization of the verbal-ideological world in the higher official socio-ideological levels, on the lower levels, on the stages of local fairs and at buffoon spectacles, the heteroglossia of the clown sounded forth, ridiculing all "languages" and dialects; there developed the literature of the *fabliaux* and *Schwänke* of street songs, folksayings, anecdotes, where there was no language-center at all, where there was to be found a lively play with the "languages" of poets, scholars, monks, knights and others, where all "languages" were masks and where no language could claim to be an authentic, incontestable face.

Heteroglossia, as organized in these low genres, was not merely heteroglossia vis-à-vis the accepted literary language (in all its various generic expressions), that is, vis-à-vis the linguistic center of the verbal-ideological life of the nation and the epoch, but was a heteroglossia consciously opposed to this literary language. It was parodic, and aimed sharply and polemically against the official languages of its given time. It was heteroglossia that had been dialogized.

Linguistics, stylistics and the philosophy of language that were born and shaped by the current of centralizing tendencies in the life of language have ignored this dialogized heteroglossia, in which is embodied the centrifugal forces in the life of language. For this very reason they could make no provision for the dialogic nature of language, which was a struggle among socio-linguistic points of view, not an intra-language struggle between individual wills or logical contradictions. Moreover, even intra-language dialogue (dramatic, rhetorical, cognitive or merely casual) has hardly been studied linguistically or stylistically up to the present day. One might even say outright that the dialogic aspect of discourse and all the phenomena connected with it have remained to the present moment beyond the ken of linguistics.

Stylistics has been likewise completely deaf to dialogue. A literary work has been conceived by stylistics as if it were a hermetic and self-sufficient whole, one whose elements constitute a closed system presuming nothing beyond themselves, no other utterances. The system comprising an artistic work was thought to be analogous with the system of a language, a system that could not stand in a dialogic interrelationship with other languages. From the point of view of stylistics, the artistic work as a whole – whatever that whole might be – is a self-sufficient and closed authorial monologue, one that presumes only passive listeners beyond its own boundaries. Should we imagine the work as a rejoinder in a given dialogue, whose style is determined by its interrelationship with other rejoinders in the same dialogue (in the totality of the conversation) – then traditional stylistics does not offer an adequate means for approaching such a dialogized style. The sharpest and externally most marked manifestations of this stylistic category – the polemical style, the parodic, the ironic – are usually classified as rhetorical and not as poetic phenomena. Stylistics locks every stylistic phenomenon into the monologic context of a given self-sufficient and hermetic utterance, imprisoning it, as it were, in the dungeon of a single context; it is not able to exchange messages with other utterances; it is not able to realize its own stylistic implications in a relationship with them; it is obliged to exhaust itself in its own single hermetic context.

Linguistics, stylistics and the philosophy of language – as forces in the service of the great centralizing tendencies of European verbal-ideological life – have sought first and foremost for *unity* in diversity. This exclusive "orientation toward unity" in the present and past life of languages has concentrated the attention of philosophical and linguistic thought on the firmest, most stable, least changeable and most mono-semic aspects of discourse – on the *phonetic* aspects first of all – that are furthest removed from the changing socio-semantic spheres of discourse. Real ideologically saturated "language consciousness," one that participates in actual heteroglossia and multi-languagedness, has remained outside its field of vision. It is precisely this orientation toward unity that has compelled scholars to ignore all the verbal genres (quotidian, rhetorical, artistic-prose) that were the carriers of the decentralizing tendencies in the life of language, or that were in any case too fundamentally implicated in heteroglossia. The expression of this hetero- as well as polyglot consciousness in the specific forms and phenomena of verbal life remained utterly without determinative influence on linguistics and stylistic thought.

Therefore proper theoretical recognition and illumination could not be found for the specific feel for language and discourse that one gets in stylizations, in *skaz*, in parodies and in various forms of verbal masquerade, "not talking straight," and in the more complex artistic forms for the organization of contradiction, forms that orchestrate their themes by means of languages – in all characteristic and profound models of novelistic prose, in Grimmelshausen, Cervantes, Rabelais, Fielding, Smollett, Sterne and others.

The problem of stylistics for the novel inevitably leads to the necessity of engaging a series of fundamental questions concerning the philosophy of discourse, questions connected with those aspects in the life of discourse that have had no light cast on them by linguistic and stylistic thought – that is, we must deal with the life and behavior of discourse in a contradictory and multi-languaged world.

Discourse in Poetry and Discourse in the Novel

For the philosophy of language, for linguistics and for stylistics structured on their base, a whole series of phenomena have therefore remained almost entirely beyond the realm of consideration: these include the specific phenomena that are present in discourse and that are determined by its dialogic orientation, first, amid others' utterances inside a *single* language (the primordial dialogism of discourse), amid other "social languages" within a single *national* language and finally amid different national languages within the same *culture*, that is, the same socio-ideological conceptual horizon.[9]

In recent decades, it is true, these phenomena have begun to attract the attention of scholars in language and stylistics, but their fundamental and wide-ranging significance in all spheres of the life of discourse is still far from acknowledged.

The dialogic orientation of a word among other words (of all kinds and degrees of otherness) creates new and significant artistic potential in discourse, creates the potential for a distinctive art of prose, which has found its fullest and deepest expression in the novel.

We will focus our attention here on various forms and degrees of dialogic orientation in discourse, and on the special potential for a distinctive prose-art.

As treated by traditional stylistic thought, the word acknowledges only itself (that is, only its own context), its own object, its own direct expression and its own unitary and singular language. It acknowledges another word, one lying outside its own context, only as the neutral word of language, as the word of no one in particular, as simply the potential for speech. The direct word, as traditional stylistics understands it, encounters in its orientation toward the object only the resistance of the object itself (the impossibility of its being exhausted by a word, the impossibility of saying it all), but it does not encounter in its path toward the object the fundamental and richly varied opposition of another's word. No one hinders this word, no one argues with it.

But no living word relates to its object in a *singular* way: between the word and its object, between the word and the speaking subject, there exists an elastic environment of other, alien words about the same object, the same theme, and this is an environment that it is often difficult to penetrate. It is precisely in the process of living interaction with this specific environment that the word may be individualized and given stylistic shape.

Indeed, any concrete discourse (utterance) finds the object at which it was directed already as it were overlain with qualifications, open to dispute, charged with value, already enveloped in an obscuring mist – or, on the contrary, by the "light" of alien words that have already been spoken about it. It is entangled, shot through with shared thoughts, points of view, alien value judgments and accents. The word, directed toward its object, enters a dialogically agitated and tension-filled environment of alien words, value judgments and accents, weaves in and out of complex interrelationships, merges with some, recoils from others, intersects with yet a third group: and all this may crucially shape discourse, may leave a trace in all its semantic layers, may complicate its expression and influence its entire stylistic profile.

The living utterance, having taken meaning and shape at a particular historical moment in a socially specific environment, cannot fail to brush up against thousands of living dialogic threads, woven by socio-ideological consciousness around the given object of an utterance; it cannot fail to become an active participant in social dialogue. After all, the utterance arises out of this dialogue as a continuation of it and as a rejoinder to it – it does not approach the object from the sidelines.

The way in which the word conceptualizes its object is a complex act – all objects, open to dispute and overlain as they are with qualifications, are from one side highlighted while from the other side dimmed by heteroglot social opinion, by an alien word about them.[10] And into this complex play of light and shadow the word enters – it becomes saturated with this play, and must determine within it the boundaries of its own semantic and stylistic contours. The way in which the word conceives its object is complicated by a dialogic interaction within the object between various aspects of its socio-verbal intelligibility. And an artistic representation, an "image" of the object, may be penetrated by this dialogic play of verbal intentions that meet and are interwoven in it; such an image need not stifle these forces, but on the contrary may activate and organize them. If we imagine the *intention* of such a word, that is, its *directionality toward the object*, in the form of a ray of light, then the living and unrepeatable play of colors and light on the facets of the image that it constructs can be explained as the spectral dispersion of the ray-word, not within the object itself (as would be the case in the play of an image-as-trope, in poetic speech taken in the narrow sense, in an "autotelic word"), but rather as its spectral dispersion in an atmosphere filled with the alien words, value judgments and accents through which the ray passes on its way toward the object; the social atmosphere of the word, the atmosphere that surrounds the object, makes the facets of the image sparkle.

The word, breaking through to its own meaning and its own expression across an environment full of alien words and variously evaluating accents, harmonizing with some of the elements in this environment and striking a dissonance with others, is able, in this dialogized process, to shape its own stylistic profile and tone.

Such is the *image in artistic prose* and the image of *novelistic prose* in particular. In the atmosphere of the novel, the direct and unmediated intention of a word presents itself as something impermissably naive, something in fact impossible, for naiveté itself, under authentic novelistic conditions, takes on the nature of an internal polemic and is consequently dialogized (in, for example, the work of the Sentimentalists, in Chateaubriand and in Tolstoy). Such a dialogized image can occur in all the poetic genres as well, even in the lyric (to be sure, without setting the tone).[11] But such an image can fully unfold, achieve full complexity and depth and at the same time artistic closure, only under the conditions present in the genre of the novel.

In the poetic image narrowly conceived (in the image-as-trope), all activity – the dynamics of the image-as-word – is completely exhausted by the play between the word (with all its aspects) and the object (in all its aspects). The word plunges into the inexhaustible wealth and contradictory multiplicity of the object itself, with its "virginal," still "unuttered" nature; therefore it presumes nothing beyond the borders of its own context (except, of course, what can be found in the treasure-house of language itself). The word forgets that its object has its own history of contradictory acts of verbal recognition, as well as that heteroglossia that is always present in such acts of recognition.

For the writer of artistic prose, on the contrary, the object reveals first of all precisely the socially heteroglot multiplicity of its names, definitions and value judgments. Instead of the virginal fullness and inexhaustibility of the object itself, the prose writer confronts a multitude of routes, roads and paths that have been laid down in the object by social consciousness. Along with the internal contradictions inside the object itself, the prose writer witnesses as well the unfolding of social heteroglossia *surrounding* the object, the Tower-of-Babel mixing of languages that goes on around any object; the dialectics of the object are interwoven with the social dialogue surrounding it. For the prose writer, the object is a focal point for heteroglot voices among which his own voice must also sound; these voices create the background necessary for his own voice, outside of which his artistic prose nuances cannot be perceived, and without which they "do not sound."

The prose artist elevates the social heteroglossia surrounding objects into an image that has finished contours, an image completely shot through with dialogized overtones; he creates artistically calculated nuances on all the fundamental voices and tones of this heteroglossia. But as we have already said, every extra-artistic prose discourse – in any of its forms, quotidian, rhetorical, scholarly – cannot fail to be oriented toward the "already uttered," the "already known," the "common opinion" and so forth. The dialogic orientation of discourse is a phenomenon that is, of course, a property of *any* discourse. It is the natural orientation of any living discourse. On all its various routes toward the object, in all its directions, the word encounters an alien word and cannot help encountering it in a living, tension-filled interaction. Only the mythical Adam, who approached a virginal and as yet verbally unqualified world with the first word, could really have escaped from start to finish this dialogic inter-orientation with the alien word that occurs in the object. Concrete historical human discourse does not have this privilege: it can deviate from such inter-orientation only on a conditional basis and only to a certain degree.

It is all the more remarkable that linguistics and the philosophy of discourse have been primarily oriented precisely toward this artificial, preconditioned status of the word, a word excised from dialogue and taken for the norm (although the primacy of dialogue over monologue is frequently proclaimed). Dialogue is studied merely as a compositional form in the structuring of speech, but the internal dialogism of the word (which occurs in a monologic utterance as well as in a rejoinder), the dialogism that penetrates its entire structure, all its semantic and expressive layers, is almost entirely ignored. But it is precisely this internal dialogism of the word, which does not assume any external compositional forms of dialogue, that cannot be isolated as an independent act, separate from the word's ability to form a concept [*koncipirovanie*] of its object – it is precisely this internal dialogism that has such enormous power to shape style. The internal dialogism of the word finds expression in a series of peculiar features in semantics, syntax and stylistics that have remained up to the present time completely unstudied by linguistics and stylistics (nor, what is more, have the peculiar semantic features of ordinary dialogue been studied).

The word is born in a dialogue as a living rejoinder within it; the word is shaped in dialogic interaction with an alien word that is already in the object. A word forms a concept of its own object in a dialogic way.

But this does not exhaust the internal dialogism of the word. It encounters an alien word not only in the object itself: every word is directed toward an *answer* and cannot escape the profound influence of the answering word that it anticipates.

The word in living conversation is directly, blatantly, oriented toward a future answer-word: it provokes an answer, anticipates it and structures itself in the answer's direction. Forming itself in an atmosphere of the already spoken, the word is at the same time determined by that which has not yet been said but which is needed and in fact anticipated by the answering word. Such is the situation in any living dialogue.

All rhetorical forms, monologic in their compositional structure, are oriented toward the listener and his answer. This orientation toward the listener is usually considered the basic constitutive feature of rhetorical discourse.[12] It is highly significant for rhetoric that this relationship toward the concrete listener, taking him into account, is a relationship that enters into the very internal construction of rhetorical discourse. This orientation toward an answer is open, blatant and concrete.

This open orientation toward the listener and his answer in everyday dialogue and in rhetorical forms has attracted the attention of linguists. But even where this has been the case, linguists have by and large gotten no further than the compositional forms by which the listener is taken into account; they have not sought influence springing from more profound meaning and style. They have taken into consideration only those aspects of style determined by demands for comprehensibility and clarity – that is, precisely those aspects that are deprived of any internal dialogism, that take the listener for a person who passively understands but not for one who actively answers and reacts.

The listener and his response are regularly taken into account when it comes to everyday dialogue and rhetoric, but every other sort of discourse as well is oriented toward an understanding that is "responsive" – although this orientation is not particularized in an independent act and is not compositionally marked. Responsive understanding is a fundamental force, one that participates in the formulation of discourse, and it is moreover an *active* understanding, one that discourse senses as resistance or support enriching the discourse.

Linguistics and the philosophy of language acknowledge only a passive understanding of discourse, and moreover this takes place by and large on the level of common language, that is, it is an understanding of an utterance's *neutral signification* and not its *actual meaning*.

The linguistic significance of a given utterance is understood against the background of language, while its actual meaning is understood against the background of other concrete utterances on the same theme, a background made up of contradictory opinions, points of view and value judgments – that is, precisely that background that, as we see, complicates the path of any word toward its object. Only now this contradictory environment of alien words is present to the speaker not in the object, but rather in the consciousness of the listener, as his apperceptive background, pregnant with responses and objections. And every utterance is oriented toward this apperceptive background of understanding, which is not a linguistic background but rather one composed of specific objects and emotional expressions. There occurs a new encounter between the utterance and an alien word, which makes itself felt as a new and unique influence on its style.

A passive understanding of linguistic meaning is no understanding at all, it is only the abstract aspect of meaning. But even a more concrete *passive* understanding of the meaning of the utterance, an understanding of the speaker's intention insofar as that understanding remains purely passive, purely receptive, contributes nothing new to the word under consideration, only mirroring it, seeking, at its most ambitious, merely the full reproduction of that which is already given in the word – even such an understanding never goes beyond the boundaries of the word's context and in no way enriches the word. Therefore, insofar as the speaker operates with such a passive understanding, nothing new can be introduced into his discourse; there can be no new aspects in his discourse relating to concrete objects and emotional expressions. Indeed the purely negative demands, such as could only emerge from a passive understanding

M. M. BAKHTIN

(for instance, a need for greater clarity, more persuasiveness, more vividness and so forth), leave the speaker in his own personal context, within his own boundaries; such negative demands are completely immanent in the speaker's own discourse and do not go beyond his semantic or expressive self-sufficiency.

In the actual life of speech, every concrete act of understanding is active: it assimilates the word to be understood into its own conceptual system filled with specific objects and emotional expressions, and is indissolubly merged with the response, with a motivated agreement or disagreement. To some extent, primacy belongs to the response, as the activating principle: it creates the ground for understanding, it prepares the ground for an active and engaged understanding. Understanding comes to fruition only in the response. Understanding and response are dialectically merged and mutually condition each other; one is impossible without the other.

Thus an active understanding, one that assimilates the word under consideration into a new conceptual system, that of the one striving to understand, establishes a series of complex interrelationships, consonances and dissonances with the word and enriches it with new elements. It is precisely such an understanding that the speaker counts on. Therefore his orientation toward the listener is an orientation toward a specific conceptual horizon, toward the specific world of the listener; it introduces totally new elements into his discourse; it is in this way, after all, that various different points of view, conceptual horizons, systems for providing expressive accents, various social "languages" come to interact with one another. The speaker strives to get a reading on his own word, and on his own conceptual system that determines this word, within the alien conceptual system of the understanding receiver; he enters into dialogical relationships with certain aspects of this system. The speaker breaks through the alien conceptual horizon of the listener, constructs his own utterance on alien territory, against his, the listener's, apperceptive background.

This new form of internal dialogism of the word is different from that form determined by an encounter with an alien word within the object itself: here it is not the object that serves as the arena for the encounter, but rather the subjective belief system of the listener. Thus this dialogism bears a more subjective, psychological and (frequently) random character, sometimes crassly accommodating, sometimes provocatively polemical. Very often, especially in the rhetorical forms, this orientation toward the listener and the related internal dialogism of the word may simply overshadow the object: the strong point of any concrete listener becomes a self-sufficient focus of attention, and one that interferes with the word's creative work on its referent.

Although they differ in their essentials and give rise to varying stylistic effects in discourse, the dialogic relationship toward an alien word within the object and the relationship toward an alien word in the anticipated answer of the listener can, nevertheless, be very tightly interwoven with each other, becoming almost indistinguishable during stylistic analysis.

Thus, discourse in Tolstoy is characterized by a sharp internal dialogism, and this discourse is moreover dialogized in the belief system of the reader – whose peculiar semantic and expressive characteristics Tolstoy acutely senses – as well as in the object. These two lines of dialogization (having in most cases polemical overtones) are tightly interwoven in his style: even in the most "lyrical" expressions and the most "epic" descriptions, Tolstoy's discourse harmonizes and disharmonizes (more often disharmonizes) with various aspects of the heteroglot socio-verbal consciousness ensnaring the object, while at the same time polemically invading the reader's belief and evaluative system, striving to stun and destroy the apperceptive background of the reader's active understanding. In this respect Tolstoy is an heir of the eighteenth century, especially of Rousseau. This propagandizing impulse sometimes leads to a narrowing-down of heteroglot social consciousness (against which Tolstoy polemicizes) to the consciousness of his immediate contemporary, a contemporary of the day and not of the epoch; what follows from this is a radical concretization of dialogization (almost always undertaken in the service of a polemic). For this reason Tolstoy's dialogization, no matter how acutely we sense it in the expressive profile of his style, sometimes requires special historical or literary commentary: we are not sure with *what* precisely a given tone is in harmony or disharmony, for this dissonance or consonance has entered into the positive project of creating a style.[13] It is true that such extreme concreteness (which approaches at time the feuilleton) is present only in those secondary aspects, the overtones of internal dialogization in Tolstoy's discourse.

In those examples of the internal dialogization of discourse that we have chosen (the internal, as contrasted with the external, compositionally marked, dialogue) the relationship to the alien word, to an alien utterance enters into the positing of the style. Style organically contains within itself indices that reach outside itself, a correspondence of its own elements and the elements of an alien context. The internal politics of style (how the elements are put together) is determined by its external politics (its relationship to alien discourse). The word lives, as it were, on the boundary between its own context and another, alien, context.

In any actual dialogue the rejoinder also leads such a double life: it is structured and conceptualized in the context of the dialogue as a whole, which consists of its own utterances ("own" from the point of view of the speaker) and of alien utterances (those of the partner). One cannot excise the rejoinder from this combined context made up of one's own words and the words of another without losing its sense and tone. It is an organic part of a heteroglot unity.

The phenomenon of internal dialogization, as we have said, is present to a greater or lesser extent in all realms of the life of the word. But if in extra-artistic prose (everyday, rhetorical, scholarly) dialogization usually stands apart, crystallizes into a special kind of act of its own and runs its course in ordinary dialogue or in other, compositionally clearly marked forms for mixing and polemicizing with the discourse of another – then in *artistic* prose, and especially in the novel, this dialogization penetrates from within the very way in which the word conceives its object and its means for expressing itself, reformulating the semantics and syntactical structure of discourse. Here dialogic interorientation becomes, as it were, an event of discourse itself, animating from within and dramatizing discourse in all its aspects.

In the majority of poetic genres (poetic in the narrow sense), as we have said, the internal dialogization of discourse is not put to artistic use, it does not enter into the work's "aesthetic object," and is artificially extinguished in poetic discourse. In the novel, however, this internal dialogization becomes one of the most fundamental aspects of prose style and undergoes a specific artistic elaboration.

But internal dialogization can become such a crucial force for creating form only where individual differences and contradictions are enriched by social heteroglossia, where dialogic reverberations do not sound in the semantic heights of discourse (as happens in the rhetorical genres) but penetrate the deep strata of discourse, dialogize language itself and the world view a particular language has (the internal form of discourse) – where the dialogue of voices arises directly out of a social dialogue of "languages," where an alien utterance begins to sound like a socially alien language, where the orientation of the word among alien utterances changes into an orientation of a word among socially alien languages within the boundaries of one and the same national language.

In genres that are poetic in the narrow sense, the natural dialogization of the word is not put to artistic use, the word is sufficient unto itself and does not presume alien utterances beyond its own boundaries. Poetic style is by convention suspended from any mutual interaction with alien discourse, any allusion to alien discourse.

Any way whatever of alluding to alien languages, to the possibility of another vocabulary, another semantics, other syntactic forms and so forth, to the possibility of other linguistic points of view, is equally foreign to poetic style. It follows that any sense of the boundedness, the historicity, the social determination and specificity of one's own language is alien to poetic style, and therefore a critical qualified relationship to one's own language (as merely one of many languages in a heteroglot world) is foreign to poetic style – as is a related phenomenon, the incomplete commitment of oneself, of one's full meaning, to a given language.

Of course this relationship and the relationship to his own language (in greater or lesser degree) could never be foreign to a historically existent poet, as a human being surrounded by living hetero- and polyglossia; but this relationship could not find a place in the *poetic style* of his work without destroying that style, without transposing it into a prosaic key and in the process turning the poet into a writer of prose.

In poetic genres, artistic consciousness – understood as a unity of all the author's semantic and expressive intentions – fully realizes itself within its own language; in them alone is such consciousness fully immanent, expressing itself in it directly and without mediation, without conditions and without distance. The language of the poet is *his* language, he is utterly immersed in it, inseparable from it, he makes use of each form, each word, each expression according to its unmediated power to assign meaning (as it were, "without quotation marks"), that is, as a pure and direct expression of his own intention. No matter what "agonies of the word" the poet endured in the process of creation, in the finished work language is an obedient organ, fully adequate to the author's intention.

The language in a poetic work realizes itself as something about which there can be no doubt, something that cannot be disputed, something all-encompassing. Everything that the poet sees, understands and thinks, he does through the eyes of a given language, in its inner forms, and there is nothing that might require, for its expression, the help of any other or alien language. The language of the poetic genre is a unitary and singular Ptolemaic world outside of which nothing else exists and nothing else is needed. The concept of many worlds of language, all equal in their ability to conceptualize and to be expressive, is organically denied to poetic style.

The world of poetry, no matter how many contradictions and insoluble conflicts the poet develops within it, is always illumined by one unitary and indisputable discourse. Contradictions, conflicts and doubts remain in the object, in thoughts, in living experiences – in short, in the subject matter – but they do not enter into the language itself. In poetry, even discourse about doubts must be cast in a discourse that cannot be doubted.

To take responsibility for the language of the work as a whole at all of its points as *its* language, to assume a full solidarity with each of the work's aspects, tones, nuances – such is the fundamental prerequisite for poetic style; style so conceived is fully adequate to a single language and a single linguistic consciousness. The poet is not able to oppose his own poetic consciousness, his own intentions to the language that he uses, for he is completely within it and therefore cannot turn it into an object to be perceived, reflected upon or related to. Language is present to him only from inside, in the work it does to effect its intention, and not from outside, in its objective specificity and boundedness. Within the limits of poetic style, direct unconditional intentionality, language at its full weight and the objective display of language (as a socially and historically limited linguistic reality) are all simultaneous, but incompatible. The unity and singularity of language are the indispensable prerequisites for a realization of the direct (but not objectively typifying) intentional individuality of poetic style and of its monologic steadfastness.

This does not mean, of course, that heteroglossia or even a foreign language is completely shut out of a poetic work. To be sure, such possibilities are limited: a certain latitude for heteroglossia exists only in the "low" poetic genres – in the satiric and comic genres and others. Nevertheless, heteroglossia (other socio-ideological languages) can be introduced into purely poetic genres, primarily in the speeches of characters. But in such a context it is objective. It appears, in essence, as a *thing*, it does not lie on the *same* plane with the real language of the work: it is the depicted gesture of one of the characters and does not appear as an aspect of the word doing the depicting. Elements of heteroglossia enter here not in the capacity of another language carrying its own particular points of view, about which one can say things not expressible in one's own language, but rather in the capacity of a depicted thing. Even when speaking of alien things, the poet speaks in his own language. To shed light on an alien world, he never resorts to an alien language, even though it might in fact be more adequate to that world. Whereas the writer of prose, by contrast – as we shall see – attempts to talk about even his *own* world in an alien language (for example, in the nonliterary language of the teller of tales, or the representative of a specific socio-ideological group); he often measures his own world by alien linguistic standards.

As a consequence of the prerequisites mentioned above, the language of poetic genres, when they approach their stylistic limit,[14] often becomes authoritarian, dogmatic and conservative, sealing itself off from the influence of extraliterary social dialects. Therefore such ideas as a special "poetic language," a "language of the gods," a "priestly language of poetry" and so forth could flourish on poetic soil. It is noteworthy that the poet, should he not accept the given literary language, will sooner resort to the artificial creation of a new language specifically for poetry than he will to the exploitation of actual available social dialects. Social languages are filled with specific objects, typical, socially localized and limited, while the artificially created language of poetry must be a

M. M. BAKHTIN

directly intentional language, unitary and singular. Thus, when Russian prose writers at the beginning of the twentieth century began to show a profound interest in dialects and *skaz*, the Symbolists (Bal'mont, V. Ivanov) and later the Futurists dreamed of creating a special "language of poetry," and even made experiments directed toward creating such a language (those of V. Khlebnikov).

The idea of a special unitary and singular language of poetry is a typical utopian philosopheme of poetic discourse: it is grounded in the actual conditions and demands of poetic style, which is always a style adequately serviced by one directly intentional language from whose point of view other languages (conversational, business and prose languages, among others) are perceived as objects that are in no way its equal.[15] The idea of a "poetic language" is yet another expression of that same Ptolemaic conception of the linguistic and stylistic world.

Language – like the living concrete environment in which the consciousness of the verbal artist lives – is never unitary. It is unitary only as an abstract grammatical system of normative forms, taken in isolation from the concrete, ideological conceptualizations that fill it, and in isolation from the uninterrupted process of historical becoming that is a characteristic of all living language. Actual social life and historical becoming create within an abstractly unitary national language a multitude of concrete worlds, a multitude of bounded verbal-ideological and social belief systems; within these various systems (identical in the abstract) are elements of language filled with various semantic and axiological content and each with its own different sound.

Literary language – both spoken and written – although it is unitary not only in its shared, abstract, linguistic markers but also in its forms for conceptualizing these abstract markers, is itself stratified and heteroglot in its aspect as an expressive system, that is, in the forms that carry its meanings.

This stratification is accomplished first of all by the specific organisms called *genres*. Certain features of language (lexicological, semantic, syntactic) will knit together with the intentional aim, and with the overall accentual system inherent in one or another genre: oratorical, publicistic, newspaper and journalistic genres, the genres of low literature (penny dreadfuls, for instance) or, finally, the various genres of high literature. Certain features of language take on the specific flavor of a given genre: they knit together with specific points of view, specific approaches, forms of thinking, nuances and accents characteristic of the given genre.

In addition, there is interwoven with this generic stratification of language a *profes-sional* stratification of language, in the broad sense of the term "professional": the language of the lawyer, the doctor, the businessman, the politician, the public education teacher and so forth, and these sometimes coincide with, and sometimes depart from, the stratification into genres. It goes without saying that these languages differ from each other not only in their vocabularies; they involve specific forms for manifesting inten-tions, forms for making conceptualization and evaluation concrete. And even the very language of the writer (the poet or novelist) can be taken as a professional jargon on a par with professional jargons.

What is important to us here is the intentional dimensions, that is, the denotative and expressive dimension of the "shared" language's stratification. It is in fact not the neutral linguistic components of language being stratified and differentiated, but rather a situation in which the intentional possibilities of language are being expropriated: these possibilities are realized in specific directions, filled with specific content, they are made concrete, particular, and are permeated with concrete value judgments; they knit together with specific objects and with the belief systems of certain genres of expression and points of view peculiar to particular professions. Within these points of view, that is, for the speakers of the language themselves, these generic languages and professional jargons are directly intentional – they denote and express directly and fully, and are capable of expressing themselves without mediation; but outside, that is, for those not participating in the given purview, these languages may be treated as objects, as typifactions, as local color. For such outsiders, the intentions permeating these languages become *things*, limited in their meaning and expression; they attract to, or excise from, such language a particular word – making it difficult for the word to be utilized in a directly intentional way, without any qualifications.

But the situation is far from exhausted by the generic and professional stratification of the common literary language. Although at its very core literary language is frequently socially homogeneous, as the oral and written language of a dominant social group, there is nevertheless always present, even here, a certain degree of social differentiation, a social stratification, that in other eras can become extremely acute. Social stratification may here and there coincide with generic and professional stratification, but in essence it is, of course, a thing completely autonomous and peculiar to itself.

Social stratification is also and primarily determined by differences between the forms used to convey meaning and between the expressive planes of various belief systems – that is, stratification expresses itself in typical differences in ways used to conceptualize and accentuate elements of language, and stratification may not violate the abstractly linguistic dialectological unity of the shared literary language.

What is more, all socially significant world views have the capacity to exploit the intentional possibilities of language through the medium of their specific concrete instancing. Various tendencies (artistic and otherwise), circles, journals, particular newspapers, even particular significant artistic works and individual persons are all capable of stratifying language, in proportion to their social significance; they are capable of attracting its words and forms into their orbit by means of their own characteristic intentions and accents, and in so doing to a certain extent alienating these words and forms from other tendencies, parties, artistic works and persons.

Every socially significant verbal performance has the ability – sometimes for a long period of time, and for a wide circle of persons – to infect with its own intention certain aspects of language that had been affected by its semantic and expressive impulse, imposing on them specific semantic nuances and specific axiological overtones; thus, it can create slogan-words, curse-words, praise-words and so forth.

In any given historical moment of verbal-ideological life, each generation at each social level has its own language; moreover, every age group has as a matter of fact its own language, its own vocabulary, its own particular accentual system that, in their turn, vary depending on social level, academic institution (the language of the cadet, the high school student, the trade school student are all different languages) and other stratifying factors. All this is brought about by socially typifying languages, no matter how narrow the social circle in which they are spoken. It is even possible to have a family jargon define the societal limits of a language, as, for instance, the jargon of the Irtenevs in Tolstoy, with its special vocabulary and unique accentual system.

And finally, at any given moment, languages of various epochs and periods of socio-ideological life cohabit with one another. Even languages of the day exist: one could say that today's and yesterday's socio-ideological and political "day" do not, in a certain sense, share the same language; every day represents another socio-ideological semantic "state of affairs," another vocabulary, another accentual system, with its own slogans, its own ways of assigning blame and praise. Poetry depersonalizes "days" in language, while prose, as we shall see, often deliberately intensifies difference between them, gives them embodied representation and dialogically opposes them to one another in unresolvable dialogues.

Thus at any given moment of its historical existence, language is heteroglot from top to bottom: it represents the coexistence of socio-ideological contradictions between the present and the past, between differing epochs of the past, between different socio-ideological groups in the present, between tendencies, schools, circles and so forth, all given a bodily form. These "languages" of heteroglossia intersect each other in a variety of ways, forming new socially typifying "languages."

Each of these "languages" of heteroglossia requires a methodology very different from the others; each is grounded in a completely different principle for marking differences and for establishing units (for some this principle is functional, in others it is the principle of theme and content, in yet others it is, properly speaking, a socio-dialectological principle). Therefore languages do not *exclude* each other, but rather intersect with each other in many different ways (the Ukrainian language, the language of the epic poem, of early Symbolism, of the student, of a particular generation of children, of the run-of-the-mill intellectual, of the Nietzschean and so on). It might even seem that the very word "language" loses all meaning in this process – for apparently there is no single plane on which all these "languages" might be juxtaposed to one another.

In actual fact, however, there does exist a common plane that methodologically justifies our juxtaposing them: all languages of heteroglossia, whatever the principle underlying them and making each unique, are specific points of view on the world, forms for conceptualizing the world in words, specific world views, each characterized by its own objects, meanings and values. As such they all may be juxtaposed to one another, mutually supplement one another, contradict one another and be interrelated dialogically. As such they encounter one another and coexist in the consciousness of real people – first and foremost, in the creative consciousness of people who write novels. As such, these languages live a real life, they struggle and evolve in an environment of social heteroglossia. Therefore they are all able to enter into the unitary plane of the novel, which can unite in itself parodic stylizations of generic languages, various forms of stylizations and illustrations of professional and period-bound languages, the languages of particular generations, of social dialects and others (as occurs, for example, in the English comic novel). They may all be drawn in by the novelist for the orchestration of his themes and for the refracted (indirect) expression of his intentions and values.

This is why we constantly put forward the referential and expressive – that is, intentional – factors as the force that stratifies and differentiates the common literary language, and not the linguistic markers (lexical coloration, semantic overtones, etc.) of generic languages, professional jargons and so forth – markers that are, so to speak, the sclerotic deposits of an intentional process, signs left behind on the path of the real living project of an intention, of the particular way it imparts meaning to general linguistic norms. These external markers, linguistically observable and fixable, cannot in themselves be understood or studied without understanding the specific conceptualization they have been given by an intention.

Discourse lives, as it were, beyond itself, in a living impulse [*napravlennost'*] toward the object; if we detach ourselves completely from this impulse all we have left is the naked corpse of the word, from which we can learn nothing at all about the social situation or the fate of a given word in life. *To study the word as such, ignoring the impulse that reaches out beyond it, is just as senseless as to study psychological experience outside the context of that real life toward which it was directed and by which it is determined.*

By stressing the intentional dimension of stratification in literary language, we are able, as has been said, to locate in a single series such methodologically heterogeneous phenomena as professional and social dialects, world views and individual artistic works, for in their intentional dimension one finds that common plane on which they can all be juxtaposed, and juxtaposed dialogically. The whole matter consists in the fact that there may be, between "languages," highly specific dialogic relations; no matter how these languages are conceived, they may all be taken as particular points of view on the world. However varied the social forces doing the work of stratification – a profession, a genre, a particular tendency, an individual personality – the work itself everywhere comes down to the (relatively) protracted and socially meaningful (collective) saturation of language with specific (and consequently limiting) intentions and accents. The longer this stratifying saturation goes on, the broader the social circle encompassed by it and consequently the more substantial the social force bringing about such a stratification of language, then the more sharply focused and stable will be those traces, the linguistic changes in the language markers (linguistic symbols), that are left behind in language as a result of this social force's activity – from stable (and consequently social) semantic nuances to authentic dialectological markers (phonetic, morphological and others), which permit us to speak of particular social dialects.

As a result of the work done by all these stratifying forces in language, there are no "neutral" words and forms – words and forms that can belong to "no one"; language has been completely taken over, shot through with intentions and accents. For any individual consciousness living in it, language is not an abstract system of normative forms but rather a concrete heteroglot conception of the world. All words have the "taste" of a profession, a genre, a tendency, a party, a particular work, a particular person, a generation, an age group, the day and hour. Each word tastes of the context and contexts in which it has lived its socially charged life; all words and forms are populated by intentions. Contextual overtones (generic, tendentious, individualistic) are inevitable in the word.

As a living, socio-ideological concrete thing, as heteroglot opinion, language, for the individual consciousness, lies on the borderline between oneself and the other. The word in language is half someone else's. It becomes "one's own" only when the speaker populates it with his own intention, his own accent, when he appropriates the word, adapting it to his own semantic and expressive intention. Prior to this moment of appropriation, the word does not exist in a neutral and impersonal language (it is not,

M. M. BAKHTIN

after all, out of a dictionary that the speaker gets his words!), but rather it exists in other people's mouths, in other people's contexts, serving other people's intentions: it is from there that one must take the word, and make it one's own. And not all words for just anyone submit equally easily to this appropriation, to this seizure and transformation into private property: many words stubbornly resist, others remain alien, sound foreign in the mouth of the one who appropriated them and who now speaks them; they cannot be assimilated into his context and fall out of it; it is as if they put themselves in quotation marks against the will of the speaker. Language is not a neutral medium that passes freely and easily into the private property of the speaker's intentions; it is populated – overpopulated – with the intentions of others. Expropriating it, forcing it to submit to one's own intentions and accents, is a difficult and complicated process.

We have so far proceeded on the assumption of the abstract-linguistic (dialectological) unity of literary language. But even a literary language is anything but a closed dialect. Within the scope of literary language itself there is already a more or less sharply defined boundary between everyday-conversational language and written language. Distinctions between genres frequently coincide with dialectological distinctions (for example, the high – Church Slavonic – and the low – conversational – genres of the eighteenth century); finally, certain dialects may be legitimized in literature and thus to a certain extent be appropriated by literary language.

As they enter literature and are appropriated to literary language, dialects in this new context lose, of course, the quality of closed socio-linguistic systems; they are deformed and in fact cease to be that which they had been simply as dialects. On the other hand, these dialects, on entering the literary language and preserving within it their own dialectological elasticity, their other-languagedness, have the effect of deforming the literary language; it, too, ceases to be that which it had been, a closed socio-linguistic system. Literary language is a highly distinctive phenomenon, as is the linguistic consciousness of the educated person who is its agent; within it, intentional diversity of speech [*raznorečivost'*] (which is present in every living dialect as a closed system) is transformed into diversity of language [*raznojazyčie*]; what results is not a single language but a dialogue of languages.

The national literary language of a people with a highly developed art of prose, especially if it is novelistic prose with a rich and tension-filled verbal-ideological history, is in fact an organized microcosm that reflects the macrocosm not only of national heteroglossia, but of European heteroglossia as well. The unity of a literary language is not a unity of a single, closed language system, but is rather a highly specific unity of several "languages" that have established contact and mutual recognition with each other (merely one of which is poetic language in the narrow sense). Precisely this constitutes the peculiar nature of the methodological problem in literary language.

Concrete socio-ideological language consciousness, as it becomes creative – that is, as it becomes active as literature – discovers itself already surrounded by heteroglossia and not at all a single, unitary language, inviolable and indisputable. The actively literary linguistic consciousness at all times and everywhere (that is, in all epochs of literature historically available to us) comes upon "languages," and not language. Consciousness finds itself inevitably facing the necessity of *having to choose a language*. With each literary-verbal performance, consciousness must actively orient itself amidst heteroglossia, it must move in and occupy a position for itself within it, it chooses, in other words, a "language." Only by remaining in a closed environment, one without writing or thought, completely off the maps of socio-ideological becoming, could a man fail to sense this activity of selecting a language and rest assured in the inviolability of his own language, the conviction that his language is predetermined.

Even such a man, however, deals not in fact with a single language, but with languages – except that the place occupied by each of these languages is fixed and indisputable, the movement from one to the other is predetermined and not a thought process; it is as if these languages were in different chambers. They do not collide with each other in his consciousness, there is no attempt to coordinate them, to look at one of these languages through the eyes of another language.

Thus an illiterate peasant, miles away from any urban center, naively immersed in an unmoving and for him unshakable everyday world, nevertheless lived in several language systems: he prayed to God in one language (Church Slavonic), sang songs in another, spoke to his family in a third and, when he began to dictate petitions to the local authorities through a scribe, he tried speaking yet a fourth language (the official-literate language, "paper" language). All these are *different languages*, even from the point of view of abstract socio-dialectological markers. But these languages were not dialogically coordinated in the linguistic consciousness of the peasant; he passed from one to the other without thinking, automatically: each was indisputably in its own place, and the place of each was indisputable. He was not yet able to regard one language (and the verbal world corresponding to it) through the eyes of another language (that is, the language of everyday life and the everyday world with the language of prayer or song, or vice versa).[16]

As soon as a critical interanimation of languages began to occur in the consciousness of our peasant, as soon as it became clear that these were not only various different languages but even internally variegated languages, that the ideological systems and approaches to the world that were indissolubly connected with these languages contradicted each other and in no way could live in peace and quiet with one another – then the inviolability and predetermined quality of these languages came to an end, and the necessity of actively choosing one's orientation among them began.

The language and world of prayer, the language and world of song, the language and world of labor and everyday life, the specific language and world of local authorities, the new language and world of the workers freshly immigrated to the city – all these languages and worlds sooner or later emerged from a state of peaceful and moribund equilibrium and revealed the speech diversity in each.

Of course the actively literary linguistic consciousness comes upon an even more varied and profound heteroglossia within literary language itself, as well as outside it. Any fundamental study of the stylistic life of the word must begin with this basic fact. The nature of the heteroglossia encountered and the means by which one orients oneself in it determine the concrete stylistic life that the word will lead.

The poet is a poet insofar as he accepts the idea of a unitary and singular language and a unitary, monologically sealed-off utterance. These ideas are immanent in the poetic genres with which he works. In a condition of actual contradiction, these are what determine the means of orientation open to the poet. The poet must assume a complete single-personed hegemony over his own language, he must assume equal responsibility for each one of its aspects and subordinate them to his own, and only

M. M. BAKHTIN

his own, intentions. Each word must express the poet's *meaning* directly and without mediation; there must be no distance between the poet and his word. The meaning must emerge from language as a single intentional whole: none of its stratification, its speech diversity, to say nothing of its language diversity, may be reflected in any fundamental way in his poetic work.

To achieve this, the poet strips the word of others' intentions, he uses only such words and forms (and only in such a way) that they lose their link with concrete intentional levels of language and their connection with specific contexts. Behind the words of a poetic work one should not sense any typical or reified images of genres (except for the given poetic genre), nor professions, tendencies, directions (except the direction chosen by the poet himself), nor world views (except for the unitary and singular world view of the poet himself), nor typical and individual images of speaking persons, their speech mannerisms or typical intonations. *Everything that enters the work must immerse itself in Lethe, and forget its previous life in any other contexts: language may remember only its life in poetic contexts (in such contexts, however, even concrete reminiscences are possible).*

Of course there always exists a limited sphere of more or less concrete contexts, and a connection with them must be deliberately evidenced in poetic discourse. But these contexts are purely semantic and, so to speak, accented in the abstract; in their linguistic dimension they are impersonal or at least no particularly concrete linguistic specificity is sensed behind them, no particular manner of speech and so forth, no socially typical linguistic face (the possible personality of the narrator) need peek out from behind them. Everywhere there is only one face – the linguistic face of the author, answering for every word as if it were his own. No matter how multiple and varied these semantic and accentual threads, associations, pointers, hints, correlations that emerge from every poetic word, one language, one conceptual horizon, is sufficient to them all; there is no need of heteroglot social contexts. What is more, the very movement of the poetic symbol (for example, the unfolding of a metaphor) presumes precisely this unity of language, an unmediated correspondence with its object. Social diversity of speech, were it to arise in the work and stratify its language, would make impossible both the normal development and the activity of symbols within it.

The very rhythm of poetic genres does not promote any appreciable degree of stratification. *Rhythm, by creating an unmediated involvement between every aspect of the accentual system of the whole* (via the most immediate rhythmic unities), destroys in embryo those social worlds of speech and of persons that are potentially embedded in the word: in any case, rhythm puts definite limits on them, does not let them unfold or materialize. Rhythm serves to strengthen and concentrate even further the unity and hermetic quality of the surface of poetic style, and of the unitary language that this style posits.

As a result of this work – stripping all aspects of language of the intentions and accents of other people, destroying all traces of social heteroglossia and diversity of language – a tension-filled unity of language is achieved in the poetic work. This unity may be naive, and present only in those extremely rare epochs of poetry, when poetry had not yet exceeded the limits of a closed, unitary, undifferentiated social circle whose language and ideology were not yet stratified. More often than not, we experience a profound and conscious tension through which the unitary poetic language of a work rises from the heteroglot and language-diverse chaos of the literary language contemporary to it.

This is how the poet proceeds. The novelist working in prose (and almost any prose writer) takes a completely different path. He welcomes the heteroglossia and language diversity of the literary and extraliterary language into his own work not only not weakening them but even intensifying them (for he interacts with their particular self-consciousness). It is in fact out of this stratification of language, its speech diversity and even language diversity, that he constructs his style, while at the same time he maintains the unity of his own creative personality and the unity (although it is, to be sure, unity of another order) of his own style.

The prose writer does not purge words of intentions and tones that are alien to him, he does not destroy the seeds of social heteroglossia embedded in words, he does not eliminate those language characterizations and speech mannerisms (potential narrator-personalities) glimmering behind the words and forms, each at a different distance from the ultimate semantic nucleus of his work, that is, the center of his own personal intentions.

The language of the prose writer deploys itself according to degrees of greater or lesser proximity to the author and to his ultimate semantic instantiation: certain aspects of language directly and unmediatedly express (as in poetry) the semantic and expressive intentions of the author, others refract these intentions; the writer of prose does not meld completely with any of these words, but rather accents each of them in a particular way – humorously, ironically, parodically and so forth;[17] yet another group may stand even further from the author's ultimate semantic instantiation, still more thoroughly refracting his intentions; and there are, finally, those words that are completely denied any authorial intentions: the author does not express *himself* in them (as the author of the word) – rather, he *exhibits* them as a unique speech-thing, they function for him as something completely reified. Therefore the stratification of language – generic, professional, social in the narrow sense, that of particular world views, particular tendencies, particular individuals, the social speech diversity and language-diversity (dialects) of language – upon entering the novel establishes its own special order within it, and becomes a unique artistic system, which orchestrates the intentional theme of the author.

Thus a prose writer can distance himself from the language of his own work, while at the same time distancing himself, in varying degrees, from the different layers and aspects of the work. He can make use of language without wholly giving himself up to it, he may treat it as semi-alien or completely alien to himself, while compelling language ultimately to serve all his own intentions. The author does not speak in a given language (from which he distances himself to a greater or lesser degree), but he speaks, as it were, *through* language, a language that has somehow more or less materialized, become objectivized, that he merely ventriloquates.

The prose writer as a novelist does not strip away the intentions of others from the heteroglot language of his works, he does not violate those socio-ideological cultural horizons (big and little worlds) that open up behind heteroglot languages – rather, he welcomes them into his work. The prose writer makes use of words that are already populated with the social intentions of others and compels them to serve his own new intentions, to serve a second master. Therefore the intentions of the prose writer are refracted, and refracted *at different angles*, depending on the degree to which the refracted, heteroglot languages he deals with are socio-ideologically alien, already embodied and already objectivized.

M. M. BAKHTIN

The orientation of the word amid the utterances and languages of others, and all the specific phenomena connected with this orientation, takes on *artistic* significance in novel style. Diversity of voices and heteroglossia enter the novel and organize themselves within it into a structured artistic system. This constitutes the distinguishing feature of the novel as a genre.

Any stylistics capable of dealing with the distinctiveness of the novel as a genre must be a *sociological stylistics*. The internal social dialogism of novelistic discourse requires the concrete social context of discourse to be exposed, to be revealed as the force that determines its entire stylistic structure, its "form" and its "content," determining it not from without, but from within; for indeed, social dialogue reverberates in all aspects of discourse, in those relating to "content" as well as the "formal" aspects themselves.

The development of the novel is a function of the deepening of dialogic essence, its increased scope and greater precision. Fewer and fewer neutral, hard elements ("rock bottom truths") remain that are not drawn into dialogue. Dialogue moves into the deepest molecular and, ultimately, subatomic levels.

Of course, even the poetic word is social, but poetic forms reflect lengthier social processes, i.e., those tendencies in social life requiring centuries to unfold. The novelistic word, however, registers with extreme subtlety the tiniest shifts and oscillations of the social atmosphere; it does so, moreover, while registering it as a whole, in all of its aspects.

When heteroglossia enters the novel it becomes subject to an artistic reworking. The social and historical voices populating language, all its words and all its forms, which provide language with its particular concrete conceptualizations, are organized in the novel into a structured stylistic system that expresses the differentiated socio-ideological position of the author amid the heteroglossia of his epoch.

NOTES

1   As recently as the 1920s, V. M. Žirmunskij [important fellow-traveler of the formalists, ed.] was writing: "When lyrical poetry appears to be authentically a work of *verbal art*, due to its choice and combination of words (on semantic as well as sound levels) all of which are completely subordinated to the aesthetic project, Tolstoy's novel, by contrast, which is free in its verbal composition, does not use words as an artistically significant element of interaction but as a neutral medium or as a system of significations subordinated (as happens in practical speech) to the communicative function, directing our attention to thematic aspects quite abstracted from purely verbal considerations. We cannot call such a *literary work* a work of *verbal art* or, in any case, not in the sense that the term is used for lyrical poetry" ["On the Problem of the Formal Method," in an anthology of his articles, *Problems of a Theory of Literature* (Leningrad, 1928, p. 173); Russian edition: "K voprosu o 'formal'nom metode'," in *Voprosy teorii literatury*, (L., 1928)].

2   Artistic prose style has been studied in Russia by the Formalists largely on these two last levels, that is, either *skaz* (Eichenbaum) or plot-informational aspects (Shklovsky) were studied as most characteristic of literary prose. [See also pp. 31–53 in this book.]

3   Such a solution to the problem was especially tempting to adherents of the formal method in poetics: in fact, the re-establishment of rhetoric, with all its rights, greatly strengthens the Formalist position. Formalist rhetoric is a necessary addition to Formalist poetics. Our

Formalists were being completely consistent when they spoke of the necessity of reviving rhetoric alongside poetics (on this, see B. M. Eichenbaum, *Literature*, [*Literatura*; Leningrad, 1927], pp. 147–148).

4   Gustav Shpet (1879–1937), outstanding representative of the neo-Kantian and (especially) Husserlian traditions in Russia; as professor at the University of Moscow for many years he influenced many (among others, the young Roman Jakobson). *M. H. note.*

5   Originally in his *Aesthetic Fragments* [*Estetičeskie fragmenty*] ; in a more complete aspect in the book *The Inner Form of the Word* [*Vnutrennjaja forma slova*] (M., 1927).

6   *Vnutrennjaja forma slova*, p. 215.

7   Viktor Vinogradov (1895–1969), outstanding linguistic and student of style in literature, a friendly critic of the Formalists, and an important theorist in his own right (especially his work on *skaz* technique). *M. H. note.*

8   V. V. Vinogradov, *On Artistic Prose* [*O xudožestvennom proze*], Moscow-Leningrad, 1930, pp. 75–106.

9   Linguistics acknowledges only a mechanical reciprocal influencing and intermixing of languages, (that is, one that is unconscious and determined by social conditions) which is reflected in abstract linguistic elements (phonetic and morphological).

10   Highly significant in this respect is the struggle that must be undertaken in such movements as Rousseauism, Naturalism, Impressionism, Acmeism, Dadaism, Surrealism and analogous schools with the "qualified" nature of the object (a struggle occasioned by the idea of a return to primordial consciousness, to original consciousness, to the object itself in itself, to pure perception and so forth).

11   The Horatian lyric, Villon, Heine, Laforgue, Annenskij and others – despite the fact that these are extremely varied instances.

12   Cf. V. Vinogradov's book *On Artistic Prose*, the chapter "Rhetoric and Poetics," pp. 75ff., where definitions taken from the older rhetorics are introduced.

13   Cf. B. M. Eichenbaum's book *Lev Tolstoj*, book I (Leningrad, 1928), which contains much relevant material; for example, an explication of the topical context of "Family Happiness."

14   It goes without saying that we continually advance as typical the extreme to which poetic genres aspire; in concrete examples of poetic works it is possible to find features fundamental to prose, and numerous hybrids of various generic types exist. These are especially widespread in periods of shift in literary poetic languages.

15   Such was the point of view taken by Latin toward national languages in the Middle Ages.

16   We are of course deliberately simplifying: the real-life peasant could and did do this to a certain extent.

17   That is to say, the words are not his if we understand them as direct words, but they are his as things that are being transmitted ironically, exhibited and so forth, that is, as words that are understood from the distances appropriate to humor, irony, parody, etc.

M. M. BAKHTIN

The Signifying Monkey

Henry Louis Gates, Jr.

Henry Louis Gates, Jr. (b. 1950)

Born in Keyser, West Virginia, Henry Louis Gates, Jr. was educated at Yale University and Clare College, Cambridge, where he received his doctorate in 1979. Gates taught at Yale University (1976–85), Cornell University (1985–90), and Duke University (1990); in 1991 he moved to Harvard University, where he is W. E. B. Du Bois Professor of the Humanities, chair of the African and African American Studies Department, and Director of the W. E. B. Du Bois Institute for African and African American Research. *Time* Magazine, which named Gates one of the 25 most influential Americans in 1997, called him "a whirlwind academic impresario." Committed to bringing African American and African history and culture to the American public, Gates regularly writes for such non-academic publications as the *New Yorker*, the *New York Times*, and the *Nation* (as well as *Sports Illustrated* and *Entertainment Weekly*). He has also been involved in several important editorial projects: Gates began the Black Periodical Fiction Project (1980), which republishes the work of forgotten African American authors; co-edited both the *Norton*

Zora Neale Hurston and the Speakerly Text

[...] Hurston, whose definition of *signify* in *Mules and Men* is one of the earliest in the linguistic literature, has made *Their Eyes Were Watching God* into a paradigmatic Signifyin(g) text. Its narrative strategies resolve that implicit tension between the literal and the figurative, between the semantic and the rhetorical, contained in standard usages of the term *signifying*. *Their Eyes* draws upon the trope of Signifyin(g) both as thematic matter and as a rhetorical strategy. Janie, as we shall see, gains her voice within her husband's store not only by daring to speak aloud where others might hear, but by engaging in that ritual of Signifyin(g) (which her husband had expressly disallowed) and by openly Signifyin(g) upon the impotency of her husband, Joe, Mayor, "I god," himself. Janie kills her husband, rhetorically, by publicly naming his impotence (with her voice) in a public ritual of Signifyin(g). His image fatally wounded, he soon succumbs to a displaced "kidney" failure.

Their Eyes Signifies upon Toomer's *Cane* in several ways. First, its plot reverses the movement of *Cane*'s plot. Whereas the settings of *Cane* move from broad open fields, through ever-diminishing physical spaces, to a circle of light in a dark and damp cellar (corresponding to the levels of self-consciousness of the central characters), *Their Eyes'* settings within its embedded narrative move from the confines of Nanny's tiny cabin in the Washburns' backyard, through increasingly larger physical structures, finally ending "on the Muck" in the Everglades, where she and her lover, Tea Cake, realize the male-female relationship for which Janie had longed so very urgently. Similarly, whereas *Cane* represents painfully unconsummated relationships, the agony of which seems to intensify in direct proportion to the diminishment of physical setting, true consummation occurs in *Their Eyes* once Janie eschews the values implied by material possessions (such as middle-class houses, especially those on which sit idle women who rock their lives away), learns to play with Tea Cake, and then moves to the swamp. The trope of the swamp, furthermore, in *Their Eyes* signifies exactly the opposite of what it does in Du Bois's *Quest for the Silver Fleece*. Whereas the swamp in Du Bois's text figures an uncontrolled chaos that must be plowed under and controlled, for Hurston the swamp is the trope of the freedom of erotic love, the antithesis of the bourgeois life and order that her protagonist flees but to which Du Bois's protagonists aspire. Whereas Du Bois's characters gain economic security by plowing up and cultivating cotton in the swamp, Janie flees the bourgeois life that Du Bois's characters realize, precisely by abandoning traditional values for the uncertainties and the potential chaos of the uncultivated, untamed swamp, where love and death linger side by side. Du Bois's shadowy figure who seems to dwell in the swamp, we recall, is oddly enough named Zora.

But *Their Eyes* is also a paradigmatic Signifyin(g) text because of its representations, through several subtexts or embedded narratives presented as the characters' discourse, of traditional black rhetorical games or rituals. It is the text's imitation of these examples of traditionally black rhetorical rituals and modes of storytelling that allows us to think of it as a speakerly text. For in a speakerly text certain rhetorical structures seem to exist primarily as representations of oral narration, rather than as integral aspects of plot or character development. These verbal rituals signify the sheer play of black language which *Their Eyes* seems to celebrate. These virtuoso displays of verbal play constitute Hurston's complex response to the New Negro poets' strictures of the use of dialect as a poetic diction. *Their Eyes Were Watching God*'s narrative Signifies upon James Weldon Johnson's arguments against dialect just as surely as Sterling A. Brown's *Southern Road* did. Indeed, we are free to think of these two texts as discursive analogues. Moreover, Hurston's masterful use of free indirect discourse (*style indirect libre*) allows her to Signify upon the tension between the two voices of Toomer's *Cane* by adding to direct and indirect speech a strategy through which she can privilege the black oral tradition, which Toomer found to be problematical and dying.

As I stated earlier, figures of play are the dominant repeated figures in the second half of *Their Eyes*, replacing the text's figures of flowering vegetation, which as we have seen repeat at least two dozen times in the first half of the text. After Janie meets Tea Cake, figures of play supplant those floral figures that appeared each time Janie dreamed of consummated love. Moreover, it is the rhetorical play that occurs regularly on the porch of his store that Janie's husband Jody prevents Janie from enjoying. As the text reads:

> Janie loved the conversation and sometimes she thought up good stories on the mule, but Joe had forbidden her to indulge. He didn't want her talking after such trashy people. "You'se Mrs. Mayor Starks, Janie. I god, Ah can't see what uh woman uh yo' sability would want tuh be treasurin' all dat gum-grease from folks dat don't even own de house dey sleep in. 'Tain't no earthly use. They's jus' some puny humans playin' round de toes uh Time."[1]

When the Signifyin(g) rituals commence – rituals that the text describes as created by "big picture talkers [who] were using a side of the world for a canvas" – Jody forces Janie to retreat inside the store, much against her will.

Eventually, however, this friction ignites a heated argument between the two, the key terms of which shall be repeated, in reverse, when Janie later falls in love with Tea Cake. Their exchange follows:

> "Ah had tuh laugh at de people out dere in de woods dis mornin', Janie. You can't help but laugh at de capers they cuts. But all the same, Ah wish mah people would git mo' business in 'em and not spend so much time on foolishness."

"Everybody can't be lak you, Jody. Somebody is bound tuh want tuh laugh and play."

"Who don't love tuh laugh and play?"

"You make out like you don't, anyhow." (p. 98)

It is this tension between work and play, between maintaining appearances of respectability and control against the seemingly idle, nonquantifiable verbal maneuvers that "produce" nothing, which becomes the central sign of the distance between Janie's unarticulated aspirations and the material aspirations signified by Jody's desire to "be a big voice," a self-designation that Jody repeats with alacrity almost as much as he repeats his favorite parenthetical, "I god."

"Play" is also the text's word for the Signifyin(g) rituals that imitate "courtship," such as the symbolic action executed by Sam Watson, Lige Moss, and Charlie Jones, which the text describes in this way: "They know it's not courtship. It's acting out courtship and everybody is in the play" (p. 105). Play, finally, is the irresistible love potion that Tea Cake administers to Janie. Tea Cake, an apparently unlikely suitor of Joe Starks's widow, since he is a drifter and is generally thought to be "irresponsible," seduces Janie by teaching her to play checkers. Responding to his challenge of a game with "Ah can't play uh lick," Tea Cake proceeds to set up the board and teach Janie the rules. Janie "found herself glowing inside. Somebody wanted her to play. Somebody thought it natural for her to play. That was even nice. She looked him over and got little thrills from every one of his good points" (p. 146). No one had taught her to play in her adulthood. The text repeats Joe's prohibition as Tea Cake's perceptive mode of seduction. As Tea Cake concludes prophetically, "You gointuh be uh good player too, after while." And "after while," Janie and Tea Cake teach each other to become "good players" in what the text depicts as a game of love.

This repeated figure of play is only the thematic analogue to the text's rhetorical play, plays of language that seem to be present essentially to reveal the complexity of black oral forms of narration. For *Their Eyes Were Watching God* is replete with storytellers, or Signifiers as the black tradition has named them. These Signifiers are granted a remarkable amount of space in this text to reveal their talents. These imitations of oral narrations, it is crucial to recall, unfold within what the text represents as Janie's framed tale, the tale of her quests with Tea Cake to the far horizon and her lonely return home. This oral narrative commences in chapter 2, while Janie and her friend, Phoeby, sit on Janie's back porch, and "the kissing, young darkness became a monstropolous old thing while Janie talked" (p. 19). Then follow almost three full pages of Janie's direct speech, "while all around the house, the night time put on flesh and blackness" (p. 23). Two paragraphs of narrative commentary follow Janie's narration; then, curiously, the narrative "fades" into "a spring-time afternoon in West Florida," the springtime of Janie's adolescence.

Without ever releasing its proprietary consciousness, the disembodied narrative voice reassumes control over the telling of Janie's story after nine paragraphs of direct discourse. We can characterize this narrative shift as from third person, to "no-person" (that is, the seemingly unmediated representation of Janie's direct speech), back to the third person of an embedded or framed narrative. This device we encounter most frequently in the storytelling devices of film, in which a first-person narrative yields, as it were, to the form of narration that we associate with the cinema. ("Kabnis," we

HENRY LOUIS GATES, JR.

remember, imitates the drama.) *Their Eyes Were Watching God* would seem to be imitating this mode of narration, with this fundamental difference: the bracketed tale, in the novel, is told by an omniscient, third-person narrator who reports thoughts, feelings, and events that Janie could not possibly have heard or seen. This framed narrative continues for the next eighteen chapters, until in chapter 20 the text indicates the end of Janie's storytelling to Phoeby, which we have overheard, by the broad white space and a series of widely spaced ellipses that I mentioned earlier.

This rather unusual form of narration of the tale-within-a-tale has been the subject of some controversy about the success or failure of Janie's depiction as a dynamic character who comes to know herself. Rather than retread that fruitless terrain, I would suggest that the subtleness of this narrative strategy allows for, as would no other mode of narration, the representation of the forms of oral narration that *Their Eyes* imitates so often – so often, in fact, that the very subject of this text would appear to be not primarily Janie's quest but the emulation of the phonetic, grammatical, and lexical structures of actual speech, an emulation designed to produce the illusion of oral narration. Indeed, each of the oral rhetorical structures emulated with Janie's bracketed tale functions to remind the reader that he or she is overhearing Janie's narrative to Phoeby, which unfolds on her porch, that crucial place of storytelling both in this text and in the black community. Each of these playful narratives is, by definition, a tale-within-the-bracketed-tale, and most exist as Significations of rhetorical play rather than events that develop the text's plot. Indeed, these embedded narratives, consisting as they do of long exchanges of direct discourse, often serve as plot impediments but simultaneously enable a multiplicity of narrative voices to assume control of the text, if only for a few paragraphs on a few pages, as Ellison explained his new narrative strategy to John Hersey.

Hurston is one of the few authors of our tradition who both theorized about her narrative process and defended it against the severe critiques of contemporaries such as Wright. Hurston's theory allows us to read *Their Eyes* through her own terms of critical order. It is useful to recount her theory of black oral narration, if only in summary, and then to use this to explicate the various rhetorical strategies that, collectively, comprise the narrative strategy of *Their Eyes Were Watching God*.

Hurston seems to be not only the first scholar to have defined the trope of Signifyin(g) but also the first to represent the ritual itself. Hurston represents a Signifyin(g) ritual in *Mules and Men*, then glosses the word *signify* as a means of "showing off," rhetorically. The exchange is an appropriate one to repeat, because it demonstrates that women most certainly can, and do, Signify upon men, and because it prefigures the scene of Signification in *Their Eyes* that proves to be a verbal sign of such importance to Janie's quest for consciousness:

"Talkin' 'bout dogs," put in Gene Oliver, "they got plenty sense. Nobody can't fool dogs much."

"And speakin' 'bout hams," cut in Big Sweet meaningly, "if Joe Willard don't stay out of dat bunk he was in last night, Ah'm gonter springle some salt down his back and sugar-cure *his* hams."

Joe snatched his pole out of the water with a jerk and glared at Big Sweet, who stood sidewise looking at him most pointedly.

"Aw, woman, quit tryin' to signify."

"Ah kin signify all Ah please, Mr. Nappy-Chin, so long as Ah know what Ah'm talkin' about."[2]

This is a classic Signification, an exchange of meaning and intention of some urgency between two lovers.

I use the word *exchange* here to echo Hurston's use in her essay, "Characteristics of Negro Expression." In this essay Hurston argues that "language is like money," and its development can be equated metaphorically with the development in the marketplace of the means of exchange from bartered "actual goods," which "evolve into coin" (coins symbolizing wealth). Coins evolve into legal tender, and legal tender evolves into "cheques for certain usages." Hurston's illustrations are especially instructive. People "with highly developed languages," she writes, "have words for detached ideas. That is legal tender." The linguistic equivalent of legal tender consists of words such as "chair," which comes to stand for "that-which-we-squat-on." "Groan-causers" evolves into "spear," and so on. "Cheque words" include those such as "ideation" and "pleonastic." *Paradise Lost* and *Sartor Resartus*, she continues, "are written in cheque words!" But "the primitive man," she argues, eschews legal tender and cheque words; he "exchanges descriptive words," describing "one act…in terms of another." More specifically, she concludes, black expression turns upon both the "interpretation of the English language in terms of pictures" and the supplement of what she calls "action words," such as "chop-axe," "sitting-chair," and "cook pot." It is the supplement of action, she maintains, which underscores her use of the word "exchange."[3]

Such an exchange, as we have seen, is that between Big Sweet and Joe Willard. As the exchange continues, not only does the characters' language exemplify Hurston's theory, but the definitions of Signifyin(g) that I have been drawing upon throughout this book are also exemplified:

"See dat?" Joe appealed to the other men. "We git a day off and figger we kin ketch some fish and enjoy ourselves, but naw, some wimmins got to drag behind us, even to de lake."

"You didn't figger Ah was draggin' behind you when you was bringin' dat Sears and Roebuck catalogue over to my house and beggin' me to choose my ruthers. Lemme tell *you* something, *any* time Ah shack up wid any man Ah gives myself de privilege to go wherever he might be, night or day. Ah got de law in my mouth."

"Lawd, ain't she specifyin'!" sniggered Wiley.

"Oh, Big Sweet does dat," agreed Richardson. "Ah knewed she had somethin' up her sleeve when she got Lucy and come along."

"Lawd," Willard said bitterly. "'My people, my people,' as de monkey said. You fool with Aunt Hagar's chillun and they'll sho discriminate you and put yo'name in de streets." (pp. 161–62)

Specifying, putting one's name in the streets, and "as de monkey said" are all figures for Signifyin(g). In *Dust Tracks on a Road*, Hurston even defines specifying as "giving a reading" in the following passage:

The bookless may have difficulty in reading a paragraph in a newspaper, but when they get down to "playing the dozens" [Signifyin(g)] they have no equal in America, and, I'd risk a

HENRY LOUIS GATES, JR.

sizable bet, in the whole world. Starting off in the first by calling you a seven-sided son-of-a-bitch, and pausing to name the sides, they proceed to "specify" until the tip-top branch of your family tree has been "given a reading."[4]

The sort of close reading that I am attempting here is also an act of specifying.

Let me return briefly to Hurston's theory of "Negro Expression" before turning to explicate rhetorical strategies at work in *Their Eyes Were Watching God.* Her typology of black oral narration, in addition to "picture" and "action" words, consists of what she calls "the will to adorn," by which she means the use of densely figurative language, the presence of "revision," which she defines as "[making] over a great part of the [English] tongue," and the use of "metaphor and simile," "the double-descriptive," and "verbal nouns." It is Hurston's sense of revision, defined as "originality [in] the modification of ideas" and "of language," as well as "reinterpretation," which I have defined in Chapter 2 as the ultimate meaning of the trope of Signifyin(g). By "revision," she also means "imitation" and "mimicry," for which she says "The Negro, the world over, is famous" and which she defines as "an art in itself." The Negro, she claims, imitates and revises, not "from a feeling of inferiority," rather "for the love of it." This notion of imitation, repetition, and revision, she maintains, is fundamental to "all art," indeed is the nature of art itself, even Shakespeare's.

Near the end of her compelling essay, Hurston argues that dialect is "Negro speech," and Negro speech, she contends throughout the essay, is quite capable of expressing the most subtle nuances of meaning, despite "the majority of writers of Negro dialect and the burnt-cork artists." "Fortunately," she concludes, "we don't have to believe them. We may go directly to the Negro and let him speak for himself." Using in large part Hurston's own theory of black oral narration, we can gain some understanding of the modes of narration at work in *Their Eyes* and thereby demonstrate why I have chosen to call it a speakerly text, a phrase that I derive both from Roland Barthes's opposition between the "readerly" and the "writerly" texts – the binarism of which I am here Signifyin(g) upon – as well as from the trope of the Talking Book, which not only is the Afro-American tradition's fundamental repeated trope but also is a phrase used by both Hurston and Ishmael Reed to define their own narrative strategies.

The "white man thinks in a written language," Hurston claims, while "the Negro thinks in hieroglyphics." By hieroglyphics, she means the "word-pictures" or the "thought pictures" as she defines these in *Their Eyes* (p. 81). It is a fairly straightforward matter to list just a few of what we might think of as Hurston's "figures of adornment," the specifically black examples of figurative language that she labels "simile and metaphor," "double-descriptives," and "verbal-nouns." Karla Holloway lists these as expressed in *Their Eyes:*

1. An envious heart makes a treacherous ear.
2. Us colored folks is branches without roots.
3. They's a lost ball in high grass.
4. She...left her wintertime wid me.
5. Ah wanted yuh to pick from a higher bush.
6. You got uh willin' mind, but youse too light behind.
7. ...he's de wind and we'se de grass.

---

8. He was a man wid salt in him.
9. ...what dat multiplied cockroach told you.
10. still-bait
11. big-bellies
12. gentlemanfied man
13. cemetary-dead
14. black-dark
15. duskin-down-dark[5]

This list certainly could be extended. Suffice it to say that the diction of both the characters' discourse and the free indirect discourse are replete with the three types of adornment that Hurston argued were fundamental to black oral narration.

In addition to these sorts of figures of adornment, *Their Eyes* is comprised of several long exchanges of direct discourse, which seem to be present in the text more for their own sake than to develop the plot. *Their Eyes* consists of a remarkable percentage of direct speech, rendered in black dialect, as if to display the capacity of black language itself to convey an extraordinarily wide variety of ideas and feelings. Frequently, these exchanges between characters extend for two or three pages, with little or no interruption from the text's narrator. When such narrative commentary does surface, it often serves to function as stage direction rather than as a traditional omniscient voice, as if to underscore Hurston's contention that it is "drama" that "permeates [the Negro's] entire self," and it is the dramatic to which black oral narration aspires. Because, as Hurston writes, "an audience is a necessary part of any drama," these Signifyin(g) rituals tend to occur outdoors, at the communal scene of oral instruction, on the porches of homes and stores.

From the novel's earliest scenes, the porch is both personified and then represented through a series of synecdoches as the undifferentiated "eyes," "mouth," and "ears" of the community. Of these three senses, however, it is the communal speaking voice – "Mouth-Almighty," as the text has it – which emerges early on as the most significant. Indeed, the first time the porch "speaks," the text represents its discourse in one paragraph of "direct quotation" consisting of ten sentences separated only by dashes, as if to emphasize the anonymous if collective voice of the community that the text proceeds to represent in several ways. Against this sort of communal narration the text pits Jody Starks, Janie's second husband, who repeatedly states that he wishes to become "a big voice." This voice, however, is the individual voice of domination. The figure of Jody's big voice comes to stand as a synecdoche of oppression, in opposition to the speech community of which Janie longs to become an integral part.

The representation of modes of black narration begins, as we have seen, with Janie's narration of her story to Phoeby, the framed tale in which most of the novel's action unfolds. Throughout this narrative, the word *voice* recurs with great frequency. Who speaks, indeed, proves to be of crucial import to Janie's quest for freedom, but who sees and who hears at all points in the text remain fundamental as well. Phoeby's "hungry listening," we recall, "helped Janie to tell her story." Almost as soon as Janie's narrative begins, however, Nanny assumes control of the text and narrates the story of Janie's genealogy, from slavery to the present, as Janie listens painfully. This quasi-slave narrative, rendered as a tale-within-a-tale, is one of the few instances of direct speech that serve as a function of the plot. Subsequent speaking narrators assume control of the narrative primarily to demonstrate forms of traditional oral narration.

These double narratives-within-the-narrative begin as soon as Janie and Jody move to Eatonville. Amos Hicks and Joe Coker engage in a brief and amusing exchange about the nature of storytelling generally and about the nature of figurative language specifically, a discussion to which we shall return. Tony Taylor next demonstrates the ironies of speech-making on the day of dedication of Jody's store, a speech that ends with requests that Janie address the community, only to be thwarted by her husband who says that "mah wife don't know nothin' 'bout no speech-makin.'" Jody's harsh actions, the narrator tell us ominously, "took the bloom off of things" for Janie. Subsequent forms of oral narration include "a traditional prayer-poem," a series of speeches, the sung communal poetry of the spirituals, but especially the front-porch Signifyin(g) rituals that serve to impede the plot. The porch is dominated by three narrators. Sam, Lige, and Walter are known as "the ringleaders of the mule-talkers," who sit for hours on the storefront porch and Signify upon Matt Bonner's yellow mule. These exchanges about the mule extend for pages (pp. 81–85, 87–96) and would seem to be present primarily to display the nature of storytelling, allowing a full range of characters' discourse to be heard.

At the end of the second mule Signification, still another tale-within-a-tale-within-a-tale unfolds, which we might think of as the allegory of the buzzards (pp. 96–97). After the second mule tale concludes with his mock funeral and mock eulogy, the disembodied narrator relates the narrative of "the already impatient buzzards," who proceed in ritual fashion to examine and disembowel the mule's carcass. This allegory, of course, serves to mock the preceding mock eulogy, complete with the speaking characters and a patterned oral ritual. This allegory, more especially, shatters completely any illusion the reader might have had that this was meant to be a realistic fiction, even though the text has naturalized the possibility of such an event occurring, if only by representing storytelling in direct speech as its principal mode of narration. Once the reader encounters the allegory of the buzzards, his or her generic expectations have been severely interrupted.

Two pages later, the text returns to more Signifyin(g) rituals, defined by the narrator as "eternal arguments," which "never ended because there was no end to reach. It was a contest in hyperbole," the narrator concludes, "carried on for no other reason" (p. 99). Sam Watson and Lige Moss then proceed to debate, for six pages, the nature of the subject and whether or not "you got to have a subjick tuh talk from, do yuh can't talk" (p. 100), and whether or not these sorts of "readings" have "points" (p. 102). Just as the two Signifiers are about to commence still another oral narration of High John de Conquer tales, three women come walking down the street and thereby generate three pages of rhetorical courtship rituals. At this point in the narrative, as at the beginning of the first mule tale, the omniscient narrator establishes the context by shifting from the past tense to the present tense, then disappears for pages and pages while the characters narrate, underscoring thereby the illusion of overhearing an event.

The most crucial of these scenes of represented speech is the devastating exchange in which Janie first speaks in public against her husband. This exchange is a Signifyin(g) ritual of the first order because Janie Signifies upon Jody's manhood, thereby ending his dominance over her and over the community, and thereby killing Jody's will to live. The exchange is marvelous. Jody begins the fatal confrontation by insulting Janie for improperly cutting a plug of tobacco:*pt* >

"I god almighty! A woman stay round uh store till she get old as Methusalem and still can't cut a little thing like a plug of tobacco! Don't stand dere rollin' yo' pop eyes at me wid yo' rump hangin' nearly to yo' knees!" (p. 121)

After a short, quick "big laugh," the crowd assembled in the store, "got to thinking and stopped. It was like somebody," the narrative continues, "snatched off part of a woman's clothes while she wasn't looking and the streets were crowded." But most remarkably of all, "Janie took the middle of the floor to talk right into Jody's face, and that was something that hadn't been done before."

Janie, as a startled Jody says, is speaking a new language, "Talkin' any such language as dat." "You de one started talkin' under people's clothes," she retorts. "Not me." Then, indeed, Janie proceeds to talk under clothes, after Jody says:

"'T'ain't no use in gettin' all mad, Janie, 'cause Ah mention you ain't no young gal no mo'. Nobody in heah ain't lookin' for no wife outa yuh. Old as you is." (p. 122)

Janie responds:

"Naw, Ah ain't no young gal no mo' but den Ah ain't no old woman neither. Ah reckon Ah looks mah age too. But Ah'm uh woman every inch of me, and Ah know it. Dat's uh whole lot more'n *you* kin say. You big-bellies round here and put out a lot of brag, but 'tain't nothin' to it but yo' big voice. Humph! Talkin' 'bout *me* lookin' old! When you pull down yo' britches, you look lak de change uh life." (pp. 122–23)

"Great God from Zion!" Sam Watson gasped. "Y'all really playin' de dozens tuhnight," the text reads, naming the sort of Signifyin(g) ritual that has occurred. "Wha-whut's dat you said?" Joe challenged, hoping that his ears had fooled him, to which lame retort "Walter taunted" in a synesthesia that the text has just naturalized for us: "You heard her, you ain't blind." Jody, we well know, now thoroughly shattered by the force of Janie's voice, soon succumbs to acute humiliation and his displaced kidney disorder. As he lies dying, Janie contemplates "what had happened in the making of a voice out of a man," the devastating synecdoche that names both Jody's deepest aspiration and his subsequent great fall.

It is striking that Janie gains her voice and becomes a speaking subject inside her husband's store. Not only does she, by speaking, defy his expressed prohibition, but the scene itself is a key repetition of the metaphors of inside and outside, which repeat frequently throughout the text and which, as I hope to show, serve as a thematic, if metaphorical, counterpart to the most striking innovation of *Their Eyes'* narrative strategy, the presence of free indirect discourse.

The repeated metaphors of inside and outside begin in the text's first chapter. Janie narrates her tale, as Phoeby listens, outside on her back porch. Janie's metaphorical and densely lyrical "outside observations," the narrator tells us, "buried themselves in her flesh." After she experiences her first orgasm, then kisses Johnny Taylor, she extends "herself outside of her dream" and goes "inside of the house." As we have seen, it is inside houses in which a series of people (first her grandmother, Nanny; then her first

HENRY LOUIS GATES, JR.

husband, Logan Killicks; then her second husband, Joe Starks) attempt to oppress her and prevent her from speaking and asserting herself. Janie dreams outdoors, in metaphors of flowering springtime, often under pear trees. When Logan insults her, the narrator says that "she turned wrongside out just standing there and feeling." Jody seduces her with dreams of "far horizons," "under the tree" and outdoors "in the scrub oaks." What Jody speaks out loud and what Janie thinks inside come to represent an opposition of such dimensions that we are not at all surprised when their final confrontation occurs. Janie, we recall, is forced to retreat inside the store when the storytelling rituals commence.

The text represents Janie's crucial if ironic scene of self-discovery rather subtly in this figurative framework of inside and outside. This coming to consciousness is not represented by a speaking scene, however; rather, it is represented in these inside-outside figures. When she finally does speak, therefore, by Signifyin(g) in the store upon Jody's impotence, the gaining of her own voice is a sign of her authority, but not a sign of a newly found unified identity. Janie's speaking voice, rather, is an outcome of her consciousness of division.[6] Indeed, hers is a rhetoric of division.

The text represents this consciousness of division in two scenes that transpire in the chapter that precedes the chapter in which she Signifies upon Jody. The text reads:

> The spirit of the marriage left the bedroom and took to living in the parlor. It was there to shake hands whenever company came to visit, but it never went back inside the bedroom again. So she put something in there to represent the spirit like a Virgin Mary image in a church. The bed was no longer a daisy-field for her and Joe to play in. It was a place where she went and laid down when she was sleepy and tired. (p. 111)

In this passage, Janie's inner feelings, "the spirit of the marriage," are projected onto outer contiguous physical spaces (the bedroom and the parlor). Her inside, in other words, is figured as an outside, in the rooms. Her bed, moreover, ceases to be a place for lovemaking, as signified by both the daisy-field metaphor and the metaphor of play (reminding us, through the repetition, of her central metaphors of dream and aspiration that repeat so often in the novel's first half). The contiguous relation of the bedroom and the parlor, both physical spaces, through which the metaphorical spirit of the marriage now moves, reveals two modes of figuration overlapping in Janie's indirectly reported thoughts for the first time – that is, one mode dependent upon substitution, the other on contiguity.[7] Clearly, the rhetorical relation among "sex" and "spirit of the marriage," and "spirit of the marriage," "bedroom," and "parlor" is a complex one.

Until this moment in the text, Janie's literacy was represented only as a metaphorical literacy. Janie's "conscious life," the text tells us, "had commenced at Nanny's gate," across which she had kissed Johnny Taylor just after experiencing her first orgasm under her "blossoming pear tree in the back-yard." In the moving passage that precedes the event but prepares us for it by describing her increasing awareness of her own sexuality, rendered in free indirect discourse, Janie names her feelings in her first metaphor: "The rose of the world was breathing out smell. It followed her through all her waking moments and caressed her in her sleep" (pp. 23–24). Janie's first language, the language of her own desire, is registered in a lyrical and metaphorical diction found in these passages of free indirect discourse. Janie has mastered, the text tells us early on, "the words of the trees and the wind" (p. 44). In this metaphorical language, "she spoke to falling seeds," as they speak to her, in lyrical metaphors, renaming "the world," for example, "a stallion rolling in the blue pasture of ether." Whereas she speaks, thinks, and dreams in metaphors, the communal voice of the porch describes her in a string of synecdoches, naming parts of her body – such as her "great rope of black hair," "her pugnacious breasts," her "faded shirt and muddy overalls" – as parts standing for the whole (p. 11).

One paragraph later, as a sign that she can name her division, the direction of her figuration reverses itself. Whereas in the first scene she projects her inner feelings onto outer physical space, in this scene she internalizes an outer physical space, her scene of oppression, the store:

> Janie stood where he left her for unmeasured time and thought. She stood there until something fell off the shelf inside her. Then she went inside there to see what it was. It was her image of Jody tumbled down and shattered. But looking at it she saw that it never was the flesh and blood figure of her dreams. Just something she had grabbed up to drape her dreams over. (p. 112)

Janie has internalized the store through the synecdoche of the shelf.[8] As Barbara Johnson summarizes the rhetorical import of this scene: "These two figural mini-narratives [represent] a kind of chiasmus, or crossover, in which the first paragraph presents an externalization of the inner, a metaphorically grounded metonymy, while the second paragraph presents an internalization of the outer, or a metonymically grounded metaphor.... The reversals operated by the chiasmus map out a reversal of the power relations between Janie and Joe."[9] When she soon speaks aloud in public against Jody and thereby redefines their relationship, it is the awareness of this willed figurative division of which her speaking voice is the sign. As the text reads, Janie "found that she had a host of thoughts she had never expressed to him, and numerous emotions she had never let Jody know about. Things packed up and put away in parts of her heart where he could never find them" (p. 112).

Janie is now truly fluent in the language of the figurative: "She had an inside and an outside now and suddenly knew how not to mix them." Three pages before she Signifies upon Jody, the text represents this fluency as follows:

> Then one day she sat and watched the shadow of herself going about tending the store and prostrating itself before Jody, while all the time she herself sat under a shady tree with the wind blowing through her hair and her clothes. Somebody near about making summertime out of lonesomeness. (p. 119)

Janie's ability to name her own division and move the parts simultaneously through contiguous spaces, her newly found and apparently exhilarating double-consciousness, is that crucial event that enables her to speak and assert herself, after decades of being defined almost exclusively by others.

The text prefigures this event. The sign that this consciousness of her own division liberates her speaking voice is Janie's first instance of voicing her feelings within the store, which occurs in the text midway between the slapping scene in which she first internally names her outside and inside (p. 112) and the scene in which she so tellingly Signifies upon Joe (pp. 121–22). Janie speaks after listening in a painful silence as Coker and Joe Lindsay discuss the merits of beating women:

> "...Tony love her too good," said Coker. "Ah could break her if she wuz mine. Ah'd break her or kill her. Makin' uh fool outa me in front of everybody."
> "Tony won't never hit her. He says beatin' women is just like steppin' on baby chickens. He claims 'tain't no place on uh woman tuh hit," Joe Lindsay said with scornful disapproval, "but Ah'd kill uh baby just born dis mawnin' fuh uh thing like dat. 'Taint nothin' but low-down spitefulness 'ginst her husband make her do it." (p. 116)

This exchange, of course, refigures the crucial scene in which Joe slaps Janie because her meal was not well prepared. Joe Lindsay's comparison in this passage of "beatin' women" and "steppin' on baby chickens" echoes Joe's proclamation to Janie that "somebody got to think for women and chillun and chickens and cows," made in their argument about who has the right "to tell" (pp. 110–11). After Joe Lindsay finishes speaking, and after his sexist remarks are affirmed as gospel by Jim Stone, Janie – for the first time – speaks out against the men's opinion about the merits of beatings. As the text states, "Janie did what she had never done before, that is, thrust herself into the conversation":

> "Sometimes God gits familiar wid us womenfolks too and talks His inside business. He told me how surprised He was 'bout y'all turning out so smart after Him makin' yuh different; and how surprised y'all is goin' tuh be if you ever find out you don't know half as much 'bout us as you think you do. It's so easy to make yo'self out God Almighty when you ain't got nothin' tuh strain against but *women and chickens*." (p. 117, emphasis added)

Janie reveals God's "inside business" to the superficial store-talkers, warning all who can hear her voice that a "surprise" lay in waiting for those who see only appearances and never penetrate to the tenor of things. Joe, we learn just four pages later, is in for the surprise of his life: the killing timbre of Janie's true inner voice. Joe's only response to this first scene of speaking is to tell his wife, "You gettin' too moufy, Janie," a veritable literalizing of the metaphor of mouth, followed by the ultimate sign of ignoring and circumventing Janie's domain, an order to her to "Go fetch me de checker-board *and* de checkers." Joe's turn to the male world of play, at Janie's expense, leads Janie to play the dozens on his sexuality and thus to his death. These metaphorical echoes and exchanges are deadly serious in Hurston's text.

Earlier in the narrative, Hicks defined the metaphorical as "co-talkin'" and says that his is "too deep" for women to understand, which explains, he says, why "Dey love to hear me talk" precisely "because dey can't understand it.... Too much co to it," he concludes (p. 59). As soon as Janie learns to name her inside and outside and to move between them, as we have seen, Jody argues that women "need tellin'" because "some-body got to think for women and chillun and chickens and cows" because a man sees "one thing" and "understands ten," while a woman sees "ten things and don't understand one" (pp. 110–11). Jody ironically accuses Janie of failing to understand how one thing can imply or be substituted for ten, thereby arguing that Janie does not understand metaphor, whereas Janie is a master of metaphor whose self-liberation awaits only the knowledge of how to narrate her figures contiguously. It is Jody who has failed to read the situation properly. As a character in *Mules and Men* argues, most people do not understand the nature of the figurative, which he characterizes as expression that "got a hidden meanin', jus' like de Bible. Everybody can't understand what they mean," he continues. "Most people is thin-brained. They's born wid they feet under the moon. Some folks is born wid they feet on de sun and they kin seek out de inside meanin' of words" (pp. 162–63). Jody, it turns out, is both thin-brained and thin-skinned, and proves to have been born with his feet under the moon. He is all vehicle, no tenor. The "inside meanings of words," of course, we think of as the tenor, or inside meaning of a rhetorical figure, while the outside corresponds to its "vehicle." Janie, as the text repeats again and again in its central metaphor for her character, is a child of the sun.

Hurston's use of free indirect discourse is central to her larger strategy of critiquing what we might think of as a "male writing." Joe Starks, we remember, fondly and unconsciously refers to himself as "I god." During the lamp-lighting ceremony (pp. 71–74), as I have suggested earlier, Joe is represented as the creator (or at least the purchaser) of light. Joe is the text's figure of authority and voice, indeed the authority *of* voice:

> "Naw, Jody, it jus' looks lak it keeps us in some way we ain't natural wid one 'nother. You'se always off talkin' and fixin' things, and Ah feels lak Ah'm jus' markin' time. Hope it soon gits over."
> "Over, Janie? I god, Ah ain't even started good. Ah told you in de very first beginnin' dat Ah aimed tuh be uh big voice. You oughta be glad, 'cause dat makes uh big woman outa you." (p. 74)

Joe says that "in de very first beginnin'" he "aimed tuh be uh big voice," an echo of the first verse of the Gospel of John: "In the beginning was the Word, and the Word was with God, and the Word was God." Joe, we know, sees himself, and wishes to be seen as the God-figure of his community. The text tells us that when speakers on formal occasions prefaced their remarks with the phrase "Our beloved Mayor," the phrase was equivalent to "one of those statements that everybody says but nobody believes like 'God is everywhere'" (p. 77). Joe is the figure of the male author, he who has authored both Eatonville and Janie's existences. We remember that when Joe lights the town's newly acquired lamp, Mrs. Bogle's alto voice sings "Jesus, the light of the world":

> We'll walk in de light, de beautiful light
> Come where the dew drops of mercy shine bright
> Shine all around us by day and by night
> Jesus, the light of the world. (p. 73)

So, when Janie Signifies upon Joe, she strips him of his hubristic claim to the godhead and exposes him, through the simile of the "change of life," as impotent and de/masculated. The revelation of the truth kills him. Janie, in effect, has rewritten Joe's text of himself, and liberated herself in the process. Janie writes herself into being by naming, by speaking herself free.... Alice Walker takes this moment in Hurston's text as the moment of revision and creates a character whom we witness literally writing herself into being, but writing herself into being in a language that imitates that idiom spoken by Janie and Hurston's black community generally. This scene, this transformation or reversal of status, is truly the first feminist critique of the fiction of the authority of the male voice, and its sexism, in the Afro-American tradition.

This opposition between metaphor and metonym appears in another form as well, that of strategies of tale-telling. Nanny narrates her slave narrative in a linear, or metonymic, manner, with one event following another in chronological order. Janie, by contrast, narrates her tale in a circular, or framed, narrative replete with vivid, startling metaphors. Janie only liberates herself by selecting alternatives exactly opposed to those advocated by Nanny, eschewing the sort of "protection" afforded by Logan Killicks and so graphically figured for Janie in her grandmother's fantasy of preaching "a great sermon about colored women sittin' on high." Only after Janie satisfies Nanny's desire, "sittin' on high" on Joe Starks's front porch, then rejecting it, will she in turn "preach" her own sermon by narrating her tale to Phoeby in a circular, framed narrative that merges her voice with an omniscient narrator's in free indirect discourse.

IV

If *Their Eyes* makes impressive use of the figures of outside and inside, as well as the metaphor of double-consciousness as the prequisite to becoming a speaking subject, then the text's mode of narration, especially its "speakerliness," serves as the rhetorical analogue to this theme. I use the word *double* here intentionally, to echo W. E. B. Du Bois's metaphor for the Afro-American's peculiar psychology of citizenship and also to avoid the limited description of free indirect discourse as a "dual voice," in Roy Pascal's term.[10] Rather than a dual voice, free indirect discourse, as manifested in *Their Eyes Were Watching God*, is a dramatic way of expressing a divided self. Janie's self, as we have seen, is a divided self. Long before she becomes aware of her division, of her inside and outside, free indirect discourse communicates this division to the reader. After she becomes aware of her own division, free indirect discourse functions to represent, rhetorically, her interrupted passage from outside to inside. Free indirect discourse in *Their Eyes* reflects both the text's theme of the doubling of Janie's self and that of the problematic relationship between Janie as a speaking subject and spoken language. Free indirect discourse, furthermore, is a central aspect of the rhetoric of the text and serves to disrupt the reader's expectation of the necessity of the shift in point of view from third person to first within Janie's framed narrative. Free indirect discourse is not the voice of both a character and a narrator; rather, it is a bivocal utterance, containing elements of both direct and indirect speech. It is an utterance that no one could have spoken, yet which we recognize because of its characteristic "speakerliness," its paradoxically written manifestation of the aspiration to the oral.

I shall not enter into the terminological controversy over free indirect discourse, except to refer the reader to the controversy itself.[11] My concern with free indirect discourse, for the purposes of this chapter, is limited to its use in *Their Eyes*.[12] I am especially interested in its presence in this text as an implicit critique of that ancient opposition in narrative theory between showing and telling, between mimesis and diegesis. The tension between diegesis, understood here as that which can be represented, and mimesis, that which Hurston repeats in direct quotations, strikes the reader early on as a fundamental opposition in *Their Eyes*. Only actions or events can be represented, in this sense, while discourse here would seem to be overheard or repeated. Hurston's use of this form of repetition creates the illusion of a direct relationship between her text and a black "real world" (which has led some of her most vocal critics to call this an anthropological text), while representation of the sort found in narrative commentary preserves, even insists upon, the difference and the very distance between them.

Free indirect discourse, on the other hand, is a third, mediating term. As Michal Ginsberg argues perceptively, "it is a *mimesis* which tries to pass for a *diegesis*."[13] But it is also, I contend, a diegesis that tries to pass for a mimesis. Indeed, it is precisely this understanding of free indirect discourse that derives from its usages in *Their Eyes Were Watching God*, simply because we are unable to characterize it either as the representation of an action (diegesis) or as the repetition of a character's words (mimesis). When we recall Hurston's insistence that the fundamental indicator of traditional black oral narration is its aspiration to the "dramatic," we can see clearly that her use of free indirect discourse is a profound attempt to remove the distinction between repeated speech and represented events. Here discourse "is not distinct from events." As Ginsberg argues, "Subject and object dissolve into each other. Representation which guaranteed the distance between them is in danger."[14] For Hurston, free indirect discourse is an equation: direct speech equals narrative commentary; representation of an action equals repetition of that action; therefore, narrative commentary aspires to the immediacy of the drama. Janie's quest for consciousness, however, always remains that for the consciousness of her own division, which the dialogical rhetoric of the text – especially as expressed in free indirect discourse – underscores, preserves, and seems to celebrate. It is this theme, and this rhetoric of division, which together comprise the modernism of this text.

A convenient way to think about free indirect discourse is that it appears initially to be indirect discourse (by which I mean that its signals of time and person correspond to a third-person narrator's discourse), "but it is penetrated, in its syntactic and semantic structures, by enunciative properties, thus by the discourse of a character,"[15] and even in Hurston's case by that of characters. In other words, free indirect discourse attempts to represent "consciousness without the apparent intrusion of a narrative voice," thereby "presenting the illusion of a character's acting out his [or her] mental state in an immediate relationship with the reader." Graham Hough defines free indirect discourse as one extreme of "coloured narrative," or narrative-cum-dialogue as in Jane Austen's fictions.[16] Hurston's use of free indirect discourse, we are free to say, is indeed a kind of "coloured narrative"! But Hurston allows us to rename free indirect discourse; near the beginning of her book, the narrator describes the communal, undifferentiated voice of "the porch" as "A mood come alive. Words walking without masters; walking altogether like harmony in a song." Since the narrator attributes these words to "the bander log" (p. 11), or the place where Kipling's monkeys sit, Hurston here gives one more, coded, reference to Signifyin(g): that which the porch (monkeys) has just done is to Signify upon Janie. If Signifyin(g) is "a mood come alive," "words walking without masters," then we can also think of free indirect discourse in this way.

HENRY LOUIS GATES, JR.

There are numerous indices whereby we identify free indirect discourse in general, among these grammar, intonation, context, idiom, register, and content; it is naturalized in a text by stream of consciousness, irony, empathy, and polyvocality.[17] The principal indices of free indirect discourse in *Their Eyes* include those which "evoke a 'voice' or presence" that supplements the narrator's, especially when one or more sentences of free indirect discourse follow a sentence of indirect discourse. Idiom and register, particularly, Hurston uses as markers of black colloquialism, of the quality of the speakerly informed by the dialect of the direct discourse of the characters. In *Their Eyes*, naturalization would seem to function as part of the theme of the developing but discontinuous self. This function is naturalized primarily by irony, empathy, and polyvocality. When it is used in conjunction with Joe Starks, irony obtains and distancing results; when it is used in conjunction with Janie, empathy obtains and an illusory identification results, an identity we might call lyric fusion between the narrator and Janie. Bivocalism, finally, or the double-voiced utterance, in which two voices co-occur, is this text's central device of naturalization, again serving to reinforce both Janie's division and paradoxically the narrator's distance from Janie. As Ginsberg concludes so perceptively, "Free indirect discourse is a way of expression of a divided self."[18]

Their Eyes employs three modes of narration to render the words or thoughts of a character. The first is direct discourse:

> "Jody," she smiled up at him, "but s'posin –"
> "Leave de s'posin' and everything else to me."

The next is indirect discourse:

> "The vision of Logan Killicks was desecrating the pear tree, but Janie didn't know how to tell Nanny that."

The third example is free indirect discourse. Significantly, this example occurs when Joe Starks enters the narrative:

> Joe Starks was the name, yeah Joe Starks from in and through Georgy. Been workin' for white folks all his life. Saved up some money – round three hundred dollars, yes indeed, right here in his pocket. Kept hearin' 'bout them buildin' a new state down heah in Floridy and sort of wanted to come. But he was makin' money where he was. But when he heard all about 'em makin' a town all outa colored folks, he knowed dat was de place he wanted to be. He had always wanted to be a big voice, but de white folks had all de sayso where he come from and everywhere else, exceptin' dis place dat colored folks was buildin' theirselves. Dat was right too. De man dat built things oughta boss it. Let colored folks build things too if dey wants to crow over somethin'. He was glad he had his money all saved up. He meant to git dere whilst de town wuz yet a baby. He meant to buy in big. (pp. 47–48)

I selected this example because it includes a number of standard indices of free indirect speech. Although when read aloud it sounds as if entire sections are in, or should be in, direct quotation, none of the sentences in this paragraph is direct discourse. There are no quotation marks here. The character's idiom, interspersed and contrasted colorfully with the narrator's voice, indicates nevertheless that this is an account of the words that Joe spoke to Janie. The sentences imitating dialect clearly are not those of the narrator alone; they are those of Joe Starks and the narrator. Moreover, the presence of the adverb *here* ("yes, indeed, right here in his pocket") as opposed to *there*, which would be required in normal indirect speech because one source would be describing another, informs us that the assertion originates within and reflects the character's sensibilities, not the narrator's. The interspersion of indirect discourse with free indirect discourse, even in the same sentence, serves as another index to its presence, precisely by underscoring Joe's characteristic idiom, whereas the indirect discourse obliterates it. Despite the third person and the past tense, then, of which both indirect and free indirect discourse consist, several sentences in this paragraph appear to report Joe's speech, without the text resorting to either dialogue or direct discourse. The principal indices of free indirect discourse direct the reader to the subjective source of the statement, rendered through a fusion of narrator and a silent but speaking character.

Exclamations and exclamatory questions often introduce free indirect discourse. The text's first few examples occur when Janie experiences the longing for love, and then her first orgasm:

> She saw a dust-bearing bee sink into the sanctum of a bloom; the thousand sister-calyxes arch to meet the love embrace and the ecstatic shiver of the tree from root to tiniest branch creaming in every blossom and frothing with delight. So this was a marriage!... Then Janie felt a pain remorseless sweet that left her limp and languid. (p. 24)

Then in the next paragraph:

> She was lying across the bed asleep so Janie tipped on out of the front door. Oh to be a pear tree – *any* tree in bloom! With kissing bees singing of the beginning of the world! She was sixteen. (p. 25)

Unlike the free indirect discourse that introduces Joe, these three sentences retain the narrator's level of diction, her idiom, as if to emphasize on one hand that Janie represents the potentially lyrical self, but on the other hand that the narrator is interpreting Janie's inarticulate thoughts to the reader on her behalf.

This usage remains fairly consistent until Janie begins to challenge, if only in her thoughts, Joe's authority:

> Janie noted that while he didn't talk the mule himself [Signify], he sat and laughed at it. Laughed his big heh, hey laugh too. But then when Lige or Sam or Walter or some of the other big picture talkers were using a side of the world for a canvas, Joe would hustle her off inside the store to sell something. Look like he took pleasure in doing it. Why couldn't he go himself sometimes? She had come to hate the inside of that store anyway. (p. 85)

Here we see Janie's idiom entering, if only in two sentences, the free indirect speech. After she has "slain" Jody, however, her idiom, more and more, informs the free indirect discourse, in sentences such as "Poor Jody! He ought not to have to wrassle in there by himself" (p. 129). Once Janie meets Tea Cake, the reader comes to expect to encounter Janie's doubts and dreams in free indirect discourse, almost always introduced by the narrator explicitly as being Janie's thoughts. Almost never, however, curiously enough,

HENRY LOUIS GATES, JR.

does Janie's free indirect discourse unfold in a strictly black idiom, as does Joe's; rather, it is represented in an idiom informed by the black idiom but translated into what we might think of as a colloquial form of standard English, which always stands in contrast to Janie's direct speech, which is foregrounded in dialect.

This difference between the representations of the level of diction of Janie's direct discourse and the free indirect discourse that the text asks us to accept as the figure of Janie's thoughts reinforces for the reader both Janie's divided consciousness and the double-voiced nature of free indirect discourse, as if the narrative commentary cannot relinquish its proprietary consciousness over Janie as freely as it does for other characters. Nevertheless, after Janie falls in love with Tea Cake, we learn of her feelings through a remarkable amount of free indirect discourse, almost always rendered in what I wish to call idiomatic, but standard, English.

It is this same voice, eventually, which we also come to associate with that of the text's narrator; through empathy and irony, the narrator begins to read Janie's world and everyone in it, through this same rhetorical device, rendered in this identical diction, even when the observation clearly is not Janie's. The effect is as if the lyrical language created by the indeterminate merging of the narrator's voice and Janie's almost totally silences the initial level of diction of the narrator's voice. Let us recall the narrator's voice in the text's opening paragraph:

> Ships at a distance have every man's wish on board. For some they come in with the tide. For others they sail forever on the horizon, never out of sight, never landing until the Watcher turns his eyes away in resignation, his dreams mocked to death by Time. That is the life of men. (p. 1)

Compare that voice with the following:

> So Janie began to think of Death. Death, that strange being with the huge square toes who lived way in the West. The great one who lived in the straight house like a platform without sides to it, and without a roof. What need has Death for a cover, and what winds can blow against him? (p. 129)

Ostensibly, these are Janie's thoughts. But compare this sentence, which is part of the narrator's commentary: "But, don't care how firm your determination is, you can't keep turning round in one place like a horse grinding sugar cane" (p. 177).

This idiomatic voice narrates almost completely the dramatic scene of the hurricane, where "six eyes were questioning *God.*" One such passage serves as an excellent example of a communal free indirect discourse, of a narrative voice that is not fused with Janie's but which describes events in the idiom of Janie's free indirect discourse:

> They looked back. Saw people trying to run in raging waters and screaming when they found they couldn't. A huge barrier of the makings of the dike to which the cabins had been added was rolling and tumbling forward.... The monstropolous beast had left his bed.... The sea was walking the earth with a heavy heel. (p. 239)

At several passages after this narration of the hurricane, the interspersed indirect discourse and free indirect discourse become extraordinarily difficult to isolate because of this similarity in idiom:

> Janie fooled around outside awhile to try and think it wasn't so.... Well, she thought, that big old dawg with the hatred in his eyes had killed her after all. She wished she had slipped off that cow-tail and drowned then and there and been done. But to kill her through Tea Cake was too much to bear. Tea Cake, the son of the Evening Sun, had to die for loving her. She looked hard at the sky for a long time. Somewhere up there beyond blue ether's bottom sat He. Was He noticing what was going on around here?...Did He *mean* to do this thing to Tea Cake and her?...Maybe it was some big tease and when He saw it had gone far enough He'd give her a sign. (pp. 263–64)

Narrative commentary and free indirect discourse, in passages such as this, move toward the indistinguishable. The final instance of free indirect discourse occurs, appropriately enough, in the novel's ultimate paragraph, in which Janie's true figurative synthesis occurs:

> The day of the gun, and the bloody body, and the courthouse came and commenced to sing a sobbing sigh out of every corner in the room; out of each and every chair and thing. Commenced to sing, commenced to sob and sigh, singing and sobbing. Then Tea Cake came prancing around her where she was and the song of the sigh flew out of the window and lit in the top of the pine trees. Tea Cake, with the sun for a shawl. Of course he wasn't dead. He could never be dead until she herself had finished feeling and thinking. The kiss of his memory made pictures of love and light against the wall. Here was peace. She pulled in her horizon like a great fish-net. Pulled it from around the waist of the world and draped it over her shoulder. So much of life in its meshes! She called in her soul to come and see. (p. 286)

Ephi Paul, in a subtle reading of various tropes in *Their Eyes* (in an unpublished essay, "My Tongue Is in My Friend's Mouth"), argues that this "final moment of transcendence" is also a final moment of control and synthesis of the opposed male and female paradigmatic tropes defined in the novel's first two paragraphs:

> The horizon that she learns about from Joe, that helps her rediscover how to "play" again with Tea Cake, has been transformed from the object of a longing gaze to a figurative "fish-net" which an active subject can pull in. While Joe's desires are, like the men of the first paragraph, "mocked to death by Time," Janie's are still alive and thriving: "The kiss of his memory made pictures of love and light against the wall." Janie finds "peace" in "his memory," just as she has always privileged her inward contemplative self over the outer active one. Yet in its own way, Janie's thriving survival of hard times has been an active process of finding a language to name her desire. The horizon as a fish-net seems to signify the synthesis of "men" and "women's" figuration, because the fish-net's "meshes" seem so like the sifting of women's memories – remembering and forgetting all that they want. So Janie has cast her horizon into a sea of possibilities and sorted out her catch of loves, naming them with an even more accurate figuration of desire. She opens her arms to "the waist of the world" and gathers in her satisfactions, rooted in her power of "feeling and thinking" for herself. (pp. 44–45)

HENRY LOUIS GATES, JR.

This merging of the opposed modes of figuration in the novel's first two paragraphs stands as an analogue of Janie's transcendent moment because of, as Paul argues,

> the male and female modes of figuration (as established in the "paradigm" of its first two paragraphs) – bringing together the horizon of change and the fish-net of memory. In her search for desire and its naming, Janie shifts back and forth between the alienation of the gazing "Watcher" and the empowerment of women believing that "the dream is the truth." She finds her satisfaction only after using Joe's horizon of "change and chance" to transform the desire she experiences alone under the pear tree; she retains the horizon long after she has dismissed Joe, because she can re-figure it to have meaning for herself. (p. 71)

To this I would only add that both the pulling in of her horizon and the calling in of her soul reveal not a unity of self but a maximum of self-control over the division between self and other. Whereas before Tea Cake Janie was forced to send a mask of herself outward, now, at novel's end, she can invite both her horizon (the figure for her desires after meeting Jody) and her soul inside herself "to come and see." She has internalized her metaphors, and brought them home, across a threshold heretofore impenetrable. This self-willed, active, subjective synthesis is a remarkable trope of self-knowledge. And the numerous sentences of free indirect discourse in this paragraph serve to stress this fact of Janie's self-knowledge and self-control. Her invitation to her soul to come see the horizon that had always before been a figure for external desire, the desire of the other, is the novel's sign of Janie's synthesis.

It is because of these dramatic shifts in the idiom in which the voice of the narrator appears that we might think of *Their Eyes* as a speakerly text. For it is clear that the resonant dialect of the character's discourse has come to color the narrator's idiom such that it resembles rather closely the idiom in which Janie's free indirect discourse is rendered. But *Their Eyes* would seem to be a speakerly text for still another reason. Hurston uses free indirect discourse not only to represent an individual character's speech and thought but also to represent the collective black community's speech and thoughts, as in the hurricane passage. This sort of anonymous, collective, free indirect discourse is not only unusual but quite possibly was Hurston's innovation, as if to emphasize both the immense potential of this literary diction, one dialect-informed as it were, for the tradition, as well as the text's apparent aspiration to imitate oral narration. One example follows:

> Most of the great flame-throwers were there and naturally, handling Big John de Conquer and his works. How he had done everything big on earth, then went up tuh heben without dying atall. Went up there picking a guitar and got all de angels doing the ring-shout round and round de throne...that brought them back to Tea Cake. How come he couldn't hit that box a lick or two? Well, all right now, make us know it. (p. 232)

Still another example is even more telling:

> Everybody was talking about it that night. But nobody was worried. The fire dance kept up till nearly dawn. The next day, more Indians moved east, unhurried but steady. Still a blue sky and fair weather. Beans running fine and prices good, so the Indians could be, *must*

be, wrong. You couldn't have a hurricane when you're making seven and eight dollars a day picking beans. Indians are dumb anyhow, always were. Another night of Stew Beef making dynamic subtleties with his drum and living, sculptural, grotesques in the dance. (p. 229)

These instances of free indirect discourse are followed in the text by straight diegesis, which retains the dialect-informed echoes of the previous passage:

> Morning came without motion. The winds, to the tiniest, lisping baby breath had left the earth. Even before the sun gave light, dead day was creeping from bush to bush watching man. (p. 229)

There are many other examples of this curious voice (see pp. 75–76, 276). Hurston, in this innovation, is asserting that an entire narration could be rendered, if not in dialect, then in a dialect-informed discourse. This form of collective, impersonal free indirect discourse echoes Hurston's definition of "a mood come alive. Words walking without masters; walking altogether like harmony in a song." The ultimate sign of the dignity and strength of the black voice is this use of a dialect-informed free indirect discourse as narrative commentary beyond that which represents Janie's thoughts and feelings alone.

There are paradoxes and ironies in speakerly texts. The irony of this dialect-informed diction, of course, is that it is not a repetition of a language that anyone speaks; indeed, it can never be spoken. As several other scholars of free indirect discourse have argued, free indirect discourse is speakerless, by which they mean "the presentation of a perspective outside the normal communication paradigm that usually characterizes language."[19] It is literary language, meant to be read in a text. Its paradox is that it comes into use by Hurston so that discourse rendered through direct, indirect, or free indirect means may partake of Hurston's "word-pictures" and "thought-pictures," as we recall she defined the nature of Afro-American spoken language. "The white man thinks in a written language," she argued, "and the Negro thinks in hieroglyphics." The speakerly diction of *Their Eyes* attempts to render these pictures through the imitation of the extensively metaphorical medium of black speech, in an oxymoronic oral hieroglyphic that is meant only for the printed page. Its obvious oral base, nevertheless, suggests that Hurston conceived of it as a third language, as a mediating third term that aspires to resolve the tension between standard English and black vernacular, just as the narrative device of free indirect discourse aspires to define the traditional opposition between mimesis and diegesis as a false opposition. And perhaps this dialogical diction, and this dialogical narrative device, can serve as a metaphor for the critic of black comparative literature whose theoretical endeavor is intentionally double-voiced as well.

If Esu's double voice is figured in *Their Eyes Were Watching God* in the dialogical basis of free indirect discourse, it manifests itself in the fiction of Ishmael Reed in the sustained attempt to critique the strategies of narration central to certain canonical Afro-American texts through parody and pastiche. Like Hurston's text, we may think of Reed's novel as double-voiced, but in an essentially different way. Reed's relation to these authors in the tradition is at all points double-voiced, since he seems to be especially concerned with employing satire to utilize literature in what Frye calls "a special function of analysis, of breaking up the lumber of stereotypes, fossilized beliefs, superstitious terrors, crank theories, pedantic dogmatisms, oppressive fashions, and all other things that impede the free movement... of society."[20] Reed, of course, seems to be most concerned with the "free movement" of writing itself. In Reed's work, parody and hidden polemic overlap, in a process Bakhtin describes as follows: "When parody becomes aware of substantial resistance, a certain forcefulness and profundity in the speech act it parodies, it takes on a new dimension of complexity via the tones of the hidden polemic.... [A] process of inner dialogization takes place within the parodic speech act."[21] This "internal dialogization" can have curious implications, the most interesting of which perhaps is what Bakhtin describes as "the splitting of double-voice discourse into two speech acts, into two entirely separate and autonomous voices." The clearest evidence that Reed in *Mumbo Jumbo* is Signifyin(g) through parody as hidden polemic is his use of the two autonomous narrative voices in *Mumbo Jumbo*, which Reed employs in the manner of and renders through foregrounding, to parody the two simultaneous stories of detective narration, that of the present and that of the past, in a narrative flow that moves hurriedly from cause to effect. In *Mumbo Jumbo*, however, the second narrative, that of the past, bears an ironic relation to the first narrative, that of the present, because it comments on the other narrative as well as on the nature of its writing itself, in what Frye describes, in another context, as "the constant tendency to self-parody in satiric rhetoric which prevents even the process of writing itself from becoming an oversimplified convention or idea."[22] Reed's rhetorical strategy assumes the form of the relationship between the text and the criticism of that text, which "serves as discourse on that text." If Hurston's novel is a Signifyin(g) structure because it seems to be so concerned to represent Signifyin(g) rituals for their own sake, then Reed's text is a Signifyin(g) structure because he Signifies upon the tradition's convention of representation.

NOTES

1   Zora Neale Hurston, *Their Eyes Were Watching God* (1937; Urbana: University of Illinois, 1978), p. 85. All subsequent references are to this edition and will be given parenthetically in the text.

2   Zora Neale Hurston, *Mules and Men: Negro Folktales and Voodoo Practices in the South* (1935; New York: Harper & Row, 1970), p. 161. Subsequent references will be given parenthetically.

3   Nancy Cunard, ed., *Negro* (1934; New York: Negro Universities Press, 1969), pp. 39–62. Reprinted in Zora Neale Hurston, *The Sanctified Church*, ed. Toni Cade Bambara (Berkeley: Turtle Island, 1981), pp. 41–78.

4   Zora Neale Hurston, *Dust Tracks on a Road: An Autobiography* (Philadelphia: J. D. Lippincott, 1942), p. 217.

5   The best discussion of the representation of black speech in Hurston's work is Karla Francesca Holloway, *A Critical Investigation of Literary and Linguistic Structures in the Fiction of Zora Neale Hurston*, Ph.D. dissertation, Michigan State University, 1978. See esp. pp. 93–94, and 101.

6   I wish to thank Barbara Johnson of Harvard University for calling my attention to this ironic mode of self-consciousness.

7   In a brilliant analysis of this scene of the novel, Barbara Johnson writes that "The entire paragraph is an externalization of Janie's feelings onto the outer surroundings in the form of a narrative of movement from private to public space. While the whole figure relates metaphorically, analogically, to the marital situation it is designed to express, it reveals the marriage

space to be metonymical, a movement through a series of contiguous rooms. It is a narrative not of union but of separation centered on an image not of conjugality but of virginity." See Barbara Johnson, "Metaphor, Metonymy, and Voice in Zora Neale Hurston's *Their Eyes Were Watching God*," in *Black Literature and Literary Theory*, ed. by H. L. Gates, Jr. (New York: Methuen, 1984), pp. 205–19. [See also pp. 257–70 in this book.]

8   Cf. Johnson: "Janie's 'inside' is here represented as a store that she then goes in to inspect. While the former paragraph was an externalization of the inner, here we find an internalization of the outer; Janie's inner self *resembles* a store. The material for this metaphor is drawn from the narrative world of contiguity; the store is the place where Joe has set himself up as lord, master, and proprietor. But here, Jody's image is broken, and reveals itself never to have been a metaphor, but only a metonymy, of Janie's dream: 'Looking at it she saw that it never was the flesh and blood *figure* of her dreams. Just something to drape her dreams over.'" Ibid.

9   Ibid.

10 See Roy Pascal, *The Dual Voice: Free Indirect Discourse and Its Functioning in the Nineteenth-Century European Novel* (Totowa, N.J.: Rowman and Littlefield, 1977), pp. 1–33.

11 See Brian McHale, "Free Indirect Discourse: A Survey of Recent Accounts," *PTL* 3 (1978): 249–87, for an excellent account of the controversy. I think the most lucid study is Michel Peled Ginsberg, "Free Indirect Discourse: Theme and Narrative Voice in Flaubert, George Eliot, and Verga," Ph.D. dissertation, Yale University, 1977. See also Stephen Ullmann, *Style in the French Novel* (Cambridge: Cambridge University Press, 1957).

12 In a sequel to this book, I would like to compare Hurston's use of free indirect discourse to that of other writers, especially Virginia Woolf.

13 Ginsberg, "Free Indirect Discourse," p. 34.

14 Ibid., p. 35.

15 Oswald Ducrot and Tzvetan Todorov, *Encyclopedic Dictionary of the Sciences of Language*, trans. by Catherine Porter (Baltimore: Johns Hopkins University Press, 1979), p. 303.

16 See Graham Hough, "Narration and Dialogue in Jane Austen," *The Critical Quarterly* xii (1970); and Pascal, *The Dual Voice*, p. 52.

17 McHale, "Free Indirect Discourse," pp. 264–80.

18 Ginsberg, "Free Indirect Discourse," p. 23.

19 Janet Holmgren McKay, *Narration and Discourse in American Realistic Fiction* (Philadelphia: University of Pennsylvania Press, 1982), p. 19.

20 Northrop Frye, *Anatomy of Criticism: Four Essays* (Princeton, N.J., 1957), p. 233. [See also pp. 97–106 in this book.]

21 Mikhail Bakhtin, "Discourse Typology in Prose," in *Readings in Russian Poetics: Formalist and Structuralist Views*, ed. Ladislav Matejka and Krystyna Pomorska (Cambridge, Mass.: MIT Press, 1971), p. 190.

22 Frye, *Anatomy of Criticism*, p. 234.

Sensational Designs

Jane Tompkins

Jane P. Tompkins (b. 1940)

Born in New York City, Jane Tompkins attended Bryn Mawr College and Yale University, where she received her Ph.D. in 1966. She taught at Temple University (1967–83) and Duke University (1984–98), before becoming a professor of English and Education at the University of Illinois at Chicago. Since 2001 Tompkins has also served as Special Assistant to the Provost for the Campus Environment, where she works to improve the university's learning environment. Tompkins's involvement in educational reform is also apparent in her autobiography, *A Life in School: What the Teacher Learned* (1996), her numerous articles on pedagogy, and her extensive work on faculty development. She has been honored as a National Humanities Center Fellow and a National Endowment for the Humanities Senior Fellow. Tompkins has contributed to four areas of literary criticism. *Reader-Response Criticism: From Formalism to Post-Structuralism* (edited, 1980) helped launched that field; ''Me and My Shadow'' (1987) signaled the advent of personal criticism; *Sensational Designs: The Cultural Work of American Fiction, 1790–1870* (1985) helped reshape ideas of canon formation; and all of these works contributed to feminist criticism.

Introduction: The Cultural Work of American Fiction

This book is the beginning of an attempt to move the study of American literature away from the small group of master texts that have dominated critical discussion for the last thirty years and into a more varied and fruitful area of investigation. It involves, in its most ambitious form, a redefinition of literature and literary study, for it sees literary texts not as works of art embodying enduring themes in complex forms, but as attempts to redefine the social order. In this view, novels and stories should be studied not because they manage to escape the limitations of their particular time and place, but because they offer powerful examples of the way a culture thinks about itself, articulating and proposing solutions for the problems that shape a particular historical moment. I believe that the works of fiction that this book examines were written not so that they could be enshrined in any literary hall of fame, but in order to win the belief and influence the behavior of the widest possible audience. These novelists have designs upon their audiences, in the sense of wanting to make people think and act in a particular way.

Consequently this book focuses primarily, though not exclusively, on works whose obvious impact on their readers has made them suspect from a modernist point of view, which tends to classify work that affects people's lives, or tries to, as merely sensational or propagandistic. *Uncle Tom's Cabin*, perhaps the most famous work of American fiction, has not until very recently drawn the attention of modern critics; Susan Warner's *The Wide, Wide World*, second only to Stowe's novel in its popular and critical success in the nineteenth century, has since dropped from sight completely; *The Last of the Mohicans*, also a best-seller in its own time, has retained critical visibility, but, like the novels by Warner and Stowe, has come to be thought of as more fit for children than for adults. Brockden Brown's novels, not at all popular when Brown was alive, subsequently gained a certain critical reputation but always with the proviso that they contained glaring artistic defects. In fact, what all of these texts share, from the perspective of modern criticism, is a certain set of defects that excludes them from the ranks of the great masterpieces: an absence of finely delineated characters, a lack of verisimilitude in the story line, an excessive reliance on plot, and a certain sensationalism in the events portrayed. None is thought to have a distinguished prose style or to reflect a concern with the unities and economies of formal construction that modern criticism seeks in great works of art. One purpose of this book is to ask why these works, many of which did not seem at all deficient to their original audiences, have come to seem deficient in the way I have just described. Another is to question the perspective from which these deficiencies spring to mind.

That perspective comes under fire in the opening chapter, which prepares the way for a consideration of non-canonical texts by investigating the processes through which canonical texts achieve their classic status. Using Hawthorne's reputation as a case in point, it argues that the reputation of a classic author arises not from the "intrinsic merit" of his or her work, but rather from the complex of circumstances that make texts visible initially and then maintain them in their preeminent position. When classic texts are seen not as the ineffable products of genius but as the bearers of a set of national, social, economic, institutional, and professional interests, then their domination of the critical scene seems less the result of their indisputable excellence than the product of historical contingencies. Through a close description of the reasons why Hawthorne's work has continued to compel our admiration, I attempt to loosen the hold his texts have exercised over American criticism, and thus to make possible the consideration of other texts, which the current canon has blotted from view.

In order to understand these neglected texts, that is, to see them, insofar as possible, as they were seen in the moment of their emergence, not as degraded attempts to pander to the prejudices of the multitude, but as providing men and women with a means of ordering the world they inhabited, one has to have a grasp of the cultural realities that made these novels meaningful. Thus, rather than asking how a given text handled the questions which have recently concerned modern critics – questions about the self, the body, the possibilities of knowledge, the limits of language – I have discussed the works of Brown, Cooper, Stowe, and Warner in relation to the religious beliefs, social practices, and economic and political circumstances that produced them. History is invoked here not, as in previous historical criticism, as a backdrop against which one can admire the artist's skill in transforming the raw materials of reality into art, but as the only way of accounting for the enormous impact of works whose force escapes the modern reader, unless he or she makes the effort to recapture the world view they sprang from and which they helped to shape. It is on this basis, that of a new kind of historical criticism, that I advance the claim that my approach yields more fruitful results than some more narrowly "literary" critical modes. Because I want to understand what gave these novels force for their initial readers, it seemed important to recreate, as sympathetically as possible, the context from which they sprang and the specific problems to which they were addressed. I have therefore not criticized the social and political attitudes that motivated these writers, but have tried instead to inhabit and make available to a modern audience the viewpoint from which their politics made sense.

This is not to say that my own attitude toward these texts is neutral or disinterested. Any reconstruction of "context" is as much determined by the attitudes and values of the interpreter as is the explication of literary works; my reading of the historical materials as well as the textual analyses I offer grow directly from the circumstances, interests, and aims that have constituted me as a literary critic. If I have from time to time accused other critics of a "presentist" bias, the same charge can be levelled against my own assumptions, which are of course no more free than theirs from the constraints of a particular historical situation. My claim is not that I am more neutral or disinterested than others, but rather that the readings I offer here provide a more satisfactory way of understanding the texts in question than the current critical consensus has.

To be specific about the interests that have motivated me: what lies behind this study is a growing awareness, on my part, of the extremely narrow confines of literary study as it is now practiced within the academy, and with that, a sense of the social implications of this exclusionary practice. Because I am a woman in a field dominated by male scholars, I have been particularly sensitive to the absence of women's writing from the standard American literature curriculum. I chose to discuss two works of domestic, or "sentimental," fiction because I wanted to demonstrate the power and ambition of novels written by women, and specifically by women whose work twentieth-century criticism has repeatedly denigrated.

Reading the scattered criticism of popular domestic novels led me to recognize – though I am certainly not the first to have done so – that the *popularity* of novels by women has been held against them almost as much as their preoccupation with "trivial" feminine concerns. And this led to the observation, again not original with me, that popular fiction, in general, at least since the middle of the nineteenth century, has been rigorously excluded from the ranks of "serious" literary works. That exclusion seems to me especially noteworthy in American literature, since the rhetoric of American criticism habitually invokes democratic values as a hallmark of greatness in American authors. When Melville calls upon that "great democratic God" and celebrates "meanest mariners, renegades, and castaways," it is cause for critical acclaim, but when the common man steps out of *Moby-Dick* or *Song of Myself* and walks into a bookstore, his taste in literature, or, as is more likely, hers, is held up to scorn. Because I think it is morally and politically objectionable, and intellectually obtuse, to have contempt for literary works that appeal to millions of people simply *because* they are popular, I chose to discuss three works of popular fiction in order to demonstrate the value of these texts: to explore the way that literature has power in the world, to see how it connects with the beliefs and attitudes of large masses of readers so as to impress or move them deeply.

I chose the texts I did because I wanted to find a way of opening up the canon not only to popular works and to works by women, but also to texts that are not usually thought to conform to a definition of imaginative literature – for example, the advice books, tract society reports, and hagiographic biographies discussed in the chapter on Susan Warner. These forms of non-fictional discourse, when set side by side with contemporary fiction, can be seen to construct the real world in the image of a set of ideals and beliefs in exactly the same way that novels and stories do. So much so that in certain instances, unless one already knows which is fiction and which fact, it is impossible to tell the difference. Finally, I have included chapters on two novels by Charles Brockden Brown because I wanted to show that texts already in the canon, which modern critics have considered artistically weak or defective, assume a quite different shape and significance when considered in light of the cultural "work" they were designed to do.

The critical perspective that has brought into focus the issues outlined here stems from the theoretical writings of structuralist and post-structuralist thinkers: Lévi-Strauss, Derrida, and Foucault; Stanley Fish, Edward Said, and Barbara Herrnstein Smith. My debt to these writers is so pervasive that I have not, with one or two exceptions, cited their work at any particular point. But the way of thinking about literature that informs the book as a whole, as well as the kinds of arguments offered in individual chapters, springs directly from my study of their work. The perspective this work affords has not only determined many of the aims and values embodied here, but has also suggested some of the tactics that I have used in interpreting the texts under discussion.

Because I was trying to understand what gave these novels traction in their original setting (i.e., what made them popular, not what made them "art"), I have looked for continuities rather than ruptures, for the strands that connected a novel to other similar texts, rather than for the way in which the text might have been unique. I have not tried to emphasize the individuality or genius of the authors in question, to isolate the sensibility, modes of perception, or formal techniques that differentiate them from

JANE TOMPKINS

other authors or from one another. Rather I have seen them, in Foucault's phrase, as "nodes within a network," expressing what lay in the minds of many or most of their contemporaries. Therefore I do not argue for the value of these texts on the grounds of their *difference* from other texts, as is normally done in literary criticism, showing how they avoid the pieties of the age and shun what is stereotyped or clichéd. My aim rather has been to show what a text had *in common* with other texts. For a novel's impact on the culture at large depends not on its escape from the formulaic and derivative, but on its tapping into a storehouse of commonly held assumptions, reproducing what is already there in a typical and familiar form. The text that becomes exceptional in the sense of reaching an exceptionally large audience does so not because of its departure from the ordinary and conventional, but through its embrace of what is most widely shared.

My own embrace of the conventional led me to value everything that criticism had taught me to despise: the stereotyped character, the sensational plot, the trite expression. As I began to see the power of the copy as opposed to the original, I searched not for the individual but for the type. I saw that the presence of stereotyped characters, rather than constituting a defect in these novels, was what allowed them to operate as instruments of cultural self-definition. Stereotypes are the instantly recognizable representatives of overlapping racial, sexual, national, ethnic, economic, social, political, and religious categories; they convey enormous amounts of cultural information in an extremely condensed form. As the telegraphic expression of complex clusters of value, stereotyped characters are *essential* to popularly successful narrative. Figures like Stowe's little Eva, Cooper's Magua, and Warner's Ellen Montgomery operate as a cultural shorthand, and because of their multilayered representative function are the carriers of strong emotional associations. Their familiarity and typicality, rather than making them bankrupt or stale, are the basis of their effectiveness as integers in a social equation.

The more I thought about the structure of these novels, the more I came to see the solving or balancing of such equations as the purpose that rationalizes their often repetitive and improbable plots. The problems these plots delineate – problems concerning the relations among people of different sexes, races, social classes, ethnic groups, economic levels – require a narrative structure different from the plots of modern psychological novels, a structure that makes them seem sensational and contrived in comparison with texts like *The Ambassadors* or *The Scarlet Letter*. But the endlessly repeated rescue scenes in *Arthur Mervyn* and *The Last of the Mohicans*, the separation of families in *Uncle Tom*, and the Job-like trials of faith in *The Wide, Wide World*, while violating what seem to be self-evident norms of probability and formal economy, serve as a means of stating and proposing solutions for social and political predicaments. The benevolent rescuers of *Arthur Mervyn* and the sacrificial mothers of *Uncle Tom's Cabin* act out scenarios that teach readers what kinds of behavior to emulate or shun; because the function of these scenarios is heuristic and didactic rather than mimetic, they do not attempt to transcribe in detail a parabola of events as they "actually happen" in society; rather, they provide a basis for remaking the social and political order in which events take place. When read in the light of its original purpose, the design of a novel like *Wieland* is no less functional than that of *The Scarlet Letter*.

In arguing for the positive value of stereotyped characters and sensational, formulaic plots, I have self-consciously reversed the negative judgments that critics have passed on these features of popular fiction by re-describing them from the perspective of an altered conception of what literature is. When literary texts are conceived as agents of cultural formation rather than as objects of interpretation and appraisal, what counts as a "good" character or a logical sequence of events changes accordingly. When one sets aside modernist demands – for psychological complexity, moral ambiguity, epistemological sophistication, stylistic density, formal economy – and attends to the way a text offers a blueprint for survival under a specific set of political, economic, social, or religious conditions, an entirely new story begins to unfold, and one's sense of the formal exigencies of narrative alters accordingly, producing a different conception of what constitutes successful characters and plots. The text succeeds or fails on the basis of its "fit" with the features of its immediate context, on the degree to which it provokes the desired response, and not in relation to unchanging formal, psychological, or philosophical standards of complexity, or truth, or correctness.

Thus, the novel's literary style, no less than its characters and plot, will seem forceful and expressive to the degree that it adopts an idiom to which a contemporary audience can respond. When little Eva says to Topsy, " 'O, Topsy, poor child, *I* love you' ... with a sudden burst of feeling, and laying her little thin, white hand on Topsy's shoulder; 'I love you because you haven't any father, or mother, or friends: – because you've been a poor, abused child! I love you, and I want you to be good,' " her style may seem saccharine or merely pathetic to us. But her language had power to move hundreds of thousands of readers in the nineteenth century because they believed in the spiritual elevation of a simple childlike idiom, in the spiritual efficacy of "sudden burst[s] of feeling," and in the efficacy of what is spiritual in general. And so when Eva ends her speech to Topsy by saying "it's only a little while I shall be with you," the comparison evoked between the doll-like Eva and the son of God does not seem absurd or contrived to Stowe's readers – it is not comparing great things with small, but affirming the potential of every person, man, woman, or child, to live and die as Christ did. Within the context of evangelical Christianity, one might say of Stowe what R. P. Blackmur said of Melville – that she habitually used words greatly.

This last point broaches, in summary fashion, an issue that goes to the heart of the present project, namely, the relationship between aesthetic value and the text's historical existence. Reconstituting the notion of value in literary works is an aim which all of these essays share. People who have read one or more of them in various forms, or heard me lecture over the last few years, almost invariably ask whether the works I am discussing are really literary or not – are they, someone always asks, really any *good*? This question, which raises theoretical issues central to my project, is the subject of the final chapter. I have postponed this discussion until the end, since any argument for changing the criteria by which we judge literary texts must depend not only on abstract reasons but on a discussion of individual cases as well.

The Novel and the Police

D. A. Miller

David A. Miller (b. 1948)

D. A. Miller received bachelor's and master's degrees from Cambridge University, and bachelor's and doctoral degrees from Yale University. After receiving his Ph.D. in 1977, Miller joined the faculty of the University of California, Berkeley, where he taught until 1989. After four years at Harvard University and seven at Columbia University, Miller returned in 2000 to Berkeley, where he is John F. Hotchkis Professor in English. His honors include fellowships from the Guggenheim Foundation and the American Council of Learned Societies. In addition to *The Novel and the Police* (1988), Miller has also written *Narrative and its Discontents: Problems of Closure in the Traditional Novel* (1981); *Bringing Out Roland Barthes* (1992); *Place for Us: Essay on the Broadway Musical* (1998); and *Jane Austen, or The Secret of Style* (2003).

Foreword: "But Officer…"

Even the blandest (or bluffest) "scholarly work" fears getting into trouble: less with the adversaries whose particular attacks it keeps busy anticipating than through what, but for the spectacle of this very activity, might be perceived as an overall lack of authorization. It is as though, unless the work at once assumed its most densely professional form, it would somehow get unplugged from whatever power station (the academy, the specialization) enables it to speak. Nothing expresses – or allays – this separation anxiety better than the protocol requiring an introduction to "situate" the work within its institutional and discursive matrix. The same nervous ritual that attests a positive dread of being asocial – of failing to furnish the proper authorities with one's papers, and vice versa – places these possibilities at an infinite remove from a writing whose thorough assimilation, courted from the start, makes it too readable to need to be read much further. If only for this reason, the moment when "explanations are in order" may rightly give rise to the desire to withhold them (like Balzac's Vautrin, whose last words to the police as they open his closets and seize his effects are "Vous ne saurez rien") long enough, at any rate, to draw attention to what is most compelling in the demand for them.

And the police? In entrusting the arresting character of my title to a term whose mere mention arouses some anxiety (not necessarily least in the law-abiding), I admit to melodramatizing – even at the risk of seeming to misname – the main concern of my work. This work centers not on the police, in the modern institutional shape they acquire in Western liberal culture during the nineteenth century, but on the ramification within the same culture of less visible, less visibly violent modes of "social control." A power that, like the police, theatrically displays its repressiveness becomes of interest here only in its relation to an extralegal series of "micro-powers" disseminating and dissembling their effects in the wings of that spectacle. Michel Foucault has called this series *discipline*, and its most pertinent general propagations include: (1) an ideal of unseen but all-seeing surveillance, which, though partly realized in several, often interconnected institutions, is identified with none; (2) a regime of the norm, in which normalizing perceptions, prescriptions, and sanctions are diffused in discourses and practices throughout the social fabric; and (3) various technologies of the self and its sexuality, which administer the subject's own contribution to the intensive and continuous "pastoral" care that liberal society proposes to take of each and every one of its charges.[1] To label all this "the police" thus anticipates moving the question of policing out of the streets, as it were, into the closet – I mean, into the private and domestic sphere on which the very identity of the liberal subject depends. Though ordinarily off-limits to the police, this sphere is nonetheless, I argue, a highly active site for the production and circulation of a complex power whose characteristically minor, fluid, and "implicit" operations distract our attention from the unprecedented density of its regulation. Were an apology required for the histrionics of, for instance, my title, it would be this: that only an ostentation of style and argument can provide the "flash" of increased visibility needed to render modern discipline a problem in its own right far more fundamental than any it invents to attach its subjects.

Yet it by no means inevitably follows that this extended understanding of policing is suitably promoted through a study of some novels by Dickens, Trollope, and Wilkie Collins. Few of course would dispute that, with Dickens, the English novel for the first time features a massive thematization of social discipline, or that, in direct and undisguised response to Dickens, Trollope and Collins develop the two most important inflections of this thematization in the "realist" and "sensation" traditions respectively.[2]

D. A. MILLER

The difficulty lies less in justifying the individual names chosen to bear the burden of the case than in understanding why the Victorian novel, however exemplified, should be particularly worthy to register such a case in the first place. The use of a fictional representation might seem to trivialize a disciplinary function that would be better illustrated in discourses whose practical orientation is immediately consequential. And the use of an outmoded representation suggests the academician's familiar retreat from the contemporary issues that, sniperlike, he targets only from the safe ground of an obsolescence. Yet perhaps no openly fictional form has ever sought to "make a difference" in the world more than the Victorian novel, whose cultural hegemony and diffusion well qualified it to become the primary spiritual exercise of an entire age. As I hope to show, the point of the exercise, relentlessly and often literally brought home as much in the novel's characteristic forms and conditions of reception as in its themes, is to confirm the novel-reader in his identity as "liberal subject," a term with which I allude not just to the subject whose private life, mental or domestic, is felt to provide constant inarguable evidence of his constitutive "freedom," but also to, broadly speaking, the political regime that sets store by this subject. Such confirmation is thoroughly imaginary, to be sure, but so too, I will eventually be suggesting, is the identity of the liberal subject, who seems to recognize himself most fully only when he forgets or disavows his functional implication in a system of carceral restraints or disciplinary injunctions. I further assume that the traditional novel – the novel that many people define their modernity by no longer reading – remains a vital consideration in our culture: not in the pious and misleading sense that, for instance, "Masterpiece Theatre" has dramatized all but one of the novels I mainly discuss, but because the office that the traditional novel once performed has not disappeared along with it. The "death of the novel" (of that novel, at any rate) has really meant the explosion everywhere of the novelistic, no longer bound in three-deckers, but freely scattered across a far greater range of cultural experience. To speak of the relation of the Victorian novel to the age of which it was, *faute de mieux*, the mass culture, is thus to recognize a central episode in the genealogy of our present.

It has become easy to show how the various decorums that determine a work of literature, from within as well as from without, are exceeded by the disseminal operations of language, narrative, or desire – so easy that the demonstration now proceeds as predictably as any other ritual. Whenever a text makes confident claims to cognition, these will soon be rendered undecidable, and whatever ideological projects it advances will in the course of their elaboration be disrupted, "internally distanciated." Full, focused psychological subjects will be emptied out and decentered as invariably as desire will resurface at the very site of its apparent containment. So common have arguments along these lines become that, even if it were true that literature exercises a destabilizing function in our culture, the current consensus that it does so does not. Yet the point of remarking what one might call (doing violence to wide differences of approach, but not to the orthodoxy in which they have come to cohere) the "subversion hypothesis" of recent literary studies cannot be to dispute the evidence of such subversion, which may well be literature's most definitive, powerful, and seductive effect. It is rather a matter of seeing how this effect tends to function within the overbearing cultural "mythologies" that will already have appropriated it.

Thus, in the case of the nineteenth-century novel, it is at present widely held that (1) though the project of this novel is to produce a stable, centered subject in a stable, centered world, (2) this project is inevitably doomed to failure. Whether the failure is greeted with philosophical resignation (to the fact that meaning can never be pinned down), political relief (that a work's suspect ideological messages don't finally hang together), or erotic celebration (of a desire that erupts when and where it is least wanted), it always gives evidence of a process that, while inherent in "the text," nonetheless remains curiously outside and deconstructive of what this text mundanely "wants to say." Even the most rigorous intentions to the contrary haven't prevented such an account of the novel from reinforcing the familiar mythological opposition between "literature" (which is compensated for its lack of power by an ability to penetrate power's ruses) and "society" (which, albeit oppressively powerful, never quite *knows* its own strength). Not only does this account help preserve for literature – as the very concept of literariness – an almost or even frankly ontological distance from the worldly discourses with which literature could otherwise be seen to collaborate. It also helps preserve the very models of social and psychological centering that, as though they had entranced even the activity of demystifying them, are tirelessly rehearsed within it. Aside from their indubitable nostalgia value, moreover, these models are largely irrelevant to a social order that is busy attaining the condition of (just for instance) the money by which it is obsessed as well as driven: its lack of particularity, the mobility of its exchange, its infinitely removed finality.

Accordingly, this book attempts to redress the "positive" achievement of nineteenth-century fiction. Just as I will argue that the theme of the police is an "alibi" for a station-house that now is everywhere, even or especially in the novel one reads at home, so I will imply the complementary claim that the novel's critical relation to society, much advertised in the novel and its literary criticism, masks the extent to which modern social organization has made even "scandal" a systematic function of its routine self-maintenance.[3] From this perspective, the enterprise of the traditional novel would no longer (or not just) be the doomed attempt to produce a stable subject in a stable world, but would instead (or in addition) be the more successful task of forming – by means of that very "failure" – a subject habituated to psychic displacements, evacuations, reinvestments, in a social order whose totalizing power circulates all the more easily for being pulverized.

* * *

The Novel and the Police

I

The frequent appearance of policemen in novels is too evident to need detecting. Yet oddly enough, the ostensive thematic of regulation thereby engendered has never impugned our belief that "of all literary genres, the novel remains the most free, the most *lawless*."[4] Though the phrase comes from Gide, the notion it expresses has dominated nearly every conception of the form. If a certain puritanical tradition, for instance, is profoundly suspicious of the novel, this is because the novel is felt to celebrate and encourage misconduct, rather than censure and repress it. A libertarian criticism may revalue this misconduct as human freedom, but it otherwise produces a remarkably similar version of the novel, which, in league with rebel forces, would bespeak and inspire various projects of insurrection. This evasive or escapist novel persists even in formalist accounts of the genre as constantly needing to subvert and make strange its inherited prescriptions. All these views commonly imply what Roger Caillois has called "the contradiction between the idea of the police and the nature of the novel."[5] For when the novel is conceived of as a successful act of truancy, no other role for the police is possible than that of a patrol which ineptly stands guard over a border fated to be transgressed. In what follows, I shall be considering what such views necessarily dismiss: the possibility of a radical *entanglement* between the nature of the novel and the practice of the police. In particular, I shall want to address two questions deriving from this entanglement. How do the police systematically function as a topic in the "world" of the novel? And how does the novel – as a set of representational techniques – systematically participate in a general economy of policing power? Registering the emergence of the modern police as well as modern disciplinary power in general, the novel of the nineteenth century seemed to me a good field in which these questions might first be posed. Practically, the "nineteenth-century novel" here will mean these names: Dickens, Collins, Trollope, Eliot, Balzac, Stendhal, Zola; and these traditions: Newgate fiction, sensation fiction, detective fiction, realist fiction. Theoretically, it will derive its ultimate coherence from the strategies of the "policing function" that my intention is to trace.

II

One reason for mistrusting the view that contraposes the notions of novel and police is that the novel itself does most to promote such a view. Crucially, the novel organizes its world in a way that already restricts the pertinence of the police. Regularly including the topic of the police, the novel no less regularly sets it against other topics of surpassing interest – so that the centrality of what it puts at the center is established by holding the police to their place on the periphery. At times, the limitations placed by the novel on the power of the police are coolly taken for granted, as in the long tradition of portraying the police as incompetent or powerless. At others, more tellingly, the marginality is dramatized as a gradual process of marginalization, in which police work becomes less and less relevant to what the novel is "really" about.

Even in the special case of detective fiction, where police detectives often hold center stage, the police never quite emerge from the ghetto in which the novel generally confines them. I don't simply refer to the fact that the work of detection is frequently transferred from the police to a private or amateur agent. Whether the investigation is conducted by police or private detectives, its sheer intrusiveness posits a world whose normality has been hitherto defined as a matter of *not needing* the police or policelike detectives. The investigation repairs this normality, not only by solving the crime, but also, far more important, by withdrawing from what had been, for an aberrant moment, its "scene." Along with the criminal, criminology itself is deported elsewhere.

In the economy of the "mainstream" novel, a more obviously circumscribed police apparatus functions somewhat analogously to define the field that exceeds its range. Its very limitations bear witness to the existence of other domains, formally lawless, outside and beyond its powers of supervision and detection. Characteristically locating its story in an everyday middle-class world, the novel takes frequent and explicit notice that this is an area that for the most part the law does not cover or supervise. Yet when the law falls short in the novel, the world is never reduced to anarchy as a result. In the same move whereby the police are contained in a marginal pocket of the representation, the work of the police is superseded by the operations of another, informal, and extralegal principle of organization and control.

Central among the ideological effects that such a pattern produces is the notion of *delinquency*. For the official police share their ghetto with an official criminality: the population of petty, repeated offenders, whose conspicuousness licenses it to enact, together with the police, a normative scenario of crime and punishment. To confine the action of the police to a delinquent milieu has inevitably the result of consolidating the milieu itself, which not only stages a normative version of crime and punishment, but contains it as well in a world radically divorced from our own. Throughout the nineteenth-century novel, the confinement of the police allusively reinforces this ideology of delinquency. We may see it exemplarily surface in a novel such as *Oliver Twist* (1838). Though the novel is plainly written as a humane attack on the institutions that help produce the delinquent milieu, the very terms of the attack strengthen the perception of delinquency that upholds the phenomenon.

A large part of the moral shock *Oliver Twist* seeks to induce has to do with the *coherence* of delinquency, as a structured milieu or network. The logic of Oliver's "career," for instance, establishes workhouse, apprenticeship, and membership in Fagin's gang as versions of a single experience of incarceration. Other delinquent careers are similarly full of superficial movement in which nothing really changes. The Artful Dodger's fate links Fagin's gang with prison and deportation, and Noah Claypole discards the uniform of a charity boy for the more picturesque attire of Fagin's gang with as much ease as he later betrays the gang to become a police informer. Nor is it fortuitous that Fagin recruits his gang from institutions such as workhouses and groups such as apprentices, or that Mr. and Mrs. Bumble become paupers "in that very same workhouse in which they had once lorded it over others."[6] The world of delinquency encompasses not only the delinquents themselves, but also the persons and institutions supposed to reform them or prevent them from forming. The policemen in the novel – the Bow Street runners Duff and Blathers – belong to this world, too. The story they tell about a man named Chickweed *who robbed himself* nicely illustrates the unity of both sides of the law in the delinquent context, the same unity that has allowed cop Blathers to call robber Chickweed "one of the family" (227). Police and offenders are conjoined in a single system for the formation and re-formation of delinquents. More than an obvious phonetic linkage connects the police magistrate Mr. Fang with Fagin himself, who avidly reads the *Police Gazette* and regularly delivers certain gang members to the police.

In proportion as Dickens stresses the coherence and systematic nature of delinquency, he makes it an *enclosed* world from which it is all but impossible to escape. Characters may move from more to less advantageous positions in the system, but they never depart

D. A. MILLER

from it altogether – what is worse, they apparently never want to. With the exception of Oliver, characters are either appallingly comfortable with their roles or pathetically resigned to them. An elsewhere or an otherwise cannot be conceived, much less desired and sought out. The closed-circuit character of delinquency is, of course, a sign of Dickens's progressive attitude, his willingness to see coercive system where it was traditional only to see bad morals. Yet one should recognize how closing the circuit results in an "outside" as well as an "inside," an "outside" precisely determined as *outside the circuit*. At the same time as the novel exposes the network that ties together the workhouse, Fagin's gang, and the police *within* the world of delinquency, it also draws a circle around it, and in that gesture, holds the line of a *cordon sanitaire*. Perhaps the novel offers its most literal image of holding the line in the gesture of *shrinking* that accompanies Nancy's contact with the "outside." "The poorest women fall back," as Nancy makes her way along the crowded pavement, and even Rose Maylie is shown "involuntarily falling from her strange companion" (302). When Nancy herself, anticipating her meeting with Rose, "thought of the wide contrast which the small room would in another moment contain, she felt burdened with the sense of her own deep shame, and shrunk as though she could scarcely bear the presence of her with whom she had sought this interview" (301). Much of the proof of Nancy's ultimate goodness lies in her awed recognition of the impermeable boundaries that separate her from Rose Maylie. It is this, as much as her love for Bill Sikes (the two things are not ultimately very different), that brings her to say to Rose's offers of help: "I wish to go back.... I must go back" (304). Righteously "exposed" in the novel, the world of delinquency is also actively occulted: made cryptic by virtue of its cryptlike isolation.

Outside and surrounding the world of delinquency lies the middle-class world of private life, presided over by Oliver's benefactors Mr. Brownlow, Mr. Losberne, and the Maylies. What repeatedly and rhapsodically characterizes this world is the contrast that opposes it to the world of delinquency. Thus, at Mr. Brownlow's, "everything was so quiet, and neat, and orderly; everybody was kind and gentle; that *after the noise and turbulence in the midst of which [Oliver] had always lived*, it seemed like Heaven itself"; and at the Maylies' country cottage, "Oliver, *whose days had been spent among squalid crowds, and in the midst of noise and brawling*, seemed to enter on a new existence" (94, 238; italics added). No doubt, the contrast serves the ends of Dickens's moral and political outrage: the middle-class standards in effect, say, at Mr. Brownlow's dramatically enhance our appreciation of the miseries of delinquency. However, the outrage is limited in the contrast, too, since these miseries in turn help secure a proper (relieved, grateful) appreciation of *the standards themselves*. It is systematically unclear which kind of appreciation *Oliver Twist* does most to foster. Much as delinquency is circumscribed by middle-class private life, the indignation to which delinquency gives rise is bounded by gratitude for the class habits and securities that make indignation possible.

The "alternative" character of the middle-class community depends significantly on the fact that it is kept free, not just from noise and squalor, but also from the police. When this freedom is momentarily violated by Duff and Blathers, who want to know Oliver's story, Mr. Losberne persuades Rose and Mrs. Maylie not to cooperate with them:

> "The more I think of it," said the doctor, "the more I see that it will occasion endless
> trouble and difficulty if we put these men in possession of the boy's real story. I am certain

it will not be believed; and even if they can do nothing to him in the end, still the dragging it forward, and giving publicity to all the doubts that will be cast upon it, must interfere, materially, with your benevolent plan of rescuing him from misery." (225)

The police are felt to obstruct an alternative power of regulation, such as the plan of rescue implies. Not to cooperate with the police, therefore, is part of a strategy of surreptitiously assuming and revising their functions. Losberne himself, for instance, soon forces his way into a suspect dwelling in the best policial manner. In a more central and extensive pattern, Oliver's diabolical half-brother Monks is subject to a replicated version of a whole legal and police apparatus. There is no wish to prosecute Monks legally because, as Mr. Brownlow says, "there must be circumstances in Oliver's little history which it would be painful to drag before the public eye" (352). Instead Brownlow proposes "to extort the secret" from Monks (351). Accordingly, Monks is "kidnapped in the street" by two of Brownlow's men and submitted to a long cross-examination in which he is overwhelmed by the "accumulated charges" (372, 378). The Bumbles are brought in to testify against him, and the "trial" concludes with his agreement to render up Oliver's patrimony and sign a written admission that he stole it.

We would call this vigilantism, except that no ultimate conflict of purpose or interest divides it from the legal and police apparatus that it supplants. Such division as does surface between the law and its supplement seems to articulate a deeper congruency, as though the text were positing something like a doctrine of "separation of powers," whereby each in its own sphere rendered assistance to the other, in the coherence of a single policing action. Thus, while the law gets rid of Fagin and his gang, the amateur supplement gets rid of Monks. Monks's final fate is instructive in this light. Retired with his portion to the New World, "he once more fell into his old courses, and, after undergoing a long confinement for some fresh act of fraud and knavery, at length sunk under an attack of his old disorder, and died in prison" (412). The two systems of regulation beautifully support one another. Only when the embarrassment that an initial appeal to the law would have created has been circumvented, does the law come to claim its own; and in so doing, it punishes on behalf of the vigilantes. A similar complicitousness obtains in the fate of the Bumbles. Although the reason for dealing with Monks privately has been to keep the secret of Oliver's parentage, it is hard to know on what basis the Bumbles are "deprived of their position" at the end, since this would imply a disclosure of their involvement in Monks's scheme to the proper authorities. Even if the confusion is inadvertent, it attests to the tacit concurrence the text assumes between the law and its supplement.

The two systems come together, then, in the connivance of class rule, but more of society is covered by the rule than outsiders such as Fagin or monsters such as Monks. Perhaps finally more interesting than the quasi-legal procedures applied to Monks are the disciplinary techniques imposed on Oliver himself. From his first moment at Mr. Brownlow's, Oliver is subject to incessant examination:

> "Oliver what? Oliver White, eh?"
> "No, sir, Twist, Oliver Twist."
> "Queer name!" said the old gentleman. "What made you tell the magistrate that your name was White?"

D. A. MILLER

"I never told him so, sir," returned Oliver in amazement.

This sounded so like a falsehood, that the old gentleman looked somewhat sternly in Oliver's face. It was impossible to doubt him; there was truth in every one of its thin and sharpened lineaments. (81)

However "impossible" Oliver is to doubt, Brownlow is capable of making "inquiries" to "confirm" his "statement" (96). The object of both interrogation and inquiry is to produce and possess a *full account* of Oliver. "Let me hear your story," Brownlow demands of Oliver, "where you come from; who brought you up; and how you got into the company in which I found you" (96). With a similar intent, when Oliver later disappears, he advertises for "such information as will lead to the discovery of the said Oliver Twist, or tend to throw any light upon his previous history" (123). It is clear what kind of narrative Oliver's "story" is supposed to be: the continuous line of an evolution. Not unlike the novel itself. Brownlow is seeking to articulate an original "story" over the heterogeneous and lacunary data provided in the "plot." It is also clear what Oliver's story, so constructed, is going to do: it will entitle him to what his Standard English already anticipates, a full integration into middle-class respectability. Another side to this entitlement, however, is alluded to in Brownlow's advertisement, which concludes with "a full description of Oliver's dress, person, appearance, and disappearance" (123). The "full description" allows Oliver to be identified and (what comes to the same thing here) *traced*. And if, as Brownlow thinks possible, Oliver has "absconded," then he will be traced *against his will*. To constitute Oliver as an object of knowledge is thus to assume power over him as well. One remembers that the police, too, wanted to know Oliver's story.

The same ideals of continuity and repleteness that determine the major articulations of this story govern the minor ones as well. The "new existence" Oliver enters into at the Maylies' cottage consists predominantly in a routine and a timetable:

> Every morning he went to a white-headed old gentleman, who lived near the little church: who taught him to read better, and to write: and who spoke so kindly, and took such pains, that Oliver could never try enough to please him. Then, he would walk with Mrs. Maylie and Rose, and hear them talk of books; or perhaps sit near them, in some shady place, and listen whilst the young lady read: which he could have done, until it grew too dark to see the letters. Then, he had his own lesson for the next day to prepare; and at this, he would work hard, in a little room which looked into the garden, till evening came slowly on, when the ladies would walk out again, and he with them: listening with such pleasure to all they said: and so happy if they wanted a flower that he could climb to reach, or had forgotten anything he could run to fetch: that he could never be quick enough about it. When it became quite dark, and they returned home, the young lady would sit down to the piano, and play some pleasant air, or sing, in a low and gentle voice, some old song which it pleased her aunt to hear. There would be no candles lighted at such times as these; and Oliver would sit by one of the windows, listening to the sweet music, in a perfect rapture. (238)

This "iterative" tense continues to determine the presentation of the idyll, whose serenity depends crucially on its legato: on its not leaving a moment blank, or out of consecutive order. "No wonder," the text concludes, that at the end of a very short time,

"Oliver had become completely domesticated with the old lady and her niece" (239). No wonder indeed, when the techniques that structure Oliver's time are precisely those of a domesticating pedagogy. Despite the half-lights and soft kindly tones, *as well as by means of them*, a technology of discipline constitutes this happy family as a field of power relations. Recalling that Blathers called Chickweed "one of the family," conjoining those who work the police apparatus and those whom it works over, we might propose a sense – only discreetly broached by the text – in which the family itself is "one of the family" of disciplinary institutions.

III

Oliver Twist suggests that the story of the Novel is essentially the story of an active regulation. Such a story apparently requires a double plot: regulation is secured in a minor way along the lines of an official police force, and in a major way in the working-through of an amateur supplement. As an example of high-realist fiction, Trollope's *The Eustace Diamonds* (1873) reverses the overt representational priorities of *Oliver Twist*. Trollope is much more concerned to explore his high-bourgeois world than he is to portray delinquency, which he seems prepared to take for granted. Thus, by way of shorthand, the novel will illustrate both the generality and the continuity of the doubly regulatory enterprise I've been discussing in Dickens. What needs regulation in *The Eustace Diamonds*, of course, is Lizzie's initial appropriation of the diamonds. The very status of the "theft" is open to question. Lizzie cannot clearly be said to "steal" what is already in her possession, and her assertion that her late husband gave her the diamonds cannot be proved or disproved. Although the family lawyer, Mr. Camperdown, is sure that "Lizzie Eustace had stolen the diamonds, as a pickpocket steals a watch," his opinion is no more a legal one than that of the reader, who knows, Trollope says, that Mr. Camperdown is "right."[7] In fact, according to the formal legal opinion solicited from Mr. Dove, the Eustace family may not reclaim the diamonds as heirlooms while there are some grounds on which Lizzie might claim them herself as "paraphernalia."

Part of what places Lizzie's theft in the interstices of the law is her position as Lady Eustace. It is not just that John Eustace refuses to prosecute on account of the consequent scandal, or that Lizzie is invited and visited by the best society. The law does not cover a lady's action here for the same reason that Mr. Camperdown is ignorant of the claim for paraphernalia:

> Up to this moment, though he had been called upon to arrange great dealings in reference to widows, he had never as yet heard of a claim made by a widow for paraphernalia. But then the widows with whom he had been called upon to deal, had been ladies quite content to accept the good things settled upon them by the liberal prudence of their friends and husbands – not greedy, blood-sucking harpies such as this Lady Eustace. (1:254)

If, as Dove's opinion shows, the legal precedents about heirlooms do not clearly define the status of Lizzie's possession of the diamonds, it is because a similar question has not previously arisen. In the world Lizzie inhabits, the general trustworthiness of widows of peers has been such that it didn't need to arise. Nor – a fortiori – have the police been much accustomed to enter this world. As Scotland Yard itself acknowledges, at a later turn in the story, "had it been an affair simply of thieves, such as thieves ordinarily are, everything would have been discovered long since; – but when lords and ladies with titles come to be mixed up with such an affair, – folk in whose house a policeman can't have his will at searching and browbeating, – how is a detective to detect anything?" (2:155).

The property whose proper ownership is put in doubt is the novel's titular instance of the impropriety that comes to rule the conduct of Lizzie, characterize her parasitical friends (Lord George, Mrs. Carbuncle, Reverend Emilius), and contaminate the otherwise decent Frank Greystock. Significantly, Lizzie's legally ambiguous retention of the diamonds opens up a series of thefts that – in certain aspects at least – resemble and prolong the initial impropriety. First, the notoriety of the diamonds in her possession attracts the attentions of professional thieves, who attempt to steal the diamonds at Carlisle, but (Lizzie's affidavit to the contrary) fail to obtain them. Their failure in turn generates a later attempt in London, in which the diamonds are successfully abstracted. In part, Trollope is no doubt using the series to suggest the "dissemination" of lawlessness. But if one theft leads to another, this is finally so that theft itself can lead to *arrest* within the circuit of the law. Subsequent thefts do not simply repeat the initial impropriety, but revise it as well, recasting it into what are legally more legible terms. The plot of the novel "passes on," as it were, the initial offense until it reaches a place within the law's jurisdiction.

Thus, the last theft is very different from the first. It involves a breaking and entering by two professional thieves (Smiler and Cann), working in collaboration with Lizzie's maid (Patience Crabstick) and at the behest of a "Jew jeweller" (Mr. Benjamin), who exports the stolen diamonds and has them recut. In short, theft finally comes to lodge in the world of delinquency: within the practice of a power that binds thieves and police together in the same degree as it isolates the economy they form from the rest of the world represented in the novel. In the circulation of this economy, nothing is less surprising than that Lizzie's maid should pass from a liaison with one of the thieves to a marriage with one of the thief-takers, or that the other thief should be easily persuaded to turn Crown's evidence. Even in terms of the common idiom they speak, police and thieves are all closer to one another than they are to Frank Greystock and Lord Fawn. Yet if theft now has the transparent clarity of pickpocketing a watch, it also has some of the inconsequence. As it is moved down to a sphere where it can be legally named, investigated, and prosecuted, it becomes – in every respect but the magnitude of the stolen goods – a *petty theft*: committed by petty thieves and policed by petit-bourgeois detectives, all of whom are confined to the peripheral world of a subplot. The impropriety which gave rise to the narrative is arrested on so different a terrain from the novel's main ground that, even after the police investigation has solved its "pretty little mystery," the larger question of Lizzie herself must remain:

> Miss Crabstick and Mr. Cann were in comfortable quarters, and were prepared to tell all that they could tell. Mr. Smiler was in durance, and Mr. Benjamin was at Vienna, in the hands of the Austrian police, who were prepared to give him up to those who desired his society in England, on the completion of certain legal formalities. That Mr. Benjamin and Mr. Smiler would be prosecuted, the latter for the robbery and the former for conspiracy to rob, and for receiving stolen goods, was a matter of course. But what was to be done with Lady Eustace? That, at the present moment, was the prevailing trouble with the police. (2:261)

Ultimately, however, it is a trouble *only* with the police. Though Lizzie is never punished by the law, never even has to appear at Benjamin and Smiler's trial, she does not quite get off the hook. For the novel elaborates a far more extensive and imposing principle of social control in what Trollope calls the "world." The coercive force of the "world" shows up best in the case of Lord Fawn, who, if asked what his prevailing motive was in all he did or intended to do, "would have declared that it was above all things necessary that he should put himself right in the eye of the British public" (2:247). Under this principle, Fawn first tries to break off his engagement to Lizzie, when it looks as though the world will disapprove of her holding on to the Eustace diamonds. Later when, in the person of Lady Glencora Palliser, the world takes up Lizzie and considers her a wronged woman, Fawn is once again willing to marry her. The coercion exercised by public opinion in the novel is purely mental, but that apparently suffices. The social order that prevents Frank Greystock from dueling with Fawn – "public opinion is now so much opposed to that kind of thing, that it is out of the question" – allows him to predict with confidence, "the world will punish him" (1:216). As Stendhal might say, society has moved from red to black: from the direct and quasi-instantaneous ceremonies of physical punishment to the prolonged mental mortifications of a diffuse social discipline. Trollope's obvious point in the novel about the instability of public opinion (taking up Lizzie to drop her in the end) should not obscure its role as a policing force. Lizzie may fear the legal consequences of her perjury at Carlisle, but what she actually suffers is the social humiliation of its being publicly known. It is enough to exile her to an untouchable *bohème* in which there is nothing to do but marry the disreputable Reverend Emilius. The Duke of Omnium, whose interest in Lizzie had extended to the thought of visiting her, is at the end quite fatigued with his fascination. "I am afraid, you know," he declares to Glencora, "that your friend hasn't what I call a good time before her" (2:375).

The understatement is profoundly consistent with the nature of discipline. What most sharply differentiates the legal economy of police power from the "amateur" economy of its supplement is precisely the latter's policy of *discretion*. It would be false to see Trollope or Dickens engaged in crudely "repressing" the policing function carried on in everyday life, since, as we have seen, the world they create exemplifies such a function. Yet it would be equally misleading to see *Oliver Twist* or *The Eustace Diamonds* advertising such a function. Though both novels draw abundant analogies between the official police apparatus and its supplementary discipline, they qualify the sameness that such analogies invite us to construe with an extreme sense of difference. When in *The Eustace Diamonds*, for example, Lizzie's gardener Andy Gowran is brought before Lord Fawn to attest to her misbehavior with Frank Greystock, he sees this situation in the legal terms of a trial: "This was a lord of Parliament, and a government lord, and might probably have the power of hanging such a one as Andy Gowran were he to commit perjury, or say anything which the lord might choose to call perjury" (2:175). But the naive exaggeration of the perception ironically repudiates the metaphor it calls into play. The metaphor is more tellingly repudiated a second time, when Fawn refuses to solicit what Gowran has to say. "He could not bring himself to inquire minutely as to poor Lizzie's flirting among the rocks. He was weak, and foolish, and, in many respects, ignorant, – but he was a gentleman" (2:177). "Gentlemanliness" is thus promoted as a kind of social security, defending the privacy of private life from its invasion by policelike practices of surveillance. Yet there is a curious gratuitousness in Fawn's principled refusal to hear Gowran. Though Gowran never makes his full disclosure to Fawn, the latter can hardly be in any doubt about its content. That he already knows what Gowran has to tell is precisely the *reason* for his shamed unwillingness to hear it. Octave Mannoni, following Freud, would speak here of a mechanism of *disavowal* (*Verleugnung*): "Je sais bien, mais quand même..." – "Of course I know, but still...."[8] By means of disavowal, one can make an admission while remaining comfortably blind to its consequences. The mechanism allows Fawn to preserve his knowledge about Lizzie together with the fantasy of his distance from the process of securing it. In more general terms, the discretion of social discipline in the Novel seems to rely on a strategy of *disavowing the police*: acknowledging its affinity with police practices by way of insisting on the fantasy of its otherness. Rendered discreet by disavowal, discipline is also thereby rendered more effective – including among its effects that "freedom" or "lawlessness" for which critics of the Novel (perpetuating the ruse) have often mistaken it. Inobtrusively supplying the place of the police in places where the police cannot be, the mechanisms of discipline seem to entail a relative *relaxation* of policing power. No doubt this manner of passing off the regulation of everyday life is the best manner of passing it on.

IV

What has been standing at the back of my argument up to now, and what I hope will allow me to carry it some steps further, is the general history of the rise of disciplinary power, such as provided by Michel Foucault in *Surveiller et punir*.[9] There Foucault documents and describes the new type of power that begins to permeate Western societies from the end of the eighteenth century. This new type of power ("new" perhaps only in its newly dominant role) cannot be identified with an institution or a state apparatus, though these may certainly employ or underwrite it. The efficacy of discipline lies precisely in the fact that it is only a *mode* of power, "comprising a whole set of instruments, techniques, procedures, levels of application, targets" (215). The mobility it enjoys as a technology allows precisely for its wide diffusion, which extends from obviously disciplinary institutions (such as the prison) to institutions officially determined by "other" functions (such as the school) down to the tiniest practices of everyday social life. This mobile power is also a modest one. Maintained well below the level of emergence of "the great apparatuses and the great political struggles" (223), its modalities are humble, its procedures minor. It is most characteristically exercised on "little things." While it thus harkens back to an earlier theology of the detail, the detail is now significant "not so much for the meaning that it conceals within it as for the hold it provides for the power that wishes to seize it" (140). The sheer pettiness of discipline's coercions tends to keep them from scrutiny, and the diffusion of discipline's operations precludes locating them in an attackable center. Disciplinary power constitutively mobilizes a tactic of tact: it is the policing power that never passes for such, but is either invisible or visible only under cover of other, nobler or simply blander intentionalities (to educate, to cure, to produce, to defend). Traditional power founded its authority in the spectacle of its force, and those on whom this power was exercised could, conversely, remain in the shade. By contrast, disciplinary power tends to remain invisible, while imposing on those whom it subjects "a principle of compulsory visibility" (187). As in Jeremy Bentham's plan for the Panopticon, a circular prison disposed about a central watchtower, surveillance is exercised on fully visible "prisoners" by unseen "guards." What this machinery of surveillance is set up to monitor is the elaborate regulation (timetables, exercises, and so on) that discipline simultaneously deploys to occupy its subjects. The aim of such regulation is to enforce not so much a norm as the normality of normativeness itself. Rather than in rendering all its subjects uniformly "normal," discipline is interested in putting in place a perceptual grid in which a division between the normal and the deviant inherently imposes itself. Concomitantly, discipline attenuates the role of actual supervisors by enlisting the consciousness of its subjects in the work of supervision. The Panopticon, where it matters less that the inmates may at any moment be watched than that they know this, only begins to suggest the extent to which disciplinary order relies on a subjectivity that, through a rich array of spiritual management techniques, it compels to endless self-examination. Throughout the nineteenth century, discipline, on the plan of hierarchical surveillance, normalization, and the development of a subjectivity supportive of both, progressively "reforms" the major institutions of society: prison, school, factory, barracks, hospital.

And the novel? May we not pose the question of the novel – whose literary hegemony is achieved precisely in the nineteenth century – in the context of the age of discipline? I have been implying, of course, that discipline provides the novel with its essential "content." A case might be made, moreover, drawing on a more somber tradition than the one exemplified in the fundamentally "comic" novels thus far considered, that this content is by no means always discreet. The novel frequently places its protagonists under a social surveillance whose explicit coerciveness has nothing to do with the euphoria of Oliver Twist's holiday in the country or the genteel understatement of Trollope's "world." In Stendhal's *Le rouge et le noir* (1830), for instance, the seminary Julien Sorel attends at Besançon is openly shown to encompass a full range of disciplinary practices. Constant supervision is secured either by Abbé Castanède's secret police or through Abbé Pirard's "moyens de surveillance."[10] Exercises such as saying the rosary, singing canticles to the Sacred Heart, "etc., etc.," are regulated according to a timetable punctuated by the monastic bell. Normalizing sanctions extend from examinations to the most trivial bodily movements, such as eating a hard-boiled egg. Part of what makes Julien's career so depressing is that he never really finds his way out of the seminary. The Hôtel de la Mole only reduplicates its machinery in less obvious ways: as Julien is obliged to note, "Tout se sait, ici comme au séminaire!" (Everything gets known, here just as much as in the seminary; 465). And the notorious drawback of being in prison is that the prisoner may not close the door on the multilateral disciplinary attempts to interpret and appropriate his crime. One scarcely needs to put great pressure on the text to see all this. The mechanisms of discipline are as indiscreet in Stendhal's presentation as his disapproval of them is explicit.

Something like that disapproval is the hallmark of all the novels which, abandoning the strategy of treating discipline with discretion, make discipline a conspicuous practice. If such novels typically tell the story of how their heroes come to be destroyed by the forces of social regulation and standardization, they inevitably tell it *with regret*. Just as Stendhal's sympathies are with Julien rather than with the directors of the seminary or the bourgeois jury that condemns him, characters like Dorothea Brooke and Tertius Lydgate seem far more admirable to George Eliot than the citizens of *Middlemarch* (1873) who enmesh them in their "petty mediums." The explicitly thematized *censure* of discipline seems to provide surer ground for retaining the opposition between the novel and the police that our readings of Dickens and Trollope put in question. The specific liabilities we have seen in that opposition when its terms were an official police and an amateur supplement cease to pertain when *both* modes of policing are opposed to the transcendent, censorious perspective taken by the novel. No longer arising from within the world of the novel, the opposition could now less vulnerably play between the world of the novel and the act of portraying it.

Yet we have already seen how the "disavowal" of the police by its disciplinary supplement allows the latter to exercise policing power at other, less visible levels and in other, more effective modes. Similarly, the novel's own repudiation of policing power can be seen not to depart from, but to extend the pattern of this discreet *Aufhebung*. Whenever the novel censures policing power, it has already reinvented it, in *the very practice of novelistic representation*. A usefully broad example of this occurs in Zola's *Nana* (1880). The prostitutes in the novel, one recalls, are in mortal terror of the police. So great is their fear of the law and the prefecture that some remain paralyzed at the doors of the cafés when a police raid sweeps the avenue they walk. Nana herself "avait toujours tremblé devant la loi, cette puissance inconnue, cette vengeance des hommes qui pouvaient la supprimer" (had always trembled before the law, that unknown authority, that male vengeance which had the power to do away with her).[11] Even amid her luxury, she "avait conservé une épouvante de la police, n'aimant pas à en entendre parler, pas plus que de la mort" (had never got over a fear of the police, whom she no more wanted to hear mentioned than she would death; 1374). The greatest anxiety is apparently inspired by the prospect of being "mise en carte": put on a police list entailing obligatory medical examination. Zola permits us no illusions about the policing of prostitution. When not seeking simply to terrorize, the *agents de moeurs* underhandedly trade their protection for sexual favors, as the experience of Nana's friend Satin shows. Yet the police procedures that are censured in the story reappear less corruptibly in Zola's method of telling it. What is *Nana* but an extended *mise-en-carte* of a prostitute: an elaborately researched "examination" sustained at the highest level by the latest scientific notions of pathology and at the lowest by the numerous "fiches" on which data is accumulated? In a larger social dimension, and with a similar prophylactic intention, Zola wants to register the Parisian *fille* no less than the police. *Nana* is the title of a file, referring both to the prostitute who resists the record and to the novel whose representational practice has already overcome this resistance.

NOTES

1   It might go without saying, but as he used to joke, it goes better with saying, that I largely find the conceptual bearings of this study in the thought of Michel Foucault, from whose personal counsel I also had opportunity to profit. Yet in announcing my project as "a Foucauldian reading of the Novel," I mean to signal, besides an intellectual debt, an intellectual gamble for

which that debt is the capital. For perhaps the most notable reticence in Foucault's work concerns precisely the reading of literary texts and literary institutions, which, though often and suggestively cited in passing, are never given a role to play within the disciplinary processes under consideration. As Foucault once put it in an interview with Roger-Pol Droit (published posthumously in *Le Monde*, September 6, 1975, p. 12), "Pour moi, la littérature était à chaque fois l'objet d'un constat, pas celui d'une analyse ni d'une réduction ni d'une intégration au champ même de l'analyse" (On every occasion I made literature the object of a report, not of an analysis and not of a reduction to, or an integration into, the very field of analysis).

2 A roughly similar triangulation might be shown to determine the corpus of nineteenth-century French fiction, where Balzac decisively sets forth the disciplinary themes and plots that, always in allusion to his achievement, will be rehearsed either hyperbolically by the feuilletonistes (Sue, du Terrail) or litotically by the realists (Flaubert, Maupassant, Zola). The first essay in this volume locates what for merely practical reasons I have confined myself to treating as the English instance within the broader context of the Western European novel.

3 Consider, from Dickens's *Bleak House*, Esther's account of her last visit, with Ada and Richard, to the Court of Chancery: "We found such an unusual crowd in the Court of Chancery that it was full to the door and we could neither see nor hear what was passing within. It appeared to be something droll, for occasionally there was a laugh, and a cry of 'Silence!' It appeared to be something interesting, for everyone was pushing and striving to get nearer. It appeared to be something that made the professional gentlemen very merry, for there were several young counsellors in wigs and whiskers on the outside of the crowd, and when one of them told the others about it, they put their hands in their pockets, and quite doubled themselves up with laughter, and went stamping about the pavement in the hall.... Our suspense was short; for a break up soon took place in the crowd, and the people came streaming out looking flushed and hot, and bringing a quantity of bad air with them. Still they were all exceedingly amused, and were more like people coming out from a Farce or a Juggler than from a court of Justice. We stood aside, watching for any countenance we knew; and presently great bundles of paper began to be carried out – bundles in bags, bundles too large to be got into any bags, immense masses of papers of all shapes, which the bearers staggered under, and threw down for the time being, anyhow, on the Hall pavement, while they went back to bring out more. Even these clerks were laughing. We glanced at the papers, and seeing Jarndyce and Jarndyce everywhere, asked an official-looking person who was standing in the midst of them, whether the cause was over. 'Yes,' he said; 'it was all up with it at last!' and burst out laughing too" (*Bleak House* [Oxford: Oxford University Press, 1948], p. 865). As it reaches its conclusion, what one reader has called Dickens's "carnivalization of bureaucracy" becomes nothing more – or less – than a carnivalization *by* bureaucracy. Esther is in no laughing mood; rather it is the professional gentlemen, the counsellors, and the clerks who "double themselves up" in amusement and who are willing to produce and receive the whole performance as Farce. Accordingly, Dickens's satire on the court cannot be described as simply a repetition of social tragedy as literary farce, since it is farce itself that must be repeated (and as what, if not the laughable, farcical protest against ever being anything but farce). This fact must cast a long shadow on the novel's efforts to satirize the court in ways not already foreseen and put to good use by the requirements of bureaucratic operation.

4 André Gide, *Les faux-monnayeurs*, in *Oeuvres complètes*, ed. L. Martin-Chauffier, 15 vols. (Paris: Nouvelle Revue Française, 1932–39), 12:268. "De tous les genres littéraires...le roman reste le plus libre, le plus *lawless*."

5 Roger Caillois, *Puissances du roman* (Marseilles: Sagittaire, 1942), p. 140.

D. A. MILLER

6   Charles Dickens, *Oliver Twist* (Oxford: Oxford University Press, 1949), p. 414. In the case of works cited more than once, page references to the edition first noted will be thereafter given parenthetically in the text.

7   Anthony Trollope, *The Eustace Diamonds*, 2 vols. in 1 (Oxford: Oxford University Press, 1973), 1:252.

8   See Octave Mannoni, "Je sais bien, mais quand même…," in his *Clefs pour l'imaginaire* (Paris: Seuil, 1969), pp. 9–33.

9   Michel Foucault, *Surveiller et punir* (Paris: Gallimard, 1975). Foucault will be cited in the English translation of Alan Sheridan, *Discipline and Punish* (New York: Pantheon, 1977).

10 Stendhal, *Le rouge et le noir*, in *Romans et nouvelles*, ed. Henri Martineau, 2 vols. (Paris: Bibliothèque de la Pléiade, 1952–55), 1:406.

11 Emile Zola, *Nana*, in *Les Rougon-Macquart*, ed. Armand Lanoux and Henri Mitterand, 5 vols. (Paris: Bibliothèque de la Pléiade, 1960–67), 2:1315.

Gender, Sexuality, and the Novel

PART VII

Introduction

When feminists such as Toril Moi credit Virginia Woolf as "the great mother and sister" of Anglo-American twentieth-century feminist criticism,[1] they seek to delineate a distinctively modern tradition of feminist theory, one that finds in the novel its distinctive literary expression. But it is also true that many of the concerns of this modern tradition are as old as English literature itself. When Chaucer's Wife of Bath asks, "Who peyntede the leon? Tel me Who!" she is railing against the covert operation of social power, its ability to mask the political basis of aesthetic representation. The Wife of Bath's belief that aesthetic representation is a vital political weapon in the social battle for minority self-expression remains at the heart of gender and sexuality studies today. In the twentieth century, gay and lesbian activists, feminists, psychoanalysts, and Foucauldian historians alike have influentially argued that gender and sexuality are primary categories of social identity; that there is no moment in social life when issues of gender and sexual identity are not at stake; and that even aesthetic activities that appear to have nothing to do with either gender or politics nonetheless are produced in and through a gender system that politicizes all representation.

In other parts of this volume we have already seen versions of the Wife of Bath's question aimed at novel theory itself. Why has theory developed as the privileged discourse of literary analysis? Why is it assumed that literary study should be objective and impersonal? Who painted the lion of novel theory? White men, Barbara Johnson and Henry Louis Gates would answer. Male academics, Jane Tompkins would say. Eve

Sedgwick asks us to formulate the answer to this question not just in terms of race, class, and gender, but in terms of sexuality as well. Her essay "Queer Performativity: Henry James's *The Art of the Novel*" (1989) relates the performance of James's queer identity in the Prefaces to his aesthetic project. In Part I, we saw that James's Prefaces served as the foundational documents for Anglo-American novel theory. James's insights into narrative technique and his discussion of the novel as a high art form led others to believe that the novel was worthy of its own aesthetic theory, which James's followers set about systematizing. By focusing on what they consider to be the objective properties of novelistic form, formalists diminish or bracket the subjectivity of novel reader and author. Sedgwick effectively undoes the transmogrification of Jamesian Preface into impersonal theory by reclaiming the autobiographical content of these writings. But importantly, she does not return us to the explicit autobiographical content of the Prefaces, James's nostalgic reflection upon the scenes and moods of his novel-writing career. Sedgwick instead revises (rather than abandons) the formalist conception of literary form by finding James's sexuality performed through form, made legible through the deployment of language that is registered by Jamesian style. On Sedgwick's view, the "narrative figures" (to use the term Tzvetan Todorov picks up from Víktor Shklovsky [see pp. 206–11]) that structure James's Prefaces convey neither the identity of the novel as a genre nor the identity of narrative per se, but the dramatic performance of Henry James's own queer identity.

What does it mean for the master of novel theory to be also "a kind of prototype of…queer performativity" (616)? As post-Foucauldian interpreters, attuned to the social control enacted through knowledge discourses, we might expect Sedgwick to argue that James's investment in conceptualizing the novel as an aesthetic object is an attempt to keep closeted his nonnormative sexual desire, an attempt to deflect critical attention on to his novels as a means of hiding from view the defining feature of his own subjectivity. But although Sedgwick is more than willing to entertain the performative function of James's aesthetic project, she also believes that James's sexuality is vividly expressed in the Prefaces for anyone who knows how to look for it. In other words, she believes that James's project of writing about his novels as aesthetic forms enables queer identity to come into view as what she elsewhere calls an open secret: by not talking directly about his subjectivity, James can perform his subjectivity. The meaning of this performance will never, on this view, be found in what the discourse is "about" but always only by the way, specifically by the way James's sexuality is conveyed through Jamesian style.

But as willing as Sedgwick is to argue for the legibility of James's sexual self-expression, she is reluctant to assign an equally legible political meaning to such involuntary self-display. Sedgwick's psychoanalytic approach to sexuality and gender leads her to challenge the tendency in identity politics to posit a clear and unambiguous relation between social discourse and political meaning. In the introduction to *Between Men* (also included in this section), she invokes the example of pornography as a social discourse whose political value has been vigorously debated among feminists. Does pornography promote female sexual degradation and violence against women? Or is it a means of female sexual liberation and social empowerment? Each position, Sedgwick points out, has its feminist supporters. In "Queer Performativity" Sedgwick notes that, in the wake of Foucault, cultural critics in general have become more tentative about assigning clear political value to social acts. Foucault's theory of power, discussed in Part

VI, puts us in an interpretative world where cultural practices are wholly mediated by hegemonic control, making it difficult to distinguish an authentic act of social rebellion from the scapegoat required by power to maintain the status quo. But Sedgwick also notes that this loss of interpretative legibility has not so much suspended political evaluation as made it both uniform and wishy-washy: no matter what aspects of culture critics are examining and no matter what the period: "The bottom line is generally the same: kinda subversive, kinda hegemonic" (619).

Sedgwick finds this stalemate an impediment to effective political action and proposes that a theoretical alternative to Foucault be worked toward. She offers as a starting point the value of Judith Butler's theory of "performativity," a psycho-political model of subjectivity that Sedgwick believes escapes the either/or binary of Foucauldian evaluation (subversive or hegemonic) and thus enables a more complex articulation of political effects. Butler, according to Sedgwick, takes for granted that individual identity can never be outside of power – that social practices will always be kinda hegemonic and kinda subversive – and then works from there to delineate the varieties of political activity available to an individual within a particular social and historical moment. Sedgwick believes that Butler's account of human consciousness offers a useful way of understanding identity as essentially defined by a border state – kinda culturally constructed and kinda personally chosen.

We can better grasp the inspiration Sedgwick finds in Butler's ideas when we look at Sedgwick's account of her own political goal in theorizing queer identity as performative. Instead of defining queer identity as something essential and exclusive to a certain minority group (which she understands as the divisive and limiting path of identity politics), Sedgwick locates queer identity on a continuum of human social experience. Queer identity is, on her view, neither unique nor autonomous but an intensification of a universal psychic condition (619). Sedgwick strives, in other words, to define queer identity as a difference in degree rather than kind, a more acute version of universal psychic functions rather than a deviation from them. Her refusal to essentialize queer identity in any way leads her explicitly to reject the project of formulating a "theory of homosexuality," or a theory "even of one 'kind' of 'homosexuality'" (616). Her interpretative ambition is instead to locate queer performativity within a general theory of human psychology, one that hypothesizes sociality and individuality as mutually defining categories, brought into relation by the psychological structure of human experience. Drawing upon research into the emotion of shame conducted by Michael Franz Basch, Francis Broucek, Donald L. Nathanson, Silvan Tomkins, and others, Sedgwick argues that the experiences of sociality and individuality come into being as imbricated "threshold" states, a dynamic liminality that positions all human identity "between sociability and introversion" (617).

Sedgwick finds this research particularly powerful because it destigmatizes shame, defining it as a key component in the structure of human experience, rather than a bad emotion in need of remedy or purge. She thus seeks to locate queer identity not just within a normative account of human psychological experience but an account of normative psychological experience that is itself rooted in anti-essentialism. The psychological theory that she draws upon does for shame what she strives to do for queer identity: to posit an essence that "delineates it without defining it or giving it content" (616). On Sedgwick's deconstructive view, shame is a "proto-affect" (610). A proto-affect is a psychological structure that, because it has no content of its own, can be deployed in the service of a variety of affects. Lacking specific content, the value of this affect lies in its form, its durable liminality: "The place of identity, the structure 'identity,' marked by shame's threshold between sociability and introversion, may be established and naturalized in the first instance *through shame*" (617). Thus for Sedgwick the signs of shame – head averted, face flushed, etc. – that communicate the individual's sense of "interrupted identification" with the social community, are indicators of the larger psychic structure fundamental to all individual experience of sociality, not just the emotion of shame. As she puts it, "shame...makes identity" (610). By this she means shame makes vivid the dynamic relation between the individual's sense of social isolation and the individual's desire to "reconstitute the interpersonal bridge." Shame thus "derives from and aims toward sociability" even as it is the condition under which "a sense of self will develop" in and through a problematic relation to this sociability (610).

Sedgwick thus interestingly offers a definition of queer identity that is in many ways similar to the definition of African American identity posited by Henry Louis Gates (see Part VI). In both cases, what most distinguishes subaltern identity is its essential inessentialness, its definition as a structure or form rather than as content. But although these two theorists both deploy deconstructive arguments in the service of identity theory, the difference between signifyin' and shame as defining terms for de-essentialized identity suggests that queer performativity and African American signifyin' may for these theorists possess, after all, other attributes beyond their shared inessentialism and liminality. As we saw in the introduction to Part VI, Gates, because he is more willing to engage in the identity politics critiqued by Sedgwick, argues for the historical particularism of African American experience, a particularism that becomes its own type of exceptionalism. Gates has, in other words, no trouble arguing that signifyin' is a linguistic practice performed better and more often by African Americans than other social groups because it derives, he believes, from political and cultural circumstances unique to African Americans. Sedgwick, by contrast, does not want to essentialize queer identity by saying that it is necessarily defined more than other social identities by shame. Nor does she want to claim, the way Gates does about African American identity, that queer identity is more theatrical or necessarily more performative than other social identities.

Sedgwick's goal is to avoid the type of essentialism embraced by Gates by developing a historical account of queer identity that would take into consideration the pragmatics of identity construction within a given culture and at a particular historical moment. In her words, she strives to show how "the structuration of shame differs strongly between cultures, between periods, and between different forms of politics" (617). Her attempt to apply Butler's more nuanced view of political cause and effect further encourages her to think not only on a large scale (differences between eras and cultures) but also on a micro-level, to take into account how the experience of queer identity can vary from "one person to another within a given culture and time" (617).

But despite her theoretical goals, Sedgwick's own application of this pragmatics yields an account of queer identity that is the opposite of nuanced, that in fact reinforces cultural stereotypes about queer identity. Her description of Jamesian sexuality, for example, relies wholly on the social practices and sexual attitudes that she believes James shares with other gay men. In keeping with the theoretical position she derives from Butler, Sedgwick argues that that these social practices hold no single or necessary political value, but are "available for the work of metamorphosis, reframing, refiguration, *trans*figuration, affective and symbolic loading and deformation" (617). But although her politics thus resist the kinda subversive, kinda hegemonic binary, the sweep of her "historical" continuum is so grand that it precludes the kind of nuanced identity formation she seeks. Her interpretation of the Prefaces relies upon the continuity she assumes between the life of gay men at the turn of the century (in England? in America? in Anglo-American contexts?) and the life of gay men at the end of the century. What is more, this continuity is derived, on her view, from the shared experience of shame, making shame not just the "first instance" of proto-affect but a primary attribute of gay identity. Sedgwick's historical approach leads her to a decidedly trans-historical conclusion: that queer identity, is, after all, "tuned most durably to the note of shame," defined by "shame-consciousness and shame-creativity" (618). Queer performativity as a theory of queer identity ends up looking kinda historical, and kinda deconstructive – but ultimately awfully essentializing.

Thus, despite her stated negative intention to refrain from offering a "theory of homosexuality" and her declared positive goal of doing "some justice to the specificity, the richness, above all the explicitness of James's particular erotics" (616), Sedgwick in fact imports to the Prefaces a single story of gay identity and psychosexual development that provides a counter-plot to James's narrative of his development as a novelist. Central to Sedgwick's account of queer identity is the shame that she says accompanies the youthful discovery of nonnormative sexual desire. According to Sedgwick, the Prefaces, written late in James's life, reinvoke this past, shamed self as part of a strategy of self-definition and mastery. James, she argues, uses the Prefaces to register the difference between that embarrassed youth and the successful writer he has since become. But, as Sedgwick observes, James does not recall this youth simply to dismiss him. On the contrary, James goes out of his way in the Prefaces to establish a relationship to him. In Sedgwick's words, "the very distance of these inner self-figurations from the speaking self of the present is marked, treasured and in fact eroticized. Their distance (temporal, figured as intersubjective, figured in turn as spatial) seems, if anything, to constitute the relished internal space of James's absorbed subjectivity" (613). On Sedgwick's view, queer sexuality does not, furthermore, just result in this particular strategy for achieving a sense of autonomy, the achievement of Jamesian authorial "narcissism" (613). It also, according to Sedgwick, provides James with a way of "cathecting or eroticizing that very shame as a way of coming into loving relation to queer or 'compromising' youth" (613). In fashioning ways to stay in touch with this past self, James re-experiences the "ecstasy-inducing" "flush of life" (James's phrase) that "the older man … *doesn't* feel" (613). James thus does not attempt to repress or work through that shameful self, but to establish an erotic relation to it. Through the Prefaces, James enjoys for himself, with himself, an inter-generational gay flirtation – and the flush of shame that accompanies this "pederastic" scenario allows for the "mutual self display" of old and new identities: the queer sexuality that both share, and which is for the older man "an explicit source of new, performatively induced authorial magnetism" (616).

I hope that this necessarily condensed summary of Sedgwick's reading of the Prefaces gives at least some sense of the dazzling conceptual complexity of her analysis. Although she may not realize the degree to which her theory of queer performativity depends upon a paradigmatic and trans-historical story about the psychosocial development of queer identity, the significances she finds in Jamesian style could not be more nuanced, complex, or surprising. Sedgwick unpacks a whole narrative of sexual development from turns of phrases and recurring images. The provocativeness of her claims about James in fact lies precisely in the *way* she derives them from the Prefaces, in her own practice of literary criticism. Sedgwick's argument about James's sexuality, in other words, would not be nearly as outrageous, perhaps hardly controversial at all, had she not made it through close reading: by attributing great meaning to small phrases, by finding sexual significance in figures of speech. A dissenting reader might feel that Sedgwick goes too far, that James's style in the Prefaces should be more simply understood as a superfluity, an adornment to meaning. But of course Sedgwick's reply to this critique would be that queer identity is performed precisely by the way, expressed through the meaning that one does not consciously communicate, giving weighty significance to even the slightest expressional gestures.

In her introduction to *Between Men* (1985), Sedgwick explicitly asks why issues of homosociality should be a literary question (591). Why shouldn't "the structure of men's relations with other men" (587) be the concern of the sociologist rather than the literary critic? The interesting answer she gives has exactly to do with the literary as a particular method of critical analysis. Sedgwick argues that cultural and political critique may be the end point of literary analysis, but that end is best achieved through the means of literary criticism, by which she means the interpretative strategies that are second nature to the literary critic. The literary critic is the interpreter who best understands that, in Sedgwick's words, "the paths of meaning" are "crabbed and oblique" (594). In possession of the knowledge that "the signifying relation of sex to power, of sexual alienation to political oppression, is not the most stable, but precisely the most volatile of social nodes" (594), the literary critic is able to attend to the complexities of the cultural field, to identify and appreciate the symbolic nature of the social text, "what it may mean for one thing to signify another" (594). While Sedgwick in theory defines the literary in a technical sense as the critical awareness of the play of signification, it is undeniable that her own critical practice achieves the kind of style, voice, and linguistic intensity that are associated with a more commonplace notion of the literary. And we can find in Sedgwick's own writing the achievement of style that can give literary criticism its own value as literature. As literary texts are increasingly esteemed by cultural theorists for their social value, the literary reemerges, it seems, as an attribute of criticism itself.

I have spent so long engaging Sedgwick not only because of the ground-breaking nature of her work, but also because she articulates a theoretical position that has caused a certain amount of gender trouble for feminists, especially those who feel that the relation between sex and power is clearer and more directly available for political reform than Sedgwick's theory allows. In the rest of this essay, I want to trace a fault line within feminist theory: the disagreement between what we can loosely call materialist and deconstructive cultural feminism. Material feminists seek to restrict the symbolic circuits of signification precisely because they believe that, without some unambiguous referential meanings, there can be no political basis for social reform or subaltern empowerment. These feminists believe that literary theory is itself part of the political problem: that it has deconstructed both efficacious subjectivity and the legibility of political value precisely at the historical moment when women and minorities had begun to realize social equality. For this school of feminism, not all social activity is equally, to invoke Sedgwick's phrase again, "available for the work of metamorphosis, reframing, refiguration, *trans*figuration, affective and symbolic loading and deformation" ("Queer Performativity," 617). On the contrary, there are many cases and social contexts, so this counter-argument goes, when a thing may overwhelmingly signify itself – especially when that thing is female empowerment. These feminists refer us to what they regard as the brute facts of material social reform. Women as property owners, as consumers with legalized and independent access to birth control, as professionals, as political officials – these are pointed to as obvious and visible manifestations of positive social change. For the materialist feminist, female access to literary authorship also belongs in this list of social progress. And feminist literary historians working from this point of view have set forth their own influential platform for the importance of novel studies, not just to literary study as a field but, more sweepingly, to any historical understanding of the evolution of female social empowerment.

From Virginia Woolf on, twentieth-century feminists have been drawn to what they consider to be the novel's defining generic feature: its particular preoccupation with making female identity visible. *Pamela, Clarissa, Jane Eyre, Tess of the D'Urbervilles, Charlotte Temple, Jane Talbot, Ruth Hall, Maggie, The Girl of the Streets, What Maisie Knew, Sister Carrie, My Antonia, Lolita* – these are of course not just the names of individuals, but girls and women whose sexuality fuels three centuries of novel writing. And it is not just that so many major novels are focused upon the sexuality of a sympathetic female protagonist. Fanny Burney, Jane Austen, Charlotte Brontë, Emily Brontë, Elizabeth Gaskell, George Eliot, Virginia Woolf, Susanna Rowson, Hannah Webster Foster, Maria Susanna Cummins, Fanny Fern, Susan Warner, Harriet Beecher Stowe, Louisa May Alcott, Charlotte Gilman, Kate Chopin, Edith Wharton, and Willa Cather are popular women novelists whose own sexuality is, so such feminists argue, expressed in and through the novel, the literary form women found best suited to their self-representation.

By the mid-nineteenth century, women so dominated a market with a seemingly insatiable appetite for female fiction that the American Nathaniel Hawthorne, filled with highbrow ambition, felt obliged to denounce the novel as a modern commodity produced by "a d—d mob of scribbling women." Hawthorne resisted such aesthetic contamination by refusing to call his fiction a novel, declaring it instead to be a species of "romance" derived from a hallowed literary father, Edmund Spenser. In 1929 Virginia Woolf looks back over two centuries of English novel writing and frames in this way the historical interest of the novel's emergence as a particularly female literary genre:

> Why, we ask at once, was there no continuous writing done by women before the eighteenth century? Why did they then write almost as habitually as men, and in the course of that writing produce, one after another, some of the classics of English fiction? And why did their art then, and why to some extent does their art still, take the form of fiction? ("Women," 580)

Woolf's questions are still live ones for the feminist cultural historians collected in this section. The different answers provided by Nancy Armstrong, Catherine Gallagher, and

Woolf herself are largely due to the different theories of culture and ideology held by each scholar, especially their differing sense of whether the female identity that the novel is so visibly about signifies itself – or instead appears to signify itself in order to signify something else.

Woolf's own theoretical position is closest to that of the material feminists I have been describing. The phrase "a room of one's own," the title of her book-length study of women's fiction, is an emblem for materialist values: when women have the same access to money and property as men, when a woman has "a room of her own and five hundred a year," she will, according to Woolf, "write a better book."[2] In "Women and Fiction" (1929), a briefer meditation on the same topic, Woolf similarly equates aesthetic achievement with social progress defined in material terms. Woolf notes how the changes in "law and custom" improved the opportunities for female self-expression. She contrasts the fifteenth-century woman, who might be "beaten and flung about the room if she did not marry the man of her parents' choice" (581), to the modern woman who enjoys political power of her own as a "voter, a wage-earner, a responsible citizen" (584).

Why will women write better novels with a room of their own and five hundred pounds a year? The obvious reply works through the question's materialist assumptions: because women will have social power and material independence, their lives will have public significance and consequence. No longer regulated to the ephemera of oral history, the privacy of domestic life, their lives will be written down – in public registers, in biographies, in histories, in newspapers, and in literature. Material changes will also provide women with the privacy and leisure time needed for writing, relieving them from the women's work that is never done, and unmooring the traditional patriarchic conceptions of the social roles available to women: wife, mother, daughter, spinster, prostitute, angel in the house. Woolf argues that at the beginning of the nineteenth century in England, "the slight changes in law and customs and manners" enabled women with literary inclinations to pursue authorship. And she further argues that these aspiring literary women inclined to a genre that itself was hardly literary at all: in Woolf's words, as the "least concentrated form of art," the novel was the "easiest thing for a woman to write" (581). If the novel's minimal formal requirements made it easy for a novice writer to master, its focus on character made it suited to the social experience of domestic women. In Woolf's words, this woman "lived almost solely in her home and her emotions"; residing "as she did in the common sitting-room, surrounded by people, a woman was trained to use her mind in observation and upon the analysis of character" (581). The nineteenth-century novel is thus for Woolf the form that best expresses the social construction of nineteenth-century female identity, both its possibilities and limitations during the period.

As material conditions for women improve, as women are allowed more social opportunities, it will, Woolf believes, become "easier" for women not just to write novels but to write good novels. This is not just because more women will have a room of their own and five hundred pounds and so the pool of literary women will increase. The surprise of Woolf's materialist position lies in the twist she gives to the causal relation between the social evolution of women and the development of the novel as a genre. As Woolf imagines the future, women who write fiction will do so no longer because it is the literary genre best suited to the limited social experience and fledgling literary abilities of women as a class; the woman of the future, free to express herself in any field of writing, will choose to write a novel because she is a novelist. And as the novel ceases to be a women's genre, as it becomes free from the social function of representing female identity, it, in turn, will develop its own autonomous identity as an art form.

Woolf's view of female social evolution comes as a surprise for those who think of her as championing not just a room of one's own for women but a room that is valuable because it is woman's own room: the figure suggests that, sequestered from male interference, female identity can at last develop in its own terms, according to its own intrinsic interests, that privacy can create authentic interiority, a female point of view. Woolf does indeed in "Women and Fiction" sometimes talk about "women's values" as if they were natural and essential. At these moments social mediation seems to be presented as a veil that women will eventually throw off: when a woman no longer looks at the world "through the eyes or through the interests of husband or brother," she will see it for herself (584). And Woolf imagines that the uncovering of female point of view has political consequences. When women paint the lion, they will "alter the established values – to make serious what appears insignificant to a man, and trivial what is to him important" (583). This reproportioning, Woolf believes, will extend to the very sentences that women will write. The standard sentence for the novel is loose, heavy, and pompous – a male sentence. Woolf advises women novelists to invent a woman's sentence, to fit the "natural shape of her thought" (583).

But even when Woolf invokes a woman's "natural" identity, her account of it is always comparative and social: a woman's point of view is made visible through its difference from a man's, its dynamic inversion of male values. Woolf ultimately believes that women can gain true independence only when they can transcend this competitive relation with men, achieving a point of view that looks through the eyes neither of a husband or brother nor an aggrieved female. As women have more genuine opportunities to participate in public life, as their experience of life increases, then so too will the female point of view expand until it encompasses the public perspective. Woolf's materialism does not culminate in the ideal of female social reformer or "gadfly to the state" (584). She imagines the ultimate evolutionary aim of women's writing as a move beyond sexual identification altogether, passing beyond the social categories of "groups and classes and races" (584) to the most generalized public vision possible, a universal vision of humanity. In the future, the best women's writing will, Woolf predicts, take the form of poetry and philosophy, modes that, in her words, "look beyond the personal and the political" to "wider questions…of our destiny and the meaning of life" (584). A room of one's own and five hundred a year will, it turns out, make women not more private but more public, allowing them the economic freedom and social opportunity to cultivate the qualities of "impersonality and dispassion" that are enjoyed already by public men.

Novels themselves will become "better," in this "golden," this "fabulous" age (585), Woolf believes, because they, too, will have evolved toward impersonality, within the limits set by genre. The novel can fulfill its own best literary identity only when it expresses an authorial vision of life that itself possesses "integrity," which for Woolf means that the novelist has achieved a point of view beyond social positionality, beyond all social mediation. Unmediated perspective is, by this logic, thus also impersonal vision: it arises from subjective experience but finds integrity, becomes abstractable, as a coherent vision of life, a philosophy. For Woolf, this philosophy should not be expressed in the novel as philosophical meditation (in the mode, say, of D. H. Lawrence or Leo Tolstoy). The integrity of the author's vision instead becomes the organizing principle of novelistic form, giving significant "shape" or structure to the novelist's depiction of the social world. If we think of any of Woolf's own novels, we can instantly understand what Woolf means by significant shape. And in "Women and Fiction," she makes clear what contributes to the novel's failure of form, the susceptibility to looseness (what Henry James called bagginess) that she deplores. On her account, the novel jeopardizes its integrity of form when it is marred by "excrescences" of sociality, which turn the novel into a litter of historical fact or "the dumping ground for the personal emotions" (584).

The complexity of Woolf's materialism and, concomitantly, her theory of the novel thus lies in her belief that the public point of view is the only truly sincere point of view. She thus judges the sincerity of a novelist's vision of life not by its detailed rendering of the author's subjective experience of life, but by the breadth of its perspective. The "spontaneous warbling" of individual self-expression that Woolf says inaugurates female literary endeavor is on this account only seemingly the expression of authentic female point of view. In fact this warbling is as much a testament to the social construction of female identity under patriarchy as the limited agency wrested by women on their own behalf. In a move that may seem surprising to present-day feminists, Woolf argues that women novelists who choose not to warble but to rail against patriarchy do not speak in a more authentic female voice but, on the contrary, through their emotion and complaint simply make vivid the extent of their male domination. As Woolf puts it:

> In *Middlemarch* and in *Jane Eyre* we are conscious not merely of the writer's character, as we are conscious of the character of Charles Dickens, but we are conscious of a woman's presence – of someone resenting the treatment of her sex and pleading for its rights. This brings into women's writing an element which is entirely absent from a man's, unless, indeed, he happens to be a working-man, a negro, or one who for some other reason is conscious of disability. It introduces a distortion and is frequently the cause of weakness. (582)

On Woolf's view, the author's felt sense of disability becomes a liability for artistic achievement: "The vision becomes too masculine or it becomes too feminine; it loses its perfect integrity and, with that, its most essential quality as a work of art" (582). In the works of George Eliot and Charlotte Brontë, Woolf finds the palpability of a woman's "presence" is itself an impediment to form, an excrescence of sociality. By giving authentic expression to their own emotion, these women fail to achieve an impersonal point of view, a point of view that could be abstracted and expressed by literary form. Woolf deplores what W. E. B. DuBois calls a "twofold instead of single point of view," which for her, as for him, is a register of the mediation of subaltern identity by power. But whereas for DuBois social protest, complaint, even song are ways for African Americans to resist mediation, to regain the integrity of their own point of view, for Woolf the emotional expression of outrage or suffering never counts as a "sincere" female point of view; it is instead itself a register of the patriarchal mediation that prevents women from attaining their own autonomous point of view, a point of view whose integrity is a precursor to and a qualification for the public vision that she believes more women will eventually be capable of achieving.

Woolf's belief in the ethical good of impersonality clearly resonates with the defenses of impersonality put forward by other author/critics in her own cultural moment, high modernists such as T. S. Eliot, Ezra Pound, and James Joyce. But the particular way Woolf defines impersonality, its particular association for her with the evolution of female identity and novelistic aesthetics into public spheres, has proven to be highly generative for feminist scholars not just in her historical moment but across the twentieth century. Nancy Armstrong, for example, prefaces *Desire and Domestic Fiction: A Political History of the Novel* (1987) with an epigraph from *A Room of One's Own*. Armstrong follows Woolf in believing that the great historical event of female authorship can only be understood in relation to the social history of ordinary female lives. At Woolf's own historical moment, the beginning of the twentieth century, the history of women's lives still remains to be written; its facts, Woolf says, are still hidden from view, "locked in old diaries, stuffed away in old drawers, half-obliterated in the memories of the aged" (580). But by 1987, when Armstrong writes, that archive has begun to emerge. Armstrong answers Woolf's question – why towards the end of the eighteenth century middle-class women began to write? – by drawing upon female conduct books, educational tracts, recreational reform theories, and Puritan treatises on household gender roles. Similar to Jane Tompkins (see Part VI), Armstrong believes that the novel is not distinguishable from these social discourses but is best understood as a preeminent gender discourse, one with powerful cultural influence. But although Tompkins and Armstrong are both ardent feminists, Armstrong's historical account of the novel's political function is more pessimistic than Tompkins'. On Armstrong's view, the novel's rise in popularity in eighteenth-century England is a function of the new strategies of social discipline emerging during this period, strategies that on her view serve the consolidation of middle-class political power. Her Foucauldian understanding of the new type of political power that emerges in this period, a social control that works, as we have discussed in Part VI, not through violence but through the power of representation, prompts Armstrong to ask if it really makes any difference whether men or women paint the lion – or whether the very notion that female identity is distinct and different from male identity isn't itself an illusion invented during the eighteenth century to promote middle-class hegemony.

For Armstrong, the determining nature of economic interests calls into question both the possibility and the desirability of any feminism that posits fundamental differences between male and female social experience. In a highly controversial move, Armstrong declares that late twentieth-century feminists who promote the notion of an essentially female identity, who argue that female identity is defined by its own point of view, who believe women speak in a voice distinct and different from men, are not only unwittingly contributing to the ideological oppression of women, but doing so by keeping alive the eighteenth-century belief that the social life of men and women is divisible into separate spheres. Armstrong herself believes, as Sedgwick in theory does, that gender has no essential or inherent qualities (either biological or cultural) but is "a purely semiotic process" (627), a "site for changing power relations between classes and cultures as well as between genders and generations" (627). The emergence of gender as a constitutive quality of human identity is a historical phenomenon, Armstrong claims, one that arises in the eighteenth century. As she puts it, "though one of the many possible functions of sexuality," gender differences became at this historical moment the culture's primary category for understanding identity, displacing in importance even "functions of generation and genealogy, which organized an earlier culture" (628).

According to Armstrong, the gendered division of labor (paid male work done out of the home vs. unpaid female work done for the family) was justified in the eighteenth-century cultural imaginary by the belief in the inherent suitability of men and women to these social spaces. Armstrong argues that separate sphere ideology developed into the view that women were inherently "at home" not only in the social space they occupied but, by extension, in their selfhood. Socially restricted from public life, women could be culturally constructed as wholly outside of public life: autonomous and private. By the nineteenth century, Armstrong claims, domestic ideology would lead to the belief that women were inherently creatures of emotion and sensibility; guided by the intrinsic "passions of the human heart" (630), women also possessed the intrinsic "qualities of mind" (622) that would enable self-governance over these passions. On Armstrong's view, the autonomous and private domestic world that was imagined as a woman's natural social space is transmogrified into the cultural notion that women in fact possess more interiority than men, that their capacity for inner life, for mental and emotional experience, is naturally more capacious and refined than that possessed by "public" men.

In a complicated but fascinating extension of her argument, Armstrong claims that although the notion of psychological identity is invented in and through separate spheres ideology, it ultimately takes over as a new cultural paradigm for all human identity, male and female alike. In Armstrong's provocative formulation, "the modern individual was first and foremost a woman" (626). Her study thus traces a historical shift in which the very basis of distinction between men and women – the essential interiority that was said to belong to women alone (622–3) – becomes the modern category for all human identity. What causes this cultural evolution? For Armstrong, the complex turnings of false ideology are simply explained by a Marxist account of class power. The middle class fosters its hegemony through the successful palliation of what are, on Armstrong's view, the real material factors that determine all social identity, male and female, private or public. By promoting a conception of universal psychological person-hood, one that imagines social beings as independent individuals, whose worth exists apart from or beyond history, birth, title, wealth, and labor, the middle class can successfully cloak the material basis of its own power.

Armstrong thus explicitly calls herself a materialist (630) – but her political theory of social power leads her to an account of the rise of the female novelist that is substantially different from Woolf's. For Armstrong, the historical emergence of the woman novelist is a result of the false ideology of female autonomy promoted by middle-class political interest. On her view, female novelists "rise" at the same time that women are permitted to imagine themselves as authorities on female conduct, female education, and female religion – a body of writing that is all directed toward cultivating the ideology of separate spheres, the notion that women exist in a realm apart and need separate social instruction. On Armstrong's view, the domestic novel contributes to female social education, by defining "what made a woman desirable" (623). According to Armstrong, these novels are, to use Woolf's term, sincere representations of female identity only in the sense that they accurately record the social conditioning of women during the period. On her reading, domestic novels construct a world in which "desire" is presented as a universal and natural property of womanhood, one in which the sexes are differentiated and linked "by the magic of sexual desire" (638). But this view of female identity and of sexuality is, Armstrong argues, an ideological snare. Domestic novels present identity as natural in order to mask the operation of social power: they turn "political information into the discourse of sexuality" (636). And by fostering the illusion that sexuality is grounded in spontaneous desire, these novels effectively serve as instruments of social control: they "coax and nudge sexual desire into conformity with the norms of heterosexual monogamy" (624).

Armstrong is thus more pessimistic than Woolf about the possibility of transcending political mediation through economic and material gains. For Armstrong, a room of one's own and five hundred pounds will only superficially give women the privacy and opportunity they need to develop their own points of view, beyond the influence of their fathers and brothers. Property and money will indeed make them socially equal to men, but whereas for Woolf the economic and social empowerment of men and women leads both sexes to the same impersonal point of view, a disinterested philosophical vision of life, on Armstrong's account such material gains lead only to a more refined condition of political oppression. As property owners with bank accounts, women can, according to Armstrong, now think of themselves as the liberal individuals described by D. A. Miller: convinced of their autonomy and free agency, they do not realize that this delusion of self-independence is the basis of their social discipline (see Part VI). Thus for Armstrong the social empowerment of women cannot, as it could for Woolf, be proven by pointing to the increased role women play in public life: "I will insist that those cultural functions which we automatically attribute to and embody as women – those, for example, of mother, nurse, teacher, social worker, and general overseer of service institutions – have been just as instrumental in bringing the new middle classes into power and maintaining their dominance as all the economic take-offs and political breakthroughs we automatically attribute to men" (639). The new roles for women in the public sphere have, in other words, aided and abetted the political operation of power rather than reforming it.

But if Armstrong and Woolf differ in their estimation of how and if women can gain social power under capitalism, they both share a vision of an ideal future when female identity will no longer be equated with novelistic expression, when the novel will cease to be regarded as the most female of literary forms. Both Armstrong and Woolf theorize that authentic female empowerment will come when women reject the psychologized identity bestowed upon them through fiction. As we have seen, Woolf believes that the novel itself can be reformed, can be reconceived to express a more philosophical vision of life (as she herself does in a work such as *The Waves*); but Woolf also suggests that, given the inherent limitations of the genre (i.e. its formal predilection for individualized and subjectivist representation of identity), women writers of the future may find it more rewarding to turn to genres that already possess this capacity for impersonality, genres such as poetry, history, and philosophy.

To Woolf's list of efficacious modes of public writing, we might add literary scholarship. The literary histories written by both Woolf and Armstrong support their respective theories of female evolution by performing the kind of nonfiction writing that both women admire. Although Woolf does not in "Women and Fiction" reflect upon her own public role as a literary critic and essayist, Armstrong makes explicit the important function she believes literary criticism plays in moving society toward a more authentic mode of female empowerment. For Armstrong, the novel is not superseded by poetry or philosophy – but by literary criticism. On her view, subject position can never be transcended through impersonality; at best it can be made visible through writing that is self-conscious about its own participation in the circulation of social power. She believes that one can begin to enact social reform through political critique, which, on her view, begins with a self-conscious awareness of the kinds of social power she herself does and does not wield as a female academic: "I want to use my power as a woman of the dominant class and as a middle-class intellectual to name what power I use as a form of power rather than to disguise it as the powerlessness of others" (639). As a literary historian and critic, Armstrong strives to undo the ideological power of novels, to lay bare the device of their political instrumentality. By using literary criticism to "name" the operation of power conducted through the novel, she hopes she will restore the "political literacy" (640) that she believes was occluded by the rise of literacy, the growth of the middle-class reading public, and the mass consumption of fiction.

When we turn to the work of Catherine Gallagher, we find a cultural history of the rise of the female novelist that resists both the ethical idealism of Woolf and the reformist mission of Armstrong. Gallagher's method in many ways brings us back to a model of nuanced and pragmatic social analysis that Sedgwick (through her enthusiasm for Butler) put forward as a theoretical ideal. Gallagher's project in *Nobody's Story* (1996) is not to distinguish good feminist politics from bad or to gauge the degree of social oppression enacted through particular literary forms. She escapes the ambivalence of the post-Foucauldian political position by refusing to regard the English cultural practices that are her object of study from any totalizing, evaluative perspective. Her analysis of "the vanishing acts of women writers in the marketplace, 1670–1820" does not, in other words, aim to judge whether these acts were politically or ethically efficacious for women, whether women were made happier by them, or became more authentically female through them. As Gallagher declares in the opening sentences of her introduction, *Nobody's Story* is not a "lament"; it does not rail against "the unjust absence of women from the eighteenth-century literary canon."[3] Nor does she strive through her literary criticism, as many of the discourse theorists in Part VI did, to turn nobodies into somebodies, to make visible to a politically enlightened contemporary audience the female point of view that was rendered invisible under seventeenth-century patriarchic oppression, to make audible in 1996 the female voice that had been silenced in 1696. As her analysis of eighteenth-century English culture makes clear, for Gallagher such politicized recovery projects get in the way of good history: the belief that female identity is any one thing for and in a particular culture – a voice, a point of view – prevents us from understanding the social pragmatics of political agency, for women and for men. For Gallagher, the political status of eighteenth-century English women, their culturally constructed identity and their social power, is socially variable and contextually nuanced. Gallagher brings to light the complex performance of "nobody" as a cultural construction. The social discourse about "nobody" is worthy of study precisely because the culture used it to perform, to invoke Sedgwick's phrase again, the "work of metamorphosis, reframing, refiguration, *trans*figuration, affective and symbolic loading and deformation."

Given the complexity Gallagher attributes to the political function of ideology at any given historical moment, she is skeptical about any historicism that posits a simple connection between past and present, that imagines sympathy or identification to be the authentic mode of historical understanding. Her introduction ends with a statement that (*contra* Jane Tompkins) stresses the distinguishability between historical analysis and personal judgment, between understanding the beliefs that characterized a culture and making those beliefs one's own: "I invite the reader to enjoy these constructions, savor their ironies, analyze their mechanisms, and discern their complex exigencies; I do not recommend *believing* in them as universal truths. 'Caveat emptor' is the motto of this study."[4] For Gallagher the complexity of historical analysis can be a source of readerly pleasure; the richness of the discursive field is something to "enjoy" and even "savor." Although Gallagher does not say that this enjoyment is made possible by the detachability of readerly judgment from cultural analysis, one might conjecture this to be the case. And although Gallagher's caveat emptor, "let the buyer beware," cleverly invokes the reader's own position within a modern literary market, unlike Armstrong, Gallagher does not ascribe to her own reader (any more than she does to English seventeenth-century readers) a particular subject position. Whatever market forces or class interests are at work on the reader of *Nobody's Story*, they do not preclude the reader's enjoyment of historical complexity as a formal pleasure, separate and distinct from the content of the cultural beliefs it records.

What drew Gallagher to the study of "nobody" and how does this cultural concept relate to the rise of the woman novelist? In part, Gallagher's study is generated by the deconstructive questions she brings to an argument like Armstrong's. If it is true that women have been socially constructed as psychological presences, as at home in their bodies and minds, then, Gallagher argues, the ideology of female presence has itself been generated out of an equally enduring and prevalent cultural belief that female identity is especially immaterial, is defined by what it lacks – that insignificance, invisibility, and nothingness are particularly female traits. Gallagher seeks to explain this paradoxical cultural discourse about women (that their somethingness derives from their nothingness) by locating it as part of a larger cultural phenomenon. Women were not, during this historical period, the only somebodies who were nobodies. As she puts it, "the 'nobodies' of my title are not ignored, silenced, erased, or anonymous women. Instead, they are literal nobodies: authorial personae, printed books, scandalous allegories, intellectual property rights, literary reputations, incomes, debts, and fictional characters."[5] Gallagher appeals neither to female identity per se, the market, or middle-class hegemony as a base of ideology. She emphasizes that women, authorship, the marketplace, and fiction "reciprocally define" one another. And it is the "layering of literary, patriarchal and economic exigencies" that puts them in potent interrelation, making the discourse of nobody available for various types of symbolic loading and transformation.[6]

Although Gallagher does not see economic forces determining ideology in any monolithic way, she does agree with Armstrong that the emergence of the book market makes professional authorship possible for women. As book writing became a potentially lucrative pursuit, the cultural status of authorship inevitably changed. It became, first of all, something that women, denied social access to other professions, were more and more tempted to pursue. As Gallagher explains, women were able to make a case for themselves as commercial authors by turning their gendered position as "nobodies" to their own economic advantage. The self-alienation required by commercial publishing was, after all, their natural condition. As modern authors, women did not claim cultural authority but its opposite: their self-abnegation and insignificance enabled them to write not as Author, but for the public. They sought not self-expression but to please others: "women writers emphasized their femininity to gain financial advantage and...in the process, they invented and popularized numerous ingenious similarities between their gender and their occupation."[7] As women developed strategies for "capitalizing on their femaleness," they "embraced and feminized" "remunerative authorship."[8] On Gallagher's view, these "vanishing acts" are thus "*conscious* artifices of the women whose works form the core of this study"(my emphasis).[9]

Gallagher's analysis of commodification makes clear that deliberately and successfully becoming a money-maker does not make a woman author any less of a nobody. Only because authorship in the period was itself conceptualized as a state of disembodiment, of dispossession, could women present themselves as qualified for the job. In her analysis of the discourse of debt and burden that women use to describe their new-found earning power, Gallagher again separates her historical account of the emergence of the woman writer from any judgment about how novel writing helped or hindered female identity per se. In demonstrating how women used what "proved profitable" for their personal gain,[10] Gallagher refrains from arguing that economically successful women were emotionally happier, or ethically better, or even more financially secure than women who were not authors. Women writers may have developed a strategy that allowed them to "thrive"[11] – but Gallagher's study also is careful to trace the discourse of anxiety that accompanies this financial success, the vulnerability, burdens, and even increased financial risks that made some popular women novelists feel more dispossessed than ever before.

The rise of the woman writer is, on Gallagher's view, related to but not itself explanatory of the rise of the novel as a literary form. In the excerpt included in this anthology, Gallagher details the changes in the law that developed in response to the commodification of authorship. Gallagher argues that the novel emerged as a successful commercial genre not because it met an inherent, human need for fiction; rather, fiction developed during this period to meet the market demand for nobodies. Her development of this original and provocative thesis carefully keeps in play the variety of social meanings "nobody" has for the novel. First and foremost is the issue of authorial property. If a novelist has simply copied his ideas from life, then in what sense are they his to sell? Ownership is easier to prove, and legal protections are easier to have, if a writer can argue that the characters in her books are "nobodies," have no social referent but are wholly products of the writer's imagination. As Gallagher explains, the cultural anxiety about the market for character, about the sales to be made by copying an individual life, fostered other types of legislation: if a novelist attempted to hold a mirror to life, he could find himself sued for slander or libel. But if characters were wholly invented, fictional "nobodies," then novelists were protected from the legal vulnerability of social reference.

While Gallagher believes that the legislation that grew up in response to market forces helps explain the incentives authors had to write novels, she goes on to argue that a full understanding of the great historical fact of fiction's emergence as not just a popular, but the dominant, modern literary mode of expression needs to take into account why the public found novels so enjoyable to read. This question is difficult to answer in part because, as she shows, it was the subject of explicit and extensive debate throughout the period. Gallagher's book follows these debates, showing how the question is formulated and reformulated throughout the eighteenth century and from different cultural perspectives within a particular historical moment. The excerpt from her book included in this anthology offers only one facet of this debate: can novels create sympathy for "nobodies"? Should a reader's engagement with fictional characters be properly thought of as sympathetic? If David Hume and other influential philosophers of the period are right, and if human sympathy is the basis of social interaction, then can and should one extend social emotions to imaginary persons (647)?

Gallagher draws out the logic by which Hume can be understood as offering a philosophical defense for the reader's sympathetic response to fictional characters. She notes that Hume defines sympathy as an act of emotional appropriation rather than identification: sympathy, on his view, "is not an emotion about someone else but is rather the process by which someone else's emotion becomes our own" (648). According to Gallagher, Hume believes that the more difference, the more "otherness" there is between the sympathizer and the sympathized, the more risk there is that the circuit of sympathy will fail. By contrast, the less distance there is between sympathizer and sufferer, the more the sympathizer can confidently imagine the sufferer to be close to herself, belonging to herself as a friend or family member, the more successful the sympathetic connection will be. On Gallagher's view, Hume's argument thus makes a case for the advantageous possessability of fictional characters: "Because they were conjectural, suppositional identities *belonging* to no one, they could be universally appropriated. A story about nobody was nobody's story and hence could be entered, occupied, identified with by anybody" (648).

The eighteenth-century defense of novelistic sympathy has resonance with the concerns of many of the twentieth-century theorists included in this volume (see especially Percy Lubbock, Wayne Booth, M. M. Bakhtin, and Nina Baym). Gallagher's book makes visible this enduring theoretical tradition not only by naming it – the novel as nobody – but also by explicitly locating it as a counter-tradition, a theory of generic identity fundamentally opposed to Ian Watt's enduring theory of formal realism. By her invocation of Watt, the father of the "rise of the novel" studies, Gallagher's accountof the rise of the female novelist usefully returns us to where our study of social discourse and the novel began (see Part VI). And we can see how her alternative criteria for deciding where and how to look for the dominant modes of social discourse within the period yield an understanding of novel form that is diametrically opposed to Watt's. Watt argues that the novel is a form defined by a minimal literariness that allows it to serve as a social discourse of individualism; unhampered by literary convention, the novel is distinguished by the specificity and wealth of its referential detail. But onGallagher's view, the novel's referential detail is better understood as precisely theregister of its achieved fictionality. She argues that truly referential discourse, representation that seeks to record the life of real persons, does not need to detail their social world because it can take that world for granted. Because a fictional character belongs to no world, its social world must be created within the world of the novel. Novelistic "realism" is thus, she maintains, paradoxically the definitive sign of fictionality: the novel's creation of "nobody *in particular*" becomes its generic mission (174). Extending Gallagher's argument, we might conclude that the novel's refinement and development of the "reality effect," to use Roland Barthes's term (see page 000 of this volume), is precisely what enables the novel to develop its own aesthetics, to emerge through the cultural debate about its artistic function as an art form. Gallagher's argument suggests that the cultural description of the novel as the least literary of forms also allowed the novel to develop as one of the most imaginative of literary forms. As an act of pure invention, as the expression of nobody's ideas, the novel, through its reality effect, can lay claim to artistic value, redefining the literary as a category by establishing a new set of conventions for the representation of nobody in the nowhere of the novel.

NOTES

1 Toril Moi, *Sexual/Textual Politics: Feminist Literary Theory* (New York: Routledge, 1985) 18.
2 Virginia Woolf, *A Room of One's Own* (1929; New York: Harcourt Brace Jovanovich, 1957) 98.
3 Catherine Gallagher, *Nobody's Story: The Vanishing Acts of Women Writers in the Marketplace, 1670–1820* (Berkeley: University of California Press, 1996) xiii.
4 Ibid. xxiv.
5 Ibid. xiii.
6 Ibid. xviii, xxii.
7 Ibid. xiii.
8 Ibid. xxiv, xiii.
9 Ibid. xviii.
10 Ibid. xxiv.
11 Ibid. xiii.

FURTHER READING

Baym, Nina. *American Women Writers and the Work of History, 1790–1860.* New Brunswick, NJ: Rutgers University Press, 1995.

Butler, Judith. *Gender Trouble: Feminism and the Subversion of Identity.* 1990. New York: Routledge, 1999.

Carby, Hazel V. *Reconstructing Womanhood: The Emergence of the Afro-American Woman Novelist.* New York: Oxford University Press, 1987.

Case, Alison A. *Plotting Women: Gender and Narration in the Eighteenth- and Nineteenth-Century British Novel.* Charlottesville: University Press of Virginia, 1999.

Castle, Terry. *The Apparitional Lesbian: Female Homosexuality and Modern Culture.* New York: Columbia University Press, 1993.

Cohen, Margaret, and Christopher Prendergast, eds. *Spectacles of Realism: Body, Gender, Genre.* Minneapolis: University of Minnesota Press, 1995.

Cohen, William A. *Sex Scandal: The Private Parts of Victorian Fiction.* Durham, NC: Duke University Press, 1996.

DuPlessis, Rachel Blau. *Writing Beyond the Ending: Narrative Strategies of Twentieth-Century Women Writers.* Bloomington: Indian University Press, 1985.

Fetterley, Judith. *The Resisting Reader: A Feminist Approach to American Fiction.* Bloomington: Indiana University Press, 1978.

Fraiman, Susan. *Unbecoming Women: British Women Writers and the Novel of Development.* New York: Columbia University Press, 1993.

Gilbert, Sandra, and Susan Gubar. *The Madwoman in the Attic: The Woman Writer and the Nineteenth-Century Literary Imagination.* 1979. New Haven: Yale University Press, 2000.

Kristeva, Julia. *Desire in Language: A Semiotic Approach to Literature and Art,* ed. Leon S. Roudiez, trans. Thomas Gora, et al. New York: Columbia University Press, 1980.

Lanser, Susan Sniader. *Fictions of Authority: Women Writers and Narrative Voice.* Ithaca, NY: Cornell University Press, 1992.

Litvak, Joseph. *Strange Gourmets: Sophistication, Theory, and the Novel.* Durham, NC: Duke University Press, 1997.

Moi, Toril. *Sexual/Textual Politics: Feminist Literary Theory.* 1985. New York: Routledge, 2002.

Poovey, Mary. *The Proper Lady and the Woman Writer: Ideology as Style in the Works of Mary Wollstonecraft, Mary Shelley, and Jane Austen.* Chicago: University of Chicago Press, 1984.

Pryse, Marjorie, and Hortense J. Spillers, eds. *Conjuring: Black Women, Fiction, and Literary Imagination.* Bloomington: Indiana University Press, 1985.

Sedgwick, Eve K., ed. *Novel Gazing: Queer Readings in Fiction.* Durham, NC: Duke University Press, 1997.

Showalter, Elaine. *A Literature of Their Own: British Women Novelists from Brontë to Lessing.* 1977; Princeton, NJ: Princeton University Press, 1999.

Spacks, Patricia M. *The Female Imagination.* New York: Knopf, 1975.

Spencer, Jane. *The Rise of the Woman Novelist: From Aphra Behn to Jane Austen.* Oxford: Blackwell, 1986.

Warhol, Robyn. *Gendered Interventions: Narrative Discourse in the Victorian Novel.* New Brunswick, NJ: Rutgers University Press, 1989.

Woolf, Virgina. *A Room of One's Own.* 1929. New York: Harcourt Brace Jovanovich, 1957.

Women and Fiction[1]

Virginia Woolf

From *Granite and Rainbow.* New York: Harcourt Brace, 1958 (1929), pp. 76–84. Copyright © 1958 by Leonard Woolf, renewed 1986 by M. T. Parsons, Executor of Leonard Sidney Woolf. Reprinted by permission of Harcourt, Inc.

(1925); *The Common Reader: Second Series* (1932); *The Death of the Moth and Other Essays* (1942); *The Moment and Other Essays* (1947); *The Captain's Death Bed and Other Essays* (1950); and the volume from which this essay is taken, *Granite and Rainbow* (1958). "Women and Fiction" was originally published in the *Forum* (March 1929).

The title of this article can be read in two ways: it may allude to women and the fiction that they write, or to women and the fiction that is written about them. The ambiguity is intentional, for in dealing with women as writers, as much elasticity as possible is desirable; it is necessary to leave oneself room to deal with other things besides their work, so much has that work been influenced by conditions that have nothing whatever to do with art.

The most superficial inquiry into women's writing instantly raises a host of questions. Why, we ask at once, was there no continuous writing done by women before the eighteenth century? Why did they then write almost as habitually as men, and in the course of that writing produce, one after another, some of the classics of English fiction? And why did their art then, and why to some extent does their art still, take the form of fiction?

A little thought will show us that we are asking questions to which we shall get, as answer, only further fiction. The answer lies at present locked in old diaries, stuffed away in old drawers, half-obliterated in the memories of the aged. It is to be found in the lives of the obscure – in those almost unlit corridors of history where the figures of generations of women are so dimly, so fitfully perceived. For very little is known about women. The history of England is the history of the male line, not of the female. Of our fathers we know always some fact, some distinction. They were soldiers or they were sailors; they filled that office or they made that law. But of our mothers, our grandmothers, our great-grandmothers, what remains? Nothing but a tradition. One was beautiful; one was red-haired; one was kissed by a Queen. We know nothing of them except their names and the dates of their marriages and the number of children they bore.

Thus, if we wish to know why at any particular time women did this or that, why they wrote nothing, why on the other hand they wrote masterpieces, it is extremely difficult to tell. Anyone who should seek among those old papers, who should turn history wrong side out and so construct a faithful picture of the daily life of the ordinary woman in Shakespeare's time, in Milton's time, in Johnson's time, would not only write a book of astonishing interest, but would furnish the critic with a weapon which he now lacks. The extraordinary woman depends on the ordinary woman. It is only when we know what were the conditions of the average woman's life – the number of her children, whether she had money of her own, if she had a room to herself, whether she had help in bringing up her family, if she had servants, whether part of the housework was her task – it is only when we can measure the way of life and the experience of life made possible to the ordinary woman that we can account for the success or failure of the extraordinary woman as a writer.

VIRGINIA WOOLF

Strange spaces of silence seem to separate one period of activity from another. There was Sappho and a little group of women all writing poetry on a Greek island six hundred years before the birth of Christ. They fall silent. Then about the year 1000 we find a certain court lady, the Lady Murasaki, writing a very long and beautiful novel in Japan. But in England in the sixteenth century, when the dramatists and poets were most active, the women were dumb. Elizabethan literature is exclusively masculine. Then, at the end of the eighteenth century and in the beginning of the nineteenth, we find women again writing – this time in England – with extraordinary frequency and success.

Law and custom were of course largely responsible for these strange intermissions of silence and speech. When a woman was liable, as she was in the fifteenth century, to be beaten and flung about the room if she did not marry the man of her parents' choice, the spiritual atmosphere was not favourable to the production of works of art. When she was married without her own consent to a man who thereupon became her lord and master, 'so far at least as law and custom could make him', as she was in the time of the Stuarts, it is likely she had little time for writing, and less encouragement. The immense effect of environment and suggestion upon the mind, we in our psycho-analytical age are beginning to realize. Again, with memoirs and letters to help us, we are beginning to understand how abnormal is the effort needed to produce a work of art, and what shelter and what support the mind of the artist requires. Of those facts the lives and letters of men like Keats and Carlyle and Flaubert assure us.

Thus it is clear that the extraordinary outburst of fiction in the beginning of the nineteenth century in England was heralded by innumerable slight changes in law and customs and manners. And women of the nineteenth century had some leisure; they had some education. It was no longer the exception for women of the middle and upper classes to choose their own husbands. And it is significant that of the four great women novelists – Jane Austen, Emily Brontë, Charlotte Brontë, and George Eliot – not one had a child, and two were unmarried.

Yet, though it is clear that the ban upon writing had been removed, there was still, it would seem, considerable pressure upon women to write novels. No four women can have been more unlike in genius and character than these four. Jane Austen can have had nothing in common with George Eliot; George Eliot was the direct opposite of Emily Brontë. Yet all were trained for the same profession; all, when they wrote, wrote novels.

Fiction was, as fiction still is, the easiest thing for a woman to write. Nor is it difficult to find the reason. A novel is the least concentrated form of art. A novel can be taken up or put down more easily than a play or a poem. George Eliot left her work to nurse her father. Charlotte Brontë put down her pen to pick the eyes out of the potatoes. And living as she did in the common sitting-room, surrounded by people, a woman was trained to use her mind in observation and upon the analysis of character. She was trained to be a novelist and not to be a poet.

Even in the nineteenth century, a woman lived almost solely in her home and her emotions. And those nineteenth-century novels, remarkable as they were, were pro-foundly influenced by the fact that the women who wrote them were excluded by their sex from certain kinds of experience. That experience has a great influence upon fiction is indisputable. The best part of Conrad's novels, for instance, would be destroyed if it had been impossible for him to be a sailor. Take away all that Tolstoi knew of war as a soldier, of life and society as a rich young man whose education admitted him to all sorts of experience, and *War and Peace* would be incredibly impoverished.

Yet *Pride and Prejudice, Wuthering Heights, Villette,* and *Middlemarch* were written by women from whom was forcibly withheld all experience save that which could be met with in a middle-class drawing-room. No first-hand experience of war or seafaring or politics or business was possible for them. Even their emotional life was strictly regulated by law and custom. When George Eliot ventured to live with Mr. Lewes without being his wife, public opinion was scandalized. Under its pressure she withdrew into a suburban seclusion which, inevitably, had the worst possible effects upon her work. She wrote that unless people asked of their own accord to come and see her, she never invited them. At the same time, on the other side of Europe, Tolstoi was living a free life as a soldier, with men and women of all classes, for which nobody censured him and from which his novels drew much of their astonishing breadth and vigour.

But the novels of women were not affected only by the necessarily narrow range of the writer's experience. They showed, at least in the nineteenth century, another characteristic which may be traced to the writer's sex. In *Middlemarch* and in *Jane Eyre* we are conscious not merely of the writer's character, as we are conscious of the character of Charles Dickens, but we are conscious of a woman's presence – of someone resenting the treatment of her sex and pleading for its rights. This brings into women's writing an element which is entirely absent from a man's, unless, indeed, he happens to be a working-man, a negro, or one who for some other reason is conscious of disability. It introduces a distortion and is frequently the cause of weakness. The desire to plead some personal cause or to make a character the mouthpiece of some personal discontent or grievance always has a distressing effect, as if the spot at which the reader's attention is directed were suddenly twofold instead of single.

The genius of Jane Austen and Emily Brontë is never more convincing than in their power to ignore such claims and solicitations and to hold on their way unperturbed by scorn or censure. But it needed a very serene or a very powerful mind to resist the temptation to anger. The ridicule, the censure, the assurance of inferiority in one form or another which were lavished upon women who practised an art, provoked such reactions naturally enough. One sees the effect in Charlotte Brontë's indignation, in George Eliot's resignation. Again and again one finds it in the work of the lesser women writers – in their choice of a subject, in their unnatural self-assertiveness, in their unnatural docility. Moreover, insincerity leaks in almost unconsciously. They adopt a view in deference to authority. The vision becomes too masculine or it becomes too feminine; it loses its perfect integrity and, with that, its most essential quality as a work of art.

The great change that has crept into women's writing is, it would seem, a change of attitude. The woman writer is no longer bitter. She is no longer angry. She is no longer pleading and protesting as she writes. We are approaching, if we have not yet reached, the time when her writing will have little or no foreign influence to disturb it. She will be able to concentrate upon her vision without distraction from outside. The aloofness that was once within the reach of genius and originality is only now coming within the reach of ordinary women. Therefore the average novel by a woman is far more genuine and far more interesting to-day than it was a hundred or even fifty years ago.

But it is still true that before a woman can write exactly as she wishes to write, she has many difficulties to face. To begin with, there is the technical difficulties – so simple, apparently; in reality, so baffling – that the very form of the sentence does not fit her. It is a sentence made by men; it is too loose, too heavy, too pompous for a woman's use. Yet in a novel, which covers so wide a stretch of ground, an ordinary and usual type of sentence has to be found to carry the reader on easily and naturally from one end of the book to the other. And this a woman must make for herself, altering and adapting the current sentence until she writes one that takes the natural shape of her thought without crushing or distorting it.

But that, after all, is only a means to an end, and the end is still to be reached only when a woman has the courage to surmount opposition and the determination to be true to herself. For a novel, after all, is a statement about a thousand different objects – human, natural, divine; it is an attempt to relate them to each other. In every novel of merit these different elements are held in place by the force of the writer's vision. But they have another order also, which is the order imposed upon them by convention. And as men are the arbiters of that convention, as they have established an order of values in life, so too, since fiction is largely based on life, these values prevail there also to a very great extent.

It is probable, however, that both in life and in art the values of a woman are not the values of a man. Thus, when a woman comes to write a novel, she will find that she is perpetually wishing to alter the established values – to make serious what appears insignificant to a man, and trivial what is to him important. And for that, of course, she will be criticized; for the critic of the opposite sex will be genuinely puzzled and surprised by an attempt to alter the current scale of values, and will see in it not merely a difference of view, but a view that is weak, or trivial, or sentimental, because it differs from his own.

But here, too, women are coming to be more independent of opinion. They are beginning to respect their own sense of values. And for this reason the subject matter of their novels begins to show certain changes. They are less interested, it would seem, in themselves; on the other hand, they are more interested in other women. In the early nineteenth century, women's novels were largely autobiographical. One of the motives that led them to write was the desire to expose their own suffering, to plead their own cause. Now that this desire is no longer so urgent, women are beginning to explore their own sex, to write of women as women have never been written of before; for of course, until very lately, women in literature were the creation of men.

Here again there are difficulties to overcome, for, if one may generalize, not only do women submit less readily to observation than men, but their lives are far less tested and examined by the ordinary processes of life. Often nothing tangible remains of a woman's day. The food that has been cooked is eaten; the children that have been nursed have gone out into the world. Where does the accent fall? What is the salient point for the novelist to seize upon? It is difficult to say. Her life has an anonymous character which is baffling and puzzling in the extreme. For the first time, this dark country is beginning to be explored in fiction; and at the same moment a woman has also to record the changes in women's minds and habits which the opening of the professions has introduced. She has to observe how their lives are ceasing to run underground; she has to discover what new colours and shadows are showing in them now that they are exposed to the outer world.

If, then, one should try to sum up the character of women's fiction at the present moment, one would say that it is courageous; it is sincere; it keeps closely to what women feel. It is not bitter. It does not insist upon its femininity. But at the same time, a woman's book is not written as a man would write it. These qualities are much commoner than they were, and they give even to second- and third-rate work the value of truth and the interest of sincerity.

But in addition to these good qualities, there are two that call for a word more of discussion. The change which has turned the English woman from a nondescript influence, fluctuating and vague, to a voter, a wage-earner, a responsible citizen, has given her both in her life and in her art a turn toward the impersonal. Her relations now are not only emotional; they are intellectual, they are political. The old system which condemned her to squint askance at things through the eyes or through the interests of husband or brother, has given place to the direct and practical interests of one who must act for herself, and not merely influence the acts of others. Hence her attention is being directed away from the personal centre which engaged it exclusively in the past to the impersonal, and her novels naturally become more critical of society, and less analytical of individual lives.

We may expect that the office of gadfly to the state, which has been so far a male prerogative, will now be discharged by women also. Their novels will deal with social evils and remedies. Their men and women will not be observed wholly in relation to each other emotionally, but as they cohere and clash in groups and classes and races. That is one change of some importance. But there is another more interesting to those who prefer the butterfly to the gadfly – that is to say, the artist to the reformer. The greater impersonality of women's lives will encourage the poetic spirit, and it is in poetry that women's fiction is still weakest. It will lead them to be less absorbed in facts and no longer content to record with astonishing acuteness the minute details which fall under their own observation. They will look beyond the personal and political relationships to the wider questions which the poet tries to solve – of our destiny and the meaning of life.

The basis of the poetic attitude is of course largely founded upon material things. It depends upon leisure, and a little money, and the chance which money and leisure give to observe impersonally and dispassionately. With money and leisure at their service, women will naturally occupy themselves more than has hitherto been possible with the craft of letters. They will make a fuller and a more subtle use of the instrument of writing. Their technique will become bolder and richer.

In the past, the virtue of women's writing often lay in its divine spontaneity, like that of the blackbird's song or the thrush's. It was untaught; it was from the heart. But it was also, and much more often, chattering and garrulous – mere talk spilt over paper and left to dry in pools and blots. In future, granted time and books and a little space in the house for herself, literature will become for women, as for men, an art to be studied. Women's gift will be trained and strengthened. The novel will cease to be the dumping-ground for the personal emotions. It will become, more than at present, a work of art like any other, and its resources and its limitations will be explored.

From this it is a short step to the practice of the sophisticated arts, hitherto so little practised by women – to the writing of essays and criticism, of history and biography. And that, too, if we are considering the novel, will be of advantage; for besides improving the quality of the novel itself, it will draw off the aliens who have been attracted to fiction by its accessibility while their hearts lay elsewhere. Thus will the novel be rid of those excrescences of history and fact which, in our time, have made it so shapeless.

So, if we may prophesy, women in time to come will write fewer novels, but better novels; and not novels only, but poetry and criticism and history. But in this, to be sure, one is looking ahead to that golden, that perhaps fabulous, age when women will have what has so long been denied them – leisure, and money, and a room to themselves.

NOTE

1   *The Forum*, March 1929.

Between Men: English Literature and Male Homosocial Desire

Eve Kosofsky Sedgwick

Eve Kosofsky Sedgwick (b. 1950)

Born in Dayton, Ohio, Eve Kosofsky Sedgwick attended Cornell University and Yale University, where she received her Ph.D. in 1975. Sedgwick taught at Boston University (1981–3), Amherst College (1984–8), and Duke University (1988–98); in 1998 she became Distinguished Professor of English at the Graduate Center of the City University of New York. A poet and visual artist, she has published *Fat Art, Thin Art* (1994), and held exhibitions at the Rhode Island School of Design, SUNY-Stony Brook, Johns Hopkins University, and Dartmouth College. Since her 1991 breast cancer diagnosis, Sedgwick has also worked as a patient advocate, among other things writing the bimonthly advice column "Off My Chest" for *MAMM Magazine: Women, Cancer, and Community* (1997–2003). Her experimental autobiography *A Dialogue on Love* (1999), focuses on her therapy sessions following her initial diagnosis. Sedgwick has received fellowships from the National Endowment for the Humanities, the National Humanities Center, and the Guggenheim Foundation, and

From *Between Men: English Literature and Male Homosocial Desire*. New York: Columbia University Press, 1985, from the Introduction, pp. 1–15, ch.1, pp. 21–7, notes, pp. 119–21. Copyright © 1985 by Columbia University Press. Reprinted by permission of Columbia University Press.

Introduction

Homosocial Desire

The subject of this book is a relatively short, recent, and accessible passage of English culture, chiefly as embodied in the mid-eighteenth- to mid-nineteenth-century novel. The attraction of the period to theorists of many disciplines is obvious: condensed, self-reflective, and widely influential change in economic, ideological, and gender arrangements. I will be arguing that concomitant changes in the structure of the continuum of male "homosocial desire" were tightly, often causally bound up with the other more visible changes; that the emerging pattern of male friendship, mentorship, entitlement, rivalry, and hetero- and homosexuality was in an intimate and shifting relation to class; and that no element of that pattern can be understood outside of its relation to women and the gender system as a whole.

"Male homosocial desire": the phrase in the title of this study is intended to mark both discriminations and paradoxes. "Homosocial desire," to begin with, is a kind of oxymoron. "Homosocial" is a word occasionally used in history and the social sciences, where it describes social bonds between persons of the same sex; it is a neologism, obviously formed by analogy with "homosexual," and just as obviously meant to be distinguished from "homosexual." In fact, it is applied to such activities as "male bonding," which may, as in our society, be characterized by intense homophobia, fear and hatred of homosexuality.[1] To draw the "homosocial" back into the orbit of "desire," of the potentially erotic, then, is to hypothesize the potential unbrokenness of a continuum between homosocial and homosexual – a continuum whose visibility, for men, in our society, is radically disrupted. It will become clear, in the course of my argument, that my hypothesis of the unbrokenness of this continuum is not a *genetic* one – I do not mean to discuss genital homosexual desire as "at the root of" other forms of male homosociality – but rather a strategy for making generalizations about, and marking historical differences in, the *structure* of men's relations with other men. "Male homosocial desire" is the name this book will give to the entire continuum.

I have chosen the word "desire" rather than "love" to mark the erotic emphasis because, in literary critical and related discourse, "love" is more easily used to name a particular emotion, and "desire" to name a structure; in this study, a series of arguments about the structural permutations of social impulses fuels the critical dialectic. For the most part, I will be using "desire" in a way analogous to the psychoanalytic use of "libido" – not for a particular affective state or emotion, but for the affective or social force, the glue, even when its manifestation is hostility or hatred or something less emotively charged, that shapes an important relationship. How far this force is properly sexual (what, historically, it means for something to be "sexual") will be an active question.

The title is specific about *male* homosocial desire partly in order to acknowledge from the beginning (and stress the seriousness of) a limitation of my subject; but there is a more positive and substantial reason, as well. It is one of the main projects of this study to explore the ways in which the shapes of sexuality, and what *counts* as sexuality, both depend on and affect historical power relationships.[2] A corollary is that in a society where men and women differ in their access to power, there will be important gender differences, as well, in the structure and constitution of sexuality.

For instance, the diacritical opposition between the "homosocial" and the "homosexual" seems to be much less thorough and dichotomous for women, in our society, than for men. At this particular historical moment, an intelligible continuum of aims, emotions, and valuations links lesbianism with the other forms of women's attention to women: the bond of mother and daughter, for instance, the bond of sister and sister, women's friendship, "networking," and the active struggles of feminism.[3] The continuum is crisscrossed with deep discontinuities – with much homophobia, with conflicts of race and class – but its intelligibility seems now a matter of simple common sense. However agonistic the politics, however conflicted the feelings, it seems at this moment to make an obvious kind of sense to say that women in our society who love women, women who teach, study, nurture, suckle, write about, march for, vote for, give jobs to, or otherwise promote the interests of other women, are pursuing congruent and closely related activities. Thus the adjective "homosocial" as applied to women's bonds (by, for example, historian Carroll Smith-Rosenberg)[4] need not be pointedly dichotomized as against "homosexual"; it can intelligibly denominate the entire continuum.

The apparent simplicity – the unity – of the continuum between "women loving women" and "women promoting the interests of women," extending over the erotic, social, familial, economic, and political realms, would not be so striking if it were not in strong contrast to the arrangement among males. When Ronald Reagan and Jesse Helms get down to serious logrolling on "family policy," they are men promoting men's interests. (In fact, they embody Heidi Hartmann's definition of patriarchy: "relations between men, which have a material base, and which, though hierarchical, establish or create interdependence and solidarity among men that enable them to dominate women.")[5] Is their bond in any way congruent with the bond of a loving gay male couple? Reagan and Helms would say no – disgustedly. Most gay couples would say no – disgustedly. But why not? Doesn't the continuum between "men-loving-men" and "men-promoting-the-interests-of-men" have the same intuitive force that it has for women?

Quite the contrary: much of the most useful recent writing about patriarchal structures suggests that "obligatory heterosexuality" is built into male-dominated kinship systems, or that homophobia is a *necessary* consequence of such patriarchal institutions as heterosexual marriage.[6] Clearly, however convenient it might be to group together all the bonds that link males to males, and by which males enhance the status of males – usefully symmetrical as it would be, that grouping meets with a prohibitive structural obstacle. From the vantage point of our own society, at any rate, it has apparently been

EVE KOSOFSKY SEDGWICK

impossible to imagine a form of patriarchy that was not homophobic. Gayle Rubin writes, for instance, "The suppression of the homosexual component of human sexuality, and by corollary, the oppression of homosexuals, is…a product of the same system whose rules and relations oppress women."[7]

The historical manifestations of this patriarchal oppression of homosexuals have been savage and nearly endless. Louis Crompton makes a detailed case for describing the history as genocidal.[8] Our own society is brutally homophobic; and the homophobia directed against both males and females is not arbitrary or gratuitous, but tightly knit into the texture of family, gender, age, class, and race relations. Our society could not cease to be homophobic and have its economic and political structures remain unchanged.

Nevertheless, it has yet to be demonstrated that, because most patriarchies structurally include homophobia, therefore patriarchy structurally *requires* homophobia. K. J. Dover's recent study, *Greek Homosexuality*, seems to give a strong counterexample in classical Greece. Male homosexuality, according to Dover's evidence, was a widespread, licit, and very influential part of the culture. Highly structured along lines of class, and within the citizen class along lines of age, the pursuit of the adolescent boy by the older man was described by stereotypes that we associate with romantic heterosexual love (conquest, surrender, the "cruel fair," the absence of desire in the love object), with the passive part going to the boy. At the same time, however, because the boy was destined in turn to grow into manhood, the assignment of roles was not permanent.[9] Thus the love relationship, while temporarily oppressive to the object, had a strongly educational function; Dover quotes Pausanias in Plato's *Symposium* as saying "that it would be right for him [the boy] to perform any service for one who improves him in mind and character."[10] Along with its erotic component, then, this was a bond of mentorship; the boys were apprentices in the ways and virtues of Athenian citizenship, whose privileges they inherited. These privileges included the power to command the labor of slaves of both sexes, and of women of any class including their own. "Women and slaves belonged and lived together," Hannah Arendt writes. The system of sharp class and gender subordination was a necessary part of what the male culture valued most in itself: "Contempt for laboring originally [arose] out of passionate striving for freedom from necessity and a no less passionate impatience with every effort that left no trace, no monument, no great work worthy to remembrance";[11] so the contemptible labor was left to women and slaves.

The example of the Greeks demonstrates, I think, that while heterosexuality is necessary for the maintenance of any patriarchy, homophobia, against males at any rate, is not. In fact, for the Greeks, the continuum between "men loving men" and "men promoting the interests of men" appears to have been quite seamless. It is as if, in our terms, there were no perceived discontinuity between the male bonds at the Continental Baths and the male bonds at the Bohemian Grove[12] or in the board room or Senate cloakroom.

It is clear, then, that there is an asymmetry in our present society between, on the one hand, the relatively continuous relation of female homosocial and homosexual bonds, and, on the other hand, the radically discontinuous relation of male homosocial and homosexual bonds. The example of the Greeks (and of other, tribal cultures, such as the New Guinea "Sambia" studied by G. H. Herdt) shows, in addition, that the structure of homosocial continuums is culturally contingent, not an innate feature of either "maleness" or "femaleness." Indeed, closely tied though it obviously is to questions of male vs. female power, the explanation will require a more exact mode of historical categorization than "patriarchy," as well, since patriarchal power structures (in Hartmann's sense) characterize both Athenian and American societies. Nevertheless, we may take as an explicit axiom that the historically differential shapes of male and female homosociality – much as they themselves may vary over time – will always be articulations and mechanisms of the enduring inequality of power between women and men.

Why should the different shapes of the homosocial continuum be an interesting question? Why should it be a *literary* question? Its importance for the practical politics of the gay movement as a minority rights movement is already obvious from the recent history of strategic and philosophical differences between lesbians and gay men. In addition, it is theoretically interesting partly as a way of approaching a larger question of "sexual politics": What does it mean – what difference does it make – when a social or political relationship is sexualized? If the relation of homosocial to homosexual bonds is so shifty, then what theoretical framework do we have for drawing any links between sexual and power relationships?

Sexual Politics and Sexual Meaning

This question, in a variety of forms, is being posed importantly by and for the different gender-politics movements right now. Feminist along with gay male theorists, for instance, are disagreeing actively about how direct the relation is between power domination and sexual sadomasochism. Start with two arresting images: the naked, beefy motorcyclist on the front cover, or the shockingly battered nude male corpse on the back cover, of the recent so-called "Polysexuality" issue of *Semiotext(e)* (4, no. 1 [1981]) – which, for all the women in it, ought to have been called the semisexuality issue of *Polytext*. It seemed to be a purpose of that issue to insist, and possibly not only for reasons of radical-chic titillation, that the violence imaged in sadomasochism is not mainly theatrical, but is fully continuous with violence in the real world. Women Against Pornography and the framers of the 1980 NOW Resolution on Lesbian and Gay Rights share the same view, but without the celebratory glamor: to them too it seems intuitively clear that to sexualize violence or an image of violence is simply to extend, unchanged, its reach and force.[13] But, as other feminist writers have reminded us, another view is possible. For example: is a woman's masochistic sexual fantasy really only an internalization and endorsement, if not a cause, of her more general powerlessness and sense of worthlessness? Or may not the sexual drama stand in some more oblique, or even oppositional, relation to her political experience of oppression?[14]

The debate in the gay male community and elsewhere over "man-boy love" asks a cognate question: can an adult's sexual relationship with a child be simply a continuous part of a more general relationship of education and nurturance? Or must the inclusion of sex qualitatively alter the relationship, for instance in the direction of exploitiveness? In this case, the same NOW communiqué that had assumed an unbroken continuity between sexualized violence and real, social violence, came to the opposite conclusion on pedophilia: that the injection of the sexual charge *would* alter (would corrupt) the

EVE KOSOFSKY SEDGWICK

very substance of the relationship. Thus, in moving from the question of sadomasochism to the question of pedophilia, the "permissive" argument and the "puritanical" argument have essentially exchanged their assumptions about how the sexual relates to the social.

So the answer to the question "what difference does the inclusion of sex make" to a social or political relationship, is – it varies: just as, for different groups in different political circumstances, homosexual activity can be either supportive of or oppositional to homosocial bonding. From this and the other examples I have mentioned, it is clear that there is not some ahistorical *Stoff* of sexuality, some sexual charge that can be simply added to a social relationship to "sexualize" it in a constant and predictable direction, or that splits off from it unchanged. Nor does it make sense to *assume* that the sexualized form epitomizes or simply condenses a broader relationship. (As, for instance, Kathleen Barry, in *Female Sexual Slavery*, places the Marquis de Sade at the very center of all forms of female oppression, including traditional genital mutilation, incest, and the economic as well as the sexual exploitation of prostitutes.)

Instead, an examination of the relation of sexual desire to political power must move along two axes. First, of course, it needs to make use of whatever forms of analysis are most potent for describing historically variable power asymmetries, such as those of class and race, as well as gender. But in conjunction with that, an analysis of representation itself is necessary. Only the model of representation will let us do justice to the (broad but not infinite or random) range of ways in which sexuality functions as a signifier for power relations. The importance of the rhetorical model in this case is not to make the problems of sexuality or of violence or oppression sound less immediate and urgent; it is to help us analyze and use the really very disparate intuitions of political immediacy that come to us from the sexual realm.

For instance, a dazzling recent article by Catherine MacKinnon, attempting to go carefully over and clear out the grounds of disagreement between different streams of feminist thought, arrives at the following summary of the centrality of sexuality per se for every issue of gender:

> Each element of the female *gender* stereotype is revealed as, in fact, *sexual*. Vulnerability means the appearance/reality of easy sexual access; passivity means receptivity and disabled resistance...; softness means pregnability by something hard.... Woman's infantilization evokes pedophilia; fixation on dismembered body parts...evokes fetishism; idolization of vapidity, necrophilia. Narcissism insures that woman identifies with that image of herself that man holds up....Masochism means that pleasure in violation becomes her sensuality.

And MacKinnon sums up this part of her argument: "Socially, femaleness means femininity, which means attractiveness to men, which means sexual attractiveness, which means sexual availability on male terms."[15]

There's a whole lot of "mean"-ing going on. MacKinnon manages to make every manifestation of sexuality mean the same thing, by making every instance of "meaning" mean something different. A trait can "mean" as an element in a semiotic system such as fashion ("softness means pregnability"); or anaclitically, it can "mean" its complementary opposite ("Woman's infantilization evokes pedophilia"); or across time, it can

"mean" the consequence that it enforces ("Narcissism insures that woman identifies....
Masochism means that pleasure in violation becomes her sensuality"). MacKinnon
concludes, "What defines woman as such is what turns men on." But what defines
"defines"? That every node of sexual experience is in *some* signifying relation to the
whole fabric of gender oppression, and vice versa, is true and important, but insufficiently exact to be of analytic use on specific political issues. The danger lies, of course,
in the illusion that we do know from such a totalistic analysis where to look for our
sexuality and how to protect it from expropriation when we find it.

On the other hand, one value of MacKinnon's piece was as a contribution to the
increasing deftness with which, over the last twenty years, the question has been posed,
"Who or what is the subject of the sexuality we (as women) enact?" It has been posed in
terms more or less antic or frontal, phallic or gyno-, angry or frantic – in short, perhaps,
Anglic or Franco-. But in different terms it is this same question that has animated the
complaint of the American "sex object" of the 1960s, the claim since the 70s for
"women's control of our own bodies," and the recently imported "critique of the
subject" as it is used by French feminists.

Let me take an example from the great ideological blockbuster of white bourgeois
feminism, its apotheosis, the fictional work that has most resonantly thematized for
successive generations of American women the constraints of the "feminine" role,
the obstacles to and the ravenous urgency of female ambition, the importance of the
economic motive, the compulsiveness and destructiveness of romantic love, and (what
MacKinnon would underline) the centrality and the total alienation of female sexuality.
Of course, I am referring to *Gone with the Wind.* As MacKinnon's paradigm would
predict, in the life of Scarlett O'Hara, it is expressly clear that to be born female is to
be defined entirely in relation to the role of "lady," a role that does take its shape and
meaning from a sexuality of which she is not the subject but the object. For Scarlett, to
survive as a woman does mean learning to see sexuality, male power domination, and
her traditional gender role as all meaning the same dangerous thing. To absent herself
silently from each of them alike, and learn to manipulate them from behind this screen
as objects or pure signifiers, as men do, is the numbing but effective lesson of her life.

However, it is *only* a white bourgeois feminism that this view apotheosizes. As in one
of those trick rooms where water appears to run uphill and little children look taller
than their parents, it is only when viewed from one fixed vantage in any society that
sexuality, gender roles, and power domination can seem to line up in this perfect chain
of echoic meaning. From an even slightly more ec-centric or disempowered perspective,
the *dis*placements and *dis*continuities of the signifying chain come to seem increasingly
definitive. For instance, if it is true in this novel that all the women characters exist in
some meaning-ful relation to the role of "lady," the signifying relation grows more
tortuous – though at the same time, in the novel's white bourgeois view, more totally
determining – as the women's social and racial distance from that role grows. Melanie is
a woman as she is a lady; Scarlett is a woman as she is required to be and pretends to be a
lady; but Belle Watling, the Atlanta prostitute, is a woman not in relation to her own role
of "lady," which is exiguous, but only negatively, in a compensatory and at the same time
parodic relation to Melanie's and Scarlett's. And as for Mammy, her mind and life, in this
view, are *totally* in thrall to the ideal of the "lady," but in a relation that excludes herself
entirely: she is the template, the support, the enforcement, of Scarlett's "lady" role, to

the degree that her personal femaleness loses any meaning whatever that is not in relation to Scarlett's role. Whose mother is Mammy?

At the precise intersection of domination and sexuality is the issue of rape. *Gone with the Wind* – both book and movie – leaves in the memory a most graphic image of rape:

> As the negro came running to the buggy, his black face twisted in a leering grin, she fired point-blank at him.... The negro was beside her, so close that she could smell the rank odor of him as he tried to drag her over the buggy side. With her own free hand she fought madly, clawing at his face, and then she felt his big hand at her throat and, with a ripping noise, her basque was torn open from breast to waist. Then the black hand fumbled between her breasts, and terror and revulsion such as she had never known came over her and she screamed like an insane woman.[16]

In the wake of this attack, the entire machinery by which "rape" is signified in this culture rolls into action. Scarlett's menfolk and their friends in the Ku Klux Klan set out after dark to kill the assailants and "wipe out that whole Shantytown settlement," with the predictable carnage on both sides. The question of how much Scarlett is to blame for the deaths of the white men is widely mooted, with Belle Watling speaking for the "lady" role – "She caused it all, prancin' bout Atlanta by herself, enticin' niggers and trash" – and Rhett Butler, as so often, speaking from the central vision of the novel's bourgeois feminism, assuring her that her desperate sense of guilt is purely superstitious (chs. 46, 47). In preparation for this central incident, the novel had even raised the issue of the legal treatment of rape victims (ch. 42). And the effect of that earlier case, the classic effect of rape, had already been to abridge Scarlett's own mobility and, hence, personal and economic power: it was to expedite her business that she had needed to ride by Shantytown in the first place.

The attack on Scarlett, in short, fully means rape, both *to her* and to all the forces in her culture that produce and circulate powerful meanings. It makes no difference at all that one constituent element of rape is missing; but the missing constituent is simply sex. The attack on Scarlett had been for money; the black hands had fumbled between the white breasts because the man had been told that was where she kept her money; Scarlett knew that; there is no mention of any other motive; but it does not matter in the least, the absent sexuality leaves no gap in the character's, the novel's, or the society's discourse of rape.

Nevertheless, *Gone with the Wind* is not a novel that omits enforced sexuality. We are shown one actual rape in fairly graphic detail; but when it is white hands that scrabble on white skin, its ideological name is "blissful marriage." "[Rhett] had humbled her, used her brutally through a wild mad night and she had gloried in it" (ch. 54). The sexual predations of white men on Black women are also a presence in the novel, but the issue of force vs. consent is never raised there; the white male alienation of a Black woman's sexuality is shaped differently from the alienation of the white woman's, to the degree that rape ceases to be a meaningful term at all. And if forcible sex ever did occur between a Black male and female character in this world, the sexual event itself would have no signifying power, since Black sexuality "means" here only a grammatic transformation of a sentence whose true implicit subject and object are white.

We have in this protofeminist novel, then, in this ideological microcosm, a symbolic economy in which both the meaning of rape and rape itself are insistently circulated.

Because of the racial fracture of the society, however, *rape and its meaning circulate in precisely opposite directions.* It is an extreme case; the racial fracture is, in America, more sharply dichotomized than others except perhaps for gender. Still, other symbolic fractures such as class (and by fractures I mean the lines along which quantitative differentials of power may in a given society be read as qualitative differentials with some other name) are abundant and actively disruptive in every social constitution. The signifying relation of sex to power, of sexual alienation to political oppression, is not the most stable, but precisely the most volatile of social nodes, under this pressure.

Thus, it is of serious political importance that our tools for examining the signifying relation be subtle and discriminate ones, and that our literary knowledge of the most crabbed or oblique paths of meaning not be oversimplified in the face of panic-inducing images of real violence, especially the violence of, around, and to sexuality. To assume that sex signifies power in a flat, unvarying relation of metaphor or synecdoche will always entail a blindness, not to the rhetorical and pyrotechnic, but to such historical categories as class and race. Before we can fully achieve and use our intuitive grasp of the leverage that sexual relations seem to offer on the relations of oppression, we need more – more different, more complicated, more diachronically apt, more off-centered – more daring and prehensile applications of our present understanding of what it may mean for one thing to signify another.

Sex or History?

It will be clear by this point that the centrality of sexual questions in this study is important to its methodological ambitions, as well. I am going to be recurring to the subject of sex as an especially charged leverage-point, or point for the exchange of meanings, *between* gender and class (and in many societies, race), the sets of categories by which we ordinarily try to describe the divisions of human labor. And methodologically, I want to situate these readings as a contribution to a dialectic within feminist theory between more and less historicizing views of the oppression of women.

In a rough way, we can label the extremes on this theoretical spectrum "Marxist feminism" for the most historicizing analysis, "radical feminism" for the least. Of course, "radical feminism" is so called not because it occupies the farthest "left" space on a conventional political map, but because it takes gender itself, gender alone, to be the most radical division of human experience, and a relatively unchanging one.

For the purposes of the present argument, in addition, and for reasons that I will explain more fully later, I am going to be assimilating "French" feminism – deconstructive and/or Lacanian-oriented feminism – to the radical-feminist end of this spectrum. "French" and "radical" feminism differ on very many very important issues, such as how much respect they give to the brute fact that everyone gets categorized as either female or male; but they are alike in seeing all human culture, language, and life as structured in the first place – structured radically, transhistorically, and essentially *similarly*, however coarsely or finely – by a drama of gender difference. (Pages 000–0 discuss more fully the particular terms by which the structuralist motive will be represented in the present study.) French-feminist and radical-feminist prose tend to

---

EVE KOSOFSKY SEDGWICK

share the same vatic, and perhaps imperialistic, uses of the present tense. In a sense, the polemical energy behind my arguments will be a desire, through the rhetorically volatile subject of sex, to recruit the representational finesse of deconstructive feminism in the service of a more historically discriminate mode of analysis.

The choice of sexuality as a thematic emphasis of this study makes salient and problematical a division of thematic emphasis between Marxist-feminist and radical-feminist theory as they are now practiced. Specifically, Marxist feminism, the study of the deep interconnections between on the one hand historical and economic change, and on the other hand the vicissitudes of gender division, has typically proceeded in the absence of a theory of sexuality and without much interest in the meaning or experience of sexuality. Or more accurately, it has held implicitly to a view of female sexuality as something that is essentially of a piece with reproduction, and hence appropriately studied with the tools of demography; or else essentially of a piece with a simple, prescriptive hegemonic ideology, and hence appropriately studied through intellectual or legal history. Where important advances have been made by Marxist-feminist-oriented research into sexuality, it has been in areas that were already explicitly distinguished as deviant by the society's legal discourse: signally, homosexuality for men and prostitution for women. Marxist feminism has been of little help in unpacking the historical meanings of women's experience of heterosexuality, or even, until it becomes legally and medically visible in this century, of lesbianism.[17]

Radical feminism, on the other hand, in the many different forms I am classing under that head, has been relatively successful in placing sexuality in a prominent and interrogative position, one that often allows scope for the decentered and the contradictory. Kathleen Barry's *Female Sexual Slavery*, Susan Griffin's *Pornography and Silence*, Gilbert and Gubar's *The Madwoman in the Attic*, Jane Gallop's *The Daughter's Seduction*, and Andrea Dworkin's *Pornography: Men Possessing Women* make up an exceedingly heterogeneous group of texts in many respects – in style, in urgency, in explicit feminist identification, in French or American affiliation, in "brow"-elevation level. They have in common, however, a view that sexuality is centrally problematical in the formation of women's experience. And in more or less sophisticated formulations, the subject as well as the ultimate object of female heterosexuality within what is called patriarchal culture are seen as male. Whether in literal interpersonal terms or in internalized psychological and linguistic terms, this approach privileges sexuality and often sees it within the context of the structure that Lévi-Strauss analyzes as "the male traffic in women."

This family of approaches has, however, shared with other forms of structuralism a difficulty in dealing with the diachronic. It is the essence of structures viewed as such to reproduce themselves; and historical change from this point of view appears as something outside of structure and threatening – or worse, *not* threatening – to it, rather than in a formative and dialectical relation with it. History tends thus to be either invisible or viewed in an impoverishingly glaring and contrastive light.[18] Implicitly or explicitly, radical feminism tends to deny that the meaning of gender or sexuality has ever significantly changed; and more damagingly, it can make future change appear impossible, or necessarily apocalyptic, even though desirable. Alternatively, it can radically oversimplify the prerequisites for significant change. In addition, history even in the residual, synchronic form of class or racial difference and conflict becomes invisible or excessively coarsened and dichotomized in the universalizing structuralist view.

As feminist readers, then, we seem poised for the moment between reading sex and reading history, at a choice that appears (though, it must be, wrongly) to be between the synchronic and the diachronic. We know that it must be wrongly viewed in this way, not only because in the abstract the synchronic and the diachronic must ultimately be considered in relation to one another, but because specifically in the disciplines we are considering they are so mutually inscribed: the narrative of Marxist history is so graphic, and the schematics of structuralist sexuality so narrative.

I will be trying in this study to activate and use some of the potential congruences of the two approaches. Part of the underpinning of this attempt will be a continuing meditation on ways in which the category *ideology* can be used as part of an analysis of *sexuality.* The two categories seem comparable in several important ways: each mediates between the material and the representational, for instance; ideology, like sexuality as we have discussed it, *both* epitomizes *and* itself influences broader social relations of power; and each, I shall be arguing, mediates similarly between diachronic, narrative structures of social experience and synchronic, graphic ones. If commonsense suggests that we can roughly group historicizing, "Marxist" feminism with the diachronic and the narrative, and "radical," structuralist, deconstructive, and "French" feminisms with the synchronic and the graphic, then the methodological promise of these two mediating categories will be understandable.

In *The German Ideology,* Marx suggests that the function of ideology is to conceal contradictions in the status quo by, for instance, recasting them into a diachronic narrative of origins. Corresponding to that function, one important structure of ideology is an idealizing appeal to the outdated values of an earlier system, in defense of a later system that in practice undermines the material basis of those values.[19]

For instance, Juliet Mitchell analyzes the importance of the family in ideologically justifying the shift to capitalism, in these terms:

> The peasant masses of feudal society had individual private property; their ideal was simply more of it. Capitalist society seemed to offer more because it stressed the *idea* of individual private property in a new context (or in a context of new ideas). Thus it offered individualism (an old value) plus the apparently new means for its greater realization – freedom and equality (values that are conspicuously absent from feudalism). However, the only place where this ideal could be given an apparently concrete base was in the maintenance of an old institution: the family. Thus the family changed from being the economic basis of individual private property under feudalism to being the focal point of the *idea* of individual private property under a system that banished such an economic form from its central mode of production – capitalism.... The working class work socially in production for the private property of a few capitalists *in the hope of* individual private property for themselves and their families.[20]

The phrase "A man's home is his castle" offers a nicely condensed example of ideological construction in this sense. It reaches *back* to an emptied-out image of mastery and integration under feudalism in order to propel the male wage-worker *forward* to further feats of alienated labor, in the service of a now atomized and embattled, but all the more intensively idealized home. The man who has this home is a different person from the lord who has a castle; and the forms of property implied in the two possessives

---

EVE KOSOFSKY SEDGWICK

(his [mortgaged] home/his [inherited] castle) are not only different but, as Mitchell points out, mutually contradictory. The contradiction is assuaged and filled in by transferring the lord's political and economic control over the *environs* of his castle to an image of the father's personal control over the *inmates* of his house. The ideological formulation thus permits a criss-crossing of agency, temporality, and space. It is important that ideology in this sense, even when its form is flatly declarative ("A man's home is his castle"), is always at least implicitly narrative, and that, in order for the reweaving of ideology to be truly invisible, the narrative is necessarily chiasmic in structure: that is, that the subject of the beginning of the narrative is different from the subject at the end, and that the two subjects cross each other in a rhetorical figure that conceals their discontinuity.

It is also important that the sutures of contradiction in these ideological narratives become most visible under the disassembling eye of an alternative narrative, ideological as that narrative may itself be. In addition, the diachronic opening-out of contradictions within the status quo, even when the project of that diachronic recasting is to conceal those very contradictions, can have just the opposite effect of making them newly visible, offering a new leverage for critique. For these reasons, distinguishing between the construction and the critique of ideological narrative is not always even a theoretical possibility, even with relatively flat texts; with the fat rich texts we are taking for examples in this project, no such attempt will be made.

Sexuality, like ideology, depends on the mutual redefinition and occlusion of synchronic and diachronic formulations. The developmental fact that, as Freud among others has shown, even the naming of sexuality as such is always retroactive in relation to most of the sensations and emotions that constitute it,[21] is *historically* important. What *counts* as the sexual is, as we shall see, variable and itself political. The exact, contingent space of indeterminacy – the place of shifting over time – of the mutual boundaries between the political and the sexual is, in fact, the most fertile space of ideological formation. This is true because ideological formation, like sexuality, depends on retroactive change in the naming or labelling of the subject.

The two sides, the political and the erotic, necessarily obscure and misrepresent each other – but in ways that offer important and shifting affordances to all parties in historical gender and class struggle.

* * *

Gender Asymmetry and Erotic Triangles

The graphic schema on which I am going to be drawing most heavily in the readings that follow is the triangle. The triangle is useful as a figure by which the "commonsense" of our intellectual tradition schematizes erotic relations, and because it allows us to condense into a juxtaposition with that folk-perception several somewhat different streams of recent thought.

René Girard's early book, *Deceit, Desire, and the Novel*, was itself something of a schematization of the folk-wisdom of erotic triangles. Through readings of major

European fictions, Girard traced a calculus of power that was structured by the relation of rivalry between the two active members of an erotic triangle. What is most interesting for our purposes in his study is its insistence that, in any erotic rivalry, the bond that links the two rivals is as intense and potent as the bond that links either of the rivals to the beloved: that the bonds of "rivalry" and "love," differently as they are experienced, are equally powerful and in many senses equivalent. For instance, Girard finds many examples in which the choice of the beloved is determined in the first place, not by the qualities of the beloved, but by the beloved's already being the choice of the person who has been chosen as a rival. In fact, Girard seems to see the bond between rivals in an erotic triangle as being even stronger, more heavily determinant of actions and choices, than anything in the bond between either of the lovers and the beloved. And within the male-centered novelistic tradition of European high culture, the triangles Girard traces are most often those in which two males are rivals for a female; it is the bond between males that he most assiduously uncovers [see pp. 000–0].

The index to Girard's book gives only two citations for "homosexuality" per se, and it is one of the strengths of his formulation not to depend on how homosexuality as an entity was perceived or experienced – indeed, on what was or was not considered sexual – at any given historical moment. As a matter of fact, the symmetry of his formulation always depends on *suppressing* the subjective, historically determined account of which feelings are or are not part of the body of "sexuality." The transhistorical clarity gained by this organizing move naturally has a cost, however. Psychoanalysis, the recent work of Foucault, and feminist historical scholarship all suggest that the place of drawing the boundary between the sexual and the not-sexual, like the place of drawing the boundary between the realms of the two genders, *is* variable, but is *not* arbitrary. That is (as the example of *Gone with the Wind* suggests), the placement of the boundaries in a particular society affects not merely the definitions of those terms themselves – sexual/nonsexual, masculine/feminine – but also the apportionment of forms of power that are not obviously sexual. These include control over the means of production and reproduction of goods, persons, and meanings. So that Girard's account, which thinks it is describing a dialectic of power abstracted from either the male/female or the sexual/nonsexual dichotomies, is leaving out of consideration categories that in fact preside over the distribution of power in every known society. And because the distribution of power according to these dichotomies is not and possibly cannot be symmetrical, the hidden symmetries that Girard's triangle helps us discover will always in turn discover hidden obliquities. At the same time, even to bear in mind the lurking possibility of the Girardian symmetry is to be possessed of a graphic tool for historical measure. It will make it easier for us to perceive and discuss the mutual inscription in these texts of male homosocial and heterosocial desire, and the resistances to them.

Girard's argument is of course heavily dependent, not only on a brilliant intuition for taking seriously the received wisdom of sexual folklore, but also on a schematization from Freud: the Oedipal triangle, the situation of the young child that is attempting to situate itself with respect to a powerful father and a beloved mother. Freud's discussions of the etiology of "homosexuality" (which current research seems to be rendering questionable as a set of generalizations about personal histories of "homosexuals")[22] suggest homo- and heterosexual outcomes in adults to be the result of a complicated play of desire for and identification with the parent of each gender: the child routes its

EVE KOSOFSKY SEDGWICK

desire/identification through the mother to arrive at a role like the father's, or vice versa. Richard Klein summarizes this argument as follows:

> In the normal development of the little boy's progress towards heterosexuality, he must pass, as Freud says with increasing insistence in late essays like "Terminable and Interminable Analysis," through the stage of the "positive" Oedipus, a homoerotic identification with his father, a position of effeminized subordination to the father, as a condition of finding a model for his own heterosexual role. Conversely, in this theory, the development of the male homosexual requires the postulation of the father's absence or distance and an abnormally strong identification by the child with the mother, in which the child takes the place of the father. There results from this scheme a surprising neutralization of polarities: heterosexuality in the male...presupposes a homosexual phase as the condition of its normal possibility: homosexuality, obversely, requires that the child experience a powerful heterosexual identification.[23]

I have mentioned that Girard's reading presents itself as one whose symmetry is undisturbed by such differences as gender; although the triangles that most shape his view tend, in the European tradition, to involve bonds of "rivalry" between males "over" a woman, in his view *any* relation of rivalry is structured by the same play of emulation and identification, whether the entities occupying the corners of the triangle be heroes, heroines, gods, books, or whatever. In describing the Oedipal drama, Freud notoriously tended to place a male in the generic position of "child" and treat the case of the female as being more or less the same, "mutatis mutandis"; at any rate, as Freud is interpreted by conventional American psychoanalysis, the enormous difference in the degree and kind of female and male power enters psychoanalytic view, when at all, as a result rather than as an active determinant of familial and intrapsychic structures of development. Thus, both Girard and Freud (or at least the Freud of this interpretive tradition) treat the erotic triangle as symmetrical – in the sense that its structure would be relatively unaffected by the power difference that would be introduced by a change in the gender of one of the participants.

In addition, the asymmetry I spoke of in the first section of the Introduction – the radically disrupted continuum, in our society, between sexual and nonsexual male bonds, as against the relatively smooth and palpable continuum of female homosocial desire – might be expected to alter the structure of erotic triangles in ways that depended on gender, and for which neither Freud nor Girard would offer an account. Both Freud and Girard, in other words, treat erotic triangles under the Platonic light that perceives no discontinuity in the homosocial continuum – none, at any rate, that makes much difference – even in modern Western society. There is a kind of bravery about the proceeding of each in this respect, but a historical blindness, as well.

Recent rereadings and reinterpretations of Freud have gone much farther in taking into account the asymmetries of gender. In France, recent psychoanalytic discourse impelled by Jacques Lacan identifies power, language, and the Law itself with the phallus and the "name of the father." It goes without saying that such a discourse has the potential for setting in motion both feminist and virulently misogynistic analyses; it does, at any rate, offer tools, though not (so far) historically sensitive ones, for describing the mechanisms of patriarchal power in terms that are at once intrapsychic (Oedipal conflict) and public (language and the Law). Moreover, by distinguishing (however incompletely) the phallus, the locus of power, from the actual anatomical penis,[24] Lacan's account creates a space in which anatomic sex and cultural gender may be distinguished from one another and in which the different paths of *men's* relations to male power might be explored (e.g. in terms of class). In addition, it suggests ways of talking about the relation between the individual male and the cultural institutions of masculine domination that fall usefully under the rubric of representation.

A further contribution of Lacanian psychoanalysis that will be important for our investigation is the subtlety with which it articulates the slippery relation – already adumbrated in Freud – between desire and identification. The schematic elegance with which Richard Klein, in the passage I have quoted, is able to summarize the feminizing potential of desire for a woman and the masculinizing potential of subordination to a man, owes at least something to a Lacanian grinding of the lenses through which Freud is being viewed. In Lacan and those who have learned from him, an elaborate meditation on introjection and incorporation forms the link between the apparently dissimilar processes of desire and identification.

Recent American feminist work by Dorothy Dinnerstein and Nancy Chodorow also revises Freud in the direction of greater attention to gender/power difference. Coppélia Kahn summarizes the common theme of their argument (which she applies to Shakespeare) as follows:

> Most children, male or female, in Shakespeare's time, Freud's, or ours, are not only borne but raised by women. And thus arises a crucial difference between the girl's developing sense of identity and the boy's. For though she follows the same sequence of symbiotic union, separation and individuation, identification, and object love as the boy, her femininity arises in relation to a person of the *same* sex, while his masculinity arises in relation to a person of the *opposite* sex. Her femininity is reinforced by her original symbiotic union with her mother and by the identification with her that must precede identity, while his masculinity is threatened by the same union and the same identification. While the boy's sense of *self* begins in union with the feminine, his sense of *masculinity* arises against it.[25]

It should be clear, then, from what has gone before, on the one hand that there are many and thorough asymmetries between the sexual continuums of women and men, between female and male sexuality and homosociality, and most pointedly between homosocial and heterosocial object choices for males; and on the other hand that the status of women, and the whole question of arrangements between genders, is deeply and inescapably inscribed in the structure even of relationships that seem to exclude women – even in male homosocial/homosexual relationships. Heidi Hartmann's definition of patriarchy in terms of "relationships between men" (see pp. 000–0), in making the power relationships between men and women appear to be dependent on the power relationships between men and men, suggests that large-scale social structures are congruent with the male-male-female erotic triangles described most forcefully by Girard and articulated most thoughtfully by others. We can go further than that, to say that in any male-dominated society, there is a special relationship between male homosocial (*including* homosexual) desire and the structures for maintaining and transmitting patriarchal power: a relationship founded on an inherent and potentially active structural congruence. For historical reasons, this special relationship may take the form

EVE KOSOFSKY SEDGWICK

of ideological homophobia, ideological homosexuality, or some highly conflicted but intensively structured combination of the two. (Lesbianism also must always be in a special relation to patriarchy, but on different [sometimes opposite] grounds and working through different mechanisms.)

Perhaps the most powerful recent argument through (and against) a traditional discipline that bears on these issues has occurred within anthropology. Based on readings and critiques of Lévi-Strauss and Engels, in addition to Freud and Lacan, Gayle Rubin has argued in an influential essay that patriarchal heterosexuality can best be discussed in terms of one or another form of the traffic in women: it is the use of women as exchangeable, perhaps symbolic, property for the primary purpose of cementing the bonds of men with men. For example, Lévi-Strauss writes, "The total relationship of exchange which constitutes marriage is not established between a man and a woman, but between two groups of men, and the woman figures only as one of the objects in the exchange, not as one of the partners."[26] Thus, like Freud's "heterosexual" in Richard Klein's account, Lévi-Strauss's normative man uses a woman as a "conduit of a relationship" in which the true *partner* is a man.[27] Rejecting Lévi-Strauss's celebratory treatment of this relegation of women, Rubin offers, instead, an array of tools for specifying and analyzing it.

Luce Irigaray has used the Lévi-Straussian description of the traffic in women to make a resounding though expensive leap of register in her discussion of the relation of heterosexual to male homosocial bonds. In the reflections translated into English as "When the Goods Get Together," she concludes: "[Male] homosexuality is the law that regulates the sociocultural order. Heterosexuality amounts to the assignment of roles in the economy."[28] To begin to describe this relation as having the asymmetry of (to put it roughly) *parole* to *langue* is wonderfully pregnant; if her use of it here is not a historically responsive one, still it has potential for increasing our ability to register historical difference.

The expensiveness of Irigaray's vision of male homosexuality is, oddly, in a sacrifice of sex itself: the male "homosexuality" discussed here turns out to represent anything but actual sex beteen men, which – although it is also, importantly, called "homosexuality" – has something like the same invariable, tabooed status for her larger, "real" "homosexuality" that incest has in principle for Lévi-Straussian kinship in general. Even Irigaray's supple machinery of meaning has the effect of transfixing, then sublimating, the quicksilver of sex itself.

The loss of the diachronic in a formulation like Irigaray's is, again, most significant, as well. Recent anthropology, as well as historical work by Foucault, Sheila Rowbotham, Jeffrey Weeks, Alan Bray, K. J. Dover, John Boswell, David Fernbach, and others, suggests that among the things that have changed radically in Western culture over the centuries, and vary across cultures, about men's genital activity with men are its frequency, its exclusivity, its class associations, its relation to the dominant culture, its ethical status, the degree to which it is seen as defining nongenital aspects of the lives of those who practice it, and, perhaps most radically, its association with femininity or masculinity in societies where gender is a profound determinant of power. The virility of the homosexual orientation of male desire seemed as self-evident to the ancient Spartans, and perhaps to Whitman, as its effeminacy seems in contemporary popular culture. The importance of women (not merely of "the feminine," but of actual women as well) in the etiology and the continuing experience of male homosexuality seems to be historically volatile (across time, across class) to a similar degree. Its changes are inextricable from the changing shapes of the institutions by which gender and class inequality are structured.

Thus, Lacan, Chodorow and Dinnerstein, Rubin, Irigaray, and others, making critiques from within their multiple traditions, offer analytical tools for treating the erotic triangle not as an ahistorical, Platonic form, a deadly symmetry from which the historical accidents of gender, language, class, and power detract, but as a sensitive register precisely for delineating relationships of power and meaning, and for making graphically intelligible the play of desire and identification by which individuals negotiate with their societies for empowerment.

NOTES

1 The notion of "homophobia" is itself fraught with difficulties. To begin with, the word is etymologically nonsensical. A more serious problem is that the linking of fear and hatred in the "-phobia" suffix, and in the word's usage, does tend to prejudge the question of the cause of homosexual oppression: it is attributed to fear, as opposed to (for example) a desire for power, privilege, or material goods. An alternative term that is more suggestive of collective, structurally inscribed, perhaps materially based oppression is "heterosexism." This study will, however, continue to use "homophobia," for three reasons. First, it will be an important concern here to question, rather than to reinforce, the presumptively symmetrical opposition between homo- and heterosexuality, which seems to be implicit in the term "heterosexism." Second, the etiology of individual people's attitudes toward male homosexuality will not be a focus of discussion. And third, the ideological and thematic treatments of male homosexuality to be discussed from the late eighteenth century onward do combine fear and hatred in a way that is appropriately called phobic. For a good summary of social science research on the concept of homophobia, see Morin and Garfinkle, "Male Homophobia."

2 For a good survey of the background to this assertion, see Weeks, *Sex*, pp. 1–18.

3 Adrienne Rich describes these bonds as forming a "lesbian continuum," in her essay, "Compulsory Heterosexuality and Lesbian Existence," in Stimpson and Person, *Women*, pp. 62–91, especially pp. 79–82.

4 "The Female World of Love and Ritual," in Cott and Pleck, *Heritage*, pp. 311–42; usage appears on, e.g., pp. 316, 317.

5 "The Unhappy Marriage of Marxism and Feminism: Towards a More Progressive Union," in Sargent, *Women and Revolution*, pp. 1–41; quotation is from p. 14.

6 See, for example, Rubin, "Traffic," pp. 182–83.

7 Rubin, "Traffic," p. 180.

8 Crompton, "Gay Genocide"; but see chapter 5 for a discussion of the limitations of "genocide" as an understanding of the fate of homosexual men.

9 On this, see Miller, *New Psychology*, ch. 1.

10 Dover, *Greek Homosexuality*, p. 91.

11 Arendt, *Human Condition*, p. 83, quoted in Rich, *On Lies*, p. 206.

12 On the Bohemian Grove, an all-male summer camp for American ruling-class men, see Domhoff, *Bohemian Grove*; and a more vivid, although homophobic, account, van der Zee, *Men's Party*.

13 The NOW resolution, for instance, explicitly defines sadomasochism, pornography, and "pederasty" (meaning pedophilia) as issues of "exploitation and violence," *as opposed to* "affectional/sexual preference/orientation." Quoted in *Heresies 12*, vol. 3, no. 4 (1981), p. 92.

14 For explorations of these viewpoints, see *Heresies*, ibid.; Snitow et al., *Powers*; and Samois, *Coming*.

15 MacKinnon, "Feminism," pp. 530–31.

16 Mitchell, *Gone*, p. 780. Further citations will be incorporated within the text and designated by chapter number.

17 For a discussion of these limitations, see Vicinus, "Sexuality." The variety of useful work that is possible within these boundaries is exemplified by the essays in Newton et al., *Sex and Class*.

18 On this, see McKeon, "'Marxism.'"

19 Juliet Mitchell discusses this aspect of *The German Ideology* in *Woman's Estate*, pp. 152–58.

20 Mitchell, *Woman's Estate*, p. 154.

21 The best and clearest discussion of this aspect of Freud is Laplanche, *Life and Death*, especially pp. 25–47. Chapter 8 title: "Adam Bede and Henry Esmond: Homosocial Desire and the Historicity of the Female."

22 On this, see Bell et al., *Sexual Preferences*.

23 Review of *Homosexualities*, p. 1077.

24 On this see Gallop, *Daughter's Seduction*, pp. 15–32.

25 Kahn, *Man's Estate*, pp. 9–10.

26 *The Elementary Structures of Kinship* (Boston: Beacon, 1969), p. 115; quoted in Rubin, "Traffic," p. 174.

27 Rubin, ibid.

28 Irigaray, "Goods," pp. 107–10.

REFERENCES FOR NOTES

1 Stephen M. Morin and Ellen M. Garfinkle, "Male Homophobia," in *Gayspeak: Gay Male and Lesbian Communication*, ed. James W. Chesebro (New York: Pilgrim Press, 1981), 117–29.

2 Jeffrey Weeks, *Sex, Politics, and Society: The Regulation of Sexuality Since 1800* (London: Longman, 1981).

3 Catharine R. Stimpson and Ethel Spector Person, eds., *Women: Sex and Sexuality* (Chicago: University of Chicago Press, 1980).

4 Nancy F. Cott and Elizabeth H. Pleck, eds., *A Heritage of Her Own: Toward a New Social History of American Women* (New York: Simon and Schuster, 1979).

5 Lydia Sargent, ed., *Women and Revolution: A Discussion of the Unhappy Marriage of Marxism and Feminism* (Boston: South End Press, 1981).

6 Gayle Rubin, "The Traffic in Women: Notes Toward a Political Economy of Sex," in *Toward an Anthropology of Women*, ed. Rayna Reiter (New York: Monthly Review Press, 1975), 157–210.

8 Louis Crompton, "Gay Genocide: From Leviticus to Hitler," in *The Gay Academic*, ed. Louie Crew (Palm Springs, Calif.: ETC Publications, 1978), 67–91.

9 Jean Baker Miller, *Toward a New Psychology of Women* (Boston: Beacon Press, 1976).

10 K. J. Dover, *Greek Homosexuality* (New York: Random House-Vintage, 1980).

11 Hannah Arendt, *The Human Condition* (Chicago: University of Chicago Press, 1958).

12 G. William Domhoff, *The Bohemian Grove and Other Retreats: A Study in Ruling-Class Cohesiveness* (New York: Harper & Row, 1974); John Van der Zee, *The Greatest Men's Party on Earth: Inside the Bohemian Grove* (New York: Harcourt Brace Jovanovich, 1974).

14 Ann Snitow, Christine Stansell, and Sharon Thompson, eds., *Powers of Desire: The Politics of Sexuality* (New York: Monthly Review Press – New Feminist Library, 1983); Samois, ed., *Coming to Power: Writing and Graphics on Lesbian S/M* (Boston: Alyson, 1982).

15 Catherine A. MacKinnon, "Feminism, Marxism, Method, and the State: An Agenda for Theory," *Signs* 7.3 (Spring 1982): 515–44.

16 Margaret Mitchell, *Gone With the Wind* (New York: Avon, 1973).

17 Martha Vicinus, "Sexuality and Power: A Review of Current Work in the History of Sexuality," *Feminist Studies* 8.1 (Spring 1982): 133–56; Judith L. Newton, Mary P. Ryan, and Judith R. Walkowitz, eds., *Sex and Class in Women's History* (London: Routledge and Kegan Paul, 1983).

18 Michael McKeon, "The 'Marxism' of Claude Lévi-Strauss," *Dialectical Anthropology* 6 (1981): 123–50.

19 Juliet Mitchell, *Women's Estate* (New York: Random House – Vintage, 1973).

21 Jean Laplanche, *Life and Death in Psychoanalysis*, trans. Jeffrey Mehlman (Baltimore: Johns Hopkins University Press, 1976).

22 Alan P. Bell, Martin S. Weinerg, and Sue Kiefer Hammersmith, *Sexual Preference: Its Development in Men and Women* (Bloomington: Indiana University Press, 1981).

23 Richard Klein, review of *Homosexualities in French Literature*, MLN 95.4 (May 1980): 1070–80.

24 Jane Gallop, *The Daughter's Seduction: Feminism and Psychoanalysis* (Ithaca, NY: Cornell University Press, 1982).

25 Coppélia Kahn, *Men's Estate: Masculine Identity in Shakespeare* (Berkeley: University of California Press, 1981).

26 Luce Irigaray, "When the Goods Get Together," in *New French Feminisms*, ed. Elaine Marks and Isabelle de Courtivron (New York: Shocken, 1981).

Queer Performativity: Henry James's *The Art of the Novel*

Eve Kosofsky Sedgwick

Eve Kosofsky Sedgwick (b. 1950)

Born in Dayton, Ohio, Eve Kosofsky Sedgwick attended Cornell University and Yale University, where she received her Ph.D. in 1975. Sedgwick taught at Boston University (1981–3), Amherst College (1984–8), and Duke University (1988–98); in 1998 she became Distinguished Professor of English at the Graduate Center of the City University of New York. A poet and visual artist, she has published *Fat Art, Thin Art* (1994), and held exhibitions at the Rhode Island School of Design, SUNY-Stony Brook, Johns Hopkins University, and Dartmouth College. Since her 1991 breast cancer diagnosis, Sedgwick has also worked as a patient advocate, among other things writing the bimonthly advice column "Off My Chest" for *MAMM Magazine: Women, Cancer, and Community* (1997–2003). Her experimental autobiography *A Dialogue on Love* (1999), focuses on her therapy sessions following her initial diagnosis. Sedgwick has received fellowships from the National Endowment for the Humanities, the National Humanities Center, and the Guggenheim Foundation, and been honored with the National Institute of Arts and Letters' Morton Dauwen Zabel

From *GLQ: Journal of Lesbian and Gay Studies*, vol. 1, no. 1, 1993, pp. 1–16. Copyright © 1993 by Gordon and Breach Science Publishers SA. All rights reserved. Used with permission.

Award for experimental writing. Sedgwick's scholarly books include: *The Coherence of Gothic Conventions* (1980; 1986); *Between Men: English Literature and Male Homosocial Desire* (1985; 1993); *Epistemology of the Closet* (1990); *Tendencies* (1993); and *Touching Feeling: Affect, Pedagogy, Performativity* (2003).

I don't remember hearing the phrase "queer performativity" used before, but it seems to be made necessary by, if nothing else, the work of Judith Butler in and since her important book *Gender Trouble*. Anyone who was at the 1991 Rutgers conference on Gay and Lesbian Studies, and heard *Gender Trouble* appealed to in paper after paper, couldn't help being awed by the productive impact this dense and even imposing work has had on the recent development of queer theory and reading – especially among the hundreds of graduate students whose "recruitment" into the gay studies, if not more simply the gay, lifestyle has been one of the most notable and fun features of the emergence of our shared discipline. Inevitably, as any theory of cultural consumption would suggest, the iteration, the citation, the *use* of Butler's formulations in the context of queer theory will prove to have been highly active and tendentious. Probably the centerpiece of Butler's recent work has been a series of demonstrations that gender can best be discussed as a form of performativity. But what that claim, in turn, "means" is performatively dependent on the uses given it. Judging from the Rutgers conference, its force so far has been in pressing toward a radical extreme of interrogation the anti-essentialist account of gender; in ratifying the apparently unique centrality of drag performance practice as – not just the shaping metaphor – but the very idiom of a tautologically heterosexist gender/sexuality system, and the idiom also of the possibility for its subversion; in broadening the notion of parody and foregrounding it as a strategy of gender critique and struggle; and more generally, in placing theater and theatrical performance at front and center of questions of subjectivity and sexuality.

There is a lot to value in all this. But as a reader I do find that the magnetism exerted on me by the notion of performativity emanates from some different places than these – also queer ones, and also, I believe, resonant with at least some concerns in Butler's writing that have proven less easy to attend to so far. I'd single out especially the relation between systemic melancholia – the melancholia she describes so suggestively as being instituted by the loss, not of particular objects of desire, but of proscribed desires themselves – the relation between that systemic melancholia and performativity. But where, then, are we to look for performativity itself? I would like the question of performativity to prove useful in some way for understanding the obliquities among *meaning*, *being*, and *doing*, not only around the examples of drag performance and (its derivative?) gendered self-presentation, but equally for such complex speech acts as coming out, for work around AIDS and other grave identity-implicating illnesses, and for the self-labelled, transversely but urgently representational placarded body of *demonstration*.

To begin with: the divided history, hence the divided reach across present and future, of this term "performativity." In many usages I am currently hearing, it seems to be filiated *only* with, motivated only by the notion of a performance in the defining instance theatrical. Yet Butler's work constitutes an invitation to, in her words, "consider gender...as...an 'act,' as it were, which is both intentional and performative, where 'performative' itself carries the double-meaning of 'dramatic' and 'non-referential'" (Butler, "Performative Acts," 272–73). "Performative" at the present moment carries the authority of two quite different discourses, that of theater on the one hand, of speech-act theory and deconstruction on the other. Partaking in the prestige of both discourses, it nonetheless, as Butler suggests, means very differently in each. The stretch between theatrical and deconstructive meanings of "performative" seems to span the polarities of, at either extreme, the *extroversion* of the actor, the *introversion* of the signifier. Michael Fried's opposition between theatricality and absorption seems custom-made for this paradox about "performativity": in its deconstructive sense performativity signals absorption; in the vicinity of the stage, however, the performative is the theatrical. But in another range of usages, a text like Lyotard's *The Postmodern Condition* uses "performativity" to mean an extreme of something like *efficiency* – postmodern representation as a form of capitalist efficiency – while, again, the deconstructive "performativity" of Paul de Man or J. Hillis Miller seems to be characterized by the *dis*linkage precisely of cause and effect between the signifier and the world. At the same time, it's worth keeping in mind that even in deconstruction, more can be said of performative speech-acts than that they are ontologically dislinked or introversively non-referential. Following on de Man's demonstration of "a radical estrangement between the meaning and the performance of any text" (298), one might want to dwell not so much on the non-reference of the performative but rather on (what de Man calls) its necessarily "aberrant"[1] relation to its own reference – the torsion, the mutual perversion as one might say, of reference and performativity.

"Performativity" is already quite a queer category, then – maybe not so surprising if we consider the tenuousness of its ontological ground, the fact that it begins its intellectual career all but repudiated in advance by its originator, the British philosopher J. L. Austin, who introduces the term in the first of his 1955 Harvard lectures (later published as *How to Do Things with Words*) only to disown it somewhere around the eighth. He disowns or dismantles "performativity," that is, as the name of a distinct category or field of utterances (that might be opposed to the "constative"); and indeed the use that deconstruction has had for "performativity" begins with the recognition of it as a property common to all utterance. Yet, as Shoshana Felman points out in *The Literary Speech Act*, Austin's own performance in these texts is anything but a simple one; and one of their sly characteristics is a repeated tropism toward – an evident fascination with – a particular class of examples of performative utterance. Presented first as pure, originary and defining for the concept; dismissed at the last as no more than "a marginal limiting case" of it if indeed either the examples or the concept can be said to "survive" the analytic operation of the lectures at all (Austin 150); nonetheless reverted to over and over as if no argument or analysis, no deconstruction or dismantlement could really vitiate or even challenge the self-evidence of their exemplary force – these sentences are what Austin's work installs in the mind *as* performativity *tout court*, even while rendering nominally unusable the concept *of* performativity *tout court*. Famously, these are a cluster of sentences in the first person singular present indicative active, about which "it seems clear that to utter the sentence (in, of course, the appropriate circumstances) is not to *describe* my doing [a thing]…or to state that I am doing it: it is to do it" (Austin 6). Examples include "I promise," "I bet…," "I bequeath…," "I christen…," "I apologize," "I dare you," "I sentence you…," and so on. But the first example Austin offers remains both his own most inveterately recurrent and his most influential: "'I do (sc. take this woman to be my lawful wedded wife)' – as uttered in the course of the marriage ceremony" (4).

The marriage ceremony is, indeed, so central to the origins of "performativity" (given the strange, disavowed but unattenuated persistence of *the exemplary* in this work) that a more accurate name for *How to Do Things with Words* might have been *How to say (or write) "I do" about twenty million times without winding up any more married than you started out.* (Short title: *I Do – Not!*) This is true both because most of the "I do"'s (or "I pronounce thee man and wife"'s) in the book are offered as examples of the different ways things can go *wrong* with performative utterances (e.g., "because we are, say, married already, or it is the purser and not the captain who is conducting the ceremony" [Austin 16]); but even more because it is *as* examples they are offered in the first place – hence as, performatively, voided in advance. *How to Do Things with Words* thus performs at least a triple gesture with respect to marriage: installing monogamous heterosexual dyadic church- and state-sanctioned marriage at the definitional center of an entire philosophical edifice, it yet posits as the first heuristic device of that philosophy *the class of things* (for instance, personal characteristics or object choices) *that can preclude or vitiate marriage*; and it constructs the philosopher himself, the modern Socrates, as a man – presented as highly comic – whose relation to the marriage vow will be one of compulsive, apparently apotropaic repetition and yet of ultimate exemption.

So, as Felman's work in *The Literary Speech Act* confirms, the weird centrality of the marriage example for performativity in general isn't exactly a sign that this train of thought is foredoomed to stultification in sexual orthodoxy. Nevertheless I am struck by the potential interest that might also lie in speculation about versions of performativity (okay, go ahead and call them 'perversions' – or 'deformatives') that might begin by placing some different kinds of utterance in the position of the exemplary. Austin keeps going back to that formula "first person singular present indicative active," for instance, and the marriage example makes me wonder about the apparently natural way the first-person speaking, acting, and pointing subject, like the (wedding) present itself, gets constituted in marriage through a confident appeal to state authority, through the calm interpellation of others present as "witnesses," and through the logic of the (heterosexual) supplement whereby individual subjective agency is guaranteed by the welding into a cross-gender dyad. Persons who self-identify as queer, by contrast, will be those whose subjectivity is lodged in refusals or deflections of (or by) the logic of the heterosexual supplement; in far less simple associations attaching to state authority; in far less complacent relation to the witness of others. The emergence of the first person, of the singular, of the present, of the active, and of the indicative are all questions, rather than presumptions, for queer performativity.

That's why I like to speculate about a performative elaboration that might begin with the example, not "I do," but, let us say, "Shame on you." "Shame on you" has several important features in common with Austin's pet examples: most notably, it names itself, it has its illocutionary force (the conferral of shame) in and by specifying its illocutionary intent. Then, like Austin's examples, it depends on the interpellation of witness.

EVE KOSOFSKY SEDGWICK

And like them too it necessarily occurs within a pronoun matrix. Unlike the "I do" set of performatives, though, its pronoun matrix begins with the second person. There is a "you" but there is no "I" – or rather, forms of the inexplicit "I" constantly remain to be evoked from the formulation "Shame on you." They can be evoked in different ways. The absence of an explicit verb from "Shame on you" records the place in which an I, in conferring shame, has effaced itself and its own agency.[2] Of course the desire for self-effacement is the defining trait of – what else? – shame. So the very grammatical truncation of "Shame on you" marks it as the product of a history out of which an I, now withdrawn, is *projecting* shame – toward another I, an I deferred, that has yet and with difficulty to come into being, if at all, in the place of the shamed second person. The verblessness of this particular performative, then, implies a first person whose singular/plural status, whose past/present/future status, and indeed whose agency/ passivity can only be questioned rather than presumed.

Why might "Shame on you" be a useful utterance from which to begin imagining *queer* performativity? Appearances are strongly against it, I admit. What's the point of accentuating the negative, of beginning with stigma, and for that matter a form of stigma – "Shame on you" – so unsanitizably redolent of that long Babylonian exile known as queer childhood? But note that this is just what the word queer itself does, too: the main reason why the self-application of "queer" by activists has proven so volatile is that there's no *way* that any amount of affirmative reclamation is going to succeed in detaching the word from its associations with shame and with the terrifying powerless-ness of gender-dissonant or otherwise stigmatized childhood. If queer is a politically potent term, which it is, that's because, far from being capable of being detached from the childhood scene of shame, it cleaves to that scene as a near-inexhaustible source of transformational energy. There's a strong sense, I think, in which the subtitle of any truly queer (perhaps as opposed to gay?) politics will be the same as the one Erving Goffman gave to his book *Stigma: Notes on the Management of Spoiled Identity.* But more than its management: its experimental, creative, performative force.

"Shame on you" is performatively efficacious because its grammar – admittedly somewhat enigmatic – *is* a transformational grammar: both at the level of pronoun positioning, as I've sketched, and at the level of the relational grammar of the affect shame itself. As described by the psychologist Silvan Tomkins, who offers by far the richest theory and phenomenology of this affect, shame effaces itself; shame points and projects; shame turns itself skin side outside; shame and pride, shame and self-display, shame and exhibitionism are different interlinings of the same glove: shame, it might finally be said, transformational shame, *is performance.* I mean theatrical performance. Performance interlines shame as more than just its result or a way of warding it off, too, though importantly it is those things. Recent work by theorists and psychologists of shame locates the proto-form (eyes down, head averted) of this powerful affect – which appears in infants very early, between the third and seventh months of life, just after the infant has become able to distinguish and recognize the face of its caregiver – at a particular moment in a particular repeated narrative. That is the moment when the circuit of mirroring expressions between the child's face and the caregiver's recognized face (a circuit which, if it can be called a form of primary narcissism, suggests that narcissism from the very first throws itself sociably, dangerously into the gravitational field of the other) is broken: the moment when the adult face fails or refuses to play its part in the continuation of mutual gaze; when, for any one of many reasons, it fails to be recognizable to, or recognizing of, the infant who has been, so to speak, "giving face" based on a faith in the continuity of this circuit. As Michael Franz Basch explains,

> The infant's behavioral adaptation is quite totally dependent on maintaining effective communication with the executive and coordinating part of the infant-mother system. The shame-humiliation response, when it appears, represents the failure or absence of the smile of contact, a reaction to the loss of feedback from others, indicating social isolation and signaling the need for relief from that condition. (765)

The proto-affect shame is thus not defined by prohibition (nor, as a result, by repression). Shame floods into being as a moment, a disruptive moment, in a circuit of identity-constituting identificatory communication. Indeed, like a stigma, shame is itself a form of communication. Blazons of shame, the "fallen face" with eyes down and head averted – and to a lesser extent, the blush – are semaphors of trouble and at the same time of a desire to reconstitute the interpersonal bridge.

But in interrupting identification, shame, too, makes identity. In fact shame and identity remain in very dynamic relation to one another, at once deconstituting and foundational, because shame is both peculiarly contagious and peculiarly individuating. Many developmental psychologists consider shame the affect that most defines the space wherein a sense of self will develop (Francis Broucek: "shame is to self psychology what anxiety is to ego psychology – the keystone affect" [369]). Nonetheless, shame both derives from and aims toward sociability.

> The shame-humiliation reaction in infancy of hanging the head and averting the eyes does not mean the child is conscious of rejection, but indicates that effective contact with another person has been broken.... Therefore, shame-humiliation throughout life can be thought of as an inability to effectively arouse the other person's positive reactions to one's communications. The exquisite painfulness of that reaction in later life harks back to the earliest period when such a condition is not simply uncomfortable but threatens life itself. (Basch 765–66)

So that whenever the actor, or the performance artist, or, I could add, the activist in an identity politics, proffers the spectacle of her or his "infantile" narcissism to a spectating eye, the stage is set (so to speak) for either a newly dramatized flooding of the subject by the shame of refused return; or the successful pulsation of the mirroring regard through a narcissistic circuit rendered elliptical (which is to say: necessarily distorted) by the hyperbole of its original cast. Shame is the affect that mantles the threshold between introversion and extroversion, between absorption and theatricality, between performativity and – performativity.

What links the currently hot topic of shame to a high-cultural figure like Henry James? Readers who have paid attention to the recent, meteoric rise of shame to its present housewife-megastar status in the firmament of self-help and popular psychology – along with that of its ingenue sidekick, the Inner Child – may be feeling a bit uneasy by this point. So, for that matter, may those used to reading about shame in the neoconservative framework that treasures shame along with guilt as, precisely, an adjunct of repression and an enforcer of proper behavior.[3] In the ways I want to be thinking about shame, the widespread moralistic valuation of this powerful affect as *good* or *bad, to be mandated* or *to be excised*, according to how one plots it along a notional axis of prohibition/permission/requirement, seems distinctly beside the point. It seems to me that the great usefulness of thinking about shame comes, by contrast, from its potential *distance* from the concepts of guilt and repression, hence from the stressed epistemologies and bifurcated moralisms entailed in every manifestation of what Foucault referred to as the repressive hypothesis. Surely then I can hardly appeal to *Toxic Shame, Healing the Shame that Binds You, or Guilt is the Teacher, Love is the Lesson*, can I, for my very methodology? Am I really going to talk about Henry James's inner child? My sense of the force and interest of the affect shame is clearly very different from what is to be found in the self-help literature, but there it is: Henry James and the inner child it must be.

Henry James undertook the New York Edition (a handsome 24-volume consolidation and revision, with new prefaces, of what he saw as his most important novels and stories to date) at the end of a relatively blissful period of literary production ("the major phase") – a blissful period poised, however, between two devastating bouts of melancholia. (The connection between melancholia and performativity, derived from Butler, with whose invocation I began this essay, needs to open out, I think, into a full-scale discussion of the connections among melancholia, mourning, disidentification, and shame – but this is a project for the future.) The first of these scouring depressions was precipitated in 1895 by what James experienced as the obliterative failure of his ambitions as a playwright, being howled off the stage at the premiere of *Guy Domville*. By 1907, though, when the volumes of the New York Edition were beginning to appear, James's theatrical self-projection was sufficiently healed that he had actually begun a new round of playwrighting and of negotiations with producers – eventuating, indeed, in performance. The next of James's terrible depressions was triggered, not by humiliation on the stage, but by the failure of the New York Edition itself: its total failure to sell, and its apparently terminal failure to evoke any recognition from any readership.

When we read *The Art of the Novel*, then (the book compiled many years later out of James's prefaces to the successive volumes of the New York Edition), we read a text that is in the most active imaginable relation to shame. Marking and indeed exulting in James's recovery from a near-fatal episode of shame in the theater, the Prefaces, gorgeous with the playful spectacle of a productive and almost promiscuously entrusted or "thrown" authorial narcissism, yet also offer the spectacle of inviting (that is, leaving themselves open to) what was in fact their and their author's immediate fate: annihilation by the blankest of non-recognizing responses from any reader. The Prefaces are way out there, in short (and in more than a couple of senses of out).

In them, at least two different circuits of the hyperbolic narcissism/shame orbit are being enacted, and in a volatile relation to each other. The first of these, as I've suggested, is the drama of James's relation to his audience of readers: in using the term "audience" here, I want to mark James's own insistent thematization of elements in this writing as specifically theatrical, with all the implications of excitement, overinvestment, danger, loss, and melancholia that the theater by this time held for him.[4] The second and related narcissism/shame circuit dramatized in the Prefaces is the perilous and productive one that extends between the speaker and his own past. James's most usual gesture in the Prefaces is to figure his relation to the past as the intensely charged relationship between the author of the Prefaces and the often much younger man who wrote the novels and stories to which the Prefaces are appended – or between either of these men and a yet younger figure who represents the fiction itself.

What undertaking could be more narcissistically exciting or more narcissistically dangerous than that of rereading, revising and consolidating one's own "collected works"? If *these*, or their conjured young author, return one's longing gaze with dead, indifferent, or even distracted eyes, what limit can there be to the shame (of him, of oneself) so incurred? Equal to that danger, however, is the danger of one's own failure to recognize or to desire them or him. Silvan Tomkins, the most important recent theorist of affect (though one whose fascinating work of the early 1960s is difficult to place in relation to the main surrounding currents – all of which he engages – of psychoanalysis, clinical and experimental psychology, and early cybernetics and systems theory), considers shame along with interest, surprise, joy, anger, distress, disgust, and contempt ("dissmell") to be the basic set of affects. He places shame, in fact, at one end of the affect polarity *shame-interest*, suggesting that the pulsations of cathexis around shame, of all things, are what either enable or disable so basic a function as the ability to be interested in the world.

> Like disgust, [shame] operates only after interest or enjoyment has been activated, and inhibits one or the other or both. The innate activator of shame is the incomplete reduction of interest or joy. Hence any barrier to further exploration which partially reduces interest…will activate the lowering of the head and eyes in shame and reduce further exploration or self-exposure.… Such a barrier might be because one is suddenly looked at by one who is strange, or because one wishes to look at or commune with another person but suddenly cannot because he is strange, or one expected him to be familiar but he suddenly appears unfamiliar, or one started to smile but found one was smiling at a stranger. (Tomkins 123)

To consider interest itself a distinct affect, and to posit an association between shame and (the [incomplete] inhibition of) interest, makes sense phenomenologically, I think, about depression, and specifically about the depressions out of which James had emerged to write his "major novels" – novels that do, indeed, seem to show the effects of a complicated history of disruptions and prodigal remediations in the *ability to take an interest*. Into such depressions as well, however, he was again to be plunged.

The James of the Prefaces revels in the same startling metaphor that animates the present-day literature of the "inner child": the metaphor that presents one's relation to one's own past as a relation*ship*, intersubjective as it is intergenerational. And, it might be added, almost by definition homoerotic. Often the younger author is present in these Prefaces as a figure in himself, but even more frequently the fictions themselves, or characters in them, are given his form. One needn't be invested (as pop psychology is) in a normalizing, hygienic teleology of *healing* this relationship, in a mawkishly essentialist overvaluation of the "child"'s access to narrative authority at the expense of that of the "adult," or in a totalizing ambition to get the two selves permanently merged into one, in order to find that this figuration opens out a rich landscape of relational positionalities – perhaps especially around issues of shame. James certainly displays no desire whatever to become once again the young and mystified author of his early productions. To the contrary, the very distance of these inner self-figurations from the speaking self of the present is marked, treasured and in fact eroticized. Their distance (temporal, figured as intersubjective, figured in turn as spatial) seems, if anything, to constitute the relished internal space of James's absorbed subjectivity. Yet for all that the distance itself is prized, James's speculation as to what different outcomes might be evoked by different kinds of overture across the distance – by different sorts of solicitation, different forms of touch, interest, and love between the less and the more initiated figure – provides a great deal of the impetus to his theoretical project in these essays. The speaking self of the Prefaces does not attempt to merge with the potentially shaming or shamed figurations of its younger self, younger fictions, younger heroes; its attempt is to love them. That love is shown to occur both in spite of shame and, more remarkably, through it.

Not infrequently, as we'll see, the undertaking to reparent, as it were, or "reissue" the bastard infant of (what is presented as) James's juvenilia is described simply as male parturition. James also reports finding in himself "that finer consideration hanging in the parental breast about the maimed or slighted, the disfigured or defeated, the unlucky or unlikely child – with this hapless small mortal thought of further as somehow 'compromising'" (80–81). James offers a variety of reasons for being embarrassed by these waifs of his past, but the persistence with which shame accompanies their repeated conjuration is matched by the persistence with which, in turn, he describes himself as cathecting or eroticizing that very shame as a way of coming into loving relation to queer or "compromising" youth. In a number of places, for example, James more or less explicitly invokes *Frankenstein* and all the potential uncanniness of the violently dis-avowed male birth. But he invokes that uncanniness in order to undo it, or at least to do something further with it, by offering the spectacle of – not his refusal – but his eroticized eagerness to recognize his progeny even in its oddness.

> The thing done and dismissed has ever, at the best, for the ambitious workman, a trick of looking dead if not buried, so that he almost throbs with ecstasy when, on an anxious review, the flush of life reappears. It is verily on recognising that flush on a whole side of "The Awkward Age" that I brand it all, but ever so tenderly, as monstrous....(99)

It is as if the ecstasy-inducing power of the young creature's "flush of life," which refers to even while evoking the potentially shaming brand of monstrosity, is the reflux of the blush of shame or repudiation the older man in this rewriting *doesn't* feel. Similarly, James writes about his mortifyingly extravagant miscalculations concerning the length of (what he had imagined as) a short story:

> Painfully associated for me has "The Spoils of Poynton" remained, until recent re-perusal, with the awkward consequence of that fond error. The subject had emerged...all suffused with a flush of meaning; thanks to which irresistible air, as I could but plead in the event, I found myself...beguiled and led on.

"The thing had 'come,'" he concludes with an undisguised sensuous pleasure but hardly a simple one, "the flower of conception had bloomed" (124). And he describes his revision of the early fictions both as his (or their?) way of "remaining *unshamed*," and in the same sentence as a process by which they have "all joyously and *blushingly* renewed themselves" (345, emphasis added). What James seems to want here is to remove the blush from its terminal place as the betraying blazon of a ruptured narcissistic circuit, and instead to put it *in* circulation – as the sign of a tenderly strengthened and indeed now "irresistible" bond between the writer of the present and the abashed writer of the past; between either of them and the queer little *conceptus.*

You can see the displacement at work in this passage from James's most extended description of his process of revision:

Since to get and to keep finished and dismissed work well behind one, and to have as little to say to it and about it as possible, had been for years one's only law, so, during that flat interregnum...creeping superstitions as to what it might really have been had time to grow up and flourish. Not least among these rioted doubtless the fond fear that any tidying-up of the uncanny brood, any removal of accumulated dust, any washing of wizened faces, or straightening of grizzled locks, or twitching, to a better effect, of superannuated garments, might let one in, as the phrase is, for expensive renovations. I make use here of the figure of age and infirmity, but in point of fact I had rather viewed the reappearance of the first-born of my progeny...as a descent of awkward infants from the nursery to the drawing-room under the kind appeal of enquiring, of possibly interested, visitors. I had accordingly taken for granted the common decencies of such a case – the responsible glance of some power above from one nursling to another, the rapid flash of an anxious needle, the not imperceptible effect of a certain audible splash of soap-and-water....

"Hands off altogether on the nurse's part!" was...strictly conceivable; but only in the light of the truth that it had never taken effect in any fair and stately...re-issue of anything. Therefore it was easy to see that any such apologetic suppression as that of the "altogether," any such admission as that of a single dab of the soap, left the door very much ajar....(337–38)

The passage that begins by conjuring the uncanniness of an abandoned, stunted, old/ young Frankenstein brood (reminiscent of the repudiated or abused children in Dickens, like Smike and Jenny Wren, whose deformed bodies stand for developmental narratives at once accelerated and frozen by, among other things, extreme material want) modulates reassuringly into the warm, overprotected Christopher Robin coziness of bourgeois Edwardian nursery ritual. The eventuality of the uncanny child's actual exposure to solitude and destitution has been deflected by an invoked domesticity. Invoked with that domesticity, in the now fostered and nurtured and therefore "childlike" child, is a new, pleasurable form of exhibitionistic flirtation with adults that dramatizes the child's very distance from abandonment and repudiation. In the place where the eye of parental care had threatened to be withheld, there is now a bath where even the nurse's attention is supplemented by the overhearing ear of inquiring and interested visitors. And in the place where the fear of solitary exposure has been warded off, there's now the playful nakedness of ablution, and a door left "very much ajar" for a little joke about the suppression of the "altogether."

This sanctioned intergenerational flirtation represents a sustained chord in *The Art of the Novel.* James describes the blandishment of his finished works in tones that are strikingly like the ones with which, in his letters, he has also been addressing Hendrik Anderson, Jocelyn Persse, Hugh Walpole, and the other younger men who at this stage

EVE KOSOFSKY SEDGWICK

of his life are setting out, with happy success, to attract him. Note in this passage (from the *Ambassadors* preface) that "impudence" is the glamorizing trait James attributes to his stories – impudence that bespeaks not the absence of shame from this scene of flirtation, but rather its pleasurably recirculated afterglow:

[the story] rejoices...to seem to offer itself in a light, to seem to know, and with the very last knowledge, what it's about – liable as it yet is at moments to be caught by us with its tongue in its cheek and absolutely no warrant but its splendid impudence. Let us grant then that the impudence is always there – there, so to speak, for grace and effect and *allure*; there, above all, because the Story is just the spoiled child of art, and because, as we are always disappointed when the pampered don't "play up," we like it, to that extent, to look all its character. It probably does so, in truth, even when we most flatter ourselves that we negotiate with it by treaty. (315)

To dramatize the story as *impudent* in relation to its creator is also to dramatize the luxurious distance between this scene and one of *repudiation*: the conceivable shame of a past self, a past production, is being caught up and recirculated through a lambent interpersonal figuration of the intimate, indulged mutual pressure of light differentials of power and knowledge.

James writes about the writing of *The American*, "One would like to woo back such hours of fine precipitation...of images so free and confident and ready that they brush questions aside and disport themselves, like the artless schoolboys of Gray's beautiful Ode, in all the ecstasy of the ignorance attending them" (25). (Or boasts of "The Turn of the Screw": "Another grain...would have spoiled the precious pinch addressed to its end" [170].) Sometimes the solicitude is ultimately frustrated, and "I strove in vain...to embroil and adorn this young man on whom a hundred ingenious touches are thus lavished" (97). The wooing in these scenes of pederastic revision is not unidirectional, however; even the age differential can be figured quite differently, as when James finds himself, on rereading *The American*, "clinging to my hero as to a tall, protective, good-natured elder brother in a rough place" (39); or says of Lambert Strether, "I rejoiced in the promise of a hero so mature, who would give me thereby the more to bite into" (310). James refers to the protagonist of "The Beast in the Jungle" as "another poor sensitive gentleman, fit indeed to mate with Stransom of 'The Altar [of the Dead]'" – adding, "my attested predilection for poor sensitive gentlemen almost embarrasses me as I march!" (246). The predilective yoking of the "I" with the surname of John Marcher, the romantic pairing off of Marcher in turn with the equally "sensitive" bachelor George Stransom, give if anything an excess of gay point to the "almost" embarrassment that is however treated, not as a pretext for authorial self-coverture, but as an explicit source of new, performatively induced authorial magnetism.

James, then, in the Prefaces is using reparenting or "reissue" as a strategy for dramatizing and integrating shame, in the sense of rendering this potentially paralyzing affect narratively, emotionally, and performatively productive. The reparenting scenario is also, in James's theoretical writing, a pederastic/pedagogical one in which the flush of shame becomes an affecting and eroticized form of mutual display. The writing subject's seductive bond with the unmerged but unrepudiated "inner child" seems, indeed, to be the condition of that subject's having an interiority at all, a spatialized subjectivity that can be characterized by absorption. Or perhaps I should say: it is a condition of his *displaying* the spatialized subjectivity that can be characterized by absorption. For the spectacle of James's performative absorption appears only in relation (though in a most complex and unstable relation) to the setting of his performative theatricality; the narcissism/shame circuit between the writing self and its "inner child" intersects with that other hyperbolic and dangerous narcissistic circuit, figured as theatrical performance, that extends outward between the presented and expressive face and its audience.

The thing I *least* want to be heard as offering here is a "theory of homosexuality." I have none and I want none. When I attempt to do some justice to the specificity, the richness, above all the explicitness of James's particular erotics, it is not with an eye to making him an exemplar of "homosexuality" or even of one "kind" of "homosexuality," though I certainly don't want, either, to make him sound as if he *isn't* gay. Nonetheless I do mean to nominate the James of the Prefaces as a kind of prototype of – not "homosexuality" – but *queerness*, or queer performativity. In this usage, "queer performativity" is the name of a strategy for the production of meaning and being, in relation to the affect shame and to the later and related fact of stigma.

I don't know yet what claims may be worth making, ontologically, about the queer performativity I have been describing here. Would it be useful to suggest that some of the associations I've been making with queer performativity might actually be features of all performativity? Or useful, instead, to suggest that the transformational grammar of "shame on you" may form only part of the performative activity seen as most intimately related to queerness, by people self-identified as queer? The usefulness of thinking about shame in relation to queer performativity, in any event, does not come from its adding any extra certainty to the question of what utterances or acts may be classed as "performative," or what people may be classed as "queer." Least of all does it pretend to define the relation between queerness and same-sex love and desire. What it does, to the contrary, is perhaps to offer some psychological, phenomenological, thematic density and motivation to what I described before as the "torsions" or aberrances between reference and performativity, or indeed between queerness and other ways of experiencing identity and desire.

But I don't, either, want it to sound as though my project has mainly to do with recuperating for deconstruction (or other anti-essentialist projects) a queerness drained of specificity or political reference. To the contrary: I'd suggest that to view performativity in terms of habitual shame and its transformations opens a lot of new doors for thinking about identity politics. Part of the interest of shame is that it is an affect that delineates identity – but delineates it without defining it or giving it content. Shame, as opposed to guilt, is a bad feeling that does not attach to what one does, but to what one is. As Donald L. Nathanson hypothesizes:

> The difference between the infant before the moment of shame (the infant in the moment of alert activity, of interest, excitement, or enjoyment) and the infant suddenly unable to function, this difference itself may be registered by the infant as a significant experience calling attention to and helping to define the self. In other words, I am suggesting that the physiological experience of the proto-affect shame is a major force in shaping the infantile self, and remains so throughout life. If this is true, then I suggest further that the adult experience of shame is linked to genitality, to self-expression, to physical appearance, to our

EVE KOSOFSKY SEDGWICK

entire construct of what it means to be lovable, initially and primarily simply because the episodes of shame experienced during the formative years (as these other psychic structures are established in the context of success and failure, of positive affect and of shame as the occasional accompaniment to failure) are crucial to the development of a sense of self. (27)[5]

Shame can only be experienced as global and about oneself, whether the invoking occasion of shame be particular or general, something one does or a way one is, one's behavior or one's smell, or even something done *to* one or something one sees done to someone else. Shame is a bad feeling attaching to what one is: one therefore *is something*, in experiencing shame. The place of identity, the structure "identity," marked by shame's threshold between sociability and introversion, may be established and naturalized in the first instance *through shame*.

It seems very likely that the structuring of associations and attachments around the affect shame is among the most telling differentials among cultures and times: not that the entire world can be divided between (supposedly primitive) "shame cultures" and (supposedly evolved) "guilt cultures," but rather that, as an affect, shame is a component (and *differently* a component) of all. Shame, like other affects, is not a discrete intra-psychic structure, but a kind of free radical that (in different people and also in different cultures) attaches to and permanently intensifies or alters the meaning of – of almost anything: a zone of the body, a sensory system, a prohibited or indeed a permitted behavior, another affect such as anger or arousal, a named identity, a script for interpreting other people's behavior toward oneself. Thus, one of the things that anyone's character or personality *is*, is a record of the highly individual histories by which the fleeting emotion of shame has instituted far more durable, structural changes in one's relational and interpretive strategies toward both self and others.

Which means, among other things, that therapeutic or political strategies aimed directly at getting rid of individual or group shame, or undoing it, have something preposterous about them: they may "work" – they certainly have powerful effects – but they can't work in the way they say they work. (I am thinking here of a range of movements that deal with shame variously in the form of, for instance, the communal *dignity* of the civil rights movement; the individuating *pride* of "Black is Beautiful" and gay pride; various forms of nativist *ressentiment*; the menacingly exhibited *abjection* of the skinhead; the early feminist experiments with the naming and foregrounding of *anger* as a response to shame; the incest survivors' movement's epistemological stress on *truth-telling* about shame; and, of course, many, many others.) The forms taken by shame are not distinct "toxic" parts of a group or individual identity that can be excised; they are instead integral to and residual in the processes by which identity itself is formed. They are available for the work of metamorphosis, reframing, refiguration, *trans*figuration, affective and symbolic loading and deformation; but unavailable for effecting the work of purgation and deontological closure.

If the structuration of shame differs strongly between cultures, between periods, and between different forms of politics, however, it differs also simply from one person to another within a given culture and time. Some of the infants, children, and adults in whom shame remains the most available mediator of identity are the ones called (a related word) shy. ("Remember the fifties?" Lily Tomlin asks. "No one was gay in the fifties; they were just shy.") *Queer*, I'd suggest, might usefully be thought of as referring in the first place to this group or an overlapping group of infants and children, those whose sense of identity is for some reason tuned most durably to the note of shame. What it is about them (or us) that makes this true remains to be specified. I mean that in the sense that I can't tell you now what it is – it certainly isn't a single thing – but also in the sense that, *for them*, it remains to be specified, is always belated: the shame-delineated place of identity doesn't determine the consistency or meaning of that identity, and race, gender, class, sexuality, appearance and abledness are only a few of the defining social constructions that will crystallize there, developing from this originary affect their particular structures of expression, creativity, pleasure, and struggle. I'd venture that queerness in this sense has, at this historical moment, *some* definitionally very significant overlap – though a vibrantly elastic and temporally convoluted one – with the complex of attributes today condensed as adult or adolescent "gayness." Everyone knows that there are some lesbians and gay men who could never count as queer, and other people who vibrate to the chord of queer without having much same-sex eroticism, or without routing their same-sex eroticism through the identity labels lesbian or gay. Yet many of the performative identity vernaculars that seem most recognizably "flushed" (to use James's word) with shame-consciousness and shame-creativity do cluster intimately around lesbian and gay worldly spaces: to name only a few, butch abjection, femmitude, leather, pride, SM, drag, musicality, fisting, attitude, zines, histrionicism, asceticism, Snap! culture, diva worship, florid religiosity, in a word, *flaming*....

And activism.

Shame interests me politically, then, because it generates and legitimates the place of identity – the *question* of identity – at the origin of the impulse to the performative, but does so without giving that identity-space the standing of an essence. It constitutes it as to-be-constituted, which is also to say, as already there for the (necessary, productive) misconstrual and misrecognition. Shame – living, as it does, on and in the capillaries and muscles of the face – seems to be uniquely contagious from one person to another. Indeed, one of the strangest features of shame (but also, I would argue, the most theoretically significant) is the way bad treatment of someone else, bad treatment *by* someone else, someone else's embarrassment, stigma, debility, blame or pain, seemingly having nothing to do with me, can so readily flood me – assuming that I'm a shame-prone person – with this sensation whose very suffusiveness seems to delineate my precise, individual outlines in the most isolating way imaginable. And the contagious-ness of shame is only facilitated by its anamorphic, protean susceptibility to new expressive grammars.

These facts suggest, I think, that asking good questions about shame and shame/performativity could get us somewhere with a lot of the recalcitrant knots that tie themselves into the guts of identity politics – yet *without* delegitimating the felt urgency and power of the notion "identity" itself. The dynamics of trashing and of ideological or institutional pogroms, like the dynamics of mourning, are incomprehensible without an understanding of shame. Survivors' guilt and, more generally, the politics of guilt will be better understood when we can see them in some relation to the slippery dynamics of shame. I would suggest that the same is true of the politics of solidarity and identification; perhaps those, as well, of humor and humorlessness. I'd also – if parenthetically – want to suggest that shame/performativity may get us a lot further with the cluster of phenomena generally called "camp" than the notion of parody will, and more too than will any opposition between "depth" and "surface." And can anyone suppose that we'll ever figure out what happened around "political correctness" if we don't see it as, among other things, a highly politicized chain reaction of shame dynamics?

It has been all too easy for the psychologists and the few psychoanalysts working on shame to write it back into the moralisms of the repressive hypothesis: "healthy" or "unhealthy," as I've pointed out, shame can be seen as *good* because it preserves privacy and decency, *bad* because it colludes with self-repression or social repression. Clearly, neither of these valuations is what I'm getting at; I want to say that *at least* for certain ("queer") people, shame is simply the first, and remains a permanent, structuring fact of identity: one that has its own, powerfully productive and powerfully social metamorphic possibilities.

The deepest interest of any notion of performativity, to me, is not finally in the challenge it makes to essentialism. Rather it lies in the alternatives it suggests to the (always moralistic) repression hypothesis. It concerns me that the force of Foucault's critique of the repression hypothesis has been radically neutralized, in much subsequent engagé criticism, by numb refusals to register the pressure of and, as it were, to participate however resistantly in what can never be more or less than the oblique and queer performance of that critique. In a myriad of ways in contemporary thought – ways in which Foucault himself was hardly unimplicated – his critique of the repression hypothesis has been all but fully recuperated in new alibis *for* the repression hypothesis: in accounts of institutional, discursive, and intrapsychic prohibitions as just so many sites for generating and proliferating – what if not repression?; in neatly symmetrical celebrations of "productive" "multiplicities" of "resistance" – to what if not to repression?; in all the dreary and routine forms of good dog/bad dog criticism by which, like good late-capitalist consumers, we persuade ourselves that deciding what we like or don't like about what's happening is the same thing as actually intervening in its production.

I seem to see this happening now in some of the uses scholars are trying to make of performativity as they think they are understanding it from Judith Butler's and other related recent work: straining eyes to ascertain whether particular performances (e.g. of drag) are really *parodic and subversive* (e.g. of gender essentialism) or just *uphold the status quo*. The bottom line is generally the same: kinda subversive, kinda hegemonic. I see this as a sadly premature domestication of a conceptual tool whose powers we really have barely yet begun to explore.

WORKS CITED

Austin, J. L. *How to Do Things with Words.* Ed. J. O. Urmson and Marina Sbisa. 2d edn. Cambridge, MA: Harvard University Press, 1975.
Basch, Michael Franz. "The Concept of Affect: A Re-Examination." *Journal of the American Psychoanalytic Association* 24 (1976): 759–78.
Broucek, Francis J. "Shame and Its Relationship to Early Narcissistic Developments." *International Journal of Psychoanalysis* 63 (1982): 369–78.
Butler, Judith. *Gender Trouble: Feminism and the Subversion of Identity.* New York: Routledge, 1990.

Butler, Judith. "Performative Acts and Gender Constitution: An Essay in Phenomenology and Feminist Theory." *Performing Feminisms: Feminist Critical Theory and Theatre*, ed. Sue-Ellen Case. Baltimore and London: Johns Hopkins University Press, 1990, 270–82.

de Man, Paul. *Allegories of Reading: Figural Language in Rousseau, Nietzsche, Rilke, and Proust*. New Haven and London: Yale University Press, 1979.

Felman, Shoshana. *The Literary Speech Act: Don Juan with J. L. Austin, or Seduction in Two Languages*. Ithaca: Cornell University Press, 1983.

Fried, Michael. *Absorption and Theatricality: Painting and Beholder in the Age of Diderot*. Berkeley: University of California Press, 1980.

Goffman, Erving. *Stigma: Notes on the Management of Spoiled Identity*. Englewood Cliffs, NJ: Prentice Hall, 1963.

James, Henry. *The Art of the Novel*. Forewd. R. W. B. Lewis. Intro. R. P. Blackmur. Boston: Northeastern University Press, 1984.

Lasch, Christopher. "For Shame: Why Americans should be wary of self-esteem." *The New Republic* 207.7, 10 August 1992: 29–34.

Litvak, Joseph. *Caught in the Act: Theatricality in the Nineteenth-Century English Novel*. Berkeley: University of California Press, 1992.

Lyotard, Jean François. *The Postmodern Condition: A Report on Knowledge*. Minneapolis: University of Minnesota Press, 1984.

Miller, J. Hillis. *Hawthorne and History: Defacing It*. Cambridge, MA: Harvard University Press, 1992.

—— *Tropes, Parables, Performatives: Essays on Twentieth-Century Literature*. Durham, NC: Duke University Press, 1991.

Nathanson, Donald L., M.D. "A Timetable for Shame." *The Many Faces of Shame*, ed. Donald L. Nathanson. New York and London: Guilford, 1987, 1–63.

Tomkins, Silvan. *The Negative Affects*. New York: Springer, 1963. Vol. 2 of *Affect Imagery Consciousness*. 4 vols. 1962–91.

NOTES

This article is taken from a longer essay on *The Art of the Novel* that is part of an ongoing project on queer performativity and shame. Timothy Gould, James Kincaid, Joseph Litvak, Michael Moon, Andrew Parker, and of course Judith Butler have been generously instrumental in my process of framing these still very tentative formulations.

1   "…far from closing off the tropological system, irony enforces the repetition of its aberration" (301).

2   It's interesting that in Latin even to say *I* am ashamed – *pudet mihi* – doesn't permit of a first-person subject.

3   Christopher Lasch writes, for instance, "Our current understanding of shame has…been distorted and diminished by attempts to distinguish it from guilt"; and he approvingly quotes the psychoanalyst Leon Wurmser's denunciation of the culture of "shamelessness": "'Everywhere there is an unrestrained exposure of one's emotions and of one's body, a parading of secrets, a wanton intrusion of curiosity.…The culture of shamelessness is also the culture of irreverence, of debunking and devaluing ideals'" (Lasch 32).

4   See Litvak, *Caught in the Act*, 195–269, for the richest description of James's account of theatricality in the novels.

5   Nathanson's collection offers an extremely useful overview of recent work on shame.

Desire and Domestic Fiction

Nancy Armstrong

Nancy Armstrong (b. 1938)

Nancy Armstrong, born in New York City, received her bachelor's degree from the State University of New York, Buffalo, and, in 1977, her doctorate from University of Wisconsin, Madison. Armstrong taught at Wayne State University (1977–86) and the University of Minnesota (1987–91) before coming to Brown University, where she is Nancy Duke Lewis Professor of Comparative Literature, English, Modern Culture and Media, and Women's Studies. Armstrong has been honored as an American Council of Learned Societies Fellow and Rockefeller Fellow; she serves as managing editor of the journal *Novel* and co-editor of the *Oxford Encyclopedia of British Literary History*. In addition to *Desire and Domestic Fiction: A Political History of the Novel* (1987), Armstrong has also written *The Imaginary Puritan: Literature, Intellectual Labor, and the Origins of Personal Life* (with Leonard Tennenhouse, 1992); *Fiction in the Age of Photography: The Legacy of British Realism* (1999); and *How Novels Think: British Fiction and the Limits of Individualism* (2004).

From *Desire and Domestic Fiction: A Political History of the Novel.* New York: Oxford University Press, 1987, Introduction, pp. 3–27, notes, pp. 261–5. Copyright © 1987 by Oxford University Press, Inc. used by permission of Oxford University Press, Inc.

Introduction: The Politics of Domesticating Culture, Then and Now

> Thus towards the end of the eighteenth century a change came about which, if I were
> rewriting history, I should describe more fully and think of greater importance than the
> Crusades or the Wars of the Roses. The middle-class woman began to write.
>
> Virginia Woolf, *A Room of One's Own*

From the beginning, domestic fiction actively sought to disentangle the language of sexual relations from the language of politics and, in so doing, to introduce a new form of political power. This power emerged with the rise of the domestic woman and established its hold over British culture through her dominance over all those objects and practices we associate with private life. To her went authority over the household, leisure time, courtship procedures, and kinship relations, and under her jurisdiction the most basic qualities of human identity were supposed to develop.

To consider the rise of the domestic woman as a major event in political history is not, as it may seem, to present a contradiction in terms, but to identify the paradox that shapes modern culture. It is also to trace the history of a specifically modern form of desire that, during the early eighteenth century, changed the criteria for determining what was most important in a female. In countless educational treatises and works of fiction that were supposedly written for women, this form of desire came into being along with a new kind of woman. And by representing life with such a woman as not only desirable but also available to virtually anyone, this ideal eventually reached beyond the beliefs of region, faction, and religious sect to unify the interests of those groups who were neither extremely powerful nor very poor. During the eighteenth century, one author after another discovered that the customary way of understanding social experience actually misrepresented human value. In place of the intricate status system that had long dominated British thinking, these authors began to represent an individual's value in terms of his, but more often in terms of *her*, essential qualities of mind. Literature devoted to producing the domestic woman thus appeared to ignore the political world run by men. Of the female alone did it presume to say that neither birth nor the accoutrements of title and status accurately represented the individual; only the more subtle nuances of behavior indicated what one was really worth. In this way, writing for and about the female introduced a whole new vocabulary for social relations, terms that attached precise moral value to certain qualities of mind.

It was at first only women who were defined in terms of their emotional natures. Men generally retained their political identity in writing that developed the qualities of female subjectivity and made subjectivity a female domain. It is fair to say that Sterne's heroes, like Fielding's Joseph Andrews, clearly declared themselves anomalous when they inverted the model and, as males, experienced life as a sequence of events that elicited sentimental responses. In this respect, they came to the reader in a form considered more appropriate for representing a female's experience than that of a male. In nineteenth century fiction, however, men were no longer political creatures so much as they were products of desire and producers of domestic life. As gender came to mark the most important difference among individuals, men were still men and women still women, of course, but the difference between male and female was

NANCY ARMSTRONG

understood in terms of their respective qualities of mind. Their psychological differences made men political and women domestic rather than the other way around, and both therefore acquired identity on the basis of personal qualities that had formerly determined female nature alone. During the course of *Wuthering Heights*, for example, one can see Heathcliff undergo a transformation that strips away the features of a Gypsy from Liverpool at the turn of the century and attributes all his behavior to sexual desire. By a similar process, Rochester loses his aristocratic bearing by the end of *Jane Eyre* to assume a role within a purely emotional network of relationships overseen by a woman. It is only by thus subordinating all social differences to those based on gender that these novels bring order to social relationships. Granting all this, one may conclude that the power of the middle classes had everything to do with that of middle-class love. And if this contention holds true, one must also agree that middle-class authority rested in large part upon the authority that novels attributed to women and in this way designated as specifically female.

In demonstrating that the rise of the novel hinged upon a struggle to say what made a woman desirable, then, I will be arguing that much more was at stake. I will consider this redefinition of desire as a decisive step in producing the densely interwoven fabric of common sense and sentimentality that even today ensures the ubiquity of middle-class power. It is my contention that narratives which seemed to be concerned solely with matters of courtship and marriage in fact seized the authority to say what was female, and that they did so in order to contest the reigning notion of kinship relations that attached most power and privilege to certain family lines. This struggle to represent sexuality took the form of a struggle to individuate wherever there was a collective body, to attach psychological motives to what had been the openly political behavior of contending groups, and to evaluate these according to a set of moral norms that exalted the domestic woman over and above her aristocratic counterpart. I am saying the female was the figure, above all else, on whom depended the outcome of the struggle among competing ideologies.

For no other reason than this could Samuel Richardson's novel *Pamela* represent a landowner's assault upon the chastity of an otherwise undistinguished servant girl as a major threat to our world as well as to hers. And Richardson could have Pamela resist such an assault only by confronting and then overthrowing the reigning notion of sexuality as articulated by Mr. B's subservient housekeeper. Scoffing at Pamela's claim that "to rob a person of her virtue is worse than cutting her throat," the housekeeper regards Mr. B's assaults as perfectly natural and states, "how strangely you talk! Are not the two sexes made for one another? And is it not natural for a gentleman to love a pretty woman? And suppose he can obtain his desires, is that so bad as cutting her throat?"[1] Clearly representing a minority position, Pamela prevails nevertheless through the novel's most harrowing scene where her master, with the help of the housekeeper, slips into bed and pins her naked body beneath him. Rather than yielding up even momentary satisfaction, this scene constitutes one of the least erotic bedroom encounters between male and female in literature:

> he kissed me with frightful vehemence; and then his voice broke upon me like a clap of thunder. Now, Pamela, said he, is the dreadful time of reckoning come, that I have threatened – I screamed out in such a manner, as never anybody heard the like. But

there was nobody to help me: and both hands were secured, as I said. Sure never poor soul was in such agonies as I. Wicked man! said I; O God! my God! this *time!* this one *time!* deliver me from this distress! or strike me dead this moment! (p. 213)

Pamela escapes with her virtue as she becomes a creature of words (she protests) and of silence (she swoons). Mr. B's attempt to penetrate a servant girl's material body magically transforms that body into one of language and emotion, into a metaphysical object that can be acquired only through her consent and his willingness to adhere to the procedures of modern love. That this is indeed the Pamela Mr. B eventually desires calls into question the whole notion of sexuality on which the housekeeper's common sense had been based.

In opening the argument of this book, I can only suggest how such a transformation occurred on a mass basis and how it revised the entire surface of social life. The nature and extent of its historical impact is only implicit in the one scene from *Pamela* that does seem genuinely erotic. In this scene, we may observe the transfer of erotic desire from Pamela's body to her words. When Richardson at last allows Mr. B to have his way with the girl, erotic desire makes its brief reappearance in the novel, not on their wedding night, but at the climax of their courtship, as Mr. B forcibly takes possession of Pamela's letters:

> Artful slut! said he, What's this to my question? – Are they [the letters] not *about* you? – If, said I, I must pluck them out of my hiding-place behind the wainscot, won't you see me? – Still more and more artful! said he – Is this an answer to my question? – I have searched every place above, and in your closet, for them, and cannot find them; so I *will* know where they are. Now, said he, it is my opinion they are about you; and I never undressed a girl in my life; but I will now begin to strip my pretty Pamela. (p. 245)

As he proceeds to probe her garters for a few more precious words, Pamela capitulates and, in a shower of tears, delivers up what he desires. Thus having displaced the conventionally desirable woman onto a written one, Richardson infuses the new body with erotic appeal. The pleasure she now offers is the pleasure of the text rather than those forms of pleasure that derive from mastering her body.

However inadequate this substitution may seem to us today, readers remain thoroughly enchanted by narratives in which a woman's virtue alone overcomes sexual aggression and transforms male desire into middle-class love, the stuff that modern families are made of. As the heirs to a novelistic culture, we are not very likely to question the whole enterprise. We are more likely to feel that the success of repeated pressures to coax and nudge sexual desire into conformity with the norms of heterosexual monogamy affords a fine way of closing a novel and provides a satisfactory goal for a text to achieve. Novels do not encourage us to doubt whether sexual desire already existed before the strategies were devised to domesticate it. Nor do novels often question the premise that such desire, if it is not so domesticated, constitutes the gravest danger – and root of all other threats – to society. And I know of no major criticism of the novel which does not at some point capitulate to the idea that sexual desire exists in some form prior to its representation and remains there as something for us to recover or liberate. It is this dominant theory of desire, I believe, that authorizes domestic fiction

NANCY ARMSTRONG

and yet conceals the role such fiction played in modern history. More to the point, in ignoring the historical dimension of desire, this theory – at once psychological and literary – has left us no way of explaining why, at the inception of modern culture, the literate classes in England suddenly developed an unprecedented taste for writing for, about, and by women.

I know of no history of the English novel that can explain why women began to write respectable fiction near the end of the eighteenth century, became prominent novelists during the nineteenth century, and on this basis achieved the status of artists during the modern period. Yet that they suddenly began writing and were recognized as women writers strikes me as a central event in the history of the novel. Ian Watt's classic study *The Rise of the Novel* ties the popularity of such writers as Defoe and Richardson to an economic individualism and Puritan ethic they shared with a substantial portion of the new reading public. But Watt's historical explanation fails to consider why "the majority of eighteenth-century novels" were written by women. When it comes time to account for Jane Austen, historical explanations elude him, and he falls back on a commonplace claim: "the feminine sensibility was in some ways better equipped to reveal the intricacies of personal relationships and was therefore at a real advantage in the realm of the novel."[2] Of late, it seems particularly apparent that such attempts to explain the history of the novel fail because – to a man – history is represented as the history of male institutions. Where women writers are concerned, this understanding of history leaves all the truly interesting questions unasked: Why the "female sensibility"? How "better equipped"? What "intricacies"? Whose "personal relationships"? Why an "advantage in the realm of the novel"? And, finally, how did all this become commonplace?

As if in response, Sandra Gilbert and Susan Gubar's *The Madwoman in the Attic* at least attempts to account for a tradition of female writers. While Watt is concerned with just how fiction played to the interests of a changing readership, Gilbert and Gubar concentrate on the authors themselves and the conditions under which they wrote. They argue that women authors, in contrast with their male counterparts, had to manage the difficult task of simultaneously subverting and conforming to patriarchal standards.[3] But when understood within this gendered frame of reference, the conditions for women's writing appear to remain relatively constant throughout history because the authors in question were women and because the conditions under which they wrote were largely determined by men. Thus, like Watt, Gilbert and Gubar virtually ignore the historical conditions that women have confronted as writers, and in so doing they ignore the place of women's writing in history. For Gilbert and Gubar, too, history takes place not in and through those areas of culture over which women may have held sway, but in institutions dominated by men. Because both these definitive histories of the novel presuppose a social world divided according to the principle of gender, neither of them can possibly consider how such a world came into being and what part the novel played in its formation. Yet these are the very questions we must consider if we want to explain why women became prominent authors of fiction during the nineteenth century in England. So long as we assume that gender transcends history, we have no hope of understanding what role women played – for better or worse – in shaping the world we presently inhabit.

To describe the history of domestic fiction, then, I will argue several points at once: first, that sexuality is a cultural construct and as such has a history; second, that written representations of the self allowed the modern individual to become an economic and psychological reality; and third, that the modern individual was first and foremost a woman. My argument traces the development of a specific female ideal in eighteenth- and nineteenth-century conduct books and educational treatises for women, as well as in domestic fiction, all of which often were written by women. I will insist that one cannot distinguish the production of the new female ideal either from the rise of the novel or from the rise of the new middle classes in England. At first, I will demonstrate, writing about the domestic woman afforded a means of contesting the dominant notion of sexuality that understood desirability in terms of the woman's claims to fortune and family name. But then, by the early decades of the nineteenth century, middle-class writers and intellectuals can be seen to take the virtues embodied by the domestic woman and to pit them against working-class culture. It took nothing less than the destruction of a much older concept of the household for industrialization to overcome working-class resistance. In time, following the example of fiction, new kinds of writing – sociological studies of factory and city, as well as new theories of natural history and political economy – established modern domesticity as the only haven from the trials of a heartless economic world. By the 1840s, norms inscribed in the domestic woman had already cut across the categories of status that maintained an earlier, patriarchal model of social relations.[4] The entire surface of social experience had come to mirror those kinds of writing – the novel prominent among them – which represented the existing field of social information as contrasting masculine and feminine spheres.[5]

This book, which links the history of British fiction to the empowering of the middle classes in England through the dissemination of a new female ideal, necessarily challenges existing histories of the novel. For one thing, it insists that the history of the novel cannot be understood apart from the history of sexuality. In dissolving the boundary between those texts that today are considered literature and those that, like the conduct books, are not, my study shows that the distinction between literary and nonliterary was imposed retrospectively by the modern literary institution upon anomalous works of fiction. It shows as well that the domestic novel antedated – was indeed necessarily antecedent to – the way of life it represented. Rather than refer to individuals who already existed as such and who carried on relationships according to novelistic conventions, domestic fiction took great care to distinguish itself from the kinds of fiction that predominated in the eighteenth and nineteenth centuries. Most fiction, which represented identity in terms of region, sect, or faction, could not very well affirm the universality of any particular form of desire. In contrast, domestic fiction unfolded the operations of human desire as if they were independent of political history. And this helped to create the illusion that desire was entirely subjective and therefore essentially different from the politically encodable forms of behavior to which desire gave rise.

At the same time and on the same theoretical grounds, my study of the novel challenges traditional histories of nineteenth century England by questioning the practice of writing separate histories for political and cultural events. Rather than see the rise of the new middle class in terms of the economic changes that solidified its hold over the culture, my reading of materials for and about women shows that the formation of the modern political state – in England at least – was accomplished largely through cultural hegemony. New strategies of representation not only revised the way in which

NANCY ARMSTRONG

an individual's identity could be understood, but in presuming to discover what was only natural in the self, they also removed subjective experience and sexual practices from their place in history. Our education does much the same thing when it allows us to assume that modern consciousness is a constant of human experience and teaches us to understand modern history in economic terms, even though history itself was not understood in those terms until the beginning of the nineteenth century. We are taught to divide the political world in two and to detach the practices that belong to a female domain from those that govern the marketplace. In this way, we compulsively replicate the symbolic behavior that constituted a private domain of the individual outside and apart from social history.

In actuality, however, the changes that allowed diverse groups of people to make sense of social experience as these mutually exclusive worlds of information constitute a major event in the history of the modern individual. It follows, then, that only those histories that account for the formation of separate spheres – masculine and feminine, political and domestic, social and cultural – can allow us to see what this semiotic behavior had to do with the economic triumph of the new middle classes. In effect, I am arguing, political events cannot be understood apart from women's history, from the history of women's literature, or from changing representations of the household. Nor can a history of the novel be historical if it fails to take into account the history of sexuality. For such a history remains, by definition, locked into categories replicating the semiotic behavior that empowered the middle class in the first place.

It is one thing to call for a study that considers the rise of the novel and the emergence of a coherent middle-class ethos as being one and the same as the formation of a highly elaborated form of female. It is quite another to account for phenomena such as writings for, by, and about women that have so far steadfastly resisted every effort of literary theory to explain their production and relevance to a moment in history. I have drawn upon the work of Michel Foucault – relying, in particular, on *The History of Sexuality*, Volume I, as well as *Discipline and Punish* – to identify the problem inherent in all but a few discussions of sexuality in literature. Foucauldian histories break up the traditional modes of historical causality in order to focus our attention on the place of language and particularly writing in the history of modern culture, as well as on the very real political interests that are served when certain areas of culture – those I am calling sexuality – remain impervious to historical investigation. I want to stress the relationship between the sexual and the political. I want to isolate some major historical changes in this relationship because – as the studies of Watt and of Gilbert and Gubar demonstrate particularly well – it is very possible to situate women's writing in history without showing the political interests that such writing served, just as it is very possible to show the politics of women's writing without acknowledging how those interests changed radically with the passage of time. Foucault, on the other hand, makes it possible to consider sexual relations as the site for changing power relations between classes and cultures as well as between genders and generations.

He offers a way out of the problem plaguing the studies of Watt and Gilbert and Gubar – the inability to historicize sexuality – by means of a double conceptual move. The first volume of his *History of Sexuality* makes sex a function of sexuality and considers sexuality as a purely semiotic process. Sexuality includes not only all those representations of sex that appear to be sex itself – in modern culture, for example, the gendered body – but also those myriad representations that are meaningful in relation to sex, namely, all the various masculine or feminine attributes that saturate our world of objects. Sexuality is, in other words, the cultural dimension of sex, which, to my way of thinking, includes as its most essential and powerful component the form of representation we take to be nature itself.[6] Thus we can regard gender as one function of sexuality that must have a history. My study of the novel will demonstrate that, with the formation of a modern institutional culture, gender differences – though one of many possible functions of sexuality – came to dominate the functions of generation and genealogy, which organized an earlier culture.

Most studies of the British novel more or less consciously acknowledge the difference between sex and sexuality, referent and representation. With almost flawless consistency, however, criticism of the novel has made this distinction only to imbed a modern truth in the referent. I find it difficult to think of a single study of the novel that does not posit an opposition between writing and desire in which desire, when written, loses at least some of its individuality, truth, purity, or power, which is nevertheless there for critics to recover. But Foucault does not accept this opposition. He asks us to think of modern desire as something that depends on language and particularly on writing. It is on this ground that his *History of Sexuality* assaults the tradition of thinking that sees modern sexuality as logically prior to its written representation. And, I should add, Gilbert and Gubar's approach to the novel resembles Watt's by positing a specific form of sexuality as natural, that is, as sex. Both studies assume this prior and essential form of sexuality is what authors subsequently represent or misrepresent (it is all the same) in fiction. It is as if their opposing accounts of the production of fiction have agreed to disagree on the relatively minor issue of whether writing operates on the side of culture to repress nature or, alternatively, brings us closer to the truth of nature. Either way sex is situated historically prior to sexuality. According to Foucault, however, sex neither was nor is already there to be dealt with in one way or another by sexuality. Instead, its representation determines what one knows to be sex, the particular form sex assumes in one age as opposed to another, and the political interests these various forms may have served.

Any representation of sex as something that has been misunderstood and must be known, something that has been repressed and must be liberated, Foucault would argue, itself operates as a component of sexuality. More than that, such representations give modern sexuality its particular political thrust, which produces rather than represses a specific form of sexuality. During the eighteenth and nineteenth centuries, as Foucault has observed, the discovery of the fact of desire hidden within the individual prompted an extensive process of verbalization that effectively displaced an eroticism that had been located on the surface of the body. The discourse of sexuality saw such forms of pleasure as a substitution for some more primary, natural, and yet phantasmagorical desire. The discovery of this repressed sexuality thus provided justification for reading and interpreting sexual behavior wherever one found it, always with the Enlightenment motive of discovering truth and producing freedom, always consequently with the very different result of enclosing sex within an individual's subjectivity.

"The notion of repressed sex is not, therefore, only a theoretical matter," Foucault insists.

NANCY ARMSTRONG

> The affirmation of a sexuality that has never been more rigorously subjugated than during the age of the hypocritical, bustling, and responsible bourgeoisie is coupled with the grandiloquence of a discourse purporting to reveal the truth about sex, modify its economy with reality, subvert the law that governs it, and change its future.[7]

It is not to wag the finger at middle-class hypocrisy that Foucault represents modern sexuality as behaving in this apparently contradictory way. Instead, he would have us see how the modern tendency that opposes desire to its verbal representation reproduces the figure of repressed sexuality. Any attempt to verbalize a form of sexuality that supposedly has been repressed in fact reproduces the distinction between essential human nature and the aspects of individual identity that have been imposed upon us by culture. This distinction does not allow us to examine culture and nature as two mutually dependent constructs that are together a political function of culture. Foucault alone shifts the investigation of sexuality away from the nature of desire to its political uses. He rejects the opposition between desire and writing in order to consider modern desire as something that depends on writing. "The question I would like to pose," Foucault explains,

> is not, Why are we repressed? but rather, Why do we say, with so much passion and so much resentment against our most recent past, against our present, and against ourselves, that we are repressed? By what spiral did we come to affirm that sex is negated? What led us to show, ostentatiously, that sex is something we hide, to say it is something we silence? (pp. 8–9)

Foucault asks us, in other words, to understand repression at once as a rhetorical figure and as a means of producing desire.

According to the same way of thinking, writing actively conceals the history of sexuality by turning repression into a narrative form. The history so produced constitutes a myth of progressive enlightenment. According to the Foucauldian hypothesis, however, our thinking is most completely inscribed within middle-class sexuality when we indulge in this fantasy, for the repressive hypothesis ensures that we imagine freedom in terms of repression, without questioning the truth or necessity of what we become with the lifting of bans. When, on the other hand, we abandon the practice of putting knowledge in a domain of nature outside of and prior to representation, we stand a chance of avoiding the tautology inherent in the notion of repression. No longer assuming that, when written, desire loses some of its individuality, truth, purity, or power, we may no longer feel strangely compelled to discover the truth about desire. Instead, we may understand desire as inseparable from its representation and understand its representation, in turn, as part of political history. In Foucault's account of the triumph of middle-class culture, the discovery of sexual repression provides an entirely new basis for understanding the relationship between one individual and another. Following his example, we can say that modern sexuality (for example, the middle-class idea that desirable femaleness was femininity) gave rise to a new understanding of sex (as the female was defined first by Darwin and then by Freud). We can also say that the representation of the individual as most essentially a sexual subject preceded the economic changes that made it possible to represent English history as the narrative unfolding of capitalism. Thus what began chiefly as writing that situated the individual within the poles of nature and culture, self and society, sex and sexuality only later became a psychological reality, and not the other way around. Foucault makes us mindful of this inversion of the normal relationship between forms of desire and the writing that represents them when he refers to the whole apparatus for producing modern individualism as "the discourse of sexuality."

But in order to describe the formation and behavior of such a discourse of sexuality in England, one must, I believe, refine Foucault's productive hypothesis to include the issue of gender. A semiotic capable of explaining virtually any form of human behavior in fact depended above all else on the creation of modern gender distinctions. These came into being with the development of a strictly female field of knowledge, and it was within this field that novels had to situate themselves if they were to have cultural authority. Even where poetry was concerned, the female ceased to represent the writers' muse and, with the Romantics, became instead a function of imagination that provided figurative language with a psychological source of meaning. And if a single cultural reflex could identify what was Victorian about Victorianism, and thus could isolate the moment when the new class system that distinguished landowner from capitalist and these from the laboring classes was securely entrenched, it was the insistence that a form of authority whose wellsprings were the passions of the human heart ultimately author- ized writing. Therefore, while strategies of gender differentiation play little role in Foucault's writing, they must be considered paramount in a study that considers the history of the British novel as the history of sexuality.

My point is that language, which once represented the history of the individual as well as the history of the state in terms of kinship relations, was dismantled to form the masculine and feminine spheres that characterize modern culture. I want to show that a modern, gendered form of subjectivity developed first as a feminine discourse in certain literature for women before it provided the semiotic of nineteenth century poetry and psychological theory. It was through this gendered discourse, more surely than by means of the epistemological debate of the eighteenth century, that the discourse of sexuality made its way into common sense and determined how people understood themselves and what they desired in others. The gendering of human identity provided the metaphysical girders of modern culture – its reigning mythology. The popular concepts of subjectivity and sensibility resembled Locke's theory that human understanding developed through an exchange between the individual mind and the world of objects, an exchange that was mediated by language. But instead of a "soul" – Locke's word for what exists before the process of self-development begins – the essential self was commonly understood in terms of gender.[8] Conduct books for women, as well as fiction in the tradition of Richardson, worked within the same framework as Locke, but they constructed a more specialized and less material form of subjectivity, which they designated as female. If the Lockean subject began as a white sheet of paper on which objects could be understood in sets of spatial relations, then pedagogical literature for women mapped out a field of knowledge that would produce a specifically female form of subjectivity. To gender this field, things within the field itself had to be gendered. Masculine objects were understood in terms of their relative economic and political qualities, while feminine objects were recognized by their relative emotional qualities.

NANCY ARMSTRONG

At the site of the household, family life, and all that was hallowed as female, this gendered field of information contested a dominant political order which depended, among other things, on representing women as economic and political objects.

Such a modification of Foucault allows one to see that sexuality has a history that is inseparable from the political history of England. To introduce their highly influential *Practical Education* in 1801, for example, Maria Edgeworth and her father Robert announce their departure from the curriculum that reinforced traditional political differences: "On religion and politics we have been silent because we have no ambition to gain partisans, or to make proselytes, and because we do not address ourselves to any sect or party."[9] In virtually the same breath, they assure readers: "With respect to what is commonly called the education of the heart, we have endeavored to suggest the easiest means of inducing useful and agreeable habits, well regulated sympathy and benevolent affections" (p. viii). Thus their proposal substitutes the terms of emotion and behavior for those of one's specific sociopolitical identity. Basing identity on the same subjective qualities that had previously appeared only in the curricula designed for educating women, the Edgeworths' program gives priority to the schoolroom and parlor over the church and courts in regulating all human behavior. In doing so, their educational program promises to suppress the political signs of identity. But, of course, to render insignificant the traditional way of naming and ranking individuals is a powerful political gesture in its own right. Perfectly aware of the political force to be exercised through education, the Edgeworths justify their program for cultivating the heart on the political grounds that it constituted a new and more effective method of policing. In their words, "It is the business of education to prevent crimes, and to prevent all those habitual propensities which necessarily lead to their commission" (p. 354).

To accomplish their ambitious political goal, the Edgeworths invoke an economy of pleasure in which the novel has been implicated since its inception in the late seventeenth century, an economy that cannot in fact be understood apart from the novel or from the criticism that grew up around the new fiction to censor and foster it simultaneously. To begin with, the Edgeworths accept the view that prevailed during the eighteenth century, which said fiction behaved subversively and misled female desire:

> With respect to sentimental stories, and books of mere entertainment, we must remark, that they should be sparingly used, especially in the education of girls. This species of reading cultivates what is called the heart prematurely, lowers the tone of the mind, and induces indifference for those common pleasures and occupations which, however trivial in themselves, constitute by far the greatest portion of our daily happiness. (p. 105)

But the same turn of mind recognizes the practical value of pleasure when it is harnessed and aimed at the right goals. Convinced that the "pleasures of literature" acted upon the reader in much the same way as the child's "taste for sugar-plums" (p. 80), the Edgeworths along with other forward-thinking educators began to endorse the reading of fiction that made social conformity seem necessary, if not entirely desirable. Although they name *Robinson Crusoe* as capable of leading immature minds astray, the Edgeworths also grant the book practical value. But they grant the book more value, curiously enough, for the very readers whom fiction most endangered: "To girls this species of reading cannot be as dangerous as it is to boys: girls must soon perceive the impossibility of their rambling about the world in quest of adventures" (p. 111). This is one of many statements that suggest how socialization was fixed to gender. It considers *Robinson Crusoe* educational for the expressed reason that women would never imagine undertaking Crusoe's economic adventures. There is also a strong possibility that early educational theorists recommended *Crusoe* over Defoe's other works because they thought women were likely to learn to desire what Crusoe accomplished, a totally self-enclosed and functional domain where money did not really matter. It was no doubt because Crusoe was more female, according to the nineteenth century understanding of gender, than either Roxana or Moll that educators found his story more suitable reading for girls than for boys of an impressionable age.

If the reading of fiction came to play an indispensable role in directing desire at certain objects in the world, it was not because such narratives as *Robinson Crusoe* administered a particularly useful dose of didacticism. Instead, I would like to pose the possibility that moral hegemony triumphed in nineteenth century England largely through consent rather than coercion; it was precisely because they were leisure-time reading that such books as *Robinson Crusoe* were important to the political struggle between the ruling classes and the laboring poor. In his study of the impact of Sunday schools on working-class culture during the nineteenth century, Thomas Walter Laqueur contends that it was through their manner of inculcating literacy and a hunger for books, not through their overt promotion of certain behavioral norms, that English Sunday schools ensured docility in regions where we would expect to find violent resistance to industrialization.[10] But these new forms of literacy seemed to intrude upon the cultural stage brandishing a double-edged sword. Education did not necessarily make newly impoverished laborers safe for an industrializing world; it could in fact have made them extremely dangerous. If education helped to produce a more tractable working class, working-class radicalism was predicated on literacy too — that is, on political pamphlets, on alternative programs for education, and even on a literature that spoke to their needs and desires rather than to those of their employers. Thus, Laqueur concludes, literacy did not simply indoctrinate the poor in the values and practices that would make them fit to inhabit an industrial world. More importantly, the total appropriation of the time during which the poor carried on traditional collective activities was essential in disarming the subversive potential of working-class literacy. Laqueur reasons that Sunday schools became an effective means of socialization not because they taught the necessity of self-sacrifice and respect for authority, but because they offered recreational programs that occupied many of the idle hours when people gathered in their customary fashion and when political plans might otherwise have been hatched.

The same principle extends, I believe, to the reading of fiction. As education became the preferred instrument of social control, fiction could accomplish much the same purpose as the various forms of recreation promoted by Sunday schools. The period following 1750 saw a new effort to regulate the free time of children and, by extension, the free time of their parents. Removing the stigma from novel reading no doubt conspired with activities promoted by Sunday schools to combat historically earlier notions of self, of family, and of pleasure. To unregulated time and pleasure was

NANCY ARMSTRONG

attributed the possibility of undermining the political order, as if, in the words of one concerned citizen, idleness alone could "fill the land with villains, render property insecure, crowd our jails with felons, and bring poverty, distress and ruin upon families."[11] But chief among the practices that the new cast of educators sought to criminalize and then to suppress were drinking, violent sport, and profligacy. The reformist policies were particularly effective in controlling the discontented laborer because those aspects of working-class culture that, in purely moral terms, most threatened the laborer's hope for salvation were also the practices that best fostered political resistance.[12]

Allon White has argued persuasively that the successful effort to push carnival and popular culture to the margins of social life was related to the victorious emergence of specifically bourgeois practices and languages, which were reinflected within a framework where they indicated an individual's degree of socialization.[13] And the novel is implicated in this process. If the production of a specifically female curriculum was an important moment in our cultural history, then the inclusion of novels within the female curriculum was also significant. Until well into the eighteenth century the reading of fiction was considered tantamount to seduction, but in the last decades of that century, certain novels were found fit to occupy the idle hours of women, children, and servants. At that point, the novel provided a means of displacing and containing long-standing symbolic practices – especially those games, festivities, and other material practices of the body that maintained a sense of collective identity. Certain novels in particular transformed all they contained into the materials of a gendered universe. And once they did so transform the signs of political identity, such signs could, as the Brontës' madwomen demonstrate, include forms of desire that challenged the norms distinguishing gender. Reading such works of fiction would still have the desirable effect of inducing a specific form of political unconscious.[14]

In formulating a theory of mass education in which fiction had a deceptively marginal role to play, the Edgeworths and their colleagues were adopting a rhetoric that earlier reformers had used to level charges of violence and corruption against the old aristocracy. They placed themselves in an old tradition of radical Protestant dissent, which argued that political authority should be based on moral superiority. At issue in the way that sexual relations were represented, according to Jacques Donzelot, "was the transition from a government of families to a government through the family."[15] Sexual relations so often provided the terms of argument that no representation of the household could be considered politically neutral. To contest the notion of a state that depended on inherited power, Puritan treatises on marriage and household governance represented the family as a self-enclosed social unit in whose affairs the state could not intervene. Against genealogy the treatises posited domesticity.[16] But in claiming sovereignty for the father over his home, they were not proposing a new form of political organization. According to Kathleen M. Davis, the Puritan doctrine of equality insisted only upon the difference of sexual roles in which the female was certainly subordinate to the male, and not upon the equality of the woman in kind. "The result of this partnership," Davis explains, "was a definition of mutual and complementary duties and characteristics." Gender was so clearly understood in oppositional terms that it could be graphically represented as such:[17]

Husband	Wife
Get goods	Gather them together and save them
Travel, seek a living	Keep the house
Get money and provisions	Do not vainly spend it
Deal with many men	Talk with few
Be "entertaining"	Be solitary and withdrawn
Be skillful in talk	Boast of silence
Be a giver	Be a saver
Apparel yourself as you may	Apparel yourself as it becomes you
Dispatch all things outdoors	Oversee and give order within

In representing the family as the opposition of complementary genders, Puritan tracts enclosed the domestic unit. If they wanted to cut it off from the genealogical tree of state and so use it to authorize the household as an independent and self-generated source of power, their moment had not yet arrived. The hegemonic potential of the model had yet to be realized at that point in time. For the Puritan household consisted of a male and female who were structurally identical, positive and negative versions of the same attributes. The female did not offer a competing form of political thinking.

Unlike the Puritan authors, the educational reformers of the nineteenth century could look back on a substantial body of writing that had represented the domestic woman in a way that authorized such a political alternative. Before it provided a common ideal for individuals who would otherwise see themselves in competition or else without any relationship at all, the household had to be governed by a form of power that was essentially female – that is, essentially different from that of the male and yet a positive force in its own right. Although certainly subject to political force, the domestic woman exercised a form of power that appeared to have no political force at all because it seemed forceful only when it was desired. It was the power of domestic surveillance. The husband who met the standards listed above passed into oblivion well before the aristocratic male ceased to dominate British political consciousness, but the domestic woman enjoyed a contrary fate. In the centuries intervening between our own day and that of the Puritan revolution, she was inscribed with values that addressed a whole range of competing interest groups and, through her, these groups gained authority over domestic relations and personal life. In this way, furthermore, they established the need for the kind of surveillance upon which modern institutions are based.

Indeed, the last two decades of the seventeenth century saw an explosion of writing that proposed to educate the daughters of numerous aspiring social groups.[18] The new curriculum promised to make these women desirable to men of a superior rank and in fact more desirable than women who had only their own rank and fortune to recommend them. The curriculum aimed at producing a woman whose value resided chiefly in her femaleness rather than in traditional signs of status, a woman who possessed psychological depth rather than a physically attractive surface, one who, in other words, excelled in the qualities that differentiated her from the male. As femaleness was redefined in these terms, the woman exalted by an aristocratic tradition of letters ceased to appear so desirable. In becoming the other side of this new sexual coin, the aristocratic woman represented surface instead of depth, embodied material instead of moral value, and displayed idle sensuality instead of constant vigilance and tireless concern for the well-being of others. Such a woman was not truly female.

But it was not until the mid-nineteenth century that the project of gendering subjectivity began to acquire the immense political influence it still exercises today. Around the 1830s, one can see the discourse of sexuality lose interest in its critique of the aristocracy as the newly organizing working classes became the more obvious target of moral reform. Authors suddenly took notice of social groups who had hardly mattered before. Reformers and men of letters discovered that politically aggressive artisans and urban laborers lacked the kind of motivation that characterized middle-class individuals. Numerous authors sought out the causes of poverty, illiteracy, and demographic change, not in the rapidly changing economic circumstances that had impoverished whole groups of people and torn their families asunder, but within those individuals themselves whose behavior was found to be at once promiscuous and insufficiently gendered. In analyzing the condition of the working classes, authors commonly portrayed women as masculine and men as effeminate and childlike. By representing the working class in terms of these personal deficiencies, middle-class intellectuals effectively translated the overwhelming political problem caused by rapid industrialization into a sexual scandal brought about by the worker's lack of personal development and self-restraint. Reformers could then step forward and offer themselves, their technology, their supervisory skills, and their institutions of education and social welfare as the appropriate remedy for growing political resistance.

In all fairness, as Foucault notes, the middle classes rarely imposed institutional constraints upon others without first trying them out on themselves. When creating a national curriculum, the government officials and educators in charge adopted one modeled on the educational theory that grew up around the Edgeworths and their intellectual circle, which can be considered the heir to the dissenting tradition.[19] It was basically the same curriculum proposed by eighteenth century pedagogues and reformers as the best way of producing a marriageable daughter. For one thing, the new curriculum drew upon the female model in requiring familiarity with British literature. By the end of the eighteenth century, the Edgeworths were among those who had already determined that the program aimed at producing the domestic woman offered a form of social control that could apply to boys just as well as to girls. And by the mid-nineteenth century, the government was figuring out how to administer much the same program on a mass basis. In forming the conceptual foundation upon which the national curriculum was based, a particular idea of the self thus became commonplace, and as gendered forms of identity determined more and more how people learned to think of themselves as well as of others, that self became the dominant social reality.

Such an abbreviated history cannot do justice to the fierce controversies punctuating the institution of a standard curriculum in England. I simply want to locate a few sites where political history obviously converged with the history of sexuality as well as with that of the novel to produce a specific kind of individual, and I do so to suggest the political implications of representing these histories as separate narratives. As it began to deny its political and religious bias and present itself instead as a moral and psychological truth, the rhetoric of reform obviously severed its ties with an aristocratic past and took up a new role in history. It no longer constituted a form of resistance but distinguished itself from political matters to establish a specialized domain of culture where apolitical truths could be told. The novel's literary status hinged upon this event. Fiction began to deny the political basis for its meaning and referred instead to the private regions of the self or to the specialized world of art, but never to the use of words that created and still maintains these primary divisions within the culture. Favored among kinds of fiction were the novels which best performed the operations of division and self-containment that turned political information into the discourse of sexuality. These novels made the novel respectable, and it is significant that they so often were entitled with female names such as Pamela, Evelina, or Jane Eyre. With this transform-ation of cultural information came widespread suspicion of political literacy, and with it, too, a mass forgetfulness that there was a history of sexuality to tell.

In this way, the emergence and domination of a system of gender differences over and against a long tradition of overtly political signs of social identity helped to usher in a new form of state power. This power – the power of representation over the thing represented – wrested authority from the old aristocracy on grounds that a government was morally obliged to rehabilitate degenerate individuals rather than to maintain their subjection through force. After the Peterloo Massacre of 1819, it was clear that the state's capacity for violence had become a source of embarrassment. Overt displays of force worked against legitimate authority just as they did against subversive factions. If acts of open rebellion had justified intervention into areas of society that the government had never had to deal with before, then the use of force on the part of the government gave credence to the workers' charges of oppression. The power of surveillance came into dominance at this moment, displacing the traditional uses of force. Like the form of vigilance that maintained an orderly household, this power did not create equality so much as trivialize the material signs of difference by translating all such signs into differences in the quality, intensity, direction, and self-regulatory capability of an individual's desire.

One could easily regard this history as yet another "just so" story were it not for the way it implicates literature and literacy in political history. Foucault's preoccupation with the power of "discourse" distinguishes his narrative from those of Marx and Freud, but the real targets of his antidisciplinary strategies are the traditional historians who ignore the hegemony of which modern literature is only one function. It is certainly possible to take issue with the way in which he collapses such categories as "history," "power," "discourse," and "sexuality." It is also right to be troubled by his failure to mention those topics that seem most germane to his argument. In the case of "sexuality," for example, there is his virtual disregard for a mode of gender differentiation that enables one sex to dominate the other, just as, in his epic study of "discipline," we must ask where is there mention of ideology or of the collective activities that resisted it? Even though he explains the formation of institutions that exercise power through knowledge, and even though he takes steps to call those institutions into question by making the political power of writing visible as such, the history Foucault tells is nevertheless a partial one.

No history of an institution – whether that of prison, hospital, and schoolroom, as Foucault describes them, or of courts, houses of parliament, and marketplace, as more conventional historians prefer – can avoid the political behavior of the disciplinary model because these histories necessarily diminish the role of the subject in authorizing the forces that govern him. Moreover, such histories tend to ignore the degree to which forms of resistance themselves determine the strategies of domination. Thus we find, in Foucault's *Discipline and Punish*, that the dismembered body of the subject composing half the scene on the scaffold disappears as the modern penal institution closes around it. The same can be said of the body of the plague victim in Foucault's account of "the birth of the clinic."[20] The history of domination over the subject's material body seems to come to an end as the state begins to control individuals through strategies of discourse rather than by means of physical violence. But to say that this body is no longer important to the history of domination does not mean that other cultural formations disappear. The panopticon, Foucault's most completely articulated figure of power, is incomplete in itself as a model of culture. It requires something on the order of "carnival," Mikhail Bahktin's figure for all the practices that, with the growth of disciplinary institutions, were entirely cast out of the domain of culture.[21]

I think we need to create other ways of talking about resistance as well, for literary criticism too easily translates carnival – and all the material practices of the body that are tolerated within its framework – into the simple absence or inversion of normative structures. If one could allow for such heterogeneity – the overlapping of competing versions of reality within the same moment of time – the past would elude the linear pattern of a developmental narrative. In the model I am proposing, culture appears as a struggle among various political factions to possess its most valued signs and symbols.[22] The reality that dominates in any given situation appears to be just that, the reality that dominates. As such, the material composition of a particular text would have more to do with the forms of representation it overcame – in the case of domestic fiction, with its defiance of an aristocratic tradition of letters and, later on, with its repudiation of working-class culture – than with the internal composition of the text per se. I would pursue this line of thought one step further and say that the internal composition of a given text is nothing more or less than the history of its struggle with contrary forms of representation for the authority to control semiosis. In this respect, there is no inside to the text as opposed to the outside, no text/context distinction at all, though we must make such distinctions for purposes of copyright laws and traditional literary analyses.

The chapters that follow demonstrate this point by constructing a history of the domestic woman as she was represented, not only in the great domestic novels, but also in texts that never developed such literary pretensions. In reading these materials, I aim neither to discover forms of repression nor to perform acts of liberation, although my argument has a definite political goal. Rather, I am committed to a productive hypothesis. I want to show how the discourse of sexuality is implicated in shaping the novel, and to show as well how domestic fiction helped to produce a subject who understood herself in the psychological terms that had shaped fiction. I regard fiction, in other words, both as the document and as the agency of cultural history. I believe it helped to formulate the ordered space we now recognize as the household, made that space totally functional, and used it as the context for representing normal behavior. In so doing, fiction contested and finally suppressed alternative bases for human relationships. In realizing this, one cannot – I think – ignore the fact that fiction did a great deal to relegate vast areas of culture to the status of aberrance and noise. As the history of this female domain is articulated, then, it will outline boldly the telling cultural move upon which, I believe, the supremacy of middle-class culture has rested. Such a history will reenact the moment when writing invaded, revised, and contained the household by means of strategies that distinguished private from social life and thus detached sexuality from political history. On the domestic front, perhaps even more so than in the courts and the marketplace, the middle-class struggle for dominance was fought and won.

While others have isolated rhetorical strategies that naturalize the subordination of female to male, no one has thoroughly examined the figure, or turn of cultural logic, that both differentiates the sexes and links them together by the magic of sexual desire. And if we simply assume that gender differentiation is the root of human identity, we can understand neither the totalizing power of this figure nor the very real interests such power inevitably serves. So basic are the terms "male" and "female" to the semiotics of modern life that no one can use them without to some degree performing the very reifying gesture whose operations we would like to understand and whose power we want to historicize. Whenever we cast our political lot in the dyadic formation of gender, we place ourselves in a classic double bind, which confines us to alternatives that are not really alternatives at all. That is to say, any political position founded primarily on sexual identity ultimately confirms the limited choices offered by such a dyadic model.[23] Once one thinks within such a structure, sexual relationships appear as the model for all power relationships. This makes it possible to see the female as representative of all subjection and to use her subjectivity as if it were a form of resistance. By inscribing social conflict within a domestic configuration, however, one loses sight of all the various and contrary political affiliations for which any given individual provides the site. This power of sexuality to appropriate the voice of the victim works as surely through inversion as by strict adherence to the internal organization of the model. It was doubtless because such a form of transgression affirmed their normative structure that middle-class intellectuals were the first to produce an extensive vocabulary of sexual crimes and perversions.

Still, there is a way in which this book owes everything to the very academic feminism it often seems to critique, for if reading women's texts as women's texts were not now a professionally advantageous thing to do, there would be no call to write a history of this area of culture. However, in view of the fact that women writers have been included in the *Norton Anthology* as part of the standard survey of British literature and also as a collection by themselves, and in view of the fact that we now have male feminists straining to hop on the bandwagon, it is time to take stock. It is time to consider why the literary institution feels so comfortable with a kind of criticism that began as a critique of the traditional canon and the interpretive procedures the canon called forth. I can only conclude that in concerning itself with writing by and representations of women, literary criticism has not destabilized successfully the reigning metaphysics of sexuality. Clearly, by generating still more words on the subject, it has invigorated the discourse that sustains such a metaphysics. And yet I am convinced that one cannot tell the history of the British novel without, at the same time, considering the history of gender formation. I know this means that in the end I will have reified the themes whose reifying behavior it is my purpose to examine; I will have turned sex into sexuality too. But recognizing this, and with a view toward demonstrating how, at crucial points in its history, the novel used a thematics of gender to appropriate political resistance, I feel it is well worth the risk to compromise theory and erode the Olympian perspective on culture that such procedures as Foucault's occasionally allow one to enjoy. To remove

NANCY ARMSTRONG

oneself from the field under consideration is finally impossible, and attempting to do so does little to show how we might use the sexual clichés of this culture to imagine some other economy of pleasure, some genuinely subversive end.

If my study of the novel clarifies only one point, then, I would like it to demonstrate the degree to which modern culture depends on a form of power that works through language – and particularly the printed word – to constitute subjectivity. According to this premise, as purveyors of a specialized form of literacy, we invariably perpetuate the hegemony I have been describing. That we do so is especially true when we make novels into literary texts where psychosexual themes control the meaning of cultural information that might otherwise represent some contrary political viewpoint. When that happens, our interpretive procedures not only conceal the process by which the novels themselves reproduce modern forms of subjectivity. Our procedures also conceal the degree to which we think and write novelistically in order to make sense of the past and of cultures different from our own. In fact, we render ourselves unconscious of the political power we ourselves exercise whenever we represent sexuality as existing prior to its representation. Grounded on a metaphysics that is yet to be widely recognized as such, and working through a highly sophisticated network of strategies by which the humanities and social sciences ground themselves on that rockbed of truth – human nature itself – sexuality continues to conceal the politics of writing subjectivity.

To avoid the female strategy of self-authorization, I will be describing the behavior of an emergent class from a historically later position which that class has empowered – from a position within that class and supported by it. I say this as a way of insisting that in constructing a history of female forms of power, I do not mean to appropriate a form of resistance but rather to reveal the operations of a class sexuality by which I have often found myself defined. At the risk of appearing dogmatic, I have at moments overstated my case and so violated the pluralistic ideology espoused by the best liberal element within my profession. I have adopted this tactic as a means of countering those who would emphasize woman's powerlessness – and we are certainly rendered powerless in specifically female ways – and therefore as a means of identifying for critical consideration that middle-class power which does not appear to be power because it behaves in specifically female ways. I will insist that those cultural functions which we automatically attribute to and embody as women – those, for example, of mother, nurse, teacher, social worker, and general overseer of service institutions – have been just as instrumental in bringing the new middle classes into power and maintaining their dominance as all the economic take-offs and political breakthroughs we automatically attribute to men. I am not, in other words, constructing a woman's history from the viewpoint of an oppressed or silent minority, for that would falsify what I do and what I am. In constructing a history of the modern woman, I want to consider the ways in which gender collaborates with class to contain forms of political resistance within liberal discourse. I want to use my power as a woman of the dominant class and as a middle-class intellectual to name what power I use as a form of power rather than to disguise it as the powerlessness of others.

To write an adequate history of domestic fiction, then, it seems to me that one must modify permanently what literary historians can say about history as well as about literature. Such scholars and critics collaborate with other historians, as well as with those who make it their business to appreciate high culture, when they locate political power primarily in the official institutions of state. For then they proceed as if there is no political history of the whole domain over which our culture grants women authority: the use of leisure time, the ordinary care of the body, courtship practices, the operations of desire, the forms of pleasure, gender differences, and family relations. As the official interpreters of the cultural past, we are trained, it appears, to deny the degree to which writing has concealed the very power it has granted this female domain. It is no doubt because each of us lives out such a paradox that we seem powerless to explain in so many words how our political institutions came to depend on the socializing practices of household and schoolroom. Yet, I contend, the historical record of this process is readily available in paperback. We call it fiction.

With this in mind, I have tried to defamiliarize the division of discourse that makes it so difficult to see the relationship between the finer nuances of women's feelings and the vicissitudes of a capitalist economy run mainly by men. My study identifies several places in cultural history where the one cannot be fully understood without the other. But I would still consider such an effort to be a frivolous demonstration of literary scholarship if it were not for the other people who are attempting to open new areas of culture to historical investigation and to provide some understanding of our own status as products and agents of the hegemony I am describing. In adopting various critical strategies, I have made no effort to be faithful to any particular theory. To my mind, such academic distinctions offer neither a trustworthy basis for making intellectual affiliations nor a solid basis for mounting an argument that concerns our own history. Rather than distinguish theory from interpretation and feminism from Marxism, deconstructionism, or formalism, I care mainly about those scholars and critics who have helped me to discover traces of the history of the present in several eighteenth and nineteenth century texts and to understand my own insights as part of the larger project now going on within those disciplines where individuals have undertaken the work of creating a new political literacy.

NOTES

1 Samuel Richardson, *Pamela, or Virtue Rewarded* (New York: W. W. Norton, 1958), pp. 111. Citations of the text are to this edition.
2 Ian Watt, *The Rise of the Novel* (Berkeley: University of California Press, 1957), p. 57.
3 Sandra M. Gilbert and Susan Gubar, *The Madwoman in the Attic: The Woman Writer and the Nineteenth Century Literary Imagination* (New Haven: Yale University Press, 1979). See especially pp. 45–92.
4 By "the patriarchal model," I mean specifically the historical phenomenon that linked the political authority of the father over the household to that of the king in a mutually authorizing relationship. On this point, for example, see Gordon J. Schochet, *Patriarchalism in Political Thought* (New York: Basic Books, 1975) and Lawrence Stone, *The Family, Sex, and Marriage in England 1500–1800* (New York: Harper and Row, 1977), pp. 239–40.
5 I draw here on David Musselwhite's argument which implicitly challenges such notions of the politics of the novel as Bahktin articulates in *The Dialogic Imagination: Four Essays*, trans. Michael Holquist (Austin: University of Texas Press, 1981). Rather than view the novel as a form that – like carnival – resisted hegemony, Musselwhite argues that the novel appropriates symbolic practices that would otherwise behave as forms of resistance. I intend to suggest that

NANCY ARMSTRONG

the politics of the novel are determined, on the one hand, by the genre's tendency to suppress allternative forms of literacy and to produce the homogenized discourse we know as polite standard English. I will push this argument further and suggest that, on the other hand, the novel's politics depend on how we use the genre today. In writing this book, I am assuming that one may expose the operations of the hegemony by reading the novel as the history of those operations. If there is any truth in this claim, then in adopting the novel's psychologizing strategies, one only perpetuates the great nineteenth century project that suppressed political consciousness. David Musselwhite, "The Novel as Narcotic," *1948: The Sociology of Literature* (Colchester, England: University of Essex, 1978), pp. 208–209.

6   In this respect, I take issue with critics whose discussion of sexuality is grounded in nature. For example, Jeffrey Weeks, in objecting to Foucault, insists that "discourse is not the only contact with the real." *Sex, Politics, and Society: The Regulation of Sexuality since 1800* (London: Longman, 1981), pp. 10–11. To refute Foucault, however, he relies on the very strategies that Foucault identifies as constituting the discourse of sexuality. Weeks nevertheless tries to cut the Gordian knot which a Foucauldian understanding of sexuality presents: "Robert Padgug has recently *written* that 'biological sexuality is the necessary precondition for human sexuality. But biological sexuality is only a precondition, a set of potentialities which is never unmediated by human reality.' That sums up the fundamental assumption of this work" (p. 11, italics mine). Along with Padgug and others, Weeks invokes a biological basis for sexuality which is transcultural and outside of history, although, admittedly, "never unmediated by human reality." Along with Foucault, I would argue that the difference between nature and culture is always a function of culture, the construction of nature being one of culture's habitual tropes of self-authorization. And I would ask if the gendered body belongs to a nature that is beyond culture, as Weeks seems to assume, then why was it not until relatively recently that the difference between male and female came to dominate representations of the biological body. Writing about seventeenth century gynecology, for example, Audrey Eccles notes that "anatomically" it was "held there was virtually no difference between the sexes, the man's penis and testicles being exactly analogous to the uterus and ovaries." *Obstetrics and Gynaecology in Tudor and Stuart England* (London: Croom Helm, 1982), p. 26. Particularly in a culture that mythologizes sex by suppressing its political dimension, the idea of natural sex, it seems to me, poses a contradiction in terms that is without doubt the purest form of ideology.

7   Michel Foucault, *The History of Sexuality*, Vol. I, *An Introduction*, trans. Robert Hurley (New York: Pantheon, 1978), p. 8. Citations of the text are to this edition.

8   In using the term "soul," Locke invokes the metaphysics of an earlier theocentric culture, but he does so in order to decenter that metaphysics and provide a material basis for individual consciousness. "I see no reason," he claims, "to believe that the soul thinks before the senses have furnished it with ideas to think on; and as those are increased and retained, so it comes, by exercise, to improve its faculty of thinking in the several parts of it; as well as, afterwards, by compounding those ideas, and reflecting on its own operations, it increases its stock, as well as facility in remembering, imagining, reasoning, and other modes of thinking." *An Essay Concerning Human Understanding*, vol. I (New York: Dover, 1959), p. 139. Locke therefore retains the term of an earlier metaphysics, but he uses it to describe subjectivity as a mode of production exactly analogous to the development of private property. It is fair to say, further, that when "soul" is supplanted by gender as the source and supervisor of the individual's development, the whole notion of subjectivity is no less metaphysical than it is in Locke's ungendered representation. The metaphysical basis for human identity – and the role of language in self-production – is simply less apparent as such.

9   Maria Edgeworth and Robert L. Edgeworth, *Practical Education*, vol. II (London, 1801), p. ix. Citations of the text are to this edition.

10 Thomas Walter Laqueur, *Religion and Respectability: Sunday Schools and Working Class Culture 1780–1850* (New Haven: Yale University Press, 1976).

11 Laqueur, p. 229.

12 In recounting the growth of restrictive laws on alehouses and the attempts to regulate leisure time, Peter Clark has written, "In 1776 John Disney blamed the spread of popular disturbances on 'unnecessary and ill-timed' assemblies in drinking houses. The same year Oxfordshire landowners called for stern measures against vagrants and disorderly alehouses, while soon after the parish vestry at Terling in Essex proclaimed that 'alehouses are the common resort of the idle and dissolute' and went on to impose a strait-jacket of controls on the village's solitary establishment." *The English Alehouse: A Social History 1200–1830* (London: Longman, 1983), p. 254.

13 Allon White, "Hysteria and the End of Carnival: Festivity and Bourgeois Neurosis," *Semiotica*, 54 (1985), 97–111.

14 Fredric Jameson argues that it is necessary for criticism to abandon "a purely individual, or merely psychological, project of salvation," in order to "explore the multiple paths that lead to the unmasking of cultural objects as socially symbolic acts." *The Political Unconscious: Narrative as a Socially Symbolic Act* (Ithaca: Cornell University Press, 1981), p. 20. [See also p. 416 in this book.] In invoking Jameson's concept from time to time, I will stress that the political unconscious is no less historical than any other cultural phenomenon. My study implicates the rise of the novel in the production of a specific form of political unconscious that suppressed the inherently political nature of kinship relations, for one thing, and of representations of women for another. Pre-Enlightenment authors seem to have been acutely aware of the politics of courtship and family relations. Removing these areas of culture from the domain of politics was a self-conscious feature of eighteenth- and nineteenth-century fiction. But the history of such semiotic process is one that our modern notion of literature systematically erases. For purposes of this study, I am particularly interested in how domestic fiction helped repress the politics of sexuality as it concealed its own political operations and how, in so doing, it differentiated itself from other fiction to earn literary status for fiction.

15 Jacques Donzelot, *The Policing of Families*, trans. Robert Hurley (New York: Pantheon, 1979), p. 92.

16 For a discussion of the paternalism that emerged in opposition to patriarchy in seventeenth century Puritan writing, see Leonard Tennenhouse, *Power on Display: The Politics of Shakespeare's Genres* (New York: Methuen, 1986), especially the chapter entitled "Family Rites." In describing the alternative to patriarchy that arose at the end of the seventeenth and beginning of the eighteenth century in aristocratic families, Randolph Trumbach opposes the term "patriarchy" to the term "domesticity," by which he refers to the modern household. This form of social organization is authorized by internal relations of gender and generation rather than by way of analogy to external power relations between monarch and subject or between God and man. *The Rise of the Egalitarian Family* (New York: Academic Press, 1978), pp. 119–63.

17 Kathleen M. Davis, "The Sacred Condition of Equality – How Original were Puritan Doctrines of Marriage?" *Social History*, 5 (1977), 570. Davis quotes this list from John Dod and Robert Cleaver, *A Godly Forme of Householde Gouernment* (London, 1614).

18 See, for example, Patricia Crawford, "Women's Published Writings 1600–1700," in *Women in English Society 1500–1800*, ed. Mary Prior (London: Methuen, 1985), pp. 211–81.

19 Brian Simon, *Studies in the History of Education 1780–1870* (London: Lawrence and Wishart, 1960), pp. 1–62.

20 In elaborating the scene on the scaffold, Foucault pays close attention to the dismembered body of the criminal in the first two chapters of *Discipline and Punish: the Birth of the Prison*, trans. Alan Sheridan (New York: Vintage, 1979). However, the material body disappears once Foucault moves into the modern period and power works not upon the body so much as

through the penetration and inscription of the subject as subjectivity. The body on the scaffold continues on in Foucauldian discourse as if it were another body, a body of knowledge, and that of an entirely different order of subject – the patient in the clinic. But in fact, as Laqueur has shown, the history of the material body does not end here. The position of the criminal on the scaffold in fact came to be occupied by the pauper's body that eighteenth century science required for the theater of anatomy, and that modern culture, by appropriating common burial grounds for private property, had placed on the market. See Foucault's *The Birth of the Clinic: An Archaeology of Medical Perception*, trans. A. M. Sheridan Smith (New York: Vintage, 1973) and Thomas Laqueur, "Bodies, Death, and Pauper Funerals," *Representations*, 1 (1983), 109–31.

21   Bakhtin's twin figures of the grotesque body and mass body offer a way of imagining an alternative social formation to our own. These figures have special appeal for people interested in researching political history from a viewpoint antagonistic to power, a viewpoint which privileges the history of the subject rather than that of the state, because Bakhtin himself obviously wanted to see in the past forms that resisted the joyless and fearful conditions of the totalitarian government under which he wrote. Thus he uses Rabelais to construct the figure of carnival that would idealize all those symbolic practices that resisted the exclusive political body organizing courtly romance. Mikhail Bakhtin, *Rabelais and his World*, trans. Helene Iswolsky (Cambridge: MIT Press, 1965). Allon White and Peter Stally-brass use the figure of carnival to trace the history of resistance into the modern period in *The Body Enclosed* (Ithaca: Cornell University Press, 1986). I wish to thank the authors for allowing me to see portions of their book while in manuscript.

22   In *The Long Revolution* (London: Chatto and Windus, 1961), Raymond Williams describes this process. (Especially see his discussion of the growth of a reading public and of a popular press, pp. 156–213). I have used, as the conceptual backbone of this book, his concept of a political revolution that took the form of a cultural revolution. Unlike Williams, however, I have focused on the process of gendering that was crucial to the triumph of a form of power based on cultural control and the dissemination of information. My work is especially concerned with how writing for and about women influenced the kind of information that was produced by "the long revolution," as well as how such writing identified the targets at which such information was directed.

23   Addressing the same issue, Cora Kaplan writes: "Masculinity and femininity do not appear in cultural discourse, anymore than they do in mental life, as purely forms at play. They are always, already, ordered and broken up through other social and cultural terms, other categories of difference. Our fantasies of sexual transgression as much as our obedience to sexual regulation are expressed through these structuring hierarchies. Class and race ideologies are, conversely, steeped in and spoken through the language of sexual differentiation. Class and race meanings are not metaphors for the sexual, or vice versa. It is better, though not exact, to see them as reciprocally constituting each other through a kind of narrative invocation, a set of associative terms in a chain of meaning. To understand how gender and class – to take two categories only – are articulated together transforms our analysis of each." "Pandora's Box: Subjectivity, Class and Sexuality in Socialist Feminist Criticism," in *Making a Difference: Feminist Literary Criticism*, ed. Gayle Greene and Coppélia Kahn (London: Routledge, 1985), p. 148.

Nobody's Story

Catherine Gallagher

Catherine M. Gallagher (b. 1945)

Catherine Gallagher was born in Denver, Colorado, and attended the University of California, Berkeley, where she received her Ph.D. in 1979. She joined the English Department faculty a year later, and was named Eggers Professor of English Literature in 1998. Gallagher has also taught at the School of Criticism and Theory, co-edited the *Cambridge Studies in Nineteenth-Century Literature and Culture* book series, and served on the editorial board of *Representations*. Her honors include National Endowment for the Humanities and Guggenheim Fellowships, election to the American Academy of Arts and Sciences, and selection as the British Academy's Mastermind Lecturer. Gallagher has written *The Industrial Reformation of English Fiction: Social Discourse and Narrative Form, 1832–67* (1985); *Nobody's Story: The Vanishing Acts of Women Writers in the Marketplace, 1670–1820* (1994); *Practicing New Historicism* (with Stephen Greenblatt, 2000); and *The Body Economic: Life, Death, and Sensation in Political Economy and the Victorian Novel* (2006). *Nobody's Story* won the James Russell Lowell Prize from the Modern Language Association.

From *Nobody's Story: The Vanishing Acts of Women Writers in the Marketplace, 1670–1820*. Oxford: Clarendon Press, 1994, from ch. 5, pp. 162–75. Copyright © 1994 by Catherine Gallagher. Reprinted by permission of Catherine Gallagher.

Nobody's Credit: Fiction, Gender, and Authorial Property in the Career of Charlotte Lennox

Thus far I have argued, first, that the heroizing of writers in the mid-eighteenth century was closely intertwined with contemporary attempts to identify the property of authorship and, second, that a new valuation of fiction emerged from this discursive nexus. Useful as this analysis may be in explaining why [Samuel] Johnson and [Charlotte] Lennox made the claims they did for fiction, it does not, however, help us understand why their claims were so readily honored. We need to ask what purposes, besides the validation of authorship itself, the advancement of fiction served. After all, it would be farfetched to suggest that readers began to prefer fiction to scandal simply because they wanted to savor the originality of a bona fide author. This section of the chapter, therefore, addresses itself to the reader's, rather than the author's, sense of propriety and its affiliations with the eighteenth-century ethical discourse about sympathy. I do not leave behind the issue of property but merely shift its location.

My discussion of the promotion of fiction through copyright disputes has tended to take the category of fiction for granted, to assume that there was always a branch of letters distinguished by its overt renunciation of particular referential truth claims. Recent historians of the novel, however, have shown that the concept of fiction, far from being a universal cultural category, developed slowly in early modern Europe, that the immediate predecessors of the novel – romances, secret histories, and memoirs – often claimed historical veracity, and that until the mid-eighteenth century, there was no widely employed means of distinguishing between a fiction and a lie. Indeed, the problem of differentiating kinds of untruth has generally plagued historians of the novel. In his introduction to *A Check List of English Prose Fiction, 1700–1739*, William Harlin McBurney admits that he included works claiming to be true as long as he judged them to be "full of improbable lies."[1] But fiction writing cannot be said to exist as a marked and recognized category in a culture until it can be effortlessly distinguished from lying. As Michael McKeon has exhaustively demonstrated, the terms for such a distinction were available in late seventeenth- and early eighteenth-century England, but they were seldom used.[2] The discourse of fiction, therefore, was awaiting not so much the requisite conceptual tools as some cultural imperative to use them.

Once we recognize that it is rare to find cultures where the category of fiction is strongly marked and valued as such, and that in British history the category does not precede but is rather coterminous with the rise of the novel, the history of that genre raises new questions. Because histories of the novel long assumed that its genealogy lay in fictional forms, they tended to focus on the issue of realism. Where, they asked, did the taste for *realistic* novelistic fiction come from? – as if a taste for fiction already existed. But once we see that the novel derives from forms that were not at the time understood to be fictional, we must address a prior question. We should ask, not why the novel became the preferred form of fiction, but why fiction became a preferred form of narrative.

Both Lennard Davis and Michael McKeon have recently helped rephrase the question in these terms, and each has contributed important answers. Davis, denying that the novel developed primarily out of the romance and asserting that its origins lay in what he calls the "news-novel matrix" – [...] points to the legal and political pressures that eventually legitimized fiction.[3] McKeon, on the other hand, adheres to the romance-novel connection and identifies a dialectical development in romance that created an imperative for verisimilitude, which is imagined to be at once fictional and "truthful," in accordance with a newly expanded idea of truth. The movement from romance to novel, according to McKeon, rests on an underlying epistemological shift from truth-as-historical-accuracy to truth-as-mimetic-simulation. It was the widespread acceptance of verisimilitude as a form of truth, rather than a form of illusion or lying, that made fiction a category and simultaneously founded the novel as a genre. Verisimilitude is the leading term in McKeon's account; there is no realized prior category of fiction to which mimetic realism is added to produce the novel. Rather, the legitimation of the verisimilar (as opposed to the historical) allowed the separation of the fictional from the historical components of the romance and the development of the former as The Novel.[4]

My own argument is deeply indebted to those of Davis and McKeon, but it focuses on some crucial, indeed definitive, aspects of the novel that they largely ignore. Fiction no doubt renounces "historical" truth claims and replaces them with mimetic ones; this axiom would hold whether the nonfictional predecessor of the novel is news, scandal, or romance. However, as we saw in the preceding chapter, the tension between factuality and verisimilitude, between history and mimesis, could have been resolved in various ways or could simply have been left unresolved as the incommensurable layers of "allegorical" representation. Fiction writers, though, did more than admit their narratives lacked historical accuracy; after all, the authors of personal satire and scandalous "allegories" had gone that far and had, on occasion, achieved a high level of verisimilitude. But they were not, properly speaking, novelists, because their stories, whether pretending to exact historical accuracy or not, claimed to be about somebody, whereas the writers of admitted fictions professed to be telling nobody's story, that is, to be telling the stories of people who never actually lived. The most radical and least explored distinction between prenovelistic and novelistic narratives is that the former often claim particular extra-textual reference for their proper names and the latter normally do not.[5] A few seventeenth- and early eighteenth-century narratives were forthrightly fictional, just as some late eighteenth-century stories insisted on their referentiality, and still others asked the reader to switch back and forth between referential and nonreferential assumptions. There was no sudden novelistic revolution that purged English narrative of somebody and replaced him or her with nobody. Nevertheless, in the middle decades of the century, fictional nobodies became the more popular and respectable protagonists.

In those decades, though, it was by no means taken for granted that everyone would want to read stories about nobody. Arabella, the heroine of Charlotte Lennox's *Female Quixote*, articulates this reluctance and expresses common eighteenth-century objections to the new kind of narrative:

> [H]e that writes without Intention to be credited, must write to little Purpose; for what Pleasure or Advantage can arise from Facts that never happened? What Examples can be afforded by the Patience of those who never suffered, or the Chastity of those who were never solicited?...When we hear a Story in common Life that raises our Wonder or Compassion, the first Confutation stills our Emotions, and however we were touched before, we then chase it from the Memory with Contempt as a Trifle, or with Indignation as an Imposture.[6]

Arabella's two main challenges – that self-proclaimed fictions can neither instruct nor *move* the hearer – are met by her interlocutor in the novel with classic mid-century assertions of the peculiar truth and pleasure of the verisimilar. But there is a mismatch between the objections and their refutation, for Arabella has asked why one should care about people who never existed, not why one should take aesthetic pleasure in a well-accomplished mimesis. To respond that the accuracy of the mimesis is the foundation of the emotional response, and the emotional response is therefore a register of artistry, is to miss the force of Arabella's question: Why introduce disbelief simply to suspend it, however artfully, in the interest of creating what Arabella calls "Compassion"?

For "Compassion," after all, was generally acknowledged to be the end of fiction. As we have often been told, fiction in the eighteenth century was believed to be an important tool for inculcating moral sentiments.[7] It was thought to allow the exercise of sympathy, that process by which one feels the joys and sufferings of another and may thereby be motivated to perform benevolent actions. Sympathy and the imagination, then, were linked in some ethical systems, and certain historians of the novel argue that the new cultural prestige of fiction depended on this link. Fiction, the argument assumes, makes it easy to appropriate another's point of view, to sympathize. But why?

Arabella's objection calls this assumption into question by pointing out that we might expect to find our emotions "stilled" if we understand that their objects do not have, and never have had, any actual existence like our own. And Arabella was by no means unique in her opinion; it is common to find early and mid-eighteenth-century commentators taking it for granted that a real hero would be easier to feel compassion for than a fictional one: "To pity a feign'd Hero," as one "novelist" expressed it, "is commendable, because it is a sure Argument that Compassion would not be wanting to a real one."[8] The link between fiction and sympathy was often made during the period in these negative terms: only someone with sympathy to spare would be able to spend any on "a feign'd Hero." Fiction was thus not always conceived as a natural stimulus to sympathy; often it was seen as a test of how far one could extend compassion. Could it be extended to a paradoxical sympathy with nobody? If so, might not the very ambiguity of the phrase "sympathizing with nobody" warn us away from such an exercise? As Arabella and a good many other eighteenth-century skeptics were fond of remarking, there is something absurd about making up people to sympathize with. Why not just sympathize with the people who were already there?

I think that there is an answer to this question, that, pace Arabella's objections, Nobody was a more likely candidate for sympathy in this period than almost anybody else. To answer Arabella, I would like to turn briefly to David Hume's *Treatise of Human Nature*, where we will find the link between fiction and sympathy that usually goes without saying. I have chosen *A Treatise* not because it was an influential work in the eighteenth century (it was not) but because literary critics are fond of quoting it to prove that eighteenth-century people believed that they naturally took on the emotional coloring of their human environment through the automatic operations of sympathy: "So close and intimate is the correspondence of human souls," wrote Hume, "that no sooner any person approaches me, than he diffuses on me all his opinions, and draws along my judgment in a greater or lesser degree."[9] Such passages have made it easy for commentators to cite Hume as an "optimistic" moral philosopher who claimed there were no obstacles to fellow feeling.[10] I will instead follow the lead of those writers who have stressed the problematic nature of Humean sympathy,[11] noting that the philosopher's discussions of the concept are intricately interlaced with his discussions of property. Property, indeed, is an important brake on the dynamic of sympathy, and it can also be identified as the invisible link between sympathy and fiction. Hume's *Treatise* reveals why fictional characters were uniquely suitable objects of compassion. Because they were conjectural, suppositional identities *belonging* to no one, they could be universally appropriated. A story about nobody was nobody's story and hence could be entered, occupied, identified with by anybody.

Significantly, Hume's most extensive discussion of sympathy is inserted into the section of the *Treatise* dealing with pride and humility, the passions that he claims take the *self* as their object. Sympathy occurs smoothly and seems automatic when its object is the joy or sorrow of a member of our own family or a business partner, someone who, in the common parlance of the time, would be said to "belong" to us; it is not a self-forgetting process. Interwoven as it is with the possibility of knowing another mind, it is nevertheless self-referring. As Hume tersely reasons: "In sympathy there is an evident conversion of an idea into an impression. This conversion arises from the relation of objects to ourself. Ourself is always intimately present to us" (p. 320). That which is originally a distant, unemotional idea, in other words, becomes present by being folded in to that which is always present to us: our "impression" of ourselves. To sympathize is to expand this impression called the self to include impressions originally experienced as mere ideas of another's self.

Sympathy, then, is not an emotion about someone else but is rather the process by which someone else's emotion becomes our own. It is the conversion of the *idea* of someone else's passion into a lively *impression* of that passion, which is indistinguishable from actually feeling the passion oneself. Sympathy does not occur immediately, but is rather accomplished in three stages: (1) certain *sense data* (melancholy looks, open wounds, mournful language) communicate an *idea* of someone else's emotional state (unhappiness); (2) that idea becomes vital, forceful, and present through the operation of one or more relational principles linking sufferer and perceiver (cause and effect, contiguity and resemblance) and is thereby converted into an *impression* (impressions differ from ideas only in force and vivacity) of the other's emotion; (3) the impression (or vivacious perception) can, under certain conditions, be "so enlivened as to become the very *sentiment* or passion" (p. 319).

Such is the process by which sense (seeing the tears of another) leads to sentiment (feeling sad oneself); and according to Hume human beings are generally vulnerable to this form of emotional contagion. But the *Treatise* also strenuously insists that the process is rarely completed. It is especially likely to remain incomplete when the original sufferer is most clearly perceived to be somebody unrelated to us. The conversion of idea into sentiment, on the other hand, is most likely to occur when all three relational principles operate in a way that obscures the "otherness" of the original sufferer. In the case of human beings, Hume says, the relational principle of resemblance always operates: other people are always to some extent like us. But this is normally an insufficient basis for sympathy. Contiguity, mere physical proximity, is a somewhat stronger relational principle, but strongest of all is cause and effect, under which Hume classifies family relations and property relations (p. 310). "All these relations, when united together," Hume explains, "convey the impression or consciousness of our own person to the idea of the sentiments or passions of others, and makes us conceive them in the strongest and most lively manner" (p. 318).

CATHERINE GALLAGHER

In short, we are most likely to experience the emotions of other people when those other people already belong to us. Sympathy is normally that process by which the emotions of those who are related to us come to be experienced by us as our own. What happens to the otherness of the other people in this process, an otherness already blurred by the relationships described? Do we become more mindful of their separate realities? Not really, and this is the paradox of Humean sympathy: another's internal state becomes "intimately present" only by losing its distinct quality of belonging to somebody else. "I cannot feel an emotion," writes Hume, "without it becoming in some sense my own." That is, when the process occurs, the very relationships of ownership on which it depends seem at once stretched out of recognizable shape and reasserted. I feel your emotion because you are already in some sense mine, but once the feeling is mine, it is no longer distinguished by being yours.

As one of Hume's commentators has pointed out, his concept of sympathy does not, strictly speaking, imply any increase in regard for the person sympathized with. Páll S. Árdal, indeed, comes up with an extreme illustration of how the process Hume calls sympathy might rather be expected to produce selfishness: if you have a desire for a glass of whiskey, he reasons, and I sympathize with you in a Humean fashion, all that's been accomplished is that I want a glass of whiskey, too.[12] The likely outcome of my sympathizing with your yearning for a glass of whiskey is thus that I will try to get one for myself, not that I will try to satisfy you. My idea of your desire may have been the original stimulus, but by the time that the idea has been enlivened into my sentiment, you have become irrelevant. This illustration may give us an odd and in some ways distorting angle on Hume's version of sympathy, but it also allows us to see how easily the process he describes under that name might be expected to aggrandize the self and its properties, even as it unsettles the concept of a bounded, stable ego.

We might argue, then, that Humean sympathy is complete when it dispenses with its original "object," the original sufferer. I sympathize with the sentiments of others by making them mine; and the conditions for such an appropriation must be there at the outset: the person who originally feels them must somehow "belong" to me. Otherwise my senses will not travel the pathway to sentiment. Hume baldly claims that at first the passions with which we eventually sympathize "appear… in *our* mind as mere ideas, and are conceived to belong to another person, as we conceive of any other matter of fact" (p. 319). In other words, as long as the emotions are "conceived to belong to another person," they are rather cold, lifeless ideas; sympathy occurs when they lose this quality of belonging exclusively to another. As long as we perceive just the evidence of someone else's sentiment, we do not feel anything; the ideas must be impressed by the imagination into that which is always intimately present to us – ourselves – in order to become sentiments.

If we grant that Humean sympathy works by appropriating emotions, by transforming them from the emotions of another (mere ideas) to our emotions (lively sentiments), we can see how property (or, more precisely, its lack) serves as the invisible link between sympathy and fiction. The body of the other person, although it conveys the original sense data and serves as the basis for all the modes of relationship that supposedly allow sympathetic identification, is also paradoxically imagined to be a barrier. It communicates but it also marks out the sentiments as belonging to somebody else and hence as being simply objective facts. Our conception of the sentiments as appropriate to *that* rather than *this* body must be overcome in the process of sympathy. This proprietary barrier of the other's body is what fiction freely dispenses with; by representing feelings that belong to no other body, fiction actually facilitates the process of sympathy. It bypasses the stage at which the sentiments perceived in other bodies are mere matters of fact and gives us the illusion of immediately appropriable sentiments, free sentiments belonging to nobody and therefore identifiable with ourselves.

In these suppositions, we can see why fictional characters would emerge as universally engaging subjectivities. Because they are unmarked by a proprietary relationship to anyone in the real world, we do not regard them with the "objective" eyes with which Hume claims we view the property of others. Although they lack all actual relation to the reader, which Hume believed was the foundation of sympathy, they similarly lack the impediment of being related to anyone else. Hence, they become a species of utopian common property, potential objects of universal identification. Another way to put this might be to say that since the stories are nobody's, everybody can have an equal interest in them. The questions that clustered around putatively "true" stories in the eighteenth century – is the story libelous? who should be allowed to tell it? whose interest does it serve to tell it this way? – vanish, and a new interest takes their place, a gratuitous and hence sympathetic, sentimental interest.

Fiction, then, stimulates sympathy because, with very few exceptions, it is easier to identify with nobody's story and share nobody's sentiments than to identify with anybody else's story and share anybody else's sentiments. But, paradoxically, we can always claim to be expanding our capacity for sympathy by reading fiction because, after all, if we can sympathize with nobody, then we can sympathize with anybody. Or so it would seem, but such sympathy remains on that level of abstraction where anybody is "nobody in particular" (the very definition of a novel character). Nobody was eligible to be the universally preferred anybody because nobody, unlike somebody, was never anybody *else*.

Hume notes that the quality of one's sympathy for a fictional character differs from that feeling elicited by people we believe to be real. The strength and duration of an impression, he argues, are partly determined by the perceiver's belief in the reality of the object; hence our sympathy with fictional entities should be relatively unstable, for all its intensity. He distinguishes between the "fervors" and "apparent agitations of the mind" that "poetic description" creates and the "firm and solid" impression left by historical narration (p. 631): "We observe...that such fictions are connected with nothing that is real. This observation makes us only lend ourselves, so to speak, to the fictions" (pp. 631–32).[13] This remark that fictional characters merely borrow our sympathy without fully claiming it gives us another hint about their peculiar efficacy, their ability to "excite" the mind without producing "that weight" (p. 631) of real entities. The lighter, temporary quality of fictional identification further separates it from the weightier but also therefore more difficult task of sympathizing with others.

Conversely, however, Hume also entertains the idea that merely imaginary objects can arouse peculiarly strong emotional responses. Admitting that the essential mechanism of sympathy, the conversion of a mere idea into an impression and then into an actual bodily sensation, might not rely on the existence of anything outside the individual's imagination, he lists several instances in which, because nobody actually feels the emotions with which one sympathizes (p. 386), the imagination is stimulated to produce sentiments "that arise by a transition from affections, which have no existence" (p. 370).[14] Since sympathy works by making sensations out of ideas, the normal empiricist trajectory from body to mind may be reversed: "The lively idea of any object always approaches its impression; and 'tis certain we may feel sickness and pain from the mere force of imagination, and make a malady real by often thinking of it" (p. 319). That Hume's exposition of sympathy should thus find an illustration in one of the eighteenth century's favorite types of tyrannical selfishness, the hypochondriac, indicates that the deeper one looks into it, the more Humean sympathy renders unreal and irrelevant its ostensible object: somebody else.

A similarly strong sense both of the impediments to sympathizing with other actual people and of the attenuation of otherness as a result of sympathy lies at the heart of the novel's most important formal trait: its overt fictionality. The very specificity and particularity of realist representation, moreover, should be viewed as confirmation, rather than obfuscation, of fiction. Those techniques that make up what Ian Watt called the novel's "formal realism" – its wealth of circumstantial and physical detail, its delineation of characters by specific class, gender, and regional characteristics, and so forth – are all overtly illusionistic confessions that the particulars of the novel character have no extra-textual existence. The character came into *fictional* existence most fully only when he or she was developed as nobody *in particular*; that is, the particularities had to be fully specified to ensure the felt fictionality of the character. A generalized character would too easily take on allegorical or symbolic reference, just as one rendered in mere "hints" would have been read at the time as a scandalous libel. Thinness of detail almost always indicated specific extra-textual reference. But the more characters were loaded with circumstantial and seemingly insignificant properties, the more the readers were assured that the text was at once assuming and making up for its reference to nobody at all. Roland Barthes has pointed out that the contingent, unmotivated detail was the code of the "real" in fiction, but he did not draw what seems to me an obvious conclusion: that realism was the code of the fictional. The very realism of the new form, therefore, enabled readers to appropriate the stories sympathetically, for readers of fiction could be, to paraphrase Burke, "acquisitive without impertinence."[15]

NOTES

1 *A Check List of English Prose Fiction, 1700–1739* (Cambridge: Harvard University Press, 1960), p. ix.
2 McKeon, *The Origins of the English Novel, 1600–1740* (Baltimore, MD: Johns Hopkins University Press, 1987), pp. 25–64.
3 *Factual Fictions: The Origins of the English Novel* (New York: Columbia University Press, 1983), pp. 25–70.
4 McKeon, esp. pp. 39–64. Recent works on the origins of the novel that inform this discussion are, in addition to the books by Lennard Davis and Michael McKeon, Robert W. Uphaus, ed., *The Idea of the Novel in the Eighteenth Century* (East Lansing, MI: Colleagues Press, 1988); J. Paul Hunter, *Before Novels: The Cultural Contexts of Eighteenth Century English Fiction* (New York: Norton, 1990); Armstrong, *Desire and Domestic Fiction*; John Bender, *Imagining the Penitentiary: Fiction and the Architecture of Mind in Eighteenth-Century England* (Chicago: University of Chicago Press, 1987); Frances Ferguson, "Rape and the Rise of the Novel," *Representations* 20 (1987): 88–112; Homer Obed Brown, "Of the Title to Things Real: Conflicting Stories," *ELH* 55 (1988): 917–54; Lennard J. Davis, *Resisting Novels: Ideology and Fiction* (New York: Methuen, 1987); Ralph W. Rader, "The Emergence of the Novel in England: Genre in History vs. History of

Genre," *Narrative* 1:1 (1993): 69–83; and Robert Folkenflik, "The Heirs of Ian Watt," *Eighteenth-Century Studies* 25:2 (1991–92): 203–17.

5   For a lucid philosophical discussion of the reference of proper names in fiction, see Richard Rorty, "Is There a Problem about Fictional Discourse?" in *Funktionen des Fiktiven* (Munich: Wilhelm Fink Verlag, 1983), pp. 67–93. Rorty concludes that a Parmenidean insistence on reference creates a problem about fiction, but that the problem would be avoided if one were consistently to view "language as behavior governed by conventions, like games, and to see 'reference' in terms of conventions which must be obeyed if one is to make a successful move in the game" (p. 71). Rorty also points out, however, that although different uses of "reference" are merely conventional, the move of claiming "no referent" constitutes the language game called "literature" in the modern period (pp. 92–93).

6   Charlotte Lennox, *The Female Quixote*, ed. Margaret Dalziel (Oxford: Oxford University Press, 1989), pp. 376–77. Subsequent quotations from this edition are cited parenthetically in the text.

7   The secondary literature on this topic is extensive. For recent studies see John Mullen, *Sentiment and Sociability: The Language of Feeling in the Eighteenth Century* (Oxford: Oxford University Press, 1988); Janet Todd, *Sensibility: An Introduction* (New York: Methuen, 1986); Fred Kaplan, *Sacred Tears: Sentimentality in Victorian Literature* (Princeton, NJ: Princeton University Press, 1987); David Marshall, *The Figure of Theater: Shaftesbury, Defoe, Adam Smith, and George Eliot* (New York: Columbia University Press, 1986), and *The Surprising Effects of Sympathy: Marivaux, Diderot, Rousseau, and Mary Shelley* (Chicago: University of Chicago Press, 1988). Although these books include many discussions of the links between eighteenth-century novels and moral sense philosophy, they tend not to ask why *fiction*, as opposed to another form of narrative, should have seemed to have a peculiar affinity with sympathetic sensibilities.

8   *The Unfortunate Duchess; or, the Lucky Gamester. A novel, founded on a true story* (London, 1739), quoted in Michael Crump, "Stranger than Fiction: The Eighteenth-Century True Story," p. 67.

9   *A Treatise of Human Nature*, ed. L. A. Selby-Bigge (Oxford: Clarendon Press, 1968), p. 592. Subsequent quotations from this edition are cited parenthetically in the text and notes.

10   See, for example, Kaplan, *Sacred Tears*, esp. pp. 18–20 and 25–27.

11   For example, Jerome Christensen, *Practicing Enlightenment: Hume and the Formation of a Literary Career* (Madison: University of Wisconsin Press, 1987). Christensen's description of Hume's alternate involvement in and detachment from the passions has helped me formulate the idea of emotional "practice." See also Carol Kay, *Political Constructions: Defoe, Richardson, and Sterne in Relation to Hobbes, Hume, and Burke* (Ithaca, NY: Cornell University Press, 1988).

12   Páll S. Árdal, *Passion and Value in Hume's Treatise* (Edinburgh: Edinburgh University Press, 1966), p. 46.

13   For other discussions of Hume and eighteenth-century fiction, see Bender, *Imagining the Penitentiary*, pp. 35–40; and John Passmore, *Hume's Intentions* (London: Duckworth, 1980), pp. 99–104.

14   Hume is referring here, not to the operations of fiction per se, but to those of the "general rules," which are "established persuasions founded on memory and custom" (p. 632). Although he claims that there is a difference between fictions and general rules, he also admits that he cannot define it (pp. 631–32).

15   Burke claims that the sympathetic interest inspired by art, combined with its representational distance from real people, allows viewers to be "inquisitive without impertinence" (*A Philosophical Enquiry into the Origins of Our Ideas of the Sublime and Beautiful*, ed. J. T. Boulton [New York: Columbia University Press, 1958], p. 53). Burke shares the period's understanding that a consciousness of the difference between representation and reality stimulates interest and emotional response.

CATHERINE GALLAGHER

PART VIII

Post-Colonialism and the Novel

Introduction

Sections V, VI, and VII of this volume have all focused on theories that seek to account for the novel as a political, historical, and social phenomenon. In one sense, post-colonialism can be viewed as offering simply another category for socially constitutive experience to be added to those already in play: class, race, gender, sexuality – and now imperialism. Yet from a different perspective, post-colonial theory may be seen as the culmination of the late twentieth-century preoccupation with identity politics in novel studies. Post-colonial theorists aim to be inclusive, to write history not just from the point of view of one social group's political interest but to take into account the whole social field. In *Culture and Imperialism* (1993), Edward Said characterizes his post-colonial project as directly inspired by the kinds of sociopolitical theorists included in earlier sections of this anthology: "If with feminists, with great cultural critics sensitive to history and class like [Raymond] Williams, with cultural and stylistic interpreters, we have been sensitized to the issues their interests raise, we should now proceed to regard the geographical division of the world...as politically charged, beseeching the attention and elucidation its considerable proportions require" (710). This new object of critical regard – the geographical division of the world – entails, Said implies, not a new way of looking but an application of the insight gained from feminist and cultural theory. The study of imperialism does not, to Said's mind, in any way eliminate or attenuate the arguments made by the different schools of political and cultural theory to which he is indebted. When Said goes on to apply a "global perspective" (712) to Jane Austen's

Mansfield Park, it yields a reading of the novel that he sees as "completing or complementing others, not discounting or displacing them" (712). Said's cooperative relation to other critics is sustainable, notably, because his object of study is not strictly congruent with the "interests" of these other theories. The global perspective is precisely that which has no single interest of its own but whose interest is defined by a multiplicity of political interests, the capacity for pluralization. Geography, in other words, has no point of view; and any point of view that might be attributable to it is an ideological effect. The "political charge" of geographical division is a projection of the political interests that structure social relations through race, class, gender, and other categories through which power operates. The global perspective turns out to be a view of nothing less than the world itself – and the pluralized categories of political interest that define that world as a social world.

"Post-Colonialism and the Novel" includes the work of Said and two other theorists, Gayatri Spivak and Franco Moretti, who share Said's desire to carry forward into their own work a theory of politics defined in terms of group interests as well as a respect for the specific identity interests championed by other cultural critics. Spivak, in her essay "Three Women's Texts and a Critique of Imperialism" (1985), tempers her critique of previous feminist scholarship by acknowledging the political gain for women's interests that such work has achieved (675). Moretti, in his *Atlas of the European Novel, 1800–1900* (1999), quarrels with Said about their respective understanding of the economy of imperialism, but he sees this disagreement as subordinate to their shared post-Marxist interest in revealing the ideological function of English geography (*Atlas*, 742). By taking as their point of departure the political effects of the modern nation-state, all three theorists seek to map a social field that includes the subaltern interests based upon race, gender, and class – but also that of social groups more historically contingent and socially variable: the native, immigrant, exile, or newly freed slave.

But for a different type of post-colonial theorist, the proliferation of subaltern interests and their dynamic interrelation pose a problem rather than a solution for the understanding of modern political culture. This unit also includes the work of a thinker who might be said to culminate in a very different way the effort to arrive at a sociopolitical account of the novel. In *The Location of Culture* (1994), Homi K. Bhabha launches a full-scale attack on the concepts of history and ideology that inform identity studies, especially the post-Marxist articulations that have played such an important role in Parts VI and VII of this anthology. Bhabha's work is (like that of Said, Spivak, and Moretti) imbued with the insights of these cultural critics. But in contrast to this group of post-colonial theorists, Bhabha's confrontation with the notion of an infinitely widened field of study (the politics of geography) with infinitely divisible political interests (all the categories of subaltern and hegemonic identity) leads him to doubt the usefulness of a theoretical paradigm that begins with a presumption of categorical stability and legibility – whether that category is history, ideology, class, or minority identity.

Bhabha calls for nothing less than a whole new theory of the modern nation-state. And he finds the inspiration for his new political theory by returning to the insights of an older literary critical tradition: deconstruction. Bhabha thus stages what we might call his own return of the repressed. As we have seen, for many of the cultural critics included in this anthology, the turn to history was a deliberate turn away from the repetition of the deconstructive insight into repetition. Deconstruction did not, of course, ever fully disappear. In Parts VI and VII, for example, qualities that deconstruction posits as a universal for all human identity become the defining characteristic of certain subaltern identities: signifyin', shame, and nobody are all terms for particular minority identities (African American, queer, female) that are defined by their essential inessentialism. But for Bhabha such a metonymic use of deconstruction is part of the larger theoretical problem he critiques: Bhabha insists that the truths of deconstruction cannot be marginalized through annexation, cannot be made equivalent to, and thus limited to, a particular subaltern identity. Bhabha instead finds in deconstruction a way to conceptualize not just subaltern identity but all post-colonial identity as constitutively structured by the emotional experience of epistemological division. On Bhabha's view, the split self is not a function of language per se; it is the condition of human knowledge and experience brought about by the modern nation-state. Bhabha's work thus might be said to build upon the cultural critics admired by Said by revealing what on Bhabha's view are the debilitating blindnesses that accompany their insights. In *The Location of Culture*, Bhabha strives to lead post-colonial theory, to use one of his favored words, "beyond" – beyond history, beyond ideology, and beyond race, class, gender, sexuality, and imperialism as constitutive categories of social identity.

Where does the novel fit into this debate within post-colonial theory? Spivak, Said, and Moretti all respectively theorize the novel's social role in ways that should now be familiar to readers of this volume. Presented by Said as an extension of the arguments put forward by Fredric Jameson and D. A. Miller, the novel is posited as an ideological instrument of political power – of English imperial power. In Said's emphatic formulation: "imperialism and the novel fortified each other to such a degree that it is impossible...to read one without in some way dealing with the other" (*Culture*, 693). Drawing on an argument advanced by Raymond Williams, Said asserts the preeminence of the novel in defining English national identity, its successful projection of the English nation as a "'knowable community'" (Said, using Williams's term, 693). The regions and neighborhoods mapped out in *Tom Jones, Pride and Prejudice, Bleak House, Middlemarch*, and *Return of the Native* (to take some of Said's examples and to add some others) "shaped the idea of England in such a way as to give it identity, presence, ways of reusable articulation" (693). Moretti echoes Said's belief that the novel, more than any other cultural form, brings into being "the modern reality" of the nation-state. "'Where,'" Moretti asks, is the nation-state?

> What does it look like? How can one *see* it?...[V]illage, court, city, valley, universe can all be visually represented – in paintings, for instance: but the nation-state? Well, the nation-state...found the novel. And vice versa: the novel found the nation-state. And being the only symbolic form that could represent it, it became an essential component of our modern culture. (*Atlas*, 737, the first ellipsis is mine, the second is Moretti's)

What is the basis of the novel's ideological preeminence? Why is the novel "the only symbolic form that could represent" the nation-state? In *The Country and the City* (1973), Williams discusses the way English novels make the nation-state visible through ideological metonymy. Jane Austen's novels, to take a favorite example, do not represent all of England, nor do they even represent the heterogeneous population of any one community. But by making vivid the interests of a few families within a particular region, Austen brings to life a social world that, because it is varied and yet unified, stratified and yet symbiotic, can be taken for a whole, can be felt to represent "English" life. The same metonymic logic that allows the novel to represent Englishness as connected to place (i.e. to a particular community or region) also encourages the view that English identity is in fact located all in one place: delimited by geographical borders, England nestles within. The novel's lavish mimetic detail gives "spatial hereness," to use Said's term, to this metonymic construction of English identity (699). And because much of this detail is devoted to the depiction of domestic life, the idea of the "within" that emerges through the novel is an idea of England as home. As Moretti says of Austen's novels, "They take the strange, harsh novelty of the modern state – and turn it into a large, exquisite home" (*Atlas*, 738).

The primary teaching of post-colonialism is that "home" comes into being in and against the "not home." It is the job of the post-colonial theorist to make visible the imperial activity by which home can be taken for granted by those who live there, revealing in the process the human cost of such domestic security. Moretti, Said, and Spivak all map the political geography of the English nation-state by looking beyond the country and the city within England to the colony and the metropolis beyond its borders. As Said puts it, "the actual geographical possession of land is what empire in the final analysis is all about":

> The geographical sense makes projections – imaginative, cartographic, military, economic, historical, or in a general sense cultural. It also makes possible the construction of various kinds of knowledge, all of them in one way or another dependent upon the perceived character and destiny of a particular geography. (699)

The novel's ability to make present English communities and to project them as a national homeland is the most obvious expression of the genre's geographical sense. But Said and Moretti also find ideological power in the novel's formal construction of space, what we might call the narrativization of novelistic space. In focusing critical attention on the novel's geographical sense, Said seeks to correct what he takes to be an omission in novel theory generally: "After Lukács and Proust, we have become so accustomed to thinking of the novel's plot and structure as constituted mainly by temporality that we have overlooked the function of space, geography, and location" (703). Moretti begins to get at what is particular to the novelistic representation of space by drawing our attention to the large scale differences between Greek romance and the English novel (*Atlas*, 740). In the romance, space is the realm of Fate, outside the control of humans (742). In the novel, space is depicted as geography, knowable objectively through mathematical measurement and also knowable subjectively by the personal sentiments projected upon it. When Darcy is supposed to be in London and yet appears in Longbourn, Elizabeth can feel that Longbourn takes on a communicative function; it has become the signifier of his love (742). In a landscape where the meaning of location seems addressed to oneself, one certainly feels at home. Said agrees with Moretti that the novel as a genre is distinguished by the personalization of space and he finds a more extreme version of this practice a work in the novels of Charles Dickens. According to Said, Dickens's novels create locations that are wholly symbolic, whose every detail serves to express a particular character's identity (*Culture*, 699). Location is in such instances more than a placeholder for subjective projection: place has no meaning outside or beyond a character's identity. (Said uses as his example Lady Deadlock in the graveyard at the end of *Bleak House*.) What is more, if identity can be figured by the novel as place, then in an extension of the metonymic logic discussed above, these symbolic locations can seem to "ground" (to use Said's term) identity (699): personal identity can, through its figuration as location, seem unified, coherent, legible – in effect, visualizable. Thus we can say that the novel's geographical projection of England as a knowable community is matched by the equally geographical presentation of individuals as knowable persons. Space within the novel thus is stratified (or even, to use Said's term, hierarchized) through its annexation to different characters (699).

But of course novels do not simply ground characters in personified landscapes and leave them there. Crucial to the novel's narrativization of space is its depiction of characters moving from one place to another. The novel as a genre is, according to Said, dedicated to "small and large dislocations and relocations" (*Culture*, 703) of characters in social space. And from the kinds of analyses conducted by Said and Moretti, we can go even further and say that the novel's strategy for depicting the movement of characters results in the spatialization of the novel itself as a literary form. Through a narrative movement that both upholds and traverses spatial boundaries, the novel itself comes to seem a "space" for representation. Rather than thinking of the novel as words on a page, the reader perceives the novel as a spatial body, a literary *form* that makes visible a place: the "world" of the characters.

Said believes that critics who understand the distinctive quality of novelistic space can make sense of works whose organizing principle might otherwise be missed. He uses as his example Austen's *Mansfield Park*, arguing that "for much of the first half of the novel the action is concerned with a whole range of issues whose common denominator, misused or misunderstood, is space" (704). According to Said, the novel resolves these confusions through Fanny's social ascension. Her successful upward mobility is presented in the novel as a rational appreciation for the "larger and better administered spaces" made possible by English imperialism (706):

> To earn the right to Mansfield Park you must first leave home as a kind of indentured servant or, to put the case in extreme terms, as a kind of transported commodity...but then you have the promise of future wealth. I think Austen sees what Fanny does as a domestic or small-scale movement in space that corresponds to the larger, more openly colonial movements of Sir Thomas, her mentor, the man whose estate she inherits. The two movements depend on each other. (706)

If Fanny's material profit accrues to her as a result of her commodification, then, Said implies, the same might be said for Sir Thomas. The economic success of both is dependent upon the capacity for physical and psychic mobility, a permanent dislocation that is a requirement of the economic conditions of life in the modern nation-state, a life that, in Moretti words, "literally drag[s] human beings out of the local dimension, and throw[s] them into a much larger one" (*Atlas*, 737). Moretti, building upon the insights of feminist critics, sees the marriage market itself as an integral component in the making of the nation-state, since it joins together "people *who belong to different*

DOROTHY HALE

counties" (736). The people who move for marriage are, of course, women – and Moretti notes that women thus "especially" carry the burden of feeling "'at home'" elsewhere, an economic practice that is ideologically constructed as a female, "spiritual" virtue (736). Moretti thus understands Jane Austen's heroines as social models for the ideological process that associates English identity with not just the "small enclave" of one's birth, but "a much wider territory" (736). Women psychically accommodate themselves to the enforced social condition of dislocation by regarding "the nation-state as a true home-land" (736).

If the theorization of novelistic space leads Moretti and Said to analyze the micro-strategies of particular novels, their claims about the historical emergence of the nation-state will hold only if they can prove that the novel's geographical sense developed at a particular historical moment. Although Moretti and Said disagree about the causal connection between the circulation of wealth within the nation-state and English imperial activity abroad (see *Atlas*, 742), they both agree that a comparative or aggregate view of English nineteenth-century novels shows how the novel helped to "consolidate" (to use Said's phrase) English identity in the nineteenth century. Precisely because he wants to emphasize the dynamism and temporality of the emergence of England as a nation-state, Said uses the term consolidation to describe the working of English nationalism. Said argues, using a term from D. C. M. Platt, that during the nineteenth century a "'departmental view'" of the English nation emerges, which Said defines as a unified vision made up of the shared assumptions about English identity voiced inde-pendently by a variety of government officials: the departmental view is "a sort of consensus about the empire held by a whole range of people responsible for it" (*Culture*, 694). Said's point is that British identity, like British power, emerged through a social process of ongoing and seemingly spontaneous agreement: precisely because it could be taken for granted, English identity "was durable and continually reinforced" (694).

According to Said, this is exactly the view of English identity presented by the nineteenth-century novel, which dislocates in order to relocate, whose plots disrupt social stability in order to enact its "reunification" (697). Said describes this narrative movement in ideological terms as the "steady, almost reassuring work done by the novel" (644). And he notes that the narrative equilibrium of the English novel is matched by the thematic depiction of English national power as wholly unthreatened: English nine-teenth-century novels "stress the continuing existence (as opposed to revolutionary overturning) of England. Moreover, they *never* advocate giving up colonies, but take the long-range view that since they fall within the orbit of British dominance, *that* dominance is a sort of norm, and thus conserved along with the colonies" (695). Said believes that as a cultural critic his work is to defamiliarize the English novel's consolidating function, first by making visible the political assumptions it holds as normative, and second by calling our attention to the political activity that the novel must render invisible or marginalize for these norms to be upheld. And for Said, it is, more than anything else, English imperialism that is absent from the novel. Even at a time when novelists were looked to for their social analyses of "the condition of England," none of these writers considered colonialization as a component of that condition (693).

Gayatri Spivak's essay, "Three Women's Texts and a Critique of Imperialism," written about a decade before *Culture and Imperialism* and *Atlas of the European Novel*, stands as an early critical attempt to conduct just the kind of ideological unmasking valued by Said and Moretti. Indeed, her theoretical assumptions are so close to Said's that the opening sentence of her essay might be mistaken for one of his: "It should not be possible to read nineteenth-century British literature without remembering that imperialism, understood as England's social mission, was a crucial part of the cultural representation of England to the English" (675). Spivak agrees with Said not only about the integral relation between English literature and English imperialism but also how the ideology of imperialism causes us to forget this relation by working through literature. The ideological power of literature lies in its ability to make us forget, to allow us to believe that political realities are located elsewhere. Spivak extends this ideological account of literature to include in her political critique the ideological function of the academic study of literature. She argues that, before the political scholarship of recent cultural historians, literary studies as a discipline contributed to what she calls the "worlding" of "the Third World." It is an ideological effect of empire, she argues, that imperialist states (presumably those with universities having departments devoted to the study of national and comparative literatures) regard native cultures as possessing "rich intact literary heritages waiting to be recovered, interpreted, and curricularized in English translation" (675).

But for all the agreement in their political investments and interests, Said and Spivak end up having different accounts of how novels perform the forgetting of imperialism. For Said, imperialism makes itself felt as the unrepresented, the vague mention, the shadowy out there, constitutively different from the hereness of home. As is indicated by her choice of texts (*Frankenstein*, *Jane Eyre*, and *The Wide Sargasso Sea*), Spivak believes that the traces of colonial violence are registered by novels despite their success at creating a "'fiction of resolution'" (Said, quoting Deirdre David, *Culture*, 697). Since on Spivak's view the reality of imperialism inscribes itself even on its own ideological products, the "forgetting" performed by literature is a fraught process, more like a gothic haunting. In the three novels she analyzes, Spivak finds nothing less than what she calls "the terrorism of the categorical imperative," the instrumental distortion of Kantian philosophy used to underwrite the imperialist project (679). In what she describes as a "travestied" appropriation of Kant, colonization is rationalized as altruism: for natives to enjoy human rights, they must first be made human; to be honored as "an end in himself," the native must first be used by the state as a means for humanization (679).

Spivak agrees with Said that the English novel works to uphold English national power, but for her the novel does not consolidate English power by taking it for granted; the novel instead actively attempts to justify the nation's imperialist pursuits. The terrorism of the categorical imperative is recoverable, Spivak believes, in novels such as *Jane Eyre* that actually make present the imperialist point of view by depicting the activity of "worlding" from that point of view. Spivak argues that Brontë presents Jane's domestic success as a direct result of her complicity in the English imperialist project. In this respect, Spivak's account of Jane sounds much like Said's account of Fanny. But whereas Said finds the colonial plot allegorized and made visible by Fanny's domestic movements, Spivak believes that Brontë's novel makes visible the human cost of Jane's upward mobility by devoting representational space to the foreign other, depicting the sacrifice of this other for the gain at home, of home. Bertha Mason is, according to Spivak, "a figure produced by the axiomatics of imperialism": "Through Bertha Mason, the white Jamaican Creole, Brontë renders the human/animal frontier as acceptably

DOROTHY HALE

indeterminate, so that a good greater than the letter of the Law can be broached" (678). Rochester can reap the gains of imperialism, in other words, by participating in an international marriage market that allows men to bring home the wealth of their "foreign" wives. As for the "foreign" wife, she may be brought to England but can never be brought home. The putative inhumanity of the alien other gives reason to the English to break the "letter of the Law" – to justify Bertha's imprisonment in the attic rather than her installation at the English hearth. Bertha's inability to be incorporated is, conveniently, her own fault. By resisting "civilization," she has simply confirmed herself to be the animal that the colonizer presumes her to be. An opening in the ruling class is thus made for Jane, whose own social dislocation (by gender and by class) has the advantage of making her perfectly mobile (like Fanny). Thus on Spivak's reading, Brontë's novel begins with Jane's dislocation in order to accomplish her relocation: Brontë's narrativization of space moves her "from the place of the counter-family to the family-in-law" (677). But it is Spivak's point that this narrative reinstatement is predicated on another, greater, narrative disjunction: Jane's narrative movement upward can only be accomplished through her narrative displacement of Bertha. Jane herself can become enfranchised, can join the English home, only because there is someone more foreign than herself who can occupy the ideological position of outsider. It is one of Spivak's important theoretical points that Brontë thus depicts the complication of feminist interests by colonial interests: women as a social group are divided against each other, separated by the incommensurable values bestowed upon female identity by class, nation, and race.

Although Spivak believes, then, that novels such as *Jane Eyre* only allow the reader to forget so much, that that the violence of imperialist ideology can be normalized but not wholly obliterated, she does not believe that Brontë's novel – or any novel written from "within" an imperialist perspective – can ameliorate this violence. She is especially critical of the suggestion that novels should attempt to overcome imperialism through the representation of the "native" point of view. For Spivak, such a notion is itself an extension of the imperialist ideology it aims to combat. The belief in the native point of view is, to her mind, no different from the belief in "rich intact literary heritages waiting to be recovered" (675). To pretend to imagine the point of view of the native other is in fact always an act of colonization, an extension of the travestied Kantian imperative that enables the representer to believe that she is altruistically speaking for the other until the other can speak for herself.

Spivak thus praises Jean Rhys, in her rewriting of *Jane Eyre*, for not imputing to Bertha an "authentic," native point of view. Spivak applauds *The Wide Sargasso Sea* for portraying Bertha as a colonized other, knowable only through the native role projected upon her by her colonizers. In Spivak's opinion, Rhys thus successfully renders Bertha as "an allegory of the general epistemic violence of imperialism, the construction of a self-immolating colonial subject for the glorification of the social mission of the colonizer" (681), which captures the complexity and divisiveness of colonial mediation. If such allegorization is depersonalizing, at least this depersonalization is in the service of imperialist demystification, which, for Spivak, is better than the opposite situation in which natives seem to be personalized only to perform as mouthpieces for their colonizers. As Rhys demonstrates through her representation of Bertha, role-playing is the only social position possible for the native brought "home" to England. Spivak thus imagines the "consolidation" of English identity as emerging not just through a shared governmental view of English power and English national identity (Said's "departmental view"); for Spivak, the unified domestic view of England's coherent national identity can emerge only in the imperialist need to negotiate a difference between home and away: "No perspective *critical* of imperialism can turn the Other into a self, because the project of imperialism has always already refracted what might have been the absolutely Other into a domesticated Other that *consolidates* the imperialist self" (683, first Spivak's emphasis, then my emphasis).

In an interesting way, Spivak's position brings us back to Said's theoretical investment in the ideological function of the absent or missing referent. But if for Said the unnamed or barely mentioned imperial English colonies are the sign of English power, if they convey a sense of English world dominance that is simply taken for granted by novelists who focus on the domestic scene, for Spivak the unrepresented has, paradoxically, the power to represent (if only by suggestion or indication) social forces outside or beyond imperial power, forces that resist incorporation precisely by remaining invisible, silent. As Spivak explains, the "absolutely Other [who] cannot be selfed" (687), who refuses even to accept the role of "native" thrust upon her by the colonizer, cannot be fathomed by the colonizer. Rhys dramatizes the difference between colonized and uncolonized "native" by contrasting Bertha with Christophine, the "native" who will not be domesticated. Although it might seem an indignity to be "driven out of the story, with neither narrative nor characterological explanation or justice" (683), in fact for Spivak Christophine's narrative dislocation is more liberating than Jane's reinscription within the imperialist plot: Christophine's banishment from the story is an act of self-preservation that enables her to breach what we might call the letter of the law of English novelistic narrative, the law of consolidation that dictates that loose ends be tied up, not disappear.

Spivak believes that Mary Shelley, writing at the beginning of the nineteenth century, fully understands the political power of representational absence. Spivak's positive account of *Frankenstein* is grounded in an appreciation of all that the novel does *not* do or say. According to Spivak, Shelley "does not speak the language of feminist individualism" (683) nor does she "deploy the axiomatics of imperialism" (684). Although she indicates the conventionality of the topos, Shelley does not participate in the strategy of imperial domestication: as Spivak emphatically states, she "*cannot* make the monster identical" with Ariel (686). And, although it is suggested that he should and might, the monster is not represented as following the path of Bertha: he is not depicted in the novel as immolating himself. On Spivak's view, to be "'lost in darkness and distance'" (Spivak, quoting *Frankenstein*) is to find a narrative space for self-possession. The monster is still in the novel but is also out of its colonizing space, out of the reach of imperialist inscription. If Brontë's novel shows how the colonial point of view divides the interests of subaltern groups, Spivak argues that Shelley effectively unites feminist and "native" interests by displaying the comparability of their marginalized positionality. The monster who is "lost in darkness and distance" is matched in Shelley's novel by the spatial position of Mrs. Saville, the English lady. Mrs. Saville resists inscription by the imperialist narrative by serving as its addressee: she "frames" the text without being "encircled" by it or "encircling" it (687). Spivak understands this liminal position as potentially liberating: the "place of both the English lady and the unnamable monster are left open by this great flawed text" (688). The novel's flaw comes from the impossibility of standing completely outside the axiomatics of imperialism, while the narrative opening is a placeholder for political critique.

When we step back from Spivak's dazzling textual readings, we may want to pose some questions about her larger theory about the role of literature in the "cultural representation of England to the English" (675). Why is it that for Spivak Brontë can be said to be a factotum of history, the follower of an "abject script" written by the "imperialist narrativization of history" (675) while Shelley, although expressing "plenty of incidental imperialist sentiment in *Frankenstein*" (684), does not "produce unquestioned ideological correlatives for the narrative structuring of the book" (684)? Said, of course, answered this question with an appeal to the linear development of English imperialism. As English imperialism rises and falls through the century, its strategies and costs become more visible. The explicit engagement of Kipling and Forster with English imperialism makes it possible, on Said's view, to look back on Austen (*Culture*, 696). What seemed so reassuring in Austen's novels can, to a later audience, defamiliarize novelistic reassurance itself, revealing its ideological basis. But this can't be Spivak's position since in her argument the chronologically earlier novel achieves the greatest defamiliarization: *Frankenstein* is published in 1818 and *Jane Eyre* not until 1847. Although Spivak's understanding of ideology may be based in a reverse chronological argument (Shelley is able to see better and more clearly because she writes at the beginning of imperialism, before its full consolidation), Spivak does not explicitly argue this position. Nor does Spivak in any direct way confront the theoretical problem of the range of insights individuals might have at any given historical moment into the workings of ideology. By referring to Shelley's politically radical parents (Mary Wollstonecraft and William Godwin), Spivak seems to imply that Shelley's upbringing put her in a position to understand better than her contemporaries (and, seemingly, other novelists writing at her historical moment or in the future), the violence and inequity upholding British nationalism – to which she refused to assent (686).

The possibility of Shelley's refusal makes Spivak's other claims about the worlding of the Third World and the linear progress of imperialist consolidation harder to believe. Shelley alone would seem to refute Spivak's sweeping claim that literature from the first half of the nineteenth century is so implicated in "producing Ariel" that it cannot also function as a site of critique. Spivak strongly insists that other social discourses of the period need to be consulted to "reopen the fracture" (683), to make visible the operation of politics in the period. In this regard, she imagines political documents to be the opposite of literary works: while the latter is the site for cultural forgetting, the former provides the positive basis for retroactive, historical remembering. Spivak repeatedly advises contemporary critics to read literary texts in relation to the "archives of imperial governance" (683). But tellingly, Spivak cannot bring herself to follow her own advice – and this is because she does not need to. Even in *Jane Eyre*, she finds the articulation of imperialist ideology and the political critique of imperialist ideology both made fully visible by the symbolic logic of the novel. Through her close readings, the novel in fact shows us all we need to know about the workings of imperialism. What her own theory does not explain, though, is why some novelists seem better able to register as critique their display of imperialist ideology.

Spivak indicates her own discomfort about this problem in a disclaimer that she makes. She will, she declares, refrain from engaging the deconstructive argument against authorship. Her work will instead bracket the category of "author," proposing instead as the "object of investigation" the "printed book." She defends this decision not on logical but on political grounds:

> We must rather strategically take shelter in an essentialism which, not wishing to lose the important advantages won by U.S. mainstream feminism, will continue to honor the suspect binary oppositions – book and author, individual and history – and start with an assurance of the following sort: my readings here do not seek to undermine the excellence of the individual artist. (675)

This is a perplexing moment in Spivak's argument, in part because it presents itself as a self-conscious clarification of her theoretical stance, even as it raises more questions than it answers about her relation both to what she calls "U.S. mainstream feminism" as well as to what she earlier in this same paragraph terms "the lessons of deconstruction" (675). Since her essay as a whole, especially her reading of *Jane Eyre*, might be understood as a critique of the "basically isolationist admiration for the literature of the female subject in Europe and Anglo-America" that is, on her view, the "high feminist norm" (675), it is difficult to say why she wants in the passage cited above to "take shelter in the essentialism" that the rest of her essay deplores. If the position is more ambivalent than this, if her argument is really that "feminist individualism" has both positive and negative political consequences, that it is both made possible by the axiomatics of imperialism (whose logic it accepts as normative) and yet ultimately challenges patriarchy (and thus wounds imperialism) through its admiration of female-authored artistic masterpieces – this argument is never made explicit. Spivak in fact falls back on a weaker, more descriptive goal: "to situate feminist individualism in its historical determination rather than simply to canonize it as feminism as such" (675).

Although Said's account of the novel's ideological function is ostensibly less problematic, grounded in his uncomplicated sense of the linear development of imperialism (the historical consolidation and decline of English imperialist power), we can in fact find in his essay the same aporia about the problem of authorial insight. He insists that "novels are not reducible to a sociological current and cannot be done justice to aesthetically, culturally, and politically as subsidiary forms of class, ideology, or interest" (*Culture*, 695). And yet his account of the development of the English novel, the whole notion of its ideological contribution to English "consolidation," lies precisely in his sense that all "individual works" (697) perform the same ideological function. Indeed, it is his main point about the English novel that its ideological function is monolithic: that the "history of the novel" is the history of "the coherence of a continuous enterprise" (697). Thus although he objects to what he has termed "the rhetoric of blame," although he seeks to distinguish himself from critics who attack a novelist such as Jane Austen "for being white, privileged, insensitive, complicit" (712), who find her politically corrupt because of her affiliation with a "slave owning society" (712), Said's own theory of ideology does not give him the conceptual tools to clarify why Austen should not be blamed.

Because Said's theory of ideology has no way of discussing authorial agency, he ends up praising Austen through the work performed by her novel: "Austen's imagination works with a steel-like rigor through a mode that we might call geographical and spatial clarification" (704). But if these same novels are acts of ideological mystification, if they also work to consolidate English identity on behalf of English imperialism, how and when do we know when the novel stops "consolidating" English national identity and starts "clarifying" its ideological operation? We find this ambivalence running throughout Said's descriptions of Austen as ideological agent. For example:

> It is no exaggeration to interpret the concluding sections of *Mansfield Park* as the coronation of an arguably unnatural (or at the very least, illogical) principle at the heart of a desired English order. The audacity of Austen's vision is disguised a little by her voice, which despite its occasional archness is understated and notably modest. (705–6)

What exactly is Austen being praised for here? That she upholds the "unnaturalness" of the English order by reproducing its logic and naturalizing it? Or is he saying that she has exposed its functioning by making visible a logic that is normally suppressed or veiled? Is she audacious because she critiques? Or is she audacious because she cleverly participates in the ideological disguise that is the *sine qua non* of imperialism?

Said tries to elide the problem of authorial agency by transferring critical attention to the role of the reader:

> Since Austen refers to and uses Antigua as she does in *Mansfield Park*, there needs to be a commensurate effort on the part of her readers to understand concretely the historical valences in the reference; to put it differently, we should try to understand *what* she referred to, why she gave it the importance she did. (707)

Said later clarifies that it is "post-colonial" readers who, "from our later perspective" (713), can decode Austen's "signifying power" (707), the particular brand of Austenian reference that Said has identified. But if Austen herself can understand enough about the operation of English imperialism to "encode" (713) it in this way, at her own cultural moment, then why couldn't there be a historical reader who might be capable of "a commensurate effort" to decode?

Said's uncertainty as to the political function of Austen's repetition of imperialist ideology (she "affirms and repeats the geographical process," 709) emerges as an explicit concern of his argument when he moves toward conclusion. As he steps back for a comprehensive view of Austen, he is left, he says, with a "paradox" that he "can in no way resolve" (712). How can we reconcile "everything we know about Austen and her values" with her apparent acceptance of "the cruelty of slavery" (712)? If her novels refer, they don't in fact *say.* For Said the visibility of imperialist logic that is registered in symbolic and abstract ways in her novels and is decodable by the reader is, apparently, a type of not saying. For Said, anything less than the direct act of speaking out against empire upholds empire. In an interesting reversal of the value accorded by Percy Lubbock, Wayne Booth, and other Anglo-American formalists to the narrative strategies of "showing" and "telling" (see Part I), Said believes that novelistic showing is never authorial telling. Showing, on Said's view, makes visible through the operation of novelistic form – and as such it can for Said be a type of expression attributable to the novel itself, even to novelistic intentionality, rather than any kind of authorial intentionality. The implication is that cultural critique cannot be accomplished by an author "showing" through her novels the operation of ideology; to present itself as a legible and effective political position, cultural critique must be directly expressed, must be expressed through the author's voice and as unambiguous social protest.

Given this position, Said can avoid blaming Austen only by instead blaming the monolithic operation of imperialism: he gets Austen off the hook by invoking a version of Spivak's "abject script." Said argues that it is anachronistic for contemporary readers to expect that Austen could have the critical perspective on imperialism that the course of history has made possible for the contemporary reader. But as we have seen, to some degree he does believe that Austen has this perspective – or else how could her novels more than other novels encode so powerfully not just the ideology of English imperialism but also its critique? The paradox that Said feels he arrives at when he attempts to sum up his understanding of Austen has in fact been prepared for by the untheorized political doubleness that throughout his argument he has attributed to the novel as a cultural form. He sees novels like *Mansfield Park* as divided between complicity and subversion: on one hand, Austen's novels perform the work of cultural forgetting by "resisting or avoiding" any reference to imperialism; on the other hand, her novels by "their formal inclusiveness, historical honesty, and prophetic suggestiveness cannot completely hide" this dominant social reality (712). By eliding the category of authorial agency, Said ends up attributing to the novels themselves an ethical sense. The work of narrative spatialization (driven by the geographical sense) is now ethically recuperated as "formal inclusiveness" – as if the novel itself were governed by a split self, the genre's bad geographical sense contributing to the ideological spatialization of narrative, and the genre's good, "historically honest" sense silently (but visibly) critiquing that ideology through formal supplementation.

The paradoxicality that Said admits only at the end of his argument and only as an irresolvable problem for his own cultural theory is taken by Homi Bhabha as the launch point for a new post-colonial theory, one that does not despair at resolving divided political interests, such as those that Said runs up against in his account of Jane Austen, because it takes the condition of self-division as the norm for life in the modern nation-state. For Bhabha, the consolidation of English identity is a much more precarious enterprise than it is for Said. The locations and dislocations upon which it depends only superficially produce a happily mobile, commodified subject, able to move smoothly from one home to the next. On Bhabha's view, geographical dislocation necessarily results in the subject's psychic and epistemological dislocation. What is more, the given of geographical dislocation splits the identity of the modern nation-state itself. The need for the nation-state to define itself by its geographical borders, borders that are themselves contestable and fluid, made and unmakeable, means that the state can never take its identity for granted. No longer authorized by a divine or royal ruler (God, Pope, king), the nation-state must produce strategies of self-authorization. Its own dislocated authority, in other words, structures its strategies of self-authorization even while it renders those strategies contingent and unstable. The result is a political world in which no group can take its authority for granted, where power is never secure: "The liminal figure of the nation-space would ensure that no political ideologies could claim transparent or metaphysical authority from themselves" (*Location*, 724).

DOROTHY HALE

The modernity of the nation-state is defined, Bhabha argues, precisely by its need to consolidate authority, to have its authority affirmed not once and for all but repeatedly and from as many quarters as possible. The strategy of self-authorization coalesces, according to Bhabha, not around the antagonism between self and other (home vs. abroad, us vs. them), but through the constitution of an ideological subject whose withinness is itself divided. The modern split subject is a result, Bhabha theorizes, of the contradictory strategies deployed by the state in service of its self-authorization. On one hand, the modern nation-state attempts to define itself as a coherent unity by appealing to the historical durability of its identity. Bhabha calls this the discourse of "nationalist pedagogy" (722). This discourse is pedagogical, on Bhabha's view, because the state positions itself as the keeper of the history that is said to be unique to this nation: the act of memorialization is achieved not just through the preservation of "native" traditions, but by indoctrinating new generations in those traditions, by teaching each new generation to call those traditions its own. Yet on the other hand, even while the state presents itself as a historically coherent entity, it simultaneously strives to define itself in terms of its "contemporaneity" (722), its relevance to those living right now, in a world that has little resemblance to life in the past. In Bhabha's vivid formulation, "The scraps, patches, and rags of daily life must be repeatedly turned into the signs of a coherent national culture, while the very act of the narrative performance interpellates a growing circle of national subjects" (722). The definition of national identity as history, as memorializable, collective experience, thus stands in tension with the definition of national identity as the now of present-day life. But as Bhabha goes on to explain it, these two strategies are not pursued discretely, as independent goods, but have a causal relation. The state's need to "perform" the unity of its people, to interpellate or "address" the "contentious, unequal interests and identities within the population" (722), generates pedagogic discourse: "the political unity of the nation consists in a continual displacement of the anxiety of its irredeemably plural modern space – representing the nation's modern territoriality is turned into the archaic, atavistic temporality of Traditionalism" (724). Bhabha calls the double ideological imperative of the state (the definition of contemporary identity as both present and past – and present because past) the "double narrative movement" or "double time" of the modern nation-state (722).

One of Bhabha's important theoretical goals is thus to replace the post-Marxist "hierarchical or binary structuring of social antagonism" (717) with a paradigm of social relation that would allow for a more heterogeneous and dynamic sense of the varieties of social division and affiliation. He proposes the term "hybridity" to describe this alternative view of the construction of identity in the post-colonial nation, and seeks, much like M. M. Bakhtin, to proliferate rather than consolidate, to make contingent rather than to essentialize the "social and textual" categories through which the inherently unstable consolidation of "nationness" is performed (717). The very specificity of the act of affiliation at any given historical moment and in any particular social context among and for individual social subjects leads Bhabha to turn his attention to the psychological experience of location, dislocation, and relocation as well as the particular cultural conditions informing that psychic experience. He thus proposes the concept of "the locality of culture" as an alternative to the theoretical understanding (invoked by

Moretti in the *Atlas of the European Novel*) of "the Western nation as an obscure and ubiquitous form of living" (718).

Of course, the idea that culture is defined by specific experiences, generated through particular locations is one that we find in Said, who takes from Raymond Williams the concept of the "structure of experience" as a way of negotiating between the determinism of ideology and the individual perception of life. Said further follows Williams in regarding literary works as offering a particularly powerful "structure of experience," powerful precisely because of literature's capacity to represent social experience as particularized. In Said's example, the ideology of the not-home emerges in English culture through its literary expression, especially its expression in novels. The contemporary critic who desires to understand this ideology is best served not by an a priori theory of imperialism, Said argues, but through an empirical engagement with, the close reading of, actual novels:

> we must accept that the structure connecting novels to one another has no existence outside the novels themselves, which means that one gets the particular, concrete experience of "abroad" only in individual novels; conversely that only individual novels can animate, articulate, embody the relationship, for instance, between England and Africa. (*Culture*, 697)

Bhabha applauds Said's recognition of the importance of "'sensuous particularity'" (*Location*, 718), something that Bhabha says he finds in Fredric Jameson's work, as well. But if we can acknowledge along with Bhabha that Said seeks to make the examination of sensuous particularity part of his theoretical enterprise, we might also add that Said's monolithic concept of ideology prevents him from realizing this goal. For Said the "structure of feeling" in each novel always amounts to the same thing: the uniform expression of imperialist ideology. Bhabha's work attacks precisely such a totalized view of the operation of political power. His own post-colonial theory seeks to go beyond the post-Marxist view of power as "animated, articulated, and embodied" (to use to Said's terms) – but not divided against itself or disrupted by other contending structures. Bhabha, on similar theoretical grounds, further distinguishes his view of social identity from subaltern theorists "who treat gender, class, or race as social totalities that are expressive of unitary collective experiences" (719). He instead provides a description of the post-colonial condition in which all personal identity comes into being through political contradiction and contestation, where every individual struggles for an epistemological certitude and a political confidence that can never be taken for granted, that must be validated again and again.

What role does the novel play in Bhabha's social theory? It plays no role – or, more accurately, it plays the same role as any other cultural form. According to Bhabha, there is no telling whether a particular literary genre speaks against power or speaks for it, because all cultural expression does both. Any literary work that attempts to represent modern life is inevitably informed by the inherent "heterogeneity of [the nation's] population" (724). The double narrative movement of the modern nation-state causes any type of cultural expression to be a "liminal signifying space" (724). If liminality suggests disempowerment, it can, on Bhabha's view, equally function as a means of minority self-authorization. In contrast to the all or nothing logic that governs Spivak's thinking about minority identity, for Bhabha the liminal signifying space can be a positive basis for the representation of minority identity. Every cultural expression produces its own liminal signifying space; liminality emerges not through the monolithic domination of minority identity, but through the proliferation of power relations within any community and at any historical moment. The novel, as liminal signifying space, thus "is *internally* marked by the discourses of minorities, the heterogeneous histories of contending peoples, antagonistic authorities and tense locations of cultural difference" (724). Whereas for Spivak the only place for the subaltern who would escape colonization is outside narrative – signified as the unrepresentable, the silent, the invisible – for Bhabha these "tense locations of cultural difference" (the novel but also potentially any other cultural expression) can become "a place from which to speak both of, and as, the minority, the exilic, the marginal and the emergent" (725).

It would be wrong, though, to think that Bhabha's concepts of hybridity and location offer an alternative to post-Marxist ideology by positing social experience as infinitely particular and thus ungeneralizable. Bhabha shares Spivak's skepticism about understanding literature, as Wayne Booth does (see Part I), as accomplishing political pluralism, as making audible a choir of liberated, multicultural voices, each singing the song of their own identity. On Bhabha's view, the "double time" of nationhood is introjected into any and all acts of self-representation. The coherence of any particular minority group is itself a narrative construction. Each group may find this coherence through a shared belief in the particular historical experience that defines it as a subgroup; but Bhabha's point is that any history of minority identity is itself a strategic narrative, one that operates according to the same double ideological imperative that structures the nation-state. The consolidation of minority identity, that is to say, also works through pedagogic discourse and by narrative interpellation. Validated through the displacement of its self-authorization, the narrative of minority identity is no more durable, no less alienated than that of the nation-state: "The subject is graspable only in the passage between telling /told, between 'here' and 'somewhere else,' and in this double scene the very condition of cultural knowledge is the alienation of the subject" (*Location*, 725).

This understanding of the "condition of cultural knowledge" means for Bhabha that the socially privileged are as much in need of authorization as the subaltern – and their discourse likewise registers this anxiety through the creation of liminal spaces. The social difference between the culturally elite and the socially disenfranchised is thus expressed through their respective versions of double narrative: "Both gentleman and slave, with different cultural means and to very different historical ends, demonstrate that forces of social authority and subversion or subalternity may emerge in displaced, even decentered strategies of signification" (721). The slave is defined by the gentleman, but the gentleman is equally defined by the slave – and it is this constitutive relation, socially multiplied, that leads Bhabha to understand liminal space as an element of narrative itself. In one of his most explicitly deconstructive formulations, he argues that that double narrative, "the ambivalence of the nation as a 'narrative' strategy," functions

As an apparatus of symbolic power [that] produces a continual slippage of categories, like sexuality, class affiliation, territorial paranoia, or "cultural difference" in the act of writing the nation. What is displayed in this displacement and repetition of terms is the nation as the measure of the liminality of cultural modernity. (718)

The double narrative of the nation-state's self authorization, its contradictory and self-splitting logic, ultimately defines national identity *as* narration: the state serves "as the measure of the liminality of cultural modernity," because the state homologically creates and enacts this liminality. The modern need to define the state as geography thus produces the condition of knowledge which, according to Bhabha, allows the nation to come into being in and through narrative. This deconstructive understanding of the nation could not be more different from Said's belief in the material base of national identity. The foundational premise of Said's argument, we remember, is that "the actual geographical possession of land is what empire in the final analysis is all about" (*Culture*, 78). For Bhabha, the actual possession of land is completely secondary to the fact that no amount of land will ever provide the nation with the external authorization that it seeks. Land is, on his view, always only a metonymic substitute for the lost transcendental signifier, the divine or royal ground of national authority. The only place for modern authority, according to Bhabha, is the liminal space created in and through narrative, through the "continual slippage" of social categories that makes social identity legible through "writing," through its representation (defined as the "passage between telling / told, between 'here' and 'somewhere else'" [725]). For Bhabha it is the deconstructive play of difference, the move between metaphor (presentness, consolidation, home, the self) and metonymy (the past, fragmentation, away, the other) that is the basis of all representation, the "double scene" that Bhabha calls "the very condition of cultural knowledge."

Bhabha's deconstructive position so thoroughly distinguishes him from the post-Marxist post-colonialists that, in addition to critiquing their view of ideology and their residual materialism, he also attacks their notion of historicism. In offering his theory of the nation as narrative, Bhabha explicitly seeks to "displace the historicism that has dominated discussions of the nation as a cultural force" (718). Through a discussion of an essay by M. M. Bakhtin, Bhabha develops what he means by a narrative rather than an historical understanding of space as place. Bhabha argues that Bakhtin (and we might add Said to this critique) has in fact himself interpellated the modern geographical sense, that Bakhtin's own analysis of novelistic space partakes of the materialist desire to ground identity (in this case generic identity) in the stability of place. In Bhabha's analysis, however, any literary effect that produces the sense of "hereness" is only one part of a narrative process that is irreducibly twofold: every successful literary evocation of hereness is won in and against the struggle against the "somewhere else." The narrative achievement of hereness is itself part of the double operation of narrative, and the representation of liminality, of constructedness, reemerges in these literary works (as we have arguably seen in our own analysis of Said and Spivak) as "displaced, even decentered strategies of signification" (721). To put it another way, if the nineteenth-century English novel is indeed defined by strategies of spatialization, this is not, on Bhabha's view, because the geographical sense successfully imbues novelistic space with ideological meaning, but because "the narrative structure of this *historical* surmounting of the 'ghostly' or the 'double' is seen in the intensification of narrative synchrony as a graphically visible position in space" (720).

The historical surmounting of the ghostly or the double is not, of course, ever accomplished once and for all, but is repeated in and as history. Bhabha believes that the double time of the modern nation-state effectively makes any particular "historical surmounting of the ghostly or the double" a symptom of narrative rather than an explanation for narrative. The structuring binary opposition of narrative can be glossed in a variety of culturally specific terms – such as, for example, the "teleology of progress" vs. the archaic past; spirit vs. body; social cohesion vs. social heterogeneity (719). But the ideological condition of knowledge will give those terms the same value, the value of "displacement and repetition," the value of the slippage between metaphor and metonymy. It is always and forever the "disjunctive time of the nation's modernity" (719) that is expressed through narrative, through the desire for the lost transcendental signifier and the reality of the proliferating, unauthorizable signifier.

Bhabha's theorization of nation as a narrative means that there is no place of epistemological security; any truth claim must be haunted by its own uncertainty. This is why, on his account, attempts to assign political value always collapse into the description of psychological states:

> the subject of modern ideology is split between the iconic image of authority and the movement of the signifier that produces the image, so that the "sign" of the social is condemned to slide ceaselessly from one position to another. It is in this space of liminality, in the "unbearable ordeal of the collapse of certainty" that we encounter once again the narcissistic neuroses of the national discourse with which I began. (725, Bhabha quoting C. Lefort)

The constitutive condition of social liminality, produced by the ahistorical, temporal repetition of signification, means we can have no knowledge of authority outside of our impossible desire to be externally authorized. The attempt at self-authorization, in other words, results in the ceaseless slide of knowledge, and on Bhabha's view the experience of this slide can be the only knowledge there is. The post-colonial theorist thus finds himself in the position of psychoanalyst, studying the affect of narrativization, the emotions produced in the social subject by his or her specific experience of the modern condition of knowledge. Yet notably, even affect emerges in Bhabha's analysis as that which is neatly split by a binary logic that is homological with narrative: the metaphoric drive toward narcissism is upset by self-fragmentation through doubt.

Bhabha offers an interesting account of how certain modern philosophies of knowledge emerge in the attempt to heal this breach, to solve the problem of narrative. He argues, for example, that ethnography gains popularity in the twentieth century precisely because it seeks to find an objective ground for self-authorization. Bhabha points out that the ethnographic belief that the individual can be split in two, can be both participant and observer, is itself a valorization of spatialization. Ethnography attempts to combat the uncertainty of narrativization through a philosophy that conceptualizes the self as spatializable. According to the ethnographer, the self can be split in two at the will of the self. The ethnographer can be both the observer of his own identity and also the identity that is observed. This is, of course, the stance adopted by theorists such as Jane Tompkins (Part V), who believe that their position within ideology does not prevent them from achieving an objective view of the historical workings of ideology.

The ethnographic belief in the " 'capacity for indefinite self-objectification,' " " 'for projecting outside itself ever-diminishing fragments of itself' " (726, Bhabha, quoting Claude Lévi-Strauss) might also be interestingly related to Spivak's psychoanalytically inflected paradigms of imperial power. The ethnographer's participation in his own self-objectification makes him less absolutely different from the colonial subjects he seeks to "world." The pursuit of self-othering, the desire to establish an impersonal relation with oneself, places the ethnographer on a continuum, somewhere between Spivak's colonial, narcissist self who projects its own identity on to the Other and Spivak's native self who will not be Othered. But of course, for Bhabha the ethnographer does not succeed in solving the problem of narrative; he simply reinscribes its operation: the space of objectification will not hold, upset by the "unbearable ordeal of the collapse of certainty" (725).

Does Bhabha believe that any type of political progress can take place within the nation as narrative? Bhabha ends his essay by addressing this question. And he mounts this answer through an analysis of specific instances of minority discourse. This discourse uses its "place to speak both of and as a minority," by critiquing the nation-state where it is most vulnerable: by throwing into question the pedagogic definition of national identity, its appeal to a defining past. From the subaltern perspective – from the point of view of the immigrant, the colonized, the ex-slave – this "native" historical past can never be one's own. The construction of national history that is carried forward marginalizes, denigrates, or omits the history of these minorities. Women and minorities thus enter into the discourse of nationhood through what Bhabha (after Derrida) calls supplementation. The supplement is that which does not " 'add up' " but which "may disturb the calculation" (729). "The supplementary strategy interrupts the successive seriality of the narrative of plurals and pluralism by radically changing their mode of articulation" (729). The result, however, is not a new calculation, not an escape from narrative, but the reconfirmation of the tentativeness of the initial calculation: "the supplementary antagonizes the implicit power to generalize, to produce the sociological solidity" (729) that is required for historical/pedagogic assertion.

While Bhabha believes that minority supplementation can lead to an acute experience of psychic alienation and social liminality (and in this regard his theory is interestingly compared to Barbara Johnson's account of female, African American identity in Part III), he does not imagine that this self-consciousness has the power to restructure knowledge, to end narrative: "The questioning of the supplement is not a repetitive rhetoric of the 'end' of society but a meditation on the disposition of space and time from which the narrative of the nation must *begin*" (730). The power of supplementarity may "renegotiate" the "times, terms and traditions through which we turn our uncertain, passing contemporaneity into the signs of history" (730). In other words, the pedagogy of the nation may ultimately be changed; what counts as a national inheritance or tradition will be modified by such renegotiation, but the structure of narrative will itself remain in place.

Bhabha thus finds in cultural expressions such as the *Handsworth Songs* a discourse of "living perplexity" (731), an acute expression of the psychological experience of living within the modern condition of narrative. Bhabha argues that this 1986 film, which contains documentary footage of the 1985 riots in Birmingham and London, presents subaltern groups whose experiences of social discrimination make it impossible for them to "celebrate the monumentality of historicist memory, the sociological totality of society, or the homogeneity of cultural experience" (731). But their identity is also not defined merely in negative relation to pedagogic discourse. For their own self-authorization, minorities must attempt to write their own narrative of the nation. And in doing so they, too, confront the double narrative of the nation; they must ask themselves, "How does one encounter the past as an anteriority that continually introduces an otherness or alterity into the present? How does one then narrate the present as a form of contemporaneity that is neither punctual nor synchronous?" (731). It may be, Bhabha implies, that a new answer will be found to this question, one that will put an end to knowledge as narrative. But in the meantime, the best that can be achieved is self-consciousness about our collective psychological condition, manifested in the specific locations of our "living perplexity."

FURTHER READING

Anderson, Benedict. *Imagined Communities: Reflections on the Origins and Spread of Nationalism.* 1983. New York: Verso, 1991.

Appiah, Kwame Anthony. "Is the Post- in Postmodernism the Post- in Postcolonial?" *Critical Inquiry* 17 (1991): 336–51.

Bhabha, Homi K, ed. *Nation and Narration.* New York: Routledge, 1990.

Brantlinger, Patrick. *Rule of Darkness: British Literature and Imperialism, 1830–1914.* Ithaca, NY: Cornell University Press, 1988.

Davis, Leith, Ian Duncan, and Janet Sorensen, eds. *Scotland and the Borders of Romanticism.* New York: Cambridge University Press, 2004.

Eagleton, Terry, Fredric Jameson, and Edward W. Said. *Nationalism, Colonialism, and Literature.* Minneapolis: University of Minnesota Press, 1990.

Fanon, Frantz. *Black Skin, White Masks.* 1952. Trans. Charles Lam Markmann. New York: Grove Press, 1965.

Gilroy, Paul. *The Black Atlantic: Modernity and Double Consciousness.* Cambridge, MA: Harvard University Press, 1993.

Hussein, Abdirahman A. *Edward Said: Criticism and Society.* New York: Verso, 2002.

McClintock, Anne. *Imperial Leather: Race, Gender and Sexuality in the Colonial Conquest.* New York: Routledge, 1995.

Said, Edward W. *Orientalism.* New York: Random House, 1978.

Spivak, Gayatri Chakravorty. "Can the Subaltern Speak?" In *Marxism and the Interpretation of Culture,* ed. Cary Nelson and Lawrence Grossberg. Urbana: University of Illinois Press, 1988, 271–313.

—— *In Other Worlds: Essays in Cultural Politics.* New York: Routledge, 1988.

Williams, Raymond. *The Country and the City.* New York: Oxford University Press, 1973.

Young, Robert. *White Mythologies: Writing History and the West.* New York: Routledge, 1990.

32

Three Women's Texts and a Critique of Imperialism

Gayatri Chakravorty Spivak

Gayatri Chakrovorty Spivak (b. 1942)

Gayatri Chakrovorty Spivak was born in Calcutta five years before India's independence from British colonial rule. She attended the Presidency College of the University of Calcutta and Cornell University, where she received her Ph.D. in 1967. Spivak has taught at the University of Iowa, the University of Texas, and the University of Pittsburgh; she is currently Avalon Foundation Professor of the Humanities at Columbia University, where she is also the Director of the Center for Comparative Literature and Society. Spivak first garnered attention with her translation of and introduction to Jacques Derrida's *Of Grammatology* (1976). She has since translated and written critical introductions to books by Bengali novelists Mahasweta Devi and Ramproshad Se. Spivak's books include *In Other Worlds: Essays in Cultural Politics* (1987); *Outside In the Teaching Machine* (1993); *Critique of Postcolonial Reason: Toward a History of the Vanishing Present* (1999); *Death of a Discipline* (2003); and *Other Asias* (2005). Significant essays include "Can the Subaltern Speak?" (1988) and the piece reprinted here, "Three Women's Texts and a Critique of Imperialism" (1985).

From *Critical Inquiry* 12, Autumn 1985, pp. 243–61. Copyright © 1985 by Gayatri Chakravorty Spivak. Reprinted by permission of Gayatri Chakravorty Spivak.

It should not be possible to read nineteenth-century British literature without remembering that imperialism, understood as England's social mission, was a crucial part of the cultural representation of England to the English. The role of literature in the production of cultural representation should not be ignored. These two obvious "facts" continue to be disregarded in the reading of nineteenth-century British literature. This itself attests to the continuing success of the imperialist project, displaced and dispersed into more modern forms.

If these "facts" were remembered, not only in the study of British literature but in the study of the literatures of the European colonizing cultures of the great age of imperialism, we would produce a narrative, in literary history, of the "worlding" of what is now called "the Third World." To consider the Third World as distant cultures, exploited but with rich intact literary heritages waiting to be recovered, interpreted, and curricularized in English translation fosters the emergence of "the Third World" as a signifier that allows us to forget that "worlding," even as it expands the empire of the literary discipline.[1]

It seems particularly unfortunate when the emergent perspective of feminist criticism reproduces the axioms of imperialism. A basically isolationist admiration for the literature of the female subject in Europe and Anglo-America establishes the high feminist norm. It is supported and operated by an information-retrieval approach to "Third World" literature which often employs a deliberately "nontheoretical" methodology with self-conscious rectitude.

In this essay, I will attempt to examine the operation of the "worlding" of what is today "the Third World" by what has become a cult text of feminism: *Jane Eyre*.[2] I plot the novel's reach and grasp, and locate its structural motors. I read *Wide Sargasso Sea* as *Jane Eyre*'s reinscription and *Frankenstein* as an analysis – even a deconstruction – of a "worlding" such as *Jane Eyre*'s.[3]

I need hardly mention that the object of my investigation is the printed book, not its "author." To make such a distinction is, of course, to ignore the lessons of deconstruction. A deconstructive critical approach would loosen the binding of the book, undo the opposition between verbal text and the bio-graphy of the named subject "Charlotte Brontë," and see the two as each other's "scene of writing." In such a reading, the life that writes itself as "my life" is as much a production in psychosocial space (other names can be found) as the book that is written by the holder of that named life – a book that is then consigned to what *is* most often recognized as genuinely "social": the world of publication and distribution.[4] To touch Brontë's "life" in such a way, however, would be too risky here. We must rather strategically take shelter in an essentialism which, not wishing to lose the important advantages won by U.S. mainstream feminism, will continue to honor the suspect binary oppositions – book and author, individual and history – and start with an assurance of the following sort: my readings here do not seek to undermine the excellence of the individual artist. If even minimally successful, the readings will incite a degree of rage against the imperialist narrativization of history, that it should produce so abject a script for her. I provide these assurances to allow myself some room to situate feminist individualism in its historical determination rather than simply to canonize it as feminism as such.

Sympathetic U.S. feminists have remarked that I do not do justice to Jane Eyre's subjectivity. A word of explanation is perhaps in order. The broad strokes of my presuppositions are that what is at stake, for feminist individualism in the age of imperialism, is precisely the making of human beings, the constitution and "interpellation" of the subject not only as individual but as "individualist."[5] This stake is represented on two registers: childbearing and soul making. The first is domestic-society-through-sexual-repro cathected as "companionate love"; the second is the imperialist project cathected as civil-society-through-social-mission. As the female individualist, not-quite/not-male, articulates herself in shifting relationship to what is at stake, the "native female" as such (*within* discourse, *as* a signifier) is excluded from any share in this emerging norm.[6] If we read this account from an isolationist perspective in a "metropolitan" context, we see nothing there but the psychobiography of the militant female subject. In a reading such as mine, in contrast, the effort is to wrench oneself away from the mesmerizing focus of the "subject-constitution" of the female individualist.

To develop further the notion that my stance need not be an accusing one, I will refer to a passage from Roberto Fernández Retamar's "Caliban."[7] José Enrique Rodó had argued in 1900 that the model for the Latin American intellectual in relationship to Europe could be Shakespeare's Ariel.[8] In 1971 Retamar, denying the possibility of an identifiable "Latin American Culture," recast the model as Caliban. Not surprisingly, this powerful exchange still excludes any specific consideration of the civilizations of the Maya, the Aztecs, the Incas, or the smaller nations of what is now called Latin America. Let us note carefully that, at this stage of my argument, this "conversation" between Europe and Latin America (without a specific consideration of the political economy of the "worlding" of the "native") provides a sufficient thematic description of our attempt to confront the ethnocentric and reverse-ethnocentric benevolent double bind (that is, considering the "native" as object for enthusiastic information-retrieval and thus denying its own "worlding") that I sketched in my opening paragraphs.

In a moving passage in "Caliban," Retamar locates both Caliban and Ariel in the postcolonial intellectual:

> There is no real Ariel-Caliban polarity: both are slaves in the hands of Prospero, the foreign magician. But Caliban is the rude and unconquerable master of the island, while Ariel, a creature of the air, although also a child of the isle, is the intellectual.

> The deformed Caliban – enslaved, robbed of his island, and taught the language by Prospero – rebukes him thus: "You taught me language, and my profit on't / Is, I know how to curse." ["C," pp. 28, 11]

As we attempt to unlearn our so-called privilege as Ariel and "seek from [a certain] Caliban the honor of a place in his rebellious and glorious ranks," we do not ask that our students and colleagues should emulate us but that they should attend to us ("C," p. 72). If, however, we are driven by a nostalgia for lost origins, we too run the risk of effacing the "native" and stepping forth as "the real Caliban," of forgetting that he is a name in a play, an inaccessible blankness circumscribed by an interpretable text.[9] The stagings of Caliban work alongside the narrativization of history: claiming to *be* Caliban legitimizes the very individualism that we must persistently attempt to undermine from within.

Elizabeth Fox-Genovese, in an article on history and women's history, shows us how to define the historical moment of feminism in the West in terms of female access to individualism.[10] The battle for female individualism plays itself out within the larger theater of the establishment of meritocratic individualism, indexed in the aesthetic field by the ideology of "the creative imagination." Fox-Genovese's presupposition will guide us into the beautifully orchestrated opening of *Jane Eyre.*

It is a scene of the marginalization and privatization of the protagonist: "There was no possibility of taking a walk that day.... Out-door exercise was now out of the question. I was glad of it," Brontë writes (*JE*, p. 9). The movement continues as Jane breaks the rules of the appropriate topography of withdrawal. The family at the center withdraws into the sanctioned architectural space of the withdrawing room or drawing room; Jane inserts herself – "I slipped in" – into the margin – "A small breakfast-room *adjoined* the drawing room" (*JE*, p. 9; my emphasis).

The manipulation of the domestic inscription of space within the upwardly mobilizing currents of the eighteenth- and nineteenth-century bourgeoisie in England and France is well known. It seems fitting that the place to which Jane withdraws is not only not the withdrawing room but also not the dining room, the sanctioned place of family meals. Nor is it the library, the appropriate place for reading. The breakfast room "contained a book-case" (*JE*, p. 9). As Rudolph Ackerman wrote in his *Repository* (1823), one of the many manuals of taste in circulation in nineteenth-century England, these low bookcases and stands were designed to "contain all the books that may be desired for a sitting-room without reference to the library."[11] Even in this already triply off-center place, "having drawn the red moreen curtain nearly close, I [Jane] was shrined in double retirement" (*JE*, pp. 9–10).

Here in Jane's self-marginalized uniqueness, the reader becomes her accomplice: the reader and Jane are united – both are reading. Yet Jane still preserves her odd privilege, for she continues never quite doing the proper thing in its proper place. She cares little for reading what is *meant* to be read: the "letter-press." *She* reads the pictures. The power of this singular hermeneutics is precisely that it can make the outside inside. "At intervals, while turning over the leaves of my book, I studied the aspect of that winter afternoon." Under "the clear panes of glass," the rain no longer penetrates, "the drear November day" is rather a one-dimensional "aspect" to be "studied," not decoded like the "letter-press" but, like pictures, deciphered by the unique creative imagination of the marginal individualist (*JE*, p. 10).

Before following the track of this unique imagination, let us consider the suggestion that the progress of *Jane Eyre* can be charted through a sequential arrangement of the family/counter-family dyad. In the novel, we encounter, first, the Reeds as the legal family and Jane, the late Mr. Reed's sister's daughter, as the representative of a near incestuous counter-family; second, the Brocklehursts, who run the school Jane is sent to, as the legal family and Jane, Miss Temple, and Helen Burns as a counter-family that falls short because it is only a community of women; third, Rochester and the mad Mrs. Rochester as the legal family and Jane and Rochester as the illicit counter-family. Other items may be added to the thematic chain in this sequence: Rochester and Céline Varens as structurally functional counter-family; Rochester and Blanche Ingram as dissimulation of legality – and so on. It is during this sequence that Jane is moved from the counter-family to the family-in-law. In the next sequence, it is Jane who restores full family status to the as-yet-incomplete community of siblings, the Riverses. The final sequence of the book is a *community of families*, with Jane, Rochester, and their children at the center.

In terms of the narrative energy of the novel, how is Jane moved from the place of the counter-family to the family-in-law? It is the active ideology of imperialism that provides the discursive field.

(My working definition of "discursive field" must assume the existence of discrete "systems of signs" at hand in the socius, each based on a specific axiomatics. I am identifying these systems as discursive fields. "Imperialism as social mission" generates the possibility of one such axiomatics. How the individual artist taps the discursive field at hand with a sure touch, if not with transhistorical clairvoyance, in order to make the narrative structure move I hope to demonstrate through the following example. It is crucial that we extend our analysis of this example beyond the minimal diagnosis of "racism.")

Let us consider the figure of Bertha Mason, a figure produced by the axiomatics of imperialism. Through Bertha Mason, the white Jamaican Creole, Brontë renders the human/animal frontier as acceptably indeterminate, so that a good greater than the letter of the Law can be broached. Here is the celebrated passage, given in the voice of Jane:

> In the deep shade, at the further end of the room, a figure ran backwards and forwards. What it was, whether beast or human being, one could not…tell: it grovelled, seemingly, on all fours; it snatched and growled like some strange wild animal: but it was covered with clothing, and a quantity of dark, grizzled hair, wild as a mane, hid its head and face. [*JE*, p. 295]

In a matching passage, given in the voice of Rochester speaking *to* Jane, Brontë presents the imperative for a shift beyond the Law as divine injunction rather than human motive. In the terms of my essay, we might say that this is the register not of mere marriage or sexual reproduction but of Europe and its not-yet-human Other, of soul making. The field of imperial conquest is here inscribed as Hell:

> "One night I had been awakened by her yells…it was a fiery West Indian night.…
>
> "'This life,' said I at last, 'is hell! – this is the air – those are the sounds of the bottomless pit! *I have a right* to deliver myself from it if I can.…Let me break away, and go home to God!'…
>
> "A wind fresh from Europe blew over the ocean and rushed through the open casement: the storm broke, streamed, thundered, blazed, and the air grew pure.…It was true Wisdom that consoled me in that hour, and showed me the right path.…
>
> "The sweet wind from Europe was still whispering in the refreshed leaves, and the Atlantic was thundering in glorious liberty.…
>
> "'Go,' said Hope, 'and live again in Europe.…You have done all that God and Humanity require of you.'" [*JE*, pp. 310–11; my emphasis]

It is the unquestioned ideology of imperialist axiomatics, then, that conditions Jane's move from the counter-family set to the set of the family-in-law. Marxist critics such as Terry Eagleton have seen this only in terms of the ambiguous *class* position of the governess.[12] Sandra Gilbert and Susan Gubar, on the other hand, have seen Bertha Mason only in psychological terms, as Jane's dark double.[13]

I will not enter the critical debates that offer themselves here. Instead, I will develop the suggestion that nineteenth-century feminist individualism could conceive of a "greater" project than access to the closed circle of the nuclear family. This is the project of soul making beyond "mere" sexual reproduction. Here the native "subject" is not almost an animal but rather the object of what might be termed the terrorism of the categorical imperative.

I am using "Kant" in this essay as a metonym for the most flexible ethical moment in the European eighteenth century. Kant words the categorical imperative, conceived as the universal moral law given by pure reason, in this way: "In all creation every thing one chooses and over which one has any power, may be used *merely as means*; man alone, and with him every rational creature, is an *end in himself*." It is thus a moving displacement of Christian ethics from religion to philosophy. As Kant writes: "With this agrees very well the possibility of such a command as: *Love God above everything, and thy neighbor as thyself*. For as a command it requires respect for a law which *commands love* and does not leave it to our own arbitrary choice to make this our principle."[14]

The "categorical" in Kant cannot be adequately represented in determinately grounded action. The dangerous transformative power of philosophy, however, is that its formal subtlety can be travestied in the service of the state. Such a travesty in the case of the categorical imperative can justify the imperialist project by producing the following formula: *make* the heathen into a human so that he can be treated as an end in himself.[15] This project is presented as a sort of tangent in *Jane Eyre*, a tangent that escapes the closed circle of the *narrative* conclusion. The tangent narrative is the story of St. John Rivers, who is granted the important task of concluding the *text*.

At the novel's end, the *allegorical* language of Christian psychobiography – rather than the textually constituted and seemingly *private* grammar of the creative imagination which we noted in the novel's opening – marks the inaccessibility of the imperialist project as such to the nascent "feminist" scenario. The concluding passage of *Jane Eyre* places St. John Rivers within the fold of *Pilgrim's Progress*. Eagleton pays no attention to this but accepts the novel's ideological lexicon, which establishes St. John Rivers' heroism by identifying a life in Calcutta with an unquestioning choice of death. Gilbert and Gubar, by calling *Jane Eyre* "Plain Jane's progress," see the novel as simply replacing the male protagonist with the female. They do not notice the distance between sexual reproduction and soul making, both actualized by the unquestioned idiom of imperialist presuppositions evident in the last part of *Jane Eyre*:

> Firm, faithful, and devoted, full of energy, and zeal, and truth, [St. John Rivers] labours for his race.... His is the sternness of the warrior Greatheart, who guards his pilgrim convoy from the onslaught of Apollyon.... His is the ambition of the high master-spirit[s] ... who stand without fault before the throne of God; who share the last mighty victories of the Lamb; who are called, and chosen, and faithful. [*JE*, p. 455]

Earlier in the novel, St. John Rivers himself justifies the project. "My vocation? My great work?... My hopes of being numbered in the band who have merged all ambitions in the glorious one of bettering their race – of carrying knowledge into the realms of ignorance – of substituting peace for war – freedom for bondage – religion for supersti- tion – the hope of heaven for the fear of hell?" (*JE*, p. 376). Imperialism and its territorial and subject-constituting project are a violent deconstruction of these oppositions.

When Jean Rhys, born on the Caribbean island of Dominica, read *Jane Eyre* as a child, she was moved by Bertha Mason: "I thought I'd try to write her a life."[16] *Wide Sargasso Sea*, the slim novel published in 1965, at the end of Rhys' long career, is that "life."

I have suggested that Bertha's function in *Jane Eyre* is to render indeterminate the boundary between human and animal and thereby to weaken her entitlement under the spirit if not the letter of the Law. When Rhys rewrites the scene in *Jane Eyre* where Jane hears "a snarling, snatching sound, almost like a dog quarrelling" and then encounters a bleeding Richard Mason (*JE*, p. 210), she keeps Bertha's humanity, indeed her sanity as critic of imperialism, intact. Grace Poole, another character originally in *Jane Eyre*, describes the incident to Bertha in *Wide Sargasso Sea*: "So you don't remember that you attacked this gentleman with a knife? ... I didn't hear all he said except 'I cannot interfere legally between yourself and your husband'. It was when he said 'legally' that you flew at him'" (*WSS*, p. 150). In Rhys' retelling, it is the dissimulation that Bertha discerns in the word "legally" – not an innate bestiality – that prompts her violent reaction.

In the figure of Antoinette, whom in *Wide Sargasso Sea* Rochester violently renames Bertha, Rhys suggests that so intimate a thing as personal and human identity might be determined by the politics of imperialism. Antoinette, as a white Creole child growing up at the time of emancipation in Jamaica, is caught between the English imperialist and the black native. In recounting Antoinette's development, Rhys reinscribes some thematics of Narcissus.

There are, noticeably, many images of mirroring in the text. I will quote one from the first section. In this passage, Tia is the little black servant girl who is Antoinette's close companion: "We had eaten the same food, slept side by side, bathed in the same river. As I ran, I thought, I will live with Tia and I will be like her.... When I was close I saw the jagged stone in her hand but I did not see her throw it.... We stared at each other, blood on my face, tears on hers. It was as if I saw myself. Like in a looking glass" (*WSS*, p. 38).

A progressive sequence of dreams reinforces this mirror imagery. In its second occurrence, the dream is partially set in a *hortus conclusus*, or "enclosed garden" – Rhys uses the phrase (*WSS*, p. 50) – a Romance rewriting of the Narcissus topos as the place of encounter with Love.[17] In the enclosed garden, Antoinette encounters not Love but a strange threatening voice that says merely "in here," inviting her into a prison which masquerades as the legalization of love (*WSS*, p. 50).

In Ovid's *Metamorphoses*, Narcissus' madness is disclosed when he recognizes his Other as his self: "Iste ego sum."[18] Rhys makes Antoinette see her *self* as her Other, Brontë's Bertha. In the last section of *Wide Sargasso Sea*, Antoinette acts out *Jane Eyre's* conclusion and recognizes herself as the so-called ghost in Thornfield Hall: "I went into the hall again with the tall candle in my hand. It was then that I saw her – the ghost. The woman with streaming hair. She was surrounded by a gilt frame but I knew her" (*WSS*, p. 154). The gilt frame encloses a mirror: as Narcissus' pool reflects the selfed Other, so this "pool" reflects the Othered self. Here the dream sequence ends, with an invocation of none other than Tia, the Other that could not be selfed, because the fracture of imperialism rather than the Ovidian pool intervened. (I will return to this difficult point.) "That was the third time I had my dream, and it ended.... I called 'Tia' and jumped and woke" (*WSS*, p. 155). It is now, at the very end of the book, that Antoinette/Bertha can say: "Now at last I know why I was brought here and what I have to do"

(*WSS*, pp. 155–56). We can read this as her having been brought into the England of Brontë's novel: "This cardboard house" – a book between cardboard covers – "where I walk at night is not England" (*WSS*, p. 148). In this fictive England, she must play out her role, act out the transformation of her "self" into that fictive Other, set fire to the house and kill herself, so that Jane Eyre can become the feminist individualist heroine of British fiction. I must read this as an allegory of the general epistemic violence of imperialism, the construction of a self-immolating colonial subject for the glorification of the social mission of the colonizer. At least Rhys sees to it that the woman from the colonies is not sacrificed as an insane animal for her sister's consolation.

Critics have remarked that *Wide Sargasso Sea* treats the Rochester character with understanding and sympathy.[19] Indeed, he narrates the entire middle section of the book. Rhys makes it clear that he is a victim of the patriarchal inheritance law of entailment rather than of a father's natural preference for the firstborn: in *Wide Sargasso Sea*, Rochester's situation is clearly that of a younger son dispatched to the colonies to buy an heiress. If in the case of Antoinette and her identity, Rhys utilizes the thematics of Narcissus, in the case of Rochester and his patrimony, she touches on the thematics of Oedipus. (In this she has her finger on our "historical moment." If, in the nineteenth century, subject-constitution is represented as childbearing and soul making, in the twentieth century psychoanalysis allows the West to plot the itinerary of the subject from Narcissus [the "imaginary"] to Oedipus [the "symbolic"]. This subject, however, is the normative male subject. In Rhys' reinscription of these themes, divided between the female and the male protagonist, feminism and a critique of imperialism become complicit.)

In place of the "wind from Europe" scene, Rhys substitutes the scenario of a suppressed letter to a father, a letter which would be the "correct" explanation of the tragedy of the book.[20] "I thought about the letter which should have been written to England a week ago. Dear Father..." (*WSS*, p. 57). This is the first instance: the letter not written. Shortly afterward:

> Dear Father. The thirty thousand pounds have been paid to me without question or condition. No provision made for her (that must be seen to)....I will never be a disgrace to you or to my dear brother the son you love. No begging letters, no mean requests. None of the furtive shabby manoeuvres of a younger son. I have sold my soul or you have sold it, and after all is it such a bad bargain? The girl is thought to be beautiful, she is beautiful. And yet...[*WSS*, p. 59]

This is the second instance: the letter not sent. The formal letter is uninteresting; I will quote only a part of it:

> Dear Father, we have arrived from Jamaica after an uncomfortable few days. This little estate in the Windward Islands is part of the family property and Antoinette is much attached to it....All is well and has gone according to your plans and wishes. I dealt of course with Richard Mason....He seemed to become attached to me and trusted me completely. This place is very beautiful but my illness has left me too exhausted to appreciate it fully. I will write again in a few days' time. [*WSS*, p. 63]

And so on.

Rhys' version of the Oedipal exchange is ironic, not a closed circle. We cannot know if the letter actually reaches its destination. "I wondered how they got their letters posted," the Rochester figure muses. "I folded mine and put it into a drawer of the desk.... There are blanks in my mind that cannot be filled up" (*WSS*, p. 64). It is as if the text presses us to note the analogy between letter and mind.

Rhys denies to Brontë's Rochester the one thing that is supposed to be secured in the Oedipal relay: the Name of the Father, or the patronymic. In *Wide Sargasso Sea*, the character corresponding to Rochester has no name. His writing of the final version of the letter to his father is supervised, in fact, by an image of the *loss* of the patronymic: "There was a crude bookshelf made of three shingles strung together over the desk and I looked at the books, Byron's poems, novels by Sir Walter Scott, *Confessions of an Opium Eater*...and on the last shelf, *Life and Letters of*...The rest was eaten away" (*WSS*, p. 63).

Wide Sargasso Sea marks with uncanny clarity the limits of its own discourse in Christophine, Antoinette's black nurse. We may perhaps surmise the distance between *Jane Eyre* and *Wide Sargasso Sea* by remarking that Christophine's unfinished story is the tangent to the latter narrative, as St. John Rivers' story is to the former. Christophine is not a native of Jamaica; she is from Martinique. Taxonomically, she belongs to the category of the good servant rather than that of the pure native. But within these borders, Rhys creates a powerfully suggestive figure.

Christophine is the first interpreter and named speaking subject in the text. "The Jamaican ladies had never approved of my mother, 'because she pretty like pretty self' Christophine said," we read in the book's opening paragraph (*WSS*, p. 15). I have taught this book five times, once in France, once to students who had worked on the book with the well-known Caribbean novelist Wilson Harris, and once at a prestigious institute where the majority of the students were faculty from other universities. It is part of the political argument I am making that all these students blithely stepped over this paragraph without asking or knowing what Christophine's patois, so-called incorrect English, might mean.

Christophine is, of course, a commodified person. "'She was your father's wedding present to me'" explains Antoinette's mother, "'one of his presents'" (*WSS*, p. 18). Yet Rhys assigns her some crucial functions in the text. It is Christophine who judges that black ritual practices are culture-specific and cannot be used by whites as cheap remedies for social evils, such as Rochester's lack of love for Antoinette. Most important, it is Christophine alone whom Rhys allows to offer a hard analysis of Rochester's actions, to challenge him in a face-to-face encounter. The entire extended passage is worthy of comment. I quote a brief extract:

> "She is Creole girl, and she have the sun in her. Tell the truth now. She don't come to your house in this place England they tell me about, she don't come to your beautiful house to beg you to marry with her. No, it's you come all the long way to her house – it's you beg her to marry. And she love you and she give you all she have. Now you say you don't love her and you break her up. What you do with her money, eh?" [And then Rochester, the white man, comments silently to himself] Her voice was still quiet but with a hiss in it when she said "money." [*WSS*, p. 130]

Her analysis is powerful enough for the white man to be afraid: "I no longer felt dazed, tired, half hypnotized, but alert and wary, ready to defend myself" (*WSS*, p. 130).

Rhys does not, however, romanticize individual heroics on the part of the oppressed. When the Man refers to the forces of Law and Order, Christophine recognizes their power. This exposure of civil inequality is emphasized by the fact that, just before the Man's successful threat, Christophine had invoked the emancipation of slaves in Jamaica by proclaiming: "No chain gang, no tread machine, no dark jail either. This is free country and I am free woman" (*WSS*, p. 131).

As I mentioned above, Christophine is tangential to this narrative. She cannot be contained by a novel which rewrites a canonical English text within the European novelistic tradition in the interest of the white Creole rather than the native. No perspective *critical* of imperialism can turn the Other into a self, because the project of imperialism has always already historically refracted what might have been the absolutely Other into a domesticated Other that consolidates the imperialist self.[21] The Caliban of Retamar, caught between Europe and Latin America, reflects this predicament. We can read Rhys' reinscription of Narcissus as a thematization of the same problematic.

Of course, we cannot know Jean Rhys' feelings in the matter. We can, however, look at the scene of Christophine's inscription in the text. Immediately after the exchange between her and the Man, well before the conclusion, she is simply driven out of the story, with neither narrative nor characterological explanation or justice. " 'Read and write I don't know. Other things I know.' She walked away without looking back" (*WSS*, p. 133).

Indeed, if Rhys rewrites the madwoman's attack on the Man by underlining of the misuse of "legality," she cannot deal with the passage that corresponds to St. John Rivers' own justification of his martyrdom, for it has been displaced into the current idiom of modernization and development. Attempts to construct the "Third World Woman" as a signifier remind us that the hegemonic definition of literature is itself caught within the history of imperialism. A full literary reinscription cannot easily flourish in the imperialist fracture or discontinuity, covered over by an alien legal system masquerading as Law as such, an alien ideology established as only Truth, and a set of human sciences busy establishing the "native" as self-consolidating Other.

In the Indian case at least, it would be difficult to find an ideological clue to the planned epistemic violence of imperialism merely by rearranging curricula or syllabi within existing norms of literary pedagogy. For a later period of imperialism – when the constituted colonial subject has firmly taken hold – straightforward experiments of comparison can be undertaken, say, between the functionally witless India of *Mrs. Dalloway*, on the one hand, and literary texts produced in India in the 1920s, on the other. But the first half of the nineteenth century resists questioning through literature or literary criticism in the narrow sense, because both are implicated in the project of producing Ariel. To reopen the fracture without succumbing to a nostalgia for lost origins, the literary critic must turn to the archives of imperial governance.

In conclusion, I shall look briefly at Mary Shelley's *Frankenstein*, a text of nascent feminism that remains cryptic, I think, simply because it does not speak the language of feminist individualism which we have come to hail as the language of high feminism within English literature. It is interesting that Barbara Johnson's brief study tries to rescue this recalcitrant text for the service of feminist autobiography.[22] Alternatively, George Levine reads *Frankenstein* in the context of the creative imagination and the nature of the hero. He sees the novel as a book about its own writing and about writing itself, a Romantic allegory of reading within which Jane Eyre as unself-conscious critic would fit quite nicely.[23]

I propose to take *Frankenstein* out of this arena and focus on it in terms of that sense of English cultural identity which I invoked at the opening of this essay. Within that focus we are obliged to admit that, although *Frankenstein* is ostensibly about the origin and evolution of man in society, it does not deploy the axiomatics of imperialism.

Let me say at once that there is plenty of incidental imperialist sentiment in *Frankenstein*. My point, within the argument of this essay, is that the discursive field of imperialism does not produce unquestioned ideological correlatives for the narrative structuring of the book. The discourse of imperialism surfaces in a curiously powerful way in Shelley's novel, and I will later discuss the moment at which it emerges.

Frankenstein is not a battleground of male and female individualism articulated in terms of sexual reproduction (family and female) and social subject-production (race and male). That binary opposition is undone in Victor Frankenstein's laboratory – an artificial womb where both projects are undertaken simultaneously, though the terms are never openly spelled out. Frankenstein's apparent antagonist is God himself as Maker of Man, but his real competitor is also woman as the maker of children. It is not just that his dream of the death of mother and bride and the actual death of his bride are associated with the visit of his monstrous homoerotic "son" to his bed. On a much more overt level, the monster is a bodied "corpse," unnatural because bereft of a determinable childhood: "No father had watched my infant days, no mother had blessed me with smiles and caresses; or if they had, all my past was now a blot, a blind vacancy in which I distinguished nothing" (*F*, pp. 57, 115). It is Frankenstein's own ambiguous and miscued understanding of the real motive for the monster's vengefulness that reveals his own competition with woman as maker:

> I created a rational creature and was bound towards him to assure, as far as was in my power, his happiness and well-being. This was my duty, but there was another still paramount to that. My duties towards the beings of my own species had greater claims to my attention because they included a greater proportion of happiness or misery. Urged by this view, I refused, and I did right in refusing, to create a companion for the first creature. [*F*, p. 206]

It is impossible not to notice the accents of transgression inflecting Frankenstein's demolition of his experiment to create the future Eve. Even in the laboratory, the woman-in-the-making is not a bodied corpse but "a human being." The (il)logic of the metaphor bestows on her a prior existence which Frankenstein aborts, rather than an anterior death which he reembodies: "The remains of the half-finished creature, whom I had destroyed, lay scattered on the floor, and I almost felt as if I had mangled the living flesh of a human being" (*F*, p. 163).

In Shelley's view, man's hubris as soul maker both usurps the place of God and attempts – vainly – to sublate woman's physiological prerogative.[24] Indeed, indulging a Freudian fantasy here, I could urge that, if to give and withhold to/from the mother a phallus is *the* male fetish, then to give and withhold to/from the man a womb might be the female fetish.[25] The icon of the sublimated womb in man is surely his productive brain, the box in the head.

GAYATRI CHAKRAVORTY SPIVAK

In the judgment of classical psychoanalysis, the phallic mother exists only by virtue of the castration-anxious son; in *Frankenstein*'s judgment, the hysteric father (Victor Frankenstein gifted with his laboratory – the womb of theoretical reason) cannot produce a daughter. Here the language of racism – the dark side of imperialism understood as social mission – combines with the hysteria of masculism into the idiom of (the withdrawal of) sexual reproduction rather than subject-constitution. The roles of masculine and feminine individualists are hence reversed and displaced. Frankenstein cannot produce a "daughter" because "she might become ten thousand times more malignant than her mate...[and because] one of the first results of those sympathies for which the demon thirsted would be children, and a race of devils would be propagated upon the earth who might make the very existence of the species of man a condition precarious and full of terror" (*F*, p. 158). This particular narrative strand also launches a thoroughgoing critique of the eighteenth-century European discourses on the origin of society through (Western Christian) man. Should I mention that, much like Jean-Jacques Rousseau's remark in his *Confessions*, Frankenstein declares himself to be "by birth a Genevese" (*F*, p. 31)?

In this overly didactic text, Shelley's point is that social engineering should not be based on pure, theoretical, or natural-scientific reason alone, which is her implicit critique of the utilitarian vision of an engineered society. To this end, she presents in the first part of her deliberately schematic story three characters, childhood friends, who seem to represent Kant's three-part conception of the human subject: Victor Frankenstein, the forces of theoretical reason or "natural philosophy"; Henry Clerval, the forces of practical reason or "the moral relations of things"; and Elizabeth Lavenza, that aesthetic judgment – "the aerial creation of the poets" – which, according to Kant, is "a suitable mediating link connecting the realm of the concept of nature and that of the concept of freedom...(which) promotes... *moral* feeling" (*F*, pp. 37, 36).[26]

This three-part subject does not operate harmoniously in *Frankenstein*. That Henry Clerval, associated as he is with practical reason, should have as his "design...to visit India, in the belief that he had in his knowledge of its various languages, and in the views he had taken of its society, the means of materially assisting the progress of European colonization and trade" is proof of this, as well as part of the incidental imperialist sentiment that I speak of above (*F*, pp. 151–52). I should perhaps point out that the language here is entrepreneurial rather than missionary:

> He came to the university with the design of making himself complete master of the Oriental languages, as thus he should open a field for the plan of life he had marked out for himself. Resolved to pursue no inglorious career, he turned his eyes towards the East as affording scope for his spirit of enterprise. The Persian, Arabic, and Sanskrit languages engaged his attention. [*F*, pp. 66–67]

But it is of course Victor Frankenstein, with his strange itinerary of obsession with natural philosophy, who offers the strongest demonstration that the multiple perspectives of the three-part Kantian subject cannot co-operate harmoniously. Frankenstein creates a putative human subject out of natural philosophy alone. According to his own miscued summation: "In a fit of enthusiastic madness I created a rational creature" (*F*, p. 206). It is not at all farfetched to say that Kant's categorical imperative can most easily be mistaken for the hypothetical imperative – a command to ground in cognitive comprehension what can be apprehended only by moral will – by putting natural philosophy in the place of practical reason.

I should hasten to add here that just as readings such as this one do not necessarily accuse Charlotte Brontë the named individual of harboring imperialist sentiments, so also they do not necessarily commend Mary Shelley the named individual for writing a successful Kantian allegory. The most I can say is that it is possible to read these texts, within the frame of imperialism and the Kantian ethical moment, in a politically useful way. Such an approach presupposes that a "disinterested" reading attempts to render transparent the interests of the hegemonic readership. (Other "political" readings – for instance, that the monster is the nascent working class – can also be advanced.)

Frankenstein is built in the established epistolary tradition of multiple frames. At the heart of the multiple frames, the narrative of the monster (as reported by Frankenstein to Robert Walton, who then recounts it in a letter to his sister) is of his almost learning, clandestinely, to be human. It is invariably noticed that the monster reads *Paradise Lost* as true history. What is not so often noticed is that he also reads Plutarch's *Lives*, "the histories of the first founders of the ancient republics," which he compares to "the patriarchal lives of my protectors" (*F*, pp. 123, 124). And his *education* comes through "Volney's *Ruins of Empires*," which purported to be a prefiguration of the French Revolution, published after the event and after the author had rounded off his theory with practice (*F*, p. 113). It is an attempt at an enlightened universal secular, rather than a Eurocentric Christian, history, written from the perspective of a narrator "from below," somewhat like the attempts of Eric Wolf or Peter Worsley in our own time.[27]

This Caliban's education in (universal secular) humanity takes place through the monster's eavesdropping on the instruction of an Ariel – Safie, the Christianized "Arabian" to whom "a residence in Turkey was abhorrent" (*F*, p. 121). In depicting Safie, Shelley uses some commonplaces of eighteenth-century liberalism that are shared by many today: Safie's Muslim father was a victim of (bad) Christian religious prejudice and yet was himself a wily and ungrateful man not as morally refined as her (good) Christian mother. Having tasted the emancipation of woman, Safie could not go home. The confusion between "Turk" and "Arab" has its counterpart in present-day confusion about Turkey and Iran as "Middle Eastern" but not "Arab."

Although we are a far cry here from the unexamined and covert axiomatics of imperialism in *Jane Eyre*, we will gain nothing by celebrating the time-bound pieties that Shelley, as the daughter of two antievangelicals, produces. It is more interesting for us that Shelley differentiates the Other, works at the Caliban/Ariel distinction, and *cannot* make the monster identical with the proper recipient of these lessons. Although he had "heard of the discovery of the American hemisphere and *wept with Safie* over the helpless fate of its original inhabitants," Safie cannot reciprocate his attachment. When she first catches sight of him, "Safie, unable to attend to her friend [Agatha], rushed out of the cottage" (*F*, pp. 114 [my emphasis], 129).

In the taxonomy of characters, the Muslim-Christian Safie belongs with Rhys' Antoinette/Bertha. And indeed, like Christophine the good servant, the subject created by the fiat of natural philosophy is the tangential unresolved moment in *Frankenstein*. The simple suggestion that the monster is human inside but monstrous outside and only provoked into vengefulness is clearly not enough to bear the burden of so great a historical dilemma.

At one moment, in fact, Shelley's Frankenstein does try to tame the monster, to humanize him by bringing him within the circuit of the Law. He "repair[s] to a criminal judge in the town and...relate[s his] history briefly but with firmness" – the first and disinterested version of the narrative of Frankenstein – "marking the dates with accuracy and never deviating into invective or exclamation.... When I had concluded my narration I said, 'This is the being whom I accuse and for whose seizure and punishment I call upon you to exert your whole power. It is your duty as a magistrate'" (F, pp. 189, 190). The sheer social reasonableness of the mundane voice of Shelley's "Genevan magistrate" reminds us that the absolutely Other cannot be selfed, that the monster has "properties" which will not be contained by "proper" measures:

> "I will exert myself [he says], and if it is in my power to seize the monster, be assured that he shall suffer punishment proportionate to his crimes. But I fear, from what you have yourself described to be his properties, that this will prove impracticable; and thus, while every proper measure is pursued, you should make up your mind to disappointment." [F, p. 190]

In the end, as is obvious to most readers, distinctions of human individuality themselves seem to fall away from the novel. Monster, Frankenstein, and Walton seem to become each other's relays. Frankenstein's story comes to an end in death; Walton concludes his own story within the frame of his function as letter writer. In the *narrative* conclusion, he is the natural philosopher who learns from Frankenstein's example. At the end of the *text*, the monster, having confessed his guilt toward his maker and ostensibly intending to immolate himself, is borne away on an ice raft. We do not see the conflagration of his funeral pile – the self-immolation is not consummated in the text: he too cannot be contained by the text. In terms of narrative logic, he is "lost in darkness and distance" (F, p. 211) – these are the last words of the novel – into an existential temporality that is coherent with neither the territorializing individual imagination (as in the opening of *Jane Eyre*) nor the authoritative scenario of Christian psychobiography (as at the end of Brontë's work). The very relationship between sexual reproduction and social subject-production – the dynamic nineteenth-century topos of feminism-in-imperialism – remains problematic within the limits of Shelley's text and, paradoxically, constitutes its strength.

Earlier, I offered a reading of woman as womb holder in *Frankenstein*. I would now suggest that there is a framing woman in the book who is neither tangential, nor encircled, nor yet encircling. "Mrs. Saville," "excellent Margaret," "beloved Sister" are her address and kinship inscriptions (F, pp. 15, 17, 22). She is the occasion, though not the protagonist, of the novel. She is the feminine *subject* rather than the female individualist: she is the irreducible *recipient*-function of the letters that constitute *Frankenstein*. I have commented on the singular appropriative hermeneutics of the reader reading with Jane in the opening pages of *Jane Eyre*. Here the reader must read with Margaret Saville in the crucial sense that she must *intercept* the recipient-function, read the letters *as* recipient, in order for the novel to exist.[28] Margaret Saville does not respond to close the text as frame. The frame is thus simultaneously not a frame, and the monster can step "beyond the text" and be "lost in darkness." Within the allegory of our reading, the place of both the English lady and the unnamable monster are left open by this great flawed text. It is satisfying for a postcolonial reader to consider this a noble resolution for a nineteenth-century English novel. This is all the more striking because, on the anecdotal level, Shelley herself abundantly "identifies" with Victor Frankenstein.[29]

I must myself close with an idea that I cannot establish within the limits of this essay. Earlier I contended that *Wide Sargasso Sea* is necessarily bound by the reach of the European novel. I suggested that, in contradistinction, to reopen the epistemic fracture of imperialism without succumbing to a nostalgia for lost origins, the critic must turn to the archives of imperialist governance. I have not turned to those archives in these pages. In my current work, by way of a modest and inexpert "reading" of "archives," I try to extend, outside of the reach of the European novelistic tradition, the most powerful suggestion in *Wide Sargasso Sea*: that *Jane Eyre* can be read as the orchestration and staging of the self-immolation of Bertha Mason as "good wife." The power of that suggestion remains unclear if we remain insufficiently knowledgeable about the history of the legal manipulation of widow-sacrifice in the entitlement of the British government in India. I would hope that an informed critique of imperialism, granted some attention from readers in the First World, will at least expand the frontiers of the politics of reading.

NOTES

1 My notion of the "worlding of a world" upon what must be assumed to be uninscribed earth is a vulgarization of Martin Heidegger's idea; see "The Origin of the Work of Art," *Poetry, Language, Thought*, trans. Albert Hofstadter (New York, 1977), pp. 17–87.

2 See Charlotte Brontë, *Jane Eyre* (New York, 1960); all further references to this work, abbreviated *JE*, will be included in the text.

3 See Jean Rhys, *Wide Sargasso Sea* (Harmondsworth, 1966); all further references to this work, abbreviated *WSS*, will be included in the text. And see Mary Shelley, *Frankenstein; or, The Modern Prometheus* (New York, 1965); all further references to this work, abbreviated *F*, will be included in the text.

4 I have tried to do this in my essay "Unmaking and Making in *To the Lighthouse*," in *Women and Language in Literature and Society*, ed. Sally McConnell-Ginet, Ruth Borker, and Nelly Furman (New York, 1980), pp. 310–27.

5 As always, I take my formula from Louis Althusser, "Ideology an Ideological State Apparatuses (Notes towards an Investigation)," *"Lenin and Philosophy" and Other Essays*, trans. Ben Brewster (New York, 1971), pp. 127–86. For an acute differentiation between the individual and individualism, see V. N. Vološinov, *Marxism and the Philosophy of Language*, trans. Ladislav Matejka and I. R. Titunik, Studies in Language, vol. 1 (New York, 1973), pp. 93–94 and 152–53. For a "straight" analysis of the roots and ramifications of English "individualism," see C. B. MacPherson, *The Political Theory of Possessive Individualism: Hobbes to Locke* (Oxford, 1962). I am grateful to Jonathan Rée for bringing this book to my attention and for giving a careful reading of all but the very end of the present essay.

6 I am constructing an analogy with Homi Bhabha's powerful notion of "not-quite /not-white" in his "Of Mimicry and Man: The Ambiguity of Colonial Discourse," *October* 28 (Spring 1984): 132. I should also add that I use the word "native" here in reaction to the term "Third World Woman." It cannot, of course, apply with equal historical justice to both the West Indian and the Indian contexts nor to contexts of imperialism by transportation.

7 See Roberto Fernández Retamar, "Caliban: Notes towards a Discussion of Culture in Our America," trans. Lynn Garafola, David Arthur McMurray, and Robert Márquez, *Massachusetts Review* 15 (Winter–Spring 1974): 7–72; all further references to this work, abbreviated "C," will be included in the text.

8 See José Enrique Rodó, *Ariel*, ed. Gordon Brotherston (Cambridge, 1967).

9 For an elaboration of "an inaccessible blankness circumscribed by an interpretable text," see my "Can the Subaltern Speak?" *Marxism and the Interpretation of Culture*, ed. Cary Nelson and Larry Grossberg (Urbana, Ill., 1988), 271–313.

10 See Elizabeth Fox-Genovese, "Placing Women's History in History," *New Left Review* 133 (May–June 1982): 5–29.

11 Rudolph Ackerman, *The Repository of Arts, Literature, Commerce, Manufactures, Fashions, and Politics* (London, 1823), p. 310.

12 See Terry Eagleton, *Myths of Power: A Marxist Study of the Brontës* (London, 1975); this is one of the general presuppositions of his book.

13 See Sandra M. Gilbert and Susan Gubar, *The Madwoman in the Attic: The Woman Writer and the Nineteenth-Century Literary Imagination* (New Haven, Conn., 1979), pp. 360–62.

14 Immanuel Kant, *Critique of Practical Reason, the "Critique of Pure Reason," the "Critique of Practical Reason" and Other Ethical Treatises, the "Critique of Judgement,"* trans. J. M. D. Meiklejohn et al. (Chicago, 1952), pp. 328, 326.

15 I have tried to justify the reduction of sociohistorical problems to formulas or propositions in my essay "Can the Subaltern Speak?" The "travesty" I speak of does not befall the Kantian ethic in its purity as an accident but rather exists within its lineaments as a possible supplement. On the register of the human being as child rather than heathen, my formula can be found, for example, in "What Is Enlightenment?" in Kant, *"Foundations of the Metaphysics of Morals," "What Is Enlightenment?" and a Passage from "The Metaphysics of Morals,"* trans. and ed. Lewis White Beck (Chicago, 1950). I have profited from discussing Kant with Jonathan Rée.

16 Jean Rhys, in an interview with Elizabeth Vreeland, quoted in Nancy Harrison, *An Introduction to the Writing Practice of Jean Rhys: The Novel as Women's Text* (Rutherford, N. J., 1988). This is an excellent, detailed study of Rhys.

17 See Louise Vinge, *The Narcissus Theme in Western European Literature Up to the Early Nineteenth Century*, trans. Robert Dewsnap et al. (Lund, 1967), chap. 5.

18 For a detailed study of this text, see John Brenkman, "Narcissus in the Text," *Georgia Review* 30 (Summer 1976): 293–327.

19 See, e.g., Thomas F. Staley, *Jean Rhys: A Critical Study* (Austin, Tex. 1979), pp. 108–16; it is interesting to note Staley's masculist discomfort with this and his consequent dissatisfaction with Rhys' novel.

20 I have tried to relate castration and suppressed letters in my "The Letter As Cutting Edge," in *Literature and Psychoanalysis; The Question of Reading: Otherwise*, ed. Shoshana Felman (New Haven, Conn., 1981), pp. 208–26.

21 This is the main argument of my "Can the Subaltern Speak?"

22 See Barbara Johnson, "My Monster/My Self," *Diacritics* 12 (Summer 1982): 2–10.

23 See George Levine, *The Realistic Imagination: English Fiction from Frankenstein to Lady Chatterley* (Chicago, 1981), pp. 23–35.

24 Consult the publications of the Feminist International Network for the best overview of the current debate on reproductive technology.

25 For the male fetish, see Sigmund Freud, "Fetishism," *The Standard Edition of the Complete Psychological Works of Sigmund Freud*, ed. and trans. James Strachey et al., 24 vols. (London, 1953–74), 21:152–57. For a more "serious" Freudian study of *Frankenstein*, see Mary Jacobus, "Is There a Woman in This Text?" *New Literary History* 14 (Autumn 1982): 117–41.

My "fantasy" would of course be disproved by the "fact" that it is more difficult for a woman to assume the position of fetishist than for a man; see Mary Ann Doane, "Film and the Masquerade: Theorising the Female Spectator," *Screen* 23 (Sept.–Oct. 1982): 74–87.

26 Kant, *Critique of Judgement*, trans. J. H. Bernard (New York, 1951), p. 39.

27 See [Constantin François Chasseboeuf de Volney], *The Ruins; or, Meditations on the Revolutions of Empires*, trans. pub. (London, 1811). Johannes Fabian has shown us the manipulation of time in "new" secular histories of a similar kind; see *Time and the Other: How Anthropology Makes Its Object* (New York, 1983). See also Eric R. Wolf, *Europe and the People without History* (Berkeley and Los Angeles, 1982), and Peter Worsley, *The Third World*, 2d edn. (Chicago, 1973); I am grateful to Dennis Dworkin for bringing the latter book to my attention. The most striking ignoring of the monster's education through Volney is in Gilbert's otherwise brilliant "Horror's Twin: Mary Shelley's Monstrous Eve," *Feminist Studies* 4 (June 1980): 48–73. Gilbert's essay reflects the absence of race-determinations in a certain sort of feminism. Her present work has most convincingly filled in this gap; see, e.g., her recent piece on H. Rider Haggard's *She* ("Rider Haggard's Heart of Darkness," *Partisan Review* 50, no. 3 [1983]: 444–53).

28 "A letter is always and *a priori* intercepted, ... the 'subjects' are neither the senders nor the receivers of messages.... The letter is constituted ... by its interception" (Jacques Derrida, "Discussion," after Claude Rabant, "Il n'a aucune chance de l'entendre," in *Affranchissement: Du transfert et de la lettre*, ed. René Major [Paris, 1981], p. 106; my translation). Margaret Saville is not made to appropriate the reader's "subject" into the signature of her own "individuality."

29 The most striking "internal evidence" is the admission in the "Author's Introduction" that, after dreaming of the yet-unnamed Victor Frankenstein figure and being terrified (through, yet not quite through, him) by the monster in a scene she later reproduced in Frankenstein's story, Shelley began her tale "on the morrow... with the words 'It was on a dreary night of November'" (*F*, p. xi). Those are the opening words of chapter 5 of the finished book, where Frankenstein begins to recount the actual making of his monster (see *F*, p. 56).

Culture and Imperialism

Edward W. Said

Edward Waid Said (1935–2003)

Born in Jerusalem to a prosperous Palestinian family, Edward Said moved with his family to Egypt after the state of Israel was founded in 1948. Said first came to the United States for preparatory school in 1951, and stayed to study at Princeton University and Harvard University, where he received his doctorate in 1964. A year earlier Said had joined the faculty at Columbia University, where he taught until his death from leukemia. Best known as an advocate of Palestinian rights, Said served as an unaffiliated member of the Palestine National Council (1977 to 1991), and wrote several critical studies, including *The Question of Palestine* (1979) and *End of the Peace Process: Oslo and After* (2000). A pianist and opera critic, Said co-founded the West-Eastern Divan Orchestra with Israeli conductor Daniel Barenboim, with whom he also wrote *Parallels and Paradoxes: Explorations in Music and Society* (2002). Said's honors include election to the American Philosophical Society and fellowships from the Guggenheim Foundation, the National Endowment for the Humanities, and the National Humanities Center. His books include *Beginnings:*

Intention and Method (1975); Orientalism (1978); Covering Islam: How the Media and the Experts Determine How We See the Rest of the World (1981); The World, the Text, and the Critic (1983); Culture And Imperialism (1993); Politics Of Dispossession (1994); Out Of Place: A Memoir (1999); Reflections on Exile and Other Essays (2001); and Humanism and Democratic Criticism (2004).

Consolidated Vision

Every novelist and every critic or theorist of the European novel notes its institutional character. The novel is fundamentally tied to bourgeois society; in Charles Morazé's phrase, it accompanies and indeed is a part of the conquest of Western society by what he calls *les bourgeois conquérants*. No less significantly, the novel is inaugurated in England by *Robinson Crusoe*, a work whose protagonist is the founder of a new world, which he rules and reclaims for Christianity and England. True, whereas Crusoe is explicitly enabled by an ideology of overseas expansion – directly connected in style and form to the narratives of sixteenth- and seventeenth-century exploration voyages that laid the foundations of the great colonial empires – the major novels that come after Defoe, and even Defoe's later works, seem not to be single-mindedly compelled by the exciting overseas prospects. *Captain Singleton* is the story of a widely travelled pirate in India and Africa, and *Moll Flanders* is shaped by the possibility in the New World of the heroine's climactic redemption from a life of crime, but Fielding, Richardson, Smollett, and Sterne do not connect their narratives so directly to the act of accumulating riches and territories abroad.

These novelists do, however, situate their work in and derive it from a carefully surveyed territorial greater Britain, and that *is* related to what Defoe so presciently began. Yet while distinguished studies of eighteenth-century English fiction – by Ian Watt, Lennard Davis, John Richetti, and Michael McKeon – have devoted considerable attention to the relationship between the novel and social space, the imperial perspective has been neglected.[1] This is not simply a matter of being uncertain whether, for example, Richardson's minute constructions of bourgeois seduction and rapacity actually relate to British military moves against the French in India occurring at the same time. Quite clearly they do not in a literal sense; but in both realms we find common values about contest, surmounting odds and obstacles, and patience in establishing authority through the art of connecting principle with profit over time. In other words, we need to have a critical sense of how the great spaces of *Clarissa* or *Tom Jones* are two things together: a domestic accompaniment to the imperial project for presence and control abroad, and a practical narrative about expanding and moving about in space that must be actively inhabited and enjoyed before its discipline or limits can be accepted.

I am not trying to say that the novel – or the culture in the broad sense – "caused" imperialism, but that the novel, as a cultural artefact of bourgeois society, and imperialism are unthinkable without each other. Of all the major literary forms, the novel is the

EDWARD W. SAID

most recent, its emergence the most datable, its occurrence the most Western, its normative pattern of social authority the most structured; imperialism and the novel fortified each other to such a degree that it is impossible, I would argue, to read one without in some way dealing with the other.

Nor is this all. The novel is an incorporative, quasi-encyclopedic cultural form. Packed into it are both a highly regulated plot mechanism and an entire system of social reference that depends on the existing institutions of bourgeois society, their authority and power. The novelistic hero and heroine exhibit the restlessness and energy characteristic of the enterprising bourgeoisie, and they are permitted adventures in which their experiences reveal to them the limits of what they can aspire to, where they can go, what they can become. Novels therefore end either with the death of a hero or heroine (Julien Sorel, Emma Bovary, Bazarov, Jude the Obscure) who by virtue of overflowing energy does not fit into the orderly scheme of things, or with the protagonists' accession to stability (usually in the form of marriage or confirmed identity, as is the case with novels of Austen, Dickens, Thackeray, and George Eliot).

But, one might ask, why give so much emphasis to novels, and to England? And how can we bridge the distance separating this solitary aesthetic form from large topics and undertakings like "culture" or "imperialism"? For one thing, by the time of World War One the British empire had become unquestionably dominant, the result of a process that had started in the late sixteenth century; so powerful was the process and so definitive its result that, as Seeley and Hobson argued toward the end of the nineteenth century, it was the central fact in British history, and one that included many disparate activities.[2] It is not entirely coincidental that Britain also produced and sustained a novelistic institution with no real European competitor or equivalent. France had more highly developed intellectual institutions – academies, universities, institutes, journals, and so on – for at least the first half of the nineteenth century, as a host of British intellectuals, including Arnold, Carlyle, Mill, and George Eliot, noted and lamented. But the extraordinary compensation for this discrepancy came in the steady rise and gradually undisputed dominance of the British novel. (Only as North Africa assumes a sort of metropolitan presence in French culture after 1870 do we see a comparable aesthetic and cultural formation begin to flow: this is the period when Loti, the early Gide, Daudet, Maupassant, Mille, Psichari, Malraux, the exoticists like Segalen, and of course Camus project a global concordance between the domestic and imperial situations.)

By the 1840s the English novel had achieved eminence as *the* aesthetic form and as a major intellectual voice, so to speak, in English society. Because the novel gained so important a place in "the condition of England" question, for example, we can see it also as participating in England's overseas empire. In projecting what Raymond Williams calls a "knowable community" of Englishmen and women, Jane Austen, George Eliot, and Mrs. Gaskell shaped the idea of England in such a way as to give it identity, presence, ways of reusable articulation.[3] And part of such an idea was the relationship between "home" and "abroad." Thus England was surveyed, evaluated, made known, whereas "abroad" was only referred to or shown briefly without the kind of presence or immediacy lavished on London, the countryside, or northern industrial centers such as Manchester or Birmingham.

This steady, almost reassuring work done by the novel is unique to England and has to be taken as an important cultural affiliation domestically speaking, as yet undocumented and unstudied, for what took place in India, Africa, Ireland, or the Caribbean. An analogy is the relationship between Britain's foreign policy and its finance and trade, a relationship which *has* been studied. We get a lively sense of how dense and complex it was from D. C. M. Platt's classic (but still debated) study of it, *Finance, Trade and Politics in British Foreign Policy, 1815–1914*, and how much the extraordinary twinning of British trade and imperial expansion depended on cultural and social factors such as education, journalism, intermarriage, and class. Platt speaks of "social and intellectual contact [friendship, hospitality, mutual aid, common social and educational background] which energized the actual pressure on British foreign policy," and he goes on to say that "concrete evidence [for the actual accomplishments of this set of contacts] has probably never existed." Nevertheless, if one looks at how the government's attitude to such issues as "foreign loans...the protection of bondholders, and the promotion of contracts and concessions overseas" developed, one can see what he calls a "departmental view," a sort of consensus about the empire held by a whole range of people responsible for it. This would "suggest how officials and politicians were likely to react."[4]

How best to characterize this view? There seems to be agreement among scholars that until about 1870 British policy was (according to the early Disraeli, for example) not to expand the empire but "to uphold and maintain it and to protect it from disintegration."[5] Central to this task was India, which acquired a status of astonishing durability in "departmental" thought. After 1870 (Schumpeter cites Disraeli's Crystal Palace speech in 1872 as the hallmark of aggressive imperialism, "the catch phrase of domestic policy")[6] protecting India (the parameters kept getting larger) and defending against other competing powers, e.g., Russia, necessitated British imperial expansion in Africa, and the Middle and Far East. Thereafter, in one area of the globe after another, "Britain was indeed preoccupied with holding what she already had," as Platt puts it, "and whatever she gained was demanded because it helped her to preserve the rest. She belonged to the party of *les satisfaits*, but she had to fight ever harder to stay with them, and she had by far the most to lose."[7] A "departmental view" of British policy was fundamentally careful; as Ronald Robinson and John Gallagher put it in their redefinition of Platt's thesis, "the British would expand by trade and influence if they could, but by imperial rule if they must."[8] We should not minimize or forget, they remind us, that the Indian army was used in China three times between 1829 and 1856, at least once in Persia (1856), Ethiopia and Singapore (1867), Hong Kong (1868), Afghanistan (1878), Egypt (1882), Burma (1885), Ngasse (1893), Sudan and Uganda (1896).

In addition to India, British policy obviously made the bulwark for imperial commerce mainland Britain itself (with Ireland a continuous colonial problem), as well as the so-called white colonies (Australia, New Zealand, Canada, South Africa, and even the former American possessions). Continuous investment and routine conservation of Britain's overseas and home territories were without significant parallel in other European or American powers, where lurches, sudden acquisitions or losses, and improvisations occurred far more frequently.

In short, British power was durable and continually reinforced. In the related and often adjacent cultural sphere, that power was elaborated and articulated in the novel, whose central continuous presence is not comparably to be found elsewhere. But we must be as fastidious as possible. A novel is neither a frigate nor a bank draft. A novel exists first as a novelist's effort and second as an object read by an audience. In time novels accumulate and become what Harry Levin has usefully called an institution of literature, but they do not ever lose either their status as events or their specific density as part of a continuous enterprise recognized and accepted as such by readers and other writers. But for all their social presence, novels are not reducible to a sociological current and cannot be done justice to aesthetically, culturally, and politically as subsidiary forms of class, ideology, or interest.

Equally, however, novels are not *simply* the product of lonely genius (as a school of modern interpreters like Helen Vendler try to suggest), to be regarded only as manifestations of unconditioned creativity. Some of the most exciting recent criticism – Fredric Jameson's *The Political Unconscious* and David Miller's *The Novel and the Police* are two celebrated examples[9] – shows the novel generally, and narrative in particular, to have a sort of regulatory social presence in West European societies. Yet missing from these otherwise valuable descriptions are adumbrations of the actual world in which the novels and narratives take place. Being an English writer meant something quite specific and different from, say, being a French or Portuguese writer. For the British writer, "abroad" was felt vaguely and ineptly to be out there, or exotic and strange, or in some way or other "ours" to control, trade in "freely," or suppress when the natives were energized into overt military or political resistance. The novel contributed significantly to these feelings, attitudes, and references and became a main element in the consolidated vision, or departmental cultural view, of the globe.

I should specify how the novelistic contribution was made and also, conversely, how the novel neither deterred nor inhibited the more aggressive and popular imperialist feelings manifest after 1880.[10] Novels are pictures of reality at the very early or the very late stage in the reader's experience of them: in fact they elaborate and maintain a reality they inherit from other novels, which they rearticulate and repopulate according to their creator's situation, gifts, predilections. Platt rightly stresses *conservation* in the "departmental view"; this is significant for the novelist, too: the nineteenth-century English novels stress the continuing existence (as opposed to revolutionary overturning) of England. Moreover, they *never* advocate giving up colonies, but take the long-range view that since they fall within the orbit of British dominance, *that* dominance is a sort of norm, and thus conserved along with the colonies.

What we have is a slowly built up picture with England – socially, politically, morally charted and differentiated in immensely fine detail – at the center and a series of overseas territories connected to it at the peripheries. The *continuity* of British imperial policy throughout the nineteenth century – in fact a narrative – is actively accompanied by this novelistic process, whose main purpose is not to raise more questions, not to disturb or otherwise preoccupy attention, but to keep the empire more or less in place. Hardly ever is the novelist interested in doing a great deal more than mentioning or referring to India, for example, in *Vanity Fair* and *Jane Eyre*, or Australia in *Great Expectations*. The idea is that (following the general principles of free trade) outlying territories are available for use, at will, at the novelist's discretion, usually for relatively simple purposes such as immigration, fortune, or exile. At the end of *Hard Times*, for example, Tom is shipped off to the colonies. Not until well after mid-century did the empire become a principal subject of attention in writers like Haggard, Kipling, Doyle, Conrad as well as in emerging discourses in ethnography, colonial administration, theory and economy, the historiography of non-European regions, and specialized subjects like Orientalism, exoticism, and mass psychology.

The actual interpretative consequences of this slow and steady structure of attitude and reference articulated by the novel are diverse. I shall specify four. The first is that, in literary history, an unusual organic continuity can be seen between the earlier narratives that are normally not considered to have much to do with empire and the later ones explicitly *about* it. Kipling and Conrad are prepared for by Austen and Thackeray, Defoe, Scott, and Dickens; they are also interestingly connected with their contemporaries like Hardy and James, regularly supposed to be only coincidentally associated with the overseas exhibits presented by their rather more peculiar novelistic counterparts. But both the formal characteristics and the contents of all these novelists' works belong to the same cultural formation, the differences being those of inflection, emphasis, stress.

Second, the structure of attitude and reference raises the whole question of power. Today's critic cannot and should not suddenly give a novel legislative or direct political authority: we must continue to remember that novels participate in, are part of, contribute to an extremely slow, infinitesimal politics that clarifies, reinforces, perhaps even occasionally advances perceptions and attitudes about England and the world. It is striking that never, in the novel, is that world beyond seen except as subordinate and dominated, the English presence viewed as regulative and normative. Part of the extraordinary novelty of Aziz's trial in *A Passage to India* is that Forster admits that "the flimsy framework of the court"[11] cannot be sustained because it is a "fantasy" that compromises British power (real) with impartial justice for Indians (unreal). Therefore he readily (even with a sort of frustrated impatience) dissolves the scene into India's "complexity," which twenty-four years before in Kipling's *Kim* was just as present. The main difference between the two is that the impinging disturbance of resisting natives had been thrust on Forster's awareness. Forster could not ignore something that Kipling easily incorporated (as when he rendered even the famous "Mutiny" of 1857 as mere waywardness, not as a serious Indian objection to British rule).

There can be no awareness that the novel underscores and accepts the disparity in power unless readers actually register the signs in individual works, and unless the history of the novel is seen to have the coherence of a continuous enterprise. Just as the sustained solidity and largely unwavering "departmental view" of Britain's outlying territories were maintained throughout the nineteenth century, so too, in an altogether literary way, was the aesthetic (hence cultural) grasp of overseas lands maintained as a part of the novel, sometimes incidental, sometimes very important. Its "consolidated vision" came in a whole series of overlapping affirmations, by which a near unanimity of view was sustained. That this was done within the terms of each medium or discourse (the novel, travel writing, ethnography) and not in terms imposed from outside, suggests conformity, collaboration, willingness but not necessarily an overtly or explicitly held political agenda, at least not until later in the century, when the imperial program was itself more explicit and more a matter of direct popular propaganda.

A third point can best be made by rapid illustration. All through *Vanity Fair* there are allusions to India, but none is anything more than incidental to the changes in Becky's fortunes, or in Dobbin's, Joseph's, and Amelia's positions. All along, though, we are made

EDWARD W. SAID

aware of the mounting contest between England and Napoleon, with its climax at Waterloo. This overseas dimension scarcely makes *Vanity Fair* a novel exploiting what Henry James was later to call "the international theme," any more than Thackeray belongs to the club of Gothic novelists like Walpole, Radcliffe, or Lewis who set their works rather fancifully abroad. Yet Thackeray and, I would argue, all the major English novelists of the mid-nineteenth century, accepted a globalized world-view and indeed could not (in most cases did not) ignore the vast overseas reach of British power. As we saw in the little example cited earlier from *Dombey and Son*, the domestic order was tied to, located in, even illuminated by a specifically *English* order abroad. Whether it is Sir Thomas Bertram's plantation in Antigua or, a hundred years later, the Wilcox Nigerian rubber estate, novelists aligned the holding of power and privilege abroad with comparable activities at home.

When we read the novels attentively, we get a far more discriminating and subtle view than the baldly "global" and imperial vision I have described thus far. This brings me to the fourth consequence of what I have been calling the structure of attitude and reference. In insisting on the integrity of an artistic work, as we must, and refusing to collapse the various contributions of individual authors into a general scheme, we must accept that the structure connecting novels to one another has no existence outside the novels themselves, which means that one gets the particular, concrete experience of "abroad" only in individual novels; conversely that only individual novels can animate, articulate, embody the relationship, for instance, between England and Africa. This obliges critics to read and analyze, rather than only to summarize and judge, works whose paraphrasable content they might regard as politically and morally objectionable. On the one hand, when in a celebrated essay Chinua Achebe criticizes Conrad's racism, he either says nothing about or overrides the limitations placed on Conrad by the novel as an aesthetic form. On the other hand, Achebe shows that he understands how the form works when, in some of his own novels, he rewrites – painstakingly and with originality – Conrad.[12]

All of this is especially true of English fiction because only England had an overseas empire that sustained and protected itself over such an area, for such a long time, with such envied eminence. It is true that France rivalled it, but, as I have said elsewhere, the French imperial consciousness is intermittent until the late nineteenth century, the actuality too impinged on by England, too lagging in system, profit, extent. In the main, though, the nineteenth-century European novel is a cultural form consolidating but also refining and articulating the authority of the *status quo*. However much Dickens, for example, stirs up his readers against the legal system, provincial schools, or the bureaucracy, his novels finally enact what one critic has called a "fiction of resolution."[13] The most frequent figure for this is the reunification of the family, which in Dickens's case always serves as a microcosm of society. In Austen, Balzac, George Eliot, and Flaubert – to take several prominent names together – the consolidation of authority includes, indeed is built into the very fabric of, both private property and marriage, institutions that are only rarely challenged.

The crucial aspect of what I have been calling the novel's consolidation of authority is not simply connected to the functioning of social power and governance, but made to appear both normative and sovereign, that is, self-validating in the course of the narrative. This is paradoxical only if one forgets that the constitution of a narrative subject, however abnormal or unusual, is still a social act *par excellence*, and as such has behind or inside it the authority of history and society. There is first the authority of the author – someone writing out the processes of society in an acceptable institutionalized manner, observing conventions, following patterns, and so forth. Then there is the authority of the narrator, whose discourse anchors the narrative in recognizable, and hence existentially referential, circumstances. Last, there is what might be called the authority of the community, whose representative most often is the family but also is the nation, the specific locality, and the concrete historical moment. Together these functioned most energetically, most noticeably, during the early nineteenth century as the novel opened up to history in an unprecedented way. Conrad's Marlow inherits all this directly.

Lukács studied with remarkable skill the emergence of history in the European novel[14] – how Stendhal and particularly Scott place their narratives in and as part of a public history, making that history accessible to everyone and not, as before, only to kings and aristocrats. The novel is thus a concretely historical narrative shaped by the real history of real nations. Defoe locates Crusoe on an unnamed island somewhere in an outlying region, and Moll is sent to the vaguely apprehended Carolinas, but Thomas Bertram and Joseph Sedley derive specific wealth and specific benefits from historically annexed territories – the Caribbean and India, respectively – at specific historical moments. And, as Lukács shows so persuasively, Scott constructs the British polity in the form of a historical society working its way out of foreign adventures[15] (the Crusades, for example) and internecine domestic conflict (the 1745 rebellion, the warring Highland tribes) to become the settled metropolis resisting local revolution and continental provocation with equal success. In France, history confirms the post-revolutionary reaction embodied by the Bourbon restoration, and Stendhal chronicles its – to him – lamentable achievements. Later Flaubert does much the same for 1848. But the novel is assisted also by the historical work of Michelet and Macaulay, whose narratives add density to the texture of national identity.

The appropriation of history, the historicization of the past, the narrativization of society, all of which give the novel its force, include the accumulation and differentiation of social space, space to be used for social purposes. This is much more apparent in late-nineteenth-century, openly colonial fiction: in Kipling's India, for example, where the natives and the Raj inhabit differently ordained spaces, and where with his extraordinary genius Kipling devised Kim, a marvelous character whose youth and energy allow him to explore both spaces, crossing from one to the other with daring grace as if to confound the authority of colonial barriers. The barriers within social space exist in Conrad too, and in Haggard, in Loti, in Doyle, in Gide, Psichari, Malraux, Camus, and Orwell.

Underlying social space are territories, lands, geographical domains, the actual geographical underpinnings of the imperial, and also the cultural contest. To think about distant places, to colonize them, to populate or depopulate them: all of this occurs on, about, or because of land. The actual geographical possession of land is what empire in the final analysis is all about. At the moment when a coincidence occurs between real control and power, the idea of what a given place was (could be, might become), and an actual place – at that moment the struggle for empire is launched. This coincidence is the logic both for Westerners taking possession of land and, during decolonization, for resisting natives reclaiming it. Imperialism and the culture associated with it affirm both the primacy of geography and an ideology about control of territory. The geographical sense makes projections – imaginative, cartographic, military, economic, historical, or in a general sense cultural. It also makes possible the construction of various kinds of knowledge, all of them in one way or another dependent upon the perceived character and destiny of a particular geography.

Three fairly restricted points should be made here. First, the spatial differentiations so apparent in late-nineteenth-century novels do not simply and suddenly appear there as a passive reflection of an aggressive "age of empire," but are derived in a continuum from earlier social discriminations already authorized in earlier historical and realistic novels.

Jane Austen sees the legitimacy of Sir Thomas Bertram's overseas properties as a natural extension of the calm, the order, the beauties of Mansfield Park, one central estate validating the economically supportive role of the peripheral other. And even where colonies are not insistently or even perceptibly in evidence, the narrative sanctions a spatial moral order, whether in the communal restoration of the town of Middlemarch centrally important during a period of national turbulence, or in the outlying spaces of deviation and uncertainty seen by Dickens in London's underworld, or in the Brontë stormy heights.

A second point. As the conclusions of the novel confirm and highlight an underlying hierarchy of family, property, nation, there is also a very strong spatial *hereness* imparted to the hierarchy. The astounding power of the scene in *Bleak House* where Lady Dedlock is seen sobbing at the grave of her long dead husband *grounds* what we have felt about her secret past – her cold and inhuman presence, her disturbingly unfertile authority – in the grave-yard to which as a fugitive she has fled. This contrasts not only with the disorderly jumble of the Jellyby establishment (with its eccentric ties to Africa), but also with the favored house in which Esther and her guardian-husband live. The narrative explores, moves through, and finally endows these places with confirmatory positive and/or negative values.

This moral commensuration in the interplay between narrative and domestic space is extendable, indeed reproducible, in the world beyond metropolitan centers like Paris or London. In turn such French or English places have a kind of export value: whatever is good or bad about places at home is shipped out and assigned comparable virtue or vice abroad. When in his inaugural lecture in 1870 as Slade Professor at Oxford, Ruskin speaks of England's pure race, he can then go on to tell his audience to turn England into a "country again [that is] a royal throne of kings; a sceptred isle, for all the world a source of light, a centre of peace." The allusion to Shakespeare is meant to re-establish and relocate a preferential feeling for England. This time, however, Ruskin conceives of England as functioning *formally* on a world scale; the feelings of approbation for the island kingdom that Shakespeare had imagined principally but not exclusively confined at home are rather startlingly mobilized for imperial, indeed aggressively colonial service. Become colonists, found "colonies as fast and as far as [you are] able," he seems to be saying.[16]

My third point is that such domestic cultural enterprises as narrative fiction and history (once again I emphasize the narrative component) are premised on the recording, ordering, observing powers of the central authorizing subject, or ego. To say of this subject, in a quasi-tautological manner, that it writes because it *can* write is to refer not only to domestic society but to the outlying world. The capacity to represent, portray, characterize, and depict is not easily available to just any member of just any society; moreover, the "what" and "how" in the representation of "things," while allowing for considerable individual freedom, are circumscribed and socially regulated. We have become very aware in recent years of the constraints upon the cultural representation of women, and the pressures that go into the created representations of inferior classes and races. In all these areas – gender, class, and race – criticism has correctly focused upon the institutional forces in modern Western societies that shape and set limits on the representation of what are considered essentially subordinate beings; thus representation itself has been characterized as keeping the subordinate subordinate, the inferior inferior.

Jane Austen and Empire

We are on solid ground with V. G. Kiernan when he says that "empires must have a mould of ideas or conditioned reflexes to flow into, and youthful nations dream of a great place in the world as young men dream of fame and fortunes."[17] It is, as I have been saying throughout, too simple and reductive to argue that everything in European or American culture therefore prepares for or consolidates the grand idea of empire. It is also, however, historically inaccurate to ignore those tendencies – whether in narrative, political theory, or pictorial technique – that enabled, encouraged, and otherwise assured the West's readiness to assume and enjoy the experience of empire. If there was cultural resistance to the notion of an imperial mission, there was not much support for that resistance in the main departments of cultural thought. Liberal though he was, John Stuart Mill – as a telling case in point – could still say, "The sacred duties which civilized nations owe to the independence and nationality of each other, are not binding towards those to whom nationality and independence are certain evil, or at best a questionable good." Ideas like this were not original with Mill; they were already current in the English subjugation of Ireland during the sixteenth century and, as Nicholas Canny has persuasively demonstrated, were equally useful in the ideology of English colonization in the Americas.[18] Almost all colonial schemes begin with an assumption of native backwardness and general inadequacy to be independent, "equal," and fit.

Why that should be so, why sacred obligation on one front should not be binding on another, why rights accepted in one may be denied in another, are questions best understood in the terms of a culture well-grounded in moral, economic, and even metaphysical norms designed to approve a satisfying local, that is European, order and to permit the abrogation of the right to a similar order abroad. Such a statement may appear preposterous or extreme. In fact, it formulates the connection between Europe's well-being and cultural identity on the one hand and, on the other, the subjugation of imperial realms overseas rather too fastidiously and circumspectly. Part of our difficulty today in accepting any connection at all is that we tend to reduce this complicated matter to an apparently simple causal one, which in turn produces a rhetoric of blame and defensiveness. I am *not* saying that the major factor in early European culture was that it *caused* late-nineteenth-century imperialism, and I am not

EDWARD W. SAID

implying that all the problems of the formerly colonial world should be blamed on Europe. I am saying, however, that European culture often, if not always, characterized itself in such a way as simultaneously to validate its own preferences while also advocating those preferences in conjunction with distant imperial rule. Mill certainly did: he always recommended that India *not* be given independence. When for various reasons imperial rule concerned Europe more intensely after 1880, this schizophrenic habit became useful.

The first thing to be done now is more or less to jettison simple causality in thinking through the relationship between Europe and the non-European world, and lessening the hold on our thought of the equally simple temporal sequence. We must not admit any notion, for instance, that proposes to show that Wordsworth, Austen, or Coleridge, because they wrote *before* 1857, actually caused the establishment of formal British governmental rule over India *after* 1857. We should try to discern instead a counterpoint between overt patterns in British writing about Britain and representations of the world beyond the British Isles. The inherent mode for this counterpoint is not temporal but spatial. How do writers in the period before the great age of explicit, programmatic colonial expansion – the "scramble for Africa," say – situate and see themselves and their work in the larger world? We shall find them using striking but careful strategies, many of them derived from expected sources – positive ideas of home, of a nation and its language, of proper order, good behavior, moral values.

But positive ideas of this sort do more than validate "our" world. They also tend to devalue other worlds and, perhaps more significantly from a retrospective point of view, they do not prevent or inhibit or give resistance to horrendously unattractive imperialist practices. No, cultural forms like the novel or the opera do not cause people to go out and imperialize – Carlyle did not drive Rhodes directly, and he certainly cannot be "blamed" for the problems in today's southern Africa – but it is genuinely troubling to see how little Britain's great humanistic ideas, institutions, and monuments, which we still celebrate as having the power ahistorically to command our approval, how little they stand in the way of the accelerating imperial process. We are entitled to ask how this body of humanistic ideas co-existed so comfortably with imperialism, and why – until the resistance to imperialism *in the imperial domain*, among Africans, Asians, Latin Americans, developed – there was little significant opposition or deterrence to empire at home. Perhaps the custom of distinguishing "our" home and order from "theirs" grew into a harsh political rule for accumulating more of "them" to rule, study, and subordinate. In the great, humane ideas and values promulgated by mainstream European culture, we have precisely that "mould of ideas or conditioned reflexes" of which Kiernan speaks, into which the whole business of empire later flowed.

The extent to which these ideas are actually invested in geographical distinctions between real places is the subject of Raymond Williams's richest book, *The Country and the City*. His argument concerning the interplay between rural and urban places in England admits of the most extraordinary transformations – from the pastoral populism of Langland, through Ben Jonson's country-house poems and the novels of Dickens's London, right up to visions of the metropolis in twentieth-century literature. Mainly, of course, the book is about how English culture has dealt with land, its possession, imagination, and organization. And while he does address the export of England to the colonies, Williams does so, as I suggested earlier, in a less focussed way and less expansively than the practice actually warrants. Near the end of *The Country and the City* he volunteers that "from at least the mid-nineteenth century, and with important instances earlier, there was this larger context [the relationship between England and the colonies, whose effects on the English imagination "have gone deeper than can easily be traced"] within which every idea and every image was consciously and unconsciously affected." He goes on quickly to cite "the idea of emigration to the colonies" as one such image prevailing in various novels by Dickens, the Brontës, Gaskell, and rightly shows that "new rural societies," all of them colonial, enter the imaginative metropolitan economy of English literature via Kipling, early Orwell, Maugham. After 1880 there comes a "dramatic extension of landscape and social relations": this corresponds more or less exactly with the great age of empire.[19]

It is dangerous to disagree with Williams, yet I would venture to say that if one began to look for something like an imperial map of the world in English literature, it would turn up with amazing insistence and frequency well before the mid-nineteenth century. And turn up not only with the inert regularity suggesting something taken for granted, but – more interestingly – threaded through, forming a vital part of the texture of linguistic and cultural practice. There were established English offshore interests in Ireland, America, the Caribbean, and Asia from the sixteenth century on, and even a quick inventory reveals poets, philosophers, historians, dramatists, statesmen, novelists, travel writers, chroniclers, soldiers, and fabulists who prized, cared for, and traced these interests with continuing concern. (Much of this is well discussed by Peter Hulme in *Colonial Encounters*.)[20] Similar points may be made for France, Spain, and Portugal, not only as overseas powers in their own right, but as competitors with the British. How can we examine these interests at work in modern England before the age of empire, i.e., during the period between 1800 and 1870?

We would do well to follow Williams's lead, and look first at that period of crisis following upon England's wide-scale land enclosure at the end of the eighteenth century. The old organic rural communities were dissolved and new ones forged under the impulse of parliamentary activity, industrialization, and demographic disloca-tion, but there also occurred a new process of relocating England (and in France, France) within a much larger circle of the world map. During the first half of the eighteenth century, Anglo-French competition in North America and India was intense; in the second half there were numerous violent encounters between England and France in the Americas, the Caribbean, and the Levant, and of course in Europe itself. The major pre-Romantic literature in France and England contains a constant stream of references to the overseas dominions: one thinks not only of various Encyclopedists, the Abbé Raynal, de Brosses, and Volney, but also of Edmund Burke, Beckford, Gibbon, Johnson, and William Jones.

In 1902 J. A. Hobson described imperialism as the expansion of nationality, implying that the process was understandable mainly by considering *expansion* as the more important of the two terms, since "nationality" was a fully formed, fixed quantity,[21] whereas a century before it was still in the process of *being formed*, at home and abroad as well. In *Physics and Politics* (1887) Walter Bagehot speaks with extraordinary relevance of "nation-making." Between France and Britain in the late eighteenth century there were two contests: the battle for strategic gains abroad – in India, the Nile delta, the Western Hemisphere – and the battle for a triumphant nationality. Both battles contrast

EDWARD W. SAID

"Englishness" with "the French," and no matter how intimate and closeted the supposed English or French "essence" appears to be, it was almost always thought of as being (as opposed to already) made, and being fought out with the other great competitor. Thackeray's Becky Sharp, for example, is as much an upstart as she is because of her half-French heritage. Earlier in the century, the upright abolitionist posture of Wilberforce and his allies developed partly out of a desire to make life harder for French hegemony in the Antilles.[22]

These considerations suddenly provide a fascinatingly expanded dimension to *Mansfield Park* (1814), the most explicit in its ideological and moral affirmations of Austen's novels. Williams once again is in general dead right: Austen's novels express an "attainable quality of life," in money and property acquired, moral discriminations made, the right choices put in place, the correct "improvements" implemented, the finely nuanced language affirmed and classified. Yet, Williams continues,

> What [Cobbett] names, riding past on the road, are classes. Jane Austen, from inside the houses, can never see that, for all the intricacy of her social description. All her discrimination is, understandably, internal and exclusive. She is concerned with the conduct of people who, in the complications of improvement, are repeatedly trying to make themselves into a class. But where only one class is seen, no classes are seen.[23]

As a general description of how Austen manages to elevate certain "moral discriminations" into "an independent value," this is excellent. Where *Mansfield Park* is concerned, however, a good deal more needs to be said, giving greater explicitness and width to Williams's survey. Perhaps then Austen, and indeed, pre-imperialist novels generally, will appear to be more implicated in the rationale for imperialist expansion than at first sight they have been.

After Lukács and Proust, we have become so accustomed to thinking of the novel's plot and structure as constituted mainly by temporality that we have overlooked the function of space, geography, and location. For it is not only the very young Stephen Dedalus, but every other young protagonist before him as well, who sees himself in a widening spiral at home, in Ireland, in the world. Like many other novels, *Mansfield Park* is very precisely about a series of both small and large dislocations and relocations in space that occur before, at the end of the novel, Fanny Price, the niece, becomes the spiritual mistress of Mansfield Park. And that place itself is located by Austen at the center of an arc of interests and concerns spanning the hemisphere, two major seas, and four continents.

As in Austen's other novels, the central group that finally emerges with marriage and property "ordained" is not based exclusively upon blood. Her novel enacts the disaffiliation (in the literal sense) of some members of a family, and the affiliation between others and one or two chosen and tested outsiders: in other words, blood relationships are not enough to assure continuity, hierarchy, authority, both domestic and international. Thus Fanny Price – the poor niece, the orphaned child from the outlying city of Portsmouth, the neglected, demure, and upright wallflower – gradually acquires a status commensurate with, even superior to, that of most of her more fortunate relatives. In this pattern of affiliation and in her assumption of authority, Fanny Price is relatively passive. She resists the misdemeanors and the importunings of others, and very occasionally she ventures actions on her own: all in all, though, one has the impression that Austen has designs for her that Fanny herself can scarcely comprehend, just as throughout the novel Fanny is thought of by everyone as "comfort" and "acquisition" despite herself. Like Kipling's Kim O'Hara, Fanny is both device and instrument in a larger pattern, as well as a fully fledged novelistic character.

Fanny, like Kim, requires direction, requires the patronage and outside authority that her own impoverished experience cannot provide. Her conscious connections are to some people and to some places, but the novel reveals other connections of which she has faint glimmerings that nevertheless demand her presence and service. She comes into a situation that opens with an intricate set of moves which, taken together, demand sorting out, adjustment, and rearrangement. Sir Thomas Bertram has been captivated by one Ward sister, the others have not done well, and "an absolute breach" opens up; their "circles were so distinct," the distances between them so great that they have been out of touch for eleven years;[24] fallen on hard times, the Prices seek out the Bertrams. Gradually, and even though she is not the eldest, Fanny becomes the focus of attention as she is sent to Mansfield Park, there to begin her new life. Similarly, the Bertrams have given up London (the result of Lady Bertram's "little ill health and a great deal of indolence") and come to reside entirely in the country.

What sustains this life materially is the Bertram estate in Antigua, which is not doing well. Austen takes pains to show us two apparently disparate but actually convergent processes: the growth of Fanny's importance to the Bertrams' economy, including Antigua, and Fanny's own steadfastness in the face of numerous challenges, threats, and surprises. In both, Austen's imagination works with a steel-like rigor through a mode that we might call geographical and spatial clarification. Fanny's ignorance when she arrives at Mansfield as a frightened ten-year-old is signified by her inability to "put the map of Europe together,"[25] and for much of the first half of the novel the action is concerned with a whole range of issues whose common denominator, misused or misunderstood, is space: not only is Sir Thomas in Antigua to make things better there and at home, but at Mansfield Park, Fanny, Edmund, and her aunt Norris negotiate where she is to live, read, and work, where fires are to be lit; the friends and cousins concern themselves with the improvement of estates, and the importance of chapels (i.e., religious authority) to domesticity is envisioned and debated. When, as a device for stirring things up, the Crawfords suggest a play (the tinge of France that hangs a little suspiciously over their background is significant), Fanny's discomfiture is polarizingly acute. She cannot participate, cannot easily accept that rooms for living are turned into theatrical space, although, with all its confusion of roles and purposes, the play, Kotzebue's *Lovers' Vows*, is prepared for anyway.

We are to surmise, I think, that while Sir Thomas is away tending his colonial garden, a number of inevitable mismeasurements (explicitly associated with feminine "lawlessness") will occur. These are apparent not only in innocent strolls by the three pairs of young friends through a park, in which people lose and catch sight of one another unexpectedly, but most clearly in the various flirtations and engagements between the young men and women left without true parental authority, Lady Bertram being indifferent, Mrs. Norris unsuitable. There is sparring, innuendo, perilous taking on of roles: all of this of course crystallizes in preparations for the play, in which something dangerously close to libertinage is about to be (but never is) enacted. Fanny, whose earlier sense of alienation, distance, and fear derives from her first uprooting, now becomes a sort of surrogate conscience about what is right and how far is too much. Yet she has no power to implement her uneasy awareness, and until Sir Thomas suddenly returns from "abroad," the rudderless drift continues.

When he does appear, preparations for the play are immediately stopped, and in a passage remarkable for its executive dispatch, Austen narrates the re-establishment of Sir Thomas's local rule:

> It was a busy morning with him. Conversation with any of them occupied but a small part of it. He had to reinstate himself in all the wonted concerns of his Mansfield life, to see his steward and his bailiff – to examine and compute – and, in the intervals of business, to walk into his stables and his gardens, and nearest plantations; but active and methodical, he had not only done all this before he resumed his seat as master of the house at dinner, he had also set the carpenter to work in pulling down what had been so lately put up in the billiard room, and given the scene painter his dismissal, long enough to justify the pleasing belief of his being then at least as far off as Northampton. The scene painter was gone, having spoilt only the floor of one room, ruined all the coachman's sponges, and made five of the under-servants idle and dissatisfied; and Sir Thomas was in hopes that another day or two would suffice to wipe away every outward memento of what had been, even to the destruction of every unbound copy of 'Lovers' Vows' in the house, for he was burning all that met his eye.[26]

The force of this paragraph is unmistakable. Not only is this a Crusoe setting things in order: it is also an early Protestant eliminating all traces of frivolous behavior. There is nothing in *Mansfield Park* that would contradict us, however, were we to assume that Sir Thomas does exactly the same things – on a larger scale – in his Antigua "plantations." Whatever was wrong there – and the internal evidence garnered by Warren Roberts suggests that economic depression, slavery, and competition with France were at issue[27] – Sir Thomas was able to fix, thereby maintaining his control over his colonial domain. More clearly than anywhere else in her fiction, Austen here synchronizes domestic with international authority, making it plain that the values associated with such higher things as ordination, law, and propriety must be grounded firmly in actual rule over and possession of territory. She sees clearly that to hold and rule Mansfield Park is to hold and rule an imperial estate in close, not to say inevitable association with it. What assures the domestic tranquility and attractive harmony of one is the productivity and regulated discipline of the other.

Before both can be fully secured, however, Fanny must become more actively involved in the unfolding action. From frightened and often victimized poor relation she is gradually transformed into a directly participating member of the Bertram household at Mansfield Park. For this, I believe, Austen designed the second part of the book, which contains not only the failure of the Edmund–Mary Crawford romance as well as the disgraceful profligacy of Lydia and Henry Crawford, but Fanny Price's rediscovery and rejection of her Portsmouth home, the injury and incapacitation of Tom Bertram (the eldest son), and the launching of William Price's naval career. This entire ensemble of relationships and events is finally capped with Edmund's marriage to Fanny, whose place in Lady Bertram's household is taken by Susan Price, her sister. It is no exaggeration to interpret the concluding sections of

Mansfield Park as the coronation of an arguably unnatural (or at very least, illogical) principle at the heart of a desired English order. The audacity of Austen's vision is disguised a little by her voice, which despite its occasional archness is understated and notably modest. But we should not misconstrue the limited references to the outside world, her lightly stressed allusions to work, process, and class, her apparent ability to abstract (in Raymond Williams's phrase) "an everyday uncompromising morality which is in the end separable from its social basis." In fact Austen is far less diffident, far more severe.

The clues are to be found in Fanny, or rather in how rigorously we are able to consider her. True, her visit to her original Portsmouth home, where her immediate family still resides, upsets the aesthetic and emotional balance she has become accustomed to at Mansfield Park, and true she has begun to take its wonderful luxuries for granted, even as being essential. These are fairly routine and natural consequences of getting used to a new place. But Austen is talking about two other matters we must not mistake. One is Fanny's newly enlarged sense of what it means to be *at home*; when she takes stock of things after she gets to Portsmouth, this is not merely a matter of expanded space.

> Fanny was almost stunned. The smallness of the house, and thinness of the walls, brought every thing so close to her, that, added to the fatigue of her journey, and all her recent agitation, she hardly knew how to bear it. *Within* the room all was tranquil enough, for Susan having disappeared with the others, there were soon only her father and herself remaining; and he taking out a newspaper – the accustomary loan of a neighbour, applied himself to studying it, without seeming to recollect her existence. The solitary candle was held between himself and the paper, without any reference to her possible convenience; but she had nothing to do, and was glad to have the light screened from her aching head, as she sat in bewildered, broken, sorrowful contemplation.
>
> She was at home. But alas! it was not such a home, she had not such a welcome, as – she checked herself; she was unreasonable.... A day or two might shew the difference. *She* only was to blame. Yet she thought it would not have been so at Mansfield. No, in her uncle's house there would have been a consideration of times and seasons, a regulation of subject, a propriety, an attention towards every body which there was not here.[28]

In too small a space, you cannot see clearly, you cannot think clearly, you cannot have regulation or attention of the proper sort. The fineness of Austen's detail ("the solitary candle was held between himself and the paper, without any reference to her possible convenience") renders very precisely the dangers of unsociability, of lonely insularity, of diminished awareness that are rectified in larger and better administered spaces.

That such spaces are not available to Fanny by direct inheritance, legal title, by propinquity, contiguity, or adjacence (Mansfield Park and Portsmouth are separated by many hours' journey) is precisely Austen's point. To earn the right to Mansfield Park you must first leave home as a kind of indentured servant or, to put the case in extreme terms, as a kind of transported commodity – this, clearly, is the fate of Fanny and her brother William – but then you have the promise of future wealth. I think Austen sees what Fanny does as a domestic or small-scale movement in space that corresponds to the larger, more openly colonial movements of Sir Thomas, her mentor, the man whose estate she inherits. The two movements depend on each other.

EDWARD W. SAID

The second more complex matter about which Austen speaks, albeit indirectly, raises an interesting theoretical issue. Austen's awareness of empire is obviously very different, alluded to very much more casually, than Conrad's or Kipling's. In her time the British were extremely active in the Caribbean and in South America, notably Brazil and Argentina. Austen seems only vaguely aware of the details of these activities, although the sense that extensive West Indian plantations were important was fairly widespread in metropolitan England. Antigua and Sir Thomas's trip there have a definitive function in *Mansfield Park*, which, I have been saying, is both incidental, referred to only in passing, and absolutely crucial to the action. How are we to assess Austen's few references to Antigua, and what are we to make of them interpretatively?

My contention is that by that very odd combination of casualness and stress, Austen reveals herself to be *assuming* (just as Fanny assumes, in both senses of the word) the importance of an empire to the situation at home. Let me go further. Since Austen refers to and uses Antigua as she does in *Mansfield Park*, there needs to be a commensurate effort on the part of her readers to understand concretely the historical valences in the reference; to put it differently, we should try to understand *what* she referred to, why she gave it the importance she did, and why indeed she made the choice, for she might have done something different to establish Sir Thomas's wealth. Let us now calibrate the signifying power of the references to Antigua in *Mansfield Park*; how do they occupy the place they do, what are they doing there?

According to Austen we are to conclude that no matter how isolated and insulated the English place (e.g., Mansfield Park), it requires overseas sustenance. Sir Thomas's property in the Caribbean would have had to be a sugar plantation maintained by slave labor (not abolished until the 1830s): these are not dead historical facts but, as Austen certainly knew, evident historical realities. Before the Anglo-French competition the major distinguishing characteristic of Western empires (Roman, Spanish, and Portuguese) was that the earlier empires were bent on loot, as Conrad puts it, on the transport of treasure from the colonies to Europe, with very little attention to development, organization, or system within the colonies themselves; Britain and, to a lesser degree, France both wanted to make their empires long-term, profitable, ongoing concerns, and they competed in this enterprise, nowhere more so than in the colonies of the Caribbean, where the transport of slaves, the functioning of large sugar plantations, and the development of sugar markets, which raised the issues of protectionism, monopolies, and price – all these were more or less constantly, competitively at issue.

Far from being nothing much "out there," British colonial possessions in the Antilles and Leeward Islands were during Jane Austen's time a crucial setting for Anglo-French colonial competition. Revolutionary ideas from France were being exported there, and there was a steady decline in British profits: the French sugar plantations were producing more sugar at less cost. However, slave rebellions in and out of Haiti were incapacitating France and spurring British interests to intervene more directly and to gain greater local power. Still, compared with its earlier prominence for the home market, British Caribbean sugar production in the nineteenth century had to compete with alternative sugar-cane supplies in Brazil and Mauritius, the emergence of a European beet-sugar industry, and the gradual dominance of free-trade ideology and practice.

In *Mansfield Park* – both in its formal characteristics and in its contents – a number of these currents converge. The most important is the avowedly complete subordination of colony to metropolis. Sir Thomas, absent from Mansfield Park, is never seen as *present* in Antigua, which elicits at most a half dozen references in the novel. There is a passage, a part of which I quoted earlier, from John Stuart Mill's *Principles of Political Economy* that catches the spirit of Austen's use of Antigua. I quote it here in full:

> These [outlying possessions of ours] are hardly to be looked upon as countries, carrying on an exchange of commodities with other countries, but more properly as outlying agricultural or manufacturing estates belonging to a larger community. Our West Indian colonies, for example, cannot be regarded as countries with a productive capital of their own...[but are rather] the place where England finds it convenient to carry on the production of sugar, coffee and a few other tropical commodities. All the capital employed is English capital; almost all the industry is carried on for English uses; there is little production of anything except for staple commodities, and these are sent to England, not to be exchanged for things exported to the colony and consumed by its inhabitants, but to be sold in England for the benefit of the proprietors there. The trade with the West Indies is hardly to be considered an external trade, but more resembles the traffic between town and country.[29]

To some extent Antigua is like London or Portsmouth, a less desirable setting than a country estate like Mansfield Park, but producing goods to be consumed by everyone (by the early nineteenth century every Britisher used sugar), although owned and maintained by a small group of aristocrats and gentry. The Bertrams and the other characters in *Mansfield Park* are a subgroup within the minority, and for them the island is wealth, which Austen regards as being converted to propriety, order, and, at the end of the novel, comfort, an added good. But why "added"? Because, Austen tells us pointedly in the final chapters, she wants to "restore every body, not greatly in fault themselves, to tolerable comfort, and to have done with all the rest."[30]

This can be interpreted to mean first that the novel has done enough in the way of destabilizing the lives of "every body" and must now set them at rest: actually Austen says this explicitly, in a bit of meta-fictional impatience, the novelist commenting on her own work as having gone on long enough and now needing to be brought to a close. Second, it can mean that "every body" may now be finally permitted to realize what it means to be properly at home, and at rest, without the need to wander about or to come and go. (This does not include young William, who, we assume, will continue to roam the seas in the British navy on whatever commercial and political missions may still be required. Such matters draw from Austen only a last brief gesture, a passing remark about William's "continuing good conduct and rising fame.") As for those finally resident in Mansfield Park itself, more in the way of domesticated advantages is given to these now fully acclimatized souls, and to none more than to Sir Thomas. He understands for the first time what has been missing in his education of his children, and he understands it in the terms paradoxically provided for him by unnamed outside forces, so to speak, the wealth of Antigua and the imported example of Fanny Price. Note here how the curious alternation of outside and inside follows the pattern identified by Mill of the outside *becoming* the inside by use and, to use Austen's word, "disposition":

> Here [in his deficiency of training, of allowing Mrs. Norris too great a role, of letting his children dissemble and repress feeling] had been grievous mismanagement; but, bad as it

was, he gradually grew to feel that it had not been the most direful mistake in his plan of education. Some thing must have been wanting *within*, or time would have worn away much of its ill effect. He feared that principle, active principle, had been wanting, that they had never been properly taught to govern their inclinations and tempers, by that sense of duty which can alone suffice. They had been instructed theoretically in their religion, but never required to bring it into daily practice. To be distinguished for elegance and accomplishments – the authorized object of their youth – could have had no useful influence that way, no moral effect on the mind. He had meant them to be good, but his cares had been directed to the understanding and manners, not the disposition; and of the necessity of self-denial and humility, he feared they had never heard from any lips that could profit them.[31]

What was wanting *within* was in fact supplied by the wealth derived from a West Indian plantation and a poor provincial relative, both brought in to Mansfield Park and set to work. Yet on their own, neither the one nor the other could have sufficed; they require each other and then, more important, they need executive disposition, which in turn helps to reform the rest of the Bertram circle. All this Austen leaves to her reader to supply in the way of literal explication.

And that is what reading her entails. But all these things having to do with the outside brought in seem unmistakably *there* in the suggestiveness of her allusive and abstract language. A principle "wanting *within*" is, I believe, intended to evoke for us memories of Sir Thomas's absences in Antigua, or the sentimental and near-whimsical vagary on the part of the three variously deficient Ward sisters by which a niece is displaced from one household to another. But that the Bertrams did become better if not altogether good, that some sense of duty was imparted to them, that they learned to govern their inclinations and tempers and brought religion into daily practice, that they "directed disposition": all of this did occur because outside (or rather outlying) factors were lodged properly inward, became native to Mansfield Park, with Fanny the niece its final spiritual mistress, and Edmund the second son its spiritual master.

An additional benefit is that Mrs. Norris is dislodged; this is described as "the great supplementary comfort of Sir Thomas's life."[32] Once the principles have been interiorized, the comforts follow: Fanny is settled for the time being at Thornton Lacey "with every attention to her comfort"; her home later becomes "the home of affection and comfort"; Susan is brought in "first as a comfort to Fanny, then as an auxiliary, and at last as her substitute"[33] when the new import takes Fanny's place by Lady Bertram's side. The pattern established at the outset of the novel clearly continues, only now it has what Austen intended to give it all along, an internalized and retrospectively guaranteed rationale. This is the rationale that Raymond Williams describes as "an everyday, uncompromising morality which is in the end separable from its social basis and which, in other hands, can be turned against it."

I have tried to show that the morality in fact is not separable from its social basis: right up to the last sentence, Austen affirms and repeats the geographical process of expansion involving trade, production, and consumption that predates, underlies, and guarantees the morality. And expansion, as Gallagher reminds us, whether "through colonial rule was liked or disliked, [its] desirability through one mode or another was generally accepted. So in the event there were few domestic constraints upon expansion."[34] Most critics have tended to forget or overlook that process, which has seemed less important to critics than Austen herself seemed to think. But interpreting Jane Austen depends on *who* does the interpreting, *when* it is done, and no less important, from *where* it is done. If with feminists, with great cultural critics sensitive to history and class like Williams, with cultural and stylistic interpreters, we have been sensitized to the issues their interests raise, we should now proceed to regard the geographical division of the world – after all significant to *Mansfield Park* – as not neutral (any more than class and gender are neutral) but as politically charged, beseeching the attention and elucidation its considerable proportions require. The question is thus not only how to understand and with what to connect Austen's morality and its social basis, but also *what* to read of it.

Take once again the casual references to Antigua, the ease with which Sir Thomas's needs in England are met by a Caribbean sojourn, the uninflected, unreflective citations of Antigua (or the Mediterranean, or India, which is where Lady Bertram, in a fit of distracted impatience, requires that William should go "'that I may have a shawl. I think I will have two shawls.'")[35] They stand for a significance "out there" that frames the genuinely important action *here*, but not for a great significance. Yet these signs of "abroad" include, even as they repress, a rich and complex history, which has since achieved a status that the Bertrams, the Prices, and Austen herself would not, could not recognize. To call this "the Third World" begins to deal with the realities but by no means exhausts the political or cultural history.

We must first take stock of *Mansfield Park*'s prefigurations of a later English history as registered in fiction. The Bertrams' usable colony in *Mansfield Park* can be read as pointing forward to Charles Gould's San Tomé mine in *Nostromo*, or to the Wilcoxes' Imperial and West African Rubber Company in Forster's *Howards End*, or to any of these distant but convenient treasure spots in *Great Expectation*, Jean Rhys's *Wide Sargasso Sea*, *Heart of Darkness* – resources to be visited, talked about, described, or appreciated for domestic reasons, for local metropolitan benefit. If we think ahead to these other novels, Sir Thomas's Antigua readily acquires a slightly greater density than the discrete, reticent appearances it makes in the pages of *Mansfield Park*. And already our reading of the novel begins to open up at those points where ironically Austen was most economical and her critics most (dare one say it?) negligent. Her "Antigua" is therefore not just a slight but a definite way of marking the outer limits of what Williams calls domestic improvements, or a quick allusion to the mercantile venturesomeness of acquiring overseas dominions as a source for local fortunes, or one reference among many attesting to a historical sensibility suffused not just with manners and courtesies but with contests of ideas, struggles with Napoleonic France, awareness of seismic economic and social change during a revolutionary period in world history.

Second, we must see "Antigua" held in a precise place in Austen's moral geography, and in her prose, by historical changes that her novel rides like a vessel on a mighty sea. The Bertrams could not have been possible without the slave trade, sugar, and the colonial planter class; as a social type Sir Thomas would have been familiar to eighteenth- and early-nineteenth-century readers who knew the powerful influence of the class through politics, plays (like Cumberland's *The West Indian*), and many other public activities (large houses, famous parties and social rituals, well-known commercial enterprises, celebrated marriages). As the old system of protected monopoly gradually disappeared and as a new class of settler-planters displaced the old absentee system, the West Indian interest lost dominance: cotton manufacture, an even more open system of trade, and abolition of the slave trade reduced the power and prestige of people like the Bertrams, whose frequency of sojourn in the Caribbean then decreased.

Thus Sir Thomas's infrequent trips to Antigua as an absentee plantation owner reflect the diminishment in his class's power, a reduction directly expressed in the title of Lowell Ragatz's classic *The Fall of the Planter Class in the British Caribbean, 1763–1833* (1928). But is what is hidden or allusive in Austen made sufficiently explicit more than one hundred years later in Ragatz? Does the aesthetic silence or discretion of a great novel in 1814 receive adequate explication in a major work of historical research a full century later? Can we assume that the process of interpretation is fulfilled, or will it continue as new material comes to light?

For all his learning Ragatz still finds it in himself to speak of "the Negro race" as having the following characteristics: "he stole, he lied, he was simple, suspicious, inefficient, irresponsible, lazy, superstitious, and loose in his sexual relations."[36] Such "history" as this therefore happily gave way to the revisionary work of Caribbean historians like Eric Williams and C. L. R. James, and more recently Robin Blackburn, in *The Overthrow of Colonial Slavery, 1776–1848*; in these works slavery and empire are shown to have fostered the rise and consolidation of capitalism well beyond the old plantation monopolies, as well as to have been a powerful ideological system whose original connection to specific economic interests may have gone, but whose effects continued for decades.

> The political and moral ideas of the age are to be examined in the very closest relation to the economic development....
> An outworn interest, whose bankruptcy smells to heaven in historical perspective, can exercise an obstructionist and disruptive effect which can only be explained by the powerful services it had previously rendered and the entrenchment previously gained....
> The ideas built on these interests continue long after the interests have been destroyed and work their old mischief, which is all the more mischievous because the interests to which they corresponded no longer exist.[37]

Thus Eric Williams in *Capitalism and Slavery* (1961). The question of interpretation, indeed of writing itself, is tied to the question of interests, which we have seen are at work in aesthetic as well as historical writing, then and now. We must not say that since *Mansfield Park* is a novel, its affiliations with a sordid history are irrelevant or transcended, not only because it is irresponsible to do so, but because we know too much to say so in good faith. Having read *Mansfield Park* as part of the structure of an expanding imperialist venture, one cannot simply restore it to the canon of "great literary masterpieces" – to which it most certainly belongs – and leave it at that. Rather, I think, the novel steadily, if unobtrusively, opens up a broad expanse of domestic imperialist culture without which Britain's subsequent acquisition of territory would not have been possible.

I have spent time on *Mansfield Park* to illustrate a type of analysis infrequently encountered in mainstream interpretations, or for that matter in readings rigorously based in one or another of the advanced theoretical schools. Yet only in the global perspective implied by Jane Austen and her characters can the novel's quite astonishing general position be made clear. I think of such a reading as completing or complementing others, not discounting or displacing them. And it bears stressing that because *Mansfield Park* connects the actualities of British power overseas to the domestic imbroglio within the Bertram estate, there is no way of doing such readings as mine, no way of understanding the "structure of attitude and reference" except by working through the novel. Without reading it in full, we would fail to understand the strength of that structure and the way it was activated and maintained in literature. But in reading it carefully, we can sense how ideas about dependent races and territories were held both by foreign-office executives, colonial bureaucrats, and military strategists and by intelligent novel-readers educating themselves in the fine points of moral evaluation, literary balance, and stylistic finish.

There is a paradox here in reading Jane Austen which I have been impressed by but can in no way resolve. All the evidence says that even the most routine aspects of holding slaves on a West Indian sugar plantation were cruel stuff. And everything we know about Austen and her values is at odds with the cruelty of slavery. Fanny Price reminds her cousin that after asking Sir Thomas about the slave trade, "There was such a dead silence"[38] as to suggest that one world could not be connected with the other since there simply is no common language for both. That is true. But what stimulates the extraordinary discrepancy into life is the rise, decline, and fall of the British empire itself and, in its aftermath, the emergence of a post-colonial consciousness. In order more accurately to read works like *Mansfield Park*, we have to see them in the main as resisting or avoiding that other setting, which their formal inclusiveness, historical honesty, and prophetic suggestiveness cannot completely hide. In time there would no longer be a dead silence when slavery was spoken of, and the subject became central to a new understanding of what Europe was.

It would be silly to expect Jane Austen to treat slavery with anything like the passion of an abolitionist or a newly liberated slave. Yet what I have called the rhetoric of blame, so often now employed by subaltern, minority, or disadvantaged voices, attacks her, and others like her, retrospectively, for being white, privileged, insensitive, complicit. Yes, Austen belonged to a slave-owning society, but do we therefore jettison her novels as so many trivial exercises in aesthetic frumpery? Not at all, I would argue, if we take seriously our intellectual and interpretative vocation to make connections, to deal with as much of the evidence as possible, fully and actually, to read what is there or not there, above all, to see complementarity and interdependence instead of isolated, venerated, or formalized experience that excludes and forbids the hybridizing intrusions of human history.

Mansfield Park is a rich work in that its aesthetic intellectual complexity requires that longer and slower analysis that is also required by its geographical problematic, a novel based in an England relying for the maintenance of its style on a Caribbean island. When Sir Thomas goes to and comes from Antigua, where he has property, that is not at all the same thing as coming to and going from Mansfield Park, where his presence, arrivals, and departures have very considerable consequences. But precisely because Austen is so summary in one context, so provocatively rich in the other, precisely because of that imbalance we are able to move in on the novel, reveal and accentuate the interdependence scarcely mentioned on its brilliant pages. A lesser work wears its historical affiliation more plainly; its worldliness is simple and direct, the way a jingoistic ditty during the Mahdist uprising or the 1857 Indian Rebellion connects directly to the situation and constituency that coined it. *Mansfield Park* encodes experiences and does not simply repeat them. From our later perspective we can interpret Sir Thomas's power to come and go in Antigua as stemming from the muted national experience of individual identity, behavior, and "ordination," enacted with such irony and taste at Mansfield Park. The task is to lose neither a true historical sense of the first, nor a full enjoyment or appreciation of the second, all the while seeing both together.

NOTES

1 Ian Watt, *The Rise of the Novel* (Berkeley: University of California Press, 1957) [see also pp. 462–80 in this book]; Lennard Davis, *Factual Fictions: The Origins of the English Novel* (New York: Columbia University Press, 1983); John Richetti, *Popular Fiction Before Richardson* (London: Oxford University Press, 1969); Michael McKeon, *The Origin of the English Novel, 1600–1740* (Baltimore: Johns Hopkins University Press, 1987).

2 J. R. Seeley, *The Expansion of England* (1884; rprt. Chicago: University of Chicago Press, 1971), p. 12; J. A. Hobson, *Imperialism: A Study* (1902; rprt. Ann Arbor: University of Michigan Press, 1972), p. 15. Although Hobson implicates other European powers in the perversions of imperialism, England stands out.

3 Raymond Williams, *The Country and the City* (New York: Oxford University Press, 1973), pp. 165–82 and *passim*.

4 D. C. M. Platt, *Finance, Trade and Politics in British Foreign Policy, 1815–1914* (Oxford: Clarendon Press, 1968), p. 536.

5 Ibid., p. 357.

6 Joseph Schumpeter, *Imperialism and Social Classes*, trans. Heinz Norden (New York: Augustus M. Kelley, 1951), p. 12.

7 Platt, *Finance, Trade and Politics*, p. 359.

8 Ronald Robinson and John Gallagher, with Alice Denny, *Africa and the Victorians: The Official Mind of Imperialism* (1961; new ed. London: Macmillan, 1981), p. 10. But for a vivid sense of what effects this thesis has had in scholarly discussion of empire, see William Roger Louis, ed., *Imperialism: The Robinson and Gallagher Controversy* (New York: Franklin Watts, 1976). An essential compilation for the whole field of study is Robin Winks, ed., *The Historiography of the British Empire-Commonwealth: Trends, Interpretations, and Resources* (Durham: Duke University Press, 1966). Two compilations mentioned by Winks (p. 6) are *Historians of India, Pakistan and Ceylon*, ed. Cyril H. Philips, and *Historians of South East Asia*, ed. D. G. E. Hall.

9 Fredric Jameson, *The Political Unconscious: Narrative as a Socially Symbolic Act* (Ithaca: Cornell University Press, 1981), [see also pp. 413–33 in this book]; David A. Miller, *The Novel and the Police* (Berkeley: University of California Press, 1988) [see also pp. 541–57 in this book]. See also Hugh Ridley, *Images of Imperial Rule* (London: Croom Helm, 1983).

10 In John MacKenzie, *Propaganda and Empire: The Manipulation of British Public Opinion, 1880–1960* (Manchester: Manchester University Press, 1984), there is an excellent account of how popular culture was effective in the official age of empire. See also MacKenzie, ed., *Imperialism and Popular Culture* (Manchester: Manchester University Press, 1986); for more subtle manipulations of the English national identity during the same period, see Robert Colls and Philip Dodd, eds., *Englishness: Politics and Culture, 1880–1920* (London: Croom Helm, 1987).

See also Raphael Samuel, ed., *Patriotism: The Making and Unmaking of British National Identity*, 3 vols. (London: Routledge, 1989).

11 E. M. Forster, *A Passage to India* (1924; rprt. New York: Harcourt, Brace & World, 1952), p. 231.

12 For the attack on Conrad, see Chinua Achebe, "An Image of Africa: Racism in Conrad's *Heart of Darkness*," in *Hopes and Impediments: Selected Essays* (New York: Doubleday, Anchor, 1989), pp. 1–20. Some of the issues raised by Achebe are well discussed by Brantlinger, *Rule of Darkness*, pp. 269–74.

13 Deirdre David, *Fictions of Resolution in Three Victorian Novels* (New York: Columbia University Press, 1981).

14 Georg Lukács, *The Historical Novel*, trans. Hannah and Stanley Mitchell (London: Merlin Press, 1962), pp. 19–88.

15 Ibid., pp. 30–63.

16 A few lines from Ruskin are quoted and commented on in R. Koebner and H. Schmidt, *Imperialism: The Story and Significance of a Political World, 1840–1866* (Cambridge: Cambridge University Press, 1964), p. 99.

17 V. G. Kiernan, *Marxism and Imperialism* (New York: St. Martin's Press, 1974), p. 100.

18 John Stuart Mill, *Disquisitions and Discussions*, Vol. 3 (London: Longmans, Green, Reader & Dyer, 1875), pp. 167–68. For an earlier version of this see the discussion by Nicholas Canny, "The Ideology of English Colonization: From Ireland to America," *William and Mary Quarterly* 30 (1973), 575–98.

19 Williams, *Country and the City*, p. 281.

20 Peter Hulme, *Colonial Encounters: Europe and the Native Caribbean, 1492–1797* (London: Methuen, 1986). See also his anthology with Neil L. Whitehead, *Wild Majesty: Encounters with Caribs from Columbus to the Present Day* (Oxford: Clarendon Press, 1992).

21 Hobson, *Imperialism*, p. 6.

22 This is most memorably discussed in C. L. R. James's *The Black Jacobins: Toussaint L'Ouverture and the San Domingo Revolution* (1938; rprt. New York: Vintage, 1963), especially Chapter 2, "The Owners." See also Robin Blackburn, *The Overthrow of Colonial Slavery, 1776–1848* (London: Verso, 1988), pp. 149–53.

23 Williams, *Country and the City*, p. 117.

24 Jane Austen, *Mansfield Park*, ed. Tony Tanner (1814; rprt. Harmondsworth: Penguin, 1966), p. 42. The best account of the novel is in Tony Tanner's *Jane Austen* (Cambridge, Mass.: Harvard University Press, 1986).

25 Ibid., p. 54.

26 Ibid., p. 206.

27 Warren Roberts, *Jane Austen and the French Revolution* (London: Macmillan, 1979), pp. 97–98. See also Avrom Fleishman, *A Reading of* Mansfield Park: *An Essay in Critical Synthesis* (Minneapolis: University of Minnesota Press, 1967), pp. 36–39 and *passim*.

28 Austen, *Mansfield Park*, pp. 375–76.

29 John Stuart Mill, *Principles of Political Economy*, Vol. 3, ed. J. M. Robson (Toronto: University of Toronto Press, 1965), p. 693. The passage is quoted in Sidney W. Mintz, *Sweetness and Power: The Place of Sugar in Modern History* (New York: Viking, 1985), p. 42.

30 Austen, *Mansfield Park*, p. 446.

31 Ibid., p. 448.

32 Ibid., p. 450.

33 Ibid., p. 456.

34 John Gallagher, *The Decline, Revival and Fall of the British Empire* (Cambridge: Cambridge University Press, 1982), p. 76.

35 Austen, *Mansfield Park*, p. 308.

EDWARD W. SAID

36 Lowell Joseph Ragatz, *The Fall of the Planter Class in the British Caribbean, 1763–1833: A Study in Social and Economic History* (1928; rprt. New York: Octagon, 1963), p. 27.
37 Eric Williams, *Capitalism and Slavery* (New York: Russell & Russell, 1961), p. 211. See also his *From Columbus to Castro: The History of the Caribbean, 1492–1969* (London: Deutsch, 1970), pp. 177–254.
38 Austen, *Mansfield Park*, p. 213.

34

The Location
of Culture

Homi K. Bhabha

Homi K. Bhabha (b. 1949)

Born in Bombay, India, Homi K. Bhabha received his bachelor's degree from Elphinstone College, University of Bombay, and his doctorate from Christ Church, Oxford. After teaching at Sussex University (1978–94) and the University of Chicago (1994–2000), Bhabha moved to Harvard University, where he is Anne F. Rothenberg Professor of English and American Literature, and chair of the Program in History and Literature. An art critic as well as a literary theorist, Bhabha has been a columnist for *Artforum* since 1995, serves on the board of INVIVA (the London International Institute of the Visual Arts), and is a special advisor to the Director of the Whitney Museum of American Art in New York. Bhabha has been honored with the Asian American Institute Milestone Award and as one of *Newsweek*'s 100 Americans to watch for the next century (1997). His books include *The Location of Culture* (1993); *The Right to Narrate* (forthcoming); and *A Measure of Dwelling: Reflections on Vernacular Cosmopolitanism* (forthcoming).

From *The Location of Culture*. London and New York: Routledge, 1994, from ch. 8, pp. 139–57, notes, pp. 266–8. Copyright © Homi K. Bhabha. Reprinted by permission of Homi K. Bhabha.

DissemiNation: Time, Narrative, and the Margins of the Modern Nation[1]

The Time of the Nation

The title of this chapter – DissemiNation – owes something to the wit and wisdom of Jacques Derrida, but something more to my own experience of migration. I have lived that moment of the scattering of the people that in other times and other places, in the nations of others, becomes a time of gathering. Gatherings of exiles and *émigrés* and refugees; gathering on the edge of 'foreign' cultures; gathering at the frontiers; gatherings in the ghettos or cafés of city centres; gathering in the half-life, half-light of foreign tongues, or in the uncanny fluency of another's language; gathering the signs of approval and acceptance, degrees, discourses, disciplines; gathering the memories of underdevelopment, of other worlds lived retroactively; gathering the past in a ritual of revival; gathering the present. Also the gathering of people in the diaspora: indentured, migrant, interned; the gathering of incriminatory statistics, educational performance, legal statutes, immigration status – the genealogy of that lonely figure that John Berger named the seventh man. The gathering of clouds from which the Palestinian poet Mahmoud Darwish asks 'where should the birds fly after the last sky?'[2]

In the midst of these lonely gatherings of the scattered people, their myths and fantasies and experiences, there emerges a historical fact of singular importance. More deliberately than any other general historian, Eric Hobsbawm[3] writes the history of the modern Western nation from the perspective of the nation's margin and the migrants' exile. The emergence of the later phase of the modern nation, from the mid-nineteenth century, is also one of the most sustained periods of mass migration within the West, and colonial expansion in the East. The nation fills the void left in the uprooting of communities and kin, and turns that loss into the language of metaphor. Metaphor, as the etymology of the word suggests, transfers the meaning of home and belonging, across the 'middle passage', or the central European steppes, across those distances, and cultural differences, that span the imagined community of the nation-people.

The discourse of national*ism* is not my main concern. In some ways it is the historical certainty and settled nature of that term against which I am attempting to write of the Western nation as an obscure and ubiquitous form of living the *locality* of culture. This locality is more *around* temporality than *about* historicity: a form of living that is more complex than 'community'; more symbolic than 'society'; more connotative than 'country'; less patriotic than *patrie*; more rhetorical than the reason of State; more mythological than ideology; less homogeneous than hegemony; less centred than the citizen; more collective than 'the subject'; more psychic than civility; more hybrid in the articulation of cultural differences and identifications than can be represented in any hierarchical or binary structuring of social antagonism.

In proposing this cultural construction of nationness as a form of social and textual affiliation, I do not wish to deny these categories their specific histories and particular meanings within different political languages. What I am attempting to formulate in this chapter are the complex strategies of cultural identification and discursive address that function in the name of 'the people' or 'the nation' and make them the immanent subjects of a range of social and literary narratives. My emphasis on the temporal dimension in the inscription of these political entities – that are also potent symbolic and affective sources of cultural identity – serves to displace the historicism that has dominated discussions of the nation as a cultural force. The linear equivalence of event and idea that historicism proposes, most commonly signifies a people, a nation, or a national culture as an empirical sociological category or a holistic cultural entity. However, the narrative and psychological force that nationness brings to bear on cultural production and political projection is the effect of the ambivalence of the 'nation' as a narrative strategy. As an apparatus of symbolic power, it produces a continual slippage of categories, like sexuality, class affiliation, territorial paranoia, or 'cultural difference' in the act of writing the nation. What is displayed in this displacement and repetition of terms is the nation as the measure of the liminality of cultural modernity.

Edward Said aspires to such secular interpretation in his concept of 'wordliness' where 'sensuous particularity as well as historical contingency...exist *at the same level of surface particularity* as the textual object itself' (my emphasis).[4] Fredric Jameson invokes something similar in his notion of 'situational consciousness' or national allegory, 'where the telling of the individual story and the individual experience cannot but ultimately involve the whole laborious telling of the collectivity itself.'[5] And Julia Kristeva speaks perhaps too hastily of the pleasure of exile – 'How can one avoid sinking into the mire of common sense, if not by becoming a stranger to one's own country, language, sex and identity?'[6] – without realizing how fully the shadow of the nation falls on the condition of exile – which may partly explain her own later, labile identifications with the images of *other* nations: 'China', 'America'. The entitlement of the nation is its metaphor: *Amor Patria; Fatherland; Pig Earth; Mothertongue; Matigari; Middlemarch; Midnight's Children; One Hundred Years of Solitude; War and Peace; I Promessi Sposi; Kanthapura; Moby-Dick; The Magic Mountain; Things Fall Apart.*

There must be a tribe of interpreters of such metaphors – the translators of the dissemination of texts and discourses across cultures – who can perform what Said describes as the act of secular interpretation.

> To take account of this horizontal, secular space of the crowded spectacle of the modern nation...implies that no single explanation sending one back immediately to a single origin is adequate. And just as there are no simple dynastic answers, there are no simple discrete formations or social processes.[7]

If, in our travelling theory, we are alive to the *metaphoricity* of the peoples of imagined communities – migrant or metropolitan – then we shall find that the space of the modern nation-people is never simply horizontal. Their metaphoric movement requires a kind of 'doubleness' in writing; a temporality of representation that moves between cultural formations and social processes without a centred causal logic. And such cultural movements disperse the homogeneous, visual time of the horizontal society. The secular language of interpretation needs to go beyond the horizontal critical gaze if we are to give 'the nonsequential energy of lived historical memory and subjectivity' its appropriate narrative authority. We need another time of *writing* that will be able to inscribe the ambivalent and chiasmatic intersections of time and place that constitute the problematic 'modern' experience of the Western nation.

HOMI K. BHABHA

How does one write the nation's modernity as the event of the everyday and the advent of the epochal? The language of national belonging comes laden with atavistic apologues, which has led Benedict Anderson to ask: 'But why do nations celebrate their hoariness, not their astonishing youth?'[8] The nation's claim to modernity, as an autonomous or sovereign form of political rationality, is particularly questionable if, with Partha Chatterjee, we adopt the postcolonial perspective:

> Nationalism...seeks to represent itself in the image of the Englightenment and fails to do so. For Enlightenment itself, to assert its sovereignty as the universal ideal, needs its Other; if it could ever actualise itself in the real world as the truly universal, it would in fact destroy itself.[9]

Such ideological ambivalence nicely supports Ernest Gellner's paradoxical point that the historical necessity of the idea of the nation conflicts with the contingent and arbitrary signs and symbols that signify the affective life of the national culture. The nation may exemplify modern social cohesion but

> Nationalism is not what it seems, and *above all not what it seems to itself.*...The cultural shreds and patches used by nationalism are often arbitrary historical inventions. Any old shred would have served as well. But in no way does it follow that the principle of nationalism...is itself in the least contingent and accidental.[10] (My emphasis)

The problematic boundaries of modernity are enacted in these ambivalent temporalities of the nation-space. The language of culture and community is poised on the fissures of the present becoming the rhetorical figures of a national past. Historians transfixed on the event and origins of the nation never ask, and political theorists possessed of the 'modern' totalities of the nation – 'homogeneity, literacy and anonymity are the key traits'[11] – never pose, the essential question of the representation of the nation as a temporal process.

It is indeed only in the disjunctive time of the nation's modernity – as a knowledge caught between political rationality and its impasse, between the shreds and patches of cultural signification and the certainties of a nationalist pedagogy – that questions of nation as narration come to be posed. How do we plot the narrative of the nation that must mediate between the teleology of progress tipping over into the 'timeless' discourse of irrationality? How do we understand that 'homogeneity' of modernity – the people – which, if pushed too far, may assume something resembling the archaic body of the despotic or totalitarian mass? In the midst of progress and modernity, the language of ambivalence reveals a politics 'without duration', as Althusser once provocatively wrote: 'Space without places, time without duration.'[12] To write the story of the nation demands that we articulate that archaic ambivalence that informs the *time* of modernity. We may begin by questioning that progressive metaphor of modern social cohesion – *the many as one* – shared by organic theories of the holism of culture and community, and by theorists who treat gender, class or race as social totalities that are expressive of unitary collective experiences.

Out of many one: nowhere has this founding dictum of the political society of the modern nation – its spatial expression of a unitary people – found a more intriguing *image* of itself than in those diverse languages of literary criticism that seek to portray the great power of the idea of the nation in the disclosures of its everyday life; in the telling details that emerge as metaphors for national life. I am reminded of Bakhtin's wonderful description of a national *vision of emergence* in Goethe's *Italian Journey*, which represents the triumph of the Realistic component over the Romantic. Goethe's realist narrative produces a national-historical time that makes visible a specifically Italian day in the detail of its passing time: 'The bells ring, the rosary is said, the maid enters the room with a lighted lamp and says: *Felicissima notte!...If one were to force a German clockhand on them, they would be at a loss*.'[13] For Bakhtin, it is Goethe's vision of the microscopic, elementary, perhaps random, tolling of everyday life in Italy that reveals the profound history of its locality (*Lokalität*), the spatialization of historical time, 'a creative humanization of this locality, which transforms a part of terrestrial space into a place of historical life for people'.[14]

The recurrent metaphor of landscape as the inscape of national identity emphasizes the quality of light, the question of social visibility, the power of the eye to naturalize the rhetoric of national affiliation and its forms of collective expression. There is, however, always the distracting presence of another temporality that disturbs the contemporaneity of the national present, as we saw in the national discourses with which I began. Despite Bakhtin's emphasis on the realist vision in the emergence of the nation in Goethe's work, he acknowledges that the origin of the nation's visual *presence* is the effect of a narrative struggle. From the beginning, Bakhtin writes, the Realist and Romantic conceptions of time coexist in Goethe's work, but the ghostly (*Gespenstermässiges*), the terrifying (*Unerfreuliches*), and the unaccountable (*Unzuberechnendes*) are consistently surmounted by the structuring process of the visualization of time: 'the necessity of the past and the necessity of its place in a line of continuous development...finally the aspect of the past being linked to the necessary future'.[15] National time becomes concrete and visible in the chronotype of the local, particular, graphic, from beginning to end. The narrative structure of this *historical* surmounting of the 'ghostly' or the 'double' is seen in the intensification of narrative synchrony as a graphically visible position in space: 'to grasp the most elusive course of pure historical time and fix it through unmediated contemplation'.[16] But what kind of 'present' is this if it is a consistent process of surmounting the ghostly time of repetition? Can this national time-space be as fixed or as immediately visible as Bakhtin claims?

If in Bakhtin's 'surmounting' we hear the echo of another use of that word by Freud in his essay on 'The "uncanny"', then we begin to get a sense of the complex time of the national narrative. Freud associates *surmounting* with the repressions of a 'cultural' unconscious; a liminal, uncertain state of cultural belief when the archaic emerges in the midst of margins of modernity as a result of some psychic ambivalence or intellectual uncertainty. The 'double' is the figure most frequently associated with this uncanny process of 'the doubling, dividing and interchanging of the self'.[17] Such 'double-time' cannot be so simply represented as visible or flexible in 'unmediated contemplation'; nor can we accept Bakhtin's repeated attempt to read the national space as achieved only in the *fullness of time*. Such an apprehension of the 'double and split' time of national representation, as I am proposing, leads us to question the homogeneous and horizontal view associated with the nation's imagined community. We are led to ask whether the *emergence* of a national perspective – of an élite or

HOMI K. BHABHA

subaltern nature – within a culture of social contestation, can ever articulate its 'representative' authority in that fullness of narrative time and visual synchrony of the sign that Bakhtin proposes.

Two accounts of the emergence of national narratives seem to support my suggestion. They represent the diametrically opposed world views of master and slave which, between them, account for the major historical and philosophical dialectic of modern times. I am thinking of John Barrell's[18] splendid analysis of the rhetorical and perspectival status of the 'English gentleman' within the social diversity of the eighteenth-century novel; and of Houston Baker's innovative reading of the 'new *national* modes of sounding, interpreting and speaking the Negro in the Harlem Renaissance'.[19]

In his concluding essay Barrell demonstrates how the demand for a holistic, representative vision of society could only be represented in a discourse that was *at the same time* obsessively fixed upon, and uncertain of, the boundaries of society, and the margins of the text. For instance, the hypostatized 'common language' which was the language of the gentleman whether he be Observer, Spectator, Rambler, 'Common to all by virtue of the fact that it manifested the peculiarities of none'[20] – was primarily defined through a process of negation – of regionalism, occupation, faculty – so that this centred vision of 'the gentleman' is so to speak 'a condition of empty potential, one who is imagined as being able to comprehend everything, and yet who may give no evidence of having comprehended anything.'[21]

A different note of liminality is struck in Baker's description of the 'radical maroonage' that structured the emergence of an insurgent Afro-American expressive culture in its expansive, 'national' phase. Baker's sense that the 'discursive project' of the Harlem Renaissance is modernist is based less on a strictly literary understanding of the term, and more on the agonistic enunciative conditions within which the Harlem Renaissance shaped its cultural practice. The transgressive, invasive structure of the black 'national' text, which thrives on rhetorical strategies of hybridity, deformation, masking, and inversion, is developed through an extended analogy with the guerilla warfare that became a way of life for the maroon communities of runaway slaves and fugitives who lived dangerously, and insubordinately, 'on the frontiers or margins of *all* American promise, profit and modes of production'.[22] From this liminal, minority position where, as Foucault would say, the relations of discourse are of the nature of warfare, the force of the people of an Afro-American nation emerges in the extended metaphor of maroonage. For 'warriors' read writers or even 'signs':

> these highly adaptable and mobile warriors took maximum advantage of local environments, striking and withdrawing with great rapidity, making extensive use of bushes to catch their adversaries in cross-fire, fighting only when and where they chose, depending on reliable intelligence networks among non-maroons (both slave and white settlers) and often communicating by horns.[23]

Both gentleman and slave, with different cultural means and to very different historical ends, demonstrate that forces of social authority and subversion or subalternity may emerge in displaced, even decentred strategies of signification. This does not prevent these positions from being effective in a political sense, although it does suggest that positions of authority may themselves be part of a process of ambivalent identification. Indeed the exercise of power may be both politically effective and psychically *affective* because the discursive liminality through which it is signified may provide greater scope for strategic manoeuvre and negotiation.

It is precisely in reading between these borderlines of the nation-space that we can see how the concept of the 'people' emerges within a range of discourses as a double narrative movement. The people are not simply historical events or parts of a patriotic body politic. They are also a complex rhetorical strategy of social reference: their claim to be representative provokes a crisis within the process of signification and discursive address. We then have a contested conceptual territory where the nation's people must be thought in double-time; the people are the historical 'objects' of a nationalist pedagogy, giving the discourse an authority that is based on the pre-given or constituted historical origin *in the past*; the people are also the 'subjects' of a process of signification that must erase any prior or originary presence of the nation-people to demonstrate the prodigious, living principles of the people as contemporaneity: as that sign of the *present* through which national life is redeemed and iterated as a reproductive process.

The scraps, patches and rags of daily life must be repeatedly turned into the signs of a coherent national culture, while the very act of the narrative performance interpellates a growing circle of national subjects. In the production of the nation as narration there is a split between the continuist, accumulative temporality of the pedagogical, and the repetitious, recursive strategy of the performative. It is through this process of splitting that the conceptual ambivalence of modern society becomes the site of *writing the nation*.

The Space of the People

The tension between the pedagogical and the performative that I have identified in the narrative address of the nation, turns the reference to a 'people' – from whatever political or cultural position it is made – into a problem of knowledge that haunts the symbolic formation of modern social authority. The people are neither the beginning nor the end of the national narrative; they represent the cutting edge between the totalizing powers of the 'social' as homogeneous, consensual community, and the forces that signify the more specific address to contentious, unequal interests and identities within the population. The ambivalent signifying system of the nation-space participates in a more general genesis of ideology in modern societies that Claude Lefort has described. For him too it is 'enigma of language', at once internal and external to the speaking subject, that provides the most apt analogue for imagining the structure of ambivalence that constitutes modern social authority. I shall quote him at length, because his rich ability to represent the *movement of* political power *beyond* the binary division of the blindness of Ideology or the insight of the Idea, brings him to that liminal site of modern society from which I have attempted to derive the narrative of the nation and its people.

> In Ideology the representation of the rule is split from the effective operation of it.... The rule is thus extracted from experience of language; it is circumscribed, made fully visible

HOMI K. BHABHA

and assumed to govern the conditions of possibility of this experience.... The enigma of language – namely that it is both internal and external to the speaking subject, that there is an articulation of the self with others which marks the emergence of the self and which the self does not control – is concealed by the representation of a place 'outside' – language from which it could be generated.... We encounter the ambiguity of the representation as soon as the rule is stated; for its very exhibition undermines the power that the rule claims to introduce into practice. This exorbitant power must, in fact, be shown, and at the same time it must owe nothing to the movement which makes it appear.... To be true to its image, the rule must be abstracted from any question concerning its origin; thus it goes beyond the operations that it controls.... Only the authority of the master allows the contradiction to be concealed, but he is himself an object of representation; presented as possessor of the knowledge of the rule, he allows the contradiction to appear through himself.

The ideological discourse that we are examining has no safety catch; it is rendered vulnerable by its attempt to make visible the place from which the social relation would be conceivable (both thinkable and creatable) by its inability to define this place without letting its contingency appear, without condemning itself to slide from one position to another, without hereby making apparent the instability of an order that it is intended to raise to the status of essence.... [The ideological] task of the implicit generalization of knowledge and the implicit homogenization of experience could fall apart in the face of the unbearable ordeal of the collapse of certainty, of the vacillation of representations of discourse and as a result of the splitting of the subject.[24]

How do we conceive of the 'splitting' of the national subject? How do we articulate cultural differences within this vacillation of ideology in which the national discourse also participates, sliding ambivalently from one enunciatory position to another? What are the forms of life struggling to be represented in that unruly 'time' of national culture, which Bakhtin surmounts in his reading of Goethe, Gellner associates with the rags and patches of everyday life, Said describes as 'the non-sequential energy of lived historical memory and subjectivity' and Lefort re-presents as the inexorable *movement of signification* that both constitutes the exorbitant image of power and deprives it of the certainty and stability of centre or closure? What might be the cultural and political effects of the liminality of the nation, the margins of modernity, which come to be signified in the narrative temporalities of splitting, ambivalence and vacillation?

Deprived of that unmediated visibility of historicism – 'looking to the legitimacy of past generations as supplying cultural autonomy'[25] – the nation turns from being the symbol of modernity into becoming the symptom of an ethnography of the 'contemporary' within modern culture. Such a shift in perspective emerges from an acknowledgement of the nation's interrupted address articulated in the tension between signifying the people as an a priori historical presence, a pedagogical object; and the people constructed in the performance of narrative, its enunciatory 'present' marked in the repetition and pulsation of the national sign. The pedagogical founds its narrative authority in a tradition of the people, described by Poulantzas[26] as a moment of becoming designated by *itself*, encapsulated in a succession of historical moments that represents an eternity produced by self-generation. The performative intervenes in the sovereignty of the nation's *self-generation* by casting a shadow *between* the people as 'image' and its signification as a differentiating sign of Self, distinct from the Other of the Outside.

In place of the polarity of a prefigurative self-generating nation 'in-itself' and extrinsic other nations, the performative introduces a temporality of the 'in-between'. The boundary that marks the nation's selfhood interrupts the self-generating time of national production and disrupts the signification of the people as homogeneous. The problem is not simply the 'selfhood' of the nation as opposed to the otherness of other nations. We are confronted with the nation split within itself, articulating the heterogeneity of its population. The barred Nation *It/Self*, alienated from its eternal self-generation, becomes a liminal signifying space that is *internally* marked by the discourses of minorities, the heterogeneous histories of contending peoples, antagonistic authorities and tense locations of cultural difference.

This double-writing or dissemi-*nation*, is not simply a theoretical exercise in the internal contradictions of the modern liberal nation. The structure of cultural liminality *within the nation* would be an essential precondition for deploying a concept such as Raymond Williams's crucial distinction between residual and emergent practices in oppositional cultures which require, he insists, a 'non-metaphysical, non-subjectivist' mode of explanation. The space of cultural signification that I have attempted to open up through the intervention of the performative, would meet this important precondition. The liminal figure of the nation-space would ensure that no political ideologies could claim transcendent or metaphysical authority for themselves. This is because the subject of cultural discourse – the agency of a people – is split in the discursive ambivalence that emerges in the contest of narrative authority between the pedagogical and the performative. This disjunctive temporality of the nation would provide the appropriate time-frame for representing those residual and emergent meanings and practices that Williams locates in the margins of the contemporary experience of society. Their emergence depends upon a kind of social ellipsis; their transformational power depends upon their being historically displaced:

> But in certain areas, there will be in certain periods, practices and meanings which are not reached for. There will be areas of practice and meaning which, almost by definition from its own limited character, or in its profound deformation, the dominant culture is unable in any real terms to recognize.[27]

When Edward Said suggests that the question of the nation should be put on the contemporary critical agenda as a hermeneutic of 'worldliness', he is fully aware that such a demand can only now be made from the liminal and ambivalent boundaries that articulate the signs of national culture, as 'zones of control *or* of abandonment, or recollection *and* of forgetting, of force *or* of dependence, of exclusiveness *or* of sharing' (my emphasis).[28]

Counter-narratives of the nation that continually evoke and erase its totalizing boundaries – both actual and conceptual – disturb those ideological manœuvres through which 'imagined communities' are given essentialist identities. For the political unity of the nation consists in a continual displacement of the anxiety of its irredeemably plural modern space – representing the nation's modern territoriality is turned into the archaic, atavistic temporality of Traditionalism. The difference of space returns as the

HOMI K. BHABHA

Sameness of time, turning Territory into Tradition, turning the People into One. The liminal point of this ideological displacement is the turning of the differentiated spatial boundary, the 'outside', into the authenticating 'inward' time of Tradition. Freud's concept of the 'narcissism of minor differences'[29] – reinterpreted for our purposes – provides a way of undertanding how easily the boundary that secures the cohesive limits of the Western nation may imperceptibly turn into a contentious *internal* liminality providing a place from which to speak both of, and as, the minority, the exilic, the marginal and the emergent.

Freud uses the analogy of feuds that prevail between communities with adjoining territories – the Spanish and the Portuguese, for instance – to illustrate the ambivalent identification of love and hate that binds a community together: 'it is always possible to bind together a considerable number of people in love, so long as there are other people left to receive the manifestation of their aggressiveness.'[30] The problem is, of course, that the ambivalent identifications of love and hate occupy the same psychic space; and paranoid projections 'outwards' return to haunt and split the place from which they are made. So long as a firm boundary is maintained between the territories, and the narcissistic wound is contained, the aggressivity will be projected on to the Other or the Outside. But what if, as I have argued, the people are the articulation of a doubling of the national address, an ambivalent *movement* between the discourses of pedagogy and the performative? What if, as Lefort argues, the subject of modern ideology is split between the iconic image of authority and the movement of the signifier that produces the image, so that the 'sign' of the social is condemned to slide ceaselessly from one position to another? It is in this space of liminality, in the 'unbearable ordeal of the collapse of certainty' that we encounter once again the narcissistic neuroses of the national discourse with which I began. The nation is no longer the sign of modernity under which cultural differences are homogenized in the 'horizontal' view of society. The nation reveals, in its ambivalent and vacillating representation, an ethnography of its own claim to being *the* norm of social contemporaneity.

The people turn *pagan* in that disseminatory act of social narrative that Lyotard defines, against the Platonic tradition, as the privileged pole of the narrated:

> where the one doing the speaking speaks from the place of the referent. As narrator she is narrated as well. And in a way she is already told, and what she herself is *telling* will not undo that somewhere else she is *told*.[31] (My emphasis)

This narrative inversion or circulation – which is in the spirit of my splitting of the people – makes untenable any supremacist, or nationalist claims to cultural mastery, for the position of narrative control is neither monocular nor monologic. The subject is graspable only in the passage between telling/told, between 'here' and 'somewhere else', and in this double scene the very condition of cultural knowledge is the alienation of the subject.

The significance of this narrative splitting of the subject of identification is borne out in Lévi-Strauss's description of the ethnographic act.[32] The ethnographic demands that the observer himself is a part of his observation and this requires that the field of knowledge – the total social fact – must be appropriated from the outside like a thing, but like a thing which comprises within itself the subjective understanding of the indigenous. The transposition of this process into the language of the outsider's grasp

– this entry into the area of the symbolic of representation/signification – then makes the social fact 'three-dimensional'. For ethnography demands that the subject has to split itself into object and subject in the process of identifying its field of knowledge. The ethnographic object is constituted 'by dint of the subject's capacity for indefinite self-objectification (without ever quite abolishing itself as subject) for projecting outside itself ever-diminishing fragments of itself'.

Once the liminality of the nation-space is established, and its signifying difference is turned from the boundary 'outside' to its finitude 'within', the threat of cultural difference is no longer a problem of 'other' people. It becomes a question of otherness of the people-as-one. The national subject splits in the ethnographic perspective of culture's contemporaneity and provides both a theoretical position and a narrative authority for marginal voices or minority discourse. They no longer need to address their strategies of opposition to a horizon of 'hegemony' that is envisaged as horizontal and homogeneous. The great contribution of Foucault's last published work is to suggest that people emerge in the modern state as a perpetual movement of 'the marginal integration of individuals'. 'What are we to-day?'[33] Foucault poses this most pertinent ethnographic question to the West itself to reveal the alterity of its political rationality. He suggests that the 'reason of state' in the modern nation must be derived from the heterogeneous and differentiated limits of its territory. The nation cannot be conceived in a state of *equilibrium* between several elements co-ordinated and maintained by a 'good' law.

> Each state is in permanent competition with other countries, other nations…so that each state has nothing before it other than an indefinite future of struggles. Politics has now to deal with an irreducible multiplicity of states struggling and competing in a limited history…the State is its own finality.[34]

What is politically significant is the effect of this finitude of the State on the liminal representation of the people. The people will no longer be contained in that national discourse of the teleology of progress; the anonymity of individuals; the spatial horizon-tality of community; the homogeneous time of social narratives; the historicist visibility of modernity, where 'the present of each level [of the social] coincides with the present of all the others, so that the present is an *essential* section which makes the essence *visible*.[35] The finitude of the nation emphasizes the impossibility of such an expressive totality with its alliance between a plenitudinous present and the eternal visibility of a past. The liminality of the people – their double-inscription as pedagogical objects and performative subjects – demands a 'time' of narrative that is disavowed in the discourse of historicism where narrative is only the agency of the event, or the medium of a naturalistic continuity of Community or Tradition. In describing the marginalistic integration of the individual in the social totality. Foucault provides a useful description of the rationality of the modern nation. Its main characteristic, he writes,

> is neither the constitution of the state, the coldest of cold monsters, nor the rise of bourgeois individualism. I won't even say it is the constant effort to integrate individuals into the political totality. I think that the main characteristic of our political rationality is the fact that this integration of the individuals in a community or in a totality results from a constant correlation between an increasing individualisation and the reinforcement of this

HOMI K. BHABHA

totality. From this point of view we can understand why modern political rationality is permitted by the antinomy between law and order.[36]

From Foucault's *Discipline and Punish* we have learned that the most individuated are those subjects who are placed on the margins of the social, so that the tension between law and order may produce the disciplinary or pastoral society. Having placed the people on the limits of the nation's narrative, I now want to explore forms of cultural identity and political solidarity that emerge from the disjunctive temporalities of the national culture. This is a lesson of history to be learnt from those peoples whose histories of marginality have been most profoundly enmeshed in the antinomies of law and order – the colonized and women.

Of Margins and Minorities

The difficulty of writing the history of the people as the insurmountable agonism of the living, the incommensurable experiences of struggle and survival in the construction of a national culture, is nowhere better seen than in Frantz Fanon's essay 'On national culture'.[37] I start with it because it is a warning against the intellectual appropriation of the 'culture of the people' (whatever that may be) within a representationalist discourse that may become fixed and reified in the annals of History. Fanon writes against that form of nationalist historicism that assumes that there is a moment when the differential temporalities of cultural histories coalesce in an immediately readable present. For my purposes, he focuses on the time of cultural representation, instead of immediately historicizing the event. He explores the space of the nation without immediately identifying it with the historical institution of the State. As my concern here is not with the history of nationalist movements, but only with certain traditions of writing that have attempted to construct narratives of the social imaginary of the nation-people, I am indebted to Fanon for liberating a certain, uncertain time of the people.

The knowledge of the people depends on the discovery, Fanon says, 'of a much more fundamental substance which itself is continually being renewed', a structure of repetition that is not visible in the translucidity of the people's customs or the obvious objectivities which seem to characterize the people. 'Culture abhors simplification,' Fanon writes, as he tries to locate the people in a performative time: 'the fluctuating movement that the people are *just* giving shape to'. The present of the people's history, then, is a practice that destroys the constant principles of the national culture that attempt to hark back to a 'true' national past, which is often represented in the reified forms of realism and stereotype. Such pedagogical knowledges and continuist national narratives miss the 'zone of occult instability where the people dwell' (Fanon's phrase). It is from this *instability* of cultural signification that the national culture comes to be articulated as a dialectic of various temporalities – modern, colonial, postcolonial, 'native' – that cannot be a knowledge that is stabilized in its enunciation: 'it is always contemporaneous with the act of recitation. It is the present act that on each of its occurrences marshalls in the ephemeral temporality inhabiting the space between the "I have heard" and "you will hear".'[38]

Fanon's critique of the fixed and stable forms of the nationalist narrative makes it imperative to question theories of the horizontal, homogeneous empty time of the

---

nation's narrative. Does the language of culture's 'occult instability' have a relevance outside the situation of anti-colonial struggle? Does the incommensurable act of living – so often dismissed as ethical or empirical – have its own ambivalent narrative, its own history of theory? Can it change the way we identify the symbolic structure of the Western nation?

A similar exploration of political time has a salutary feminist history in 'Women's time'.[39] It has rarely been acknowledged that Kristeva's celebrated essay of that title has its conjunctural, cultural history, not simply in psychoanalysis and semiotics, but in a powerful critique and redefinition of the nation as a space for the emergence of feminist political and psychic identifications. The nation as a symbolic denominator is, according to Kristeva, a powerful repository of cultural knowledge that erases the rationalist and progressivist logics of the 'canonical' nation. This symbolic history of the national culture is inscribed in the strange temporality of the future perfect, the effects of which are not dissimilar to Fanon's occult instability.

The borders of the nation Kristeva claims, are constantly faced with a double temporality: the process of identity constituted by historical sedimentation (the pedagogical); and the loss of identity in the signifying process of cultural identification (the performative). The time and space of Kirsteva's construction of the nation's finitude is analogous to my argument that the figure of the people emerges in the narrative ambivalence of disjunctive times and meanings. The concurrent circulation of linear, cursive and monumental time, in the same cultural space, constitutes a new historical temporality that Kristeva identifies with psychoanalytically informed, feminist strategies of political identification. What is remarkable is her insistence that the gendered sign can hold together such exorbitant historical times.

The political effects of Kristeva's multiple women's time leads to what she calls the 'demassification of difference'. The cultural moment of Fanon's 'occult instability' signifies the people in a fluctuating movement *which they are just giving shape to*, so that postcolonial time questions the teleological traditions of past and present, and the polarized historicist *sensibility* of the archaic and the modern. These are not simply attempts to invert the balance of power within an unchanged order of discourse. Fanon and Kristeva seek to redefine the symbolic process through which the social imaginary – nation, culture or community – becomes the subject of discourse, and the object of psychic identification. These feminist and postcolonial temporalities force us to rethink the sign of history *within* those languages, political or literary, which designate the people 'as one'. They challenge us to think the question of community and communication *without* the moment of transcendence: how do we understand such forms of social contradiction?

Cultural identification is then poised on the brink of what Kristeva calls the 'loss of identity' or Fanon describes as a profound cultural 'undecidability'. The people as a form of address emerge from the abyss of enunciation where the subject splits, the signifier 'fades', the pedagogical and the performative are agonistically articulated. The language of national collectivity and cohesiveness is now at stake. Neither can cultural homogeneity, or the nation's horizontal space be authoritatively represented within the familiar territory of the *public sphere*: social causality cannot be adequately understood as a deterministic or overdetermined effect of a 'statist' centre; nor can the rationality of political choice be divided between the polar realms of the private and the public. The narrative of national cohesion can no longer be signified, in Anderson's words, as a 'sociological solidity'[40] fixed in a 'succession of *plurals*' – hospitals, prisons, remote villages – where the social space is clearly bounded by such repeated objects that represent a naturalistic, national horizon.

Such a pluralism of the national sign, where difference returns as the same, is contested by the signifier's 'loss of identity' that inscribes the narrative of the people in the ambivalent, 'double' writing of the performative and the pedagogical. The movement of meaning *between* the masterful image of the people and the movement of its sign interrupts the succession of plurals that produce the sociological solidity of the national narrative. The nation's totality is confronted with, and crossed by, a supplementary movement of writing. The heterogeneous structure of Derridean supplementarity in *writing* closely follows the agonistic, ambivalent movement between the pedagogical and performative that informs the nation's narrative address. A supplement, according to one meaning, 'cumulates and accumulates presence. It is thus that art, *technē*, image, representation, convention, etc. come as supplements to nature and are rich with this entire cumulating function'[41] (pedagogical). The *double entendre* of the supplement suggests, however, that

[It] intervenes or insinuates itself *in-the-place-of*....If it represents and makes an image it is by the *anterior* default of a presence...the supplement is an adjunct, a subaltern instance....As substitute, it is not simply added to the positivity of a presence, it produces no relief....Somewhere, something can be filled up of *itself*...only by allowing itself to be filled through sign and proxy.[42] (performative)

It is in this supplementary space of doubling – *not plurality* – where the image is presence and proxy, where the sign supplements and empties nature, that the disjunctive times of Fanon and Kristeva can be turned into the discourses of emergent cultural identities, within a non-pluralistic politics of difference.

This supplementary space of cultural signification that opens up – and holds together – the performative and the pedagogical, provides a narrative structure characteristic of modern political rationality: the marginal integration of individuals in a repetitious movement between the antinomies of law and order. From the liminal movement of the culture of the nation – at once opened up and held together – minority discourse emerges. Its strategy of intervention is similar to what British parliamentary procedure recognizes as a supplementary question. It is a question that is supplementary to what is stated on the 'order paper' for the minister's response. Coming 'after' the original, or in 'addition to' it, gives the supplementary question the advantage of introducing a sense of 'secondariness' or belatedness into the structure of the original demand. The supplementary strategy suggests that adding 'to' need not 'add up' but may disturb the calculation. As Gasché has succinctly suggested, 'supplements...are pluses that compensate for a minus in the origin.'[43] The supplementary strategy interrupts the successive seriality of the narrative of plurals and pluralism by radically changing their mode of articulation. In the metaphor of the national community as the 'many as one', the *one* is now both the tendency to totalize the social in a homogeneous empty time, and the repetition of that minus in the origin, the less-than-one that intervenes with a metonymic, iterative temporality.

One cultural effect of such a metonymic interruption in the representation of the people, is apparent in Julia Kristeva's political writings. If we elide her concepts of women's time and female exile, then she seems to argue that the 'singularity' of woman – her representation as fragmentation and drive – produces a dissidence, and a distanciation, within the symbolic bond itself which demystifies 'the *community* of language as a universal and unifying tool, one which totalises and equalises'.[44] The minority does not simply confront the pedagogical, or powerful master-discourse with a contradictory or negating referent. It interrogates its object by initially withholding its objective. Insinuating itself into the terms of reference of the dominant discourse, the supplementary antagonizes the implicit power to generalize, to produce the sociological solidity. The questioning of the supplement is not a repetitive rhetoric of the 'end' of society but a meditation on the disposition of space and time from which the narrative of the nation must *begin*. The power of supplementarity is not the negation of the preconstituted social contradictions of the past or present; its force lies – as we shall see in the discussion of *Handsworth Songs* that follows – in the renegotiation of those times, terms and traditions through which we turn our uncertain, passing contemporaneity into the signs of history.

Handsworth Songs[45] is a film made by the Black Audio and Film Collective during the uprisings of 1985, in the Handsworth district of Birmingham, England. Shot in the midst of the uprising, it is haunted by two moments: the arrival of the migrant population in the 1950s, and the emergence of a black British people in the diaspora. And the film itself is part of the emergence of a black British cultural politics. Between the moments of the migrants' arrival and the minorities' emergence spans the filmic time of a continual displacement of narrative. It is the time of oppression and resistance; the time of the performance of the riots, cut across by the pedagogical knowledges of State institutions. The racism of statistics and documents and newspapers is interrupted by the perplexed living of Handsworth songs.

Two memories repeat incessantly to translate the living perplexity of history into the time of migration: first, the arrival of the ship laden with immigrants from the ex-colonies, just stepping off the boat, always just emerging – as in the fantasmatic scenario of Freud's family romance – into the land where the streets are paved with gold. This is followed by another image of the perplexity and power of an emergent peoples, caught in the shot of a dreadlocked rastafarian cutting a swathe through a posse of policemen during the uprising. It is a memory that flashes incessantly through the film: a dangerous repetition in the present of the cinematic frame; the edge of human life that translates what will come next and what has gone before in the writing of History. Listen to the repetition of the time and space of the peoples that I have been trying to create:

> In time we will demand the impossible in order to wrestle from it that which is possible, In time the streets will claim me without apology, In time I will be right to say that there are no stories... in the riots only the ghosts of other stories.

The symbolic demand of cultural difference constitutes a history in the midst of the uprising. From the desire of the possible in the impossible, in the historic present of the riots, emerge the ghostly repetitions of other stories, the record of other uprisings of people of colour: Broadwater Farm; Southall; St Paul's, Bristol. In the ghostly repetition of the black woman of Lozells Rd, Handsworth, who sees the future in the past. There

HOMI K. BHABHA

are no stories in the riots, only the ghosts of other stories, she told a local journalist: 'You can see Enoch Powell in 1969, Michael X in 1965.' And from the gathering repetition she builds a history.

From across the film listen to another woman who speaks another historical language. From the archaic world of metaphor, caught in the movement of the people she translates the time of change into the ebb and flow of language's unmastering rhythm: the successive time of instantaneity, battening against the straight horizons, and then the flow of water and words:

> I walk with my back to the sea, horizons straight ahead
> Wave the sea way and back it comes,
> Step and I slip on it.
> Crawling in my journey's footsteps
> When I stand it fills my bones.

The perplexity of the living must not be understood as some existential, ethical anguish of the empiricism of everyday life in 'the eternal living present', that gives liberal discourse a rich social reference in moral and cultural relativism. Nor must it be too hastily associated with the spontaneous and primordial *presence* of the people in the liberatory discourses of populist *ressentiment*. In the construction of this discourse of 'living perplexity' that I am attempting to produce we must remember that the space of human life is pushed to its incommensurable extreme; the judgement of living is perplexed; the topos of the narrative is neither the transcendental, pedagogical idea of History nor the institution of the State, but a strange temporality of the repetition of the one in the other – an oscillating movement in the governing *present* of cultural authority.

Minority discourse sets the act of emergence in the antagonistic *in-between* of image and sign, the accumulative and the adjunct, presence and proxy. It contests genealogies of 'origin' that lead to claims for cultural supremacy and historical priority. Minority discourse acknowledges the status of national culture – and the people – as a contentious, performative space of the perplexity of the living in the midst of the pedagogical representations of the fullness of life. Now there is no reason to believe that such marks of difference cannot inscribe a 'history' of the people or become the gathering points of political solidarity. They will not, however, celebrate the monumentality of historicist memory, the sociological totality of society, or the homogeneity of cultural experience. The discourse of the minority reveals the insurmountable ambivalence that structures the *equivocal* movement of historical time. How does one encounter the past as an anteriority that continually introduces an otherness or alterity into the present? How does one then narrate the present as a form of contemporaneity that is neither punctual nor synchronous? In what historical time do such configurations of cultural difference assume forms of cultural and political authority?

NOTES

1   In memory of Paul Moritz Strimpel (1914–87): Pforzheim–Paris–Zurich–Ahmedabad–Bombay–Milan–Lugano.

2   Quoted in E. Said, *After the Last Sky* (London: Faber, 1986).

3   I am thinking of Eric Hobsbawm's great history of the 'long nineteenth century', particularly *The Age of Capital 1848–1875* (London: Weidenfeld & Nicolson, 1975) and *The Age of Empire 1875–1914* (London: Weidenfeld & Nicolson, 1987). See especially some of the suggestive ideas on the nation and migration in the latter volume, ch. 6.

4   E. Said, *The World, The Text and The Critic* (Cambridge, Mass.: Harvard University Press, 1983), p. 39.

5   F. Jameson, 'Third World literature in the era of multinational capitalism', *Social Text* (Fall 1986), p. 69 and *passim*.

6   J. Kristeva, 'A new type of intellectual: the dissident', in T. Moi (ed.) *The Kristeva Reader* (Oxford: Blackwell, 1986), p. 298.

7   E. Said, 'Opponents, audiences, constituencies and community', in H. Foster (ed.) *Postmodern Culture* (London: Pluto, 1983), p. 145.

8   B. Anderson, 'Narrating the nation', *The Times Literary Supplement* 4341 (13 June 1986), p. 659.

9   P. Chatterjee, *Nationalist Thought and the Colonial World: A Derivative Discourse* (London: Zed, 1986), p. 17.

10   E. Gellner, *Nations and Nationalism* (Oxford: Basil Blackwell, 1983), p. 56.

11   Ibid., p. 38.

12   L. Althusser, *Montesquieu, Rousseau, Marx* (London: Verso, 1972), p. 78.

13   M. Bakhtin, *Speech Genres and Other Late Essays*, C. Emerson and M. Holquist (eds), V. W. McGee (trans.) (Austin: University of Texas Press, 1986), p. 31.

14   Ibid., p. 34.

15   Ibid., p. 36 and *passim*.

16   Ibid., pp. 47–9.

17   S. Freud, 'The "uncanny"', *Standard Edition*, XVII, J. Strachey (ed.) (London: Hogarth Press, 1974), p. 234. See also pp. 236, 247.

18   J. Barrell, *English Literature in History, 1730–1780* (London: Hutchinson, 1983).

19   H. A. Baker, Jr, *Modernism and the Harlem Renaissance* (Chicago: Chicago University Press, 1987), esp. chs 8–9.

20   Barrell, *English Literature*, p. 78.

21   Ibid., p. 203.

22   Baker, *Modernism*, p. 77.

23   R. Price, *Maroon Societies*, quoted in Baker, *Modernism*, p. 77.

24   C. Lefort, *The Political Forms of Modern Society* (Cambridge: Cambridge University Press, 1986), pp. 212–14; my emphasis.

25   A. Giddens, *The Nation State and Violence* (Cambridge: Polity, 1985), p. 216.

26   N. Poulantzas, *State, Power, Socialism* (London: Verso, 1980), p. 113.

27   R. Williams, *Problems in Materialism and Culture* (London: Verso, 1980), p. 43. I must thank Prof. David Lloyd of the University of California, Berkeley, for reminding me of Williams's important concept.

28   E. Said, 'Representing the colonized', *Critical Inquiry*, vol. 15, no. 2 (winter 1989), p. 225.

29   S. Freud, 'Civilization and its discontents', *Standard Edition* (London: Hogarth Press, 1961), p. 114.

30   Ibid.

31   J.-F. Lyotard and J.-L. Thebaud, *Just Gaming*, W. Godzich (trans.) (Manchester: Manchester University Press, 1985), p. 41.

32   C. Lévi-Strauss, *Introduction to the Work of Marcel Mauss*, F. Baker (trans.) (London: Routledge, 1987). Mark Cousins pointed me in the direction of this remarkable text. See his review in *New Formation*, no. 7 (spring 1989). What follows is an account of Lévi-Strauss's argument to be found in section 11 of the book, pp. 21–44.

33 M. Foucault, *Technologies of the Self*, H. Gutman et al. (eds) (London: Tavistock, 1988).

34 Ibid., pp. 151–4. I have abbreviated the argument for my convenience.

35 L. Althusser, *Reading Capital* (London: New Left Books, 1972), pp. 122–32. I have, for convenience, produced a composite quotation from Althusser's various descriptions of the ideological effects of historicism.

36 Foucault, *Technologies*, pp. 162–3.

37 F. Fanon, *The Wretched of the Earth* (Harmondsworth: Penguin, 1969). My quotations and references come from pp. 174–90.

38 J.-F. Lyotard, *The Postmodern Condition*, G. Bennington and B. Massumi (trans.) (Manchester: Manchester University Press, 1984), p. 22.

39 J. Kristeva, 'Women's time', in T. Moi (ed.) *The Kristeva Reader* (Oxford: Blackwell, 1986), pp. 187–213. This passage was written in response to the insistent questioning of Nandini and Praminda in Prof. Tshome Gabriel's seminar on 'syncretic cultures' at the University of California, Los Angeles.

40 Anderson, 'Narrating the nation', p. 35.

41 J. Derrida, *Of Grammatology*, G. C. Spivak (trans.) (Baltimore, Md: Johns Hopkins University Press, 1976), pp. 144–5. Quoted in R. Gasché, *The Tain of the Mirror* (Cambridge, Mass.: Harvard University Press, 1986), p. 208.

42 Derrida, *Of Grammatology*, p. 145.

43 Gasché, *Tain of the Mirror*, p. 211.

44 Kristeva, 'Women's time', p. 210. I have also referred here to an argument to be found on p. 296.

45 All quotations are from the shooting script of *Handsworth Songs*, generously provided by the Black Audio and Film Collective.

35

Atlas of the European Novel, 1800–1900

Franco Moretti

Franco Moretti (b. 1950)

Born in Sondrio, Italy, Franco Moretti received his doctorate from the Università di Roma in 1972. Moretti taught at the Università di Salerno (1979–83) the Università di Verona (1983–90), and Columbia University (1990–2000); since 2000 he has been the Danily C. and Laura Louise Bell Professor of English and Comparative Literature at Stanford University, where he is also founding director of the Center for the Study of the Novel. Moretti, who writes in both Italian and English, has published *Signs Taken for Wonders* (1983); *The Way of the World* (1987); *Opere mondo* (1994; *Modern Epic*, 1995); and *Atlante del romanzo europeo 1800–1900* (1997; *Atlas of the European Novel 1800–1900*, 1998). Since 2001 he has served as general editor for *Il romanzo* (*The Novel*), a five-volume collection which re-conceptualizes the novel as both a complex, formally diverse literary system, and a worldwide, culturally transformative social phenomenon.

The Novel, the Nation-State

Home-land

Let me begin with a map of very well-known novels: figure 35.1, which shows the places where Jane Austen's plots (or more exactly, their central thread, the heroine's story) begin and end. *Northanger Abbey*, for instance, begins at Fullerton and ends at Woodston; *Sense and Sensibility*, at Norland Park and at Delaford; and so on for the others (except *Persuasion*, whose endpoint is left rather vague). Please take a few moments to look at the figure, because in the end this is what literary geography is all about: you select a textual feature (here, beginnings and endings), find the data, put them on paper – and then you look at the map. In the hope that the visual construct will be more than the sum of its parts: that it will show a shape, a pattern that may *add* something to the information that went into making it.

And a pattern does indeed emerge here: of exclusion, first of all. No Ireland; no Scotland; no Wales; no Cornwall. No 'Celtic fringe', as Michael Hechter has called it;[1] only England: a much smaller space than the United Kingdom as a whole. And not even all of England: Lancashire, the North, the industrial revolution – all missing. Instead, we

Figure 35.1.   Jane Austen's Britain.

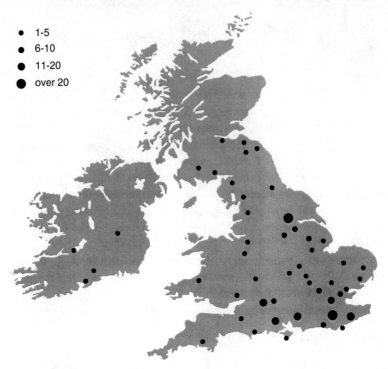

● 1-5
● 6-10
● 11-20
● over 20

Figure 35.2. 'Estate poems' 1650–1850. Estate poems – which describe and celebrate a country estate – are most frequent in the southern counties of England where Austen's novels typically take place, while the 'Celtic periphery' is again virtually absent.

have here the much older England celebrated by the 'estate poems' of topographical poetry: hills, parks, country houses…(figure 35.2). It's a first instance of what literary geography may tell us: two things at once: what *could* be in a novel – and what actually *is* there. On the one hand, the industrializing 'Great' Britain of Austen's years; on the other, the small, homogeneous England of Austen's novels.

A small England, I have said. Smaller than the United Kingdom, to be sure; and small for us, now. Less so, however, at the turn of the eighteenth century, when the places on the map were separated by a day, or more, of very uncomfortable travel. And since these places coincide with the residences of the heroine (the beginning), and that of her husband-to-be (the ending), the distance between them means that Austen's plots join together – 'marry' – people *who belong to different counties*. Which is new, and significant: it means that these novels try to represent what social historians refer to as the 'National Marriage Market': a mechanism that crystallized in the course of the eighteenth century, which demands of human beings (and especially of women) a new mobility: physical, and even more so *spiritual* mobility. Because it is clear that a large marriage market can only work if women feel 'at home' – in figure 35.1, many of the names indicate homes – not only in the small enclave of their birth, but in a much wider territory.[2] If they can feel the nation-state as a true home-land – and if not the nation-state as a whole, at least its 'core area', as social geography calls it: the wealthiest, most populated area (and the safest one, where a young woman may move around without fear). *Northanger Abbey*:

> Charming as were all Mrs. Radcliffe's works, and charming even as were the works of all her imitators, it was not in them perhaps that human nature, at least in the midland counties of England, was to be looked for. Of the Alps and the Pyrenees, with their pine forests and their vices, they might give a faithful delineation; and Italy, Switzerland, and the south of France, might be as fruitful in horrors as they were represented. Catherine dared not doubt beyond her own country, and even of that, if hard pressed, would have yielded the northern and western extremities [the Celtic Fringe!]. But in the central part of England there was surely some security for the existence even of a wife not beloved, in the laws of the land, and the manner of the age...
>
> Northanger Abbey, 25[3]

But in the central part of England... There is no better title for the map of Austen's novels. And as for Radcliffe's imitators, figure 35.3 shows the wide gulf separating the world of the Gothic from that of Catherine Morland.

Literary sociology has long insisted, as we know, on the relationship between the novel and capitalism. But Austen's space suggests an equally strong affinity (first pointed out by Benedict Anderson, in *Imagined Communities*) between the novel and the geopolitical reality of the nation-state. A modern reality, the nation-state – and a curiously elusive one. Because human beings can directly grasp most of their habitats: they can embrace their village, or valley, with a single glance; the same with the court, or the city (especially early on, when cities are small and have walls); or even the universe – a starry sky, after all, is not a bad image of it. But the nation-state? 'Where' is it? What does it look like? How can one *see* it? And again: village, court, city, valley, universe can all be visually represented – in paintings, for instance: but the nation-state? Well, the nation-state... found the novel. And viceversa: the novel found the nation-state. And being the only symbolic form that could represent it, it became an essential component of our modern culture.

Some nation-states (notably England/Britain and France) already existed, of course, long before the rise of the novel: but as 'potential' states, I would say, rather than actual ones. They had a court at the center, a dynasty, a navy, some kind of taxation – but they were hardly integrated systems: they were still fragmented into several local circuits, where the strictly *national* element had not yet affected everyday existence. But towards the end of the eighteenth century a number of processes come into being (the final surge in rural enclosures; the industrial take-off; vastly improved communications; the unification of the national market; mass conscription) that literally drag human beings out of the local dimension, and throw them into a much larger one. Charles Tilly speaks of a new value for this period – 'national loyalty' – that the state tries to force above and against 'local loyalties'.[4] He is right, I believe, and the clash of old and new loyalty shows also how much of a *problem* the nation-state initially was: an unexpected coercion, quite unlike previous power relations; a wider, more abstract, more enigmatic dominion – *that needed a new symbolic form in order to be understood.*

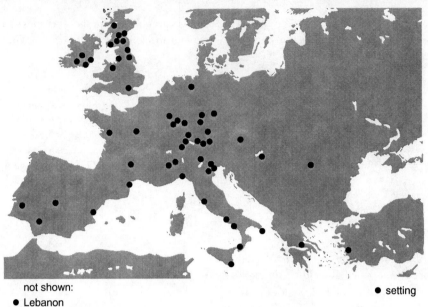

not shown:
● Lebanon
● Ceylon

● setting

Figure 35.3. British Gothic tales 1770–1840. In this sample of nearly sixty texts, the highest concentration of Gothic tales is to be found in the triangle comprised between the Rhine, the Black Forest, and the Harz (the region of the pact with the Devil): a geographical distribution that was probably influenced by the enormous number of Gothic texts written in German. In general, Gothic stories were initially set in Italy and France; moved north, to Germany, around 1800; and then north again, to Scotland, after 1820. Except for one tale located in Renaissance London, no other story takes place inside Austen's English space.

And here, Austen's novelistic geography shows all its intelligence. In a striking instance of the problem-solving vocation of literature, her plots take the painful reality of territorial uprooting – when her stories open, the family abode is usually on the verge of being lost – and rewrite it as a seductive journey: prompted by desire, and crowned by happiness. They take a *local* gentry, like the Bennets of *Pride and Prejudice*, and join it to the *national* elite of Darcy and his ilk.[5] They take the strange, harsh novelty of the modern state – and turn it into a large, exquisite home.

England and its Double

Marriage market, then. Like every other market, this also must take place somewhere, and figure 35.4 shows where: London, Bath, the seaside. Here people meet to complete their transactions, and here is also where all the trouble of Austen's universe occurs: infatuations, scandals, slanders, seductions, elopements – disgrace. And all of this happens because the marriage market (again, like every other market) has produced its own brand of swindlers: shady relatives, social climbers, speculators, seducers, déclassé aristocrats...

It makes sense, then, that this figure should be the inverse of figure 35.1. Look at them: the former is an introverted, rural England: an island within an island. The latter opens up to the sea, the great mix of Bath, and London, the busiest city in the

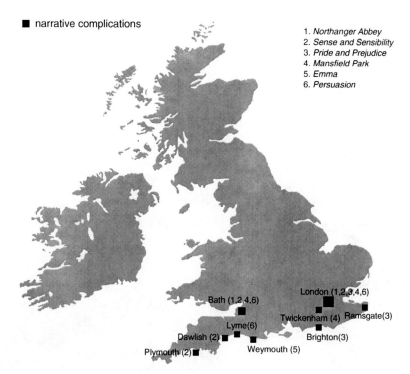

- narrative complications

1. *Northanger Abbey*
2. *Sense and Sensibility*
3. *Pride and Prejudice*
4. *Mansfield Park*
5. *Emma*
6. *Persuasion*

London (1,2,3,4,6)
Bath (1,2,4,6)
Twickenham (4) Ramsgate(3)
Lyme(6)
Dawlish (2)
Brighton(3)
Plymouth (2)
Weymouth (5)

Figure 35.4.   Jane Austen's Britain.

world. In one, a scattered distribution of independent estates: in the other, an ellipse with one focus in London, and the other in Bath. There, homes; here, cities: and cities that are all real, whereas those homes were all fictional: an asymmetry of the real and the imaginary – of geography, and literature – that will recur throughout the present research.[6]

Two Englands, where different narrative and axiological functions are literally 'attached' to different spaces (figure 35.5): and which one will prevail? The élite that has preserved its rural and local roots – or the mobile, urbanized group of seducers? In the language of the age: Land, or Money? We know Austen's answer: Land (preferably, with plenty of Money). But more significant than the final choice between the two spaces is the preliminary fact that Austen's England *is not one*. The novel functions as the symbolic form of the nation-state, I said earlier: and it's a form that (unlike an anthem, or a monument) not only does not conceal the nation's internal divisions, *but manages to turn them into a story.* Think of the two Englands of figure 35.5: they form a field of narrative forces, whose reiterated interplay defines the nation *as the sum of all its possible stories.* London, or the painful complications of life; the countryside, or the peace of closure; the seaside, and illicit emotions; Scotland, for secret lovers; Ireland and the Highlands, who knows, perhaps lands of the Gothic…

Austen's England; what an invention. And I say invention deliberately, because today the spatial scope of her novels may strike us as obvious, but historically it wasn't obvious at all. Readers needed a symbolic form capable of making sense of

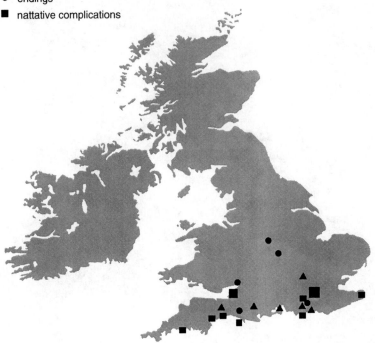

Figure 35.5. Jane Austen's Britain.

the nation-state, I have often repeated; they needed it, yes – but, before Austen, no one had really come up with it. Look at figure 35.6: the travels of the heroine and the other main characters in Amelie Opie's *Adeline Mowbray*. Space, here, is so stretched as to be almost shapeless: in one novel, the heroine and the other characters travel as much as in Austen's six novels taken together (figure 35.7) – a choice which has its own *raison d'être* (a woman who defies current morality will suffer an endless *via crucis*: in Lisbon, in Perpignan, in Richmond, in London...), but that certainly cannot turn the nation into a symbolic 'home'. Or again, look at figure 35.8: the 'excellent tale of *Manouvering*', as Scott calls it in the preface to *Ivanhoe*. Here, we have the opposite configuration to Opie's: the two heroines are motionless, in Devon, inside two neighboring estates – while their men sail all over the world. A very simple, very clear division of the narrative universe: women at home, and men abroad (while the nation is again lost from sight).

Austen's geography is really different: it's a middle-sized world, much larger than Edgeworth's estate, and much smaller than Opie's Atlantic. It is the typically *intermediate* space of the nation-state, 'large enough to survive and to sharpen its claws on its neighbors, but small enough to be organized from one center and to feel itself as an entity', as Kiernan once put it.[7] A contingent, intermediate construct (large enough... small enough...): and perhaps, it is also because she saw this new space that Austen is still read today, unlike so many of her rivals.

In Austen's middle-sized world, the notion of 'distance' acquires in its turn a new meaning. In Opie, or Edgeworth (or Susannah Gunning, Mary Charlton, Barbara Hofland, Selina Davenport: in fact, in most sentimental fiction), distance is an absolute, ontological category: the loved one is Here – or Away. At Home, or in the Wide World. Present, or Absent (and probably Dead). It's still the atmosphere of Greek romances: space as a mythical force, against whose power of separation human beings (and especially women, from whose viewpoint the story is told) have only one weapon: constancy. They must remain what they are, despite all distance; they must remain loyal, patient – *faithful*.

Against this veritable ideology of space, Austen's heroines discover concrete, Relative Distance. Willoughby, Darcy, are twenty miles away, forty, sixty; so is London, or Portsmouth. Maybe there will be a visit, maybe not, because it takes time and effort to travel forty miles. But this moderate uncertainty shows that distance has been brought down to earth: it can be measured, understood; it is no longer a function of Fate, but of sentiment. It is one more way to attach a meaning to the national space, by literally 'projecting' emotions upon it. When Darcy, who should be in London, shows up at Longbourn, 'a smile of delight added lustre to [Elizabeth's] eyes' (*Pride and Prejudice*, 53). If he has come this far...

'The recent losses in the West India estate'

England, Great Britain, the national marriage market, London, Bath, the Celtic fringe... And the colonies? Edward Said, 'Jane Austen and Empire':

> In *Mansfield Park*, [...] references to Sir Thomas Bertram's overseas possessions are threaded through; they give him his wealth, occasion his absences, fix his social status at home and abroad, and make possible his values [...]
>
> What sustains this life materially is the Bertram estate in Antigua [...] no matter how isolated and insulated the English place (e.g., Mansfield Park), it requires overseas sustenance [...] The Bertrams could not have been possible without the slave trade, sugar, and the colonial planter class.[8]

The Bertrams could not have been possible... I like the directness of the claim, but disagree with it. I disagree, that is, not with the fact that the British colonies were very profitable, and very ruthlessly run: but with the idea that the English ruling class would 'not have been possible' without them. Take Antigua away, suggests Said, and Sir Bertram disappears: no 'wealth', no 'social status at home and abroad', no 'values', no 'material support', no 'sustenance'. But is this truly the case?

The argument, here, has clearly two sides: the economic role of the British empire – and its fictional representation. On the former, which is far from my field of work, I can only say that I have been convinced by those historians for whom the colonies played certainly a significant, but not an *indispensable* role in British economic life.[9] And this is even truer for the gentry of Northamptonshire (the country of Mansfield Park), which according to Stone and Stone, between 1600 and 1800 engaged in business activities (including colonial investment) in a percentage that oscillated *between one and two percent*.

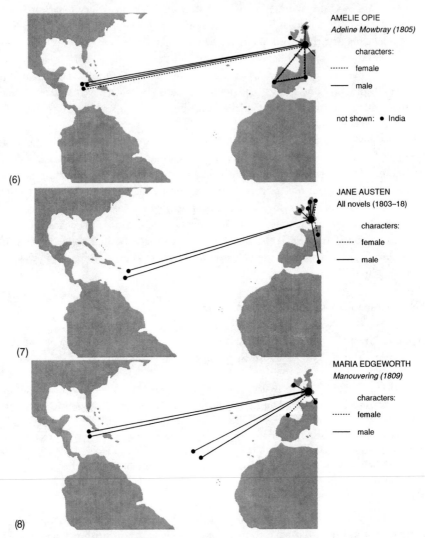

Figures 35.6–8. Britain and the world. In early nineteenth-century sentimental novels the international (and especially Atlantic) space takes the form of long retrospective narratives that focus on the (predominantly male) subplots: wars at sea, long-distance trade, Indian nabobs, West Indian planters…

Compared to her contemporaries, Austen markedly increases the central (and 'English') axis of the plot, so that the significance of the international subplot is accordingly reduced.

> The degree to which local landed elites were composed of men enriched in any way by business activities was always negligible. […] Evidence of infiltration, interaction, marriage, entrepreneurship, and other kinds of intermingling were fairly low up to 1879.[10]

Thus economic history. And if we then turn to *Mansfield Park* itself, Said's thesis becomes even more dubious. Early in the novel, when Bertram's older son runs into debt, his gambling 'robs Edmund for ten, twenty, thirty years, perhaps for life, of more than half the income which ought to be his' (*Mansfield Park*, 3). On the other hand, the 'recent losses in the West India estate', that are mentioned in the very same page, leave no trace on the life at Mansfield Park: losses or not, everything remains exactly the same. Perhaps that estate was not so indispensable after all? And then, here is Bertram, back from Antigua:

> It was a busy morning with him. Conversation with any of them occupied but a small part of it. He had to reinstate himself in all the wanted concerns of his Mansfield life, to see his steward and his bailiff – to examine and compute – and, in the intervals of business, to walk into his stables and his gardens, and nearest plantations.
>
> *Mansfield Park*, 20

To examine and compute, to walk into stables and plantations, to meet the steward and the bailiff (who are in charge of managing the estate, of collecting rents, and of financial affairs in general)... All signs of large economic interests *in Britain*, and most likely near Mansfield Park itself. Said's picture seems exactly reversed: modest colonial profits – and large national ones. And yet, when all is said, Bertram *does* indeed leave for Antigua, and stays away for a very long time. If Antigua is not essential to his finances – why on earth does he go?

He goes, not because he needs the money, but because Austen needs him out of the way. Too strong a figure of authority, he intimidates the rest of the cast, stifling narrative energy, and leaving Austen without a story to tell: for the sake of the plot, he must go. It is the difference, as Russian Formalists would say, between the 'function' and the 'motivation' of a narrative episode: between the *consequences* of Bertram's absence (the play, the flirt between Edmund and Mary, Maria's adultery: in short, *virtually the entire plot of the novel*), and its premises: which are far less important, because (as in Freudian 'rationalization', which is a very similar concept) one 'reason' can always be replaced by another without much difficulty.

Bertram goes to Antigua, then, not because he must go *there* – but because *he must leave Mansfield Park*. But it's nevertheless to Antigua that he goes, and I must still account for Austen's specific motivation of her plot. And then, in sentimental novels at the turn of the century, the colonies are a truly ubiquitous presence: they are mentioned in two novels out of three, and overseas fortunes add up to one third, if not more, of the wealth in these texts (figure 35.9). Why this insistence? Could it be a 'realistic' feature of nineteenth-century narrative, as Said suggests for Jane Austen?

Possibly. But, frankly, these fictional fortunes are so out of proportion to economic history that I suspect them to be there not so much because of reality, but for strictly *symbolic* reasons. Because Jamaica, or Bengal, remove the production of wealth to faraway worlds, in whose effective reality most nineteenth-century readers were probably not 'at all interested' (like Fanny's cousins: see *Mansfield Park*, 21).[11] The way in which colonial fortunes are introduced – a few hasty commonplaces, period – is itself a good clue to the real state of affairs; and as for the colonies themselves, *not one of the thirteen novels of figure 35.9 represents them directly*; at most, we get a retrospective (and dubious) tale like Rochester's in *Jane Eyre*. This is the mythic geography – *pecunia ex machina* – of a wealth

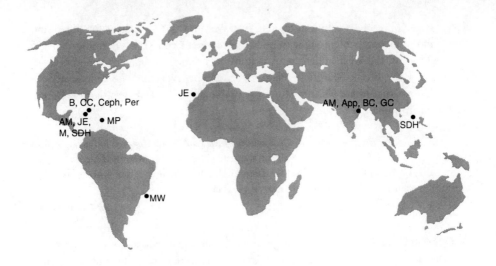

Novels included:

AM	Amelie Opie *Adeline Mowbray*	JE	Charlotte Bronte *Jane Eyre*
App	Amelie Opie *Appearance Was Against Her*	M	Maria Edgeworth *Manouvering*
B	Maria Edgeworth *Belinda*	MP	Jane Austen *Mansfield Park*
BC	Mrs Ross *The Balance of Comfort*	MW	Barbara Hofland *The Merchant's Widow*
CC	anonymous *The Castle on the Cliff*	Per	Jane Austen *Persuasion*
Ceph	anonymous *Cephisa*	SDH	Emily Eden *The Semi-Detached House*
GC	Susannah Gunning *The Gypsy Countess*		

Figure 35.9. Colonial wealth in British sentimental novels.

that is not really produced (nothing is ever said of work in the colonies), but magically 'found' overseas whenever a novel needs it. And so, among other things, the link between the wealth of the élite and the 'multitude of labouring poor' of contemporary England can be easily severed: the élite is cleared, innocent. Which is a wonderful thing to know, for heroines that want to marry into it – and even better, of course, in the decades of the harshest class struggle of modern British history.

Disavowal: this is the true meaning of figure 35.9. It is not economic history that explains it, but ideology: an ideology that *projects*, literally, an uncomfortable reality away from Britain. And indeed…

NOTES

1 Michael Hechter, *Internal Colonialism. The Celtic Fringe in British National Development, 1836–1966*, University of California Press, Berkeley–Los Angeles 1975.

2 Austen's space is of course too obviously *English* to be truly representative of the *British* nation. In this respect, Edgeworth's *The Absentee* (1812), or Ferrier's *Marriage* (1818), that deal with Ireland and Scotland as well as England, provide a more complete geographical setting (although in the end Edgeworth and Ferrier return to the idea of the nation within the nation, relinquishing the corruption of England for Ireland and Scotland respectively). The point is that England has long enjoyed an ambiguous and privileged position within the

United Kingdom: *part* of it (like Scotland, Ireland, Wales) – but a *dominant* part, that claims the right to stand in for the whole. Austen's geo-narrative system is an extremely successful version of this opaque overlap of England and Britain.

3 Narrative passages are identified by the title of the text, followed by the number of the chapter.

4 Charles Tilly, *Coercion, Capital, and European States*, Blackwell, Cambridge–Oxford 1990, p. 107.

5 On the two gentries, see Lawrence Stone and Jeanne C. Fawtier Stone, *An Open Elite? England 1540–1880*, Oxford University Press, 1986, passim.

6 Why do novels so often mix real geographical sites and imaginary locations? Are the latter needed for some *specific* narrative function? Are there, in other words, events that tend to happen in real spaces – and others that 'prefer' fictional ones? It is early to give a definitive answer, but Austen's novels certainly suggest that fictional spaces are particularly suited to happy endings, and the wish-fulfillment they usually embody. By contrast, the more pessimistic a narrative structure becomes, the more infrequent are its imaginary spaces.

7 V. G. Kiernan, 'State and Nation in Western Europe', *Past and Present*, July 1965, p. 35.

8 Edward Said, *Culture and Imperialism*, Knopf, New York 1993, pp. 62, 85, 89, 94. [See also pp. 691–715 in this book.]

9 In general, the key historical question (somewhat removed from *Mansfield Park* itself) is whether colonial profits financed the industrial revolution or not: and whether, as a consequence, the take-off of European capitalism would have been at all possible without colonial possessions. On this point, the arguments I have found most persuasive are those by Patrick K. O'Brien ('The Costs and Benefits of British Imperialism', *Past and Present*, 120, 1988), V. G. Kiernan (*Imperialism and its Contradictions*, Routledge, New York–London 1995), and Paul Bairoch (*Economics and World History*, Chicago University Press, 1993); although Robin Blackburn's *The Making of New World Slavery. From the Baroque to the Modern* (Verso, London 1997), which I read when this book had already been finished, made me reconsider several things.

Kiernan (who is, of course, a vitriolic critic of British imperialism) argues for instance that 'the spoils of Bengal [...] *may* have percolated by devious channels into Lancashire mills, but not quite as promptly [as to start the industrial revolution]': and he then proceeds to point out that if early industrialists 'had little access to the big money, they had, however [given the modest financial needs of the industrial take-off] equally little need of it' (pp. 54–5). As for Paul Bairoch, the thesis that the exploitation of the Third World financed the industrial revolution is for him one of the 'myths' of economic history, and his own conclusions turn the argument on its head: 'during the 18th and 19th centuries colonization was primarily a result of industrial development and not vice versa' (p. 82). As Bairoch himself explains at length, however, the myth is so widely accepted because 'if the West did not gain much from colonialism, it does not mean that the Third World did not lose much' (p. 85). In other words, although the Third World did not contribute much to the industrial revolution, the latter, by contrast, had catastrophic effects on the Third World itself (as in the case of de-industrialization, to which Bairoch devotes an entire chapter of his book).

For his part, Blackburn shows in great detail the exceptional profits arising out of West Indian slave plantations, and summarizes his findings in the following way: 'We have seen that the pace of capitalist industrialization in Britain was decisively advanced by its success in creating a regime of extended primitive accumulation and battening upon the super-exploitation of slaves in the Americas. Such a conclusion certainly does not imply that Britain followed some optimum path of accumulation in this period [...] nor does our survey lead to the conclusion that New World slavery produced capitalism. What it does show is that exchanges with the slave plantations helped British capitalism to make a breakthrough to industrialism and global economy ahead of its rivals' (p. 572).

10   Stone and Fawtier Stone, *An Open Elite?* pp. 141, 189. See also the chart on p. 141.

11   Around 1800, *The Lady's Magazine* devotes hundreds of pages to tales and 'anecdotes' of the colonial world – but provides only a couple of genuine news items.

Novel Reader

Introduction

This anthology finds its ending by asking its own reader to begin again: to reconfigure the essays gathered between its covers according to the investment each has in conceptualizing the role of the novel reader. Classifier, craftsman, connoisseur, scholar, ethical judge, scientist, privileged knower, phantasmal projection, questing epistemological subject, pleasure seeker – do these various constructions of the novel reader have anything in common? A reconsideration of the role of the reader can offer some resolution to the issues that define novel theory as a field – but not in the sense of a wind-up or solution. The category of novel reader resolves the field in the sense that it brings into sharper focus the philosophical assumptions that distinguish the theoretical approaches gathered in this anthology: the fact that almost every essay has claims to make about novel readers, whether or not these claims are self-consciously presented as theoretical propositions, means that the category of novel reader can function as a lens to compare the underlying assumptions that guide each theory of the novel. The task of this volume is not, not even here at its own end, to solve the problem of novel theory but to make legible the rich problematic that is novel theory.

While many of the selections in this volume thus could be reprinted under the heading of "Novel Readers," there is a strong rationale for signaling out three particular essays, all from books published in the second half of the twentieth century and each highly influential in the decade in which it was published: Wolfgang Iser's *The Implied Reader* (1974); Nina Baym's *Novels, Readers, and Reviewers* (1984); and Garrett Stewart's

Dear Reader (1996). Each of these books makes the novel reader an explicit object of investigation – and therefore, when taken together, the essays included in this unit can give us an idea of where twentieth-century novel theory ends up when the experience of novel reading is taken as the beginning of theoretical inquiry. Wolfgang Iser, for example, believes that his focus on the reader leads to a significant revision of the neo-Aristotelian theory that is the direct inspiration for his own project: Wayne Booth's *The Rhetoric of Fiction* (1961; see Part II). Iser derives his title, *The Implied Reader*, from an idea put forward by Booth, the idea that an implied communicative relation is objectified in the narrative strategies of fiction. Iser is persuaded by Booth that "'The author creates, in short, an image of himself and another image of his reader; he makes his reader, as he makes his second self, and the most successful reading is one in which the created selves, author and reader, can find complete agreement.'"[1] But although Iser agrees that "In the act of reading, we are to undergo a kind of transformation,"[2] his own sense of the quality and complexity of readerly response leads him to correct what he perceives as a mistake Booth makes about the act of communication through fiction. Fiction is not, for Iser, a subset of rhetoric. Iser argues that the Boothian understanding of rhetoric is too narrowly equated with forensic argumentation to serve as a paradigm for fiction. "Rhetoric," Iser argues, "if it is to be successful, needs a clearly formulated purpose, but the 'new province of writing' that Fielding is trying to open up to his readers is in the nature of a promise, and it can only rouse the expectations necessary for its efficacy if it is not set out in words."[3]

Iser's point is not that fiction eventually masters the conventions of rhetoric, developing to have a clearly formulated purpose, effectively set out in words. On the contrary, Iser argues that to think of fiction as a type of rhetoric is to miss all that is particular to fiction as a communicative mode. Fiction, he argues, communicates in its own way, through techniques that are peculiar to it – and these techniques are characterized precisely by the quality of implicitness, what an early critic like Percy Lubbock called fiction's capacity for "showing" (see Part I). It is the work of Iser's theory to make explicit these implicit strategies – and to argue further that novelistic implicitness results in readerly implication. Iser's primary thesis is that novelistic communication is overwhelmingly distinguished by a single property: the reader's felt sense of his or her own participation in the spontaneous discovery of meaning, a participation that has been wholly prepared for by the novel itself. In Iser's words, "The reader must be made to feel for himself the new meaning of [i.e. the kind of meaning that is new to] the novel. To do this he must actively participate in bringing out the meaning and this participation is an essential precondition for communication between the author and the reader."[4]

Nina Baym and Garrett Stewart join Iser in the attempt to analyze why novelistic "meaning" seems especially linked to readerly participation; why, to put it another way, a reader's understanding of what a novelist is trying to communicate through a given novel is inseparable from that reader's felt sense of investment in the act of reading that novel. Stewart's theory explicitly draws on the work of both Iser and Booth as he follows their respective attempts to define the types of readerly responses constructed by novels, focusing his project on what he believes is the particular type of readerly induction conducted by what he calls "classic fiction," the great tradition of English nineteenth-century novels. Stewart ambitiously defends and updates the notion of the implied reader through an engagement with what can only be called the major schools of literary theory (deconstruction, New Historicism, feminism, Marxism), all of which have either explicitly attacked the theory of a unified reader response or simply dismissed it as a naive hold-over from formalism.[5] Nina Baym, in contrast to Iser and Stewart, takes an empirical and historical approach to the novel reader – which makes it all the more interesting that her study yields a portrait of the novel reader that is compatible with Iser's and Stewart's. Baym discovers that, at a certain time (in the first half of the nineteenth century) and in a certain place (the United States), novel reading was considered to be overwhelmingly, even dangerously, engaging. The novel attracted a mass audience who craved the intense feelings of interest and excitement that they found consistently delivered in its pages.

But if Baym's historical and empirical approach to the novel ends in upholding by different means the phenomenological account of readerly experience offered by Iser and Stewart, we should also note that Iser and Stewart both imagine their respective projects as, in their own senses of the term, historical. For each, the phenomenology of readerly experience takes place in and through a particular novel's representation of social norms, norms that are historically sensitive. As Iser and Stewart both understand it, the experience of the novel reader is the experience of history, history that the novel itself brings to life. A closer look at each theory will clarify these investments.

Novels, Readers, and Reviewers: Responses to Fiction in Antebellum America takes up a question familiar to readers of this volume: why does the novel "triumph" as a literary form? As a historian of American culture, Baym particularly wants to know why the novel triumphed in the US. Her project is motivated in large part by her disagreement with what at the time of her writing was an entrenched critical belief: that antebellum American society was hostile to fiction – a misconception, on her view, projected by modern scholars who too readily accepted and perpetuated the Puritan attacks on fiction. Baym forcefully argues that such a misunderstanding of American literary culture could develop and persist only by wholly ignoring what the reading public of the time actually said and did. Her research overwhelmingly proves that antebellum America, at least from 1800 on, was in fact obsessed with novels. It devoured fiction authored at home and abroad. Some of this writing was produced by authors who were considered at the time to be great, but much of it was produced by authors who were known not to be great – and yet were nonetheless regarded as providers of readerly gratification.

The seemingly insatiable appetite for novels spawned a culture industry devoted to reviewing, advertising, and publishing fiction. Baym conjectures that the answer to her question, why the novel triumphed as a literary form, lies in this archive. In the belief that the most direct account of the appeal of this new genre is to be found in novel reviews, she focuses her study on those written for major American periodicals, magazines that had large readerships and wide purchase in antebellum culture, especially between 1840 and 1860. The importance of understanding the triumph of the novel in terms of readerly effects is thus presented by Baym as a historical finding. The historical record can be corrected, in other words, simply through the empirical examination of public documents, available to any researcher who cares to track them down. Her own investigation encompasses more than 2,000 reviews.[6] There are, of course, limitations to any archive. In her case, the archive inevitably privileges a certain kind of reader, the professional "magazinist," the novel reader who reads novels in order to write about them. But Baym argues persuasively for the historical value of the liminality that

DOROTHY HALE

characterizes this professional position: part of the magazinist's job is to understand the difference between his professional opinion and that of the common reader. He (or less often, she) sets about to educate that common reader, to refine literary taste – and thus many of these published reviews provide insight into the values held by the professional reader as well as those attributed to the recreational reader, not to mention the reviewer's sense of whether and how these two different set of values might be commensurable.

It is one of Baym's specific historical claims that the material conditions under which novels were produced structured the relationship between elite and common reader in a significantly new way. While professional reviewers from this period might imagine themselves as fulfilling the time-honored function of social betterment (the education of the public by the elite), Baym contends that at this particular historical moment the cultural role of the literary elite has deeply and irrevocably altered. Whereas the cultural elite would in previous eras attempt "a change of taste in an existing audience," the novel's mass publication and distribution introduces nothing less than "a change in the makeup of the audience for the written word" (782). Baym lists the technological innovations between 1830 and 1840 that lead to this expansion of literacy: "improvements in papermaking, typesetting, and printing machinery, along with the railroad and the steamboat, put books within the physical and financial reach of a vast segment of an increasingly literate population."[7] She argues that the expansion of the reading public and the emergence of that public as novel readers means that American literary taste is, for the first time, being shaped from the bottom up: "To follow the public instead of leading it, to surrender critical judgment to the extent of permitting a low literary mode to assume cultural significance, involved critics in new and difficult professional decisions" (781).

Baym supports this claim by citing testimony from the daunted elite, who increasingly acknowledge, albeit grudgingly, that the popular taste for novels can be neither resisted nor ignored. Baym describes a wonderful instance of what we can only term social evolution: the adjustment in consciousness made by the cultural elite in an attempt to stave off cultural obsolescence. Baym quotes a *Graham's* reviewer, writing in 1854, who observes that, in a world where the public wants only to read novels, even " 'The opponents of novel writing have turned novelists' " (783). Baym also points out the irony of the minister reviewer, writing for the *Christian Examiner* in 1853, who "looks back nostalgically to a social era when books were out of public reach and the ability to own and read them conferred power and prestige. Now, in contrast, the minister is dependent on a reading public that gets its information about ministers from novels" (782).

Baym's primary point is that the novel was from its advent, and remains essentially, a popular form. Serious novels became possible, but only as an adaptation of the popular mode and only after "the novel had … establish[ed] itself as *the* form of the times" (783). What made the novel so popular? The material and technological changes that Baym describes could have easily made available books of lyric poetry or travel narratives: why the novel? The reviewers she studies also ask this question – and it is an interesting historical fact that they tend to provide an ahistorical answer to their own historical question. According to an 1848 *Graham's* review, "Fiction has exercised an important influence over the public from the earliest ages of the world … It will not do to despise that which is so indestructible, and which everywhere exercises such powerful influence" (786, Baym's ellipsis). Baym summarizes this as the appeal to a "basic psycho-logical reality of the human love for fiction, which all critics understood to be the bedrock of the novel's amazing success" (787). In general defenses of fiction, the novel is regarded as the culmination of the mode: "The literature of fiction is the only permanent flower of the imagination...No man's nerves tingle when he hears the name of Aristotle. But to think of Fielding, and Scott, and Dickens, is like grasping a warm hand or leaning against a beating heart" (787, Baym, quoting from *Harper's* [1860], Baym's ellipsis). Tingling nerves, warm hands, beating hearts – if the novel represented the highest cultivation of the love of fiction, the human relations it promoted were experienced as distinctively corporeal. Cultural authorities of the time pondered the ultimate social effects of the imaginary bodily engagement that fiction promoted. Did the emotive power of the novel result in a superior socialization of novel readers, making them more sympathetic (training them to grasp other warm hands out of brotherly love)? Or did the imaginary experience of emotional connection foster only self-gratification, encouraging novel readers to substitute imaginary human contact for real social engagement (788)?

But if the social effects of fiction were ambiguous, the peculiar power of the novel as a literary form was not. According to Baym, there was overwhelming unanimity (from professional reviewers and ordinary readers alike) about what constituted the appeal of the novel as a literary form: its capacity to absorb its reader. According to Baym, the popularity of the novel was due to what audiences found to be its superior capacity for generating readerly interest and excitement, or, more accurately, for generating readerly interest as excitement, as a mental activity that incited intense emotional engagement, so much so that the act of reading itself seems a bodily experience. Baym notes that the qualities of absorbing interest, uncommon power, vigor, and vivacity are everywhere associated with the novel's effects but rarely if ever theorized by reviewers of the time in aesthetic terms (790–1). When reviewers are self-conscious about what the novel is or should be, they have more lofty goals in mind, which usually have to do with the novel's capacity to promote serious social purposes. Reviewers praise the novel for its "com-prehensive" vision, to "embrace all that man ever did, and all that man ever knew" (786). But Baym interestingly observes that even serious novels are judged unsuccessful if they lack the qualities of energy and excitement, if they fail, in other words, to give the readerly satisfactions that are the hallmark of novelistic endeavor (791).

The experience of novelistic power is described, Baym notes, in terms that evoke the paradox of appetite. Readers find in the novel a superior satisfaction of their desire to be excited – but finding satisfaction in a particular novel whets the appetite for more such satisfactions. No matter how many novels one reads, the experience of novel reading does not diminish in intensity: in fact it is precisely the reliability of the novel's gratification that prompts the reader to pick up another and another and another. The novel reader is thus dependent upon novels in the sense that she requires a continuous fix, a fresh supply – and she is also like an addict in the sense that she craves the experience of being "absorbed," the sense of being overcome, overpowered by the vivacity of the reading experience (790). The novel makes the reader's nerves tingle not just because he or she feels in touch with the author's warm hand or beating heart, but because she feels herself being touched: the best type of novel "seizes upon the feelings with a stronger grasp" (790, Baym quoting the *Christian Examiner* [1853]). The reading experience is thus understood as an enjoyable overwhelming of the self, the pleasure of reaction rather than initiation. But this surrender, Baym convincingly argues, works paradoxically to instill in the reader a certain feeling of empowerment. In a line of analysis that resonates with Eve Sedgwick's account of Henry James's relation to his own works of fiction (see Part III of this volume), Baym emphasizes, "Power is thus experienced as power *over* the reader; but power works too by creating interest *in* the reader, so that the reader too becomes strong" (790). On this view, reading is a type of transfer: the reader is overwhelmed by the novel only to be reinspirited by the qualities of energy, vigor, and vivacity that define it.

Baym emphasizes, like many of the cultural historians in this volume, that she is simply reporting what her research has revealed about the beliefs of the period. In her preface she declares, "I do not discuss the correctness of reviewer evaluations, for I am not interested in their judgments so much as in the criteria on which judgments were allegedly based."[8] This disclaimer stands as a version of the "caveat emptor" invoked by Catherine Gallagher as the "motto" of *Nobody's Story*. Gallagher cautions her reader not to take the cultural constructions of her historical study as "universal truths" to be "*believed*"(see Part VII).[9] But for a different type of theorist, such historical testimony is a provocation to judgment, a potential truth claim to be tested. Wolfgang Iser and Garrett Stewart are both interested in figuring out what can in fact be believed about the reading experience offered by novels. Although Iser and Stewart use less corporeal terms to define the readerly experience, they both begin with an assumption that resonates with Baym's findings: that novel reading performs a particular kind of emptying out of the reader in order to construct an intensely satisfying experience of interested engagement. Both Iser and Stewart believe that the position of interest that novels create for their readers is a formal component of the novel itself, a structure available to all readers, whether a person reads *Pamela* at the moment of publication in England or two centuries later in Thailand. The difference in their approach from Baym's can perhaps be summed up by this formulation of Stewart's: "there are no statistics that can genuinely round up the Victorian (or any other) general reader... [S]ocial history of the so-called reading public is not a study of the reader, let alone *a* reader, until it is informed by precisely that phenomenological detour, routed by language, along whose groves, when people read, readers emerge, generated in process."[10]

To say that each novel produces its reader is decidedly not to say that all novels produce the same reader. Iser and Stewart both believe that a particular novel's construction of readerly interest, its capacity to be absorbing, is culturally and historically relative, inseparable from the particular social context from which that particular literary work emerged. Iser and Stewart thus do not imagine that their phenomenological approach is opposed to a historical approach to novel reading. The two methods will seem irreconcilable, on their view, only if history is understood as something outside or beyond literary works. Iser and Stewart both instead believe that history is best known through the pages of a novel. On this view, to read a novel of 1820 is to know 1820. Reading a novel from 1820 puts the modern reader in direct contact with the attitudes and values of a past culture – and, even more particularly, allows her to inhabit these values (even if only momentarily or in a qualified manner) through the specific way that novels construct the reading experience. Stewart expresses the notion of novelistic history in this way, "You don't have to have been there" in order to experience a past culture as a "'reading event.'"[11] Iser goes so far as to posit traditional historiography as a pale version of the living history made available through novels. Through the example of *Vanity Fair*, Iser asserts, "*the novel* continues to be effective even today, though the *social conditions* it describes are only of historical interest" (766, my emphasis). "Historical interest" is what has no readerly interest, what has not been made available to the experience of the reader. "If the past has been kept alive," Iser continues, "this is primarily due to the structural pattern through which the events are conveyed to the reader" (766).

The novel's particular way of conveying events to the reader thus, on Iser's view, distinguishes it as the historical artifact (better than buildings, better than government records, better than poetry) that brings the values of the past to life. Iser himself does not argue for the novel's power comparatively; he does not seek to show how its production of reader involvement is different from the experience of reading other literary genres or encountering other historical objects. But from comments Iser makes in his introduction, we can conclude that his belief in the novel's preeminent capacity for keeping the past alive has to do with the genre's intense preoccupation with the social concerns of the day: "Like no other art form before it, the novel was concerned directly with social and historical norms that applied to a particular environment, and so it established an immediate link with the empirical reality familiar to its readers."[12] It is the "link" that the novel establishes between reader and empirical reality that is the basis of its historical significance: the novel makes the past come alive not just because it reproduces a view of a past reality but because it *connects* its reader to that empirical reality by relating it to *her own* experience of life.

This theory of readerly experience gains interest and complexity as Iser details how this linkage works. In contrast to Ian Watt, who emphasizes the plenitude of novelistic mimesis, attributing to the genre an empirical reality that seems, especially in contrast to earlier literary conventions of representation, full and complete, Iser emphasizes the felt insufficiency of the novel's mimetic representation. He argues that the very impossibility of representing empirical reality in a complete way draws the reader's attention to the "process of selection" used by the author to delimit the empirical world.[13] Iser further argues that the reader's awareness about the implicit and covert values that organize the novel's representation of the empirical world leads her to reflect upon her own experience of life itself. She comes to understand novel reading as a homology for the way she experiences the world. The principles of selectivity that underlie the novel are, she discovers, at work in the world outside the novel. The ramifications of this revelation are, Iser believes, historically determined. An eighteenth-century author will pose one solution (say, the solution of choosing good authorities to guide moral life) while a twentieth-century author will pose another solution (perhaps that moral choice is wholly subjective). But in all eras, Iser theorizes, the novel destabilizes social convention simply by exposing its covert operation: "Norms are social regulations, and when they are transposed into the novel they are automatically deprived of their pragmatic nature. They are set in a new context which changes their function, insofar as they no longer act as social regulations but as a subject of discussion which, more often than not, ends in a questioning rather than a confirmation of their validity."[14]

For Iser, then, the novel makes the past come to life by producing in the reader a self-conscious understanding first of the social regulations that guided life in the past and second of the illusory quality of her own empirical experience of life, an experience that is equally structured by covert norms. Importantly, this is not a revelation that happens once and for all, at a given moment in the reading experience. The link between the reader's experience of the relation between the novel world and her own world structures the reader's entire experience of any given novel. Iser argues that the novel performs what we might call (although he does not) the deconstruction of empirical security, a performance that has its effect as a process. (To work out this connection, see especially J. Hillis Miller, pages 242–56 of this volume.) Iser argues that the realist novel positions its reader as an empirical observer of a social world – and then works to unmoor that vision by changing the reader's position, not once but frequently. The most obvious way that position is changed is through a shift in point of view. But, importantly, for Iser the reader's positionality is not only connected to spatial effects. The novel can convey the constructedness of knowledge through a whole array of narrative techniques: irony, narratorial opinion, free indirect discourse, elision. The author's conception of how to position his reader and the narrative choices available to him will coincide, according to Iser, with the philosophical beliefs of his era. Iser sums up the general historical trajectory of these epistemological possibilities as follows: in the eighteenth century, the reader is "guided" by the author and "cast in a specific role"; in the nineteenth century, the reader, asked to inhabit multiple roles, comes to the revelation that society itself has "imposed a part on him"; and in the twentieth century the reader learns that the patterning that produces epistemological legibility exists not in the world but within perception itself.[15]

Iser coins a new meaning for the term "discovery" to describe the type of active receptiveness required by the novel. The novel's signal generic feature is to make the reader feel she has "spontaneously" arrived at the philosophical views put forward through the novel.[16] Discovery is possible only through readerly absorption, the reader's willingness to be positioned by the novel. But the process of absorption that Iser describes is of a different order from that experienced by Baym's novel addict. Iser's reader equally surrenders to the novel, but the novel throws him back upon himself. Of course, in Baym's analysis the experience of readerly abandonment also returned the reader to herself: the felt sense of her own interest leaves her feeling more alive. But for Iser the felt interest of reading a novel produces a self-consciousness in the reader about the operation of interest itself: interest as a philosophical condition, defined by different ages in terms of morality, politics, or epistemology. And while Iser stresses the historical relativity of these views, their revelation in and through the experience of novel reading gives them, on his account, a certain type of commonality: novels produce if not out-and-out social critics, then at least skeptics, who, as a result of their experience of the deconstruction of empiricism, question the source and "validity" of social regulations.[17]

If we turn to "The Reader as a Component Part of the Realist Novel: Esthetic Effects in Thackeray's *Vanity Fair*," the chapter from *The Implied Reader* included in this volume, we can see more clearly how Iser understands the phenomenology of readerly discovery as a historical process. In other words, we can see how Thackeray's narrative strategies work to lead the reader to discover the philosophical views that Iser believes typify Thackeray's era. Thackeray establishes multiple roles for the reader first of all by proliferating judgment about the morality of the characters' thought and behavior: characters judge the world differently – and the narrator judges differently from any of the characters. This moral and ethical instability is intensified by the novel's lack of a clear "hero," which typically provides the "basic focal point of orientation" (767–8). Without a sympathetic relation to one character, we are not "placed" in relation to the world of the novel, meaning we do not identify with a character, imagining ourselves "in their place" (768). Instead, Thackeray keeps the reader mobile, requiring her to position and reposition herself in relation to expressed opinions, evaluating for herself the persuasiveness or shortcomings of the characters and narrators who express their judgments about the events that constitute the novel's plot.

Iser's understanding of the nineteenth-century novel's investment in the criteria for moral judgment leads to a fresh account of the narrator in *Vanity Fair*. Considered by Henry James and others as a fatal disruption of the novel's mimetic project, Thackeray's self-conscious narrator is, for Iser, not a hindrance to readerly discovery but a facilitator of it: "we get involved because we react to the viewpoints advanced by the narrator" (767). The liveliness of the narrator in fact functions as a "continual endeavor to stimulate the reader's mind" (772), prompting the reader to emulate the narrator – not in the content of his opinions, but in the number of "viewpoints" he possesses and in the energy this amount affords him. *Vanity Fair* further "stimulates the reader into forming judgments of his own" (768) by asking the reader not just to think in and against the characters' and narrator's explicit opinions, but beyond these opinions: to "visualize the possibilities which they have not thought of" (775). The process of instantiation and distantiation, in other words, leads the reader to a meta-understanding of the operation of social norms in the period: that nineteenth-century English society is defined by role playing. But this is only half his discovery. Since "the narrative can only be completed through the cooperation of the reader (which is allowed for in the text), then the borderline between fiction and reality becomes increasingly hazy, for the reader can scarcely regard his own participation as fictional" (771). The experience of past as present, of history as a living reality, is for Iser what "activates" (776) the reader. Being "compelled...to view things for himself and discover his own reality" (776), the reader is led from the experience of reading Thackeray's novels to consider his experience of his world, the world outside the novel.

Although in this analysis of Thackeray Iser quotes Booth approvingly, it is important to recognize where Iser's conception of the novel reader differs from Booth's. For Booth, a person prepares for reading by evacuating his social self, by setting aside the beliefs he holds in everyday life, by absenting the everyday self who "goes about paying bills, repairing leaky faucets, and failing in generosity and wisdom" (773, Iser quoting Booth). The ideal reader in Booth's model is one who "must subordinate my mind and heart to the book" (773, Iser quoting Booth). But for Iser, the process of readerly "discovery" can only work through the experience of upset and surprise – and this can only come about if the reader brings to the text the beliefs and practices that constitute his everyday life, beliefs and practices about which novel reading makes him self-conscious.

Put this way, Iser's theory of novelistic discovery might be said to share as much with Russian formalism as with the Chicago School. For Víktor Shklovsky, the literary work also took the reader through a process, culminating in the reader's recognition of the social conventions that he had mistaken for empirical reality. But there is an important difference between Iserian discovery and Shklovskian defamiliarization. Shklovsky believes that literature restores perception, that its narrative techniques clear away social convention, enabling the reader to feel anew the stoniness of the stone.[18] But for Iser, the defamiliarization performed by the novel deconstructs the belief that reality is perceived through any kind of direct, sensory contact. As we have seen, for Iser the reader is led by fiction to a position of philosophical critique. Novel reading provides the reader with what can only be called new experience, which Iser describes as "something unexpected which necessitates a readjustment." This exposure results in what Iser, borrowing from Henry James, terms an "enlargement of experience."[19] But this new experience, importantly, is processed by the reader as a negative relation to her past experience: enlargement is experienced as a self-consciousness about the inadequacy of one's past understanding: "the reader discovers the meaning of the text, taking negation as his starting-point; he discovers a new reality through fiction which, at least in part, is different from the world he himself is used to; and he discovers the deficiencies inherent in prevalent norms and in his own restricted behavior." In Iser's theory, as in Shklovsky's, the novel's meaning thus "revolves around a basic divergence from the familiar." But rather than having empiricism restored through the literary defamiliarization of social convention, Iser's reader feels that it is the act of reading itself that allows him to "free himself – even if only temporarily – from what he is and escape from the restrictions of his own social life."[20] This freedom is the freedom of contemplation, of the condition of "discovery" enabled by the structures of novel reading. This is why Iser calls the radical skepticism afforded by the novel an "esthetic experience," implying that it can not be sustained when one returns to the world of leaky faucets and bill-paying.[21]

Garrett Stewart's *Dear Reader: The Conscripted Audience in Nineteenth-Century British Fiction* (1996) is also deeply concerned with novel reading as an aesthetic experience – but for Stewart novel reading does not culminate in a privileged form of social awareness but begins with an awareness that novel reading itself is a special kind of social activity. Stewart believes that readers of classic novels, then and now, come to reading with self-conscious expectations about what Iser might call the "norms" of novel reading. Iser's reader discovers in the process of reading that the world represented in its pages has been structured by organizing principles; but Stewart's reader assumes from the outset that novels are acts of communication rather than empirical worlds. According to Stewart, the reader comes to novels with socially and historically conditioned expectations about what it means to be a novel reader. The contemporary reader who picks up a work of classic English fiction expects that the novel will vigorously, even self-consciously, accomplish its goal of communication by scripting the reader's response. The reader of classic fiction thus comes to a particular novel knowing that it assumes the reader's willingness to be led. In Stewart's words, the reader of classic fiction, as the "true worker of the literary work," is "slotted for response, zoned for construction."[22] Stewart is closer to Iser than he is to Booth in his understanding of what it means to become a worker of the literary work. The novel reader does not purge himself of the everyday self that he is, does not cease to be the man who pays bills and fixes faucets. But Stewart differs from Iser in an important way, too: whereas Iser formulates the link between the reader's world and the world of novel reading as that based upon deep, experiential continuity, Stewart theorizes this linkage as defined by the experience of ontological discontinuity, of experiential division and doubleness.

Stewart thus gives us a different account of what it means for a novel reader to seek the experience of being "taken in," what he also calls being "absorbed."[23] "The reader is a drastic abstraction of the self, spirited away from self-identity by text, a subjective construction spun out from moment to moment...on the read, not just opened, page."[24] Stewart's novel reader, like Baym's reader, seeks to be overcome by the experience of reading; but if Baymian absorption results in the paradox of readerly self-strengthening, for Stewart the experience of reading produces the sense of a self split in two. The self that comes into being through the aesthetic experience of reading exists in dynamic and negative relation to the reader's nonreading identity: "Fictional reading leeches identity in the name of identification."[25] The "drastic abstraction of the self" comes about through the experience of vampirish siphoning off: as the reader performs acts of identification invited by the novel, her nonreading self becomes abstracted because in and through the reading experience she perceives her identity as alienable. Noncoincidence thus becomes the defining relation of the two states of being (both the performance of novel reading and as this performance splits the self). If this doubleness is what allows the novel reader to perform the acts of identification prepared for her by the text, it also prevents her from wholly identifying herself with those identifications. Indeed, it is the very condition of doubleness (created through novel reading) that novelistic identification cannot enact. For Stewart, the novel can figure an audience response, can "recruit" the "very reading it requires," but can never "fully characterize, let alone dictate, its own effect...The fictional text can only strive – only contrive – to model and so mandate, without ever being able to monitor, your response."[26] The abstracted self that is reserved from reading, by reading, is a by-product of the particular kind of readerly absorption cultivated by the novel: "Depending, as literary reading always does, on social subjects at least fractionally estranged from themselves by their gravitation to fictional life stories, the high station of literature is inseparable from its internal destabilization."[27] From the position of the abstracted self, readerly identification will always be experienced as a type of "conscription" by the text, however much self-initiated and self-pursued.

Conscription might be thought of as Iserian discovery – but with the reader's "negative" positionality now theorized as an emotional component of the self-consciousness brought on through reading.[28] For Iser, novel reading is felt to be a "spontaneous" experience that leads to the enlargement of readerly experience through self-conscious, self-critical understanding; for Stewart, conscription is never unselfconscious: the reader is never not aware that her "input is a predigested function of the text's output," and it is this self-consciousness about the text's capacity for conscripting the reader that splits her in two, allowing her to enjoy being "drafted by the text, written with," because she also maintains a self outside "the closed circuit of conscripted response."[29] Readerly surrender is possible precisely because the reader knows that she does not surrender everything, that readerly conscription is a voluntary condition, a "contract" that can be broken at any time, most apparently by closing the book, but also by stopping the "work" of reading by day-dreaming, free association, generally thinking otherwise – and thereby failing to occupy the zones for self-construction.

If one feels that Iser's theory is most illuminating when describing the narrative techniques of realist novels such as *Vanity Fair*, Stewart's more complex formulation of readerly experience seems applicable to classic novels of every sort, from realist to gothic. Indeed, it could be said that the proof of the theoretical pudding is for Stewart in the close readings he conducts of specific novels, readings that account for the bulk of

Dear Reader's 400 pages. Stewart's textual engagements span the nineteenth century, ranging from Mary Shelley to Bram Stoker, from Jane Austen to Oscar Wilde. The chapter on Mary Shelley included in this anthology should be understood as representative of the way Stewart reads – but should not be understood as presenting the only sorts of thematics he reads for. I've selected this chapter rather than any other because Stewart finds in Shelley's novel a figuration of the abstracted reader that helps illuminate this concept as a theoretical basis. *Frankenstein* shows its reader, Stewart argues, that, "dependent as it is on your surrender to the deputized agents of narrative identification, textual transmission must evacuate consciousness before invading (and replacing) it" (794). In following his reading of *Frankenstein*, we can better understand how conscription works through the voluntary surrender of self.

The narrative strategy that Stewart focuses on is also that which interests Gayatri Spivak: the addresses within the story world to story-world readers who are never represented as receiving those addresses. For Spivak, Shelley's narrative technique creates a place within the novel free from social inscription, a way for the subaltern (women, the colonized) to escape the roles in which they are cast by the operation of hegemonic power relations (see pages 683–7 of this volume). By contrast, Stewart understands this narrative strategy as part of Shelley's strategy of readerly conscription. He argues that the place of the reader in the story world is evoked in order to be absented – and absented in order to then be inhabited by the reader of *Frankenstein*. According to Stewart, Shelley's novel figures the dynamic and complex process of readerly identification: the doubling of readerly identity through the split attention created through novel reading. On his description, Shelley's narrative technique "circumscribes" attention "while leaving it blank" (794), thereby bringing the reader, through the experience of displacement, to the discovery that "your most engaged reading takes place in your own absence, or in other words takes your place" (795).

Frankenstein goes even further to mount a self-conscious defense of the cultural and psychological importance of literature generally and gothic literature in particular: "the Creature, as a mere structure of intertexts and inscriptions can turn out, at another level, to be reinscribing – and in the process conscripting – the rationalized (and here championed) irrationality of audience response" (802). The reader's willingness to surrender to gothic fascination, to be absorbed by this frightening tale, is positioned by the novel as a corrective to Victor Frankenstein's youthful rejection of precisely such tales. By contrasting the productive value of her own artistic creation to the destructive value of Frankenstein's, Shelley, according to Stewart, justifies the "constructive anxieties of fairy tale or gothic narrative" which develop in the reader "a healthy sense of mystery, a responsible timidity before the unknown" (801). Shelley's defense of the gothic resonates with Stewart's larger claim about the defense of fiction more generally performed by novels through their readers. If Catherine Gallagher emphasizes the strictly historical nature of her study of fiction, setting forward "caveat emptor" (let the buyer beware) as the motto of *Nobody's Story*, Stewart's phenomenology of novel reading theorizes a self-reflexive reader whose self-awareness inscribes its own caution as part of the reading experience: "Let the reader be aware, beware."[30] Doubled and doubling, readerly self-consciousness (the reader's bewareness of the text's invasive power) is the defining condition of awareness. As if to mark his difference from cultural histories of the novel, Stewart entitles his epilogue "Caveat Lector."

How does Stewart himself conduct the project of historicizing a novel such as *Frankenstein*? Especially since his reading of this gothic novel is driven by psychoanalytic concepts and vocabulary, the rhetorical cues that he attributes to Shelley's novel may seem more post-modern than classic. For example, when Stewart contemplates the significance of the novel's representation of letters that are written and yet portrayed in the story world as never read, his analysis echoes Shoshana Felman's Lacanian reading of *The Turn of The Screw* (pp. 316–28). Stewart's point, that the reader intercepts the letter in place of the narrator, leads him to conclude, as Felman similarly concludes about James, that the novel represents "certain characters who not only live their lives so that they may become narratable, or in the absence of such life stories seek out the narratives of others to fill the void, but who await final engagement and understanding through the rerun of all such experience as *read*."[31] If a skeptical reader demurs, asking how such a modern attitude can in fact be held by Shelley, avant the Lacanian letter (avant even Freud and modern psychology) – then the power of Stewart's position is to argue – how do you know? Stewart wants to challenge precisely the preconceptions about history and culture that nonliterary readers have about a period – and more generally the assumption that chronological progress is cultural progress, that Anglo-American civilization develops superior knowledge as it develops through history. On Stewart's view, a historical understanding of what a person or culture thought at a particular time and place should start with the attitudes about literature and reading inscribed in novels. It is the literary nature of this experience that allows the reader not to "place" events on a historical time line but to be in the historical place made present by the novel in its attempts to write its reader, to "place" its reader rhetorically. The "reading event" is "not determined strictly by the social history of its day" and is transferable through novelistic rhetoric to the contemporary reader who can "work to re-create rather than merely 'place'" that event.[32]

Thus for Stewart, unlike Iser, novels are not just reflections of large-scale changes in philosophy but are themselves potential agents of that change. Writing after Foucault, Stewart recognizes that the phenomenology of novel reading is not insulated from ideology – although it is his strong point that ideological meaning and values can neither be predicted by nor reduced to the hegemonic values of the age, even if certain novels and periods might indeed further those values in more or less straightforward ways. What a novel takes from culture is "only half the picture, and very little of the story, if it is not correlated with what the narrative sends back into cultural circulation through the very form of its own discourse" (796). The microanalysis of a novel's rhetorical conscription of the reader is thus itself an act of historiography that is necessary to any ideological understanding of a particular place and time: "the cultural logic of interpellation is a logic only manifest in fiction according to literature's own logistics: a set of minutely calibrated verbal strategies devised *by* narrative rather than a blanket fact *about* narrative."[33]

Although Stewart may at times seem to imply that the reader's freedom to determine the nature of history through novels places the reader outside of history altogether, this is not the point Stewart himself wants to make, nor is there anything in his argument that logically insists on this position. In fact, Stewart goes out of his way in the conclusion to *Dear Reader* to stress the compatibility between his own theory of reader response and the more explicitly Foucaldian ideological analyses of social power put

DOROTHY HALE

forward by critics such as D. A. Miller.[34] Stewart suggests that the phenomenological effects that his book has devoted itself to describing are ones that can be in turn recruited by social power. Because the belief in the particularity and exceptionalism of novel reading (the belief that readers bring to the novel) is not just a literary but also a social belief, it can be mobilized for political interests. Stewart does not, then, argue, as Iser does, that novel reading leads to truthful insight. The aesthetic moment of social freedom posited by Iser has no place in Stewart's theory. On the contrary, Stewart believes that the feeling of aesthetic exceptionalism, the belief that novel reading yields a privileged kind of knowledge, is itself a readerly effect promoted by the classic novel. To close a nineteenth-century novel is to feel that one reenters a world where one can "go about unwritten, unsubjected, where one has a "communal (hence present) rather than focal (because absent) place."[35] The classic novel's success at figuring reading as a literary experience, an interpretative world apart, thus works to remimeticize, as it were, the social world. The every day world to which the reader returns is perceived as the world where a person lives an unabsorbing (because unscripted) quotidian life, fixing leaky faucets and paying bills. Whatever reading the classic novel has taught the reader about the phenomenology of the literary reading experience and the life of the past, when she stops reading she is left to discover other truths, by other means.

NOTES

1   Wolfgang Iser, *The Implied Reader: Patterns of Communication in Prose Fiction from Bunyan to Beckett* (Baltimore: Johns Hopkins University Press, 1974) quoting Booth, 30.
2   Ibid.
3   Ibid.
4   Ibid.
5   Garrett Stewart, *Dear Reader: The Conscripted Audience in Nineteenth-Century British Fiction* (Baltimore, MD: Johns Hopkins University Press, 1996). See especially pp. 21–4 of his introduction.
6   Nina Baym, *Novels, Readers, and Reviewers: Responses to Fiction in Antebellum America* (Ithaca, NY: Cornell University Press, 1984) 14.
7   Ibid. 19.
8   Ibid. 7.
9   Catherine Gallagher, *Nobody's Story: The Vanishing Acts of Women Writers in the Marketplace, 1670–1820* (Berkeley: University of California Press, 1996) xxiv.
10 Stewart, *Dear Reader* 10.
11 Ibid. 6.
12 Iser, *The Implied Reader* xi.
13 Ibid. xii.
14 Ibid.
15 Ibid. xiii–xiv.
16 Ibid. xiii, xiv.
17 Ibid. xii.
18 Víktor Shklovsky, "Art as Technique," in *Russian Formalist Criticism: Four Essays*, ed. and trans. Lee T. Lemon and Marion J. Reis (1917; Lincoln: University of Nebraska Press, 1965) 12.
19 Iser, *The Implied Reader* 58.
20 Ibid. xii.

21   Ibid. 58.
22   Stewart, *Dear Reader* 7.
23   Ibid.
24   Ibid. 10.
25   Ibid. 396.
26   Ibid. 12, 19.
27   Ibid. 396.
28   Iser, *The Implied Reader* xii.
29   Stewart, *Dear Reader* 8.
30   Ibid. 396.
31   Ibid. 118.
32   Ibid. 6.
33   Ibid. 22.
34   Ibid. 397.
35   Ibid. 400.

FURTHER READING

Eco, Umberto. *The Role of the Reader: Explorations in the Semiotics of Texts.* Bloomington: Indiana University Press, 1979.

Fetterley, Judith. *The Resisting Reader: A Feminist Approach to American Fiction.* Bloomington: Indiana University Press, 1978.

Fish, Stanley. *Is There a Text in this Class? The Authority of Interpretive Communities.* Cambridge, MA: Harvard University Press, 1980.

——- "Why No One's Afraid of Wolfgang Iser." *Diacritics* 11.1 (Spring 1981): 2–13.

Hamilton, Craig A., and Ralf Schneider. "From Iser to Turner and Beyond: Reception Theory Meets Cognitive Criticism." *Style* 36.4 (Winter 2002): 640–58.

Holland, Norman N. *The Dynamics of Literary Response.* 1968. New York: Oxford University Press, 1989.

Holub, Robert C. *Reception Theory: A Critical Introduction.* New York: Methuen, 1984.

Iser, Wolfgang. *The Act of Reading: A Theory of Aesthetic Response.* Baltimore, MD: Johns Hopkins University Press, 1978.

Jauss, Hans Robert. *Aesthetic Experience and Literary Hermeneutics,* trans. Michael Shaw. Minneapolis: University of Minnesota Press, 1982.

Phelan, James. *Reading People, Reading Plots: Character, Progression, and the Interpretation of Narrative.* Chicago: University of Chicago Press, 1989.

Prince, Gerald. *Narratology: The Form and Functioning of Narrative.* New York: Mouton, 1982.

Rabinowitz, Peter. *Before Reading: Narrative Conventions and the Politics of Interpetation.* 1987. Columbus: Ohio State University Press, 1998.

Radway, Janice. *Reading the Romance: Women, Patriarchy, and Popular Literature.* 1984. Chapel Hill: University of North Carolina Press, 1991.

Riquelme, John Paul, ed. *On the Writings of Wolfgang Iser.* Special Issue of *New Literary History* 31.1 (Winter 2000).

Suleiman, Susan, and Inge Crosman, eds. *The Reader in the Text: Essays on Audience and Interpretation.* Princeton, NJ: Princeton University Press, 1980.

Tompkins, Jane P., ed. *Reader-Response Criticism: From Formalism to Post-Structuralism.* Baltimore, MD: Johns Hopkins University Press, 1980.

The Implied Reader

Wolfgang Iser

Wolfgang Iser (b. 1926)

Wolfgang Iser was born in Marienberg, Germany, and educated at the universities of Leipzig, Tübingen, and Heidelberg, where he received his Ph.D. in 1950. After teaching English literature at the universities of Glasgow, Heidelberg, Würzburg, and Cologne, Iser joined the new University of Konstanz, where he remained from 1967 until 1991; since 1978 Iser has also taught at the University of California, Irvine. Together with Hans Robert Jauss, Iser developed what became known as the "Konstanz School" of reception theory, which holds that reading is an interactive experience. Iser articulated this idea in *Der implizite Leser* (1972; translated as *The Implied Reader,* 1974), and *Der Akt des Lesens: Theorie ästhetischer* (1976; translated as *The Act of Reading: A Theory of Aesthetic Response,* 1978). In his more recent work, including *Prospecting: From Reader Response to Literary Anthropology* (1989), and *The Range of Interpretation* (2000), Iser (who now writes in English) has expanded his focus to consider the effect of reading and the nature of readers. Iser is a Fellow of the Heidelberg Academy of Arts and Sciences and the Academia Europea, an Honorary Foreign Fellow of the American Academy of Arts and Sciences, and the recipient of the Werner Heisenberg Medal.

From *The Implied Reader: Patterns of Communication in Prose Fiction from Bunyan to Beckett.* Baltimore and London: Johns Hopkins University Press, 1974 (1972), from ch. 5, pp. 101–20. Copyright © 1974 by the Johns Hopkins University Press. Reprinted with permission of the Johns Hopkins University Press.

The Reader as a Component Part of the Realistic Novel: Esthetic Effects in Thackeray's *Vanity Fair*

I

"You must have your eyes forever on your Reader. That alone constitutes...Technique!"[1] Ford Madox Ford's exhortation to the novelist draws attention to one of the few basic rules that have governed the novel throughout its relatively short history. This awareness as a prerequisite for steering the reader has always exerted a fundamental influence on the form of the narrative. From the start the novel as a 'genre' was virtually free from traditional constraints and so the novelists of the eighteenth century considered themselves not merely as the creators of their works but also as the law-makers.[2] The events they devise also set out the standards regarded as necessary for judging the events; this is shown clearly by Defoe and Richardson in their prefaces and commentaries, and especially by Fielding in the innumerable essays with which he permeates his narrative. Such interventions are meant to indicate how the author wants his text to be understood, and also to make the reader more deeply aware of those events for the judgment of which his own imagination has to be mobilized. With the author manipulating the reader's attitude, the narrator becomes his own commentator and is not afraid to break into the world he is describing in order to provide his own explanations. That this is a deliberate process is demonstrated by a sentence from Fielding's *Tom Jones:* "And this, as I could not prevail on any of my actors to speak, I myself was obliged to declare."[3]

And so the novel as a form in the eighteenth century is shaped by the dialogue that the author wishes to conduct with his reader. This simulated relationship gives the reader the impression that he and the author are partners in discovering the reality of human experience. In this reader-oriented presentation of the world, one can see an historical reflection of the period when the possibility of a priori knowledge was refuted, leaving fiction as the only means of supplying the insight into human nature denied by empirical philosophy.

The author–reader relationship, which was thus developed by the eighteenth-century novel, has remained a constant feature of narrative prose and is still in evidence even when the author seems to have disappeared and the reader is deliberately excluded from comprehension. While Fielding offers this reassurance to his readers: "I am, indeed, set over them for their own good only, and was created for their use, and not they for mine,"[4] Joyce, at the other end of the scale drops only the ironic information that the author has withdrawn behind his work, "paring his fingernails."[5] The reader of modern novels is deprived of the assistance which the eighteenth-century writer had given him in a variety of devices ranging from earnest exhortation to satire and irony. Instead, he is expected to strive for himself to unravel the mysteries of a sometimes strikingly obscure composition. This development reflects the transformation of the very idea of literature, which seems to have ceased to be a means of relaxation and even luxury, making demands now on the capacity of understanding because the world presented seems to have no bearing on what the reader is familiar with. This change did not happen suddenly. The stages of transition are clearly discernible in the nineteenth century, and one of them is virtually a half-way point in the development: the so-called 'realistic' novel. An outstanding example of this is Thackeray's *Vanity Fair.* Here, the author–reader relationship is as different from the eighteenth-century 'dialogue' as it is from the twentieth-century demand that the reader find for himself the key to a many-sided puzzle. In Thackeray, the reader does have to make his own discoveries, but the author provides him with unmistakable clues to guide him in his search.

The first stage in our discussion must be to modify the term 'author'. We should distinguish, as Wayne Booth does in his *Rhetoric of Fiction*, between the man who writes the book (author), the man whose attitudes shape the book (implied author), and the man who communicates directly with the reader (narrator): "The 'implied author' chooses, consciously or unconsciously, what we read;...he is the sum of his own choices.... This implied author is always distinct from the 'real man' – whatever we may take him to be – who creates a superior version of himself, a 'second self', as he creates his work."[6] The narrator, of course, is not always to be identified with the implied author. In the novels of the nineteenth century it happens again and again that the narrator moves even further and further away from the implied author by virtue of being an actual character in the story itself. Traces of this kind of narrator are already apparent in Dickens's novels, and in Thackeray's *Vanity Fair* he is a complete character in his own right. It is almost as if the implied author, who devised the story, has to bow to the narrator, who has a deeper insight into all the situations. What the implied author describes is interpreted by the narrator to a degree far beyond what one might normally deduce from the events. One is bound to ask the purpose of this clear though sometimes complex separation between narration and commentary, especially in a 'realistic' novel which is supposed to represent reality as it is. The justification lies in the fact that even a realistic novel cannot encompass total reality. As Arnold Bennett once remarked: "You can't put the whole of a character into a book."[7] If the limitations of the novel are such that one cannot reveal a complete character, it is even more impossible to try to transcribe complete reality. And so even a novel that is called realistic can present no more than particular aspects of a given reality, although the selection must remain implicit in order to cloak the author's ideology.

II

Thackeray's *Vanity Fair* is also governed by this principle, which is clearly reflected by the different titles of the original version and the final one. The first, consisting of eight chapters, was called "Pen and Pencil Sketches of English Society," indicating that the reality described was meant primarily as a reproduction of social situations; the final version, "Vanity Fair," is concerned less with depicting social situations than with offering a judgment of them. This quality is commented on by Thackeray himself in a letter written a few years after the publication of *Vanity Fair:* "...the Art of Novels is...to convey as strongly as possible the sentiment of reality – in a tragedy or a poem or a lofty drama you aim at producing different emotions; the figures moving, and their words sounding, heroically."[8] "Sentiment of reality" implies that the novel does not represent reality itself, but aims rather at producing an idea of how reality can be experienced. Thus *Vanity Fair* not only offers a panorama of contemporary reality but also reveals the way in which the abundance of details has been organized, so that the reader can participate in the organization of events and thus gain the "sentiment of reality." This is the reason why the novel continues to be effective even today, though the social conditions it describes are only of historical interest. If the past has been kept alive, this is primarily due to the structural pattern through which the events are conveyed to the reader: the effect is gained by the interplay between the implied author who arranges the events, and the narrator who comments on them. The reader can only gain real access to the social reality presented by the implied author, when he follows the adjustments of perspective made by the narrator in viewing the events described. In order to ensure that the reader participates in the way desired, the narrator is set up as a kind of authority between him and the events, conveying the impression that understanding can only be achieved through this medium. In the course of the action, the narrator takes on various guises in order to appear as a fully developed character and in order to control the distance from which the reader has to view the scenes unfolded before him.

At the start of the novel, the narrator introduces himself as "Manager of the Performance,"[9] and gives an outline of what the audience is to expect. The ideal visitor to 'Vanity Fair' is described as a "man with a reflective turn of mind";[10] this is an advance indication of what the reader has to accomplish, if he is to realize the meaning of the proceedings. But at the same time, the Manager promises that he has something for everyone: "Some people consider Fairs immoral altogether, and eschew such, with their servants and families: very likely they are right. But persons who think otherwise, and are of a lazy, or a benevolent, or a sarcastic mood, may perhaps like to step in for half an hour, and look at the performances. There are scenes of all sorts: some dreadful combats, some grand and lofty horse-riding, some scenes of high life, and some of very middling indeed; some love-making for the sentimental, and some light comic business."[11] In this way the Manager tries to entice all different types of visitors to enter his Fair – bearing in mind the fact that such a visit will also have its after-effects. When the reader has been following the narrator for quite some time, he is informed: "This, dear friends and companions, is my amiable object – to walk with you through the Fair, to examine the shops and the shows there; and that we should all come home after the flare, and the noise, and the gaiety, and be perfectly miserable in private."[12] But the reader will only feel miserable after walking through the Fair if, unexpectedly, he has come upon himself in some of the situations, thereby having his attention drawn to his own behavior, which has shone out at him from the mirror of possibilities. The narrator is only pretending to help the reader – in reality he is goading him. His reliability is already reduced by the fact that he is continually donning new masks: at one moment he is an observer[13] of the Fair, like the reader; then he is suddenly blessed with extraordinary knowledge, though he can explain ironically that "novelists have the privilege of knowing everything";[14] and then, toward the end, he announces that the whole story was not his own at all,[15] but that he overheard it in a conversation.[16] At the beginning of the novel the narrator is presented as Manager of the Performance, and at the end he presents himself as the reporter of a story which fell into his hands purely by chance. The further away he stands from the social reality depicted, the clearer is the outline of the part he is meant to play. But the reader can only view the social panorama in the constantly shifting perspectives which are opened up for him by this Protean narrator. Although he cannot help following the views and interpretations of the narrator, it is essential for him to understand the motivations behind this constant changing of viewpoints, because only the discovery of the motivations can lead to the comprehension of what is intended. Thus the narrator regulates the distance between reader and events, and in doing so brings about the esthetic effect of the story. The reader is given only as much information as will keep him oriented and interested, but the narrator deliberately leaves open the inferences that are to be drawn from this information. Consequently, empty spaces are bound to occur, spurring the reader's imagination to detect the assumption which might have motivated the narrator's attitude. In this way, we get involved because we react to the viewpoints advanced by the narrator. If the narrator is an independent character, clearly separated from the inventor of the story, the tale of the social aspirations of the two girls Becky and Amelia takes on a greater degree of objectivity, and indeed one gains the impression that this social reality is not a mere narration but actually exists. The narrator can then be regarded as a sort of mediator between the reader and the events, with the implication that it is only through him that the social reality can be rendered communicable in the first place.

III

The narrator's strategy can be seen even more clearly in his relations with the characters in the novel and with the reader's expectations. *Vanity Fair* has as the subtitle, *A Novel without a Hero*, which indicates that the characters are not regarded as representing an ideal, exemplary form of human conduct, as established by the conventions of the eighteenth-century novel. Instead, the reader's interest is divided between two figures who, despite the contrast in their behavior, can under no circumstances be regarded as complementary or even corrective. For Becky, no price is too high for the fulfillment of her social ambitions; her friend Amelia is simple and sentimental. And so right at the beginning we are told:

> As she is not a heroine, there is no need to describe her person; indeed I am afraid that her nose was rather short than otherwise, and her cheeks a great deal too round and red for a heroine; but her face blushed with rosy health, and her lips with the freshest of smiles, and she had a pair of eyes which sparkled with the brightest and honestest good-humour, except indeed when they filled with tears, and that was a great deal too often; for the silly thing would cry over a dead canary-bird; or over a mouse, that the cat haply had seized upon; or over the end of a novel, were it ever so stupid.[17]

The details of such a description serve only to trivialize those features that were so important in the hero or heroine of the traditional novel. These details give the impression that something significant is being said about the person described, but the succession of clichés, from the round red cheeks and sparkling eyes to the soft-hearted sentimentality, achieve their purpose precisely by depriving the character of its representative nature. But if Amelia is deprived of traditional representative qualities and is not to be regarded as the positive counterpart to the unscrupulous, sophisticated Becky, then the novel denies the reader a basic focal point of orientation. He is prevented from sympathizing with the hero – a process which till now had always provided the nineteenth-century reader with his most important means of access to the events described – as typified by the reaction of a reviewer to Charlotte Brontë's *Jane Eyre*: "We took up *Jane Eyre* one winter's evening, somewhat piqued at the extravagant commendations we had heard, and sternly resolved to be as critical as Croker. But as we read on we forgot both commendations and criticism, identified ourselves with Jane in all her troubles, and finally married Mr. Rochester about four in the morning."[18] In contrast, *Vanity Fair* seems bent on breaking any such direct contact with the characters, and indeed the narrator frequently goes out of his way to prevent the reader from putting himself in their place.

This occurs predominantly through the narrator's comments on the particular patterns of behavior developed by Amelia and Becky in critical situations. He reveals the motives behind their utterances, interpolating consequences of which they themselves are not aware, so that these occasions serve to uncover the imbalance of the characters.[19] Often the behavior of the characters is interpreted far beyond the scope of the reactions shown and in the light of knowledge which at best could only have been revealed by the future.[20] In this way the reader is continually placed at a distance from the characters. As Michel Butor once pointed out, in a different context: "If the reader is put in the place of the hero, he must also be put in the hero's immediate present; he cannot know what the hero does not know, and things must appear to him just as they appear to the hero."[21] In *Vanity Fair*, however, the characters are illuminated by a knowledge to which they themselves have no access. They are constantly kept down below the intellectual level of the narrator, whose views offer the reader a far greater stimulus to identification than do the characters themselves. This detachment from the characters is part of the narrator's avowed intention: "…as we bring our characters forward, I will ask leave, as a man and a brother, not only to introduce them, but occasionally to step down from the platform, and talk about them: if they are good and kindly, to love them and shake them by the hand; if they are silly, to laugh at them confidentially in the reader's sleeve: if they are wicked and heartless, to abuse them in the strongest terms which politeness admits of."[22] The characters in this novel are completely hedged in by such judgments, and the reader sees all their actions only when they have been refracted by the narrator's own critical evaluations. The immensity of his presence makes it impossible for the reader to live their lives with them, as did the reviewer we have quoted, during his reading of *Jane Eyre*. The actual gap between the characters' actions and the narrator's comments stimulates the reader into forming judgments of his own – thereby bridging the gaps – and gradually adopting the position of critic himself.

It is mainly this intention that shapes the composition of the characters, and there are two dominant techniques to be observed. The first part of the novel reproduces letters which Becky and Amelia write to each other. The letter makes it possible to reveal the most intimate thoughts and feelings to such a degree that the reader can learn from the correspondents themselves just who they are and what makes them 'tick'. A typical example is Becky's long letter telling Amelia all about her new surroundings at the Crawley family's country seat. Becky's impressions end with the spontaneous self-revelation: "I am determined to make myself agreeable."[23] Fitting in with present circumstances remains her guiding principle throughout her quest for social advancement. Such a wish is so totally in keeping with her own character that the maneuvers necessary for its fulfillment constitute for Becky the natural way to behave. Thus we see that in society, self-seeking hypocrisy has become second nature to man. In the letters, however, Becky's self-esteem remains so constant that she is clearly quite unaware of her two-facedness. The obvious naiveté of such self-portraits is bound to provoke the reader into critical reaction, and the heading of the chapter that reproduces Becky's letter is already pointing in this direction, for the unmistakably ironic title is: "Arcadian Simplicity."[24] Thus the self-revelation of the letter actually justifies the narrator for not taking the character as it is, but setting it at a critical distance so that it can be seen through. Elsewhere we read: "Perhaps in Vanity Fair there are no better satires than letters."[25] But the intention of the satire is for the reader himself to uncover, for the narrator never offers him more than ironic clues. The narrator's keen concern to give the impression that he never commits himself to ultimate clarity reveals itself at those times when he accidentally reaches an 'understanding' with his reader, but then remembers that such an exchange of experiences goes beyond the limits of his narrative: "...but we are wandering out of the domain of the story."[26]

The second technique designed to rouse the critical faculties of the reader is revealed in Amelia's almost obsessive habit of "building numberless castles in the air...which Amelia adorned with all sorts of flower-gardens, rustic walks, country churches, Sunday schools, and the like."[27] This day-dreaming is typical of Amelia,[28] who devises these beautiful visions as an escape from the narrow confines of her social existence. Her whole outlook is governed by expectations that generally arise out of chance events in her life and are therefore as subject to fortuitous change as the social situations she gets into. The dependence of these often very sentimental day-dreams on the circumstances of the moment shows not only the fickleness of her behavior but also the disorientated nature of her desires, the fulfillment of which is inevitably frustrated by the apparently superior forces of her environment. The projection of hopes which cannot be realized leads to an attitude which is as characteristic of Amelia as it is of Becky, who for different motives also covers up what she really is, in order to gain the social position she hankers after.[29] Despite the difference in their motives, both Amelia's and Becky's lives are largely governed by illusions, which are shown up for what they are by the fact that whenever they are partially realized, we see how very trivial the aspirations really were.[30] The characters themselves, however, lack this awareness, and this is hardly surprising, as their ambitions or longings are often roused by chance occurrences which are not of sufficient lasting importance to give the characters a true sense of direction. Becky certainly has greater drive in her quest for social advancement, and one would therefore expect a greater degree of continuity in her conduct; but this very ambition requires that she should adapt her conduct to the various demands made by the different strata of society; and this fact in turn shows how malleable and therefore illusory are the conventions of social life. What is presented in Becky's life as continuity should not be confused with the aspirations of the eighteenth-century hero, who went forth in order to find out the truth about himself; here it is the expression of the many-sided sham which is the very attribute of social reality.

When the narrator introduces his characters at the beginning of the novel, he says of Becky: "The famous little Becky Puppet has been pronounced to be uncommonly flexible in the joints, and lively on the wire."[31] As the characters cannot free themselves from their illusions, it is only to be expected that they should take them for unquestionable reality. The reader is made aware of this fact by the attitude of the narrator, who has not only seen through his 'puppets', but also lets them act on a level of consciousness far below his own. This almost overwhelming superiority of the narrator over his characters also puts the reader in a privileged position, though with the unspoken but ever-present condition that he should draw his own conclusions from the extra knowledge imparted to him by the narrator. There is even an allegory of the reader's task at one point in the novel, when Becky is basking in the splendor of a grand social evening:

> The man who brought her refreshment and stood behind her chair, had talked her character over with the large gentleman in motley-coloured clothes at his side. Bon Dieu! it is awful, that servants' inquisition! You see a woman in a great party in a splendid saloon, surrounded by faithful admirers, distributing sparkling glances, dressed to perfection, curled, rouged, smiling and happy: – Discovery walks respectfully up to her, in the shape of a huge powdered man with large calves and a tray of ices – with Calumny (which is as fatal as truth) behind him, in the shape of the hulking fellow carrying the wafer-biscuits, Madam, your secret will be talked over by those men at their club at the public-house to-night.... Some people ought to have mutes for servants in Vanity Fair – mutes who could not write. If you are guilty, tremble. That fellow behind your chair may be a Janissary with a bow-string in his plush breeches pocket. If you are not guilty, have a care of appearances: which are as ruinous as guilt.[32]

This little scene contains a change of standpoints typical of the way in which the reader's observations are conditioned throughout this novel. The servants are suddenly transformed into allegorical figures with the function of uncovering what lies hidden beneath the façades of their masters. But the discovery will only turn into calumny from the standpoint of the person affected. The narrator compares the destructive effect of calumny with that of truth and advises his readers to employ mutes, or better still illiterate mutes, as servants, in order to protect themselves against discovery. Then he brings the reader's view even more sharply into focus, finally leaving him to himself with an indissoluble ambiguity: if he feels guilty, because he is pretending to be something he is not, then he must fear those around him as if they were an army of Janissaries. If he has nothing to hide, then the social circle merely demands of him to keep up appearances; but since this is just as ruinous as deliberate hypocrisy, it follows that life in society imposes roles on all concerned, reducing human behavior to the level of play-acting. All the characters in the novel are caught up in this play, as is expressly shown by the narrator's own stage metaphor at the beginning and at the end. The key word for the reader is 'discover', and the narrator continually prods him along the road to discovery, laying a trail of clues for him to follow. The process reveals not only the extent to which Becky and Amelia take their illusions for reality but also – even more strikingly – the extent to which reality itself is illusory, since it is built on the simulated relationships between people. The reader will not fail to notice the gulf between 'illusion' and 'reality', and in realizing it, he is experiencing the esthetic effect of the novel: Thackeray did not set out to create the conventional illusion that involved the

WOLFGANG ISER

reader in the world of the novel as if it were reality; instead, his narrator constantly interrupts the story precisely in order to prevent such an illusion from coming into being. The reader is deliberately stopped from identifying himself with the characters. And as the aim is to prevent him from taking part in the events, he is allowed to be absorbed only to a certain degree and is then jerked back again, so that he is impelled to criticize from the outside. Thus the story of the two girls serves to get the reader involved, while the meaning of the story can only be arrived at by way of the additional manipulations of perspective carried out by the narrator.

This 'split-level' technique conveys a far stronger impression of reality than does the illusion which claims that the world of the novel corresponds to the whole world. For now the reader himself has to discover the true situation, which becomes clearer and clearer to him as he gets to know the characters in their fetters of illusion. In this way, he himself takes an active part in the animation of all the characters' actions, for they seem real to him because he is constantly under obligation to work out all that is wrong with their behavior. In order that his participation should not be allowed to slacken, the individual characters are fitted out with different types and degrees of delusion, and there are even some, like Dobbin, whose actions and feelings might mislead one into taking them for positive counterparts to all the other characters. Such a false assumption is certainly perceived, even if not intended, by the narrator, who toward the end of the novel addresses the reader as follows: "This woman [i.e., Amelia] had a way of tyrannising over Major Dobbin (for the weakest of all people will domineer over somebody), and she ordered him about, and patted him, and made him fetch and carry just as if he was a great Newfoundland dog.... This history has been written to very little purpose if the reader has not perceived that the Major was a spooney."[33] What might have seemed like noble-mindedness was in fact the behavior of a nincompoop, and if the reader has only just realized it, then he has not been particularly successful in the process of 'discovering'.

The esthetic effect of *Vanity Fair* depends on activating the reader's critical faculties so that he may recognize the social reality of the novel as a confusing array of sham attitudes, and experience the exposure of this sham as the true reality. Instead of being expressly stated, the criteria for such judgments have to be inferred. They are the blanks which the reader is supposed to fill in, thus bringing his own criticism to bear. In other words, it is his own criticism that constitutes the reality of the book. The novel, then, is not to be viewed as the mere reflection of a social reality, for its true form will only be revealed when the world it presents has, like all images, been refracted and converted by the mind of the reader. *Vanity Fair* aims not at presenting social reality, but at presenting the way in which such reality can be experienced. "To convey as strongly as possible the sentiment of reality" is Thackeray's description of this process, which he regarded as the function of the novel. If the sense of the narrative can only be completed through the cooperation of the reader (which is allowed for in the text), then the borderline between fiction and reality becomes increasingly hazy, for the reader can scarcely regard his own participation as fictional. He is bound to look on his reactions as something real, and at no time is this conviction disputed. But since his reactions are real, he will lose the feeling that he is judging a world that is only fictional. Indeed, his own judgments will enhance the impression he has that this world is a reality.

How very concerned Thackeray was to confront the reader with a reality he himself considered to be real is clear from the passage already quoted, in which the narrator tells the reader that his object is to walk with him through the Fair and leave him "perfectly miserable" afterward. Thackeray reiterates this intention in a letter written in 1848: "my object...is to indicate, in cheerful terms, that we are for the most part an abominably foolish and selfish people...all eager after vanities...I want to leave everybody dissatisfied and unhappy at the end of the story – we ought all to be with our own and all other stories."[34] For this insight to take root in the reader, the fictional world must be made to seem real to him. Since, in addition, the reader is intended to be a critic of this world, the esthetic appeal of the novel lies in the fact that it gives him the opportunity to step back and take a detached look at that which he had regarded as normal human conduct. This detachment, however, is not to be equated with the edification which the moral novel offered to its readers. Leaving the reader perfectly miserable after his reading indicates that such a novel is not going to offer him pictures of another world that will make him forget the sordid nature of this one; the reader is forced, rather, to exercise his own critical faculties in order to relieve his distress by uncovering potential alternatives arising out of the world he has read about. "A man with a reflective turn of mind" is therefore the ideal reader for this novel. W. J. Harvey has remarked, in a different context:

> A novel...can allow for a much fuller expression of this sensed penumbra of unrealized possibilities, of all the what-might-have-beens of our lives. It is because of this that the novel permits a much greater liberty of such speculation on the part of the reader than does the play. Such speculation frequently becomes, as it does in real life, part of the substantial reality of the identity of any character. The character moves in the full depth of his conditional freedom; he is what he is but he might have been otherwise. Indeed the novel does not merely *allow* for this liberty of speculation; sometimes it *encourages* it to the extent that our sense of conditional freedom in this aspect becomes one of the ordering structural principles of the entire work.[35]

IV

The aspect of the novel which we have discussed so far is the narrator's continual endeavor to stimulate the reader's mind through extensive commentaries on the actions of the characters. This indirect form of guidance is supplemented by a number of remarks relating directly to the expectations and supposed habits of the novel-reader. If the fulfillment of the novel demands a heightened faculty of judgment, it is only natural that the narrator should also compel the reader – at times quite openly – to reflect on his own situation, for without doing so he will be incapable of judging the actions of the characters in the novel. For this process to be effective, the possible reader must be visualized as playing a particular role with particular characteristics, which may vary according to circumstances. And so just as the author divides himself up into the narrator of the story and the commentator on the events in the story, the reader is also stylized to a certain degree, being given attributes which he may either accept or reject. Whatever happens he will be forced to react to those ready-made qualities ascribed to him. In this manner the double role of the author has a parallel in that of the reader, as W. Booth has pointed out in a discussion on the narrator:

...the same distinction must be made between myself as reader and the very often different self who goes about paying bills, repairing leaky faucets, and failing in generosity and wisdom. It is only as I read that I become the self whose beliefs must coincide with the author's. Regardless of my real beliefs and practices, I must subordinate my mind and heart to the book if I am to enjoy it to the full. The author creates, in short, an image of himself and another image of his reader; he makes his reader, as he makes his second self, and the most successful reading is one in which the created selves, author and reader, can find complete agreement.[36]

Such an agreement can, however, be reached along widely differing lines, for instance through disagreement – i.e., a subtly instituted opposition between reader and narrator – and this is what happens in *Vanity Fair*.

When the narrator pretends to be at one with the reader in evaluating a certain situation, the reverse is usually the case. For instance, he describes an old but rich spinster who is a member of the great Crawley family, into which Becky is going to marry, in fulfillment of her social aspirations:

> Miss Crawley was...an object of great respect when she came to Queen's Crawley, for she had a balance at her banker's which would have made her beloved anywhere. What a dignity it gives an old lady, that balance at the banker's! How tenderly we look at her faults if she is a relative (and may every reader have a score of such), what a kind good-natured old creature we find her!...How, when she comes to pay us a visit, we generally find an opportunity to let our friends know her station in the world! We say (and with perfect truth) I wish I had Miss MacWhirter's signature to a cheque for five thousand pounds. She wouldn't miss it, says your wife. She is my aunt, say you, in an easy careless way, when your friend asks if Miss MacWhirter is any relative. Your wife is perpetually sending her little testimonies of affection, your little girls work endless worsted baskets, cushions, and footstools for her. What a good fire there is in her room when she comes to pay you a visit, although your wife laces her stays without one!...Is it so, or is it not so?[37]

By using the first person plural, the narrator gives the impression that he is viewing through the reader's eyes the many attentions paid to the old lady with the large bank balance; for the reader such conduct is scarcely remarkable – indeed it is more the expression of a certain *savoir vivre*. By identifying himself with this view, the narrator seems to reinforce rather than to oppose this attitude, which is symptomatic of human nature. But in pretending merely to be describing 'natural' reactions, he is in fact seeking to trap the reader into agreeing with him – and as soon as this is accomplished, the reader realizes for himself the extent to which consideration of personal gain shapes the natural impulses of human conduct.

In this way, the difference between the reader and the characters in the novel is eliminated. Instead of just seeing through them, he sees himself reflected in them, so that the superior position which the narrator has given him over the pretences and illusions of the characters now begins to fade. The reader realizes that he is similar to those who are supposed to be the objects of his criticism, and so the self-confrontations that permeate the novel compel him to become aware of his own position in evaluating that of the characters. In order to develop this awareness, the narrator creates situations in which the characters' actions correspond to what the reader is tricked into regarding as natural, subsequently feeling the irresistible urge to detach himself from the proceedings. And if the reader ignores the discreet summons to observe himself, then his critical attitude toward the characters becomes unintentionally hypocritical, for he forgets to include himself in the judgment. Thackeray did not want to edify his readers, but to leave them miserable,[38] though with the tacit invitation to find ways of changing this condition for themselves.

This predominantly intellectual appeal to the mind of the reader was not always the norm in the realistic novel. In Dickens, for example, emotions are aroused in order to create a premeditated relationship between the reader and the characters.[39] A typical illustration of this is the famous scene at the beginning of *Oliver Twist*, when the hungry child in the workhouse has the effrontery (as the narrator sees it) to ask for another plate of soup.[40] In the presentation of this daring exploit, Oliver's inner feelings are deliberately excluded, in order to give greater emphasis to the indignation of the authorities at such an unreasonable request.[41] The narrator comes down heavily on the side of authority, and can thus be quite sure that his hard-hearted attitude will arouse a flood of sympathy in his readers for the poor starving child. The reader is thus drawn so far into the action that he feels he must interfere. This effect, not unlike the tension at a Punch and Judy show, enables Dickens to convey contemporary reality to his readers. He follows traditional practice insofar as he brings about a total involvement of the reader in the action. In Thackeray things are different. He is concerned with preventing any close liaison between reader and characters. The reader of *Vanity Fair* is in fact forced into a position outside the reality of the novel, though the judgment demanded of him is not without a tension of its own, as he is always in danger of sliding into the action of the novel, thereby suddenly being subjected to the standards of his own criticism.

The narrator does not aim exclusively at precipitating his reader into such situations of involuntary identification with the characters. In order to sharpen the critical gaze, he also offers other modes of approach, though these demand a certain effort at discrimination on the part of the reader – for instance, when he wishes to describe, at least indirectly, the various aspects of the important love affair between Amelia and Osborne:

> The observant reader, who has marked our young Lieutenant's previous behaviour, and has preserved our report of the brief conversation which he has just had with Captain Dobbin, has possibly come to certain conclusions regarding the character of Mr. Osborne. Some cynical Frenchman has said that there are two parties to a love-transaction: the one who loves and the other who condescends to be so treated. Perhaps the love is occasionally on the man's side; perhaps on the lady's. Perhaps some infatuated swain has ere this mistaken insensibility for modesty, dullness for maiden reserve, mere vacuity for sweet bashfulness, and a goose, in a word, for a swan. Perhaps some beloved female subscriber has arrayed an ass in the splendour and glory of her imagination; admired his dullness as manly simplicity; worshipped his selfishness as manly superiority; treated his stupidity as majestic gravity, and used him as the brilliant fairy Titania did a certain weaver at Athens. I think I have seen such comedies of errors going on in the world. But this is certain, that Amelia believed her lover to be one of the most gallant and brilliant men in the empire: and it is possible Lieutenant Osborne thought so too.[42]

Apparently simple situations are taken apart for the reader and split up into different facets. He is free to work his way through each one and to choose whichever he thinks

WOLFGANG ISER

most appropriate, but whether this decision favor the image of the cynical Frenchman or that of the infatuated swain, there will always remain an element of doubt over the relationship under discussion. Indeed the definite view that Amelia has of her relationship with Osborne acts as a warning to the reader, as such a final, unambiguous decision runs the risk of being wrong.

The reader is constantly forced to think in terms of alternatives, as the only way in which he can avoid the unambiguous and suspect position of the characters is to visualize the possibilities which they have not thought of. While he is working out these alternatives the scope of his own judgment expands, and he is constantly invited to test and weigh the insights he has arrived at as a result of the profusion of situations offered him. The esthetic appeal of such a technique consists in the fact that it allows a certain latitude for the individual character of the reader, but also compels specific reactions – often unobtrusively – without expressly formulating them. By refusing to draw the reader into the illusory reality of the novel, and keeping him at a variable distance from the events, the text gives him the illusion that he can judge the proceedings in accordance with his own point of view. To do this, he has only to be placed in a position that will provoke him to pass judgments, and the less loaded in advance these judgments are by the text, the greater will be the esthetic effect.

The "Manager of the Performance" opens up a whole panorama of views on the reality described, which can be seen from practically every social and human standpoint. The reader is offered a host of different perspectives, and so is almost continually confronted with the problem of how to make them consistent. This is all the more complicated as it is not just a matter of forming a view of the social world described, but of doing so in face of a rich variety of viewpoints offered by the commentator. There can be no doubt that the author wants to induce his reader to assume a critical attitude toward the reality portrayed, but at the same time he gives him the alternative of adopting one of the views offered him, or of developing one of his own. This choice is not without a certain amount of risk. If the reader adopts one of the attitudes suggested by the author, he must automatically exclude the others. If this happens, the impression arises, in this particular novel, that one is looking more at oneself than at the event described. There is an unmistakable narrowness in every standpoint, and in this respect the reflection the reader will see of himself will be anything but complimentary. But if the reader then changes his viewpoint, in order to avoid this narrowness, he will undergo the additional experience of finding that his behavior is very like that of the two girls who are constantly adapting themselves in order to ascend the social scale. All the same, his criticism of the girls appears to be valid. Is it not a reasonable assumption then that the novel was constructed as a means of turning the reader's criticism of social opportunism back upon himself? This is not mentioned specifically in the text, but it happens all the time. Thus, instead of society, the reader finds himself to be the object of criticism.

V

Thackeray once mentioned casually: "I have said somewhere it is the unwritten part of books that would be the most interesting."[43] It is in the unwritten part of the book that

---

the reader has his place – hovering between the world of the characters and the guiding sovereignty of the "Manager of the Performance." If he comes too close to the characters, he learns the truth of what the narrator told him at the beginning: "The world is a looking-glass, and gives back to every man the reflection of his own face."[44] If he stands back with the narrator to look at things from a distance, he sees through all the activities of the characters. Through the variableness of his own position, the reader experiences the meaning of *Vanity Fair*. Through the characters he undergoes a temporary entanglement in the web of his own illusions, and through the demand for judgment he is enabled to free himself from it and to get a better view of himself and of the world.

And so the story of the two girls and their social aspirations forms only one aspect of the novel, which is continually supplemented by views through different lenses, all of which are trained on the story with the intention of discovering its meaning. The necessity for these different perspectives indicates that the story itself does not reveal direct evidence as to its meaning, so that the factual reality depicted does not represent a total reality. It can only become total through the *manner* in which it is observed. Thus the narrator's commentary, with its often ingenious provocations of the reader, has the effect of an almost independent action running parallel to the story itself. Herein lies the difference between Thackeray and the naturalists of the nineteenth century, who set out to convince their readers that a relevant 'slice of life' was total reality, whereas in fact it only represented an ideological assumption which, for all the accuracy of its details, was a manipulated reality.

In *Vanity Fair* it is not the slice of life, but the means of observing it that constitute the reality, and as these means of observation remain as valid today as they were in the nineteenth century, the novel remains as 'real' now as it was then, even though the social world depicted is only of historical interest. It is in the preoccupation with different perspectives and with the activation of the reader himself that *Vanity Fair* marks a stage of transition between the traditional and what we now call the 'modern' novel. The predominant aim is no longer to create the illusion of an objective outside reality, and the novelist is no longer concerned with projecting his own unambiguous view of the world onto his reader. Instead, his technique is to diversify his vision, in order to compel the reader to view things for himself and discover his own reality. The author has not yet withdrawn "to pare his fingernails," but he has already entered into the shadows and holds his scissors at the ready.

NOTES

1   Ford Madox Ford, "Techniques," *The Southern Review* I (1935): 35. The dots are part of the original text and are used by Ford to accentuate "Technique."
2   See Henry Fielding, *Joseph Andrews* (Everyman's Library) (London, 1948), "Author's Preface": xxxii; and *Tom Jones* (Everyman's Library) (London, 1962), II, 1: 39; also Samuel Richardson, *Clarissa, or The History of a Young Woman Comprehending the most Important Concerns of Private Life* (The Shakespeare Head Edition) (Oxford, 1930–31), VII: 325.
3   Fielding, *Tom Jones*, III, 7: 93.
4   Ibid., II, 1: 39.

5 James Joyce, *A Portrait of the Artist as a Young Man* (London, 1966), p. 219. The full sentence reads: "The artist, like the God of creation, remains within or behind or beyond or above his handiwork, invisible, refined out of existence, indifferent, paring his fingernails."

6 Wayne C. Booth, *The Rhetoric of Fiction* (Chicago, 1961), pp. 74 f. and 151. [See also pp. 154–83 in this book.] Kathleen Tillotson, *The Tale and the Teller* (London, 1959), p. 22, points out that Dowden, in 1877, had already differentiated between the author as an historical person and the author as narrator. He calls the narrator of George Eliot's novel "that second self who writes her books."

7 Quoted by Miriam Allott, *Novelists on the Novel* (Columbia Paperback) (New York, 1966), p. 290; see also Hans Blumenberg, "Wirklichkeitsbegriff und Möglichkeit des Romans," in *Nachahmung und Illusion* (Poetik und Hermeneutik, I), ed. H. R. Jauss (Munich, 1964), pp. 21 f.

8 William Makepeace Thackeray, *The Letters and Private Papers*, ed. Gordon N. Ray (London, 1945), II: 772 f. For an historical discussion on the relationship between commentary and story, see Geoffrey Tillotson, *Thackeray the Novelist* (University Paperbacks) (London, 1963), pp. 209 ff.

9 William Makepeace Thackeray, *Vanity Fair*, I (The Centenary Biographical Edition), ed. Lady Ritchie (London, 1910), p. liii.

10 Ibid., p. liv.

11 Ibid., for the irony of the author's commentary, see Ulrich Broich, "Die Bedeutung der Ironie für das Prosawerk W. M. Thackerays unter besonderer Berücksichtigung von 'Vanity Fair'" Dissertation, Bonn, 1958, p. 78.

12 Thackeray, *Vanity Fair*, I: 225.

13 This comes out strikingly in his remark at the end of the novel: "Ah! *Vanitas Vanitatum!* which of us is happy in this world?" Thackeray, *Vanity Fair*, II: 431; there are also less striking instances, when the author pretends that he does not quite know what is happening in the minds of his characters; *Vanity Fair*, I: 236.

14 Ibid., p. 29.

15 See Thackeray, *Vanity Fair*, II: 344. This is the first definite statement that the author "the present writer of a history of which every word is true" makes the personal acquaintance of important characters in his novel at the ducal Court of Pumpernickel.

16 Ibid., p. 404. John Loofbourow, *Thackeray and the Form of Fiction* (Princeton, 1964), p. 88, suggests: "In *Vanity Fair*, the Commentator is a dimension of dissent."

17 Thackeray, *Vanity Fair*, I: 6.

18 Quoted by Kathleen Tillotson, *Novels of the Eighteen-Forties* (Oxford Paperbacks, 15) (Oxford, 1961), pp. 19 f.

19 See Thackeray, *Vanity Fair*, I: 67, 94 f., 108 f., 146, 210 ff., 214, passim.

20 Ibid., pp. 20, 26 f., 32, 37 f., 291, 296 f.; II: 188, passim.

21 Michel Butor, *Repertoire*, transl. H. Scheffel (Munich, 1965), II: 98.

22 Thackeray, *Vanity Fair*, I: 95 f.

23 Ibid., p. 120.

24 Ibid., pp. 112 ff.

25 Ibid., p. 227.

26 Ibid., II: 31.

27 Ibid., I: 146.

28 Ibid., pp. 37, 39 f., 145, 317 f.; II: 39 f., 277 f., 390, 401, 408, and 423 f.

29 Ibid., II: 151 f., 209, passim.

30 Ibid., p. 188.

31 Ibid., I: lv. On Becky the puppet, see H. A. Talon, *Two Essays on Thackeray* (Dijon, no date), pp. 7 f.

32   Thackeray, *Vanity Fair*, II: 112.

33   Ibid., p. 399. Re the character of Dobbin, see Talon, *Two Essays*, p. 31; re the name, see J. A. Falconer, "Balzac and Thackeray," *English Studies* 26 (1944/45): 131.

34   Thackeray, *The Letters and Private Papers*, II: 423.

35   W. J. Harvey, *Character and the Novel* (London, 1965), p. 147.

36   Booth, *The Rhetoric of Fiction*, pp. 137 f.

37   Thackeray, *Vanity Fair*, I: 103 f.

38   Ibid., p. 225, and Thackeray, *The Letters and Private Papers*, II: 423.

39   "Make 'em laugh; make 'em cry; make 'em wait" was the principle underlying Dickens's novels; see Kathleen Tillotson, *Novels of the Eighteen-Forties*, p. 21.

40   See Charles Dickens, *The Adventures of Oliver Twist* (The New Oxford Illustrated Dickens) (London, 1959), pp. 12 f.

41   Ibid., pp. 13 f. – especially p. 14, with the ironic comments of the author.

42   Thackeray, *Vanity Fair*, I: 145. A key to such passages lies in the reflections conveyed to the reader near the beginning of the novel, as to whether what follows should be narrated in the "genteel ... romantic, or in the facetious manner" (I: 59). Thus the author opens up a view of other modes of narration which would inevitably show the events in a different light. In this way, the author indicates to the reader what consequences are linked with a change in perspective.

43   Thackeray, *The Letters and Private Papers*, III: 391.

44   Thackeray, *Vanity Fair*, 1: 12.

WOLFGANG ISER

Novels, Readers, and Reviewers

Nina Baym

Nina Baym (b. 1936)

Born in Princeton, New Jersey, Nina Baym received her bachelor's degree from Cornell University, master's from Radcliffe University, and, in 1963, her doctorate from Harvard University. A year later she joined the faculty of the University of Illinois at Urbana-Champaign, where she is Swanlund Chair and Center for Advanced Study Professor of English, as well as Jubilee Professor of Liberal Arts and Sciences. Baym has been honored with the Modern Language Association's Jay Hubbel Medal for lifetime achievement in American literary study, and fellowships from the Guggenheim Foundation and the National Endowment for the Humanities. She has written critical introductions for numerous nineteenth-century American novels and served as general editor for the *Norton Anthology of American Literature*. Baym's books include *Novels, Readers, and Reviewers: Responses to Fiction in Antebellum America* (1984); *Feminism and American Literary History: Essays* (1992); *American Women Writers and the Work of History, 1790–1860* (1995); and *American Women of Letters and the Nineteenth-Century Sciences: Styles of Affiliation* (2002).

From *Novels, Readers, and Reviewers: Responses to Fiction in Antebellum America*. Ithaca, NY, and London: Cornell University Press, 1984, from ch. 2, pp. 26–43. Copyright © 1984 by Cornell University. Used by permission of the publisher, Cornell University Press.

The Triumph of the Novel

No doubt American life in the colonial, revolutionary, and early national periods was inhospitable to fiction. Religious conviction, pragmatic values, and the hardships of settlement life certainly cooperated to make fiction seem a dispensable if not shameful luxury. No doubt, too, American novelists or would-be novelists in the second quarter of the nineteenth century and beyond continued to have a hard time making a living by writing. But for American readers it appears that novels had carried the day long before 1850.

In July 1827 the *North American* described the times as an "age of novel writing." Life before novels was hard to imagine. "We of the present generation can hardly estimate our own good fortune," the reviewer said. "Thrice blessed is the man who first devised these agreeable fictions. The press daily, nay hourly, teems with works of fiction, of no contemptible quality." Less cheerfully, it observed in April 1831 that "novels have broken upon us in a deluge." Throughout the period journals testified that a huge number of novels was available. *Knickerbocker* in January 1836 referred to the "numerous attempts at novel writing with which the American press has of late been burdened," and it commented the next month that "the press is at this juncture so prolific in novels, romances, *et id genus omne*, that to give each the time it deserves for a perusal, would not only consume the entire day, but take largely from the hours usually devoted to sleep." In June 1843 it appealed to its readers, "Think, O think, ye great multitudes of novel-readers that no man can number."

The *New York Review* (July 1840) mentioned "floods" of novels. The *Ladies' Repository* (April 1843) observed that "this age is most prolific in works of fiction. Scarcely a newspaper falls under the eye that does not announce the forthcoming of a new novel"; it wrote again (May 1847) that novels "swarm America as did the locusts in Egypt"; and it used the same image two months later: novels "drop down by millions all over our land." The *American Review* (April 1843) complained about "tens of thousands of miserably written, and worsely printed novels, that have been floating, in pamphlet form, thick as autumn leaves over the country" and referred more matter-of-factly (October 1848) to the "hundreds of novels, published every year." The *Christian Examiner* wrote of a "deluge" of novels "poured upon us from all lands" and again of a "tide" of novels (March 1845, May 1845).

Harper's library of "select" novels issued its 167th volume in April 1852 (the series eventually exceeded 600 titles). The *North American* in April 1856 described "heaps of fictitious works which load the shelves of booksellers" and in October of that year echoed *Knickerbocker* of two decades earlier: "the works of novel writers follow one another in such quick succession, that an immense amount of reading is forced upon those who would keep up with the times in this branch of literature." In September 1859 the *Atlantic* noted that the British Museum had accumulated more than twenty-seven thousand novels written since the publication of *Waverley*. The *Christian Examiner* for January 1860 began a review essay on novels of the previous year with this summary statement: "novel-reading may be misused, but argument for or against it is quite worn-out and superfluous. The great supply which the last year furnished only proved the demand. In Mr. Carlyle's phrase, the 'all devouring fact' itself has eaten up and quite ended the old palaver of fine objections to it, and of fine defences of it." It went on to observe that 1859 was "emphatically a novel-writing year, and we hold it a good sign of the times that so many of its fictions are of such excellent quality."

Though much of this commentary expresses enthusiasm, the language of tide, flood, deluge, and inundation also suggests uneasiness. The novel phenomenon caught reviewers by surprise. Not only was it a new form, it was a popular one; and it was an unprecedented cultural event for the masses to be determining the shape of culture. To follow the public instead of leading it, to surrender critical judgment to the extent of permitting a low literary mode to assume cultural significance, involved critics in new and difficult professional decisions. But the tide, as their language expressed it, really could not be resisted, because successful authorship depended on selling, and novels were what the public was buying.

There are references throughout the reviews to the public appetite for novels. A writer in the *North American* for October 1823 remarked that "a Waverley novel once or twice a year has grown into such a second nature of our intellectual constitutions, that the rising generation must be at a loss to know what their elder brothers and sisters talked about, before such things existed." "We live in such a novel-reading age," *Knickerbocker* said in September 1838, "that every work of romance, possessing more than ordinary excellence, is seized on with avidity, and made popular at once." Less generously, the *Literary World* for June 24, 1848, said that "the great vice of the age in literature is the novel. The whole world is mad for this style of writing." The *Ladies' Repository* complained in April 1843 that novels "are devoured by thousands, nay millions, of men, women, and children" and in January 1845 that "the popular reading of the day consists almost entirely in works of fiction." The *Christian Examiner* (July 1843) called novels the "favorite reading of the day," and the *North American* (December 1849) described them as "the most popular mode of communication with the public."

In July 1840 the *New York Review* asserted that "for every single reader of any work purely didactic, a popular story counts its hundreds." This hardly surprising public preference for novels over lessons is frequently noted and explains in part the qualified endorsement the genre received from reviewers. Those who read novels might not read anything else. According to the *Ladies' Repository* for January 1845, "it is romance reading, more than everything else put together, that has so universally corrupted the taste of the present age. If a man writes a book – a work of profound study and solid merit, no body will read it." The *Southern Literary Messenger* for September 1849 described novel readers as "an enormous class, who have neither leisure, nor inclination, for graver and more solid studies." *Harper's* (June 1853) observed that "hundreds of readers who would sleep over a sermon, or drone over an essay, or yield a cold and barren assent to the deductions of an ethical treatise, will be startled into reflection, or won to emulation, or roused into effort, by the delineations they meet with in a tale which they opened only for the amusement of an hour." The *Christian Examiner* (September 1855) observed, with reference to Dickens's *Hard Times* and Gaskell's *North and South*, that "it is easier to read a novel than to study political economy or theology, and while there are few who are willing to toil along the hard and difficult path of truth, there are thousands ready to lounge along the broad highway."

Some reviewers claimed that the novel had lowered the level of public taste, but more commonly they recognized that public taste itself was something new, since in prior ages taste had been the prerogative of an elite. Attributing the rise of the novel to the emergence of a large class of new readers, they tended to approach it, if not as a cultural improvement, at least as a cultural opportunity. *North American*, writing on Dumas in January 1843, attributed the popularity of novels to "the increase of the reading public, consequent on the diffusion of education and the cheapness of paper and print." Six months later, reviewing novels by Fredrika Bremer, it described novel reading as "the most common recreation in civilized lands." The *Democratic Review* in July 1846 characterized novels as "a mark of an advanced state of society, as far as the masses of people are concerned."

In short, the novel was thought to have originated as the chosen reading of the newly literate masses, and its dominant position represented less a change of taste in an existing audience than a change in the makeup of the audience for the written word. "As we read these records of ministerial life," a reviewer for the *Christian Examiner* commented on novels concerning ministers, "the mind naturally reverts to olden times. ...We see at a glance into what entirely new conditions society has fallen. Then the minister made himself felt; he was a man of power; he was far more erudite than those around him; the means of acquiring knowledge was far less than now.... The printing press had not achieved its present miracles of art, and public libraries were unknown" (November 1853). The minister-reviewer looks back nostalgically to a social era when books were out of public reach and the ability to own and read them conferred power and prestige. Now, in contrast, the minister is dependent on a reading public that gets its information about ministers from novels. "No department of literature has more direct bearing upon the popular mind than that of fiction" (*Sartain's*, September 1850).

If an educated elite was to reassert its role as arbiter of taste, then it had to establish some control over novels, and this effort was described as an attempt to raise their quality. An early statement of this intention appears in the *North American* for July 1825, in an essay predicting that a new type of novel, focused on ordinary life, would "become exceedingly numerous....A large proportion of them will have a considerable circulation, and consequent influence upon the public opinion, taste, and morals. It follows, further, that it is the duty of reviewers to exercise a strict *surveillance* over this department of literature...and endeavor to give a beneficial direction to a force, that they cannot resist if they would." Speaking of and to "the wise and the good," the *Christian Examiner* (July 1843) said, "there is no case in which they are more bound to use their judgments for the benefit of the unwise, the impetuous, the unthinking, the susceptible, than in the scrutiny of the favorite reading of the day." And a reviewer in the *Home Journal* (March 24, 1855) said, "it is futile to attempt to prevent the young, and many not young, from the perusal of works of fiction. There is a powerful fascination in such productions which ensures to them multitudinous readers in this reading age.... Indeed, I question the utility, while I cannot but mark the utter inefficiency, of the wholesale and indiscriminate proscription of fictitious literature by many well-meaning persons. They meet a natural demand in our intellectual natures which must be gratified. They address the imagination, the most powerful and influential faculty of the mind; and, instead of denouncing everything in this class of literature, we should seek rather to select and provide pure and wholesome aliment in this form for the mental appetite of the young."

Reviewers were joined by novelists in this attempt to make better novels. And by January 1860 the *Christian Examiner* could record some success. "We doubt if readers now-a-days could be content with fiction which serves merely an idle hour's amusement....It is gratifying to find the class of readers on the increase, who, while seeking genial entertainment and recreation from the novelist, will make still larger demands for wholesome sentiment, free and foodful thought, and good impulse to believing the true and doing the right." We should not mistake this praise from a Unitarian journal as referring only to pious, didactic works of fiction by sentimental American women; the remark occurs in a general review of novels including *The Virginians* and *Adam Bede* as well as works by Wilkie Collins and Charles Reade – major figures by "our" standards as well as those of the day. The reviewer was describing a perceived development in the novel's form: novel readers were becoming more sophisticated and, rather than moving on to more weighty forms of literature, were either welcoming or being persuaded to welcome a more weighty type of novel.

Along with an access of "wholesomeness," another change noted by reviewers was a diversification of subgenres; as "the novel" extended its hegemony it absorbed other types of literature and hence began to fracture internally. The tendency of the age, *Graham's* wrote in reviewing Charles Kingsley's *Hypatia* in April 1854, was to present everything in novel form. "We have political novels, representing every variety of political opinion – religious novels, to push the doctrines of every religious sect – philanthropic novels, devoted to the championship of every reform – socialist novels, philosophic novels, metaphysical novels, even railway novels.... The opponents of novel writing have turned novelists." The *Graham's* reviewer was not pleased with this development, considering it the proper function of the novelist "to create or imitate individual character, to invent incident, to represent manners, and to convey the cosmopolitan and comprehensive sympathies of the observer of human life." Even these criteria, however, represent an enlargement of expectations for the novel in comparison to pre-Waverley days. That more and more novels written in these years were "serious" seems certain. Otherwise, no writer who aspired to greatness could have cast ambition in the form of a novel. In effect, however, the "serious novel" developed as a subtype of a popular form, and for this to happen the novel had first to establish itself as *the* form of the times.

"Novels are one of the features of our age," *Putnam's* wrote in October 1854. "We know not what we would do without them....Do you wish to instruct, to convince, to please? Write a novel! Have you a system of religion or politics or manners or social life to inculcate? Write a novel! Would you have the 'world' split its sides with laughter, or set all the damsels in the land a-breaking their hearts? Write a novel! Would you lay bare the secret workings of your own heart, or have you a friend to whom you would render that office? Write a novel!... And lastly, not least, but loftiest...would you make money? Then, in Pluto's and Mammon's name! Write a novel!" The reference to the novel as a way to wealth is not merely jocular. Discussions of Sir Walter Scott regularly commented on the amount of money his novels made, and clearly the chance of becoming rich as well as famous as a novelist introduced a new element to authorship. Indeed, the novel was responsible for a new idea of professional authorship, and the aspiring novelist, even a "serious" one, launched a career with expectations that owed much to the possibilities of the novel as a popular form.

Accordingly, though uneasiness about the attractiveness of the novel is expressed in many reviews, and though a great many novels were reviewed unfavorably, most summary statements about the novel as a genre are finally favorable. To fly in the face of a clear public preference would be, in America, to doubt "the people," and this relatively few reviewers were prepared to do, especially in journals that themselves were aspiring to mass circulation. Among the twenty-one publications that make up my pool, only the Methodist *Ladies' Repository* took a theoretical position of hostility to the novel as a form.

This Cincinnati-based magazine announced in its second issue (February 1841) that "in some instances a desire has been expressed for some '*good moral tales*'; but such wishes cannot be granted. This periodical must be the vehicle of truth, and not of tales." In January 1843 it editorialized, "nothing can be more killing to devotion than the perusal of a book of fiction." In March 1843 it featured an essay on novel reading that linked the love of novels to original sin: "Our mental constitution is originally and naturally diseased. It loves undue excitement." The measure of a novel's pernicious effect was precisely the degree to which it afforded pleasure; that which was popular was necessarily pleasurable and necessarily evil. The habit of novel reading would go far not only "to destroy the taste for useful studies, but also to *destroy* the *power* of severe mental *application*." By giving false pictures of life, novels made readers, especially young women readers, unfit "for the arduous duties and stern realities of life" and also had a tendency "to weaken the barriers of virtue" by "introducing impure scenes and ideas into pure minds." As we will see, the general campaign to raise the quality of novels involved an attempt to make them reflect the stern realities of life and hence in effect to make them less pleasurable, and criticisms like this one frequently occur with respect to particular novels. But only the *Ladies' Repository* condemned the entire genre.

At the same time, the *Ladies' Repository* constantly testified to the number of novels published and the popularity of the genre by its complaints as well as the frequency with which it published antinovel essays and editorials. And it is with more than a little amusement that one observes the appearance, in 1849, of a serial written by the editor, Rev. B. F. Tefft. This historical work, called *The Shoulder-Knot*, was thought by everybody but the editor himself to be a novel. "It is certainly gratifying," he sputtered in December 1849, "to find that there is such a general hostility to fiction, that history itself, if written with a little less than ordinary dullness, excites suspicion.... There seem to be some amongst us, and those of some pretensions to knowledge, who do not appear to know when they are reading facts and when fiction.... Because the story is somewhat romantic, they can hardly credit it as a reality." And so on. "To allay all fears, now and for ever, respecting the historical character of our story, we will here plainly say, that we have gathered our materials, by a very extensive course of reading, from more than one hundred volumes of authentic history.... If we know what fiction is, we never wrote a word of it in our life, and we never shall."

Whatever it was, *The Shoulder-Knot* did the *Ladies' Repository* good, as Tefft made clear in July 1852 when he announced his resignation from the editorship: "complaint was raised against my Shoulder-Knot articles, and it was roundly but childishly asserted, sometimes by persons of official consequence, and by a great many of no

NINA BAYM

consequence, that a continuance of the series would infallibly break down the work. Well, reader, it is now enough to say, that the series was continued, in the face of a great deal of shallow but mischievous talk; and the result was, that, while my annual gain had then averaged about *eleven hundred a year*, the next year's *increase* was over *five thousand names.*"

The journal's no longer pure stand against novels was further weakened in the 1850s by the appearance of numerous so-called religious novels that it felt obliged to notice from time to time and found difficult to condemn. And finally, in January 1859, it reviewed a novel called *The Methodist* at great length and with a full critical vocabulary. "It may be thought, however, rather a bold step, and perhaps some will say an ill-advised one, to attempt to use the emotional exercises of religion, and their various manifestations, to give interest to a romance, and to employ Methodist class meeting, love-feasts, and revivals as the machinery of a novel. But this our author has done – with all gravity and good taste – without cant or bombast or sickly sentimentalisms – and done it successfully." The issue is no longer whether religion can accommodate the novel, but whether the novel can accommodate religion.

So much for the *Ladies' Repository*, to which I have devoted this space in order to give voice to the antinovel faction in reviews of this era. It was joined by other sectarian journals, of smaller circulation; and certainly segments of the populace remained opposed to novel reading throughout the period. But in all the other periodicals in my sample, only a handful of attacks on the novel as a type can be found, and all of them before 1850. In the Unitarian *Christian Examiner* for March 1845 there is a jab at "that kind of literature of which so large a proportion is worthless, and a larger still detrimental," but this occurs in a favorable review of Fredrika Bremer's novels. Another essay in the *Christian Examiner* (May 1845) attacks cheap literature, primarily fiction, but insists "it is impossible we should be understood in these remarks as deprecating all works of imagination; pronouncing them all deleterious and immoral; opening a crusade against the whole department of fictitious composition"; rather, the complaint is only against "the abuse of this department." Another essay (January 1847) starts out as a pure attack on novels as such: "it is surprising that so many, even of the influential and conscientious, are apparently insensible to these appalling dangers; surprising, that parents and teachers of the young do not discern the sure process of corruption which goes on, under the ministry of reckless novelists, in the heart of our community." But after this opening, the essay becomes a conscientious review of seventeen current novels, many of which it praises. And though, to be sure, the *Christian Examiner* always preferred novels full of morality and uplift, this is the last attack on novels as such in its pages.

In the nonsectarian publications, hostility is even sparser. The *Southern Literary Messenger* wrote in February 1842 of the "pernicious influence of this fascinating species of productions" but limited its criticism to "highly wrought fictions," the forerunner of the "sensation novel" of the late 1850s and 1860s. In July 1843, in a review otherwise favorable to novels, the *North American* described the taste for novels as unhealthy. The *American Review* complained in May 1845 that novels "have done more than all other causes combined to corrupt our taste, and degenerate our literature." The *Literary World* for December 16, 1847, argued that, though the genre had possibilities, when one assigned literary rank by the "ordinary and average products" of a form, then "novel-writing, a field that lies open to all, and whose fruits may be gathered with less of labor and previous tillage than any other kind, is so overrun with the poorer sort of laborers, that it seems impossible to set much store by it." Note the class implications of this comment. Novels are easier to write than other forms because the genre has fewer rules to learn and master. Thus anybody can write one. Produced by the people as well as for them, the novel's origins destine it for artistic mediocrity.

Few journals were willing to adopt the antidemocratic view expressed in the *Literary World*. The novel form was much more frequently praised than censured, and it was praised for many accomplishments. The favorable note sounds as early as the second year of the *North American Review*'s publishing history; in July 1816 it wrote that modern novels (in which "fiction is brought home to daily occurrences and observations") "give the reader more freedom and play, than he is allowed in any other kind of composition." Reviewing the Waverley novels in April 1831, it rhapsodized that the novel "will embrace all that man ever did, and all that man ever knew; nothing is above it nor beneath it; it includes with perfect ease and gracefulness all varieties of science, information, profession, and character; and as it does not restrain or oppress the writer, it is not likely to change, except by improvement." In connection with Cooper's novels (January 1838) it stated simply, "to write a good novel, we hold to be one of the highest efforts of genuis." "The novel, indeed," it said in a review of *Dombey and Son* (October 1849), "is one of the most effective, if not most perfect forms of composition, through which a comprehensive mind can communicate itself to the world, exhibiting, as it may, through sentiment, incident, and character, a complete philosophy of life, and admitting a dramatic and narrative expression of the abstract principles of ethics, metaphysics, and theology. Its range is theoretically as wide and deep as man and nature.... It is the most difficult of all modes of composition." "The successful novel of the present day is strictly a work of art" (October 1856); "fiction has become more and more an art" (October 1859).

Other periodicals took the same line. The *New York Mirror* (April 16, 1836), listing the most eminent contemporary writers in England and America, named eighteen novelists out of a total of thirty writers. On December 28, 1839, it said, "that species of invention which alone could body forth the infinite variety of modern society – the novel – requires much peculiar to its period, and all that the mind has ever possessed of original power." The association of the novel with the age recurs in other journals. "The novel is the characteristic literary effort of the present age. It is more. It is its creature and impression" (*Southern Literary Messenger*, May 1854). "The man, who shall build in living literature a monument of this teeming nineteenth century, will find the novel a far fitter form of structure than the poem" (*Putnam's*, March 1855).

More universal claims were made for novels and novelists by many critics. "Fiction has exercised an important influence over the public from the earliest ages of the world.... It will not do to despise that which is so indestructible, and which everywhere exercises such powerful influence" (*Graham's*, May 1848). The *Democratic Review* in February 1852 described fiction as "a department of literature in which it is as honorable as it is difficult to excell" and referred to the "superiority of prose fictions over all other kinds of literature, in inculcating healthy truths and healthy sentiments. Nowhere else can satire be so well directed, fancies so aptly expressed, observations so effectually presented, and style so happily varied, as in fiction." *Harper's* in June 1853 said that "considered merely as artist productions, we are disposed to place the ablest and finest works of fiction in a very high rank among the achievements of human intellect," and an Easy Chair for February 1860 said flatly that "the literature of fiction is the only permanent flower of the imagination....No man's nerves tingle when he hears the name of Aristotle. But to think of Fielding, and Scott, and Dickens, is like grasping a warm hand or leaning against a beating heart....The scope of fiction is as broad as Life and Imagination, and its influence is finer and profounder than that of all other literature." *Harper's*, of course, was published by the house of Harper and Brothers, whose prosperity was founded on cheap issues of foreign novels. It was not disinterested, but neither was any journal that aimed for a large, general audience.

"Life offers nothing better than a good novel" (*Literary World*, July 29, 1848). The *American Review* for December 1849, discussing Jane Austen, commented that "if all literary fiction could be withdrawn and forgotten, and its renovation prohibited, the greatest part of us would be dolts, and what is worse, unfeeling, ungenerous, and under the debasing dominion of the selfishness of simple reason." In October 1854 *Putnam's* ran a major essay called "Novels; Their Meaning and Mission," which stated that these days "novels are judged as art products....Novels are now, many of them, the productions of men of the highest intellectual and moral worth, and are at present more generally read, and probably exercise a greater influence than any or all other forms of literature together." The *Home Journal* (November 10, 1855) praised Dickens and Thackeray as "the two greatest artists of our time." And *Knickerbocker* (September 1859) said that novels constitute "the favorite department, at present, with both readers and writers. There are novels in every style, suited to every taste, treating of every topic, revealing all conditions of life, discussing all branches of learning, rambling through every field of speculation, ordaining the principles of Church and State as easily as the rationale of manners, demolishing and reconstructing society, penetrating all mysteries, unfolding, in short, all the facts and all the wonders of the world which have been since creation, and which shall be while destiny be accomplished. The mission of the novelist is to depict society, and when we reflect that the ideas of all thinkers, the visions of all poetic dreamers, the diverse schemes suggested by love, by ambition, by benevolence, and the multiplied hopes and purposes of all classes of persons are combined and work and ravel together in what may be called the mind of the community, it ceases to surprise us that the domain of the novelist embraces every department of human thought."

This rhetoric sublimates, elevates, or otherwise purifies the basic psychological reality of the human love for fiction, which all critics understood to be the bedrock of the novel's amazing success. "Fiction," according to the *Christian Examiner* for March 1842, "has its origins in man's dissatisfaction with the present state of things, and his yearning after something higher and better, in effort to realize those innate ideas of the beautiful, the grand, and the good, which have no counterpart in the actual world." A more secular approach appeared in the March 1850 issue of *Sartain's*, which described the love of "narratives of adventure or delineations of character" as a "passion." It was "in vain to utter general fulminations against so natural a taste. It were as wise to attempt to extinguish love, or hope, or curiosity." These three earthly passions underlie the novel's power: love for the characters, hope for their

---

good fortune, curiosity as to the outcome of their story. "The appetite for narrative has a solid foundation in the social nature, and must endure. Works of imagination will ever find hearts eager to be made to throb with sympathy for the joys and woes, the physical and moral struggles, of humanity" (*North American*, January 1851). "There is nothing more universal than the taste for fiction, nothing in which all persons more universally agree than love for the imaginative, the marvellous, the ideal – for those incidents and traits of character which transcend the common place realities of life, and find their only home in the regions of the fancy and imagination" (*New York Ledger*, March 19, 1859). "In its essence," according to *Harper's* Easy Chair (February 1860), "story-telling is the earliest desire and the simplest instinct.... Fiction is a final fact of human education, and is no more to be explained or defended than the sunset or the rose."

These accounts of the love of fiction converge from different starting points. In the *Home Journal, Christian Examiner*, and *New York Ledger* we see a sort of idealism, where fiction is a corrective to real life; in the other journals we observe something more like realism, where fiction is faithful to real life; but both approaches root the love of fiction in social emotions. Whether these be the desire for connection with the social body or with an ideal world, they are always the yearning of self toward something beyond it.

But this is not the whole story. Throughout these statements of praise we may also note an emphasis on freedom and scope for both writer and reader, in implied contrast to other, more restrictive, literary forms. Even though relatively few of the multitude of novels read and enjoyed might reach the pinnacles of artistry envisioned in some of the reviews, almost all of them seemed to gesture toward a kind of personal enhancement. Novels, in some way, attract because they gratify the self. The hostility of the *Ladies' Repository* in this review from April 1843 is founded on such an assumption: "in a well-written fiction there is interwoven so much that is beautiful and fascinating, that young persons often feel themselves bound to the page as by enchantment. The descriptions ...are so high wrought that they cannot fail to please. And then rare adventures by land and sea, hairbreadth escapes, sudden reverses of fortune, heart-rending separations, and miraculous meetings, in connection with high wrought portraitures of peerless beauty, and extravagant delineations of character, all have a tendency to gratify by excitement.... The mind becomes ungovernable."

In gratifying the self, novels foster self-love and a tendency to self-assertion that make the mind ungovernable and thus jeopardize the agencies of social and psychological control. That most readers of novels (and virtually all those who read novels only) were thought to be women and youth made particularly ominous the implications of a novel reading based on self-gratification as opposed to social feelings. Not only in the *Ladies' Repository*, but in other journals as well, reviews of individual novels showed concern about the novel's potential for creating social and personal disruption. The ideal novel would negotiate the claims of the individual writer and individual reader and of the social order: as *Knickerbocker* said, "the diverse schemes suggested by love, by ambition, by benevolence, and the multiplied hopes and purposes of all classes of persons are combined and work and ravel together in what may be called the mind of the community." In such a novel, the competing and legitimate claims of individuals and the commonality might be resolved.

NINA BAYM

Rather clearly, reviewers considered those novels superior that weighted the claims of the commonality higher than those of the individual. The preference led them to favor what would come to be called the realistic novel, the type that enforces the primacy of the social world by presenting it as natural fact. Those novels that frankly catered to individual fantasy were described, and dismissed, as less serious works. But reviewers were not alone in a preference for the socializing over the individualizing potential of novels. Many authors had an interest in seeing that "better" novels according to society's lights were written, and by no means were these authors exclusively older males, in whom the existing social structure invested power at all levels of life. It was, after all, George Eliot whose anonymous critique in the *Westminster Review* attacked "silly novels" by silly women novelists. Her comments were quoted and discussed in several American journals. *Godey's* in April 1857 quoted this segment of her essay: the silly novel's "greatest deficiencies are due hardly more to the want of intellectual power than to the want of those moral qualities that contribute to literary excellence – patient diligence, a sense of the responsibility involved in publication, and an appreciation of the sacredness of the writer's art." No schoolmaster could have said it better: the religiosity and didacticism of Eliot's idea for fiction corresponds well with the idea of the better novel held by reviewers. Here is the historical moment at which the novel becomes divided within itself, as a subgenre of inevitably limited appeal seeks to emerge from, and claim the prerogative of, the popular form. This is a trend that has continued unabated into our own time, even to the point where the "serious" novel is now openly intended to be unreadable and exists as the occasion of elite academic and critical commentary, yet anticipates a sale of millions of copies.

Indeed, from the vantage point of the contemporary scene the nineteenth-century American reviewers really appear quite broad-minded, looking favorably on a far greater number and wider range of authors than we have permitted to survive in the canon. They never assumed, though they might have feared, that popularity implied poor novelistic quality, and they were prepared to appreciate novels that fell considerably below their own sense of the highest standard. Further, and more significant, if one attempts to extract from all the varieties of praise those terms that persist, one finds a lexicon for individual novels somewhat different from those propounded in the more self-conscious and generalized descriptions of the ideal work.

The concept behind many different words seems to be something connected to *energy*. Here are phrases from the *Home Journal*: "this interesting story will enhance her reputation," "her books are always deeply interesting," "a spirited and well-wrought tale, displaying vigor and discrimination," "deeply interesting," "one of the most spirited and powerful of female novelists," "the incidents are of thrilling interest, and the characters sustained with power," "the story unfolds itself with absorbing interest." *Arthur's Home Journal*, an exponent of didactic fiction, nevertheless praised books that possessed "uncommon power," "vigor of intellectual grasp," or fertility, vigor, power, and vivacity. *Godey's*, designed for women and girls, praised Hoffman's *Grayslaer* (August 1840) as an exciting, interesting, and vigorous production "full of graphic description and stirring incidents," and *Love's Progress* as "a narrative full of interest." The phrases "full of interest" and "stirring incidents" recur in its reviews.

The *Literary World*, reviewing *The Tenant of Wildfell Hall* (August 12, 1848), saw the secret of the writer's "power" as "vigor of thought, freshness and naturalness of expression, and remarkable reality of description. No matter how untrue to life her scene or character may be, the vividness and fervor of her imagination is such that she instantly *realizes* it." The first issue of *Harper's* (June 1850) described Edward Grayson's *Standish the Puritan* as a "narrative of very considerable interest and power" and referred to the "vigor" of its satire. In January 1855 one of its reviews said that *The Lost Heiress* by E. D. E. N. Southworth depicted events with "great power" whose "vigor of conception and brilliancy of description make it one of the most readable novels of the season." The *New York Ledger* described the novels of Anne S. Stephens (June 5, 1858) as "of absorbing interest," containing dramatic fire, intense vitality, and vividness that "enchain the reader's attention."

Taking the opposite tack, *Putnam's* for November 1856 criticized four morally worthy novels for the absence of interest and power: *Household Mysteries* was "not highly exciting, and yet agreeable"; *The Fashionable Life* showed "the strongest religious sensibilities and the kindest intentions in the writer, but [was] quite destitute of originality or power"; *Helen Lincoln* possessed "few remarkable or striking qualities"; *Elmwood* was "a sensible story" that displayed "the most respectable talent without calling for much remark either in the way of praise or blame." Even in the *Christian Examiner*, the journal most consistently devoted to fiction at once decorous and weighty, these judgments appear. George Sand, it admitted, "writes always with beauty, often with singular power" (March 1847). It preferred *The Shady Side* because it had "more power and genius" than two other novels about ministers: "it seizes upon the feelings with a stronger grasp, and makes much greater demands on the reader's sympathies" (November 1853). Melville's *Israel Potter* was faulted (May 1855) because the main character "lacks those elements which arrest and enchain the reader's sympathies; and, at the best, it is only a feeble delineation of a very commonplace person."

Examples of this sort could be greatly multiplied. Whole novels, parts of novels, and novelists were assessed as vigorous or feeble, powerful or tame. Power and vigor were always good, feebleness and tameness always bad, quite independently of any other variables such as the type of novel, the acceptability of its morality, the gender of the author. Domestic fiction was usually not of the first rank because it was difficult to make powerful stories about household routine; but those who succeeded in doing so won high praise. The French novelists were fiercely excoriated because their vicious morality was conveyed in works of extraordinary power, on account of which they were hugely (and deservedly, the reviewers grimly admitted) popular. Women writers were supposed to be less capable of literary artistry because they belonged to the weaker sex. But this theoretical presumption often failed in practice: Ann Stephens, E. D. E. N. Southworth, George Sand, Charlotte Brontë, and Emily Brontë were all exceptions, and their works were praised.

What does the concept of power mean here, and why is it so favorably assessed? It was never defined or discussed, but its desirability in novels and its essential relation to their success were taken for granted. It seems to be a property of writers or texts that calls out a complementary response in readers, a response called "interest." The greater the power of the text, the greater the reader's interest, which at its height becomes enchantment, absorption, or fascination. Power is thus experienced as power *over* the reader; but power works by creating interest *in* the reader, so that the reader too becomes strong. Interest refers less to intellect than emotions; as the dictionary puts it, interest is "excitement of feeling, accompanying special attention to some object." The objects of interest in the novel are the story and its agents, who by virtue of their resemblance to human events and human beings have the capacity to create an interest beyond that of any other literary genre. Interest in the novel is a kind of excitement.

So the explanation for the success of the novel lies in the inherent power of the form to generate reader excitement. Novels that succeed realize their formal potential. Such a potential, it should be noted, has little to do with the additional capacity of the novel to – as the *North American* had written – embrace all that man ever did, and all that man ever knew; to include with perfect ease and gracefulness all varieties of science, information, profession, and character. Or with its capacity, according to another review in that journal, to exhibit through sentiment, incident, and character a complete philosophy of life, and to admit a dramatic and narrative expression of the abstract principles of ethics, metaphysics, and theology. These undoubted desiderata were always ancillary. And their ancillary status always left a trace of bad faith in reviews that hoped to utilize the immense popularity of the novel for "higher" aims.

38 Dear Reader

Garrett Stewart

Garrett Stewart (b. 1945)

Garrett Stewart was born in Detroit, Michigan, and educated at the University of Southern California and Yale University. After receiving his doctorate in 1971, Stewart taught at Boston University (1971–6) and the University of California, Santa Barbara (1976–93); since 1993 he has been the James O. Freedman Professor of Letters at the University of Iowa. Stewart's honors include Guggenheim and National Endowment for Humanities Fellowships. His books include *Dear Reader: The Conscripted Audience in Nineteenth-Century British Fiction* (1996); *Between Film and Screen: Modernism's Photo Synthesis* (1999); and *The Look of Reading 1514–1990* (forthcoming).

From *Dear Reader: The Conscripted Audience in Nineteenth-Century British Fiction.* Baltimore and London: Johns Hopkins University Press, 1996, from ch. 5, pp. 113–26, notes, pp. 417–18. Copyright © 1996 by the Johns Hopkins University Press. Reprinted with permission of the Johns Hopkins University Press.

In the Absence of Audience: Of Reading and Dread in Mary Shelley

What do the least gothic novel ever written, *Persuasion*, and the most famous gothic novel ever written, *Frankenstein*, have in common? If nothing of substance, then the question turns us to form. Yet since there is no obvious structural resemblance, either, between Austen's omniscience and Shelley's dramatized frame tale, the question pays off only if it gets us to some deeper notion of narrative formation – or, more particularly, to the structure of reading fashioned by such formal determinants.

Well before the transitional pre-Victorian figure of Mary Shelley, with her whole-hearted renewal of gothic materials, what Austen's comic realism has already managed to do is to draw off from the gothics flourishing in her day a formula that subtends their narrative peculiarities: a psychodynamic of novelistic reading per se which the lurid excess of the gothics was bound to maximize. Intensified in that melodramatic mode is the rhythm of contemplative (often moralizing) calm after narrative storm. In this way late-eighteenth-century gothic plotting tends to rehearse on its way toward closure the evolutionary outmoding of its very genre: the metamorphosis from sensation to sensibility. This takes place even as the latter mode retains – in Austen, for instance, and in *Persuasion* as much as in *Northanger Abbey* – something of the same pronounced emotional curvative which, though perfected in the gothics, came to seem inherent in the very temporality of narrative fiction.

Mary Shelley, of course, taps the gothic conventions in a more direct manner, while at the same time returning to the epistolary roots of Austenian realism for a full-blown but still curiously disembodied version of that "whomsoever it may concern" structure manifested by the respectively psychological and apocalyptic ironies of framing in *Frankenstein* and *The Last Man*. In the process, Shelley's stress is laid on credibility and dissemination as much as on rhetorical heightening and the necessities of resolution. The gothic atmospheres and mechanisms of the literary vernacular emerge *within* the plot of *Frankenstein*, for instance, as they have come to it: mediated and transmitted many times over, processed and dispensed, in a word *received*. Where Austen inherits and reworks the narrativity of late-eighteenth-century gothic plotting, its arcs of suspense, tribulation, subsidence, and evaluative retrospect, Shelley's revisionary emphasis falls more on its discourse in circulation: its overwrought paths of access between narrators and narratees. In Shelley as much as in Austen, therefore, you are not just implicated but schooled as coparticipant in that work of plotting which takes its bearings from the present modulation, rather than the mere promise, of response.

To linger even momentarily over the structural contrast between these two early nineteenth-century writers is to grasp in short order the breadth of effect opened up within the force field of conscription between, at one pole, the work of submerged interpolation in Austen (the marginalized "dear reader") and, at the other, the frame-ups of extrapolation in Shelley (the circumferential zones of reception). If Austen's gothic flirtations in *Northanger Abbey* enlist a melodramatic format which, in loose alliance with the shape of provincial romance, helped further codify for the history of fiction the reciprocal demands of anticipation and closure, Shelley's unabashed gothic plotting is a transgressive or deviant storytelling that pitches to crisis the narrative contract itself, psychologizing (under far more extreme narrative circumstances than in Austen) the very motives for the dispensing and receiving of stories. Furthermore, where Austen in *Northanger Abbey* checks the excesses of the gothic within the sphere of its acknowledged and harmless appeal, Shelley in *Frankenstein* chronicles the aftermath of the gothic's more dangerous exile from the mind's regimen. She does so through the withholding of supernatural narrative affect altogether from her hero, thereby constructing a mentality doomed by its very difference from the reader's own. As much as Austen's texts, therefore, Shelley's too are embroiled in the psychosocial protocols of literary acculturation. So that, once again, the analysis of narrative structures confronts most directly the workings of culture, and fiction's place in it, by staying alert to the structuration of the reading agency not only laid out by story but replayed by reading.

Yet such an agency, I stress again, is by no means the solid bourgeois citizen, the stabilized monolithic presence, of recent reductive accounts – but instead the very absenting of subjectivity both demanded and dramatized by the fictional text. Dependent as it is on your surrender to the deputized agents of narrative identification, textual transmission must evacuate consciousness before invading (and replacing) it. In this sense, Shelley's two major frame tales, *Frankenstein* (1818) and *The Last Man* (1826), undergo their own textuality, enact their own becoming-text, by invoking an attention whose personification they finally obliterate. They thereby subsume the scenario of reception under that aspect of reading which they can conscript but, beyond a certain point, never hope to specify. Everything about storytelling and transcription in them, everything about textual processing, everything about the transmissive function of language, everything, in short, about their own narrative impulse and textual premise comes forward toward that moment they attempt to circumscribe while leaving blank: the moment, plausible in one, impossible in the other, of their own reading. For one is a gothic thriller whose feverish stenographer lives on, and as if only, to tell of what he has heard and seen; the other a tour de force of dystopian futurism whose last author, sole survivor of a universal plague, has no conceivable readers left.

Mary Shelley's two most interesting novels serve therefore, in a revealing symmetry, to test the phenomenological bounds of fictional address as a function not only of textual circulation but of linguistic and cultural, even racial, continuance. What the nineteenth-century fiction industry takes for granted – namely, the normal routes of reception – Shelley instead takes to a denaturalizing limit. The very transmission of human consciousness in language is at stake in the rhetoric of her narratives. She wrote two novels, that is, in which the situation of the reader, even though in different ways emptied out of the text, is necessary to complete the thematic of storytelling within that text: a reader whose attention alone fulfills the communicative and confessional impulses of the characters themselves. Equally in *Frankenstein* and *The Last Man*, the story will out only if the reader's enacted absence is overridden – or underwritten – by textual activation, in short by reading.

In *Frankenstein*, the fated Creature, denied progeny, is able to leave behind no more than a story, which he tells to and through Victor Frankenstein, also the dying last of his family line, who in turn unfolds his version of the story to a ship's captain named Walton, who then transcribes it in a journal appended to letters that are, though read (at least by us), never definitively received by the sister back in England to whom they are addressed. Where narrative thus operates in *Frankenstein*, for Victor and his Creature alike, as an ultimately posthumous transmission to an always deferred present from a fatal past, operates in other words as a surrogate posterity, in *The Last Man* there is no one left alive to inherit the story of worldwide annihilation. It is a story that comes to us not by way of mystical vision but by way of a telepathically transcribed document from the future discovered by the Shelleys in the cave of the Cumaean Sybil. Narrative becomes the sole relic of the human race: an epic in the wake of culture itself. It is not read posthumously by those who outlive its events, for their number is none, but read proleptically by those (any of us) whom its very writing will (already) have outlasted. In *Frankenstein*, then, the reader receives the narrative of deviant creation as the event's only legacy. In *The Last Man*, the reader receives the text of racial extirpation as that eventuality's only solace, before rather than after the fact. In neither case, however, is the reader actually there to do so. Taken together as experiments in reading, these two texts jointly explore – by exaggerating from opposite directions – a phenomenological intuition one might phrase as follows: a sense that your most engaged reading takes place in your own absence, or in other words takes your place.

"With What Interest and Sympathy I Shall Read!"

No reader can miss the fact that Mary Shelley's *Frankenstein* is a novel preoccupied with storytelling and transcription, shaping itself by subsidiary narratives of all sorts – journals and confessional accounts framed and redoubled by the narrative event of epistolary broadcast. That the novel, in structure even more than in episode, is as much about reading as about writing, about narrative consumption as about narrative production, is perhaps less obvious. And this is because reading is most pointedly thematized by what we might call its encompassing absence. The issue only grows clear by the end. Even with Victor's entire narrative retold, and the Creature's within it, by Walton to his sister, the completed story never arrives at a *narrated* destination. Its frame functions, instead, more as an open bracket. Certainly you don't "see" the posted documents being read. There is no presentation of them by the butler, no parlor of breathless perusal, in short no *mise en scène* of receipt. All you can be sure of is that the letters, enclosing Walton's journal of Victor's story, have somehow made it your way.

But they do so – as at one level who could doubt? – only as they fade from documentary to fictional status: the first letter realistically placed and dated, except for the "editorial" avoidance of the year ("St. Petersburg, Dec. IIth, 17—), and then formally signed ("Your affectionate brother, R. Walton"); the second shifted toward the quasi-mystical ("Archangel"); the third merely dated, without site of origin, and mechanically initialed ("R.W."); the fourth, again without salutation or place of origin, dated in three stages (as if now by pure narrative chronology) and then yielding place to no closing signature.[1] All that follows, twenty-four chapters later, is the eventual subsumption of epistolary narrator to novelistic character within the omniscient stage direction "Walton, in continuation." With more typographical cueing than in Austen, literary history is again telescoped by the local evocation of generic precursors. Like the Creature made rather than born, demonically cobbled together, the novelistic mode is pieced out before our eyes, born of epistolary directness, midwifed by a framing structure that remains vectored beyond plot's own closure. Walton disappears "in continuation," never to return in proper (or signatory) persona, but only to have his transcriptive role absorbed by the reading audience's own reactions. And just as there is no one there to sign off on the story, so there is no one seen to sign *for it*, as it were, in receipt. Mrs. Saville is nowhere to be found except in the address of the discourse, playing mere narratee in contrast to your role as reader. You therefore intercept the letters (the transcript of Frankenstein's extended monologue enclosed with the last of them) in her place, in place of the civilized reader "tutored and refined by books and retirement from the world" (letter 4:27).

Moreover, the chain of reception, and hence the psychology of reading, does not stop there. It doubles back on itself when even the scribe of Frankenstein's story wants part of the action at the receiving end: "This manuscript will doubtless afford you the greatest pleasure," Walton writes to his sister, "but to me, who know him [Victor] and hear it from his own lips – with what interest and sympathy shall I read it in some future day!" (4:29). In an ethos of internalized narrative energy, vicariousness goes deep.[2] As we began to see with Austen, reading becomes not just an extension of but a model for human experience, which Shelley's text seems to recognize as *vicarious at its source*. From the ranks of fictional characters, all of whom are narrated, emerge certain characters who not only live their lives so that they may become narratable, or in the absence of such life stories seek out the narratives of others to fill the void, but who await final engagement and understanding through the rerun of all such experience *as read*. With Dickens and the Brontës and Eliot still waiting in the wings of nineteenth-century narrative, here already is the emergent valence of the novel as Victorian cultural establishment. When, in the reading of *Frankenstein*, fiction structures desire in the form of its secondary processing *as story*, narrative has overstepped the bounds of art or commodity to become a prosthesis of social subjecthood.

Even to suspect as much is to question the newer methodological terrains of literary study, including the contested grounds of the proper disciplinary object itself: text versus context, as if the two were not structurally contiguous. Now is therefore a timely moment in these pages to italicize one corrective emphasis of this chapter – and of those to come. I want to insist that what a narrative artifact, as rhetorical construct, takes from the discourses of its culture – let us say in Shelley's case, for starters, the science-versus-poetry debate, evolutionary anxiety, gynophobia, class tensions, a dubious stance toward the romantic sublime, and so forth – is only half the picture, and very little of the story, if it is not correlated with what the narrative sends back into cultural circulation through the very form of its own discourse. This is to say that the critical reading of literature, precisely as an act of historical recovery, deserves the name only if it keeps its eye on rhetorical interplay as well as mimetic subtext, on fiction's "interface" with its reading subjects as well as on its image of their (other) social (because discursive) imbrications.

Reading, Revival, Reanimation

Read as literary construct, then, *Frankenstein* conflates two traditions of the British novel as Shelley has inherited them. First, it borrows those evidentiary mechanisms of the eighteenth-century text that were often attached as prefatory editorial footwork to prose fictions. Second, this device is crossbred in Shelley's novel with the epistolary mode of writing-to-the-moment. In this way the "editor," taking on the role of empassioned "correspondent," melds the corroborative with the affective dimension of textual force.

GARRETT STEWART

The romantic transformation to which Shelley's inherited materials is submitted, however, results at the structural level from the arrest of the epistolary circuit, on the one hand, and, on the other, from the avoidance of its more overtly rhetorical derivative in the "dear reader" formula. Straddling these models, the vocative phrase "My dear Sister" (letter 3:21) appears in only one letter – as if serving a strictly rhetorical rather than epistolary function.

As such, this residuum of address is only part of a broad rhetorical campaign whereby the extrapolative force of the novel, the managed output of its fictional effect, is programmed in part through the novel's literary-historical input, as detailed in a variety of prefatory allusions having to do with the general literary topography of the period as well as with certain specific source texts. Anticipating how the "sentiments" of the novel may "affect the reader" (xiv), the preface assures the audience that the story is bent on "avoiding the enervating effects of the novels of the present day" (xiv). It cannot be missed that the binary opposition thus insinuated offers as the relevant counter to such fiction the surcharged and energizing novel, a text revived and reviving – the novel, in a word, *reanimated*. A fable emerges. Despite the moralizing condemnation of Victor's overambitious trespass upon forbidden ground, he seeks what Shelley achieves: the vivification of an inert form. And like Shelley, no matter how violent his deviant inventiveness, he can promise in the end, as he does to Walton, an "apt moral" (letter 4:28) in reward. The deliberate links throughout the text between Victor's laboratory exertions and the labor of fictional invention on Shelley's part serve to confirm this. They offer, by their supposed candor about the creative process, a check on the disingenuousness of this forcefully cautionary, because scarcely enervating, tale. For it is a tale about the allowable limits of what one is tempted to call regenerative pastiche, the very process that brought it about in the first place.

For all its avowed solicitude concerning the reader, though, there is no structural room in *Frankenstein* for the direct solicitation of the audience. One notes, by contrast, Mary Shelley's later short story, "Transformations" (1830), a supernatural narrative of doubling and physical malformation, pride and psychic transgression, very much in the mold of the 1818 novel. Without the distancing of the novel's frame, however, disallowing as it does all direct authorial address, the second paragraph of Shelley's story stalls upon its own reasons for being: "Why tell a tale of impious tempting of Providence, and soul-subduing humiliation? Why, answer me, ye who are wise in the secrets of human nature!"[3] Such an apostrophe, in the traditional combination of imperative and vocative, is the sort of interpolation ruled out by the dramaturgy (without commentary) of narration in *Frankenstein*. Instead, Shelley works a wholesale extrapolation of response displaced from the absent Mrs. Saville upon that individual reader who must proceed under the aegis of an *intended* but not necessarily achieved attention.

And the fable continues – as the story of a formative reading that blurs borders between plot and its preconditions in imaginative vulnerability. Just as textual reception awaits the narrative at or beyond its outer edge, so too, deep within the plot's chronological prehistory, can the will to reading be traced all the way back to the constitutive inclinations of narrative's desiring agents. "My education was neglected, yet I was passionately fond of reading." Thus Walton writes in the autobiographical mode (letter 1:16), yet giving anticipatory voice to the Creature's story as well. Eavesdropping later at the de Lacey cottage, the Creature will be initiated first into language, then into its cultural productions (Goethe, Plutarch, Milton), by his listening in on a quintessential family scene of hearthside reading aloud. In a more radical way than that in which the phrase is ordinarily taken, the Creature is *humanized by reading*. Yet this reading is placed in ironic juxtaposition to that undertaken by both his creators, Victor as well as Shelley. Victor's case is perhaps the clearest, by being the most extreme and complete. Whereas Mary Shelley, Walton, and the Creature each narrate as they have been programmed to do by their reading, indeed narrate an experience that would never have emerged in the same way but for their reading, it is Victor, spurred to creation by what he has (and hasn't) read, who is the only character to take charge explicitly of his own narration in an editorial role, as we are about to see, helping to guide its desired reading. In this, as in many other ways, he is of course very close to Mary Shelley as author and editor of her own published manuscript. The fecund monstrosities of her tale come to seem as terrible to her, so she would pretend, as Victor's brain-child does to him, a "hideous progeny" (xii) like his "hideous narration" (23:188) later.

Such a figurative crossing between discourse and story, between textual and anatomical invention, is subsequently reversed when metaphors of verbal creativity are incorporated into the language of transgressive creation – rather than narrative itself figured as monstrosity. Not only does Victor accuse himself (by the phrasal doubling of hendiadys) of being the "miserable origin and author" (10:96) of the Creature, but he refuses to make the same mistake twice, to "compose a female" (18:143), as if it were to be an act, again, of authorship rather than laboratory magic. This link between black magic and aesthetic conjuration is further tightened by the manner in which the compositional will to invention and the labors of the laboratory are conflated in Victor's own mind near the end of his story to Walton. "Frankenstein discovered that I made notes concerning his history; he asked to see them and then himself corrected and augmented them in many places" (24:199), his editorial rigor devoted "principally" to the task of "giving the life and spirit to the conversations he held with his enemy" (24:199). Not content to have breathed life into a pastiche, a random assemblage, of body parts, Victor now tries to animate the prose that records it. His will to power persists, that is, across two levels of "compositional" energy. Finally, too, the language of aberration and deformity surfaces in his description of this editorial purpose: " 'Since you have preserved my narration,' said he, 'I would not that a mutilated one should go down to posterity' " (24:199) – that "posterity" by which the created and printed text alone, not its homologous Creature, is bid to replicate itself. Narrative mutilation, biological malformation – these are the paired defaults of "authorship" in Shelley's novel, from a negotiation between which all audience response must be processed.

Thus is confirmed a running parallel between the genesis plot and the story of its own literary generation. Just as Victor sutures together the Creature, so does Shelley, assembling her creation *Frankenstein*, also assemble the man for whom it is named: a composite, as he is, of two figures from the German ghost stories that Shelley read aloud with Percy Shelley, Byron, and Polidori.[4] Along with the effects of conversation about Erasmus Darwin and his reputed experiments in spontaneous animation (x), these stories coalesce in Shelley's unconscious, invade her dreams, and spawn the script of unholy creation that becomes, upon waking, her tale. Out of discrepant body parts, a humanoid shape; out of discrepant pieces, a newly articulated narrative, a narrative galvanized by the spark of creative inspiration: such is the offspring of writer and hero

GARRETT STEWART

alike. Moreover, Shelley's dream (from the preface) of an artificial man, an artifice of life, stands to the novel as a whole – embryonically – as do Frankenstein's feverish conceptions to the confessional tale he ends up having to tell, reread, edit, and revitalize.

In this way the prefatory explanations of what James would call the "germ" of the text relate indirectly to the most deeply receded text-within-the-text of the story proper, a microcosm of its own gestation. This analogue of conception embedded in the resulting narrative is inscribed – under proscription – in the form of Victor's journal, containing his notes for the assembly and animation of the Creature. As the ur-text within this nest of tales, transcripts, and transmissions – a text stolen by the Creature shortly after the inception of his consciousness (15:124), never quoted from, and never seen again – it is the origin under erasure of all that follows. Providing for the Creature a primal reading lesson, the unfolded mystery of his origination, for us it is instead the unreadable journal within that read journal-like transcription that constitutes the largest part of the novel: the story of a constructed Creature within that creative construction – here, explicitly, a dreamlike dictation from the unconscious – which is fiction itself.

To pursue the comparison between Walton's journal and Victor's, tunneling back together, as they do, toward the mysterious inception of the story in Shelley's own reading, is to confirm the literary-historical overtones of her "progeny" trope. For the process of its gestation plays out in advance the nature of its fictionalized plot: the *making up*, in two senses, of a new hybrid form. I have suggested that at some level the reading that brings the Creature to compelled and compelling voice, the reading aloud at the de Lacey cottage, is what "humanizes" him. So, too, with the reading by Mary Shelley that went into his imaginative composition. Reframed thrice over by the novel's layered textual dissemination, the Creature erupts as a perversely fashioned organic entity in every sense *brought alive by reading*. Shelley's, Victor's, the cottagers', the Creature's own, Walton's, Mrs. Saville's prospectively, and finally, in the moment of extrapolation from all of them, your own.

"To Encounter Your Unbelief"

Everything points toward this emphasis on the nerved and sinewy grip of textual fascination upon an audience, including a sequence of derailed private narratives near the end of the novel that follow out – without being able to follow through on – Victor's final attempts, before he meets Walton, to confess in narrative form the mayhem he has indirectly perpetrated. His first effort seems designed to return his guilt over beastly creation to its progenitorial source, but his father "changed the subject of our conversation" (22:177). Next, as if to substitute for sexual initiation, he has assured Elizabeth that she will hear a tale of terrible explanation on her wedding morn (22:183). What is promised is the almost black-comic equivalent of a nineteenth-century male's coming clean about his unchaste past. Yet Elizabeth does not live long enough to hear what she might well suppose to be a sexual secret – meeting instead the Creature in the flesh. Where the urge to create was a sublimation of desire that deferred marriage in the first place, now the urge to "compose" the story in retrospect is all that is left of the maker's libido. To give yourself over in turn, as reader, to this central narrative logic with your own desire for the rest of the tale is thus to wed yourself to a fraught textual eros.

Once Elizabeth's murder has forestalled disclosure, Victor proceeds instead to give a "deposition" (23:189) to the local magistrate: a receiving agent stationed to externalize the self-policing that confession entails. And you don't hear a word of Victor's disclosure to this unnamed civil servant. You don't hear it because you know it full well. It is precisely, and in detail, the novelized story up to this point, all the events of plot without the extended discourse by which you have been led to interpret them. This circumscribed absence of an already familiar story, this ellipsis of recapitulation, is thus a hole in the narrative filled up, *pars pro toto*, by the narrative as a whole: another, more encompassing version (like the account of monstrous conception in Victor's unread journal) of a *mise en abyme* under erasure.

At first "incredulous," the magistrate is soon "attentive and interested" (23:189). At some points he would "shudder with horror; at others a lively surprise, unmingled with disbelief" characterizes his reactions. Just before the close of the novel, this figure of attention offers a retroactive sketch of your own reading, in all its Coleridgean "suspension of disbelief," as well as of the transferential investments that flow from that reading without passing over into credence. The hair-raising details of Victor's "deposition" are cordoned off from the magistrate's official role. To the surprise and frustration of Victor, a surprise – as we will see – bred of his own deprivations in the realm of fantasy, nothing he has said seems *actionable*. He calls for the "seizure and punishment" (23:190) of his monstrous creation, but his auditor has emerged from the story as merely, in effect, his reader, not his confessor, let alone his disciplinary agent. "He had heard my story with that half kind of belief that is given to a tale of spirits and supernatural events; but when he was called upon to act officially in consequence, the whole tide of his incredulity returned" (23:190). It is clear now that the magistrate did not "credit my narrative" – except, of course, as just that: a riveting narrative. Asked to go further into credulity, he "reverted to my tale as the effects of delirium" (23:190).

In its elided replay of the plot to this stage, this mere "tale" also sends us back to one of the novel's founding dramatic ironies. For it shows Victor punished in his failed confession to the magistrate by the very response on the latter's part – gothic fascination – whose possibility for Victor himself was abrogated in childhood, thus leading to his transgression and its narrative in the first place. Following on from (in order of disclosure across frame and tale) the interdict of Walton's father against his son's activating his book-fed fantasies of a seafaring life, and in turn Alphonse Frankenstein's contemptuous forbidding of Victor's reading in medieval science, there is the subsequent revelation of a textual proscription (or at least neutralization) earlier yet in the disentangled chronology of the plot. By way of explanation for his lack of squeamishness in rooting about among corpses in the graveyard, Victor recalls precisely what set him apart in childhood from the chain – that putatively humanizing nexus – of narrative reception passing now from the Creature through Victor to Walton and on to you. Or not so precisely, since the admission seems dragged out of a language that has no ready words for it. "In my education my father had taken the greatest precautions that my mind should be impressed with no supernatural horrors" (4:50). In what sense not "impressed"? Inured or altogether protected? Did the excitation of fantasy get tamed by reason or warded off by proscription?

Shelley's vulnerability to circumlocution, though not to nightmare, is seldom devolved upon Victor to more deviously revealing effect. Here is the core of her psychic

GARRETT STEWART

diagnosis, yet it comes to us swathed symptomatically in the character's own self-protective obscuration. Even as Victor continues in what may seem a stiffly explicit diction, still the recalled interdict (or corrective discipline?) is filtered through the blurred screen of internalized denial: "I do not ever remember to have trembled at a tale of superstition or to have feared the apparition of a spirit" (4:50). Grammar abets his evasion through its own ambivalence. Does he remember never trembling? Or simply never let himself remember? If the former, is it a maintained childhood taboo or a gradual debility that has sustained his exemption from all gothic aggravation, his exclusion from the fostering romanticism of the negative sublime? Whether or not such a "tale" was any more available to Victor as a child than the visitations of specters, the basic privation is clear. With the father's own scare tactics amounting either to an outlawing of natural instinct or to a kind of aversion therapy through neutralized affect, here is how Victor's antiromantic childhood helps him in a starkly literal sense, and in a sweeping parody of Wordsworthian gestational maturation, to *father the man*. "Darkness had no effect upon my fancy, and a churchyard was to me merely the receptacle of bodies deprived of life" (4:50). An ounce of unadvised parental prevention ends up requiring an adult male's dead weight in cemetery refuse as raw material for an unhinged creative cure.

Indeed, Victor introduces this whole passage on the blocked imaginative passage of his childhood in a way that shows his "recourse to death" (4:50), his graveyard forays, as a displacement of a once denied access to the perturbations of the "supernatural tale" onto his present lust for forbidden thrills. The dead metaphors of this self-characterization demonstrate, in other words, how he has become, in the fever of dubious creation, his own electrified ghoul: a frenzied agent "animated by an almost supernatural enthusiasm" (4:50), without which his loathsome scavenging would have been "almost intolerable" (4:50). Denied a child's normal focus, and outlet, for imaginative unrest, never allowed the constructive anxieties of fairy tale or gothic narrative, Victor's arrested fictional development – ironically leaving him unprepared for the inefficacy of his later confession when taken as just such a tale of superstition – is an impoverishment from which the novel as a whole defends its readers. Portrayed in Victor's case is a kind of trauma by exclusion: the scarring *avoidance* of a narrative opportunity – or its potency – which (as with Shelley's novel, and others like it) might have indued a healthy sense of mystery, a responsible timidity before the unknown. Instead, the deficit of Victor's earliest reading comes to haunt him now, like the return of the repressed, in the form of the nameless magistrate's purely *readerly* interest in his tale.

The novel reader's more sophisticated response must be extrapolated by contrast. That Victor suffers for our interest as well as for his sins is the tried and tired logic of catharsis. The structure of Shelley's novel explores a fuller psychodrama. In between Walton's feeding off of the hero's suffering (Walton dependent, insatiable, passively snared by identification) and the foregrounded evacuation of the sister's response – in between the voracious and the unspoken – opens the zone of your potential critical distance as well as your complicity. At the other end of the century, the revival of the gothic genre takes up where these inferences in *Frankenstein* leave off. The socializing symbiosis of narrative and response that we will investigate in Dickens, the Brontës, Eliot, Meredith, and the other high Victorian novelists gives way in certain *fin de siècle* novels to an even less acquiescent sense of textual reception. In Bram Stoker's *Dracula*, for instance, the absentation that is reading, together with its annexation of otherness, becomes actively devouring. To engage with a text is figured there as a no longer passive dependency, derivative and harmlessly vicarious, but rather as a labor akin to vampirism itself, not animating the text so much as drawing off its life into the void of response.

In pursuing such implications, my last chapter will return more systematically to the mode of reading sketchily attempted here. For what we have seen with Shelley's text is how a novel that proceeds by "deconstructing" its own most famous creation, the Creature, as a mere structure of intertexts and inscriptions can turn out, at another level, to be reinscribing – and in the process conscripting – the rationalized (and here championed) irrationality of audience response. In certain bellwether texts at century's end, that is, as before them in *Frankenstein*, textual self-referentiality develops simultaneously as reader reflex. After all (we have been reminding ourselves), this is exactly the path by which literary form engages culture: not by imitation so much as by a rhetoric of participation.

NOTES

1 Mary Shelley, *Frankenstein* (New York: American Library, 1963). All subsequent references will be noted parenthetically by chapter and page number.

2 Here one might follow out a recent suggestion by Peter Brooks about narrative interaction. Having pursued Roland Barthes's notion of "contract narrative" with illuminating results in *Reading for the Plot*, Brooks expands further on the psychodynamic of such narrative exchanges in a chapter on *Frankenstein* in *Body Work*, where the relation between Walton and Mrs. Saville is conceived on the "transferential" model: "As a 'subject supposed to know,' the listener is called upon to 'supplement' the story…, to articulate and even enact the meaning of the desire it expresses in ways that may be foreclosed to the speaker" (200). Though Brooks doesn't mention this, Mrs. Saville's structured silence as narrative recipient may contribute to the sense that she fills the role of therapeutic sounding board in this fable of vicarious interchange. Moreover, it is Walton's own anticipation of one day taking up the role of reader rather than narrator of the story which may imply his urge for an imaginative access otherwise "foreclosed" by his role as storyteller. Only by reading, perhaps, can he "articulate and even enact the meaning of the desire" he has begun by half confessing on his own part, half reporting on Victor's.

3 Charles E. Robinson, ed., *Mary Shelley: Collected Tales and Stories* (Baltimore: Johns Hopkins University Press, 1976), 121.

4 The protagonist of the *History of the Inconstant Lover*, "when he thought to clasp the bride to whom he had pledged his vows, found himself in the arms of the pale ghost of her whom he had deserted" (viii–ix). Anticipating Victor's dream of his mother's corpse replacing his fiancée, Elizabeth, in his arms (5:57), this fictional prototype also captures the ambivalence of erotic desire and marital drive in Victor's whole story. Then there was "the tale of the sinful founder of his race" – the very periphrasis for paternity offering a proleptic hint – "whose miserable doom it was to bestow the kiss of death on all the younger sons of his fated house" (ix). Prefigured here is the negating effect of Frankenstein on all his "progeny," both the natural children he fails to have and that monstrous issue he seeks to eradicate.

INDEX

Abrams, M. H. 173–4
  The Mirror and the Lamp 163
abstract potentiality 398–402
Achebe, Chinua 697
Ackerman, Rudolph: *Repository* 677
Addison, Joseph 475
Adorno, Theodor W.: *The Ageing of Modern Music* 407
Aeschylus 472
aesthetic happiness, in Girard's *Deceit, Desire and the Novel* 290, 291
African American identity
  and Gates 13, 454–9, 511–33, 563
  and the Harlem Renaissance 721
  see also Johnson, Barbara
Alcott, Louisa May 566
allegory, and modernism 408–12
Althusser, Louis 352, 354–5, 428, 719
American fiction
  Baym on antebellum 13, 750–3, 780–91
  Tompkins on nineteenth-century 445–8, 536–40
  see also African American identity

American Review 785, 787
Amis, Kingsley: *Lucky Jim* 273
Amory, Thomas: *John Bunkle* 104
analytical psychology 109
anatomies 104, 105
Anderson, Benedict 719, 729, 737
Anglo-American novel theory 15
Anichkov, E. V. *Ceremonial Songs of Spring* 43
antinomies 355
  Jameson on 426–8
aphasia: Jakobson on metaphor/metonymy and 258–9, 264
Apuleius 102, 104
Arabian Nights 373
Arendt, Hannah 589
Aristotle 14, 141, 142, 144, 165, 330, 752
  and Chatman 187
  and the Chicago School 109, 110, 111–12, 114, 115
  and novelistic discourse 488
  and realism 467
  Rhetoric 261
  see also neo-Aristotelianism

Armstrong, Nancy 4, 9, 11, 443, 566
  biographical details 621
  Desire and Domestic Fiction 7, 13, 570–3,
    621–40
Arnold, Matthew 693
art, and allegory 409
Arthur's Home Journal 789
Athenaeus: *Deipnosophoists* 103
The Atlantic Monthly 66, 780
Auerbach, Erich: *Mimesis* 265–6
Augustine, St. 101
  City of God 415
Austen, Jane 7, 10–11, 98, 102, 179, 566,
    625, 759
  American Review on 787
  and Emily Brontë 99
  and geography 735–44
  and Gothic fiction 793–4
  and ideas 101
  and impersonal narration 177
  and Johnson's Rule 114, 152–3
  Mansfield Park 654–5, 658–9, 665, 666,
    699, 703–13, 741–3
  and moral action 141, 142, 148, 150–3
  Northanger Abbey 100, 150–1, 735, 737, 793–4
  Persuasion 153, 735, 793
  and post-colonialism 10, 13, 654, 656–7,
    658–9, 664–6, 693, 696, 697, 701,
    703–13
  Pride and Prejudice 114, 151–2, 582, 656,
    738, 741
  Sense and Sensibility 152, 735
  Woolf on 581, 582
  and Woolf 10–11
Austin, J. L.: *How to Do Things with Words* 607–8
autobiography 100–1

Bagehot, Walter: *Physics and Politics* 702
Baker, Houston 721
Bakhtin, M. M. 4, 6, 8, 12, 16, 208, 253,
    576, 637
  biographical details 481–2
  "Discourse in the Novel" 448–54, 481–509
  "Epic and Novel" 449
  *The Formal Method of Literary
    Scholarship* 448–9
  and Gates 454, 456, 457
  on parody 532–3
  and post-colonialism 667, 720–1, 723
  Problems of Dostoevsky's Poetics 449

Bakhtin Circle 449
Bal, Mieke: *Narratology* 192
Balzac, Honoré de 10, 12, 83, 179, 240,
    336, 545
  and imperialism 697
  Jameson on 355–6, 357, 414, 419–28
  La Vieille Fille 421–2, 423–8
  Le Chef d'oeuvre inconnu 384
  Le Père Goriot 474
  Les Paysans 421, 428
  Lukács on 350–1, 352, 356, 381, 383, 384,
    386–7, 388–9, 392, 393, 402, 424, 425
  and realism 466, 476
Baroque art/literature, and allegory 409–10,
    411
Barrell, John 721
Barry, Kathleen: *Female Sexual Slavery* 591, 595
Barthes, Roland 3, 6, 8, 14, 187, 199–202,
    203, 274, 331, 332, 340, 517
  biographical details 229–30, 235–6
  "From Work to Text" 199, 200–1, 235–41
  and Jameson 352, 414
  and narratology 189–90
  and psychoanalytic theory 275–7, 279,
    280, 283
  "The Reality Effect" 199–200, 229–34, 577
Basch, Michael 562, 610
Bataille, Georges 237
Baym, Nina 13, 576
  Novels, Readers and Reviewers 748, 749,
    750–3, 755, 758, 779–91
Beattie, James 120
Beckett, Samuel 412
  Molloy 400, 404
Beebe, Maurice 172, 173
Behn, Aphra 469, 478
belief, and reader objectivity 171–6
Bely, Andrey: *Kotik Latayev* 33
Benjamin, Walter 5, 11, 279, 332, 346,
    354, 407, 412, 437, 443
  and allegory 409–11
  biographical details 361–2
  and Jameson 356, 358, 359, 419, 430
  The Storyteller 346–9, 355, 356, 359, 361–78
Benn, Gottfried 400, 401, 404, 405, 412
  Static Poems 405
Bennett, Arnold 371
Bentham, Jeremy 554
Benveniste, Emile 206, 209
Bergson, Henri 407

Berkeley, George 467, 468
Besant, Walter 24
Bhabha, Homi 7, 12–13
 biographical details 716
 The Location of Culture 655–6, 666–73, 716–31
The Bible 106
Bielinski, V. G. 381, 389, 390
Bildungsroman 365
black women, in Hurston's *Their Eyes Were Watching God* 266–9
Blackburn, Robin: *The Overthrow of Colonial Slavery* 711
Blackmur, R. P. 540
Blin, Georges 211
Bloch, Ernst 374, 421
Bloomsbury Group 579
Boas, George 212
Boccaccio, Giovanni: *Decameron* 101, 155, 190–1, 208, 212–13, 214–18, 424
Boethius: *Consolation of Philosophy* 104
Booth, Wayne 4–5, 6, 108–9, 115–17, 576
 biographical details 154
 and Chatman 187
 "Emotions, Beliefs and the Reader's Objectivity" 116–17
 and Iser 756
 and Lukács 347, 351–2
 and post-colonialism 665, 669
 The Rhetoric of Fiction 116–17, 154–79, 351–2, 749, 765, 772–3
Borrow, George 104
 Lavengro 98
Boswell, John 601
bovarysm, in Girard's *Deceit, Desire and the Novel* 297, 306
Bray, Alan 601
Brecht, Bertolt 163
Brod, Max 411
Brodhead, Richard: "Sparing the Rod" 443
Brontë, Anne: *The Tenant of Wildfell Hall* 789–90
Brontë, Charlotte 13, 114, 566, 581, 686, 790
 Jane Eyre 272, 569, 582, 623, 660–1, 663, 664, 675, 677–80, 682, 686, 687, 688, 695, 768
 Villette 582
Brontë, Emily 12, 566, 581, 790
 Wuthering Heights 98–9, 582, 623

Brooks, Peter 7, 11, 274
 biographical details 329–30
 "Freud's Masterplot" 275–9, 285, 292, 329–41
 and Girard 285–6, 288
Broucek, Francis 562, 610
Brown, Charles Brockden 536, 537, 538
Brown, Sterling A.: *Southern Road* 513
Bullough, Edward 163
Bunyan, John 469, 473, 478
 Pilgrim's Progress 99–100, 472, 679
Burke, Edmund 426, 651, 702
Burke, Kenneth 109
Burnet, Gilbert: *History of His Own Time* 470
Burney, Fanny 141, 566
 Cecilia 151
 Evelina 148–50, 151, 272
Burns, Robert 100
Burton, Robert: *Anatomy of Melancholy* 98, 103–4, 167
Butler, Joseph 468
Butler, Judith 562, 564, 573, 619
 Gender Trouble 606
 "Performative Acts" 607
Butler, Samuel: *The Way of All Flesh* 101, 102
Butor, Michel 208, 768
Byron, George Gordon, Lord 798
Byzantine art, and allegory 409

Caillois, Roger 545
Camus, Albert 175, 176, 693
Carlyle, Thomas 100, 478, 581, 693, 701
 Sartor Resartus 98, 104, 516
Carmichael, Stokely 267
Carroll, Lewis: *Alice* books 103
Castiglione, Baldassare 103
Cather, Willa 566
Catholicism, and reader objectivity 173, 174, 175
Cervantes, Miguel de 12
 "The Curious Impertinent" 311–12, 313
 Don Quixote 34, 38, 40, 47, 100, 104
  Girard on 291, 295, 296, 297, 298, 299, 302–3, 311–12, 313
  Jameson on 418
  and storytelling 365, 372
characterization, and the romance 99
characterological consciousness, and Marxism 8–9

Charlton, Mary 741
Chateaubriand, François-René, comte de 339, 494
  Life of Rancé 237
Chatman, Seymour 450
  biographical details 219
  Story and Discourse 186, 186–7, 192, 194–5, 196, 219–28
Chatterjee, Partha 719
Chaucer, Geoffrey 103, 466, 478, 560
Chekhov, Anton 99, 158
Chernyshevski, N. G. 389, 390
Chesterton, G. K. 176, 385
Chicago School 4, 6, 108–17, 756
  and Barthes 201
  and the genre approach to the novel 12
  and neo-Aristotelianism 109, 112, 113, 117
  and novelistic unity 9
  and reader response theory 109–13, 117
  see also Booth, Wayne; Crane, R. S.;
    Rader, Ralph
Chodorow, Nancy 600, 602
Chopin, Kate 566
Christian Examiner 751, 752–3, 780–1, 782, 783, 785, 787, 790
class
  in Austen's *Mansfield Park* 710–11
  and domestic fiction 635, 637–8, 639
  and homosociality 588, 589
  and identity politics 454–5
  middle-class domestic fiction 570–3
  and nineteenth-century American novels 448
Cohen, Ralph 142
Cohn, Dorrit 8, 192
  Transparent Minds 273
Coleridge, Samuel Taylor 120, 172, 473, 601
Colet, Louise 162
Collins, Wilkie 542, 545, 783
colonial wealth, in British sentimental novels 743–744
commodification
  Gallagher on authorship and 575
  Jameson on modern novel and 356
Communist Manifesto 357
concrete potentiality 399–402
conditional mood, and narrative discourse 215–16
confessions 100–1, 104, 105

Conrad, Joseph 12, 423, 581, 696, 697, 707
  Heart of Darkness 710
  Lord Jim 100, 273
Cooper, James Fenimore 537, 786
  The Last of the Mohicans 536, 539
Corday, Charlotte 230–1
Corvo, Baron (Frederick Rolfe) 171
covert narrators 194, 220–1
Crane, R. S. 108, 114, 115, 117, 141
  biographical details 119
  and Chatman 187
  The Concept of Plot and the Plot of Tom Jones 110–11, 113, 119–36, 142
  Critics and Criticism: Ancient and Modern 109, 114
  theory of reader response 109–13
critical theory 4
Croce, Benedetto 414
Crompton, Louis 589
Cross, W. L. 121
cultural anthropology 109
cultural history 13
cultural studies 252
Cumberland, Richard: *The West Indian* 710
Cummins, Maria Susanna 566
Czar Maximilian (Russian folk drama) 44

Dante Alighieri 171, 173, 350, 383
Darwin, Charles 629
Darwin, Erasmus 798
Darwish, Mahmoud 717
Daudet, Alphonse 693
Davenport, Selina 741
David, Deirdre: *Culture* 660
Davis, Lennard 645–6, 692
deconstruction 2, 3, 4, 5, 7, 11, 196–203
  and identity politics 455–6
  and novel readers 750
  and post-colonialism 655–6
  and psychoanalytic theory 281
defamiliarization 15, 16, 20, 27, 29
  of character 23–4
  and human perception 24–5
  and J. Hillis Miller's theory of narrative performance 197, 198
  and novel readers 757
  in Sterne's *Tristram Shandy* 20–1, 45–50
Defoe, Daniel 98, 161, 625, 696
  and formal realism 477, 478
  language and prose style 475, 476

Moll Flanders 101, 252, 440, 469,
    473–4, 692, 698
and the novel form 463, 464, 465, 467
and novel readers 764
and plot 466
Robinson Crusoe 468, 469, 631–2, 692, 698
and space 473–4
and time 472
use of proper names 469, 470
Deleuze, Gilles and Guattari, Félix:
    The Anti-Oedipus 416–17
Deloney, Thomas 98
Democratic Review 786–7
Dennis, John 475
De Quincey, Thomas 104
Derrida, Jacques 14, 245, 254,
    538, 717, 729
Descartes, René 208, 465, 466, 467, 468
description, and narrative 230–1
desire
    Armstrong on domestic fiction and 622–40
    Brooks on desire for the end 331, 332
    J. Hillis Miller and desire for reference 196
    Sedgwick on homosocial desire 565–6,
        587–90
    see also triangular desire
detective fiction 545
dialect
    in Hurston's *Their Eyes Were Watching
        God* 517–18
    and literary language 505
dialogue
    and discourse 253, 492–4
    and stylistics 491–2
Dickens, Charles 10, 12, 19, 70, 114, 176, 542,
    545, 582
    and authorial objectivity 157
    Bleak House 656, 658, 699
    Dombey and Son 697, 786
    Great Expectations 278, 339–40, 695, 710
    Hard Times 695, 781
    and James Joyce 169
    Little Dorrit 100, 450
    and Mary Shelley 796, 801
    and narrative voice 251, 252, 254
    and novel readers 752, 787
    Oliver Twist 272, 546–50, 552, 554, 555, 774
    Our Mutual Friend 250
    Pickwick Papers 243, 244–5, 246, 247,
        250–1, 252

and post-colonialism 657–8, 693, 702
Sketches by Boz 251
Dinnerstein, Dorothy 600, 602
disciplinary power 542, 553–4, 636–7
discourse
    Bakhtin on discourse in the novel 448–54,
        481–509
    indirect 243–55
    and narrative 209–10, 214–18
    and narratology 193–5
    see also social discourse
Disraeli, Benjamin 694
distortion, and psychopathology 404–5
Döblin, Alfred 399
Dobrolyubov, N. A. 389, 390
domestic fiction: Armstrong on 570–3, 622–40
Donzelot, Jacques 633
Dos Passos, John 399
Dostoevsky, F. M. 12, 191, 208, 272, 390
    The Brothers Karamazov 122, 156–7
    Crime and Punishment 170–1
    The Eternal Husband 309–11, 312, 313
    The House of the Dead 406
    and Leskov 367, 376
    A Raw Youth 309
    and realism 476
    and triangular desire 307–11
double voice 15
    Gates on 459
Dover, K. J.: *Greek Homosexuality* 589, 601
dramatization, and fiction writing 91–2
Dreiser, Theodore: *Sister Carrie* 356–7, 422–3
Dubois, W. E. B. 266, 458, 525, 569
    Quest for the Silver Fleece 512–13
Dujardin, Edouard 177
Dumas, Alexandre 240
Dworkin, Andrea: *Pornography: Men
        Possessing Women* 595

Eagleton, Terry 678, 679
Edgeworth, Maria 741
    and Edgeworth, Robert: *Practical
        Education* 631–2, 633, 635
educational reform, and gender 631–7, 635
Egyptian Book of the Dead 106
eighteenth-century fiction 12, 13, 98
    and the Chicago School 113, 119
    and gender 622, 624–5
    and Mary Shelley 793
    moral action novels 141–53

eighteenth-century fiction (*cont'd*)
    and novel readers 764–5, 767
    and overseas travel 692
    and sexuality 623–4
    and sympathy 645, 647–51
    Watt on realism and the novel form 438–9,
        463–78
Eisler, Hanns 407
Eliot, George 10, 70, 71, 104, 251,
        545, 566
    Adam Bede 783
    and authorial objectivity 157
    critique in the *Westminster Review* 789
    Daniel Deronda 273
    and imperialism 693, 697
    and Mary Shelley 796, 801
    Middlemarch 250, 555, 569, 582, 656
    Woolf on 581, 582
Eliot, T. S. 173, 400
    The Cocktail Party 400–1
Elton, Oliver 121
Emerson, Ralph Waldo 88
Empson, William 336
Engels, Friedrich 386–7
English identity, and post-colonialism 656–7,
        659, 662, 666, 693
the Enlightenment 415
epistolary technique 179, 796–7
Erasmus, Desiderius 102, 103
erotic triangles: gender asymmetry and
        597–602
ethnography, and post-colonialism 671–2
external and internal mediation: Girard
        on 287, 299, 305–7

fairy tales
    Propp's *Morphology* of 23–4, 55–63
    and storytelling 373–5
Fanon, Frantz: "On national culture" 727–8,
        729
Faulkner, William 172, 176, 339, 356
    Absalom, Absalom! 115
    Lukács on 398, 400
    The Sound and the Fury 400
Felman, Shoshana 8, 9, 10, 11, 14, 347
    biographical details 315–16
    and Girard 274–5, 285–6, 288, 291
    The Literary Speech Act 607, 608
    "Turning the Screw of Interpretation" 10,
        279–86, 315–27, 760

feminism
    French 594–5, 596
    Marxist 595, 596–7
    materialist 7, 565–6, 567
    and narratology 192
    and novel readers 750
    radical 594–5
    and reading sex or reading history 594–7
    and sexual meaning 588, 590–4
    Spivak and feminist individualism 664,
        675–7, 678–9, 685
    and women writers 566
Fern, Fanny 566
Fernbach, David 601
fiction
    Gallagher on 575, 649–50
    and the novel 98, 101–2
    use of the term 11
FID *see* free indirect discourse (FID)
Fielding, Henry 98, 141, 692
    Amelia 125, 142, 160, 470
    and gender 622
    Jonathan Wild 160
    Joseph Andrews 160
    language and prose style 475–6
    and moral action 141, 142, 147, 148
    and the novel form 364, 464, 467
    and novel readers 752, 764, 787
    and objectivity 157, 159–60, 161, 179
    Shamela 473
    and space 474
    Tom Jones 100, 110–11, 113, 114, 119–36,
        141, 142, 147, 148, 160, 473, 476, 656,
        692, 764
    use of proper names 469–70
first-person narration 269–70
    and indirect style 227
    and James 25, 27, 82–3
    Lubbock on 93–5
Fish, Stanley E. 316, 538
Flaubert, Gustave 4, 12, 103, 313, 581
    and author objectivity 157, 158–9, 162
    Barthes on 199, 200, 230, 231, 232, 234, 240
    and imperialism 697
    and indirect style 224, 226–7
    Jameson on 414, 419
    Lukács on 381, 382, 383
    Madame Bovary 100, 105, 155–6, 157, 224,
        226–7, 232, 265, 272
    Girard on 290, 296–7, 298, 299, 303

and realism 464, 476
Sentimental Education 162, 372, 381, 397
Ford, Ford Madox 161, 764
formal realism 441, 477–8, 651
formalism 2, 4, 5, 6, 7, 11, 186
  and Bakhtin 448
  Jamesian tradition of 24–6
  and theories of genre 12
  see also Chicago School; Russian formalism
Forster, E. M. 155, 172, 471, 663
  Howards End 710
  A Passage to India 696
Foster, Hannah Webster 566
Foucault, Michel 14, 538, 539, 601, 619, 721
  and disciplinary power 542, 553–4, 636–7
  Discipline and Punish 627, 637, 727
  The History of Sexuality 627–30, 631
  and performativity 561–2
  on the rationality of the modern
    nation 726–7
  and the repressive hypothesis 611
  theory of social power 442–5, 447, 760–1
Fox-Genovese, Elizabeth 676–7
free indirect discourse (FID) 195, 450
  in Hurston's *Their Eyes Were Watching
    God* 521–2, 524–32
free/tagged indirect style 221–7
Frege, Gottlob 209
French feminism 594–5, 596
French fiction, and realism 463–4, 476
French imperialism 693, 697, 698, 703
French Revolution, and Balzac 426
Freud, Sigmund 14, 212, 285, 553, 597, 629
  "Beyond the Pleasure Principle" 275–9,
    332–41
  and Girard 289
  and homosexuality 598–9, 600, 601
  The Interpretation of Dreams 281, 326–7
  and Marxist theory 353–4
  and post-colonialism 720, 725
  and psychopathology 403
  "The Theme of the Three Caskets" 333
  "The Uncanny" 334
  and the unconscious 274, 280–2
  "The Unconscious" 281, 353
Fried, Michael 607
Frye, Northrop 5, 471
  Anatomy of Criticism 28–9, 97–106
  biographical details 97
  and Booth 115

and Chatman 187
and the genre approach to the novel 12
and Jameson 355
on parody 533
Furetière, Antoine 464, 478

Gallagher, Catherine 7, 13, 453, 566
  biographical details 644
  Nobody's Story 573–7, 644–51, 753, 759
Gallagher, John 694, 709
Gallop, Jane: *The Daughter's Seduction* 595
Gasché, R. 729
Gaskell, Elizabeth 254, 566, 693, 702
  Cranford 243–4, 246–8, 250, 251
  North and South 781
Gates, Henry Louis, Jr. 6, 13, 270, 560
  biographical details 511–12
  "Criticism in the Jungle" 266
  and Sedgwick 563
  The Signifying Monkey 454–9, 511–33
Gaultier, Jules de: *Bovarysm* 297
Gellner, Ernest 719, 723
gender and sexuality 2, 4, 5, 560–77
  in Hurston's *Their Eyes Were Watching
    God* 265–9
  and nineteenth-century American
    novels 448
  and post-colonialism 655
  and queer performativity 5, 561–5
  and social discourse 453–4
  see also Armstrong, Nancy; feminism;
    Gallagher, Catherine; Sedgwick, Eve
    Kosofsky; women writers; Woolf,
    Virginia
Genet, Jean: *Notre-Dame des Fleurs* 336
Genette, Gérard 192, 193, 239, 450
genre theory 12, 187
  and discourse 501
  Frye on 98–106
  and psychological realism 272–3
  and Watt on the rise of the novel 441
Gerstäcker, Friedrich 363
Gibbon, Edward 702
Gibson, Walter 172
Gide, André 381, 399, 412, 544, 693
  The Immoralist 304
Gilbert, Sandra and Gubar, Susan: *The
    Madwoman in the Attic* 595, 625, 627,
    628, 678, 679
Gilman, Charlotte 566

Ginsberg, Michal 526, 527
Giotto di Bondone 409
Girard, René 5, 9, 12, 13, 15–16, 274–5, 444
    biographical details 294
    Deceit, Desire and the Novel 285, 294–314,
        597–9
global perspective, and post-colonialism
        654–5
Godey's 789
Godwin, William 663
    Caleb Williams 446
Goethe, Johann Wolfgang von 157, 383, 388,
        392, 395–6
    Italian Journey 720, 723
Goffman, Erving: *Stigma: Notes on the
        Management of Spoiled Identity* 609
Gogol, N. V. 40
    Dead Souls 34
    The Inspector General 43–4
Goncharov, I. A., *Oblomov* 34
Gorki, Maxim 373, 388, 391, 392, 406
Gothic fiction 738, 793–4
    see also Shelley, Mary
Gotthelf, J. 363, 364
Graham's 751–2, 783, 786
grammar of narrative 212–18
grammatical model of subjectivity 198–9
Grayson, Edward: *Standish the Puritan* 790
Greek homosexuality 589
Green, T. H. 471, 477
Greimas, A. J. 355, 426, 427
Griboyedov, A. S.: *Wit Works Woe* 44
Griffin, Susan: *Pornography and Silence* 595
Griffith, D. W. 473
Grimmelshausen, Hans von 478
Guattari, Félix *see* Deleuze, Gilles and
        Guattari, Félix
Gubar, Susan *see* Gilbert, Sandra and Gubar,
        Susan
Gunning, Susannah 741

Haggard, H. Rider 696
Handsworth Songs 672–3, 730–1
Hardy, Thomas 114, 476, 696
    "The Pedigree" 249
    Return of the Native 656
Harlem Renaissance 721
Harper's 781, 787, 788, 790
Harris, Jocelyn 148
Harris, Wilson 682

Hartmann, Heidi 588, 590, 600
Harvey, W. J. 772
hatred: in Girard's *Deceit, Desire and the
        Novel* 299–301
Hauff, Wilhelm 378
Hawthorne, Nathaniel 536–7, 566
    The House of the Seven Gables 100
    The Scarlet Letter 539
Hazlitt, William 478
Head, Richard 478
Hebel, Johann Peter 363, 364, 373, 376
    "Unexpected Reunion" 369
Hechter, Michael 735
Hegel, G. W. F. 427
Hegelianism, and Lukács 2, 382
Heidegger, Martin 380, 397, 401, 406, 410
Heimann, Moritz 373
Helms, Jesse 588
Hemingway, Ernest 176
Herder, J. G. 415
Herdt, G. H. 589
hereness: Bhabha on 670
Herodotus: *Histories* 366
Herzen, Alexander 389, 391
Hesse, Hermann: *Siddhartha* 165
heteroglossia: Bakhtin on 449, 450, 451–2, 485,
        489, 490–1, 492, 495, 498–9, 500, 503,
        505–6, 507–8, 509
historical novels 100
historical studies 12
historicism
    and Marxism 414–15
    see also New Historicism
historiography, and storytelling 369–70, 371
Hitler, Adolf 401
Hobbes, Thomas 468, 469
Hobsbawm, Eric 717
Hobson, J. A. 693, 702
Hoffmann, E. T. A.: *Kater Murr* 40
Hofland, Barbara 741
Hofmannsthal, Hugo von 398, 408
Hogg, James: *Confessions of a Justified Sinner* 104
Holland, Norman 340
Holloway, Karla 517
Home Journal 782–3, 787, 789
Homer 34, 120, 171, 401, 406, 478
    Odyssey 105, 156, 157
homosexuality
    and erotic triangles 597–602
    and homosocial desire 587–8, 589, 590–1

and queer performativity 562
and triangular desire 310–11
homosociality: Sedgwick on 565–6, 586–602
hooks, bell (Gloria Watkins) 267–8
Hopkins, Gerard Manley: "The Habit of
    Perfection" 173, 174
Hough, Graham 526
Hulme, Peter: *Colonial Encounters* 702
Humboldt, K. W. von 490
Hume, David 159, 468, 470, 576
    Treatise of Human Nature 647–51
Hurston, Zora Neale
    Dust Tracks on a Road 516–17
    Mules and Men 512, 515, 524
    Their Eyes Were Watching God
        Gates on 456–9, 512–32, 533
        Johnson on 202–3, 261–70, 352, 522
Huxley, Aldous 102, 103
    Brave New World 101
    Point Counterpoint 101
hybridity, and post-colonialism 7, 667
hyperbole 253
hypotyposis: Barthes on 232–3

Icelandic Sagas 100, 106
identity politics *see* African American identity
ideology
    Bakhtin on 450–1
    and Jameson 352, 354, 358, 414, 417, 426,
        430
    and Lukács 349–50, 395, 403, 405
    and Marxism 344
imperialism 13
    Moretti on 655
    Said on 655, 660, 664–6, 692–713
    Spivak on 655, 660–4, 674–88
impersonal narration 211
    morality of 176–9
impersonality: Woolf on women writers
        and 570, 573, 584
implied authors 116
    and narrators 765, 766
implied readers 116, 749
    Booth on 159–63
incest, and textual energy in narrative 339
India, and British imperialism 694
indirect discourse: Miller on 243–55
indirect tagged/free style 221–7
individualism
    Bakhtin on cultural individualism 449

in D. A. Miller's *The Novel and the Police*
    441–2
James's radical individualism and J. Hillis
    Miller's philosophy of identity 198
in Tompkins' *Sensational Designs* 447
and Watt on the rise of the novel 437–41
information, and storytelling 365–6
internal dialogism: Bakhtin on 449–50,
    451–2, 495, 497–9
internal mediation: Girard on 287, 288,
    299, 309
Irigaray, Luce 601, 602
irony, and indirect discourse 243–55
Iser, Wolfgang 10, 753–7, 758
    biographical details 763
    The Implied Reader 748, 749, 750, 755–7,
        763–76

Jacobsen, J. P.: *Niels Lyhe* 411
Jakobson, Roman 202, 207
    on metaphor and metonymy 258–9, 264,
        337
James, C. L. R. 711
James, Henry 4, 5, 10, 12, 14–15, 18, 19, 98,
    103, 211, 470, 696, 799
    The Ambassadors 25, 26, 73, 75–85, 173,
        539, 615
    The American 66, 615
    "The Art of Fiction" 24–5, 346
    The Art of the Novel 611–16
    and Bakhtin 449
    biographical details 65
    and Booth 116
    and characterological consciousness 8, 9
    and Chatman 187
    and formalism 24–6
    and Gates 455
    and the "house of fiction" metaphor 24,
        69, 437–8
    and ideas 101
    and Lubbock 27, 86
    and Marxist theory 346, 354, 356
    and J. Hillis Miller's theory of narrative
        performance 198
    New York Prefaces 19, 25, 26, 66–85,
        317–18
        and queer performativity 561, 563–4,
            611–16
    and novel readers 753, 757
    and novelistic unity 9

James, Henry (*cont'd*)
  The Portrait of a Lady 15, 26, 66–75, 122,
      273, 290, 291, 437
  Roderick Hudson 25, 66, 346
  on romance and realism 28
  and Thackeray 756
  and third-person narration 25–6
  and Todorov 186
  The Turn of the Screw 275, 284, 316–27,
      615, 760
  and *The Whole Family: A Novel by Twelve
      Authors* 167
  The Wings of the Dove 76, 83
  and Woolf 569
James, William 19
Jameson, Fredric 4, 5, 9, 10, 12, 346, 437
  biographical details 413–14
  Marxism and Form 352
  The Political Unconscious 344, 352–9,
      413–30, 436, 695
  and post-colonialism 656, 668, 718
  and storytelling 11–12, 352
  and Tompkins 446
  see also narrative
Johnson, Barbara 7, 8, 9, 11, 14, 274, 522,
      560, 672, 683
  biographical details 257
  A World of Difference 202–3, 257–70,
      352, 353
Johnson, James Weldon 513
  Autobiography of an Ex-Colored Man 266
Johnson, Samuel 645
  and "Johnson's Rule" 113, 114, 143, 148,
      152–3
Jones, Alexander 318
Jones, William 702
Jonson, Ben
  The Silent Woman 128
  Volpone 128
Joyce, James 4, 114, 356
  "The Dead" 223
  Dubliners 101, 225
  "Eveline" 222, 224–5
  Finnegans Wake 105–6
  and formal realism 477
  Lukács on 381, 397, 399, 404, 412
  narrators 221
  and novel readers 764
  and objectivity 171, 176, 177, 178

A Portrait of the Artist As A Young Man
      101, 169
  Ulysses 105, 141, 169, 175, 223, 395, 396
Jünger, Ernst 401

Kafka, Franz 178, 254–5, 356
  The Castle 406, 411
  Lukács on 397, 400, 405, 406–7, 410, 411–12
  The Trial 406, 411–12
Kahn, Coppélia 600
Kames, Henry Home, Lord: *Elements of
      Criticism* 468
Kant, Immanuel 281, 660, 679, 685–6
Keats, John 581
Keller, Gottfried 386
Kermode, Frank 331
Kerr, Alfred 402
Kierkegaard, Søren 401
  Either/Or 104, 254
Kiernan, V. G. 740
Kilwardby, Robert 212
Kingsley, Charles
  Hypatia 783
  The Water-Babies 103
Kinkead-Weekes, Mark 141
Kipling, Rudyard 99, 373, 663, 702, 707
  Kim 696, 704
Klein, Richard 601
Knickerbocker 780, 781, 787, 788
Koeppen, Wolfgang: *Das Treibhaus* 400
Kristeva, Julia 718
  "Women's Time" 728–9, 730

La Calprenède, Gautier de 478
Lacan, Jacques 14, 254, 281, 285, 319, 320, 324,
      330, 337
  and the centered subject 418–19
  and erotic triangles 599–600, 602
  and feminism 594
  "The Instance of the Letter in the
      Unconscious" 274
Laclos, Pierre Choderlos de 476
Ladies' Repository 780, 781, 784–5, 788
La Fayette, Marie-Madeleine, Madame de 476
Lakoff, George 261
Lamb, Charles 441, 478
Landor, Walter Savage: *Imaginary
      Conversations* 103
language
  Bakhtin on 448–9, 451, 452–3

Bakhtin on discourse in poetry and the
   novel 492–509
Bakhtin on modern stylistics and the
   novel 483–92
Barthes on 200, 201, 231, 236
and realist novels 464–6
Saussure's structuralist theory of 187–9,
   192–3, 201, 274
Todorov on literature and 206–18
Lanser, Susan Sniader 8
Laqueur, Thomas Walter 632
Latin American culture, and Retamar's
   "Caliban" 676
Lawrence, D. H. 172, 569
Lefort, Claude 723–4, 725
Leibniz, G. W. 490
Lennox, Charlotte 645
   The Female Quixote 646–7
Lesage, Alain 464
Leskov, Nikolai 347, 362, 363–4,
   371, 373, 378
   "A Propos of the Kreutzer Sonata" 376
   "The Alexandrite" 370, 377
   "The Deception" 366, 367
   "The Enchanted Pilgrim" 374–5
   "Kotin the Provider and Platonida" 375
   Lady Macbeth of Mzensk 375
   "The Steel Flea" 367–8
   Tales from Olden Times 376
   "The Voice of Nature" 375–6
   "The White Eagle" 366
   "Why Are Books Expensive in Kiev?" 363–4
Lévi-Strauss, Claude 295, 330, 538, 595,
   601, 672, 725–6
Levin, Harry 695
Levine, George 683–4
liminal signifying space: Bhabha on 668–70,
   721, 724–6
linguistic structuralism 187–9, 192–3, 201
and Bakhtin 448–9
and psychoanalytic theory 274, 275–7,
   279, 280, 282, 283
Literary World 781, 785–6, 787, 789–90
Locke, John 465, 467, 468, 470, 472, 476, 630
   Essay Concerning Human Understanding 474–5
Loti, Pierre 693
Lubbock, Percy 3, 4, 8, 12, 18, 576, 749
   biographical details 86
   and Booth 115
   and Chatman 187

The Craft of Fiction 19, 26–8, 29, 86–96,
   194, 273, 356
and Crane 110
and post-colonialism 665
Lucian 102
Lukács, György 2, 4, 5, 279, 340, 436, 657, 703
and Bakhtin 448
biographical details 379–80, 394–5
and historicization 12
"The Ideology of Modernism" 345–6,
   351–2, 356, 357, 394–42
and Jameson 354, 356, 358, 359, 424, 425
and novelistic unity 9
and realist novels 10
and storytelling 347
   Studies in European Realism 345–6, 350–1,
      379–93
   The Theory of the Novel 349–52, 359, 371–2,
      437, 449
Lyly, John 469, 475
Lyotard, Jean-François: *The Postmodern
   Condition* 607, 725

MacKinnon, Catherine 591–2
Macmillan's Magazine 66
Macrobius: *Saturnalia* 103
magazines: Baym on reviews in 750–3, 780–91
Magny, Claude-Edmonde 211
male homosociality: Sedgwick on 565–6,
   586–602
Mallarmé, Stéphane 240
Malraux, André 693
Man, Paul de 261, 607
Manley, Mary de la Rivière 469
Mann, Thomas 178, 356, 381, 388, 401, 406
   Doctor Faustus 408
   Lotte in Weimar 395, 396
Mannoni, Octave 553
Mansfield, Katherine 99
   "The Garden Party" 226
Marcus, Steven 250–1
marriage, and performativity 608
Marx, Karl 14
   The German Ideology 596
Marxism 2, 4, 5, 6, 7, 11, 344–59
and Bakhtin 448
Barthes on 236, 239
and characterological consciousness 8–9
and feminism 595, 596–7
and the genre approach to the novel 12

Marxism (*cont'd*)
and middle-class domestic fiction 571
and narratology 192
and novel readers 750
and the novel as referential lure 10
and objective social value 344–5,
353, 358
and the political unconscious 344, 352–9,
413–30, 436
and psychoanalysis 11, 279
and social discourse 44, 436–7, 439, 440,
450–1
see also Benjamin, Walter; Jameson,
Fredric; Lukács, György
materialist feminism 7, 565–6, 567
Maupassant, Guy de 693
Mauriac, François: *Knot of Vipers* 175
McBurney, William Harlin: *A Check List of
English Prose Fiction* 645
McKeon, Michael 645, 646, 692
meaning of life: Benjamin on storytelling
and 348–9
medieval art, and allegory 409
Melville, Herman 540
Israel Potter 790
Moby Dick 98, 104, 105, 538
memory, and storytelling 370–1
Menippean satire 102–4
Meredith, George 801
The Egoist 98
metaphor/metonymy distinction 202–3,
258–70, 277, 330, 337, 338, 525
The Methodist 785
Michelet, Jules 230–1, 234
Middle Ages
and realism 464, 466
and social discourse 437
Miklashevsky, Vladimir 52
Mill, John Stuart 101, 693, 700, 701
Principles of Political Economy 708
Miller, D. A. 6–7, 8, 9, 14, 572, 761
biographical details 541
and post-colonialism 656
The Novel and the Police 441–5, 453,
541–55, 695
and Tompkins 446–7, 448
Miller, J. Hillis 8, 9, 11, 203, 274, 607, 755
biographical details 242
"Indirect Discourses and Irony" 196–8, 199,
243–55, 286–7

Milton, John 466
Paradise Lost 173, 174, 516, 686
Mitchell, Juliet 596–7
Mitchell, Margaret: *Gone with the Wind* 592–4,
598
modernism/modernity 12
and allegory 408–12
Girard on 286, 288–9
Lukács on the ideology of 345–6, 351–2,
356, 357, 394–42
and the nation 718–19
and potentiality 398–400
and psychopathology 402–5
and social discourse 437
and time 407–8
Moi, Toril 560
Molière (Jean-Baptiste Poquelin): *Don
Juan* 312–13
Montaigne, Michel de 101, 366
Essays 167
Montherlant, Henri Millon de 404
moral action novels 141–53
Moravia, Alberto: *The Indifferent Ones* 399
Morazé, Charles 692
Moretti, Franco 7, 13, 14
Atlas of the European Novel 655, 656–7, 658–9,
668, 734–44
biographical details 734
and Spivak 660
Morris, William 99, 100
Murasaki, Lady 581
musical criticism, and modernism 407
Musil, Robert 303, 356, 397–8, 399, 402, 403,
405, 410, 412
The Man without Qualities 400
The Writer in our Age 406
Musset, Alfred de 162

Nabokov, Vladimir 162–3
Nairn, Tom: *The Break-up of Britain* 429
names of characters, in realist novels 468–70
narcissism
and the nation 725
and performativity 609–10, 611–12, 614
and queer performativity 564
in Rhys's *Wide Sargasso Sea* 680–1, 683
narrated monologue 224
narration
covert narrators 194, 220–1
in Shelley's *Frankenstein* 794–6

in Thackeray's *Vanity Fair* 765–77
see also first-person narration; third-person
   narration
narrative 11
   and description 230–1
   and discourse 209–10, 214–18
   grammar of 212–18
   and Jameson 352, 353, 355
   and Johnson 203
   and psychoanalytic theory 278–9, 279–86,
     291, 316–27, 330–2, 338–41
   and resemblance 330
narrative devices, in Hurston's *Their Eyes Were
   Watching God* 514–19
narrative voice 251–2, 254
narratology 2, 4, 5, 7–8, 189–99, 201, 330
Nathanson, Donald L. 562, 616–17
nation-space: Bhahba on 722–7
nation-states: Moretti on the novel and 735–44
national literatures 12, 13
nationalism: Jameson on 429–30
naturalism
   and modernism 402
   and realism 383–5, 405–6, 477
Nazism 401
Negelein, Julius von: *Germanische Mythologie* 55
neo-Aristotelianism, and the Chicago
   School 109, 112, 113, 117
neutrality, and authorial objectivity 157–64
New Historicism 750
New York Ledger 788, 790
New York Mirror 786
New York Review 780, 781
Newman, Christopher 26
Newman, John Henry: *Apologia* 101
Newton, Isaac 472
Nietzsche, Friedrich 301, 416
nihilism, and impersonal narration 177
nineteenth-century fiction
   Baym on reviews and readers of 748, 749,
     750–3, 779–91
   and classic novels 757, 761
   D. A. Miller on social control and 541–55
   and novel readers 765
   Tompkins on 445–8, 536–40
   Woolf on women and 581–3
Noctes Ambrosianae 104
Nodier, Charles 364
North American Review 780, 781, 782, 785, 786,
   788, 791

Norton Anthology 638
novel readers 748–61
   and discovery 755, 757, 770
   reader response theory 2, 7, 14, 109–13, 117
   see also Baym, Nina; Iser, Wolfgang; reader
     objectivity; Stewart, Garrett
novelistic discourse 508–9
   stylistics of 483–92
Nussbaum, Martha C.: *Love's Knowledge* 273

objectivity 155–79
   of authors 155–63
   and impersonal narration 176–9
   and literary form 27, 117
   of readers 163–76
obligative mood, and narrative discourse 215
Oedipal triangle, in Girard's *Deceit, Desire and
   the Novel* 289, 598–9
Oedipus complex
   and *The Anti-Oedipus* 416–17
   in Rhys's *Wide Sargasso Sea* 681–2
Opie, Amelie 740–1
   Adeline Mowbray 740
optative mood, and narrative discourse 215
Origen: *On First Principles* 374
Orwell, George 702
Ovid: *Metamorphoses* 680

parable, and irony 253
parody: Bakhtin on 532–3
Pascal, Roy 450, 525
Pater, Walter 243
   Marius the Epicurean 122
patriarchy, and homosociality 588–9, 600–1
Paul, Ephi: "My Tongue Is in My Friend's
   Mouth" 530–1
Pavese, Cesare 399
Pavlov, I. 403
Peacock, Thomas Love 98, 102, 103, 104
perception, and defamiliarization 24–5
performativity *see* queer performativity
personality, dissolution of 401–2
perspective, and Marxism 345–6
Peterloo Massacre (1819) 636
Petronius 102, 103
   Satyricon 475
phallogocentrism 254
Phelan, James 8
philosophical realism, and the novel form
   464–5, 474–5, 476–7

Picard, Raymond 236
pictorial books, and fiction writing 92–3
Plato 103, 254, 337, 471
    Symposium 589
Platt, D. C. M. 659, 694
plot
    and Brooks's "Freud's Masterplot" 278
    and Fielding's *Tom Jones* 120–36
    and nineteenth-century American
        fiction 539, 540
    and realist novels 466–7
Plutarch: *Lives* 686
Poe, Edgar Allan 99, 373, 378
    "The Man That Was Used Up" 424
poetic discourse: Bakhtin on 483, 486,
        498–501, 506–8
poetic theory 4
poetry, and metaphor 259
point of view 9, 10, 210–11, 357
    and Bakhtin 439, 449
    and formalism 24, 27, 29
    history and 438, 454
    Iser on 755
    and Tompkins 447
    Watt and James 427–8
Polanyi, Michael 141
policing in novels: Miller on 441–5, 453,
        541–55
political theory 4
the political unconscious: Jameson on 413–30
polysemy 208
pornography, and sexual politics 590, 591
post-colonialism 2, 4, 6, 7, 10, 13, 654–73
    and *Frankenstein* 14
    and location 657–8, 666, 667
    and novelistic unity 9
    and social discourse 453–4
    see also Bhabha, Homi; Moretti, Franco; Said,
        Edward; Spivak, Gayatri Chakravorty
post-structuralism 11, 199, 273–4
    and historicism 416
    and nineteenth-century American
        fiction 538
    and psychoanalytic theory 273–4, 275–9,
        281–2, 284–5, 288
    and social discourse 448
postmodernism, and nineteenth-century
        American culture 447–8
potentiality, and modernism 398–402
Pouillon, Jean 211

Poulantzas, N. 429, 723
Pound, Ezra 171, 173
power
    disciplinary 542, 553–4, 636–7
    social 442–5, 447, 560, 561–2, 567,
        572, 760–1
predictive mood, and narrative discourse
        215–16
Prévost, Jean: *La Création chez Stendhal* 305
Propp, Vladímir 5, 19, 22–4, 28, 111, 331
    biographical details 54
    and Jameson 355, 420
    Morphology of the Folktale 23–4, 55–63
    and psychoanalytic theory 272, 280
    and Todorov 186, 187, 190, 198, 199, 330
Proust, Marcel 4, 12, 104, 210, 239, 240,
        470, 657, 703
    The Captive 311, 312
    Lukács on 381
    Remembrance of Things Past 306–7, 407
    and triangular desire 305–7, 308, 309,
        310–11
psychoanalysis 2, 5, 7, 11,
        109, 272–92
    and *The Anti-Oedipus* 416–17
    Barthes on 236
    and homosexuality 598–601
    and Marxist theory 11, 353–4
    and narratology 192
    and Shelley's *Frankenstein* 684–5
    see also Brooks, Peter; Felman, Shoshana;
        Girard, René
psychological realism 272–3
psychopathology, and modernism 402–5
Puritanism
    and gender 633–4
    and novel reading 625, 750
Pushkin, Alexander
    Evgeny Onegin 52
    Tales of Belkin 34
Putnam's 783, 786, 787, 790

queer performativity: Sedgwick on 5, 561–5,
        605–19
Quintilian 103

Rabelais, François 102, 103, 104, 469
race
    and African American identity 13,
        454–9, 511–33, 563

in Hurston's *Their Eyes Were Watching God* 266–9
and post-colonialism 655
and sexuality 593–4
Racine, Jean 208
Rader, Ralph 108–9, 113–15
  biographical details 140
  and eighteenth-century moral action novels 140–53
radical feminism 594–5
Ragatz, Lowell: *The Fall of the Planter Class in the British Caribbean* 711
rape, and *Gone with the Wind* 593–4
Raynal, Guillaume-Thomas-François, Abbé 702
Reade, Charles 783
reader objectivity 163–76
  and abstract forms 166
  and belief 171–6
  and cause-effect 165–6
  and combinations and conflicts of interests 169–71
  and conventional expectations 166
  and intellectual interest 164–5
  and practical interests 167–9
  and "promised" qualities 166–7
reader response theory 2, 7, 14, 109–13, 117
Reagan, Ronald 588
the Real: Jameson on Marxism and 345, 353, 354, 355, 357
realism 10, 12, 357–8, 463–78
  American 446–8
  formal 441, 477–8, 651
  and French fiction 463–4, 476
  Gallagher on 576–7
  Jameson on 418, 419
  language and prose style 474–6
  Lukács on European realism 383–93
  and names of characters 468–70
  and naturalism 383–5, 405–6, 477
  and novel readers 755, 774, 776
  and particularity of character 467–70
  philosophical 464–5, 474–5, 476–7
  and plot 466–7
  and space 473–4
  and time 470–3
  Watt on realism and the novel form 441, 463–78
Reed, Ishmael 517, 532–3
  Mumbo Jumbo 533

referential illusion 234
referential lure 9, 10, 274, 443, 457
Reid, Thomas 465, 468
religious allegory, in Kafka's works 411–12
Rembrandt 463, 468
Retamar, Roberto Fernández: "Caliban" 676
Reviews: Baym on novel readers and 748, 749, 750–3
Reynolds, Sir Joshua 468
rhetorical discourse: Bakhtin on 488
Rhys, Jean: *Wide Sargasso Sea* 660, 661–2, 675, 680–3, 686, 688, 710
Richards, I. A. 172
Richardson, Samuel 12, 625, 630, 692
  Clarissa 114, 143–7, 272, 273, 469, 472–3, 474, 692
  and formal realism 477, 478
  language and prose style 475, 476
  and the novel form 364, 464, 465, 467
  and novel readers 764
  Pamela 104, 141, 143, 144, 147, 152, 440, 468, 469, 474, 623–4
  and plot 466
  Sir Charles Grandison 147–8, 474
  and space 474
  and time 472–3
  use of proper names 469, 470
Richetti, John 692
Robinson, Ronald 694
Rodó, José Enrique 676
Rolfe, Frederick *see* Corvo, Baron (Frederick Rolfe)
romances 99–100, 101, 104, 105
Romanticism 100
Ronsard, Pierre de 260
Rougemont, Denis de 311
Rousseau, Jean-Jacques 101
  Confessions 297, 336, 685
  Discourse on the Origins of Inequality 334
  La Nouvelle Héloïse 254, 336, 339
  and Tolstoy 498
Rowbotham, Sheila 601
Rowson, Susanna 566
Rubin, Gayle 601, 602
Ruskin, John 699
Russian folk drama, and Sterne's *Tristram Shandy* 44–5
Russian formalism 19–24, 28, 186, 190, 192, 207, 210, 743
  and Bakhtin 449

Russian formalism (*cont'd*)
   and novel readers 756–7
   and psychoanalytic theory 280
Russian realism: Lukács on 389–92
Rutgers Conference on Gay and Lesbian
      Studies 606

Sacks, Sheldon 141, 142
Sade, Donatien-Alphonse-François,
      marquis de 591
Said, Edward 9, 13, 538
   and Bhabha 668, 670, 718, 723, 724
   biographical details 691–2
   Culture and Imperialism 654–5, 656, 657–9,
      664–6, 670, 691–713
   "Jane Austen and Empire" 741–3
   and Spivak 659–60, 662
   and the "structure of experience" 668
Salomon, Ernst von: *The Questionnaire* 401
Saltykov-Shchedrin, N. 389
Sand, George 790
Sappho 581
Sartain's 782, 787–8
Sartre, Jean-Paul 156, 157, 158, 159
   La Nausée 331–2
   L'Enfance des hommes illustres 332
   Les Mots 332
satire 98
   Menippean 102–4
Saussure, Ferdinand de
   and Bakhtin 448–9, 485
   linguistic theory 14, 187–9, 192–3, 201, 274
Scarron, Paul 464
Scheler, Max: *Ressentiment* 300–1
Schiller, J. von 370
Schlegel, Friedrich 254
Schmitt, Carl 401
Schönberg, Arnold 407
Schorer, Mark 161
scientism 3
Scott, Sir Walter 10, 12, 19, 70, 99, 100, 696
   on Fielding 120
   and imperialism 696, 698
   and impersonal narration 177
   Ivanhoe 740
   Lukács on 388, 392
   and novel readers 752, 787
   and professional authorship 783–4
   Waverley novels 100, 780, 786
Scudéry, Madeleine de 475

Sedgwick, Eve Kosofsky 5, 14, 560–6, 570, 573
   Between Men 565–6, 586–602
   biographical details 586–7, 605–6
   "Queer Performativity: Henry James's *The
      Art of the Novel*" 561–5, 605–19, 753
Seeley, J. R. 693
self-authorization, and post-colonialism 670,
      671
self-consciousness: Bakhtin on 451–2
sentimental novels: Tompkins on 446, 448,
      537–40
sexual politics, and sexual meaning 590–4
sexuality 2, 4, 5, 569–77
Shaftesbury, Anthony Ashley Cooper, 3rd Earl
      of: *Essay on the Freedom of Wit and Humour*
      467–8
Shakespeare, William 71, 144, 312, 383, 385,
      403, 699
   King Lear 172, 174, 175
   The Merchant of Venice 333
   Othello 163
   and reader objectivity 162, 169–70, 172,
      174–5
   and realism 466, 472, 473
   Troilus and Cressida 249
shame, and queer performativity 562–3,
      609–11, 612, 616–19
Shelley, Mary
   Frankenstein 14, 613, 660, 662–3, 675, 683–8,
      759–60, 793–802
   The Last Man 793, 794, 795
   "Transformations" 797
Shelley, Percy Bysshe 798
Shklovsky, Víktor 5, 8, 9, 12, 15–16, 18, 19–22,
      443
   "Art as Technique" 19–20
   and Bakhtin 448
   biographical details 31–2
   and Crane 109–10, 111
   and James 24
   and Lubbock 26–7, 29
   and Lukács 351
   and J. Hillis Miller's theory of narrative
      performance 197, 198
   and novel readers 756–7
   and Propp 23–4
   and psychoanalytic theory 274, 280
   on Sterne's *Tristram Shandy* 20–2, 32–52,
      190, 196, 351
   Theory of Prose 19

and Todorov 186, 187, 190, 191, 207,
330, 561
Sholokhov, Mikhail 390, 401
Shpet, Gustav 487–8
Sidney, Sir Philip 98, 469, 475
Arcadia 472, 473
signification 188–9, 201
and Marxism 353–4
and post-colonialism 671
and psychoanalytic theory 274, 275–7, 279,
280, 282, 283, 319–20, 327
and signifying in Hurston's *Their Eyes Were
Watching God* 512–14, 515–17, 519–20,
521, 528, 533
Smith, Barbara H. 331, 538
Smith-Rosenberg, Carroll 588
Smollett, Tobias 470, 692
social discourse 2, 4, 13, 436–59
and Foucault's theory of social power 442–5,
447
and Marxism 436–7, 439, 440, 442
see also Bakhtin, M. M.; Miller, D. A.;
Tompkins, Jane; Watt, Ian
*Social Formalism: The Novel in Theory from Henry
James to the Present* (Hale) 3–4
social theory 5
sociohistorical approaches to the novel 12
Socrates 254
Sophocles 397
Oedipus 122
Southern Literary Messenger 781, 785, 786
Southey, Robert: *Doctor* 104
Southworth, E. D. E. N. 790
space
and post-colonialism 658–9, 722–7
and realist novels 437–8, 473–4
The Spectator 468
speech types, and stylistics 484–5
Spengler, Oswald 380, 471
Spenser, Edmund 466, 566
"The Faerie Queene" 472
Spivak, Gayatri Chakravorty 13, 656, 657, 759
and Bhabha 669, 670
biographical details 674
and feminist individualism 664
"Three Women's Texts and a Critique of
Imperialism" 14, 655, 659–60, 674–88
Stein, Gertrude: *Melanctha* 167
Stendhal (Henri Beyle) 12, 303–5, 307, 308,
309, 313, 403, 545

De l'Amour 303, 304–5, 307
and imperialism 698
The Italian Chronicles 304
Memoirs of a Tourist 301
The Red and the Black 297–9, 305, 306,
474, 554–5
Stephens, Anne S. 790
stereotyped characters, and nineteenth-
century American fiction
539–40
Sterne, Laurence 12, 166, 470, 692
A Sentimental Journey 40–1
Tristram Shandy 20–2, 32–53, 98, 104, 105,
141, 190, 336, 351
Stevenson, Robert Louis 70, 378
Stewart, Garrett 7, 8
biographical details 792
Dear Reader 14, 748–9, 749–50, 753,
757–61, 792–802
Stoker, Bram 759
Dracula 801–2
story and discourse, and narratology 193–5
storytelling 11–12, 346–9, 355, 356, 359,
361–78
and death 368–9, 370, 371
and fairy tales 373–5
and historiography 369–70, 371
and information 365–6
and memory 370–1
and the novel 364–5, 372–3
and realism 419
in Shelley's *Frankenstein* 794, 795
and the short story 368
see also Leskov, Nikolai
Stowe, Harriet Beecher 566
Uncle Tom's Cabin 446, 536, 537, 539, 540
stratification of language, and discourse
501–4, 507, 508
stream of consciousness technique 101, 105,
177, 211, 395, 399, 404
and narratology 192
and Surrealism 405
and time 471
structuralism 2, 4, 5, 186–9, 190, 236
and Bakhtin 448
and the Chicago School 117
and deconstruction 199–200
and feminism 595, 596
and nineteenth-century American
fiction 538

structuralism (cont'd)
  see also linguistic structuralism; post-
      structuralism
stylistics: Bakhtin on modern stylistics and
      the novel 483–92
subjectivity
  and abstract potentiality 398–400
  Benjamin on storytelling and 347–8
  and the centred subject 418–19
  and deconstruction 197–9
  and domestic fiction 630, 639
  and gender 622–3
  Jameson on 357
  in *Jane Eyre* 675–6
  and queer performativity 564, 608, 613,
      615–16
  and time 407–8
Sunday schools, and novel reading 632–3
supplementation, and post-colonialism 672
Surrealism 405, 412
Swift, Jonathan 102, 103, 389
  "Description of the Morning" 475
  Gulliver's Travels 43, 98, 101, 102, 105
Symbolists, and the language of poetry 501
sympathy: eighteenth-century discourse
      on 645, 647–51
synonymy, and polysemy 208

tagged style, indirect 221–7
technological change, and individualism 440
Tefft, B. F.: *The Shoulder-Knot* 784
the Text: Barthes on 236–41
textual determinant: Jameson on 358
Thackeray, William Makepeace 12, 161, 251,
      693, 787
  Vanity Fair 695, 696–7, 703, 754, 755–7,
      758, 765–77
third-person narration 269–70
  and indirect style 227
  and James 25–6
Tillotson, Kathleen 159
Tilly, Charles 737
time
  and modernism 407–8
  and realist novels 437–8, 470–3
  realist and Romantic conceptions of 720
  women's time 728
Todorov, Tzvetan 5, 8, 189, 334, 425, 561
  biographical details 205

on narrative structure and
      transformation 330–1, 338, 340, 355
  The Poetics of Prose 186, 190–2, 198–9,
      205–18, 272
  and psychoanalytic theory 274
  and Russian formalists 186, 190
Tolstoy, Leo 4, 10, 12, 19, 37, 43, 103, 176, 569
  Anna Karenina 87–9, 90, 91, 272
  Bakhtin on 494, 497–8
  Lukács on 381, 383, 386, 388–9, 390–1,
      392, 397
  War and Peace 207, 381, 581–2
"Tom Thumb": Russian version of 43
Tomkins, Silvan 562, 609, 612
Tomlin, Lily 617
Tompkins, Jane 9, 13, 451, 454–5, 560
  biographical details 535
  Sensational Designs 445–8, 453, 535–40
Toomer, Jean: *Cane* 512, 513
tragedy 123
transference, and psychoanalytic theory
      280–1, 324–7, 334, 339
transrelative mood, and narrative
      discourse 216
triangular desire, in Girard's *Deceit, Desire and
      the Novel* 15, 287–92, 295–313
Tristan and Isolde 311
Trollope, Anthony 99, 100, 254, 470, 542,
      545, 554
  The Eustace Diamonds 550–4, 555
  narrative voice of 251–2
  The Warden 243, 246, 247, 248–9, 250
Turgenev, Ivan 19, 67
  A Nest of Gentlefolk 34

the unconscious
  and Marxism 353–4
  and psychoanalytic theory 274, 280–2,
      286, 340–1
unitary language: Bakhtin on discourse
      and 489–91
unity of the novel 9–10

Valéry, Paul 206, 211, 246, 304
  and storytelling 368, 377
vaniteux: Girard on triangular desire and
      287–8, 298, 302, 307, 311
Varro 102, 103

verisimilitude: Barthes on 232–4
Victorian novels: Miller on social power
      and 443, 444–5
Villemessant (founder of *Le Figaro*) 365
Vinogradov, Viktor 488
Virgil 385
Volney, C.: *Ruins of Empires* 686, 702
Voltaire (François-Marie Arouet)102, 103
   Candide 101

Walker, Alice 524–5
Walton, Izaak: *The Compleat Angler* 103, 104
Warhol, Robyn 7–8
Warner, Susan 566
   The Wide, Wide World 446, 536, 537, 538, 539
Watkins, Gloria *see* hooks, bell (Gloria
    Watkins)
Watt, Ian 4, 449, 454, 651, 692
  biographical details 462
  and novel readers 754
  The Rise of the Novel 13, 436–42, 453,
    462–78, 576, 625, 627, 628
Weeks, Jeffrey 601
Wellerisms 252
West, Jessamyn 159
Westminster Review 789
Wharton, Edith 4, 566
White, Allon 633
Whorf, Benjamin 216
Wilberforce, William 703
Wilde, Oscar 759
Williams, Eric: *Capitalism and Slavery* 711
Williams, Raymond 654, 693, 706, 724
  The Country and the City 656, 701–2
Wolf, Eric 686
Wolfe, Thomas 397

Wollstonecraft, Mary 663
women writers
  American reviews on 790
  Armstrong on 570–3
  and domestic fiction 622, 625–40
  and feminists 566
  Gallagher on 574–7
  and nineteenth-century
    American fiction 537–8
  Woolf on 567–73, 579–85
Woolf, Virginia 4, 7, 114, 560,
    566–73
  biographical details 579–80
  and impersonal narration 177
  and indirect style 223, 226
  and Jane Austen 10–11
  Mrs Dalloway 226, 683
  A Room of One's Own 570, 622
  To the Lighthouse 175, 265
  The Waves 572
  "Women and Fiction" 567–73,
    572–3, 579–85
Wordsworth, William 100, 220, 701
Worsley, Peter 686
Wright, Richard 266
Wundt, W. 55

Yeats, W. B. 173
Young, Edward: *Conjectures on Original
    Composition* 466

Zola, Émile 345, 383, 384, 385,
    386–8, 391, 545
  and formal realism 477
  Nana 555

CPSIA information can be obtained at www.ICGtesting.com
Printed in the USA
BVOW06s1539271013

334709BV00004B/25/P